D0742213

ILIOS the city and country of the TROJANS

Heinrich SCHLIEMANN

Troy As It Appears After the Excavations of 1879.
The View is taken from the Bridge on the ancient Scamander.
The Theatre is in the hills to the left which border the Valley of the Simois.
The hills to the right, which belong to the same plateau,
dominate the Plain of the Scamander. Behind Hissarlik extends the site of Novum Ilium.
To the right of Hissarlik are Dr. Schliemann's houses and magazines.

ILIOS the city and country of the
TROJANS

The results of researches and discoveries

on the site of Troy and throughout the

Troad in the years 1871, 72, 73, 78, 79

Including an autobiography of the author

BENJAMIN BLOM, *New York and London*

TO

THE RIGHT HONOURABLE

SIR AUSTEN HENRY LAYARD, G.C.B., D.C.L.,

THE PIONEER IN RECOVERING THE LOST HISTORY OF THE

ANCIENT CITIES OF WESTERN ASIA

BY MEANS OF THE PICKAXE AND THE SPADE,

IN ACKNOWLEDGEMENT OF HIS KIND AND EFFECTIVE AID TO THE

EXCAVATIONS ON THE SITE OF TROY,

AS AMBASSADOR TO THE SUBLIME PORTE,

THIS WORK IS RESPECTFULLY AND GRATEFULLY

Dedicated

BY

THE AUTHOR.

First Published 1881
Reissued 1968 by
Benjamin Blom, Inc., Bronx, New York 10452
and 56 Doughty Street, London, W.C. 1
Library of Congress Catalog Card Number 68-21229
Printed in the United States of America

CONTENTS.

NOTE.—Special attention is also called to Professor Max Müller's Dissertation on the 卐 and 卍 at pages 346–349.

MAPS AND PLANS

AT THE END OF THE BOOK.

ILLUSTRATIONS.

DIAGRAM

SHOWING THE SUCCESSIVE STRATA OF REMAINS ON THE
HILL OF HISSARLIK.

Mètres. Feet (abt.).   *Surface.*

Mètres	Feet	Stratum
2	6	Stratum of the 7th City, the Aeolic Ilium.
2	6½	Remains of the 6th, the Lydian City.
2		Stratum of the 5th City.
4	13	
3		Stratum of the 4th City.
7	23	
3		Stratum of the 3rd, the Burnt City (the Homeric Ilios).
10	33	
4 to 6		Stratum of the 2nd City.
13½	45	
to	to	Stratum of the 1st City.
16	52½	

Native rock.—Its present height above the sea is 109½ feet. Its present height above the plain at the foot of the hill is consequently 59½ feet, but it may probably have been 16 or 20 feet more at the time of the Trojan war, the plain having increased in height by the alluvia of the rivers and the detritus of vegetable and animal matter.

COMPARATIVE TABLE OF FRENCH AND ENGLISH MEASURES,
EXACT AND APPROXIMATE.

Metric.	Inches.	Ft.	Inch.	Approximate.
Millimètre .	0·0393708	,,	0·03937	·04 or $\frac{1}{25}$ of inch.
Centimètre .	0·393708	,,	0·39371	·4 ,, $\frac{2}{5}$,,
Décimètre .	3·93708	,,	3·9371	4 inches.
Mètre .	39·3708	3	3·3708	$3\frac{1}{4}$ feet.
2	78·7416	6	6·7416	$6\frac{1}{2}$,,
3	118·1124	9	10·1124	10 ,,
4	157·4832	13	1·4832	13 ,,
5	196·8540	16	4·8540	$16\frac{1}{3}$,,
6	236·2248	19	8·2248	$19\frac{2}{3}$,,
7	275·5956	22	11·5956	23 ,,
8	314·9664	26	2·9664	$26\frac{1}{4}$,,
9	354·3372	29	6·3372	$29\frac{1}{2}$,,
10	393·7089	32	9·7080	33 ,,
11	433·0788	36	1·0788	36 (12 yds.)
12	472·4496	39	4·4496	$39\frac{1}{3}$ feet.
13	511·8204	42	7·9204	$42\frac{2}{3}$,,
14	551·1912	45	11·1912	46 ,,
15	590·5620	49	2·5620	$49\frac{1}{4}$,,
16	620·9328	52	5·9328	$52\frac{1}{2}$,,
17	669·3036	55	9·3036	$55\frac{3}{4}$,,
18	708·6744	59	0·6744	59 ,,
19	748·0452	62	4·0452	$62\frac{1}{3}$,,
20	787·416	65	7·4160	$65\frac{2}{3}$,,
30	1181·124	98	5·124	$98\frac{1}{2}$,,
40	1574·832	131	2·832	$131\frac{1}{4}$,,
50	1968·54	164	0·54	164 ,,
100	3937·08	328	1·08	328 (109 yds.)

N.B.—The following is a convenient approximate rule :—" To turn *Mètres* into *Yards*, add 1–11th to the number of Mètres."

PREFACE.

——◦◦◦——

A book like the present, certain to be so long talked of *after* (*Nachrede*), has no real need of a *Preface* (*Vorrede*). Nevertheless, as my friend Schliemann insists on my introducing it to the public, I put aside all the scruples which, at least according to my own feeling, assign to me only an accessory position. A special chance allowed me to be one of the few eye-witnesses of the last excavations at Hissarlik, and to see the "Burnt" City emerge, in its whole extent, from the rubbish-heaps of former ages. At the same time I saw the Trojan land itself, from week to week, waking up out of its winter's sleep, and unfolding its natural glories in pictures ever new, ever more grand and impressive. I can therefore bear my testimony, not only to the labours of the indefatigable explorer, who found no rest until his work lay before him fully done, but also to the truth of the foundations, on which was framed the poetical conception that has for thousands of years called forth the enchanted delight of the educated world. And I recognize the duty of bearing my testimony against the host of doubters, who, with good or ill intentions, have never tired of carping alike at the trustworthiness and significance of his discoveries.

It is now an idle question, whether Schliemann, at the beginning of his researches, proceeded from right or wrong presuppositions. Not only has the result decided in his favour, but also the method of his investigation has proved to be excellent. It may be, that his hypotheses were too bold, nay arbitrary; that the enchanting picture of Homer's immortal poetry proved somewhat of a snare to his fancy; but this fault of imagination, if I may so call it, nevertheless involved the secret of his success. Who would have undertaken such great works, continued through so many years,—have spent such large means out of his own fortune,—have dug through layers of *débris* heaped one on the other in a series that seemed almost endless, down to the deep-lying virgin soil,—except a man who was penetrated with an assured, nay an enthusiastic conviction? The Burnt City would still have lain to this day hidden in the earth, had not imagination guided the spade.

But severe enquiry has of itself taken the place of imagination. Year by year the facts have been more duly estimated. The search for truth—for the whole truth and nothing but the truth—has at last so far relegated the intuitions of poetry to the background, that I—a naturalist habituated to the most dispassionate objective contemplation (*mit der Gewohnheit der kältesten Objectivität*) felt myself forced to remind my friend, that the poet was not a poet only, that his pictures must also have had an objective foundation, and that nothing ought to deter us from bringing the reality, as it presented itself to us, into relation with the old legends formed upon definite recollections of the locality and of the events of the olden time. I rejoice that the book, as it now lies before us, fully satisfies both requirements : while it gives a true and faithful description of the discoveries and of the conditions of the land and the place, it everywhere links together the threads, which allow our imagination to bring the personal agents into definite relations with actual things.

The excavations at Hissarlik would have had an imperishable value, even if the *Iliad* had never been sung. Nowhere else in the world has the earth covered up so many remains of ancient settlements lying upon one another, with such rich contents within them. When we stand at the bottom of the great funnel, which has opened up the heart of the hill-fortress, and the eye wanders over the lofty walls of the excavations, beholding here the ruins of dwellings, there the utensils of the ancient inhabitants, at another spot the remnants of their food, every doubt as to the antiquity of this site soon vanishes. A mere dreamy contemplation is here excluded. The objects present such striking peculiarities as to position and stratification, that the comparison of their properties, whether among themselves, or with other remote discoveries, is of necessity forced upon us. One cannot be otherwise than realistic (*objectiv*), and I have pleasure in testifying that Schliemann's statements satisfy every demand of truthfulness and accuracy. Whoever has himself made an excavation knows that minor errors can hardly be avoided, and that the progress of an investigation almost always corrects some of the results of earlier stages of the enquiry. But at Hissarlik the correction was simple enough to guarantee the accuracy of the general result, and what is now offered to the world may be placed, in respect of the authenticity of the facts, beside the best researches of archæology. Besides, an error in verifying the position of any object could in each case relate to details only ; the great mass of results cannot be affected thereby.

The simple investigation of the fortress-hill of Hissarlik suffices to prove with complete exactness the succession of the settlements, of which Schliemann now supposes seven. But order of succession is not yet chronology. From the former we learn what is older and what later, but not how old each separate stratum is. This question involves a comparison with other like places, or at least objects, the date of which is well established ; in other words, interpretation. But, with interpretation, uncertainty also begins. The archæologist is seldom in the position of being able to support his interpretation by the identity of all the objects found. And especially, the farther the comparisons have to be fetched, the less is it possible to calculate that discoveries will correspond in their totality. Attention is therefore directed to single objects, just as the palæontologist seeks for characteristic shells (*Leitmuscheln*), to determine the age of a geological stratum. But experience has shown how uncertain are the *Leitmuscheln* of archæology. The human intellect invents identical things at different places, and different things at the same place. Certain artistical or technical forms are developed simultaneously, without any connection or relation between the artists or craftsmen. I recal the case of the *maeander* ornament, which appears in Germany quite late, probably not till the time of the Roman emperors, but presents itself much later still in Peru and on the Amazon, where it appears as yet inadmissible to regard it as imported. Local fashions and artistic forms are so far from being uncommon, that the expert sometimes recognizes the source of the discovery from a single piece.

In the case of Hissarlik, the strata which can be defined according to their whole character occur very near the surface. Under the Greek City (Novum Ilium), and the wall which is probably Macedonian, the excavator comes upon objects, especially upon pottery which, according to its form, material, and painting, belongs to what is called the Archaic period of Greek art. Then begins the Pre-historic age, in the narrower sense of the term. Dr. Schliemann has endeavoured, on good grounds, to show that the Sixth City, reckoning upwards, should be ascribed, in accordance with tradition, to the Lydians, and that we may recognize in its artistic forms an approximation to Etrurian or Umbrian pottery. But the deeper we go, the fewer correspondences do we find. In the Burnt City we occasionally meet with one or another object, which reminds us of Mycenae, of Cyprus, of Egypt, of Assyria; or probably rather, which points to a like origin, or at least to similar models. Perhaps we shall succeed in multiplying these connecting links, but as yet so little is known of all these relations, that the adaptation of a foreign chronology to the new discoveries seems in the highest degree dangerous.

An example full of warning as to this sort of casuistical archæology is furnished by the latest attack upon Dr. Schliemann by a scholar at St. Petersburg. Because Hissarlik offers certain points of correspondence with Mycenae, and the latter again with South Russia, this scholar therefore concludes that the South Russian chronology must also be the measure for Hissarlik, and that both Mycenae and Hissarlik are to be referred to roving hordes of Heruli in the third century after Christ. Going right to the opposite extreme, other scholars have been inclined to ascribe the oldest " cities " of Hissarlik to the Neolithic Age, because remarkable weapons and utensils of polished stone are found in them. Both these conceptions are equally unjustified and inadmissible. To the third century after Christ belongs the surface of the fortress-hill of Hissarlik, which still lies above the Macedonian wall; and the oldest " cities "—although not only polished stones but also chipped flakes of chalcedony and obsidian occur in them—nevertheless fall within the Age of Metals. For even in the First City, utensils of copper, gold, nay even silver, were dug up.

It is beyond doubt that no Stone People, properly so-called, dwelt upon the fortress-hill of Hissarlik, so far as it has been as yet uncovered. A progressive development of such a people to a higher metallic civilization can no more be spoken of here, than at any other point of Asia Minor hitherto known. Implements of polished stone are also found elsewhere in Asia Minor—as, for example, in the neighbourhood of the ancient Sardes—but it is not yet proved that they belong to the "Stone Age." Probably this people immigrated at a period of their development, at which they had already entered on the "Metal Age." Were we to take for the foundation of the discussion what first suggests itself, the frequent occurrence of nephrite and jadeite, we might suppose that the immigration took place from the borders of China, and that, when the people reached the Hellespont, they had already acquired a high degree of technical dexterity and of finished manufacture.

It may be an accident that even in the oldest city two stone hammers have been found with holes bored through them, whereas in no other spot of all Asia Minor, so far as I know, has any similar object occurred. In any case the art of stone-working was already far advanced, and the story of the foundation of Ilium, as sketched out in the *Iliad*, exactly coincides with the discoveries. The few skulls also, which were saved out of the lower "cities," have this in common, that without exception they present the character (*habitus*) of a more civilized people; all savage peculiarities, in the stricter sense, are entirely wanting in them.

It is strange enough that this race, according to all appearance, *had no iron*. Although there occasionally occur native red iron-stones, which have evidently been used, yet every object which was originally regarded as an iron instrument has proved, on closer investigation, not to be iron.

No less strange is it that even in the Burnt City *no proper sword has anywhere been found*. Weapons of copper and bronze occur frequently— lance-heads, daggers, arrow-heads, knives, if we may designate these as weapons—but no swords. Corresponding to this deficiency is another in the case of ornaments, which to us Occidentals is still more striking,— I mean the *absence of the fibula* (the buckle of the brooch). Among the copper and bronze pins are many which, judging from their size and curvature, may be regarded as pins for dress; but no single fibula in our sense has occurred. I was always of opinion, that the abundance of fibulæ in the northern discoveries is explained by the greater necessity for fastening the garments tighter in colder climates. The Roman provincial fibula, which in the northern countries is all but the most frequent object in the discoveries of the Imperial age, falls even in Italy quite into the background. But the fact that, among a race so rich in metals as the ancient Trojans, absolutely no fibula has occurred, is certainly a sign of very high antiquity, and a sure mark of distinction from the majority of Western discoveries which have been adduced in comparison. The same may be said, in passing, of the *absence of lamps* in the ancient "cities."

The pottery presents many more points of correspondence with that of the West. To be sure I could not cite any place where the whole of the pottery found agreed with that of any one of the older cities upon Hissarlik. It is not till the Sixth City that we find, as Dr. Schliemann has very convincingly proved, manifold relations with the Etruscan vases; and I might still further remark, that not a few of the forms which occur at Hissarlik in clay are executed in Etruria in bronze.

In this connection I may also refer, as *Leitmuscheln*, to the Etruscan beaked pitchers, which have been dug up in the heart of Germany and Belgium. In most of the pre-historic cities of Hissarlik there are terra-cottas just like those which are frequently met with in Hungary and Transylvania, in eastern and middle Germany, nay even in the pile-dwellings of Switzerland. I myself possess, through the kindness of Dr. Victor Gross, fragments of black polished clay bowls from the Lake of Bienne, the inner surfaces of which are covered with incised geometrical patterns, filled with white earth, such as I brought away from the oldest city of Hissarlik. Quite lately I was present at the excavation of a great conical barrow, conducted by Prof. Klopfleisch in the territory of Anhalt: the greater number of the clay vessels discovered there had broad wing-shaped excrescences with perpendicular perforations, and very large and particularly broad handles, which were put on quite low down close to the bottom, like those met with in the Burnt City. I have before alluded to the similarity of the little animal figures, the ornamented stamps, and other terra-cottas in Hungary. The strange perforated incense-vessels (lanterns) of Hissarlik find numerous analogies in the burial-grounds of Lusatia and Posen.

I am not prepared to affirm that these are proofs of a direct connection. That question can only be reviewed when the countries of the Balkan peninsula shall have been more thoroughly investigated archæologically, a thing which is urgently to be desired. But even if a real connection should appear, the question will still remain open, whether the current of civilization set from Asia Minor to Eastern Europe, or the inverse way; and, since the former is presumptively the more probable, little would be gained hence for the chronology of Hissarlik.

Much might be brought in here, as, for instance, the hooked cross (Suastika), the Triquetrum, the circular and spiral decoration, the wave-ornament; but I pass by these, as being widely-diffused marks, which, as we learn from experience, furnish little support for the determination of time. On the other hand, I cannot entirely refrain from touching on a point, on which I do not completely agree with Schliemann. I refer to our *Face-Vases*, such as occur plentifully in Pomerellen and East Pomerania, as far as Posen and Silesia, in a region distinctly defined. I cannot deny that there is a great resemblance between them and the Trojan "Owl-Vases," though I also admit that the "Owl's Face" does not occur upon them. But as to this matter I am disposed somewhat to modify my friend's expression. So far as I see, there is not a single Trojan Face-Vase, which can be said to have a true Owl's Head, or in which the part of the vase referred to can be regarded as completely in the form of a bird. As a matter of Natural History, the type of the form modelled on this upper part is human, and it is only within the human outlines and proportions that the nose and the region of the eyes are owl-formed. The ear, on the other hand, is always put on like that of a man, never like that of an owl. I do not deny that the form of the face often represents the owl-type, and I have no objection to make against the connection with the γλαυκῶπις, but I should not like to extend the likeness to a larger surface than around the eyes and the upper part about the nose : the ears, and the mouth (where it occurs), as well as the breasts, are exclusively human. And so—only still more in the human form—are also the Face-Urns of Pomerellen. I do not therefore give up the hope that a certain connection may yet be discovered; but, if so, I am prepared to find that our Face-Urns will have to be assigned to a much later period than those of Troy.

My conclusion is this: that the discoveries at Hissarlik will not be explained by those made in the North or the West, but, inversely, that we must test our collections by Oriental models. For Hissarlik also, the probable sources of connection lie East and South; but their determination requires new and far more thorough studies in the fields of the Oriental world, hitherto so scantily reaped. It was not the *Iliad* itself that first brought the Phoenicians and the Ethiopians into the Trojan legendary cycle; the discoveries at Hissarlik themselves, in placing before our eyes ivory, enamel, figures of the hippopotamus, and fine works in gold, point distinctly to Egypt and Assyria. It is there that the chronological relations of Hissarlik must find their solution.

Meanwhile, however, there stands the great hill of ruins, forming for realistic contemplation a phenomenon quite as unique as the "Sacred Ilios" for poetical feeling. It has not its like. Never once in any other heap of ruins is a standard given by which to judge it. Therefore it will not fit into the Procrustean bed of systematizers (*Schematiker*). *Hinc illae irae.* This excavation has opened for the studies of the archæologist a completely new theatre—like a world by itself. Here begins an entirely new science.

And in this unique hill there is a Stratum, and that one of the deepest—according to Schliemann's present reckoning, the Third from the bottom,—which especially arrests our attention. Here was a great devouring fire, in which the clay walls of the buildings were molten and made fluid like wax, so that congealed drops of glass bear witness at the present day to the mighty conflagration. Only at a few places are cinders left, whose structure enables us still to discover what was burnt,—whether wood or straw, wheat or pease. A very small part of this city has upon the whole escaped the fire; and only here and there in the burnt parts have portions of the houses remained uninjured beneath the rubbish of the foundering walls. Almost the whole is burnt to ashes. How enormous must have been the fire that devoured all this splendour ! We seem to hear the crackling of the wood, the crash of the tumbling buildings ! And, in spite of this, what riches have been brought to light out of the ashes ! Treasures of gold, one after another, presented themselves to the astonished eye. In that remote time, when man was so little advanced in the knowledge of the earth and of his own power, in that time when, as the poet tells us, the king's sons were shepherds, the possession of such treasures of the precious metals, and that in the finest and most costly workmanship, must have become famous far and wide. The splendour of this chieftain must have awakened envy and covetousness; and the ruin of his high fortress can signify nothing else than his own downfall and the destruction of his race.

Was this chieftain PRIAM? Was this city SACRED ILIOS? No one will ever fathom the question, whether these were the names which men used when the celebrated king still looked out from his elevated fortress over the Trojan Plain to the Hellespont. Perhaps these names are only the poet's inventions. Who can know? Perhaps the legend had handed down no more than the story of the victorious enterprise of war undertaken from the West, to overthrow the kingdom and the city. But who will doubt that on this spot a terrible conquest was really won in fight against a garrison, who not only defended themselves, their families, and their houses, with weapons of stone and bronze, but who also had great wealth in gold and silver, ornaments and furniture, to protect? It is in itself of little consequence to quarrel about the names of these men or of their city. And yet the first question that rises to every one's lips, to-day as in the time of Homer, is this:—Who and whence among mankind were they? Though the severe enquirer may refuse them names, though the whole race may glide past before the judgment-seat of science like the ghosts of Hades,—yet for us, who love the colours of daylight, the dress of life, the glitter of personality, for us PRIAM and ILIUM will remain the designations upon which our thoughts fasten, as often as they concern themselves with the events of that period. It was here, where Asia and Europe for the first time encountered in a war of extermination (*in völkerfressendem Kampfe*); it was here that the only decisive victory was won in fight, which the West gained over the East on the soil of Asia, during the whole time down to Alexander the Great.

And now, under our eyes, this site has been again disclosed. When those men whom we call the Classics wrote, the burnt abodes lay hidden beneath the ruins of succeeding settlements. To the question—"Where was Ilium?"—no one had an answer. Even the legend had no longer a locality. It must assuredly have been otherwise when the poem had its origin. Whether we call the poet Homer, or substitute in his place a host of nameless bards,—when the poetic tale originated, the tradition must still have been preserved upon the spot, that the royal fortress had stood exactly on this mountain spur. It is in vain to dispute with the poet his knowledge of the place by his own eyesight. Whoever the "divine bard" was, he must have stood upon this hill of Hissarlik—that is, the Castle- or Fortress-Hill—and have looked out thence over land and sea. In no other case could he possibly have combined so much truth to nature in his poem. I have described, in a brief essay,[1] the Trojan country as it is, and compared it with what the *Iliad* says of it, and I believe I may call any one to bear witness, whether it is possible that a poet living at a distance could have evolved out of his own imagination so faithful a picture of the land and people as is embodied in the *Iliad*.

To this is to be added another consideration. The *Iliad* is not merely an Epic which sings of human affairs: in the conflict of men the great circle of the Olympic gods takes part, acting and suffering. Hence it happened that the *Iliad* became the special religious book, the Bible of

---

[1] See Appendix I., *Troy and Hissarlik*.

the Greeks and partly of the Romans. This must not be overlooked. Therefore I have especially called attention to the fact, that the theatre for the action of the gods has been drawn much larger than for the men. The range of these poems extends far beyond the Plain of Troy. Its limit is there, where the eye finds its boundary, on the lofty summits of Ida and the peak of Samothrace, where the clouds have birth and the storms make their home. Who could have lighted upon such a story of the gods with this fineness of localizing, except one who had himself beheld the mighty phenomena of nature which are here displayed? Who, that had not gazed on them in their alternate course for days and weeks together?

The question of the *Iliad* is not simply the old question—*Ubi Ilium fuit?* No, it embraces the whole. We must not sever the story of the gods from the story of the men. The poet who sang of Ilium painted also the picture of the whole Trojan country. Ida and Samothrace, Tenedos and the Hellespont, Callicolone and the Rampart of Herakles, the Scamander and the memorial tumuli of the heroes—all this appeared before the view of the enraptured hearer. All this is inseparable. And therefore it is not left to our choice, where we should place Ilium. Therefore we must have a place, which answers to all the requirements of the poetry. Therefore we are compelled to say :—*Here*, upon the fortress-hill of Hissarlik, —*here*, upon the site of the ruins of the Burnt City of Gold,—*here was Ilium.*

And therefore thrice happy the man to whose lot it has fallen to realize in the maturity of manhood the dreams of his childhood, and to unveil the Burnt City. Whatever may be the acknowledgement of contemporaries, no one will be able to rob him of the consciousness, that he has solved the great problem of thousands of years. A barbarous government, which weighed as a heavy burthen on the land, has upon the whole kept down the condition of the surface of the country and the habits of human life in the Troad at the same level as when it imposed its yoke. Thus, much has been preserved which elsewhere would probably have been destroyed by daily cultivation. Schliemann was able to make his excavations, as it were, in a virgin soil. He had the courage to dig deeper and still deeper, to remove whole mountains of rubbish and *débris ;* and at last he saw before him the treasure sought and dreamt of, in its full reality. And now the treasure-digger has become a scholar, who, with long and earnest study, has compared the facts of his experience, as well as the statements of historians and geographers, with the legendary traditions of poets and mythologers. May the work which he has terminated become to many thousands a source of enjoyment and instruction, as it will be to himself an everlasting glory!

RUDOLF VIRCHOW.

BERLIN, *September 10th,* 1880.

ILIOS.

INTRODUCTION.

§ I. Early and Commercial Life : 1822 to 1866.

If I begin this book with my autobiography, it is not from any feeling of vanity, but from a desire to show how the work of my later life has been the natural consequence of the impressions I received in my earliest childhood; and that, so to say, the pickaxe and spade for the excavation of Troy and the royal tombs of Mycenae were both forged and sharpened in the little German village in which I passed eight years of my earliest childhood. I also find it necessary to relate how I obtained the means which enabled me, in the autumn of my life, to realize the great projects I formed when I was a poor little boy. But I flatter myself that the manner in which I have employed my time, as well as the use I have made of my wealth, will meet with general approbation, and that my autobiography may aid in diffusing among the intelligent public of all countries a taste for those high and noble studies, which have sustained my courage during the hard trials of my life, and which will sweeten the days yet left me to live.

I was born on the 6th of January, 1822, in the little town of Neu Buckow, in Mecklenburg-Schwerin, where my father,[1] Ernest Schliemann, was Protestant clergyman, and whence, in 1823, he was elected in that capacity to the parish of the village of Ankershagen between Waren and Penzlin, in the same duchy. In that village I spent the eight following years of my life; and my natural disposition for the mysterious and the marvellous was stimulated to a passion by the wonders of the locality in which I lived. Our garden-house was said to be haunted by the ghost of my father's predecessor, Pastor von Russdorf; and just behind our garden was a pond called "das Silberschälchen," out of which a maiden was believed to rise each midnight, holding a silver bowl. There was also in the village a small hill surrounded by a ditch, probably a pre-historic

---

[1] Deceased in November 1870, at the age of 90 years.

burial-place (or so-called *Hünengrab*);[2] in which, as the legend ran, a robber knight in times of old had buried his beloved child in a golden cradle. Vast treasures were also said to be buried close to the ruins of a round tower in the garden of the proprietor of the village. My faith in the existence of these treasures was so great that, whenever I heard my father complain of his poverty, I always expressed my astonishment that he did not dig up the silver bowl or the golden cradle, and so become rich. There was likewise in Ankershagen a medieval castle, with secret passages in its walls, which were six feet thick, and an underground road, which was supposed to be five miles long, and to pass beneath the deep lake of Speck; it was said to be haunted by fearful spectres, and no villager spoke of it without terror.[3] There was a legend, that the castle had once been inhabited by a robber knight of the name of Henning von Holstein, popularly called "Henning Bradenkirl," who was dreaded over the whole country, for he plundered and sacked wherever he could. But, to his vexation, the Duke of Mecklenburg gave safe-conducts to many of the merchants who had to pass by his castle. Wishing to wreak vengeance upon the duke, Henning begged him to do him the honour of a visit. The duke accepted the invitation, and came on the appointed day with a large retinue. But a cowherd, who was cognizant of Henning's design to murder his guest, hid himself in the underwood on the roadside, behind a hill a mile distant from our house, and lay in wait for the duke, to whom he disclosed his master's murderous intention, and the duke accordingly returned instantly. The hill was said to have derived its present name, "Wartensberg" or "Watch-mount," from the event. Henning, having found out that his design had been frustrated by the cowherd, in revenge fried the man alive in a large iron pan, and gave him, when he was dying, a last kick with his left foot. Soon after this the duke came with a regiment of soldiers, laid siege to the castle, and captured it. When Henning saw that there was no escape for him, he packed all his treasures in a box and buried it close to the round tower in his garden, the ruins of which are still standing, and he then committed suicide. A long line of flat stones in our churchyard was said to mark the malefactor's grave, from which for centuries his left leg used to grow out, covered with a black silk stocking.[4] Nay, both the sexton Prange and the sacristan Wöllert swore that, when boys, they had themselves cut off the leg and used its bone to knock down pears from the trees, but that, in the beginning of the present century, the leg had suddenly stopped growing out. In my childish simplicity I of course believed all

---

[2] This sepulchre still exists, and when I lately revisited Ankershagen I strongly recommended its present proprietor, the excellent Mr. E. Winckelmann, and his accomplished lady, whose bountiful hospitality I here gratefully acknowledge, to excavate it, on the ground that they would in all probability find there, not indeed a golden cradle, yet very interesting prehistoric antiquities.

[3] In this very same castle, the famous German translator of Homer, J. H. Voss, passed very

unhappy days as tutor. See Dr. Fr. Schlie, *Schliemann und seine Bestrebungen*, who cites W. Herbst, *Johann Heinrich Voss*, i. p. 46.

[4] According to the tradition, one of these legs had been buried just before the altar. Strange to say, when some years ago the church of Ankershagen was being repaired, a single leg-bone was found at a small depth before the altar, as my cousin the Rev. Hans Becker, the present clergyman of Ankershagen, assures me.

this; nay, I often begged my father to excavate the tomb or to allow me to excavate it, in order to see why the foot no longer grew out.

A very deep impression was also made upon my mind by the terra-cotta relief of a man on the back wall of the castle, which was said to be the portrait of Henning Bradenkirl himself. As no paint would stick to it, popular belief averred that it was covered with the blood of the cow-herd, which could not be effaced. A walled-up fireplace in the saloon was indicated as the place where the cowherd had been fried on the iron pan. Though all pains were said to have been taken to obliterate the joints of that terrible chimney, nevertheless they always remained visible; and this too was regarded as a sign from heaven, that the diabolic deed should never be forgotten.

I also believed in a story that Mr. von Gundlach, the proprietor of the neighbouring village, Rumshagen, had excavated a mound near the church, and had discovered in it large wooden barrels containing Roman beer.

Though my father was neither a scholar nor an archæologist, he had a passion for ancient history. He often told me with warm enthusiasm of the tragic fate of Herculaneum and Pompeii, and seemed to consider him the luckiest of men who had the means and the time to visit the excavations which were going on there. He also related to me with admiration the great deeds of the Homeric heroes and the events of the Trojan war, always finding in me a warm defender of the Trojan cause. With great grief I heard from him that Troy had been so completely destroyed, that it had disappeared without leaving any traces of its existence. My joy may be imagined, therefore, when, being nearly eight years old, I received from him, in 1829, as a Christmas gift, Dr. Georg Ludwig Jerrer's *Universal History*,[5] with an engraving representing Troy in flames, with its huge walls and the Scaean gate, from which Aeneas is escaping, carrying his father Anchises on his back and holding his son Ascanius by the hand; and I cried out, "Father, you were mistaken: Jerrer must have seen Troy, otherwise he could not have represented it here." "My son," he replied, "that is merely a fanciful picture." But to my question, whether ancient Troy had such huge walls as those depicted in the book, he answered in the affirmative. "Father," retorted I, "if such walls once existed, they cannot possibly have been completely destroyed: vast ruins of them must still remain, but they are hidden away beneath the dust of ages." He maintained the contrary, whilst I remained firm in my opinion, and at last we both agreed that I should one day excavate Troy.

What weighs on our heart, be it joy or sorrow, always finds utterance from our lips, especially in childhood; and so it happened that I talked of nothing else to my playfellows, but of Troy and of the mysterious and wonderful things in which our village abounded. I was continually laughed at by every one except two young girls, Louise[6] and Minna[7]

[5] Nürnberg, 1828.
[6] Louise Meincke has been, since 1838, the happy wife of the Rev. E. Frölich, and is now living at Neu Brandenburg, in Mecklenburg.
[7] Minna Meincke married, in 1846, the excellent farmer Richers, and is now living happily at Friedland, in Mecklenburg.

Meincke, the daughters of a farmer in Zahren, a village only a mile distant from Ankershagen; the former of whom was my senior by six years, the latter of my own age. Not only did they not laugh at me, but, on the contrary, they always listened to me with profound attention, especially Minna, who showed me the greatest sympathy and entered into all my vast plans for the future. Thus a warm attachment sprang up between us, and in our childish simplicity we exchanged vows of eternal love. In the winter of 1829–30 we took lessons in dancing together, alternately at my little bride's house, at ours, and in the old haunted castle, then occupied by the farmer Mr. Heldt, where, with the same profound interest, we contemplated Henning's bloody bust, the ominous joints of the awful fireplace, the secret passages in the walls, and the entrance to the underground road. Whenever the dancing-lesson was at our house, we would either go to the cemetery before our door, to see whether Henning's foot did not grow out again, or sit down in admiration before the church-registers, written by the hand of Johann Chr. von Schröder and Gottfriederich Heinrich von Schröder, father and son, who had occupied my father's place from 1709 to 1799; the oldest records of births, marriages, and deaths inscribed in those registers having a particular charm for us. Or we would visit together the younger Pastor von Schröder's daughter,[8] then eighty-four years of age, who was living close to us, to question her about the past history of the village, or to look at the portraits of her ancestors,[9] of which that of her mother, Olgartha Christine von Schröder, deceased in 1795, was our special delight, partly because we thought it a masterpiece of workmanship, partly because it resembled Minna.

We also often visited the village tailor Wöllert,[10] who was one-eyed, had only one foot, and was for this reason called " Peter Hüppert," or Hopping Peter. He was illiterate, but had such a prodigious memory that he could repeat my father's sermon word by word after having heard it in church. This man, who might possibly have become one of the greatest scholars of the world, had he had a university education, was full of wit, and excited our curiosity to the utmost by his inexhaustible stock of anec- dotes, which he told with a wonderful oratorical skill. Thus, to give but one of them : he told us how, being desirous to know whither the storks migrated for the winter, he had, in the time of my father's predecessor, Pastor von Russdorf, caught one of the storks which used to build their nests on our barn, and had fastened round its foot a piece of parchment, on which, at his request, the sexton Prange had written that he himself, the sexton, and Wöllert the tailor, at the village of Ankershagen in Meck- lenburg-Schwerin, humbly begged the proprietor of the barn, on which

[8] Deceased in 1844, at the age of 98.

[9] By the kind efforts of Miss Ida Frölich, the accomplished daughter of Mrs. Louise Frölich, all these portraits—five in number—have lately become my property, and I have assigned to them the place of honour in my library, facing the Acropolis of Athens. At the death of Miss von Schröder, these portraits had passed over into the possession of my father's successor, Pastor Con- radi, who had bequeathed them to the church of Ankershagen, but he ceded them to me in order to use the proceeds for presenting to that church, while he still lived, a more durable object, namely, a silver calyx.

[10] Deceased in 1856.

the stork had its nest in the winter, to inform them of the name of his country. When the stork was again caught by him in the spring, another parchment was found attached to its foot, with the following answer in bad German verse :—

> " Schwerin Mecklenburg ist uns nicht bekannt,
> Das Land wo sich der Storch befand
> Nennt sich Sankt Johannes-Land."

" We do not know Schwerin Mecklenburg: the country where the stork was is called Saint John's Land."

Of course we believed all this, and would have given years of our life to know where that mysterious Saint John's Land was to be found. If this and similar anecdotes did not improve our knowledge of geography, at least they stimulated our desire to learn it, and increased our passion for the mysterious.

From our dancing-lessons neither Minna nor I derived any profit at all, whether it was that we had no natural talent for the art, or that our minds were too much absorbed by our important archæological investigations and our plans for the future.

It was agreed between us that as soon as we were grown up we would marry, and then at once set to work to explore all the mysteries of Ankershagen ; excavating the golden cradle, the silver basin, the vast treasures hidden by Henning, then Henning's sepulchre, and lastly Troy ; nay, we could imagine nothing pleasanter than to spend all our lives in digging for the relics of the past.

Thanks to God, my firm belief in the existence of that Troy has never forsaken me amid all the vicissitudes of my eventful career; but it was not destined for me to realize till in the autumn of my life, and then without Minna—nay, far from her—our sweet dreams of fifty years ago.

My father did not know Greek, but he knew Latin, and availed himself of every spare moment to teach it me. When I was hardly nine years old, my dear mother died : this was an irreparable misfortune, perhaps the greatest which could have befallen me and my six brothers and sisters.[11] But my mother's death coincided with another misfortune, which resulted in all our acquaintances suddenly turning their backs upon us and refusing to have any further intercourse with us. I did not care much about the others ; but to see the family of Meincke no more, to separate altogether from Minna—never to behold her again—this was a thousand times more painful to me than my mother's death, which I soon forgot under my overwhelming grief for Minna's loss. In later life I have undergone many great troubles in different parts of the world, but none of them ever caused me a thousandth part of the grief I felt at the tender age of nine years for my separation from my little bride. Bathed in tears and alone, I used to stand for hours each day before Olgartha von Schröder's portrait, remembering in my misery the happy

---

[11] My two brothers are dead. Of my four sisters only the eldest, Elise, is unmarried. The second, Doris, was the happy wife of the late secretary Hans Petrowsky in Roebel (Mecklenburg) ; the third, Wilhelmine, is the happy wife of Professor Wilhelm Kuhse in Dillenburg (Hesse-Cassel) ; and the fourth, Louise, is the happy wife of the teacher Martin Pechel in Dargun (Mecklenburg).

days I had passed in Minna's company. The future appeared dark to me; all the mysterious wonders of Ankershagen, and even Troy itself, lost their interest for a time. Seeing my despondency, my father sent me for two years to his brother, the Reverend Friederich Schliemann,[1] who was the pastor of the village of Kalkhorst in Mecklenburg, where for one year I had the good fortune of having the candidate Carl Andres[2] from Neu Strelitz as a teacher; and the progress I made under this excellent philologist was so great that, at Christmas 1832, I was able to present my father with a badly-written Latin essay upon the principal events of the Trojan war and the adventures of Ulysses and Agamemnon. At the age of eleven I went to the Gymnasium at Neu Strelitz, where I was placed in the third class. But just at that time a great disaster befel our family, and, being afraid that my father would no longer have the means of supporting me for a number of years, I left the gymnasium after being in it only three months, and entered the *Realschule* of the same city, where I was placed in the second class. In the spring of 1835 I advanced to the first class, which I left in April 1836, at the age of fourteen, to become apprentice in the little grocer's shop of Ernest Ludwig Holtz,[3] in the small town of Fürstenberg in Mecklenburg-Strelitz.

A few days before my departure from Neu Strelitz, on Good Friday 1836, I accidentally met Minna Meincke, whom I had not seen for more than five years, at the house of Mr. C. E. Laué.[4] I shall never forget that interview, the last I ever had with her. She had grown much, and was now fourteen years old. Being dressed in plain black, the simplicity of her attire seemed to enhance her fascinating beauty. When we looked at each other, we both burst into a flood of tears and fell speechless into each other's arms. Several times we attempted to speak, but our emotion was too great; neither of us could articulate a word. But soon Minna's parents entered the room, and we had to separate. It took me a long time to recover from my emotion. I was now sure that Minna still loved me, and this thought stimulated my ambition. Nay, from that moment I felt within me a boundless energy, and was sure that with unremitting zeal I could raise myself in the world and show that I was worthy of her. I only implored God to grant that she might not marry before I had attained an independent position.

I was employed in the little grocer's shop at Fürstenberg for five years and a half; for the first year by Mr. Holtz, and afterwards by his successor, the excellent Mr. Theodor Hückstaedt.[5] My occupation consisted in retailing herrings, butter, potato-whiskey, milk, salt, coffee, sugar, oil, and candles; in grinding potatoes for the still, sweeping the shop, and the like employments. Our transactions were on such a small scale, that our aggregate sales hardly amounted to 3000 thalers, or £450 annually; nay, we thought we had extraordinary luck when we sold two

---

[1] Deceased in 1861.

[2] Candidate Carl Andres is now librarian of the Grand-ducal library and keeper of the Museum of Antiquities in Neu Strelitz.

[3] Deceased in 1836.

[4] Mr. Laué died in 1860, but Mrs. Laué, now eighty-four years old, is still living at Neu Strelitz, where the author lately saw her.

[5] Th. Hückstaedt died in 1872, but the little grocer's business is continued by his excellent widow and her son-in-law, Mr. Meyer.

pounds' worth of groceries in a day. There I of course came in contact only with the lowest classes of society. I was engaged from five in the morning till eleven at night, and had not a moment's leisure for study. Moreover I rapidly forgot the little that I had learnt in childhood; but I did not lose the love of learning; indeed I never lost it, and, as long as I live, I shall never forget the evening when a drunken miller came into the shop. His name was Hermann Niederhöffer. He was the son of a Protestant clergyman in Roebel (Mecklenburg), and had almost completed his studies at the Gymnasium of Neu Ruppin, when he was expelled on account of his bad conduct. Not knowing what to do with him, his father apprenticed him to the farmer Langermann in the village of Dambeck; and, as even there his conduct was not exemplary, he again apprenticed him for two years to the miller Dettmann at Güstrow. Dissatisfied with his lot, the young man gave himself up to drink, which, however, had not made him forget his Homer; for on the evening that he entered the shop he recited to us about a hundred lines of the poet, observing the rhythmic cadence of the verses.[6] Although I did not understand a syllable, the melodious sound of the words made a deep impression upon me, and I wept bitter tears over my unhappy fate. Three times over did I get him to repeat to me those divine verses, rewarding his trouble with three glasses of whiskey, which I bought with the few pence that made up my whole fortune. From that moment I never ceased to pray God that by His grace I might yet have the happiness of learning Greek.

There seemed, however, no hope of my escaping from the hapless and humble position in which I found myself. And yet I was relieved from it, as if by a miracle. In lifting a cask too heavy for me, I hurt my chest; I spat blood and was no longer able to work. In despair I went to Hamburg, where I succeeded in obtaining a situation with an annual salary of 180 marks, or £9 sterling: first in the grocer's shop of Lindemann junior, on the Fishmarket in Altona; and afterwards in that of E. L. Deycke junior, at the corner of the Mühren and Matten-Twiete in Hamburg. But as I could not do the heavy work, owing to my weakness in the chest, I was found useless by my employers, and was turned away from each place, after having occupied it for only eight days. Seeing the impossibility of filling a situation as grocer's shopman, and prompted by want to engage in any work, however humble,

---

[6] This Hermann Niederhöffer is now 66 years old, and is living in easy circumstances at Roebel, where the author lately saw him, and instantly recognized him by the pathos with which he declaimed Homer, as well as by other circumstances. Having been born in 1813, he was twenty-four years of age when, in 1837, he entered the little shop of Ernest Ludwig Holtz, at Fürstenberg, where the author was apprenticed. He remained for seven years afterwards, making in all ten years, a journeyman miller, working successively at a great many different places in Germany. Having in 1844 returned to his family at Roebel, through the influence of his relations he obtained employment as communal clerk at Wredenhagen, and remained for four years in that capacity, until in 1848 the magistrate of Roebel gave him the office of collector on a turnpike road. In this employment he at once married an excellent wife, who induced him to give up intoxicating liquors, so that he retained the same place for thirty-one years, only leaving it in the spring of 1879, when he retired to Roebel. Wonderful to say, in spite of all the vicissitudes of his eventful life, he has forgotten neither his Homer nor his Virgil, and still declaims them with the same warm enthusiasm as he did forty-three years ago in the shop at Fürstenberg.

merely to earn my food, I endeavoured to obtain employment on board a ship, and at the recommendation of a very kind-hearted shipbroker, Mr. J. F. Wendt, a native of Sternberg in Mecklenburg, who when a child had been brought up with my late mother, I succeeded in obtaining a situation as cabin-boy on board the little brig *Dorothea*, commanded by Captain Simonsen, owned by the merchants Wachsmuth and Kroogmann of Hamburg, and bound for La Guayra in Venezuela.

I had always been poor, but never yet so utterly destitute as at that time; I had even to sell my only coat in order to buy a blanket. On the 28th of November, 1841, we left Hamburg with a fair wind; but in a few hours it turned contrary, and we were accordingly detained for three days in the river Elbe, near Blankenese, until on the 1st of December the wind again became fair. On that day we passed Cuxhaven and entered the open sea, but we had no sooner reached Heligoland than the wind returned to the west, and remained there up to the 12th of December. We were continually tacking, but made little or no progress, until in the night of the 11th–12th December we were shipwrecked in a fearful storm off the island of Texel, on the bank called "de Eilandsche Grond." After escaping innumerable dangers, and having been tossed about by the fury of the elements for nine hours in a very small open boat, the crew, consisting of nine men, were all saved. I shall always remember with gratitude to Heaven the joyful moment when our boat was thrown by the surf on a bank close to the shore of the Texel, and all danger was over. I did not know the name of the land we had been cast upon, but I perceived that it was a foreign country. I felt as if on that bank a voice whispered to me that the tide in my earthly affairs had come, and that I had to take it at its flood. My belief was confirmed when, on the very day of our arrival, my little box, containing a few shirts and stockings, as well as my pocket-book with the letters of recommendation for La Guayra procured for me by Mr. Wendt, was found floating on the sea and was picked up, while all my comrades and the captain himself lost everything. In consequence of this strange event, they gave me the nickname of "Jonah," by which I was called as long as we remained at the Texel. We were kindly received there by the consuls Sonderdorp and Ram, who proposed to send me, together with the rest of the crew, by way of Harlingen, back to Hamburg. But I declined to return to Germany, where I had been so overwhelmingly unfortunate, telling them that I regarded it as my destiny to remain in Holland, that I intended to proceed to Amsterdam to enlist as a soldier, for I was utterly destitute, and saw, for the moment, no other means of obtaining a living. At my urgent request, therefore, Messrs. Sonderdorp and Ram paid 2 guilders (3s. 4d.) for my passage to Amsterdam.

The wind having now changed to the south, the little vessel by which I was forwarded had to stay a day at the town of Enkhuyzen, and it took us no less than three days to reach the capital of Holland. For want of clothes I suffered fearfully on this passage. Fortune did not smile on me at first at Amsterdam: winter had set in; I had no coat, and was suffering cruelly from the cold. My intention to enlist as a soldier could not be realized so soon as I had imagined; and the few florins which I had collected as alms on the island of Texel and in Enkhuyzen, as well as the two florins which I obtained from Mr. Quack, the consul for Mecklenburg at Amsterdam, were soon spent in the tavern of Mrs. Graalman in the Ramskoy at Amsterdam, where I had taken my lodgings. As my means of living were entirely exhausted, I feigned illness and was taken into the hospital. From this terrible situation I was released by the kind shipbroker already mentioned, Mr. Wendt[7] of Hamburg, to whom I had written from the Texel, informing him of my shipwreck and my intention to try my fortune at Amsterdam. By a lucky chance my letter reached him when he was sitting at a dinner party with numerous friends. The account of the disaster which had befallen me excited universal compassion, and a subscription which he at once raised for me produced the sum of 240 florins (£20), which he sent me through Consul Quack. At the same time, he recommended me to the excellent Consul-General of Prussia at Amsterdam, Mr. W. Hepner,[8] who procured me a situation in the office of Mr. F. C. Quien.[9]

In my new situation my work consisted in stamping bills of exchange and getting them cashed in the town, and in carrying letters to and from the post-office. This mechanical occupation suited me, for it left me time to think of my neglected education.

First of all I took pains to learn to write legibly, and this I succeeded in doing after twenty lessons from the famous calligraphist Magnée, of Brussels. Afterwards, in order to improve my position, I applied myself to the study of modern languages. My annual salary amounted only to 800 francs (£32), half of which I spent upon my studies; on the other half I lived—miserably enough, to be sure. My lodging, which cost 8 francs a month, was a wretched garret without a fire, where I shivered with cold in winter and was scorched with the heat in summer. My breakfast consisted of rye-meal porridge, and my dinner never cost more than two-pence. But nothing spurs one on to study more than misery and the certain prospect of being able to release oneself from it by unremitting work. Besides, the desire of showing myself worthy of Minna created and developed in me a boundless courage. I applied myself with extraordinary diligence to the study of English. Necessity taught me a method which greatly facilitates the study of a language. This method consists in reading a great deal aloud, without making a translation, taking a lesson every day, constantly writing essays upon subjects of interest, correcting these under the supervision of a teacher, learning them by heart, and repeating in the next lesson what was corrected on the previous day. My memory was bad, since from my childhood it had not been exercised upon any object; but I made use of every moment, and even stole time for study.

---

[7] My benefactor J. F. Wendt died in January 1856.

[8] Consul Hepner died in 1870.

[9] The commercial house of F. C. Quien still exists at Amsterdam, under the same name. The founder of the house is dead, but his two sons, Charles and George Quien, who were already partners in the house when the author first entered it at the beginning of 1842, are both still alive.

In order to acquire a good pronunciation quickly, I went twice every Sunday to the English church, and repeated to myself in a low voice every word of the clergyman's sermon. I never went on my errands, even in the rain, without having my book in my hand and learning something by heart; and I never waited at the post-office without reading. By such methods I gradually strengthened my memory, and in three months' time found no difficulty in reciting from memory to my teacher, Mr. Taylor, in each day's lesson, word by word, twenty printed pages, after having read them over three times attentively. In this way I committed to memory the whole of Goldsmith's *Vicar of Wakefield* and Sir Walter Scott's *Ivanhoe.* From over-excitement I slept but little, and employed my sleepless hours at night in going over in my mind what I had read on the preceding evening. The memory being always much more concentrated at night than in the day-time, *I found these repetitions at night of paramount use.* Thus I succeeded in acquiring in half a year a thorough knowledge of the English language.

I then applied the same method to the study of French, the difficulties of which I overcame likewise in another six months. Of French authors I learned by heart the whole of Fénelon's *Aventures de Télémaque* and Bernardin de Saint Pierre's *Paul et Virginie.* This unremitting study had in the course of a single year strengthened my memory to such a degree, that the study of Dutch, Spanish, Italian, and Portuguese appeared very easy, and it did not take me more than six weeks to write and speak each of these languages fluently.

Whether from my continual readings in a loud voice, or from the effect of the moist air of Holland, my complaint in the chest gradually disappeared during my first year's residence in Amsterdam, and it has never returned. But my passion for study caused me to neglect my mechanical occupation in the office of Mr. F. C. Quien, especially as I began to consider it beneath me. My principals would give me no promotion; they probably thought that a person who shows his incapacity for the business of a servant in an office proves thereby his unfitness for any higher duties. At last, however, through the intercession of my worthy friends, Louis Stoll[10] of Mannheim and J. H. Ballauf[11] of Bremen, I had on the 1st of March, 1844, the good fortune to obtain a situation as correspondent and book-keeper in the office of Messrs. B. H. Schröder & Co. of Amsterdam,[1] who engaged me at a salary of 1200 francs (£48); but when they saw my zeal, they added 800 francs a year more by way of encouragement. This generosity, for which I shall ever be grateful to them, was in fact the foundation of my prosperity; for, as I thought that I could make myself still more useful by a knowledge of Russian, I set to work to learn that language also. But the only Russian books I could procure were an old grammar,

---

[10] Mr. L. Stoll is still flourishing at Mannheim.

[11] Deceased in 1873.

[1] The house of B. H. Schröder and Co. of Amsterdam still exists and continues to flourish.

Mr. B. H. Schröder died in 1849, but Mr. Henry Schröder, the same who personally engaged me on the 1st of March, 1844, and who was then already a partner in the house, is still one of its principals.

a lexicon, and a bad translation of *Les Aventures de Télémaque*. In spite of all my enquiries, I could not find a teacher of Russian, since, with the exception of the Russian Vice-Consul, Mr. Tannenberg, who would not consent to give me lessons, there was no one in Amsterdam who understood a word of the language. So I betook myself to the study of it without a master, and, with the help of the grammar, I learned the Russian letters and their pronunciation in a few days. Then, following my old method, I began to write short stories of my own composition, and to learn them by heart. As I had no one to correct my work, it was, no doubt, extremely bad; but I tried at the same time to correct my mistakes by the practical exercise of learning the Russian *Aventures de Télémaque* by heart. It occurred to me that I should make more progress if I had some one to whom I could relate the adventures of Telemachus; so I hired a poor Jew for four francs a week, who had to come every evening for two hours to listen to my Russian recitations, of which he did not understand a syllable.

As the ceilings of the rooms of the common houses in Holland consist of single boards, people on the ground-floor can hear what is said in the third storey. My recitations therefore, delivered in a loud voice, annoyed the other tenants, who complained to the landlord, and twice while studying the Russian language I was forced to change my lodgings. But these inconveniences did not diminish my zeal, and in the course of six weeks I wrote my first Russian letter to Mr. Vasili Plotnikoff, the London agent for the great indigo-dealers, Messrs. M. P. N. Malutin Brothers,[2] at Moscow, and I found myself able to converse fluently with him and the Russian merchants Matweieff and Froloff, when they came to Amsterdam for the indigo auctions. After I had completed my study of the Russian language, I began to occupy myself seriously with the literatures of the languages I had learned.

In January, 1846, my worthy principals sent me as their agent to St. Petersburg. Here, as well as in Moscow, my exertions were in the very first two months crowned with the fullest success, which far exceeded the most sanguine expectations of my employers and myself. No sooner had I rendered myself indispensable to Messrs. B. H. Schröder & Co. in my new career, and thus obtained a practically independent position, than I hastened to write to the friend of the Meincke family, Mr. C. E. Laué of Neu Strelitz, describing to him all my adventures, and begging him to ask Minna at once for me in marriage. But, to my horror, I received a month later the heartrending answer, that she was just married. I considered this disappointment at the time as the greatest disaster which could have befallen me, and I was for some time utterly unfit for any occupation and sick in bed. I constantly recalled to mind all that had passed between Minna and myself in early childhood, all our sweet dreams and vast plans, for the ultimate realization of which I now saw such a brilliant chance before me; but how could I think of

---

[2] The three brothers Malutin have been long dead, but the commercial house continues to flourish under the same name.

realizing them without her participation? Then again I bitterly accused myself for not having demanded her in marriage before proceeding to St. Petersburg; but again I recollected that I could not have done so without exposing myself to ridicule, because while in Amsterdam I was only a clerk, and my position was a dependent one, subject to the caprice of my employers; besides, I was not sure of succeeding at St. Petersburg, where instead of success I might have made a complete failure. I fancied that neither could she be happy with anyone else besides me, nor that I could possibly ever live with another wife but her. Why then should fate be so cruel as to tear her from me when, after having for sixteen long years striven to reach her, I seemed at last to have succeeded in attaining her? It had indeed happened to Minna and me as it often happens to us in our sleep, when we dream that we are pursuing some-body and can never catch him, because as often as we reach him he escapes us again. I thought I could never get over the misfortune of losing Minna as the partner of my life; but time, which heals all wounds, at last healed mine, so that, although I remained for years mourning for her, I could at least continue my mercantile pursuits without further interruption.

In my very first year at St. Petersburg my operations had already been so successful, that in the beginning of 1847 I was inscribed in the Guild as a wholesale merchant. But, in spite of my new functions, I remained in connection with Messrs. B. H. Schröder and Co. of Amsterdam, whose agency I kept for nearly eleven years. As I had acquired in Amsterdam a thorough knowledge of indigo, my transactions were almost exclusively limited to that article; and, as long as my fortune was below 200,000 frs. (£8000), I never gave credit except to merchants of the very first standing. Thus I had to content myself at first with very small profits, but my business was a perfectly safe one.

Not having heard of my brother, Louis Schliemann, who in the beginning of 1849 had emigrated to California, I went thither in the spring of 1850, and found that he was dead. Happening, therefore, to be in California when, on the 4th of July, 1850, it was made a State, and all those then resident in the country became by that very fact naturalized Americans, I joyfully embraced the opportunity of becoming a citizen of the United States.

At the end of 1852 I established a branch-house at Moscow for wholesale dealing in indigo, first under the direction of my excellent agent, Mr. Alexei Matweieff, and after his death under the direction of his servant Jutchenko, whom I raised to the dignity of a merchant of the Second Guild, considering that an able servant may easily become a good director, whilst a director can never become a good servant.

As I was always overwhelmed with work at St. Petersburg, I could not continue my linguistic studies there, and it was not until the year 1854 that I found it possible to acquire the Swedish and Polish languages.

Divine Providence protected me marvellously, and on more than one occasion I was saved from apparently certain destruction by a mere accident. All my life long I shall remember the morning of the 4th of

October, 1854. It was at the time of the Crimean war. The Russian ports being blockaded, all the merchandise intended for St. Petersburg had to be shipped to the Prussian ports of Memel or Königsberg, thence to be forwarded overland. Some hundreds of chests of indigo, as well as large quantities of other goods, had been thus shipped by Messrs. J. Henry Schröder & Co. of London [3] and Messrs. B. H. Schröder & Co. of Amsterdam, on my account, by two steamers to my agents, Messrs. Meyer & Co. of Memel, to be sent on by the latter overland to St. Petersburg. I had just returned from the indigo auctions at Amsterdam in order to see after my goods at Memel, and had arrived late in the evening of the 3rd of October at the Hôtel de Prusse in Königsberg, when, happening to look out of the window of my bedroom on the following morning, I saw the following ominous inscription, written in large gilt letters on the tower of the gate close by, called " das Grüne Thor :" [4]—

> " Vultus fortunae variatur imagine lunae,
> Crescit decrescit, constans persistere nescit."

Though I am not superstitious, the inscription made a profound impression upon me, and I was seized with a kind of panic, as though an unknown disaster were hanging over me. In continuing my journey by the mail-coach, I was horror-stricken to learn, at the first station beyond Tilsit, that the whole city of Memel had been consumed on the previous day by a fearful conflagration; and I saw this but too well confirmed on my arrival before the city, which resembled an immense graveyard on which blackened walls and chimneys stood out like tombstones, mournful monuments of the fragility of human things. Almost in despair, I ran among the smouldering ruins in search of Mr. Meyer. At last I found him, and asked him whether my goods were safe: by way of answer, he pointed to his smouldering warehouses and said, "There they are buried." The blow was tremendous: by eight and a half years' hard labour in St. Petersburg I had only saved 150,000 thalers, or £22,500, and this was now all lost. But no sooner had I acquired the certainty that I was ruined, than I recovered my presence of mind. It gave me great comfort to think that I had no debts to pay, for it was only at the beginning of the Crimean war, and business being then very unsafe, I had bought only for cash. So I thought Messrs. Schröder of London and Amsterdam would give me credit, and I felt confident that I should make up the loss in course of time. In the evening, when on the point of leaving by the mail for St. Petersburg, I was telling my misfortune to the other passengers, when a bystander suddenly asked me my name, and, having heard it, exclaimed : " Schliemann is the only man who has not lost anything! I am Meyer & Co.'s first clerk. Our warehouse being

---

[3] The house of Messrs. J. Henry Schröder and Co. of London and Hamburg, with whom I have had the good fortune to be in connection now for thirty-four years, is one of the richest and most eminent commercial houses in the world. The senior partner, the venerable Baron John Henry von Schröder, now ninety-six years old, the founder of the celebrated house of benevo-lence *das Schrödersche Stift*, still manages the Hamburg house; his partner is the very able Mr. Vogler. The London house is managed by the venerable Baron J. H. W. Schröder, jun., and his very able partners Mr. Henry Tiarks and Mr. von der Meden.

[4] This gate was pulled down in August 1864, in consequence of municipal improvements.

crammed full of goods when the steamers arrived with his merchandise, we were obliged to build close to it a wooden barrack, in which all his property lies perfectly safe."

The sudden transition from profound grief to great joy is difficult to bear without tears: I was for some minutes speechless; it seemed to me like a dream and incredible that I alone should have escaped unhurt from the universal ruin. But so it was. The strangest thing was that the fire had originated in Meyer & Co.'s stone warehouse, at the northern extremity of the town, whence, owing to a furious gale which was blowing from the north at the time, the flames rapidly spread over the whole city; whereas, under the protection of the same storm, the wooden barrack remained unhurt, though it was not more than a couple of yards north of the warehouse. My goods having thus been preserved, I speedily sold them to great advantage; turned the money over and over again; did a large business in indigo, dyewoods, and war material (saltpetre, brimstone, and lead); and, as capitalists were afraid to do much business during the Crimean war, I was able to realize large profits, and more than doubled my capital in a single year. I was greatly assisted in my transactions during the Crimean war by the great tact and ability of my agent, my dear friend Mr. Isidor Lichtenstein, senior, partner in the house of Messrs. Marcus Cohn & Son at Königsberg, and his junior partner, Mr. Ludwig Leo, who forwarded all my transit goods to me with a promptitude really wonderful.

My wish to learn Greek had always been great, but before the Crimean war I did not venture upon its study, for I was afraid that this language would exercise too great a fascination over me and estrange me from my commercial business; and during the war I was so overwhelmed with work, that I could not even read the newspapers, far less a book. When, however, in January 1856, the first tidings of peace reached St. Petersburg, I was no longer able to restrain my desire to learn Greek, and at once set vigorously to work, taking first as my teacher Mr. Nicolaos Pappadakes and then Mr. Theokletos Vimpos, both from Athens, where the latter is now archbishop. I again faithfully followed my old method; but in order to acquire quickly the Greek vocabulary, which seemed to me far more difficult even than the Russian, I procured a modern Greek translation of *Paul et Virginie*, and read it through, comparing every word with its equivalent in the French original. When I had finished this task, I knew at least one-half the Greek words the book contained, and after repeating the operation I knew them all, or nearly so, without having lost a single minute by being obliged to use a dictionary. In this manner it did not take me more than six weeks to master the difficulties of modern Greek, and I next applied myself to the ancient language, of which in three months I learned sufficient to understand some of the ancient authors, and especially Homer, whom I read and re-read with the most lively enthusiasm.

I then occupied myself for two years exclusively with the literature of ancient Greece; and during this time I read almost all the classical authors cursorily, and the *Iliad* and *Odyssey* several times. Of the

Greek grammar, I learned only the declensions and the verbs, and never lost my precious time in studying its rules ; for as I saw that boys, after being troubled and tormented for eight years and more in schools with the tedious rules of grammar, can nevertheless none of them write a letter in ancient Greek without making hundreds of atrocious blunders, I thought the method pursued by the schoolmasters must be altogether wrong, and that a thorough knowledge of the Greek grammar could only be obtained by practice,—that is to say, by the attentive reading of the prose classics, and by committing choice pieces of them to memory. Following this very simple method, I learnt ancient Greek as I would have learnt a living language. I can write in it with the greatest fluency on any subject I am acquainted with, and can never forget it. I am perfectly acquainted with all the grammatical rules without even knowing whether or not they are contained in the grammars ; and whenever a man finds errors in my Greek, I can immediately prove that I am right, by merely reciting passages from the classics where the sentences employed by me occur.[5]

Meanwhile my mercantile affairs in St. Petersburg and Moscow went on steadily and favourably. I was very cautious in my business; and although I received severe blows during the fearful commercial crisis of 1857, they did not hurt me much, and even in that disastrous year I made, after all, some profits.

In the summer of 1858 I renewed with my friend, Professor Ludwig von Muralt,[6] in St. Petersburg, my study of the Latin language, which had been interrupted for nearly twenty-five years. Now that I knew both modern and ancient Greek, I found the Latin language easy enough, and soon mastered its difficulties.

I therefore strongly recommend all directors of colleges and schools to introduce the method I have followed; to do away with the abominable English pronunciation of Greek, which has never been in use outside of England ; to let children first be taught modern Greek by native Greek professors, and only afterwards begin ancient Greek

---

[5] I hear with pleasure from my honoured friend Professor Rudolf Virchow of Berlin, that he learned the classical languages in a similar way ; he writes to me on the subject as follows : " Up to my thirteenth year I took private lessons in a small Pomeranian town. My last teacher there was the second clergyman, whose custom was to make me translate and write a great deal extemporaneously ; on the other hand, he did not let me learn by heart a single grammatical rule in the stricter sense of the word. In this way the learning of the ancient languages afforded me so much pleasure, that I also very frequently made translations for myself which had not been set me as a task. When I was sent to the Gymnasium at Coslin, the director was so highly pleased with my Latin that, until my departure from the school, I remained his particular favourite. On the other hand, the teacher of Greek, Professor Grieben, who had studied theology, could so little conceive how any one could make a good Greek translation without a literal knowledge of Buttmann's Grammar, that he openly accused me of deceit ; even when in spite of all his vigilance he could not detect me in any illicit expedient, he nevertheless pursued me with his suspicions until my *examen abiturientis*. At this he examined me out of the Greek text of the New Testament ; and, when I passed successfully, he declared to the assembled teachers, who unanimously bestowed upon me a favourable testimony, that he had to decide against me, since I did not possess the maturity of morals required for the University. Fortunately this protest remained without effect. Having passed the examination, I sat down in my room and learned Italian without any assistance."

[6] Professor von Muralt is now living at Lausanne, in Switzerland.

when they can speak and write the modern language with fluency, which it can hardly take them more than six months to do. The same professors can teach the ancient language, and by following my method they will enable intelligent boys to master all its difficulties in a year, so that they will not only learn it as a living language, but will also understand the ancient classics, and be able to write fluently on any subject they are acquainted with.

This is no idle theory, but a stubborn fact, which therefore ought to be listened to. It is a cruel injustice to inflict for years upon an unhappy pupil a language of which, when he leaves college, as a general rule he knows hardly more than when he first began to learn it. The causes of this miserable result are, in the first place, the arbitrary and atrocious pronunciation of Greek usual in England;[7] and in the second place the erroneous method employed, according to which the pupils learn to disregard the accents entirely, and to consider them as mere impediments, whereas the accents constitute a most important auxiliary in learning the language. What a happy effect would be produced on general education, and what an enormous stimulus would be given to scientific pursuits, if intelligent youths could obtain in eighteen months a thorough knowledge of modern Greek, and of that most beautiful, most divine, and most sonorous language, which was spoken by Homer and Plato, and could learn the latter as a living tongue, so as never to forget it! And how easily, at how small an expense, could the change be made! Greece abounds with highly-educated men, who have a thorough knowledge of the language of their ancestors, who are perfectly acquainted with all the classics, and who would gladly and at moderate salaries accept places in England or America. How greatly the knowledge of modern Greek assists the student in mastering ancient Greek I could not illustrate better than by the fact, that I have seen here in Athens office-clerks who, feeling no inclination for commerce, have left the counting-house, settled down to study, and been able in four months' time to understand Homer, and even Thucydides.

Latin should, in my opinion, be taught not before, but after, Greek.

In the year 1858 I thought I had money enough, and wished to retire from commercial pursuits. I travelled in Sweden, Denmark, Germany, Italy, and Egypt, where I sailed up the Nile as far as the Second Cataracts. I availed myself of this opportunity to learn Arabic, and I afterwards travelled across the desert from Cairo to Jerusalem. I visited Petra, and traversed the whole of Syria; and in this manner had abundant opportunity of acquiring a practical knowledge of Arabic, the deeper study of which I continued afterwards in St. Petersburg. After leaving Syria I visited Smyrna, the Cyclades, and Athens, in the summer of 1859, and I was on the point of starting for the island of Ithaca when

---

[7] To say the least, Greek was pronounced 892 years ago precisely as it is now in Greece, since all the Greek words borrowed by the Russian language, when in 988 A.D. Russia adopted the Greek religion, are pronounced in Russian just as they are now pronounced in Greece. The same may be said of the Greek names which occur in the cuneiform inscriptions of the time of the Seleucids.

I was seized with fever. At the same time I received information from St. Petersburg that a merchant, Mr. Stepan Solovieff, who had failed, owing me a large sum of money, and with whom I had agreed that he should repay it in the course of four years by annual instalments, not only had not made his first payment, but had brought a suit against me in the Commercial Court. I therefore hurried back to St. Petersburg, was cured of fever by the change of air, and promptly gained my cause. But my antagonist appealed to the Senate, where no lawsuit can be terminated in less than three and a half or four years; and my presence on the spot being necessary, I went into business once more, much against my will, and on a much larger scale than before. My imports from May to October 1860 reached as high a sum as £500,000. Besides indigo and olive oil, I also in 1860 and 1861 embarked largely in cotton, which gave great profits, owing to the Civil War in the United States of America, and the blockade of the Southern ports. But when cotton became too dear, I abandoned it, and in its stead went into tea, the importation of which by sea was permitted from May 1862 and onwards. My first tea order to Messrs. J. Henry Schröder and Co. of London was for 30 chests; and when these were advantageously disposed of, I imported 1000, and afterwards 4000 and 6000 chests. I also bought of Mr. J. E. Günzburg of St. Petersburg, who was withdrawing from the trade in goods, his whole stock of tea, at a cheap rate, and gained in the first six months £7000 on my transactions in that commodity. But when in the winter of 1862–1863 the insurrection broke out in Poland, and the Jews, profiting by the disorder then prevailing there, smuggled immense quantities of tea into Russia, I could not stand this competition, being obliged to pay the high import duty. I therefore retired again from the tea trade, but it took me a long time to sell at a small profit the 6000 chests which had remained on my hands. But my staple commodity always remained indigo; for, as I knew the article well, and was always favoured by Messrs. John Henry Schröder and Co. of London with choice and cheap purchases, and as I also imported large quantities direct from Calcutta, and never confided the sale of indigo to clerks or servants, as others did, but always stood myself in my warehouse, and showed and sold it personally and wholesale to the indigo dealers, I had no competition to fear, and my net profit on this article was on an average £10,000 annually, with 6 per cent. interest on the capital employed.

Heaven continued to bless all my mercantile undertakings in a wonderful manner, so that at the end of 1863 I found myself in possession of a fortune such as my ambition had never ventured to aspire to. But in the midst of the bustle of business I never forgot Troy, or the agreement I had made with my father and Minna in 1830 to excavate it. I loved money indeed, but solely as the means of realizing this great idea of my life. Besides, I had recommenced business much against my will, and merely in order to have some occupation and distraction while the tedious lawsuit with the merchant who had attacked me was going on. When therefore his appeal had been rejected by the Senate, and I had received from him the last payment, in December 1863, I began to liquidate my business. But before devoting myself entirely to archæology, and to the realization of the dream of my life, I wished to see a little more of the world. So I started in April, 1864, for Tunis, to investigate the ruins of Carthage, and went thence, by way of Egypt, to India. I visited in succession the island of Ceylon, Madras, Calcutta, Benares, Agra, Lucknow, Delhi, the Himalaya Mountains, Singapore, and the island of Java, and stayed for two months in China, where I visited Hong Kong, Canton, Amoy, Foochoo, Shanghai, Tin-Sin, Peking, and the Great Wall. I then went to Yokohama and Jeddo in Japan, and thence crossed the Pacific Ocean in a small English vessel to San Francisco in California. Our passage lasted fifty days, which I employed in writing my first work, *La Chine et le Japon.*[8] From San Francisco I went, by way of Nicaragua, to the Eastern United States, travelled through most of them, visited Havannah and the city of Mexico, and in the spring of 1866 settled down in Paris to study archæology, henceforth with no other interruption than short trips to America.

§ II. First Visits to Ithaca, the Peloponnesus, and Troy: 1868, 1870.

At last I was able to realize the dream of my life, and to visit at my leisure the scene of those events which had always had such an intense interest for me, and the country of the heroes whose adventures had delighted and comforted my childhood. I started therefore, in April 1868, by way of Rome and Naples, for Corfu, Cephalonia, and Ithaca. This famous island I investigated carefully; but the only excavations I made there were in the so-called Castle of Ulysses, on the top of Mount Aëtos. I found the local character of Ithaca to agree perfectly with the indications of the *Odyssey*, and shall have occasion to describe this island more fully in the subsequent pages.

I afterwards visited the Peloponnesus, and particularly examined the ruins of Mycenae, where it appeared to me that the passage in Pausanias[9] in which the Royal Sepulchres are mentioned, and which has now become so famous, had been wrongly interpreted; and that, contrary to the general belief, those tombs were not at all understood by that writer to be in the lower town, but in the Acropolis itself. I visited Athens, and started from the Piraeus for the Dardanelles, whence I went to the village of Bounarbashi, at the southern extremity of the Plain of Troy. Bounarbashi, together with the rocky heights behind it, called the Bali Dagh, had until then, *in recent times*, been almost universally considered to be the site of the Homeric Ilium; the springs at the foot of that village having been regarded as the two springs mentioned by Homer,[10] one of which sent forth warm, the other cold water. But, instead of only two springs, I found thirty-four, and probably there are forty, the site of them being called by the Turks Kirk-Giös,—that is to say, "forty eyes;" moreover, I found in all the springs a uniform temperature of 17° centigrade, equal to 62°·6 Fahrenheit. In addition to this, the distance of Bounar-

---

[8] Paris, 1866, Librairie Centrale.   [9] Paus. ii. 16, § 4.   [10] *Il.* xxii. 147–156.

bashi from the Hellespont is, in a straight line, eight miles, whilst all the indications of the *Iliad* seem to prove that the distance between Ilium and the Hellespont was but very short, hardly exceeding three miles. Nor would it have been possible for Achilles to have pursued Hector in the plain round the walls of Troy, had Troy stood on the summit of Bounarbashi. I was therefore at once convinced that the Homeric city could not possibly have been here. Nevertheless, I wished to investigate so important a matter by actual excavations, and took a number of workmen to sink pits in hundreds of different places, between the forty springs and the extremity of the heights. But at the springs, as well as in Bounarbashi and everywhere else, I found only pure virgin soil, and struck the rock at a very small depth. At the southern end of the heights alone there are some ruins belonging to a very small fortified place, which I hold with the learned archæologist, my friend Mr. Frank Calvert, United States Vice-Consul at the Dardanelles, to be identical with the ancient city of Gergis. Here the late Austrian Consul, G. von Hahn, made some excavations, in May 1864, in company with the astronomer Schmidt, of Athens. The average depth of the *débris* was found not to exceed a foot and a half; and Von Hahn, as well as myself, discovered there only fragments of inferior Hellenic pottery of the Macedonian time, and not a single relic of archaic pottery. The walls too of this little citadel, in which so many great luminaries of archæology have recognized the walls of Priam's Pergamus, have been erroneously called Cyclopean.

Bounarbashi having thus given negative results, I next carefully examined all the heights to the right and left of the Trojan Plain, but my researches bore no fruits until I came to the site of the city called by Strabo New Ilium,[1] which is at a distance of only three miles from the Hellespont, and perfectly answers in this, as well as in all other respects, to the topographical requirements of the *Iliad*. My particular attention was attracted to the spot by the imposing position and natural fortifications of the hill called HISSARLIK, which formed the north-western corner of Novum Ilium, and seemed to me to mark the site of its Acropolis as well as of the Pergamus of Priam. According to the measurement of my friend M. Émile Burnouf, honorary director of the French School at Athens, the elevation of this hill is 49°·43 mètres or 162 ft. above the level of the sea.

In a hole dug here at random by two villagers, some twenty-five years ago, on the brink of the northern slope, in a part of the hill which belonged to two Turks of Koum-Kaleh, there was found a small treasure of about 1200 silver staters of Antiochus III.

The first recent writer who asserted the identity of Hissarlik with the Homeric Troy was Maclaren.[2] He showed by the most convincing arguments that Troy could never have been on the heights of Bounarbashi, and that, if it ever existed, Hissarlik must mark its site. But already

---

[1] Or, to use his exact phrase, "the present Ilium," the Ilium of his day, τὸ νῦν Ἴλιον, ἡ νῦν πόλις, τὸ σημερινὸν Ἴλιον.

[2] *Dissertation on the Topography of the Plain of Troy*, Edinburgh, 1822; and *The Plain of Troy described*, Edinburgh, 1863.

before him, Dr. Edw. Dan. Clarke[3] had declared himself against Bounar-bashi, and thought that the Homeric city had been at the village of Chiblak, a theory afterwards adopted by P. Barker Webb.[4] Such weighty authorities as George Grote,[5] Julius Braun,[6] and Gustav von Ecken-brecher,[7] have also declared in favour of Hissarlik. Mr. Frank Calvert further, who began by upholding the theory which placed Troy at Bounarbashi, became, through the arguments of the above writers, and particularly, it appears, through those of Maclaren and Barker Webb, a convert to the Troy-Hissarlik theory and a valiant champion of it. He owns nearly one-half of Hissarlik, and in two small ditches he had dug on his property he had brought to light before my visit some remains of the Macedonian and Roman periods; as well as part of the wall of Hellenic masonry, which, according to Plutarch (in his Life of Alexander), was built by Lysimachus. I at once decided to commence excavations here, and announced this intention in the work *Ithaque, le Péloponnèse et Troie*, which I published at the end of 1868.[8] Having sent a copy of this work, together with a dissertation in ancient Greek, to the University of Rostock, that learned body honoured me with the diploma of Doctor of Philosophy. With unremitting zeal I have ever since endeavoured to show myself worthy of the dignity conferred on me.

In the book referred to I mentioned (p. 97) that, according to my interpretation of the passage of Pausanias (ii. 16, § 4) in which he speaks of the Sepulchres at Mycenae, the Royal Tombs must be looked for in the Acropolis itself, and not in the lower town. As this inter-pretation of mine was in opposition to that of all other scholars, it was at the time refused a hearing; now, however, that in 1876 I have actu-ally found these sepulchres, with their immense treasures, on the very site indicated by me, it would seem that my critics were in the wrong and not myself.

Circumstances obliged me to remain nearly the whole of the year 1869 in the United States, and it was therefore only in April 1870 that I was able to return to Hissarlik and make a preliminary excavation, in order to test the depth to which the artificial soil extended. I made it at the north-western corner, in a place where the hill had increased considerably in size, and where, consequently, the accumulation of *débris* of the Hellenic period was very great. Hence it was only after digging 16 ft. below the surface, that I laid bare a wall of huge stones, 6½ ft. thick, which, as my later excavations have shown, belonged to a tower of the Macedonian epoch.

---

[3] *Travels in various Countries of Europe, Asia, and Africa;* London, 1812.

[4] *Topographie de la Troade ;* Paris, 1844.

[5] *Hist. of Greece;* 4th edit. London, 1872, i. pp. 305, 306.

[6] *Geschichte der Kunst in ihrem Entwicklungs-gange,* Wiesbaden, 1856 ; and *Homer und sein Zeitalter,* Heidelberg, 1856–1858, ii. pp. 206–274.

[7] *Die Lage des Homerischen Troja ;* Düssel-dorf, 1875.

[8] In French, published by C. Reinwald, 15 rue des Saints Pères, Paris; in German, by F. A. Brockhaus, Leipzig.

§ III. First Year's Work at Hissarlik : 1871.

In order to carry on more extensive excavations I needed a firman from the Sublime Porte, which I only obtained in September 1871, through the kind offices of my friends the United States Minister Resident at Constantinople, Mr. Wyne McVeagh, and the late dragoman of the United States Legation, Mr. John P. Brown.

At length, on the 27th of September, I made my way to the Dardanelles, together with my wife, Sophia Schliemann, who is a native of Athens and a warm admirer of Homer, and who, with glad enthusiasm, joined me in executing the great work which, nearly half a century ago, my childish simplicity had agreed upon with my father and planned with Minna. But we met with ever-recurring difficulties on the part of the Turkish authorities, and it was not until the 11th of October that we could fairly commence our work. There being no other shelter, we were obliged to live in the neighbouring Turkish village of Chiblak, a mile and a quarter from Hissarlik. After working with an average number of eighty labourers daily up to the 24th of November, we were compelled to cease the excavations for the winter. But during that interval we had been able to make a large trench on the face of the steep northern slope, and to dig down to a depth of 33 ft. below the surface of the hill.

We first found there the remains of the later Aeolic Ilium, which, on an average, reached to a depth of $6\frac{1}{2}$ ft. Unfortunately we were obliged to destroy the foundations of a building, 59 ft. long and 43 ft. broad, of large wrought stones, which, by the inscriptions found in or close to it, which will be given in the chapter on the Greek Ilium, seems to have been the Bouleuterion or Senate House. Below these Hellenic ruins, and to a depth of about 13 ft., the *débris* contained a few stones, and some very coarse hand-made pottery. Below this stratum I came to a large number of house-walls, of unwrought stones cemented with earth, and, for the first time, met with immense quantities of stone implements and saddle-querns, together with more coarse hand-made pottery. From about 20 ft. to 30 ft. below the surface, nothing was found but calcined *débris*, immense masses of sun-dried or slightly-baked bricks and house-walls of the same, numbers of saddle-querns, but fewer stone implements of other kinds, and much better hand-made pottery. At a depth of 30 ft. and 33 ft. we discovered fragments of house-walls of large stones, many of them rudely hewn ; we also came upon a great many very large blocks. The stones of these house-walls appeared as if they had been separated from one another by a violent earthquake. My instruments for excavating were very imperfect : I had to work with only pickaxes, wooden shovels, baskets, and eight wheelbarrows.

§ IV. Second Year's Work at Hissarlik : 1872.

I returned to Hissarlik with my wife at the end of March 1872, and resumed the excavations with 100 workmen. But I was soon able to increase the number of my labourers to 130, and had often even 150 men at work. I was now well prepared for the work, having been

provided by my honoured friends, Messrs. John Henry Schröder & Co.
of London, with the very best English wheelbarrows, pickaxes, and
spades, and having also procured three overseers and an engineer, Mr.
A. Laurent, to make the maps and plans. The last received monthly
£20, the overseers £6 each and my servant £7 4s.; whilst the daily
wages of my common labourers were 1 fr. 80 c., or about 18 pence
sterling. I now built on the top of Hissarlik a wooden house, with three
rooms and a magazine, kitchen, &c., and covered the buildings with
waterproof felt to protect them from the rain.[9]

No. 1.   Troy as seen from Koum Kioi, in June 1879.

On the steep northern slope of Hissarlik, which rises at an angle
of 45°, and at a perpendicular depth of 46½ ft. below the surface, I
dug out a platform 233 ft. wide, and found there an immense number of
poisonous snakes; among them remarkably numerous specimens of the
small brown adder called *antelion* (ἀντήλιον), which is hardly thicker
than an earthworm, and gets its name from the vulgar belief, that the
person bitten by it only survives till sunset.

I first struck the rock at a depth of about 53 ft. below the surface of
the hill, and found the lowest stratum of artificial soil to consist of very
compact *débris* of houses, as hard as stone, and house-walls of small
pieces of unwrought or very rudely cut limestone, put together so that
the joint between two of the stones in a lower layer is always covered by
a single stone in the course above it. This lowest stratum was succeeded
by house-walls built of large limestone blocks, generally unwrought, but
often rudely cut into something resembling a quadrangular shape. Sometimes I came upon large masses of such massive blocks lying close upon
one another, and having all the appearance of being the broken walls
of some large building. There is no trace of a general conflagration,
either in this stratum of buildings built with large stones or in the
lowest layer of *débris*; indeed, the multitudinous shells found in these
two lowest strata are uninjured, which sufficiently proves that they have
not been exposed to a great heat. I found in these two lowest strata the

---

[9] These houses are seen in the views on the subsequent pages, No. 5 on p. 29, &c.

same stone implements as before, but the pottery is different. The pottery differs also from that in the upper strata.

As the cutting of the great platform on the north side of Hissarlik advanced but slowly, I began on the 1st of May a second large trench from the south side; but the slope being there but slight, I was forced to give it a dip of 14°. I here brought to light, near the surface, a pretty bastion, composed of large blocks of limestone, which may date from the time of Lysimachus. The southern part of Hissarlik has been formed principally by the *débris* of the later or Novum Ilium, and for this reason Greek antiquities are found here at a much greater depth than on the top of the hill.

As it was my object to excavate TROY, which I expected to find in one of the lower cities, I was forced to demolish many interesting ruins in the upper strata; as, for example, at a depth of 20 ft. below the surface, the ruins of a pre-historic building 10 ft. high, the walls of which consisted of hewn blocks of limestone perfectly smooth and cemented with clay. The building evidently belonged to the fourth of the enormous strata of *débris* in succession from the virgin soil; and if, as cannot be doubted, each stratum represents the ruins of a distinct city, it belonged to the fourth city. It rested on the calcined bricks and other *débris* of the third city,[10] the latter being apparently marked by the ruins of four different houses, which had succeeded each other on the site, and of which the lowest had been founded on remnants of walls or loose stones of the second city. I was also forced to destroy a small channel made of green sandstone, 8 in. broad and 7 in. deep, which I found at a depth of about 36 ft. below the surface, and which probably served as the gutter of a house.

With the consent of Mr. Frank Calvert, I also began on the 20th of June, with the help of seventy labourers, to excavate in his field on the north side of Hissarlik,[1] where, close to my large platform and at a perpendicular depth of 40 ft. below the plateau of the hill, I dug out of its slope another platform, about 109 ft. broad, with an upper terrace and side galleries, in order to facilitate the removal of the *débris*. No sooner had I commenced the work than I struck against a marble triglyph with a splendid metope, representing Phoebus Apollo and the four horses of the Sun.[2] This triglyph, as well as a number of drums of Doric columns which I found there, can leave no doubt that a temple of Apollo of the Doric order once existed on the spot, which had, however, been so completely destroyed that I did not discover even a stone of its foundations *in situ*.

When I had dug this platform for a distance of 82 feet into the hill, I found that I had commenced it at least 16½ ft. too high, and I therefore abandoned it, contenting myself with cutting into its centre a trench

---

[10] In my former work, *Troy and its Remains*, this burnt city, which I hold to be the Ilium of Homer, was reckoned as the *second* from the virgin soil. The reasons for now reckoning it .the *third* will be given at the proper place.

[1] See the large trench marked v on the north side to the right of point c, on Plan I. (of Troy).

[2] See the engraving and description in the chapter on the Greek Ilium.

26 ft. wide at the top and 13 ft. wide at the bottom.[3] At a distance of 131 ft. from the slope of the hill, I came upon a great wall, 10 ft. high

No. 2. Front View of Walls belonging to the First and Second Cities.

The wall B is built of large blocks joined with small ones; its courses are sloping, and appear to have followed the dip of the ancient soil. The wall A is still more ancient; it is an *abomurus* or retaining wall, and has served to sustain the slope of the hill.

and 6½ ft. thick (see No. 2, B), the top of which is just 34 ft. below the surface. It is built in the so-called Cyclopean manner, of large blocks joined together with small ones : it had at one time been much higher, as the quantity of stones lying beside it seemed to prove. It evidently belonged to the city built with large stones, the second in succession from the virgin soil. At a depth of 6 ft. below this wall I found a retaining wall of smaller stones (see No. 2, A), rising at an angle of 45°. This latter wall must of course be much older than the former: it evidently served to support the slope of the hill, and it proves beyond any doubt that, since its erection, the hill had increased 131 ft. in breadth and 34 ft. in height. As my friend Professor A. H. Sayce was the first to point out, this wall, A, is built in exactly the same style as the house-walls of the first and lowest city, the joint between two of the stones in the lower layer being always covered by a third in the upper layer. Accordingly, in agreement with him, I do not hesitate to attribute this wall to the first city. The *débris* of the lower stratum being as hard as stone, I had very great difficulty in excavating it in the ordinary way, and I found it easier to undermine it by cutting it vertically, and with the help of windlasses and enormous iron levers, nearly 10 ft. in length and 6 in. in circumference, to loosen and so break it down in fragments 16 ft. high, 16 ft. broad, and 10 ft. thick. But I found this manner of excavating very dangerous, two workmen having been buried alive under a mass of *débris* of 2560 cubic feet, and having been saved as by a miracle. In consequence of this accident I gave up the idea of running the great platform 233 ft. broad through the whole length of the hill, and decided on first digging a trench, 98 ft. wide at the top and 65 ft. at the bottom.[4]

As the great extent of my excavations rendered it necessary for me to work with no less than from 120 to 150 labourers, I was obliged, on the 1st of June, on account of the harvest season, to increase the daily wages to 2 francs. But even this would not have enabled me to collect the requisite number of men, had not the late Mr. Max Müller, German Consul at Gallipoli, sent me 40 workmen from that place. After the 1st

[3] See this trench marked w in the middle of the large trench v, to the right of point c on Plan I. (of Troy).

[4] See No. 4, p. 28, to the right ; also Sectional Plan III. at the end of the volume, the letters X–Y on this plan marking the east side of this great trench, which is indicated by the same letters on Plan I. (of Troy).

of July, however, I easily procured a constant supply of 150 workmen. Through the kindness of Mr. Charles Cookson, English Consul at Constantinople, I secured 10 hand-carts, which are drawn by two men and pushed by a third. I thus had 10 hand-carts and 88 wheelbarrows to work with, in addition to which I kept 6 horse-carts, each of which cost 5 francs or 4s. a day, so that the total cost of my excavations amounted to more than 400 francs (£16) a day. Besides screw-jacks, chains and windlasses, my implements consisted of 24 large iron levers, 108 spades, and 103 pickaxes, all of the best English manufacture. I had three capital

No. 3. The Great Tower of Ilium, seen from the S.E. The top is 8 M. (26 ft.) below the surface of the hill: the foundation is on the rock, 14 M. (46¼ ft.) deep: the height of the Tower is 20 ft.

foremen, and my wife and myself were present at the work from sunrise to sunset; but our difficulties increased continually with the daily augmenting distance to which we had to remove the *débris*. Besides this, the constant strong gale from the north, which drove a blinding dust into our eyes, was exceedingly troublesome.

On the south side of the hill, where on account of the slight natural slope I had to make my great trench with an inclination of 76°, I discovered, at a distance of 197 ft. from its entrance, a great mass of masonry, consisting of two distinct walls, each about 15 ft. broad, built close

together, and founded on the rock at a depth of 46½ ft. below the surface.
Both are 20 ft. high ; the outer wall slopes on the south side at an angle
of 15°, and is vertical on the north side. The inner wall falls off at an
angle of 45° on its south side, which is opposite to the north side of the
outer wall. There is thus a deep hollow between the two walls. The
outer wall is built of smaller stones cemented with clay, but it does
not consist of solid masonry. The inner wall is built of large unwrought
blocks of limestone; it has on the north side solid masonry to a depth
of only 4 ft., and leans here against a sort of rampart 65½ ft. broad and
16½ ft. high, partly composed of the limestone which had to be removed
in order to level the rock for building the walls upon it. These two walls
are perfectly flat on the top, and have never been higher; they are 140 ft.
long, their aggregate breadth being 40 ft. on the east and 30 ft. at the
west end. The remnants of brick walls and masses of broken bricks,
pottery, whorls, stone implements, saddlequern-stones, &c., with which
they were covered, appear to indicate that they were used by the inhabitants of the third or burnt city, as the substructions of a great tower;
and I shall therefore, to avoid misunderstanding, call these walls, throughout the present work, " the Great Tower," though they may originally
have been intended by their builders for a different purpose. The accompanying engraving (No. 3) gives a sketch of the two walls as they looked
when they were first brought to light and when they still appeared to
be one solid mass of masonry. A much better view of these two great
walls is given by the engraving No. 144.

§ V.   Third Year's Work at Hissarlik : 1873.

I ceased excavating on the 14th of August, 1872, and resumed my
operations, in company with my wife, on the 1st of February of the
following year. In the preceding autumn, by the side of my two wooden
buildings, we had built a house for ourselves composed of stones brought
to light in my excavations, and had made the walls 2 ft. thick ;[5] but we
were compelled to let our foremen occupy it, as they were not sufficiently
provided with clothes and wrappers, and would otherwise have perished
during the great cold of the winter. My poor wife and myself, therefore,
suffered very much, since the icy north wind, which recals Homer's frequent mention of the blasts of Boreas, blew with such violence through
the chinks of our house-walls, which were made of planks, that we were
not even able to light our lamps in the evening; and although we had
fire on the hearth, yet the thermometer showed −4° Réaumur or 23°
Fahrenheit, while the water which stood near the hearth froze into solid
masses. During the day we could to some degree bear the cold by working in the excavations, but in the evenings we had nothing to keep us
warm except our enthusiasm for the great work of discovering Troy.[6]

---

[5] See engraving No. 9, p. 34, the house to
the right, represented also on No. 10, p. 35, on
which the house to the left is one of the wooden
buildings removed hither.

[6] For the sake of convenience, I shall throughout this work use the name "Troy," specially
employing it to denote the burnt city, the third
in succession from the virgin soil, whatever may
be the name which will be ultimately given to
it by the scientific world.

Once we had the narrowest possible escape from being burnt alive. The stones of our fireplace rested merely upon the boards of the floor, and, whether through a crevice in the cement between the stones or from some other cause, one night the floor took fire; and when I accidentally awoke at 3 o'clock, I found flames extending over a large part of it. The room was filled with dense smoke, and the north wall was just beginning to catch fire; a few seconds would have sufficed to burn a hole into it, and the whole house would then have been in flames in less than a minute, for a high north gale was blowing on that side. I did not, however, lose my presence of mind. Pouring the contents of a bath upon the burning wall, I at once stopped the fire in that direction. Our cries awoke a labourer who was asleep in the adjoining room, and he called the foremen from the stone house to our assistance. Without losing a moment they fetched hammers, iron levers, and pickaxes: the floor was broken up, torn to pieces, and quantities of damp earth thrown upon it, as we had no water. But, as the lower beams were burning in many places, a quarter of an hour elapsed before we got the fire under and all danger was at an end.

For the first three weeks I had an average number of 100 workmen only, but on the 24th of February we were able to increase the number to 158, and later on to 160, which remained our average number of labourers up to the last.

Besides continuing the excavations on the north side in the field of Mr. Frank Calvert, I opened another trench, 42½ ft. broad, on the same side, at the eastern end of the large platform,[7] upon which I had to throw the greater part of the *débris* which was dug up, as it would have been difficult to carry it to a greater distance. I also dug in a north-westerly direction, from the south-eastern corner of the ancient city.[8]

As the hill at this point has only a very gradual slope, I was compelled to give the new trench a considerable dip, but nevertheless was able to make eight side passages for removing the *débris*. Experience had shown me that much precious time was lost in breaking down an earthen wall with long iron levers driven in by a ram, and that it was much more profitable and less dangerous for the workmen to keep the earthen wall always at an ascending angle of 55°, since they can then dig as occasion requires, and cut away the *débris* from below with pickaxes.

In this new trench I had first to break through a wall 10 ft. thick, consisting of large blocks of marble, most of which were drums of Corinthian columns cemented with lime; then I had to pierce the wall of Lysimachus, which was also 10 ft. thick, and built of large hewn stones. Besides this, we had to cut our way through two Trojan walls, the first 5¼ ft. thick, and the second 10 ft.; both consisting of stones joined together with earth.[9] While making this excavation I found a great

---

[7] See No. 4 to the left, and on Plan I. (of Troy) the letters P P to the south of point C.

[8] See on Plan I. (of Troy) the trench z–z

and on Sectional Plan IV. the points z–z.

[9] See *ibid.*

number of large earthen wine-jars ($\pi i\theta o\iota$), from $3\frac{1}{3}$ to $6\frac{2}{3}$ ft. high and from 2 to 4 ft. wide, as well as numerous drums of Corinthian columns

No. 4. Trojan Buildings on the north side.   To the right, the Great Trench cut through the whole Hill; as the excavations appeared in June 1873.   At its beginning, to the right and left, is visible part of the great Outer Wall.

and other sculptured blocks of marble.   All these marbles must have belonged to the Hellenic buildings, the southern wall of which I laid bare to a distance of 285½ ft.[10]   At first this wall is composed of small stones joined with cement, and it rests upon well-hewn blocks of limestone ; further on it consists solely of this latter masonry.   The direction of the wall, and hence of the whole building, is east south-east.

Three inscriptions, which I found among its ruins,[11] and one of which states that it was set up in the ἱερόν – that is to say, in the temple— leave no doubt that this was the temple of the Ilian Athené, the πολι-οῦχος θεά, for it is only this sanctuary that could have been called simply τὸ ἱερόν on account of its size and importance, which surpassed that of all the other temples of Novum Ilium.

No. 5. The Excavations below the Temple of Athené. From the East.
As the excavations appeared in April 1873.

Its foundations nowhere extended to a greater depth than 6½ ft.   The floor, which consisted of large slabs of limestone resting upon double layers of hewn blocks of the same material, was frequently covered with only a foot of vegetable soil, and never with more than 3¼ ft. of it. This explains the total absence of entire sculptures ; for whatever sculptures there were in or upon the temple could not sink into the ground on the summit of the hill when the building was destroyed, and they therefore remained on the surface for many centuries, till they were broken up by religious zeal or out of sheer mischief.   Hence we can easily explain the enormous mass of fragments of statues which cover the entire hill.   In order to bring Troy itself to light, I was forced to sacrifice the ruins of this temple, of which I left standing only some parts of the north and south walls.[1]

---

[10] See Sectional Plan IV., line z–z, and Plan I. (of Troy) under the same letters.

[11] They will be given in the chapter on the

Greek Ilium.

[1] See the woodcuts No. 5, No. 7, and Sectional Plan IV., points z–z in the upper row, marked U.

Just below the south wall of the temple I brought to light the remains of a small round cellar, 3½ ft. in diameter and about 2½ ft. high, which stood beneath the foundations, and must therefore be older than the temple. It was built of chalk and stones, but the inner side had been daubed over with a kind of varnish or glaze, and had a glossy appearance. This small cellar was filled with fragments of Greek terra-cottas, among which, however, I found six small vases almost uninjured.

Below the temple, at a depth of from 23 to 26 ft. beneath the surface, I discovered a house with eight or nine chambers:[2] its walls consist of small stones cemented with earth, from 19⅔ to 25½ in. thick. Several of these walls were 10 ft. high, and on some of them could be seen large patches of a plaster made of yellow or white clay. In most of the rooms the floors had been of wood; in one only I found a floor of unhewn slabs of limestone.

By the side of the house, as well as in its larger apartments, I found a great quantity of human bones, but only two skeletons, which must be those of warriors, for they were found at a depth of 23 ft., with fragments of helmets on or near their heads. Unfortunately the fragments are so small and corroded, that the helmets cannot be put together again; but their upper portions ($\phi\acute{a}\lambda o\iota$) were well preserved, and a drawing of one of them will be given in its place. My honoured friend, Professor Rudolf Virchow of Berlin, has kindly made exact drawings of these skulls, which will be given in the chapter on the Third, the burnt City, together with his dissertation on them. By the side of one of the skeletons, I found a large lance-head, of which I shall also give a drawing.

The quantity of pottery found in and around this house was really enormous. It deserves particular mention that, when the Temple of Athené was built, the site on which it stood was artificially levelled, and a considerable portion of it was cut away. This is proved by the calcined ruins of the burnt city which are here found immediately below the foundations of the temple, whereas elsewhere two distinct strata of débris, 16 ft. deep, intervene between the Hellenic city and the burnt city.

On the east side of the house was a sacrificial altar of a very primitive description, which is turned to the N.W. by W., and consists of a slab of slate-granite about 5¼ ft. long and 5½ ft. broad.[3] The upper part of the stone is cut into the form of a crescent, probably to facilitate the slaughter of the animal which was intended for sacrifice. About 4 ft. below the sacrificial altar I found a channel made of slabs of green slate, which probably served to carry off the blood. The altar stood on a pedestal of bricks but very slightly burnt, and was surrounded by an enormous quantity of similar bricks and wood-ashes to a height of 10 feet. Both the sacrificial stone and its pedestal were daubed over with a white crust of clay, which upon the pedestal was nearly an inch thick.

Below the level of the altar and the pre-historic house already mentioned, I came upon walls of fortification[4] and very ancient houses,[5]

---

[2] See the engraving No. 7.
[3] See the engraving No. 6.
[4] See Plan of Troy on the south side, in the

two places marked f, h.
[5] See No. 7 to the left, just below the overhanging marble block.

the walls of which are still partially covered with a coating of clay and white colour, all bearing traces of a terrible conflagration, which had

No. 6.   Great Altar for Sacrifices, found in the depths of the Temple of Athené. (1 : 25 actual size.)
As the altar appeared in 1873.

so completely destroyed everything in the chambers, that we only occasionally found charred fragments of pottery among the red and yellow wood-ashes with which the spaces were filled. Curiously enough, other house-walls were again found below : these must be still older than those above; like them, they show indications of having been exposed to a great heat.

In fact, this labyrinth of ancient house-walls, built one above another and discovered under the Temple of Athené erected by Lysimachus, is unique, and presents the archæologist with the richest materials for investigation. The greatest difficulty connected with the discovery, however, is afforded by one-of the above-mentioned walls of fortification, 11¾ ft. high, which runs through the labyrinth from W.N.W. to E.S.E. This is likewise built of stones joined together with earth, and is 6 ft. broad at the top and 12 ft. broad at the foot. It does not stand directly upon the native rock, nor was it built till the rock had gradually become covered with a layer of earth 1¾ ft. in thickness. Running parallel with this wall of fortification, only 2½ ft. from it and at the same depth, there is a wall 2 ft. high, which is likewise built of stones cemented with earth.[6]

The chamber at the greatest depth to which I have excavated is 10 ft. high and 11¼ ft. wide; but it may have been higher: its length I have not been able to ascertain. One of the compartments of the

---

[6] See Plan I. (of Troy), on the south side, in the places marked *f*, *h*.

uppermost houses, below the Temple of Athené and belonging to the third, the burnt city, appears to have been used as a magazine for storing

No. 7. Trojan Buildings discovered in, the depths of the Temple of Athené; as they appeared in June 1873.

Altar and Substruction.

corn or wine, for there are in it nine enormous earthen jars ($\pi\iota\theta o\iota$) of various forms, about $5\frac{3}{4}$ ft. high and $4\frac{3}{4}$ ft. across, their mouths being from

$29\frac{1}{2}$ to $35\frac{1}{4}$ in. broad.[7] Each of them has four handles, $3\frac{3}{4}$ in. broad, and the clay of which they are made is as much as $2\frac{1}{4}$ in. thick. Upon the

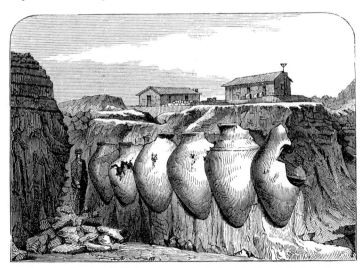

No. 8. The Magazine, with its Colossal Jars, in the depths of the Temple of Athené; as it appeared in June 1873.

south side of the jars I found a wall of fortification, 26 ft. long and 10 ft. high, built of sun-dried bricks, which, though thoroughly baked in the conflagration, were exceedingly fragile.

In the middle of March I also commenced a large excavation close to my wooden house and to the west of the Great Tower.[8] I found near the surface the ruins of a large house of the Greek period, which extended to a depth of $6\frac{1}{2}$ ft. It must have belonged to a great man, perhaps a high priest, for the floors of the rooms were made of large slabs of red stone excellently polished. Below this Greek house I found, as usual, a layer of *débris* with but few stones; then a number of house-walls composed of small stones joined together with earth; and beneath these again immense masses of burnt and partly-vitrified bricks. At last, at the depth of 30 ft. below the surface, I brought to light a street $17\frac{1}{4}$ ft. wide, paved with stone flags, from $4\frac{1}{4}$ to 5 ft. long and from 35 in. to $4\frac{1}{2}$ ft. broad, which runs down very abruptly in a south-westerly direction towards the Plain.[9] The slope of the street is so great that, while on the north side, so far as it is there uncovered, it is only 30 ft. below the surface of the hill, at a distance of 33 ft. further to the south it already lies as low as 37 ft. under the ground.

This well-paved street led me to conjecture that a large building must at one time have stood at the end of it, at a short distance on the north-

---

[7] In the view, No. 8, six of the jars are shown, and a seventh (broken) is outside the trench to the right. The two largest of all are out of view, on the other side of the wall of the magazine.

[8] See No. 9 to the left.

[9] See No. 10 and No. 13, and Plan I. (of Troy), *a*.

east side, and I therefore immediately set 100 men to dig through the ground lying in front of it in that direction. I found the street covered to a height of from 7 to 10 ft. with yellow, red, or black wood-ashes,

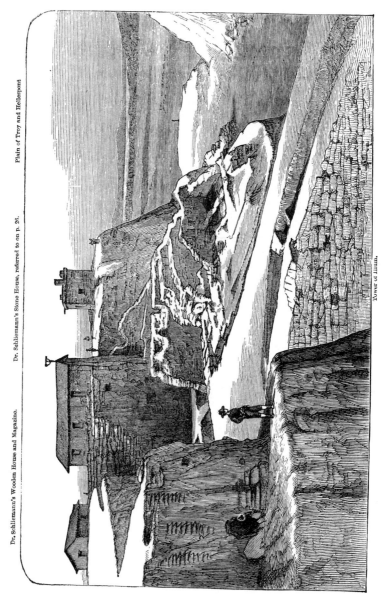

No. 9. The Tower of Ilium, the Gate, and the Ruins of a large House; looking North along the cutting through the whole Hill. The excavations as they appeared in May 1873.

mixed with thoroughly-burnt and often partly-vitrified fragments of bricks and stones. Above this thick layer of *débris* I came upon the ruins of a large building composed of stones cemented with earth, of which I only broke away as much as was necessary to clear the street with its

Samothrace.
Imbros.

Dr. Sculimann's Stone House and Barrack.

Plain of Troy, seen through the Great Trench.

Later but pre-Hellenic Buildings, partly over the ruins of the House of the Town-chief or King.

Hellespont.
Plain of Troy.
Scamander.

Greek Tower (where the man stands).

a. Place where the largest Treasure was found.

Wall of Troy, Gate, and Paved Road to the Plain.

Paved Road.

The Great Tower.

No. 10. The Great Trench on the North-west side, the Gate and Paved Road, the Great Tower, City Wall, part of the House of the Town-chief or King, and the walls of a Tower of the Greek age; from the South-east. The excavations as they appeared in June 1873.

parapets.[10] Proceeding thus in a north-easterly direction, I brought to light two large gateways, standing 20 ft. apart, and in each of them a

No. 11.

No. 12.

Nos. 11, 12. Copper Bolts; found exactly in the middle (No. 11) of the first (No. 12) of the second Gates.

long copper bolt, which had no doubt served to fasten the wooden wings of the gates, and of which I give drawings. The first gateway is 12¼ ft. wide, and is formed by two projections of the side-wall, one of which stands out to a distance of 2½ ft., the other to a distance of 2¾ ft.; both are 3¼ ft. high and 3¾ ft. broad. The pavement of large flags ends at the first gate, whence to the second gate—for a distance of 20 ft.—the street is very roughly paved with large unhewn stones.[1] The pavement has probably become uneven through the fall of the walls of the great tower, which must once have crowned the Gates, and of whose existence the masses of calcined rubbish, from 7 to 10 ft. deep, which covered the passage, furnish the most evident proofs. It is clear that wood entered largely into the construction of these walls, not only from the large masses of wood-ashes, but also from the fact that the large red flags of the street, though they looked fresh and solid when first brought to light, speedily crumbled away when exposed to the air; a circumstance which can only be explained by the intense heat to which they had been subjected.

Like the first gate, the second gate is also formed by two projections in the wall, which are 2 ft. high, more than 3 ft. broad, and project about 2½ ft.

I cleared the street as far as 5 ft. to the north-east of the second gate, but did not venture to proceed further, as this could not have been done without breaking down more of the walls of the large house erected upon the *débris* with which it is covered to the depth of from 7 to 10 ft. This house is, of course, of later date than the double gate; but still I considered it of great interest to archæology, the more so as it covered the ruins of extensive and more ancient buildings to the right and left of the gate. These latter are on a level with the double gate, and, as that to the north-west seems to be the largest building of the burnt city, the third in succession from the virgin soil, I believed it to be the mansion of the last chief or king of the town. The correctness of this opinion appears to be corroborated by the large number of treasures I subsequently discovered in or close to it. The more recent house had been erected when the ruins of the more ancient houses were completely covered with ashes and burnt *débris,* as is obvious from the fact that the more recent walls run in all directions above the more ancient ones, never standing directly upon them, and frequently separated from them by a layer of calcined rubbish, from 7 to 10 ft. deep. The ruined walls of the lower as well as of the upper houses are built of stones joined together with earth; but the walls of the lower houses are much thicker and more solidly built than those of the upper one. It is plain that the more

---

[10] See No. 10.   [1] See No. 10 and No. 13, and the place marked *a* on Plan I. (of Troy).

recent house was not built till the street was covered up, to a depth of from 7 to 10 ft., by the ruins and *débris* of the fallen buildings.

From these and other considerations, I wished to preserve as much as possible of both the ancient and the more recent buildings, the more

No. 13. The Double Gate, Tower of Ilium, and part of the House of the Town-chief or King; seen from the North-west. The excavations as they appeared in June 1873.

so as I feared my statements in regard to them might be disbelieved. Consequently, after clearing the double gate, I left the ruins of both buildings *in situ*, and removed the *débris* from those chambers only of the ancient houses which could be excavated without injury to the building above them. I found in them a vast quantity of pottery of the most interesting character, which will be made known to the reader in the proper place.

The great cold did not last long, and we had afterwards splendid weather. The nights however were cold up to the middle of March, and the thermometer frequently fell to the freezing-point towards morning, whereas during the day the heat of the sun was already beginning to be troublesome, the thermometer often showing 18° Réaumur (72½° Fahrenheit) in the shade at mid-day. From about the 1st of March we heard the perpetual croaking of millions of frogs in the surrounding marshes, and in the second week of March the storks returned. One of the many discomforts of our life in the wilderness we inhabited was the hideous shrieking of innumerable owls, which built their nests in the holes of my trenches; their shrieks had a weird and horrible sound, and were especially intolerable at night.

Up to the beginning of May 1873, I had believed that the hill of Hissarlik, where I was excavating, marked the site of the Trojan citadel only; and it certainly is the fact that Hissarlik was the Acropolis of Novum Ilium.[2] I therefore imagined that Troy was larger than the latter town, or at least as large; but I thought it important to discover the precise limits of the Homeric city, and accordingly I sank twenty shafts as far down as the rock, on the west, south-west, south-south-east, and east of Hissarlik, directly at its foot or at some distance from it, on the plateau of the Ilium of the Greek colony. As I found in these shafts no trace of fragments either of pre-historic pottery or of pre-historic house-walls, and nothing but fragments of Hellenic pottery and Hellenic house-walls; and as, moreover, the hill of Hissarlik has a very steep slope towards the north, the north-east, and the north-west, facing the Hellespont, and is also very steep on the west side towards the Plain, the city could not possibly have extended in any one of these directions beyond the hill itself. It therefore appears certain that the ancient city cannot have extended on any side beyond the primeval plateau of Hissarlik, the circumference of which is indicated on the south and south-west by the Great Tower and the double gate; and on the north-west, north-east, and east, by the great boundary wall.

The shafts which I sank beyond the hill are all indicated by letters, A to U, on the Plan of the Hellenic Ilium, on which it is also stated at what precise depth in each of them the rock was struck; and of the seven deepest shafts sections are given. I therefore call particular attention to this Plan.[3] I also call particular attention to the tombs which I came upon in the shafts which are marked D, O, and R on the Plan of

---

[2] I reluctantly give the later Ilium the epithet Novum, because the city existed for at least 1000 years, and its site has been a desert for perhaps 1400 years. All classical writers (except Strabo) call it simply Ilium.

[3] See Plan II. at the end of the volume.

Novum Ilium. Each of these three tombs was cut out of the rock and covered with flat slabs: each contained a corpse; but the corpses were all so much damaged, that the skulls crumbled to dust when exposed to the air. The tombs evidently belonged to persons of small means and of a late date, since what little pottery was found in them was of a very inferior description and evidently of the Roman period. But the fact that in three out of the twenty shafts, which I sank at random on the site of Novum Ilium, tombs were discovered, seems to denote with great probability that the inhabitants of that city buried their dead, or at least a large portion of them, within the precincts of the town. Cremation however was also in use with them, since in the first trench I opened, in April 1870, I struck upon an urn of the Roman period, filled with ashes of animal matter intermixed with remnants of calcined bones, which are evidently those of a human body. I did not find any other burnt bodies in the strata of Novum Ilium, but it must be remembered that I only excavated in Hissarlik, which does not cover a twenty-fifth part of the later city.[4] Hissarlik moreover was the Acropolis of Novum Ilium and contained the principal temples, in consequence of which it is likely that it was considered sacred ground, in which no burials were allowed. Hence it is very probable that, if systematic excavations were made in the lower city, many sepulchres and funeral urns would be found.

The inhabitants of the five pre-historic cities of Hissarlik seem generally to have burnt the dead, as I found in 1872 two tripod-urns with calcined human remains on the virgin soil in the first city; and in 1871, 1872, and 1873, a vast number of large funeral urns, containing human ashes, in the third and fourth cities. I found no bones however except a single tooth, and on one occasion among the ashes a human skull, which is well preserved, with the exception of the lower jaw, which is missing: as I found a brooch of bronze along with it, I suppose it may have belonged to a woman. I am also indebted to Prof. Virchow for drawings of this skull, which will be given, together with his dissertation on it and the other skulls, in the chapter on the Third, the burnt City.

It is true that nearly all the pottery found in the pre-historic ruins of Hissarlik is broken, and that there is hardly one large vessel out of twenty which is not in fragments; nay, in the first two cities the pottery has all been shattered by the weight and pressure of the stones with which the second city was built. But still, even if all the funeral urns with human ashes ever deposited in Hissarlik had been well preserved, yet, judging from the fragments of them—in spite of the abundance of these fragments—I can hardly think that I could have found even a thousand entire urns. It is, therefore, evident that the inhabitants of the five pre-historic cities of Hissarlik buried only a small part of their funeral urns in the city itself, and that we must look for their principal necropolis elsewhere.

Whilst these important excavations were going on, I neglected the trenches on the north side, and only worked there when I had workmen to

---

[4] See Plan II. (of the Hellenic Ilium).

spare. But I brought to light here the prolongation of the great wall which I agree with Prof. Sayce in attributing to the second stone city.[5]

Wishing to investigate the fortifications on the west and north-west sides of the ancient city, in the beginning of May 1873 I also commenced making a trench, 33 ft. broad and 141 ft. long, on the north-west side of the hill, at the very point where I had made the first trench in April 1870.[6] I broke first through an Hellenic circuit-wall, probably that which, according to Plutarch in his Life of Alexander, was built by Lysimachus, and found it to be 13 ft. high and 10 ft. thick, and to consist of large hewn blocks of limestone. Afterwards I broke through an older wall, $8\frac{3}{4}$ ft. high and 6 ft. thick, composed of large blocks cemented with earth. This second wall is attached to the large wall which I brought to light in April 1870, and the two form two sides of a quadrangular Hellenic tower,[7] a third wall of which I had to break through later on.

This part of the hill was evidently much lower in ancient times, as seems to be proved not only by the wall of Lysimachus, which must at one time have risen to a considerable height above the surface of the hill, whereas it is now covered by $16\frac{1}{2}$ ft. of rubbish, but also by the remains of the Hellenic period, which are here found to a great depth. It appears, in fact, as if the rubbish and *débris* of habitations had been thrown down on this side for centuries, in order to increase the height of the place.

In order to hasten the excavations on the north-west side of the hill, I cut a deep trench from the west side also,[8] in which, unfortunately, I struck obliquely the circuit-wall of Lysimachus, here 13 ft. high and 10 ft. thick, and was consequently compelled to remove a double quantity of stones to force a way through it. But I again came upon the ruins of large buildings of the Hellenic and pre-Hellenic periods, so that this excavation could only proceed slowly. Here at a distance of 69 ft. from the declivity of the hill, at a depth of 20 ft., I struck an ancient enclosure-wall, 5 ft. high, with a projecting battlement, which, on account of its comparatively modern structure and small height, must belong to a post-Trojan period. Behind it I found a level place, paved partly with large flags of stone, partly with stones more or less hewn; and after this a wall of fortification, 20 ft. high and 5 ft. thick, built of large stones and earth, which ran below my wooden house, but $6\frac{1}{2}$ ft. above the Trojan circuit-wall, which starts from the Gate.[9]

While following up this circuit-wall, and bringing more and more of it to light, close to the ancient building and north-west of the Gate, I struck upon a large copper article of the most remarkable form, which attracted my attention all the more, as I thought I saw gold behind it.[10] On the top of it was a layer of red and calcined ruins, from $4\frac{3}{4}$ to $5\frac{1}{4}$ ft. thick, as hard as stone, and above this again the above-mentioned wall of

---

[5] See the Sectional Plan III. x, v.

[6] This trench is just in front of the reader in the view No. 10, p. 35; it is also represented on the Sectional Plan No. IV., z', West, and on the Plan I. (of Troy) under the letter z'.

[7] See No. 10 (p. 35) in the trench below the standing man.

[8] See on the Plan I. (of Troy) the trench marked R to the west of the gate.

[9] See this Trojan wall, marked *b*, to the north-west of the gate on Plan I. (of Troy).

[10] The precise spot of this important discovery is marked Δ on Plan I. (of Troy).

fortification (5 ft. broad and 20 ft. high), built of large stones and earth, which must have been erected shortly after the destruction of Troy. In order to secure the treasure from my workmen and save it for archæology, it was necessary to lose no time; so, although it was not yet the hour for breakfast, I immediately had *païdos* called. This is a word of uncertain derivation, which has passed over into Turkish, and is here employed in place of ἀνάπαυσις, or time for rest. While the men were eating and resting, I cut out the Treasure with a large knife. This required great exertion and involved great risk, since the wall of fortification, beneath which I had to dig, threatened every moment to fall down upon me. But the sight of so many objects, every one of which is of inestimable value to archæology, made me reckless, and I never thought of any danger. It would, however, have been impossible for me to have removed the treasure without the help of my dear wife, who stood at my side, ready to pack the things I cut out in her shawl, and to carry them away. All the different articles of which this Treasure was composed will be described at the proper place in the precise order in which they were taken out of the ruins. I here only give a general view of the whole (No. 14).

As I found all these articles together, in the form of a rectangular mass, or packed into one another, it seems certain that they were placed on the city wall in a wooden chest. This supposition seems to be corroborated by the fact that close by the side of these articles I found a copper key. It is therefore possible that some one packed the treasure in the chest, and carried it off, without having had time to pull out the key; when he reached the wall, however, the hand of an enemy, or the fire, overtook him, and he was obliged to abandon the chest, which was immediately covered, to a height of 5 ft., with the ashes and stones of the adjoining house.[11]

Perhaps the articles found a few days previously in a room of the chief's house, close to the place where the Treasure was discovered, belonged to this unfortunate person. These articles consisted of a helmet and a silver vase, with a cup of electrum, which will be described in the chapter on this Third City.

On the thick layer of *débris* which covered the Treasure, the builders of the new city erected a fortification-wall already mentioned, composed of large hewn and unhewn stones and earth. This wall extended to within $3\frac{1}{4}$ ft. of the surface of the hill.

That the Treasure was packed together at a moment of supreme peril appears to be proved, among other things, by the contents of the largest silver vase, consisting of nearly 9000 objects of gold, which will be described in the subsequent pages. The person who endeavoured to save the Treasure had, fortunately, the presence of mind to place the silver vase, with the valuable articles inside it, upright in the chest, so that nothing could fall out, and everything has been preserved uninjured.

---

[11] But as in 1878 and 1879 I found, at a distance of but a few yards from the spot where this treasure was discovered, four more treasures, which must evidently have fallen from an upper storey of the town-chief's house, I now rather think that the same may have been the case with the large treasure.

Hoping to find more treasures here, I pulled down the upper wall, and I also broke away the enormous block of *débris* which separated my western and north-western trenches[1] from the great massive walls which I used to call the "Tower." But to do this I had to pull down the

No. 14. General View of the Treasure. (Depth, 28 ft.) *a.* Key of the Treasure Chest. *b.* The Golden Diadems, Fillet, Ear-rings, and small Jewels. *c.* Silver "Talents" and Vessels of Silver and Gold. *d.* Silver Vases and curious Plate of Copper. *e.* Weapons and Helmet-crests of Copper or Bronze. *f.* Copper Vessel. *g.* Copper Cauldron. *h.* Copper Shield.

larger of my wooden houses, and to bridge over the Gates, so as to facilitate the removal of the *débris*. I found there many interesting

---

[1] See Plan I. (of Troy); also on Nos. 9 and 10 the block in front, and on No. 13 on the left side.

antiquities; more especially three silver dishes ($\phi\iota\acute{a}\lambda\alpha\iota$), 1 ft. 9 in. below
the place where the Treasure was discovered: two of them were broken in
pieces by the labourer's pickaxe; the third is entire. That the. Treasure
itself escaped injury from the pickaxes, was due to the large copper vessel,
which projected in such a way that I could cut everything out of the
hard *débris* with a knife.

I now perceived that the trench which I had made in April 1870
had exactly struck the right point for excavating,[2] and that, if I had
only continued it, I should, in a few weeks, have uncovered the most
remarkable buildings in Troy; whereas, by abandoning it, I had to make
colossal excavations from east to west, and from north to south, through
the entire hill, in order to find them.

We discontinued the excavations on the 17th of June, 1873.

In December of the same year the Turkish authorities of Koum
Kaleh seized many gold ornaments which two of my workmen had
found in three different places in the preceding March, whilst working
for me in the trenches of Hissarlik, at a depth of nearly 30 ft. below the
surface of the hill. Most of these jewels were contained in a vase with
an owl's head. Unfortunately one of the workmen had got his part of the
booty melted down by a goldsmith at Ren Kioi, and made into ornaments after the present Turkish fashion. All these gold ornaments, both
genuine and re-made, are now in the Imperial Museum at Constantinople.
The genuine ones will be represented and explained in the subsequent
pages; and it will be seen that they are nearly all of the same type as
those contained in the great treasure discovered by me, though similar
types had never before been found elsewhere.

In the beginning of 1874, Mr. F. A. Brockhaus of Leipzig published,
in German, an account of my excavations and discoveries at Troy, under
the title of *Troianische Alterthümer*, of which a translation in French by
Mr. Alexander R. Rangabé, Ambassador of Greece at Berlin, appeared
simultaneously. Both editions were accompanied by an Atlas containing
218 photographs, representing nearly 4000 of the objects discovered in
the excavations, together with a minute description of each of them. The
English translation of the same work, made by Miss Dora Schmitz and
edited by Mr. Philip Smith, was published by Mr. John Murray of London,
in November 1874, under the title of *Troy and its Remains*.

§ VI. INTERVAL IN THE WORK AT TROY: EXCAVATIONS AT MYCENAE: 1874–1877.

Having obtained from the Greek Government permission to excavate
at Mycenae, I began operations there in February 1874, by sinking thirty-
four shafts in its Acropolis; and I had just discovered the site of the
ancient Royal Sepulchres mentioned by Pausanias, when I was interrupted

---

[2] See No. 10, p. 35, the trench just in front, below the standing man. The same trench is
marked z' on Plan I.

in my explorations by the legal proceedings instituted against me at Athens by the Turkish Government, which claimed one-half of my collection of Trojan antiquities. The lawsuit lasted for a year, when the Court decided that I should pay the Turkish Government an indemnity of £400 in settlement of their claims. But instead of £400 I sent, in April 1875, £2000 to the Turkish Minister of Public Instruction, for the benefit of the Imperial Museum, expressing my great desire always to remain on friendly terms with them, and explaining to them that they stood as much in need of a man like myself as I stood in need of them. My donation was so kindly received by H. H. Safvet Pasha, then Minister of Public Instruction, that I was emboldened to go to Constantinople at the end of December 1875, to solicit a new firman for the exploration of Troy. By the powerful assistance of my honoured friends, H. E. the United States Minister Resident Mr. Maynard, H. E. the Italian Ambassador Count Corti, H. H. Safvet Pasha, and particularly by the unremitting zeal and undaunted energy of H. E. the Great Logothete Aristarches Bey, I was on the point of obtaining my firman, when my request was suddenly rejected by the Council of State.

But H. E. the Great Logothete Aristarches Bey having introduced me to H. E. the late Rashid Pasha,[3] then Minister of Foreign Affairs, a man of high culture, who had been for five years Governor of Syria, I had no difficulty in inspiring him with a warm enthusiasm for Troy and its remains, so that he went himself to H. H. the Grand Vizier, Mahmoud-Nedim Pasha, spoke warmly in my favour, and obtained from him an order that the firman should be given me without delay. I received my firman accordingly at the end of April 1876, and at once proceeded to the Dardanelles to continue my excavations. But I there found the Governor-General, Ibrahim Pasha, totally averse to the continuation of the works, probably because ever since I had stopped them, in June 1873, he had been in the habit of himself giving a sort of firman to the numerous travellers who came to see my excavations, and this of course would have ceased had I resumed my operations. Having kept me therefore for nearly two months at the Dardanelles, under the pretence that he had not yet received the confirmation of my firman, he at last allowed me to recommence the excavations, but gave me as guardian a certain Izzet Effendi,[4] whose sole office it was to throw obstacles in my way. Seeing the utter impossibility of going on, I returned to Athens, and wrote a letter to the *Times* (published 24th of July, 1876), in which I denounced Ibrahim Pasha's conduct before the tribunal of the civilized world. The article having been reproduced by the Constantinople papers, he was transferred in October 1876 to another Vilayet.

I could then have recommenced the excavations at Troy; but at the end of July I had begun to excavate again at Mycenae, and could not give up my work there until I had thoroughly explored all the royal

---

[3] Rashid Pasha was murdered in June, 1876.
[4] This Izzet Effendi has lately been exiled on account of gross embezzlement of government monies.

tombs. The really wonderful success which attended my excavations, the immense and marvellous treasures with which I enriched the Greek nation, are well known; for all ages to come travellers from all parts of the world will flock to the Greek capital to see here in the Mycenae Museum the result of my disinterested labours. The publication of my work on Mycenae in English and German occupied the whole of 1877; the French edition kept me busy until the summer of 1878, and it was only in July of that year that I was able to think of continuing the excavations at Troy. But my firman of April 1876 having been given for two years only, it had now expired, and a new firman had to be procured; many fresh difficulties, too, had arisen which I could never have overcome without the aid of my honoured friend Sir Austen Henry Layard, Ambassador of her Britannic Majesty at Constantinople, who smoothed away all my difficulties with the Turkish Government, obtained for me a more liberal firman than that which I had had before, and always cheerfully lent me his powerful assistance whenever I applied for it, which sometimes happened as often as twice a day during the progress of the excavations. I therefore fulfil a most agreeable duty in now thanking his Excellency publicly and most cordially for all the services he has rendered me, without which I could never have brought my work to a close. But my new firman not being ready till September 1878, I had time to make a more thorough exploration of the island of Ithaca.

§ VII. Exploration of Ithaca : 1878.

I regret to say that systematic excavations for archæological purposes are altogether out of the question here. I began my researches in the valley called Polis, which is in the northern part of the island, and has generally been considered as the site of the Homeric capital of Ithaca: first, on account of its name, which is the Greek word for city; second, on account of its splendid harbour, at a distance of only two miles from a small island now called Mathitarió, which, being the only one in the strait between Ithaca and Cephalonia, has naturally always been identified with the Homeric island of Asteris, behind which the suitors of Penelope lay in wait for Telemachus on his return from Pylos and Sparta.[5] As a fourth reason for the identity of Polis with the site of the capital of Ithaca, I may mention an acropolis which a traveller fancies he can perceive on the very steep rock, at a height of about 400 ft., on the north side of the port. My first care was to climb up to it, and I found it to consist of a very irregular calcareous rock, which had evidently never been touched by the hands of man, and can most certainly never have served as a work of defence. But as seen from below, this rock has the shape of a fortress. It is still at the present day called "castron" here, and in like manner it must in remote antiquity have been called "Polis," the original meaning of this word having been "acropolis." Thus there can be no

---

[5] *Od.* iv. 844-847:

ἔστι δέ τις νῆσος μέσσῃ ἁλὶ πετρήεσσα,
μεσσηγὺς Ἰθάκης τε Σάμοιό τε παιπαλοέσσης,

Ἀστερίς, οὐ μεγάλη· λιμένες δ᾽ ἔνι ναύλοχοι
αὐτῇ
ἀμφίδυμοι· τῇ τόνγε μένον λοχόωντες Ἀχαιοί.

doubt that the name of this valley is derived—not, as has hitherto been thought, from a real city, but merely from an imaginary fortress.

Besides, this valley is the most fertile spot in Ithaca, and it can therefore never have been used for the site of a city; in fact, no case has ever occurred in Greece where a city was built on fertile land, and least of all can such have been the case on the rocky island of Ithaca, where arable land is so exceedingly rare and precious. If, therefore, there had been a city at Polis, it could only have been built on the surrounding rocky heights, the pointed or abrupt and always irregular shape of which precludes the idea that they can have ever been inhabited by men. Colonel Leake[6] mentions an old ruin on the south side of the port; it still exists, but is nothing else than a Christian church of the Middle Ages.

I visited and carefully measured the island of Mathitarió. Its length is 586 ft.; its breadth varies between 108 ft. and 176 ft. On account of these small dimensions, it cannot possibly be identified with the Homeric Asteris, which, as the poet says, had two ports, each of them with two entrances. But still I have no reason to question that the sight of Mathitarió may have given to Homer the idea of his imaginary Asteris. On the island are the ruins of a tower and three buildings, one of which is said to have been a school-house, which would explain the name Mathitarió. The ruins can hardly be more than a couple of centuries old.

Though for all these reasons I was perfectly convinced that no city can ever have occupied the fertile valley of Polis, yet I thought it in the interest of science to investigate the matter by actual excavations. With the permission of the owner of the land, Mr. N. Metaxas Zannis, I sunk many shafts there; but in nearly all of them I struck the natural rock at a depth of 10 to 13 ft., except in the middle of the valley, which seems to have been hollowed out to a great depth by a mountain torrent. Fragments of rudely-made black or white Greek pottery and pieces of tiles were all I found. There were only a few fragments of archaic pottery, for which I could claim the date of the sixth century B.C. Tombs are sometimes found on the neighbouring heights, but, as is proved by the pottery and coins contained in them, they are of the third, fourth, or fifth century B.C. Of the same period are also the antiquities found in a cavern to the right of the port of Polis: for an inscription found there, I can with certainty claim the date of the sixth or even the seventh century B.C.[7] Therefore, the supposition that Polis is the site of the Homeric capital of Ithaca must now be definitely abandoned.

I afterwards carefully surveyed the remaining northern part of the island, but I nowhere found the site of an ancient town, except in the environs of the small building of cyclopean masonry, usually called the "School of Homer," which the owner of the property, the priest Sp. Vretó, has, in his pious zeal, lately converted into a small church. But unfortunately he left in it the thick layer of *débris* it contained, which has now become the pavement of the church. Had he cleared it out and

---

[6] *Travels in Northern Greece.*   [7] See my *Mycenae*, p. 78.

carefully collected the potsherds, we might probably at once have found in these the key to the date of the building. He refused me permission to excavate in the church, but allowed me to do so in the adjoining fields, where a number of rock-hewn house-foundations and remnants of cyclopean walls testified to the existence of an ancient settlement. I dug there a great many holes, but always struck the native rock at less than 3 ft., and sometimes even at a depth of less than 12 in. : thus there can be no doubt that a town existed here in classical times, and most probably it is the very town mentioned by Scylax, *Per.* 34, and Ptolemy, iii. 14. 13.

I proceeded thence to Mount Aëtos, situated on the narrow isthmus, hardly one mile wide, which joins Northern and Southern Ithaca. I believed the ancient city to have been at the northern foot of that mountain, and to have extended all over the small ridge which crosses the hollow between it and Mount Merovúni to the south of it. But I discovered I had been mistaken, for I found everywhere the purest virgin soil, except on the very crest of the ridge, where, near the chapel of Hagios Georgios, I found a very small plain with an accumulation of artificial soil 10 ft. deep. I dug there two long trenches, in one of which I brought to light a terrace-wall 7 ft. high, consisting of huge polygonal blocks well fitted together; to compare this wall to the modern terrace-walls which surround it, is to compare a giant's work to a work of dwarfs. Of pottery I found there nothing but a few fragments of black Greek vases. Having here also failed in my researches, I most carefully explored Mount Aëtos, which rises to a height of 600 ft. from the sea, and has on its artificially but rudely levelled summit a platform of triangular form, with two large cisterns and a small one, and remnants of six or seven small cyclopean buildings, which were either separate houses or, more probably, chambers of the large cyclopean mansion which is said to have stood there, and is commonly called "the Castle of Ulysses." There can hardly be any doubt that in the same manner as the Acropolis of Athens was widened by Cimon,[8] who took in a large portion of its north-eastern slope and filled up the lower space with stones and *débris,* the level summit of Mount Aëtos was extended to the north and south-west by a huge cyclopean wall still existing, the space between the top and the wall being filled up with stones and *débris.* Thus the summit formed a level quadrangular platform, 166 ft. 8 in. long by 127 ft. 4 in. broad, so that there was on the summit ample room for a large mansion and courtyard. To the north and south of the circuit-wall are towers of cyclopean masonry, from each of which a huge wall of immense boulders runs down. But at a certain distance these two walls begin to form a curve, and ultimately join each other. Two more cyclopean walls run down from the top—the one in an easterly, the other in a south-easterly direction—and join the curve formed by the two first-named walls. Lastly, I have to mention a huge circuit-wall about 50 ft. below the upper circuit-wall. This wall has fallen on the west side, but is in a marvellous state of preservation on the other sides. To

---

[8] Pausanias, i. 28, § 3.

increase the strength of the place, the foot of the rock has been cut away so as to form a perpendicular wall of rock 20 ft. high. Three gates can be recognized in the walls.

Between all these cyclopean walls there once stood a city, which may have contained 2000 houses, either cut out in the rock or built of cyclopean masonry. Of 190 of these houses I have been able to find the ruins more or less well preserved. I measured twelve of them, and found them between 21 ft. and 63 ft. long, and from 15 ft. to 20 ft. broad. The usual size of the rudely-cut stones is 5 ft. in length, 4 ft. 8 in. in breadth, and 2 ft. in thickness. The size of these stones by far exceeds that of the stones in the cyclopean houses I discovered at Mycenae and Tiryns. Some of the houses consisted of only one room; others had four or even six chambers. From below not one of the houses is visible; and as the peasants of Ithaca thought them to be mere heaps of stones, they did not point them out to foreigners, who might ascend Mount Aëtos a hundred times without noticing any one of them, for the slopes of Aëtos ascend at an angle of 35°, and they are thus 7° steeper than the upper cone of Mount Vesuvius. It is therefore exceedingly difficult and fatiguing to ascend Mount Aëtos, the more so as it is full of pointed rocks, and overgrown with thorny underwood and thistles. Besides, the path by which the peasants lead strangers to the top does not pass near any of the better-preserved cyclopean houses; it passes only a few foundations, in which even the best archæologist might fail to recognize remnants of houses unless he had seen the better-preserved buildings. For all these reasons even Colonel Leake only saw "some terrace walls and some foundations of buildings on the side of Aëtos;" and from this remark of his no one could have expected to find here the ruins, more or less well preserved, of 190 houses of Ithaca's most ancient capital, which had, however, long before Colonel Leake, been identified by William Gell.[9] This cyclopean capital is unique in the world, and every admirer of Homer ought to come out to see it. Visitors ought to take as their guide the peasant Nicólaos Psarrós, whom I have repeatedly shown over the ancient city. He lives at the foot of Mount Aëtos, close to the chapel of Hagios Georgios.

For two weeks I excavated with thirty workmen in those cyclopean buildings: but fragments of pottery, which has no resemblance to any of the Mycenean pottery, but is much like that from the two most ancient cities at Troy; fragments of most curious tiles with impressed ornaments; also two with a sort of written characters for which I cannot claim a high antiquity; further, the fragments of a very ancient and most curious handmill—these were the only results of all my labour. But I must wonder that I have succeeded in finding even thus much, because on account of the steep slope no accumulation of *débris* was possible here, and the heavy winter rains have for ages swept all remnants of ancient industry into the sea. The heat on Mount Aëtos is overwhelming, on account of the rocks and stones, which get hot in the sun.

---

[9] *The Geography and Antiquities of Ithaca;* London, 1807.

I need hardly say that the drawing which Sir W. Gell gives in his *Ithaca* of the Palace of Ulysses is altogether imaginary.

I also commenced excavating the stalactite grotto near the little port of Dexia, which is generally identified with the port of Phorkys, where Ulysses was landed by the Phaeacians, the grotto being rightly considered to be identical with the Homeric Grotto of the Nymphs, in which Ulysses, assisted by Athené, hid his treasures. But having opened a trench just before the little altar, down to the rock, without even finding a potsherd, I abandoned this ungrateful excavation. The grotto is very spacious, and it exactly answers the description of Homer, who says " that it has two entrances, one on its north side for men, and one on its south side for the immortal gods, for no man can enter by the divine door." [10] All this is true; but by the entrance for the gods he means the artificially cut hole in the vault of the grotto, which must have served as a chimney to carry off the smoke of the sacrificial fires. From this chimney to the bottom of the grotto the depth is 56 ft., and, of course, no man can enter by this way. But for ages the proprietors of the field seem to have utilized this chimney to get rid of some of the stones which abound here, for the grotto is filled with small stones to the depth of 5 or 6 ft. From the vault of the grotto hang innumerable stalactites, which gave to Homer the idea of the stone urns and amphoræ, and the stone frames and looms on which the Nymphs wove purple-coloured mantles and veils.[1] I most carefully explored the whole southern portion of Ithaca. The town of Vathy, the present capital of Ithaca, is not yet a hundred years old, and the complete absence of ancient potsherds on the flat soil seems to prove that there was no city or village on the site in ancient times. Before Vathy was founded, the city was on a rocky height about one mile further south. On the site of the old town I found but a very small accumulation of *débris*, and no trace of ancient pottery.

Near the south-eastern extremity of the island, about 4½ miles from Vathy, are a number of rooms like stables, averaging 25 ft. in length and 10 ft. in breadth, partly rock-cut, partly formed by cyclopean walls of very huge rudely-wrought stones, which must have given to Homer the idea for the twelve pig-sties built by the divine swineherd Eumaeus.[2] To the east of these stables, and just in front of them, thousands of very common but most ancient potsherds indicate the existence of an ancient rustic habitation, which Homer appears to have described to us as the house and station of Eumaeus.[3] This is the more probable, as at a very

---

[10] See *Od.* xiii. 109–112. The whole passage (102–112) is:

αὐτὰρ ἐπὶ κρατὸς λιμένος τανύφυλλος ἐλαίη,
ἀγχόθι δ' αὐτῆς ἄντρον ἐπήρατον ἠεροειδές,
ἱρὸν Νυμφάων αἳ Νηϊάδες καλέονται.
ἐν δὲ κρητῆρές τε καὶ ἀμφιφορῆες ἔασιν
λάϊνοι· ἔνθα δ' ἔπειτα τιθαιβώσσουσι μέλισσαι·
ἐν δ' ἱστοὶ λίθεοι περιμήκεες, ἔνθα τε νύμφαι
φάρε' ὑφαίνουσιν ἁλιπόρφυρα, θαῦμα ἰδέσθαι,
ἐν δ' ὕδατ' αἰενάοντα. δύω δέ τέ οἱ θύραι εἰσίν,
αἱ μὲν πρὸς Βορέαο, καταιβαταὶ ἀνθρώποισιν,

αἱ δ' αὖ πρὸς Νότου εἰσὶ θεώτεραι· οὐδέ τι κείνῃ
ἄνδρες ἐσέρχονται, ἀλλ' ἀθανάτων ὁδός ἐστιν.

[1] See vv. 105–108 in the passage just cited.

[2] *Od.* xiv. 13, 14:

ἔντοσθεν δ' αὐλῆς συφεοὺς δυοκαίδεκα ποίειν
πλησίον ἀλλήλων, εὐνὰς συσίν·

[3] *Od.* xiv. 5–10:

τὸν δ' ἄρ' ἐνὶ προδόμῳ εὗρ' ἥμενον, ἔνθα οἱ αὐλή
ὑψηλὴ δέδμητο, περισκέπτῳ ἐνὶ χώρῳ,
καλή τε μεγάλη τε, περίδρομος· ἥν ῥα συβώτης
αὐτὸς δείμαθ' ὕεσσιν ἀποιχομένοιο ἄνακτος,

short distance to the south of this site, and near the sea, is a white cliff
with a perpendicular descent of 100 ft., which to the present day is called
Korax, "the Raven Rock," to which Homer refers when he represents
Ulysses as challenging Eumaeus "to precipitate him from the great rock"
if he finds that he is telling lies.[4] Below the Korax, in a recess, is a
natural and always plentiful spring of pure water, which tradition identifies with Homer's fountain of Arethusa, where the swine of Eumaeus were
watered.[5] I excavated in the stables, as well as in front of them on the
site of the rustic habitation ; I found the stables filled with stones, but
on the site of the house I struck the rock at a depth of 1 ft., and found
there fragments of very interesting, most ancient, unpainted pottery,
also of archaic pottery with red bands, and masses of broken tiles of a
later period.

I found in my excavations at the foot of Mount Aëtos two coins of
Ithaca, having on one side a cock with the legend ΙΘΑΚΩΝ, and on the
other side a head of Ulysses with a conical cap or pilidion ; also two coins
of Agathocles of Syracuse. These latter coins are here frequently found
and abundantly offered for sale. Corinthian and Roman coins are also
very frequent here. According to Aristotle[6] and Antigonus Carystius,[7] no
hare can live on Ithaca. But, on the contrary, hares are more abundant
here than on any other Greek island, it being next to impossible to hunt
them on the steep slopes of the huge mountains overgrown with thorny
underwood.

I may add that Ithaca is, like Utica, a Phoenician word, and means
"colony." According to Homer, Poseidon was the grandfather of Laertes,
and Mr. Gladstone appears, therefore, to be right in holding that the
descent from Poseidon always means "descent from the Phoenicians."

I strongly recommend a visit to Ithaca, not only to all admirers of
Homer, but also to all those who wish to see the ancient Greek type of
men and great female beauty. Visitors should not omit when at Vathy,
the capital of Ithaca, to call upon my friend Mr. Aristides Dendrinos, to
whom and to whose amiable lady, Mrs. Praxidea Dendrinos, I here make
my warmest acknowledgment for their bountiful hospitality. Mr. Dendrinos is the most wealthy man in Ithaca, and will at all times be happy
to assist travellers with his advice. He has a son Telemachus and a
daughter Penelope.

§ VIII. Fourth Year's Work at Troy : 1878.

I recommenced my excavations at Troy towards the end of September
1878, with a large number of workmen and several horse-carts, having
previously built felt-covered wooden barracks, with nine chambers for
my own accommodation and that of my overseers, servants, and visitors.

νόσφιν δεσποίνης καὶ Λαέρταο γέροντος,
ῥυτοῖσιν λάεσσι, καὶ ἐθρίγκωσεν ἀχέρδῳ.
    [4] *Od.* xiv. 398–400 :
εἰ δέ κε μὴ ἔλθῃσιν ἄναξ τεός, ὡς ἀγορεύω,
δμῶας ἐπισσεύας βαλέειν μεγάλης κατὰ πέτρης,
ὄφρα καὶ ἄλλος πτωχὸς ἀλεύεται ἠπεροπεύειν.

    [5] *Od.* xiii. 407–410 :
δήεις τόν γε σύεσσι παρήμενον· αἳ δὲ νέμονται
πὰρ Κόρακος πέτρῃ, ἐπί τε κρήνῃ Ἀρεθούσῃ,
ἔσθουσαι βάλανον μενοεικέα καὶ μέλαν ὕδωρ
πίνουσαι, τά θ' ὕεσσι τρέφει τεθαλυῖαν ἀλοιφήν.
    [6] *Hist. An.* viii. 27. 2.   [7] *Hist., Mir.* 11.

I also built a wooden barrack, which served both as a storehouse for antiquities and as a small dining-hall, together with a wooden magazine, in
which the antiquities were preserved, which were to be divided between
the Imperial Museum and myself, and of which the Turkish delegate
had the key; also a wooden magazine for my implements, wheelbarrows,
hand-carts, and other machinery for excavating; besides a small stone
house for the kitchen, a wooden house for my ten gensdarmes, and a stable
for the horses.[8]   All these buildings were erected on the north-west
slope of Hissarlik, which here descends at an angle of 75° to the plain.
The site of my barracks is, according to M. Burnouf's measurement,
25·55 mètres = 84 ft. above the level of the sea; consequently 23·88 m.
= 78 ft. below the summit of Hissarlik.

The ten gensdarmes, to whom I paid £20 10s. monthly, were all
refugees from Roumelia, and were of great use to me, for they not
only served as a guard against the brigands by whom the Troad was
infested, but they also carefully watched my labourers whilst they were
excavating, and thus forced them to be honest.

How necessary the ten gensdarmes were to me could not have been
better proved than by the fight which took place a short time after my
departure in the village of Kalifatli, only twenty minutes' walk from
Hissarlik, between the peasants and a large number of armed Circassians,
who in the night attacked the house of a villager reputed to possess
10,000 frs.   The villager ascended the terrace of his house and cried
for assistance, whereupon his neighbours hurried out with their rifles
and killed two of the assailants, but unfortunately lost two of their own
number—the brother-in-law and son-in-law of the demarch of Kalifatli.

The wages of my three overseers were from £5 to £10 monthly; those
of the common workmen, 2 frs. or 20 pence daily; the three carpenters
received 3¼ frs. or 2s. 7d.; the wheelwright 5 frs. or 4s. a day.   But the
highest wages of all were paid to my servant, who thought he was
indispensable, and therefore refused to serve for less than 300 frs. or £12
monthly; but he made at least twice as much out of his wine and bread-
store, of which his brother was the manager, for he sold to my labourers
on credit, and, as he was my paymaster, he always got back his money
easily and could never lose.

My endeavours were now principally directed to the excavation of
the large building to the west and north-west of the gate, and of the
north-eastern prolongation of the gateway.[9]   I had always identified the
large building with the residence of the last chief or king of Troy, because
in it, or close to it, had been found not only the large treasure I myself
discovered, but also the treasure which had been concealed from me
by my labourers and seized by the Turkish authorities, besides a vast
quantity of Trojan pottery; but I now maintain that identity with more
assurance than ever, having again discovered in it, or close to it, three
small treasures and a large one of gold jewels.   Of these the first was
found and excavated on the 21st of October, in the presence of seven

---

[8] See the frontispiece, to the right.
[9] See on No. 10, p. 35, the whole block in front; also the block on which the two houses stand.

officers of H.M.S. *Monarch,* in a chamber in the north-east part of the building, at a depth of 26 ft. 5 in. below the surface of the mound. It was contained in a broken hand-made terra-cotta vessel, which lay in an oblique position about 3 ft. above the floor, and must have fallen from an upper storey.

I give a drawing of the town-chief's house in the chapter on the Third City. Its longest wall runs parallel with the great external wall of the city, and is 53 ft. 4 in. long and 4 ft. 4 in. high; it consists of smaller and larger stones joined together with clay. Near the north-western extremity of this wall, and just 3 ft. above the ground, I found, in a layer of grey wood-ashes, two more small treasures, both contained in broken hand-made terra-cotta vases, of which the one lay in an oblique, the other in a horizontal position, from which circumstance I conclude that both had fallen from an upper part of the house; the orifices of the vases nearly touched each other. Only 3 ft. from this discovery, but on the house-wall itself, and at a depth of 26 ft. below the surface of the ground, a larger treasure of bronze weapons and gold jewels was found. All the objects contained in these four treasures, as well as all the other antiquities discovered in these excavations, will be described in the subsequent pages, as well as the gold ornaments found elsewhere.

I also continued excavating on the site of my former platform, on the north side of the hill,[10] but, on account of the winter rains, was obliged to stop the works on the 26th of November. According to the stipulations of my firman, I had to give up two-thirds of all the objects I found to the Imperial Museum, and carried off only one-third myself.

§ IX. Fifth Year's Work at Troy and the Heroic Tumuli, and Exploration of the Troad : 1879.

I went to Europe, and returned to the Dardanelles towards the end of February 1879. Having again procured the services of ten gensdarmes or zaptiehs and 150 workmen, I recommenced the excavations on the 1st of March. Up to the middle of March I suffered cruelly from the north wind, which was so icy cold that it was impossible to read or write in my wooden barracks, and it was only possible to keep oneself warm by active exercise in the trenches. To avoid taking cold, I went, as I had always done, very early every morning on horseback to the Hellespont to take my sea-bath, but I always returned to Hissarlik before sunrise and before the work commenced.[1] Two of my gensdarmes always served me as a guard in the bathing excursions, or whenever I absented myself from

---

[10] See No. 4 to the left ; also Plan I. (of Troy) between the points x and c.

[1] These rides in the dark were not without accidents. Travellers to the Troad will see a large block missing from the northern edge of the bridge of Koum Kioi. This stone was broken out when once in the dark I rode too near the edge, and I was precipitated with my horse into the bushes below. The horse having fallen upon me, I could not extricate myself from beneath it ; and my gensdarmes having gone ahead, could not hear my cries. A whole hour I was in this desperate position, till at last my gensdarmes, not seeing me coming to my usual bathing-place at Karanlik, returned and extricated me. Since that accident I always alight before passing a Turkish bridge, and lead my horse over by the bridle.

Hissarlik. But the cold weather did not last longer than a fortnight, and after that we had a succession of fine weather. The storks appeared in the beginning of March.

At the end of March I was joined at Hissarlik by my honoured friends Professor Rudolf Virchow of Berlin, and M. Émile Burnouf of Paris, Honorary Director of the French School at Athens; the latter having been sent to Troy on a scientific mission by the French Government, at the initiative of M. Jules Ferry, the Minister of Public Instruction. Both assisted me in my researches to the utmost of their ability. Professor Virchow studied the flora, fauna, and geological characteristics of the Plain of Troy, as well as the condition of the ruins and *débris* brought to light in the course of my excavations; and M. Burnouf, who is an excellent engineer and painter, made all the plans and maps, as well as many of the sketches contained in this book. He also studied the geology of the Plain of Troy, as well as the several layers of *débris* at Hissarlik.

My endeavours were this time principally directed towards bringing to light the entire circuit of the walls, and I therefore excavated to the east and south-west of the gate[2] (which, according to M. Burnouf's measurement, is 41·10 mètres = 135 ft. 2 in. above the level of the sea, and 8·33 m. = 27 ft. 5 in. below the surface of the hill), and to the north-west and north of the house of the chief, as well as to the east of my great northern trench.[3] It being especially important to preserve the houses of the burnt city, I gradually excavated the ruins of the three upper cities horizontally, layer by layer, until I reached the easily-recognizable calcined *débris* of the third or burnt city. Having brought down to one level the whole space I intended to explore, I began at the extremity of the area, excavating house by house, and gradually proceeding with this work in the direction of the northern slope, where the *débris* had to be shot. In this manner I was able to excavate all the houses of the third city without injuring their walls. But of course all that I could bring to light of them were the substructions, or first storeys, 3 to 10 ft. high, built of bricks or of stones cemented with earth. The great number of jars they contain can hardly leave any doubt that these served as cellars; though at first sight it is difficult to explain the scarcity of doorways, of which visitors will see but few. But it appears that these lower parts of the houses were entered by wooden stairs or ladders from above; regular openings for the doors, however, exist in all the rooms and chambers of the large building to the west and north-west of the gate.

Professor Virchow calls attention to the fact that, in an architectural point of view, the condition of this third city is the exact prototype of the kind of building which still characterizes the villages of the Troad. It was only when his medical practice[4] had introduced him into the interior of the present houses that he was able to understand the architectural details of those of the ancient state. The characteristic of the architecture is, that in most cases the lower part of the houses has no

---

[2] See Plan I. (of Troy).
[3] See Sectional Plan III., x, y.
[4] I give in Appendix V. Professor Virchow's

interesting account of his medical practice in the Troad.

entrance, and is surrounded by a stone wall. The upper storey, which is built of quadrangular sun-dried bricks, serves as the habitation for the family ; the lower one, which is entered by stairs or ladders from above, serves as a storehouse. Whenever the ground-floor has a door, it is also very frequently used as a stable for the cattle. When, as often happens also at the present day, modern houses of this kind fall into ruin, the ruins present precisely the same aspect as those of the third or burnt city of Hissarlik. The stones of the walls of the first storey of the Trojan houses present no trace of having been wrought ; they have come from the easily-obtainable natural strata of the tertiary fresh-water limestone of the neighbouring ridge. The rooms enclosed by these Trojan house-walls contain those gigantic terra-cotta jars which often stand in whole rows, representing a considerable fortune by their huge size, which is so great that a man can stand upright in each of them.

Streets also were scarce ; for besides the broad street of the gate, I brought to light only one street 4 ft. broad, paved with large flags, which bear the marks of the intense heat to which they have been exposed. This street may be seen just above the ruins of the second city, on the east side of my great trench ;[5] there is, besides, a passage 2 ft. broad, between the Trojan houses running off at right angles from the street d to the N.E. I further excavated to the east and south-east of the "Great Tower," where I was forced to destroy a number of house-walls close to the magazine containing the nine great jars discovered in 1873,[6] in order to unearth the city wall and its connection with the two gigantic stone walls called by me "the Great Tower." All this has been accomplished. My excavations to the south, south-west, west, north-west, and north of the gates, have also enabled me to uncover the city wall in these directions ; so that it is now disclosed in its entire circuit, except where it has been cut through by my great trench. In the course of these researches I found, in the presence of Professor Virchow and M. Burnouf, on the slope of the north-western part of the wall another treasure, consisting of gold ornaments, which will be described hereafter.

Outside the city wall on the east side, I discovered a great many house-walls, but scarcely any antiquities, which circumstance appears to prove that the suburb was inhabited by the poorer class. The south-east corner of the city presents no signs of the great conflagration.

I dug about one-half of my great trench down to the limestone rock, and thus laid bare three parallel house-walls[7] of the first settlers on Hissarlik. I also dug a deep drain for the discharge of the rain-water.

Although H.E. Munif Effendi, the Minister of Public Instruction, had already in January 1879 consented to H.E. Sir Henry Layard's request that a firman should be granted me for the exploration of the Tumuli, the so-called heroic tombs of the Troad, I had the very greatest difficulty in obtaining it. I was however powerfully aided by Sir Henry Layard and my honoured friend Mr. Ed. Malet, Minister Plenipotentiary during

---

[5] This street is marked d on Plan I. (of Troy).

[6] See No. 8, p. 33.

[7] See Plan III. f, between M and N.

his absence, as well as by H.E. Count Hatzfeldt, the German Ambassador at Constantinople, who assisted me at the request of Professor Virchow, and the firman at last arrived on the 17th of April. I immediately started to explore the two largest tumuli of the Troad, the Besika Tepeh and the Ujek Tepeh, as well as four smaller ones. These excavations will be described at length in the chapter on the Tumuli.

In company with Professor Virchow, I again visited the village of Bounarbashi, and the heights behind it, the Bali Dagh, which have had for nearly a hundred years the undeserved honour of being identified with the site of the Homeric Ilium.

Professor Virchow fully agrees with me that the circuit-walls of the little Acropolis — which, according to M. Burnouf's measurement, is 144·36 mètres = 472 ft. above the level of the sea, and in which so many great modern luminaries in archæology have seen the walls of Priam's Pergamus—have never deserved to be called "Cyclopean." He was the first to observe, from the peculiar manner in which the stones of the walls have been wrought, that they have been slowly shaped (*abgesplittert*) with an iron pick-hammer, and must consequently belong to a comparatively late period. As above mentioned, these ruins probably mark the site of Gergis, where, according to Xenophon,[8] Queen Mania kept her treasures. I showed him that the average depth of the accumulation of *débris* in the little Acropolis is only 1 ft. 6 in., and that only Hellenic pottery is found there. He recognized the *agora* of the little town in a recess of amphitheatrical form, in which the ruins of four rows of stone seats may still be seen. It is strange that this *agora* never fell under the notice of any one before, and that it was reserved for the keen eye of Professor Virchow to discover it.

We also visited the springs[9] of Bounarbashi,[10] which, according to M. Burnouf's measurement, are 27·77 mètres = 91 ft. above the level of the sea, and in which the defenders of the Bounarbashi theory recognize two springs only—one lukewarm, the other icy cold—in order to force them into agreement with those described by Homer, near which Hector was killed by Achilles: "But they dashed forward by the watch-tower and the wind-beaten fig-tree always along the wall, on the chariot road, until they reached the two fair-flowing springs, where the twin sources of the eddying Scamander bubble up: for the one flows with lukewarm water, from which clouds of steam arise as from a burning fire; the other runs forth in summer like hail or cold snow, or as from frozen water."[11]

---

[8] *Hist. Gr.*, iii. 1, § 15: Ταῦτα δὲ ποιήσας Σκῆψιν καὶ Γέργιθα ἐχυρὰς πόλεις κατέσχεν, ἔνθα καὶ τὰ χρήματα μάλιστα ἦν τῇ Μανίᾳ. "When he (Meidias) had done this, he took possession of the fortified cities of Scepsis and Gergis, where Mania chiefly kept her treasures."

[9] As before mentioned, I counted here thirty-four springs; but as the spot where they rise is called Kirk-Giös, or "forty eyes," there are probably forty springs here.

[10] Bounarbashi means "head of the springs." Clarke (i. p. 109) reminds us that in Wales there is a Pen tre fynnyn, which means "head of the three springs."

[11] *Il.* xxii. 145-152:

οἳ δὲ παρὰ σκοπιὴν καὶ ἐρινεὸν ἠνεμόεντα
τείχεος αἰὲν ὑπὲκ κατ' ἀμαξιτὸν ἐσσεύοντο·
κρουνὼ δ' ἵκανον καλλιρρόω, ἔνθα δὲ πηγαί
δοιαὶ ἀναΐσσουσι Σκαμάνδρου δινήεντος.
ἣ μὲν γάρ θ' ὕδατι λιαρῷ ῥέει, ἀμφὶ δὲ καπνός
γίγνεται ἐξ αὐτῆς, ὡσεὶ πυρὸς αἰθομένοιο.
ἣ δ' ἑτέρη θέρεϊ προρέει εἰκυῖα χαλάζῃ,
ἢ χιόνι ψυχρῇ, ἢ ἐξ ὕδατος κρυστάλλῳ.

Professor Virchow found in two of the springs a temperature of 16°·8 centigrade (62°·24 Fahrenheit), in a third 17° (62°·6 Fahrenheit), in a fourth 17°·4 (63°·32 Fahrenheit). The last spring rises in a swamp, and, as Professor Virchow explains, is for this reason slightly warmer, the water being stagnant. On the other hand, the spring which shows 17° runs at once into a little rivulet formed by other sources higher up, and it appears, therefore, to be a little colder; the two springs of 16°·8 were tested as they bubbled forth from beneath the rock: and thus, Virchow says, it is quite intelligible that, the difference of temperature of the water in the swamp and of the running water in the rivulet being still more marked in winter than in spring or summer, vapour might be seen to rise from the former and not from the latter.

I further visited, in company with the same friend, the vast ruins of Alexandria-Troas on the coast nearly opposite Tenedos.[1] We went from thence to the hot springs called Ligia Hammam, in a valley to the south-east; the height above the sea is 85 ft., according to Virchow. The water is saline and ferruginous, and its temperature is 150° Fahrenheit, according to Barker Webb;[2] according to Clarke,[3] only 142° Fahrenheit. The numerous ancient ruins in the valley leave no doubt that the springs were very celebrated in antiquity. The baths are much frequented in summer for rheumatic and cutaneous affections. We passed the night in the prosperous Turkish village of Kestamboul, which commands a magnificent view of Mount Chigri (called in Turkish " Chigri Dagh ") and the Aegean Sea. Next we ascended Mount Chigri (its height above the sea is 1639 ft. according to Virchow), passing on our way the ancient quarries near the village of Koch-Ali-Ovassi. We saw there seven columns which had been cut whole out of the granite rock, each 38 ft. 6 in. long, the diameter at the top being 4 ft. 6 in., and 5 ft. 6 in. at the base. They appear to have been destined for Alexandria-Troas, as they are exactly similar to the three which lie there on the beach.

On the top of Mount Chigri we greatly admired the vast Hellenic ruins supposed by Mr. Calvert to mark the site of Neandria, whilst others identify them with Cenchreae. The fortress, which has the unusual length of 1900 paces, and is 520 paces broad, is considered to be very ancient,

---

[1] In opposition to the common belief, I think that this city was not founded by Antigonus, but that it was only enlarged by him, for Strabo (xiii. pp. 593, 604) expressly states that "its site was formerly called ' Sigia,' and that Antigonus, having colonized it with the inhabitants of Chrysa, Cebrene, Neandria, Scepsis, Larissa, Colonae, Hamaxitus, and other cities, named it Antigonia." He further states that it was afterwards embellished by Lysimachus, who named it, in honour of Alexander the Great, "Alexandria-Troas." Julius Caesar was so much pleased with its site, that, according to Suetonius (Jul. Caes. 79), he intended to make it the capital of the Roman Empire. According to Zosimus (ii. 30) and Zonaras (xiii. 3), Constantine the Great had the same idea before he chose Byzantium: he intended to build his new capital μεταξὺ Τρῳάδος (Alexandria) καὶ τῆς ἀρχαίας Ἰλίου, according to Zosimus; ἐν Σιγαίῳ (sic), according to Zonaras. Under Hadrian, the celebrated orator Herodes Atticus was governor of the city. Several portions of the gigantic aqueduct which he built, and to the cost of which his father Atticus contributed three millions of drachmas of his own money, still exist. Alexandria-Troas is also mentioned in Holy Scripture (by the name of Troas) as one of the cities which were visited by St. Paul (Acts xx. 5). Its extensive Byzantine ruins leave no doubt that it was inhabited till the end of the Middle Ages. It is now called " Eski-stambul " (i.e. the Old City).

[2] Topographie de la Troade, p. 131.

[3] Travels in various Countries of Europe, Asia, and Africa, i. 148.

and parts of it are assigned to the same epoch as Tiryns and Mycenae. But we could not discover in it anything which might claim a high antiquity; besides, pre-historic cities are always very small. The walls average 10 ft. in breadth, and consist of two parallel walls of regular horizontal courses of granite blocks cut into a wedge-like shape, with their broad end turned outside, the space between the two walls, as well as the interstices between the blocks, being filled up with small stones. To this sort of masonry, which can also be seen in the famous Acropolis of Assos, we did not think ourselves justified in attributing a greater antiquity than the Macedonian period, the more so as the stones have been worked with an iron pick-hammer. Some parts of the walls we saw were composed of polygonal stones well fitted together, but they equally failed to convey to us an idea of high antiquity. In fact, I could point out in Greece a number of walls formed of polygonal stones, which we know to have been erected in Macedonian times; as, for instance, the substructions of some of the tombs in the ancient cemetery of the Hagia Trias at Athens and the fortifications on Salamis. The walls of the fortress on Mount Chigri are for the most part well preserved, but in many places they are more or less destroyed. I attribute this to the roots of the trees which grow between the small stones and must have dislocated the large blocks. Professor Virchow does not think this explanation insufficient, but prefers to ascribe the destruction of the walls to earthquakes. It deserves to be noticed that the bare rock crops out in all parts of the fortress, and that there is no accumulation of *débris;* only here and there I saw a late Roman potsherd and some fragments of bricks of a late date.

We next visited the small Turkish town of Iné, on the Scamander, 304 ft. above the sea, the name of which is probably a corruption of *Aenea*.[4] However this may be, it appears evident that Iné occupies the site of an ancient town, perhaps of Scamandria, as Mr. Calvert thinks, for many fragments of ancient sculptures are to be seen there, and masses of fragmentary pottery peep out of the clay walls of the houses, a good many of the fragments being Hellenic. From Iné we went to the prettily-situated town of Beiramich, which stands on a plateau on the banks of the Scamander, 516 ft. above the sea according to Virchow, whence we proceeded to the neat village of Evjilar, situated 864 ft. above the sea: the name Evjilar means "village of the hunters." This also stands on the bank of the Scamander, whose width varies here from 40 to 66 ft., while the water is hardly a foot deep. We had with us three gensdarmes on horseback and two on foot, the country being unsafe.

Thence we ascended the mountains of Ida, which are covered with a beautiful forest of oak and pine,[5] intermingled with chestnut-trees,

---

[4] There being silver-mines near Iné (see Chandler, i. 142; Pococke, iii. p. 160; and Lechevalier, *Voyage dans la Troade*, p. 128), it is highly probable that, instead of ἡ Νέα κώμη (καὶ ἀργύρια), between Polichna and Palaescepsis, we ought to read in Strabo, xiii. p. 603, according to the parallel passage, xii. p. 552, Αἴνεα or Ἔνεα κώμη (see Groskurd, ii. pp. 480 and 580). Pliny, *H. N.* ii. 96, 97, v. 30. 30, and Steph. Byz. p. 487, who mention Nea, seem to have taken it from Strabo, p. 603. A. Pauly, *Real Encyclopädie*, s. v. "Nea."

[5] *Il.* xi. 494:

πολλὰς δὲ δρῦς ἀζαλέας, πολλὰς δέ τε πεύκας.

plane-trees, limes, and the like. The rain, which came down in torrents,
prevented us from reaching the summit of Gargarus, which is 5750 ft.
above the level of the sea. We could only get as far as the sources
of the Scamander, which are 4056 ft. below the top of the mountain.
The principal source, which according to Virchow's measurement is
1694 ft. above the level of the sea, dashes forth in a stream about 7 ft.
broad from a natural cavern, in a nearly vertical rock wall, from 250
to 300 ft. high, which is composed of a coarse crystalline marble. It falls
at once almost vertically 60 to 70 ft. over projecting blocks of rock, and
after a course of 200 ft. it is joined by a small stream, formed by the
waters of three smaller but still abundant sources, and a number of very
small ones rising out of crevices in the rock close to the large one, as well
as by a large rivulet which is supplied from the melted snow, and has but
very little water in summer. At about 200 ft. from the great cavern, five
or six paces from the river-bed, is a small cavity, evidently the same as
that of which P. Barker Webb[6] speaks, and from which there once ran a
copious source of warm water; but now, and probably for many years past,
this cave is dry, the spring having bored another channel through the
rock considerably below it, and close to the Scamander, into which it flows.
This source had, according to Virchow's observations, a temperature of
60°·44 Fahrenheit, the air being at 58°·64; and the water of the Scamander, as it flows from the cavern, 47°·12. Professor Virchow[7] observes :
" Although in the *Iliad*[8] the Scamander is mentioned as one of the rivers
which rise from the Ida range, yet a certain doubt has prevailed as to the
exact place of its origin. It appears to me that this doubt is due to the
statements of Demetrius of Scepsis, who, among the various peaks of the
Ida, indicated the Cotylus as the place of the sources of the Scamander,
while the presumptions of the *Iliad* essentially refer to Mount Gargarus.
Here a grove and an altar were consecrated to Zeus ;[9] and here he was
wont to stay.[10] And when the Scamander is indicated as the son of Zeus,
where else could his source be, but on Mount Gargarus ? Though, according to Hercher,[1] the repeated addition, ὃν ἀθάνατος τέκετο Ζεύς,[2] may be
rejected as a later interpolation, there remains the epithet διιπετέος
ποταμοῖο, which occurs three times ;[3] and even if the beginning of the
twelfth book of the *Iliad*, where the Scamander is called δῖος,[4] should not
be genuine, yet the divine character of the river-god is expressly testified
in the Μάχη παραποτάμιος, Heré calling him ἀθάνατον θεόν,[5] and Achilles
διοτρεφές.[6] In the imagination of the poet the river and the river-god
blend together into a single personality, and the origin of both is referred,
as it were, to the great weather-god on Mount Gargarus."
    We returned to Evjilar, and proceeded thence, by way of Erenlü
(780 ft. above the sea), Bujuk Bounarbashi, and Aiwadjik, to Behrahm,
the ancient Assos, whence we returned in an open boat to the Plain of

[6] *Topographie de la Troade*, p. 46.
[7] *Beiträge zur Landeskunde der Troas*, p. 36.
[8] xii. 19-21.
[9] *Il.* viii. 48.
[10] *Il.* xiv. 157, 158.

[1] *Phil. und histor. Abh. der k. Akad. d. Wis-
sensch.* ; Berlin, 1875, p. 105.
[2] *Il.* xiv. 434 ; xxi. 2 ; xxiv. 693.
[3] *Il.* xvii. 263 ; xxi. 268, 326.
[4] xii. 21.   [5] xxi. 380.   [6] xxi. 223.

Troy. According to Virchow's measurement, Bujuk Bounarbashi is 907, Aiwadjik is 871, and the Acropolis of Assos 615 ft. above the level of the sea. I fully agree with Colonel Leake, that the ruins of Assos give the most perfect idea of a Greek city that we can now find anywhere. Its circuit-walls are better built, and are in a far better state of preservation, than those of any other Greek city now existing. They are, on an average, 8 ft. 4 in. thick, and consist of wrought stones, either square or wedge-shaped, which are put together precisely like those of the walls of the great fortress on Mount Chigri; the interior of the walls, as well as the interstices between the stones, being filled with small stones. Wherever the wall consists of square blocks, these are intersected at regular distances by long wedgelike blocks, which serve to consolidate them in their position. All the stones show the most evident marks of having been worked with an iron pick-hammer, and consequently cannot claim a very remote antiquity. Professor Virchow agrees with me in thinking that, although some parts of the walls may belong to the sixth century B.C., yet by far the larger part of them has been built in Macedonian times.

In company with Professor Virchow and M. Burnouf, I also made an excursion through the Doumbrek valley to Mount Kara Your and Mount Oulou Dagh, the former of which is, according to M. Burnouf's measurement, 209 m. = 686 ft. above the level of the sea, and has hitherto had the honour of being identified with Mount Callicolone, mentioned twice

No. 15. The Plain of the Simois, seen from the border of the Southern Swamp. To the left, the Heights between the Simois and the Hellespont; to the right, the Plateau between the Simois and the Thymbrius; in the background, the Oulou Dagh.

by Homer.[7] But, as the poet makes the war-god leap alternately from Ilium to Callicolone, and from Callicolone to Ilium, Professor Virchow considers it to be implied that Callicolone must be visible from Ilium; and Mount Kara Your not fulfilling this condition, he identifies Mount Oulou Dagh with the Homeric Callicolone, this being the only other great height in the neighbourhood of the Simois; besides, Hissarlik and nearly every point of the Plain of Troy can be seen from this mount, which is not the case with Mount Kara Your. Mount Oulou Dagh is, according to M. Burnouf's measurement, 429·80 m. = 1409 ft. above the level of the sea.

We also visited the ruins of the ancient town of Ophrynium, now

---

[7] *Il.* xx. 52, 53:   and xx. 151:

ὀξὺ κατ' ἀκροτάτης πόλιος Τρώεσσι κελεύων   οἳ δ' ἑτέρωσε κάθιζον ἐπ' ὀφρύσι Καλλικολώνης.
ἄλλοτε πὰρ Σιμόεντι θέων ἐπὶ Καλλικολώνῃ·

Palaeo-Kastron, which stood between Cape Rhoeteum and the village of Ren Kioi, on a lofty height overhanging the Hellespont; hence its name (from ὀφρύς). Its Acropolis is about the same size as Hissarlik. Remnants of the wall are visible on three sides, with traces of two towers; there was probably no wall on the fourth side, this being protected by the precipice. Within the Acropolis are remains of several buildings. The lower town appears to have extended to the valley on the south side of the Acropolis, where several heaps of stones appear to mark the sites of houses; but all the fragments of pottery I could gather there and in the Acropolis are of the Hellenic period. As to the identity of the place with Ophrynium, the coins found on the spot leave no doubt. The site of Ophrynium is erroneously marked on Admiral Spratt's map to the east of Ren Kioi, two miles distant from its real position.

We also visited the rocky height opposite the Bali Dagh, on the east side of the Scamander. We found there on the north-west, north, north-east, east, and south-east sides of the summit large fragmentary walls, which, to judge from the huge heaps of stones on either side of them, appear to have had a height of 20 ft. or more; they consist of unwrought stones joined together with small ones. The largest blocks contained in the walls are 3 ft. long, and about 1½ ft. in breadth and height; but in general the stones are much smaller. Within the walls may be traced some foundations of houses. Many more foundations can be detected on the plateau below the summit as well as down the whole slope, where the lower city appears to have extended. The hill runs in an almost vertical line on the south and west sides towards the Scamander. On account of the many inequalities of ground in the little Acropolis, as well as in the lower city, the rains have so completely swept away every vestige of artificial *débris*, that the bare rock everywhere protrudes, and no excavations are possible. In spite of the most careful examination, I could not find a single fragment of pottery either on the Acropolis or in the lower town. On the slope on the north side is a tumulus of loose stones, which has lost its conical shape. The ruins of this ancient Acropolis and city are marked on Admiral Spratt's map of 1840, but they had been indicated to him by Mr. Frank Calvert, who discovered them.

I give here an extract from the speech which Professor Virchow made on his return to Berlin from his expedition to the Troad, before the Berlin Society for Anthropology, Ethnology, and Pre-historic Archæology, on the 20th of June, 1879:—

"That part of the citadel-hill of Hissarlik in which the calcined ruins of the '*burnt* city' were found had at the time of my departure from the Troad been cleared away, in a considerable number of places, down to the virgin soil. At one place we reached the rock itself, on which the most ancient city had been built. In the midst of the great trench Schliemann had left standing a mighty block, which, as long as it holds together, will indicate to visitors the original level of the surface. It forms a large quadrangular column, which rises between 8 and 9 mètres (26 ft. 4 in. to 29 ft. 7 in.) above the level of the ground on which the town-chief's house stands. But below this latter level one may dig 6, 8, nay 10 mètres

No. 16.   Troy as seen from the Hellenic Theatre.   The Swamp to the right has been formed by the waters of the Simois and by those of the Springs below the Walls of Novum Ilium.   In the background to the right is the Plain of the Scamander.   View taken after the excavations in 1879.

(19 ft. 9 in., 26 ft. 4 in., or 32 ft. 10 in.), before penetrating through all the layers of ruin. Thus the aggregate depth of all the strata of *débris*,

from the surface to the rock itself, amounts to nearly 20 mètres (66 ft.). The whole of this depth consists of the remains of ancient habitations. There is nothing in or about it which could give the impression of having belonged to anything else.

"Its situation is as follows: on the last spur of a tertiary mountain-ridge, which projects from the volcanic mountains on the east towards the Scamander, and rises perhaps 100 ft. above the plain, there has been heaped up a series of layers of *débris*, in which it is easy to recognize the stratification of the settlements which have succeeded each other. These masses of *débris* have indeed grown to an incredible height. But the very circumstance, that perhaps nowhere else in the world has an accumulation of this kind been hitherto discovered—an accumulation consisting of such a mass of *débris* of successive settlements—proves that an extraordinarily long time must have elapsed from the foundation of the first settlement to the destruction of the last. Whatever opinion may be formed of the manner in which the successive buildings were constructed, for the masses of *débris* to have attained such a depth more time is undoubtedly needed than we are justified in accepting for the formation of the mounds of ruins at any other place whatever in the world. If one wishes to make a comparison, at the best a certain parallel might be found in the Assyrian mounds, in which, owing to the great quantity of bricks that entered into their construction, the dissolving masses of clay have attained a very extraordinary bulk. A certain comparison is also presented by the excavations on the Palatine Mount at Rome. But the accumulations at Hissarlik are distinguished from all others by the fact, that there exists here *a larger series of successive heterogeneous stratifications* than in any other known spot; and these, by their whole nature and condition, testify to repeated changes in the population. Their duration cannot, indeed, be calculated by definite numbers of years; but we nevertheless gain a chronological basis from the enclosed material, which exists in rich abundance.

"How long the aforesaid block can resist the influences of the weather, I dare not say. At all events, it will for a long time to come give testimony, not only to the gigantic height of these masses of ruins, but also, as I believe, to the incredible energy of the man, who has with his own private means succeeded in removing such enormous masses of earth. If you could see what mounds of earth (in the full sense of the word) had to be dug away and removed, in order to have a view of the lower layers, you would indeed scarcely believe that a single man in the course of a few years could have accomplished so great an under-taking. On this occasion I would stand up for Schliemann against a reproach which, though plausible in itself, falls to the ground on closer consideration—the reproach that he has not excavated from the surface, layer by layer, so as to obtain a complete plan for each successive period.

"There is no doubt that the manner in which he has excavated, by making at once a large trench through the whole hill, has had, in the highest degree, a destructive effect on the upper layers. In those near the surface were portions of temples of the Hellenic period, columns, triglyphs, and all kinds of marble fragments, thrown together *pêle-mêle*. Nevertheless, with great care and attention, such as that with which the excavations at Olympia are carried on, it might perhaps have been possible to have reconstructed a temple, at least in part. But Schliemann felt no interest in a temple belonging to a period far too late for him. I may also say that, after having seen a considerable proportion of the fragments, I doubt whether, if all had been brought together, an essential gain would have been contributed to the history of art or to science. I allow that it has been a kind of sacrilege. Schliemann has cut the temple (of Athené) right in two; the building material has been thrown aside and partly again buried; it will not be easy for any one, even with the largest expenditure, to collect it again. But, undoubtedly, if Schliemann had proceeded in such a way as to remove the ruins stratum by stratum from the surface, he would, owing to the vastness of the task, not even to-day have reached

No. 17.   Troy seen from the South-east side.   This point of view has been taken from the Plateau between the Simois and the Thymbrius, above the Theatre in Novum Ilium.   View taken in 1879.

the layers in which the principal objects were found. He only reached them by at once extracting the nucleus of the great hill.

"The hill of Hissarlik has indeed increased, in the course of time, not only in height, but also *in breadth and thickness*, through the masses of *débris* removed and thrown aside by successive generations, in order to obtain a site on which they could build. Since the excavations in this direction have now been carried on systematically, chronological conclusions may be drawn with the greatest precision from the accumulation of the *débris*, which show in the vertical trenches a series of stratifications lying the one upon the other, and falling off obliquely. Such conclusions could hardly have been arrived at, if the strata, which lie one upon the other, but do not always continue on the same level, had been simply taken off in succession.

" Near the surface, we see in one place the foundations of the temple, in another the wall composed of regular layers of wrought stones of the Alexandrian time, the so-called wall of Lysimachus. Its situation is highly characteristic. In the vertical trenches made through the outer circumference of the hill may be seen successive slanting layers of *débris*, from which it may easily be perceived that the *débris* had been thrown over the slope of the hill.   On these accumulations the wall has been

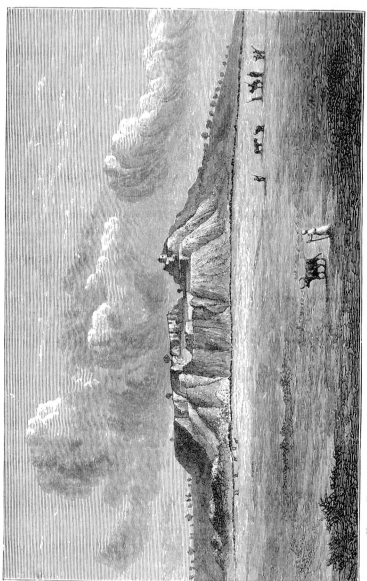

No. 18. Troy as it appeared after the Excavations of 1871–1873.   The northern side, viewed from the bank of the ancient Scamander.

erected:[8] it does not stand upon the primitive rock, but on the material which has been thrown down sideways, and indeed in places where there

---

[8] See the Section given in the chapter on the Greek Ilium.

is no rock at all below. It may thus be understood that the surface of
the hill has manifestly increased in width from settlement to settlement.
The circumference of the hill went on continually enlarging in the course
of time. In this way it has increased to dimensions which, in height as well
as in width, very far exceed those of the 'burnt city.' This latter forms,
in the midst of the whole, a proportionately small central part. The
successive cities became continually larger and larger, and extended their
radius. Our attention was first called to this by our own work in order
to bring to light the 'burnt city.' The *débris* was taken out from the
midst, and carried to the side; but as the slope was here, it was carried
through a trench, which had been cut radially through the hill, to the
brink of the slope, and was there thrown over. Thus the mass of earth
partly slid down the slope, and partly remained lying on it, while only
the larger stones rolled down into the plain. By these means the hill
visibly and continually increased, and, as seen from below, it appeared to
be always growing larger and larger. It now looks, I believe, more stately
than ever it did before. The various trenches and accumulations have
given the hill the appearance of something which very much resembles a
large fortress. The hill thus artificially excavated is now in the following
condition. Apart from the single trenches, the exterior covering of the
ancient hill still remains at its original height, whereas the interior is
excavated. Standing on the circuit-walls, one looks down into a sort
of large cauldron, at the bottom of which lies the 'burnt city,' with
its walls and foundations visible as on a plan. In this way the visitor
is in a position to become acquainted with the peculiar nature of the
constructions.

"This is in so far of great interest for those philologists who wish to
investigate how far the indications of Homer agree with the existing conditions: for example, with reference to the course run three times round
the city by Hector and Achilles. The question is no longer, as hitherto,
about the whole hill of Hissarlik, but only about the central part of it,
which really represents the ancient settlement. This latter is much
smaller than the whole content and circumference of Hissarlik itself. I
must, however, lay stress on the fact, that in comparison with the
Acropolis on the Bali Dagh, even this smaller part would still represent a
considerable town, which far exceeds the settlement on Bounarbashi."

As on my last journey to England and Germany I have heard it
repeatedly stated that, carried away by ambition, I am ruining myself in
my archæological explorations, to the prejudice of my children,[9] who will
be penniless after my death, I find it necessary to assure the reader that,
although on account of my present scientific pursuits I am bound to keep
aloof from all sorts of speculation and am compelled to content myself
with a small interest on my capital, I still have a yearly income of £4000
as the net proceeds of the rents of my four houses in Paris, and £6000

---

[9] I have four children: a son, Sergius, born
in 1855, and daughter, Nadeshda, born in 1861,
by my first wife; and a son, Agamemnon, born in
1878, and daughter, Andromache, born in 1871,
by my second wife.

interest on my funded property, making in all £10,000; whilst, inclusive of the large cost of my excavations, I do not spend more than £5000 a year, and am thus able to add £5000 annually to my capital. I trust, therefore, that on my death I shall leave to each of my children a fortune large enough to enable them to continue their father's scientific explorations without ever touching their capital. I avail myself of this opportunity to assure the reader that, as I love and worship science for its own sake, I shall never make a traffic of it. My large collections of Trojan antiquities have a value which cannot be calculated, but they shall never be sold. If I do not present them in my lifetime, they shall at all events pass, in virtue of my last will, to the Museum of the nation I love and esteem most.

I cannot conclude this introduction without expressing my warmest thanks to my honoured friends Mr. Frank Calvert, Consul of the United States of America; Mr. Paul Venizelos, Consul of Greece; Mr. Emilio Vitali, Consul of Italy; and Mr. Nicolaos Didymos, first dragoman and political agent of the Turkish Government at the Dardanelles, for all the kindness they have shown and all the valuable services they have rendered me during the long period of my excavations at Hissarlik. I also warmly thank my friends, Doctor F. Imhoof Blumer of Winterthur and Mr. Achilles Postolaccas, keeper of the National Collection of Coins at Athens: the former for the great kindness he has shown me in getting photographed for me all the different Ilian coins he had at his disposal; the latter for the great friendship he has shown me in superintending the drawing of these coins, as well as of all the Ilian coins contained in the collection under his charge; also for the learned dissertation he has written for me on the Ilian coins and medals, which will appear in the chapter on Novum Ilium.

CHAPTER I.

THE COUNTRY OF THE TROJANS (οἱ Τρῶες).

§ I. The Extent of the Trojan Land. The Troad (ἡ Τρῳάς, sc. γῆ).

In interpreting the Homeric geography of the Troad, Strabo[1] rightly says: "The coast of the Propontis extends from the district of Cyzicus, and the neighbourhood of the Aesepus and the Granicus, to Abydus and Sestus; the land around Ilium, and Tenedos, and Alexandria-Troas from Abydus to Lectum:[2] but above all these lies the mountain-range of Ida, which extends to Lectum. But from Lectum to the river Caïcus[3] and (the promontory of) Canae there follows the country around Assos,[4] and Adramyttium, and Atarneus,[5] and Pitane,[6] and the Elaitic Gulf;[7] opposite all of which stretches the island of the Lesbians: then follows immediately the district of Cyme, as far as the Hermus[8] and Phocaea, which forms the beginning of Ionia and the end of Aeolis. Such being the localities, the poet gives us to understand that, from the district of the Aesepus and the present province of Cyzicene to the river Caïcus, the Trojan rule extended, divided into eight or even nine parts, according to the dominions; but the mass of auxiliary troops is counted among the confederates."

Thus the Homeric Troad comprised the north-western part of the later Mysia, between the rivers Aesepus and Caïcus: this is fully confirmed by the poet, who makes Achilles mention in conversation with Priam that Priam's dominion comprises all that is bounded to the north-west (ἄνω) by Lesbos and to the north-east (καθύπερθεν) by Phrygia and the Hellespont. All the nations which inhabit this dominion are called Trojans (Τρῶες) by Homer, although he sometimes appears to designate under this name more especially the inhabitants of Ilium and its immediate environs.

---

[1] xiii. p. 581: Ἀπὸ δὲ τῆς Κυζικηνῆς καὶ τῶν περὶ Αἴσηπον τόπων καὶ Γράνικον, μέχρι Ἀβύδου καὶ Σηστοῦ, τὴν τῆς Προποντίδος παραλίαν εἶναι συμβαίνει· ἀπὸ δὲ Ἀβύδου μέχρι Λεκτοῦ τὰ περὶ Ἴλιον, καὶ Τένεδον, καὶ Ἀλεξάνδρειαν τὴν Τρωάδα· πάντων δὴ τούτων ὑπέρκειται ἡ Ἴδη τὸ ὄρος, μέχρι Λεκτοῦ καθήκουσα· ἀπὸ Λεκτοῦ δὲ μέχρι Καΐκου ποταμοῦ καὶ τῶν Κανῶν λεγομένων ἐστὶ τὰ περὶ Ἄσσον, καὶ Ἀδραμύττιον, καὶ Ἀταρνέα, καὶ Πιτάνην, καὶ τὸν Ἐλαϊτικὸν κόλπον· οἷς πᾶσιν ἀντιπαρήκει ἡ τῶν Λεσβίων νῆσος· εἶθ' ἑξῆς τὰ περὶ Κύμην, μέχρις Ἕρμου καὶ Φωκαίας, ἥπερ ἀρχὴ μὲν τῆς Ἰωνίας ἐστί, πέρας δὲ τῆς Αἰολίδος. Τοιούτων δὲ τῶν τόπων ὄντων, ὁ μὲν ποιητὴς ἀπὸ τῶν περὶ Αἴσηπον τόπων, καὶ τῶν περὶ τὴν νῦν Κυζικηνὴν χώραν, ὑπαγορεύει μάλιστα τοὺς Τρῶας ἄρξαι μέχρι τοῦ Καΐκου ποταμοῦ διῃρημέ- νους κατὰ δυναστείας εἰς ὀκτὼ μερίδας, ἢ καὶ ἐννέα· τὸ δὲ τῶν ἄλλων ἐπικούρων πλῆθος ἐν τοῖς συμμάχοις διαριθμεῖται.

[2] Τὸ Λεκτόν, now called Cape Baba or Santa Maria. Here Heré, in company with Hypnos, first touches the Trojan land on her way to Ida (Il. xiv. 283, 284: Ἴδην δ' ἱκέσθην . . . Λεκτόν, ὅθι πρῶτον λιπέτην ἅλα).

[3] Now Ak-Su, or Bochair, Bakir, Bacher.

[4] Now Behram or Bearahm.

[5] Now Dikeli Kioi.

[6] Now Sanderli.

[7] Now the Gulf of Sanderli or of Fokia.

[8] This river is now called Gedis or Ghiediz Tschai.

We shall follow Buchholz [9] in describing in the following order the eight or nine smaller dominions of which the Troad was composed :—

I. Dominion of Pandarus.[10]
II. Dominion of Adrestus and Amphius.[1]
III. Dominion of Asius.[2]
IV. Dominion of Aeneas (Dardania).[3]
V. Dominion of Hector (Troy in the more narrow sense).[4]

The following districts are further mentioned in Homer :—

VI. Dominion of Altes (the Leleges).[5]
VII. Dominion of the Cilicians, viz. :
    a. Dominion of Eëtion.[6]
    b. Dominion of Mynes.[7]
    c. Dominion of Eurypylus (the Ceteians).[8]

§ II. Mountains of the Troad.

Mount Ida (ἡ Ἴδη,[9] τὰ Ἰδαῖα ὄρη [10]) still retains its ancient name. Its Homeric epithets are ὑψηλή (high [1]), πολυπίδαξ (rich in fountains [2]); and from its abundance of game it is also called the mother or nourisher of wild animals (μήτηρ θηρῶν [3]). It extends through Western Mysia in many branches from south-west to north-east. On account of its manifold ramifications, it was compared by the ancients to a centipede (scolopendra).[4] One of its principal branches extends along the northern coast of the Gulf of Adramyttium, and runs out into the promontory of Lectum ;[5] the other extends in a westerly direction along the river Aesepus, and terminates at the city of Zeleia :—" those who inhabited Zeleia at the lowest foot of Ida." [6] In Ida rise the rivers Rhesus, Heptaporus, Caresus, Rhodius, Grenicus (Granicus), Aesepus, Scamander, and Simois :—" Then Poseidon and Apollo took counsel to destroy the wall, turning against it all the rivers that flow from the mountains of Ida into the sea—Rhesus, Heptaporus, Caresus, Rhodius, Grenicus, and Aesepus, divine Scamander also and Simois." [7] As already stated, the highest summit of Ida is Mount Gargarus, now called Kaz Dagh, 5750 ft. above the level of the sea. On Gargarus was " a temenos sacred to Zeus,

[9] *Homerische Kosmographie und Geographie*, von Dr. E. Buchholz; Leipzig, 1871.
[10] *Il.* ii. 824–827.   [1] *Il.* ii. 828 834.
[2] *Il.* ii. 835–839.   [3] *Il.* ii. 819–823.
[4] *Il.* ii. 816–818.   [5] *Il.* xxi. 86, 87.
[6] *Il.* vi. 396, 397 ; ii. 692.
[7] *Il.* xix. 296.   [8] *Od.* xi. 519–521.
[9] *Il.* viii. 207 ; xiii. 13.
[10] *Il.* viii. 170.
[1] *Il.* xiv. 293 : Ἴδης ὑψηλῆς.
[2] *Il.* viii. 47 ; xiv. 157, 283, 307 ; xv. 151 ; xx. 59, 218 ; xxiii. 117.
[3] *Il.* viii. 47 :
Ἴδην δ' ἵκανεν πολυπίδακα μητέρα θηρῶν, . . .
[4] Strabo, xiii. p. 583 : πολλοὺς δ' ἔχουσα

πρόποδας ἡ Ἴδη καὶ σκολοπενδρώδης οὖσα τὸ σχῆμα . . .
[5] Strabo, xiii. p. 605 : ἡ γὰρ ἀπὸ τοῦ Λεκτοῦ ῥάχις ἀνατείνουσα πρὸς τὴν Ἴδην ὑπέρκειται τῶν πρώτων τοῦ κόλπου μερῶν, . . .
[6] *Il.* ii. 824, 825 :
οἳ δὲ Ζέλειαν ἔναιον ὑπαὶ πόδα νείατον Ἴδης, ἀφνειοί, πίνοντες ὕδωρ μέλαν Αἰσήποιο, . . .
[7] *Il.* xii. 17–22 :
δὴ τότε μητιόωντο Ποσειδάων καὶ Ἀπόλλων τείχεος ἀμαλδῦναι, ποταμῶν μένος εἰσαγαγόντες ὅσσοι ἀπ' Ἰδαίων ὀρέων ἅλαδε προρέουσιν, Ῥῆσός θ' Ἑπτάπορός τε Κάρησός τε Ῥοδίος τε Γρήνικός τε καὶ Αἴσηπος δῖός τε Σκάμανδρος καὶ Σιμόεις, ὅθι πολλὰ βοάγρια καὶ τρυφάλειαι.

and a fragrant altar."[8]   Mount Gargarus is further mentioned three times by Homer.[9]

According to P. Barker Webb,[10] the summit of Gargarus consists of actinolithic schist, nearly all the rest of the mountain being of mica-schist. This schist is accompanied by immense deposits of primitive white compact calcareous rock. Here are the sources of the Scamander, which, as I have related above, I visited in company with Professor Virchow. According to Webb, travellers have penetrated for a distance of 200 mètres (658 ft.) into the cavern, from which the principal source dashes forth, without reaching its fountain. Tchihatcheff's measurements [1] make the sources 650 mètres (2138 ft.) above the level of the sea. The mica-schist of Gargarus has a somewhat greenish colour; it sometimes contains a little asbestus. In the lower part of the mountain this schist assumes a different aspect; and under its new form, which is that of the true mica-schist, it extends exclusively from the top of Gargarus as far as the village of Saliklar Kioi. This primitive rock extends to the plain on the north side of the river, where the hills have some elevation.

Turning now to the South, we seé a country very different from that we have just left. Alexandria-Troas is built on an ashy syenite, composed of the three usual elements, among which the felspar predominates; it gives its colour to the whole mass, in spite of a quantity of crystals of blackish mica. The syenite extends through the whole country to the east of Alexandria-Troas, as far as Iné or Ené. The valley of Ligia Hammam is formed of schist surrounded on all sides by syenite. Between Kemalli and Iné are the silver mines already referred to. P. Barker Webb goes on to say : "Descending the hill about 200 mètres, we found ourselves on a volcanic tufa, which was succeeded at first by columns of phonolith, and then by trachyte, as far as Iné. At a distance of two hours from Iné the syenite meets a series of trap and basaltic rocks. Not far from Iné is the curious conical hill called Iné Tepeh, or Suran Tepeh, which has been thought by some to be an artificial tumulus; but in reality it is nothing else than an isolated mass of basalt, which rises abruptly in the midst of the plain. The valley of Beiramich, as well as the other valleys which converge there, are composed of the secondary limestone of the Troad. Several chains of hills penetrate into it towards the south; they consist entirely of basaltic or trap rock, and rise from the great centre of ancient volcanoes around Assos. The largest of the lateral valleys is that of Aiwadjik, already mentioned, three hours to the south-west of Beiramich. About halfway

---

[8] *Il.* viii. 48 :

Γάργαρον, ἔνθα τέ οἱ (Ζηνί) τέμενος βωμός τε θυήεις.

[9] *Il.* xv. 152, 153 :

εὗρον δ' εὐρύοπα Κρονίδην ἀνὰ Γαργάρῳ ἄκρῳ ἥμενον.

(They found the wide-thundering son of Kronos enthroned on the peak of Gargarus.)

xiv. 292, 293 :

῞Ηρη δὲ κραιπνῶς προσεβήσετο Γάργαρον ἄκρον ῎Ιδης ὑψηλῆς ·

(Heré quickly ascended Gargarus, the summit of lofty Ida.)

xiv. 352 :

ὣς ὃ μὲν ἀτρέμας εὗδε πατὴρ ἀνὰ Γαργάρῳ ἄκρῳ,

. . . (So he the father slept quietly on the height of Gargarus.)

[10] *Topographie de la Troade ancienne et moderne* ; Paris, 1844, p. 129.

[1] *Asie Mineure : Description physique, statistique, et archéologique de cette contrée* ; Paris, 1853-69, pt. i.

between the two towns rises a beautiful conical hill called Kara-Euli, which stands isolated in the plain. Its sides, which resemble walls, are formed of basaltic columns, presenting to the eye a thousand elegant shapes. Having passed the mountain, we had before and around us a thousand varieties of trachyte and other rocks of igneous origin, with volcanic agglomerations and tufa. Sometimes pretty large masses of hardened schistose clay alternate, striated with variegated colours, in company with jasper and jaspoide thermantide. Aiwadjik is built on a height of volcanic rock, and its walls are composed of the same material. Among the stones of the walls we noticed a very strange white tufa, which was probably cut from a neighbouring quarry. Wherever we looked, the country appeared to have been overturned by the action of ancient volcanoes until we arrived at Assos. At Mantasha, distant an hour from Assos, on the road to Aiwadjik, the ruins of a castle may be seen on the top of a small hill, which has the appearance of an extinct volcano. We also noticed towards the sea a current of trachyte lava of considerable length. As tufas and conglomerates are found there, it is highly probable that it was a submarine volcano, whose scoriae, ashes, and pumice-stone have been carried away by the water. We nevertheless felt a great pleasure in still observing volcanic remains and erratic masses of obsidian strewn here and there on the surface of the current. The summit on which Assos is situated is a spur of that of Mantasha, though the former is much higher and occupies a much greater space. From the top, where we now see the ruins of the citadel of Assos, currents of trachyte extend in various directions, similar to those at Nemi, near Rome, principally in the direction of Adramyttium. This country also recals to mind, though on a larger scale, the volcanic hill of Radicofani in Tuscany; and the resemblance was increased by our finding in the rock the mineral which Thomson calls *florite*, and which by the German mineralogists is termed *hyalite*. Though the volcano is no longer active, we saw evident signs of internal subversions of the soil and of the frequent earthquakes which ravage this country."[2]

"In the Troad there is no primordial volcanic formation; the principal part of the volcanic districts is situated in the south. We find there at every step thermal fountains and an abundance of salt-water springs, the intimate relation of which to the phenomena of volcanic eruptions has been so often observed by geologists; nay, these hot springs are so numerous, that the vapours produced by the hot water have made some authors say that they spread a thick cloud as far as the extremity of the Gulf of Adramyttium."[3] "The lowlands, and that part which is properly called the Plain of Troy, are interrupted by frequent elevations, we might almost say by slight undulations of the ground, formed by the spurs of Mount Ida, which terminate imperceptibly on the sea-coast. Towards Dardania and Cebrenia, the mountainous ridges of Ida rise one

---

[2] P. Barker Webb, *Topogr. de la Troade*; Paris, 1844, pp. 135–137.
[3] *Ibid.*, p. 129.

above the other, covered with pine-trees. The basaltic rocks of the Bali Dagh attach these ridges to the syenite mountains behind Alexandria-Troas, in the midst of which rise those conical masses which are visible to so great a distance at sea." [4]

Between the two affluents of the Simois, which meet at the village of Doumbrek, there is, according to the investigations of Professor Virchow and M. Burnouf, an extensive mass of diluvium, composed of quartz, diorite, serpentine, trachyte, &c., more or less rounded. The vegetation consists principally of arbutus, andrachnés, and pines, which increase in size with the height of the mountain ridges. There is a group of tangled heights formed of quartzose mica-schist, where the pines are of noble dimensions. There is a rivulet in every dale. The dales become more and more hollow, and it is difficult to advance owing to the shrubs which cover the slopes. The *Oulou Dagh* is now reached; it is a long ridge, belonging to a range of Ida, whose height is 429·80 m. = 1409 ft. The Oulou Dagh consists essentially of a somewhat laminated serpentine: on its roundish conical surface we see many steeply-raised enormous masses of snow-white quartz and brown ferruginous quartzite, which lie pretty accurately in the direction of north and south. The mountain-ridge maintains this character as far as the Kara Your; only from hence the ridge extending towards Chiblak and Hissarlik consists of tertiary limestone.

From the Oulou Dagh may be seen to the west a large part of the Troad, Ida, Lesbos, the Kara Dagh, the islands of Tenedos, Imbros, and Samothrace, the Plain of Troy, Hissarlik, and the confluence of the Simois and Scamander. The descent is easy by the mountain ridge; there is a good road through the pines, which form here and there beautiful tufts. These woods are now cultivated for sale by Turcomans, whose graves may be seen here and there.

Following the ridge, the *Kara Your* is reached. This mountain, which is 209 mètres = 686 ft. high, forms the eastern extremity of the plateau which separates the basin of the Simois from that of the Thymbrius. From the Kara Your we enjoy a fine view over the basin of the Thymbrius as far as the heights of Bounarbashi, with all its undulations; but Hissarlik is not visible from hence.

I may here remind the reader that Mount Kara Your has hitherto been held to be identical with the Homeric Callicolone; but that, as Troy is not visible from it, I have now, at the suggestion of Professor Virchow, and in accordance with Burnouf's view, transferred that honour to the Oulou Dagh, which fulfils this apparently indispensable condition. I must however remark that Strabo, on the authority of Demetrius of Scepsis, evidently believed in the identity of the Kara Your with the Homeric Callicolone, for he states it to be only 5 stadia from the Simois and 10 stadia from Ἰλιέων Κώμη, which distances perfectly agree with the situation of the Kara Your, but not with that of the Oulou Dagh.[5]

---

[4] P. Barker Webb, *op. cit.* p. 129.

[5] Strabo, xiii. p. 597: ὑπὲρ δὲ τῆς Ἰλιέων κώμης δέκα σταδίοις ἐστὶν ἡ Καλλικολώνη, λόφος τις, παρ' ὃν ὁ Σιμόεις ῥεῖ, πεντασταδίον διέχων.

I remind the reader, once for all, that the

Professor Virchow, moreover, pointed out to me on the Kara Your the foundations of an ancient building, perhaps a temple, whereas there are no traces of buildings on the Oulou Dagh.

The plateau between Kara Your and the village of Chiblak is desert, uncultivated, destitute of wood, and full of ravines. Here and there are some bushes on a sort of very meagre prairie. In proportion as you advance to the west the soil becomes limestone; but the vegetation is the same, except the pines, which cease with the schist.

Of *Promontories*, I have in the first place to mention *Cape Lectum*, opposite Lesbos, which is the westernmost peak of Ida, and the extreme southern point of the Trojan dominion. In Strabo's time the altar was still shown here, which, according to tradition, had been erected by Agamemnon to the twelve gods;[6] but this very mention of a definite number of the gods shows that its origin must belong to a later period. Here, as before stated, Heré, in company with Hypnos, on their way to Mount Gargarus, first reached the Trojan shore.[7] It is also mentioned by Herodotus.[8]

Next comes the famous *Cape Sigeum*, which forms the north-western point of all Asia, at the entrance of the Hellespont, opposite to the city of Eleusa on the southern extremity of the Thracian Chersonesus. It is now called Cape Yeni Shehr. According to M. Burnouf's measurement, the height of Cape Sigeum is 77·20 mètres = 252 ft. above the level of the sea. On this cape (and not, as is erroneously shown on Admiral Spratt's map, on the high plateau to the S.S.W. of it) was situated the ancient city of Sigeum: in the first place because there is here an accumulation of ancient *débris* 6 ft. deep, whereas there is none at all on the neighbouring plateau; and secondly because Sigeum had a port, which did in fact exist immediately to the east of the promontory, whilst there is none at the foot of the plateau. The city was destroyed by the Ilians soon after the overthrow of the Persian empire, and it no longer existed in Strabo's time.[9] Like the whole ridge of which it forms the north-eastern extremity, this promontory consists of limestone, and falls off very abruptly towards the sea. It is now crowned by the village of Yeni Shehr, which is inhabited exclusively by Christians, and stands on the *débris* and ruins of the ancient city of Sigeum.

In a direct line to the east of Cape Sigeum is *Cape Rhoeteum*, now called In Tepeh, on the Hellespont. The distance between these two promontories is, according to Strabo,[10] 60 stadia; but this is one of the

---

stadium of 600 Greek feet was the tenth part of the English geographical mile. In other words, 10 stadia = 1 geog. mile = 1 minute of a degree at the Equator.

[6] Strabo, xiii. p. 605: ἐπὶ δὲ τῷ Λεκτῷ βωμὸς τῶν δώδεκα θεῶν δείκνυται, καλοῦσι δ' Ἀγαμέμνονος ἵδρυμα·

[7] *Il.* xiv. 283, 284:
Ἴδην δ' ἱκέσθην . . . .
Λεκτόν, ὅθι πρῶτον λιπέτην ἅλα·

[8] ix. 114.

[9] Mela, i. 18. 3; Plin. *H. N.* v. 33; *Serv. ad Aen.* ii. 312; τὸ Σίγειον, Herod. v. 65, 94; Thucyd. viii. 101; Strabo, xiii. p. 595; Ptol. v. 23; Steph. Byz. p. 597. Strabo, xiii. p. 603, calls it also ἡ Σιγείας ἄκρα. The town τὸ Σίγειον is also called Σίγη by Hecataeus, p. 208; Scylax, p. 36.

[10] xiii. p. 595: ἔστι δὲ τὸ μῆκος τῆς παραλίας ταύτης ἀπὸ τοῦ Ῥοιτείου μέχρι Σιγείου καὶ τοῦ Ἀχιλλέως μνήματος εὐθυπλοούντων ἑξήκοντα σταδίων.

many proofs that the geographer never visited the Troad, the real distance
being only 30 stadia, which is given by Pliny.[1] On this cape formerly
stood the town of Rhoeteum (τὸ ‘Ροίτειον).[2] It is not a promontory in the
proper sense of the word, but an elevated rocky shore with several peaks,
of which the highest, according to M. Burnouf's measurement, is only
168 ft. high. For this reason it is also called by Antipater Sidonius
‘Ροιτηίδες ἀκταί.[3] It is spoken of as the "Rhoetea litora" by Virgil.[4]
Rhoeteum is also mentioned by Livy.[5] On a lower peak of this promontory is the tumulus attributed by tradition to Ajax, of which I shall
treat hereafter. It deserves particular notice that the names of the two
capes, Σίγειον and ‘Ροίτειον, do not occur in Homer, and that he only
once mentions them where we read that, although the sea-shore was
broad, yet it could not contain all the ships, and the people were
crowded; they had therefore drawn them up in rows, and had filled
the long mouth of the whole shore as far as it was enclosed by the
promontories.[6]

§ III. RIVERS OF THE TROAD.

(a) The *Simois* (ὁ Σιμόεις), now called Doumbrek Su, rises, according
to Homer, on Mount Ida, but more precisely on the Cotylus. Virchow,[7]
who investigated this river together with me, writes of this river as
follows : " In its beginning it is a fresh mountain-brook. Its sources lie
eastward of the wooded mountains of the Oulou Dagh. From numerous
little watercourses, which partly bubble forth from the rock, and some of
which form little torrents, two rivulets are at first formed. The larger
and longer them flows in a valley gap, between a prominent spur of the
Oulou Dagh, separated from the principal mount by a deep, green meadow
valley, and a spur of the tertiary mountain ridge, which descends from
Ren Kioi towards Halil Eli, nearly parallel with the ridge of Rhoeteum.
The shorter and more southerly rivulet gathers the water from the Kara
Your and the mountain ridge which joins it to the Oulou Dagh. Both
rivulets join not far above Doumbrek Kioi and form the Doumbrek Su
(Simois), which is midway between a small river and a large rivulet. Its
bed, which is deeply cut throughout, and proceeds now in shorter, now in
longer windings, is at Doumbrek perhaps from 12 to 30 yards wide; but
on the 11th of April the water covered only part of the bottom of this
bed, and nowhere did its depth exceed 6 inches. We could wade through
it without any difficulty. The current is rapid; the bottom is covered
with small pebbles, now and then also with somewhat larger rounded
stones from the Oulou Dagh.[8] The valley itself is small, but very fertile.

---

[1] *H. N.* v. 33: "fuit et Aeantium, a Rhodiis
conditum, in altero cornu, Ajace ibi sepulto, xxx.
stad. intervallo a Sigeo."

[2] Herodot. vii. 43; Scylax, p. 35; Steph.
Byz. p. 577; Mela, i. 18. 5; Plin. *H. N.* v. 33;
Thucyd. iv. 52, viii. 101.

[3] *Anthol. Gr.* ii. p. 24, ed. Jacobs; i. p. 254,
No. 146, ed. Tauchnitz.

[4] *Aen.* vi. 595, and Plin. *H. N.* v. 33.

[5] xxxvii. 37.

[6] *Il.* xiv. 33–36 :

οὐδὲ γὰρ οὐδ' εὐρύς περ' ἐὼν ἐδυνήσατο πάσας

αἰγιαλὸς νῆας χαδέειν, στείνοντο δὲ λαοί·
τῷ ῥα προκρόσσας ἔρυσαν, καὶ πλῆσαν ἁπάσης
ἠϊόνος στόμα μακρόν, ὅσον συνεέργαθον ἄκραι.

[7] *Beiträge zur Landeskunde der Troas*, pp.
92–96.

[8] In the celebrated passage where the Scamander summons the Simois to battle against
Achilles, it is said (*Il.* xxi. 311–314):

ἀλλ' ἐπάμυνε τάχιστα, καὶ ἐμπίπληθι ῥέεθρα
ὕδατος ἐκ πηγέων, πάντας δ' ὀρόθυνον ἐναύλους,
ἵστη δὲ μέγα κῦμα, πολὺν δ' ὀρυμαγδὸν ὄρινε
φιτρῶν καὶ λάων, ἵνα παύσομεν ἄγριον ἄνδρα . . .

If we then pass the mountain ridge which crosses the valley below Doum-brek Kioi, and descend on its gradually sloping west side to the region of Halil Eli, which abounds with trees and fruit, we find the little river scarcely larger at this village. Here also we ride through it without the horses' feet getting wet above the ankles. The clearness of the water permits us to see the bottom covered with small pebbles and gravel. At a short distance below the village, which is situated on its right bank, the little river divides into two arms. The right or northern arm, after having received the 'Rain-brook of Ren Kioi,'—a very small and incon-siderable rivulet, which has only an intermittent flow of water,—forms a large swamp in which it disappears. On the other hand, the left or southern arm approaches more and more to the mountain ridge which ex-tends from Kara Your past Chiblak towards Hissarlik, and it flows pretty near the lower edge of its slope. At first, as long as it flows through the 'Plain,' it has a somewhat deeper bed, whose banks are frequently under-mined and fall off every here and there 5 or 6 ft.; its breadth varies, but it hardly anywhere exceeds 20 ft. Here and there groups of willows and other bushes grow on the bank and on small islands in the river-bed; a rich vegetation of shrubs, especially of tamarisks and *Vitex agnus-castus*,[9] extends along its banks. But further on, in proportion as the little river approaches the foot of the mountain ridge, it divides into more and more arms, whose course, as one easily sees, must be very irregular. One after the other disappears in the large and deep swamp, which, connected at many points with the northern swamp, extends as far as the foot of His-sarlik, and occupies the larger part of the so-called Plain of the Simois. Whilst the ramification of by-rivulets and their disappearance in the great swamp causes a continual diminution of the volume of running water, there nevertheless still remains a 'main arm,' which continues its course along the ridge. We could still follow it up along the three springs of Troy, though it was there reduced to a little rivulet of 4 to 5 paces in breadth, and with an insignificant, though still rapid, current. Of these three springs, all of which are marked on our Map of the Troad, the first, which runs from a stone-enclosure and has a temperature of $14°·6$ Celsius $= 58°·28$ Fahr., is immediately below the ruins of the ancient city wall. The second, whose stone-enclosure is destroyed, and a third, with a well-preserved stone-enclosure and a double outlet, having a temperature of $14°·3$ to $15°$ Celsius $= 57°·74$ to $59°$ Fahr., are within a quarter of a mile from the first spring.

"At the west end of the great swamp formed by the waters of the Simois, a short stream gathers again, and pours into the Kalifatli Asmak. The spot where the gathering of the water takes place is pretty nearly in a straight line drawn from Hissarlik to the In Tepeh Asmak; that is to say, at the point on the western edge of the swamp which is farthest from Hissarlik. Apparently without any preparation, there is almost immedi-ately a large broad river-bed, with many windings, between steep banks from 6 to 8 ft. high; this river-bed is interrupted by numerous islands,

---

[9] ἄγνος = ἄγονος means *sine semine* (Theo-phrast. i. p. 264). In the *Iliad* (xi. 105) the shrub is called λύγος, διὰ τὸν περὶ τὰς ῥάβδους αὐτῆς εὔτονον (Dioscorides). See *Od.* ix. 427; x. 166. *Hymn. ad Dionys.* 13, ed. Miquel, p. 37.

but every here and there it is pretty deep. After a course of scarcely
10 minutes the stream empties into the eastern bend of the Kalifatli
Asmak, a little above the place where an artificial ditch leads from the
Kalifatli Asmak to the In Tepeh Asmak, above a stone bridge which here
spans the Kalifatli Asmak in the direction of Koum Kioi. No water can
flow through the ditch except during the inundations."

The Simois is mentioned seven times in the *Iliad*. Thus the poet says :
" But when they (Heré and Athené) approached Troy and the two flowing
streams, where the Simois and Scamander mingle their currents, there
Heré, the white-armed goddess, stopped the horses, releasing them from
the chariot, and she poured a thick cloud around them, and the Simois
sprouted ambrosia for their pasture."[10] Again : " Simois also, where many
ox-hide shields and crested helms fell down in the dust."[1] Again : " Black
as a storm, Ares cried on the other side, now shouting shrilly to the
Trojans from the citadel, now running along the Simois unto Callicolone."[2] Again : " He (Scamander) grew yet more furious against
the son of Peleus, and, lifting high the crested wave of (his) stream,
shouted to the Simois."[3] Again : " Descending from Ida along the
banks of the Simois."[4] Lastly : " The dread battle-shout of Trojans
and Achaeans was left alone ; and many times did the fight sway hither
and thither over the plain, as they pointed against each other their
brazen spears between Simois and the floods of Xanthus."[5] The river
is also mentioned by Aeschylus,[6] Ptolemy,[7] Stephanus Byzantinus,[8]
Mela,[9] Pliny,[10] Horace,[1] Propertius,[2] and Virgil.[3]

The identity of this river with the Simois of Homer is confirmed by
Strabo,[4] who states, on the authority of Demetrius of Scepsis :

" From the mountains of Ida two ridges advance to the sea, the one

---

[10] *Il.* v. 773–776:
ἀλλ' ὅτε δὴ Τροίην ἷξον ποταμώ τε ῥέοντε,
ἧχι ῥοὰς Σιμόεις συμβάλλετον ἠδὲ Σκάμανδρος
ἔνθ' ἵππους ἔστησε θεὰ λευκώλενος Ἥρη
λύσασ' ἐξ ὀχέων, περὶ δ' ἠέρα πουλὺν ἔχευεν·

[1] *Il.* xii. 22, 23:
καὶ Σιμόεις, ὅθι πολλὰ βοάγρια καὶ τρυφάλειαι
κάππεσον ἐν κονίῃσι . . .

[2] *Il.* xx. 52, 53:
ὀξὺ κατ' ἀκροτάτης πόλιος Τρώεσσι κελεύων,
ἄλλοτε πὰρ Σιμόεντι θέων ἐπὶ Καλλικολώνῃ.

[3] *Il.* xxi. 305–307:
      . . . ἀλλ' ἔτι μᾶλλον
χώετο Πηλεΐωνι, κόρυσσε δὲ κῦμα ῥόοιο
ὑψόσ' ἀειρόμενος, Σιμόεντι δὲ κέκλετ' ἀΰσας . . .

[4] *Il.* iv. 475:
Ἴδηθεν κατιοῦσα παρ' ὄχθῃσι Σιμόεντος . . .

[5] *Il.* vi. 1–4:
Τρώων δ' οἰώθη καὶ Ἀχαιῶν φύλοπις αἰνή·
πολλὰ δ' ἄρ' ἔνθα καὶ ἔνθ' ἴθυσε μάχη πεδίοιο,
ἀλλήλων ἰθυνομένων χαλκήρεα δοῦρα,
μεσσηγὺς Σιμόεντος ἰδὲ Ξάνθοιο ῥοάων.

[6] *Agamemnon*, v. 696, ed. Tauchnitz.
[7] v. 2. 3.   [8] P. 601.   [9] i. 18. 3.
[10] *H. N.* v. 33.   [1] *Epod.* 13. 21.   [2] iii. 1. 27.
[3] *Aen.* i. 618 ; v. 262, 473.
[4] Strabo, xiii. p. 597: ἀπὸ δὲ τῆς κατὰ

τοὺς τόπους Ἰδαίας ὀρεινῆς δύο φησὶν ἀγκῶνας
ἐκτείνεσθαι πρὸς θάλατταν, τὸν μὲν εὐθὺ Ῥοιτείου τὸν δὲ Σιγείου, ποιοῦντας ἐξ ἀμφοῖν γραμ-
μὴν ἡμικυκλιώδη· τελευτᾶν δ' ἐν τῷ πεδίῳ,
τοσοῦτον ἀπέχοντας τῆς θαλάττης ὅσον τὸ νῦν
Ἴλιον. τοῦτο μὲν δὴ μεταξὺ τῆς τελευτῆς τῶν
λεχθέντων ἀγκώνων εἶναι, τὸ δὲ παλαιὸν κτίσμα
μεταξὺ τῆς ἀρχῆς· ἀπολαμβάνεσθαι δ' ἐντὸς
τό τε Σιμοείσιον πεδίον δι' οὗ ὁ Σιμόεις φέρεται,
καὶ τὸ Σκαμάνδριον δι' οὗ Σκάμανδρος ῥεῖ. τοῦτο
δὲ καὶ ἰδίως Τρωϊκὸν λέγεται, καὶ τοὺς πλείστους
ἀγῶνας ὁ ποιητὴς ἐνταῦθα ἀποδίδωσι· πλατύτε-
ρον γάρ ἐστι, καὶ τοὺς ὀνομαζομένους τόπους
ἐνταῦθα δεικνυμένους ὁρῶμεν, τὸν ἐρινεόν, τὸν
τοῦ Αἰσυήτου τάφον, τὴν Βατίειαν, τὸ τοῦ Ἴλου
σῆμα. οἱ δὲ ποταμοὶ ὅ τε Σκάμανδρος καὶ ὁ
Σιμόεις, ὁ μὲν τῷ Σιγείῳ πλησιάσας ὁ δὲ τῷ
Ῥοιτείῳ, μικρὸν ἔμπροσθεν τοῦ νῦν Ἰλίου συμβάλλουσιν, εἶτ' ἐπὶ τὸ Σίγειον ἐκδιδόασι καὶ
ποιοῦσι τὴν στομαλίμνην καλουμένην. διείργει
δ' ἑκάτερον τῶν λεχθέντων πεδίων ἀπὸ θατέρου
μέγας τις αὐχὴν τῶν εἰρημένων ἀγκώνων ἐπ'
εὐθείας, ἀπὸ τοῦ νῦν Ἰλίου τὴν ἀρχὴν ἔχων
συμφυὴς αὐτῷ, τεινόμενος δ' ἕως τῆς Κεβρηνίας καὶ ἀποτελῶν τὸ ϵ γράμμα πρὸς τοὺς
ἑκατέρωθεν ἀγκῶνας.

terminating in the promontory of Rhoeteum, the other in that of Sigeum;
they form with it a semicircle, but terminate in the Plain at the same
distance from the sea as Novum Ilium. This city, therefore, lies between
the two extremities of the ridges already named, but the ancient town
between their starting-points; but the inner space comprises as well the
Plain of the Simois, through which the Simois flows, as the Plain of the
Scamander, through which the Scamander flows. The latter is properly
called the Trojan Plain, and the poet makes it the theatre of most of the
battles; for it is broader, and here we see the places mentioned by the
poet,—the fig hill, the tomb of Aesyetes, the Batieia, and the tumulus of
Ilus. But the rivers Scamander and Simois, of which the one approaches
Sigeum, the other Rhoeteum, join at a short distance below Ilium, and
discharge near Sigeum, where they form the so-called *Stomalimne*. The
two above-mentioned plains are separated by a long neck of land, which
issues directly from the two ridges already named; beginning from the
projection on which Novum Ilium is situated, and attaching itself to it
(συμφυὴς αὐτῷ), this neck of land advances (southward) to join Cebrenia,
thus forming with the two other chains the letter **Є**."

The description of Pliny[5] agrees with that of Strabo: "dein portus
Achaeorum, in quem influit Xanthus Simoenti junctus: stagnumque prius
faciens Palaescamander."

The identity of this river with the Homeric Simois is further confirmed by Virgil, who tells us that Andromache, after Hector's death,
had again married Helenus, another son of Priam, who became king
of Chaonia:

> "Ante urbem in luco falsi Simoentis ad undam
> Libabat cineri Andromache, Manesque vocabat
> Hectoreum ad tumulum, viridi quem cespite inanem
> Et geminas causam lacrymis sacraverat aras."[6]

Thus Hector's tomb was in a grove near the Simois; but, according to
Strabo,[7] Hector's tomb was in a grove at Ophrynium, and this is also
confirmed by Lycophron in his *Cassandra*. But Ophrynium is in close
proximity to the river of which we are now speaking, and which, from
this and all other testimonies, can be none other than the Simois.

As the present name of the Simois, *Doumbrek*, is believed not to be a
Turkish word, some take it for a corruption of the name Thymbrius, and
use it to prove that the river—which runs through the north-eastern
valley of the Plain of Troy, and falls into the Kalifatli Asmak (the ancient
bed of the Scamander) in front of Ilium—is the Thymbrius, and cannot
possibly be the Simois.

To this I reply, that there is no example of a Greek word ending in *os*
being rendered in Turkish by a word ending in *k*; further that Doumbrek
must certainly be a corruption of the two Turkish words طوك برق
Don barek. *Don* signifies "ice," and *barek* "possession" or "habitation:"
the two words therefore mean much the same thing as "containing ice,"

---

and the name might be explained by the fact, that the inundations caused by the Simois are frequently frozen over in winter, when the whole north-eastern plain forms a sheet of ice.

But if in classical times this river was called Simois, there can be no doubt whatever of its identity with the Homeric Simois, because—as MacLaren [8] justly observes—in all parts of the world rivers have preserved their names with wonderful persistency in the midst of linguistic change and political revolution. An ancient name may indeed be lost, but, if it still exists, it would be difficult to conceive how it could possibly be transferred from one river to another.

No ford of the Simois is mentioned in the *Iliad*, though the armies must have passed the river constantly in marching to or from the plain between this river and the Scamander, where all the battles were fought. But though the Simois may perhaps have had a slightly larger quantity of water in ancient times, before the invention of water-mills, it can never have been of much consequence. Therefore, there was no need to speak of a ford.

(b) The *Thymbrius*, called ὁ Θύμβριος by Strabo [9] and Eustathius,[10] is a small river, which originates in the immediate vicinity of Mount Kara Your, and receives the drainage of ten or twelve valleys, pouring at a right angle into the Scamander opposite Bounarbashi. Its present name is Kemar Su, from the Greek word καμάρα (*vault*), and the Turkish word "su" (*water*), the river being crossed, at about 3 miles above its confluence, by a Roman aqueduct. Homer does not mention this river at all, though he mentions the town of Thymbré.[1]

The site of this ancient town corresponds with the farm at Akshi Kioi on the banks of the Thymbrius, the proprietor of which, Mr. Frank Calvert, has made excavations there, and has found inscriptions which can leave no doubt of its identity. The whole place is strewn with archaic Hellenic potsherds. The height of the site above the level of the sea, at the place where Mr. Calvert's farmhouse stands, is, according to M. Burnouf's measurements, 63·35 mètres or 207 ft. Strabo states that close to the confluence of the Thymbrius and Scamander, and at a distance of 50 stadia from Novum Ilium, stood the famous temple of the Thymbrian Apollo,[2] which, as my friend Professor A. H. Sayce, who lately visited the Troad, remarks,[3] must be identical with the almost entirely artificial mound of Hanaï Tepeh, which I have excavated in company with Mr. Calvert, and of which I shall treat hereafter. According to M. Burnouf's measurement, the height of the Hanaï Tepeh is 87·75 mètres = 285 ft. above the level of the sea; the confluence of the Thymbrius and the Scamander being 24·5 mètres = 80 ft. 5 in. The distance given by Strabo is perfectly correct.

M. Burnouf makes the following remarks upon the river:—"The

---

[8] *Observations on the Topography of the Plain of Troy.* See Barker Webb, *Topographie de la Troade,* p. 47.

[9] xiii. p. 598.

[10] *Ad Hom. Il.* x. 430.

[1] *Il.* x. 430:

πρὸς Θύμβρης δ' ἔλαχον Λύκιοι Μυσοί τ' αγέ ρωχοι.

("Towards Thymbré the Lycians and the lordly Mysians had their place allotted.")

[2] xiii. p. 598: πλησίον γάρ ἐστι τὸ πεδίον ἡ Θύμβρα καὶ ὁ δι' αὐτοῦ ῥέων ποταμὸς Θύμβριος, ἐμβάλλων εἰς τὸν Σκάμανδρον κατὰ τὸ Θυμβραίου Ἀπόλλωνος ἱερόν.

[3] In the *Academy,* Oct. 18, 1879.

Thymbrius flows in the hollow of a valley between the hills of Akshi
Kioi and the heights to the south. It is about 30 ft. broad. Its banks
are steep; it is perfectly limpid, and is overshadowed by large trees. Its
banks, which are from 10 to 12 ft. high, show two very distinct layers:
first, a modern alluvium, consisting of earth washed down by the rains
from the hills; secondly, below this, a thick layer of plastic clay,
analogous to that which forms the soil of the plain of the Scamander.
The confluence of the Thymbrius and the Scamander is not difficult to
determine,[4] since the banks are high. During the inundations, the
great polygon formed by the Thymbrius, the Scamander, and the hills to
the east, becomes covered with water, which runs with great impetuosity
in an easterly direction; inundates the swamp (now rendered salubrious)
to the north of Akshi Kioi; pours into the large bed of the Kalifatli
Asmak, which is identical with the ancient bed of the Scamander; and
forms other streams, which flow in the same direction. On the 18th of
May, 1879, we saw this whole plain covered with dead trees and branches,
which had been carried away in the same direction, and caught by the
bushes of the agnus-castus and tamarisk."

(c) The *Scamander* (ὁ Σκάμανδρος, as it was called in the language of
men, according to Homer, but *Xanthus*, "the yellow stream," as it was
termed by the gods[5]) is the modern Mendere, a plain corruption of the
name Scamander.

The punning etymology of Eustathius[6] makes Σκάμανδρος, σκάμμα
ἀνδρὸς (Ἡρακλέους) τὸν Ξάνθον ἐκ γῆς προήγαγεν, since "the excavation
of the man (Heracles) brought the Xanthus forth out of the earth." This,
of course, is mere trifling; but the termination of the name is one which
we find in many of the river-names of Asia Minor, such as Maeander,
Alander, and the like. It is possible that the title by which the river
was known in the language of the gods—that is, of the Greek settlers—
was a translation of its native name.

As before mentioned,[7] Homer makes the Scamander rise from two
springs—one lukewarm, the other cold—close to the city wall; while
in another passage, already quoted, he correctly makes it rise in Mount
Ida. I have already described its sources from my own inspection of
them.[8] Strabo asserts, on the authority of Demetrius of Scepsis—who,
as he says, was a native of the country—that the Scamander flows from a
single source in Mount Cotylus, one of the peaks of Ida, about 120 stadia
above Scepsis, and that the Granicus and Aesepus originate from the
same mountain from several springs, in such close proximity to the
source of the Scamander, that all are within a space of 20 stadia, the
Scamander flowing in a westerly, the two others in a northerly direction,
and the length of the Aesepus being about 500 stadia.[9] He confirms the

---

[4] This means that the banks of the river are
not obliterated, and do not confound themselves
with the plain.
[5] *Il.* xx. 73, 74:
. . . . ποταμὸς βαθυδίνης,
ὃν Ξάνθον καλέουσι θεοί, ἄνδρες δὲ Σκάμανδρον.
[6] *Ad Il.* xx. 74.   [7] See p. 55.   [8] See p. 58.
[9] Strabo, xiii. p. 602: ἔμπειρος δ᾽ ὢν τῶν

τόπων, ὡς ἂν ἐπιχώριος ἀνήρ, ὁ Δημήτριος τοτέ
μὲν οὕτως λέγει περὶ αὐτῶν· "ἔστι γὰρ λόφος
τις τῆς Ἴδης Κότυλος· ὑπέρκειται δ᾽ οὗτος ἑκατόν που καὶ εἴκοσι σταδίοις Σκήψεως, ἐξ οὗ ὅ
τε Σκάμανδρος ῥεῖ καὶ ὁ Γρανικος, καὶ Αἴσηπος,
οἱ μὲν πρὸς ἄρκτον καὶ τὴν Προποντίδα, ἐκ
πλειόνων πηγῶν συλλειβόμενοι, ὁ δὲ Σκάμανδρος
ἐπὶ δύσιν ἐκ μιᾶς πηγῆς· πᾶσαι δ᾽ ἀλλήλαις

fact that the Scamander and Simois meet, and says that the Scamander falls into the Hellespont near Sigeum: "But the rivers Scamander and Simois, of which the former approaches Sigeum, the latter Rhoeteum, join a little below Novum Ilium and fall into the sea at Sigeum, where they form the so-called Stomalimne "[10] (*i.e.* "lake at the mouth ").

He further says that: " A little beyond lies the village of the Ilians ('Ιλιέων Κώμη), where the ancient Ilium is believed to have formerly stood, 30 stadia distant from the present city." [1] And again : "There are neither hot springs in this place, nor is the source of the Scamander here, but in the mountains; and there are not two sources, but only one. It seems therefore that the hot springs have disappeared, but that the cold spring escapes from the Scamander by a subterranean channel, and rises again in this place (before 'Ιλιέων Κώμη); or else that this water is merely called a source of the Scamander, because it is near to it: for several sources of one and the same river are so called." [2]

The length of the Scamander from its sources to its mouth in the Hellespont close to Koum Kaleh is, according to G. von Eckenbrecher,[3] in a straight line 10 German miles[4] (= 47 English miles nearly); according to Tchihatcheff,[5] 20 French leagues. The sources of the Scamander are 650 mètres (2138 ft.) above the sea; the fall of the current is on an average 21 mètres (=69 ft.) to the league, which is equal to 30 ft. per mile.[6] But the fall varies with the locality: thus from the sources to the district of Iné (Ené), and even to Bounarbashi, the fall of the river is very rapid, but further on it is comparatively insignificant.

M. Burnouf, who has studied the ancient and modern beds of the Scamander with great care, sends me the following note on the subject:— " At the time of inundation the Scamander bursts with great impetuosity through its narrow pass between the rocks of Bounarbashi, carrying with it sand and gravel, which it heaps up over pretty large spaces of ground, and which are sufficient to modify its course. Its course is therefore changeable: it takes a fixed direction only after its confluence with the Thymbrius, which, when I measured it at the end of May, was 24½ mètres (80 ft. 5 in.) above the sea. This elevation is highly important from all points of view, because it gives the slope of the Plain of

---

πλησιάζουσιν, ἐν εἴκοσι σταδίων περιεχόμεναι διαστήματι· πλεῖστον δ᾽ ἀφέστηκεν ἀπὸ τῆς ἀρχῆς τὸ τοῦ Αἰσήπου τέλος, σχεδόν τι καὶ πεντακοσίους σταδίους."

[10] xiii. p. 597: οἱ δὲ ποταμοὶ ὅ τε Σκάμανδρος καὶ ὁ Σιμόεις, ὁ μὲν τῷ Σιγείῳ πλησιάσας, ὁ δὲ τῷ Ῥοιτείῳ, μικρὸν ἔμπροσθεν τοῦ νῦν Ἰλίου συμβάλλουσιν, εἶτ᾽ ἐπὶ τὸ Σίγειον ἐκδιδόασι καὶ ποιοῦσι τὴν Στομαλίμνην καλουμένην.

[1] xiii. p. 597: Ὑπὲρ δὲ τούτου μικρὸν ἡ τῶν Ἰλιέων κώμη ἐστίν, ἐν ᾗ νομίζεται τὸ παλαιὸν Ἴλιον ἱδρῦσθαι πρότερον, τριάκοντα σταδίους διέχον ἀπὸ τῆς νῦν πόλεως.

[2] Strabo, xiii. p. 602: οὔτε γὰρ θερμὰ νῦν ἐν τῷ τόπῳ εὑρίσκεται, οὐθ᾽ ἡ τοῦ Σκαμάνδρου πηγὴ ἐνταῦθα, ἀλλ᾽ ἐν τῷ ὄρει, καὶ μία, ἀλλ᾽ οὐ δύο. τὰ μὲν οὖν θερμὰ ἐκλελεῖφθαι εἰκός, τὸ δὲ ψυχρὸν

κατὰ διάδυσιν ὑπεκρέον ἐκ τοῦ Σκαμάνδρου κατὰ τοῦτ᾽ ἀνατέλλειν τὸ χωρίον, ἢ καὶ διὰ τὸ πλησίον εἶναι τοῦ Σκαμάνδρου καὶ τοῦτο τὸ ὕδωρ λέγεσθαι τοῦ Σκαμάνδρου πηγήν· οὕτω γὰρ λέγονται πλείους πηγαὶ τοῦ αὐτοῦ ποταμοῦ.

[3] *Die Lage des Homerischen Troja*, p. 4.

[4] The German mile, of 15 to the degree, is equal to 4 English geographical miles, or nearly 4⅔ statute miles.

[5] *Asie Mineure : Description physique, statistique, archéologique*, &c., p. 78.

[6] In his calculation Tchihatcheff has no doubt taken into account all the windings of the Scamander, because, if the fall of the current were to be reckoned in a straight line from the sources, it would exceed 46 feet per mile.

Troy.   In order to obtain the average slope in each mètre, it is sufficient
to take on our Map the distance in a straight line from the confluence
of the Thymbrius to the shore of the sea near the Stomalimne, and to
divide this distance by 24 m. 50 cent.   In this way we shall obtain the
number of millimètres to each mètre, representing the average slope of
the plain.   In order to obtain the fall of the river, it is necessary to
follow all its sinuosities on the map.   The number of mètres thus obtained
will be greater; nevertheless, when divided by 24 m. 50 cent., the result
gives a considerable average rapidity to the stream.   During the inundation this rapidity is much greater, because the elevation of 24 m. 50 cent.
would be brought to at least 26 m. 50 cent., or 27 mètres, by the rise of
the waters.   During the inundation the Thymbrius carries a considerable
quantity of water, because in spite of its high banks its bed is then full
of water, which overflows into the plain.   At its confluence, the Scamander has a breadth of about 150 mètres = 492 ft.   Its banks are not
so high as those of the Thymbrius, because there is no upper alluvial
layer, as in the banks of the latter.   Thus the lower part of the valley
of the Thymbrius is elevated by about 2 mètres above the plain of the
Scamander at the same place.   The altitude of the plain of the Scamander
at its confluence is 27 m. 22 cent. = 90 ft. 9 in.   After its confluence, the
present bed of the Scamander becomes more contracted; the river flows
from thence between two steep banks of plastic clay.   At the ferry near
Kalifatli these banks are about 1 mètre = 3 ft. 4 in. high; the breadth of
the river there is only about 30 m. = 98 ft. 5 in.; it is deep in its whole
breadth.   At the bridge of Koum Kaleh the bed of the Scamander has
a breadth of 117 mètres = 384 ft., of which—in the middle season between
the rising of the waters and the drought—about one-half is occupied
by the water.

   "The ancient bed of the Scamander, which is identical with the
Kalifatli Asmak, is characterized by fallen banks, want of level ground,
and little hills of alluvial sand, while the new bed has steep banks,
and no alluvial sandhills except at Koum Kaleh, near its mouth.   The
accumulations of sand and gravel have nearly obliterated the ancient
bed for some distance below the confluence of the Thymbrius.   The
westerly winds have extended these sands on the east side of the plain;
their rotatory currents have heaped them up in the form of small hills
along almost the whole length of the ancient bed.   I have myself witnessed
such a phenomenon.   The last inundation had left a layer, a fraction of
an inch deep, on the submerged lands; the sun had dried it, and the
wind, which carried the sand away towards the east, formed of it small
heaps round the bushes of the ancient bed of the Scamander, and brought
the clay of the plain again to light.   The translocation of the river-bed
has been favoured by the configuration of the soil.   The spurs of the
heights on the east side of the Plain have in their lower part a projection,
which slopes down to the river and forms there a steep bank, while the
small plains between them terminate in a swamp.   In front of Novum
Ilium the ancient bed of the Scamander passes between a bank of this
kind and a somewhat elevated hill of alluvial river-sand, after which the

bed again extends and has a breadth of not less than 200 m. = 656 ft.
A little further down it encounters the slope which descends from
Hissarlik towards the west, and which forces it to make a bend almost
at a right angle; afterwards comes another bend, which brings it back
to its first direction. In fact,
in front of Troy, the plain rises
suddenly, forming from *b* to *b* a
sort of bank, 5 ft. high at least;
from this point the ancient bed
proceeds straight towards the
bridge below Hissarlik.

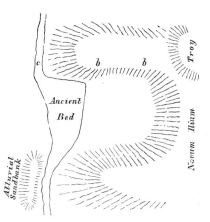

" At the bridge the plain is
15 m. = 49 ft. 2 in. above the
level of the sea; the breadth of
the ancient bed is there 93 mètres
= 305 ft. A shaft sunk at this
spot on the right bank has proved
that the bed of the river was
once larger, and that it has been
narrowed by the accumulation of
the sand of the river. This sand

No. 19.   Plan showing the ancient Bed of the Scamander
in front of Troy.

contains no marine deposits; it
is composed of the detritus of the rocks which form the massive block of
Mount Ida. The space comprised between the bridge in front of Hissarlik
and the small hill, which we hold to be identical with the *Tumulus
of Ilus*, presents most interesting features. About 500 m. = 1640 ft.
below the bridge, there rises on the left bank of the ancient bed of the
Scamander a large hill of river-sand, the western part of which is
covered with ruins and *débris*, which mark the site of an ancient town;
remnants of the wall are still extant. Very probably this is Polium,
which, according to Strabo, the Astypalaeans, who inhabited the city of
Rhoeteum, built on the Simois; it was afterwards called Polisma. Not
being built on a place fortified by nature, it was soon destroyed.[7]

" It is true that this site is not exactly on the Simois, but immediately in front of its mouth in the ancient bed of the Scamander.
The site is now partly occupied by the miserable village of Koum Kioi
(Village of Sand), which is not inhabited in summer on account of the
pestilential air; on the eastern part of the site is a Turkish cemetery.
Between this cemetery and the ancient Scamander is flat ground, a sort
of lagoon, which extends to the river. On the east side of the ancient
Scamander is the plain of the Simois, which runs out to the former river
in a bank, 2 mètres = 6 ft. 7 in. higher than the left bank. Immediately
below this is the confluence of the Simois with the ancient Scamander.
As the latter bends suddenly at this spot to the west, its bed appears to
be the continuation of the Simois, which flows from the east: this fact has

[7] Strabo, xiii. p. 601 : πρῶτοι μὲν οὖν ᾿Αστυ-   πρὸς τῷ Σιμόεντι Πόλιον, ὃ νῦν καλεῖται Πόλισμα,
παλαιεῖς, οἱ τὸ ῾Ροίτειον κατασχόντες, συνῴκισαν   οὐκ ἐν εὐερκεῖ τόπῳ· διὸ κατεσπάσθη ταχέως.

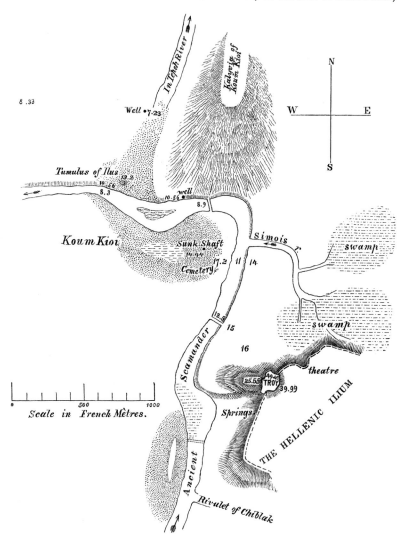

caused the error of the topographers, who make the Simois run directly
to the sea through the bed of the river In Tepeh Asmak. In this bend
the bank of the ancient bed of the Scamander, on the side of Koum Kioi,

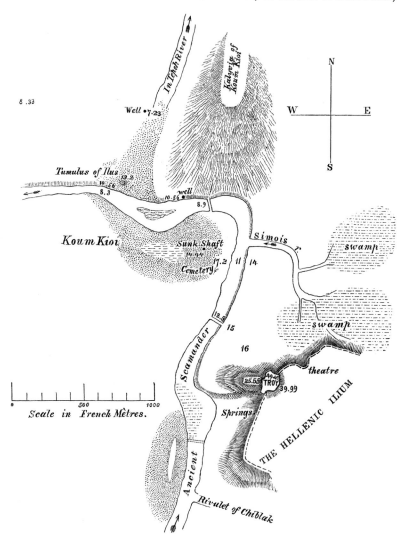

No. 20. The Dunes of the Ancient Scamander.

The confluence of the Simois and the Ancient Scamander is between Troy and the hill to the north-east of Koum
Kioi. The plain of the Simois is there 2 mètres higher than the plain of the Scamander. In front of
this confluence is a large dune of sand, which has been cut through by the river between Koum Kioi and the
Tomb of Ilus; the depression between the plain (8·33 mètres) and the hill of the Kalyvia gave a passage
to the river, which then discharged itself into the bed of the In Tepeh. Between the Tumulus of Ilus and this
bed of the In Tepeh can be seen the sand which has filled up this depression. (The numbers indicate the
altitudes in mètres.)

is effaced and confounded with the plain; on the opposite side it has a
high bank. The land which terminates in this steep bank rises gradually

towards the hills of In Tepeh, and opposes an insuperable barrier to the waters of the Simois. Afterwards comes the bridge of Koum Kioi, to the north of the alluvial hill of river-sand. A shaft sunk near the cemetery reached the plastic clay on a level with the plain, and proved that the hill of sand at Koum Kioi is really formed by fluvial deposits.

"To the north of the bridge of Koum Kioi the bank is 10 mètres 56 c. = 34 feet 8 inches above the level of the sea, and the soil maintains this elevation for a distance of about 1000 mètres = 3281 feet to the west. This plateau terminates in the remnant of a conical tumulus which, from its situation, must be identical with the Tomb of Ilus, repeatedly referred to in the *Iliad*. But the shaft sunk in it has given no proof of its claim to be a sepulchre; it rather appears to have been a mere hill of river-sand, which has been transformed by tradition into a tumulus. In its present ruined state this tumulus is only 1 m. = 3 ft. 4 in. high; but the soil on which it stands consists of river-sand, and is more than 2 m. = 6 ft. 7 in. above the mean height of the water. For a distance of more than 200 m. = 656 ft. to the west of the Tomb of Ilus, the bank of the ancient Scamander consists of river-sand; afterwards it assumes again its ordinary character of plastic clay. There is therefore on this spot a barrier of sand, through which the river has dug its bed. From the Tomb of Ilus this barrier extends to the north for a space of more than 500 m. = 1640 ft. in length, and of a great breadth. This space of ground is under cultivation, but the poverty and scantiness of its grain offer a striking contrast to the rich crops which are grown on the clay of the plain to the east and west. At a distance of 500 m. = 1640 ft. is a well on the border of this field of sand; the altitude of this well is no more than 7 m. 23 cent. = 23 ft. 9 in. above the sea—that is to say, it is lower than the level of the river, which at the Tomb of Ilus is 8 m. 30 cent. = 27 ft. 3 in. above the sea. It is therefore evident that, if this sand were removed, the surface of the clay below it would form a large channel, through which the river would flow off. This depression in the ground terminates in the bed of the In Tepeh Asmak. It may therefore be admitted, with very great probability, that at the time when the hillocks of river-sand at Koum Kioi and the Tomb of Ilus had not yet obstructed the ancient Scamander, its waters flowed to the north and poured through the present bed of the In Tepeh into the sea. This invasion of the sand has forced the river to bore its new bed to the west. This conclusion has the more probability, as the general level of the great plain, to the west of the In Tepeh Asmak, is higher than the surface of the sandy depression.

"If, at the time of the Trojan war, the principal stream of the Scamander occupied the large river-bed, which still serves to carry its waters during the period of inundation, the change just described must have taken place a short time afterwards. This appears to be conclusively shown from the word *Stomalimne* (pool at the mouth) employed by Strabo, because this word shows that there was the mouth of a river in the *Stomalimne* at the time of this geographer, or at least at that of Demetrius of Scepsis (about 180 B.C.).

" Below the Tomb of Ilus, the ancient Scamander flows between very high vertical banks, which indicate that the bed is relatively of recent formation. At the wooden bridge above the *Stomalimne*, the altitude of the plain is not more than 2 m. 77 c. = 8 ft. 10 in.; the breadth of the ancient Scamander is there 45 m. = 147 ft. 8 in.

"The *Stomalimne* is a pool about 800 m. = 2625 ft. long and 200 to 300 m. = 656 to 984 ft. broad on the average. Into this pool flow the waters of the Kalifatli Asmak, which is identical with the ancient Scamander. This pool communicates by a narrow channel with the Hellespont, and its water is brackish. The clay of the plain extends on the right of the pool to the sea, and borders it with vertical banks. On the left of the pool—that is to say, on the west side—the clay ceases about 300 m. = 984 ft. short of the sea-shore; the space which follows forms a triangular neck of land, which terminates at the channel of the *Stomalimne*. This neck of land is an undulating sandbank, the hollows or cavities of which are 50 centimètres = 1 ft. 8 in. above the level of the sea, whilst its projections are from 1 to 2 mètres = 3 ft. 4 in. to 6 ft. 7 in. above the sea-level. I sank a shaft 1 mètre = 3 ft. 4 in. deep into one of these hollows, and thus penetrated *below* the level of the sea. The upper layer, which consisted of grey sand, is only 2 centimètres deep; after that comes a dark blue sand mixed with many roots of plants; below this I found pure dark blue sand, of older date and a marshy character. These layers are obviously produced by river silt; they contain no marine deposits, and no stones. The space occupied by this undulating sandbank is very small; the soil of it appears to be formed in the same manner as the alluvium of Koum Kaleh, but apparently it cannot extend further into the sea, because the current of the Hellespont tends to maintain it in its actual limits. The shaft, having been dug below the level of the sea, gradually filled with water up to that level : this water was at first turbid, but it soon became clear, and had a hardly perceptible brackish taste; it therefore did not come from the sea, but from the *Stomalimne*."

Professor Virchow also affirms that he has found in the Plain of Troy nothing which tells in favour either of a marine formation of the soil, or of the growth and increase of the plain towards the Hellespont. In a long and learned dissertation he[8] proves beyond any doubt that the hydrography of the Plain of Troy must have been at the time of Pliny and Strabo much the same as it is now, and that when, in following up the Trojan coast from south to north, Pliny[9] says,—"Scamander amnis navigabilis, et in promontorio quondam Sigeum oppidum. Dein portus Achaeorum, in quem influit Xanthus Simoenti junctus : stagnumque prius faciens Palaescamander,"—he cannot mean by the *ancient* Scamander any other river but the In Tepeh Asmak; by the "Xanthus Simoenti junctus" the Kalifatli Asmak, into which in his time, as now, the Simois flowed ; and by "Scamander" the great river near Sigeum.

Professor Virchow says : " There can be no doubt whatever that the

---

[8] *Landeskunde*, &c., pp. 124–140.　　[9] *H. N.* v. 33.

volume of water which once flowed in the bed of the Kalifatli Asmak was much larger than that which now flows in it, even at the period of the inundations. Its bed answers so well to a great and powerfully working stream, that the present river appears only as a residue of its former wealth. Where was formerly water, there are now broad edges of bank overgrown with bushes, and now and then showing deeply-indented borders. In places here and there are still deep bays, of whose origin the present current offers no explanation. In many places, especially on the left bank, are rows of sand-hills, which must once have been formed by alluvium; they are at present so high that even their foot is never reached by the water. The common sources of the Asmak in the Duden swamp, close to Akshi Kioi, are not copious enough to feed a large river. Now, in the region of the confluence of the Thymbrius and further down, broad and for the most part dry water-beds branch off from the Scamander, extending to the Kalifatli Asmak close to those sources, and even now, at the time of high water, receiving the overflowing water of the Scamander. But even these merely temporary affluents are not sufficient to make the Kalifatli Asmak so impetuous as it must once have been, judging by the testimony of its banks. This could only happen again, if the main volume of the Scamander were let into it. Has this ever taken place? A glance at Spratt's map shows in fact that the main ' winter-bed,' which leads from the confluence of the Thymbrius to the Kalifatli Asmak, is the direct continuation of the Scamander, as this river is seen after having flowed around the Bali Dagh and entered the Plain. If the line of the river-course, the direction of which is here almost directly to the north, be prolonged, it comes in a straight line to the sources in the Duden. Nothing, therefore, is more probable than that the Scamander once took this course, and that the Kalifatli Asmak represents the further course of the Scamander at that time. Later on it may have displaced this bed by its own alluvial deposits, and may have pierced a new bed more to the west through the Plain."

Further on,[10] Professor Virchow thinks it perfectly certain that, immediately below Koum Kioi, the ancient Scamander (in the bed of the Kalifatli Asmak) turned eastward, and that it poured into the Hellespont, by the bed of the In Tepeh Asmak, on the east side of the Plain, close to the promontory of Rhoeteum. He thinks that the deep sandy depression found by M. Burnouf below Koum Kioi, between the Kalifatli and the In Tepeh Asmak, marks the ancient bed of the Scamander. He holds such a communication to be the more probable, as the In Tepeh Asmak is far too broad and deeply cut for him to suppose that it could possibly have been formed by the northern arm of the Simois, which is a most insignificant rivulet. This rivulet may have flowed later into the In Tepeh Asmak, perhaps at a time when the communication between the ancient Scamander (Kalifatli Asmak) and the In Tepeh Asmak had already been closed, but most certainly it was never strong enough to produce the bed of the latter. Professor Virchow

---

[10] *Landeskunde*, &c., pp. 136, 137, 170.

adds:[11] "The Kalifatli, in that part of its course which extends from between Hissarlik and Kalifatli to the junction of the Simois, has a bed just so broad, that it is not inferior to the present bed of the Scamander itself, and no other river in the Troad approaches it even remotely, and *this fact has been overlooked by nearly all critics.*" Professor Virchow[1] further says: "Regarding the alluvial deposits in the Plain, Maclaren[2] has advanced an important argument. He proceeds from the soundings made by the English Admiralty in the Hellespont, which are indicated on their map. Following these, he has drawn along the coast of the Hellespont three curves, which connect together the depths of one, two, and three fathoms respectively. These lines are not parallel with the coast, but they nearly join at the mouth of the Scamander; they recede from the coast before the *Stomalimne,* and still more before the In Tepeh Asmak, and again approach each other, as well as the coast, at the neck of land before Rhoeteum. There is, besides, the difference produced in the form of the coast-line by the curves of one and two fathoms; that is to say, they are bent inward to the south, whereas the three fathoms' line forms a curve which is on the north bent forward to the Hellespont, and projects far beyond the coast and the neck of land. Immediately behind it the depth of the water amounts to 10, 12, 16, and 19 fathoms. Maclaren concludes from this that the mass of alluvium, which has raised the bottom of the Hellespont, cannot have been produced by the present Scamander, but must be attributed to a time when this river flowed first through the In Tepeh Asmak, and later through the *Stomalimne;* that the Hellespont, whose current has a velocity of two miles an hour, carries its own alluvial material and a large part of that of the Scamander into the Aegean Sea, but the counter-current along the Trojan coast, which sometimes, especially with west and south-west winds, is very strong, distributes a certain quantity of the material along the coast as far as Rhoeteum; and that, if the mouth of the Scamander had always been at the present place, the lines of depths would be parallel with the coast-line. To this it may be replied, that we cannot at once admit Maclaren's supposition, that the depth of the Hellespont once was nearly as great on the coast as in the midst of this channel, and that the present difference in depth has been produced solely by alluvial deposits. On the other hand, we have some safe indications, which show the fact of the alluvial deposits, as well as their direction. As such I consider three phenomena:—1. The bar of sand before the mouth of the In Tepeh Asmak,[3] which has exactly the direction of the Hellespont current, for it is joined on the east side to Rhoeteum, and proceeds thence for a long distance westward. 2. The sandbanks at the mouth of the Scamander. 3. The sandy plain which projects into the Hellespont, on which Koum Kaleh is situated, and which extends in a south-westerly direction to the foot of the tumulus of Achilles. It appears to me that

---

[11] *Landeskunde,* &c., p. 138.
[1] *Ibid.* p. 143 ff.

[2] Charles Maclaren, *The Plain of Troy described;* Edinburgh, 1863, p. 46.
[3] Virchow, *Landeskunde,* &c., p. 144.

these facts prove, not only that there exists a perceptible alluvium, but also that the easterly stream is the one which decides its formation. If it depended principally on the westerly or south-westerly counter-current, neither would exist the neck of land of Koum Kaleh, nor the sand-bar of the In Tepeh Asmak. Here comes in another circumstance which must not be underrated, namely, the direction and force of the wind. I may cite two observations which I consider to be sufficiently certain. One is the motion of the sand at the citadel of Koum Kaleh, which proves the predominance of an easterly or north-easterly direc-tion of the wind, in accordance with the direction and current of the Hellespont. The other is the position of the trees on Rhoeteum and on the lower section of the Plain. The trunks of all these trees (Valonea oaks) are uniformly inclined towards the west-south-west. This is in accordance with Maclaren's [4] statement that the wind formerly called Ventus Hellespontinus blows for at least ten months in the year down the Hellespont. This direction of the wind explains sufficiently why the sand is carried along the coast in a westerly direction, and why in the course of time it has accumulated more and more below and before Sigeum, so as to form there the neck of land of Koum Kaleh. The coast-marsh proper, therefore, remains protected against an accumulation of sand, unless—as in the *Stomalimne*—the sea itself washes away part of the marshy soil. Indeed my investigations in the *Stomalimne* have proved that not only is there no alluvium, but rather a *washing away of the marshy soil*, which is partially replaced by sea-sand, but that there is no formation of dunes. This washing away takes place on the west side of the *Stomalimne;* it testifies to the powerful agency of the water in the direction of the Hellespont current. I must, therefore, acknowledge that Maclaren's arguments must not be rated so low as might appear. If it is found that, notwithstanding the force of the easterly current of water and wind, the three fathoms' line before the In Tepeh Asmak extends in a convex curve far into the Hellespont, and indeed also far beyond the neck of land of Rhoeteum, this would tell decidedly for the view, that much alluvium has once been brought down by the In Tepeh Asmak, and perhaps also by the stream of the *Stomalimne*, provided of course the raising of the Hellespont bottom be due to sand and other alluvium. This has not been proved, but it is probable. In no case can I admit that this raising could have been produced by deposits of the water of the Hellespont which comes down from the Propontis. While, therefore, I do not hesitate to admit the existence of sand accumulations at the coast as certain, and for some distance from the coast in the Hellespont itself as probable, still I can infer but little from this as to the formation of the coast-land. Strabo says, indeed, with much assurance:[5] 'The Scamander and Simois, uniting in the plain, and bringing down a great quantity of mud, bank up the sea-coast, and form a blind mouth, salt-water lagoons, and marshes.'

---

[4] *Loc. cit.* p. 215.

[5] Strabo, xiii. p. 595: συμπεσόντες γὰρ ὅτε Σιμόεις καὶ ὁ Σκάμανδρος ἐν τῷ πεδίῳ πολλὴν καταφέροντες ἰλύν, προσχοῦσι τὴν παραλίαν, καὶ τυφλὸν στόμα τε καὶ λιμνοθαλάττας καὶ ἕλη ποιοῦσι.

But nowhere on the coast can there be shown an increase of the soil by real mud (ἰλύς), except in the In Tepeh Asmak itself, namely in its upper part. The mud which reaches the Hellespont is soon cleared of its clayey ingredients; what remains is clean quicksand. This sand can change or fill up the mouths of the rivers, and can thereby cause the damming up of the water; but except at the neck of land of Koum Kaleh, it has exercised no immediate influence on the growth of the coast-land, at least not so long as the coast-marsh has existed. In order, therefore, to obtain a somewhat sure basis for the question of the alluvial formations, it appeared to us necessary to investigate the soil of the Plain itself at various places."

Professor Virchow [6] commenced his investigations by digging a number of holes; the first to the right of the bridge which spans the Kalifatli Asmak near Hissarlik. To a depth of 1·25 mètres, he found a very compact blackish soil, and below it coarse sand, among which small pieces of quartz, flakes of mica, blackish grains and coarser fragments of rock, were conspicuous. There were no remains of shells. He dug the second hole in the flat dune-like hill on the left bank of the Kalifatli Asmak near Koum Kioi, on which is a Turkish cemetery. He found there to a depth of 2 mètres nothing but coarse sand of a dark colour, consisting principally of angular grains of quartz mixed with mica, and some coarser but smoothed pebbles of rock; no trace of shells. He dug the third hole in a place near the road to Koum Kaleh, where the zone of the Valonea oak-trees ceases, and where the coast-marsh proper begins. He found there to a depth of 1 mètre very rich dark clay, of which the banks of the Kalifatli Asmak are also composed. He dug a fourth hole in the dry overgrown bed of the In Tepeh Asmak, close to the little neck of land at the south-west corner of Rhoeteum. Here he found the same compact clammy rich black earth, to a depth of 1 mètre 10 centimètres; there were no stones in it, but a great number of rounded pieces of baked bricks. He dug a fifth hole 1 mètre deep to the west of Kalifatli, in a filled-up channel of the Scamander. The soil consisted there of fine sand near the surface and of coarse sand below; the latter was mixed with a fine clayish sand, and small grains of quartz, partly rounded and partly angular, as well as with large mica-flakes and coarse small stones, for the most part angular, but rounded at the corners. In *none* of these holes was found any trace of a marine formation. Professor Virchow having taken samples of the sand from all these holes, and having had them analysed in Berlin, they were all found to consist of quartz-bearing syenite. This, in his opinion, solves the question as to the origin of the alluvial layers in the plain, for the Scamander flows above Evjilar through a broad zone of syenite which is in process of disintegration.[7] A similar region, also drained by the Scamander, is situated on the north-east part of the Chigri Dagh. CONSEQUENTLY THE ALLUVIUM OF THE PLAIN OF TROY IS ESSENTIALLY THE PRODUCT OF THE HIGHER MOUNTAINS, ESPECIALLY OF IDA. At the period of inundation the Scamander

---

[6] *Landeskunde der Troas*, pp. 146–154.   [7] See Tchihatcheff, *loc. cit.* t. i. p. 359.

carries away not only the primary products of the disintegrated syenite, but perhaps the larger part of the mud which the river brings to the lower plain originates in the older deposits of the upper plain between Iné and Beiramich. Here the Scamander and its numerous affluents are continually tearing and carrying away fresh parts of the banks. Its water, which is perfectly clear at its source, and which at Evjilar still shows no turbidity, appears in the lower plain turbid and yellowish, so that the name of Xanthus is here perfectly suitable. This change in its appearance, therefore, occurs during the course of the river through the upper plain, and the suspended matter which causes the muddy appearance belongs for the most part to the freshly-dissolved masses of a very ancient alluvium, which was formed in the upper plain at a time when it was still a lake. By thus proving that the alluvial soil of the lower plain is essentially of a syenitic origin, every possibility at once disappears of attributing to the other rivers and rivulets any determining part whatever in the conveyance of the alluvial deposits. Neither the Bounarbashi Su, nor the Kemar Su, nor the Kalifatli Asmak, can be taken into consideration, unless indeed they might occasionally again put in motion the alluvium already deposited by the Scamander. The fact is of very special importance, that the silt of all the Asmaks— of the Kalifatli Asmak, of the old Scamander-bed to the west of Kalifatli, and especially of the In Tepeh Asmak—is derived from the upper mountains. It is not the material of the Oulou Dagh, such as the Simois carries away, which can possibly have filled up the In Tepeh Asmak; the syenitic admixtures of the clay, which I took from the ancient bed of this Asmak, now filled up, point distinctly to its having been covered by the mud of the Scamander. The Plain of the Kalifatli Asmak also consists, below a later layer of a fine clayish deposit, of the same coarse sand, which now, as before, the Scamander alone brings down from the high mountains. Nay, the quicksand of the *Stomalimne*, though of much finer grain, has nothing of maritime origin except an admixture of shells; and for the rest, this quicksand is just such a syenitic sand as that of the Plain,—river-sand, carried into the Hellespont, but thrown by it on the land.[8]

Professor Virchow[9] goes on to say : " However satisfactory this result is in itself, it is but of little use for the chronological question. Only in the In Tepeh Asmak I found fragments of bricks in the silt of the river-bed, which bore witness to the comparative lateness of this silting up, which must, therefore, have taken place when brick-baking men already had their habitations in the Plain. I observe here that these brick fragments occurred not only on the surface, but also below. On this side, therefore, there can exist no evidence against the opinion that *the In Tepeh Asmak has ceased to be a real outlet only in a relatively modern time.*"

The result of the investigations of Virchow and Burnouf, that except in its hydrography the Plain of Troy has undergone hardly any material change since the Trojan war, is identical with that which Prof. P. W.

---

[8] Mauduit, *Découvertes dans la Troade*, p 136.   [9] *Op. cit.* p. 153.

Forchhammer [10] obtained by the explorations he made in 1839 in company with Lieutenant (now Admiral) T. A. B. Spratt: " We reject," he says, "as utterly erroneous the theories, that the lower plain may have been formed by a post-Homeric alluvium, and that the latter may have covered up a pretended port, which once extended for a long distance into the land. Both these theories are decidedly contradicted by the facts, and they are not in any way corroborated by the Homeric poems. It would be perfectly inexplicable how vertical banks, from 6 to 10 ft. high, could have been built up by the alluvial soil on the sides of the rivers after their prolongation and at the eastern end of the strand, while the lagoons were not filled up by them, but were nevertheless separated from the Hellespont by a sandbank. Homer, who mentions the large lagoon, neither knows of a port in the neighbourhood of the Greek camp, nor alludes to its existence by a single word. On the contrary, many passages in the *Iliad* [1] prove that the Greek camp was on the actual shore of the sea or of the Hellespont. Scylax rightly states the distance from Novum Ilium to the sea to be 25 stadia. The plain in its present condition is, in all essential features, old Priam's ancient kingdom and the battle-field of Hector and Achilles."

I may also cite here what I wrote on the same subject twelve years ago: [2] " I followed the seashore to the west towards the promontory of Sigeum, investigating most attentively the nature of the soil, in order to see whether it might be, as Strabo asserts, of an alluvial formation later than the Trojan war. The gradual elevation of the heights of In Tepeh appeared to me at once to refute the supposition that a gulf could ever have existed there, and I became fully convinced of this on seeing the high vertical banks of the little rivers In Tepeh Asmak and Kalifatli Asmak near their mouths in a swampy soil. If the soil of the plain had been produced by the alluvium of the present rivers and rivulets, their banks could not have had a perpendicular height of from 6 to 10 ft., in places where the ground is marshy and loose. Besides, the large deep lagoons on the shore of the plain make it impossible that the Plain of Troy could have been formed, either entirely or partially, by alluvial soil; because, if the rivers had deposited alluvial soil to the profit of the plain, these deep lagoons would have been filled up first. The great *Stomalimne*, or lagoon and swamp, of which Strabo [3] speaks, still exists, and doubtless it is now neither larger nor smaller than in the time of that geographer, because the water which evaporates from the lagoon is immediately replaced by infiltration from the sea. The current of the Hellespont, moreover, which runs at the rate of two miles an hour, carries away the alluvial matter of the rivers, and deposits it on the shallow grounds to the left outside the Hellespont, at a distance of several kilomètres from the Plain of Troy; and this same current must at all times have prevented the growth of the shore."

[10] *Topographische und physiographische Be- schreibung der Ebene von Troia*, p. 28.
[1] *Il.* ii. 92, 152 ; viii. 501 ; xiii. 682 ; xiv. 31 ; xviii. 66 ; xix. 40 ; xxiii. 59 ; xxiv. 12.
[2] *Ithaque, le Péloponnèse et Troie ;* Paris, 1869, p. 208.
[3] xiii. p. 595.

In his learned dissertation[4] on *The Asiatic Coast of the Hellespont,* Mr. Frank Calvert, who has been for twenty years a resident on the Dardanelles, proves beyond any doubt the cessation of the growth of the land on the coast, and the gradual invasion of the sea upon the land. After having cited a number of instances where the waters of the Hellespont have washed away portions of land on the Asiatic coast above the Plain of Troy, he writes: "The present effect of the Hellespont on the alluvium of the rivers which discharge into it, may in its consequence be compared with the impetuous current of a large river at the mouth of an affluent. Since on the sea-front of Sultanieh Kaleh[5] and Koum Kaleh,[6] at the mouths of the rivers Rhodius and Scamander, no increase has taken place, it is thereby clearly proved that no growth of the coast has occurred since 1453 and 1659. If the hypothesis of the disappearance of a large part of the alluvial neck of land of Nagara (Abydus) since the time of Xerxes is admitted, then the proportion can, on the ground of historical testimonies, be dated back to a much earlier period; namely, to 480 B.C. The natural geological testimony presented by the crumbling sea-washed slopes of the coast, and the narrow strand close to the river-mouths and their deltas, especially near the promontories of Sigeum and Rhoeteum, proves that the destructive agency of the sea has been in activity long before the historical time, whilst the recession of the deltas would show that this is to be attributed to a change in the relative level of land and sea. The change is not limited to the Hellespont. An investigation of the whole northern coast of the Gulf of Volo in 1875 has proved that, in those comparatively quiet waters which have no current, the sea has advanced on the land. If it is admitted that the alluvial coast between the promontories of Sigeum and Rhoeteum marks the site of the Greek camp and the Naustathmos, then in my opinion the testimony of geology proves that the coast-line was, at the time of the Trojan war, not different from what it is now."

I may here still further mention that those, who assume from the *Iliad* the existence of a deep gulf in the plain at the time of Homer, do not, in my opinion, rightly interpret the passages they quote, where the poet states that "they marched in front of the deep shore,"[7] and again, that "they filled the long mouth of the whole shore, as much as the promontories enclosed."[8] He evidently intends merely to describe the low shore of the Hellespont, shut in as it is by Capes Sigeum and Rhoeteum ; that is to say, by the heights of In Tepeh. Again, the words —"But the eddying Scamander will carry you to the broad bosom of the sea"[9]—cannot make us think of a real gulf; besides, the word εὐρύς means in the *Iliad* "broad" and not "deep:" εὐρὺς κόλπος can therefore mean nothing else but the broad or the vast expanse of the sea.

---

[4] Frank Calvert, *Ueber die asiatische Küste des Hellespont,* vorgelegt in der Sitzung der Berliner Anthropol. Gesellschaft am 20 Decbr. 1879, p. 39.

[5] The fort in the town of the Dardanelles, built in 1453.

[6] Built, according to Mr. Calvert, in 1659.

[7] *Il.* ii. 92 :
ἠϊόνος προπάροιθε βαθείης ἐστιχόωντο.

[8] *Il.* xiv. 35, 36 :
. . . . καὶ πλῆσαν ἁπάσης
ἠϊόνος στόμα μακρόν, ὅσον συνεέργαθον ἄκραι.

[9] *Il.* xxi. 124, 125 :
. . . . ἀλλὰ Σκάμανδρος
οἴσει δινήεις εἴσω ἁλὸς εὐρέα κόλπον.

I have myself always maintained, not only the identity of the Kalifatli Asmak with the ancient Scamander, but also that the latter once turned at Koum Kioi into the bed of the In Tepeh Asmak, through which it fell into the Hellespont close to the promontory of Rhoeteum.[10] That the ancient Scamander had this course and no other, appears evident from Homer; for, had it occupied its present bed at the time of the Trojan war, it would have flowed through the Greek camp, and Homer would have had abundant opportunity of speaking of so important a fact. As he never mentions a river in the camp, we must infer that he did not know that there was any there. But there are several passages in the *Iliad* which prove that in the poet's mind the Greek camp was to the *left* and not to the right of the Scamander, as would have been the case if the river had then had its present course. When, for instance, Priam on his visit to Achilles passes the Tomb of Ilus and immediately afterwards reaches the ford of the Scamander, where he waters his horses and mules,[1] the Greek camp is necessarily to the left of the river, and this is clearly also the case when, on his return from the Greek camp, he again reaches the ford of the Scamander and drives his chariot to the city, while the cart drawn by mules follows with the corpse of Hector.[2] I may further cite the passage where, Hector being wounded, his companions lift him in their arms and carry him from the battle-field, where his charioteer stands with the splendid chariot and the swift horses, which bring him back deeply groaning to the town. But when they reached the ford of the broad-flowing Xanthus born of Zeus, they lifted him from the chariot, laid him on the ground, and poured water over him.[3] As W. Christ[4] justly remarks, this passage can leave no doubt that, on his way to Ilium, Hector had necessarily to pass the Scamander (or Xanthus), for it cannot possibly be admitted that the charioteer could have deviated from the shorter and more direct road to reach the river, in order to pour water over the dangerously wounded hero.

That the Greek camp was to the left of the Scamander, and that this river flowed between the town and the camp, is further proved by the passage where, after Patroclus had cut off the foremost Trojan troops, he drove them back again to the ships, baffled their attempts to gain the town, and attacked and killed them between the ships, the river, and the high walls of Troy.[5]

My theory that the Scamander, after its confluence with the Simois, flowed into the Hellespont to the east of the Greek camp, has been

---

[10] See my *Troy and its Remains*, pp. 72, 73.

[1] *Il.* xxiv. 349-351 :

οἳ δ' ἐπεὶ οὖν μέγα σῆμα παρὲξ Ἴλοιο ἔλασσαν,
στῆσαν ἄρ' ἡμιόνους τε καὶ ἵππους, ὄφρα πίοιεν,
ἐν ποταμῷ.

[2] *Il.* xxiv. 692 :

ἀλλ' ὅτε δὴ πόρον ἷξον ἐϋρρεῖος ποταμοῖο,
and 696, 697 :

οἳ δ' εἰς ἄστυ ἔλων οἰμωγῇ τε στοναχῇ τε
ἵππους, ἡμίονοι δὲ νέκυν φέρον.

[3] *Il.* xiv. 428-436 :

τὸν δ' ἄρ' ἑταῖροι
χερσὶν ἀείραντες φέρον ἐκ πόνου, ὄφρ' ἵκεθ' ἵππους
ὠκέας, οἵ οἱ ὄπισθε μάχης ἠδὲ πτολέμοιο

ἕστασαν ἡνίοχόν τε καὶ ἅρματα ποικίλ' ἔχοντες·
οἵ τόν γε προτὶ ἄστυ φέρον βαρέα στενάχοντα.

ἀλλ' ὅτε δὴ πόρον ἷξον ἐϋρρεῖος ποταμοῖο,
Ξάνθου δινήεντος, ὃν ἀθάνατος τέκετο Ζεύς,
ἔνθα μιν ἐξ ἵππων πέλασαν χθονί, κὰδ δέ οἱ ὕδωρ
χεῦαν·

[4] W. Christ, *Topographie der Troianischen Ebene*, p. 203.

[5] *Il.* xvi. 394-398 :

Πάτροκλος δ' ἐπεὶ οὖν πρώτας ἐπέκερσε φάλαγγας,
ἂψ ἐπὶ νῆας ἔεργε παλιμπετές, οὐδὲ πόληος
εἴα ἱεμένους ἐπιβαινέμεν, ἀλλὰ μεσηγύς
νηῶν καὶ ποταμοῦ καὶ τείχεος ὑψηλοῖο
κτεῖνε μεταΐσσων, . . .

warmly defended as far back as 1852 by the late gifted scholar Julius Braun, in his learned dissertation *Homer und sein Zeitalter*.[6] W. Christ [7] nevertheless thinks that the Scamander must have flowed on the west side of the Greek camp, because all the principal battles are in the plain between the Scamander and Simois, where the armies alternately pursue each other to the town or to the ships, without any mention being made of their having to cross the rivers. But Homer is an epic poet, and no historian; he writes with poetical licence, not with the minute accuracy of a geographer, and we must be thankful to him for giving us the general outlines of the topography of the plain. From the passages quoted above, where the ford of the Scamander is mentioned, it is clear that this river had to be passed in order to reach the Greek camp, which lay to the left of it. The poet further alludes [8] to the confluence of the Simois and Scamander immediately in front of Troy; he repeatedly and most distinctly describes the principal battles as taking place on the plain between the two rivers and the city; but to demand from him also a description of the manner in which the armies passed the Scamander, is asking, I think, too much from an epic poet. The passage to which W. Christ refers [9] can only mean the plain between the Scamander, the Simois, and Troy. In a passage already referred to [10] the Greek ships are said to fill the whole shore between the two promontories of Sigeum and Rhoeteum. But this may well be said of a camp which extended from Cape Sigeum eastward, and was only separated from the opposite cape by the breadth of the river.

The Homeric epithets of the Scamander are ἠϊόεις,[11] which signifies *high-banked*, from ἠϊών, used in Homer only of the sea-shore; εὔρροος,[1] *fair-flowing*; δινήεις,[2] *eddying*; μέγας ποταμὸς βαθυδίνης,[3] *the great deep-eddying river*; βαθύρροος ἀργυροδίνης,[4] *deep-flowing with silvery eddies*; εὔρροος ἀργυροδίνης,[5] *fair-flowing with silvery eddies*; δῖος, *divine*.[6] Its banks were steep and high;[7] and live bulls and hard-hoofed horses were sacrificed to it.[8] The Scamander was said to have been born of Zeus,[9] and had its priest in Troy, who was venerated by the people as a god,[10] which leads us to suppose that the river-deity had a temple or at least an altar in the town. He was called Xanthus by the gods, and assisted at the assembly of the gods on Olympus;[11] he took part in the battle of the gods before Troy;[1] he made great inundations;[2] and, as at the present day, his banks were abundantly covered with elms, willows, tamarisks, lotus, bulrushes, and cyprus-grass.[3]

---

[6] Heidelberg, 1856–1858.
[7] *Topogr. d. Troian. Ebene*, p. 202.
[8] *Il.* v. 774–778. [9] *Il.* vi. 4.
[10] *Il.* xiv. 35, 36. [11] *Il.* v. 36.
[1] *Il.* xiv. 433; xxi. 130; xxiv. 693.
[2] *Il.* xiv. 434; xxi. 2, 8; xxiv. 694.
[3] *Il.* xx. 73; xxi. 329, 603.
[4] *Il.* xxi. 8. [5] *Il.* xxi. 130.
[6] *Il.* xii. 21. [7] *Il.* xxi. 171, 175, 200.
[8] *Il.* xxi. 131, 132:

. . . . . . ᾧ δὴ δηθὰ πολέας ἱερεύετε ταύρους,
ζωοὺς δ᾽ ἐν δίνῃσι καθίετε μώνυχας ἵππους.

[9] *Il.* xiv. 434; xxi. 2; xxiv. 693.
[10] *Il.* v. 77:

Δολοπίονος, ὅς ῥα Σκαμάνδρου
ἀρητὴρ ἐτέτυκτο, θεὸς δ᾽ ὣς τίετο δήμῳ, . . .

[11] *Il.* xx. 5–40 and 73, 74.
[1] *Il.* xx. 73, 74.
[2] *Il.* xxi. 234–242.
[3] *Il.* xxi. 350–352:

καίοντο πτελέαι τε καὶ ἰτέαι ἠδὲ μυρῖκαι,
καίετο δὲ λωτός τ᾽ ἰδὲ θρύον ἠδὲ κύπειρο,ν
τὰ περὶ καλὰ ῥέεθρα ἅλις ποταμοῖο πεφύκειν.

I may add, that nothing seems to me better to show the great importance which the Trojans attached to this river, and the veneration which they had for it, than the fact that Hector, the most powerful champion of Ilium, compares himself to the Scamander, and gives to his son Astyanax the name of "Scamandrius," or the Scamandrian.[4]

Herodotus says that when the army of Xerxes reached the Scamander, it was the first stream they had crossed since leaving Sardis, the water of which failed them, and did not suffice to satisfy the thirst of the men and cattle, and that the Persian monarch afterwards ascended into the Pergamus of Priam,[5] in order to see it. This account of Herodotus appears to be no exaggeration; for, although the Scamander has a large volume of water in winter and spring, it is in the dry season generally reduced to a very slender and shallow brook. I have seen it several times, and the last time in September and October 1878, so dried up that there was no stream at all in the Plain of Troy, nothing in fact but a series of pools of stagnant water. This is by no means a rare occurrence; nay, the villagers of Kalifatli, Yeni Shehr, and Yeni Kioi assured me that in dry summers, and on an average once in three years, there is in August and September no flowing water whatever in the river in the Plain of Troy. They also asserted that this always occurs in the late summer or autumn, if in April and May there have been in the mountains of Ida abundant rains, which melt away the snow, and these have been followed by a long-protracted drought. If the army of Xerxes reached the Scamander when in such a condition, it is no wonder that its water did not suffice for the men and animals. This condition of the Scamander is described with some exaggeration by Lucan, who says that Caesar had unconsciously passed the winding Xanthus on a surface of dry sand, and had safely put his foot among the deep grass.[6]

In the time also of Pomponius Mela, the Roman geographer, who flourished during the reign of the Emperor Claudius (41–54 A.D.), the Scamander and Simois were considered to possess no other importance than that of the reminiscences attached to them; for he observes, in speaking of them, "Fama quam natura majora flumina."[7] This very just observation stands in striking contrast with the statement of Pliny,[8] who, twenty-five or thirty years later, mentioning the objects he saw from his ship when passing the coast of the Troad, speaks of the Scamander as "amnis navigabilis." Now, to call the Scamander a "navigable river" is simply a bad joke, because even in winter it is not navigable for small

---

[4] *Il.* vi. 402, 403 :
τόν ῥ' Ἕκτωρ καλέεσκε Σκαμάνδριον, αὐτὰρ οἱ ἄλλοι
'Αστυάνακτ' · οἶος γὰρ ἐρύετο Ἴλιον Ἕκτωρ.

[5] vii. 43 : 'Απικομένου δὲ τοῦ στρατοῦ ἐπὶ τὸν Σκάμανδρον, ὃς πρῶτος ποταμῶν, ἐπεί τε ἐκ Σαρδίων ὁρμηθέντες ἐπεχείρησαν τῇ ὁδῷ, ἐπέλιπε τὸ ῥέεθρον οὐδ' ἀπέχρησε τῇ στρατιῇ τε καὶ τοῖσι κτήνεσι πινόμενος, ἐπὶ τοῦτον δὴ τὸν ποταμὸν ὡς ἀπίκετο Ξέρξης, ἐς τὸ Πριάμου Πέργαμον ἀνέβη ἵμερον ἔχων θεήσασθαι.

[6] *Pharsal.* ix. 974 :
" Inscius in sicco serpentem pulvere rivum

Transierat, qui Xanthus erat; securus in alto
Gramine ponebat gressus."

[7] *De Situ Orbis*, i. 18.

[8] *H. N.* v. 33 : "Troadis primus locus Hamaxitus : dein Cebrenia : ipsaque Troas, Antigonia dicta ; nunc Alexandria, colonia Romana. Oppidum Nee, Scamander amnis navigabilis, et in promontorio quondam Sigeum oppidum. Dein Portus Achaeorum, in quem influit Xanthus Simoenti junctus : stagnumque prius faciens Palaescamander."

boats, on account of its strong current and many sandbanks. The Roman naturalist commits also an obvious error in making the Xanthus and the Scamander two distinct rivers, and mentioning besides a Palaescamander. It has been repeatedly asserted by scholars who never visited the Troad, that, as Pliny mentions the navigable Scamander before the promontory of Sigeum, he cannot possibly mean anything else than the artificial channel by which part of the waters of the rivulet called the Bounar-bashi Su run into the Bay of Besika. This channel, however, is only from 13 to 20 ft. broad, and its depth is from 1 to 4 ft.; but it is much less still at its mouth. It would therefore be a ridiculous parody to call it an " amnis navigabilis." Hence I perfectly agree with Professor Virchow that Pliny cannot mean by his Scamander any other river than the present Scamander; by the " Xanthus Simoenti junctus," the Kali-fatli Asmak, into which the Simois still flows, and the bed of which, as we have before explained, is identical with that of the ancient Scamander; lastly, by Palaescamander, the In Tepeh Asmak, by which the ancient Scamander once fell into the Hellespont close to Cape Sigeum.[9]

(d) The *In Tepeh Asmak*[10] " runs along the eastern border of the plain in a parallel line with the Rhoeteum ridge, and falls into the Hellespont at a distance of about 600 ft. to the north of In Tepeh, the tumulus attri-buted to Ajax. According to Akerblad[1] and Forchhammer,[2] the mouth of the In Tepeh Asmak is called by the inhabitants Karanlik-Limani (Port of Karanlik, which word means ' darkness '). But this is an error, for by this name is designated, not the mouth of the In Tepeh Asmak, but a small bay or creek immediately to the east of the projecting neck of land of Rhoeteum; it is encompassed by a rampart-like border of the tertiary ridge, and is thus pretty well concealed : hence its name. Here, as I have said, I always took my morning bath in the dark. Maclaren[3] holds the mouth of the In Tepeh Asmak to be identical with the Portus Achaeorum mentioned by several ancient writers.[4] This mouth is separated from the Hellespont by a vast, flat sandbank, which Pro-fessor Virchow estimates to be 230 paces long, and which is connected on the east side with the projecting neck of land of Rhoeteum. From its mouth to the bridge,[5] which is 72 paces long, the In Tepeh Asmak becomes a river of importance. It preserves its breadth for some distance, but its banks and borders are covered with a richer vegetation ; the rushes, which are very hard and pointed, become higher and thicker ; here and there the wild vine (*Vitis vinifera*) slings its long branches among them ; tall shrubs of Asphodel and an odoriferous Arte-misia occupy the higher and dry places. At some fifty paces above the

---

[9] Büchner, *Homerische Studien*, i. ii. Progr. Schwerin, 1871, 1872, endeavours to prove (i. p. 15) that Pliny held the channel of the Bounar-bashi Su, which empties itself into the Bay of Besika, to be the Scamander, the Mendere or present Scamander the Xanthus Scamander, and the Kalifatli Asmak the Palaescamander. E. Brentano, *Alt-Ilion im Dumbrekthal*, p. 8, pro-poses to read the passage in Pliny : " Xanthus Simoenti junctus stagnumque prius faciens, Pa-laescamander."

[10] I extract this interesting description of the In Tepeh Asmak from R. Virchow, *Beiträge zur Landeskunde der Troas*, pp. 82–92.

[1] Lechevalier, *op. cit.*, t. ii. p. 244, note.

[2] Forchhammer, *Topogr. und physiogr. Be-schreibung der Ebene von Troia*, p. 12.

[3] Maclaren, *op. cit.*, p. 41.

[4] As *e.g.* by Pliny, *H. N.*, v. 33.

[5] See the Map of the Troad.

bridge the open water-current in the river-bed becomes narrow, and it soon disappears under a rich vegetation of reeds, rushes, and Typha. It appears again here and there, but covers itself with a thick veil of water-ranunculus. Still further on may be seen in the river-current solid islands, of greater or less length, partly covered with vegetation, as well as masses of ground projecting into the river from the banks which are here higher, so that the width of the river-bed becomes quite out of proportion to the breadth of the water-current. About ten minutes' walk above the first bridge is a second stone bridge, but it is short and low. Soon afterwards the watercourse appears only as a small ditch; finally it becomes altogether dammed up by rushes and harder soil. This is the case somewhat below the high ground which projects from the south-west corner of Rhoeteum, and which can easily be recognized by a couple of sheep-folds which stand on it, and which belong to Koum Kioi. Here the ancient river-bed, which is easily recognized by its sloping banks, is still 42 paces broad, but is entirely dry, except on its right border a ditch-like watercourse 4 to 5 ft. broad, which has no current. It is still cut like a trough, but the surface is unequal, being here and there slightly hilly, and in general somewhat higher in the middle than on the sides. It is covered with grass interspersed with clover (λωτός) and numerous blue flowers of the Gynandriris; there are still here and there thick beds of rushes. A short distance farther upwards the trough is still more filled up, and on the further side of the above-mentioned high ground the old river-bed can no longer be distinctly recognized." Professor Virchow goes on to say: "I have described the nature of the In Tepeh Asmak thus fully, in order to put an end to the uncertainty regarding the extent, the character, and the connection of that river. It will be seen from this description that at present *this Asmak is a dead, stagnant watercourse*, whose upper bed is more and more overgrown, and whose lower part is only kept open by the flowing in of the Hellespont. *It is no longer an outflowing, but rather an inflowing stream* (inlet Inwike). What water it receives, except at the time of the inundations, can only be rain-water."

(e) *The Bounarbashi Su.*—The principal part of the water which composes this rivulet comes from the 34 or, more probably, 40 springs at the foot of the heights of Bounarbashi, which I visited and explored in company with Professor Virchow.[6] The first three of them are in close proximity; a little further north are two more, and the others rise within a distance of about 1700 ft. Their waters form a rivulet from 3 to 6 ft. deep and 13 to 20 ft. broad. It is joined at once by a very small affluent, which comes from the valleys to the east of the Bali Dagh. "In its further course," says Professor Virchow,[7] "it forms a series of large swamps, which have been most accurately described by M. Forchhammer.[8] The rivulet of Bounarbashi," he adds, "notwithstanding its turning off by the artificial channel, provides, during its short course,

[6] See p. 55.
[7] *Beiträge zur Landeskunde der Troas*, pp. 114–119.
[8] P. W. Forchhammer, *Topogr. und physiogr. Beschr. der Ebene von Troia*, p. 15; compare Maclaren, p. 123.

four large basins with a lasting supply of water even during the summer. Apart from the infiltration through the compact soil at the sources themselves, we find to the east of Ujek Tepeh a large tank, which is deep in the middle and overgrown with reeds and rushes; even in the height of summer it is navigated by fishing boats. Further down, at Yerkassi Kioi, is a smaller swamp with abundance of water. There is a similar swamp in the valley through which the canal is cut. In the rainy season, the same rivulet (the Bounarbashi Su), by means of the winter-stream of the original bed, the so-called Lisgar, fills also a vast swamp in a sinuosity of the promontory of Yeni Shehr below Hagios Demetrios Tepeh. This swamp dries up in summer, and it was in August overgrown with high dry reeds.

"The winter-stream (just mentioned) of the 'rivulet,' as Forchhammer calls the Bounarbashi Su in a very significant manner, is in his opinion[9] identical with the original bed, which existed before the artificial channel to the Aegean Sea was cut. That ancient bed is partly cut deep in the clayey soil, and partly it spreads over the flat surface with undefined borders. But even in these flat places its limits do not change from year to year. While the stream prefers in winter the already existing bed to any other course over higher ground, in summer it all the more preserves the course impressed on the clayey soil, the clay becoming by the heat almost as hard as stone. In the hard clayey soil of the level parts of this winter-bed small artificial channels were visible, whose age may perhaps be considerable. This winter-stream of the Bounarbashi Su discharges in two places into the Scamander above Yeni Shehr, and pours with it into the Hellespont.

"From this description it is apparent that the whole west side of the Plain along the Ujek and Sigeum ridges is full of the swamps of the Bounarbashi Su, and this is still more evident from Spratt's map. These swamps occupy all the sinuosities of the coast-line and encroach to a great extent on the Plain, so that they leave only in its southern part a small portion of land for tillage; and even this is also exposed to the inundations of the Scamander. One can best view all this by following up the road which leads from Kalifatli to Yerkassi Kioi and Ujek Kioi. On the 22nd of April it was in the following condition:— Having passed a field still very wet from the last inundation, and covered in places where it had dried up with a rich crumbling crust, I first came to two small arms of the Bounarbashi Su, which are close together, and in which there was open, but scarcely flowing, dirty water; a half-ruined bridge leads over them. To the right (north) these arms were lost in a vast swamp thickly overgrown with luxuriant water-plants. To the left, where the swamp was not less extensive, old reeds still stood, double a man's height. Through this swamp a long winding road leads over a ruined stone dyke. On the west side we reach another small stone bridge, spanning with a single short arch the excavated canal below. Somewhat turbid but still transparent water

---

[9] *Topogr. und physiogr. Beschr. der Ebene von Troia*, p. 14.

flows through it in a rapid current.   Immediately beyond it, on the western bank, firm soil is reached."

Considering the series of swamps and particularly the ancient water-beds of the Bounarbashi Su further down, Professor Virchow[10] thinks the construction of the artificial canal to the Aegean Sea cannot claim a high antiquity.   In fact, various conjectures have been made as to its age. It was first spoken of by Wood,[1] who supposed it to have been excavated by a Turkish governor.   Hunt,[2] who travelled in the Troad in 1801, says he heard from the peasants, that eighty years before (that is, in 1720) the canal had been made by a Sultana of the Serail, who was at that time proprietor of the estate, and that it had been afterwards restored by Hassan Pasha.   The Turks of Yerkassi Kioi assured Lechevalier[3] that the Kapudan Pasha Hassan had built a mill and baths in the neighbouring valley, and they had themselves been employed in the excavation of the new canal.   Lechevalier thinks that the water of the Bounarbashi Su had formerly been led off to Alexandria-Troas by the aqueduct of Herodes Atticus.   Barker Webb[4] also says that Hassan Pasha el Ghazi led the water of the Bounarbashi Su through an old canal which he restored and which moves a mill.   Mauduit[5] is of opinion that the canal has been restored at different periods, but that it already existed at the time of Xerxes, and that at the time of Demetrius of Scepsis it led off all the water of the Bounarbashi Su (called by him Scamander) into the Aegean Sea.   Forchhammer[6] shares the opinion that the canal is very ancient.   Colonel Leake[7] did not venture to decide whether it was a work of the ancients or of the Turks.   But I think we find the best answer to the question in the alluvium deposited by this channel, which covers a space about one mile and a half long and broad, and has thus already filled up by far the larger portion of the Bay of Besika.   That a small rivulet like this channel should form such immense alluvial deposits in a hundred years is out of the question; in my opinion, a long number of centuries is required.   This canal is, as before mentioned, from 13 to 20 ft. broad, and from 1 to 4 ft. deep.   It is cut for a long distance in the rock.

Virchow[8] says: "As M. Forchhammer rightly observes in the passage quoted above, the ancient water-beds of the Bounarbashi Su are partly very deeply impressed; and, I might add, they are impressed so deeply that we cannot well suppose them to have been preserved so for thousands of years.   This can best be seen by following the road from Yeni Kioi down to the ferry of the Scamander.   A long turning is first made to the north round the Lisgar; then the road leads round a spur of the ridge towards a couple of bridges on which we cross two such watercourses.   When I first came there, I thought, especially at the

---

[10] *Beiträge zur Landeskunde der Troas*, p. 118.

[1] *Essay on the Original Genius and Writings of Homer*; London, 1775, p. 326.

[2] Walpole, *Memoirs relating to European and Asiatic Turkey*; London, 1817, p. 135.

[3] Lechevalier, *Voyage de la Troade en 1785, 1786*, ii. p. 193.

[4] Barker Webb, at other places, p. 34, notes.

[5] A. F. Mauduit, *Découvertes dans la Troade*; Paris et Londres, 1840, pp. 132, 215.

[6] Forchhammer, *op. cit.* p. 26.

[7] *Journal of a Tour in Asia Minor*, p. 293.

[8] *Landeskunde*, &c., p. 118.

eastern bridge, that I saw a stately river before me. As far as I could see on both sides there was before us a broad bed, with but slight windings, filled with open water and sharply-cut banks, presenting on a small scale the image of the Scamander which is close by. But a further investigation showed that this bed had no continuity; even at the time of high water it was connected with the Bounarbashi Su only by the swamps and the inundating water. This water, however, had not been brought down by the Bounarbashi Su, but by the Scamander, which inundates its left bank in certain fixed places. The three principal places where this occurs are accurately marked on Spratt's map, just as I found them to be. The first is not far below Bounarbashi, where, after its entry into the Plain, the Scamander makes its first great bend to the west and forms the islands. The second is opposite the Ujek Tepeh, and indeed in a distinctly-marked connection with the great reedy swamp of the Bounarbashi Su. The third is much farther down, opposite Yeni Kioi; it fills the swamps of the Lisgar district and the adjoining low ground.

"Properly speaking, the proportion of the Bounarbashi Su to the Scamander is very similar to that of the Kalifatli Asmak. Both of them are indebted for their existence, in a large degree, to the powerful 'brother.' If it were not for the artificial canal to Besika Bay, the water of the Bounarbashi Su would also pour entirely into the Plain, and it would fill the watercourses further down which are now dry, just as the water of the Duden sources fills the bed of the Kalifatli Asmak. There should, therefore, be also a name 'Bounarbashi Asmak.' The name Su is only suitable if the artificial canal with its flowing water is referred to."

Another canal, which has evidently required even greater labour, has, at an unknown period, been cut across the promontory of Sigeum between Yeni Kioi and Hagios Demetrios Tepeh. According to Forchhammer,[9] the length of this canal is 3000 ft., its depth more than 100 ft., and its upper width about 100 ft. At present it is filled up 10 to 15 ft. deep with earth, so that it is of no use whatever. It had evidently been made to drain the waters of the Lisgar and the winter inundation of the Bounarbashi Su."

Before the artificial canal was cut, and before the Scamander had its present course, the Bounarbashi Su ran along the heights of Sigeum and fell into the Hellespont. As in this position, and also on account of its insignificance, it in no way interfered with the movement of the armies, it is not mentioned by Homer.

(*f*) Of the *Kalifatli Asmak*—which, with Virchow, Burnouf, and Calvert, I hold to be identical with the ancient bed of the Scamander—I have already spoken at some length. It is enough to add here, that one arm of it rises in the Duden swamp[10] on Mr. Calvert's farm of Akshi Kioi, while another arm starts from the point where the Scamander and

---

9 Forchhammer, *op. cit.* p. 20.
10 This swamp, which formerly covered an area of about 250 acres, has by the exertions of Mr. Calvert and his engineer, Mr. Stoney, been dried up and converted into most valuable land; the three springs which produced it still exist

Thymbrius meet. The latter arm, which is broad and deep, brings at the time of the floods an immense volume of water from the Scamander, and joins the former arm at a short distance to the north of the Duden swamp. There can hardly be any doubt that this is the ancient bed of the Scamander. At a short distance to the north of the confluence of the Scamander and Thymbrius there is a second channel, and a little further on a third, through which the Scamander now sends its surplus waters into the Kalifatli Asmak. In all three channels, but particularly in the last one, may be seen countless trunks of uprooted trees, which have been carried down the stream by the force of the current. The Kalifatli Asmak has scarcely any current except in the winter months; in the dry season it consists of a long series of pools of stagnant water.

(g.) The river *Rhesus* (ὁ Ῥῆσος[11]) was called Rhoïtes (Ῥοείτης) in the time of Strabo, who says, however, on the authority of Demetrius of Scepsis, that possibly the river which flows into the Granicus might be identical with the Rhesus of Homer.[1]

(h.) The river *Heptaporus* (ὁ Ἑπτάπορος[2]), according to Strabo,[3] flowed 180 stadia to the north of Adramyttium.

(i.) The river *Caresus* (ὁ Κάρησος[4]) originated at Maloüs, between Palaescepsis and Achaeum, on the coast opposite Tenedos, and fell into the Aesepus.[5]

(j.) The river *Rhodius* (ὁ Ῥοδίος[6]) is, in all probability, the small river which falls into the Hellespont at the Dardanelles.[7] According to Strabo, it fell into the Hellespont between Abydus and Dardanus; opposite its mouth, on the Thracian Chersonesus, was the Dog's-tumulus (*Cynossema*, Κυνὸς σῆμα or Κυνόσσημα), the pretended tomb of Hecuba. Strabo further states that, according to others, the Rhodius fell into the Aesepus.[8] Elsewhere Strabo says that the Rhodius fell into the Aenius; he remarks at the same time that it came from Cleandria and Gordus.[9]

(k.) The *Granicus* (ὁ Γρήνικος[10]) rises in Mount Cotylus, one of the peaks of Ida.[1] It flows to the north-east through the district of Adrasteia, and falls into the Propontis opposite the island of Ophiusa (now Afzia).[2] On the banks of this river Alexander the Great defeated the army of Darius (334 B.C.)

(l.) The *Aesepus* (ὁ Αἴσηπος[3]) rises also in Mount Cotylus,[4] receives the Caresus, as before stated, passes to the north-east of Zeleia, and

---

[11] *Il.* xii. 20.

[1] xiii. 602: ὁ μὲν Ῥῆσος ποταμὸς νῦν καλεῖται Ῥοείτης, εἰ μὴ ἄρα ὁ εἰς τὸν Γράνικον ἐμβάλλων Ῥῆσός ἐστιν.

[2] *Il.* xii. 20.

[3] xiii. p. 603: Ἀδραμυττίου δὲ διέχει πρὸς ἄρκτον ἑκατὸν καὶ ὀγδοήκοντα σταδίους.

[4] *Il.* xii. 20.

[5] Strabo, xiii. p. 603: Κάρησος δ' ἀπὸ Μαλοῦντος ῥεῖ, τόπου τινος κειμένου μεταξὺ Παλαισκήψεως καὶ Ἀχαίου τῆς Τενεδίων Περαίας· ἐμβάλλει δὲ εἰς τὸν Αἴσηπον.

[6] *Il.* xii. 20.

[7] E. Buchholz, *Homer. Kosmogr. und Geogr.* p. 310.

[8] xiii. p. 595: μεταξύ τε (Ἀβύδου καὶ Δαρδάνου) ὁ Ῥοδίος ἐκπίπτει ποταμός, καθ' ὃν ἐν τῇ Χερρονήσῳ τὸ Κυνὸς σῆμά ἐστιν, ὅ φασιν Ἑκάβης εἶναι τάφον· οἱ δὲ τὸν Ῥοδίον εἰς τὸν Αἴσηπον ἐμβάλλειν φασίν.

[9] xiii. p. 603: Ῥοδίος δὲ ἀπὸ Κλεανδρίας καὶ Γόρδου ἃ διέχει τῆς καλῆς πεύκης ἑξήκοντα σταδίους· ἐμβάλλει δ' εἰς τὸν Αἴνιον.

[10] *Il.* xii. 21.

[1] Strabo, xiii. p. 602: ἔστι γὰρ λόφος τις τῆς Ἴδης Κότυλος· ἐξ οὗ ὅ τε Σκάμανδρος ῥεῖ καὶ ὁ Γράνικος καὶ Αἴσηπος.

[2] E. Buchholz, *Homer. Kosmogr. und Geogr.* p. 311.

[3] *Il.* xii. 21.

[4] Strabo, xiii. p. 602, just cited.

falls into the Propontis opposite the island of Halone, the present Aloni.[5]

(*m.*) The *Selleïs* (ὁ Σελλήεις[6]) flowed in the neighbourhood of Arisbe. Strabo says : " Of the rivers the poet makes the Selleïs flow near Arisbe, if indeed Asius came from Arisbe and the river Selleïs."[7]

(*n.*) The *Practius* (ὁ Πράκτιος[8]) flowed between Abydus and Lampsacus. Strabo says : " The Practius is also a river, but a city (of this name), as some have thought, is not to be found. This river flows also between Abydus and Lampsacus."[9]

(*o.*) The *Satnioïs* (ὁ Σατνιόεις), to which the poet gives the epithet ἐΰρρείτης (with a fair current[10]), is now called Tuzlatchai, that is to say, " Salt river : " it rises in Ida, flows in a westerly direction through the southernmost part of the Troad, and falls into the Aegean Sea between Larissa and Hamaxitus.[1]

§ IV. The Climatology of the Troad.

If we consider the Homeric Troad to extend from the coast of the Propontis and the district of Cyzicus to the Caïcus, it would lie between 40° 30′ and 39° N. latitude ; Novum Ilium being in latitude 39° 53′ : its climate therefore must be almost identical with that of Constantinople, which lies only 1° 7′ further to the north. According to Tchihatcheff,[2] the mean temperature of Constantinople is 14°·27 Celsius = 57°·70 Fahrenheit ; while that of Rome, which lies in the same latitude, is 15°·04 = 59°·30 Fahrenheit, that of Barcelona 17° = 62°·60 Fahrenheit.

Table of the mean Number of Days of the Four Cardinal Winds; of fine Days; of rainy Days; and of more or less cloudy Days in the Years 1847, 1848, and 1854.[3]

Months.	North.	East.	South.	West.	Fine days.	Rainy days.	Cloudy days.
January . . .	20	2	6	–	6	12	14
February . . .	11	1	12	1	4	2½	21
March	19	1	6	2	8	8½	15
April	9	1	14	4	17	10	9
May	19	1	9	2	13	4½	12
June	15	1	9	–	16	3½	10
July	23	1	4	1	14	3	13
August . . .	21	4	4	–	21	3	8
September . .	22	–	6	1	9	8	15
October . . .	21	4	7	1	11	4½	13
November . . .	19	–	7	2	6	10½	14
December . . .	18	1	7	1	5	16½	14
Total numbers.	217	17	91	15	130	86½	158

[5] E. Buchholz, *Homer. Kosmogr. und Geogr.* p. 311.

[6] *Il.* ii. 838, 839 :
Ἄσιος Ὑρτακίδης, ὃν Ἀρίσβηθεν φέρον ἵπποι, αἴθωνες, μεγάλοι, ποταμοῦ ἀπὸ Σελλήεντος.

[7] Strabo, xiii. p. 590 : τῶν δὲ ποταμῶν τὸν μὲν Σελλήεντά φησιν ὁ ποιητὴς πρὸς τῇ Ἀρίσβῃ ῥεῖν· εἴπερ ὁ Ἄσιος Ἀρίσβηθέν τε ἧκε καὶ ποταμοῦ ἀπὸ Σελλήεντος.

[8] *Il.* ii. 835 :
οἱ δ' ἄρα Περκώτην καὶ Πράκτιον ἀμφενέμοντο.

[9] xiii. p. 590 : ὁ δὲ Πράκτιος ποταμὸς μέν ἐστι, πόλις δ' οὐχ εὑρίσκεται, ὥς τινες ἐνόμισαν· ῥεῖ δὲ καὶ οὗτος μεταξὺ Ἀβύδου καὶ Λαμψάκου.

[10] *Il.* vi. 34 : Σατνιόεντος ἐΰρρείταο. See also xiv. 445 and xxi. 87.

[1] E. Buchholz, *Homer. Kosmogr. und Geogr.* p. 354.

[2] P. de Tchihatcheff, *Asie Mineure*: II. *Climatologie et Zoologie*, pp. 35–37.

[3] P. de Tchihatcheff, *Ibid.* p. 44.

It will be seen from this table that the north wind predominates very decidedly, except in February and April. Thus in January it is on an average nearly three times more frequent than all the other winds taken together; in March it is a quarter more frequent than the rest; in May, November, and December, almost twice as frequent; in July, more than three times as frequent; and in August, twice as frequent.

These north winds blow nearly always with great violence, and they caused us much suffering during the whole period of our excavations at Troy.

The rainy season here is in December, January, and February. From the beginning of April to the end of October it hardly ever rains, and in the many summers I passed in the Troad I experienced hardly any rain except in the shape of an occasional thunderstorm.

The winters are seldom very severe in the Troad; the cold generally does not set in before January. It is seldom so cold that the rivers freeze. I have seen the Kalifatli Asmak frozen over in the winter of 1873, but never the Scamander or Simois. But it appears that even the Hellespont has sometimes been frozen over, since the straits were frozen in 739 [4] and 753 [5] A.D., while in 755 A.D. both the Bosphorus and the Hellespont are reported to have been covered with ice.[6] Tchihatcheff,[7] from whom I take this information, mentions further two occasions when the Bosphorus was frozen during the reign of the Emperor Romanus (919-944 A.D.), one in 1011 and one in 1068; also one in 1620 A.D.

No traveller has studied the climate of the Troad with more attention and accuracy than P. Barker Webb, who expresses himself in the following terms:[8]—"The Troad being placed in the delicious temperature of Northern Asia, its winters are tempered by the south winds which blow from the Mediterranean; the summer heat is also modified by the regular return of the Etesian winds, which are poetically described by Homer under the image of Boreas traversing the Thracian Sea. The fertility of the fields and valleys, continually irrigated by the waters which descend from Mount Ida, so rich in springs; the variety of the soil, now flat, now mountainous; the abundance of the rivers; the neighbourhood of the sea; the charming and picturesque landscape, which Nature alone has had the care of forming, without Art having any share in it,—all pleases the eye and strikes the imagination: in one word, the situation of this country, considered as a whole, is such that Nature leaves nothing to desire. In fact, if this country had a more enlightened government, if it were under a less barbarous rule, few countries in the world could be compared with it, whether for the richness and variety of its products, or for the abundance of all that is necessary for human life. We may say the same of the whole of Asia Minor, which was celebrated for the luxury and the riches of its ancient inhabitants; but Phrygia in particular appears to have been in a high degree favoured by Heaven. Its forests

---

[4] Von Hammer-Purgstall, *Gesch. des Osm. Reichs*, 2nd ed. vol. ii. p. 784.
[5] Glycas, ed. Bon., p. 493.
[6] Theophanes, ed. Bon., vol. i. pp. 540 and 670.

[7] *Asie Min. : Descr. phys.* p. 70.
[8] *Topographie de la Troade ancienne et moderne,* pp. 110, 111.

Yeni Sheir on Sigeum Pr.

Island of Imbros.   Mount Saoce of Samothrace.   The Ægean Sea.   Koum Kaleh.   Lighthouse.   Peninsula of Gallipoli.

Hellespont.

Simois.

Mounds of Achilles and Patroclus.   To the right of the Gamola is the old bed of the Scamander.

No. 21A.   VIEW OF THE NORTHERN PART OF THE PLAIN OF TROY, FROM THE HILL OF HISSARLIK.

THE CHAIN OF MOUNT IDA.

Village of Chiblak.

Mount Gargarus (Kaz Daghi).

Altar.

Excavations in the Temple.

No. 21B. VIEW OF THE SOUTH-EASTERN PART OF THE PLAIN OF TROY, FROM THE HILL OF HISSARLIK.

and pasture-lands are greener than those of the neighbouring countries of Europe, and the fertility of its soil is by no means inferior to that of the rest of Asia : add to this that it has neither the rigorous winters of the former nor the scorching heat of the latter. What is missing here is man. *Desunt manus poscentibus arvis!* The want of population has changed these very blessings into as many misfortunes; nay, this want of men is the cause of those pestilential miasmata which have rendered endemic in this country the sickness represented by Homer under the image of the arrows cast by the wrath of Apollo. The aspect of the country is in the highest degree picturesque: sometimes it reminds an Englishman of the landscapes of his own country. This resemblance is due as much to the form of the fields enclosed by verdant hedges, as to the trees which are scattered here and there without symmetry, now isolated, now in detached groups; and this gives to the whole the appearance of a park, or of a large space of ground destined to please the eye of the traveller by its variety. There are but few vineyards here; what is chiefly cultivated is grain."

§ V.   PANORAMIC VIEW OF THE PLAIN OF TROY.

I might add, that the Plain of Troy itself is even more favoured than the surrounding country in the exuberant fertility of its soil and the glorious beauty of its landscape. I beg the reader to accompany me at sunset in spring to the summit of Hissarlik, in order that he may convince himself how greatly the Trojans were favoured above other men in the beautiful situation of their city.[9] Immediately before us extends the plain bordered by the Simois and the Kalifatli Asmak, the ancient Scamander, which was the theatre of the principal battles of the *Iliad* and the scene of so many heroic actions. It is covered with grain and innumerable yellow or red flowers. It ends at the confluence of the two rivers, a mile distant, close to the village of Koum Kioi, whose small terraced houses much resemble the mud hovels of the Egyptian fellahs. The ridge to the right of this village, clothed with Valonea oaks, runs out on the north-east into the promontory of Rhoeteum, on a lower height of which, to the left, our eyes discern the tumulus which tradition attributes to Ajax; its summit is, according to Burnouf's measurement, 40·22 metres = 131 ft. above the sea. To the north of this tumulus lies the site of an ancient city, 8 m. = 26 ft. 8 in. above the level of the sea, according to Burnouf's measurement. It is strewn with fragments of ancient pottery and sculptured splinters of white marble. Near the seashore rises a small mound, which, according to Pausanias,[10] must be the tumulus to which tradition pointed as the original tomb of Ajax. I shall revert to it in the description of the Heroic tumuli.[11]   Close to this tumulus lies a mutilated marble statue of a warrior, draped and of colossal size. In all probability the spot marks the site of the ancient city of Aeanteum, which is not mentioned by Strabo, but is alluded to by Pliny,[1] who says that it no longer existed in his time.

---

[9] See the View, No. 21A.   [10] i. 35. 5.   [11] See Chapter XII. (on the Tumuli).   [1] *H. N.* v. 33.

On the promontory of Rhoeteum, 250 m. = 820 ft. to the east of the great tumulus of Ajax, are numerous traces of an ancient city, probably Rhoeteum, which is repeatedly mentioned by Strabo,[2] and still existed in the time of Pliny.[3] A little further to the east and north-east are four more small artificial tumuli, on the height which descends to a miniature port now called "Karanlik" (darkness). Fragments of marble columns and pottery abound here. I agree with Mr. Calvert that the above-mentioned city of Aeanteum must have extended as far as this, and that Karanlik marks its port, and perhaps at the same time the port of Rhoeteum.

Close to the height of Rhoeteum, and parallel with it, is the deep bed of the In Tepeh Asmak, into which the Scamander once flowed a little to the north-east of Koum Kioi. We cannot discern from hence the tumulus of Ilus, where the Scamander formerly bent to the north-east or east, as it is too low. The eye follows for some distance to the north-west the present bed of the Kalifatli Asmak, until we lose sight of it among the oaks with which the plain is covered; but we can distinctly trace its course to the north as far as its mouth by the two rows of trees with which the banks of the Scamander are lined. To the left of its mouth we see the little town of Koum Kaleh, with its two white minarets and its citadel surrounded with high walls, which can now be easily scaled, the wind having accumulated immense masses of sand on its eastern side. Koum Kaleh was a thriving and flourishing city before the town of the Dardanelles was built, which cannot be much more than a hundred years ago; indeed, the masses of marble which have been lavished on its mosques and its fountains, now dried up, testify to its former opulence. Fragments of ancient marbles, as well as stone tombs, which are sometimes dug up in Koum Kaleh or its neighbourhood, lead me to think that it marks the site of the ancient city of Achilleum (τὸ Ἀχίλλειον), which, according to Herodotus,[4] was built by the Mytilenaeans. It is mentioned by Strabo as having been destroyed by the Ilians,[5] and by Pliny,[6] who says that it no longer existed in his time. M. Burnouf observes to me: "The current of the Hellespont does not prevent the accumulation of alluvial soil at Koum Kaleh, because (1) the fort is almost buried under the sand which the north and north-east winds heap up there: (2) the current of the Scamander forms before Koum Kaleh horizontal mounds of sand, where the swamp changes little by little, by the effect of the vegetation, into vegetable earth: (3) there are deposits of sand at the mouth of the Scamander, which are on a level with the surface of the sea; though it appears that they cannot grow higher, since the wind carries away their crest when it emerges and becomes dry: (4) behind Koum Kaleh, on the side of the Aegean, is a lagoon of salt water, which tends to fill up and appears to have once been connected with the sea. In short, the whole neck of land of Koum Kaleh seems to be of recent formation; the sea must once have washed the foot of Cape Sigeum. But probably this neck of land, in its present condition, already existed in the Trojan time, for such a formation requires ages."

---

[2] xiii. pp. 595, 597, 601, 602.   [3] *H. N.* v. 33.   [4] v. 94.   [5] xiii. pp. 600, 604.   [6] *H. N.* v. 33.

To the south-west of Koum Kaleh we see Cape Sigeum, crowned with the Christian village of Yeni Shehr, 252 ft. above the sea, and its many windmills; and immediately to the east of it two tumuli, one of which is attributed to Achilles, the other to Patroclus. Looking further on, we see the beautiful blue Hellespont, bordered on the north by the Thracian Chersonesus, which runs out to a point, crowned by a lighthouse, the site probably of the ancient Elaeus (Ἐλαιοῦς) mentioned by Thucydides.[7] Further to the north-west, we see in the Aegean Sea, and at a distance of about 23 miles from Cape Sigeum, the island of Imbros. It is about 23 miles in circumference, and in ancient times had on its east side a city of the same name. Above Imbros rises the high mountain of the island of Samothrace, on the top of which Poseidon sat, and gazed with wonder at the battles before Troy: from thence he overlooked the Greek fleet, the city of Troy, and Mount Ida.[8] According to the Scholiast (on this passage) and Pliny;[9] this mountain was called Σαώκη: it is 5000 ft. high. Pliny adds, with absurd exaggeration, which seems a copyist's error: "Samothrace attollitur monte Saoce x. mill. passuum altitudinis." A little more to the west we discern, at a distance of 119 miles, the beautiful cone of Mount Athos, called Ἀθόως by Homer,[10] Ἄθως and Ἄθων by other classic writers[11] (now Monte Santo), the highest and most eastern ridge by which the Macedonian peninsula of Chalcidice penetrates into the Aegean Sea. Pliny[1] states that it extends for 75 Roman miles into the sea, and that its circumference is 150 miles. Strabo[2] compares its form to a woman's breast.

A severe critic of mine has declared that Mount Athos is only visible from Hissarlik at sunset in early autumn;[3] but I can assure the reader that this is an utter mistake, as the mountain is visible from Hissarlik all the year round at sunset, whenever the weather is clear.

According to Herodotus,[4] Xerxes, during his expedition to Greece, dug a canal through the neck of land which joins Athos to the Chalcidic peninsula. The promontory was also called Acte.[5] Mount Athos is now celebrated for its monasteries, of which there are said to be 34 (32 Greek and 2 Russian), and for the ancient MSS. preserved in their libraries.

Returning to the Plain of Troy and turning our eyes to the north-west, west, and south-west, we see immediately before us the broad bed of the ancient Scamander (now the Kalifatli Asmak); then the Christian village of Kalifatli, with its wooden church steeple; further on, the lines of trees which flank the course of the present bed of the Scamander; then fields of grain, followed by vast swamps, which are impassable except in the very driest season of the year, and even then only in a few places. There are, however, three bridges in these swamps, by which

---

[7] viii. 102, 107.

[8] Il. xiii. 11–14:
καὶ γὰρ ὃ θαυμάζων ἧστο πτόλεμόν τε μάχην τε
ὑψοῦ ἐπ᾽ ἀκροτάτης κορυφῆς Σάμου ὑληέσσης
Θρηϊκίης· ἔνθεν γὰρ ἐφαίνετο πᾶσα μὲν Ἴδη,
φαίνετο δὲ Πριάμοιο πόλις καὶ νῆες Ἀχαιῶν.

[9] H. N. iv. 12, 23.   [10] Il. xiv. 229.

[11] See Tzschucke, and Mela, ii. 2, 10.

[1] H. N. iv. 10, 17. Pliny exaggerates the length of Athos, which is actually about 40 English miles.

[2] vii. p. 331.

[3] B. Stark, Jenaer Literatur Zeitung, 1874, No. 23.

[4] vii. 23. See also Diodor. xi. 1, and Plin. H. N. iv. 10, 17.   [5] Thucydides, iv. 109.

they may always be crossed, except during the period of inundation and for some time afterwards. These large sheets of stagnant water, helped by the decomposition of the animal and vegetable matter contained in them, produce pestilential miasmata, which engender much sickness and especially intermittent fevers.

We learn from ancient authors that swamps existed in the Plain of Troy throughout antiquity, even at a time when the population was numerous and powerful. There was even a swamp immediately below the walls of Troy itself, for Ulysses says to Eumaeus:[6] "But when we reached the city and the high wall, we lay down in full armour around the citadel, in the midst of the thick shrubs, among the rushes and the swamp." But the swamps must have largely increased since the disappearance of the industrious population which formerly inhabited the Troad. Renewed prosperity and cultivation can alone remove the majority of the endemic diseases which are due to them.

The Trojan plain, which is about two hours' ride in breadth, is bounded on the west by the shores of the Aegean Sea, which are, on an average, 131 ft. high, and upon which we see first a conical hill, not unlike a tumulus in appearance. This is called Hagios Demetrios Tepeh, "the hill of Saint Demetrius," on account of an open chapel dedicated to that saint, which has been built at the foot of the hill, fragments of sculptured white marble having been used for the purpose. Many other sculptured marble blocks lie close by, and evidently mark the site of an ancient Greek temple, which, as Mr. Sayce justly observes,[7] must in all probability have been dedicated to Demeter, who—like nearly all other Greek deities—has been metamorphosed into a saint of no real existence, or absurdly confounded with a real one.[8] But here people have not even gone to the trouble of changing the name more than was necessary in order to alter the feminine gender into the masculine (Δημήτηρ into Δημήτριος). I explored the tumulus and shall revert to it later on.

A little further to the south-west lies the large Christian village of Yeni Kioi, in a splendid situation on the cliff, 203 ft. high, and over-hanging the sea. But in spite of its high situation, it is, owing to its close neighbourhood to the swamps, more infested by fever than any other place in the Troad; it even sometimes happens that all the inhabitants of Yeni Kioi are fever-stricken at the same time.[9]

---

[6] *Odys.* xiv. 472–475 :

ἀλλ' ὅτε δή ῥ' ἱκόμεσθα ποτὶ πτόλιν αἰπύ τε τεῖχος,
ἡμεῖς μὲν περὶ ἄστυ κατὰ ῥωπήϊα πυκνά,
ἂν δόνακας καὶ ἕλος, ὑπὸ τεύχεσι πεπτηῶτες
κείμεθα, νὺξ δ' ἄρ' ἐπῆλθε κακὴ Βορέαο πεσόντος.

[7] *Athenæum*, Oct. 4th, 1879.

[8] Thus, for example, Saint Nicholas has taken the place and functions of Poseidon. Many of the chapels or churches dedicated to him occupy the site where a sanctuary or temple of the Greek god once stood ; and just as in old times the sailors invoked the assistance of Poseidon to grant them a fair wind or to save them from

danger, so the Greek sailors of our own time invoke Saint Nicholas to the same effect.

[9] Without possessing the slightest knowledge of medicine, I became celebrated in the Troad as a physician, owing to the quantity of quinine and tincture of arnica I had brought with me and dispensed liberally. In all the villages of the Troad, the priest is the parish doctor; and as he himself possesses no medicines, and is ignorant of their properties, besides having an innate dislike to cold water and all species of washing, he never uses any other means than bleeding, which of course never cures, and often kills the poor creatures he takes in charge.

To the south-east of this village is the military farm of Yerkassi, with its ruined mosque and minaret ; and further south, on the heights, the lofty tumulus called Ujek Tepeh, which is 83 ft. high, and thus by far the highest of all the tumuli in the Troad. Those who would place Troy at Bounarbashi erroneously identify it with the tomb of Aesyetes. I have thoroughly explored it, and shall describe it in detail in the following pages.

To the north-west of Ujek Tepeh, we see high up on the shore the tumulus called Besika Tepeh, which I also explored, and of which I shall speak hereafter. Of this tumulus, however, we can merely catch the top, as it is screened from our view by the intervening hills and tall oaks. Immediately to the west of Besika Tepeh is a small promontory, which has the shape of a castle, and is for this reason called " Palaeocastron." I visited it in company with Professor Virchow. We found there the foundations of one or two modern buildings, but no accumulation of *débris* and no fragments of pottery,—those everlasting and indestructible witnesses of ancient settlements. Here begins the far-stretching Bay of Besika, in front of which lies the island of Tenedos, still called by its ancient name, but by the Turks Bogdsha-Adassi. It is distant about 40 stadia from the mainland.[10] Pliny[1] gives its distance from Lesbos as 56 Roman miles, and from Sigeum as 12½ miles.

This island appears to have been celebrated in ancient times, together with Chryse[2] and Cilla,[3] for its worship of the Sminthian Apollo : " Hear me, O God of the silver bow, thou that guardest Chryse and most holy Cilla, and rulest Tenedos with might, Sminthean Apollo ; if ever I roofed for thee an acceptable shrine, or if ever I burnt for thee fat thighs of bulls or goats, fulfil for me this wish."[4]

Tenedos is now celebrated for its excellent wine, which is not mentioned in Homer.

Returning again to the Plain of Troy, our eyes wander in a southerly direction,[5] for the distance of a two hours' ride, as far as the Turkish village of Bounarbashi and the heights to the right and left of it ; this village rises up with its white minaret, and behind it, at a great distance, Mount Chigri, which I have mentioned before. To the north-east of Bounarbashi we again recognize the Scamander by the masses of trees with which its banks are lined ; here to the south of its confluence with the Thymbrius is its best ford. As I have said before, from the temple

---

[10] Strabo, xiii. p. 604.

[1] *H. N.* v. 31, 140.

[2] Chryse was a city on the coast of the Troad, situated on a hill near Thebe, in the neighbourhood of Adramyttium, with a temple of the Sminthian Apollo in a sacred grove. It was the home of Chryseïs: *Iliad*, i. 390, 452 ; Ovid, *Metam.* xiii. 174 ; Strabo, xiii. pp. 605, 611. Pliny, *H. N.* v. 32, says, " fuit et Polymedia civitas, et Chrysa et Larissa alia Smintheum templum durat ;" but he can of course only mean the later Chryse, which was near Hamaxitus (Strabo, xiii. p. 612), the ancient city having utterly disappeared in Strabo's time.

[3] Cilla was in the valley of Thebe in the Troad, on the river Cillaeus, at the foot of Mount Cillaeus (part of the range of Ida): Strabo, xiii. pp. 612, 618 ; Pliny, *H. N.* v. 30 ; Herodotus, i. 149 ; Ovid, *Metam.* xiii. 174.

[4] *Il.* i. 37–41 :

κλῦθί μευ, ἀργυρότοξ᾽, ὃς Χρύσην ἀμφιβέβηκας
Κίλλαν τε ζαθέην, Τενέδοιό τε ἶφι ἀνάσσεις,
Σμινθεῦ. εἴ ποτέ τοι χαρίεντ᾽ ἐπὶ νηὸν ἔρεψα,
ἢ εἰ δή ποτέ τοι κατὰ πίονα μηρί᾽ ἔκηα
ταύρων ἠδ᾽ αἰγῶν, τόδε μοι κρήηνον ἐέλδωρ·

[5] See the View, No. 21B, opposite p. 103.

of the Thymbrian.Apollo, at the confluence, to Novum Ilium is, according to Strabo,[6] 50 stadia. At a mile's distance in a north-westerly direction lies the beautiful estate belonging to my friend Mr. Calvert, the old name of which—Akshi Kioi or Batak (which latter means "swamp")—has now been changed into Thymbra. It deserves the change of name, for not only is it bounded by the river Thymbrius, but it stands, as before stated, on the site of the ancient Thymbra. It also comprises the site of an early settlement, on a small hill to the north of Mr. Calvert's farm-house. This site is covered with fragments of ordinary Greek pottery, and in regard to position, distance, &c., corresponds so closely with the statements of Strabo, that it must certainly be his Ἰλιέων Κώμη, where, on the authority of Demetrius of Scepsis, he places the Homeric Troy. At the foot of the hill are, curiously enough, the three springs of water already described, which produced the Duden swamp, now dried up, of which I have spoken before. The temperature of these springs is, according to Professor Virchow's measurement, 68°-71°·60 Fahr.

I have explored the site of Ἰλιέων Κώμη, but found it to consist simply of coarse gravel sand; there is no accumulation of *débris*; and the scanty potsherds lie on the surface of the ground. Demetrius of Scepsis may have been deceived by the appearance of the soil; he may have supposed the Trojan walls to be hidden under a small natural rampart, which projects to some distance and encloses the site in some places; but it really consists of nothing but gravel and sand. Mr. Calvert has excavated a number of tombs close to this site. If we may judge from the contents of the tombs, they would belong to poor villagers. Another curiosity of the estate is the tumulus of Hanaï Tepeh, of which I shall treat hereafter.

Between the estate and Hissarlik are small heights covered with oaks, low shrubs, and bushes. At a short distance to the south rises a tumulus called Pasha Tepeh, which has been excavated by Mrs. Schliemann, and which I shall describe hereafter.[7] To the north-east of it is the Turkish village of Chiblak or Tchiplak (a word which means "naked"), with its minaret lately built with the stones I excavated at Hissarlik. This tumulus is situated on a neck of land which projects thence in a westerly direction for half a mile further into the Plain of Troy, and whose last spur dominates the swamp of the Kalifatli Asmak. On this sort of promontory Webb[8] places ancient Troy. But his map is in confusion, for he says that this promontory is to the east of Ilium and to the south-east of Chiblak, whereas it is to the south of the former and to the west of the latter. Webb[9] supposes that there were two springs at the foot of the site, which formed a swamp. But there are no springs; there are only low lands which are inundated at the period of the high waters. He commits a further error in making the Kalifatli Asmak come from Chiblak, and in identifying the tumulus of Aesyetes with Besika Tepeh. The facts are, as M. Burnouf writes to me, that

[6] xiii. p. 598.
[7] See Chapter XII.
[8] P. Barker Webb, *Topographie de la Troade*, p. 55.
[9] *Ibid.* p. 55.

the little promontory consists of a horizontal limestone rock 290 mètres
= 951 ft. long by 16 to 90 mètres = 52 to 295 ft. broad; the two lower
spurs, *b* and *c*, advance from it to the north-west and south-west. (See
the Plan, No. 22.) On the hill A′ are to be found only a few fragments
of red modern pottery. Advancing towards A, the quantity of vase-
fragments increases, but the pottery is the same, wheel-made, and dull
red. There is no fragment of
hand-polished pottery, no fragment of a saddle-quern, or of
other ancient objects. The
accumulation of *débris* here
and there hardly amounts to
1 inch; below it is the naked
rock. But there are fragments of white or coloured
marble, some of which are
sculptured.

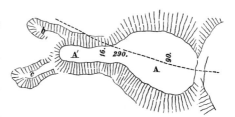

No. 22.   The Hill which extends from Pasha Tepeh, in the
form of a small promontory, to the Plain.

The hill is crossed by the footpath which leads from Kalifatli by Pasha
Tepeh to Chiblak. In the dale at the southern foot of the hill is the little
rivulet of Chiblak, which is hardly 3 ft. wide, and generally dry; it passes
in front of the little promontory A′, feeds the reeds in the plain, and discharges into the Kalifatli Asmak at about 300 mètres = 984 ft. below the
village of this name. To the south-east of Chiblak Mount Gargarus, now
called Kaz Dagh, lifts up its head in the far distance. Immediately to
the south-west, south, and east, is the site of Novum Ilium, the walls of
which may still be traced in a number of places. Its extent would imply
that it may have had from 40,000 to 50,000 inhabitants. The accumulation of *débris* on its site is generally from 6 to 16 ft. deep. The surface
is covered with Hellenic and Roman potsherds, as well as with fragments
of marble sculptures and columns, which testify to the ancient magnificence of the town.

As before explained, the hill of Hissarlik is the spur of a continuous
ridge, which Strabo well describes by the words συνεχὴς ῥάχις,[10] because
it runs for 12 miles in an easterly direction. It is partly covered with
oaks, and apparently terminates in Mount Oulou Dagh, which I have tried
to identify with the Homeric Callicolone. Between this ridge and the
heights of Rhoeteum is the beautiful plain called Halil Ovasi, from 1 to
1½ mile in breadth and 4 miles in length, which is traversed by the
Simois, and extends to the foot of the hill upon which are the ruins
of Ophrynium: in this valley, which forms part of the great Plain of
Troy, at a distance of 2½ miles, lies the Turkish village of Halil Eli.
Another branch of the same valley extends from this village along the
Simois to beyond the pretty Turkish village of Doumbrek, which is at
a distance of 8 miles from Hissarlik. This second valley is of wonderful
fertility; its orchards are full of peach-trees, almond-trees, pear-trees,
and the like.

In the steep rocky slope close to Hissarlik, a large theatre has been

[10] Strabo, xiii. p. 599.

excavated, with a stage 197 ft. broad, and apparently capable of containing 5000 persons. To judge from the fragments of sculptured marble I have dug up there, it appears to belong to the Macedonian time. It was probably built by Lysimachus, and was one of the favours he conferred upon Novum Ilium.[11]

Immediately to the east of this theatre, directly below the ruins of the town-wall of Novum Ilium, and exactly 365 mètres or 399 yds. from Hissarlik, is the spring, whose water has, as before mentioned, a temperature of 14°·6 Celsius (58°·28 Fahrenheit). It is enclosed to a height of 6½ ft. by a wall of large stones joined with cement, 9¼ ft. in breadth, and in front of it there are two stone troughs for watering cattle. A second spring, which is likewise still below the ruins of the ancient town-wall, is exactly 725 mètres (793 yds.) distant from Hissarlik. It had a similar enclosure of large stones, 7 ft. high and 5 ft. broad, and has the same temperature. But it is out of repair: all the stones of the enclosure have been taken away by the villagers for building purposes, and the water no longer runs through the stone pipe, but along the ground before it reaches the pipe. After these two springs, exactly 945 mètres or 1033 yds. from Hissarlik, is a third spring. It is copious and runs out through two stone pipes placed side by side in an enclosure composed of large stones joined with earth, which rises to a height of 7 ft. and is 23 ft. broad. The temperature of the spring is from 14°·3 to 15° Celsius (57°·74 to 59° Fahr.). In front of the spring are six stone troughs, placed so that the superfluous water runs from the first through all the others. All these enclosures and troughs are of Turkish masonry and manufacture. These three springs were of course insufficient for the vast population of Novum Ilium; a large quantity of water was consequently brought also from the Upper Thymbrius by the great aqueduct already mentioned, which still spans the lower course of that river.

§ VI. Zoology of the Troad.

Barker Webb writes:[1] "The zone of forests with which the Gargarus is surrounded is probably in the same state of wild nature in which it was at the time of the Trojan war; even at a much more advanced stage of civilization it preserved the same aspect, for Libanius informs us that the mountains of Ida were inhabited by a peculiarly wild species of bear;[2] nay, Cresconius Corippus, at a later period, describes the same wild scene as existed at the time of Homer and as still exists to-day.[3] These forests are peopled by bears, wolves, and a race of animals, probably jackals, which, we hear, pursue their prey in bands. Mount Ida is still the μήτηρ θηρῶν (mother of wild beasts), and, if we believe the inhabitants of the country, even tigers are sometimes seen there."

I will here make some extracts from Tchihatcheff[4] on the Zoology of the Troad: "Jackal (Chacal) is a Persian word. The wolf, described by Aristotle and Pliny under the name of θώς, is identical with the jackal.

[11] Strabo, xiii. p. 593.
[1] Topographie de la Troade, p. 113.
[2] Libanius, Epist. 146.
[3] Flavii Crescon. Coripp. Johannidos.
[4] Asie Mineure: Descr. phys. p. 592 ff.

The lion, so well known to Homer, in the time of Herodotus[5] still inhabited the country between the rivers Nestus[6] and Achelous[7] (between the present Missolonghi and Salonica), so that he calls it infested by lions. Aristotle[8] reproduces the delimitation of the country inhabited by lions as drawn by Herodotus. Parthenius,[9] who lived about 50 B.C., says that the hunter Euanippus hunted lions and boars in Thessaly. Aelian,[10] who flourished in the beginning of the third century of our era, mentions lions and bears on Mount Pangaeus in Thrace. An Homeric hymn[11] mentions lions, panthers, bears, and wolves on Mount Ida. According to Aelian,[1] there were lions in Armenia. According to Constantine Porphyrogenitus,[2] lions existed in Cappadocia. The medals of Tarsus represent a lion devouring a bull. It appears that the lion had already in the time of Hadrian (117–138 A.D.) left the districts which it had inhabited in Europe. Lions were still seen in Asia Minor in the sixteenth century of our era; but they have now completely deserted the peninsula. We learn from the Bible,[3] that lions were very common in Palestine and Syria. That they were bold enough to attack, not only flocks guarded by shepherds, but wayfarers on the roads, is shown by the lions killed by Samson (Judg. xiv. 5, 6) and by David (1 Sam. xvii. 34), and by the lion that slew the disobedient prophet (1 Kings xiii. 24). The lion is a constant image of strength and courage, violence and oppression, in innumerable passages, especially of Job, the Psalms, the Proverbs, and the Prophets; and he is the symbol of the tribe of Judah, and of the Messiah himself (Gen. xlix. 9; Rev. v. 5). The retrograde movement of the lion seems at first sight the more difficult to explain, as the countries which it inhabited underwent an immense decrease of population. But the cause is to be found in this very decrease of population and domestic animals. Panthers are no longer found in the Troad, but they are still seen in the environs of Smyrna. Boars are very frequent in all the mountains of Phrygia and in those of the Troad, which appear to have been one of the most ancient residences of this pachyderm. But it must be distinctly understood that our domestic pig does not descend from the *Sus scropha*, or boar, but from the wild pig of India.

"Horses are very numerous in the Troad. We know from the testimony of Homer that Asia Minor and Thrace were celebrated for their horses. According to the Bible,[4] Solomon (1000 B.C.) had 12,000 horsemen; Isaiah (700 B.C.) speaks of the cavalry of the Israelites, and mentions the horse as serving for agricultural purposes. Asses, mules, oxen, goats, camels, and sheep, are equally plentiful. The wool of Phrygia and of Miletus was very celebrated in antiquity, for Aristophanes thrice[5] mentions that the Athenians imported their wool for the manufacture of cloth from Phrygia and Miletus. Herodotus[6] represents

---

[5] Herodotus, vii. 126.
[6] The present Karasu or Maïsto, to the east of Salonica.
[7] Probably the Aspropotamus, in Livadia.
[8] *Hist. Animal.* viii. 28.
[9] Ed. Passau; Leipzig, 1824.
[10] *Hist. Animal.* iii. 13.

[11] *Hymn. in Venerem*, vv. 69, 199.
[1] *Hist. Animal.* xvii. 31.
[2] *De Themat.*, i. *Th m. Armeniacum.*
[3] Jeremiah v. 6; xlix. 19; Solomon's Song, iv. 8.   [4] 2 Chronicles, i. 14.
[5] In *Av.*, verse 493; in *Lysist.*, verse 730; and in *Ran.*, verse 549.   [6] v. 49.

Phrygia as the richest country in the world for flocks. Appian informs us that on the shores of the Pontus the abundance of cattle was so great that, when Lucullus besieged Amisus (Samsoun), the price of an ox was 1 drachma (about 1 franc), and that of other animals in proportion.

"Of the eight different species of oxen only the ox (*Bos taurus*) and the buffalo (*Bos bubalus*) are found in Asia Minor. Independently of the little advanced state of industry and agriculture, the development of the bovine race finds in this country rather unfavourable conditions, owing to its mountainous formation and the nature of its pasture-grounds. These are generally composed of an herbage more or less short, which is excellent for sheep, goats, and even horses, but not good for oxen. Milk, cheese, and meat, being furnished here almost exclusively by sheep and goats, the use of the ox is limited to the needs of agriculture; and as this is here but very little developed, the number of oxen and buffaloes is naturally inconsiderable. Varro[7] mentions very wild bulls (*perferi boves*) in Dardania (the Troad), as well as in Thrace and Media; but these certainly do not remind us of the present bulls of Asia Minor, which are so quiet and inoffensive.

"Aelian[8] informs us that the laws of Phrygia condemned to death any one who killed an ox destined for the plough. This proves either the great scarcity of this animal, or the great development of agriculture. Varro,[9] Pliny,[10] Valerius Maximus,[1] and Columella,[2] also inform us that the ancients had such a respect for the ox, as indispensable for agriculture, that they decreed death to any one who killed one.

"The buffalo is very common, and frequently serves instead of oxen for the labours of agriculture. Of camels, the only species found here is the *Camelus Bactrianus*. That this species was known in Assyria, which has close relations with Asia Minor, is proved by the appearance of the two-humped camel among the tributes brought to king Shalmaneser III. (B.C. 840), on the famous black obelisk in the British Museum. This animal seems to have been unknown in Asia Minor and Greece in high antiquity, for Herodotus[3] attributes the victory of Cyrus over Croesus at Sardis to the presence of camels in the Persian army, which were unknown until then, and the sight of which frightened the Lydian cavalry.

"The stag (*Cervus elaphus*) is rare, whereas the deer (*Cervus dama*) and the roebuck (*Cervus capriolus*) are very abundant. Of *gazelles*, the *Antilope Dorcas* is the most frequent.

"The *ornithological Fauna* is very rich, but little known. Crows, ravens, partridges (both red and grey), quails, as well as storks, are very abundant. The part which the stork plays in the physiognomy of the landscape is particularly due to the respect shown to him: this respect is such that he is everywhere inviolable, and his presence is regarded as a good omen. According to Rosenmüller, the word *Chasidah*, by which the stork is named in the Bible, signifies 'pious.'"

---

[7] *De Re Rust.* ii. 11.   [8] *Hist. Animal.* xii. 54.   [9] *De Re Rust.* ii. 5.
[10] *H. N.* viii. 70. 4.   [1] viii. 8.   [2] *De Re Rust.* vi.   [3] i. 79, 80.

I must mention, however, that the storks build their nests only on the houses of Turks, or on walls and trees, never on the houses of the Christians; for while the former have a sort of veneration for the stork, the latter call it the sacred bird of the Turks, and do not suffer it to build nests on their houses. The Turks, on the contrary, can never have too many storks' nests on their houses. There are houses in Bounarbashi with four, six, eight, ten, and even twelve storks' nests on one and the same flat roof.

Cranes do not remain in the Troad during the summer, but migrate northward in immense swarms in March, and return in August to more congenial climes. As Homer never mentions storks, though they must have been at all times plentiful in the Troad, I am inclined to think that he includes under the word γέρανοι both storks and cranes. Nothing can be more beautiful than his description of the passage of these birds: "The Trojans went with clanging and noise like birds; as when the clanging of the cranes rises in the face of heaven, who, after having escaped the winter and the tremendous rain, fly with loud cries over the streams of Ocean, bearing murder and destruction to the Pygmaean race." [4]

There are various species of vultures in the Plain of Troy, but only one species of eagle. This has a very dark plumage, nearly black, in consequence of which M. Burnouf holds it to be identical with the Homeric περκνός, of which the poet says: "Zeus, the counsellor, heard him (Priam), and forthwith sent an eagle, the king of birds, a dark bird of chase, which men also call percnos." [5]

There is also a small bird in the plain with a beautiful plumage, which M. Burnouf holds to be identical with the Homeric Cymindis, called Chalcis by the gods. The reader will remember that Sleep, in the shape of this bird, sat hidden in the foliage among the boughs of a pine-tree.[6] Owls are here even still more plentiful than in Athens. Some species of them have a beautiful plumage; they used to make

---

[4] Il. iii. 2–6:

Τρῶες μὲν κλαγγῇ τ' ἐνοπῇ τ' ἴσαν, ὄρνιθες ὥς,
ἠΰτε περ κλαγγὴ γεράνων πέλει οὐρανόθι πρό,
αἵ τ' ἐπεὶ οὖν χειμῶνα φύγον καὶ ἀθέσφατον
    ὄμβρον,
κλαγγῇ ταί γε πέτονται ἐπ' Ὠκεανοῖο ῥοάων,
ἀνδράσι Πυγμαίοισι φόνον καὶ κῆρα φέρουσαι.

[5] Il. xxiv. 314–316:

ὣς ἔφατ' εὐχόμενος, τοῦ δ' ἔκλυε μητίετα Ζεύς.
αὐτίκα δ' αἰετὸν ἧκε, τελειότατον πετεηνῶν,
μόρφνον θηρητῆρ', ὃν καὶ περκνὸν καλέουσιν.

There can be no doubt that μορφνός means dark-coloured (μέλας); according to Hesychius, it is related to ὄρφνη, which appears to be confirmed by the word περκνός (also πέρκος in Aristotle), because the verb περκάζειν, which has the same root, is used for grapes which are beginning to turn black.

[6] Il. xiv. 289–291:

ἔνθ' ἧστ' ὄζοισιν πεπυκασμένος εἰλατίνοισιν,
ὄρνιθι λιγυρῇ ἐναλίγκιος, ἥν τ' ἐν ὄρεσσιν
χαλκίδα κικλήσκουσι θεοί, ἄνδρες δὲ κύμινδιν.

The Scholiast of Venice, interpreting the name Χαλκίς, says (ad Iliad. xiv. 291): "Some people say that Χαλκίς is the mother of the Corybantes" (οἱ δὲ τὴν μητέρα τῶν Κορυβάντων Χαλκίδα φασίν). He adds that, according to the traditions, this bird was nothing else but a metamorphosed heroine, and that its name was derived either from its copper-coloured plumage, or from the circumstance that, during her lifetime, the heroine dwelt at Chalcis in Euboea. As we shall see in the subsequent pages, the Corybantes were celebrated metallurgists in the service of Rhea and practised divination on the island of Samothrace. Professor Sayce observes to me, that, "if κύμινδις in the language of men—that is, in the language of the natives—had the same meaning as the Greek Χαλκίς or 'bronze-coloured,' we might compare it with σκάμανδρος, the Greek equivalent of which was ξανθός, and derive them both from a root or stem skamand, signifying 'yellow.'"

their nests in the holes of my trenches, and annoyed us a great deal, particularly at night, by their doleful and hideous cries.

Snakes are very frequent in the Troad ; in fact, so much so that, were it not for the storks which eat them, the Plain would abound with them. There are a great many different species of snakes, and among them many are very poisonous ; but, as before mentioned, the most poisonous of all is said to be a small adder, not larger than a worm, which is called ἀντήλιον by the present Trojans, probably because they fancy that a person bitten by it can only live till sunset. The pools of the Plain of Troy abound with water-snakes, some of which are said to be venomous. As tortoises are not eaten, both land and water tortoises are very abundant; in fact, it would not be difficult to catch some hundreds of them in a day.

All the water-pools in the Plain of Troy are also very rich in annelids of the sucker class, particularly in medicinal leeches and horse-leeches ; the former, indeed, are so plentiful that an oke = 2½ lbs. troy is sold for 10 francs = 8s. sterling, so that a pound of leeches would cost only 3s. 2d.

The devouring locusts (Grillus migratorius) are very common. They sometimes make their devastating visits for several years in succession. Very common also is the Kermes (Coccus ilicis), which inhabits the evergreen oak (Quercus ilex) and the Quercus coccifera.

I am indebted to Professor Virchow for the following report on the Conchylia which he has brought from the Troad. He collected them partly in his excursions in the Troad, partly in my excavations. The report was read on the 17th of June, 1879, by Herr von Martens, at the session of the Gesellschaft naturforschender Freunde at Berlin.

"1. LAND SNAILS.—Hyalina hydatina (Rossm.), found at Koum Kaleh, at the mouth of the Scamander. Helix vermiculata (Müll.). Helix Taurica (Kryncki ; radiosa, Ziegler ; Rossmässler, fig. 456), from the Ida mountains. Helix figulina (Parr). Helix variabilis (Drap). Another Helix of the group of the Xerophils. Helix Cantiana (Montague), near Koum Kaleh. Buliminus tuberculatus (Turton), also from Koum Kaleh. Buliminus Niso (Risso ; seductilis, Ziegler): this species was hitherto supposed not to be found in Asia Minor. Stenogyra decollata (L.).

"2. FRESHWATER CONCHYLIA.—Limnaea auricularia (L.), from the Scamander. Melanopsis praerosa (L.), var. Ferussaci (Roth.); numerous in the Bounarbashi Su. Melanopsis costata (Oliv.), found on the strand of the Hellespont near Rhoeteum. Neritina Syriaca, var. Trojana (Charpentier) ; found in the Bounarbashi Su, together with M. praerosa.

"3. MARINE CONCHYLIA. (H., on the shore of the Hellespont near Rhoeteum. A., collected alive in the Gulf of Adramyttium, at Assos.)—H. Conus Mediterraneus (Hwass). H. Columbella rustica (L.). H. A. Nassa neritea (L.). H. Cerithium vulgatum, var. pulchellum (Phil.). H. Cerithium Mediterraneum (Desh.). H. Cerithium scabrum (Olivi). H. A. Trochus articulatus (Lamarck as Monodonta) A. Trochus divaricatus (L.). H. Trochus albidus (Gmelin ; Biasolettii, Phil.). H. Trochus Adriaticus (Phil.). H. Patella Tarentina (Salis ; Lam.). H. Dentalium Tarentinum (Lam.). H. Anomia cepa (L.). Pecten glaber (L., from the Dardanelles).

H. A. *Mytilus edulis* (L.). H. *Mytilus minimus* (Poli). A. *Cardita sulcata* (Brug.). H. *Cardium edule* (L.), var. *rusticum* (Lam.). H. *Lucina leucoma* (Turt.; *lactea*, auct.). H. *Cytherea Chione* (L.). H. *Venus verrucosa* (L.). *Venus gallina* (L.), in the sand of the serail at Constantinople. H. *Tapes decussatus* (L.). *Tapes aureus* (Maton). H. *Mactra stultorum* (L.). H. *Donax trunculus* (L.). H. *Tellina tenuis* Dacosta, mouth of the Scamander. H. *Tellina fragilis* (L.).

"In the excavations at Troy were found:—

"*Murex trunculus* (L.). *Purpura haemastoma* (L.). *Columbella rustica*. *Cerithium vulgatum*, var. *spinosum* (Philippi). *Cypraea lurida* (L.). *Trochus articulatus* (Lam.). *Patella caerulea* (L.). *Ostrea lamellosa* (Brocchi). *Spondylus gaederopus* (L.). *Pecten glaber* (L.). *Pecten glaber*, var. *sulcatus* (Born). *Pectunculus pilosus* (L.). *Pectunculus violascens* (Lam.). *Mytilus edulis* (L.), var. *Galloprovincialis* (Lam.); very numerous. *Cardium edule* (L.), var. *rusticum* (Lam.); very numerous. *Venus verrucosa* (L.). *Tapes decussatus* (L.). *Solen marginatus* (Pulteney; *vagina*, auct.).

"*Murex trunculus* and *Purpura haemastoma* have probably served for the manufacture of purple. This is the more likely, as precisely these two occur in peculiarly sharp angular fragments, such as are not found at present either on the seashore or in kitchen-middens. But, as Aristotle and Pliny expressly state, the purple-fish were violently broken for the manufacture of purple. *Murex trunculus* is the very kind which was already found in 1811 by Lord Valentia, and later by Dr. Wilde (1839–1840), in the ruins of Tyre, and was recognized as the purple-fish; it was found also in the Morea by Bory St. Vincent. *Purpura haemastoma* serves the fishermen of Minorca at the present day for marking their shirts. It was used by Lacaze-Duthiers for his well-known researches on purple; but as far as we know, no specimen of it, preserved from antiquity, had hitherto been known. This Trojan specimen is therefore of capital interest. We may conclude from the statement of Aristotle [7] that the industry of purple-dyeing flourished on the coast of the Troad, as well as that a large species of purple-fish was found near Sigeum. The knowledge of purple among the Greeks goes back to a very remote period, as is proved by numerous passages in the Homeric poems, which mention purple, sometimes in its proper sense for dyeing garments, sometimes in certain well-known passages, as the colour of very heterogeneous objects.

"Most of the other cochleae and conchylia found in the excavations have doubtless served the Trojans or Ilians as food. Cerithium, Trochus, Patella, Ostrea, Spondylus, Pecten, Cardium, Venus, Tapes, and Solen, are precisely the kinds which the inhabitants of the Mediterranean coasts are still fond of using for food; as well as the inhabitants of the islands in the Aegean Sea, [8] of Dalmatia, of the eastern coast of Italy, and of Southern France. In some parts of the Upper Adriatic, even the ancient Greek names of these cochleae and conchylia are preserved.

---

[7] *Hist. Animal.* v. 15.   [8] See Tournefort's *Travels into the Levant*, Lond. 1718.

Thus *Cerithium vulgatum* is called *strombolo* in the fish-market of Spalatro. By the *strombos* of the ancient Greeks we are to understand this peculiar species, and not the general conception of a cochlea with spiral convolutions.   It is therefore of interest to find the *Cerithium* among the antiquities of Troy.   The ancient authors took their statements on sea-animals essentially from the mouths of fishermen and lovers of delicacies ; but such only know and name what is of practical interest to them. How important the cochleae and conchylia were as food to the ancient Greeks we see from the comedies, as well as from the *Deipnosophistae* of Athenaeus.   On the other hand, it appears strange that we find no mention made of them in the *Iliad* and *Odyssey.*   A passage in the *Iliad*,[9] which compares the mortally-wounded Hebriones, precipitated from his chariot, to a diver who searches for τήθεα, has indeed been referred to oysters; but as this word does not occur again in Homer, whereas the very similar τήθυον means in Aristotle and others merely ascidia (ἀσκίδια, acephalous molluscs), which still serve on the Mediterranean coast as food for men, that interpretation is at least doubtful. The Homeric poems describe chiefly the royal festive meals of sacrificial meats, not the daily food of the common people.   We hesitate to regard as remains of food only the *Columbella*, on account of its smallness ; the *Trochus articulatus*, on account of its good preservation ; and the *Pectunculus*, on account of its perforation, which may perhaps be artificial. These species may have been used as ornaments or toys."

§ VII.   The Flora of the Troad.[10]

" Most of the plains and hills of the Troad abound with trees, particularly with that kind of oak which yields the valonea (from βάλανος, ' acorn '), called *Quercus aegilops*.   The road from Bounarbashi to Alexandria-Troas leads through an almost uninterrupted forest of these oaks, mixed here and there with some nettle-trees (*Celtis Tournefortii*).   If left to its natural development, this oak grows majestically ; but as the oaks are annually beaten with poles in order to knock off the acorns, they are often much deformed.   The acorns are gathered a little before maturity ; they are thrown into heaps, and after a slight fermentation the acorn detaches itself from the cup.   Only this latter is used.   It is exposed to the air, and as soon as it is completely dry it can be used for tanning.   This is the most important produce of the Troad, and is largely exported to England.   There is another variety of oak, the leaves of which have both surfaces of an identical green colour, and scarcely at all villous (*Quercus trojana*, Nob.).   On all the low and barren hills flourish two other kinds of oak, the *infectoria* and the *coccifera*, or rather *Quercus pseudo-coccifera*, which rarely exceed the size of a shrub.   The former of these shrubs produces the gall-nut or oak-apple of commerce,

---

[9] xvi. 746, 747 :
εἰ δή που καὶ πόντῳ ἐν ἰχθυόεντι γένοιτο,
πολλοὺς ἂν κορέσειεν ἀνὴρ ὅδε τήθεα διφῶν.
[10] Not being a botanist myself, I think I cannot do better than quote here a translation of the

learned dissertation which the accomplished botanist P. Barker Webb gives on the flora of the Troad : *Topographie de la Troade ancienne et moderne*, pp. 115–123.

which is nothing else than an excrescence in the form of a walnut, produced by the sting of an insect; the latter yields the small red grains of the dyers, produced by a similar cause: but in the Troad none of these objects are used, or even gathered.

" Homer is an admirable painter of the beauties of physical nature. One of his characteristic qualities is to sketch by a few masterly strokes the most simple objects and the distinct qualities of each object. He describes to us the Plain of the Scamander, where the Greek army was drawn up in battle array—'they stood on Scamander's flowery meadow.' [1] He tells us that it was covered with flowers, just as we see it now. When the soldiers return to their tents, they give their horses the *Lotus* and *Apium*, with which the swamps are covered.[2] When Hephaestus, yielding to the prayers of Heré, kindles a great fire on the banks of the Scamander, 'the elms, the willows, and the tamarisk-shrubs burned; and the lotus burned too, and the reeds, and the gallingale, which grew abundantly about the fair streams of the river.' [3] In another passage [4] we find also mentioned the μυρίκαι and the δόνακες (*Tamarix Gallica* and *Arundo donax*), which grew near the river. See besides in the *Iliad* (vi. 39; [5] xxi. 18,[5] 242 [6]); *Odyssey* (xiv. 474 [7]), and the description of the nuptials of Zeus and Heré in the *Iliad*.[8] All the plants named there by the poet still exist.

" The ἐρώδιαι of Homer are now called ῥοδοδάφνη, but more frequently πικροδάφνη in modern Greek (*Nerium Oleander*, Lin.). They are found everywhere on the banks of rivers or in dry river-beds, side by side with the *Platanus orientalis*, the *Vitex Agnus-castus*, and the aforesaid *Tamarix Gallica*, called μυρίκη by the poet."

Webb says: " Though the year was on its decline, we still saw in flower, on the top of Gargarus, a dianthus, sp. n., and a centaurea with yellow flowers. These two plants flourished on the top of Gargarus, where the long duration of the snow stops even the vegetation of the pines. Near them was an exceedingly beautiful purple-coloured garlic, and several other interesting vegetables, which were no longer in flower. A little farther down we found the ground covered with the autumn crocus, *Colchicum autumnale et variegatum*, and *Ophrys spiralis*, but less abundantly.

" In some places the ground was entirely covered with these plants, and presented to our eyes the flowery couch on which the nuptials of

---

[1] *Il.* ii. 467 :
ἔσταν δ' ἐν λειμῶνι Σκαμανδρίῳ ἀνθεμόεντι . . .

[2] *Il.* ii. 775–777 :
ἵπποι δὲ παρ' ἅρμασιν οἷσιν ἕκαστος,
λωτὸν ἐρεπτόμενοι ἐλεόθρεπτόν τε σέλινον
ἕστασαν.

[3] *Il.* xxi. 350–352 :
καίοντο πτελέαι τε καὶ ἰτέαι ἠδὲ μυρῖκαι,
καίετο δὲ λωτός τε ἰδὲ θρύον ἠδὲ κύπειρον,
τὰ περὶ καλὰ ῥέεθρα ἅλις ποταμοῖο πεφύκειν.

[4] *Il.* x. 466, 467 :
θῆκεν ἀνὰ μυρίκην· δέελον δ' ἐπὶ σῆμά τ' ἔθηκεν,
συμμάρψας δόνακας μυρίκης τ' ἐριθηλέας ὄζους, . . .

[5] μυρίκη, tamarisk.

[6] πτελέη, elm.   [7] δόναξ, reed.

[8] *Il.* xiv. 346–351 :
Ἦ ῥα, καὶ ἀγκὰς ἔμαρπτε Κρόνου παῖς ἣν παράκοιτιν.
τοῖσι δ' ὑπὸ χθὼν δῖα φύεν νεοθηλέα ποίην,
λωτόν θ' ἑρσήεντα ἰδὲ κρόκον ἠδ' ὑάκινθον
πυκνὸν καὶ μαλακόν, ὃς ἀπὸ χθονὸς ὑψόσ' ἔεργεν.
τῷ ἔνι λεξάσθην, ἐπὶ δὲ νεφέλην ἕσσαντο
καλὴν χρυσείην· στιλπναὶ δ' ἀπέπιπτον ἔερσαι.

"The son of Cronus clasped his consort in his arms; and under them divine earth put forth the new-blown grass, and dewy lotus, and crocus and hyacinth thick-spread and soft, which shut them off aloft from the ground. Thereon they lay veiled in a beautiful golden cloud, and glistering dewdrops fell from it."

Jove were accomplished.[9] The Homeric descriptions are always founded on reality, and show that Homer was a most accurate observer as well as an inimitable poet. His verses describe admirably the cloud of dew which enveloped the mountain; they are likewise the result of observation and truth.[10] We are indeed at a loss which to admire most, the beauty of the allegory or the fidelity of the description.

"In the second zone of forests, the only plant which we saw in flower as far as Evjilar, in the shade of the pine-trees, was the *Adenocarpus divaricatus*, which is not found at a lesser elevation. We found there the *Quercus crinita*, which did not reappear after Kuchunlu Tepeh, and around the Bali Dagh an almond-tree, which Jaubert and Spach have called *Amygdalus Webbii*.

"We have already mentioned one of the most important productions of the rural economy in this plain; that is to say, the valonea, or fruit of the *Quercus aegilops*. In the fields we see the women working the soil with their families, and at every step on the roads we encounter their little carts, which have the shape of the ancient chariots, and quietly return laden with the produce of the soil. Around the Greek villages is gathered a certain quantity of excellent wine, and especially at Giaur Kioi and Yeni Kioi. If the red wine of Tenedos were carefully made, it would not be inferior to that grown in France. It must also be said that they have not in this country the bad habit, which prevails nearly everywhere in the Morea, of mixing rosin or pitch with the wine to preserve it. From these ingredients the wine gets a taste which is highly disagreeable to any one not accustomed to it. Nevertheless this habit must date from a very remote antiquity, for we know from the most ancient monuments that the fruit of the pine has at all times been sacred to Dionysus.

"On the banks of the Simois, and particularly in the village of Doumbrek, the Turks themselves cultivate the vine; they make of the grapes either a sort of syrup, called *petmez*, or a kind of preserve. They also dry the grapes in the sun, and thus preserve them as provision for the winter. Grapes, water-melons, and several other fruits, form a large part of their food in summer. They cultivate the *Solanum Melongena* and the *Sesamum orientale*, from which they know how to prepare an excellent oil. They spread on their bread the grains of this plant, mixed with those of the *Nigella damascena*. Homer mentions this habit in the *Batrachomyomachia*. They also cultivate the *Hibiscus esculentus*, which they vulgarly call Bamiá, as well as chick-pease, kidney-beans, lentils, and various other leguminous plants. The cultivation of cotton, wheat, and Indian corn is the most profitable. According to Sibthorpe, the yellow variety of Indian corn is the commonest. They also gather here cocoons of silk, which they work rudely enough. We observed that, as regards the cultivation of the fig-tree, they always employ the ancient method of caprification. The pomegranate attains a great development, and almost all trees appear to thrive in this climate."

I may here add that Homer mentions a field of wheat under the very walls of Troy.[1]

---

[9] See the preceding note [8].   [10] *Il.* xiv. 347–351.   [1] *Il.* xxi. 602: πεδίον πυροφόρον.

CHAPTER II.

ETHNOGRAPHY OF THE TROJANS: THEIR SEVERAL DOMINIONS
IN THE TROAD: TOPOGRAPHY OF TROY.

§ I. ETHNOGRAPHY OF THE TROJANS.

WE have the testimony of Herodotus [1] that the Trojans were Teucrians. This is confirmed by the tradition preserved by Apollodorus, that from Electra, the daughter of Atlas, were born by Zeus Iasion and Dardanus. Now Iasion, having fallen in love with Demeter and intending to violate the goddess, was killed by a thunderbolt. Dardanus, grieving for his brother's death, left the island of Samothrace, and crossed to the opposite continent. Here reigned Teucer (Τεῦκρος), son of the river Scamander and a Nymph of Ida, from whom the inhabitants of the country were called Teucrians. Having been adopted by the king, he married his daughter Bateia, received part of the land, built the city of Dardanus, and, after Teucer's death, named the whole country Dardania.[2]

In the time of Herodotus, the inhabitants of the city of Gergis [3] were still considered a remnant of the ancient Teucrians,[4] who, in company with the Mysians, had crossed the Bosphorus into Europe before the time of the Trojan war, and, after conquering all Thrace, had pressed forward till they came to the Ionian Sea (the modern Adriatic), while southward they reached as far as the river Peneus.[5] According to some writers, these Mysians appear to have been Thracians, who had come into Asia from Europe.[6] Others, and among them Herodotus,[7] seem to have looked upon the Mysians as a genuine Asiatic race, closely akin to the Lydians, whose language the Mysian tongue greatly resembled. According to Xanthus,[8] the Mysian dialect was akin both to the Lydian and the Phrygian (μιξολύδιος καὶ μιξοφρύγιος).[9] By the Roman poets the names Teucrians and Trojans are employed as

---

[1] ii. 118; v. 13.
[2] Apoll. iii. 12, § 1: Ἠλέκτρας δὲ τῆς Ἄτλαντος καὶ Διὸς Ἰασίων καὶ Δάρδανος ἐγένοντο. Ἰασίων μὲν οὖν, ἐρασθεὶς Δήμητρος καὶ θέλων καταισχῦναι τὴν θεόν, κεραυνοῦται, Δάρδανος δὲ ἐπὶ τῷ θανάτῳ τοῦ ἀδελφοῦ λυπούμενος, Σαμοθρᾴκην ἀπολιπὼν εἰς τὴν ἀντίπερα ἤπειρον ἦλθε. Ταύτης δὲ ἐβασίλευε Τεῦκρος ποταμοῦ Σκαμάνδρου καὶ νύμφης Ἰδαίας · ἀφ' οὗ καὶ οἱ τὴν χώραν νεμόμενοι Τεῦκροι προσηγορεύοντο. Ὑποδεχθεὶς δὲ ὑπὸ τοῦ βασιλέως καὶ λαβὼν μέρος τῆς γῆς καὶ τὴν ἐκείνου θυγατέρα Βάτειαν, Δάρδανον ἔκτισε πόλιν, τελευτήσαντος δὲ Τεύκρου τὴν χώραν ἅπασαν Δαρδανίαν ἐκάλεσε.

[3] In all probability the small city on the Bali Dagh behind Bounarbashi.
[4] Herod. v. 122 and vii. 43.
[5] Herod. vii. 20: μήτε τὸν Μυσῶν τε καὶ Τευκρῶν, τὸν πρὸ τῶν Τρωϊκῶν γενόμενον, οἳ διαβάντες ἐς τὴν Εὐρώπην κατὰ Βόσπορον, τούς τε Θρήϊκας κατεστρέψαντο πάντας καὶ ἐπὶ τὸν Ἰόνιον πόντον κατέβησαν μέχρι τε Πηνειοῦ ποταμοῦ τὸ πρὸς μεσαμβρίης ἤλασαν.
[6] Strabo, iii. pp. 295, 303; viii. p. 572: cf. Xanth. Lyd. Frag. 8.
[7] Herod. i. 171.   [8] Frag. 8.
[9] Rawlinson's History of Herodotus, iv. p. 23, note 5.

equivalents:[10] on the other hand, the Roman prose-writers generally use the word *Trojani*.[1]

It is curious that, whilst Herodotus always calls the old Trojans of epic poetry Teucrians, the Attic tragedians and the Roman poets call them Phrygians, although the Trojans and Phrygians are represented as completely distinct in the Homeric *Hymn to Aphrodité*, where this goddess says to Anchises: "Otreus is my sire, famous of name, if anywhere thou hearest it, who reigns over all well-fortified Phrygia; and both your language and mine I know well, for a Trojan nurse nourished me in the palace; she nurtured me, taking me as a little baby from my mother: thus I know indeed your language well." [2] The name Hector is Phrygian;[3] so also are Paris and Scamandrius, for the Greek Alexandros and Astyanax seem to be Phrygian appellations.[4] Moreover, the Phrygians are merely mentioned in the *Iliad* as allies of the Trojans from distant Ascania,[5] and there is little indication of any more intimate relationship. Hecuba, however, was a Phrygian princess,[6] and her brother lived in Phrygia on the banks of the Sangarius.[7] According to Strabo[8] and Stephanus Byzantinus, the Phrygians were Thracians. Herodotus reports that the Macedonians preserved a tradition, according to which the Phrygians had once been their neighbours, but that they had afterwards emigrated to Asia Minor.[9] The Lydian Xanthus[10] asserts that this emigration did not occur till after the Trojan war; but Conon[1] makes it take place as early as ninety years before this war, under King Midas. On the other hand, several testimonies have been preserved to us as to the affinity existing between the Phrygians and the Armenians. In the expedition of Xerxes, both these nations appear under one commander-in-chief and with the same armament; nay, Herodotus[2] adds that the Armenians were descendants of the Phrygians. Eudoxus[3] confirms this, and mentions, in addition, the similarity of the two languages. So too we find subterranean dwellings in use among both the Phrygians and the Armenians.[4] Finally, both nations were actually considered as identical,[5] the Armenians being said to have come from Western Phrygia.

But the Assyrian inscriptions make it clear that no Aryans were settled eastward of the Halys before the eighth century B.C. Armenia was inhabited by a non-Aryan race, which has left behind it many still undeciphered inscriptions at Van and its neighbourhood, until the close of the Assyrian monarchy, and there are no traces of Aryan inha-

---

[10] Virgil, *Aen.* i. 172; v. 265; xii. 137. Horace, *Od.* iv. 6, 15. Ovid. *Met.* xii. 66.

[1] Cic. *Div.* ii. 39; Livy, i. 1.

[2] Ὕμνος εἰς Ἀφροδίτην, 111–116:

Ὀτρεὺς δ' ἐστὶ πατὴρ ὄνομα κλυτός, εἴπου ἀκούεις,
ὃς πάσης Φρυγίης εὐτειχήτοιο ἀνάσσει.
γλῶσσαν δ' ὑμετέρην καὶ ἡμετέρην σάφα οἶδα,
Τρωὰς γὰρ μεγάρῳ με τροφὸς τρέφεν · ἡ δὲ διαπρὸ
σμικρὴν παῖδ' ἀτίταλλε, φίλης παρὰ μητρὸς ἑλοῦσα.
ὡς δ' ἤτοι γλῶσσάν γε καὶ ὑμετέρην εὖ οἶδα.

[3] Hesychius, s. v. Δαρεῖος.

[4] *Il.* vi. 402; Strabo, xiv. pp. 680, 681
[5] *Il.* ii. 863.   [6] *Il.* xvi. 718, 719.
[7] *Il.* xvi. 717.
[8] Strabo, vii. p. 295, and x. p. 471.
[9] Herodotus, vii. 73.
[10] Strabo, xiv. p. 680.
[1] *Ap.* Photium, p. 130, Bekk.
[2] Herod. vii. 73.
[3] *Ap.* Steph. Byz. s. v. Ἀρμενία; and Eustath. ad Dion. *Per.* 694.
[4] Vitruv. ii. 1, 5; Xenoph. *Anab.* iv. 5, 25; Diod. xiv. 28.
[5] Cramer, *Anecd. Graec.*; Oxon. iv. p. 257.

bitants in Armenia until a much later period. Even the Aryan Medes did not occupy the country to the south of the Caspian until the eighth century B.C. The Assyrians first became acquainted with them in the reign of Shalmaneser III. (B.C. 840), when they lived far to the east, the non-Aryan Parsuas or Parthians intervening between them and Assyria. It is not till the age of Rimmon-nirari, about 790 B.C., that they had advanced into the country known to the classical geographers as Media Rhagiana. All the proper names mentioned on the Assyrian monuments as belonging to the natives of the districts east of the Halys continue to be non-Aryan up to the last, and the language of the modern Iron or Ossetes in the Caucasus is, like the Kurdish, a member of the Iranic or Persian stock.[6] An examination of the Phrygian words preserved in classical writers and inscriptions, which has been made by Fick,[7] has shown that, while the language was related to Thracian and Lydian, it was so closely allied to Greek as to be fitly termed its sister, both Greek and Phrygian presupposing a common parent-language. Professor E. Curtius in his *History of Greece* had already pointed out a close connection between the Greeks and the Phrygians upon other grounds, while Plato[8] long ago recognized the affinity between the languages of the two nations. The Phrygian legends of Midas and Gordius formed part of Greek mythology, and the royal house of the Pelopids was made to come with all its wealth from the golden sands of the Pactolus.[9] The Armenian language, on the other hand, stands apart by itself, and belongs rather to the Asiatic branch of the Aryan family of speech than to the European.

It deserves particular attention that the Teucrian name is nowhere connected in Homer with Troy or its people. But as they had a city Gergis, Gergithus, or Gergetha, in the Troad, we may perhaps connect the name with that of the Homeric Gargarus[10] as well as with Gorgythion, who, with Cebriones, is mentioned by Homer as a natural son of Priam.[1] The poet thus gives, as Grote[2] remarks, a sort of epical recognition to both Gergis and Cebren. It must, however, be remarked that *Teucer* (*Teucros*), the celebrated archer, was according to legend the son of the Trojan princess Hesioné, whom she bore to Telamon.[3]

According to a tradition which we find in Strabo, the Teucrians immigrated from Crete into the Troa settle down in the place where they born. This is said to have happened ne host of field-mice came forth from the leather of their arms and utensils. Th themselves, and called the range of Ida in Crete. Strabo adds that this tradit

---

[6] Sayce, *Principles of Comparative Philology,* 2nd edit. p. 391.

[7] *Die ehemalige Spracheinheit Europa's*, 1873.

[8] *Cratylus*, 410 A.

[9] A. H. Sayce, *Contemporary Review*, December 1878.

[10] *Il.* viii. 48; xiv. 292, 352; xv. 152.

elegiac poet Callinus (about 660 B.C.), and after him by many others.[4] So,
e g., by Ovid.[5]

It appears from this legend that the Teucrians were credited with
having introduced into the Troad the worship of the Sminthian Apollo,
who had a celebrated temple at Chrysa near Hamaxitus. Strabo distinctly
says that Chrysa was said to be the spot where the newly-arrived Teu-
crians were attacked by the field-mice. ($\Sigma\mu\iota\nu\theta\sigma\varsigma$, it may be added, is said
by the Venetian Scholiast on the *Iliad* to have meant a field-mouse, both
in the Cretan and in the Aeolian dialects.[6]) Others, however, denied the
legend, maintaining that Teucer, the primitive ancestor of the Teucrians,
had immigrated from Attica.[7]

I may mention here that the name of the Tekkri, believed to be
identical with that of the Teucrians, figures in the mural paintings of
Medinet-Abou among the confederate nations, which in the thirteenth
century B.C. invaded Egypt during the reign of Ramses III.[8]

The connection of the Teucrians with Crete seems to be confirmed by
the similarity of certain geographical names, such as those of Mount Ida
and the city named Pergamus.[9]

Grote says: " From the Teucrian region of Gergis and from the
Gergithes near Kyme sprang the original Sibylline prophecies, and the
legendary Sibyl, who plays so important a part in the tale of Aeneas.
The myth of the Sibyl, whose prophecies are supposed to be heard in
the hollow blast bursting from obscure caverns and apertures in the
rocks,[10] was indigenous among the Gergithian Teucrians, and passed from
the Kymaeans in Aeolis, along with the other circumstances of the tale
of Aeneas, to their brethren the inhabitants of Kumae in Italy. The date
of the Gergithian Sibyl, or rather the circulation of her supposed prophecies, is placed under the reign of Croesus, a period when Gergis was
thoroughly Teucrian. Her prophecies, though embodied in Greek verses,
had their root in a Teucrian soil and feelings; and the promises of future
empire, which they so liberally make to the fugitive hero escaping from
the flames of Troy into Italy, become interesting from the remarkable way in which they were realized by Rome. The date of this Gergithian Sibyl, or of the prophecies passing under her name, is stated
by Heracleides of Pontus, and there seems no reason for calling it
in question." [11]

According to Herodotus, the Paeonians prided themselves upon being
Teucrian colonists from Troy.[1] The descent of the Paeonians from the
Teucrians is confirmed by Strabo,[2] whilst others held them to have been
descended from the Phrygians.[3] It is important to notice that in Homer
we find Paeonians from the Axius fighting on the same side as their

[4] Strabo, xiii. p. 604.
[5] *Metamorph.* xiii. 705.
[6] Grohmann, *Apollo Smintheus und die Bedeu-
der Mäuse in der Mythologie;* Prag. 1862.
abo, xiii. p. 604.
ois Lenormant, *Les Antiquités de la
is,* 1876, p. 75.
iv. 12, 20.

[10] Virgil, *Æneid.* vi. 43–45:
" Excisum Euboicae latus ingens rupis in antrum,
Quo lati ducunt aditus centum, ostia centum :
Unde ruunt totidem voces, responsa Sibyllae."
[11] Grote's *History of Greece,* i. 310, 311.
[1] Herodot. v. 13.
[2] Fragm. Palat. Vatic. 37, ed. Tafel.
[3] Eustath. *ad Hom. Il.* ii. 848.

Trojan kinsmen.[4]   Their expedition to Perinthus on the Propontis, according to the statement of Herodotus, must have taken place at a very early epoch.[5]   To the east of the Axius, Crestonia and Bisaltia were once Paeonian possessions;[6] to the west Emathia was formerly called Paeonia;[7] while Pieria and Pelagonia had originally a Paeonian population.[8]   In Pieria was a city named Pergamus.[9]   Pliny[10] calls the Eordians a Paeonian nation; and it is evident from Lycophron[1] that they were of Phrygian race.   They are doubtless the Mysians, whom Hellanicus[2] calls neighbours of the Macedonians.   To these Eordians the name of the river Eordaïcus,[3] the present Deval or Devol, doubtless belongs; it is near the lake of Lychnidus, where we also find traces of the Phrygians.[4]

Homer has no knowledge of Dardanus having immigrated from Samothrace, Arcadia, or Italy; he only knows him as a son of Zeus, and as having his origin in Dardania.   He conceived the Troad to be inhabited by a non-Hellenic population,—Trojans, Dardanians, Cilicians, Lelegians, and Pelasgians.   Of these, the Dardani or Dandani (Dardanians) of Iluna (Ilion) are mentioned, together with the Leka (possibly the Lycians) and the peoples of Pedasa (Pedasus), the Masu (Mysians), and the Akerit (perhaps the Carians), in the poem of Pentaur in the "Sallier" hieratic papyrus, preserved in the British Museum, among the confederates who came to the help of the Hittites (or Khita) under the walls of Kadesh, on the Orontes, in the fifth year of Ramses II. (cir. 1333-1300 B.C.).   There was therefore at that period a kingdom of the Dardanians, one of whose principal towns was Ilion, a kingdom which ranked among the most powerful of Asia Minor, and sent its warriors into Syria to do battle with the Egyptian troops for the defence of Asia.   This agrees admirably with what Greek tradition says of the power of Troy.   This poem of Pentaur is also to be seen engraved on the walls of the temples of Luxor and Karnak at Thebes.   It deserves particular attention that in the mural paintings and inscriptions in the temple of Medinet-Abou at Thebes, among the confederates against Ramses III., about 1200 B.C., instead of the Dardanians, who do not appear at all, only the Teucrians (Tekkri) are mentioned.[5]

According to Forbiger, the Trojans were a Thracian race, who had immigrated at a remote period into the Troad and had there intermarried with the Phrygians, who until then inhabited the region.[6]   This appears to be confirmed by Strabo, who mentions at a distance of only 40 stadia from Lampsacus a temple of great sanctity dedicated to the Mother of

---

[4] *Il.* ii. 848–850; xvi. 287–291; xvii. 348–353; xxi. 139.

[5] Herodot. v. 1, 2.

[6] Strabo, *Fragm.* 40.

[7] Polyb. xxiv. 8; Liv. xl. 3; Justin. vii. 1.

[8] Strabo, *Fragm.* 37; Eustath. *ad Il.* i. 1.

[9] Herodot. vii. 112.

[10] *H. N.* iv. 17.   [1] Alexandra.

[2] *Ap.* Constant. Porphyrogen. *de Them.* ii. 2, p. 48; Schol. *ad Hom. Il.* xiii. 3.

[3] Arrian. *Alexand. Anabas.* i. 5, 9.

[4] Pauly's *Real-Encyclopädie*, s. v. "Phryges."

[5] François Lenormant, in the *Academy* of 21st and 28th March, 1874.   Professor Sayce writes to me: "Brugsch-Bey, however, has proposed different identifications for these names. He makes the Tekkri the Zygritae of the Caucasus, the Leka the Ligyes, the Dardani the Dardanians of Kurdistan (Herodot. i. 189), the Masu the inhabitants of Mount Masius, and Pedasa the town of Pidasis, while he reads ' Iluna' as Maluna.—*Egypt under the Pharaohs* (Eng. transl., vol. ii. p. 129, 2nd ed.)"

[6] Pauly's *Real-Encyclopädie*, s. v. "Troas."

the Gods, surnamed the sanctuary of Rhea.[7] In another passage he says: "The Berecynthians, a Phrygian race, and the Phrygians generally, as well as those of the Trojans who live in the district of Ida, worship Rhea, and celebrate orgies in her honour, calling her the Mother of the Gods, and Agdistis, and the great Phrygian goddess, adding, according to the localities, the epithets Idaean, Dindymene, Sipylene, Pessinuntis, and Cybele (Cybebe)."[8] He further states that the country near the junction of the Hellespont and the Propontis was originally inhabited by the Bebrycians,[9] who had immigrated from Thrace;[1] also that a great many Thracian names existed in the Troad. "On Lesbos (he says) was a city Arisba, whose lands are now possessed by the Methymnaeans, and there is in Thrace a river Arisbus, on which live the Thracian Cebrenians.[2] There are indeed many similar names common to the Thracians and the Trojans: for instance, the Scaeans, a certain Thracian race, the river Scaeus, the Scaean wall, and the Scaean gate; the Xanthians in Thrace, and the river Xanthus at Troy; Rhesus, a river at Troy, and Rhesus, king of the Thracians. The poet also mentions another person of identical name with the Asius,[3] who was an uncle of Hector the tamer of horses, Hecuba's full brother, and son of Dymas, who resided in Phrygia on the river Sangarius."[4]

I may here add that, according to Stephanus Byzantinus,[5] there was a city Ilium in Thrace; further, that Strymo was the daughter of the river Scamander, wife of Laomedon and mother of Priam,[6] whilst Strymon was a great river in Thrace;[7] further, that the name of the powerful Trojan province Dardania also existed in Thrace, the island of Samothrace having originally borne this name.[8]

In the *Iliad* the Thracians are allies of the Trojans.[9] According to Dionysius of Halicarnassus,[10] the Trojans were Greeks. The Dardanians play an important part in the *Iliad;* to the descendants of their prince

---

[7] xiii. p. 589: οἱ δ' ἀπὸ τετταράκοντα τῆς Λαμψάκου σταδίων δεικνύουσι λόφον, ἐφ' ᾧ μητρὸς θεῶν ἱερόν ἐστιν, ἅγιον τῆς Ῥέης ἐπικαλούμενον.

[8] x. p. 469: οἱ δὲ Βερέκυντες Φρυγῶν τι φῦλον καὶ ἁπλῶς οἱ Φρύγες καὶ τῶν Τρώων οἱ περὶ τὴν Ἴδην κατοικοῦντες Ῥέαν μὲν καὶ αὐτοὶ τιμῶσι καὶ ὀργιάζουσι ταύτῃ, μητέρα καλοῦντες θεῶν καὶ Ἄγδιστιν καὶ Φρυγίαν θεὸν μεγάλην, ἀπὸ δὲ τῶν τόπων Ἰδαίαν καὶ Δινδυμήνην καὶ Σιπυλήνην καὶ Πεσσινουντίδα καὶ Κυβέλην [Κυβήβην].   [9] Strabo, xiii. p. 586.

[1] Strabo, vii. p. 295 ; xii. p. 542.

[2] I here call attention to the name of the ancient city of Cebrene in the Troad.

[3] Here Strabo evidently means by the former Asius the son of Hyrtacus, the leader of the troops from Abydos, of whom he speaks at p. 585, whilst at p. 586 he tells us that the district of Abydus was held by the Bebrycians, a Thracian race (pp. 295, 542), and was subsequently occupied by Thracians, who had probably newly immigrated. All, therefore, that he shows us by the name Asius is, that it existed in Thrace and in Phrygia.

[4] Strabo, xiii. p. 590: ἦν δὲ καὶ ἐν Λέσβῳ πόλις Ἀρίσβα, ἧς τὴν χώραν ἔχουσι Μηθυμναῖοι· ἔστι δὲ καὶ ποταμὸς Ἄρισβος ἐν Θρᾴκῃ, ὥσπερ εἴρηται, καὶ τούτου πλησίον οἱ Κεβρήνιοι Θρᾷκες. πολλαὶ δ' ὁμωνυμίαι Θρᾳξὶ καὶ Τρωσίν, οἷον Σκαιοὶ Θρᾷκές τινες καὶ Σκαιὸς ποταμὸς καὶ Σκαιὸν τεῖχος καὶ ἐν Τροίᾳ Σκαιαὶ πύλαι· Ξάνθιοι Θρᾷκες, Ξάνθος ποταμὸς ἐν Τροίᾳ· Ἄρισβος ὁ ἐμβάλλων εἰς τὸν Ἕβρον, Ἀρίσβη ἐν Τροίᾳ· Ῥῆσος ποταμὸς ἐν Τροίᾳ, Ῥῆσος δὲ καὶ ὁ βασιλεὺς τῶν Θρᾳκῶν. ἔστι δὲ καὶ τῷ Ἀσίῳ ὁμώνυμος ἕτερος παρὰ τῷ ποιητῇ Ἄσιος "ὃς μήτρως ἦν Ἕκτορος ἱπποδάμοιο, αὐτοκασίγνητος Ἑκάβης, υἱὸς δὲ Δύμαντος, ὃς Φρυγίην ναίεσκε ῥοῆς ἐπὶ Σαγγαρίοιο."

[5] S. v. Ἴλιον.

[6] Apollodor. iii. 2, 3.

[7] Stat. *Theb.* v. 188 ; Steph. Byz. s. v. Μίεζα.

[8] Pausanias, vii. 4; Steph. Byzant. s. v. Δαρδανία.

[9] *Il.* x. 434, 435 ; xx. 484, 485.

[10] *Antiq. Rom.* i. 62: ὡς μὲν δὴ καὶ τὸ Τρωϊκὸν γένος Ἑλληνικὸν ἀρχῆθεν ἦν, δεδήλωταί μοι.

Aeneas is predicted the future dominion over Troy: "But now the mighty Aeneas shall reign over the Trojans, and his sons' sons, who shall be born hereafter."[1] The genealogy of the royal house of Dardania presents, as Aldenhoven[2] observes, some strange names, which make him think that they are of Phrygian origin.

I think it not out of place to cite here the following words of Grote:[3] "According to the Trojan legend, it was under proud Laomedon, son of Ilus, that Poseidon and Apollo underwent, by command of Zeus, a temporary servitude; the former building the walls of the town, the latter tending the flocks and herds. When their task was completed, they claimed the stipulated reward; but Laomedon angrily repudiated their demand, and even threatened to cut off their ears, to tie them hand and foot, and to sell them in some distant island as slaves.[4] He was punished for this treachery by a sea-monster, whom Poseidon sent to ravage his fields and to destroy his subjects. Laomedon publicly offered the immortal horses given by Zeus to his father Tros, as a reward to any one who would destroy the monster. But an oracle declared that a virgin of noble blood must be surrendered to the monster, and the lot fell upon Hesioné, daughter of Laomedon himself. Herakles, arriving at this critical moment, killed the monster by the aid of a fort built for him by Athené and the Trojans,[5] so as to rescue both the exposed maiden and the people; but Laomedon, by a second act of perfidy, gave him mortal horses in place of the matchless animals which had been promised. Thus defrauded of his due, Herakles equipped six ships, attacked and captured Troy, and killed Laomedon,[6] giving Hesioné to his friend and auxiliary Telamon, to whom she bore the celebrated archer Teucros.[7] A painful sense of this expedition was preserved among the inhabitants of the historical town of Ilium, who offered no worship to Herakles."[8]

I have cited all this in order to show that a link of connection seems to have existed between Troy and Phoenicia, for, as Mr. Gladstone has ingeniously endeavoured to show,[9] a connection with Poseidon frequently denotes Phoenician associations; and further, as Müllenhof has proved, in his *Deutsche Alterthumskunde*,[10] Herakles is the representative of the Phoenicians. This has also been pointed out by Professor Sayce, who says: "The whole cycle of myths grouped about the name of Herakles points as clearly to a Semitic source as does the myth of Aphrodité and Adonis."[1]

The Homeric Cilicians (Κίλικες) of the Troad inhabited the plain of the Hypoplakian Thebes, and appear, according to Strabo,[2] to have been of the same race as the inhabitants of the later Cilicia.

---

[1] *Il.* xx. 307, 308:
νῦν δὲ δὴ Αἰνείαο βίη Τρώεσσιν ἀνάξει
καὶ παίδων παῖδες, τοί κεν μετόπισθε γένωνται.
[2] *Ueber das neuentdeckte Troia.*
[3] *History of Greece,* i. p. 264.
[4] *Il.* vii. 452, 453; xxi. 451–456; Hesiod. *ap.* Schol. Lycophr. 393.
[5] *Il.* xx. 145; Dionys. i. 52.
[6] *Il.* v. 640–642.

[7] Diodorus, iv. 32–49.   Compare Schol. Venet. *ad Iliad.* viii. 284.
[8] Strabo, xiii. p. 596.
[9] See his Preface to my *Mycenae,* pp. viii. and xxiv.
[10] W. Christ, *Die Topographie der Troian. Ebene,* p. 225.
[1] *Contemporary Review,* December 1878.
[2] Strabo, viii. p. 376; xiv. p. 676.

The Leleges (Λέλεγες) are often brought into connection with the
Carians. In fact, according to Herodotus,[3] the former was merely the
ancient name of the latter; Homer, however, mentions the Leleges and
Carians as two distinct peoples. But we also find the Leleges in Greece,
as a very ancient and wide-spread race, dating from a pre-Hellenic time.
They are mentioned by Homer side by side with the Pelasgians.[4] The
little troop of Leleges, of whom the *Iliad* speaks, occupied the district
to the east of Cape Lectum.[5]

Regarding the Pelasgians, I think I cannot do better than give
here an extract from a letter of Professor Sayce published in the
Academy of the 25th of January, 1879: "I do not intend to dispute
the existence of tribes called by the Greeks Pelasgians. But to turn
these into a particular race or people is quite a different matter. It is
true that Greek writers, from Homer and Hesiod downward, mention
Pelasgians, but if we examine their statements we find that the term is
used in two (or perhaps three) senses: firstly, as denoting a certain Greek
tribe which inhabited Thessaly during the heroic age; and secondly, as
equivalent to our own term 'pre-historic.' In the first sense it is used
twice in the *Iliad* (ii. 681 and xvi. 233). In two other Homeric
passages of later date (*Il.* x. 429; *Od.* xix. 177), the name has passed
into the region of mythology, and a way has accordingly been prepared
for the use of it by later writers to denote those populations of Greece
and its neighbourhood which we should now call pre-historic, or whose
origin and relationship were unknown. (For this employment of the
word, see Herodotus, i. 146; i. 56; ii. 56; viii. 44; vii. 94; ii. 51; v. 26;
vi. 138.) The name is more especially applied to the natives of Thrace,
who seem to have belonged to the Illyrian stock (see Herodotus, i. 56;
Thucydides, iv. 109). It is probable, therefore, that there were tribes on
the coastland of Thrace who were known as Pelasgians; and, since the
same name is also found in Mysia (*Il.* ii. 840-3), it is probable that it was
a word of general meaning, like so many of the names of early Greek
ethnology, and accordingly applied to tribes of different origin and race.
Hence Pischel's etymology, which makes Πελασγός a compound of the
roots we have in πέραν and εἶμι (*ya*), and so meaning 'the further-
goers' or 'emigrants,' becomes very probable.

"We now know enough of the languages of Italy, Greece, Albania,
and Asia Minor, to be able to lay down that, although all probably
belonging to the Indo-European stock, they are as distinct from one
another as Latin and Greek. Indeed, it is still doubted by some philologists whether Albanian should be classed as an Aryan language at all.
However this may be, I am quite willing to allow that it is very probably
a descendant of the ancient Illyrian or Thracian, and I will not quarrel
with any one who wishes to call the latter Pelasgian. But it must be
remembered that we know nothing about the Pelasgian language or

---

[3] Herodot. i. p. 171.

[4] *Il.* x. 429; Hecat. *ap.* Strab. vii. p. 321,
xii. p. 572.

[5] Strabo, xiii. p. 605: ἡ γὰρ ἀπὸ τοῦ Λεκτοῦ

ῥάχις, ἀνατείνουσα πρὸς τὴν Ἴδην, ὑπέρκειται
τῶν πρώτων τοῦ κόλπου μερῶν· ἐν οἷς πρῶτον
τοὺς Λέλεγας ἱδρυμένους ὁ ποιητὴς πεποίηκεν.

languages; and that, if the ancient Thraco-Illyrian is to be called Pelasgian, the latter term must be closely defined. In the oldest passages of Homer where it occurs, it is applied to Achaean Greeks, not to barbarous Thracians; in later Greek literature, it is merely synonymous with 'pre-historic;' while in modern times it has served as the watch-word of all kinds of obsolete theories and pre-scientific fancies."

Strabo informs us that after the Trojan war the whole Troad, from Cyzicus to the Caïcus, was Aeolized; that is to say, it was occupied by colonies formed by Peloponnesian Achaeans and Aeolian Boeotians, who had been driven from their homes by the Dorian invasion. As Mr. Gladstone judiciously observes, Homer was not aware of the existence of Aeolians, only of Aeolids. But in the later Greek tradition we have numerous notices of Aeolians as settled in various parts of Greece. In Homer a variety of persons and families, holding the highest stations and playing important parts in the early history, are descended from or connected with Aeolus, a mythical eponymist, but of an Aeolian tribe he is ignorant.[6]

According to Thucydides,[7] the Dorian invasion of the Peloponnesus took place 80 years, according to Strabo[8] 60 years—that is, two generations—after the Trojan war; according to Pausanias,[9] in the time of Orestes. Pausanias seems probably to be in the right, for the dynasty of the Pelopids appears to have ceased at Mycenae with the death of Aegisthus, which occurred in the eighth year after the murder of Agamemnon,[10] and thus about eight years after the Trojan war; in fact, tradition says that Agamemnon's son Orestes reigned in Arcadia and Sparta, but not that he succeeded his father. Only a fearful political revolution and catastrophe, such as the Dorian Invasion, could have prevented Orestes from becoming king in Mycenae, which was the richest and most powerful State of Greece, and belonged to him as the only son of the glorious and universally lamented Agamemnon. Strabo[11] says that Orestes began the emigration, that he died in Arcadia, and that his son Penthilus came as far as Thrace; whilst his other son, Archelaus, brought the Aeolian colony into the district of Cyzicus, in the neighbourhood of Dascylium. But Gras, the youngest son of Archelaus, penetrated as far as the river

---

[6] *Homeric Synchronism*, p. 74.

[7] i. 12.   [8] xiii. p. 582.

[9] viii. 5, § 1.

[10] *Od.* iii. 305–307:

ἑπτάετες δ᾽ ἤνασσε (Αἴγισθος) πολυχρύσοιο
    Μυκήνης·
τῷ δὲ οἱ ὀγδοάτῳ κακὸν ἤλυθε δῖος Ὀρέστης
ἄψ ἀπ᾽ Ἀθηνάων, κατὰ δ᾽ ἔκτανε πατροφονῆα.

[11] xiii. p. 582: Ὀρέστην μὲν γὰρ ἄρξαι τοῦ στόλου, τούτου δ᾽ ἐν Ἀρκαδίᾳ τελευτήσαντος τὸν βίον διαδέξασθαι τὸν υἱὸν αὐτοῦ Πενθίλον, καὶ προελθεῖν μέχρι Θρᾴκης ἑξήκοντα ἔτεσι τῶν Τρωικῶν ὕστερον, ὑπ᾽ αὐτὴν τὴν τῶν Ἡρακλειδῶν εἰς Πελοπόννησον κάθοδον· εἶτ᾽ Ἀρχέλαον υἱὸν ἐκείνου περαιῶσαι τὸν Αἰολικὸν στόλον εἰς τὴν νῦν Κυζικηνὴν τὴν περὶ τὸ Δασκύλιον· Γρᾶν δὲ τὸν υἱὸν τούτου τὸν νεώτατον προελθόντα μέχρι

τοῦ Γρανίκου ποταμοῦ καὶ παρεσκευασμένον ἄμεινον περαιῶσαι τὸ πλέον τῆς στρατιᾶς εἰς Λέσβον καὶ κατασχεῖν αὐτήν· Κλεύην δὲ τὸν Δώρου καὶ Μαλαόν, καὶ αὐτοὺς ἀπογόνους ὄντας Ἀγαμέμνονος, συναγαγεῖν μὲν τὴν στρατιὰν κατὰ τὸν αὐτὸν χρόνον καθ᾽ ὃν καὶ Πενθίλος, ἀλλὰ τὸν μὲν τοῦ Πενθίλου στόλον φθῆναι περαιωθέντα ἐκ τῆς Θρᾴκης εἰς τὴν Ἀσίαν, τούτους δὲ περὶ τὴν Λοκρίδα καὶ τὸ Φρίκιον ὄρος διατρίψαι πολὺν χρόνον, ὕστερον δὲ διαβάντας κτίσαι τὴν Κύμην τὴν Φρικωνίδα κληθεῖσαν ἀπὸ τοῦ Λοκρικοῦ ὄρους. Τῶν Αἰολέων τοίνυν καθ᾽ ὅλην σκεδασθέντων τὴν χώραν, ἣν ἔφαμεν ὑπὸ τοῦ ποιητοῦ λέγεσθαι Τρωικήν, οἱ ὕστερον οἱ μὲν πᾶσαν Αἰολίδα προσαγορεύουσιν οἱ δὲ μέρος, καὶ Τροίαν οἱ μὲν ὅλην οἱ δὲ μέρος αὐτῆς, οὐδὲν ὅλως ἀλλήλοις ὁμολογοῦντες.

Granicus, led the larger part of his troops over to Lesbos, and occupied this island. Penthilus then brought his expedition over from Thrace to the Troad, and was followed by other descendants of Agamemnon. The Roman geographer further says that, the Aeolians having spread over the whole country called Trojan by the poet, the whole was by some later writers called Aeolis, whilst others call only part of it by this name.

Strabo informs us that Abydos was first occupied by Milesian colonists in the reign and by the permission of the Lydian king Gyges (cir. 698-660 B.C.), to whom the whole Troad and the neighbouring territory belonged. A promontory near Dardanus was called after him, Gygas.[1] Neither Strabo nor any other classical author tells us when this Lydian dominion in the Troad commenced. But, as I shall describe at length in the subsequent pages, I found in my excavations at Hissarlik, at an average depth of from 6 to 7 ft. below the surface of the ground, and just between the ruins of Novum Ilium and the *débris* of the latest pre-historic city, a mass of pottery which, both in shape and fabric, has the very greatest resemblance to the most ancient Etruscan pottery, whilst it has no similarity whatever either to any of the pre-historic pottery or to that of Novum Ilium. Professor Sayce calls my attention to the fact, that two terra-cotta cones, inscribed with the Cypriote character *mo* and found at a depth of 3 mètres, exactly correspond in size, shape, and material with a cone found by the late Mr. George Smith under the floor of Assur-bani-pal's palace at Kouyunjik. This cone must have been brought by an embassy sent to Nineveh by Gyges about B.C. 665, when, according to the inscriptions, the Assyrians heard the name of Lydia for the first time, and became acquainted with the districts westward of the Halys.

Now we read in Herodotus:[2] "In the reign of Atys, son of Manes, there was a great famine throughout all Lydia. The Lydians bore the calamity patiently for some time, but, seeing that it did not stop, they set to work to devise remedies for the evil. Various expedients were discovered by various persons; dice and huckle-bones and ball, and all such games, were invented, with the exception of tables, the invention of which

---

[1] xiii. p. 590: Ἄβυδος δὲ Μιλησίων ἐστὶ κτίσμα ἐπιτρέψαντος Γύγου τοῦ Λυδῶν βασιλέως· ἦν γὰρ ἐπ' ἐκείνῳ τὰ χωρία καὶ ἡ Τρῳὰς ἅπασα, ὀνομάζεται δὲ καὶ ἀκρωτήριόν τι πρὸς Δαρδάνῳ Γύγας.

[2] Herodot. i. 94, ed. George Rawlinson: ἐπὶ Ἄτυος τοῦ Μάνεω βασιλέος σιτοδηίην ἰσχυρὴν ἀνὰ τὴν Λυδίην πᾶσαν γενέσθαι· καὶ τοὺς Λυδοὺς τέως μὲν διάγειν λιπαρέοντας, μετὰ δέ, ὡς οὐ παύεσθαι, ἄκεα δίζησθαι, ἄλλον δὲ ἄλλο ἐπιμηχανᾶσθαι αὐτῶν. ἐξευρεθῆναι δὴ ὧν τότε καὶ τῶν κύβων καὶ τῶν ἀστραγάλων καὶ τῆς σφαίρης καὶ τῶν ἀλλέων πασέων παιγνιέων τὰ εἴδεα πλὴν πεσσῶν· τούτων γὰρ ὧν τὴν ἐξεύρεσιν οὐκ οἰκηιοῦνται Λυδοί. ποιέειν δὲ ὧδε πρὸς τὸν λιμὸν ἐξευρόντας, τὴν μὲν ἑτέρην τῶν ἡμερέων παίζειν πᾶσαν, ἵνα δὴ μὴ ζητέοιεν σιτία, τὴν δὲ ἑτέρην σιτέεσθαι παυομένους τῶν παιγνιέων. τοιούτῳ τρόπῳ διάγειν ἐπ' ἔτεα δυῶν δέοντα εἴκοσι. ἐπεὶ

τε δὲ οὐκ ἀνιέναι τὸ κακόν, ἀλλ' ἐπὶ μᾶλλον ἔτι βιάζεσθαι, οὕτω δὴ τὸν βασιλέα αὐτῶν δύο μοίρας διελόντα Λυδῶν πάντων κληρῶσαι, τὴν μὲν ἐπὶ μονῇ, τὴν δὲ ἐπὶ ἐξόδῳ ἐκ τῆς χώρης, καὶ ἐπὶ μὲν τῇ μένειν αὐτοῦ λαγχανούσῃ τῶν μοιρέων ἑωυτὸν τὸν βασιλέα προστάσσειν, ἐπὶ δὲ τῇ ἀπαλλασσομένῃ τὸν ἑωυτοῦ παῖδα, τῷ οὔνομα εἶναι Τυρσηνόν. λαχόντας δὲ αὐτῶν τοὺς ἑτέρους ἐξιέναι ἐκ τῆς χώρης, καταβῆναι ἐς Σμύρνην καὶ μηχανήσασθαι πλοῖα, ἐς τὰ ἐσθεμένους τὰ πάντα, ὅσα σφι ἦν χρηστὰ ἐπίπλοα, ἀποπλέειν κατὰ βίου τε καὶ γῆς ζήτησιν, ἐς ὃ ἔθνεα πολλὰ παραμειψαμένους ἀπικέσθαι ἐς Ὀμβρικούς, ἔνθα σφέας ἐνιδρύσασθαι πόλιας καὶ οἰκέειν τὸ μέχρι τοῦδε. ἀντὶ δὲ Λυδῶν μετονομασθῆναι αὐτοὺς ἐπὶ τοῦ βασιλέος τοῦ παιδός, ὅς σφεας ἀνήγαγε· ἐπὶ τούτου τὴν ἐπωνυμίην ποιευμένους ὀνομασθῆναι Τυρσηνούς.

they do not claim as theirs. The device adopted against the famine was to give up one day so entirely to playing as not to feel any want of food, and the next day to eat and to stop the games. In this manner they continued for eighteen years. As the affliction lasted and even became more grievous, the king divided the nation in half, and made the two portions draw lots, the one to stay, the other to emigrate from the country; he would remain king of those whose lot it should be to remain behind, whilst his son Tyrsenus should be the leader of the emigrants. When they had drawn lots, those who had to emigrate went down to Smyrna and built themselves vessels, in which they put all needful stores; after that they sailed away in search of land and sustenance. After having sailed past many countries, they reached Umbria, where they built cities for themselves and fixed their residence. Instead of Lydians they called themselves after the name of the king's son, who led the colony, Tyrsenians."

In these Tyrsenians the general voice of antiquity saw the Etruscans, though Dionysius of Halicarnassus, the contemporary of Strabo, maintained that neither in language, religion, laws, nor customs was there any similarity between the Lydians and Etruscans. But so firmly convinced of the relationship were most of the ancients that, according to Tacitus,[3] in the time of Tiberius deputies from Sardis recited before the Roman Senate a decree of the Etruscans, declaring their consanguinity, on the ground of the early colonization of Etruria by the Lydians. Mommsen,[4] Corssen, and other authorities, however, now agree with Dionysius. The fact that the great cities of Etruria were inland and not maritime shows that they could not have been founded by a people who came by sea; and the native name of the Etruscans, the Rasena, is evidently identical with the Rhaeti of the Rhaetian Alps, whose language, according to Livy (v. 33), was similar to that of the Etruscans. Now, Etruscan inscriptions have been found as far north as Botzen, the phonology of which belongs to an earlier period in the history of the Etruscan language than the phonology of the inscriptions found in Etruria proper. Moreover, no relationship can be discovered between the Etruscan language, which is agglutinative, and the remains of the Lydian language, which are Aryan. If, nevertheless, the connection between Etruria and Lydia is still maintained,[5] considering the striking resemblance of the curious pottery found at Hissarlik immediately below the ruins of Novum Ilium, with the most ancient pottery found in the cemeteries of Felsina,[6] Villanova,[7] and Volterra,[8] I think it possible that there may have been a Lydian settle-

---

[3] *Annal.* iv. 55.

[4] *Römische Geschichte*, i. 9. Mommsen suggests that the notion of a connection between Etruria and Lydia arose out of a confusion between the Tursenni (more properly Rasena), corrupted by Greek pronunciation into Tyrrheni, and the Lydian Tyrrheni, whose name, according to Xanthus, was really Torrhebi.

[5] See George Dennis, *Cities and Cemeteries of Etruria*, i. pp. xxxv. *sq.*

[6] Giovanni Gozzadini, *di alcuni Sepolcri della Necropole Felsinea*, p. 6.

[7] Giovanni Gozzadini, *la Necropole di Villanova* (1870), p. 33.

[8] L. Pigorini, *Bullettino di Paletnologia*, anno i. Nos. 4 and 5, April and May 1875. Plate iii. Nos. 3 *a* and 3 *b*.

ment on Mount Hissarlik contemporary with the colonization of Etruria by the Lydians (1044 B.C.), and that the Lydian dominion may have been established over the whole Troad at the same epoch.

Of other nations which may have sojourned for a short time in the Troad, I may name the Trerians, whom Strabo mentions once as neighbours of the Thracians.[9] They invaded the north coast of Asia Minor in the seventh century B.C. in company with the Cimmerians,[10] and even took Sardis, which had been already taken by the Cimmerians.[1] But in another passage Strabo states that the Trerians were a Cimmerian people;[2] and again in another he says that the Trerians were also called Cimmerians, or a tribe of them.[3] According to Aristotle, the Cimmerians settled in Antandros on the Gulf of Adramyttium, at the foot of Ida, and remained there a hundred years. This appears to be confirmed by Pliny[4] and Stephanus Byzantinus,[5] according to whom the town was formerly called Cimmeris and Edonis. Alcaeus[6] calls it a city of the Leleges; Herodotus[7] and Conon[8] call it a Pelasgian city.

How fearfully the Troad must have been devastated by these invasions, we may conclude from the statement of a Greek historian, that the district of Lampsacus had formerly been called Bebrycia, but that the Bebrycians had disappeared through the frequent wars.[9]

I have further to mention the Gauls or Galatians, who, in 279 B.C., passed over into Asia Minor, partly by the Hellespont, partly by the Thracian Bosporus,[10] and spread such terror by their devastations that, according to Livy,[1] "the coast of the Hellespont was given up to the Trocmi, the Tolistoboji obtained Aeolis and Ionia, the Tectosagi the inland parts of Asia, and they exacted tribute from all Asia within Taurus, while they chose their own abode about the river Halys,—so that at last even the kings of Syria did not refuse to give them tribute." But these Galatians seem not to have stopped for any length of time in the Troad, for otherwise Strabo would have known the fact through Demetrius of Scepsis, who flourished but a hundred years after the invasion of the Gauls. But as Strabo is silent on the subject, and only mentions the Gauls as living quietly in the country on the Halys, south of Paphlagonia, we may consider it as certain that they did not stay in the Troad.

---

[9] i. p. 59; but it must be distinctly understood that Strabo nowhere mentions that the Trerians settled for any length of time in the Troad; he only speaks of their constant invasions.   [10] xii. p. 573.

[1] xiii. p. 627. Professor Sayce calls my attention to the fact that, "according to the Assyrian inscriptions, the Gimirrai or Cimmerians invaded Lydia in the time of Gyges, who sent two of their chiefs in chains to Assurbani-pal, the Sardanapalus of the Greeks (about B.C. 665). Subsequently Gyges assisted Psammetichus of Egypt in shaking off the Assyrian yoke, in consequence of which, says Assur-banipal, the gods punished him by causing him to be defeated and beheaded in battle by the Cimmerians. His son and successor, Ardys, again

sent tribute to Nineveh. See also *Od.* xi. 14–19."   [2] xiv. p. 647.
[3] i. p. 61.   [4] *H. N.* v. 32.
[5] S. v. Κίμμερος.   [6] *Ap.* Strabo, xiii. p. 606.
[7] vii. 42.   [8] *Narr.* 41.
[9] Charon *in* Schol. *ap. Rhod.* 2, 2.
[10] Memnon Heracl. *ap.* Phot. i. 1.
[1] See Wernsdorf, *de Republ. Galatt.* i. p. 15. Liv. xxxviii. 16: "Trocmis Hellesponti ora data, Tolistoboji Aeolida atque Ioniam, Tectosagi mediterranea Asiae sortiti sunt, et stipendium tota cis Taurum Asia exigebant, sedem autem ipsi sibi circa Halyn flumen ceperunt,—ut Syriae quoque ad postremum reges stipendium dare non abnuerent." The Trocmi, Tolistoboji, and Tectosages were the three races or clans of the Gauls.

I shall not speak in this place of the passage of the Persians, Macedonians, Romans, &c., through the Troad; I have enumerated only those nations of whose sojourn or devastation in this country tradition or history has preserved some record. It will be seen in the following pages that the ruins at Hissarlik bear testimony to the settlements of at least five different nations, which have succeeded each other on the site in remote pre-historic ages. In fact the passage of nations to and fro on this spot could not have been better described than by Mr. Gladstone:[2]—
"It appears as if the Hellespont and the immediate neighbourhood of the Bosphorus had formed a sort of hinge, upon which turned the fortunes and movements of mankind from a very remote period. Consequently I am not surprised when I see how some powerful cause has determined the course of events actually exhibited in historical times. I am not at all surprised to find at Hissarlik the marks of an extraordinary interest attaching to that neighbourhood, and of a great number of successive races, beginning with the earliest recorded periods of civilized settlement, endeavouring to lodge themselves upon this particular spot. To me it involves no paradox, because I think it greatly supported and confirmed by what we have seen since in respect to the desirableness of that spot, and its importance in connection with the movements of races. The very circumstances of climate and soil may, I apprehend, be considered as rendering it a very eligible site, and therefore there is nothing strange to me in finding that a number of different peoples should have planted themselves upon the hill of Hissarlik within the course of a certain number of centuries."

I also cite here what Mr. Philip Smith[3] has written on the subject:

"Apart even from its traditional claim to be the Ilium of Homer, Hissarlik lay in the track of the primitive migrations of the Indo-European race from their cradle in the East to their settlement in the West; and not of one migration only, but of their passage to and fro between the shores of Asia and of Europe; as well as upon the path of their commerce and military expeditions, after they were settled in their homes. For, lest we be misled by the arbitrary distinction between the continents, which is stereotyped in the names of Asia and Europe —that is, East and West—it must be borne in mind that the Hellespont and Bosporus (as the latter name expresses) were *ferries* rather than sundering seas, and the islands of the Aegean were stepping-stones. The close affinities of the early settlers on both shores had long since been proved; and, in particular, the presence of the great Pelasgo-Hellenic or Graeco-Italic family had been traced on both. The very ancient habitation of the north-western parts of Asia Minor by the Ionians—the Oriental name of the whole Hellenic race—long before their traditional colonization from the peninsula of Hellas—had been maintained by Ernst Curtius twenty years ago,[4] and more fully esta-

---

[2] At the Royal Institute of British Architects, 30th April, 1877; see Sessional Papers, 1876–1877, No. 12.

[3] See my *Troy and its Remains*, p. 364.
[4] Curtius, *Die Ionier vor der Wanderung*; Berlin, 1855.

blished by recent Egyptologers [5]—thus confirming the most ancient ethnic record, that the *Isles of the Gentiles* were divided among the families of the *Sons of Javan*." [6]

§ II. The several Dominions of the Troad. [7]

1. *The Dominion of Pandarus.*—This possession of the Lycians extended along the Aesepus to Zeleia; its inhabitants are called wealthy (ἀφνειοί). Their leader is Pandarus, son of Lycaon, the excellent archer. [8]

Cities.—The only city mentioned by the poet is Zeleia, situated on the Aesepus at the last spur of Ida. According to Strabo, [9] it was at a distance of 80 stadia from the nearest sea (the Propontis) into which the Aesepus falls, and 190 stadia from (the post-Homeric) Cyzicus.

2. *The Dominion of Adrestus and Amphius, sons of Merops.*—This dominion bordered on the preceding, as is shown by Homer, [10] as well as by Strabo: "Below Zeleia, on the sea, on this side of the Aesepus, was situated the plain of Adresteia." [1] The leaders of the Adresteans are Adrestus and Amphius, sons of Merops, though elsewhere Amphius is called the son of Selagus.

Cities.—Three are mentioned by the poet :—

a. *Adresteia* (ἡ ᾿Αδρήστεια) was situated between Priapus and Parium. [2]

b. *Apaesus* (ἡ ᾿Απαισός), [3] also called Paesos (ἡ Παισός), [4] was situated between Lampsacus and Parium on the river Paesus. Strabo says that the city was destroyed and that its inhabitants had settled in Lampsacus, [5] because they were Milesians, like the Lampsacenes, which is confirmed by Anaximenes. [6]

c. *Pityeia* (ἡ Πιτύεια) [7] was situated in Pityûs, a district of the territory of Parium, at the foot of a mountain overgrown with pines, between Priapus and Parium, close to the town of Linum on the sea,

---

[5] Chabas, *Études sur l'Antiquité historique;* Paris, 1872, p. 190.

[6] "Genesis x. 4, 5. The essential letters of the Hebrew name יון are identical with the Greek ΙΩΝ (Ion), and both are equivalent to the *Yavanas*, the 'younger race' of the old Aryan traditions, who migrated to the West, while the elder branch remained in the East. See the *Student's Ancient History of the East*, Chapter xx., on the Nations of Asia Minor, which contains a discussion of the Hellenic affinities of the Phrygians and Trojans in particular."

[7] In the geography of the several dominions of the Troad I have adopted the order followed by E. Buchholz in his excellent work, *Homerische Kosmographie und Geographie*, and I have to a large extent profited by his details ; but as regards Ilium, I have not used his work at all.

[8] *Il.* ii. 824–827:

οἳ δὲ Ζέλειαν ἔναιον ὑπαὶ πόδα νείατον ᾿Ίδης,
ἀφνειοί, πίνοντες ὕδωρ μέλαν Αἰσήποιο,
Τρῶες· τῶν αὖτ᾿ ἦρχε Λυκάονος ἀγλαὸς υἱός,
Πάνδαρος, ᾧ καὶ τόξον ᾿Απόλλων αὐτὸς ἔδωκεν.

[9] Strabo, xiii. p. 587: ᾿Η μὲν δὴ Ζέλεια ἐν τῇ παρωρείᾳ τῇ ὑστάτῃ τῆς ᾿Ίδης ἐστίν, ἀπέ-

χουσα Κυζίκου μὲν σταδίους ἐνενήκοντα καὶ ἑκατόν, τῆς δ᾿ ἐγγυτάτω θαλάττης καθ᾿ ἣν ἐκδίδωσιν Αἴσηπος ὅσον ὀγδοήκοντα.

[10] *Il.* ii. 828–830:

οἳ δ᾿ ᾿Αδρήστειάν τ᾿ εἶχον καὶ δῆμον ᾿Απαισοῦ,
καὶ Πιτύειαν ἔχον καὶ Τηρείης ὄρος αἰπύ·
τῶν ἦρχ᾿ ᾿Αδρηστός τε καὶ ῎Αμφιος λινοθώρηξ.

[1] xii. p. 565: τῇ δὲ Ζελείᾳ ὑποπέπτωκε πρὸς θαλάττῃ ἐπίταδε τοῦ Αἰσήπου τὸ τῆς ᾿Αδρηστείας πεδίον.

[2] Strabo, xiii. p. 588: ἡ μὲν οὖν πόλις (ἡ ᾿Αδρήστεια) μεταξὺ Πριάπου καὶ Παρίου.

[3] *Il.* ii. 828.

[4] *Il.* v. 612:

καὶ βάλεν ῎Αμφιον, Σελάγου υἱόν, ὅς ῥ᾿ ἐνὶ Παισῷ ναῖε.

[5] Strabo, xiii. p. 589: ἐν δὲ τῷ μεταξὺ Λαμψάκου καὶ Παρίου Παισὸς ἦν πόλις καὶ ποταμός· κατέσπασται δ᾿ ἡ πόλις, οἱ δὲ Παισηνοὶ μετῴκησαν εἰς Λάμψακον, Μιλησίων ὄντες ἄποικοι καὶ αὐτοὶ καθάπερ καὶ οἱ Λαμψακηνοί.

[6] Strabo, xiv. p. 635: ᾿Αναξιμένης γοῦν ὁ Λαμψακηνὸς οὕτω φησίν, ὅτι—Μιλήσιοι συνῴκησαν—῎Αβυδον, ῎Αρισβαν, Παισόν.

[7] *Il.* ii. 829.

where the Linusian cochleae were fished up, which were considered the best of all sorts of cochleae.[8] But others maintained that Pityeia was only the ancient name of Lampsacus.[9]

3. *The Dominion of Asius.*—This dominion extended along the coast of the Troad, from Percoté to Abydos. Asius, son of Hyrtacus,[10] was the ruler of this district; under his command was the contingent of the Thracian city of Sestos on the Hellespont.[1]

Of *Cities* Homer mentions three in this dominion:—

a. Percoté (ἡ Περκώτη),[2] of which its present name, Borgas or Bergas, may be a corruption. Its ancient name was also Percopé.[3]

b. Abydos (ἡ Ἄβυδος),[4] at the narrowest part of the Hellespont, which, according to Herodotus,[5] was there only 7 stadia broad; but in reality the breadth of the strait is here 10 stadia. Abydos was situated opposite to Sestos, though slightly to the south-east. A little to the north of the city Xerxes passed the Hellespont on a bridge of boats, in 480 B.C. Of Abydos no ruins are extant; only fragments of pottery or marble mark its site. It is at a distance of 3 miles from the present town of Dardanelles. On the site of Abydos are two nearly conical natural hills, both of which may have once been fortified, but the opinion of some travellers,[6] that they are composed of *débris*, is altogether erroneous; they consist of purely natural soil.

c. Arisbé (ἡ Ἀρίσβη), not far from the Selleïs,[7] was the residence of Asius, and has in the poems the epithets "divine" (δῖα)[8] and "well-built" (ἐϋκτιμένη).[9]

4. *The Dominion of Aeneas (Dardania).*—Strabo defines Dardania as follows:—"On the further side of Abydos come the districts around Ilium, the sea-shore as far as Lectum, the land of the Trojan Plain, and the district at the side of Mount Ida subject to Aeneas."[10] Again: "The mountain-border (of the Trojan Plain) is narrow; on one side it extends in a southerly direction to the district around Scepsis, on the other side to the north as far as the Lycians of the district of Zeleia: this plain the poet puts under the dominion of Aeneas and the Antenorids, and calls it Dardania."[1] This dominion was therefore long and narrow; it ex-

---

[8] Strabo, xiii. p. 588: Πιτύα δ' ἐστὶν ἐν Πιτυοῦντι τῆς Παριανῆς ὑπερκείμενον ἔχουσα πιτυῶδες ὄρος μεταξὺ δὲ κεῖται Παρίου καὶ Πριάπου καὶ Λίνον χωρίον ἐπὶ θαλάττῃ, ὅπου οἱ Λινούσιοι κοχλίαι ἄριστοι τῶν πάντων ἁλίσκονται.

[9] Steph. Byz. and Etym. Mag. s. v. Λάμψακος; Schol. *Apoll. Rhod.* i. 933; Orph. *Arg.* 488; Plin. *H. N.* v. 32: "Lampsacum antea Pityusa dictum." This is also implied in the story told in Herodotus, vi. 37, the point of which is missed by the historian, who does not seem to have heard that Pityeia or Pityusa was reputed to have been the ancient name of Lampsacus.

[10] *Il.* ii. 837, 838:
τῶν αὖθ' Ὑρτακίδης ἦρχ' Ἄσιος, ὄρχαμος ἀνδρῶν, Ἄσιος Ὑρτακίδης.

[1] *Il.* ii. 836.

[2] *Il.* ii. 835; xi. 229; xv. 548.

[3] Steph. Byz. s. v. Περκώτη: Περκώτη καὶ πάλαι Περκώπη πόλις Τρωάδος.

[4] *Il.* ii. 836.

[5] vii. 34: ἔστι δὲ ἑπτὰ στάδια ἐξ Ἀβύδου ἐς τὴν ἀπαντίον.

[6] Richter, *Wallfahrten im Morgenlande*, p. 435.

[7] *Il.* ii. 838, 839:
Ἀρίσβηθεν . . .
ποταμοῦ ἀπὸ Σελλήεντος.
Comp. xii. 96, 97.

[8] *Il.* ii. 836; xxi. 43: δῖαν Ἀρίσβην.

[9] *Il.* vi. 13: ἐϋκτιμένη ἐν Ἀρίσβη.

[10] xiii. p. 592: Ἔξω δὲ Ἀβύδου τὰ περὶ τὸ Ἴλιον ἐστι, τά τε παράλια ἕως Λεκτοῦ καὶ τὰ ἐν τῷ Τρωϊκῷ πεδίῳ καὶ τὰ παρώρεια τῆς Ἴδης τὰ ὑπὸ τῷ Αἰνείᾳ.

[1] xiii. p. 596: τούτου δ' ἡ μὲν παρώρειός ἐστι στενή, τῇ μὲν ἐπὶ τὴν μεσημβρίαν τεταμένη μέχρι τῶν κατὰ Σκῆψιν τόπων, τῇ δ' ἐπὶ τὰς ἄρκτους μέχρι τῶν κατὰ Ζέλειαν Λυκίων. ταύτην δ' ὁ ποιητὴς ὑπ' Αἰνείᾳ τάττει καὶ τοῖς Ἀντηνορίδαις, καλεῖ δὲ Δαρδανίαν.

tended between Priam's dominion and that of the Meropids, being bordered on one side by the Hellespont, on the other by the Leleges and Cilicians. Its inhabitants, called Dardanians (Δαρδάνιοι[2] or Δάρδανοι),[3] were a race kindred with the Trojans, and are sometimes confounded with them: thus, for instance, Euphorbus, son of Panthoüs, a Trojan, is called a Dardanian.[4]

Of *Cities* we can only mention Dardania, built by Dardanus at the foot of Ida before sacred Ilium was founded in the plain.[5] In the time of Strabo it had utterly disappeared.[6] It has of course nothing in common with the later Dardanus, which—as excavations lately made there at my request by the military governor of the Dardanelles have shown—has left a layer of *débris* hardly 2½ ft. deep, in which nothing but fragments of Greek potsherds are found. It therefore appears certain that it was built by the Aeolian Greeks. It lies on the shore of the Hellespont, as Strabo[7] rightly remarks, at a distance of 70 stadia from Abydos, and, according to Pliny,[8] 70 stadia from Rhoeteum.

5. *The Dominion of Altes.*[9]—We find also in Homer that a troop of Leleges had settled in the Troad, on the river Satnioïs near Cape Lectum: thus they seem to have dwelt between the dominion of the Cilicians and that of the Dardanians.[10] Their king was Altes, father of Laothoë, who bore Lycaon, and father-in-law to Priam.[1]

Of *Cities* I can only mention *Pedasus* (ἡ Πήδασος) on the Satnioïs, with the epithets " lofty " (αἰπήεσσα),[2] " high-towered " or " high-walled " (αἰπεινή).[3] It was destroyed by Achilles,[4] and is supposed, as I have before observed, to be mentioned on the Egyptian monuments under the name of Pidasa.

6. *The Dominion of the Cilicians.*—

a. The Dominion of Eëtion (the Theban Cilicia)[5] extends between the district of Lyrnessus occupied by the Cilicians and the Leleges. The description given by Homer of Thebé[6] has led to the general belief

---

[2] *Il.* ii. 819:
Δαρδανίων αὖτ' ἦρχεν ἐὺς παῖς 'Αγχίσαο
Αἰνείας . . . .
[3] *Il.* iii. 456, vii. 348:
κέκλυτέ μευ, Τρῶες, καὶ Δάρδανοι ἠδ' ἐπίκουροι.
[4] *Il.* xvi. 807:
    . . . . Δάρδανος ἀνήρ,
Πανθοΐδης Εὔφορβος, ...
[5] *Il.* xx. 215–218:
Δάρδανον αὖ πρῶτον τέκετο νεφεληγερέτα
    Ζεύς,
κτίσσε δὲ Δαρδανίην, ἐπεὶ οὔπω "Ιλιος ἱρή
ἐν πεδίῳ πεπόλιστο, πόλις μερόπων ἀνθρώπων,
ἀλλ' ἔθ' ὑπωρείας ᾤκεον πολυπίδακος "Ιδης.
[6] xiii. p. 592: νῦν μὲν γὰρ οὐδ' ἴχνος πόλεως
σώζεται αὐτόθι.
[7] xiii. p. 595: ἡ πόλις ἡ Δάρδανος, διέχουσα
τῆς 'Αβύδου ο' σταδίους.
[8] *H. N.* v. 33: "a Rhoeteo Dardanium oppidum parvum abest stadia lxx."
[9] Deviating here from the order followed by E. Buchholz, *Homer. Kosm. und Geogr.*, I shall first speak of the dominions of the Leleges and the Cilicians, and afterwards of the dominion of

Troy proper, as this latter will occupy a large space.
[10] Strabo, xiii. p. 605: ἡ γὰρ ἀπὸ τοῦ Λεκτοῦ ῥάχις ἀνατείνουσα πρὸς τὴν "Ιδην ὑπέρκειται τῶν πρώτων τοῦ κόλπου μερῶν, ἐν οἷς πρῶτον τοὺς Λέλεγας ἱδρυμένους ὁ ποιητὴς πεποίηκεν.
[1] *Il.* xxi. 84–86:
    . . . . μινυνθάδιον δέ με μήτηρ
γείνατο Λαοθόη, θυγάτηρ "Αλταο γέροντος,
"Αλτεω ὃς Λελέγεσσι φιλοπτολέμοισιν ἀνάσσει.
[2] *Il.* xxi. 87:
("Αλτης) Πήδασον αἰπήεσσαν ἔχων ἐπὶ Σατνιόεντι.
[3] *Il.* vi. 34, 35:
ναῖε δὲ Σατνιόεντος ἐϋρρείταο παρ' ὄχθας
Πήδασον αἰπεινήν.
[4] *Il.* xx. 92:
πέρσε δὲ ('Αχιλλεὺς) Λυρνησσὸν καὶ Πήδασον.
[5] Strabo, xiii. p. 586: ἡ τῶν Κιλίκων διττή, ἡ μὲν Θηβαϊκὴ ἡ δὲ Λυρνησσίς.
[6] *Il.* vi. 396, 397:
'Ηετίων, ὃς ἔναιεν ὑπὸ Πλάκῳ ὑληέσσῃ
Θήβῃ ὑποπλακίῃ, Κιλίκεσσ' ἄνδρεσσιν ἀνάσσων.

that there was a mountain called Plakos, at the foot of which the city was situated. But Strabo knows no such mountain; he says: "But in the interior, 50 stadia further on, is the now deserted Thebé, which the poet puts below the ' wooded Plakos,' but there is here neither a Plakos nor a Plax, nor is there a forest above it though it adjoins Ida." [7]

Cities. (a) Thebé (ἡ Θήβη) was situated 60 stadia to the north-west of Adramyttium,[8] between the latter and Cariné.[9] It was the capital of Eëtion; hence its epithet "*sacred city of Eëtion.*" [10] It is called "flourishing" (εὐναιετάωσα) and "high-gated" (ὑψίπυλος), and was destroyed by Achilles.[11] It was a fortified place, for Homer speaks of its walls.[1]

Mr. Gladstone [2] has sought to show that under Thothmes III., whose reign is computed to have extended over the first half of the sixteenth century B.C. (or 1600-1550), when the power of the great Egyptian Empire reached its climax, it embraced most of the populations of Greece, where Thothmes put his own sons as governors in the places he had conquered. He calls attention to the fact, that the Thébe of Eëtion is connected in the *Iliad* with special excellence of horses; that it is the sacred city of Eëtion; and that lastly it has lofty gates (ὑψίπυλος).[3] It is surely remarkable, he adds, that we find all these three characteristics reproduced in the Cadmean Thebes of Boeotia. It is sacred (ἱερὰ πρὸς τείχεα Θήβης).[4] It is most closely associated with the horse; for to the Cadmeans alone, besides the Trojans, does Homer give the designation κέντορες ἵππων.[5] It is also remarkable for its gates, being the seven-gated Thebes.[6] Both cities, too, were rich. The Thébe of Eëtion is εὐναιετάουσα, or "a flourishing city;" while the Cadmean Thebes is εὐκτίμενον πτολίεθρον, "a well-built fortress," [7] and εὐρύχορος, "an extensive (?) city." [8] These three pointed characteristics, as well as the fourth, all belonged to the mighty city of Thebes in Egypt. This had a hundred gates; this horsed 20,000 chariots; and was eminently a sacred city, for she was the centre of the worship of Amun.[9]

Recent researches, however, seem to show that the identifications with Greek tribes proposed for geographical names occurring in the Egyptian inscriptions are untenable. The chief support for Mr. Gladstone's views

---

[7] Strabo, xiii. p. 614: ἐν δὲ τῇ μεσογαίᾳ ἀπὸ πεντήκοντα σταδίων ἐστὶν ἡ Θήβη ἔρημος, ἥν φησιν ὁ ποιητής, " ὑπὸ Πλάκῳ ὑληέσσῃ " οὔτε δὲ Πλάκος ἢ Πλὰξ ἐκεῖ τι λέγεται, οὔθ' ὕλη ὑπέρκειται καίτοι πρὸς τῇ Ἴδῃ.

[8] Strabo, xiii. p. 612: διέχουσι δὲ Ἀδραμυττίου σταδίους ἡ μὲν (Θήβη) ἑξήκοντα, ἡ δὲ (Λυρνησσὸς) ὀγδοήκοντα καὶ ὀκτὼ ἐπὶ θάτερα.

[9] Herod. vii. 42: ἀπὸ δὲ ταύτης (Καρίνης) διὰ Θήβης πεδίου ἐπορεύετο, Ἀδραμύττειόν τε πόλιν καὶ Ἄντανδρον τὴν Πελασγίδα παραμειβόμενος.

[10] *Il.* i. 366:
ἐς Θήβην ἱερὴν πόλιν Ἠετίωνος.

[11] *Il.* vi. 415, 416:
ἐκ δὲ πόλιν πέρσεν (Ἀχιλλεὺς) Κιλίκων εὐναιε-
τάωσαν
Θήβην ὑψίπυλον.

[1] *Il.* ii. 691: τείχεα Θήβης.
[2] *Homeric Synchronism*, p. 137.
[3] *Ibid.* p. 158.   [4] *Il.* iv. 378.
[5] *Il.* iv. 391.
[6] *Il.* iv. 406; *Od.* xi. 263.
[7] *Il.* ii. 505; vi. 415.   [8] *Od.* xi. 265.
[9] *Homer. Synchr.*, pp. 158, 159. Regarding the form of the name, we may add, that whilst the city of Eëtion is always called Thebé in the singular, this was also the *proper* form for the Egyptian city, whose original name (namely, the name of its sacred quarter, to the east of the Nile) was T-APE. The Greeks assimilated the name to that of Thebes (Θῆβαι) in Boeotia; but this city, as we see in Homer, is also called Thebé (Θήβη).

consequently falls to the ground. Since the Cadmeans of Boeotian Thebes were a Phoenician colony, it is probable that the origin of the name of the city must be sought in the Semitic languages. On the other hand, Egyptian Thebes derived its name from the Egyptian *ta-apiu*, the plural of *ta-ap*, "the little house," a title originally given to one only of the quarters of the city. According to Varro (*de Re Rust.* iii. 1, 16), "the Aeolian Boeotians" and the Sabines called hills *tebae* or *thebae*.

(β) Chrysé (ἡ Χρύση), already desolate in Strabo's time, was situated close to Thebé, and belonged to the possessions of Eëtion, as is evident from the fact that Chryseïs was captured by Achilles when he destroyed Thebé.[10] It had a temple of Apollo Smintheus, of which the father of Chryseïs was the priest.[1] It was situated on the sea, and had a port in which Ulysses landed when he brought Chryseïs back to her father with a hecatomb for the god. As Strabo remarks, it is to be distinguished from the *later* Chrysa, near Hamaxitus, which had also a temple of the Sminthian Apollo, but no port.[2] The temple of this god, which Pliny [3] mentions here, can consequently refer only to the later place.

(γ) Cillé (Κίλλη), situated also in the Theban plain on the small river Cillaeus, at the foot of Mount Cillaeus and in the neighbourhood of Antandros, was founded by Pelops, son of Tantalus, and had a celebrated temple of the Cillaean Apollo, which still existed in Strabo's time.[4]

b. The Dominion of Mynes appears to have been limited to the city of Lyrnessus (Λυρνησσός), called also the city of Mynes by Homer,[5] destroyed by Achilles, who here captured Briseïs.[6] Hither Aeneas fled, pursued by Achilles.[7] It was situated in the Plain of Thebé, 88 stadia from Adramyttium, and is described by Strabo as fortified by nature, but deserted.[8] Fellowes [9] believed he had found its ruins four miles from Karavaren.

c. The Dominion of Eurypylus is difficult to define. He was leader of a troop of Keteioi (οἱ Κήτειοι), whose identity with the Hittites of the Old Testament, the Kheta of the Egyptian monuments and the Khattai of the Assyrian inscriptions, has been most ingeniously maintained by

---

[10] *Il.* i. 366, 367 :
ᾠχόμεθ' ἐς Θήβην, ἱερὴν πόλιν 'Ηετίωνος
τὴν δὲ διεπράθομεν τε καὶ ἤγομεν ἐνθάδε πάντα.

[1] *Il.* i. 37–39 :
κλῦθί μευ, ἀργυρότοξ', ὃς Χρύσην ἀμφιβέβηκας
. . . .
Σμινθεῦ.

[2] Strabo, xiii. p. 612: 'Η δὲ Χρῦσα ἐπὶ θαλάττῃ πολίχνιον ἦν ἔχον λιμένα, πλησίον δὲ ὑπέρκειται ἡ Θήβη · ἐνταῦθα δ' ἦν καὶ τὸ ἱερὸν τοῦ Σμινθέως Ἀπόλλωνος καὶ ἡ Χρυσηΐς ἠρήμωται δὲ νῦν τὸ χωρίον τελέως · εἰς δὲ τὴν νῦν Χρῦσαν τὴν κατὰ Ἀμαξιτὸν μεθίδρυται τὸ ἱερόν, τῶν Κιλίκων τῶν μὲν εἰς τὴν Παμφυλίαν ἐκπεσόντων τῶν δὲ εἰς Ἀμαξιτόν· οἱ δ' ἀπειρότεροι τῶν παλαιῶν ἱστοριῶν ἐνταῦθα τὸν Χρύσην καὶ τὴν Χρυσηΐδα γεγονέναι φασὶ καὶ τὸν Ὅμηρον τούτου τοῦ τόπου μεμνῆσθαι· ἀλλ' οὔτε λιμήν ἐστιν ἐνταῦθα, ἐκεῖνος δέ φησιν "οἱ δ' ὅτε δὴ λιμένος πολυβενθέος ἐντὸς ἵκοντο." [3] *H. N.* v. 32. 3.

[4] Homer, *Il.* i. 38. Herodot. i. 149. Strabo,

xiii. p. 612: πλησίον οὖν τῆς Θήβης ἔτι νῦν Κίλλα τις τόπος λέγεται, ἐν ᾧ Κιλλαίου Ἀπόλλωνος ἔστιν ἱερόν · παρραρρεῖ δ' αὐτῷ ἐξ Ἴδης φερόμενος ὁ Κιλλαῖος ποταμός. Ovid, *Met.* xiii. 174. Plin. *H. N.*, v. 32, says that it no longer existed in his time.

[5] *Il.* xix. 296 :
πέρσεν δὲ πόλιν θείοιο Μύνητος·

[6] *Il.* ii. 690, 691 :
τὴν (Βρισηΐδα) ἐκ Λυρνησσοῦ ἐξείλετο πολλὰ μογήσας,
Λυρνησσὸν διαπορθήσας.

[7] *Il.* xx. 191, 192 :
ἔνθεν δ' ἐς Λυρνησσὸν ὑπέκφυγες · αὐτὰρ ἐγὼ τὴν πέρσα μεθορμηθείς.

[8] xiii. p. 612: ἐνταῦθα γὰρ καὶ ἡ Θήβη καὶ ἡ Λυρνησσός, ἐρυμνὸν χωρίον· ἔρημοι δ' ἀμφότεραι· διέχουσι δὲ Ἀδραμυττίου σταδίους ἡ (Θήβη) μὲν ἑξήκοντα ἡ (Λυρνησσὸς) δὲ ὀγδοήκοντα καὶ ὀκτὼ ἐπὶ θάτερα. See also Diod. v. 49 ; Plin. *H. N.* v. 26 and 32. [9] Excursus, in *Asia Minor*, p. 39.

Mr. Gladstone.[10] His arguments lead to the conclusion that the Keteioi "come from outside the circle of the earlier Trojan alliances, and therefore from Lycia, and the countries of the Mysoi and Kilikes."[1] Strabo says :[2] "Just as the land of the Cilicians is twofold, the Theban and the Lyrnessian, to which may also be reckoned the domain of Eurypylus, coming next to the territory of Lyrnessus." And again :[3] "According to Homer, Eurypylus reigned in the country on the Caïcus, so that perhaps a part of the Cilicians also was subject to him." And further :[4] "But it can only be a question of probabilities if any one endeavours to determine from the poet the exact frontier to which the Cilicians and Pelasgians extended, as well as the Keteioi between them who were under Eurypylus. As to the Cilicians and the subjects of Eurypylus, we have already stated the probability ; and how they were bounded, especially by the districts on the Caïcus."

It is on account of Strabo's first statement, which makes the Keteioi under Eurypylus border upon Lyrnessus, that their territory has been noticed here.

7. *The Dominion of the Homeric Arimi* (οἱ Ἄριμοι).—The Arimi seem to be a mythic people, who have been searched for in various regions. They are only once mentioned by Homer : "The earth groaned under their feet, as when the god of thunder, Zeus, in wrath strikes the land of the Arimi around Typhöeus, where the bed of Typhöeus is said to be."[5] According to Strabo, this land of the Arimi was identical with the Catakekaumené (or "burnt land") possessed by the Mysians and Lydians.[6] In another passage he states that by some the burnt land is believed to be in Lydia in the environs of Sardis ; by others in Cilicia or in Syria, by some on the Pithecussae (monkey-islands), who said, at the same time, that monkeys were called Arimi by the Tyrrhenians.[7] I may here mention that the present Island of Ischia, in the Gulf of Naples, was once called Pithecusa, Aenaria or Inarimé. Strabo also cites the opinion of Posidonius, according to which "the Arimi are not the inhabitants of a certain district of Syria, of Cilicia, or of any other country, but the inhabitants of all Syria, who are called Aramaei. But perhaps they were called Arimaei or Arimi by the Greeks."[8]

[10] *Homeric Synchronism*, pp. 121, 127, 171, 174, 177, 180, 184.

[1] *Ibid.* p. 183.

[2] xiii. p. 586 : καθάπερ καὶ ἡ τῶν Κιλίκων διττή, ἡ μὲν Θηβαϊκὴ ἡ δὲ Λυρνησσίς· ἐν αὐτῇ δ' ἂν λεχθείη ἡ ὑπὸ Εὐρυπύλῳ ἐφεξῆς οὖσα τῇ Λυρνησσίδι.

[3] xiii. p. 616 : ὅτι ἐν τοῖς περὶ τὸν Κάϊκον τόποις φαίνεται βεβασιλευκὼς καθ' "Ομηρον ὁ Εὐρύπυλος, ὥστ' ἴσως καὶ τῶν Κιλίκων τι μέρος ἦν ὑπ' αὐτοῦ.

[4] xiii. p. 620 : εἰκοτολογεῖν δ' ἐστι κἂν εἴ τις τὸν ἀκριβῆ ζητεῖ κατὰ τὸν ποιητὴν ὅρον μέχρι τίνος οἱ Κίλικες διέτεινον καὶ οἱ Πελασγοὶ καὶ ἔτι οἱ μεταξὺ τούτων Κήτειοι λεγόμενοι οἱ ὑπὸ τῷ Εὐρυπύλῳ. περὶ μὲν οὖν τῶν Κιλίκων καὶ τῶν ὑπ' Εὐρυπύλῳ τὰ ἐνόντα εἴρηται, καὶ διότι [ἐπὶ] τὰ περὶ τὸν Κάϊκον μάλιστα περατοῦνται.

[8] *Il.* ii. 781–783 :
γαῖα δ' ὑπεστενάχιζε Διῒ ὥς τερπικεραύνῳ
χωομένῳ, ὅτε τ' ἀμφὶ Τυφωέῖ γαῖαν ἱμάσσῃ
εἰν Ἀρίμοις, ὅθι φασὶ Τυφωέος ἔμμεναι εὐνάς.

[6] xii. p. 579 : καὶ δὴ καὶ τὰ περὶ τὸν Τυφῶνα πάθη ἐνταῦθα μυθεύουσι καὶ τοὺς Ἀρίμους καὶ τὴν Κατακεκαυμένην ταύτην εἶναι φασιν.

[7] xiii. p. 626 : ἄλλοι δ' ἐν Κιλικίᾳ, τινὲς δ' ἐν Συρίᾳ πλάττουσι τὸν μῦθον τοῦτον, οἱ δ' ἐν Πιθηκούσσαις, οἳ καὶ τοὺς πιθήκους φασὶ παρὰ τοῖς Τυρρηνοῖς ἀρίμους καλεῖσθαι.

[8] xvi. p. 784 : λέγει δὲ καὶ τοὺς Ἀρίμους ὁ ποιητής, οὕς φησι Ποσειδώνιος δέχεσθαι δεῖν μὴ τόπον τινα τῆς Συρίας ἢ τῆς Κιλικίας ἢ ἄλλης τινος γῆς, ἀλλὰ τὴν Συρίαν αὐτὴν Ἀραμαῖοι γὰρ οἱ ἐν αὐτῇ· τάχα δ' οἱ Ἕλληνες Ἀριμαίους ἐκάλουν ἢ Ἀρίμους.

8. *The Dominion of the Pelasgians* (οἱ Πελασγοί).—I finally mention here the dominion of the Asiatic Pelasgians, who were under the command of Hippothoüs and Pylaeus, sons of Lethus,[9] and occupied the district of the Aeolian coast from the river Caïcus up to the Ionian frontier. Their chief city was Larissa (ἡ Λάρισσα, Λάρισα), which Strabo places in the neighbourhood of Cyme, for he says:[10] "But the Pelasgians we have reason to place next to them (the Cilicians) and the subjects of Eurypylus, as well from the indications of Homer as from other information. For the poet says : 'Hippothoüs led the tribes of the spear-practised Pelasgians, who dwelt on the fertile soil of Larissa—these were led by Hippothoüs and Pylaeus, the offspring of Ares, both sons of the Pelasgian Lethus, the son of Teutamus.' Hereby he indicates a considerable multitude of Pelasgians, because he speaks, not of 'a tribe,' but 'of tribes,' and puts their seat in Larissa. Now there are many Larissas, but we must assume one in the neighbourhood; and we should be most right in supposing the one near Cyme. For there are three, but the one near Hamaxitus lies directly in sight of Ilium, and very near it, about 200 stadia distant, so that it could not have been rightly said that Hippothoüs fell in the fight over Patroclus 'far from Larissa;' but this would rather have been rightly said of the Larissa near Cyme, because there are about 1000 stadia between that Larissa and Ilium."

9. *The Dominion of Priam, Ilium, and the Country belonging to it.*— For the extent of this dominion we have Strabo's statement: "Below it (Aeneas's dominion of Dardania), and nearly parallel with it, is Cebrenia, consisting for the most part of table-land. But there was once a city Cebrené. Demetrius supposes that here was the limit of the country about Ilium subject to Hector, which thus extended from the naustathmus to Cebrenia."[1]

Of *Cities* belonging to this dominion, we know from the poems only Ilios (ἡ Ἴλιος) and Thymbré (ἡ Θύμβρη). The latter is only once mentioned by the poet: "But towards Thymbré encamped the Lycians and the haughty Mysians, and the Phrygians, tamers of horses, and the Maeonians with their horsehair crests."[2] Strabo erroneously supposed that Homer spoke here, not of the city of Thymbra, but of the plain of Thymbra, for he says: "But near to it (Ilium) is the plain

---

[9] *Il.* ii. 840–843.

[10] Strabo, xiii. p. 620: τοὺς δὲ Πελασγοὺς εὔλογον τούτοις ἐφεξῆς τιθέναι ἔκ τε τῶν ὑφ' Ὁμήρου λεγομένων καὶ ἐκ τῆς ἄλλης ἱστορίας. ὁ μὲν γὰρ οὕτω φησίν "'Ἱππόθοος δ' ἄγε φῦλα Πελασγῶν ἐγχεσιμώρων, τῶν οἳ Λάρισαν ἐριβώλακα ναιετάασκον· τῶν ἦρχ' Ἱππόθοός τε Πύλαιός τ' ὄζος Ἄρηος, υἷε δύω Λήθοιο Πελασγοῦ Τευταμίδαο." ἐξ ὧν πλῆθός τε ἐμφαίνει ἀξιόλογον τὸ τῶν Πελασγῶν (οὐ γὰρ φῦλον, ἀλλὰ φῦλα ἔφη) καὶ τὴν οἴκησιν ἐν Λαρίσῃ φράζει · πολλαὶ μὲν οὖν αἱ Λάρισαι, δεῖ δὲ τῶν ἐγγύς τινα δέξασθαι, μάλιστα δ' ἂν τὴν περὶ Κύμην ὑπολάβοι τις ὀρθῶς · τριῶν γὰρ οὐσῶν ἡ μὶν καθ' Ἀμαξιτὸν ἐν ὄψει τελέως ἐστὶ τῷ Ἰλίῳ, καὶ ἐγγὺς

σφόδρα ἐν διακοσίοις που σταδίοις, ὥστ' οὐκ ἂν λέγοιτο πιθανῶς ὁ Ἱππόθοος πεσεῖν ἐν τῷ ὑπὲρ Πατρόκλου ἀγῶνι "τῆλ' ἀπὸ Λαρίσης," ταύτης γε, ἀλλὰ μᾶλλον τῆς περὶ Κύμην · χίλιοι γάρ που στάδιοι μεταξύ.

[1] Strabo, xiii. p. 596: ὑπὸ δὲ ταύτῃ Κεβρηνία, πεδιὰς ἡ πλείστη, παράλληλός πως τῇ Δαρδανίᾳ · ἦν δὲ καὶ πόλις ποτὲ Κεβρήνη. ὑπονοεῖ δ' ὁ Δημήτριος μέχρι δεῦρο διατείνειν τὴν περὶ τὸ Ἴλιον χώραν τὴν ὑπὸ τῷ Ἕκτορι, ἀνήκουσαν ἀπὸ τοῦ ναυστάθμου μέχρι Κεβρηνίας.

[2] *Il.* x. 430, 431 :
πρὸς Θύμβρης δ' ἔλαχον Λύκιοι Μυσοί τ' ἀγέρωχοι
καὶ Φρύγες ἱππόδαμοι καὶ Μῄονες ἱπποκορυσταί.

of Thymbra and the river Thymbrius, which flows through it and falls into the Scamander close to the temple of the Thymbrian Apollo, at a distance of 50 stadia from Novum Ilium."[3] Stephanus Byzantinus[4] and Pliny[5] understood the poet rightly, for they mention Thymbra as a town.

The other city of Priam's dominion, whose fame and fate gave birth to Homer's immortal poems, demands a separate notice.

§ III. THE CITY OF ILIOS, ILIUM, OR TROY.

ILIUM, or TROY, the residence of Priam, the city besieged by the Greek army under Agamemnon, is called Ἴλιος and Τροίη by the poet, who frequently uses the latter name both for the city and the land belonging to it, calling it ἐριβῶλαξ ("fat and fertile"). Ἴλιος, on the other hand, is only used for the city; but the oldest form was evidently Ϝίλιος, with the Vau or Digamma.[6] The neuter, Ἴλιον, occurs only once in Homer,[7] in consequence of which Aristarchus considers the passage as a later interpolation.[8] But the tragic poets[9] having adopted it, it was also used commonly by the prose-writers.[10] The Latin writers use the corresponding forms, Ilium and Troja, the latter being preferred by the poets, for the reason that Ilium could not fit into an hexameter verse. Morritt[11] thinks that Ἰλήϊον is derived from Ἴλη, turma, and that the πεδίον Ἰλήϊον was the Campus Martius of Troy, which he believes to have been in the open plain about Arablar.[1]

The city has in Homer the following epithets: εὐρυάγυια,[2] "with broad streets;" ἐϋκτίμενον (πτολίεθρον),[3] and ἐϋδμητος,[4] "well built;" εὐναιόμενον (πτολίεθρον),[5] "well inhabited" or "flourishing;" ἐρατεινή,[6] "pleasant" or "elegant;" εὔπωλος,[7] "rich in foals;" μέγα (ἄστυ),[8] "great;" εὐτείχεος,[9] "enclosed by good walls;" ὀφρυόεσσα,[10] "beetling;"

---

[3] xiii. p. 598 : πλησίον γάρ ἐστι τὸ πεδίον ἡ Θύμβρα καὶ ὁ δι' αὐτοῦ ῥέων ποταμὸς Θύμβριος, ἐμβάλλων εἰς τὸν Σκάμανδρον κατὰ τὸ Θυμβραίου Ἀπόλλωνος ἱερόν, τοῦ δὲ νῦν Ἰλίου καὶ πεντήκοντα σταδίους διέχει.

[4] S. v. Θύμβρη.

[5] H. N. v. 33.

[6] See, for instance, Il. xx. 216 : κτίσσε δὲ Δαρδανίην, ἐπεὶ οὔπω Ἴλιος ἱρή . . .

[7] Il. xv. 70, 71 :
. . . . εἰσόκ' Ἀχαιοί
Ἴλιον αἰπὺ ἕλοιεν Ἀθηναίης διὰ βουλάς.

[8] See also Steph. Byz. s. v. Ἴλιον.

[9] Soph. Phil. 454, 1200 ; Eurip. Andr. 400 ; Troad. 25, 145, 511 ; Or. 1381.

[10] Herod. ii. 117, 118 ; Scylax, 35 ; Plato, Legg. iii. 682, and others.

[11] Apud Robert Walpole, Memoirs relating to European and Asiatic Turkey, edited from manuscript journals ; London, 1817, p. 578.

[1] R. Virchow, Beiträge zur Landeskunde der Troas, p. 46.

[2] Il. ii. 141:
οὐ γὰρ ἔτι Τροίην αἱρήσομεν εὐρυάγυιαν ;
ii. 12 :
νῦν γάρ κεν ἕλοι πόλιν εὐρυάγυιαν.

[3] Il. xxi. 433:
Ἰλίου ἐκπέρσαντες ἐϋκτίμενον πτολίεθρον.
Il. iv. 33:
Ἰλίου ἐξαλαπάξαι ἐϋκτίμενον πτολίεθρον.

[4] Il. xxi. 516:
μέμβλετο γὰρ οἱ τεῖχος ἐϋδμήτοιο πόληος.

[5] Il. xiii. 380:
Ἰλίου ἐκπέρσῃς εὐναιόμενον πτολίεθρον.

[6] Il. v. 210:
ὅτε Ἴλιον εἰς ἐρατεινήν.

[7] Il. v. 551 ; Od. ii. 18, xiv. 71 :
Ἴλιον εἰς εὔπωλον.

[8] Il. ii. 332, 803 :
ἄστυ μέγα Πριάμοιο.

[9] Il. ii. 113 :
Ἴλιον ἐκπέρσαντ' εὐτείχεον ἀπονέεσθαι.

[10] Il. xxii. 410, 411 :
. . . . ὡς εἰ ἅπασα
Ἴλιος ὀφρυόεσσα πυρὶ σμύχοιτο κατ' ἄκρης.

αἰπύ[1] and αἰπεινή,[2] "steep" or "lofty;" ἠνεμόεσσα,[3] "exposed to the wind;" ἱρή,[4] "sacred." It had an Acropolis called the Pergamos (ἡ Πέργαμος), which was in a more elevated position than the town, and had the epithets ἱερή,[5] "sacred," and ἄκρη,[6] "highest point." Here was Priam's beautiful habitation, built of polished stone, with fifty chambers in which his sons slept with their wedded wives; while opposite, within the court, on an upper floor, were twelve chambers, likewise of polished stone, and close to each other, in which Priam's sons-in-law slept with their chaste wives.[7] Before the doors of this palace was the Agora.[8] Here was also the well-built dwelling of Hector,[9] as well as the beautiful dwelling of Paris, which he had himself built, aided by the best builders of the fertile realm of Troy:—" They made him a chamber, a hall, and a court, close to the residences of Priam and Hector in the Acropolis." [10] Here, moreover, was the Temple of Pallas Athené, the tutelar deity of Troy,[1] with a statue of the goddess, probably of wood, in a sitting posture; for unless it had been sitting, the priestess Theano could not have deposited Hecuba's *peplos* on its knees.[2] Here was also a temple of Apollo,[3] from which the god is represented as looking down.[4] It further appears that Zeus had a temple or at least an altar here, on which Hector sacrificed the thighs of oxen.[5] In the poet's imagination the hill of the Pergamos appears to

[1] *Il.* xv. 71: Ἴλιον αἰπύ (this verse has been already quoted).

[2] *Il.* xiii. 772, 773:
νῦν ὤλετο πᾶσα κατ' ἄκρης
. . . . . . Ἴλιος αἰπεινή.
Il. xv. 215:
Ἰλίου αἰπεινῆς πεφιδήσεται, οὐδ' ἐθελήσει
ἐκπέρσαι . . . .
Il. xvii. 327, 328:
Αἰνεία, πῶς ἂν καὶ ὑπὲρ θεὸν εἰρύσσαισθε
Ἴλιον αἰπεινήν.
[3] *Il.* viii. 499, xii. 115:
ἂψ ἀπονοστήσειν προτὶ Ἴλιον ἠνεμόεσσαν.
Il. xiii. 724:
Τρῶες ἐχώρησαν προτὶ Ἴλιον ἠνεμόεσσαν.
Il. xviii. 174:
οἱ δ' ἐρύσσασθαι ποτὶ Ἴλιον ἠνεμόεσσαν.
Il. xxiii. 64:
Ἕκτορ' ἐπαΐσσων προτὶ Ἴλιον ἠνεμόεσσαν.
Il. xxiii. 297:
ἵνα μή οἱ ἔποιθ' ὑπὸ Ἴλιον ἠνεμόεσσαν.
[4] *Il.* vi. 448:
ἔσσεται ἦμαρ, ὅτ' ἄν ποτ' ὀλώλῃ Ἴλιος ἱρή.
Il. xxiv. 27:
ἀλλ' ἔχον, ὥς σφιν πρῶτον ἀπήχθετο Ἴλιος ἱρή.
Od. xvii. 293:
. . . . . πάρος δ' εἰς Ἴλιον ἱρὴν
ᾤχετο . . . .
Il. xxi. 128:
φθείρεσθ' εἰσόκεν ἄστυ κιχείομεν Ἰλίου ἱρῆς . . .
[5] *Il.* v. 446:
Περγάμῳ εἰν ἱερῇ, ὅθι οἱ νηός γ' ἐτέτυκτο.
[6] *Il.* v. 460:
ὣς εἰπών, αὐτὸς μὲν ἐφέζετο Περγάμῳ ἄκρῃ.
[7] *Il.* vi. 242-250:
ἀλλ' ὅτε δὴ Πριάμοιο δόμον περικαλλέ' ἵκανεν,
ξεστῆς αἰθούσῃσι τετυγμένον—αὐτὰρ ἐν αὐτῷ

πεντήκοντ' ἔνεσαν θάλαμοι ξεστοῖο λίθοιο,
πλησίοι ἀλλήλων δεδμημένοι· ἔνθα δὲ παῖδες
κοιμῶντο Πριάμοιο παρὰ μνηστῇς ἀλόχοισιν.
κουράων δ' ἑτέρωθεν ἐναντίοι ἔνδοθεν αὐλῆς
δώδεκ' ἔσαν τέγεοι θάλαμοι ξεστοῖο λίθοιο,
πλησίοι ἀλλήλων δεδμημένοι· ἔνθα δὲ γαμβροὶ
κοιμῶντο Πριάμοιο παρ' αἰδοίῃς ἀλόχοισιν.
[8] *Il.* vii. 345, 346:
Τρώων αὖτ' ἀγορὴ γένετ' Ἰλίου ἐν πόλει ἄκρῃ
δεινή, τετρηχυῖα, παρὰ Πριάμοιο θύρῃσιν.
[9] *Il.* vi. 370:
. . . . . Ἕκτωρ
αἶψα δ' ἔπειθ' ἵκανε δόμους εὐναιετάοντας.
[10] *Il.* vi. 313-317:
Ἕκτωρ δὲ πρὸς δώματ' Ἀλεξάνδροιο βεβήκει
καλά, τά ῥ' αὐτὸς ἔτευξε σὺν ἀνδράσιν, οἵ τότ'
ἄριστοι
ἦσαν ἐνὶ Τροίῃ ἐριβώλακι τέκτονες ἄνδρες·
οἵ οἱ ἐποίησαν θάλαμον καὶ δῶμα καὶ αὐλήν
ἐγγύθι τε Πριάμοιο καὶ Ἕκτορος ἐν πόλει ἄκρῃ.
[1] *Il.* vi. 88:
νηὸν Ἀθηναίης γλαυκώπιδος ἐν πόλει ἄκρῃ.
[2] *Il.* vi. 302, 303:
ἡ δ' ἄρα πέπλον ἑλοῦσα Θεανὼ καλλιπάρῃος,
θῆκεν Ἀθηναίης ἐπὶ γούνασιν ἠϋκόμοιο.
[3] *Il.* v. 445, 446:
Αἰνείαν δ' ἀπάτερθεν ὁμίλου θῆκεν Ἀπόλλων
Περγάμῳ εἰν ἱερῇ, ὅθι οἱ νηός γ' ἐτέτυκτο.
[4] *Il.* vii. 20, 21:
. . . . τῇ δ' ἀντίος ὤρνυτ' Ἀπόλλων,
Περγάμου ἔκ κατιδών, Τρώεσσι δὲ βούλετο νίκην.
[5] *Il.* xxii. 169-172:
. . . . . ἐμὸν δ' ὀλοφύρεται ἦτορ
Ἕκτορος, ὅς μοι πολλὰ βοῶν ἐπὶ μηρί' ἔκηεν
Ἴδης ἐν κορυφῇσι πολυπτύχου, ἄλλοτε δ' αὖτε
ἐν πόλει ἀκροτάτῃ . . . .

have formed a slope; for Cassandra—probably on leaving Priam's house, which was itself in the Acropolis—still ascends the Pergamos.[6]

Ilium was surrounded by a strong wall (as is shown by its epithet εὐτείχεος), which was built by Poseidon and Apollo; for the former says, "They will forget the wall which I and Phoebus Apollo built with much pain for the hero Laomedon."[7] But according to another passage it was built by Poseidon alone, for he says to Apollo: "Do you not remember all the wrong we two suffered for Ilium, alone of all the gods, when for a year we served proud Laomedon by Jove's command, for a fixed hire, and he assigned our labours? I indeed built for the Trojans round about the city a wall broad and very fair, that the town might be impregnable, whilst thou, Phoebus, didst tend the oxen with twisted horns and crooked gait in the glens of woody Ida, with its many dales."[8]

These walls were provided with parapets[9] and towers, for a watch-tower (σκοπιή)[10] is mentioned; also another tower different from that of the Scaean Gate.[1] On one side of the city, close to the wall, was the Erineos, or wild fig-tree; but the word was understood by Strabo to mean a rugged stony place (probably a small hill) covered with wild fig-trees;[2] so that he thinks Andromache was right in saying to Hector, "Array the troops by the *erineos*, for there the city can most easily be scaled, and the assault on the wall is the most practicable."[3] Andromache adds: "For three times have the most valiant chiefs come and assailed this point, those with the two Ajaxes and famous Idomeneus, as well as those with the Atreidae and the mighty son of Tydeus."[4] But this being the only passage where Homer mentions the wall as of easiest access on this side, or that a fight had occurred here, some commentators have assigned the event to a time before the Trojan war. The *Cypria* of Stasinus describes it as having taken place when the embassy of the Greeks had been unsuccessful. But it appears very likely that the poet had this very same weak place in view, when he makes Patroclus thrice endeavour to scale a corner or buttress of the wall, whence he is as many times repulsed by Apollo, who stood on a tower.[5] The Erineos is further mentioned when Achilles and Hector pass it in their course round the city;[6] and here also it appears to be close to the walls.

---

[6] *Il.* xxiv. 699:
. . . . . Πέργαμον εἰσαναβᾶσα.
[7] *Il.* vii. 452, 453:
τοῦ δ' ἐπιλήσονται, τὸ ἐγὼ καὶ Φοῖβος Ἀπόλλων
ἥρῳ Λαομέδοντι πολίσσαμεν ἀθλήσαντες.
[8] *Il.* xxi. 441–449:
. . . . . οὐδέ νυ τῶνπερ
μέμνηαι, ὅσα δὴ πάθομεν κακὰ Ἴλιον ἀμφὶς
μοῦνοι νῶϊ θεῶν, ὅτ' ἀγήνορι Λαομέδοντι
πὰρ Διὸς ἐλθόντες θητεύσαμεν εἰς ἐνιαυτὸν
μισθῷ ἔπι ῥητῷ· ὁ δὲ σημαίνων ἐπέτελλεν.
ἦ τοι ἐγὼ Τρώεσσι πόλιν πέρι τεῖχος ἔδειμα,
εὐρύ τε καὶ μάλα καλόν, ἵν' ἄρρηκτος πόλις εἴη·
Φοῖβε, σὺ δ' εἰλίποδας ἕλικας βοῦς βουκολέεσκες
Ἴδης ἐν κνημοῖσι πολυπτύχου ὑλησέσσης.
[9] *Il.* xxii. 3:
κεκλιμένοι καλῇσιν ἐπάλξεσιν . . . .

[10] *Il.* xxii. 145:
οἱ δὲ παρὰ σκοπιὴν καὶ ἐρινεὸν ἠνεμόεντα.
[1] *Il.* xvi. 700:
εἰ μὴ Ἀπόλλων Φοῖβος ἐϋδμήτου ἐπὶ πύργου.
[2] xiii. p. 598: τραχύς τις τόπος καὶ ἐρινεώδης,
τῷ μὲν ἀρχαίῳ κτίματι ὑποπέπτωκεν.
[3] *Il.* vi. 433, 434:
λαὸν δὲ στῆσον παρ' ἐρινεόν, ἔνθα μάλιστα
ἄμβατός ἐστι πόλις, καὶ ἐπίδρομον ἔπλετο τεῖχος.
[4] *Il.* vi. 435–437:
τρὶς γὰρ τῇ γ' ἐλθόντες ἐπειρήσανθ' οἱ ἄριστοι
ἀμφ' Αἴαντε δύω καὶ ἀγακλυτὸν Ἰδομενῆα
ἠδ' ἀμφ' Ἀτρείδας καὶ Τυδέος ἄλκιμον υἱόν.
[5] *Il.* xvi. 702, 703:
τρὶς μὲν ἐπ' ἀγκῶνος βῆ τείχεος ὑψηλοῖο
Πάτροκλος, τρὶς δ' αὐτὸν ἀπεστυφέλιξεν Ἀπόλλων.
[6] *Il.* xxii. 145, just cited.

But in a third passage we see the Trojans rushing near the tomb of Ilus, through the middle plain, past the Erineos, longing to reach the town. Here therefore this hill is described as lying on the usual line of march of both armies.[7]

There was no impediment to running all round the city wall, for Achilles pursued Hector three times with flying speed about the city.[8] It has often been contended that the preposition περί (around) has in this passage the signification of παρά (near); and that, consequently, the course of the two heroes was along the wall of Troy, between the two springs and the Scamander. But this interpretation is inadmissible, for Homer represents the course of the two heroes as beyond the two springs.[9] That this meaning and no other must be attributed to the poet, is clearly proved by the passage in which he describes Achilles as dragging the body of Hector three times περί (around) the sepulchre of Patroclus.[10] Besides, throughout antiquity the passage was understood to mean that the race had been all round the city, as Virgil proves by saying:

"Ter circum Iliacos raptaverat Hectora muros."[1]

Strabo, again, in speaking of Novum Ilium, says that the flight of Hector round the city is improbable, for no one could run round that town on account of the adjoining ridge, but one could have run freely round the ancient city.[2] I may further mention that my friend Dr. G. von Eckenbrecher calls attention to Aristotle,[3] "who cites the pursuit of Hector as an example of how the poet had judiciously taken advantage of the impossible, to excite greater astonishment. He must therefore have understood the poet as intending to describe that the heroes ran three times round the city, for otherwise there would not have been a trace of impossibility in the pursuit of Hector. It has been maintained very improperly that Virgil, in the 12th Aeneid, very accurately imitates Hector's flight; that he consequently must have understood Homer to describe a course *before* and not *round* Troy, because he makes Aeneas and Turnus run, not *round* Laurentum, but in five circles *before* the city. It is evident that Virgil here imitates Homer, but it is just as evident that he endeavours to distinguish himself from him, in order not to serve up to the readers of Homer what they were acquainted with; nay, he intended to furnish something new, and he has done this with extraordinary art. Thus, although he might understand Homer just as all other ancients did, he could very well change the race round the town into a race before it.[4] But it ought to be well understood

---

[7] *Il.* xi. 166–168:

οἱ δὲ παρ' Ἴλου σῆμα παλαιοῦ Δαρδανίδαο,
μέσσον κὰπ πεδίον παρ' ἐρινεὸν ἐσσεύοντο
ἱέμενοι πόλιος.

[8] xxii. 165:

ὡς τὼ τρὶς Πριάμοιο πόλιν περιδινηθήτην.

[9] *Il.* xxii. 157:

τῇ ῥα παραδραμέτην, φεύγων, ὁ δ' ὄπισθε διώκων.

[10] *Il.* xxiv. 16, 17:

τρὶς δ' ἐρύσας περὶ σῆμα Μενοιτιάδαο θανόντος
αὖτις ἐνὶ κλισίῃ παυέσκετο.

[1] *Aeneid.* i. 483.

[2] xiii. p. 599: οὐδ' ἡ τοῦ Ἕκτορος δὲ περιδρομὴ ἡ περὶ τὴν πόλιν ἔχει τι εὔλογον· οὐ γάρ ἐστι περίδρομος ἡ νῦν διὰ τὴν συνεχῆ ῥάχιν· ἡ δὲ παλαιὰ ἔχει περιδρομήν.

[3] *Poetica*, xxv.: παράδειγμα ἡ τοῦ Ἕκτορος δίωξις. The passage, *Poetica*, xxiv.—τὰ περὶ τὴν Ἕκτορος δίωξιν—does not concern this question, for it treats of the difference between what can be represented on the stage and in the Epos.

[4] The plain fact that Virgil understood Homer just as we do, and as all the ancients did, is shown by the above-cited passage.

that, with him, *Aeneas was embarrassed in his running by a wound he had received shortly before;* whilst, in Homer, Achilles is the pursuer in his full strength, which makes him superior in swiftness to all other heroes. Thus, with Virgil, a repeated circular run on a level ground without impediment is possible, but this would have been impossible in the case of Achilles and Hector."[5]

I may add here that the run round Hissarlik is very easy, and may be accomplished without any diminution of speed. The only steep place is near the theatre, but here—as is seen in the Frontispiece and the view No. 16—the footpath ascends obliquely with a gentle slope. In this respect therefore, as in all others, the Homeric text is well adapted to Hissarlik.

Of Gates the poet only mentions that one which faces the plain, and which he alternately calls the Dardanian and Scaean Gate (Σκαιαὶ Πύλαι). It has always been believed that the latter name is due to the position of the gate to the left hand of the augur, who turned his face towards midnight, that is the north, and consequently had the evening or west side to his left. But the celebrated Orientalist, the late Professor Martin Haug of Munich, who read in the Trojan inscriptions the name of a god or hero Sigo or Siko, maintained[6] that the name of the Trojan Gate is by no means the adjective σκαιός, but contains the name of the same god or hero, which he also finds in the name Scamander, as well as in the Trojan promontory, Sigeum; in Sigia, the original name of the site of Alexandria-Troas; in Sichaeus, the husband of Dido, who was visited by the Trojan Aeneas; and in Sigon, a city of Phoenicia mentioned by Arrian.[7]

Dr. Franz Eyssenhardt sends me an interesting dissertation on the subject of the Trojan Gate,[8] of which I here give the translation:

"The ancient critics (Schol. A V on *Iliad.* viii. 58) have rightly observed that, in mentioning the *Gates* (Πύλαι) of the city, Homer employs the word differently from the later classical writers; for he means by the plural the two wings of the gate, and, consequently, but one gate. When Priam looks on the battle from the wall, he orders the watchmen to keep 'the gates' open, in order that the fugitives might escape into the city.[9] Antenor alone, leaning against the beech-tree, awaits Achilles;[10] and Hector also waits close to it at the Scaean Gate.[11] Hence it is evident that 'the gates' can be no other than the Scaean Gate. But this gate again, as has already been observed by the ancients (Schol. *ad Iliad.* v. 789; ix. 354), is identical with the Dardanian Gate; for where this latter is mentioned, it is also close to the frequently-mentioned beech-tree, which is close to the city wall. If, therefore, having regard to these passages, it cannot be doubted

---

[5] *Die Lage des Homerischen Troia*, pp. 24, 25.

[6] See his letter on "Trojan Inscriptions" in the *Beilage zur Augsburg. Allgemeinen Zeitung*, Feb. 1, 1874.

[7] *Anab.* ii. 13. 8.

[8] *Sammlung Wissenschaftlicher Vorträge*, von Rud. Virchow und Fr. von Holtzendorff; 1875, Ser. x., Heft 229.

[9] *Il.* xxi. 531, 532:
πεπταμένας ἐν χερσὶ πύλας ἔχετ' εἰσόκε λαοὶ
ἔλθωσι προτὶ ἄστυ πεφυζότες.

[10] *Il.* xxi. 549: φηγῷ κεκλιμένος.

[11] *Il.* xxii. 5, 6:
Ἕκτορα δ' αὐτοῦ μεῖναι ὀλοὴ Μοῖρ' ἐπέδησεν,
Ἰλίου προπάροιθε πυλάων τε Σκαιάων.

that Homer gives only one gate to the sacred Ilios, there is a still more evident proof of this in the account of the last combat of Hector with Achilles. Hector is pursued by Achilles round the city; but whenever he approaches the Dardanian Gate, he is prevented by Achilles from escaping beneath the wall or into the city.[1] It is self-evident that this could only be said if Troy had but one gate."

This Scaean Gate had over it a tower, often mentioned in the *Iliad*, where it is called *the great tower of Ilium*[2] and the *divine tower*;[3] but this latter epithet may perhaps refer to its divine origin, as having been built by Poseidon, or by Apollo and Poseidon. It deserves to be mentioned that, when Homer does not use the plural of πύργος figuratively, he generally means by it the walls of defence.

There is also mentioned, close to the city wall, a chariot-road (ἀμαξιτός,[4] sc. ὁδός), which appears to have led from the Scaean Gate to the two sources of the Scamander. These sources were at a short distance from the Scaean Gate and the Erineos, probably on the other side of the road: one of them had lukewarm water, from which smoke rose as if from burning fire; the water of the other was in summer as "cold as hail or as winter-snow, or as water frozen to ice." Close to the two sources were beautiful stone washing-troughs, in which the Trojan women formerly, in the time of peace, before the arrival of the Greek army, had used to wash their clothes.[5] Close to the city wall, and probably close to the two springs, was a swamp overgrown with thick shrubs, bushes, and reeds.[6] I may remark here that swamps appear to be further indicated in the lower plain, near the Greek camp, by the reeds which Ulysses broke, and with which he made a mark on a tamarisk,[7] as well as by the heron (a bird which lives in swamps), whose cries Ulysses and Diomedes hear on leaving the camp.[8]

I have further to mention the tree (φηγός), which stood before the Scaean Gate, and which is mentioned seven times in the *Iliad*. It was a *high tree and sacred* to Zeus;[9] it is also called *the very beautiful φηγός of the aegis-bearing Zeus*.[10] On this φηγός sat Athené and Apollo, in the

---

[1] *Il.* xxii. 194–196 :
δσσάκι δ' ὁρμήσειε πυλάων Δαρδανιάων
ἀντίον ἀΐξασθαι, ἐϋδμήτους ὑπὸ πύργους,
εἴ πως οἱ καθύπερθεν ἀλάλκοιεν βελέεσσιν.

[2] *Il.* vi. 386 :
ἀλλ' ἐπὶ πύργον ἔβη μέγαν Ἰλίου.

[3] *Il.* xxi. 526 :
Ἑστήκει δ' ὁ γέρων Πρίαμος θείου ἐπὶ πύργου.

[4] *Il.* xxii. 146 :
οἱ δὲ . . . .
τείχεος αἰὲν ὑπὲκ κατ' ἀμαξιτὸν ἐσσεύοντο.

[5] *Il.* xxii. 147–156 :
κρουνὼ δ' ἵκανον καλλιῤῥόω, ἔνθα τε πηγαί
δοιαὶ ἀναΐσσουσι Σκαμάνδρου δινήεντος·
ἡ μὲν γάρ θ' ὕδατι λιαρῷ ῥέει, ἀμφὶ δὲ καπνός
γίγνεται ἐξ αὐτῆς, ὡς εἰ πυρὸς αἰθομένοιο·
ἡ δ' ἑτέρη θέρεϊ προρέει εἰκυῖα χαλάζη,
ἢ χιόνι ψυχρῇ, ἢ ἐξ ὕδατος κρυστάλλῳ·
ἔνθα δ' ἐπ' αὐτάων πλυνοὶ εὐρέες ἐγγὺς ἔασιν
καλοὶ λαΐνεοι, ὅθι εἵματα σιγαλόεντα

πλύνεσκον Τρώων ἄλοχοι, καλαί τε θύγατρες
τὸ πρὶν ἐπ' εἰρήνης, πρὶν ἐλθεῖν υἷας Ἀχαιῶν.

[6] *Od.* xiv. 472–475 :
ἀλλ' ὅτε δή ῥ' ἱκόμεσθα ποτὶ πτόλιν αἰπύ τε
　τεῖχος,
ἡμεῖς μὲν περὶ ἄστυ κατὰ ῥωπήϊα πυκνά
ἂν δόνακας καὶ ἕλος, ὑπὸ τεύχεσι πεπτηῶτες
κείμεθα.

[7] *Il.* x. 466, 467 :
　. . . . δέελον δ' ἐπὶ σῆμά τ' ἔθηκεν,
συμμάρψας δόνακας μυρίκης τ' ἐριθηλέας ὄζους.

[8] *Il.* x. 274–277 :
τοῖσι δὲ δεξιὸν ἧκεν ἐρωδιὸν ἐγγὺς ὁδοῖο
Παλλὰς Ἀθηναίη· τοὶ δ' οὐκ ἴδον ὀφθαλμοῖσιν
νύκτα δι' ὀρφναίην, ἀλλὰ κλάγξαντος ἄκουσαν·
χαῖρε δὲ τῷ ὄρνιθ' Ὀδυσεύς, ἠρᾶτο δ' Ἀθήνη.

[9] *Il.* vii. 60 :
φηγῷ ἐφ' ὑψηλῇ πατρὸς Διὸς αἰγιόχοιο.

[10] *Il.* v. 693 :
εἷσαν ὑπ' αἰγιόχοιο Διὸς περικαλλέϊ φηγῷ.

shape of vultures (*Vultur barbatus*), to enjoy the sight of the battle.[1] Under this φηγός the wounded Sarpedon is deposited by his companions.[2] Here also Hector and Agamemnon awaited each other.[3] Leaning on this φηγός, Apollo, enveloped in fog, encourages Agenor to fight against Achilles.[4] Buchholz[5] mentions that, according to Miquel,[6] φηγός is not a beech, as has been generally understood, but an oak (*Quercus esculus*), whilst Euchholz recognizes in it a chestnut-tree (*Fagus castanea*),[7] and Braun[8] a valonea-oak.

Professor Virchow,[9] in a learned dissertation on the Trojan φηγός, seems rather to incline to the opinion that the tree meant is the *Carpinus Betulus*, L., which in Germany is vulgarly called *Buche* (beech). "I found it," he says, "everywhere in the Troad; in the plain as well as in the mountains. In opposition to the real or red beech, it is called white beech or small beech (*Weiss-Hage-*, or *Hain-buche*), which even in Germany reaches a height of 70 ft. In ancient times the opinion seems to have been prevalent that the φηγός of the *Iliad* was an oak-tree. In favour of this are the accounts of the existence of very ancient φηγοί before Ilium. Theophrastus[10] mentions 'the φηγοί at Ilium on the tomb of Ilus,' among the trees which were known for their great age, being already spoken of by the 'mythologists.' In manifest connection with this remark of Theophrastus, Pliny[1] expresses himself in the following manner in a passage in which he treats of very ancient trees: 'Juxta urbem (Ilium) quercus, in Ili tumulo tunc satae dicuntur, cum coepit Ilium vocari.' Here apparently φηγούς has been rendered by *quercus*. But, whatever value may be attributed to the statement or to the translation, at all events the question is here of a number of trees, and we cannot derive from it a decision as to the *one* φηγός before Ilium."

Behind Ilium extended a plateau called the Ilian or Ileïan Plain (Πεδίον Ἰλήϊον),[2] whence the heights of Ida, overgrown with shrubs, could easily be reached.[3] From these heights flowed a river, probably the Scamander, in which Agenor thought to bathe if he could escape from Achilles.[4]

Below the wall in the plain was a wheat-field, of which I have spoken before. At a distance from Troy, near the Simois, was the hill called Callicolone. Ares, like a black storm, commands the Trojans, shouting

---

[1] *Il.* vii. 58–60 :

κὰδ δ' ἄρ' Ἀθηναίη τε καὶ ἀργυρότοξος Ἀπόλλων
ἑζέσθην, ὄρνισιν ἐοικότες αἰγυπιοῖσιν
φηγῷ ἐφ' ὑψηλῇ πατρὸς Διὸς αἰγιόχοιο.

[2] *Il.* v. 692, 693 :

οἱ μὲν ἄρ' ἀντίθεον Σαρπηδόνα δῖοι ἑταῖροι
εἷσαν ὑπ' αἰγιόχοιο Διὸς περικαλλέϊ φηγῷ.

[3] *Il.* xi. 170, 171 :

ἀλλ' ὅτε δὴ Σκαιάς τε πύλας καὶ φηγὸν ἵκοντο,
ἔνθ' ἄρα δὴ ἵσταντο, καὶ ἀλλήλους ἀνέμιμνον.

[4] *Il.* xxi. 547-549 :

ἐν μέν οἱ κραδίῃ θάρσος βάλε, πὰρ δέ οἱ αὐτὸς
ἔστη, ὅπως θανάτοιο βαρείας Κῆρας ἀλάλκοι,
φηγῷ κεκλιμένος· κεκάλυπτο δ' ἄρ' ἠέρι πολλῇ.

[5] E. Buchholz, *Homer. Kosm. und Geogr.* pp. 322, 323.

[6] *Homer. Flora.*

[7] *Flora Homer.*, Progr. p. 14.

[8] Jul. Braun, *Homer und sein Zeitalter*, S. 9.

[9] *Beiträge zur Landeskunde der Troas*, pp. 72–78.

[10] Theophrasti Eresii *de Hist. Plant.*, iv. 14 : φηγοὺς δὲ τὰς ἐν Ἰλίῳ τὰς ἐπὶ τοῦ Ἴλου μνήματος.

[1] "Cajus Plinius Secundus, *Histor. Natur.* (ed. Bipont. 1783), xvi. 88."

[2] *Il.* xxi. 558 : φεύγω πρὸς πεδίον Ἰλήϊον, ὄφρ' ἂν ἵκωμαι.

[3] *Il.* xxi. 559 : Ἴδης τε κνημούς, κατά τε ῥωπήϊα δύω.

[4] *Il.* xxi. 560 : ἑσπέριος δ' ἂν ἔπειτα λοεσσάμενος ποταμοῖο.

now from the Acropolis of Troy, now from Callicolone.[5] The Trojans, thus excited to battle by Ares, stood on the θρωσμὸς πεδίοιο, which is generally translated by "hill in the plain." But this translation is, in my opinion, altogether wrong: first, because there is no separate elevation in the Plain of Troy; secondly, because philologically the words can only mean "rising of the plain;" and, thirdly, because the sense of the three Homeric passages in which these words occur does not admit of such a translation. We read in the *Iliad*:[6] "Awake, O son of Tydeus; why dost thou indulge in sleep all night? Hearest thou not how the Trojans are encamped ἐπὶ θρωσμῷ πεδίοιο, near the ships, and that now but a small space keeps them off?" In another passage[7] we read: "The Trojans drew up ἐπὶ θρωσμῷ πεδίοιο, around great Hector and blameless Polydamas." In both these passages the θρωσμὸς πεδίοιο is the site of the Trojan camp, on the right bank of the Scamander, already referred to in the Eighth Book (vv. 489-492), where we read as follows: " Illustrious Hector then called an assembly of the Trojans, having conducted them apart from the ships on (the bank of) the eddying river, in a clear space where the ground was free from corpses; and, alighting from their horses, they listened to his speech."[8] In these verses no suggestion is made that the site of the Trojan camp, on the bank of the Scamander, was higher than the plain. We find the words θρωσμὸς πεδίοιο a third time in the *Iliad*: " Thus, O son of Peleus, around thee, insatiable of battle, stood the Achaeans armed, beside their curved ships, and the Trojans, on the other hand, ἐπὶ θρωσμῷ πεδίοιο."[9] Here also the words indicate the site of the Trojan camp, which has been previously described in *Il*. xviii. 256: " In the plain near the ships, for we are far away from the wall"—showing that the site of the camp was in the level plain near the ships. I call particular attention to the fact that, in these three cases, the poet mentions the site of the Trojan camp in opposition to the site of the Greek camp, which latter was situated on the shore of the Hellespont. Consequently the only possible translation of the θρωσμὸς πεδίοιο would be " the Upper Plain," which rises a little, but has no elevations in the shape of hills.

Before the city, but a little sideways from the Plain of Troy, there stood in a free space a high tumulus, called by men Batieia, whilst the gods called it the sepulchre of the swift Myriné; here the Trojans and their auxiliaries arrayed their troops.[10] Myriné, according to Strabo, was

---

[5] *Il*. xx. 51-53:

αὖε δ' Ἄρης ἑτέρωθεν, ἐρεμνῇ λαίλαπι ἶσος,
ὀξὺ κατ' ἀκροτάτης πόλιος Τρώεσσι κελεύων,
ἄλλοτε πὰρ Σιμόεντι θέων ἐπὶ Καλλικολώνῃ.

[6] x. 159-161:

Ἔγρεο, Τυδέος υἱέ· τί πάννυχον ὕπνον ἀωτεῖς;
οὐκ ἀΐεις, ὡς Τρῶες ἐπὶ θρωσμῷ πεδίοιο
εἵαται ἄγχι νεῶν, ὀλίγος δ' ἔτι χῶρος ἐρύκει;

[7] *Il*. xi. 56, 57:

Τρῶες δ' αὖθ' ἑτέρωθεν ἐπὶ θρωσμῷ πεδίοιο,
Ἕκτορά τ' ἀμφὶ μέγαν καὶ ἀμύμονα Πουλυδά-
μαντα.

[8] *Il*. viii. 489-492:

Τρώων αὖτ' ἀγορὴν ποιήσατο φαίδιμος Ἕκτωρ.

νόσφι νεῶν ἀγαγών, ποταμῷ ἔπι δινήεντι,
ἐν καθαρῷ, ὅθι δὴ νεκύων διεφαίνετο χῶρος.
ἐξ ἵππων δ' ἀποβάντες ἐπὶ χθόνα μῦθον ἄκουον.

[9] *Il*. xx. 1-3:

ὣς οἱ μὲν παρὰ νηυσὶ κορωνίσι θωρήσσοντο
ἀμφὶ σέ, Πηλέος υἱέ, μάχης ἀκόρητον Ἀχαιοί,
Τρῶες δ' αὖθ' ἑτέρωθεν ἐπὶ θρωσμῷ πεδίοιο.

[10] *Il*. ii. 811-815:

ἔστι δέ τις προπάροιθε πόλεος αἰπεῖα κολώνη,
ἐν πεδίῳ ἀπάνευθε, περίδρομος ἔνθα καὶ ἔνθα,
τὴν ἦ τοι ἄνδρες Βατίειαν κικλήσκουσιν,
ἀθάνατοι δέ τε σῆμα πολυσκάρθμοιο Μυρίνης·
ἔνθα τότε Τρῶές τε διέκριθεν ἠδ' ἐπίκουροι.

held, from her epithet πολύσκαρθμος ("racer"), to be one of the Amazons; this epithet being given to horses from their swiftness, and Myriné was so called from her swiftness in driving the chariot.[1] But Professor Sayce tells me that he fancies Myriné to be identical with the Amazon Smyrna, that is, a name of Artemis-Cybele, the Amazons having been in the first instance the priestesses of this Asiatic goddess. Myriné was the name of a town in Lemnos, as well as of another on the coast of Mysia, 40 stadia to the south of Grynion, and Smyrna or Samorna was an old appellation of Ephesus, whose foundation was ascribed to the Amazons. Myrrha, a name of the Oriental Aphrodité, is but a form of Smyrna, n being assimilated to the preceding r.

Homer further mentions the tumulus of Aesyetes, from the top of which Polites, son of Priam, trusting to the rapidity of his feet, sat waiting until the Achaeans should rush forward from the ships.[2] This tumulus must therefore necessarily be sought between Ilium and the Greek camp. The son of Aesyetes, Alcathoüs, was married to the daughter of Anchises, Hippodameia.[3]

At a certain distance before Ilium was, as already stated, the confluence of the Scamander and the Simois, as well as the ford of the Scamander; and near them was the tumulus of Ilus, crowned with a pillar, against which Paris leant when he shot an arrow at Diomedes and wounded him.[4] This position of the monument is also proved by the agora which Hector held far from the ships, on the bank of the Scamander,[5] and close by the tumulus of Ilus.[6] It was between the Greek camp and the Scamander, for the thousand watch-fires of the Trojan camp were seen between the ships and the river.[7] But it must be distinctly understood that, as the tumulus of Ilus was situated between the Greek camp and the Scamander, it was of necessity on or near its *left* bank, which is an important circumstance in determining the topography of the Plain of Troy. There is, however, another passage which appears to contradict this again; for Priam, on his way to visit Achilles, first passes the tumulus of Ilus, and then reaches the ford of the Scamander, where he waters his mules and horses.[8] It appears further to be contradicted by the passage where it is stated that Hector,

---

[1] Strabo, xii. p. 573: ἐν δὲ τῷ Ἰλιακῷ πεδίῳ κολώνη τις ἔστιν ἣν ἱστοροῦσι μίαν εἶναι τῶν Ἀμαζόνων ἐκ τοῦ ἐπιθέτου τεκμαιρόμενοι· εὐσκάρθμους γὰρ ἵππους λέγεσθαι διὰ τὸ τάχος κἀκείνην οὖν πολύσκαρθμον διὰ τὸ ἀπὸ τῆς ἡνιοχείας τάχος.

[2] Il. ii. 791–794:
εἴσατο δὲ φθογγὴν υἷϊ Πριάμοιο Πολίτῃ,
ὃς Τρώων σκοπὸς ἷζε, ποδωκείῃσι πεποιθώς,
τύμβῳ ἐπ' ἀκροτάτῳ Αἰσυήταο γέροντος,
δέγμενος ὁππότε ναῦφιν ἀφορμηθεῖεν Ἀχαιοί.

[3] Il. xiii. 427–429:
ἔνθ' Αἰσυήταο διοτρεφέος φίλον υἱόν,
ἥρω' Ἀλκάθοον—γαμβρὸς δ' ἦν Ἀγχίσαο,
πρεσβυτάτην δ' ὤπυιε θυγατρῶν Ἱπποδάμειαν.

[4] Il. xi. 369–372:
αὐτὰρ Ἀλέξανδρος, Ἑλένης πόσις ἠϋκόμοιο,
Τυδεΐδῃ ἔπι τόξα τιταίνετο, ποιμένι λαῶν,

στήλῃ κεκλιμένος ἀνδροκμήτῳ ἐπὶ τύμβῳ
Ἴλου Δαρδανίδαο, παλαιοῦ δημογέροντος.

[5] Il. viii. 489, 490:
Τρώων αὖτ' ἀγορὴν ποιήσατο φαίδιμος Ἕκτωρ,
νόσφι νεῶν ἀγαγών, ποταμῷ ἔπι δινήεντι.

[6] Il. x. 414, 415:
Ἕκτωρ μὲν μετὰ τοῖσιν, ὅσοι βουληφόροι εἰσίν,
βουλὰς βουλεύει θείου παρὰ σήματι Ἴλου.

[7] Il. viii. 560–563:
τόσσα μεσηγὺ νεῶν ἠδὲ Ξάνθοιο ῥοάων
Τρώων καιόντων πυρὰ φαίνετο Ἰλιόθι πρό.
χίλι' ἄρ' ἐν πεδίῳ πυρὰ καίετο, πὰρ δὲ ἑκάστῳ
εἵατο πεντήκοντα σέλᾳ πυρὸς αἰθομένοιο.

[8] Il. xxiv. 349–351:
οἱ δ' ἐπεὶ οὖν μέγα σῆμα παρὲξ Ἰλίοιο ἔλασσαν,
στῆσαν ἄρ' ἡμιόνους τε καὶ ἵππους, ὄφρα πίοιεν,
ἐν ποταμῷ.

who was fighting on the left of the battle on the bank of the Scamander, knew nothing of the slaughter[9] which was going on near the
tumulus of Ilus, where, according to *Il.* xi. 369-379, Diomedes had been
wounded by Paris.

From all the indications of the *Iliad* we see that the station of the
ships (Naustathmos) and the camp of the Greek army extended along the
low shore of the Hellespont, between Cape Sigeum and Cape Rhoeteum.
The distance between these two heights is erroneously stated by Strabo[10]
to be 60 stadia, whilst Pliny[1] gives it rightly as 30 stadia. As before
explained, the Scamander must have fallen into the Hellespont through
the bed of the present In Tepeh Asmak, close to Cape Rhoeteum.
The 1186 Greek ships were drawn up on the beach, but the available
space being too narrow, they were placed in several lines, one behind the
other, and used partly as the camp and fortifications, the sterns being
turned towards the land. To prevent the ships' keels becoming rotten,
they were put on stone supports (ἔχματα);[2] but nevertheless, after nine
years, the wood and the ropes of the ships began to rot.[3] The troops
of each tribe lay with their commander behind their ships, which served
them as a protection. The ships which had first come to land were
drawn furthest up the shore and formed the first line; the later comers
were arranged in the second or third line.[4] At the two extremities of
the first rank were the ships and camps of Achilles and Ajax; the former
to the right, at the foot of Cape Sigeum, the latter on the opposite side.[5]
To the right of Ajax would have been the Athenians, if the verse in
Il. ii. 558 had been genuine, where it is stated that Ajax placed his
ships where the Athenian phalanxes stood.[6] But this verse was already
in ancient times considered to have been interpolated by Solon or
Pisistratus on political grounds. The Athenian fleet under Menestheus
appears to have been further on in this line towards the centre, for
they defended that part of the rampart which was attacked by Hector
and Sarpedon; that is to say, at the middle gate.[7] Further on in the
same line appear to have also been the ships of the Boeotians,[8] to the

---

[9] *Il.* xi. 497-499:

.... οὐδέ πω Ἕκτωρ
πεύθετ', ἐπεί ῥα μάχης ἐπ' ἀριστερὰ μάρνατο
πάσης,
ὄχθας πὰρ ποταμοῖο Σκαμάνδρου.

[10] xiii. p. 595: ἔστι δὲ τὸ μῆκος τῆς παραλίας
ταύτης ἀπὸ τοῦ Ῥοιτείου μέχρι Σιγείου καὶ τοῦ
Ἀχιλλέως μνήματος εὐθυπλοούντων ἑξήκοντα
σταδίων.

[1] *Il. N.* v. 33: "fuit et Aeantium, a Rhodiis
conditum, in altero cornu, Ajace ibi sepulto,
xxx. stad. intervallo a Sigeo, et ipso statione
classis suae."

[2] *Il.* xiv. 410:

.... τά ῥα πολλά, θοάων ἔχματα νηῶν.

[3] *Il.* ii. 134, 135:

ἐννέα δὴ βεβάασι Διὸς μεγάλου ἐνιαυτοί,
καὶ δὴ δοῦρα σέσηπε νεῶν καὶ σπάρτα λέλυνται.

[4] *Il.* xiv. 30-34:

πολλὸν γάρ ῥ' ἀπάνευθε μάχης εἰρύατο νῆες

θῖν' ἐφ' ἁλὸς πολιῆς· τὰς γὰρ πρώτας πεδίονδε
εἴρυσαν, αὐτὰρ τεῖχος ἐπὶ πρύμνησιν ἔδειμαν.
οὐδὲ γὰρ οὐδ' εὐρύς περ ἐὼν ἐδυνήσατο πάσας
αἰγιαλὸς νῆας χαδέειν, στείνοντο δὲ λαοί.

[5] *Il.* vi. 6-9:

ἣ ῥ' ἐν μεσσάτῳ ἔσκε γεγωνέμεν ἀμφοτέρωσε,
ἠμὲν ἐπ' Αἴαντος κλισίας Τελαμωνιάδαο,
ἠδ' ἐπ' Ἀχιλλῆος, τοί ῥ' ἔσχατα νῆας ἐΐσας
εἴρυσαν, ἠνορέῃ πίσυνοι καὶ κάρτεϊ χειρῶν.

[6] *Il.* ii. 558:

στῆσε δ' ἄγων ἵν' Ἀθηναίων ἵσταντο φάλαγγες.

[7] *Il.* xii. 331, 332:

τοὺς δὲ ἰδὼν ῥίγησ' υἱὸς Πετεῶο Μενεσθεύς·
τοῦ γὰρ δὴ πρὸς πύργον ἴσαν κακότητα φέροντες.

[8] *Il.* xiii. 685-689:

ἔνθα δὲ Βοιωτοὶ καὶ Ἰάονες ἑλκεχίτωνες,
Λοκροὶ καὶ Φθῖοι καὶ φαιδιμόεντες Ἐπειοί
σπουδῇ ἐπαΐσσοντα νεῶν ἔχον, οὐδ' ἐδύναντο
ὦσαι ἀπὸ σφείων φλογὶ εἴκελον Ἕκτορα δῖον·
οἱ μὲν Ἀθηναίων προλελεγμένοι.

left of whom stood the Phoceans.[9] Thus the Athenians were succeeded by the Phoceans, and further on to the right followed the Boeotians; the last in this line to the right being the Myrmidons under Achilles.

It is difficult to determine the order of the ships in the second rank, the indications contained in the *Iliad* being too slight. Lenz[10] supposed that in this line were the Locrians under Ajax, the son of Oïleus, the Dulichians, Epeians, and so forth; for, according to the passage already quoted,[1] they were near the foremost row, whilst, according to another passage,[2] they were near the rear line. Agamemnon, Ulysses, and Diomedes are stated to have drawn their ships on shore far from the battle:[3] they must therefore have been in the last line, which, as Lenz supposes, they filled up by themselves. In the middle of this line was the little fleet of Ulysses.[4] Before this last was the Agora, which served as the place for the public assemblies, the council, the military tribunal, and the sacrifices:[5] here were the altars of the gods,[6] especially that of Zeus Panomphaeos, on which, when in great distress, Agamemnon sacrifices a fawn.[7] This Agora must have extended into the second line of ships, for the whole Greek army is frequently called hither to an assembly. As the people sat in the Agora, there must have been seats of stones or turf.[8] Nestor's ships and tents must have been in the hindmost line, as it is expressly stated that his tent was on the shore.[9] It appears very probable that Menelaus was encamped close to his brother, Agamemnon. According to the Boeotia (or Catalogue of Ships), Menelaus came with the sixty ships of the Lacedaemonians, who arrayed themselves separately (ἀπάτερθε); that is to say, they were not mixed up with Agamemnon's troops, but formed a band by themselves. Between the ships were many lanes and roads,[10] of which, as Lenz suggests, the chief ones may probably have extended between the three lines of ships, while a great number of lanes run crosswise between the ships.

There were, writes Lenz,[1] no tents such as are now in use; but all the troops had huts,[2] which were probably of wood and earth with a thatch

---

[9] *Il.* ii. 525, 526:

οἳ μὲν Φωκήων στίχας ἵστατον ἀμφιέποντες,
Βοιωτῶν δ' ἔμπλην ἐπ' ἀριστερὰ θωρήσσοντο.

[10] C. G. Lenz, *Die Ebene von Troia*; Neu Strelitz, 1798, p. 193.   [1] *Il.* xiii. 685–689.

[2] *Il.* x. 110–113:

ἠδ' (ἐγείρομεν) Αἴαντα ταχὺν καὶ Φυλέος ἄλκιμον
υἱόν.
ἀλλ' εἴ τις καὶ τούσδε μετοιχόμενος καλέσειεν,
ἀντίθεόν τ' Αἴαντα καὶ Ἰδομενῆα ἄνακτα ·
τῶν γὰρ νῆες ἔασιν ἑκαστάτω, οὐδὲ μάλ' ἐγγύς.

[3] *Il.* xiv. 29–31:

Τυδεΐδης Ὀδυσεύς τε καὶ Ἀτρείδης Ἀγαμέμνων.
πολλὸν γάρ ῥ' ἀπάνευθε μάχης εἰρύατο νῆες
θῖν' ἔφ' ἁλὸς πολιῆς.

[4] *Il.* viii. 222–226:

στῆ δ' ἐπ' Ὀδυσσῆος μεγακήτεϊ νηΐ μελαίνῃ,
ἥ ῥ' ἐν μεσσάτῳ ἔσκε, γεγωνέμεν ἀμφοτέρωσε ·
ἠμὲν ἐπ' Αἴαντος κλισίας Τελαμωνιάδαο,
ἠδ' ἐπ' Ἀχιλῆος · τοί ῥ' ἔσχατα νῆας ἐΐσας
εἴρυσαν, ἠνορέῃ πίσυνοι καὶ κάρτεϊ χειρῶν.

[5] *Il.* xix. 172–174:

. . . τὰ δὲ δῶρα ἄναξ ἀνδρῶν Ἀγαμέμνων

οἰσέτω ἐς μέσσην ἀγορήν, ἵνα πάντες Ἀχαιοὶ
ὀφθαλμοῖσιν ἴδωσι, σὺ δὲ φρεσὶ σῇσιν ἰανθῇς.

[6] *Il.* xi. 808:

. . . τῇ δὴ καί σφι θεῶν ἐτετεύχατο βωμοί.

[7] *Il.* viii. 249, 250:

πὰρ δὲ Διὸς βωμῷ περικαλλέϊ κάββαλε νεβρόν,
ἔνθα πανομφαίῳ Ζηνὶ ῥέζεσκον Ἀχαιοί.

[8] *Il.* ii. 86–99.

[9] *Il.* xi. 618–622:

οἳ δ' ὅτε δὴ κλισίην Νηληϊάδεω ἀφίκοντο,
. . . . τοὶ δ' (Νέστωρ καὶ Μαχάων) ἱδρῶ ἀπεψύ-
χοντο χιτώνων,
στάντε ποτὶ πνοιὴν παρὰ θῖν' ἁλός.

[10] *Il.* x. 66:

πολλαὶ γὰρ ἀνὰ στρατόν εἰσι κέλευθοι.

[1] C. G. Lenz, *Die Ebene von Troia*, pp. 200–203.

[2] *Il.* xvi. 155, 156:

Μυρμιδόνας δ' ἄρ' ἐποιχόμενος θώρηξεν Ἀχιλλεύς,
πάντας ἀνὰ κλισίας σὺν τεύχεσιν ·
and *Il.* xxiii. 111, 112:

οὐρῆάς τ' ὤτρυνε καὶ ἀνέρας ἀξέμεν ὕλην
πάντοθεν ἐκ κλισιῶν.

of rushes. The chief had probably his tent in the foremost line of his troops: this is certain as regards the tent of Ulysses, in front of which a lane passed, and the Agora commenced. All the tents or huts of the chiefs must have been more or less like that of Achilles, which is described in the 24th book of the *Iliad*. It was surrounded by an enclosure of posts, and had a gate which shut with a bar.[3] Inside, around the hut, was a court, in the midst of which stood an altar, for here Achilles prayed to Zeus and poured out libations of wine.[4] The hut proper, called οἶκος,[5] and μέλαθρον,[6] but usually κλισίη, was surrounded by an open vestibule, which rested on posts, and was called πρόδομος[7] and αἴθουσα,[8] from which the hall[9] was entered by an opening called πρόθυρον[10] or θύρα.[1] The hall was probably decorated with trinkets won as booty.[2] In this sense we may probably explain the *glittering walls* in the tent of Idomeneus.[3] Behind the hall were chambers, which served partly for storing the treasures, partly as a habitation for the female slaves and concubines; here also Achilles and Patroclus had their separate chambers.[4] The huts had a thatch of woolly rushes.[5] There must, besides, have been in the court sheds for chariots and stables for the horses, of which Achilles possessed a whole stud;[6] also stables for oxen, sheep, goats, and swine, as for meat-eaters like the Greeks a considerable stock of cattle was indispensable.

Near the ships of Ulysses, and along the shore as far as those of Agamemnon, there must have been a considerable space; for the races with horses and chariots, as well as the other funeral games to the memory of Patroclus, were held there. Here also was an elevated seat

---

[3] *Il.* xxiv. 452–456:
ἀμφὶ δέ οἱ μεγάλην αὐλὴν ποίησαν ἄνακτι
σταυροῖσιν πυκινοῖσι· θύρην δ' ἔχε μοῦνος ἐπιβλής
εἰλάτινος, τὴν τρεῖς μὲν ἐπιῤῥήσσεσκον Ἀχαιοί,
τρεῖς δ' ἀναοίγεσκαν μεγάλην κληῖδα θυράων,
τῶν ἄλλων· Ἀχιλεὺς δ' ἄρ' ἐπιῤῥήσσεσκε καὶ οἶος.

[4] *Il.* xvi. 231, 232:
εὔχετ' ἔπειτα στὰς μέσῳ ἕρκεϊ, λεῖβε δὲ οἶνον
οὐρανὸν εἰσανιδών· Δία δ' οὐ λάθε τερπικέραυνον.

[5] *Il.* xxiv. 471, 472:
. . . . . γέρων δ' ἰθὺς κίεν οἴκου,
τῇ ῥ' Ἀχιλεὺς ἵζεσκε διΐφιλος.

[6] *Il.* ix. 639, 640:
. . . . . σὺ δ' ἵλαον ἔνθεο θυμόν,
αἴδεσσαι δὲ μέλαθρον.

[7] *Il.* xxiv. 673, 674:
οἱ μὲν ἄρ' ἐν προδόμῳ δόμου αὐτόθι κοιμήσαντο,
κῆρυξ καὶ Πρίαμος, πυκινὰ φρεσὶ μήδε' ἔχοντες.

[8] *Il.* xxiv. 643, 644:
ἦ ῥ', Ἀχιλεὺς δ' ἑτάροισιν ἰδὲ δμωῇσι κέλευσεν
δέμνι' ὑπ' αἰθούσῃ θέμεναι καὶ ῥήγεα καλά.

[9] *Il.* xxiv. 647:
αἱ δ' ἴσαν ἐκ μεγάροιο δάος μετὰ χερσὶν
ἔχουσαι, . . .

[10] *Il.* xix. 211, 212:
ὅς μοι ἐνὶ κλισίῃ δεδαϊγμένος ὀξέϊ χαλκῷ
κεῖται, ἀνὰ πρόθυρον τετραμμένος.

[1] *Il.* xxiv. 571, 572:
ὣς ἔφατ', ἔδεισεν δ' ὁ γέρων καὶ ἐπείθετο μύθῳ·
Πηγείης δ' οἴκοιο λέων ὣς ἆλτο θύραζε.

[2] *Il.* xxiii. 558–561:
Ἀντίλοχ', εἰ μὲν δή με κελεύεις οἴκοθεν ἄλλο
Εὐμήλῳ ἐπιδοῦναι, ἐγὼ δέ κε καὶ τὸ τελέσσω.
δώσω οἱ θώρηκα τὸν Ἀστεροπαῖον ἀπηύρων,
χάλκεον, ᾧ πέρι χεῦμα φαεινοῦ κασσιτέροιο.

[3] *Il.* xiii. 261:
. . . . ἐν κλισίῃ πρὸς ἐνώπια παμφανόωντα.

[4] *Il.* ix. 663–669:
αὐτὰρ Ἀχιλλεὺς εὗδε μυχῷ κλισίης εὐπήκτου·
τῷ δ' ἄρα παρκατέλεκτο γυνή, τὴν Λεσβόθεν
ἦγεν,
Φόρβαντος θυγάτηρ Διομήδη καλλιπάρῃος.
Πάτροκλος δ' ἑτέρωθεν ἐλέξατο· πὰρ δ' ἄρα καὶ τῷ
Ἶφις ἐϋζωνος, τήν οἱ πόρε δῖος Ἀχιλλεύς
Σκύρον ἑλὼν αἰπεῖαν, Ἐνυῆος πτολίεθρον.
οἳ δ' ὅτε δὴ κλισίῃσιν ἐν Ἀτρεΐδαο γένοντο, . . .
Il. xxiv. 675, 676:
αὐτὰρ Ἀχιλλεὺς εὗδε μυχῷ κλισίης εὐπήκτου·
τῷ δ' ἄρα Βρισηῒς παρελέξατο καλλιπάρῃος.

[5] *Il.* xxiv. 450, 451:
. . . . ἀτὰρ καθύπερθεν ἔρεψαν
λαχνήεντ' ὄροφον λειμωνόθεν ἀμήσαντες.

[6] *Il.* xxiv. 281:
ἵππους δ' εἰς ἀγέλην ἔλασαν θεράποντες ἀγαυοί.
Il. ii. 775–778:
. . . . ἵπποι δὲ παρ' ἅρμασιν οἷσιν ἕκαστος,
λωτὸν ἐρεπτόμενοι ἐλεόθρεπτόν τε σέλινον,
ἕστασαν, ἅρματα δ' εὖ πεπυκασμένα κεῖτο ἀνάκτων
ἐν κλισίης.

(περιωπή),[7] as in Nestor's tent, from the top of which Idomeneus looked on at the games. Here on the projecting shore were raised the tumulus of Patroclus and at a later period that of Achilles.[8] There was also an ancient sepulchral monument, or goal of a hippodrome, consisting of the trunk of a tree with two white stones on either side,[9] and near it a road hollowed out by the winter rain.[10]

For nine years the ships of the Greeks appear to have been their sole fortification, but then, after the first battle of the *Iliad*, by the advice of Nestor, a common tumulus was erected in front of the ships over the ashes of all the dead, to which was joined a high wall with towers, and before it was dug a deep moat.[1] The wall was built of earth, into which were rammed trunks of trees and stones to give it greater solidity.[2] It had wooden towers,[3] and in or close to them were gates.[4] On the wall and the towers were breastworks (ἐπάλξεις), which projected from the wall like steps (κρόσσαι); also buttresses (στῆλαι, προβλῆτες), serving to protect and consolidate the wall.[5] There seem to have been only three gates. Between the wall and the moat was a path,[6] in front of which a stockade or thick row of palisades was stuck into the edge of the moat, in order to render the approach still more difficult to the enemy.[7]

I have further to mention the wall of Herakles (τεῖχος ἀμφίχυτον Ἡρακλῆος),[8] called also σκοπιή,[9] a sort of rampart which the Trojans and Pallas Athené had erected for the protection of Herakles, lest the sea-monster which threatened Hesioné with destruction should pursue him from the beach to the plain. It therefore appears to have been near the shore.

---

[7] *Il.* xxiii. 451 :
ἧστο γὰρ ἐκτὸς ἀγῶνος ὑπέρτατος ἐν περιωπῇ.

[8] *Il.* xxiii. 125, 126 :
κὰδ δ' ἄρ' ἐπ' ἀκτῆς βάλλον ἐπισχερώ, ἔνθ' ἄρ' Ἀχιλλεύς
φράσσατο Πατρόκλῳ μέγα ἠρίον ἠδὲ οἷ αὐτῷ.
Od. xxiv. 80–82 :
ἀμφ' αὐτοῖσι δ' ἔπειτα μέγαν καὶ ἀμύμονα τύμβον
χεύαμεν Ἀργείων ἱερὸς στρατὸς αἰχμητάων,
ἀκτῇ ἔπι προὐχούσῃ, ἐπὶ πλατεῖ Ἑλλησπόντῳ.

[9] *Il.* xxiii. 327–333 :
ἕστηκε ξύλον αὖον, ὅσον τ' ὄργυι', ὑπὲρ αἴης,
ἢ δρυὸς ἢ πεύκης· τὸ μὲν οὐ καταπύθεται ὄμβρῳ,
λᾶε δὲ τοῦ ἑκάτερθεν ἐρηρέδαται δύο λευκώ
ἐν ξυνοχῇσιν ὁδοῦ, λεῖος δ' ἱππόδρομος ἀμφίς·
ἤ τευ σῆμα βροτοῖο πάλαι κατατεθνηῶτος,
ἢ τό γε νύσσα τέτυκτο ἐπὶ προτέρων ἀνθρώπων,
καὶ νῦν τέρματ' ἔθηκε ποδάρκης δῖος Ἀχιλλεύς.

[10] *Il.* xxiii. 418–421 :
αἶψα δ' ἔπειτα
στεῖνος ὁδοῦ κοίλης ἴδεν Ἀντίλοχος μενεχάρμης.
ῥωχμὸς ἔην γαίης, ᾗ χειμέριον ἀλὲν ὕδωρ
ἐξέρρηξεν ὁδοῖο, βάθυνε δὲ χῶρον ἅπαντα.

[1] *Il.* vii. 327–347, 435–441.

[2] *Il.* xii. 28, 29 :
. . . . ἐκ δ' ἄρα πάντα θεμείλια κύμασι πέμπεν
φιτρῶν καὶ λάων, τὰ θέσαν μογέοντες Ἀχαιοί.

[3] *Il.* xii. 35, 36 :
τότε δ' ἀμφὶ μάχη ἐνοπή τε δεδήει
τεῖχος ἐϋδμητον, κανάχιζε δὲ δούρατα πύργων.

[4] *Il.* vii. 338, 339 :
πύργους ὑψηλούς, εἶλαρ νηῶν τε καὶ αὐτῶν.
ἐν δ' αὐτοῖσι πύλας ποιήσομεν εὖ ἀραρυίας·
and 436–438 :
ἄκριτον ἐκ πεδίου, ποτὶ δ' αὐτὸν τεῖχος ἔδειμαν
πύργους θ' ὑψηλούς, εἶλαρ νηῶν τε καὶ αὐτῶν.
ἐν δ' αὐτοῖσι πύλας ἐνεποίεον εὖ ἀραρυίας.

[5] *Il.* xii. 258–260 :
κρόσσας μὲν πύργων ἔρυον, καὶ ἔρειπον ἐπάλξεις,
στήλας τε προβλῆτας ἐμόχλευον, ἃς ἄρ' Ἀχαιοὶ
πρώτας ἐν γαίῃ θέσαν ἔμμεναι ἔχματα πύργων.

[6] *Il.* ix. 67, 87; xii. 64–66, 145; xviii. 215, 228; xx. 49.

[7] *Il.* xii. 63–66 : see also 54–57; vii. 941; ix. 350.

[8] *Il.* xx. 145–148 :
τεῖχος ἐς ἀμφίχυτον Ἡρακλῆος θείοιο,
ὑψηλόν, τό ῥά οἱ Τρῶες καὶ Παλλὰς Ἀθήνη
ποίεον, ὄφρα τὸ κῆτος ὑπεκπροφυγὼν ἀλέαιτο,
ὁππότε μιν σεύαιτο ἀπ' ἠΐονος πεδίονδε.

[9] *Il.* xx. 136, 137 :
ἀλλ' ἡμεῖς μὲν ἔπειτα καθεζώμεσθα κιόντες
ἐκ πάτου ἐς σκοπιήν.

CHAPTER III.

THE HISTORY OF TROY.

As Mr. Gladstone [1] rightly remarks, the Dardanian name in the *Iliad* is the oldest of all those names, found in the Poems, which are linked by a distinct genealogy with the epoch of the Trojan war. As already stated, Dardanus was called the son of Zeus by Electra, daughter of Atlas, and was further said to have come from Samothrace, or from Arcadia, or from Italy; [2] but Homer mentions nothing of this. Dardanus founded Dardania in a lofty position on the slope of Mount Ida; for he was not yet powerful enough to form a settlement in the plain. He married Bateia, an Idaean nymph, [3] daughter of Teucer, son of the river Scamander, and begat Ilus and Erichthonius, who became the richest of all mortal men. He had in his pastures three thousand mares, the offspring of some of whom, by Boreas, produced twelve colts of supernatural swiftness. [4] Having married Astyoche, daughter of the river Simois, he had by her a son called Tros. [5] This latter, who became the eponym of the Trojans, had by his wife Calirrhoë, daughter of the Scamander, three sons, called Ilus, Assaracus, and Ganymedes, and a daughter, called Cleopatra. [6] Ganymedes having become the most beautiful of mankind was carried away by the gods, and made the cup-

---

[1] *Homeric Synchronism*, p. 122.

[2] Hellanicus, *Fragm.* 129, ed. Didot; Dionys. Hal. i. 50–61; Apollodor. iii. 12. 1; Schol. *Iliad.*, xviii. 486; Varro, *ap.* Servium *ad Virgil. Aeneid.* iii. 167; Cephalon. Gergithius *ap.* Steph. Byz. s. v. 'Αρίσβη.

[3] *Il.* xx. 215–218:

Δάρδανον αὖ πρῶτον τέκετο νεφεληγερέτα Ζεύς
κτίσσε δὲ Δαρδανίην· ἐπεὶ οὔπω Ἴλιος ἱρή
ἐν πεδίῳ πεπόλιστο, πόλις μερόπων ἀνθρώπων,
ἀλλ' ἔθ' ὑπωρείας ᾤκεον πολυπίδακος Ἴδης.

Apollodorus, iii. 12. 1: Δάρδανος δὲ ἐπὶ τῷ θανάτῳ τοῦ ἀδελφοῦ λυπούμενος, Σαμοθρᾴκην ἀπολιπών, εἰς τὴν ἀντίπερα ἤπειρον ἦλθε. Ταύτης δὲ ἐβασίλευε Τεῦκρος ποταμοῦ Σκαμάνδρου καὶ Νύμφης Ἰδαίας, ἀφ' οὗ καὶ οἱ τὴν χώραν νεμόμενοι Τεῦκροι προσηγορεύοντο. Ὑποδεχθεὶς δὲ ὑπὸ τοῦ βασιλέως καὶ λαβὼν μέρος τῆς γῆς καὶ τὴν ἐκείνου θυγατέρα Βάτειαν, Δάρδανον ἔκτισε πόλιν. τελευτήσαντος δὲ Τεύκρου, τὴν χώραν ἅπασαν Δαρδανίαν ἐκάλεσε.

[4] *Il.* xx. 219–229:

Δάρδανος αὖ τέκεθ' υἱὸν Ἐριχθόνιον βασιλῆα,
ὃς δὴ ἀφνειότατος γένετο θνητῶν ἀνθρώπων·

τοῦ τρισχίλιαι ἵπποι ἕλος κάτα βουκολέοντο
θήλειαι, πώλοισιν ἀγαλλόμεναι ἀταλῇσιν.
τάων καὶ Βορέης ἠράσσατο βοσκομενάων·
ἵππῳ δ' εἰσάμενος παρελέξατο κυανοχαίτῃ,
αἳ δ' ὑποκυσσάμεναι ἔτεκον δυοκαίδεκα πώλους.
αἳ δ' ὅτε μὲν σκιρτῷεν ἐπὶ ζείδωρον ἄρουραν·
ἄκρον ἐπ' ἀνθερίκων καρπὸν θέον, οὐδὲ κατέκλων,
ἀλλ' ὅτε δὴ σκιρτῷεν ἐπ' εὐρέα νῶτα θαλάσσης,
ἄκρον ἐπὶ ῥηγμῖνα ἁλὸς πολιοῖο θέεσκον.

[5] Apollodorus, iii. 12. 2: Γενομένων δὲ αὐτῷ (Δαρδάνῳ) παίδων Ἴλου καὶ Ἐριχθονίου· Ἴλος μὲν οὖν ἄπαις ἀπέθανεν· Ἐριχθόνιος δὲ διαδεξάμενος τὴν βασιλείαν, γήμας Ἀστυόχην τὴν Σιμόεντος, τεκνοῖ Τρῶα.

Il. xx. 230:

Τρῶα δ' Ἐριχθόνιος τέκετο Τρώεσσιν ἄνακτα.

[6] Apollodorus, iii. 12. 2: οὗτος (Τρώς) παραλαβὼν τὴν βασιλείαν, τὴν μὲν χώραν ἀφ' ἑαυτοῦ Τροίαν ἐκάλεσε. Καὶ γήμας Καλιρρόην τὴν Σκαμάνδρου, γεννᾷ θυγατέρα μὲν Κλεοπάτραν, παῖδας δὲ Ἴλον καὶ Ἀσσάρακον καὶ Γανυμήδην.

Il. xx. 231, 232:

Τρωὸς δ' αὖ τρεῖς παῖδες ἀμύμονες ἐξεγένοντο,
Ἶλός τ' Ἀσσάρακός τε καὶ ἀντίθεος Γανυμήδης.

bearer of Zeus,[7] who gave to Tros, as the price of the youth, a team of immortal horses.[8]   From Ilus and Assaracus the Trojan and Dardanian lines diverge : the former proceeding from Ilus to Laomedon, Priam and Hector ; the latter from Assaracus to Capys, Anchises and Aeneas.[9]

Ilus went to Phrygia, where he arrived during the games instituted by the king, in which he took part, and, having conquered in wrestling, received from the king, as his prize of victory, fifty youths and fifty maidens. The king also gave him, in accordance with an oracle, a cow of many colours, directing him to build a city in the place where the animal should lie down. Ilus therefore followed the cow, which lay down on the hill of the Phrygian Áté, where he built Ilium. Having prayed to Zeus to give him a favourable sign, on the following day he saw lying before his tent the Palladium, which had fallen from heaven (διϊπετές). It was three cubits (4½ ft.) long, its feet were joined ; in its right hand it held an uplifted lance, in its left a distaff and spindle.[10]

In Homer Áté is represented as the personified power of infatuation and delusion, and is the pernicious eldest daughter of Zeus.[11]   She is strong and swift ;[1] Hesiod mentions her among the children of Eris ;[2] she walks with her light soft feet over the heads of men.[3]   At the birth of Herakles she caused even her own father, Zeus, to swear an over-hasty oath, in consequence of which he seized her by the hair in his wrath and cast her out of Olympus, swearing a mighty oath that

---

[7] Il. xx. 233–235 :
ὃς (Γανυμήδης) δὴ κάλλιστος γένετο θνητῶν
     ἀνθρώπων ·
τὸν καὶ ἀνηρείψαντο θεοὶ Διῒ οἰνοχοεύειν,
κάλλεος εἵνεκα οἷο, ἵν' ἀθανάτοισι μετείη.
Apollodorus, iii. 12. 2: τοῦτον μὲν οὖν διὰ κάλλος ἀναρπάσας Ζεὺς δι' ἀετοῦ, θεῶν οἰνοχόον ἐν οὐρανῷ κατέστησεν.
At first Ganymedes is mentioned as cup-bearer of the gods, and particularly of Zeus, in the place of Hebe (see Virgil, Aeneid. i. 28); afterwards, especially since Pindar, he is said to have been beloved by Zeus, κάλλεος εἵνεκα. In the same way, in Odys. v. 121, Orion, in Odys. xv. 251, Kleitos, and in Apollod. iii. 2, 4 (see Il. xi. 1) Tithonus, is carried off by Eos on account of his beauty.

[8] Hellanicus, Fragm. 146. Apollodorus, ii. 5, 9: Ταύτην ('Ησιόνην) ἰδὼν ἐκκειμένην Ἡρακλῆς, ὑπέσχετο σώσειν αὐτήν, εἰ τὰς ἵππους παρὰ Λαομέδοντος λήψεται, ἃς ὁ Ζεὺς ποινὴν τῆς Γανυμήδους ἁρπαγῆς ἔδωκε.
Il. v. 265–267 :
τῆς γάρ τοι γενεῆς, ἧς Τρωΐ περ εὐρύοπα Ζεὺς
δῶχ' υἷος ποινὴν Γανυμήδεος · οὕνεκ' ἄριστοι
ἵππων, ὅσσοι ἔασιν ὑπ' ἠῶ τ' ἠέλιόν τε.

[9] Il. xx. 236–240 :
Ἶλος δ' αὖ τέκεθ' υἱὸν ἀμύμονα Λαομέδοντα;
Λαομέδων δ' ἄρα Τιθωνὸν τέκετο Πρίαμόν τε,
Λάμπον τε Κλυτίον θ' Ἱκετάονά τ' ὄζον Ἄρηος ·
Ἀσσάρακος δὲ Κάπυν · ὃ δ' ἄρ' Ἀγχίσην τέκε
     παῖδα ·

αὐτὰρ ἔμ' Ἀγχίσης, Πρίαμος δ' ἔτεχ' Ἕκτορα
δῖον.

[10] Apollodorus, iii. 2, 3 : Ἶλος δὲ εἰς Φρυγίαν ἀφικόμενος, καὶ καταλαβὼν ὑπὸ τοῦ βασιλέως αὐτόθι τεθειμένον ἀγῶνα, νικᾷ πάλιν · καὶ λαβὼν ἆθλον πεντήκοντα κούρους καὶ κόρας τὰς ἴσας, δόντος αὐτῷ τοῦ βασιλέως κατὰ χρησμὸν καὶ βοῦν ποικίλην, καὶ φράσαντος, ἐν ᾧπερ ἂν αὐτῇ κλιθῇ τόπῳ, πόλιν κτίζειν, εἵπετο τῇ βοΐ. Ἡ δὲ ἀφικομένη ἐπὶ τὸν λεγόμενον τῆς Φρυγίας Ἄτης λόφον, κλίνεται · ἔνθα πόλιν κτίσας Ἶλος, ταύτην μὲν Ἴλιον ἐκάλεσε. Τῷ δὲ Διῒ σημεῖον εὐξάμενος αὐτῷ τι φανῆναι, μεθ' ἡμέραν τὸ διϊπετὲς Παλλάδιον πρὸ τῆς σκηνῆς κείμενον ἐθεάσατο. Ἦν δὲ τῷ μεγέθει τρίπηχυ, τοῖς δὲ ποσὶ συμβεβηκός, καὶ τῇ μὲν δεξιᾷ δόρυ διηρμένον ἔχον, τῇ δὲ ἑτέρᾳ ἠλακάτην καὶ ἄτρακτον.

[11] Il. xix. 91–93 :
πρέσβα Διὸς θυγάτηρ Ἄτη, ἣ πάντας ἀᾶται,
οὐλομένη, τῆς μέν θ' ἁπαλοὶ πόδες · οὐ γὰρ ἐπ'
     οὔδει
πίλναται, ἀλλ' ἄρα ἥγε κατ' ἀνδρῶν κράατα
     βαίνει.

[1] Il. ix. 505–507 :
ἡ δ' Ἄτη σθεναρή τε καὶ ἀρτίπος · οὕνεκα πάσας
πολλὸν ὑπεκπροθέει, φθάνει δέ τε πᾶσαν ἐπ' αἶαν
βλάπτουσ' ἀνθρώπους.

[2] Theogonia, 230 :
Δυσνομίην, Ἄτην τε, συνήθεας ἀλλήλῃσιν.

[3] Il. xix. 91–93, just cited. See also Rhianus, ap. Stob. Mor. iv. p. 54.

she should not return thither; and she quickly fell on the works of men.[4]

The tradition cited above from Apollodorus is confirmed by Lycophron[5] as well as by Eustathius,[6] Hesychius,[7] and Stephanus Byzantinus.[8] From all these authorities my friend Professor Otto Keller[9] has concluded with certainty "the existence of a Phrygian goddess Até, her worship on the hill of Hissarlik as well as on a second hill on the river Rhyndacus, and her idol which fell from heaven.[10] The Ilian Athené, who originated from this Até, appears on a medal as an especially Phrygian goddess, wearing the Phrygian cap. She is distinguished from the common Greek Até or infatuation, who is a mere abstraction, by the epithet ἡ Φρυγία. Probably she was related to the Phrygian god Atis (Attis or Atys). Owing to the similarity in the sound of their names, after the conquest of the land by the Greeks, Até and Athené were combined, and thus originated the peculiar Athené Ilias with the Phrygian cap, spear, torch, and owl. The non-Hellenic torch was replaced by the distaff and spindle. In the Ephesian Artemis we see before us a very non-Hellenic, but genuine Asiatic goddess, confounded with an Hellenic goddess; nay, a goddess overloaded with symbols of maternity confounded with a virgin goddess. We have examples of the remoulding of the names of Asiatic deities in a Greek form, amongst others, in Eileithyia-Yoledeth, Moledeth, Mylitta ; or in Apollo Ismenius, who is the Phoenician Eshmun ; for the common etymology from the Indo-European *ish*, ' desire,' is not satisfactory. Even the Zeus Meili-

---

[4] *Il.* xix. 126–131 :

αὐτίκα δ᾽ εἷλ᾽ Ἄτην κεφαλῆς λιπαροπλοκάμοιο,
χωόμενος φρεσὶν ᾗσι, καὶ ὤμοσε καρτερὸν ὅρκον
μή ποτ᾽ ἐς Οὔλυμπόν τε καὶ οὐρανὸν ἀστερόεντα
αὖτις ἐλεύσεσθαι Ἄτην, ἣ πάντας ἀᾶται.
ὣς εἰπὼν ἔρριψεν ἀπ᾽ οὐρανοῦ ἀστερόεντος
χειρὶ περιστρέψας · τάχα δ᾽ ἵκετο ἔργ᾽ ἀνθρώπων.

[5] *Alexandra*, 28–30 :

ἡ δ᾽ ἔνθεον σχάσασα βακχεῖον στόμα,
Ἄτης ἀπ᾽ ἄκρων βουπλανοκτίστων λόφων,
τοιῶν δ᾽ ἀπ᾽ ἀρχῆς ἦρχ᾽ Ἀλεξάνδρα λόγων.

See Schol. Vindobon. I. *ap.* Bachmann, p. 15 : λόφος πρὸ τοῦ ἐκαλεῖτο καὶ Ἄλιος (probably instead of Ἄτιος) ; and Tzetzes : ἄτης ἤγουν βλάβης, ἢ ὄνομα ὄρους, λόφον ἄτης καὶ βουπλανόκτιστον τὴν Τροίαν λέγει . . . . Δάρδανος δὲ κατακλυσμοῦ γεγονότος ἐκ Σαμοθράκης εἰς τὴν ἀντιπέρα γῆν περαιοῦται καὶ τὴν νῦν Τροίαν ἔμελλε κτίζειν. Χρησμὸς δὲ τοῦτον κωλύει κτίζειν τὸν λόφον τοῦτον εἰπὼν βλάβην γενέσθαι τοῦτον τοῖς αὐτὸν κατοικήσασιν. ἐν Πριήπῳ δὲ ἐμαντεύσατο. ἔχρησε δὲ αὐτῷ ὁ Πριηπαῖος Ἀπόλλων μὴ κτίζειν τὸν λόφον τοῦτον, ἄτης γὰρ αὐτὸν ἔφη. διὸ καὶ Δάρδανος κωλυθεὶς αὐτὸν οὐκ ἔκτισεν, ἀλλὰ τὴν ὑπὸ τὴν Ἴδην Δαρδανίαν, πρότερον Σκαμάνδρου λόφον καλουμένην, βασιλεύοντος τότε τῶν Τρωϊκῶν μερῶν Τεύκρου τοῦ Σκαμάνδρου καὶ Ἰδαίας νύμφης. οὗ Σκαμάνδρου τὴν θυγατέρα Βάτειαν λαβὼν ὁ Δάρδανος, ἣν καὶ ὁ Λυκόφρων Ἀρίσβην λέγει, γεννᾷ Ἴλον καὶ Ἐριχθόνιον · ὧν

Ἴλος ἄπαις τελευτᾷ, Ἐριχθόνιος δὲ ἐξ Ἀστυόχης τῆς Σιμόεντος γεννᾷ Τρῶα. Τρωὸς καὶ Καλλιρρόης τῆς Σκαμάνδρου Ἴος (sic) καὶ ἕτεροι. Ὃς Ἴλος εἰς Φρυγίαν ἐλθὼν καὶ ἀγῶνα ὑπὸ τοῦ βασιλέως τεθειμένον εὑρὼν νικᾷ πάλην, καὶ λαβὼν ἐκ τοῦ βασιλέως ἄθλον ν κόρας καὶ ν κόρους, ἐκ χρησμοῦ εἵπετο βοΐ πλανηθείσῃ ἐκ Μυσίας, ἥτις ἀφικομένη ἐπὶ τὸν λεγόμενον τῆς Φρυγίας Ἄτης λόφον κατακλίνεται, ἔνθα πόλιν κτίσας ὁ Ἴλος Ἴλιον ἐκάλεσε.

[6] Eustath. *ad Il.* xix. 136 : φασὶ δὲ εἰς Ἴλιον κατενηνέχθαι ῥιφεῖσαν τὴν Ἄτην, διὸ καὶ Ἄτης λόφος ἐκεῖ, οὗ ὁ Λυκόφρων μέμνηται. τοῦτο δὲ ἀστείως πέπλασται διὰ τὰς μεγάλας ἄτας, ὡς ἐκ Διὸς οἱ Τρῶες ἔπαθον. Schol. *in Il.* i. 591 : λόφον Ἄτης ἐν Τροίᾳ παρὰ Λυκόφρονι, ἔνθα ὑπὸ Διὸς ἐκείνη ἐρρίφη, ὡς καὶ ἐν τοῖς Ἀπίωνος καὶ Ἡροδώρου δηλοῦται.

[7] S. v. Ἀτιόλοφος· οὕτως τὸ Ἴλιον (Ἴλεον cod.) ἐκαλεῖτο πρῶτον.

[8] Ἴλιον πόλις Τρωάδος ἀπὸ Ἴλου, ἥν οἱ Τρῶες Ἄτην (ἄτην in the MS.) ἐκάλουν καὶ Ἄτης λόφον· δευτέρα (αὐτῆς λόφοι δύο in the MS.) ἐν τῇ Προποντίδι παρὰ Ῥυνδάκῳ ποταμῷ.

[9] *Die Entdeckunj Ilion's zu Hissarlik* ; Freiburg, 1875.

[10] Schol. *ad Il.* i. 591 : ἔνθα ὑπὸ Διὸς ἐκείνη ἐρρίφη ; also Apollodorus, iii. 12, and Diodorus, *Fragm.* 14, p. 640 ; Wessel. a διϊπετές.

chios, with his soft name, is only the Hellenic mask of the terrible Moloch, greedy of human sacrifices.

" Now with regard to the cow of many colours, this animal is quite in its place in the tradition of the foundation of the temple of the Ilian Athené. Nay, it may serve as an authentic proof of the genuineness and antiquity of the legend, which is told us by Apollodorus, and was certainly not invented by him. The legend of which we speak is common Indo-European property.[1]   Horses, stags, bears, and bulls designate the place where churches and monasteries are to be built; these animals direct also the building of castles, cities, and colonies. A god-sent animal is wont to show the wandering army their place of settlement.   Sacred cows indicate by standing still the place for church building.[2]   We find similar legends in Friedreich.[3]   To this class belong, the legend of the Opicians who were guided by a bull, and the peculiar rite of drawing the furrows with a plough whereby Roman cities were consecrated.   A cow also showed Cadmus, when he came from Asia, the site where Thebes was to be erected : *this cow had on each side a white mark in the form of the full moon.*[4]   A cow, probably *likewise a symbol of the moon goddess*, was the symbol on the coins of the Cilician cities of Tarsus, Mallus, and Soloi, likewise of Side.[5]   We also see the cow on the medals of the neighbouring Cyzicus.[6]   Marquardt[7] refers this to Persephone.   We think we are not mistaken in understanding the cow of many colours, which indicated the site of Troy, as the sacred symbol of Athené or Até, the goddess of Night or the Moon.   The fifty boys and fifty girls who follow the moon-cow are nothing else than the fifty weeks of the year.[8] From the Ilian coins, on which is represented the sacrifice of a cow before the statue of Athené Ilias, we infer that the cow was chosen as the sacrificial animal of that goddess,[9] which seems also to be proved from Homer.[10]   Thus for every one who does not wilfully shut his eyes we have furnished the proof that the legend of the foundation of Ilium is by no means a frivolous or childish invention of Apollodorus, but an ancient legend of primitive growth, which is devised with beautiful symbolism, and relates to the peculiarities of the worship of the Ilian Athené. Nay, this legend also contains a very interesting topographical notice concerning the hill of Até, a notice which has not been understood either by the narrators themselves, or till now by the commentators.

---

[1] See H. B. Schindler, *Aberglaube des Mittelalters*, p. 265.

[2] Vernaleken, *Apensagen*, 316.

[3] *Symbolik und Mythologie der Natur*, p. 498.

[4] Pausanias, ix. 12, § 1 : Λέγεται δὲ καὶ ὅδε ὑπ' αὐτῶν λόγος, ὡς ἀπιόντι ἐκ Δελφῶν Κάδμῳ τὴν ἐπὶ Φωκέων βοῦς γένοιτο ἡγεμὼν τῆς πορείας, τὴν δὲ βοῦν ταύτην παρὰ βουκόλων εἶναι τῶν Πελάγοντος ὠνητήν· ἐπὶ δὲ ἑκατέρᾳ τῆς βοὸς πλευρᾷ σημεῖον ἐπεῖναι λευκόν, εἰκασμένον κύκλῳ τῆς σελήνης, ὁπότε εἴη πλήρης· ἔδει δὲ ἄρα Κάδμον καὶ τὸν σὺν αὐτῷ στρατὸν ἐνταῦθα οἰκῆσαι κατὰ τοῦ θεοῦ τὴν μαντείαν, ἔνθα ἡ βοῦς

ἔμελλε καμοῦσα ὀκλάσειν· ἀποφαίνουσιν οὖν καὶ τοῦτο τὸ χωρίον.

[5] Brandis, *Münzwesen in Vorderasien*, p. 354.

[6] Mionnet, Nos. 168, 308, 410 ; see also Sestini, *Descr. d. Stateri Ant.* p. 54.

[7] *Cyzicus und sein Gebiet*, p. 134.

[8] See E. Gerhard, *Prodromus*, p. 167.

[9] Müller, Wieseler, and Oesterley, *D. A. K.* ii. 21, 222 ; Sestini, *Descr. Num.* vii. 3, p. 396 ; Pellerin, *R. et V.* ii. 31. 3.

[10] *Il.* vi. 93, 94 :

καί οἱ ὑποσχέσθαι δυοκαίδεκα βοῦς ἐνὶ νηῷ ἤνις ἠκέστας, ἱερευσέμεν, εἴ κ' ἐλεήσῃ.

To this the medieval legends of the saints offer hundreds of parallels, which German science has only lately understood in the sense in which, as I have shown, it must be understood in the legend of the hill of Até."

Thus, according to the tradition, sacred Ilios was built by Ilus, who married Eurydice, daughter of Adrastus. His son Laomedon married, as some said, Strymo, daughter of the Scamander, according to others Plakia, daughter of Atreus or of Leucippos; his sons were Tithonus, Lampon, Clytius, Hicetaon, Podarces; his daughters, Hesione, Cilla, and Astyoche.[1] As already stated, it was under Laomedon that the walls of Troy were built by Poseidon alone,[2] or by him and Apollo,[3] and also that the city was attacked and captured by Herakles, who killed the king and all his sons except Podarces. Herakles having allowed Hesioné to choose from among them whomsoever she wished, she chose Podarces; but Herakles demanded that he should first be sold as a slave, allowing her to buy him afterwards with whatever she pleased. He was therefore sold, and Hesioné bought him back with her veil, in consequence of which he was called Priam (Πρίαμος, from πρίασθαι, "to purchase," particip. πριάμενος).[4]

Grote[5] says: "As Dardanus, Trôs, and Ilos are respectively eponyms of Dardania, Troy, and Ilium, so Priam is eponym of the Acropolis Pergamum. Πρίαμος is in the Aeolic dialect Πέρραμος (Hesychius): upon which Ahrens remarks, 'caeterum ex hac Aeolica nominis forma apparet, Priamum non minus arcis Περγάμων eponymum esse, quam Ilum urbis, Troëm populi; Πέργαμα enim a Περίαμα natum est, ι in γ mutato.'"[6]

I may here remind the reader that there were several cities of a similar name; first the celebrated Pergamon in the Mysian province of Teuthrania, and then Pergamus in Crete, considered by Cramer[7] to be identical with the present Perama on the north side of the island. According to Virgil,[8] this latter city was founded by Aeneas.

Priam married the Phrygian princess Hecabé (Lat. Hecuba), daughter of Cisseus, who is a very distinguished character in the *Iliad*. By

---

[1] Apollodorus, iii. 2, 3 : Ἴλος δὲ γήμας Εὐρυδίκην τὴν Ἀδράστου, Λαομέδοντα ἐγέννησεν · ὃς γαμεῖ Στρυμὼ τὴν Σκαμάνδρου · κατὰ δέ τινας, Πλακίαν τὴν Ἀτρέως, κατ᾽ ἐνίους δέ, Λευκίππου · καὶ τεκνοῖ παῖδας μὲν Τιθωνόν, Λάμπωνα, Κλύτιον, Ἱκετάονα, Ποδάρκην · θυγατέρας δέ, Ἡσιόνην, καὶ Κίλλαν καὶ Ἀστυόχην.

[2] Il. xxi. 442–449 :
μέμνηαι, ὅσα δὴ πάθομεν κακὰ Ἴλιον ἀμφίς
μοῦνοι νῶϊ θεῶν, ὅτ᾽ ἀγήνορι Λαομέδοντι
πὰρ Διὸς ἐλθόντες θητεύσαμεν εἰς ἐνιαυτόν
μισθῷ ἔπι ῥητῷ · ὃ δὲ σημαίνων ἐπέτελλεν.
ἦ τοι ἐγὼ Τρώεσσι πόλιν πέρι τεῖχος ἔδειμα,
εὐρύ τε καὶ μάλα καλόν, ἵν᾽ ἄρρηκτος πόλις εἴη ·
Φοῖβε, σὺ δ᾽ εἰλίποδας ἕλικας βοῦς βουκολέεσκες
Ἴδης ἐν κνημοῖσι πολυπτύχου ὑλησσσης.

[3] Il. vii. 449–453 :
τεῖχος ἐτειχίσσαντο νεῶν ὕπερ, ἀμφὶ δὲ τάφρον

ἤλασαν, οὐδὲ θεοῖσι δόσαν κλειτὰς ἑκατόμβας ;
τοῦ δ᾽ ἦ τοι κλέος ἔσται ὅσον τ᾽ ἐπὶ κίδναται ἠώς ·
τοῦ δ᾽ ἐπιλήσονται, τὸ ἐγὼ καὶ Φοῖβος Ἀπόλλων
ἥρῳ Λαομέδοντι πολίσσαμεν ἀθλήσαντες.

[4] Apollodorus, ii. 6. 4 : καὶ ταύτῃ (Ἡσιόνῃ) συγχωρεῖ τῶν αἰχμαλώτων, ὃν ἤθελεν ἄγεσθαι. Τῆς δὲ αἱρουμένης τὸν ἀδελφὸν Ποδάρκην, ἔφη δεῖν πρῶτον αὐτὸν δοῦλον γενέσθαι, καὶ τότε, τί ποτε δοῦσαν ἀντ᾽ αὐτοῦ, λαβεῖν αὐτόν. Ἡ δέ, πιπρασκομένου, τὴν καλύπτραν ἀφελομένη τῆς κεφαλῆς ἀντέδωκεν · ὅθεν Ποδάρκης Πρίαμος ἐκλήθη.

[5] *History of Greece*, i. p. 265.

[6] Ahrens, *De Dialecto Aeolica*, 8. 7, p. 56 ; compare *ibid*. 28. 8, p. 150, περρ̀ ἀπάλω.

[7] Cramer, *Desc. of Anc. Greece*, iii. p. 383.

[8] *Aen*. iii. 133.

her and other women he had fifty sons and twelve daughters.[9] Among the sons were Hector,[10] Paris, Deïphobus, Helenus, Troïlus, Polites, Polydorus; among the daughters, Laodice, Creüsa, Polyxena, and Cassandra, were the most distinguished. The birth of Paris was preceded by formidable presages; for Hecuba dreamed that she was delivered of a firebrand, and Priam, on consulting the soothsayers, was informed that the son about to be born would cause the destruction of Troy. Accordingly he was exposed on Mount Ida, was brought up by shepherds, and was finally recognized and adopted by his parents.[1] He was distinguished for beauty and strength, and was a courageous defender of the flocks and shepherds, for which reason he was called Alexandros (defender of men).[2]   By his wife Oenone, daughter of the river Cebren, he had a son Corythus.[3] To Paris came the three goddesses, Heré, Aphrodité, and Athené, that he might decide the dispute which had arisen among them at the nuptials of Thetis and Peleus, as to which of them was the most beautiful. Paris awarded the prize to Aphrodité, who had promised him the most beautiful of women for his wife; in consequence of which Heré and Athené became the bitter enemies of Troy.[4] Paris then built ships and went on a visit to Sparta, where he was hospitably received by Menelaus, whose wife Helen he carried off, together with large treasures, under the protection of Aphrodité,[5] and returned by way of Egypt and Phoenicia to Troy.[6] Menelaus found universal sympathy among the Greek chiefs. Ten years were spent in equipping the expedition destined to avenge the outrage. By the united efforts of all the Greek chiefs a force was at length assembled at Aulis in Boeotia, consisting of 1186 ships and more than 100,000 men, under the command of the ἄναξ ἀνδρῶν, Agamemnon, king of Mycenae. This force outnumbered by more than ten to one any that the Trojans could oppose to it, and was superior to the defenders of Troy even with all her allies included.[7]

---

[9] Il. vi. 242–250:

ἀλλ' ὅτε δὴ Πριάμοιο δόμον περικαλλέ' ἵκανεν,
ξεστῆς αἰθούσῃσι τετυγμένον—αὐτὰρ ἐν αὐτῷ
πεντήκοντ' ἔνεσαν θάλαμοι ξεστοῖο λίθοιο,
πλησίοι ἀλλήλων δεδμημένοι· ἔνθα δὲ παῖδες
κοιμῶντο Πριάμοιο παρὰ μνηστῆς ἀλόχοισιν.
κουράων δ' ἑτέρωθεν ἐναντίοι ἔνδοθεν αὐλῆς
δώδεκ' ἔσαν τέγεοι θάλαμοι ξεστοῖο λίθοιο,
πλησίοι ἀλλήλων δεδμημένοι· ἔνθα δὲ γαμβροί
κοιμῶντο Πριάμοιο παρ' αἰδοίης ἀλόχοισιν.

[10] Grote, History of Greece, vol. i. p. 265, remarks: "Hector was affirmed, both by Stesichorus and Ibykus, to be the son of Apollo (Stesichorus, ap. Schol. Ven. ad Iliad. xxiv. 259; Ibyci Fragm. xiv. ed. Schneidewin): both Euphorion (Fr. 125, Meincke) and Alexander Aetolus follow the same idea. Stesichorus further stated, that after the siege Apollo had carried Hekabé away into Lykia to rescue her from captivity (Pausanias, x. 27. 1). According to Euripides, Apollo had promised that she should die in Troy (Troad. 427). By Sappho, Hector was given as a surname of Zeus, Ζεὺς Ἕκτωρ (Hesychius, s. v.

Ἕκτορες). A prince belonging to the regal family of Chios, anterior to the Ionian settlement, as mentioned by the Chian poet Iôn (Pausanias, vii. 3. 3), was so called."

[1] Apollodorus, iii. 11. 5; Hyg. Fab. 91; Ovid, Her. xvi. 45, and 359; Homer, Il. iii. 325, xii. 93; Serv. ad Virg. Aen. v. 370.

[2] Apollodorus, iii. 12. 5; Schol. Hom. Il. iii. 325.

[3] Tzetz. ad Lycophr. 57; Conon, Narr. 22; Parthen. Erot. 34.

[4] Serv. ad Virg. Aen. i. 27; Il. xxiv. 25; Tzetz. ad Lycophr. 93.

[5] Hom. Il. iii. 46–49, 144; vii. 350–363; Apollodorus, iii. 12. 6. See also Paus. iii. 22. 2; also in the argument of the Cyprian Poem (comp. Aeschyl., Agamemnon, 534).

[6] Hom. Od. iv. 228; Il. vi. 291; Herod. ii. 113.

[7] Il. ii. 128. As Grote remarks, Uschold makes the total as great as 135,000 men (Geschichte des Troianischen Krieges, p. 9; Stuttgart, 1836).

After many hindrances, the fleet at last reached the shore of the Plain of Troy. The Trojans had gathered troops from all the districts of their own country between the Aesepus and the Caïcus, as well as allies from various parts of Asia Minor and Thrace: Carians, Mysians, Lycians under Sarpedon, Maeonians, Phrygians, Thracians, Paeonians, and Alizonians.[8] But the Trojans in vain opposed the landing; they were routed and driven within their walls. After this, the war was carried on with little vigour for nine years, during which the Greeks seem to have occupied their time principally in attacks on neighbouring cities. Thus Achilles stormed Thebé, Lyrnessus, Pedasus, Lesbos, and other places, twelve towns on the coast and eleven in the interior. "Ten years was," as Grote[9] remarks, "the fixed epical duration of the siege of Troy, just as five years was the duration of the siege of Kamikus by the Kretan armament, which came to avenge the death of Minos.[10] Ten years of preparation, ten years of siege, and ten years of wandering for Odysseus, were periods suited to the rough chronological dashes of the ancient epic, and suggesting no doubts nor difficulties with the original hearers. But it was otherwise when the same events came to be contemplated by the historicising Greeks, who could not be satisfied without either finding or inventing satisfactory bonds of coherence between the separate events. Thucydides tells us that the Greeks were less numerous than the poets have represented, and that, being moreover very poor, they were unable to procure adequate and constant provisions: hence they were compelled to disperse their army, and to employ a part of it in cultivating the Chersonese, a part in marauding expeditions over the neighbourhood. Could the whole army have been employed at once against Troy (he says), the siege would have been much more speedily and easily concluded.[1] If the great historian could permit himself thus to amend the legend in so many points, we might have imagined that a simpler course would have been to include the duration of the siege among the list of poetical exaggerations, and to affirm that the real siege had lasted only one year instead of ten. But it seems that the ten years' duration was so capital a feature in the ancient tale, that no critic ventured to meddle with it."

The *Iliad* describes the events of the war in the tenth year during a period of fifty-one days. It begins with the wrath of Achilles, of which

---

[8] See the Catalogue of the Trojans, *Il.* ii. 815–877.

[9] *History of Greece*, i. p. 274.

[10] Herodotus, vii. 170. Ten years is a proper mythical period for a great war to last. The war between the Olympic gods and the Titan gods lasts ten years (Hesiod, *Theogon.* 636): compare δεκάτῳ ἐνιαυτῷ (Hom. *Od.* xvi. 17).

[1] Thucyd. i. 11: Αἴτιον δ' ἦν οὐχ ἡ ὀλιγανθρωπία τοσοῦτον, ὅσον ἡ ἀχρηματία· τῆς γὰρ τροφῆς ἀπορίᾳ τόν τε στρατὸν ἐλάσσω ἤγαγον, καὶ ὅσον ἤλπιζον αὐτόθεν πολεμοῦντα βιοτεύσειν, ἐπειδή τε ἀφικόμενοι μάχῃ ἐκράτησαν (δῆλον δέ· τὸ γὰρ ἔρυμα τῷ στρατοπέδῳ οὐκ ἂν ἐτειχίσαντο), φαίνονται δ' οὐδ' ἐνταῦθα πάσῃ τῇ δυνάμει χρησάμενοι, ἀλλὰ πρὸς γεωργίαν τῆς Χερσονήσου τραπόμενοι καὶ λῃστείαν τῆς τροφῆς ἀπορίᾳ· ἦ καὶ μᾶλλον οἱ Τρῶες αὐτῶν διεσπαρμένων τὰ δέκα ἔτη ἀντεῖχον βίᾳ τοῖς ἀεὶ ὑπολειπομένοις ἀντίπαλοι ὄντες· περιουσίαν δὲ εἰ ἦλθον ἔχοντες τροφῆς, καὶ ὄντες ἀθρόοι ἄνευ λῃστείας καὶ γεωργίας ξυνεχῶς τὸν πόλεμον διέφερον, ῥᾳδίως ἂν μάχῃ κρατοῦντες εἷλον, οἵγε καὶ οὐκ ἀθρόοι, ἀλλὰ μέρει τῷ ἀεὶ παρόντι ἀντεῖχον· πολιορκίᾳ δ' ἂν προσκαθεζόμενοι ἐν ἐλάσσονί τε χρόνῳ καὶ ἀπονώτερον τὴν Τροίαν εἷλον· ἀλλὰ δι' ἀχρηματίαν τά τε πρὸ τούτων ἀσθενῆ ἦν, καὶ αὐτά γε δὴ ταῦτα ὀνομαστότατα τῶν πρὶν γενόμενα δηλοῦται τοῖς ἔργοις ὑποδεέστερα ὄντα τῆς φήμης καὶ τοῦ νῦν περὶ αὐτῶν διὰ τοὺς ποιητὰς λόγον κατεσχηκότος.

Apollo was the originating cause, from eagerness to avenge the injury which his priest Chryses had suffered from Agamemnon. Under the influence of his anger, Achilles refuses to put on his armour, and keeps his Myrmidons in the camp. The other Greek chiefs vainly strove to make amends for this hero's absence. The humiliation which they underwent was severe; they were many times defeated by Hector and the Trojans, and driven to their ships. At last the fearful distress of the Greeks aroused the anxious and sympathising Patroclus, who extorted a reluctant consent from Achilles to allow him and the Myrmidons to avert the last extremity of ruin. Patroclus was killed by Hector, when Achilles, forgetting his anger, drove the Trojans with great slaughter within their walls, and killed Hector, with whose funeral the *Iliad* ends.

Then—to follow the story from the allusions in Homer, and from later epic poets and mythologists—there came from Thrace to the relief of the Trojans the beautiful warlike queen of the Amazons, Penthesileia, with a band of her countrywomen; but she too was slain by the invincible arm of Achilles.

The dismayed Trojans were again animated with hope by the arrival of Memnon,[2] son of Tithonus and Eös, the most stately of living men, with a troop of Aethiopians, who at first made great havoc among the Greeks, and killed even the hero Antilochus, son of Nestor; but at last Memnon himself was slain by Achilles in single combat. After proving, by a series of most ingenious arguments, that in all probability Memnon was the leader of the Keteioi or Hittites, Mr. Gladstone[3] adds: "Now, if Memnon were leader of the Keteioi, it may be observed, in the first place, that this country lay far eastward in the same parallel of latitude as Southern Greece; and he might therefore, with ample consistency, be called by the poet, son of the Morning. And most certainly the Homeric statement, that Memnon was the famous son of the Morning, would be in thorough accordance both with the poet's geographical idea of the East and sunrise, which the *Odyssey* by no means carries far towards the south, and with the fame to which the Khita (Keteioi), as the resolute and somewhat successful opponents of the vast Egyptian power, may well have attained." Memnon's tomb was shown on a hill near the mouth of the Aesepus in the Propontis.[4]

Soon after Memnon's death, Achilles himself was slain near the Scaean Gate by an arrow from the quiver of Paris.[5] According to Dictys Cretensis (iii. 29), the murder took place in the temple of Apollo at Thymbra, whither Achilles had gone to marry Polyxena.[6]

[2] *Odyss.* xi. 522:
κεῖνον δὴ κάλλιστον ἴδον μετὰ Μέμνονα δῖον.
See also *Od.* iv. 187; Pindar, *Pyth.* vi. 31. Aeschylus (*ap.* Strab. xv. p. 728) conceives Memnon as a Persian, who had come from Susa.

According to Ctesias, the expedition under Memnon was sent by the king of Assyria to the relief of his vassal, Priam of Troy. Ctesias pretended to have got this information from the royal archives. According to Diodorus (ii. 22 and iv. 77), the Egyptians asserted that Memnon had come from Egypt.

[3] *Homeric Synchronism*, p. 178.

[4] Strabo, xiii. p. 587: ὑπὲρ δὲ τῆς ἐκβολῆς τοῦ Αἰσήπου σχεδόν τι . . . . σταδίους κολωνὸς ἔστιν, ἐφ᾽ ᾧ τάφος δείκνυται Μέμνονος τοῦ Τιθωνοῦ.

[5] *Il.* xxii. 360; Soph. *Philoct.* 334; Virgil, *Aen.* vi. 56.

[6] See Philostratus, *Her.* 19. 11; Hyginus, *Fab.* 107, 110; Q. Smyrnæus, iii. 50; Tzetzes, *ad* Lycophr. 307.

The Greeks learned from Helenus, son of Priam, whom Ulysses had captured in ambuscade,[7] that Troy could not be taken unless both Philoctetes and Neoptolemus, the son of Achilles, joined the besiegers. The former had been left on Lemnos at the beginning of the campaign, having been stung in the foot by a serpent, and having become intolerable to the Greeks from the stench of the wound. But he had still the peerless bow and arrows of Herakles, which were said to be essential to the capture of Troy. He was brought by Diomedes to the Greek camp, and healed by Machaon;[8] he fought bravely against the Trojans, and killed Paris in single combat with one of the arrows of Herakles. Ulysses fetched Neoptolemus from Scyros, whilst the Trojans were reinforced by Eurypylus, king of the Keteioi (or Khita), on the Caïcus, who was son of Telephus and Astyoché, sister of Priam. He came with a large band and killed Machaon, but was himself slain by Neoptolemus.[9] This son of Achilles drove the Trojans back with great slaughter within their walls, from whence they never again came forth to give battle.[10]

But nevertheless Troy was to remain impregnable so long as it retained the Palladium, which—as we have before said—had been given by Zeus to the founder of the city, Ilus. Ulysses, however, having disguised his person with miserable clothes and self-inflicted wounds, introduced himself into the city, and found means to carry away the Palladium by stealth. He was recognized only by Helen, who concerted with him means for the capture of the town.[1] A final stratagem was resorted to. At the suggestion of Athené, Epeius and Panopeus constructed a hollow wooden horse, capacious enough to contain a hundred men. In this horse the most eminent of the Greek heroes concealed themselves, whilst the whole Greek army, having burnt their tents and pretended to give up the siege, sailed away with their ships, which they anchored behind Tenedos. Overjoyed to see themselves finally relieved, the Trojans issued from the city and wondered at the stupendous horse, on which was written, that it was dedicated to Athené by the departing Greeks. They were long at a loss what to do with it; and the anxious heroes from within heard their consultations, as well as the voice of Helen, when she pronounced the name of each hero, counterfeiting the accent of his wife's voice.[2] Some desired to bring it into the city and to dedicate it to the gods; others advised distrust of the enemy's legacy. Laocoön, the priest of Poseidon, came with his two sons, and, in his indignation, thrust his spear against the horse. The sound revealed that the horse was hollow; but at the same moment Laocoön

---

[7] Soph. *Philoct.* 604.

[8] Sophocles (*Philoct.* 1437, 1438) makes Herakles send Asklepius to the Greek camp to heal the wound.

[9] Pausanias, iii. 26, § 7.

[10] *Odyss.* xi. 510–520 ; Quint. Smyrn. vii. 533–544, viii. 201.

[1] Arctinus, *ap.* Dionys. Halic. i. 69 ; Hom. *Od.* iv. 244–264 ; Virg. *Aen.* ii. 161–167 ; Quint.

Smyrn. x. 351–360. With this legend about the Palladium may be compared, as Grote suggests, the Roman legend respecting the Ancilia (Ovid, *Fasti*, iii. 381).

[2] *Odyss.* iv. 275–289 ; *Aen.* ii. 13–20. Stesichorus gave, as Grote states, in his 'Ιλίου Πέρσις, the number of heroes in the wooden horse as 100. (Stesichor. *Fragm.* 26, ed. Kleine ; compare Athenaeus, xiii. p. 610.)

and one of his sons perished miserably, two monstrous serpents having been sent by Heré out of the sea to destroy them. The Trojans, terrified by this spectacle, and persuaded by the perfidious counsels of the traitor Sinon—who had been expressly left behind by the Greeks to give them false information—were induced to drag the fatal fabric into their city; and, as the gate was not broad enough to admit it, they even made a breach in their own wall. Thus the horse was introduced into the Acropolis, and placed in the Agora before Priam's palace. But even now opinions were divided; many demanding that the horse should be cut in pieces, others advising that it should be dragged to the highest point of the Acropolis, and thrown thence on the rocks below. The strongest party, however, insisted on its being dedicated to the gods, as a token of gratitude for their deliverance.[3]

After sunset the Greek fleet returned to the shore of the Plain of Troy, and awaited the preconcerted signal. Whilst the Trojans indulged in riotous festivities, Sinon kindled the fire-signal and assisted the concealed heroes to open the secret door in the horse's belly, out of which they descended. The city was now assailed from within and without, and was completely sacked and destroyed, nearly the whole population being slain. Priam, who had vainly sought refuge at the altar of Zeus Herkeios, was killed by Neoptolemus. His son Deïphobus, who, after the death of his brother Paris, had become the husband of Helen, was attacked by Ulysses and Menelaus: he defended his house desperately, but was finally overcome and slain. Thus Menelaus at length won back his wife.[4]

---

[3] *Odys.* viii. 492, xi. 523 ; the Argument of the 'Ιλίου Πέρσις of Arctinus, p. 21 ; Bacchylides and Euphorion, *ap.* Servium, *ad Aen.* ii. 201.

Grote, *History of Greece*, i. 280, says : " Both Sinon and Laocoön originally came from the old epic poem of Arctinus, though Virgil may perhaps have immediately borrowed both them, and other matters in his second book, from a poem passing under the name of Pisander. (Macrob. *Saturn.* v. 2 ; Heyne, *Excurs.* 1 *ad Aen.* ii.; Welcker, *Der epische Cyclus*, p. 97.) In Quintus Smyrnaeus (xii. 366), the Trojans torture and mutilate Sinon to extort from him the truth ; his endurance, sustained by the inspiration of Heré, is proof against the extremity of suffering, and he adheres to his false tale. This is probably an incident of the old epic, though the delicate taste of Virgil, and his sympathy with the Trojans, induced him to omit it. Euphorion ascribed the proceedings of Sinon to Ulysses ; he also gave a different cause for the death of Laocoön. (*Fragm.* 35, 36, p. 55, ed. Düntz, in the *Fragments of Epic Poets after Alexander the Great*.) Sinon is ἑταῖρος 'Οδυσσέως in Pausanias, x. 27. 1."

[4] *Odys.* viii. 492-520 :

ἀλλ' ἄγε δὴ μετάβηθι, καὶ ἵππου κόσμον ἄεισον,
δουρατέου, τὸν 'Επειὸς ἐποίησεν σὺν 'Αθήνῃ,
ὅν ποτ' ἐς ἀκρόπολιν δόλον ἤγαγε δῖος 'Οδυσσεύς,
ἀνδρῶν ἐμπλήσας, οἳ Ἴλιον ἐξαλάπαξαν.
αἵ κεν δή μοι ταῦτα κατὰ μοῖραν καταλέξῃς,

αὐτίκα καὶ πᾶσιν μυθήσομαι ἀνθρώποισιν,
ὡς ἄρα τοι πρόφρων θεὸς ὤπασε θέσπιν ἀοιδήν.
ὣς φάθ', ὃ δ' ὁρμηθεὶς θεοῦ ἤρχετο, φαῖνε δ' ἀοιδήν,
ἔνθεν ἑλὼν ὡς οἱ μὲν ἐϋσσέλμων ἐπὶ νηῶν
βάντες ἀπέπλειον, πῦρ ἐν κλισίῃσι βαλόντες,
'Αργεῖοι, τοὶ δ' ἤδη ἀγακλυτὸν ἀμφ' 'Οδυσῆα
εἴατ' ἐνὶ Τρώων ἀγορῇ κεκαλυμμένοι ἵππῳ ·
αὐτοὶ γάρ μιν Τρῶες ἐς ἀκρόπολιν ἐρύσαντο.
ὣς ὃ μὲν ἑστήκει, τοὶ δ' ἄκριτα πόλλ' ἀγόρευον,
ἥμενοι ἀμφ' αὐτόν · τρίχα δέ σφισιν ἥνδανε βουλή,
ἠὲ διαπλῆξαι κοῖλον δόρυ νηλέϊ χαλκῷ,
ἢ κατὰ πετράων βαλέειν ἐρύσαντας ἐπ' ἄκρης,
ἠὲ ἐᾶν μέγ' ἄγαλμα θεῶν θελκτήριον εἶναι,
τῇ περ δὴ καὶ ἔπειτα τελευτήσεσθαι ἔμελλεν ·
αἶσα γὰρ ἦν ἀπολέσθαι, ἐπὴν πόλις ἀμφικαλύψῃ
δουράτεον μέγαν ἵππον, ὅθ' εἴατο πάντες ἄριστοι
'Αργείων Τρώεσσι φόνον καὶ κῆρα φέροντες.
ἤειδεν δ' ὡς ἄστυ διέπραθον υἷες 'Αχαιῶν
ἱππόθεν ἐκχύμενοι, κοῖλον λόχον ἐκπρολιπόντες.
ἄλλον δ' ἄλλῃ ἄειδε πόλιν κεραϊζέμεν αἰπήν,
αὐτὰρ 'Οδυσσῆα προτὶ δώματα Δηϊφόβοιο
βήμεναι, ἠΰτ' Ἄρηα, σὺν ἀντιθέῳ Μενελάῳ.
κεῖθι δὴ αἰνότατον πόλεμον φάτο τολμήσαντα
νικῆσαι καὶ ἔπειτα διὰ μεγάθυμον 'Αθήνην.

But the story of Helen and of the Trojan war was differently told by the priests of Memphis to Herodotus, who gives us the following account of it (Herodotus, translated by Rawlinson, ii. 113-121): "The priests, in answer to my enquiries on the subject of Helen, informed me

Thus Troy was destroyed, as Aeschylus says : the altars, the temples,

of the following particulars." [Here Rawlinson (p. 184) justly observes that the fact of Homer having believed that Helen went to Egypt only proves that the story was not invented in the time of Herodotus, but was current long before.] "When Alexander had carried off Helen from Sparta, he took ship and sailed homewards. On his way across the Aegean, a gale arose, which drove him from his course and took him down to the sea of Egypt. Hence, as the wind did not abate, he was carried on to the coast, when he went ashore, landing at the Salt-pans, in that mouth of the Nile which is now called the Canobic. At this place there stood upon the shore a temple, which still exists, dedicated to Hercules. If a slave runs away from his master, and taking sanctuary at this shrine gives himself up to the god, and receives certain sacred marks upon his person, whosoever his master may be, he cannot lay hand on him. This law still remained unchanged to my time. Hearing, therefore, of the custom of the place, the attendants of Alexander deserted him and fled to the temple, where they sat as suppliants. While there, wishing to damage their master, they accused him to the Egyptians, narrating all the circumstances of the rape of Helen and the wrong done to Menelaus. These charges they brought, not only before the priests, but also before the warden of that mouth of the river, whose name was Thônis. As soon as he received the intelligence, Thônis sent a message to Proteus, who was at Memphis, to this effect: 'A stranger is arrived from Greece; he is by race a Teucrian, and has done a wicked deed in the country from which he is come. Having beguiled the wife of the man whose guest he was, he carried her away with him, and much treasure also. Compelled by stress of weather, he has now put in here. Are we to let him depart as he came, or shall we seize what he has brought?' Proteus replied, 'Seize the man, be he who he may, that has dealt thus wickedly with his friend, and bring him before me, that I may hear what he will say for himself.' Thônis, on receiving these orders, arrested Alexander, and stopped the departure of his ships; then, taking with him Alexander, Helen, the treasures, and also the fugitive slaves, he went up to Memphis. When all were arrived, Proteus asked Alexander, 'who he was, and whence he had come.' Alexander replied by giving his descent, the name of his country, and a true account of his late voyage. Then Proteus questioned him as to how he got possession of Helen. In his reply Alexander became confused, and diverged from the truth, whereon the slaves interposed, confuted his statements, and told the whole history of the crime. Finally, Proteus delivered judgment as follows: 'Did I not regard it as a matter of the utmost consequence, that no stranger driven to my country

by adverse winds should ever be put to death, I would certainly have avenged the Greek by slaying thee. Thou basest of men,—after accepting hospitality, to do so wicked a deed! First, thou didst seduce the wife of thy own host; then, not content therewith, thou must violently excite her mind and steal her away from her husband. Nay, even then thou wert not satisfied, but, on leaving, thou must plunder the house in which thou hadst been a guest. Now then, as I think it of the greatest importance to put no stranger to death, I suffer thee to depart; but the woman and the treasures I shall not permit to be carried away. Here they must stay till the Greek stranger comes in person and takes them back with him. For thyself and thy companions, I command thee to be gone from my land within the space of three days; and I warn you that, otherwise, at the end of that time you will be treated as enemies.' Such was the tale told me by the priests concerning the arrival of Helen at the court of Proteus. It seems to me that Homer was acquainted with this story; and, while discarding it, because he thought it less adapted for epic poetry than the version which he followed, showed that it was not unknown to him. This is evident from the travels which he assigns to Alexander in the *Iliad*—and let it be borne in mind that he has nowhere else contradicted himself—making him to be carried out of his course on his return with Helen, and after diverse wanderings come at last to Sidon in Phoenicia. The passage is in the Bravery of Diomed (*Iliad*, vi. 289–292), and the words are as follows :—

' There were the robes, many coloured, the work of Sidonian women :
They from Sidon had come, what time god-shaped Alexander
Over the broad sea brought, that way, the high-born Helen.'

ἔνθ' ἔσαν οἱ πέπλοι παμποίκιλοι, ἔργα γυναικῶν
Σιδονίων, τὰς αὐτὸς Ἀλέξανδρος θεοειδὴς
ἤγαγε Σιδονίηθεν, ἐπιπλὼς εὐρέα πόντον,
τὴν ὁδὸν ἣν Ἑλένην περ ἀνήγαγεν εὐπατέρειαν.

" In the *Odyssey* also the same fact is alluded to, in these words (*Odyss.* iv. 227–230) :—

' Such, so wisely prepared, were the drugs that her stores afforded,
Excellent gift which once Polydamna, partner of Thônis,
Gave her in Egypt, where many the simples that grow in the meadows,
Potent to cure in part, in part as potent to injure.'

τοῖα Διὸς θυγάτηρ ἔχε φάρμακα μητιόεντα
ἐσθλά, τά οἱ Πολύδαμνα πόρεν, Θῶνος παράκοιτις,
Αἰγυπτίη, τῇ πλεῖστα φέρει ζείδωρος ἄρουρα
φάρμακα, πολλὰ μὲν ἐσθλὰ μεμιγμένα πολλὰ δὲ λυγρά.

and the population perished.[5] Antenor—having rejected with indigna-

Menelaus, too, in the same poem, thus addresses Telemachus (*Odyss.* iv. 351, 352):—

'Much did I long to return, but the gods still
     kept me in Egypt—
Angry because I had failed to pay them their
     hecatombs duly.'

Αἰγύπτῳ μ' ἔτι δεῦρο θεοὶ μεμαῶτα νέεσθαι
ἔσχον, ἐπεὶ οὔ σφιν ἔρεξα τεληέσσας ἑκατόμβας.

"In these places Homer shows himself acquainted with the voyage of Alexander to Egypt, for Syria borders on Egypt, and the Phoenicians, to whom Sidon belongs, dwell in Syria. From these various passages, and from that about Sidon especially, it is clear that Homer did not write the *Cypria*: for there it is said that Alexander arrived at Ilium with Helen on the third day after he left Sparta, the wind having been favourable, and the sea smooth; whereas in the *Iliad*, the poet makes him wander before he brings her home. Enough, however, for the present of Homer and the *Cypria*. I made enquiry of the priests, whether the story which the Greeks tell about Ilium is a fable, or no. In reply they related the following particulars, of which they declared that Menelaus had himself informed them. After the rape of Helen, a vast army of Greeks, wishing to render help to Menelaus, set sail for the Teucrian territory; on their arrival they disembarked, and formed their camp, after which they sent ambassadors to Ilium, of whom Menelaus was one. The embassy was received within the walls, and demanded the restoration of Helen, with the treasures which Alexander had carried off, and likewise required satisfaction for the wrong done. The Teucrians gave at once the answer, in which they persisted ever afterwards, backing their assertions sometimes even with oaths, to wit, that neither Helen nor the treasures claimed were in their possession; both the one and the other had remained, they said, in Egypt; and it was not just to come upon them for what Proteus, king of Egypt, was detaining. The Greeks, imagining that the Teucrians were merely laughing at them, laid siege to the town, and never rested until they finally took it. As, however, no Helen was found, and they were still told the same story, they at length believed in its truth, and despatched Menelaus to the court of Proteus. So Menelaus travelled to Egypt, and on his arrival sailed up the river as far as Memphis, and related all that had happened. He met with the utmost hospitality, received Helen back unharmed, and recovered all his treasures. After this friendly treatment, Menelaus, they said, behaved most unjustly towards the Egyptians; for as it happened that at the time when he wanted to take his departure he was detained by the wind being contrary, and as he found this obstruction continue, he had recourse to a most wicked expedient. He seized,

they said, two children of the people of the country, and offered them up in sacrifice. When this became known, the indignation of the people was stirred, and they went in pursuit of Menelaus, who, however, escaped with his ships to Libya, after which the Egyptians could not say whither he went. The rest they knew full well, partly by the enquiries which they had made, and partly from the circumstances having taken place in their own land, and therefore not admitting of doubt. Such is the account given by the Egyptian priests, and I am myself inclined to regard as true all they say of Helen from the following considerations:—If Helen had been at Troy, the inhabitants would, I think, have given her up to the Greeks, whether Alexander consented to it or no. For surely neither Priam nor his family could have been so infatuated as to endanger their own persons, their children, and their city, merely that Alexander might possess Helen. At any rate, if they determined to refuse at first, yet afterwards, when so many of the Trojans fell in every encounter with the Greeks, and Priam, too, in each battle lost a son, or sometimes two or three, or even more, if we may credit the epic poets, I do not believe that even if Priam himself had been married to her he would have declined to deliver her up, with the view of bringing the series of calamities to a close. Nor was it as if Alexander had been heir to the crown, in which case he might have had the chief management of affairs, since Priam was already old. Hector, who was his elder brother, and a far braver man, stood before him, and was the heir to the kingdom on the death of their father Priam. And it could not be Hector's interest to uphold his brother in his wrong, when it brought such dire calamities upon himself and the other Trojans. But the fact was that they had no Helen to deliver, and so they told the Greeks, but the Greeks would not believe what they said; Divine Providence, as I think, so willing, that, by their utter destruction, it might be made evident to all men that when great wrongs are done by men the gods will surely visit them with great punishments. Such, at least, is my view of the matter. When Proteus died, Rhampsinitus, the priests informed me, succeeded to the throne." Rawlinson (p. 190) thinks this is evidently the name of a king Ramses of the 19th dynasty, and probably of Ramses III. This supposition is confirmed by Brugsch (*Hist. of Egypt*), who shows that Ramses III. was called *Ramessu pa Nuter*, i.e. "Ramses the god" —a name at once convertible into Rhampsinitus, and also that the robbing of the treasury is quite consistent with events in this king's reign related in an Egyptian papyrus.

    [5] Aeschyl. *Agamemnon*, 527, 528:
        Βωμοὶ δ' ἄϊστοι καὶ θεῶν ἱδρύματα,
        καὶ σπέρμα πάσης ἐξαπόλλυται χθονός.

tion the suggestion of some Trojans to slay Ulysses and Menelaus, when, previous to the war, they had come as ambassadors to Troy and were his guests, and having moreover publicly defended them—was always regarded favourably by the Greeks; and he as well as Aeneas were allowed to escape with their families. But there is a version, according to which they had betrayed the city to the Greeks, and a panther's skin hung out of Antenor's door was the signal to the besiegers to spare the house.[6] Hector's son, Astyanax, was cast from the top of the wall and killed. Priam's daughter, Polyxena, was immolated by Neoptolemus on the tomb of Achilles. According to the tradition, Achilles had fallen in love with her; the Trojans had promised to give her to him on the condition that he should make peace, but, when he came to negociate it, he was treacherously wounded by Paris. When dying, therefore, he had demanded that, after the capture of Troy, Polyxena should be sacrificed on his sepulchre, which was done by his son.[7] According to another version, Polyxena had fled to the Greek camp after the death of Achilles, and had immolated herself with a sword on the tomb of her lover.[8] Her sister, Cassandra, had sought refuge in the temple and at the altar of the Ilian Athené, whose statue she embraced. Here Ajax, son of Oïleus, made an attempt to violate her, and he seized her so that the idol fell. This sacrilegious deed caused universal indignation among the Greeks, who could hardly be restrained from stoning Ajax to death; he only saved himself by escaping to the altar of the goddess.[9] But he had drawn both on himself and his country the grievous wrath of Athené. Whilst he himself miserably perished on his homeward voyage, a terrible pestilence broke out in Locris. The oracle of Apollo having been consulted, the god said that the wrath of Athené could only be appeased if the Locrians sent annually two noble virgins to Ilium, to do menial service in the temple of the goddess. This the Locrians scrupulously performed until shortly before the time of Plutarch.[10]

Neoptolemus received as his prize both Andromache and Helenus. After his death, Helenus became king of Chaonia, and married Andromache, whom the Molossian kings considered as their heroic mother.[1] Antenor went by sea with a body of Eneti or Veneti from Paphlagonia, who were allies of Troy, into the inner part of the Adriatic Gulf, where he vanquished the neighbouring barbarians, and founded Patavium, the present Padua. The Veneti (founders of Venice) were said to owe their origin to this immigration.[2]

As to the fate of Aeneas, the traditions were manifold. We hear of

---

[6] Grote (*History of Greece*, i. p. 281) remarks that this symbol of treachery also figured in the picture of Polygnotus, but that a different story appears in Schol. *ad Iliad*. iii. 206.

[7] Serv. *ad Virg. Aen.* iii. 322.

[8] Philostr. *Her.* xix. 11 : see also *Vit. Apollon.* iv. 16 ; Tzetz. *ad Lycophr.* 323.

[9] Arctinus, 'Ιλίου Πέρσις in the *Excerpta* of Proclos ; see Welcker, *Ep. Cycl.* ii. pp. 185 and 522. See also the representation on the chest of Cypselus, in Pausanias, v. 19. 1 ; Euripides,

Troad. 69.

[10] Timaeus Siculus, *ap.* Tzetz. *Lycophr.* 1145 ; Callimachus, *ap.* Schol. *ad Il.* xiii. 66 ; Welcker, *Griech. Frag.* i. p. 164 ; Plutarch, *Ser. Numin. Vindict.* p. 557, with the citation from Euphorion or Callimachus; Düntzer, *Epicc. Vett.* p. 118.

[1] Virg. *Aen.* iii. 294–490 ; Pausanias, i. 11. 1, ii. 23. 6 ; Lesches, *Fragm.* 7 (ed. Düntzer), *ap.* Schol. *Lycophr.* 1263 ; see also Schol. ad 1232.

[2] Strabo, v. 212 ; Ovid, *Fasti*, iv. 75 ; Liv. i. 1, xxxix. 22 ; Servius, *ad Aeneid.* i. 242.

him, as Grote[3] observes, " at Aenus in Thrace, in Pallene, at Aeneia in
the Thermaic Gulf, in Delos, at Orchomenus and Mantineia in Arcadia;
in the islands of Cythera and Zacynthus; in Leucas and Ambracia, at
Buthrotum in Epirus, on the Solentine peninsula and various other
places in the southern region of Italy; at Drepana and Segesta in Sicily,
at Carthage, at Cape Palinurus, Cumae, Misenum, Caieta, and finally
in Latium, where he lays the first humble foundation of the mighty
Rome and her empire.[4] But Aeneas was, like Hector, worshipped as a
god[5] in Novum Ilium; and we have the remarkable statement of the
Lesbian Menecrates, that Aeneas, 'having been wronged by Paris, and
stripped of the sacred privileges which belonged to him, avenged himself
by betraying the city, and then became one of the Greeks.'[6]   One
tale among many respecting Aeneas, and that too the most ancient of all,
thus preserved among the natives of the Troad, who worshipped Aeneas
as their heroic ancestor, was that, after the capture of Troy, he continued
in the country as king of the remaining Trojans, on friendly terms with
the Greeks."

This tale appears to be fully confirmed by Homer, who informs us, in
the first place, that Aeneas always bore a grudge against Priam, because
he did not appreciate him, though he was one of the most valiant of his
men;[7] in the second place, that Aeneas and his descendants should reign
over the Trojans.   He gives us this latter information in the prophetic
words which he puts into the mouth of Poseidon, a god who is always
favourable to the Greeks, and even fights for them, but who here saves
the Trojan or rather Dardanian Aeneas from certain death; nay, even the
implacable Trojan-hating goddess Heré assents to the proceeding: "Well,
let us snatch him (Aeneas) from death, lest Jove be wroth if Achilles
slays him. It is destined to him to escape, that the race of Dardanus
should not perish without descendants and be forgotten,—of Dardanus
whom the son of Kronos loved most of all the children whom he begat by
mortal women.   For the race of Priam has now become odious to the
son of Kronos; now, therefore, shall the power of Aeneas rule over the
Trojans, and his sons' sons, who shall hereafter be born."[8]

---

[3] History of Greece, i. p. 292.

[4] Dionys. Halic. Ant. Rom. i. 48–54; Heyne,
Excurs. 1 ad Aeneid. iii. De Aeneae Erroribus, and
Excurs. 1 ad Aeneid. v.; Conon, Narr. 46; Livy,
xi. 4; Steph. Byz. s. v. Aἴνεια. The inhabitants
of Aeneia on the Thermaic Gulf worshipped him
with great solemnity as their heroic founder
(Pausan. iii. 22. 4; viii. 12. 4). The tomb of
Anchises was shown on the confines of the Arca-
dian Orchomenus and Mantineia (compare Steph.
Byz. s. v. Κάφυαι), under the mountain called
Anchisia, near the temple of Aphrodité. On the
discrepancies respecting the death of Anchises,
see Heyne, Excurs. 17 ad Aen. iii. Segesta in
Sicily claimed to be founded by Aeneas (Cicero,
Verr. iv. 33).

[5] Lycophron, 1208, and Schol.; Athenagoras,
Legat. 1; Inscription in Clarke's Travels, vol. ii.
p. 86: Οἱ Ἰλιεῖς τὸν πάτριον θεὸν Αἰνείαν.

Lucian. Deorum Concil. c. 12, i. 111, p. 534,
ed. Hemst.

[6] Menecrat. ap. Dionys. Hal. i. 48: Ἀχαιοὺς
δ' ἀνίη εἶχε (after the burial of Paris) καὶ
ἐδόκεον τῆς στρατιῆς τὴν κεφαλὴν ἀπηράχθαι.
Ὅμως δὲ τάφον αὐτῷ δαίσαντες, ἐπολέμεον γῇ
πάσῃ ἄχρις Ἴλιος ἑάλω, Αἰνείεω ἐνδόντος. Αἰ-
νείης γὰρ ἄτιτος ἐὼν ὑπὸ Ἀλεξάνδρου καὶ ἀπὸ
γερέων ἱερῶν ἐξειργόμενος, ἀνέτρεψε Πρίαμον,
ἐργασάμενος δὲ ταῦτα, εἷς Ἀχαιῶν ἐγεγόνει.

[7] Il. xiii. 460, 461:
[Αἰνείας] αἰεὶ γὰρ Πριάμῳ ἐπεμήνιε δίῳ
Οὕνεκ' ἄρ' ἐσθλὸν ἐόντα μετ' ἀνδράσιν οὔ τι τί-
        εσκεν.

[8] Il. xx. 300–308:
ἀλλ' ἄγεθ', ἡμεῖς πέρ μιν ὑπὲκ θανάτου ἀγάγωμεν,
μή πως καὶ Κρονίδης κεχολώσεται, εἴ κεν Ἀχιλ-
        λεὺς
τόν δὲ κατακτείνῃ· μόριμον δέ οἵ ἐστ' ἀλέασθαι,
        [ὄφρα

Again, Poseidon tells Aeneas that he has nothing to dread from any other Greek than Achilles.[9] I here call particular attention to another passage in the *Iliad*,[10] in which Achilles taunts Aeneas with being a candidate for the throne of Troy after the death of Priam.

Strabo, who rejects all other traditions regarding Aeneas, infers from this clear Homeric statement that Aeneas remained at Troy, that he reigned there after the extinction of Priam's dynasty, and that his sons and their descendants reigned after him.[1] If, therefore, we accept it as an historical truth, that Troy was rebuilt after its destruction, and that Aeneas and his descendants reigned over it, we find nothing extraordinary in the fact that the Locrian maidens were periodically sent to Ilium, and that this custom should have been continued for such a long number of centuries. Mr. Gladstone[2] holds that "Poseidon's prophecy has every sign of being founded on what actually occurred immediately after the Troïca; and for this reason, that it was a tradition most unlikely to be invented. The part taken by Aeneas in the war was not one of high distinction; and his character, cold and timid, was one very far removed from the sympathies of the poet and his countrymen; he appears as the representative of the Dardanian branch, with a sidelong jealous eye towards the predominating Ilian house of Priam. It is a statement by no means congenial to the general purpose of the poem, which next after Achilles glorifies the Achaians, and, after the Achaians, the house of Priam. But, on the other hand, nothing could be more probable or more natural than that, after the Greeks had withdrawn, some social or political order should be established in Troas, and that its establishment should be effected, after the ruin of the house of Priam, under the surviving representative of the family which probably was a senior branch, and which manifestly stood next in influence and power. We are nowhere told that Dardanié was, like so many other cities, destroyed in the war. The friendship of Poseidon possibly indicates its possession of some foreign alliance or sympathy, not enjoyed by the Trojans proper, whom Poseidon hated; and if it be replied that such a sovereignty was more likely to be in Dardanié than in a rebuilt Ilion, I answer that this is just what the text seems to contemplate, for it says that the might of Aeneas shall reign, not in Troy, but over the Trojans (*Troessin anaxei*), and the Troës are the people of the Troad (see *e.g. Il.* ii. 824-826)."

Grote[3] says that these "passages regarding Aeneas have been construed by various able critics to refer to a family of philo-Hellenic

---

ὄφρα μὴ ἄσπερμος γενεὴ καὶ ἄφαντος ὄληται
Δαρδάνου, ὃν Κρονίδης περὶ πάντων φίλατο παί-
　　δων,
οἳ ἔθεν ἐξεγένοντο γυναικῶν τε θνητάων.
ἤδη γὰρ Πριάμου γενεὴν ἤχθηρε Κρονίων·
νῦν δὲ δὴ Αἰνείαο βίη Τρώεσσιν ἀνάξει
καὶ παίδων παῖδες, τοί κεν μετόπισθε γένωνται.
　　[9] *Il.* xx. 339:
οὐ μὴν γάρ τίς σ᾽ ἄλλος Ἀχαιῶν ἐξεναρίξει.
　　[10] *Il.* xx. 178-181:
Αἰνεία, τί σὺ τόσσον ὁμίλου πολλὸν ἐπελθὼν
ἔστης; ἦ σέ γε θυμὸς ἐμοὶ μαχέσασθαι ἀνώγει

ἐλπόμενον Τρώεσσιν ἀνάξειν ἱπποδάμοισιν
τιμῆς τῆς Πριάμου;
　　[1] Strabo, xiii. p. 608: "Ὅμηρος μέντοι συνη-
γορεῖν οὐδετέροις ἔοικεν, οὐδὲ τοῖς περὶ τῶν
ἀρχηγετῶν τῆς Σκήψεως λεχθεῖσιν· ἐμφαίνει
γὰρ μεμενηκότα τὸν Αἰνείαν ἐν τῇ Τροίᾳ καὶ
διαδεδεγμένον τὴν ἀρχὴν καὶ παραδεδωκότα παισὶ
παίδων τὴν διαδοχὴν αὐτῆς, ἠφανισμένου τοῦ
τῶν Πρισμιδῶν γένους.
　　[2] *Homeric Synchronism*, p. 34.
　　[3] *History of Greece*, i. p. 291.

or semi-Hellenic Aeneadae, known even in the time of the early singers
of the *Iliad* as masters of some territory in or near the Troad, and
professing to be descended from, as well as worshipping, Aeneas." The
Scepsian critic Demetrius, a contemporary of Crates and Aristarchus
(about 180 B.C.),[4] who wrote a Commentary in thirty books on the Homeric
catalogue of the Trojans,[5] and whose arguments are in nearly every point
adopted by Strabo, who did not visit the Troad himself—this Demetrius
informs us that Scamandrius, the son of Hector, and Ascanius, the son
of Aeneas, were founders of his native town, which had been originally
situated above the city of Cebren, on one of the highest ranges of Ida,
near Polichne, and was subsequently transferred by them 60 stadia lower
down, to the site where it stood in his time : these two families are said
by Demetrius to have reigned there for a long time. Demetrius believed
that the ancient town (Palaescepsis) had been the royal residence of
Aeneas, as it was situated midway between his dominion and Lyrnessus,
whither he had fled when pursued by Achilles.[6] But, as has been said
before, this conjecture of Demetrius is not admitted by Strabo, who
believed that Aeneas and his descendants reigned in Troy. According to
one passage in Strabo,[7] Novum Ilium and the Temple of Athené were
built during the dominion of the Lydian kings, and therefore at some
period later than 720 B.C. ; but, according to another passage in the same
author,[8] it was only built under Croesus (560-546 B.C.). But we shall
be able to show in the subsequent pages that this chronology is
altogether erroneous, because the pottery found in my trenches at
Hissarlik proves that the site has continued to be inhabited.

Novum Ilium was situated on a low height in the plain ; that is to
say, nearly in its centre, because the ridge whose western spur it occupies
extends almost to the middle of the plain. This western spur is surrounded on three sides by the plain, into which it slopes gradually on
the west and south sides, whereas to the north and north-east it falls
off at an angle of 45° ; it is, according to M. Burnouf's measurement,
49·43 mètres = 162 ft. above the level of the sea.

The distance from Novum Ilium in a straight line to the Hellespont
is, according to Scylax,[9] 25 stadia, but in reality it is rather more
than 3 miles, and to Cape Sigeum 4 miles.

It was inhabited by Aeolic Greeks, and remained a town of incon-
siderable power, until after the time of Alexander the Great, and even
until the period of the Roman dominion, as we see from the fact that
Rhoeteum, Sigeum, and Achilleum, though situated at distances of
between 3 and 4 miles from it, were all independent of Ilium.[10] But,
nevertheless, it was raised into importance by the legendary reverence

---

[4] Strabo, xiii. p. 609.

[5] Strabo, xiii. p. 603.

[6] Strabo, xiii. p. 607 ; Homer, *Iliad.* xx. 188–
191 ; Nicolaus *ap.* Steph. Byz. s. v. Ἀσκανία.

[7] xiii. p. 601.

[8] xiii. p. 593 ; according to the reading of
κατὰ Κροῖσον, restored by Kramer (from two
MSS.) for the κατὰ χρησμόν of the MSS.

[9] § 95 : Ἐντεῦθεν δὲ Τρωὰς ἄρχεται, καὶ πόλεις
Ἑλληνίδες εἰσὶν ἐν αὐτῇ αἵδε· Δάρδανος, Ῥοίτειον, Ἴλιον (ἀπέχει δὲ ἀπὸ τῆς θαλάττης στάδια
κὲ) καὶ ἐν αὐτῇ ποταμὸς Σκάμανδρος.

[10] Herodotus, v. 94, 95. See his account of the
war between the Athenians and Mitylenaeans
about Sigeum and Achilleum.

attached to it, as being the only place which ever bore the sacred name immortalized by Homer. Athené had her temple in the Pergamus of Novum Ilium, and was worshipped as the tutelary deity of the city, just as she had been worshipped in the Pergamus of the Homeric Ilium. The Ilians maintained that at its capture by the Achaean troops their city had not been entirely destroyed, but that it had always remained inhabited, and had never ceased to exist.[1] The proofs produced by the Ilians for the identity of their city with the ancient one, were, as Grote [2] remarks, testimonies which few persons in those ages were inclined to question, when combined with the identity of name and general locality, nor does it seem that any one did question them, except Demetrius of Scepsis and Hestiaea of Alexandria-Troas, who from mere jealousy and envy contested the universally acknowledged identity, and of whom I shall presently have occasion to speak.

Polemon was a native of Novum Ilium, and wrote a description (περιήγησις) of the city. He flourished at the end of the third and beginning of the second centuries B.C., and was therefore earlier than Demetrius of Scepsis. He noticed in Novum Ilium the identical altar of Zeus Herkeios on which Priam had been slain, as well as the identical stone upon which Palamedes had taught the Greeks to play at dice.[3] Hellanicus, who was born on the day of the naval battle of Salamis (480 B.C.), and was therefore a contemporary of Herodotus, wrote a special work on Troy (called Τρωϊκά), in which he testified to the identity of Novum Ilium with the Homeric Ilium, for which assertion Strabo (or rather Demetrius followed by Strabo) gratuitously attributes to him an undue partiality for the Ilians.[4]

Herodotus says that Xerxes, in his expedition to Greece, ascended into the "Pergamon of Priam, because he had a longing to behold the place. Having seen everything and enquired into all particulars of the Homeric siege, he sacrificed to Athené, the tutelary goddess of Ilium, (his magnificent offering of) a thousand oxen (ten hecatombs), while the Magians poured libations to the heroes slain at Troy. The night after, a panic fell upon the camp: but in the morning they started at daylight, and skirting on the left hand the towns of Rhoeteum, Ophrynium, and Dardanus (which borders on Abydos), and on the right the Teucrians of Gergis, they reached Abydos."[5] It has been

---

[1] Strabo, xiii. p. 600 : λέγουσι δ' οἱ νῦν Ἰλιεῖς καὶ τοῦτο, ὡς οὐδὲ τελέως ἠφανίσθαι συνέβαινεν τὴν πόλιν κατὰ τὴν ἅλωσιν ὑπὸ τῶν Ἀχαιῶν, οὐδ' ἐξελείφθη οὐδέποτε.

[2] History of Greece, i. p. 298.

[3] Polemon, Fragmenta, 32, ed. Didot.

[4] Strabo, xiii. p. 602 : Ἑλλάνικος δὲ χαριζόμενος τοῖς Ἰλιεῦσιν, οἷος ἐκείνου θυμός, συνηγορεῖ τὸ τὴν αὐτὴν εἶναι πόλιν τὴν νῦν τῇ τότε.

[5] Herodotus, vii. 43 : ἐπὶ τοῦτον δὴ τὸν ποταμὸν ὡς ἀπίκετο Ξέρξης, ἐς τὸ Πριάμου Πέργαμον ἀνέβη, ἵμερον ἔχων θεήσασθαι. θεησάμενος δὲ καὶ πυθόμενος κείνων ἕκαστα τῇ Ἀθηναίῃ τῇ Ἰλιάδι ἔθυσε βοῦς χιλίας, χοὰς δὲ οἱ μάγοι τοῖσι ἥρωσι ἐχέαντο. ταῦτα δὲ ποιησαμένοισι νυκτὸς

φόβος ἐς τὸ στρατόπεδον ἐνέπεσε. ἅμα ἡμέρῃ δὲ ἐπορεύετο ἐνθεῦτεν, ἐν ἀριστερῇ μὲν ἀπέργων Ῥοίτειον πόλιν καὶ Ὀφρύνειον καὶ Δάρδανον, ᾗπερ δὴ Ἀβύδῳ ὅμουρός ἐστι, ἐν δεξιῇ δὲ Γέργιθας Τευκρούς.

It is out of place to speak here of the topography ; but in making this quotation from Herodotus, I cannot forego the opportunity of explaining the foregoing chapter (42), which is difficult to understand: Ἐποιέετο δὲ τὴν ὁδὸν ἐκ τῆς Λυδίης ὁ στρατὸς ἐπί τε ποταμὸν Κάϊκον καὶ γῆν τὴν Μυσίην, ἀπὸ δὲ Κάϊκου ὁρμεώμενος, Κάνης ὄρος ἔχων ἐν ἀριστερῇ, διὰ τοῦ Ἀταρνέος ἐς Καρίνην πόλιν· ἀπὸ δὲ ταύτης διὰ Θήβης πεδίου ἐπορεύετο, Ἀτραμύττειόν τε πόλιν καὶ Ἄντανδρον

generally maintained in modern times, by those who dispute the identity of Novum Ilium with the Homeric Troy, that the place called by Herodotus the Pergamon of Priam must be different from Novum Ilium; but, as Grote[6] rightly observes, the mention of the Ilian Athené identifies them as the same.

Eckenbrecher[7] ingeniously observes that "Herodotus cannot but have identified the Aeolic Ilium with the Homeric city, because in Book i. c. 5, he calls the latter merely 'Ilion,' without an epithet, just as we should designate the present Rome and the Rome of the ancient Romans by the same name. This," he argues, "appears evident when we compare this passage, where the historian says that the Persians traced their enmity against Greece from the conquest of Ilium, with the passage in Book ii. c. 10. We see also," he continues, "that Xerxes

τὴν Πελασγίδα παραμειβόμενος· τὴν Ἴδην δὲ λαβὼν ἐς ἀριστερὴν χέρα ἤϊε ἐς τὴν Ἰλιάδα γῆν· καὶ πρῶτα μέν οἱ ὑπὸ τῇ Ἴδῃ νύκτα ἀναμείναντι βρονταί τε καὶ πρηστῆρες ἐπεισπίπτουσι, καί τινα αὐτοῦ ταύτῃ συχνὸν ὅμιλον διέφθειραν. "The march of the army, after leaving Lydia, was directed upon the river Caïcus and the land of Mysia. Beyond the Caïcus the road, leaving Mount Cana upon the left, passed through the Atarnean plain, to the city of Carina. Quitting this, the troops advanced across the plain of Thebé, passing by Adramyttium and Antandrus, the Pelasgic settlement; then, keeping Mount Ida upon the left hand, they entered the Trojan territory. As they bivouacked during the night at the foot of Ida, a storm of thunder and lightning burst upon them, and killed a great many of them."

But if the Persian army had come by the ordinary road, crossing the ridge which extends from Ida westward and terminates in Cape Lectum, the true Ida must have been left considerably to the right. It is therefore generally thought that either Herodotus has made a mistake, or—as, among others, G. Rawlinson (Hist. of Herodotus, iv. p. 42, footnote) suggests—he has given the name of Ida to the highlands which close in the valley of the Scamander on the left, lying west and south of Bounarbashi. But this theory appears to us as unacceptable as that of P. Barker Webb (Topographie de la Troade, p. 134), who endeavours to make us believe that the Persian army, in coming by the ordinary way, might have had the true Mount Ida to its left, for he says: "To the south of the promontory of Lectum, the coast slopes rapidly to the east and north-east, and forms with the opposite shore the Gulf of Adramyttium. From this conformation of the gulf, which is not exactly marked on any modern map, it results that the Gargarus, instead of being situated, as is generally supposed, in the centre of Phrygia, approaches much more to the Gulf of Adramyttium, and appears almost to tower above it. Thus Herodotus's account of Xerxes, who on his march from Sardis to the

Hellespont left the Gargarus to his left, a statement which appears strange to many people, is true to the real position of Mount Ida." This statement is altogether inconsistent with the existing facts.

I can accept as the only right explanation that of Professor Virchow, who writes to me: "As Herodotus expressly states that Xerxes entered the territory of Ilium having Mount Ida to his left, I can but conclude from this that Xerxes went from Adramyttium northward, and penetrated from the east into the Plain of Beiramich; that is, nearly by the road taken by Tchihatcheff. The only doubt which could arise would be the mention of Antandros, which appears to have been situated more to the west. But the expression παραμειβόμενος admits of the interpretation that he passed by Antandrus; namely, that he passed by it to his left. Otherwise he must have taken his way across the high mountains. On the eastern road he passed round Ida, which remained to his left, and descended from the heights into the valley of the Scamander. As he must have gone from Iné through the defile into the Plain of Troy, he had Bounarbashi to his left." Professor Virchow adds that for this reason the small city on the Bali Dagh can, in his opinion, not be Gergis, because Herodotus (vii. 43) distinctly states that on the day after his visit to Ilium Xerxes went forward, passing to his left Rhoeteum, Ophrynium, and Dardanus, which borders on Abydos, but to his right the Teucrians of Gergis (ἅμα ἡμέρῃ δὲ ἐπορεύετο ἐνθεῦτεν, ἐν ἀριστερῇ μὲν ἀπέργων Ῥοίτειον πόλιν καὶ Ὀφρύνειον καὶ Δάρδανον, ἥπερ δὴ Ἀβύδῳ ὅμουρός ἐστι, ἐν δεξιῇ δὲ Γέργιθας Τευκρούς). As Xerxes passed at the foot of the Bali Dagh, it would appear strange indeed that Herodotus should have mentioned Gergis, not before but after Ilium, if the little city on that mountain were identical with Gergis.

[6] History of Greece, i. p. 298.

[7] G. von Eckenbrecher, Die Lage des Homerischen Troia; Düsseldorf, 1875, p. 34.

considered the Ilion of his time (that of Herodotus, Hellanicus, and
Strabo) as the Homeric Ilion, because we are told (vii. 43) that he
ascended to Priam's Pergamon, which he could not possibly think to be
situated anywhere else but in Ilion."

A further proof of the certainty which people felt regarding the
identity of ancient Troy with Novum Ilium is furnished by Xenophon,
who relates that the Lacedaemonian admiral Mindarus, while his fleet
lay at Abydos, went up himself to Ilium to sacrifice to Athené, and
saw from thence the naval battle between the squadron of Dorieus and
the Athenians, near the shore off Rhoeteum.[8]

Though the dominion of Novum Ilium was still very unimportant
during the interval between the Peloponnesian war and the Macedonian
invasion of Persia, and did not even extend to the neighbouring Hellespont, yet the city was garrisoned as a strong position. We see this from
the account given by Plutarch:[9] "Ilion was taken by Herakles on account
of the horses of Laomedon; it was also taken by Agamemnon by means
of the wooden horse; for the third time it was taken by Charidemus,
because, a horse having fallen in the gate, the Ilians could not promptly
shut it." This is confirmed by Polyaenus,[10] who says : " When the Ilians
sacked the city of Charidemus, he got hold of a slave, who had come to
plunder, and by great presents he induced him to betray the city (Novum
Ilium). But in order that he might appear faithful to the watchmen
of the gates, he gave him many sheep and slaves to bring in, twice
or three times. The watchmen, having distributed these, allowed him
often to go out in the night, and with him more men to bring in the
booty. Charidemus seized and bound those who had come with the
man, dressed his own armed men in their clothes, and gave them, with
the rest of the booty, a horse, as if it had been captured. But the
watchmen, in order to receive the horse, opened the whole gate. The
soldiers rushed in together with the horse, killed the watchmen, and,
having encountered the rest of the force, stormed the city. If we may
make the jest, Ilion was taken for the second time by the stratagem
of a horse."

This Charidemus can certainly be no other than the notorious merce-
nary chief, who flourished in the time of Philip II. (B.C. 359–336). We
know him principally from the speech of Demosthenes against Aristo-

[8] *Hellenica*, i. 1, 4 : Μίνδαρος δὲ κατιδὼν τὴν
μάχην ἐν Ἰλίῳ θύων τῇ Ἀθηνᾷ, ἐβοήθει ἐπὶ τὴν
θάλατταν · καὶ καθελκύσας τὰς ἑαυτοῦ τριήρεις
ἀπέπλει, ὅπως ἀναλάβοι τὰς μετὰ Δωριέως.

[9] *Life of Sertorius*, i. : ἑάλω δὲ τὸ Ἴλιον ὑφ'
Ἡρακλέους διὰ τὰς Λαομέδοντος ἵππους, καὶ ὑπὸ
Ἀγαμέμνονος διὰ τοῦ Δουρείου προσαγορευθέντος
ἵππου, τρίτον δ' ὑπὸ Χαριδήμου, τὰς πύλας, ἵππου
τινὸς ἐμπεσόντος, ἀποκλεῖσαι ταχὺ τῶν Ἰλιέων
μὴ δυνηθέντων.

[10] *Strategic.* iii. 14 : Χαρίδημος, Ἰλιέων λεη-
λατούντων αὐτοῦ τὴν πόλιν, οἰκέτην Ἰλιέα προελθόντα ἐπὶ λείαν συλλαβών, μεγάλοις δώροις
ἔπεισε προδοῦναι τὴν πόλιν. Ἵνα δὲ πιστὸς
φανείη τοῖς φυλάττουσι τὰς πύλας, ἔδωκεν αὐτῷ

πολλὰ πρόβατα καὶ ἀνδράποδα δίς που καὶ τρὶς
ἀγαγεῖν. Οἱ δὲ φύλακες, ταῦτα νειμάμενοι,
συνεχώρουν αὐτῷ πολλάκις ἐξιέναι νύκτωρ, καὶ
σὺν αὐτῷ ἄνδρας πλείονας τὴν λείαν περιελαύ-
νοντας. Χαρίδημος τοὺς μὲν σὺν αὐτῷ συλλαβὼν
ἔδησε· τὰ δὲ τούτων ἱμάτια περιβαλὼν ἰδίοις
ἀνδράσιν ὡπλισμένοις, ἔδωκεν αὐτοῖς τά τε ἄλλα
τῆς λείας καὶ ἵππον ὡς αἰχμάλωτον. Οἱ φύλακες,
ἵνα δέξαιντο τὸν ἵππον, πᾶσαν τὴν πύλην ἀνέῳξαν.
Οἱ στρατιῶται, τῷ ἵππῳ συνεισπεσόντες, τούς τε
φύλακας ἀπέκτειναν καὶ τὴν λοιπὴν δύναμιν
δεξάμενοι τῆς πόλεως ἐκράτησαν, ὥστε, εἰ χρή
τι καὶ παῖξαι, δεύτερον ἑάλω τὸ Ἴλιον πάλιν
ἵππῳ καταστρατηγούμενον.

crates, in which the capture of Ilium is confirmed, but without particulars as to how it happened. Dismissed by Timotheus, he took service in Asia Minor with Memnon and Mentor, who desired to liberate their brother-in-law Artabazus, who had been taken prisoner by Autophradates. The capture of Ilium by him must therefore have taken place about 356 B.C. From this event, therefore, it appears certain that at that time Novum Ilium was a fortified city.

When Alexander the Great crossed the Hellespont, he sent his army from Sestos to Abydos under Parmenio; and, after having offered solemn sacrifices at the tomb of Protesilaus at Elaeus in the Chersonese, he crossed over to the shore of the Plain of Troy. Having ascended to Ilium, he sacrificed to Athené, made libations to the heroes, hung up his armour in the temple of the goddess, and took in exchange some of the sacred arms which had been preserved from the Trojan war. Such was his veneration for these Trojan arms, that he had them carried before him in battle by his lifeguardsmen. He also offered at Ilium, in the temple of Zeus Herkeios, sacrifices to Priam, begging him to relax his wrath against the race of Neoptolemus, to which he, Alexander, belonged.[1]

Dicaearchus composed a separate work respecting this sacrifice of Alexander (περὶ τῆς ἐν Ἰλίῳ θυσίας).[2]

Plutarch tells us that Alexander, after having passed the Hellespont, ascended to Ilium, sacrificed to Athené, and made offerings to the shades of the heroes, and, after having anointed with oil the funeral column of Achilles, he ran, as was customary, stark naked round the tomb with his companions, put a wreath of flowers on it, and felicitated Achilles on having had during his life a true friend, and, after his death, a great herald of his glory. As he was walking through the city (Ilium) and examining its curiosities, some one asked him if he wished to see the lyre of Alexander (Paris); he answered that he cared but very little about that, but that he desired to see the lyre of Achilles, to which he had chanted the glory and the deeds of great men.[3]

---

[1] Arrian. Alexand. Anab. i. 11. 5–8: ἐλθὼν δὲ ἐς Ἐλαιοῦντα θύει Πρωτεσιλάῳ ἐπὶ τῷ τάφῳ τοῦ Πρωτεσιλάου, ὅτι καὶ Πρωτεσίλαος πρῶτος ἐδόκει ἐκβῆναι ἐς τὴν Ἀσίαν τῶν Ἑλλήνων τῶν ἅμα Ἀγαμέμνονι ἐς Ἴλιον στρατευσάντων · καὶ ὁ νοῦς τῆς θυσίας ἦν ἐπιτυχεστέραν οἷ γενέσθαι ἢ Πρωτεσιλάῳ τὴν ἀπόβασιν.

Παρμενίων μὲν δὴ τῶν πεζῶν τοὺς πολλοὺς καὶ τὴν ἵππον διαβιβάσαι ἐτάχθη ἐκ Σηστοῦ ἐς Ἄβυδον · καὶ διέβησαν τριήρεσι μὲν ἑκατὸν καὶ ἑξήκοντα, πλοίοις δὲ ἄλλοις πολλοῖς στρογγύλοις. Ἀλέξανδρον δὲ ἐξ Ἐλαιοῦντος ἐς τὸν Ἀχαιῶν λιμένα κατᾶραι ὁ πλείων λόγος κατέχει, καὶ αὐτόν τε κυβερνῶντα τὴν στρατηγίδα ναῦν διαβάλλειν καὶ ἐπειδὴ κατὰ μέσον τὸν πόρον τοῦ Ἑλλησπόντου ἐγένετο, σφάξαντα ταῦρον τῷ Ποσειδῶνι καὶ Νηρηΐσι σπένδειν ἐκ χρυσῆς φιάλης ἐς τὸν πόντον. λέγουσι δὲ καὶ πρῶτον ἐκ τῆς νεὼς σὺν τοῖς ὅπλοις ἐκβῆναι αὐτὸν ἐς τὴν γῆν τὴν Ἀσίαν καὶ βωμοὺς ἱδρύσασθαι ὅθεν τε

ἐστάλη ἐκ τῆς Εὐρώπης καὶ ὅπου ἐξέβη τῆς Ἀσίας Διὸς ἀποβατηρίου καὶ Ἀθηνᾶς καὶ Ἡρακλέους · ἀνελθόντα δὲ ἐς Ἴλιον τῇ τε Ἀθηνᾷ θῦσαι τῇ Ἰλιάδι, καὶ τὴν πανοπλίαν τὴν αὑτοῦ ἀναθεῖναι ἐς τὸν νεών, καὶ καθελεῖν ἀντὶ ταύτης τῶν ἱερῶν τινα ὅπλων ἔτι ἐκ τοῦ Τρωϊκοῦ ἔργου σωζόμενα. καὶ ταῦτα λέγουσιν ὅτι οἱ ὑπασπισταὶ ἔφερον πρὸ αὐτοῦ ἐς τὰς μάχας. θῦσαι δὲ αὐτὸν καὶ Πριάμῳ ἐπὶ τοῦ βωμοῦ τοῦ Διὸς τοῦ Ἑρκείου λόγος κατέχει, μῆνιν Πριάμου παραιτούμενον τῷ Νεοπτολέμου γένει, ὃ δὴ ἐς αὐτὸν καθῆκεν.

[2] Dicaearch. Fragm. p. 114, ed. Fuhr; Athenaeus, xiii. p. 693.

[3] Plutarch. Alexand. xv.: Ἀναβὰς δ' εἰς Ἴλιον, ἔθυσε τῇ Ἀθηνᾷ, καὶ τοῖς ἥρωσιν ἔσπεισε. Τὴν δ' Ἀχιλλέως στήλην ἀλειψάμενος λίπα, καὶ μετὰ τῶν ἑταίρων συναναδραμὼν γυμνός, ὥσπερ ἔθος ἐστίν, ἐστεφάνωσε, μακαρίσας αὐτόν, ὅτι καὶ ζῶν φίλου πιστοῦ, καὶ τελευτήσας μεγάλου κή-

I may also call attention to the valuable inscription [4] which proves the liberality of Antiochus Soter towards the Ilian Athené in 278 B.C. The inscriptions Nos. 3601 and 3602 also attest that Panathenaic games were solemnized at Ilium in honour of the Ilian Athené by the Ilians, conjointly with various other cities in the neighbourhood.[5]

We read in Strabo :[6] " It is said that the city of the present Ilians was until then a small market-town, and that it had a small and insignificant temple of Athené. But Alexander, having ascended to it after the victory on the Granicus, adorned the temple with offerings, raised the town to the rank of a city, commanded the wardens to enlarge it by new buildings, and declared the city free and exempt from all taxes. At a later time, after the conquest of the Persian empire, he sent to Ilium a very kind letter, promising to make it a large city, to make its temple very celebrated, and to institute sacred games in the city. After his death, Lysimachus did much for the city, surrounded it with a wall 40 stadia in circuit, built a temple, and increased the population by adding to it the inhabitants of the old neighbouring cities, which were in decay. Alexander felt a great interest in the Ilians, both on account of his relationship, and because of his admiration for Homer. There has been handed down a corrected edition of the Homeric poems, called ' the edition of the casket ' (ἐκ τοῦ νάρθηκος), because Alexander revised and annotated these poems with the aid of the pupils of Callisthenes and Anaxarchus, and preserved them in a richly ornamented casket, which he had found in the Persian treasury. Alexander's great kindness towards the Ilians proceeded, therefore, in the first place from his veneration for the poet,

---

ρυκος ἔτυχεν. 'Εν δὲ τῷ περιϊέναι καὶ θεᾶσθαι τὰ κατὰ τὴν πόλιν, ἐρομένου τινὸς αὐτόν, εἰ βούλεται τὴν 'Αλεξάνδρου λύραν ἰδεῖν, ἐλάχιστα φροντίζειν ἐκείνης ἔφη. τὴν δ' 'Αχιλλέως ζητεῖν, ᾗ τὰ κλέα καὶ τὰς πράξεις ὕμνει τῶν ἀγαθῶν ἀνδρῶν ἐκεῖνος.

[4] No. 3595 in Boeckh's *Corpus Inscriptionum Graec.* :

. . . . βασιλεὺς 'Αντίοχος . . . . τὴμ μὲν ἱέρειαν καὶ τοὺς ἱερονόμους καὶ τοὺς πρυτάνεις εὔξασθαι τῇ 'Αθηνᾷ τῇ 'Ιλιάδι . . . (ἐπὶ δὲ ταῖς εὐχαῖς τῇ μὲν 'Αθηνᾷ συντελεσάτωσαν τὴν νομιζομένην καὶ πάτ(ριον θυ)σίαν οἵ τε ἱερονόμοι . . . . (στῆσαι δ' αὐτοῦ εἰ)κόνα χρυσῆν ἐφ' ἵππου ἐν τῷ ἱερῷ τῆς 'Αθηνᾶς ἐν τῷ ἐπιφα-(νεστάτῳ τόπῳ) . . . . καὶ ἐπιγράψαι· 'Ο δῆμος ὁ ('Ιλιέων βασιλέα 'Αντί)οχον . . . . εὐσεβείας ἕνεκεν τῆς εἰς τὸ ἱερό(ν, εὐεργέτην καὶ σω)τῆρα γεγονότα τοῦ δήμου, κ. τ. λ.

[5] The inscription No. 3601 is much damaged. Boeckh says of it : " Decretum Ilii atque urbium vicinarum, quae cum Ilio sacrorum communionem habebant de ratione sollemnium et ludorum instituendorum scitum. Haec sollemnia arbitror fuisse Panathenaea, quae et ipsa, minora quidem vs. 11 nominata sunt." The inscription No. 3602 is : 'Ιλιεῖς καὶ αἱ) πόλεις α(ἱ κ)ο(ιν)ω(νοῦ)σαι (τῆς θυ)σίας καὶ τοῦ ἀγῶνος καὶ τῆς πανηγύρεως . . . . Δημητρίου 'Ιλιάδα, καλῶς καὶ ἐ(ν)δό(ξ)ως κανηφορήσασαν, (εὐσ)εβείας ἕνεκεν τῆς πρὸς τὴν θεάν.

[6] xiii. p. 593, 10–20, and p. 594, 30 : Τὴν δὲ τῶν 'Ιλιέων πόλιν τῶν νῦν τέως μὲν κώμην εἶναί φασι τὸ ἱερὸν ἔχουσαν τῆς 'Αθηνᾶς μικρὸν καὶ εὐτελές, 'Αλέξανδρον δὲ ἀναβάντα μετὰ τὴν ἐπὶ Γρανίκῳ νίκην ἀναθήμασί τε κοσμῆσαι τὸ ἱερὸν καὶ προσαγορεῦσαι πόλιν καὶ οἰκοδομίαις ἀναλαβεῖν προστάξαι τοῖς ἐπιμεληταῖς ἐλευθέραν τε κρῖναι καὶ ἄφορον· ὕστερον δὲ μετὰ τὴν κατάλυσιν τῶν Περσῶν ἐπιστολὴν κατατέμψαι φιλάνθρωπον, ὑπισχνούμενον πόλιν τε ποιῆσαι μεγάλην καὶ ἱερὸν ἐπισημότατον καὶ ἀγῶνα ἀποδείξειν ἱερόν· μετὰ δὲ τὴν ἐκείνου τελευτὴν Λυσίμαχος μάλιστα τῆς πόλεως ἐπεμελήθη καὶ νεὼν κατεσκεύασε καὶ τεῖχος περιεβάλετο ὅσον τετταράκοντα σταδίων, συνῴκισέ τε εἰς αὐτὴν τὰς κύκλῳ πόλεις ἀρχαίας ἤδη κεκακωμένας.

'Εκεῖνος γὰρ κατὰ συγγενείας ἀνανέωσιν ὥρμησε προνοεῖν αὐτῶν, ἅμα καὶ φιλόμηρος ὤν· φέρεται γοῦν τις διόρθωσις τῆς 'Ομήρου ποιήσεως, ἡ ἐκ τοῦ νάρθηκος λεγομένη, τοῦ 'Αλεξάνδρου μετὰ τῶν περὶ Καλλισθένη καὶ 'Ανάξαρχον ἐπελθόντος καὶ σημειωσαμένου τινά, ἔπειτα καταθέντος εἰς νάρθηκα ὃν ηὗρεν ἐν τῇ Περσικῇ γάζῃ πολυτελῶς κατεσκευασμένον· κατά τε δὴ τὸν τοῦ ποιητοῦ ζῆλον καὶ κατὰ τὴν συγγένειαν τὴν ἀπὸ τῶν Αἰακιδῶν τῶν ἐν 'Ανδρομάχην ἱστοροῦσι βασιλεῦσαι τὴν "Εκτορος γενομένην γυναῖκα, ἐφιλοφρονεῖτο πρὸς τοὺς 'Ιλιέας ὁ 'Αλέξανδρος.

and secondly from his relationship with the Aeacids, the kings of the Molossians, among whom, as is said, Andromache also reigned, who was once the wife of Hector."

But Strabo informs us that, when the Romans first went over to Asia and expelled Antiochus the Great from this side of the Taurus (190-189 B.C.), Demetrius of Scepsis, being then a youth, visited Ilium, and saw the city so much in decay, that there were not even tiles on the roofs of the houses.[7] He further states that, according to Hegesianax, the Galatians, having come over from Europe, went up to Ilium in search of a fortified place; but that they left it immediately, because the town had no walls of defence.[8] But this statement is thoroughly inconsistent with, and in contradiction to, the statement made by Strabo, a dozen lines before;[9] for he had there informed us that Lysimachus, after the death of Alexander, paid great attention to Ilium, surrounded it with a wall 40 stadia in circumference, and settled in Ilium the inhabitants of the ancient cities around, which were in a state of decay. Besides, the passages in Livy (xxxv. 43; xxxvii. 9) and Polybius (v. 78, 111) prove beyond all doubt that Novum Ilium was fortified and defensible about 218 B.C.

Livy informs us[10] that Antiochus the Great went up from the sea to Novum Ilium, to sacrifice to the Ilian Athené (190 B.C.); and further, that the Roman Consul Livius went up thither to sacrifice to the same goddess.

We read in Justin[11] that, in the first Roman expedition to Asia, there was a reciprocal exchange of joy between the Ilians and the Romans, as if between parents and children after a long separation.

Eckenbrecher[1] mentions the statement of Ennius,[2] that when the Romans, under the command of Cornelius Scipio Asiaticus, approached the Trojan shore, they exclaimed, at the first glimpse of Troy:—

"O patria, o divom domus Ilium, et incluta bello
Pergama."

The Romans, who were proud of their origin from Ilium and Aeneas, treated the city of their heroic ancestors with signal munificence, adding to its domain the adjacent territories of Sigeum, Rhoeteum, and Gergis, as well as the whole coast from the Peraea (or

---

[7] But, as M. Burnouf ingeniously observes to me, this does not necessarily mean that the houses had had tiles, and that for want of reparation they were without them. It may imply as well that the houses were poor buildings, which were not even covered with tiles, but had only terraces of clay mixed with straw.

[8] Strabo, xiii. p. 594: Καὶ τὸ Ἴλιον δ' ὃ νῦν ἔστι κωμόπολίς τις ἦν, ὅτε πρῶτον Ῥωμαῖοι τῆς Ἀσίας ἐπέβησαν καὶ ἐξέβαλον Ἀντίοχον τὸν μέγαν ἐκ τῆς ἐντὸς τοῦ Ταύρου. φησὶ γοῦν Δημήτριος ὁ Σκήψιος, μειράκιον ἐπιδημήσας εἰς τὴν πόλιν κατ' ἐκείνους τοὺς καιρούς, οὕτως ὠλιγωρημένην ἰδεῖν τὴν κατοικίαν ὥστε μηδὲ κεραμωτὰς ἔχειν τὰς στέγας· Ἡγησιάναξ δὲ

τοὺς Γαλάτας περαιωθέντας ἐκ τῆς Εὐρώπης ἀναβῆναι μὲν εἰς τὴν πόλιν δεομένους ἐρύματος, παρὰ χρῆμα δ' ἐκλιπεῖν διὰ τὸ ἀτείχιστον.
[9] Ibid. xiii. p. 593.   [10] xxxv. 43.
[11] Justin. xxxi. 8: "Tanta laetitia omnium fuit, quanta esse post longum tempus inter parentes et liberos solet. Juvabat Ilienses, nepotes suos, occidente et Africa domita, Asiam et avitum regnum vindicare. Optabilem ruinam Trojae dicentes, ut tam feliciter renasceretur. Contra Romanos, avitos Lares et incunabula majorum ac deorum simulacra inexplicabile desiderium videndi tenebat."
[1] Die Lage des Homerischen Troia, p. 37
[2] Annal. 14. 9, ed. P. Merulae.

continental territory) of Tenedos, southward of Sigeum, to the confines of Dardanus.[3] The Sigeans would not submit to this loss of autonomy, and their city was therefore destroyed by the Ilians.[4] A like fate appears to have befallen the neighbouring city of Achilleum.

"The dignity and power of Ilium being thus," as Grote[5] remarks, "prodigiously enhanced, we must find it but natural that the Ilieans assumed to themselves exaggerated importance, as the recognized parents of all-conquering Rome. Partly, we may naturally suppose, from the jealousies thus aroused on the part of their neighbours at Scepsis and Alexandria-Troas,—partly from the pronounced tendency of the age (in which Kratês at Pergamus, and Aristarchus at Alexandria, divided between them the palm of literary celebrity) towards criticism and illustration of the old poets,—a blow was now aimed at the mythical legitimacy of Ilium."

The two leaders in this new "Trojan war"—the attempt to destroy the traditional glory of Ilium—were, first, Demetrius of Scepsis, a most laborious Homeric critic, who, as already stated, had written thirty books of Commentaries on the Trojan Catalogue in the *Iliad*, and who was ambitious of proving that his native city, Scepsis, had also been the royal residence of Aeneas: and, secondly, Hestiaea,[6] an authoress of Alexandria-Troas, who had also written comments on the *Iliad*, and had made researches as to whether the Trojan war could have taken place before Novum Ilium. Both declared that there was no space for the great exploits related in the *Iliad*, the plain which now separates this city from the Hellespont having been formed since the Trojan war by the alluvium of the rivers. Further, that Polites, who, relying on the swiftness of his feet, sat as a scout on the top of the tumulus of Aesyetes, to watch when the Greek army should rush forward from the ships, must have been a fool, as he could have observed the movements of the Greek army much better from the much higher Acropolis of Ilium, without needing his swift feet; and that the still extant tumulus of Aesyetes is situated five stadia from Novum Ilium, on the road to Alexandria-Troas. Further, that the race of Hector and Achilles could not have taken place, it being impossible to run round Novum Ilium on account of the adjoining ridge, but that they could have run round the ancient town.[7] They admitted that no trace was

---

[3] Strabo, xiii. p. 600: Κατέσκαπται δὲ καὶ τὸ Σίγειον ὑπὸ τῶν Ἰλιέων διὰ τὴν ἀπείθειαν, ὑπ᾽ ἐκείνοις γὰρ ἦν ὕστερον ἡ παραλία πᾶσα ἡ μέχρι Δαρδάνου, καὶ νῦν ὑπ᾽ ἐκείνοις ἔστι.
Livy, xxxviii. 39.

[4] I may remind the reader that Dardanus, on the promontory of Gygas, between Rhoeteum and the present city of the Dardanelles, was an Aeolic settlement, and had therefore no title to legendary reverence as the special sovereignty of Aeneas, which Grote (*Hist. of Greece*, i. p. 301) erroneously attributes to it. He evidently confounds it with Dardanié, which was situated far from Dardanus, on the slope of Ida, and of which no trace was extant in the time of Demetrius

(see Strabo, xiii. p. 592).

[5] *History of Greece*, i. 301.

[6] Hestiaea is cited repeatedly in the Homeric Scholia (Schol. Venet. *ad Iliad.* iii. 64 ; Eustath. *ad Iliad.* ii. 538).

[7] Strabo, xiii. p. 599 : παρατίθησι δ᾽ ὁ Δημήτριος καὶ τὴν Ἀλεξανδρίνην Ἑστίαιαν μάρτυρα, τὴν συγγράψασαν περὶ τῆς Ὁμήρου Ἰλιάδος, πυνθανομένην εἰ περὶ τὴν νῦν πόλιν ὁ πόλεμος συνέστη, καὶ . . . τὸ Τρωϊκὸν πεδίον, ὃ μεταξὺ τῆς πόλεως καὶ τῆς θαλάττης ὁ ποιητὴς φράζει· τὸ μὲν γὰρ πρὸ τῆς νῦν πόλεως ὁρώμενον πρόχωμα εἶναι τῶν ποταμῶν ὕστερον γεγονός. ὅ τε Πολίτης "ὃς Τρώων σκοπὸς ἷζε ποδωκείῃσι πεποιθώς, τύμβῳ ἐπ᾽ ἀκροτάτῳ Αἰσυήταο γέροντος,"

left of ancient Troy, but they found this quite natural; for the towns all around having been desolated, but not entirely destroyed, whilst the ancient city had been completely destroyed, its stones had been used for their restoration. Thus, for example, they asserted that Archaeanax of Mitylene had built the walls of Sigeum with the stones of Troy.[8] Demetrius maintained that ancient Ilium was identical with the " Village of the Ilians " ('Ιλιέων Κώμη), the site of which he indicates exactly, for he says that it was 30 stadia from Novum Ilium, and 10 stadia from the hill of Callicolone, which latter was at a distance of 5 stadia from the Simois.[9] Strabo does not tell us whether Hestiaea concurred in the opinion of Demetrius, that Troy was identical with 'Ιλιέων Κώμη.

But all these objections are futile. In treating of the Topography, I think I have proved that, except the course of the rivers, the Plain of Troy cannot have undergone any essential change since the time of the Trojan war, and that the distance from Novum Ilium to the Hellespont must then have been the same as it is now. With regard to the tumulus of Aesyetes, Hestiaea and Demetrius are perfectly right in saying, that the Greek camp must have been more readily seen from the summit of the Pergamus than from a sepulchral mound on the road to Alexandria-Troas, 5 stadia from Novum Ilium. For Alexandria-Troas lies to the south-west of Ilium, and the road to it, which is distinctly marked by the ford of the Scamander at its entrance into the Plain of Troy, goes direct south as far as Bounarbashi, whereas the Hellespont and the Greek camp were north of Ilium. But to the south of Ilium, exactly in the direction in which the road to Alexandria-Troas must have been, I see before me, as I stand on Hissarlik, a tumulus 33 ft. high and 131 yds. in circumference, and, according to an exact measurement which I have made, 1017 yds. from the southern city wall. This, therefore, must necessarily be the sepulchral mound which Hestiaea and Demetrius indicate, but they evidently assume its identity with the sepulchre of Aesyetes, merely in order to prove the situation of this tumulus to be in a straight line between the Greek camp and the Village of the Ilians ('Ιλιέων Κώμη), and the latter to be the site of Troy. The tumulus of Aesyetes was probably situated at the present village of Koum Kioi, not far from the confluence of the Scamander and the Simois, for the remains of a tumulus several feet in height are still to be seen there. The tumulus said by Hestiaea

μάταιος ἦν. καὶ γὰρ εἰ ἐπ' ἀκροτάτῳ ὅμως [ἀπὸ] πολὺ ἂν μείζονος ὕψους τῆς ἀκροπόλεως ἐσκόπευεν ἐξ ἴσου σχεδόν τι διαστήματος, μὴ δεόμενος μηδὲν τῆς ποδωκείας τοῦ ἀσφαλοῦς χάριν· πέντε γὰρ διέχει σταδίους ὁ νῦν δεικνύμενος τοῦ Αἰσυήτου τάφος κατὰ τὴν εἰς 'Αλεξάνδρειαν ὁδόν· οὐδ' ἡ τοῦ "Εκτορος δὲ περίδρομὴ ἡ περὶ τὴν πόλιν ἔχει τι εὔλογον· οὐ γάρ ἐστι. περίδρομος ἡ νῦν διὰ τὴν συνεχῆ ῥάχιν· ἡ δὲ παλαιὰ ἔχει περιδρομήν.

[8] Strabo, xiii. p. 599: Οὐδὲν δ' ἴχνος σώζεται τῆς ἀρχαίας πόλεως. εἰκότως· ἅτε γὰρ ἐκπεπορθημένων τῶν κύκλῳ πόλεων, οὐ τελέως δὲ κατεσπασμένων, ταύτης δ' ἐκ βάθρων ἀνατετραμμένης, οἱ λίθοι πάντες εἰς τὴν ἐκείνων ἀνάληψιν μετηνέχθησαν. 'Αρχαιάνακτα γοῦν φασι τὸν Μιτυληναῖον ἐκ τῶν ἐκεῖθεν λίθων τὸ Σίγειον τειχίσαι.

[9] Strabo, xiii. p. 597: Ὑπὲρ δὲ τούτου μικρὸν ἡ τῶν 'Ιλιέων κώμη ἐστίν, ἐν ᾗ νομίζεται τὸ παλαιὸν "Ιλιον ἱδρῦσθαι πρότερον, τριάκοντα σταδίους διέχον ἀπὸ τῆς νῦν πόλεως, ὑπὲρ δὲ τῆς 'Ιλιέων κώμης δέκα σταδίοις ἐστὶν ἡ Καλλικολώνη, λόφος τις, παρ' ὃν ὁ Σιμόεις ῥεῖ πενταστάδιον διέχων.

and Demetrius to be that of Aesyetes is now called Pasha Tepeh. It has been excavated by Mrs. Schliemann, and I shall take occasion to speak of it more fully.[10] From the above indications of the distances, we easily see that Demetrius held Mount Kara Your, which I have already described, to be the Homeric Callicolone, and that, as before stated, his Ἰλιέων Κώμη must have occupied the site of a low hill on Mr. Calvert's farm, to the north-east of Thymbra, and just in front of the swamp, now dried up, which used to be called the Duden swamp. A few coarse Hellenic potsherds mark the site of an ancient village there, but there is no accumulation of *débris*. The statement of Demetrius is gratuitous, that Troy had disappeared without leaving a trace, its stones having been employed for the reconstruction of other cities, and especially for the walls of Sigeum. If, as I hope to prove, Hissarlik marks the site of Troy, the Trojan walls lay already buried upwards of 20 ft. below the surface of the ground when Sigeum was built, in the seventh century B.C. ; and, as no vestiges of the ancient city were visible above ground, people thought, of course, that even the ruins had entirely vanished:—" etiam periere ruinae." Thus it also happens that Strabo, who never visited the Troad, adopts, as Grote[11] remarks, the unsupported hypothesis of Demetrius, as if it were an authenticated fact; distinguishing pointedly between Old and New Ilium, and even censuring Hellanicus for having maintained the received local faith. But it appears certain that the theory of Hestiaea and Demetrius was not adopted by any other ancient author, excepting Strabo. Polemon, who, as before mentioned, was a native of Ilium, could not possibly have accepted their theory that Ilium was not the genuine Troy, for his work describing the localities and relics of Ilium implies their identity as a matter of course.

Novum Ilium continued to be universally considered and treated as the genuine Homeric Troy. According to Strabo,[1] " Novum Ilium was much damaged by the Roman rebel Fimbria, who besieged and conquered it in the Mithridatic war (85 B.C.). Fimbria had been sent as quaestor with the consul Valerius Flaccus, who was elected commander-in-chief against Mithridates. But having excited a revolt, and having murdered Valerius in Bithynia, Fimbria made himself commander-in-

---

[10] See the chapter on the Heroic Tumuli.

[11] *History of Greece*, i. p. 302.

[1] xiii. 594 : εἶτ᾽ ἐκάκωσαν αὐτὴν πάλιν οἱ μετὰ Φιμβρίου ᾿Ρωμαῖοι λαβόντες ἐκ πολιορκίας ἐν τῷ Μιθριδατικῷ πολέμῳ. συνεπέμφθη δὲ ὁ Φιμβρίας ὑπάτῳ Οὐαλερίῳ Φλάκκῳ ταμίας προχειρισθέντι ἐπὶ τὸν Μιθριδάτην· καταστασιάσας δὲ καὶ ἀνελὼν τὸν ὕπατον κατὰ Βιθυνίαν αὐτὸς κατεστάθη κύριος τῆς στρατιᾶς, καὶ προελθὼν εἰς ᾿Ίλιον, οὐ δεχομένων αὐτὸν τῶν ᾿Ιλιέων ὡς λῃστήν, βίαν τε προσφέρει καὶ δεκαταίους αἱρεῖ· καυχωμένου δ᾽ ὅτι ἣν ᾿Αγαμέμνων πόλιν δεκάτῳ ἔτει μόλις εἷλε τὸν χιλιόναυν στόλον ἔχων καὶ τὴν σύμπασαν ᾿Ελλάδα συστρατεύουσαν, ταύτην αὐτὸς δεκάτῃ ἡμέρᾳ χειρώσαιτο, εἶπέ τις τῶν ᾿Ιλιέων " οὐ γὰρ ἦν ᾿Έκτωρ ὁ ὑπερμαχῶν τῆς πόλεως." τοῦτον μὲν οὖν ἐπελθὼν Σύλλας κατέλυσε, καὶ

τὸν Μιθριδάτην κατὰ συμβάσεις εἰς τὴν οἰκείαν ἀπέπεμψε, τοὺς δ᾽ ᾿Ιλιέας παρεμυθήσατο πολλοῖς ἐπανορθώμασι. καθ᾽ ἡμᾶς μέντοι Καῖσαρ ὁ θεὸς πολὺ πλέον αὐτῶν προὐνόησε ζηλώσας ἅμα καὶ ᾿Αλέξανδρον . . . ὁ δὲ Καῖσαρ καὶ φιλαλέξανδρος ὢν καὶ τῆς πρὸς τοὺς ᾿Ιλιέας συγγενείας γνωριμώτερα ἔχων τεκμήρια, ἐπερρώσθη πρὸς τὴν εὐεργεσίαν νεανικῶς· γνωριμώτερα δέ, πρῶτον μὲν ὅτι ᾿Ρωμαῖος, οἱ δὲ ᾿Ρωμαῖοι τὸν Αἰνείαν ἀρχηγέτην ἡγοῦνται, ἔπειτα ὅτι ᾿Ιούλιος ἀπὸ ᾿Ιούλου τινὸς τῶν προγόνων· ἐκεῖνος δ᾽ ἀπὸ ᾿Ιούλου τὴν προσωνυμίαν ἔσχε ταύτην, τῶν ἀπογόνων εἷς ὢν τῶν ἀπὸ Αἰνείου. χώραν τε δὴ προσένειμεν αὐτοῖς καὶ τὴν ἐλευθερίαν καὶ τὴν ἀλειτουργησίαν αὐτοῖς συνεφύλαξε καὶ μέχρι νῦν συμμένουσιν ἐν τούτοις.

chief of the army and marched against Ilium. When the Ilians refused
to receive him, as being a brigand, he attacked the city by force and took
it in ten days. When he glorified himself upon having overpowered in
ten days the city which Agamemnon, with his fleet of a thousand ships
and the whole power of Hellas, had hardly been able to conquer in the
tenth year, one of the Ilians said : 'It happened because we had no
Hector to fight for the city.' Fimbria was soon attacked and destroyed
by Sulla, who by the treaty of peace with Mithridates allowed the latter
to return to his country, and who consoled the Ilians by making many
improvements in their city. In our time the divine (Julius) Caesar
did yet more for Ilium, partly because he imitated Alexander (the
Great) . . . ; but Caesar also felt a juvenile impulse for his beneficence,
both as an admirer of Alexander and because he had still more evident
proofs of his relationship with the Ilians. Those proofs were the more
notorious, first because he was a Roman, and the Romans hold Aeneas to
be their ancestor; next because it was from Iulus, one of his ancestors,
that he was called Julius, but he had received his name, as being one
of the descendants of Aeneas, from Iulus [the son of Aeneas, Ascanius,
who, according to an old legend, was called Iulus]. For those reasons he
allotted lands to them, and confirmed their freedom and exemption from
state taxes, and these privileges have remained to them until now."

But Appian[2] relates the conquest of Ilium by Fimbria differently.
He says : " The Ilians, being besieged by Fimbria, applied to Sulla, who
told them that he would come, and ordered them meanwhile to tell
Fimbria that they had given themselves up to Sulla. When Fimbria
heard this, he praised them as being already friends of the Romans,
requested them to receive him as he was also a Roman, and ironically
referred to the affinity existing between the Romans and the Ilians. But
when he entered the city, he murdered all who came in his way, burned
the whole city, and in various ways shamefully treated those who had
gone as ambassadors to Sulla. He neither spared the sanctuaries nor
those who had fled to the temple of Athené, for he burned them together
with the temple. He also pulled down the walls, and went round on
the following day, to see whether anything of the town still remained
standing. The town suffered more than under Agamemnon, and perished
root and branch by the hand of a kinsman ; not a house of it was saved,
nor a temple nor an idol. But the statue of Athené, called the Palladium,
which is held to have fallen from heaven, some believe was found unhurt,

---

[2] i. pp. 364, 365 : Ἰλιεῖς δὲ πολιορκούμενοι
πρὸς αὐτοῦ κατέφυγον μὲν ἐπὶ Σύλλαν, Σύλλα
δὲ φήσαντος αὐτοῖς ἥξειν, καὶ κελεύσαντος ἐν
τοσῷδε Φιμβρίᾳ φράζειν ὅτι σφᾶς ἐπιτετρόφασι
τῷ Σύλλᾳ, πυθόμενος ὁ Φιμβρίας ἐπήνεσε μὲν ὡς
ἤδη Ῥωμαίων φίλους, ἐκέλευσε δὲ καὶ αὐτὸν ὄντα
Ῥωμαῖον ἔσω δέχεσθαι, κατειρωνευσάμενός τι
καὶ τῆς συγγενείας τῆς οὔσης ἐς Ῥωμαίους Ἰλιεῦσιν. ἐσελθὼν δὲ τοὺς ἐν ποσὶ πάντας ἔκτεινε
καὶ πάντα ἐνεπίμπρη, καὶ τοὺς πρεσβεύσαντας ἐς
τὸν Σύλλαν ἐλυμαίνετο ποικίλως, οὔτε τῶν ἱερῶν
φειδόμε ος οὔτε τῶν ἐς τὸν νεὼν τῆς Ἀθηνᾶς

καταφυγόντων, οὓς αὐτῷ νεῷ κατέπρησεν. κατέ-
σκαπτε δὲ καὶ τὰ τείχη, καὶ τῆς ἐπιούσης ἡρεύνα
περιὼν μή τι συνέστηκε τῆς πόλεως ἔτι. ἡ μὲν
δὴ χείρονα τῶν ἐπὶ Ἀγαμέμνονι παθοῦσα ὑπὸ
συγγενοῦς διολώλει, καὶ οἰκόπεδον οὐδὲν αὐτῆς
οὐδ' ἱερὸν οὐδ' ἄγαλμα ἔτι ἦν · τὸ δὲ τῆς Ἀθηνᾶς
ἕδος, ὃ Παλλάδιον καλοῦσι καὶ διοπετὲς ἡγοῦνται, νομίζουσί τινες εὑρεθῆναι τότε ἄθραυστον,
τῶν ἐπιπεσόντων τειχέων αὐτὸ περικλυψάντων,
εἰ μὴ Διομήδης αὐτὸ καὶ Ὀδυσσεὺς ἐν τῷ Τρωϊκῷ
ἔργῳ μετήνεγκαν ἐξ Ἰλίου.

having been covered by the walls which fell upon it, unless Diomedes and Ulysses carried it away from Ilium in their exploit at Troy." Appian adds that this happened at the very end of the 173rd Olympiad (that is, in 84 B.C.). This account of the complete destruction of Ilium, as given by Appian, who flourished at the time of Antoninus Pius, seems hardly credible, more especially as Strabo, who lived at the time of Julius Caesar and Augustus (nearly 200 years earlier than Appian), and was almost a contemporary of the event, only knew that Ilium had been damaged, but not that it had been destroyed root and branch.

According to Suetonius, Julius Caesar even intended to make Ilium the capital of the Roman empire;[3] and in the well-known ode of Horace,[4] to which we shall have occasion to recur, a like plan is attributed to Augustus.

Meyer[5] mentions a passage in Nicolaus of Damascus,[6] according to which " Julia, daughter of Augustus, unexpectedly came by night to Ilium, and in passing the Scamander, which had overflowed and was very rapid, she had a narrow escape of being drowned. Julia's husband, Agrippa, punished the Ilians by imposing upon them a fine of a hundred thousand denarii, for not having made provision for the safety of the princess; but they had not been able to do so, as they were totally ignorant of Julia's intention to visit their city. It was only by long exertions that Nicolaus succeeded in procuring the remission of the fine, by the intercession of Herodes."

Julia's son, Caius Caesar, who was the adoptive son of his grandfather Augustus, and became governor of Asia at nineteen years of age, must also have visited Ilium, taken a deep interest in it, and lavished favours upon it; for in an inscription found on the spot he is called the kinsman, the benefactor, and the patron of Ilium.[7]

Ovid[8] also mentions his own visit to Ilium.

According to Tacitus,[9] Nero, when still a boy (53 A.D.), made a speech in the Forum of Rome, in Greek, in favour of the Ilians. He spoke with so much eloquence of the descent of the Romans from Troy, that Claudius exempted the inhabitants from all public taxes. Suetonius informs us that Claudius freed the Ilians for ever from all tribute, after having read aloud an old Greek letter of the Roman Senate and People, who offered to King Seleucus friendship and alliance only on condition that he would grant to their kinsmen, the Ilians, freedom from all taxes and imposts of every kind.[10]

Eckenbrecher[1] quotes the statement of Tacitus,[2] that " the Ilians were

[3] Suetonius, *Caes.* 79.

[4] Horat. *Carm.* iii. 3. See Ch. IV. pp. 204, 205.

[5] Eduard Meyer, *Geschichte von Troas;* Leipzig, 1877, p. 96.

[6] *De Vita sua:* Fragm. 3, ed. Müller and Dindorf.

[7] The inscription is given in the chapter on Novum Ilium.

[8] *Fast.* vi. 421 :

" Creditur armiferae signum coeleste Minervae
Urbis in Iliacae desiluisse juga :
Cura videri fuit, vidi templumque locumque,
Hoc superest illi : Pallada Roma tenet."

[9] *Annal.* xii. 58.

[10] Suet. *Claud.:* " Iliensibus, quasi Romanae gentis auctoribus, tributa in perpetuum remisit, recitata vetere epistola Graeca senatus populique Romani, Seleuco regi amicitiam et societatem ita demum pollicentis, si consanguineos suos, Ilienses ab omni genere immunes praestitisset."

[1] G. von Eckenbrecher, *Die Lage des Homerischen Troia,* p. 39.

[2] *Annal.* iv. 55 : " Ne Ilienses quidem, cum parentem urbis Romae Trojam referrent, nisi antiquitatis gloria pollebant.'

only important through the glory of their antiquity, because they claimed Troy as the parent of Rome; and, he adds, this proves that Tacitus recognized the ancient glory of the Ilians, and thus the identity of their city with the Homeric Troy." He further mentions, that "Pliny[3] speaks of the historical Ilium, calling it the fountain of all celebrity." He also cites the testimony of Pomponius Mela,[4] who calls the Ilium of his time "Urbs bello excidioque clarissima." Eckenbrecher further mentions that "in like manner the identity of the historical Ilium with the Homeric Ilium is acknowledged by Dionysius Periegetes (cir. 270 A.D.), the orator Aristides[5] (150 A.D.), Stephanus (de Urbe), and Suidas (in voce)."

The Ilian coins, with the names and effigies of Roman emperors and empresses, and the legend "Hector of the Ilians," or "Priam of the Ilians," are additional proofs that the identity of Novum Ilium with Homeric Troy continued to be recognized.[6]

The Emperor Caracalla showed his veneration for sacred Ilium, the cradle of the ancestors of Rome, in a unique manner. He offered, with his army, funeral sacrifices at the tomb of Achilles and honoured it by races, which he and his army ran in arms around it. After that he rewarded his soldiers with money, as if they had accomplished a great feat, and had really conquered the ancient Ilium themselves; and he also erected a bronze statue of Achilles.[7]

According to Herodian,[8] "Caracalla first visited all the remains of Ilium (by which we are of course to understand all the relics which were shown by the Ilians as those of ancient Troy), and then went to the tomb of Achilles, and having adorned it sumptuously with wreaths and flowers, he again imitated Achilles. Being in want of a Patroclus, he did as follows: one of his freedmen, Festus by name, was his most intimate friend and keeper of the imperial archives. This Festus died when Caracalla was at Ilium: as some people said, he was poisoned in order that he might be buried like Patroclus; as others said, he died from illness. Caracalla ordered the funeral, and that a great pile of wood should be heaped up for the pyre. Having put the body in the midst, and having slaughtered all kinds of animals, he kindled the fire, and taking a cup he made

---

[3] *H. N.* v. 33 : "Ac mille quingentis passibus remotum a portu Ilium immune—unde omnis rerum claritas." I remark here once for all that for all quotations from Pliny I have used the edition of M. E. Littré; Paris, 1860.

[4] i. 18.

[5] ii. 369 ; ed. Dindorf: ἐνθυμεῖσθαι χρὴ καὶ λέγειν—ὅτι ἑάλω μὲν Ἴλιος, ἡ δυνατωτάτη τῶν ἐν τῇ Ἀσίᾳ πόλις κατ' ἐκείνους τοὺς χρόνους, ἀλλ' ὅμως οἰκεῖται νῦν Ἴλιος.

[6] See the description of the Ilian coins in the chapter on Novum Ilium.

[7] Dio Cassius, lxxvii. 16 : καὶ τὸν Ἑλλήσποντον οὐκ ἀκινδύνως διαβαλών, τόν τε Ἀχιλλέα καὶ ἐναγίσμασι, καὶ περιδρομαῖς ἐνοπλίοις καὶ ἑαυτοῦ καὶ τῶν στρατιωτῶν ἐτίμησε, καὶ ἐπὶ τούτῳ ἐκείνοις τε, ὡς καὶ μέγα τι κατωρθωκόσι, καὶ τὸ Ἴλιον ὡς ἀληθῶς αὐτὸ τὸ ἀρχαῖον ᾑρηκόσι, χρήματα ἔδωκε, καὶ αὐτὸν τὸν Ἀχιλλέα χαλκοῦν

[8] Herodian, iv. 8, §§ 4, 5 : Ἐπελθὼν δὲ πάντα τὰ τῆς πόλεως ['Ιλίου] λείψανα, ἧκεν ἐπὶ τὸν Ἀχιλλέως τάφον, στεφάνοις τε κοσμήσας καὶ ἄνθεσι πολυτελῶς πάλιν Ἀχιλλέα ἐμιμεῖτο. ζητῶν τε καὶ Πάτροκλόν τινα ἐποίησέ τι τοιοῦτον. ἦν αὐτῷ τις τῶν ἀπελευθέρων φίλτατος, Φῆστος μὲν ὄνομα, τῆς δὲ βασιλείου μνήμης προεστώς. οὗτος ὄντος αὐτοῦ ἐν Ἰλίῳ ἐτελεύτησεν, ὡς μέν τινες ἔλεγον, φαρμάκῳ ἀναιρεθεὶς ἵν' ὡς Πάτροκλος ταφῇ, ὡς δὲ ἕτεροι ἔφασκον, νόσῳ διαφθαρείς. τούτου κομισθῆναι κελεύει τὸν νέκυν, ξύλων τε πολλῶν ἀθροισθῆναι πυράν· ἐπιθείς τε αὐτὸν ἐν μέσῳ καὶ παντοδαπὰ ζῷα κατασφάξας ὑφῆψέ τε, καὶ φιάλην λαβὼν σπένδων τε τοῖς ἀνέμοις εὔχετο. πάνυ τε ὢν ψιλοκόρσης, πλόκαμον ἐπιθεῖναι τῷ πυρὶ ζητῶν ἐγελᾶτο· πλὴν ὧν εἶχε τριχῶν ἀπεκείρατο.

libations to the winds and prayed. As he was very bald-headed and tried to put a lock of hair on the fire, he was laughed at; only he cut off all the hair he had." I shall show in the subsequent pages that Caracalla erected in honour of Festus the tumulus now called Ujek Tepeh, which is the largest in the Troad.[9]

When Constantine the Great decided upon building a new capital for his vast empire, which was definitively to replace ancient Rome, he intended at first to found Nova Roma in the land of the ancient ancestors of the Romans. According to Zosimus, he chose a site between Alexandria-Troas and the ancient Ilium (μεταξὺ Τρῳάδος καὶ τῆς ἀρχαίας Ἰλίου); according to Zonaras, on Sigeum (ἐν Σιγαίῳ, sic). There he laid the foundations of the city; and part of the wall had already been built when he gave the preference to the much more suitable Byzantium.[10] Meyer[1] mentions that "the statue of Constantine, which was erected on the porphyry column (the 'burnt column' of Stamboul), is said to have originally been a statue of Apollo which stood in Ilium." [2]

I am indebted to my friend Dr. Carl Henning, the learned assistant of his Majesty the Emperor of Brazil, for a copy of a letter of the Emperor Julian, the manuscript of which he has discovered in the Harleian Library, 5610.[3] I give it here word for word, as it is a most important contribution to the history of Novum Ilium:

---

[9] See the description of this tumulus in the chapter on the Heroic Tumuli.

[10] Zosimus, ii. 30; Zonaras, Ann. p. 5, ed. Venet.; compare E. Meyer, Geschichte von Troas, pp. 96, 97.

[1] E. Meyer, Gesch. von Troas, p. 97.

[2] Zonaras, p. 6, C.: λέγεται δὲ καὶ Ἀπόλλωνος εἶναι στήλην τὸ ἄγαλμα, καὶ μετενεχθῆναι ἀπὸ τῆς ἐν Φρυγίᾳ πόλεως τοῦ Ἰλίου.

[3] Dr. Henning has published this inedited letter in the Hermes, vol. ix. pp. 257–266: Πηγάσιον ἡμεῖς οὔποτ᾽ ἂν προσήκαμεν ῥᾳδίως, εἰ μὴ σαφῶς ἐπεπείσμεθα, ὅτι καὶ πρότερον εἶναι δοκῶν τῶν Γαλιλαίων ἐπίσκοπος ἠπίστατο σέβεσθαι καὶ τιμᾶν τοὺς θεούς. οὐκ ἀκοὴν ἐγώ σοι ταῦτα ἀπαγγέλλω τῶν πρὸς ἔχθραν καὶ φιλίαν λέγειν εἰωθότων, ἐπεὶ καὶ ἐμοὶ πάνυ διετεθρύλητο τὰ τοιαῦτα περὶ αὐτοῦ, καὶ νὴ τοὺς θεοὺς ᾤμην οὕτω χρῆναι μισεῖν αὐτόν, ὡς οὐδένα τῶν πονηροτάτων. ἐπεὶ δὲ κληθεὶς εἰς τὸ στρατόπεδον ὑπὸ τοῦ μακαρίτου Κωνσταντίου ταύτην ἐπορευόμην τὴν ὁδόν, ἀπὸ τῆς Τρῳάδος ὄρθρου βαθέος διαναστάς, ἦλθον εἰς τὸ Ἴλιον περὶ πληθουσαν ἀγοράν. ὁ δὲ ὑπήντησε καὶ βουλομένῳ τὴν πόλιν ἱστορεῖν (ἦν γάρ μοι τοῦτο πρόσχημα τοῦ φοιτᾶν εἰς τὰ ἱερά) περιηγητής τε ἐγένετο καὶ ἐξενάγησέ με πανταχοῦ. ἄκουε τοίνυν ἔργα καὶ λόγους ἀφ᾽ ὧν ἄν τις εἰκάσειεν οὐκ ἀγνώμονα τὰ πρὸς τοὺς θεοὺς αὐτόν. ἡρῷόν ἐστιν Ἕκτορος ὅπου χαλκοῦς ἕστηκεν ἀνδριὰς ἐν ναΐσκῳ βραχεῖ. τούτῳ τὸν μέγαν ἀντέστησαν Ἀχιλλέα κατὰ τὸ ὕπαιθρον. εἰ τὸν τόπον ἐθεάσω, γνωρίζεις δήπουθεν ὃ λέγω. τὴν μὲν οὖν ἱστορίαν δι᾽ ἣν ὁ μέγας Ἀχιλλεὺς ἀντιτεταγμένος αὐτῷ πᾶν τὸ ὕπαιθρον κατείληφεν, ἔξεστί σοι τῶν περιηγητῶν ἀκούειν. ἐγὼ δὲ

καταλαβὼν ἐμπύρους ἔτι, μικροῦ δέω φάναι λαμπροὺς ἔτι τοὺς βωμοὺς καὶ λιπαρῶς ἀληλιμμένην τὴν τοῦ Ἕκτορος εἰκόνα, πρὸς Πηγάσιον ἀπιδών ᾽τί ταῦτα᾽ εἶπον ᾽Ἰλιεῖς θύουσιν;᾽ ἀποπειρώμενος ἠρέμα πῶς ἔχει γνώμης. ὁ δέ ᾽καὶ τί τοῦτο ἄτοπον, ἄνδρα ἀγαθὸν ἑαυτῶν πολίτην, ὥσπερ ἡμεῖς᾽ ἔφη ᾽τοὺς μάρτυρας, εἰ θεραπεύουσιν;᾽ ἡ μὲν οὖν εἰκὼν οὐχ ὑγιής. ἡ δὲ προαίρεσις ἐν ἐκείνοις ἐξεταζομένη τοῖς καιροῖς ἀστεία. τί δὴ τὸ μετὰ τοῦτο; ᾽βαδίσωμεν᾽ ἔφην ᾽ἐπὶ τὸ τῆς Ἰλιάδος Ἀθηνᾶς τέμενος.᾽ ὁ δὲ καὶ μάλα προθύμως ἀπήγαγέ με καὶ ἀνέῳξε τὸν νεών, καὶ ὥσπερ μαρτυρούμενος ἐπέδειξέ μοι πάντα ἀκριβῶς σῶα τὰ ἀγάλματα, καὶ ἔπραξεν οὐδὲν ὧν εἰώθασιν οἱ δυσσεβεῖς ἐκεῖνοι πράττειν, ἐπὶ τοῦ μετώπου τὸ ὑπόμνημα τοῦ δυσσεβοῦς σκιαγραφοῦντες, οὐδὲ ἐσύριττεν, ὥσπερ ἐκεῖνοι, αὐτὸς καθ᾽ ἑαυτόν· ἡ γὰρ ἄκρα θεολογία παρ᾽ αὐτοῖς ἐστι δύο ταῦτα, συρίττειν τε πρὸς τους δαίμονας καὶ σκιαγραφεῖν ἐπὶ τοῦ μετώπου τὸν σταυρόν. δύο ταῦτα ἐπηγγειλάμην εἰπεῖν σοι· τρίτον δὲ ἐλθὸν ἐπὶ νοῦν οὐκ οἶμαι χρῆναι σιωπᾶν. ἠκολούθησέ μοι καὶ πρὸς τὸ Ἀχίλλειον ὁ αὐτός, καὶ ἀπέδειξε τὸν τάφον σῶον· ἐπεπύσμην δὲ καὶ τοῦτον ὑπ᾽ αὐτοῦ διεσκάφθαι. ὁ δὲ καὶ μάλα σεβόμενος αὐτῷ προσῄει. ταῦτα εἶδον αὐτός. ἀκήκοα δὲ παρὰ τῶν νῦν ἐχθρῶς ἐχόντων πρὸς αὐτόν, ὅτι καὶ προσεύχοιτο λάθρᾳ καὶ προσκυνοίη τὸν Ἥλιον. ἆρα οὐκ ἂν ἐδέξω με καὶ ἰδιώτην μαρτυροῦντα; τῆς περὶ τοὺς θεοὺς διαθέσεως ἑκάστου τίνες ἂν εἶεν ἀξιοπιστότεροι μάρτυρες αὐτῶν τῶν θεῶν; ἡμεῖς ἂν ἱερέα Πηγάσιον ἐποιούμεθα, εἰ συνεγνώκειμεν αὐτῷ τι περὶ τοὺς θεοὺς δυσσεβές; εἰ δὲ ἐν ἐκείνοις τοῖς χρόνοις εἴτε δυναστείας ὀρεγόμενος εἴθ᾽, ὅπερ

" We should never easily have had anything to do with Pegasius, had we not been convinced that formerly, whilst he appeared to be a bishop of the Galileans, he knew how to respect and honour the gods. I tell you this, not because I heard it from those who are wont to speak from sentiments of enmity or friendship—and indeed a very great many such rumours were current about him and came to my ears, and, by the gods, I thought that he deserved to be hated more than the most depraved wretches. But when, being called by the late Constantius to the camp, I went by that road, I started from (Alexandria) Troas very early in the morning and reached Ilium at the time of full market (between nine and ten in the morning). He came to meet me, and he became my guide, as for one who wished to know the city (this being my pretext for visiting the temples), and led me about everywhere to show me the curiosities.

" Listen, then, to facts and words from which one may suppose him to be not regardless of the gods. There is a sanctuary of Hector, where a bronze statue stands in a small chapel. Opposite to him they have put up Achilles in the open air. If you have seen the place, you will well understand what I say. You may hear from the guides the legend on account of which great Achilles has been placed opposite to him, and occupies the whole space in the open air. Happening to find the altars still burning, and I might almost say still in a blaze, and Hector's statue anointed with fat, I looked at Pegasius and said : ' What is the meaning of these sacrifices of the Ilians ? '—sounding him in a delicate way in order to learn how his feelings were. He answered : ' What is there unbecoming if they do homage to a good man, their citizen, just as we do to the martyrs ? ' It is true the statue is not uninjured ; but the good will of (the Ilians) in respect of those times, if it is looked into, is comely. What, then, happened afterwards ? ' Let us go,' I said, ' into the sacred precincts (the *temenos*) of the Ilian Athené.' He also most willingly led the way, opened to me the temple, and, as if calling me to witness, he showed me all the statues perfectly well preserved, and he did none of the things those impious men are wont to do, who make on the forehead [4] the memorial of the impious (one), nor did he hiss to himself (*i.e.* ' aside '), like those (men), for their high theology consists in these two things, hissing against the daemons [5] and making the sign of the cross on the

πρὸς ἡμᾶς ἔφη πολλάκις, ὑπὲρ τοῦ σῶσαι τῶν θεῶν τὰ ἔδη τὰ ῥάκια ταῦτα περιαμπέσχετο καὶ τὴν ἀσέβειαν μέχρι ὀνόματος ὑπεκρίνατο (πέφηνε γὰρ οὐδὲν οὐδαμοῦ τῶν ἱερῶν ἠδικηκὼς πλὴν ὀλίγων παντάπασι λίθων ἐκ καταλύματος, ἵνα αὐτῷ σώζειν ἐξῇ τὰ λοιπά), τοῦτο ἐν λόγῳ ποιούμεθα καὶ οὐκ αἰσχυνόμεθα ταῦτα περὶ αὐτὸν πράττοντες ὅσαπερ Ἀφόβιος ἐποίει καὶ οἱ Γαλιλαῖοι πάντες προσεύχονται πάσχοντα ἰδεῖν αὐτόν; εἴ τι μοι προσέχεις, οὐ τοῦτον μόνον ἀλλὰ καὶ τοὺς ἄλλους οἵ μετατέθεινται τιμήσεις, ἵν' οἱ μὲν ῥᾷον ὑπακούσωσιν ἡμῖν ἐπὶ τὰ καλὰ προκαλουμένοις, οἱ δ' ἧττον χαίρωσιν. εἰ δὲ τοὺς αὐτομάτους ἰόντας ἀπελαύνοιμεν, οὐδεὶς ὑπακούσεται ῥᾳδίως παρακαλοῦσιν.

[4] σκιαγραφοῦντες, *i.e.* making the sign of the cross in mere show with the finger; like σκιαμαχοῦντες, making the mere movements of fighting.

[5] My friend the Honourable Alexander Rangabé, Ambassador of Greece at Berlin, reminds me that the term δαίμονες was at that time applied to the ancient gods who were identified with the devils. The Christians, consequently, hissed to themselves in order to avert their energy, like now in the Greek church, when the priest baptizes a child, he blows thrice into the baptismal water and spits thrice on the child, in order to avert the power of the devils from it.

forehead. These two things I desired to tell you; a third, which comes to my mind, I think I must not conceal. The same Pegasius followed me also to the Achilleum, and showed me the sepulchre unhurt, for I had heard also that he had excavated this tomb. But he approached it even with great reverence.

"All this I saw myself. But I have heard from those who are now inimically disposed against him, that in secret he prays to and worships the sun. Would you not accept my testimony, even as a private man? Of the sentiments which each one has regarding the gods, who could be more credible witnesses than the gods themselves? Should we have made Pegasius a priest if we had known him to have been impious towards the gods? But if in those times, whether aspiring to power, or, as he often told us, desiring to preserve the temples of the gods, he wrapped those rags around (his body) and feigned impiety in name (for he has shown that he never did mischief to anything at all in the sanctuaries, except some few stones which he took out from an inn [or perhaps *ruin*, the word κατάλυμα being derived from the verb καταλύω] in order to be able to save the rest); is it worth while to speak about it, and should we not be ashamed to treat him just as Aphobius did and as all the Galileans pray to see him treated? If you listen at all to me, you will honour not him alone, but also the others who go over (from Christianity to heathenism), in order that these may follow us easily when we summon them to the good way, and that the others (the Christians) may rejoice the less. But if we drive away those who come of themselves, nobody will readily follow when we invite them."[6]

---

[6] Dr. Henning says, in his comments on this letter: "The MS. of this letter is of the fourteenth century: it is preserved in the British Museum. The person to whom the letter is addressed is not mentioned; he appears to have been a friend of the Emperor, and, perhaps, as governor of some province, to have made remonstrances with Julian for having given probably an influential sacerdotal position to Pegasius, who was suspected of Christianity and had been formerly a (false) Christian. Julian defends himself, and shows how, when as prince he visited Ilium, he had had occasion to recognize the heathen sentiments of that false Christian, though a Christian bishop. Julian wrote the letter as emperor; that is, between 361 and 363 A.D. First of all, this letter offers us an important supplement to the history of Novum Ilium, the existence of which, so far as I know, could only be followed up to about 350 A.D. by the coins. In the middle of the fourth century Julian came, on his way to the camp of Constantius, from Troas ('Αλεξάνδρεια ἡ Τρωάς) to Ilium. Here he is led round through the city and the temples by Pegasius. He shows him τὸ ἡρῷον Ἕκτορος, with its bronze statue ἐν ναΐσκῳ βραχεῖ, and τὸν μέγαν 'Αχιλλέα ἀντιτεταγμένον αὐτῷ κατὰ τὸ ὕπαιθρον. On the altars still glow fire-brands of the sacrifices made by the Ilians. Pegasius then leads Julian to the τέμενος of the Ilian Athené

(Herodotus, vii. 43; Xenoph. *Hell.* i. 1. 4; Arrian. *Anab.* i. 11. 7; Plutarch, *Alexander*): he opens the temple and shows him all the statues of the gods intact. He also shows him the Achilleum, and proves to him that the tomb is uninjured. At the time of this visit, and, as Julian states nothing to the contrary, at the time when this letter was written, *i.e.* between 361 and 363 A.D., the Lysimachian Ilium, which had so frequently suffered, but which had become prosperous again under the Roman emperors, must have existed still, with all its temples and curiosities. In spite of all edicts against the worship of the ancient gods, it must still have been under the first Christian emperors a place of pilgrimage for the heathen world, for Julian speaks of the Periegetae as of professional guides for strangers. The city, with all its temples, was indeed more than neglected by the emperors; but nevertheless we find it treated better than other cities, if we remember that by an edict of the year 324, repeated in 341, the service of the Hellenic worship of the gods was prohibited in the East (Mücke, *Julianus*, ii. 73), the temples themselves were confiscated (326), and many of them were then destroyed, partly by order of the authorities, partly with their express or tacit consent. Julian finds very credible what Pegasius assures him, that he was nothing but a false Christian (and that as such

Nothing is known to us of the further history of Novum Ilium, but, as the latest coins I found there are of Constantius II., there can be no doubt that it decayed with the prevalence of Christianity, the destruction of its temples, and the consequent cessation of the pilgrimages to their shrines. Meyer[7] mentions, however, that by Constantinus Porphyrogennetus[8] (A.D. 911–959) most cities of the Troad are cited as bishoprics: Adramyttium, Assos, Gargara, Antandros, Alexandria-Troas, Ilium, Dardanus, Abydos, Lampsacus; Parium even as the seat of an archbishop. But there being no Byzantine potsherds or Byzantine ruins on the site of Ilios, the bishopric of Ilium may probably have been on another site.

---

he had become ἐπίσκοπος τῶν Γαλιλαίων, probably in Ilium, and with the superintendence over the confiscated temples), in order to be able the better to preserve these monuments from destruction. It is true that Pegasius, in order to save the principal objects, was obliged to do some trifling damage in the temples; and if he, in his devotion to the ancient gods and their worship, was forced to make this sacrifice to the destructive rage of the Christians, how then may not a Christian fanatic, as bishop or governor, have raged?"

Henning then proves by a learned discussion that Julian's visit to Novum Ilium must have taken place either in December 354, or in September–October 355.

[7] Eduard Meyer, *Die Geschichte der Troas*, p. 97.

[8] *De Cerem.*, ii. 54, pp. 792, 794.

CHAPTER IV.

THE TRUE SITE OF HOMER'S ILIUM.

THE problem of the real site of the Homeric Ilium slept during the Middle Ages, and attracted no attention after the Renaissance. The few travellers, who visited the Troad since the sixteenth century, either recognized the Homeric Ilium in the ruins of Alexandria-Troas,[1] or limited their researches to a very superficial inspection of the Plain of Troy or only of its coast.[2]

In 1785 and 1786 the Troad was visited by Lechevalier,[3] who was aided in his researches by the architect Cazas, and patronized by Count Choiseul-Gouffier, then French ambassador at Constantinople. At that time the science of archæology was only in its first dawn. Egyptology did not yet exist; the cities of Assyria were not yet discovered; pre-historic antiquities were still unknown; excavations for scientific purposes were a thing unheard of; the study of Sanscrit had not yet begun; the science of comparative philology had not yet been created; nay, philology was limited to a stammering play on Latin words, from which all languages

---

[1] So Pietro Beloni, *Observations de plusieurs Singularités et Choses remarquables trouvées en Grèce, Asie, Judée, Égypte, etc.*, par Pierre Belon, du Mans, 1588 ; and Pietro della Valle, *Les fameux Voyages de P. J. V., surnommé l'illustre Voyageur*, Paris, 1670. See Lechevalier, *Voyage de la Troade*, ii. pp. 157, 158; I. Spon and G. Wheeler, *Voyage d'Italie, etc.* A la Haye, 1724 ; see also Buchholz, *Homer. Kosmogr. und Geogr.* p. 330.

[2] Sandys, *Descr. of the Turk. Empire ;* London, 1627. He could only remain one day on the shore of the Plain of Troy, the country being infested by robbers. Grelot (*Relation d'un Voyage de Constantinople*, 1680) professes to have seen the Plain of Troy as well as the Xanthus and Simois from Cape Sigeum: see Lechevalier, *Voyage de la Troade*, ii. pp. 158, 159 ; Le Bruyn, *Voyage au Levant.* Buchholz mentions for curiosity's sake Lady Mary Wortley Montague, an enterprising English traveller, who, on her journey to the Hellespont and Constantinople, stopped with her vessel at Cape Sigeum, and went —the *Iliad* in her hand—up to its top, whence she perceived the tumulus of Achilles, Cape Rhoeteum with the tumulus of Ajax, and the Simois with the Scamander (Lady Mary Wortley Montague, *Briefe während ihrer Reisen in Europa, Asien, und Afrika.* 3 Theile und Nachträge ; Leipzig,

1763-1767 : a translation of her well-known English work). Buchholz also mentions Pococke (*Beschreibung des Morgenlandes und einiger anderer Länder*, German ed. by Breyer and Scheber, Erlangen, 1790, 1791, a translation of the well-known English work) as the first who in the year 1739 made thorough researches in the Plain of Troy, determined the situation of its various heroic tombs, saw the valley of the Thymbrius and the confluence of the Scamander and Simois. Buchholz, p. 331, also mentions Wood (*Essay on the Original Genius and Writings of Homer*, London, 1769, 4 ; 1770, 4 ; 1775, 4), who discovered the sources of the Scamander, believing them to be those of the Simois ; also Chandler (*Travels in Asia Minor*, Oxford, 1775), who fixed the position of the heroic tombs with categorical certainty. I may further mention F. A. G. Spohn, *Comment. Geogr. Crit. de agro Trojano in carminibus Homericis descripto*, Lipsiae 1814; but he had no personal knowledge of the Troad, and endeavours to fix all the sites by the indications of Homer. Neither did Alexander Pope know the Troad personally, but nevertheless he made a Map of Troy and its environs (before he translated the *Iliad*).

[3] *Voyage de la Troade*, 3 tomes, 3ᵉ édit. ; Paris, Dentu, An. x. 1802.

were thought to be derived, except by those who held the fond fancy that Hebrew was the primitive speech of the whole human race; and no one had an idea of the descent of our race from the highlands above India, which indeed was still almost a *terra incognita*. Since there were no archæologists, there was no archæological criticism. When, therefore, Lechevalier [4] made his romantic pilgrimage in search of Ilium, and learnt intuitively, without even touching the ground with the spade, and as if by divine inspiration,—just as Virgil says:

> " Hic Dolopum manus, hic saevus tendebat Achilles;
> Classil us hic locus, hic acie certare solebant," [5]—

that Priam's Pergamus had been on the hill at the extremity of the heights of Bali Dagh; that the city had extended over the heights as far down as the village of Bounarbashi, which marked the site of the Scaean Gate; and that the *forty cold* springs at the foot of the village were the *two* sources of the Scamander, of which he described the one as *warm*, with volumes of steam arising from it, in order to make it agree with the Homeric indication; [6]—when further he affirmed that the rivulet Bounarbashi Su, formed by the forty springs, was the Scamander (*arentem Xanthi cognomine rivum*), and made this river appear on his map of the Plain of Troy almost as broad as the real Scamander, which he called Simois, declaring the Doumbrek Su (Simois) to be the Thymbrius;—when finally, in order to put his system in perfect accord with the indications of the *Iliad*, he represented his Scamander as joining his Simois at Koum Kioi, and falling into the Hellespont close to Cape Rhoeteum; [7]— his theories were almost unanimously adopted, and his imaginary identifications produced in the scientific world a far greater sensation than any real discovery in later times.

Lechevalier's theories found an especially warm defender in Count Choiseul-Gouffier, [8] French ambassador at Constantinople, in whose service he was, and who himself visited the Plain of Troy and confirmed all his discoveries. Choiseul-Gouffier says that the sources of the Scamander at Bounarbashi are still in the same condition as they were in Homer's time; [9] that one is warm and the other cold; [10] that the village of Bounarbashi is situated on the hill Batieia; [1] that the Scaean Gate was a little above Bounarbashi, on the upper part of that hill; that the Erineos can be easily recognized; [2] that the site of Troy is covered with ancient *débris*, and that foundations of an ancient settlement can be traced; [3] finally, that the tumulus of Ujek Tepeh is the sepulchre of Aesyetes. [4] Choiseul-Gouffier admits, with Lechevalier, that the ancient Scamander fell into the Hellespont at the foot of Cape Rhoeteum, for so he also represents

---

[4] *Voyage de la Troade*, 3 tomes, 3ᵉ édit.; Paris, Dentu, An. x. 1802. Lechevalier's *Beschreibung der Ebene von Troia, mit Anmerkungen von Dalzel, aus dem Englischen, von Dornedden*; Leipzig, 1792.

[5] *Aeneid.* ii. 29.

[6] *Il.* xxii. 147–152.

[7] See the map in his work above mentioned.

[8] *Voyage pittoresque de la Grèce*, tome ii. livraison ii.; Paris, 1820. See Buchholz, *Homer. Kosmogr. und Geogr.* p. 333.

[9] See C. G. Lenz, *Die Ebene von Troia, nach dem Grafen Choiseul-Gouffier*; Neu Strelitz, 1798, p. 26.   [10] *Ibid.* p. 59.

[1] *Ibid.* p. 31.   [2] *Ibid.* p. 34.

[3] *Ibid.* p. 44.   [4] *Ibid.* pp. 54, 55.

it on his map:[5] this last appears to be the single right view that these two travellers hit upon.

The theory of Lechevalier and Choiseul-Gouffier, that ancient Troy was situated on the heights of Bounarbashi, was at the end of the last century violently opposed by Jacob Bryant,[6] who declares the war of Troy to be a myth, but maintains that Homer had in view a real space of ground for his tragedy: this theatre of the Trojan war he places near Cape Lectum and the city of Hamaxitus.

Messrs. Hawkins, Sibthorpe, Lyston, and Dallaway, travellers to the Plain of Troy, mentioned by Lechevalier,[7] adopted his theory. This Troy-Bounarbashi theory was further adopted by the following writers:—

Heyne, *Excurs. ad Iliad.*, lib. vi.

Carl Gotthold Lenz, *Die Ebene von Troia;* Neu Strelitz, 1798.

J. B. S. Morritt, in his answer to Jacob Bryant, *A Vindication of Homer,* York, 1798; and *Some Observations upon the Vindication of Homer,* Eton, 1799.

Wm. Franklin, *Remarks and Observations on the Plain of Troy, made during an Excursion in June,* 1799; London, 1800.

William Gell, *The Topography of Troy and its Vicinity;* London, 1801.

Hawkins, in the *Edinburgh Transactions,* vol. iv.

Robert Walpole, *Memoirs relating to European and Asiatic Turkey,* London, 1817, adopts the observations made on the Troad by P. Hunt, who puts Troy at Bounarbashi.

Otto Friedrich von Richter, *Wallfahrten im Morgenlande;* Berlin, 1822.

Colonel W. M. Leake, *Journal of a Tour in Asia Minor;* London, 1824, p. 277 ff.

Von Prokesch-Osten, *Erinnerungen aus Aegypten und Kleinasien,* iii. 1–117, Wien, 1829–1831; and *Denkwürdigkeiten und Erinnerungen aus dem Orient,* i. pp. 137 ff., Stuttgart, 1836–1837.

Field-Marshal Count von Moltke has also declared in favour of the Troy-Bounarbashi theory; *Briefe über Zustände und Begebenheiten in der Türkei aus den Jahren* 1835 *bis* 1839; Berlin, Posen, und Bromberg, bei E. S. Mittler, 1841, pp. 167–172. Moltke says: "We who are no scholars suffer ourselves to be simply guided by a military instinct to the spot, which, in old times as well as now, would be colonized, if an inaccessible citadel were to be founded." For these details of Field-Marshal Count von Moltke's judgment, I am indebted to my friend Dr. G. von Eckenbrecher.

Sir Charles Fellowes, *Excursion in Asia Minor,* 1838.

Charles Texier, *Description de l'Asie Mineure,* i.; Paris, 1839.

---

[5] *Ibid.* See map at the end of the work *Voyage pittoresque de la Grèce,* &c.; and C. G. Lenz, *Die Ebene von Troia,* &c.: also Lechevalier, *Voyage de la Troade,* &c. The maps of Lechevalier and Choiseul-Gouffier are perfectly identical, for both are nothing but copies of the map made by the architect Cazas. (See Lenz, *Die Ebene von Troia,* &c. p. xii.)

[6] *Observations upon a Treatise entitled a "Description of the Plain of Troy,"* by M. Lechevalier, Eton, 1795; and *Dissertation concerning the War of Troy and the Expedition of the Grecians as described by Homer,* London, 1796.

[7] *Voyage de la Troade,* ii. 212.

Henry W. Acland, *The Plains of Troy;* Oxford, 1839.

Forbiger, ‘*Handbuch der alten Geographie,* ii. p. 149.

Mauduit, *Découvertes dans la Troade;* Paris et Londres, 1840.

Lieutenant, now Admiral, T. A. B. Spratt, as well as Commander Thomas Graves, follow the same theory in their map of the Troad, 1840. I cannot refrain from making on this occasion a warm acknowledgment to both Admiral Spratt and Commander Graves for the immense service they have rendered to science by their most excellent map of the Troad. Nothing has escaped the close scrutiny they gave to every spot, in order to produce as complete a map of the plain and the hills falling into it as was possible, as a basis for the future study of Homeric Topography. For all previous maps were mere compilations of many travellers' journeys, and so in many points very erroneous and confusing, as well as deficient in giving the necessary geographical details. Every ruin, however small, is marked on this map, which can hardly ever be excelled.

P. W. Forchhammer, *Topographische und physiographische Beschreibung der Ebene von Troja,* published in English, in the *Journal of the Royal Geographical Society,* vol. xii., 1842, and republished in German, Kiel, 1850; also in the *Allgemeine Zeitung,* 1874, Beilage zu No. 93; also in his *Daduchos, Einleitung in das Verhältniss der hellenischen Mythen,* Kiel, 1875; also in the *Augsburger Allgemeine Zeitung,* Beilage zu No. 92, 1875; and his *Scamandros* in the *Jahrbücher für class. Philologie,* Jahrgang xxii. 1876.

Friedr. Gottlieb Welcker, *Kleine Schriften,* vol. ii. pp. 41, 44 ff.; Bonn and Elberfeld, 1844–1867.

Heinrich Kiepert, *Memoir über die Construction der Karte von Kleinasien;* Berlin, 1854.

G. W. F. Howard (Lord Carlisle), *Diary in Turkish and Greek Waters;* London, 1854.

Sir J. C. Hobhouse (Lord Broughton), *Travels in* 1810, London, 1813 (new edition, London, 1855), who puts Troy near Alexandria-Troas.

J. G. von Hahn, *Ausgrabungen auf der Homer. Pergamos;* Leipzig, 1864. He excavated on the heights above Bounarbashi in May 1864, and says, in conclusion, that he does not believe in a real Troy, but thinks Homer has adapted his poems to the site of Bounarbashi.

M. G. Nikolaïdes, *Topographie et Plan stratégique de l'Iliade;* Paris, 1867.

L. W. Hasper, *Beiträge zur Topographie der Homerischen Ilias,* Brandenburg, 1867; also, *Das alte Troia und das Schlachtfeld der Homerischen Helden,* Glogau, 1868; also, *Ueber die Lage des alten Ilium,* Leipzig, 1873; also, *Das negative Resultat der Ausgrabungen Schliemann's auf Hissarlik, und Beweis dass der Sänger der Ilias Troia auf Bali Dagh erbaut angenommen habe,* Berlin, 1874.

Henry Fanshawe Tozer, *Researches in the Highlands of Turkey;* London, 1869, p. 337.

Ernst Curtius, *Griechische Geschichte,* 4th edition, Berlin, 1874; also in his Lecture at Berlin in November 1871.

E. Buchholz, *Homerische Kosmographie und Geographie*; Leipzig, 1871.

E. Isambert, *Itinéraire descriptif*; Paris, 1873.

A. Conze, *Troianische Ausgrabungen*, in the *Preuss. Jahrbücher*, xxxiv., Berlin, 1874; and xxxv. p. 398, 1875.

George Perrot, *Excursion à Troie et aux Sources du Menderé; Extrait de l'Annuaire de l'Association pour l'Encouragement des Études grecques en France*, 1874.

G. d'Eichthal, *Le Site de Troie selon Lechevalier ou selon Schliemann*; Paris, 1875.

B. Stark, in the *Jenaer Literaturblätt*, No. 23, 1874; also *Nach dem Griechischen Orient, Reisestudien*, 1875, *Jenaer Lit. S.* 156; *Augsburger Allgemeine Zeitung*, Beilage No. 8, Arad. 5, S. 601; *Literar. Central-blatt*, S. 1131.

L. Vivien de Saint-Martin, *L'Ilion d'Homère, l'Ilium des Romains*; *Revue Archéologique*, Nouvelle Série, xxix.; Paris, 1875.

George Rawlinson, *History of Herodotus*; London, 1875. See the map in vol. iv. p. 43.

S. Ch. Schirlitz, in Ersch and Gruber's *Allgemeine Encyklopädie*, mentions further, among the explorers of the Troad, Dodwell and Forster, whose dissertations and theories are unknown to me.

Of those who adopt other theories, different from the sites of Bounar-bashi and Novum Ilium (Hissarlik)—

Dr. E. D. Clarke, *Travels in various Countries of Europe, Asia, and Africa*, Pt. i. London, 1812, endeavours to identify the village of Chiblak with Ilium and with the village of the Ilians ('Ιλιέων Κώμη).

Major J. Rennell, *Observations on the Topography of the Plain of Troy*, London, 1814; and later, H. N. Ulrichs, *Rheinisches Museum*, 3 Jahrg., pp. 573 ff., translated into English by Dr. Patrick Colquhoun, *An Excursus on the Topography of the Homeric Ilium*, in the *Transactions of the Royal Society of Literature*, vol. v.;—identify the site of Troy with 'Ιλιέων Κώμη, which they put on the height of *Akshi Kioi*, the farm of Mr. Calvert.

P. Barker Webb, *Topographie de la Troade*, Paris, 1844, identifies a site to the west of the village of Chiblak with the Homeric Troy.

H. Gelzer, *Eine Wanderung nach Troia*, Basel, 1873, does not decide in favour of any particular site; cf. *Literar. Centralblatt*, S. 1556 (1874).

E. Brentano, *Alt-Ilion im Dumbrekthal.*, Frankfurt am Main, 1877, endeavours to show that the Homeric Troy was on a hill in the Doumbrek valley, between the villages of Halil Eli and Ren Kioi, but he will never make a single convert to his impossible theory.

R. Hercher, *Ueber die Homerische Ebene von Troia*, Berlin, 1875, seems to believe that a real Troy never existed.

O. Frick, *Zur Troischen Frage*, in the *Jahrb. für class. Phil.*, 1876, pp. 289 ff., does not venture to pronounce in favour of a particular site, and thinks the discussion on the subject not yet far enough advanced.

L. von Sybel, *Ueber Schliemann's Troia*, Marburg, 1875, holds the same opinion.

To these I must add seven scholars, whose opinions on the subject are unknown to me:—

Virlet d'Aoust, *Description topographique et archéologique de la Troade,* 1873.

A. de Longpérier, *Compte Rendu,* 2, p. 94; *Revue Archéol.,* 27, p. 328.

Karl Henning, *Neu-Ilion,* in the *Hermes,* 9, p. 25; and in the *Archäolog. Zeitung,* p. 186, 1875.

C. Aldenhoven, *Ueber das neuentdeckte Troja; Im Neuen Reich,* i. p. 569, 1874.

August Steitz, *Die Lage des Homerischen Troia,* in the *Jahrbücher für classische Philologie,* ed. Alfr. Fleckeisen, Jahrgang xxi., Band iii.; Leipzig, 1875.

E. Mehlis, *Schliemann's Troja und die Wissenschaft,* in the German periodical *Das Ausland;* Stuttgart, 1875.

Julius Rieckler, *Ueber Schliemann's Ausgrabungen, Verhandlungen deutscher Philologen und Schulmänner;* Tübingen, 1876.

The following scholars have recognized the identity of Novum Ilium with the site of the Homeric Troy:—

C. Maclaren, *Dissertation on the Topography of the Plain of Troy,* Edinburgh, 1822; and *The Plain of Troy described,* Edinburgh, 1863.

G. von Eckenbrecher, *Ueber die Lage des Homerischen Ilion,* in the *Rheinische Museum,* Neue Folge, vol. ii. pp. 1 ff. 1842; and *Die Lage des Homerischen Troia,* Düsseldorf, 1875.

George Grote, *History of Greece;* London, 1846, 1st edition, vol. i.

Julius Braun, *Geschichte der Kunst in ihrem Entwicklungsgange,* Wiesbaden, 1856; and *Homer und sein Zeitalter,* Heidelberg, 1856-8.

Dr. L. Schmitz, in Dr. W. Smith's *Dictionary of Greek and Roman Geography,* art. Ilium; London, 1857.

Wm. Büchner, *Jahresbericht über das Gymnasium Fridericianum;* Schwerin, 1871 and 1872.

Émile Burnouf, *Revue des Deux Mondes,* du 1er Janvier, 1874, and *Mémoires de l'Antiquité,* Paris, 1878.

Philip Smith, *Discoveries at Troy,* in the *Quarterly Review,* April 1874.

C. T. Newton, *Dr. Schliemann's Discoveries at Ilium Novum;* Lecture before the Society of Antiquaries, April 30th, 1874; *Academy,* 1874, No. 173.

Frank Calvert, who was formerly an adherent of the Troy-Bounarbashi theory, became a convert to the Troy-Hissarlik theory, which he now energetically defends (see his *Contributions towards the Ancient Geography of the Troad;* also *Trojan Antiquities,* arts. i. ii.; *The Athenæum,* 1874, Nov. 7 and 14, London).

Ph. Déthier, *Une Partie du Trésor troyen au Musée de Constantinople* (*Revue Arch.* 31, p. 416), 1874; also *Nouvelle Trouvaille faite à Ilium-Hissarlik,* 1874.

Otto Keller, *Die Entdeckung Ilions zu Hissarlik,* Freiburg, 1875; also *Ueber die Entdeckung Trojas durch H. Schliemann,* Beilage zur *Allgemeinen Zeitung,* Nos. 344, 345, 1874.

Felix Ravaisson de Molien, *Revue Archéologique*, 26, p. 404; cf. *Arcad.* 26, p. 326.

Stephen Salisbury, *Troy and Homer, Remarks on the Discoveries of Dr. H. Schliemann in the Troad;* Worcester, 1875.

G. A. Lauria, *Troia, uno Studio;* Napoli, 1875.

W. Christ, *Topographie der Troianischen Ebene*, München, 1874; also *Troja und die Troade*, i.–iii., in the *Allgemeine Zeitung*, 1875, Drittes Quartal, Beilage zu Nos. 196, 197, 198.

Maxime du Camp, *L'Emplacement de l'Ilion d'Homère, d'après les plus récentes Découvertes;* Paris, 1875.

François Lenormant, *Les Antiquités de la Troade et l'Histoire primitive des Contrées grecques;* Paris, 1876.

F. Schlie, *Wissenschaftliche Beurtheilung der Funde Schliemanns in Hissarlik*, Schwerin, 1876; also *Schliemann und seine Bestrebungen*, Schwerin, 1876.

W. E. Gladstone, *Homer's Place in History*, in the *Contemporary Review*, 1874; *Homeric Synchronism*, London, 1876; and *Homer*, London, 1878, enthusiastically defends the Troy-Hissarlik theory.

Eduard Meyer, *Geschichte von Troas;* Leipzig, 1877.

A. H. Sayce, in his letters to the *Athenæum* and the *Academy*, October 1879, and in the *Contemporary Review*, December 1878.

I have finally to mention the great authority of Professor Rudolf Virchow, who assisted me in my excavations at Hissarlik, from the 4th of April till the 4th of May, 1879, and who energetically opposes the Troy-Bounarbashi theory, and enthusiastically declares in favour of the identity of Hissarlik with the Homeric Troy. See his Lectures in the session of the Berlin Anthropological Society of the 26th of June and the 12th of July, 1879; in the Anthropological Congress at Strassburg on the 13th of August, and at Amsterdam on the 16th of September, of the same year: also his excellent work, *Beiträge zur Landeskunde der Troas*, Berlin, 1879.

The principal argument of the defenders of the Troy-Bounarbashi theory is that immediately below the village are the two springs of Homer—one lukewarm, the other cold; but this argument falls to the ground before the fact already mentioned, that there are not two but forty springs, all of which are cold and have a temperature of from $62°·24$ to $62°·6$ Fahr. Besides, as already stated, the Scamander originates, not in the Plain of Troy, but at a distance of twenty hours' journey from Hissarlik, in the range of Ida, from a cold spring, which has a temperature of $47°·12$ Fahr. About 200 ft. from this source, the river is joined by the water of a spring which has a temperature of $60°·44$ Fahr., and might perhaps, in comparison with the other spring, be called lukewarm. Perhaps Homer had heard of this lukewarm spring and the cold spring of the Scamander, and the poet may have brought them from Ida down to the Plain in order to introduce his beautiful verses (*Il.* xxii. 147-152). He clearly states (*Il.* xii. 19-21) that the Scamander flows from Mount Ida. That he had not in his mind the springs of Bounarbashi, is also clearly shown by the statement, that close to the two sources were large washing troughs of stone, in which the Trojan women used to wash their clothes in the time of peace, before the arrival of the Greek army,[5] because the Bounarbashi springs being, in a straight line, at a distance of eight miles from the Hellespont and there being no regular siege, but only battles in the plain, there would have been no cause for them to stop washing at the springs on account of the war, as the advancing enemy could be seen at a great distance off in the plain. Consequently, this passage proves that, in the mind of the poet, the distance between the Greek camp and Troy was but very short.

I must further absolutely deny the truth of the statement made by Choiseul-Gouffier[6] and Ernst Curtius,[7] that the site of Troy on the heights of Bounarbashi is covered with ancient ruins. I take Virchow and Burnouf, who accompanied me all over those heights, as witnesses, that not only are there no ruins whatever of ancient buildings, but even that there are no ancient potsherds or fragments of bricks, and that the ground is everywhere uneven, full of pointed or abrupt rocks and nowhere artificially levelled, so that the site can never have been inhabited by men. I also cite the weighty testimony of the late Austrian Consul-General, J. G. von Hahn, who, with the celebrated astronomer Julius Schmidt, excavated during the whole of May, 1864, in the little city at the southern extremity of those heights (the Bali Dagh), and who, on stopping the work, writes as follows:[8]—"I can only confirm the testimony of Von Bröndsted, that the whole locality does not show the slightest trace of a great city ever having existed here, which ought to have extended over the wide northern slope of the Bali Dagh, from the foot of the Acropolis to the springs of Bounarbashi. In spite of our zealous researches, we could not discover there—besides the tumuli—any sign which might point to a former human settlement, *not even* fragments of ancient pottery or bricks, those never-failing and consequently inevitable witnesses of an ancient establishment. No fragments of columns or other building stones, no ancient freestone, nowhere in the native rock a quarried bed of any such stone, nowhere any artificial levelling of the rock; everywhere the natural soil, which has never been touched by the hand of man." I may here repeat, that my thorough exploration of the heights of Bounarbashi in August 1868 gave the same results. I excavated in hundreds of places at the springs, in Bounarbashi itself, and on the land between that village and the Scamander, as well as on the declivities wherever I found earth. I struck the rock almost everywhere at a depth of from 2 to 3 feet, without ever finding the slightest vestige of bricks or pottery.[9]

With regard to the walls brought to light by J. G. von Hahn and

---

[5] *Il.* xxii. 153–156 :
ἔνθα δ' ἐπ' αὐτάων πλυνοὶ εὐρέες ἐγγὺς ἔασιν
καλοὶ λαΐνεοι, ὅθι εἵματα σιγαλόεντα
πλύνεσκον Τρώων ἄλοχοι καλαί τε θύγατρες
τὸ πρὶν ἐπ' εἰρήνης, πρὶν ἐλθεῖν υἷας Ἀχαιῶν.

[6] *Voyage pittoresque de la Grèce*, ii. ; Paris,

1820, p. 44.

[7] Lecture at Berlin, in November 1871.

[8] J. G. von Hahn, *Die Ausgrabungen auf der Homerischen Pergamos* ; Leipzig, 1864, p. 33.

[9] See my *Ithaque, le Péloponnèse et Troie* ; Paris, 1869, pp. 151, 161, 162 ; and above, p. 19.

Julius Schmidt in the little city at the extremity of the Bali Dagh, in which so many great luminaries of archæology have seen the cyclopean walls of Priam's Pergamus, and which Ernst Curtius[10] holds to be contemporaneous with the cyclopean walls of Tiryns and Mycenae, which latter are universally considered to be the most ancient specimens extant of cyclopean masonry;—nearly all these walls are low retaining walls, formed of comparatively small quadrangular, or nearly quadrangular, slabs; there are also a few small straight walls of square blocks or polygons on the north side, a portion of one of which my friend Admiral Spratt represents in the vignette of his map; there is also a fragment of wall of square hewn blocks in the south-west corner: but we have no right whatever to call these walls, or any part of them, "cyclopean;" for this epithet can only refer to the gigantic, never to the lilliputian. In a hundred different places in Greece I can point out walls of well-fitted polygons, of which we know with certainty that they are of the Macedonian period, or at least of the latter part of the fifth century B.C. But I will here only name two places which can be easily seen by those who visit Athens: namely, the tombs in the Hagia Trias at Athens, some of the substructions of which consist of well-fitted polygons; and the fortifications on the island of Salamis, which show the same masonry.[1] Unhewn boulders, rough quarried stones, and those which had a polygonal cleavage due to their structure, were often used for convenience by builders, who were quite able to work quadrangular blocks, as is proved by walls in which the former kinds are placed above the latter.[2] Walls of polygons have for the last twenty years come into extensive use in Sweden and Norway, as substructions of railway bridges; and if any one in Sweden were to call this masonry "cyclopean walls," the people there would laugh just as the Athenians would laugh if the fortifications in Salamis or the substructions in Hagia Trias were called by that name.

As to the chronology of the little city on the Bali Dagh, we have fortunately two data for its determination: first, by the manner in which the stones have been worked; and, secondly, from the pottery. On all the stones of the walls, without exception, the blows of the stonecutters' iron pick-axes are conspicuous, and therefore, in my opinion, no part of them can claim a higher antiquity than the fourth or fifth century B.C. As a witness to my statement I cite the authority of Professor Rudolf Virchow, who was the first to discover that all the stones had been worked with iron pick-axes, and who expresses himself as follows:[3]—

---

[10] Lecture at Berlin, in November 1871.

[1] Émile Burnouf, *La Ville et l'Acropole d'Athènes*, pp. 192, 193.

[2] E. H. Bunbury, *Cyclopean Remains in Central Italy*, in the *Classical Museum*, 1845, vol. ii. pp. 147 et seq.; and the article MURUS in Dr. Wm. Smith's *Dictionary of Greek and Roman Antiquities.* My friend, the writer of that article, informs me that he noticed, at the sea-side, a wall built up of boulders of concrete from a sea-wall washed down during the preceding winter, which had a most curious resemblance

to "cyclopean" walls, both of the rough-square and polygonal type; and there are hundreds of such cases of rough materials still used from motives of convenience.

[3] In his Lecture at the session of the Berlin Anthropological Society, 20th June, 1879: "Die ganze Art der Fundation (der kleinen Acropolis am Südende des Bali Dagh) entspricht nicht dem was man von einer so alten Stadt erwarten müsste, und es ist wohl unzweifelhaft, dass die wohlbehauenen Quadern, auf denen noch die Hiebe der Steinhauer zu sehen sind, mit guten

" The whole character of the foundations (of the little Acropolis at the southern extremity of the Bali Dagh) does not correspond with what one would have expected from so ancient a place, and there can be no doubt that the well-cut blocks, on which the blows of the stonecutters can be still seen, have been worked with good iron instruments. Whoever compares this place with what presents itself at Hissarlik, cannot doubt that it belongs to a much later period, and that, at the highest date, it approaches the time of Alexander."

I further cite the testimony of Mr. Frank Calvert, as well as that of Professor A. H. Sayce and Mr. F. W. Percival, all of whom acknowledge, from their own inspection, that the stones of all the walls of the little city have been worked with iron pick-hammers, and that, consequently, these walls must belong to a comparatively late period.[4]

As a fifth most trustworthy authority for the comparatively late date of the walls on the Bali Dagh, I cite the pottery contained in the *very scanty* accumulation of *débris* inside the walls. No wall of any city or acropolis in the world can be more ancient than the most ancient potsherds contained in the place enclosed by them : nay, the strongest walls may be broken away, or may, in the course of time, crumble away and disappear ; but not so the fragments of pottery, because they are indestructible. The pottery I found in the royal sepulchres at Mycenae is acknowledged by all competent authorities to date from between 1200 and 1500 B.C., and it is still as well preserved, and looks as fresh, as if it had been made yesterday ; and, if it remained buried for millions of years more, it would hardly have a different appearance. The whole site of Mycenae is strewn with fragments of most ancient pre-historic pottery, which have probably been exposed for 3000 years to the open air ; nevertheless they are as solid as if they had been but recently made, and their painted colours have lost but little of their original brightness. In the potsherds, therefore, contained in the *débris* inside of walls, we must necessarily find two *termini* for the age of the walls themselves. Now, Von Hahn and Schmidt found in their excavations on the Bali Dagh, in May 1864, only one small headless figure of terra-cotta, four tubes of clay, a common clay pitcher, two clay lamps, some clay vessels, fragments for the most part of black-glazed pottery, some copper coins of the second and third centuries B.C., and some fragments of house-walls of a late and poor Hellenic masonry.[5] I obtained the same results in the excavations I made there in August 1868.[6] I did not find one archaic potsherd, nor one of those whorls with incised ornamentation, of which I found so many thousands at Hissarlik ; in fact, no pottery to which archæology could attribute a higher antiquity than the fourth or fifth century B.C. We therefore obtained, by the exploration of the site, and particularly by

Eiseninstrumenten gearbeitet wurden. Wenn man diese Stelle vergleicht mit dem, was in Hissarlik hervortritt, so zweifelt man nicht, dass sie einer viel späteren Periode augehört und höchstens sich der Zeit Alexanders nähert."

[4] A. H. Sayce, in his Letters from the Troad, in the *Athenæum* of October 4th, 1879 ; from Smyrna, in the *Academy* of 18th October ; and from Oxford, in the same journal of 8th November.

[5] J. G. von Hahn, *Ausgrabungen auf der Homerischen Pergamos*, pp. 22, 23.

[6] See my *Ithaque, le Péloponnèse et Troie*, pp. 169, 170 ; and above, p. 19.

its pottery, the same chronology for the walls which we obtain by the characteristic working of the stones themselves,—namely, the fourth or fifth century B.C. Besides, the accumulation of *débris* is but very insignificant: in many places in the little Acropolis the bare rock crops out; nowhere did I strike the rock at a greater depth than 5 feet, and *generally at a few inches below the surface.* I beg the reader to compare these results with those obtained at Hissarlik, where the accumulation of *débris* is from 52 to 53 ft. deep!

I may here mention that, as Homer makes Hector and Achilles run three times round the city of Troy,[7] it is a necessary condition that such a course should be physically possible. But if the heights of Bounarbashi mark the site of Troy, such a course is perfectly impossible, because the hill of the little Acropolis on the Bali Dagh—(which, according to the measurement of the astronomer Schmidt,[8] is 472 ft. above the sea, and according to M. Burnouf's measurement 144·36 mètres, which equally makes 472 ft.)—falls off very abruptly to the north-east, the east, and particularly to the south. Now, as the heroes must have run down on the south side to make the circuit of the city, I went myself down by this side, which falls off at first at an angle of 45°, and afterwards at an angle of about 25°; thus I was forced to crawl backward on all fours: it took me a quarter of an hour to come down, and I carried away the conviction that no mortal being, not even a goat, has ever been able to run swiftly down a slope which descends at an angle of 25°; and that Homer never intended to make us believe that Hector and Achilles, in making the circuit of the city, could have run down this impossible descent.

I may add that neither from the Bali Dagh, nor from any other point of the heights of Bounarbashi attributed by Lechevalier and his followers to Troy, can Mount Ida be seen; but this is at variance with Homer, who represents Zeus as looking down from the top of Mount Gargarus on the city of Troy.[9]

Further, the heights of Bounarbashi belong to the lower range of Mount Ida. If Troy had been situated on those heights, Homer could not have expressly stated that it was built *in the plain,* in opposition to the first Trojan settlement, Dardanié, which, as he says, was built on the declivity of Ida rich in springs.[10] Plato confirms the account that the first Trojan settlement was on the heights of Ida, whence they built Ilium in a wide and beautiful plain, on a hill which was not high, and close to which were rivers pouring down their waters from the heights of Ida.[1] The position of Hissarlik, on a low hill almost in the midst of the splendid Plain of Troy, agrees perfectly with this important statement of

[7] *Il.* xxii. 165, 166:
ὣς τὼ τρὶς Πριάμοιο πόλιν περιδινηθήτην
καρπαλίμοισι πόδεσσι· θεοὶ δέ τε πάντες ὁρῶντο.
[8] J. G. von Hahn, *Ausgrabungen,* &c., p. 7.
[9] *Il.* viii. 51, 52:
αὐτὸς (Ζεὺς) δ' ἐν κορυφῇσι (Γαργάρου) καθέζετο
κύδεϊ γαίων,
εἰσορόων Τρώων τε πόλιν καὶ νῆας Ἀχαιῶν.

[10] *Il.* xx. 216–218:
κτίσσε δὲ Δαρδανίην, ἐπεὶ οὔ πω Ἴλιος ἱρὴ
ἐν πεδίῳ πεπόλιστο, πόλις μερόπων ἀνθρώπων,
ἀλλ' ἔθ' ὑπωρείας ᾤκεον πολυπίδακος Ἴδης.
[1] Plato, *De Legibus,* iii. 682, ed. G. Stallbaum:
Κατῳκίσθη δή, φαμέν, ἐκ τῶν ὑψηλῶν εἰς μέγα
τε καὶ καλὸν πεδίον Ἴλιον, ἐπὶ λόφον τινὰ οὐχ
ὑψηλὸν καὶ ἔχοντα ποταμοὺς πολλοὺς ἄνωθεν ἐκ
τῆς Ἴδης ὡρμημένους.

Plato; whereas the heights of Bounarbashi, which touch this Plain only on their small northern side, and are on all other sides connected with the higher range of Ida, are utterly opposed to and in contradiction with it. As to the objection made by the adherents of the Troy-Bounarbashi theory, that "the high mount of Bali Dagh behind Bounarbashi offers the most appropriate situation for a fortified city, and that for this reason—without the slightest ancient authority and in opposition to the distinct indications of Homer, and to the firm belief of all antiquity that Priam's city was in the plain—we must transfer it to that mount,"—this objection is (as Eckenbrecher[2] rightly observes) "untenable." He adds: "Mycenae, Tiryns, Athens, Rome, were built on low hills, Thebes[3] altogether in the plain. Why, then, was not the citadel of Athens built close by on Mount Lycabettus, which towers high above the hill of the Acropolis?"

"Nor must it," as Mr. Philip Smith observes to me, "be forgotten, throughout the whole argument, that the theory of Lechevalier is a mere *hypothesis*, born from the fancy of a modern traveller, *without the slightest historical or traditional foundation*. The whole *onus probandi*, therefore, lies upon its advocates, and nothing but an overwhelming body of evidence for this new invention can prevail against that historical and traditional *right of possession* by Novum Ilium, which is even sounder in archæology than it is proverbially in law. Every new discovery in modern scholarship is daily tending to restore the authority of historical tradition, in opposition to the theories of sceptical enquirers."

I must further repeat here, that the distance between the forty springs of Bounarbashi and the Hellespont is in a straight line eight miles, and from the little Acropolis, held to be identical with Priam's Pergamus, to the Hellespont is upwards of nine miles; whilst all the battles and all the marches to and fro in the *Iliad* justify the supposition that the distance between the city and the Greek camp cannot have exceeded three miles. Let us consider for instance the first battle, which, according to Pope's calculation, is on the twenty-third day of the *Iliad*. In the night, Zeus orders the God of Dreams to go to Agamemnon, and induce him to arm the Greeks, promising him that he shall now take Troy.[4] At the first dawn, Agamemnon orders the Greeks to assemble in the Agora; he tells his dream to the other chiefs, and, wishing to sound their intentions, he proposes to them to return to their country:[5] the troops, with loud cries, disperse among the ships and make preparations to set them afloat.[6] Ulysses restrains the troops, persuades them to remain, and they assemble for the second time in the Agora,[7] where long speeches are made by Ulysses, Nestor, and Agamemnon.[8] At last they decide to remain; the warriors disperse again through the camp to prepare the morning meal,

---

[2] G. von Eckenbrecher, *Die Lage des Homer-ischen Troja;* Düsseldorf, 1875, p. 23.

[3] M. Burnouf observes to me that, properly speaking, Thebes is not built in the plain, but on the Cadmea, which by a series of heights is connected with Mount Helicon.

[4] *Il.* ii. 8–15:

βάσκ' ἴθι, οὖλε ὄνειρε, θοὰς ἐπὶ νῆας Ἀχαιῶν·
ἐλθὼν ἐς κλισίην Ἀγαμέμνονος Ἀτρεΐδαο

πάντα μάλ' ἀτρεκέως ἀγορευέμεν ὡς ἐπιτέλλω.
θωρῆξαί ἑ κέλευε κάρη κομόωντας Ἀχαιούς
πανσυδίῃ· νῦν γάρ κεν ἕλοι πόλιν εὐρυάγυιαν
Τρώων· οὐ γὰρ ἔτ' ἀμφὶς Ὀλύμπια δώματ'
ἔχοντες
ἀθάνατοι φράζονται· ἐπέγναμψεν γὰρ ἅπαντας
Ἥρη λισσομένη, Τρώεσσι δὲ κήδε' ἐφῆπται.

[5] *Il.* ii. 48–140.   [6] *Il.* ii. 142–154.
[7] *Il.* ii. 182–210.   [8] *Il.* ii. 284–393.

which they then eat.[9]   Agamemnon sacrifices a fat ox to Zeus, and assembles all the chiefs for this ceremony.[10]   Nestor makes another speech, after which Agamemnon orders the heralds to summon the troops to draw up in order of battle;[1] and the army is arrayed before their camp in the Plain of the Scamander.[2]

Iris gives notice of this to the Trojans, who arm themselves, open all the gates of the city, rush out with a great noise,[3] and array their army at the tumulus of Batieia.[4]   The two armies meet in the plain;[5] but the plain could not have been large, because from the tower of the Scaean Gate Helen recognizes the chiefs of the Greeks and recounts their names to Priam.[6]   The Greek army could not have been farther off than half a mile, since one must be very keen-sighted in order to recognize men at that distance.

Paris challenges Menelaus to single combat.   Hector makes a speech, and Menelaus makes another.[7]   Hector despatches heralds to Troy to fetch live lambs, whilst Agamemnon sends his herald Talthybius to the Greek camp for the same purpose.[8]   As the Greek army could not be further distant than half a mile, at most, from the Scaean Gate, it would have been at least seven miles and a half from the camp, if Troy had been on the heights of Bounarbashi, with its gate—as Curtius supposes—on the site of this village.   In this case Talthybius could not have come back in less than six hours with the live lamb.   But his absence is so short, that the poet does not even mention it; hence it is evident that the distance which this herald had to go was very short.

Solemn sacrifices are offered, and solemn oaths are taken;[9] the single combat takes place; Paris is vanquished by Menelaus, and carried away by Aphrodité.[10]   Pandarus shoots an arrow at Menelaus and wounds him;[1] a long colloquy takes place between Agamemnon and Menelaus;[2] Machaon, skilful in the art of healing, dresses the wound.[3]

Agamemnon makes numerous speeches to encourage the Greek chiefs; and at last the battle begins.   Athené leads the impetuous Ares out of the battle, and makes him sit down on the bank of the Scamander.[4]   The Trojans are driven back to the walls of Troy.[5]   They are excited to battle by Apollo and Ares.[6]   During the battle, the wounded as well as the booty taken from the enemy are continually carried to Troy and to the Greek camp: arms, chariots, and horses.[7]   The Greeks *retire backwards* before the victorious Trojans;[8] they are repulsed as far as the Naustathmus, because they are represented as fighting near the ships.[9]

---

[9] *Il.* ii. 394–401.   [10] *Il.* ii. 402–433.   [3] *Il.* iv. 208–219.   [4] *Il.* v. 35, 36.

[1] *Il.* ii. 441–454.   [2] *Il.* ii. 464, 465.   [5] *Il.* v. 37 :

[3] *Il.* ii. 786–810; iii. 1–9.

[4] *Il.* ii. 811–815.

Τρῶας δ' ἔκλιναν Δαναοί· ἕλε δ' ἄνδρα ἕκαστος ἡγεμόνων.

[5] *Il.* iii. 15.   [6] *Il.* iii. 166–235.   [6] *Il.* v. 460–470.

[7] *Il.* iii. 67–75, 86–94, 97–110.   [7] *Il.* v. 325–663, 668, 669.

[8] *Il.* iii. 116–120 :   [8] *Il.* v. 699–702 :

Εκτωρ δὲ προτὶ ἄστυ δύω κήρυκας ἔπεμπεν
καρπαλίμως ἄρνας τε φέρειν Πρίαμόν τε καλέσσαι.
αὐτὰρ ὃ Ταλθύβιον προΐει κρείων Ἀγαμέμνων
νῆας ἔπι γλαφυρὰς ἰέναι, ἠδ' ἄρν' ἐκέλευεν
οἰσέμεναι· ὃ δ' ἄρ' οὐκ ἀπίθησ' Ἀγαμέμνονι δίῳ.

Ἀργεῖοι δ' ὑπ' Ἄρηϊ καὶ Ἕκτορι χαλκοκορυστῇ
οὔτε ποτὲ προτρέποντο μελαινάων ἐπὶ νηῶν
οὔτε ποτ' ἀντεφέροντο μάχῃ, ἀλλ' αἰὲν ὀπίσσω
χάζονθ'.

[9] *Il.* iii. 268–301.   [10] *Il.* iii. 355–382.   [9] *Il.* v. 791 :

[1] *Il.* iv. 104–140.   [2] *Il.* iv. 155–191.

νῦν δὲ ἑκὰς πόλιος κοίλης ἐπὶ νηυσὶ μάχονται.

The Greeks must in their turn have had the advantage, for we again
see a terrible battle between them and the Trojans in the plain between
the Scamander and the Simois. The Greeks recede again ;[10] and Hector
goes up to Troy to order sacrifices to the gods.[1] He appears to arrive
there during the space of time occupied by the touching scene and the
beautiful colloquy between Glaucus and Diomedes.[2] Hector has long
conversations with his mother, with Paris, and with Helen ; he looks for
his wife Andromaché ; he meets her and has a very long and affecting
conversation with her, after which comes the pathetic scene with his son.[3]
Hector returns to the battle in company with Paris, and it appears that
they reach the army immediately after having gone out of the Scaean
Gate.[4] Indeed the troops must have been before the Scaean Gate, because
Athené and Apollo, who had taken the form of two vultures, sit down on
the high beech-tree (φηγός) to enjoy the spectacle of the warriors, whose
thick lines are seated, bristling with helmets, shields, and spears.[5] As we
have seen before, this tree was near the Scaean Gate.[6] Hector and Paris
kill several enemies ;[7] then Hector provokes the bravest of the Greeks to
single combat.[8] There is a pause, because nobody dares to oppose himself
to Hector ; then a speech of Menelaus, who offers to fight with him ; then
speeches of Agamemnon and Nestor.[9] Nine heroes offer themselves to
fight with Hector ; they draw lots ; the lot falls on Ajax, son of Telamon,
who rejoices and puts on his glancing armour.[10] Then follow the speeches
of the two adversaries ;[11] they fight till night falls, and then exchange
presents.[1] The Greeks return to their camp ; the chiefs assemble in the
tent of Agamemnon, where the king slaughters an ox ; the animal is
skinned, cut up, and roasted ; and after this has been done, the evening
meal is taken.[2]

Let us now once more review the multitude of incidents on this single
day : first, at daybreak, the general assembly in the Greek camp ; the
long speech of Agamemnon ; then the dispersion of the troops to set the
ships afloat ; the long speeches of three heroes ; the meal is prepared ;
Agamemnon sacrifices an ox to Zeus ; the new speech of Nestor ; finally,
Agamemnon orders the army to be put in battle array. But this
variety of acts and speeches must have occupied at least four hours ;
therefore it is ten in the morning when the troops advance in the Plain

---

[10] Il. vi. 107 :
'Αργεῖοι δ' ὑπεχώρησαν, λῆξαν δὲ φόνοιο.
[1] Il. vi. 111–115.   [2] Il. vi. 119–235.
[3] Il. vi. 254–493.
[4] Il. vii. 1–7 :
ὣς εἰπὼν πυλέων ἐξέσσυτο φαίδιμος Ἕκτωρ,
τῷ δ' ἅμ' 'Αλέξανδρος κί' ἀδελφεός· ἐν δ' ἄρα
θυμῷ
ἀμφότεροι μέμασαν πολεμίζειν ἠδὲ μάχεσθαι.
ὣς δὲ θεὸς ναύτῃσιν ἐελδομένοισιν ἔδωκεν
οὖρον, ἐπεί κε κάμωσιν ἐϋξέστῃς ἐλάτῃσιν
πόντον ἐλαύνοντες, καμάτῳ δ' ὑπὸ γυῖα λέλυνται,
ὣς ἄρα τὼ Τρώεσσιν ἐελδομένοισι φανήτην.
[5] Il. vii. 58–62 :
κὰδ δ' ἄρ' 'Αθηναίη τε καὶ ἀργυρότοξος 'Απόλλων
ἑζέσθην, ὄρνισιν ἐοικότες αἰγυπιοῖσιν,
φηγῷ ἐφ' ὑψηλῇ πατρὸς Διὸς αἰγιόχοιο,

ἀνδράσι τερπόμενοι· τῶν δὲ στίχες εἵατο πυκναί,
ἀσπίσι καὶ κορύθεσσι καὶ ἔγχεσι πεφρικυῖαι.
[6] Il. vi. 237 :
Ἕκτωρ δ' ὡς Σκαιάς τε πύλας καὶ φηγὸν ἵκανεν.
[7] Il. vii. 8–16 :
ἔνθ' ἑλέτην ὃ μὲν υἱὸν 'Αρηϊθόοιο ἄνακτος,
Ἄρνῃ ναιετάοντα Μενέσθιον, ὃν κορυνήτης
γείνατ' 'Αρηΐθοος καὶ Φυλομέδουσα βοῶπις·
Ἕκτωρ δ' Ἠϊονῆα βάλ' ἔγχεϊ ὀξυόεντι
αὐχέν' ὑπὸ στεφάνης εὐχάλκου, λῦσε δὲ γυῖα
Γλαῦκος δ' Ἱππολόχοιο πάϊς, Λυκίων ἀγὸς ἀνδρῶν,
'Ιφίνοον βάλε δουρὶ κατὰ κρατερὴν ὑσμίνην
Δεξιάδην, ἵππων ἐπιάλμενον ὠκειάων,
ὦμον· ὃ δ' ἐξ ἵππων χαμάδις πέσε, λύντο δὲ γυῖα.
[8] Il. vii. 67–91.   [9] Il. vii. 96–160.
[10] Il. vii. 161–225.   [11] Il. vii. 226–243.
[1] Il. vii. 244–312.   [2] Il. vii. 313–336.

of the Scamander. They approach so near to the Scaean Gate, that Helen recognizes the Greek chiefs. Paris challenges Menelaus to single combat; there are speeches of Hector and Menelaus; heralds are sent to Troy and to the Greek camp to fetch live lambs; then come the solemn sacrifice and single combat. Numerous speeches are made by Agamemnon. The Greeks drive the Trojans back to the walls of Troy, and they are repulsed in their turn; *but they retire backward to the ships.* The Greeks must have again advanced, for a fearful battle takes place in the plain between the Scamander and the Simois. The Greeks retreat again. Hector goes to Troy; there are long speeches by him, by Hecuba, by Paris, by Helen, and by Andromaché. The Greeks must have advanced again, for Hector and Paris are in their presence when they go out of the Scaean Gate; then come the speeches of Hector, of Menelaus, of Nestor; the single combat terminated by the night; and finally the return of the Greeks to their camp.

Thus the distance between the city and the Greek camp has been traversed at least *six* times in the space of time from ten in the morning to seven in the evening—namely, twice by the herald who fetched the lamb, and at least four times by the army—and even once *backwards;* and all these marches and countermarches could be made in spite of the enormous consumption of time occasioned by the numerous speeches, the sacrifices, the different battles, and the two single combats. It is, therefore, evident that the distance between the Greek camp and Troy was assumed to be very short, and *less* than 3 miles. Bounarbashi is 8 miles from the shore of the Hellespont: if, therefore, Troy had been on the heights of Bounarbashi, at least 50 miles would have been traversed from ten in the morning to seven in the evening, in spite of all the loss of time produced by the different causes which I have enumerated.

Lechevalier and his adherents find all this possible, relying on the principle that Homér, as a poet, exaggerates, and that the warriors of the heroic times would have been able, or were believed to be able, to accomplish superhuman feats. But if we put aside the intervention of the gods, Homer is, as Webb [3] remarks, very exact about facts: "When he tells us that Achilles, if Poseidon gave him a good passage, would be in Phthia (a distance of 200 miles) in three days,[4] and that the ships of Nestor and Diomedes, with winds constantly favourable, sailed from Troy to Argos (a distance of 300 miles) in four days,[5] he speaks to us not of an heroic but of a very common passage, for Herodotus counts for a day of navigation 700 stadia (70 geog. miles), and, for a day and a night together, 1300 stadia.[6] Telemachus and Pisistratus, in a chariot with two swift

---

[3] P. Barker Webb, *Topographie de la Troade,* p. 170.

[4] *Il.* ix. 363 :

ἤματί κε τριτάτῳ Φθίην ἐρίβωλον ἱκοίμην.

[5] *Od.* iii. 180–182 :

τέτρατον ἦμαρ ἔην, ὅτ᾽ ἐν Ἄργεϊ νῆας ἐΐσας
Τυδεΐδεω ἕταροι Διομήδεος ἱπποδάμοιο
ἔστασαν.

[6] Herodotus, iv. 86 : Μεμέτρηται δὲ ταῦτα

ὧδε · νηῦς ἐπίπαν μάλιστά κη κατανύει ἐν μακρημερίῃ ὀργυιὰς ἑπτακισμυρίας, νυκτὸς δὲ ἑξακισμυρίας. ἤδη ὦν ἐς μὲν Φᾶσιν ἀπὸ τοῦ στόματος (τοῦτο γάρ ἐστι τοῦ Πόντου μακρότατον) ἡμερέων ἐννέα πλόος ἐστὶ καὶ νυκτῶν ὀκτώ · αὗται ἕνδεκα μυριάδες καὶ ἑκατὸν ὀργυιέων γίνονται, ἐκ δὲ τῶν ὀργυιέων τουτέων στάδιοι ἑκατὸν καὶ χίλιοι καὶ μύριοί εἰσι.

horses, took two days to go from Pylos to Sparta, a distance of 50 miles.[7]
No doubt it would have been easier for Telemachus to have gone to
Sparta in half a day, than for the Greeks and Trojans to have accom-
plished the task imposed upon them by the system of Lechevalier." [8]

On the day after the *first* battle of the *Iliad*, the herald Idaeus
is sent by the Trojans at daybreak into the Greek camp to propose an
armistice, for the burial of the dead.[9] He concludes the armistice, and
brings the news back to Troy; the Trojans begin to collect the
dead bodies and wood to burn them, and then only does the sun
rise.[10] But how long can it have been between the first dawn of the
morning and sunrise? Certainly not more than an hour and a half.
This is only consistent if we suppose Troy to have been at Hissarlik, for,
if it had been at Bounarbashi, the herald would have had at least 16 miles
to walk, and he could not have done this in less than five hours, for—as
Eckenbrecher[1] observes—any one who has read Homer, even superficially,
will certainly not suppose that the herald could have gone on horseback
or in a chariot, for, if this had been the case, the poet would have mentioned it explicitly; but on the contrary he expressly says, " Early in the
morning let Idaeus go to the hollow ships," [2] and " Early in the morning
Idaeus went to the hollow ships;" [3] and again " Idaeus went back to
sacred Ilium." [4] Eckenbrecher[5] adds that Welcker,[6] the warmest defender
of the Troy-Bounarbashi theory, suggests that the herald might have
run; there being so much running in the *Iliad*, and the poet endowing
his heroes with superhuman power : " But wherever he does this it
is to make them appear more heroic and more sublime, and not to
make them ridiculous. Can the herald, who has to conclude the armistice
for burying the dead, be conceived of as running at a trot for four hours !
Then we must suppose that, if Troy had been at Bounarbashi, still three
hours at least would have been occupied in concluding the armistice, in
its proclamation, in the preparation for the setting out of the armies
and in their long march, before both armies could have met. *Therefore,
at least seven hours would have been required to execute that which Homer*

---

[7] *Od.* iii. 484–497 and iv. 1 :
μάστιξεν δ' ἐλάαν, τὼ δ' οὐκ ἄκοντε πετέσθην
ἐς πεδίον, λιπέτην δὲ Πύλου αἰπὺ πτολίεθρον.
οἱ δὲ πανημέριοι σεῖον ζυγὸν ἀμφὶς ἔχοντες.
δύσετό τ' ἠέλιος σκιόωντό τε πᾶσαι ἀγυιαί,
ἐς Φηρὰς δ' ἵκοντο, Διοκλῆος ποτὶ δῶμα,
υἱέος Ὀρσιλόχοιο, τὸν Ἀλφειὸς τέκε παῖδα.
ἔνθα δὲ νύκτ' ἄεσαν, ὃ δὲ τοῖς πὰρ ξείνια θῆκεν.
ἦμος δ' ἠριγένεια φάνη ῥοδοδάκτυλος Ἠώς,
ἵππους τε ζεύγνυντ' ἀνά θ' ἅρματα ποικίλ'
    ἔβαινον,
ἐκ δ' ἔλασαν προθύροιο καὶ αἰθούσης ἐριδούπου.
μάστιξεν δ' ἐλάαν, τὼ δ' οὐκ ἄκοντε πετέσθην.
Ἷξον δ' ἐς πεδίον πυρηφόρον, ἔνθα δ' ἔπειτα
ἦνον ὁδόν · τοῖον γὰρ ὑπέκφερον ὠκέες ἵπποι.
δύσετό τ' ἠέλιος σκιόωντό τε πᾶσαι ἀγυιαί,
οἱ δ' ἷξον κοίλην Λακεδαίμονα κητώεσσαν, . . .

[8] There is no carriage-road over Mt. Taygetus,
which Telemachus and Pisistratus must necessarily have crossed ; and there are no signs that

there has ever been such a road. Thus to go in
a chariot from Pherae (now Calamata) across
those mountains has at all times been impossible.
But Homer, who probably did not know the
locality, supposed it to be possible.

[9] *Il.* vii. 381 :
ἠῶθεν δ' Ἰδαῖος ἔβη κοίλας ἐπὶ νῆας.

[10] *Il.* vii. 421–423 :
ἠέλιος μὲν ἔπειτα νέον προσέβαλλεν ἀρούρας,
ἐξ ἀκαλαρρείταο βαθυρρόου Ὠκεανοῖο
οὐρανὸν εἰσανιών · οἱ δ' ἤντεον ἀλλήλοισιν.

[1] *Die Lage des Homerischen Troja*, p. 29.

[2] *Il.* vii. 372 :
ἠῶθεν δ' Ἰδαῖος ἴτω κοίλας ἐπὶ νῆας.

[3] *Il.* vii. 381, *sup. cit.*

[4] *Il.* vii. 413 :
ἄψορρον δ' Ἰδαῖος ἔβη προτὶ Ἴλιον ἱρήν.

[5] *Die Lage des Homer. Troja*, p. 29.

[6] *Kleine Schriften*, Band ii. p. xviii.

mentions as having been done, at the most, in one hour and a half. This proves that *the distance, at which Homer considers his Troy to be from the Hellespont, is more than four times less than the distance of Bounarbashi from the sea-coast at the Trojan epoch.*"

On the third day, after sunset,[7] Hector causes the Trojans to encamp on the bank of the Scamander,[8] and orders oxen, sheep, and wine to be brought quickly from the city:[9] the animals and the wine, as well as bread, are immediately brought from Troy.[10] Oxen and sheep move slowly, especially in the night, but nevertheless they arrive καρπαλίμως, *promptly.* The Trojans slaughter the animals, and sacrifice to the gods.[1] But the Trojan camp was close to the Tumulus of Ilus,[2] on the left bank of the Scamander, since the thousand watch-fires of the Trojans were seen between the Greek camp and the river;[3] the Tumulus of Ilus was also close to the *ford* of the Scamander.[4] The Trojan camp, then, being at the Tumulus of Ilus, on the left bank of the Scamander, near its ford, was, as we have seen, near Troy; and this is further proved by the poet's statement, that their watch-fires were burning before Ilium (Ἰλιόθι πρό). Now the proximity of this same Trojan camp to the Greek ships, on the shore of the Hellespont, could not be better indicated than by the passage in which Agamemnon is represented as looking from his tent on to the plain; when he is alarmed at seeing the watch-fires of the Trojan camp which *burn before Ilium,* and at hearing the sound of the Trojan flutes and pipes and the hum of the warriors.[5]

Now, if Troy had been at Bounarbashi, the Trojan camp, which is described by the poet as being very near Ilium, must be supposed to have been at a distance of 7 miles from the Greek camp. But what mortal ear can hear musical sounds or the hum of men at such a distance? The same may be said of the Ἰλιέων Κώμη, which is nearly as far from the Hellespont as Bounarbashi, and which has besides the disadvantage that it cannot be seen from the shore, being screened from view by the intervening heights.

On the day on which the third great battle took place, which is the twenty-eighth day of the *Iliad* according to Pope's calculation,

---

[7] *Il.* viii. 485-488 :
ἐν δ' ἔπεσ' Ὠκεανῷ λαμπρὸν φάος ἠελίοιο,
ἕλκον νύκτα μέλαιναν ἐπὶ ζείδωρον ἄρουραν.
Τρωσὶν μέν ῥ' ἀέκουσιν ἔδυ φάος, αὐτὰρ Ἀχαιοῖς
ἀσπασίη τρίλλιστος ἐπήλυθε νὺξ ἐρεβεννή.

[8] *Il.* viii. 489-491 :
Τρώων αὖτ' ἀγορὴν ποιήσατο φαίδιμος Ἕκτωρ,
νόσφι νεῶν ἀγαγών, ποταμῷ ἔπι δινήεντι,
ἐν καθαρῷ, ὅθι δὴ νεκύων διεφαίνετο χῶρος.

[9] *Il.* viii. 505, 506 :
ἐκ πόλιος δ' ἄξεσθε βόας καὶ ἴφια μῆλα
καρπαλίμως, οἶνον δὲ μελίφρονα οἰνίζεσθε.

[10] *Il.* viii. 545, 546 :
ἐκ πόλιος δ' ἄξαντο βόας καὶ ἴφια μῆλα
καρπαλίμως, οἶνον δὲ μελίφρονα οἰνίζοντο.

[1] *Il.* viii. 548-550 :
ἕρδον δ' ἀθανάτοισι τεληέσσας ἑκατόμβας,
κνίσην δ' ἐκ πεδίου ἄνεμοι φέρον οὐρανὸν εἴσω
ἡδεῖαν.

[2] *Il.* x. 414, 415 :
Ἕκτωρ μὲν μετὰ τοῖσιν, ὅσοι βουληφόροι εἰσίν,
βουλὰς βουλεύει θείου παρὰ σήματι Ἴλου.

[3] *Il.* viii. 560-563 :
τόσσα μεσηγὺ νεῶν ἠδὲ Ξάνθοιο ῥοάων
Τρώων καιόντων πυρὰ φαίνετο Ἰλιόθι πρό.
χίλι' ἄρ' ἐν πεδίῳ πυρὰ καίετο, πὰρ δὲ ἑκάστῳ
εἴατο πεντήκοντα σέλαι πυρὸς αἰθομένοιο.

[4] *Il.* xxiv. 349-351 :
οἳ δ' ἐπεὶ οὖν μέγα σῆμα παρὲξ Ἴλοιο ἔλασσαν,
στῆσαν ἄρ' ἡμιόνους τε καὶ ἵππους, ὄφρα πίοιεν,
ἐν ποταμῷ.
But this passage, in contradiction to the foregoing, makes it appear that the tomb of Ilus was on the right bank of the Scamander.

[5] *Il.* xi. 11-13 :
ἤ τοι ὅτ' ἐς πεδίον τὸ Τρωϊκὸν ἀθρήσειεν,
θαύμαζεν πυρὰ πολλὰ τὰ καίετο Ἰλιόθι πρό,
αὐλῶν συρίγγων τ' ἐνοπὴν ὅμαδόν τ' ἀνθρώπων.

sunrise[6] and noon[7] are mentioned. In the afternoon the Greeks drive the Trojans to the Scaean Gate;[8] but the former are again driven back to the ships, where a terrible carnage takes place.[9] The Trojans are again repulsed,[10] but they drive back the Greeks a second time to the ships,[1] where there is a fearful slaughter. Patroclus drives the Trojans to the walls of Troy, and tries three times to scale it;[2] the Greeks fight until evening before the Scaean Gate.[3] Thus, in this third battle, as in the first, the Greeks go at least four times in one afternoon over the space between the camp and Troy, in spite of the long battles at the ships, in the plain, and under the walls of Troy.

There is another passage which proves the short distance between Troy and the Greek camp. Priam begs Achilles to grant an armistice of eleven days for the funeral of Hector, for, he says, the city is shut up too closely by the siege, and they must fetch the wood afar from the mountains.[4] The old king would certainly not have had to complain of this, had Troy been at Bounarbashi, or at Ἰλιέων Κώμη; for as both these places—the heights of the former as well as the hill of the latter—are connected with the higher wooded range of Mount Ida, the Trojans could have quietly fetched their wood, without fear of being troubled by the Greeks.

The defenders of the Troy-Bounarbashi theory lay much stress on the passage where, in the battle at the ships, Poseidon reproaches the Greeks, and says that formerly, before the retirement of Achilles, the Trojans never for a moment dared to meet the Greeks in open battle, whereas now they fight *far from the city* at the hollow ships;[5]—again, on the passage where Polydamas advises the Trojans, when they had withdrawn from the Greek camp, to retire to the city, and not to remain all the night in the plain near the ships, because " we are *far from the walls of Troy;* "[6]—also on the passage in which Ulysses, when lying with his companions in ambush in the reeds and bushes before the walls of Troy, says to them: " We have gone very *far from the ships.*"[7]   But we do not

---

[6] *Il.* xi. 1, 2 :
Ἠὼς δ' ἐκ λεχέων παρ' ἀγαυοῦ Τιθωνοῖο
ὤρνυθ', ἵν' ἀθανάτοισι φόως φέροι ἠδὲ βροτοῖσιν.

[7] *Il.* xi. 84–86 :
ὄφρα μὲν ἠὼς ἦν καὶ ἀέξετο ἱερὸν ἦμαρ,
τόφρα μάλ' ἀμφοτέρων βέλε' ἥπτετο, πῖπτε δὲ
λαός ·
ἦμος δὲ δρυτόμος περ ἀνὴρ ὡπλίσσατο δεῖπνον.

[8] *Il.* xi. 166–170 :
οἳ δὲ παρ' Ἴλου σῆμα παλαιοῦ Δαρδανίδαο,
μέσσον κὰπ πεδίον, παρ' ἐρινεὸν ἐσσεύοντο
ἱέμενοι πόλιος · ὁ δὲ κεκληγὼς ἕπετ' αἰεὶ
Ἀτρείδης, λύθρῳ δὲ παλάσσετο χεῖρας ἀάπτους.
ἀλλ' ὅτε δὴ Σκαιάς τε πύλας καὶ φηγὸν ἵκοντο.

[9] *Il.* xii. 35 to xiv. 439.

[10] *Il.* xv. 6–8 :
στῆ δ' ἄρ' ἀναΐξας, ἴδε δὲ Τρῶας καὶ Ἀχαιούς,
τοὺς μὲν ὀρινομένους τοὺς δὲ κλονέοντας ὄπισθεν,
Ἀργείους, μετὰ δέ σφι Ποσειδάωνα ἄνακτα.

[1] *Il.* xv. 343–345 :
ὄφρ' οἳ τοὺς ἐνάριζον ἀπ' ἔντεα, τόφρα δ' Ἀχαιοὶ

τάφρῳ καὶ σκολόπεσσιν ἐνιπλήξαντες ὀρυκτῇ
ἔνθα καὶ ἔνθα φέβοντο, δύοντο δὲ τεῖχος ἀνάγκῃ.

[2] *Il.* xvi. 702, 703 :
τρὶς μὲν ἐπ' ἀγκῶνος βῆ τείχεος ὑψηλοῖο
Πάτροκλος . . . . .

[3] *Il.* xviii. 453 :
πᾶν δ' ἦμαρ μάρναντο περὶ Σκαιῇσι πύλῃσιν.

[4] *Il.* xxiv. 662, 663 :
οἶσθα γὰρ ὡς κατὰ ἄστυ ἐέλμεθα, τηλόθι δ' ὕλη
ἀξέμεν ἐξ ὄρεος, μάλα δὲ Τρῶες δεδίασιν.

[5] *Il.* xiii. 105–107 :
ὣς Τρῶες τὸ πρίν γε μένος καὶ χεῖρας Ἀχαιῶν
μίμνειν οὐκ ἐθέλεσκον ἐναντίον, οὐδ' ἠβαιόν.
νῦν δὲ ἑκὰς πόλιος κοίλης ἐπὶ νηυσὶ μάχονται.

[6] *Il.* xviii. 254–256 :
ἀμφὶ μάλα φράζεσθε, φίλοι · κέλομαι γὰρ ἐγώγε
ἄστυδε νῦν ἰέναι, μὴ μίμνειν Ἠῶ δῖαν
ἐν πεδίῳ παρὰ νηυσίν · ἑκὰς δ' ἀπὸ τείχεος
εἰμέν.

[7] *Od.* xiv. 496 :
λίην γὰρ νηῶν ἑκὰς ἤλθομεν.

see how it can be inferred from these passages that there must have been a great distance between the Greek camp and Troy ; for in the first the question is of the Trojans fighting at the ships, and therefore at the farthest possible point from Troy between the city and the Greek camp ; in the second passage they are close by this farthest point ; and in the third passage Ulysses, in ambush under the very walls of Troy, is as far as he can be from the camp, speaking of the space between it and Troy. Thus, the adverb ἑκάς is in all three cases used only relatively, and it need by no means indicate a really long distance, especially as the whole *Iliad* shows the space between Troy and the Greek camp to have been but very short. I may add that in a war, such as was carried on between the Greeks and Trojans, the distance between the Hellespont and Hissarlik can be and ought to be considered as relatively *great*.

The short distance between Ilium and the Greek camp appears also to be indicated by the short run which Dolon had to make, to reach the ships.[8] We further recognize the short distance, when, in the last battle, the Trojans being arrayed between the Greek camp and the Scamander, Athené excites the Greeks by her cries from the wall of the camp and from the shore, whilst Ares excites the Trojans by his cries from the height of the Acropolis.[9] It must be remembered that the Trojan camp was at that time in close proximity to the ships.

Against Bounarbashi we have also the passage in the Πατρόκλεια,[10] where Patroclus, after having driven back the Trojans to the ships, does not allow them to return to the town, *but kills them between the ships, the wall (of the city), and the Scamander*. This passage shows three important facts : in the first place, that the distance between the city, the Scamander, and the Greek camp, was but very short ; in the second place, that the Scamander was between the city and the Greek camp ; and, thirdly, that Troy could consequently not be situated at Bounarbashi, as the Scamander would not have intervened between it and the Greek camp.

The Troy-Bounarbashi theorists further maintain that, at the time of the Trojan war, Hissarlik was close to the Hellespont, the whole lower plain being a much later formation ; and that, consequently, there was no room for the battles described in the *Iliad*. They refer to the beforementioned Hestiaea, who, according to Strabo,[1] made the same objection ; and also to Herodotus,[2] who says that the land about Ilium (that is, the

---

[8] *Il.* x. 337-369.

[9] *Il.* xx. 51, 52 :

αὖε δ᾽ Ἄρης ἑτέρωθεν, ἐρεμνῇ λαίλαπι ἶσος,
ὀξὺ κατ᾽ ἀκροτάτης πόλιος Τρώεσσι κελεύων.

[10] *Il.* xvi. 394-398 :

Πάτροκλος δ᾽ ἐπεὶ οὖν πρώτας ἐπέκερσε φάλαγγας,
ἂψ ἐπὶ νῆας ἔεργε παλιμπετές, οὐδὲ πόληος
εἴα ἱεμένους ἐπιβαινέμεν, ἀλλὰ μεσηγύς
νηῶν καὶ ποταμοῦ καὶ τείχεος ὑψηλοῖο
κτεῖνε μεταΐσσων, πολέων δ᾽ ἀπετίνυτο ποινήν.

[1] xiii. p. 599 : παρατίθησι δ᾽ ὁ Δημήτριος καὶ τὴν Ἀλεξανδρίνην Ἑστίαιαν μάρτυρα, τὴν συγγράψασαν περὶ τῆς Ὁμήρου Ἰλιάδος, πυνθανομένην εἰ περὶ τὴν νῦν πόλιν ὁ πόλεμος συνέστη,

καὶ . . . τὸ Τρωϊκὸν πεδίον, ὃ μεταξὺ τῆς πόλεως καὶ τῆς θαλάττης ὁ ποιητὴς φράζει· τὸ μὲν γὰρ πρὸ τῆς νῦν πόλεως ὁρώμενον πρόχωμα εἶναι τῶν ποταμῶν ὕστερον γεγονός.

[2] ii. 10 : τῶν γὰρ οὐρέων τῶν εἰρημένων τῶν ὑπὲρ Μέμφιν πόλιν κειμένων τὸ μεταξὺ ἐφαίνετό μοι εἶναί κοτε κόλπος θαλάσσης, ὥσπερ γε τὰ περὶ Ἴλιον καὶ Τευθρανίην καὶ Ἐφεσόν τε καὶ Μαιάνδρου πεδίον, ὥστε εἶναι σμικρὰ ταῦτα μεγάλοισι συμβαλέειν. The parallel is unlucky for the theory, since the geology of Egypt proves Herodotus to be utterly wrong in his *assumption* (for it is nothing more—and the same is true of the Plain of Troy) that the Nile-valley was formed

historical Ilium) appears to him to have once been a gulf filled up by the alluvium of the rivers, like part of the Nile valley. But I have given numerous reasons which lead to the conclusion that the Plain of Troy must probably be older even than the Hellespont, and that it must have extended at the Trojan epoch just as far towards the latter as it does now. Moreover, Herodotus does not say that in his opinion the plain was formed after the Trojan war; and, as Eckenbrecher[3] ingeniously remarks, " How could he have expressed such an opinion, as the historical Ilium is in his view identical with the Homeric Ilium, which fact necessarily involves the supposition that the plain existed at the Trojan epoch ? "

The defenders of the Troy-Bounarbashi theory further cite the testimony of the orator Lycurgus,[4] who says in his speech against Leocrates, accused of treachery after the battle of Chaeronea: " Who has not heard that Troy, the greatest city of its time, and sovereign of all Asia, after having been destroyed by the Greeks, has remained uninhabited ever since ? " " But how "—asks Eckenbrecher[5]—" could Lycurgus suppose this *to be universally* known, as there must have been not a few persons who knew nothing about it ; for instance, the Ilians of his time, who (with Hellanicus and others) had the firm conviction that the site of their city was identical with the Homeric Troy ? This question can only be solved by the right interpretation of the word ' uninhabited ' (ἀοίκητος) ; and, fortunately, Lycurgus himself assists us in explaining it ; for he says also in his speech, that through the treachery of Leocrates Athens had been in danger of becoming ' uninhabited ' (ἀοίκητον ἂν γενέσθαι). Does he mean by this, the danger of *literally no one* living in Athens? No, he can only have meant, in danger of *becoming deserted, desolate, dead*, which expressions we use in speaking of a ruined city, just as the modern Venetians have been heard to say ' non v' è più Venezia.' We see, then, that the word ' uninhabited ' was used in Greek in this sense ; and we may therefore understand it so in the passage in which Lycurgus applies it to Troy. In this way we remove the inconsistency involved in this passage by translating the word ' uninhabited,' and do away with the proof that the site of the Homeric Troy had never been inhabited after its destruction. For the rest, Strabo[6] cites the words of Lycurgus, after having given Homer's authority for the complete destruction of the city, in order to show, as he says, that this was also acknowledged in later times. The confirmation of Troy's complete destruction (κατεσκάφη) contained in the words of Lycurgus served Strabo for his purpose, for the sake of which he cannot have laid any absolute stress on the words that the city of the Ilians (which he here calls Troy) remained ' uninhabited ' (ἀοίκητον οὖσαν); for even a city *which has literally not a single inhabitant* need not on this account be destroyed:

by the gradual filling up of a chasm, like that of the Red Sea, by the alluvial deposits of the river in the course of centuries.

[3] *Die Lage des Homerischen Troja*, p. 57.

[4] Lycurg. *in Leocratem*, p. 62, ed. Carol. Scheibe: τὴν Τροίαν τίς οὐκ ἀκήκοεν, ὅτι

μεγίστη γεγενημένη τῶν τότε πόλεων καὶ πάσης ἐπάρξασα τῆς ᾿Ασίας, ὡς ἅπαξ ὑπὸ τῶν ῾Ελλήνων κατεσκάφη, τὸν αἰῶνα ἀοίκητός ἐστι;

[5] *Die Lage des Homer. Troja*, p. 41.

[6] xiii. p. 601.

it can easily be seen that Strabo only adds the final words in order to conclude the phrase of Lycurgus."

Eckenbrecher [7] further says, in defence of Hissarlik against Bounarbashi: "The prophecy of Juno in the Ode of Horace *Justum ac tenacem, &c.,*[8] has been cited as a decisive proof against Novum Ilium. Welcker [9] maintains: 'We cannot wish for a more conclusive testimony, that Ilium was not rebuilt on the ancient site, than this threat of Juno, that the Capitol would only exist and that Rome would only dominate, *dum Priami Paridisque busto Insultet armentum et catulos ferae Celent inultae:*'—

> ' Dum longus inter saeviat Ilion
> Romamque pontus, qualibet exsules
> In parte regnanto beati:
> Dum Priami Paridisque busto
>
> ' Insultet armentum et catulos ferae
> Celent inultae, stet Capitolium
> Fulgens triumphatisque possit
> Roma ferox dare jura Medis.'

"We reply: Juno promises (1) that the Romans shall reign happily, so long as the wide sea shall roar between Ilium and Rome; and (2) that the Capitol shall gloriously stand, and Rome shall be victorious, so long as on the tumulus of Priam and Paris herds shall trample and wild beasts shall with impunity conceal their brood. In the first part of this prophecy is contained a guarantee for the eternal duration of the Capitol; for it is said that Rome's happy dominion, which is unimaginable without the existence of the Capitol, will last *as long as the sea shall roar between Ilium and Rome*, that is, eternally. Now, Juno would have made a *contradictio in adjecto*, if she had said in the second part of her promise, that the eternal standing of the Capitol was uncertain; but she would have said this if she had designated the length of the duration of the Capitol's existence, not by a thing which must last eternally, like the roaring of the sea, but by something which might perhaps not last eternally. She must therefore have thought, that the herds and wild animals must continue for ever to trample on the sepulchre of Priam and Paris: thus these graves are supposed to be at a spot, perhaps in the secluded dales of Mount Ida, where pasturing herds and wild animals are presumed to remain for ever. What has been said of the latter would therefore give the same sense as we might perhaps express by saying: 'As long as cows are pasturing on the Alps, and chamois climb about on their rocks;' thus this promise purports nothing else than:—the victorious power shall be eternal. There is nothing else, therefore, in this passage; not a trace of a proof against the identity of Novum Ilium with the Homeric Ilium. But we should impute to Horace an absurd mode of writing, if, in the second part of the promise—which, like the first, he introduces by *dum*, 'as long as'—he intended to express a condition which was not necessarily to be fulfilled, like the condition contained in the first part; that is, which was not to be fulfilled in case the Romans built a city on the site of

---

[7] *Die Lage des Homer. Troja*, pp. 42–46.   [8] Horat. *Carm.* iii. 3.
[9] Welcker, *Kleine Schriften*, Band iv. p. 19.

those tombs, whereas it would be fulfilled if they did not do this. He must have supposed, however, that in the latter case herds and wild animals would be eternally on those tumuli. He would, therefore, use the image of the pasturing flocks and wild animals as an image of eternity. Those who pretend to find in the second part of the promise[10] the condition that no city must ever be built on the site of ancient Troy, ought not to be surprised, that with *our* mode of explanation, we attribute this meaning to Horace.

" But our Ode contains yet more than the promise of Juno which we have discussed. It is said later on :

> ' Sed bellicosis fata Quiritibus
> Hac lege dico: ne nimium pii
> Rebusque fidentes avitae
> Tecta velint reparare Trojae.'

With reference to this we must say : If indeed these words were to be understood to prescribe that Troy should never be rebuilt, as the condition of the victorious grandeur of Rome, Horace's opinion would certainly be expressed by saying, that it had never been rebuilt—that is, the site of Homeric Troy had never again borne human habitations; that that site, therefore, was different from that on which, in Horace's time, stood the great and flourishing city of Ilium. But Juno's words are not necessarily to be understood as containing this condition. They may also be interpreted, not altogether to prohibit building again on the site of Priam's Troy, but merely to enjoin that this should not be done with *exaggerated* piety (*ne nimium pii*), and with exaggerated confidence in the secure power of Rome. I believe indeed that, considering the circumstances, we must say that Horace meant his words to be understood in this manner : because, had he been understood to make it the condition of Rome's greatness, that the site of Priam's Troy should never be again built upon, then every one would have concluded from this Ode, either that Juno had prophesied falsely, or that—by the rebuilding of Troy— Rome had already for centuries worked at its own perdition ; for, according to the popular belief as well as in the opinion of the most distinguished men, on the site of Priam's Troy stood a city of Troy, which the Romans had with bountiful liberality for centuries been endeavouring to raise to a highly flourishing condition. We must therefore explain Horace only to have intended to rebuke *the exaggerated piety*, &c. displayed in the restoration of Troy, and *not* its restoration generally. Suetonius perhaps gives us the explanation of the poet's motive for saying this in such emphatic words. He tells us, in fact, that shortly before Caesar's assassination there had been a strong and universally diffused rumour, that he intended to transfer the centre of gravity of the Roman power to Ilium.[11] How much this was to the Roman taste [or rather a favourite idea of certain emperors] we see from the fact, that at a later time Constantine the Great, before establishing Constantinople at Byzantium,

---

[10] See above.

[11] Suetonius, *Julius Caesar*, 79 : " varia fama percrebuit migraturum Alexandriam vel Ilium, translatis simul opibus imperii, exhaustaque Italia delectibus, et procuratione urbis amicis permissa."

had in all seriousness selected the environs of Ilium for his new capital.[1] Such plans may also have hovered in the air at the time of Augustus, and may have induced Horace, who held them to be pernicious, to express himself in the sharpest manner.[2] For the rest, the adherents of Bounarbashi have overlooked the fact, that no one at Rome ever at any time thought of building a Troy outside Novum Ilium, on any site believed to be identical with Priam's Troy, in opposition to Novum Ilium. It therefore could not occur to Horace's mind to warn them against *that* scheme.

"Like Horace, Aeschylus[3] is also most unjustly cited against Novum Ilium. He says no more than that Troy had been destroyed and its site deserted,[4] and that Athené had taken possession of the Trojan land as a portion of booty ($\lambda \acute{a} \chi o s$) for the children of Theseus.[5] If we suppose that by this is meant only a portion of the Trojan land, it does not follow that that land, as Welcker maintains, should be thought to be excluded from all kinds of profane use (and therefore from the building of houses). And which portion of the Trojan land was it ? Welcker indeed knows very precisely that it was the region of Bounarbashi, but he does not make it clear to us how he knows this.

" Just as little as the adherents of Bounarbashi can appeal to Aeschylus, so little can they appeal to Lucan's *Pharsalia*.[6] It is evident that Lucan makes Caesar visit the Ilium of his time and hold it to be the Homeric city. Of this the verse

'Circuit exustae nomen memorabile Trojae'

can hardly leave any doubt, because on the coast of Troy there existed only the city called Ilium or Troy, and no other of this name. But it is self-evident that Caesar could not have found there ruins of the *ancient* Pergamus and the wall of Phoebus Apollo, and this bears as little on the subject as the trees and brakes which grew on the Pergamus, as now on the Acrocorinthus and many another Acropolis, whilst the city which belongs to it lives and bears its ancient name. Let us also remember Caesar's solemn vow made on the sacred precincts :[7]

'Restituam populos, grata vice moenia reddent
Ausonidae Phrygibus, Romanaque Pergama surgent,'

of which promise Lucan says[8] that it has been fulfilled—

'Votaque thuricremos *non irrita* fudit in ignes ;'

which cannot refer to anything else than the numerous good acts and

---

[1] Gibbon, c. 17. Constantine had even begun to erect on the chosen site important and sumptuous buildings, which afterwards fell to pieces.

[2] See also Loebell, *Ueber das Principat des Augustus*, in Raumer's *Histor. Taschenbuch*, 1834.

[3] Welcker, *Kleine Schriften*, Band iv. p. 17.

[4] Aeschylus, *Agamemnon*, vv. 524–528 :

ἀλλ' εὖ νιν ἀσπάσασθε, καὶ γὰρ οὖν πρέπει,
Τροίαν κατασκάψαντα τοῦ δικηφόρου
Διὸς μακέλλῃ, τῇ κατείργασται πέδον.

βωμοὶ δ' ἄϊστοι καὶ θεῶν ἱδρύματα,
καὶ σπέρμα πάσης ἐξαπόλλυται χθονός.

[5] *Eumenides*, 397–402 :

πρόσωθεν ἐξήκουσα κληδόνος βοήν,
ἀπὸ Σκαμάνδρου γῆν καταφθατουμένη,
ἣν δῆτ' Ἀχαιῶν ἄκτορές τε καὶ πρόμοι,
τῶν αἰχμαλώτων χρημάτων λάχος μέγα,
ἔνειμαν αὐτόπρεμνον εἰς τὸ πᾶν ἐμοί,
ἐξαίρετον δώρημα Θησέως τόκοις.

[6] ix. 961.   [7] Lucan. *Pharsal.* ix. 998, 999.

[8] *Pharsal.* ix. 989.

favours, by which—as we notoriously know from history—Julius Caesar endeavoured to raise the Ilium of his time to a flourishing condition."

I may here add that the site of Bounarbashi is in contradiction with the hydrographical foundations of our map, in consequence of which all the adherents of the Troy-Bounarbashi theory must submit to a radical renaming of the rivers of the plain.

It has been argued against the identity of Novum Ilium with the Homeric Troy that, if the latter had been so near the ships, the Trojans would not have needed to encamp in the plain. But it was Hector's intention to attack the Greeks the moment they should try to put their ships afloat and to go on board, for he supposed they had such a design.[9] By encamping at the tumulus of Ilus he saved a march of a mile and a half, and kept his warriors under arms instead of dispersed in the city.

When the battle is raging near Troy, Ajax is afraid that those of the Greeks who had remained in the camp at the ships might be discouraged at seeing their comrades repulsed by Hector.[10] *The distance appears, therefore, to have been so short that they could see each other.* Virgil,[11] the most veracious narrator of traditions, and Quintus Smyrnaeus,[1] represent the Trojan women as looking at the Greek fleet from the walls, and hearing the cries of the Greeks when they rushed from the camp. These are merely instances of the views of these two later authors with regard to the distance and the relative situation of the city and the camp. But it must be supposed that people at the camp and in Ilium perceived each other only very imperfectly, for otherwise there could be no reason why Polites—who, confiding in his speed, sat as scout on the tumulus of Aesyetes (which we may suppose to have been near Koum Kioi)—should have watched when the Greeks would rush forth from their ships.[2]

The legend of the Trojan wooden horse is undoubtedly nothing but a sacred symbol. Euphorion, in the rationalizing spirit of the later Greeks, supposed this horse to have been nothing else than a Grecian ship called ἵππος, "the horse."[3] So too Pausanias pronounced that the Trojan horse must have been in point of fact a battering-engine, because to admit the literal narrative would be to impute utter childishness to the defenders of the city.[4] Keller[5] suggests that "it probably refers to an oracle; let us call to mind the numerous Sibyls in Asia Minor, at Sardis, Erythrae, and Samos,[6] as well as the oracle of the wooden walls of Athens, which signified its ships." But the Trojan horse, as Grote[7] says, with its

---

[9] *Il.* viii. 508–511 :

ὥς κεν παννύχιοι μέσφ' ἠοῦς ἠριγενείης
καίωμεν πυρὰ πολλά, σέλας δ' εἰς οὐρανὸν ἵκῃ,
μή πως καὶ διὰ νύκτα κάρη κομόωντες Ἀχαιοί
φεύγειν ὁρμήσωνται ἐπ' εὐρέα νῶτα θαλάσσης.

[10] *Il.* xvii. 637–639 :

οἴ που δεῦρ' ὁρόωντες ἀκηχέδατ', οὐδ' ἔτι φασίν
Ἕκτορος ἀνδροφόνοιο μένος καὶ χεῖρας ἀάπτους
σχήσεσθ', ἀλλ' ἐν νηυσὶ μελαίνῃσιν πεσέεσθαι.

[11] Aeneid. ii. 460–462 :

"Turrim in praecipiti stantem summisque sub astra

Eductam tectis, unde omnis Troia videri
Et Danaûm solitae naves et Achaica castra."

[1] ix. 75 :

Τρῶες δ' εὖτ' ἐπύθοντο βοὴν καὶ λαὸν ἰδόντο,
θάμβησαν.

[2] *Il.* ii. 791–794, already cited.

[3] *Fragmenta*, 34, *ap.* Düntzer, *Fragmenta Epic. Graec.* p. 55.

[4] Grote, *History of Greece*, i. p. 285.

[5] *Die Entdeckung Ilion's zu Hissarlik*, p. 16.

[6] Aelian. *Var. Hist.* xii. 35.

[7] *Hist. of Greece*, i. p. 305.

accompaniments, Sinon and Laocoön, is one of the capital and indispensable events in the epic: Homer, Arctinus, Lesches, Virgil, and Quintus Smyrnaeus, all dwell upon it emphatically as the proximate cause of the capture of Troy.

I mention the Trojan horse here, in order to show that those who invented or supported the legend can only have had the idea that it was dragged to a Pergamus situated at a very short distance from the Greek camp, but they cannot possibly have supposed that such an immense machine, full of warriors, could have been dragged for eight miles through the plain, and then for more than one mile up the steep rocks of the Bali Dagh to the Pergamus. The adherents of the Bounarbashi theory maintain that the passage in the *Odyssey*[8]—which refers to the consultation as to whether the great horse, which had been dragged into the Acropolis, should be thrown down on the stones at its foot—can only be referred to the little Acropolis on the Bali Dagh, with its deep and steep slope, and not to Hissarlik. But we see no reason for this, because the slope of Hissarlik is on the north, north-west, and north-east side at an angle of 45°; and the city had, besides, high walls. We must therefore understand that it was proposed to drag the horse to the edge of the wall and to throw it thence on the stones below; there is not the slightest reason to suppose that Homer must necessarily have meant here very high, almost perpendicular, pointed cliffs.

At the time of Demetrius of Scepsis the little Acropolis on the Bali Dagh, behind Bounarbashi, was probably still standing. It was strategically well situated; but nevertheless, though envious and jealous of Novum Ilium, he did not, like the modern explorers, dare to proclaim its identity with the Homeric Ilium. He preferred to instal a poor unfitly situated little village in the legendary rights of the ancient Ilium, because that name at least appeared to cling to it. Nobody dared in antiquity to shake the tradition of a name,—an example of caution which should be a warning to us.[9]

W. Christ[10] cites B. Stark of Heidelberg,[1] whose enthusiasm for his Troy-Bounarbashi theory goes so far that, without paying any attention whatever to the ancient testimonies, he puts the Ἰλιέων Κώμη of Demetrius close to Bounarbashi.

Grote[2] observes: "Theophrastus, in noticing old and venerable trees, mentions the φηγοί (*Quercus aesculus*) on the tomb of Ilus at Ilium, without any doubt of the authenticity of the place (*De Plant.* iv. 14); and his contemporary, the harper Stratonikos, intimates the same feeling, in his jest on the visit of a bad Sophist to Ilium during the festival of the Ilieia (Athenaeus, viii. p. 351) The same may be said respecting the author of the tenth epistle ascribed to the orator Aeschines

---

[8] *Od.* viii. 506–509:
. . . . τρίχα δέ σφισιν ἥνδανε βουλή,
ἠὲ διαπλῆξαι κοῖλον δόρυ νηλέϊ χαλκῷ,
ἢ κατὰ πετράων βαλέειν ἐρύσαντας ἐπ' ἄκρης,
ἢ ἐάαν μέγ' ἄγαλμα θεῶν θελκτήριον εἶναι.

[9] Otto Keller, *Die Entdeckung Ilion's zu Hissarlik*, p. 27.
[10] *Die Topographie der Trojan. Ebene*; München, 1874.
[1] *Reise nach dem griechischen Orient*, p. 166.
[2] *History of Greece*, i. p. 299.

(p. 737), in which his visit of curiosity to Ilium is described—as well as about Apollonius of Tyana, or the writer who describes his life and his visit to the Troad; it is evident that he did not distrust the ἀρχαιολογία of the Ilians, who affirmed their town to be the real Troy (Philostr. *Vit. Apol. Tyan.* iv. 11). The goddess Athené of Ilium was reported to have rendered valuable assistance to the inhabitants of Kyzikus, when they were besieged by Mithridates, commemorated by inscriptions set up in Ilium" (Plutarch, *Lucullus*, 10).

Grote[3] also finds an important argument for the identity of Novum Ilium with the Homeric Troy in the above-mentioned periodical sending of the Locrian maidens to Ilium, to do menial service in the temple of Athené, as an expiation of the sin of their hero Ajax, son of Oileus. He thinks that the sending of these virgins could not possibly have been commenced under the dominion of the Persians, as Strabo[4] says: but, on the contrary, he finds in it a proof that Ilium always existed, and, consequently, that it had never ceased to be inhabited. I may add that, according to another passage in Strabo,[5] the Ilians maintained that the annual sending of Locrian virgins to Ilium had commenced soon after the capture of Troy, and that the city had neither been totally destroyed by the besieging Greek army nor had it ever been (entirely) deserted. The history of the city could not have been anywhere better preserved than by its inhabitants.

As the hill of Hissarlik, under whatever essential aspect we may examine it, answers to the indications of the *Iliad* in regard to the situation of ancient Ilium, the fact that a city of the same name existed here in later times tends rather to confirm than to enfeeble its right to be considered identical with the city celebrated by the poet. The identity of name is a strong presumption in favour of the coincidence of position. It must also be considered, that the interest which the ancients felt for the Troy of Homer was far greater even than ours; that they had plentiful sources of information which are lost to us; and that they were consequently far better prepared for a thorough examination of the site *ubi Troja fuit* than we are. The Ilians were Aeolic Greeks,[6] who had immigrated into the Troad[7] and had no doubt got mixed up with the remaining Trojans, and who adhered with fervent zeal to the worship of the Ilian Athené and to that of the heroes who had fallen in the war, to whom, as we have seen,[8] funeral services were celebrated as

---

[3] *History of Greece*, i. p. 282.

[4] xiii. p. 601: τὰς δὲ Λοκρίδας πεμφθῆναι Περσῶν ἤδη κρατούντων συνέβη.

[5] xiii. p. 600: Λέγουσι δ' οἱ νῦν Ἰλιεῖς καὶ τοῦτο ὡς οὐδὲ τελέως ἠφανίσθαι συνέβαινεν τὴν πόλιν κατὰ τὴν ἅλωσιν ὑπὸ τῶν Ἀχαιῶν, οὐδ' ἐξελείφθη οὐδέποτε· αἱ γοῦν Λοκρίδες παρθένοι μικρὸν ὕστερον ἀρξάμεναι ἐπέμποντο κατ' ἔτος.

[6] Herodotus, v. 122: (Ὑμέης) καταλιπὼν τὴν Προποντίδα ἐπὶ τὸν Ἑλλήσποντον ἦγε τὸν στρατόν, καὶ εἷλε μὲν Αἰολέας πάντας, ὅσοι τὴν Ἰλιάδα νέμονται, εἷλε δὲ Γέργιθας τοὺς ὑπολειφθέντας τῶν ἀρχαίων Τευκρῶν.

Pausanias, i. 35. 4: λόγον δὲ τῶν μὲν Αἰολέων τῶν ὕστερον οἰκησάντων Ἴλιον ἐς τὴν κρίσιν τὴν ἐπὶ τοῖς ὅπλοις ἤκουσα.

Pausanias, viii. 12. 9: τούτου δὲ συντελοῦσιν ἐς πίστιν Αἰολέων οἱ Ἴλιον ἐφ' ἡμῶν ἔχοντες, κ. τ. λ.

Grote, *History of Greece*, i. p. 296, also cites Αἰολεὺς ἐκ πόλεως Τρωάδος, the title proclaimed at the Olympic games (Paus. v. 8. 3): like Αἰολεὺς ἀπὸ Μουρίνας, from Myrina in the more southerly region of Aeolis, which we find in the list of victors at the Charitesia, at Orchomenus in Boeotia (Boeckh, *Corp. Inscrip. Graec.* No. 1583).

[7] See p. 128.

[8] See pp. 180, 181.

late as the time of the Emperor Julian. Everything therefore here contributed to keep alive the reminiscences of the Trojan war and its locality.

Not only did an ancient and venerable city stand on Hissarlik: this city was also so rich and powerful that there could not easily be in the Plain of Troy a second equally important city; it must therefore have been regarded as the capital of the Trojan dominion.[9]

"The legendary faith (in the identity of Novum Ilium with the Homeric Ilium) subsisted before, and continued" (as Grote[10] says) "afterwards, notwithstanding the topographical difficulties. Hellanicus, Herodotus, Mindarus, the guides of Xerxes, and Alexander, had not been shocked by them: the case of the latter is the strongest of all, because he had received the best education of his time under Aristotle —he was a passionate admirer and constant reader of the *Iliad*—he was, moreover, personally familiar with the movements of armies, and lived at a time when maps, which began with Anaximander, the disciple of Thales, were at least known to all who sought instruction. Now if, notwithstanding such advantages, Alexander fully believed in the identity of Ilium, unconscious of the topographical difficulties, much less would Homer himself, or the Homeric auditors, be likely to pay attention to them, at a period, five centuries earlier, of comparative rudeness and ignorance, when prose records as well as geographical maps were totally unknown." Grote further cites the argument of Major Rennell:[1] "Alexander is said to have been a passionate admirer of the *Iliad*, and he had an opportunity of deciding on the spot how far the topography was consistent with the narrative. Had he been shown the site of Bounarbashi for that of Troy, he would probably have questioned the fidelity either of the historical part of the poems or of his guides. It is not within credibility, that a person of so correct a judgment as Alexander could have admired a poem which contained a long history of military details and other transactions that could not physically have an existence. What pleasure could he receive, in contemplating as subjects of history, events which could not have happened? Yet he did admire the poem, and *therefore must have found the topography consistent;* that is, Bounarbashi, surely, was not shown to him for Troy."

Grote further mentions the testimony of Arrian, "who, though a native of Nicomedia, holding a high appointment in Asia Minor, and remarkable for the exactness of his topographical notices, describes the visit of Alexander to Ilium, without any suspicion that the place with all its relics was a mere counterfeit. Aristides, Dio Chrysostom, Pausanias, Appian, and Plutarch, hold the same language."[2]

---

[9] W. Christ, *Die Topographie der Trojanischen Ebene;* München, 1874. "If not *Troy*, what is this city but its *double?*"—*Quarterly Review,* April 1874, p. 559.

[10] *History of Greece,* i. p. 305.

[1] *Observations on the Plain of Troy,* p. 128.

[2] Arrian. *Anab.* i. 11; Appian, *Mithridat.* c. 53; Aristides, *Oratio,* 43; *Rhodiaca,* p. 820 (Dindorf, p. 369). The curious *Oratio* xi. of Dio Chrysostom, in which he writes his new version of the Trojan war, is addressed to the inhabitants of Ilium. Grote adds: "But modern writers seem for the most part to have taken up the supposition from Strabo as implicitly as he took it from Demetrius. They call Ilium by the disrespectful appellation of *New* Ilium, while the traveller in the Troad looks for *Old* Ilium as if it were the unquestionable spot where Priam had lived and moved; the name is even formally enrolled on the best maps of the ancient Troad."

(211)

CHAPTER V.

THE FIRST PRE-HISTORIC CITY ON THE HILL OF HISSARLIK.

As I have explained in the preceding pages,[1] I ascertained by the twenty shafts sunk on the site of Novum Ilium, which are accurately indicated on the Plan of the Hellenic Ilium,[2] that the ruins of none of the pre-historic cities, which succeeded each other here in the course of ages, exceeded the precincts of the hill of Hissarlik, which forms its north-west corner, and served as its Acropolis. This Acropolis, like the Acropolis of old Troy, was called Pergamum.[3] Here were the temples of the gods,[4] among which the sanctuary of Athené, the tutelary deity of the city, was of great celebrity. The Ilians, who firmly believed in the ancient tradition that their town occupied the very site of ancient Troy, were proud to show in their Pergamum the house of Priam as well as the altar of Zeus Herkeios, where that unhappy old man had been slain,[5] and the identical stone on which Palamedes had taught the Greeks to play at dice.[6] They were so totally ignorant of archæology, that they took it as an undoubted fact, that the Trojans had walked on the very same surface of the soil as themselves, and that the buildings they showed were all that remained of the ancient city. It never occurred to their minds that ruins could exist except on the surface. As they had no cellars, so they had no excavations to make; but still they once certainly made an excavation, because there is a well[7] in the Acropolis, which is walled up with stones and chalk, and was evidently dug by the later Ilians. This well has been dug with great trouble through numbers of pre-historic house-walls. By a strange chance it has been pierced, at a depth of about 30 ft. below the surface, through the thick walls of a house, which is the largest house in the burnt city, and which I firmly hold to be the mansion of its chief or king, because, as mentioned in the preceding pages, in or close to it I found nine smaller or larger treasures. But they dug with great pains through these house-walls without even noticing them, for, had they noticed them, they might have raised pretensions to archæology; they might perhaps have excavated the whole mansion, and might have felt inclined to proclaim it as the real house of Priam, instead of the building which they showed 28 or 30 ft. above it, on the surface of the hill. With the same indifference they dug on, and, having pierced through several still more

[1] P. 38.
[2] The shafts are marked by the letters A to V on Plan II.
[3] Herodotus, vii. 43: τὸ Πέργαμον. The form in Homer is always ἡ Πέργαμος. The Tragic poets use also the plural, τὰ Πέργαμα.
[4] The Inscriptions authenticate, besides Athené, a temple of Zeus Polieus at Novum Ilium (Boeckh, Corp. Inscr., No. 3599).
[5] Grote, History of Greece, i. p. 298.
[6] Polemon Perieget. Frag. xxxi.; ed. L. Preller.
[7] This well is marked a z on Plan I. (of Troy).

ancient house-walls, they at last, at a depth of 53 ft., reached the rock, into which they sunk their shaft deep enough to get water. The Ilians dug this well from above, whereas in describing the results of my excavations I shall commence from below.

The rock consists of soft limestone.

The first inhabitants of these sacred precincts did not take the trouble to remove the black earth which covered this rock to the depth of 8 in.; but they laid on it the foundations of their houses, of which three walls, composed of small uncut stones joined with earth, may be seen in my great trench, which passes from north to south through the whole hill.[8] On some of these walls the well-smoothed clay coating, with which they were once covered, is still preserved.

I have hitherto attributed the enormous layer of *débris*, 23 ft. deep, which covers the rock and precedes the burnt city, to only one nation, and have called those vast ruins the First City on the hill of Hissarlik.[9] But the pottery contained in the lowest stratum, from 6 to 7 ft. thick, is so vastly, so entirely different from that of the subsequent layer, 16 ft. thick; and further—as Professor A. H. Sayce, who recently visited the Troad, has ingeniously observed—the architecture of the house-walls in these two strata is so widely different,—that I cannot but acknowledge, in agreement with him, that the first city must have been destroyed or abandoned, and again built over by another people.

To my great regret, I have been able to excavate comparatively little of these two lowest cities, as I could not bring them to light without completely destroying the burnt city, the third in succession from the virgin soil, the ruins of which rest upon the second city. For this reason also I can only give the depth of the ruins of the first city[10] approximately, as from 6 to 7 ft.: in some places it may be a little less, in others a little more. Thus, for instance, the depth of the *débris* of the first city is 9 ft. in two places in which M. Burnouf has most carefully examined them. He found them to consist of:

	Thickness.
1. The limestone rock:	
2. The layer of black earth	20 centimètres deep.
3. Dark blue plastic clay	3 „ „
4. Light grey plastic clay	3½ „ „
5. Dark blue plastic clay	8½ „ „
6. Black earth	6 „ „
7. Dark blue clay mixed with grey clay	8 „ „
8. Mixture of the preceding earth with traces of charcoal . .	26 „ „
9. Yellow clay	9 „ „
10. Dark blue clay mixed with much charcoal	13 „ „
11. Yellowish clay, much mixed with grey clay and black earth, traces of charcoal	20 „ „
12. Layer of mixed earth between two brown clayish laminæ . .	10 „ „
13. Earth mixed with all these elements and with stones . . . 1	50 „ „
	2 mètres 77 ctm.

Then follow the buildings of the Second City.

[8] See Plan III. (marked *f f f* in Section of the Great Central Trench, x–y), also Plan I. (of Troy), on which they are likewise marked *f f* in the Great Trench, x–y.

[9] See my *Troy and its Remains*, pp. 148–156.

[10] These ruins of the first city are marked N on Plan III. (Section of the Great Central Trench).

M. Burnouf remarks that these layers are frequently interrupted by large cakes of clay (in French, *galettes*) or groups of them, which were in general use with the inhabitants of the first three, and even of the first four, pre-historic cities. He explains that these clay cakes were used to consolidate and to level the layers of *débris*, because as they dried they became so hard that the heaviest walls could be erected upon them. He adds that the layer of *débris* of the first city often contains single stones, small deposits of brown or black ashes, as well as mussels and oyster shells, but few cockles and bones. The layers of *débris* slope with the hill towards the north.

This first city was evidently not destroyed by fire, for I never found there blackened shells or other marks of a great fire.

Now, with regard to walls of defence, there are none in the excavated part of it which I could with any probability attribute to this first city; only on the north-east side of the hill, at a distance of 133 ft. from its slope, I brought to light a retaining wall of white stones,[1] which, in agreement with Burnouf and Sayce, I can attribute only to this first city, because at a depth of 50 ft. it ascends, at an angle of 45°, 6 ft. below the ruined city wall built of large blocks joined with small stones,[2] and it must, therefore, have been built a very long time before the latter, which we ascribe, with every probability, to the second city.

It appears that this first city had either no regular walls of defence, or, as is more likely, its walls appeared not strong enough for the second nation, which built, not only its walls, but even its houses, of much larger stones. Professor Sayce suggests that the entrance to this first city was not on the south-west side, where the second settlers built their gate, but that it must have been on the west side, where the hill slopes gently at an angle of 70° to the plain. I think this highly probable.

In treating of the objects of human industry found in the *débris*, I begin with the most important—Pottery,—because it is the cornucopia of archæological wisdom for those dark ages, which we, vaguely groping in the twilight of an unrecorded past, are wont to call pre-historic. Indeed, " the art of making pottery seems," as Mr. A. W. Franks[3] judiciously observes, " to have been practised by mankind from very early times. It is even a question whether it was not known to the primitive inhabitants of Europe, in those early ages when the mammoth and reindeer still lived in the plains of France. The invention of pottery in China is referred by native writers to the legendary Emperor Hwang-ti, who is stated to have commenced his reign of 100 years in 2697 B.C. A subsequent emperor, Yu-ti-shun (2255 B.C.), is stated to have himself made pottery before he ascended the throne. The potter's wheel was known in Egypt at an early period, having probably been invented as early as the 6th Egyptian dynasty."

Of all the imitative arts the working in clay was naturally the most

---

[1] See on the engraving, No. 2, the retaining wall marked A.

[2] See the wall B on the same engraving.

[3] *Introduction to his Catalogue of a Collection of Oriental Porcelain and Pottery;* London, 1878.

ancient, as modelling of course precedes casting, carving, or painting. The pre-historic peoples, who inhabited the hill of Hissarlik, made of baked clay all utensils for everyday life and for depositing the remains of the dead. Instead of wooden or stone coffins they used funeral urns of terra-cotta. Instead of cellars, chests, or boxes, they had large jars (πίθοι), from 4 to 7 ft. high, which were dug into the ground, so that only the mouth was visible, and were used either for the preservation of food, or as reservoirs for oil, wine, or water. Instead of wash-tubs, they used large terra-cotta bowls; of terra-cotta were all their vessels used for cooking, eating, and drinking; of terra-cotta even were their hooks for hanging up clothes, the handles of their brushes, their *ex-votos*, and the weights of their fishing-nets. Thus we cannot be astonished at finding in the *débris* of their cities such large masses of broken pottery, among which, however, there is no trace of tiles. It therefore appears certain that, just like the houses of the present inhabitants of the Troad, the houses of all the five pre-historic cities, which succeeded each other here, were covered with flat roofs of beams on which was heaped a thick layer of clay as protection against the rain.

If, as we judge of the degree of civilization of a country by its literature, and particularly by its newspapers, it were possible to judge of the degree of civilization of a pre-historic people by the greater or less perfection of their pottery, then we might conclude, that of all the peoples which have succeeded each other here, that of the first city was by far the most civilized, because its pottery shows, both in fabric and shape, by far the most advanced art. But I am far from maintaining this theory; I shall only cite facts. To this early people the potter's wheel was already known, but it was not in common use,

because all the bowls and plates, as well as all the larger vessels, are invariably hand-made. We may say the same of nearly all the smaller vases, among which, however, we now and then find one which has most undoubtedly been turned on the potter's wheel, as, for instance, the vase No. 23, which is of a dim black colour and globular form, so that it cannot stand without being supported.[4] Like most vases of a similar shape in this first city, it has on each

No. 23. Globular Vase, with double tubular holes on either side for suspension. (About 1 : 4 actual size. Depth, 48 ft.)

side two long vertical tubular holes for suspension by a string. We

---

[4] This vase is in my collection in the South Kensington Museum, where every one can convince himself that it is wheel-made: this, however, can be also clearly seen in the engraving.

see this same system on the accompanying fragments of a lustrous-black hand-made vase (Nos. 24 and 25).

This system of double vertical tubular holes for suspension, which was in common use in the first city, has been but very rarely found elsewhere.

No. 24. Fragment of a Vase, with two tubular holes on each side for suspension.
(About half actual size. Depth, about 48 ft.)

The Museum of Saint Germain-en-Laye contains a fragment of a dark-brown vase, with two vertical tubular holes, found in a cavern in Andalusia, which in fabric resembles some of the pottery of the first city at Hissarlik. There are also three fragments of vases, with two vertical tubular holes, found in Dolmens, the locality of which is not indicated ; further, the casts of two more such fragments, of which the originals, preserved in the Museum of Vannes, were found in the Dolmen of Kerroh, at Loc-mariaker. There has also been found in Denmark, in a sepulchre of the Stone age, a similar vase, with two vertical tubular holes on each side for suspension ; it is preserved in the Royal Museum of Nordiske Oldsager in Copenhagen, and is repre-sented among the vases of the Stone age, in J. J. A. Worsaae's *Nordiske Oldsager*, p. 20, No. 100. This Danish vase is covered with a lid, having on each side two corresponding perforations, through which the strings were passed : in this way the vase could be shut quite close.

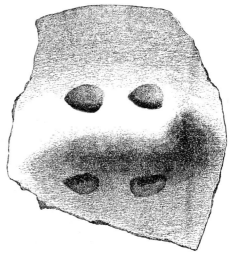

No. 25.   Fragment of a Vase, with two tubular holes for suspension on each side. (Nearly actual size. Depth, 48 ft.)

Similar vase-covers, with two tubular holes for suspension on each side, are frequent in this first city. The accompanying engraving represents two such vase-covers, of which the

No. 26.   No. 27.

Nos. 26, 27.   Vase Covers, with vertical tubular holes for suspension.
(About half actual size. Depth, 48 ft.)

one standing upright has on its top four perforated projections, in the form of feet, and a fifth not perforated in the middle. The other, which stands on its head, has an equal number of such foot-like protuberances, of which only one on each side is perforated: this latter, therefore, belongs to a vase with only one vertical tubular hole for suspension on each side.

I may add that the five fragments of vases found in French Dolmens, as well as the Danish vase, have only the system for suspension in common with those of the first city at Hissarlik; the fabric and clay are altogether different.

A very great number of the bowls and some of the vases of the first city had, on the inner side of the rim, an incised linear ornamentation, which was filled up with white chalk, so as to strike the eye. To this class of bowls belong the fragments Nos. 28 and 29, the ornamentation of which appears to have been borrowed from weaving patterns. The fragment No. 31 is the rim of a shallow basin with a perforated handle. Many others have an incised linear ornamentation on the outside of the rim, like Nos. 30, 32, 33, and 34, of which that on No. 32 appears also to be a textile pattern. No. 35 is the bottom of a vase decorated with incisions.

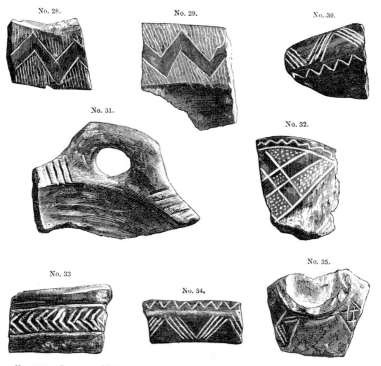

No. 28.   No. 29.   No. 30.

No. 31.

No. 32.

No. 33

No. 34.

No. 35.

Nos. 28–35.   Fragments of Pottery, ornamented with linear and other patterns filled with white chalk.
(About half actual size. Depth, 46 to 53 ft.)

The ornamentation of No. 33, which is very common, appears to be borrowed from the fish-spine. Very curious is the incised ornamentation on

the fragment No. 36, which resembles an owl's face in monogram, but
I am far from suggesting that the potter who made it intended to
represent an owl. It is however, as M. Burnouf remarks, easy to follow
upon the vases the series of forms gradually passing over from the owl-
head to this monogram. He calls attention to the bundle of vertical lines
to the right, which in his opinion are meant to represent female hair.

Most of the bowls have on the two sides, as in Nos. 37 and 38, slight
projections in the rim with *horizontal* tubular holes, which—in proportion

No. 36. Fragment of a Bowl, with an ornamentation
filled with white chalk.
(About half actual size. Depth, 48 ft.)

No. 37. Lustrous-black Bowl, with two horizontal
tubular holes for suspension.
(About 1 : 4 actual size. Depth, 45 ft.)

No. 38. Lustrous-black Bowl, with long horizontal tubular rings for suspension on the rim.
(About 1 : 4 actual size. Depth, about 48 ft.)

to the size of the vessel—are from 2 to 4 in. long, and which likewise
served for suspending the bowls.

The fragments with tubular holes (on p. 218) belong to large bowls,
on account of which the holes are much wider, as the heavy weight of
the vessels, when filled, necessitated a strong cord.

On some bowls these protuberances, containing the tubular holes for
suspension, are ornamented, as in Nos. 40 and 42, with deep impressed
furrows, so that they have the shape of a hand with the fingers clenched.

In the tubular hole of a fragment of a bowl in my possession, my
friend the professor of chemistry, Xavier Landerer, late of the University
of Athens, found the remnants of the cord which had served for suspending the vase. He ascertained these remnants to be of an organic
nature; they burned, he says, like tinder or like the fibres of a thread
or cord. On examination through a microscope, they proved to be the
remains of a twisted linen cord.

With the exception of the vase No. 23—which, as already stated, is of a dull black—and of Nos. 40 and 42, which are of a yellow colour—all the

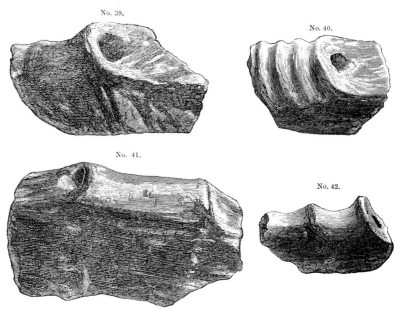

No. 39.

No. 40.

No. 41.

No. 42.

Nos. 39-42. Fragments of Pottery, with tubular holes for suspension.
(About half actual size.   Depth, 46 to 52 ft.)

above fragments and bowls are of a lustrous black; and the larger they are, so much the thicker are they in many places, so that, for instance, at the lower end of the rim and in the base the clay is often rather more than half an inch thick.   Although the rich shining deep black colour of these bowls, enhanced as it is by its contrast to the fantastic rim-ornamentation filled with white chalk, is really fascinating to the eye and looks like a mirror, yet on close examination we find the surface of the bowls, both outside and inside, very uneven.   But this could hardly be otherwise, as they are all hand-made, and were polished with stones of porphyry, diorite, or jasper, expressly cut for the purpose, of which I found a great quantity in this first city as well as in all the four successive pre-historic cities of Hissarlik.   Fair specimens of these polishing stones are seen in the chapter on the Third, the burnt City, under Nos. 648–651, to which I refer.   (See p. 444.)

The unevenness of the surfaces of the pottery may also be accounted for by the ingredients of which these vessels are composed; for, when fractured, we see that the clay has been mixed with coarsely-pounded granite, the mica of which shows its presence by the numerous small flakes glittering like gold or silver.   Professor Landerer, who examined some of the fragments chemically, found in them, besides granite, gneiss and quartz.   It appears therefore evident, that this most ancient and highly curious pottery of the first city was fabricated in the same way as the pre-historic pottery found in Mecklenburg, of which my friend the celebrated archæologist, Dr. Lisch of Schwerin, writes to me as follows:— " As to the manufacture of clay vessels in the heathen time, numerous thorough investigations have been made in Mecklenburg for the last fifty years. First, the core of the vessel was made by hand of common clay, which was thoroughly kneaded with pounded granite and mica. For this reason, there are many urns which have a rough surface, owing to the protruding little stones. But the interior surface of these urns was covered smoothly with clean clay. The pounded granite was required in order that the form of the vessel might be preserved in the fire, because otherwise it would have collapsed. This mode of manufacture is also proved by the sparkles of mica which may be seen on the surface. Then the core of the vessel was dried or slightly baked. When this had been done, the whole external surface of the vessels was coated with clay, from which all the coarser particles had been separated by water, so as to establish a smooth surface and to fill up all the gaps. Hence we may explain the astonishing and otherwise inexplicable phenomenon, that fragments of such vessels show in the interior a granular, on the exterior a clean smooth surface. After this, the ornamentation was cut in or impressed, and the finished vessel was dried or baked *at an open fire*, in which operation many vessels were coloured coal-black by the soot or smoke. The black colour is vegetable, which can be easily proved if a fragment of such coal-black pottery is put into a potter's oven, because it is evaporated by the heat and leaves *no* metallic residuum, whilst, by strong baking, the clay of the fragment becomes perfectly brick-red. For the rest, no trace has ever been found of a pre-historic potter's oven. The surface of many vessels may finally have been polished with bones or smooth stones. Brick-kilns and potters' ovens were only introduced into Mecklenburg in the twelfth century A.D., whilst in the Roman provinces on the Rhine they existed as early as the third century A.D., or earlier, as is testified by the numerous Roman bricks and vessels. I may add, that pottery which has been baked in a potter's oven always gives a ringing sound when touched by a hard object, whilst pottery which has been baked at an open fire always gives a dull sound."

Professor Virchow writes to me : " The preparation of the black terracotta vessels has in our Berlin Anthropological Society been the subject of many and long discussions. It has been proved that the most common mode of preparing them is, by slow burning in shut-up places, to produce much smoke, which enters into the clay and impregnates it. The black colour can be made of any intensity that is desired. The Hissarlik vessels have certainly been made in this way."

M. Burnouf remarks to me that for baking pottery thoroughly a great heat is required, generally as much as 800–1600° Celsius = 1472–2944° Fahrenheit, a heat which can never be attained in the open air.

Be this as it may, the rich lustrous deep black colour of the bowls of the first city must have been produced by a peculiar process. M. Landerer is of opinion that it must have been produced by an abundance of pine-soot, with which the vessels were coloured at the second baking in the open fire. On examining with a microscope the white chalk with which the incised ornamentation is filled, he found in it the remains of linen cords.

Professor Landerer calls my attention to the fact, that the colour of the Hellenic terra-cotta vases is *coal black*, which was produced in the following manner :—" Before the baking, the vases were oiled over with tar (πίσσα), or perhaps with the pissa asphalt of Herodotus,[5] which occurs on the island of Zacynthus. In the baking the rosin was changed into the finest coal, which got attached to the exterior layer of clay of the vases and produced their black varnish."

There are also terra-cotta vessels in the first city with four perforations for suspension on each side in the rim, as is illustrated by the accompanying engraving No. 43.

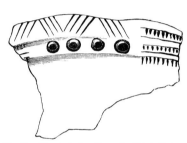

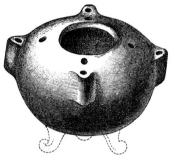

No. 43. Fragment of a Vase of polished black Earthenware, with incised pattern filled with white chalk. (About half actual size. Depth, 46 ft.)

No. 44. Tripod Vase, with four tubular holes and four holes in the rim for suspension. (Actual size. Depth, 52 ft.)

Another fine specimen of this sort is represented by the little hand-made globular tripod No. 44, which has not been covered over with fine clean clay, and has its surface therefore very rude and unequal. Gold-like or silver-like sparkles of the mica contained in the clay may be seen glittering on the outside as well as on the inside. The fracture at its base is surrounded by an incised circle, which can leave no doubt that, after the vase was made, a piece of clay on which three feet were modelled

[5] iv. 195: εἴη δ' ἂν πᾶν, ὅκου καὶ ἐν Ζακύνθῳ ἐκ λίμνης καὶ ὕδατος πίσσαν ἀναφερομένην αὐτὸς ἐγὼ ὥρεον· εἰσὶ μὲν καὶ πλεῦνες αἱ λίμναι αὐτόθι, ἡ δ' ἂν μεγίστη αὐτέων, ἑβδομήκοντα ποδῶν πάντῃ, βάθος δὲ διόργυιός ἐστι· ἐς ταύτην κοντὸν κατιεῖσι, ἐπ' ἄκρῳ μυρσίνην προσδήσαντες, καὶ ἔπειτα ἀναφέρουσι τῇ μυρσίνῃ πίσσαν, ὀδμὴν μὲν ἔχουσαν ἀσφάλτου, τὰ δ' ἄλλα, τῆς Πιερικῆς πίσσης ἀμείνω· ἐσχέουσι δὲ ἐς λάκκον ὀρωρυγμένον ἀγχοῦ τῆς λίμνης· ἐπεὰν δὲ ἀθροίσωσι συχνήν, οὕτω ἐς τοὺς ἀμφορέας ἐκ τοῦ λάκκου καταχέουσι. ὅ, τι δ' ἂν ἐσπέσῃ ἐς τὴν λίμνην, ὑπὸ γῆν ἰὸν, ἀναφαίνεται ἐν τῇ θαλάσσῃ.

Dr. Chandler (*Travels*, ii. pp. 367, 368) thus describes the " tar-springs " (as he calls them) of Zante: " The tar is produced in a small valley, about two hours from the town, by the sea, and encompassed with mountains, except towards the bay. The spring, which is most distinct and apt for inspection, rises on the further side, near the foot of the hill. The well is circular, and 4 or 5 ft. in diameter. A shining film like oil, mixed with scum, swims on the top. You remove this with a bough, and see the tar at the bottom, 3 or 4 ft. below the surface. . . . The water is limpid, and runs off with a smart current. . . . We filled some vessels with tar by letting it trickle into them from the boughs which we immersed ; and this is the method used to gather it from time to time into pits, where it is hardened by the sun, to be barrelled when the quantity is sufficient." (George Rawlinson, *History of Herodotus*, iii. pp. 169, 170.)

was attached here. This supposition is also confirmed by the circular depression in the middle of the fracture. The vase before us, therefore, has been a tripod. Round the body we see, at equal distances from each other, four vertical tubular holes for suspension, and four perforations in the rim in the same direction. I have not found the cover to this vase, but it must naturally have been similar to that represented under No. 26. As these lids have four perforations, they could well be fastened on by means of four strings, one of which was passed through each of the tubular holes and the corresponding holes in the rim and in the cover; at the other end of each string a knot had previously been made, which remained at the lower end of the tubular holes and prevented the strings from slipping. A similar contrivance is seen in the gold boxes found by me in the royal sepulchres at Mycenae.[6] A similar contrivance is also presupposed in the box which Areté, wife of king Alcinoüs, fills with presents for Ulysses, for she recommends him : " Look now thyself to the lid and tie quickly a knot on it, lest any one should rob thee on the way, when thou reposest again in sweet slumber, sailing in the black ship." [7] Homer says in the verses immediately following:—" Moreover when the much-enduring divine Ulysses heard this, he forthwith fitted on the lid, and quickly put upon it a manifold knot, which venerable Circe had once prudently taught him." [8]

Telemachus, preparing for his voyage to Sparta, bids his nurse Euryclea fill twelve amphorae with wine and fit them all with lids; but these would need to be very close-fitting for liquors.[9] Such lids for amphorae were also found by me in the royal tombs at Mycenae.[10]

Fragments of similar vases with four holes at each side for suspension were found in the caves at Inzighofen, on the Upper Danube.[1] There are other vases with only one perforation on each side in the rim, like No. 45, which has all round it an ornamentation forming five ovals filled up with dots. Again, other vases have on each side of the body only one vertical tubular hole for suspension, like No. 46, which has also two female breasts. This vase is also hand-made, but of green colour; its clay is only 2-10ths in. thick, and therefore finer than that of the larger vases or bowls. The pretty little vase No. 47 is also hand-made, and has only one perforated projection on each side.

In the collection of pre-historic antiquities found in Thera, below three layers of pumice-stone and volcanic ashes, and preserved in the French School at Athens, there are two very rude hand-made vases of cylindrical form, with one vertical tubular hole on each side for suspen-

---

[6] See my *Mycenae*, p. 205, No. 318; p. 206, No. 319 ; p. 207, Nos. 321, 322.

[7] *Odyss.* viii. 443–445 :

αὐτὸς νῦν ἴδε πῶμα, θοῶς δ' ἐπὶ δεσμὸν ἴηλον,
μή τίς τοι καθ' ὁδὸν δηλήσεται, ὁππότ' ἂν αὖτε
εὕδῃσθα γλυκὺν ὕπνον, ἰὼν ἐν νηὶ μελαίνῃ.

[8] *Odyss.* viii. 446–448 :

αὐτὰρ ἐπεὶ τό γ' ἄκουσε πολύτλας δῖος 'Οδυσσεύς,
αὐτίκ' ἐπήρτυε πῶμα, θοῶς δ' ἐπὶ δεσμὸν ἴηλεν
ποικίλον, ὅν ποτέ μιν δέδαε φρεσὶ πότνια Κίρκη.

[9] *Odyss.* ii. 349–353 :

μαῖ', ἄγε δή μοι οἶνον ἐν ἀμφιφορεῦσιν ἄφυσσον
ἡδύν, ὅτις μετὰ τὸν λαρώτατος, ὃν σὺ φυλάσσεις
κεῖνον ὀϊομένη, τὸν κάμμορον, εἴ ποθεν ἔλθοι
διογενὴς 'Οδυσεὺς θάνατον καὶ κῆρας ἀλύξας.
δώδεκα δ' ἔμπλησον, καὶ πώμασιν ἄρσον ἅπαντας.

[10] See my *Mycenae*, p. 256, Nos. 373 and 374.

[1] Ludwig Lindenschmit, *Die Vaterländischen Alterthümer der Hohenzollerschen Sammlungen ;* Mainz, 1860. Plate xxvi., Nos. 7, 8.

sion; and a pear-shaped vase in the same collection has an identical system for suspension. These Thera antiquities are thought by archæologists to date from the sixteenth or seventeenth century B.C., but it

No. 45. Cup with an incised ornamentation. (About 1 : 4 actual size. Depth, 45 ft.)

No. 47. Lustrous dark-brown
Vase, with tubular rings for suspension. (About 1 : 4 actual
size. Depth, 48 ft.)

No. 46. Globular Vase, with two breasts and two perforated projections for suspension. (1 : 4 actual size. Depth, 45 ft.)

deserves attention that most of the Thera pottery has rudely-painted ornaments, whilst there is no trace of painting at Hissarlik.

In the Assyrian Collection of the British Museum there are three vases, found at Nimroud, which have the same system of one vertical tubular hole on each side. There is also, in the collection of Babylonian antiquities, the fragment of a hand-made slightly-baked vase, which has the same vertical tubular holes for suspension. The same system also exists on a vase from Cyprus in the Louvre, as well as on a vase in the Museum of St. Germain-en-Laye, found in a Dolmen; again, on a fragment of a vase in the collection of Count Szechenyi Bela in Hungary,[2] and on a small vase marked No. 1094, in the Grand Ducal Antiquarium of Schwerin. This latter vase was found in a conical tomb (*Hünengrab*) near Goldenitz, in Mecklenburg. Professor Virchow calls my attention to an urn with three vertically perforated excrescences on the sides and at the foot,—having thus, properly speaking, three double tubular holes for suspension with a string. This urn was found at Dehlitz, near Weissenfels, on the river Saale, in Germany.[3] But I have not found this system anywhere else.

It must be distinctly understood that I speak here solely of vases with *vertical* tubular rings or holes for suspension, and *not* of vases

---

[2] Dr. Joseph Hampel, *Catalogue de l'Exposition préhistorique des Musées de Province et des Collections particulières de la Hongrie;* Buda-Pesth, 1876, p. 71, fig. 55.

[3] See the *Sessional Report of the Berlin Society of Anthropology, Ethnology, and Pre-historic Archæology,* of Nov. 28, 1874, p. 7.

having projections with horizontally placed rings, because these occur on a vase found in the Lake-dwellings of the Stone age at the station of Estavayer;[4] on four vases found in Dolmens in France, and preserved in the Museum of St. Germain-en-Laye; on some fragments of vases in the same Museum; on vases in the Egyptian Collection in the British Museum; on two vases of the Stone age in the Museum at Copenhagen;[5] on several vases in the Collection of German Antiquities in the British Museum; on one from Cyprus in the South Kensington Museum; on several vases found in the excavations at Pilin in Hungary;[6] and on many vases in the Grand Ducal Antiquarium of Schwerin. Similar vases with horizontal tubular holes for suspension are frequently found in Germany, and the Märkisches Museum in Berlin contains many of them. Professor Virchow also has in his own collection some fine specimens of such vases found in the extensive excavations he has made, in company with his accomplished daughter Adèle and his son Dr. Hans Virchow, in the vast pre-historic graveyard of Zaborówo, in the province of Posen.

I lay stress on the fact, that vases with vertical tubular holes for suspension are a very great rarity except at Hissarlik, where they occur by thousands in all the five pre-historic cities, whilst vases with horizontal tubular holes only occur here on bowls in the first city and in none of the subsequent ones.

On the other hand, Mr. Calvert and I found in our excavations in the tumulus of Hanaï Tepeh, only three miles to the south of Hissarlik,[7] vases with *horizontal* tubular holes exclusively; also bowls with the same system as those in the first city on Hissarlik: but the horizontal tubular holes are not in the rim itself, as here, but much below it; and thus the people to whom the Hanaï Tepeh antiquities belonged must have been altogether different from the inhabitants of any one of the five cities at Hissarlik, for it is impossible that one and the same people could make such perfectly different pottery.

Nos. 48 and 49 represent the feet of hand-made lustrous-black vessels; they are hollow, and have three and sometimes four round holes. I

No. 48. No. 49.

Nos. 48, 49. Two feet of Terra-cotta Vessels. (About half actual size. Depth, 47 to 52 ft.)

gathered many similar vase-feet, but never an entire vessel of this kind. I call particular attention to the great resemblance of these feet,

[4] Dr. Ferd. Keller, *Établissements Lacustres;* Zürich, 1876, Pl. xviii. No. 5, décrits par Dr. V. Gross.

[5] J. J. A. Worsaae, *Nordiske Oldsager* (1859), Pl. 19, Nos. 95 and 98, and Pl. 20, No. 99.

[6] Dr. Joseph Hampel, *Catalogue*, &c. p. 130,

fig. 130, and p. 41, fig. 28: and *Antiquités préhistoriques de la Hongrie;* Esztergom, 1877, Plate xviii. figs. 2, 5, 8, 9, 11, 12; Plate xix., fig. 11; Pl. xx., figs. 4, 8, 19; Pl. xxi., fig. 9; Pl. xxii., figs. 2, 3.

[7] See Mr. Calvert's Paper in his Appendix.

Nos. 48 and 49, to those of the censers found in German tombs, of which there are many in the Märkisches Museum in Berlin, and some, found in the graveyard of Zaborówo, in the collection of Professor Virchow. The lower part of No. 50 is a similar foot, on which I have glued the fragment of another object of cylindrical form which does not belong to it. This latter object is of terra-cotta and of unknown use; the top of it is also restored: and it has a striking resemblance to two objects of terra-cotta found at Pilin in Hungary.[8] Feet of vessels like Nos. 48 and 49, but without holes, are very frequent.

No. 51 represents a very pretty lustrous hand-made red goblet with one handle; it was in fragments, but I have been able to put it together. Fragments of another such goblet, which I have

No. 50. Curious Vessel, use unknown (perhaps a Censer), placed on the foot of another vessel. (About 1 : 4 actual size. Depth, 45 ft.)

No. 51. Pretty lustrous red Cup with one handle. (About 1 : 4 actual size. Depth, 48 ft.)

under my eyes whilst writing this, show precisely the same mode of manufacture as that which I have described above for the large bowls, with the sole difference, that here red clay was used, and that, as M. Landerer explains to me, the cup, immediately before its second baking in an open fire, was repeatedly dipped in a wash of fine red clay containing much peroxide of iron, which has produced the varnish-like glazing.

I would here call particular attention to the fact, that the goblet No. 51 represents more or less exactly the form of all the goblets of terra-cotta found by me at Mycenae and Tiryns.[9] Those found there in the royal tombs, and which are the most ancient, are of a light-green colour, with curious black painted ornaments; those found in the lowest strata outside the tombs are of a single colour, light green; a little higher up follow the same kind of goblets of a uniform bright-red colour; and others which, on a light-red dead ground, have an ornamentation of numerous painted parallel dark-red circular bands; these, again, are succeeded by unpainted goblets of white clay. These latter must have been in use for ages, for they occur in such large masses, that I could

[8] Dr. Joseph Hampel, *Antiquités préhistoriques de la Hongrie;* Esztergom, 1877, Plate xx., Nos. 18 and 20.

[9] See my *Mycenae,* p. 70, No. 83; p. 71, Nos. 84 and 88.

have gathered thousands of such goblet-feet.   Except the light-green goblets with the black ornamentation, I found all these kinds of goblets of the same shape also in my excavations at Tiryns.[1]   But in the sepulchres of Mycenae I found five golden cups of exactly the same form as that before us (No. 51) from the first city of Hissarlik.[2]   Now, it deserves very particular attention, that fourteen goblets of exactly the same form were found in a sepulchre at Ialysus in Rhodes, and are now in the British Museum.   The only difference is, that these latter have a painted ornamentation representing mostly the cuttle-fish (sepia), though spirals are also depicted, as well as that curious sea-animal which so frequently occurs on the other pottery of Mycenae,[3] but never on the Mycenean goblets.   While speaking of painting, I may make the important remark : *that neither the inhabitants of the first city, nor those of the four succeeding pre-historic cities at Hissarlik, had any idea of pigments, and that,—except a single terra-cotta box found in the third city, on which the keen eye of my honoured friend, Mr. Chas. T. Newton, has recognized a cuttle-fish, painted with dark-red clay on a light-red dead ground, and two small bowls of terra-cotta from the fourth city, in which a large cross is painted with dark-red clay ;—except also the small rude idols of white marble on which the face of an owl is roughly drawn with black clay ;—there is no trace of painting on any object ever found in any one of the five pre-historic cities at Hissarlik.*

Of similar goblets found elsewhere I can only mention a cup found in Zaborówo in Professor Virchow's collection and another found at Pilin,[4] which have some resemblance to this in shape ; but the difference is that the cups from Zaborówo and Pilin have not the wide foot which is peculiar to the goblet before us, as well as to all those found at Mycenae. Besides, their handles are much longer.

No. 52 represents a very small pitcher with one handle; it has neither been covered inside nor outside with prepared clay, and is, therefore, very rude.

No. 53.

No. 54.

No. 52.
Miniature Pitcher.
(Half actual size.
Depth, about 50 ft.)

Nos. 53, 54.   Fragment of a lustrous dark-grey Vessel.   No. 53, outside; No. 54, inside.
(About 1:4 actual size.   Depth, 50 ft.)

[1] See my *Mycenae*, p. 70.
[2] See my *Mycenae*, p. 233, No. 343, and p. 350, No. 528.
[3] See my *Mycenae*, No. 213, *a, b*, p. 138.
[4] Joseph Hampel, *Antiquités préhistoriques de la Hongrie ;* Esztergom, 1877, Plate xix. fig. 3.

I further show under No. 53 the outside, and under No. 54 the inside, of a fragment of a large hand-made vase, which has impressed wave-patterns on both sides.

No. 55 is a fragment of black terra-cotta, probably part of a box, to which it served as an ornament; it is decorated with lines and three or four rows of dots, which are filled with white chalk. As appears from

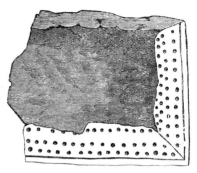

No. 55.   Fragment of Terra-cotta, perhaps part of a box, found on the primitive rock.
(About half actual size.   Depth, 53 ft.)

the upper and the lower side, and from the two perforations, it may have been the setting and decoration of a wooden jewel-casket. It is made with so much symmetry, and looks so elegant, that I at first thought it was of ebony inlaid with ivory.

Of terra-cottas from the first city I further give here, under Nos. 56

No. 56.   Jug.   (About 1 : 4 actual size.   No. 57.   Jug.   (About 1 : 3 actual size.
Depth, 45 ft.)   Depth, 45 ft.)

and 57, engravings of two lustrous-black pitchers; both have a globular base, and have been put together from fragments. No. 58 represents a lustrous-black pitcher of terra-cotta, with three female breasts and incised linear patterns, which was found at a depth of 52 ft.

All the terra-cottas hitherto represented are uninjured by moisture; some others, however, have become soft from damp. Thus, for instance, I found upon the rock, at a depth of 51½ ft., in a small tomb-like recess, formed and protected by three stones 26 in. long and 18 in. broad, two funeral urns of a very remarkable form, with three long feet, and filled with human ashes. The urns are hand-made, and consist, as usual, of coarse clay, mixed with silicious earth and pounded granite, containing much mica; they have, apparently, been baked only once very imperfectly at an open fire, and were not covered over with fine clay; nevertheless, owing to the oxide of iron contained in their clay, they have a dull red colour. They have suffered so much from moisture, that, in spite

No. 58. Pretty lustrous-black Pitcher of Terra-cotta, with three female breasts and incised linear patterns. (Nearly half actual size. Depth, 52 ft.)

of every care and precaution, I could not get them out without breaking them up completely; but as I had collected all the fragments, I could easily restore both of them.

No. 59. Tripod Urn, containing human ashes and the bones of an embryo. (About 1 : 8 actual size. Depth, 51½ ft.)

The accompanying engraving, No. 59, represents the larger of the two, in which I found among the human ashes the bones of an embryo of six months, from which the entire skeleton has been restored by my friend, the celebrated surgeon Aretaeos of Athens, who maintains that the preservation of these small bones was only possible on the supposition that the mother had made a premature birth and died from its effect; that her body was burnt, and the unburnt embryo put with her ashes into the funeral urn, where I found it.

No. 60 is the engraving of a large common hand-made vase with two handles, the original brick colour of its clay having acquired a brownish hue by age. No. 61 is a small hand-made red vase of a very curious shape. No. 62 is a hand-made lustrous-black bowl, without tubular holes for suspension; bowls of this description are very common in the first city.

No. 60. Hand-made Vase. (About 1 : 6 actual size. Depth, 49¼ ft.)

I may further mention a hand-made vase of globular shape, ornamented with an incised pattern of zigzag lines, similar to that on two

No. 61. Hand-made Vase. (About 1 : 4 actual
size. Depth, 50 ft.)

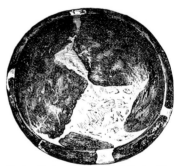

No. 62. Hand-made lustrous-black Bowl. (About
1 : 4 actual size. Depth, 46 ft.)

vases of the Stone age in the Museum at Copenhagen,[5] with the difference that on this Trojan vase the zigzag lines are accompanied on each side by a row of deep dots.

Of the terra-cotta whorls, of which I found many thousands in the

[5] See J. J. A. Worsaae, *Nordiske Oldsager*, Pl. xx. Nos. 99 and 100.

débris of the third, fourth, and fifth cities, I could collect comparatively few in the strata of the first and second cities, and particularly in that of the first, of which I am now treating. Those which I gathered in the first city are either unornamented, and in this case they have a uniform lustrous-black colour and have more or less the shape of a cone or of two cones joined at the bases (see Nos. 1806 and 1807), or they are ornamented

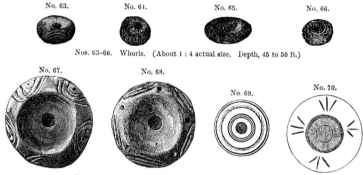

No. 63.   No. 64.   No. 65.   No. 66.

Nos. 63–66. Whorls. (About 1 : 4 actual size. Depth, 45 to 50 ft.)

No. 67.   No. 68.

No. 69.

No. 70.

Nos. 67–70. Whorls. (About half actual size. Depth, 48 to 52 ft.)

with incisions (see Nos. 63–70); and in this case they are very flat, and resemble the wheels of the Turkish country-carts. Thus a whorl of this first city may easily be recognized from among thousands of others found in the subsequent cities.

As we see on only a few of these whorls traces that they have been used, I suppose that they served as offerings to the tutelary deity of the city, who may have had the character of Athené Ergané, and may have been regarded as the protecting divinity of female handiwork, and particularly of women engaged in spinning and weaving. That such a goddess was adored in Ilium, we may gather with all probability from the legend before recorded,[6] that the builder of the city, Ilus, was rewarded by Zeus with a favourable sign, consisting of the Palladium which fell from heaven, with a distaff and a spindle in one hand and a lance in the other; for the distaff and spindle can probably mean nothing else than the goddess's allegorical character as *Ergané*. I am far from maintaining that Ilus ever existed, or that he might have founded this first city. If he really built a city here, it would probably be the third in succession; but the strange coincidence of the legend of Athené with the distaff, and the numerous whorls found here, makes me think that the worship of Athené Ergané was not instituted by the builder of the third city, but that a goddess of an identical character, though probably of a different name, had a cultus here ages before the third city was built.

The ornamentation on the whorls is incised, and, as on the vases, it is filled up with white chalk to strike the eye. I abstain from discussing whether this ornamentation may be symbolical or not; I will only say that the patterns of the whorls, of the shape of those represented

---

[6] See p. 153.

under Nos. 1817-1820, are found in the terramare of Italy, in Lake-
dwellings of the Stone age. Through the kindness of my friend, Professor
Giuseppe G. Bianconi of Bologna, I have received the drawings of ten
such whorls, which are preserved in the Museum of Modena, having
been found in the terramare of that district: among them are six which
have the same ornamental carvings that I found upon whorls in my
excavations at Hissarlik. The same friend has also sent me the drawings
of 18 similar whorls found in the graves of the cemetery of Villanova,
and now in the museum of Count Gozzadini at Bologna. As the Count
found an "aes rude" in one of the graves, he thinks that the cemetery
must belong, like it, to the time of King Numa, that is, to about 700 B.C.;
De Mortillet,[7] however, ascribes a much greater age to the cemetery.
But at all events, 15 of the 18 drawings lying before me have a
modern appearance, compared with the 10 whorls in the Museum of
Modena, or with the whorls found at Hissarlik, even in the latest pre-
historic city; for not only the ornamentation, but the forms also of
the whorls, are much more elaborate.

The comparison of these 18 whorls with those from Hissarlik con-
vinces me, therefore, that Count Gozzadini is right in ascribing no greater
age to the cemetery than 700 B.C. Two terra-cotta whorls, likewise with
incised ornamentation, now in the Museum of Parma, were found in
the terramare of Castione and Campeggine.[8] From 300 to 400 terra-
cotta whorls were found in the Lake habitations of the Stone age at
the station of Moeringen on the Lake of Bienne in Switzerland,[9] some
of which have incised ornamentation. Among these ornamented terra-
cotta whorls are several with patterns similar to some of those found
at Hissarlik, but in general all the whorls from the Lake of Bienne
appear to be much more elaborate and much more modern than those of
Hissarlik.

A terra-cotta whorl without ornamentation was also found in the
cemetery of Zywietz near Oliva.[1] There are also a great many unorna-
mented terra-cotta whorls in the Museum of Neu Strelitz, of which
Mr. Carl Andres is the learned keeper, and which was kindly shown to
me by Dr. Goetz; as well as in the Museum of Neu Brandenburg, which
was kindly shown to me by its keeper, the high forester Julius Müller,
Senator Gustav Brückner, and Mr. Conrad Siemerling; and in the Grand
Ducal Antiquarium of Schwerin, of which my honoured friend, the learned
Miss Amalie Buchheim, is the keeper. But there are in all these three
Museums some terra-cotta whorls in the form of discs with an incised
ornamentation, such as we find at Troy. From the photographs which
Dr. Joseph Hampel, the learned keeper of the archæological department
in the Hungarian National Museum at Buda-Pesth, had the kindness to
send me, I see that there are exhibited in that museum 11 terra-cotta
whorls, found in the excavations at Szihalom, in the county of Borsod

---

[7] *Le Signe de la Croix*, pp. 88, 89.   [8] *Ibid.*
[9] Ferd. Keller, *Établissements Lacustres*, by
Dr. V. Gross, p. 18, Pl. xxii.
[1] Dr. Lissauer, *Beiträge zur westpreussischen*

Urgeschichte, Plate iii., fig. 8. Professor Virchow informs me that terra-cotta whorls without ornamentation are frequently found in
Germany.

in Hungary, and attributed to the Stone age.   Of these 11 whorls, represented on Plate x. Nos. 22–32, one, No. 30, has an impressed or incised ornamentation.[2]

The Collection of Mexican Antiquities in the British Museum contains a large number of similar whorls, for the most part of conical shape, many of them with ornaments, which may be inscriptions; but this ornamentation runs all round the cone, and is not on its base, as in the whorls of Hissarlik.   Some of these whorls are more or less flat; a few are painted blue.   So far as I know, ornamented terra-cotta whorls have never yet been found in Greece.   Unornamented ones, on the other hand, are frequent there.   At Mycenae I found about 300 whorls of stone, and but very few of terra-cotta.   A terra-cotta whorl, ornamented with an incised decoration, found in the pre-historic villages below three layers of pumice-stone and volcanic ashes on the Island of Thera, is in the small collection of antiquities in the French School at Athens.

In this first, as well as in all the four succeeding pre-historic cities of Hissarlik, there are also very numerous small discs of terra-cotta, from $1\frac{1}{2}$ to 3 in. in diameter, with a hole drilled through the centre.   As they are slightly convex on one side, and on the other slightly concave, and as the edges are very rudely cut, there can be no doubt that they were cut out of broken pottery.   Those of the first city have the pretty lustrous dark-black colour peculiar to the pottery of the primitive settlers.   There can hardly be any doubt that these discs were used with the distaff, in spinning as well as in weaving, as weights for the thread.[3]

Similar discs, with the same characteristics, proving that they were cut out of broken pottery, have been also found at Szihalom; two of them, exhibited in the National Hungarian Museum, are represented on Plate ix., Nos. 2 and 4 of the photographs of the collections.   Another such disc, found at Magyarad, in the county of Hont, is represented under No. 37 on Plate xiii. in Joseph Hampel's *Antiquités préhistoriques de la Hongrie.*

No. 71 is the fragment of a very rude figure of terra-cotta.   No. 72

No. 71.   Fragment of a rude figure of Terra-cotta.
(About half actual size. Depth, 46 ft.)

No. 72.   Terra-cotta Fragment, lustrous red, with
impressed ornamentation.
(Actual size. Depth, 52 ft.)

[2] As Dr. Hampel informs me that the photographic plates are on sale, I shall always refer to them.

[3] I may here call attention to the fact, that the spinning-wheel is a modern invention, commonly ascribed to the year 1530.

represents a perfectly flat bright-red fragment of terra-cotta, 6 millimètres (about a quarter of an inch) thick, which I found myself, in the presence of M. Burnouf, in the very lowest *débris* of the first city, and which, I think, is the only specimen of perfectly baked terra-cotta I ever found at Hissarlik, except of course the large jars, which are always thoroughly baked, and the pottery of the third or burnt city, most of which has been thoroughly baked by the intense heat of the conflagration. In fact, the clay of the fine red goblet No. 51 is only 4 millimètres (about one-sixth of an inch) thick, and yet only 1 millimètre of it is really baked on either side, while in the middle there remain 2 millimètres of clay quite unbaked. As the fragment No. 72 is quite flat, it cannot belong to a vase. Professor Rhousopoulos suggests that it may have belonged to a wooden casket, on which it served as an ornament. The ornamentation of branches and concentric circles is very characteristic: it looks, as Prof. Sayce observes to me, Hittite and Babylonian. This piece exhibits perhaps the finest clay I ever found at Hissarlik; but nevertheless, when observed through a powerful lens, it is not free from small stones.

No. 73 is a very rude flat figure of marble. I found about half-a-dozen figures in this first city, of the very same shape and fabric, but all of

No. 73. Rude flat Idol of Marble.
(About half actual size.
Depth, 50 ft.)

them without a trace of any incision. I, therefore, should never have thought them to be figures at all, were it not that more than 500, of nearly the same flat form—on many of which a bird-like face, female breasts, a girdle, or female hair, are rudely incised—were found by me in the third, fourth, and fifth pre-historic cities. On a great many others the bird's face is rudely drawn with black clay on the white figures. It is therefore highly probable that a similar face had once been drawn on all the figures on which it is not incised, but that in the course of ages it has been effaced by the dampness of the *débris*. As all these rude figures represent the same form, there can be no doubt that they are idols of a female goddess, the patron deity of the place, whether she may have been called Até or Athené, or have had any other name; nay, there appears to be the highest probability that all of them are copies of the celebrated primeval Palladium, to which was attached the fate of Troy, and which was fabled to have fallen from heaven (see p. 153).

According to the legend, the feet of this Palladium were joined together, and they could not possibly be more joined than on these idols, on which the whole inferior part of the body is represented as a hemispherical lump. I may here call attention to the fact, that the form which the ancients commonly gave to some deities in the inferior part of the body, as for instance to the statues of Hermes, served to indicate their stability in the place where they were preserved. In like manner Victory was represented without wings, when the idea of its permanence was to be expressed.

Mr. Gladstone calls attention to the fact, that we find in Homer but one clear instance of an image for religious worship. The solemn procession in the 6th *Iliad* carries the dedicated veil or robe to the temple of Athené on the summit of the hill, where the priestess Theano receives it, and deposits it on the knees of the goddess :

$$\Theta\hat{\eta}\kappa\epsilon\nu\ '\text{A}\theta\eta\nu\alpha\text{i}\eta\varsigma\ \epsilon\pi\text{i}\ \gamma\text{o}\text{ú}\nu\alpha\sigma\iota\nu\ \dot{\eta}\ddot{\upsilon}\kappa\text{ó}\mu\text{o}\iota\text{o}.^4$$

Thus it is evident that the poet imagined the Palladium to have been in a sitting posture, and of human form, just as all idols were represented in his time, and widely different from the hideous and barbaric idols I find at Hissarlik, even in the latest of the five pre-historic cities. It may be observed that the famous figure of Niobé on Mount Sipylus, which is alluded to in the 24th book of the *Iliad* (614-617), and which probably was originally intended to represent the goddess Cybelé, was likewise in a sitting posture. I readily believe with Mr. Gladstone,[5] that statues would have been more mentioned by the poet had they been common, and that they were rare or to the poet unattractive; probably of wood. Pausanias[6] mentions in certain temples wooden statues of gods (Xoana), as well as statues formed of other materials (including clay), less durable than stone and marble, or than bronze : the use of these materials prevailed especially in primitive times. Such objects were called *daidala*, and it was from them, Pausanias thinks, that the personal name Daidalos afterwards arose.[7] It was only by degrees that they came to represent the human form at all.[8] Only by degrees, too, they assumed the character of works of art. Indeed, if we survey the world all over at the present day, it is singular to notice how little and how rarely marked religious worship and true beauty have been associated together in images.

The idols of Hissarlik are certainly ruder than the rudest ever found in Greece or elsewhere. However barbarous the idols of Mycenae and Tiryns may be, they are nevertheless masterpieces of art in comparison with these Trojan idols. The conception of the human form as an organic whole, a conception we meet with at the very dawn of creative Greek art, nowhere appears. " The Trojan artist began," as Mr. Newton ingeniously remarks, " as these primitive sculptures denote, with something even more elementary than Shakspeare's manikin made after supper out of a cheeseparing; and that which gradually converted this manikin into an organic form was the instinct of Greek genius trained and developed by the contact with more civilized races around, and imbibing ideas of Egyptian and Assyrian art through traffic with the Phoenicians."[9]

---

[4] *Il.* vi. 297–303.

[5] *Homeric Synchronism*, pp. 65, foll.

[6] Paus. viii. 17, § 2: τοῖς δὲ ἀνθρώποις τὸ ἀρχαῖον, ὁπόσα καὶ ἡμεῖς καταμαθεῖν ἐδυνήθημεν, τοσάδε ἦν ἀφ' ὧν ξόανα ἐποιοῦντο, ἔβενος, κυπάρισσος, αἱ κέδροι, τὰ δρύϊνα, ἡ μῖλαξ, ὁ λωτός· τῷ δὲ Ἑρμῇ τῷ Κυλληνίῳ τούτων μὲν ἀπὸ οὐδενός, θύου δὲ πεποιημένον τὸ ἄγαλμά ἐστιν.

[7] Paus. ix. 3, § 2: ἐπὶ ταύταις ταῖς διαλλαγαῖς Δαίδαλα ἑορτὴν ἄγουσιν, ὅτι οἱ πάλαι τὰ ξόανα

ἐκάλουν δαίδαλα. ἐκάλουν δέ, ἐμοὶ δοκεῖν, πρότερον ἔτι ἢ Δαίδαλος ὁ Παλαμάονος ἐγένετο 'Αθήνησι· τούτῳ δὲ ὕστερον ἀπὸ τῶν δαιδάλων ἐπίκλησιν γενέσθαι δοκῶ καὶ οὐκ ἐκ γενετῆς τεθῆναι τὸ ὄνομα.

[8] Preface of Siebelis to Pausanias; Leipzig, 1822, pp. xii. seqq.

[9] Mr. C. T. Newton's Lecture on the 30th April, 1874, before the Society of Antiquaries in London.

Nos. 74 and 75 represent saddle-querns of trachyte, of which the strata of *débris* of all the pre-historic cities of Hissarlik contain many

No. 74. Saddle-quern of Trachyte. (About 1 : 5 actual size. Depth, 48 to 53 ft.)

No. 75. Saddle-quern of Trachyte. (About 1 : 5 actual size. Depth, 48 to 53 ft.)

hundreds. I found a large number of similar saddle-querns in my excavations at Mycenae. They occur sometimes, but rarely, in Silesia and Saxony, made of trachyte; and they are, as my friend M. Alexandre Bertrand, Director of the Museum of St. Germain-en-Laye, assures me, but very seldom found in the Dolmens of France. Another friend, Dr. Giustiniano Nicolucci, of Isola del Liri in Italy, states[1] that similar saddle-querns have also been found in the terramare of the Stone and Bronze ages in Italy. A saddle-quern similar to No. 75, but of mica-slate, was found in the excavations at Magyarad, in the county of Hont in Hungary, and is in the collection of B. Nyáry Jenó.[2] The hand-mills found in Mecklenburg, and preserved in the Grand Ducal Antiquarium at Schwerin, are of granite, from 2 to 3 ft. long and 1 to 2 ft. broad, with smaller ones of the same form for bruising the grain. Dr. Lisch believes that the rudely-cut stones of globular form (like Nos. 80 and 81, on p. 236) were used as pestles for the same purpose.

The Trojan saddle-querns are either of trachyte, like the two above, or of basaltic lava, but by far the larger number are of the former material. They are of oval form, flat on one side and convex on the other, and resemble an egg cut longitudinally through the middle. Their length is from 7 to 14 and even as much as 25 in.; the very long ones are usually crooked longitudinally; their breadth is from 5 to 14 in. The grain was bruised between the flat sides of two of these querns; but only a kind of groats can have been produced in this way, not flour; the

---

[1] *Armi ed Utensili in Pietra della Troade;* Napoli, 1879, p. 16.

[2] Joseph Hampel, *Antiquités préhistoriques de la Hongrie;* Plate xiii., No. 38.

bruised grain could not have been used for making bread.   In Homer we
find it used for porridge,[3] and also for strewing on the roasted meat.[4]

No. 76.   Implement of Basalt ; probably a Mortar.
(About 1 : 5 actual size. Depth, 48 to 53 ft.)

No. 77.   Pestle of compact Limestone.
(Half actual size. Depth, 45 to 48 ft.)

Pliny[5] confirms the fact, that the grain was merely bruised and boiled to
pap, or eaten in form of dumplings (*offae*).

No. 76, which is of basaltic lava, has a globular
cavity, and may probably have been used as a mortar.
The implement No. 77 no doubt served as a pestle.
Mr. Thomas Davies, F.G.S., of the British Museum, who
kindly assisted me at the recommendation of my friend
Professor Nevil Story-Maskelyne, late keeper of the
Mineral Department in the British Museum, holds the
pear-shaped pestle No. 77 to be compact limestone ; its
colour is greyish .mixed with yellow.   The instrument
No. 78, which seems likewise to be a pestle, is of
granite.

A mortar of granite similar to No. 76 is in the
Museum of St. Germain-en-Laye ; it was found in Denmark.   M. Bertrand holds it to have been used to break
copper ore in order to detach pieces of it for making arrow-heads.

No. 78.   Instrument
of Granite. (Half
actual size.
Depth, 45 to 48 ft.)

---

[3] *Il.* xviii. 558-560 :
κήρυκες δ' ἀπάνευθεν ὑπὸ δρυΐ δαῖτα πένοντο,
βοῦν δ' ἱερεύσαντες μέγαν ἄμφεπον· αἱ δὲ
   γυναῖκες
δεῖπνον ἐρίθοισιν λεύκ' ἄλφιτα πολλὰ πάλυνον.
[4] *Od.* xiv. 76, 77 :
ὀπτήσας δ' ἄρα πάντα φέρων παρέθηκ' 'Οδυσῆϊ
θέρμ' αὐτοῖς ὀβελοῖσιν· ὃ δ' ἄλφιτα λευκὰ
   πάλυνεν.

[5] *H. N.* xviii. 19 : " Pulte autem, non pane,
vixisse longo tempore Romanos manifestum,
quoniam inde et pulmentaria hodieque dicuntur.
Et Ennius antiquissimus vates obsidionis famem
exprimens, offam eripuisse plorantibus liberis
patres commemorat. Et hodie sacra prisca, atque
natalium, pulta fritilla conficiuntur ; videturque
tam puls ignota Graeciae fuisse, quam Italiae
polenta."

No. 79 represents a beautifully polished implement, which, according to Mr. Davies, consists of hæmatite; it was probably used for polishing large terra-cotta vessels.

No. 79. Implement of Stone for polishing. (Half actual size. Depth, 45 to 50 ft.)

No. 80. Round Stone for bruising Corn. (Half actual size. Depth, 45 to 52 ft.)

Rudely-cut, nearly globular stone instruments, like Nos. 80 and 81, are very numerous in all the four lower pre-historic cities; nay, I do

No. 81. Round Stone for bruising Corn. (Half actual size. Depth, 45 to 52 ft.)

not exaggerate when I affirm that I could have collected thousands of them. They are, according to Mr. Davies, of basaltic lava, granite, quartz, diorite, porphyry, or other sorts of stone, and only in one instance of silex.

Similar instruments are found in the cave-dwellings of the Dordogne, as well as in the Dolmens in France; and many specimens of these are preserved in the Museum of St. Germain-en-Laye. They are very numerous in the most ancient Swiss Lake habitations, and particularly in those of the Lake of Constance, where all of them are of hard sandstone. A number of rudely-cut globular stone instruments, similar to Nos. 80 and 81, were found in the excavations at Szihalom, and are exhibited in the National Hungarian Museum at Buda-Pesth.[6] In the opinion of my friend, Professor Ludwig Lindenschmit, founder and director of the celebrated Museum of Mainz, these implements were the most ancient

[6] See Plate x., Nos. 52–54, 57–60 of the photographs of the National Hungarian Museum at Buda-Pesth.

millstones of the simplest kind, and were employed for bruising the grain on the plates of sandstone which abound in the Lake habitations.[7]

The same rudely-cut round stones occur also in the pre-historic villages in Thera.[8] Professor Virchow, M. Burnouf, and Dr. Nicolucci [9] concur in Professor Lindenschmit's opinion, that they served for bruising grain or other substances.

Not less abundant than the round corn-bruisers are implements more or less in the form of Nos. 82 and 83, which are of diorite, and represent

No. 82.   Stone Instrument for bruising or polishing.
(Half actual size.   Depth, 45 to 50 ft.)

No. 84.   Stone Implement, with a furrow running
lengthwise round.   (Half actual size.
Depth, 45 to 50 ft.)

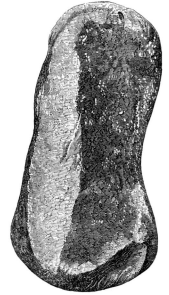

No. 83.   Rude Stone Hammer.   (Half actual size.
Depth, 45 to 50 ft.)

No. 85.   Axe of Diorite.   (Half actual size.
Depth, 45 to 48 ft.)

[7] L. Lindenschmit, Die Vaterländischen Alterthümer, pp. 172, 173, 178, and Plate xxvii.
No. 8.

[8] See the small collection of Thera antiquities
in the French School at Athens.

[9] Dr. G. Nicolucci, Armi ed Utensili in Pietra
della Troade, pp. 16, 17.

two of the best specimens. Instruments like No. 82 may probably have served, as Nicolucci suggests, for smoothing the clay of the large vases, perhaps also for crushing the coarse particles contained in the clay, or for bruising the granite, with which the latter was mixed. No. 83 is a rude primitive hammer, both ends of which are much worn down, and testify to the long use which has been made of it. From its large size and heavy weight we are induced to think that it was merely grasped by the hand, and could not have been fastened in a cloven wood handle. I repeat that these are two of the best specimens, for there are in the first four pre-historic cities thousands of similar but far ruder implements, of diorite, granite, silicious rock, hornblende, gneiss, and other sorts of stone.

No. 84 is an implement of granite, of oval form, with a deep furrow running lengthwise round it. It resembles a stone implement found in Denmark which is in the Museum of Copenhagen, and is represented in J. J. A. Worsaae's *Nordiske Oldsager*, Pl. xviii. No. 87, among the objects of the Stone age. These objects appear to have served as weights for looms or fishing-nets.

I now come to the axes or *celts*,[10] of which I have been able to collect more than 500 in the first four pre-historic cities of Hissarlik.

Mr. Thomas Davies, who examined them carefully, declares them to consist of blue serpentinous rock, green gabbro-rock, black slaty rock, dark-green hornstone, black or grey diorite, jadeite and jade (nephrite). Of the five celts of the first city of which I here give the engravings, No. 85 consists of black diorite ; No. 88, of jadeite ; Nos. 86, 87, and 89, of jade (nephrite).

No. 89.

No. 88.

No. 87.

No. 86.

Nos. 86–89. Axes of Jadeite and Jade (Nephrite). (About half actual size. Depth, about 45 to 52 ft.)

" The axe was," as my honoured friend the celebrated anthropologist, Sir J. Lubbock, rightly remarks,[1] " pre-eminently the implement of antiquity. It was used in war and in the chase, as well as for domestic purposes, and great numbers of celts have been found in the Lake-dwellings at Wangen (Lake of Constance) and Concise (Lake of Neuf-

---

[10] Readers not conversant with archæology may be informed that this word is not derived from the Celtic people, but from *celtis*, " a chisel." " This word, however," as Mr. John Evans (*Ancient Stone Implements of Great Britain*, p. 50) observes, " is an ἅπαξ λεγόμενον in this sense, being only found in the Vulgate translation of Job, chap. xix. v. 24. It also occurs in a quotation of the passage by St. Jerome, in his *Epist. ad Pammachium*. (See *Athenæum*, June 11, 1870.)

The usual derivation given is *a coelando*, and it is regarded as the equivalent of *coelum*. The first use of the term that I have met with, as applied to antiquities, is in Beger's *Thesaurus Brandenburgicus* (vol. iii. p. 418), 1696, where a bronze celt, adapted for insertion in its haft, is described under the name of *Celtes*."

[1] *Pre-historic Times;* London, 1878, 4th edit. pp. 95–97 and 194.

chatel). With a few exceptions they were small, especially when compared with the magnificent specimens from Denmark; in length they varied from one to six inches, while the cutting edge had generally a width of from fifteen to twenty lines."

This is also the usual proportion of the axes at Hissarlik, but there are a few whose cutting edge, like that of No. 87, is only about four and a half lines. The manner in which these axes were made is described in a masterly way by Sir John Lubbock:[2]—"After having chosen a stone, the first step was to reduce it by blows with a hammer to a suitable size. Then grooves were made artificially, which must have been a very tedious and difficult operation, when flint knives, sand, and water were the only available instruments. Having carried the grooves to the required depth, the projecting portions were removed by a skilful blow with a hammer, and the implement was then sharpened and polished on blocks of sandstone. The axes were then fastened into the handles. To us, accustomed as we are to the use of metals, it seems difficult to believe that such things were ever made use of; we know, however, that many savages of the present day have no better tools. Yet with axes such as these, and generally with the assistance of fire, they will cut down large trees and hollow them out into canoes. The piles used in the Swiss Stone age Lake-habitations were evidently, from the marks of the cuts on them, prepared with the help of stone axes; and in the Danish peat-bogs, several trees have been found with the marks of stone axes and of fire upon them; and in one or two cases, stone celts have even been found lying at the side. In the excavations known as Grimes' Graves, again, a basalt hatchet was found, which had evidently been used for excavating the gallery, as shown by the marks still distinctly visible on the walls. One use of the American tomahawk was to crush bones for the sake of the marrow; and it is most probable that the ancient stone axes also served the same purpose. In many cases the axes themselves bear ample marks of long-continued use. That they were also weapons of war is probable, not only on à priori grounds, but also because they have frequently been found in the graves of chiefs, associated with bronze daggers. About the year 1809, a large cairn in Kircudbrightshire, popularly supposed to be the tomb of a King Aldus M'Galdus, was removed by a farmer. When the cairn had been removed, the workmen came to a stone coffin of very rude workmanship, and, on removing the lid, they found the skeleton of a man of uncommon size. The bones were in such a state of decomposition, that the ribs and vertebræ crumbled into dust on attempting to lift them. The remaining bones, being less decayed, were taken out, when it was discovered that one of the arms had been almost separated from the shoulder by a stroke of a stone axe, and that a fragment of the axe still remained in the bone. The axe was of greenstone, a material which does not occur in this part of Scotland. There were also found with the skeleton a ball of flint, about 3 in. in diameter, which was perfectly round

---

[2] *Pre-historic Times;* London, 1878, 4th edit. pp. 95-97 and 194.

and highly polished, and the head of an arrow, also flint, but not a particle of any metallic substance. We know also the North American stone axe or tomahawk served not merely as an implement, but also as a weapon, being used both in the hand and also as a missile."

I am indebted to my friend Professor H. Fischer of Freiburg, for the discovery that I have thirteen axes of jade in my Trojan collection. Having read in my former publication [3] that I had found axes of very hard transparent greenstone, he insisted upon my getting them carefully examined. Professor Maskelyne, to whom I applied, was good enough to have the specific gravities of the different specimens determined for me in the usual way; namely, by weighing them successively in air and in water, so as to determine the ratio of the weight of the stone to that of an equal bulk of water. This was done by his assistant, Mr. Thomas Davies. The result was that the specific gravity of twelve of my green transparent axes and of one white transparent axe lies between 2·91 and 2·99, and that, consequently, all thirteen are of jade (nephrite). Mr. Davies remarked to me at the same time that, " in association with the implements or arms of jade found in Brittany, some turquoise beads have been discovered.[4] This mineral is not at present found *in situ* in Europe, and thus we have here additional evidence of the probability of these substances having been procured from Eastern countries."

Professor Maskelyne writes to me : " Now I tell you that your thirteen Hissarlik jade implements are to me of the highest interest. They are so for the reason that now for the first time have I seen true white jade as the material of a stone implement, and that too in association with the regular green jade, which is not so rare a material.[5] This is interesting ; and so is the Hissarlik locality, altogether apart from the Homeric bearings of it, and

'Immortal dreams that could beguile
The blind old man of Scio rocky isle.'

The presence of the white jade is interesting as pointing to the locality whence it came ; its association with its green brother is interesting as helping to confirm this indication. In fact, it is a very great probability that the Kúen-lún mountains produced the mineral of which these implements are made, and that they came from Khotan by a process of primeval barter, that must have nursed a trade capable of moving onward over the ' roof of the world ' perhaps, or less probably by Cashmere, Afghanistan, and Persia, into the heart of Europe. If the Pamir and the region north of the Hindoo Kush was the route, this primitive stream of commerce may have flowed along the course of the Oxus before that great artery of carrying power had become diverted by the geological upheaval of Northern Persia from its old course to the Caspian. I have always wondered why jade ceased to be a prized material and an article of commerce so soon as civilization laid hold of our race. The Assyrians and

---

[3] *Troy and its Remains*, p. 21.

[4] For example, the pendant of a necklace made of callaïs (turquoise) found in a Dolmen called " Mancer-H'roëk," in the locality Loc-

mariaker in Morbihan, Brittany.

[5] Professor Maskelyne informs me that he has since met with another celt of white jade (in Mr. Franks's hands), found in Crete.

Egyptians hardly, if the latter at all, knew jade. Yet jade implements have been dug up in Mesopotamia of primeval type, and the commerce that transported these implements in far distant times bore them as far as Brittany. The Assyrians and the Egyptians, like all other peoples, have valued green stones. Green jasper and Amazon stone, and even plasma, were known and appreciated; why not then jade also? My answer would be, that they could not get it. Unlike the Chinese, who have always kept it in honour because they had it at their gate, the Mesopotamian and Egyptian artists did not know jade, or only knew it as coming accidentally to hand, perhaps as the material of a pre-historic weapon.[6] We need to know more than we do of the pre-historic movements of the human race, to be able to say whether the region of the Pamir and of Eastern Turkestan was once more densely peopled, was in fact more habitable, than to-day is the case; but I am strongly inclined to believe that a geological change is at the bottom of the disappearance of jade from among the valued materials of the archaic, the ancient, and the medieval ages, down to within three hundred or four hundred years from this time. If the upheaval of the regions, along which this commerce flowed, has rendered them less habitable, has planted deserts where once men dwelt with flocks, has made regions of ice where once winter was endurable,— has, finally, diverted from its course a great river, that bore a commerce, or at least fertilized the route of a commerce,— there may be an explanation of the drying up of the stream of that commerce itself.

" The Hissarlik locality for such an interesting find of so many and such beautiful jade implements has an interest also in this, that the geographical importance of the Hellespont, as the Bridge from Asia to Europe, seems to have brought to that spot the opportunity of selection and an abundance of material. I am writing to you perhaps some dreams more dreamy, you will think perhaps, than any of the dreams I wrote of in my first page. At any rate, while you are giving realistic life to the ancient tale of Troy, strive to do something, too, for this more venerable witness to the brotherhood and the intercommunication of the human race in the age rather of Kronos than of Zeus. Was it the jade-stone that Kronos swallowed ?"

Professor Fischer writes to me, that "as far as my knowledge goes jade (nephrite) axes only occur in South Italy (Calabria), in the Lake-dwellings of Switzerland and the Lake of Constance, the Lake of Starnberg near Munich, and the ancient settlement of Blasingen (between Freiburg and Basel, and therefore far from Lake-dwellings); further a small chisel of jade (nephrite) is said to have been found in the district of Nördlingen." He adds that " Professor Damour, who made most active researches in France, could discover there only one jade (nephrite) axe, of which the locality where it was found is unknown ; it was sold in

---

[6] With reference to this remark of Prof. Maskelyne, I may mention that, according to Brugsch-Bey, *battle-axes with stone heads* were among the spoils brought home by Thutmes III., together with weapons and armour of bronze, and works of art in gold and silver, from the highly civilized states of Western Asia. (*Hist. of Egypt*, vol. i. p. 405, Engl. trans., 2nd ed.)

Rheims, and the quality of the jade resembles that of the Swiss Lake-dwellings."

Professor Fischer is amazed at hearing that among my thirteen Hissarlik jade axes there is a white one,[7] for he had as yet only seen axes of green jade; he knows raw white jade abundantly from Turkestan (at least, yellowish, greyish, and greenish white), besides perfectly white from China; but no trace of axes was discovered by the travellers of his acquaintance who explored the jade quarries of Turkestan. The Siberian jade has a bright grass-green colour; the New Zealand jade for the most part a more dark green colour. There is besides a very dark green jade in Asia, which must be native somewhere in Asia (perhaps in Turkestan), and of which Timur's tombstone in Samarkand is made. Professor Fischer received fragments of the latter from the late Professor Barbot de Marny of St. Petersburg, who knocked them off with his own hand in the mosque, of course at the danger of his life.

Professor Fischer says in conclusion that my thirteen Hissarlik jade axes come from the farthest eastern point at which polished jade axes have been found, and expresses the wish that before the end of his life the fortune might be allotted to him of finding out what people brought them to Europe.[8]

---

[7] This white jade axe, of which I shall have to speak later on, was found at a depth of 6½ ft. below the surface, and must therefore belong to the latest pre-historic city of Hissarlik; for in the subsequent settlement, which from the pottery I hold to be an ancient Lydian one, I never found stone implements.

[8] Mr. Thomas Davies kindly gave me the following note, which he had communicated to the translator of Keller's *Lake Dwellings*, and which appeared in the Appendix to the second edition of that work issued by Messrs. Longmans. It has been reproduced in the *Geological Magazine*, Decade II. vol. v. No. 4, April 1878. I deem it too interesting not to give it here.

"Note on 'Jadeite' and 'Jade.' By Thomas Davies, F.G.S.

"Jadeite (Damour).

"Specific gravity, 3·28 to 3·4; hardness, 6·5 to 7. Colours milky-white, with bright green veins and splotches, greenish-grey, bluish-grey, clear grey and translucent as chalcedony, orange-yellow, smoky-green passing to black, apple-green, sometimes emerald-green, all the green tints as a rule much brighter than in the Oriental jade, also, but rarely, of violet shades. Texture from compact to crypto-crystalline, and distinctly crystalline, sometimes coarsely so; fibro-lamellar, opaque to. translucent and sometimes transparent.

"Thin splinters will fuse in the flame of a spirit-lamp. Damour, from analyses made by him, suggests its affinities to the epidotes.

"*Localities.*—Central Asia, and particularly China; also as articles worked by the Aztecs, Mexico.

"Oriental Jade (Damour).

"Specific gravity, 2·96 to 3·06; hardness, 5·5 to 6·5. Colours white and white variously tinted, greenish-grey, many shades of green. Texture mostly compact, rarely crypto-crystalline.

"Found chiefly in Central Asia, particularly in China and on its borders. Also in New Zealand and the Pacific Islands generally.

"Specific gravity of upwards of 100 specimens from New Zealand determined by myself have been within the limits of 3·00 to 3·02, by far the larger number giving 3·01.

"Oceanic Jade (Damour).

"Specific gravity, 3·18; hardness, 5·5 to 6·5. Of this variety I possess no personal experience, the large number of objects of jade which have come under my observation not having yielded me one example. Damour, however, who examined four specimens, states that in its aspect and general characters—with the exception of its density—it much resembles the Oriental jade. It, however, possesses a somewhat silky lustre, due to exceedingly delicate fibres which traverse the mass. I have met with this structure frequently however in the jade from New Zealand, which possessed the density of 3·01. From an analysis Damour refers it to the pyroxene group, whereas the Oriental is referable to hornblende. Vars. Tremolite or Actinolite.

"Found in New Caledonia and Marquise Island, Pacific.

"None of these minerals to my knowledge have been met with *in situ* in Europe, though the British Museum possesses a fragment of unworked Oriental jade purporting to have been found in Turkey"—probably, as Mr. Maskelyne suggests, an error for Turkestan.

The mineralogist, Professor Ferd. Roemer of Breslau, writes to me that "in the choice of the material for stone weapons, particularly stone axes, the *tenacity* of the stone was more decisive than its hardness, and that consequently jade (nephrite), diorite, and serpentine were chosen by preference. In Silesia and in other parts of Germany, diorite and serpentine were by preference the material for stone axes. Serpentine has no great hardness, but it is solid, and it does not break into splinters when struck upon. Jade (nephrite) is the most tenacious of all stones. Even with very heavy hammers it is exceedingly difficult to crush pieces of it. For this reason jade (nephrite) and the nearly related jadeite were the most appreciated material in pre-historic times."

Professor Maskelyne adds: "Jade being so exceedingly tough, the axes must have been cut with the assistance of emery. Jade may be approximately described as amorphous or uncrystallized hornblende, which is a magnesium and calcium silicate."

According to Sir John Lubbock,[9] Professor von Fellenberg states that jade (nephrite) and jadeite are found only in Central Asia, New Zealand, and South America.[10] In another passage [11] Sir John Lubbock informs us that in the great tumulus called Mont St. Michel, at Carnac in Brittany, there were found, besides a large number of other stone axes, eleven jade celts, and 110 beads, mostly of callaïs, but no trace of metal.

Of my thirteen jade axes only the three represented under Nos. 86, 87, and 89, were found in the first city; No. 88, which has been engraved with them, is of jadeite, and belongs also to this first city. To those who wish to know more of jade (nephrite) I recommend Prof. Fischer's celebrated work.[1]

There also frequently occurs in the four lower pre-historic cities of Hissarlik a curious implement of the same kind of stone as the axes, and of the same shape, with the sole difference that at the lower end, where the edge ought to be, it is blunt, perfectly smooth, and from a quarter to half an inch thick. Such an implement, found at a depth of 46 ft., is represented by No. 90. Mr. Davies, who examined it, finds it to be of diorite. These implements, which are rarely found elsewhere, are, as Professor Virchow of Berlin and Mr. A. W. Franks of the British Museum believe, thought to have been used as polishers.

No. 90. Curious Stone Implement. (Nearly half actual size. Depth, 46 ft.)

Axes are found in nearly all countries, and are almost everywhere of nearly the same shape.[2]

---

[9] *Pre-historic Times*, p. 82.

[10] Professor Virchow observes to me that jade (nephrite) has never been found in South America in a natural state, but only worked out into implements.

[11] *Pre-historic Times*, p. 167.

[1] Heinrich Fischer, *Nephrit und Jadeit nach ihren mineralogischen Eigenschaften, sowie nach ihrer urgeschichtlichen und ethnographischen Bedeutung;* Stuttgart, 1875.

[2] *Smithsonian Contributions to Knowledge*, No. 287, Washington, 1876; the *Arch. Coll. of the U. S. Nat. Museum*, p. 17.

Idem, No. 259, *Explor. of Aboriginal Remains of Tennessee*, pp. 51 and 142. See further *Archivos do Museu Nacional do Rio de Janeiro*, Rio de

Under Nos. 91 and 92 I represent two well-polished perforated axes found in the first city, of which the former, according to Mr. Davies, is of

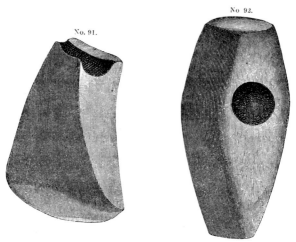

No. 91.   No 92.

Nos. 91, 92.   Two polished perforated Axes.   (About half actual size.   Depth, 45 to 52 ft.)

hæmatite, the latter of porphyry. Similar perforated axes, either with two sharp edges, or with only one, like No. 92, occur in all the four lowest pre-historic cities of Hissarlik. Mr. Davies, who examined a number of them, found them to consist of diorite, porphyry, silicious rock, hæmatite, hornblende, gneiss, crystalline limestone, blue serpentine, gabbro-rock, &c. Whence the pre-historic peoples of Hissarlik obtained all these varieties of stones, I have not been able to find out. Diorite they may have got from the valley of the Rhodius, where, as Mr. Calvert informs me, it is plentiful.

Like the axes described above, these perforated axes were evidently used for domestic purposes as well as for battle-axes. They are exceedingly rare in the Swiss Lake-habitations; in fact, no entire specimens have ever been found there. The two halves of such an axe, which Lindenschmit[3] represents, were found in the Lake-dwellings at the station of Wangen, in the Lake of Constance. The same author also represents entire perforated axes of basalt and serpentine,[4] one of which was found at Linz, the other at Hohenzollern. Similar perforated axes are also found in Denmark, in the settlements of the Stone age, as well as in England, Germany, Livonia, Courland, &c.[5] Two axes like No. 92 were found by Professor Virchow in the pre-historic graveyard at Zaborówo and are preserved in his collection. They are very plentiful

Janeiro, 1876, Pl. i.; Joseph Hampel, *Antiquités préhistoriques de la Hongrie*, Plate iii. For the stone axes found at Szihalom, see Pl. x. of the photographs taken of the objects exhibited in the National Hungarian Museum. Similar stone axes are contained in all the collections of pre-historic antiquities; I shall therefore not quote

more of them here.

[3] *Die Vaterländischen Alterthümer*, Pl. xxvii., Nos. 12 and 13.

[4] *Ibid.*, Pl. xliii., Nos. 3 and 11.

[5] J. J. A. Worsaae, *Nordiske Oldsager*, Pl. xiii. John Evans, *The Ancient Stone Implements;* London, 1872, pp. 75, 129, 163, 164.

in Hungary.[6] Professor Roemer asks me if the pre-historic peoples of Hissarlik knew of the emery of Naxos, as quartz (silicious rock), onyx, corneol, &c., cannot be polished without emery. Professor Sayce remarks to me that emery is also found in the Gümush Dagh, the range of mountains which runs along the northern bank of the Maeander in the extreme south of Lydia.

As to the perforations, my friend Mr. John Evans is of opinion that they were drilled with a stick by means of sand; whilst Professor Maskelyne holds that the hard stones were probably perforated with a drill of bronze or stone, or even perhaps of wood, worked by a bow. This, fed with emery and water, would gradually bore a hole. Professor Virchow observes to me that experiments made in drilling with a stick by means of sand have repeatedly been made with perfect success.

That the perforating of the hard stones was an exceedingly difficult operation for the pre-historic inhabitants of Hissarlik, could not be better proved than by the great number of hammers, and in a few instances also axes, in which the operation of boring had been commenced on both sides (sometimes on one side only), but was abandoned when a hole had been bored the depth of a quarter or half an inch. In several instances the operation of boring had been merely begun, and was abandoned when the holes were only a line or two deep. But nearly all the hammers of this kind were found in the *débris* of the third and fourth pre-historic cities. In the first city, which now occupies us, only one hammer of a whitish limestone was found, in which the boring had been commenced but abandoned. Similar hammers, in which the drilling of holes had been commenced and abandoned, are found in Denmark in the settlements of the Stone age;[7] they are also, as Professor Virchow informs me, frequently found in Germany, and he has one from Zaborówo in his own collection. They are further found in Hungary[8] and England.[9]

Lindenschmit[1] says: "The rarity, nay the absence, of entire specimens of completely perforated axes (in the Swiss Lake-dwellings) may perhaps be rather explained by the supposition, that they were used chiefly as arms, which, on the destruction of the settlement at the hands of warriors, must have disappeared, either with them in the battle itself, or on their return to the forests."

Under Nos. 93–98 I give engravings of double-edged saws of white and brown flint or chalcedony. They consist of flat, sharp, indented pieces of these kinds of stone. Those of which one side only is indented, as in No. 96, were inserted into pieces of wood or of staghorn and cemented with pitch, of which traces still remain on one or two specimens; but that the double-edged saws were inserted in a like manner appears improbable. They seem to have been used for sawing bones. Similar

[6] Jos. Hampel, *Antiquités préhistoriques de la Hongrie*, Pl. iv.; also see Pl. x. of the photographs of the National Hungarian Museum, Nos. 66, 67, representing the finds at Szihalom.

[7] J. J. A. Worsaae, *Nordiske Oldsager*, Pl. xii.

No. 33.

[8] Joseph Hampel, *Antiquités préhistoriques de la Hongrie*, Pl. iv. Nos. 3, 4, 6.

[9] John Evans, *Stone Implements*, pp. 217, 218.

[1] *Die Vaterländischen Alterthümer*, p. 179.

flint saws are found in the cave-dwellings in the Dordogne; some are
preserved in the Museum of St. Germain-en-Laye; they are also found

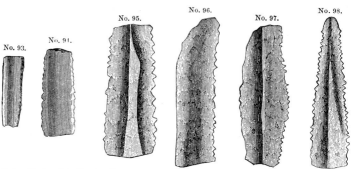

Nos. 93–98.   Single and double-edged Saws of Flint or Chalcedony.   (Nearly 2:3 actual size.   Depth, 45 to 52 ft.)

in the Swiss Lake-habitations of the Stone age.[2]   Two such saw-knives
were found at Bethsaur near Bethlehem, and are preserved in the British
Museum, where I also noticed other saws of the same kind found in
India, in the Collection of Indian Antiquities.   Similar saws of silex,
found in pre-historic tombs in Mecklenburg, are preserved in the Museum
of Neu Brandenburg and in the Grand Ducal Antiquarium at Schwerin.
The keeper of the former, Mr. Julius Müller, suggests that they may
have been used for cutting sinews, hides, and bones.   Similar flint saws
are also found in Denmark.[3]

At Hissarlik these double or single edged saws of silex or chalcedony
are so plentiful in all the four lower pre-historic cities, that I have been
able to collect nearly a thousand of them.   In the latest pre-historic city
I only found two such, of very large size.   Double-edged flint saws, of
the shape of No. 98, occurred only twice or three times.   They may
probably have been used as arrow-heads; for regularly-shaped arrow-
heads, such as I found in the Royal Sepulchres at Mycenae,[4] do not exist
here.   Abundant at Hissarlik, but less frequent than the saw-knives, are
the knives of silex or chalcedony, of the same size as the saws, having
either only one or two sharp edges.   Such knives are also found
abundantly in the habitations of the Stone age in Scandinavia,[5] in the
Swiss Lake-habitations,[6] in the cave-habitations in the Dordogne,[7] in
Mecklenburg as well as elsewhere in Germany, and in many other places
and countries; as, for instance, in Hungary.[8]   Flakes of silex or chalcedony are still used to the present day in immense quantities all over
Asia Minor for the corn-shellers or threshing-boards (in modern Greek,

[2] Lindenschmit, *Die Vaterländischen Alterthümer*, p. 179, Plate xxvii. No. 18 ; Sir J. Lubbock,
Pre-historic Times, p. 107 ; V. Gross, *Établissements Lacustres*, Pl. i. No. 4.

[3] A. P. Madsen, *Antiquités préhistoriques du
Danemarc*; Copenhagen, 1872, Plate xxiv. Nos.
5–8, 12–15.

[4] See my *Mycenae*, p. 272, No. 435.

[5] J. J. A. Worsaae, *Nordiske Oldsager*, Pl. xv.

No. 61 ; A. P. Madsen, *Antiquités préhistoriques
du Danemarc*, Pl. xviii. Nos. 25–28 ; Lubbock,
Pre-historic Times, p. 89.

[6] Lindenschmit, *Die Vaterländischen Alterthümer*, p. 179, Pl. xxviii. Nos. 19–23.

[7] Large masses of these are preserved in the
Museum of St. Germain-en-Laye.

[8] Joseph Hampel, *Antiquités préhistoriques de
la Hongrie*, Pl. i.

δοκάνι). These are in the form of sledges, and consist of two heavy wooden planks 6½ ft. long, and at one end 2 ft., at the other 1 ft. 4 in., broad. In the lower side of these corn-shellers an immense number of holes are made, about 2 in. long, in which the flint flakes are fastened lengthwise, so that all are in the direction of the boards. These flints have the length of those I find at Hissarlik, but they are much thicker, and none of them has a sharp or an indented edge. These machines are drawn by a horse over the ears of corn spread on the threshing-floor ; they are also used for chopping up straw.

Much less abundant are the flakes or knives of obsidian, though they occur in all the four lowest pre-historic cities at Hissarlik. All of them are two-edged, and some are so sharp that one might shave with them. Such obsidian flakes or knives are sometimes found together with the common flint flakes, but only in those countries where obsidian occurs in a natural state. That such knives of flint or obsidian were once in general use, seems to be proved by the fact, that here and there the Jews to the present day circumcise their children with such knives.

Now, as to the place whence the pre-historic peoples of Hissarlik obtained their silex and chalcedony. These stones, as Mr. Calvert assures me, are found near Koush-Shehr at Sapgee, about 20 miles to the east of Hissarlik, where they are still worked for the manufacture of the Turkish threshing-boards. The same friend informs me that he found obsidian of a coarse nature near Saragik ; he further calls my attention to the statement of Barker Webb (*De Agro Troiano*, p. 42), that he observed the mineral near Mantescia, on the road from Assos to Aivajik—one hour from the former place. Professor Virchow found chalcedony contained in the volcanic layers near the Foulah Dagh [9] in the Troad.

It deserves particular notice that, *except the little knives and saw-knives, no implements or arms of silex were ever found at Hissarlik.*

No. 99 represents a pretty little disc of greenish sandstone, with a projecting border and a round hole in the centre ; its use is unknown.

No. 99. Flat perforated Stone. (Half actual size.
Depth, about 48 ft.)

No. 100. Fragment of a Bowl, with
a pair of eyes. (About half actual size.
Depth, about 48 ft.)

No. 100 represents in outline a fragment of a lustrous-black bowl, which, like No. 36, seems to represent an owl's face in monogram. Prof. Sayce asks, " Is it not for warding off the evil eye ? Compare the Etruscan vases."

[9] See *Zeitschrift für Ethnologie* (*Berliner Anthropolog. Gesellschaft*, Band xi. S. 272).

Of whetstones, such as Nos. 101 and 102, only a few were found in the first city; they are much more frequent in the three following cities.

No. 101.

No. 102.

Nos. 101, 102. Whetstones of Green and Black Slate. (Half actual size. Depth, 40 to 52 ft.)

Nearly all are perforated at one end for suspension. Mr. Davies pronounces them all to consist of indurated slate. Two similar whetstones have been found in Egyptian sepulchres; one of them is in the Egyptian Collection in the Louvre; the other appears in the Egyptian Collection in the British Museum, with the notice that it was found in a tomb of the Twentieth Dynasty. Many such whetstones, found in England, are also in the British Museum, where the ancient Peruvian Collection likewise contains some specimens of them. Two such whetstones, found at Szihalom, are in the Hungarian National Museum at Buda-Pesth.[10] Prof. Virchow informs me that similar whetstones also occur in Germany.

No. 103. A Mould of Mica-slate for casting arrow-heads of a very curious form.
(About half actual size. Depth, 46 ft.)

The accompanying mould No. 103 consists, according to Prof. Landerer, of mica-slate. It forms a trapezium 3 in. long, 1½ in. broad at one end and 1·8 in. at the other, and half an inch thick. It has three moulds for casting pointed instruments of a kind such as have never yet occurred anywhere, and which, in my opinion, can be nothing else than arrow-heads, though the only species of arrow-heads I discovered in this first city as well as in the two succeeding ones are vastly different.

My friend Mr. Carlo Giuliano, the celebrated London goldsmith and jeweller of antiques — who showed me the great kindness of repeatedly visiting my Trojan collection and explaining to me, for three hours at a time, how all the metallic work, and particularly how the jewels, were made by the pre-historic peoples—holds it to be impossible that the objects to be cast in these moulds could have been intended for breast- or hair-pins. He agrees with me that they were intended for arrow-heads: this view appears also to be confirmed by the barbs on one of them. It seems still more difficult to explain the use of the triangular object represented by the fourth mould. Professor Sayce asks me, "Was it not intended for a bead?" For casting all the objects represented here, two such

10 See Pl. x., Nos. 82 and 83, of the photographs of the collection.

mould-stones, each of them having exactly the same beds, were fastened together by means of a small round stick, which was put into the round hole ; then the metal was poured through the openings on the small sides of the stones into the beds, and was left there till it had become cold.

Under Nos. 104–111 I represent curious objects of pure copper. The head of No. 104 is in the form of a spiral ; that of No. 105 is quite flat.

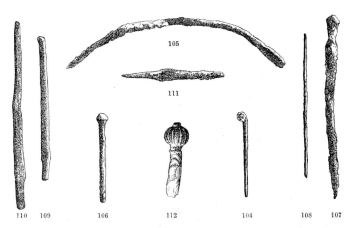

Nos. 104–112. Punches, Brooches, and Arrow-head of Copper, also a Silver Brooch.
(Half actual size. Depth, 45 to 53 ft.)

Nos. 106 and 107 have heads of globular form, and are in the form of nails ; but they can of course never have been used as such, being far too long and thin and fragile to be driven into wood.   One of those found in this first city is 7 in. long.   They can consequently only have served as brooches and hair-pins, and were the ancient predecessors of the fibulæ invented ages later.   Similar primitive brooches are very numerous in the first four pre-historic cities of Hissarlik, but only in the first two cities are they of copper ; in the two later cities they are of bronze.   They are also of bronze in the ancient Lake-habitations in the Lake of Bourget.   A certain number found in that lake are pre-served in the Museum of St. Germain-en-Laye, the director of which, M. Alexandre Bertrand, attributes to them the date of from 600 to 500 B.C. Brooches of bronze of the same shape, but much more elaborate, were found in the Lake-dwellings at Moeringen and Auvernier.[1]   Needles with two pointed ends, like No. 108, were found at Szihalom in Hungary ;[2] they are also very plentiful in Germany, Denmark, and elsewhere.   There are a great many such primitive brooches of bronze, both of the form of No. 104 with a head in the form of a spiral, and of that of Nos. 106 and 107, in the Grand Ducal Antiquarium of Schwerin ; they were all found in the Mecklenburg sepulchral mounds called " Hünengraber," and in many other ancient sites in Germany.   Miss Adèle Virchow has collected a

[1] Victor Gross, *Deux Stations Lacustres ;* Neuveville, 1878, Pl. viii., Nos. 12 and 13.

[2] See Pl. x., Nos. 7 and 16, of the photographs

of the Pre-historic Collection of the National Hungarian Museum.

number of brooches, like Nos. 104 and 107, in her excavations in the graveyard of Zaborówo.

Nos. 109 and 110 are declared by Mr. Giuliano to be punches, the lower ends of which were inserted in wooden handles. No. 111, 1·6 in. long, is in the usual form of the arrow-head, such as I have found in the *débris* of the three lower cities; indeed, I never found a differently shaped arrow-head there. A similar arrow-head appears to have been found in the excavations at Szihalom in Hungary.[3]

All these brooches, punches, and arrows have evidently been cast, though only in the third city have I found a mould for such arrows, never one for brooches or punches. No. 112 is a fragmentary brooch of silver.

In the accompanying group the copper punch, No. 113, as well as the copper brooches, Nos. 114 and 115, are from the second city.[4] The rest

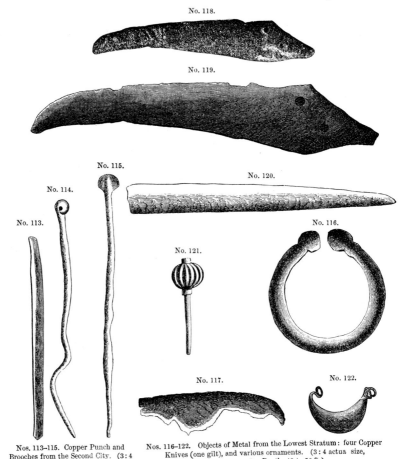

Nos. 113–115. Copper Punch and Brooches from the Second City. (3 : 4 actual size. Depth, 35 to 42 ft.)

Nos. 116–122. Objects of Metal from the Lowest Stratum: four Copper Knives (one gilt), and various ornaments. (3 : 4 actua size, but No. 119, 2 : 5. Depth, 43 to 50 ft.)

---

[3] See Plate x., No. 20, of the photographs of the Collection in the National Museum at Buda-Pesth.

[4] They are given here, as they happen to have been engraved on the same block with the other objects.

of the metal objects are from the first city. No. 116 represents a copper bracelet, but it is so small that it can only have fitted the arm of a little child. Nos. 117, 118, and 119 are copper knives; the first is much broken; in the larger end of the two latter may be seen the two or three holes of the pins with which they were fixed in the handles of wood or bone.

My friend Mr. W. Chandler Roberts, F.R.S., assayer at the Royal Mint, and Professor of Metallurgy in the Royal School of Mines, kindly analysed the metals of this first city, and wrote for me the following valuable report on the subject :—

" I also analysed with much care small portions of implements found at depths of over 40 ft.

" No. 120 is a knife-blade (depth 45 ft.) on the surface of which there are thin flakes of metal that cupellation showed to be gold. The knife had evidently been gilded, a fact which proves that the artificer who made it possessed much metallurgical knowledge and technical skill.

" Analysis showed that copper was present to the extent of 97·4 per cent. in the metallic state, the rest of the metal being in the form of green carbonate and red oxide of copper; for the blade was so corroded at the end that it was impossible to entirely eliminate these substances. Tin, however, was certainly *not* present in appreciable quantity; so that the implement must be regarded as having been originally formed of unalloyed *copper*.

" The nail or pin, No. 105 (depth 46 ft.), was also much corroded, but a cleaned portion gave on analysis :—

97·83 per cent. copper.
0·21 „ „ tin.
0·90 „ „ iron.
   Traces of nickel and cobalt.
———
98·94

" A portion from the end of No. 115 (depth 42 ft.), also a nail or pin, contained :—

98·20 per cent. copper.
0·75 „ „ iron.
0·13 „ „ sulphur.
   Trace of tin.
———
99·08

" The metal in the three last cases is much harder than modern commercial copper, a fact which may be accounted for by its impurities not having been removed by refining.[5] There is every probability that the presence of a small quantity of tin in No. 105 is accidental, more especially since specimens of commercial copper have been found to contain such an amount.

" If then we may assume that the several implements were used as nails and knives, it would appear that they belong to a pre-Bronze age, and that the makers of them were not familiar with the fact that copper is hardened by the addition of tin."

---

[5] While this book is passing through the press, I have received information of a most interesting discovery in America of weapons and implements of *copper hardened by a natural* alloy of *rhodium*, for an account of which I am deeply indebted to the discoverer, Mr. A. J. Duffield. (See his Appendix.)

It deserves particularly to be remarked that No. 120 is the only gilded object I ever found in any one of the pre-historic cities of Hissarlik, whereas the art of gilding bronze was in general use at Mycenae.[6] But the Mycenean goldsmith was not able to gild silver; whenever, therefore, objects of silver were to be plated with gold, he first plated them with bronze and then gilded the latter.[7]

No. 121 represents a silver brooch, the head of which is ornamented with flutings; but it is much deteriorated by the chloride, and must have been originally much longer. Of silver also is the curious pendant of an ear-ring, No. 122, which in form resembles a primitive ship, and which was suspended in the ear by means of a thin wire. I should not have thought it to be an ear-ring at all, had it not been for the number of similar pendants of gold found by me in the third city. Certainly this object (No. 122) looks much like a fibula, of which only the pin is missing. But for that purpose the silver leaf is far too thin, and this is still much more the case with the gold ear-rings of a similar shape found in the third or burnt city, all of which are made of very thin gold leaf. There was found, besides, in the stratum of the first city, a silver wire.

Of copper lances or battle-axes no trace was discovered; I only found a quadrangular copper bar 10 in. long, which runs out into an edge at one end, and may have been used as a weapon. Of other objects of copper worth enumerating, I may mention a plain ring. Of other metals, lead was now and then found in small quantities.

We, therefore, find in use among these primitive inhabitants of the most ancient city on Hissarlik, together with very numerous stone implements and stone weapons, the following metals: gold, silver, lead, copper, but no iron; in fact, no trace of this latter metal was ever found by me either in any of the pre-historic cities of Troy, or at Mycenae.

Nothing, I think, could better testify to the great antiquity of the pre-historic ruins at Hissarlik and at Mycenae, than the total absence of iron. It is true that Hesiod distinctly states that iron was discovered later than copper and tin, for, in speaking of the peoples who were ancient even in his day, he says that they used bronze, and not iron.[8] But still, in order to show how old the knowledge of iron and steel was, he represents Gaea as making a sickle for Kronos of greyish glittering steel,[9] and he gives to Herakles, besides armour of gold and greaves of bronze, a sword of iron and a helmet of steel.[10] Lucretius distinctly confirms the three ages :—

> " Arma antiqua, manus, ungues, dentesque fuerunt
> Et lapides, et item sylvarum fragmina rami,
> Posterius ferri vis est aerisque reperta,
> Sed prior aeris erat, quam ferri cognitus usus." [1]

---

[6] See my *Mycenae*, p. 283.

[7] *Ibid.* pp. 216, 217, Nos. 327, 328; p. 240, No. 348, and many others.

[8] Hesiod., *Opp. et Dies*, vv. 149, 150 :
τοῖς δ᾽ ἦν χάλκεα μὲν τεύχεα, χάλκεοι δέ τε οἶκοι,
χαλκῷ δ᾽ εἰργάζοντο · μέλας δ᾽ οὐκ ἔσκε σίδηρος.

[9] Hesiod., *Theogonia*, vv. 161, 162 :
αἶψα δὲ (Γαῖα) ποιήσασα γένος πολιοῦ ἀδάμαντος,
τεῦξε μέγα δρέπανον καὶ ἐπέφραδε παισὶ φίλοισιν.

[10] Hesiod., *Scut. Heracl.* vv. 122–138.

[1] Vv. 1282–1285.

Hostmann[2] also cites Terentius Varro[3] and Agatharchides[4] as adopting the same theory. But it deserves attention that before the Deluge, in the seventh generation from Adam, according to the Book of Genesis,[5] Tubal Cain was simultaneously master in various kinds of work of *bronze* and *iron*.[6] According to Hostmann, iron is only mentioned thirteen times in the whole Pentateuch, whereas brass, by which is here at all events to be understood bronze (that is to say, the mixture of tin and copper), is mentioned forty-four times.

The question now arises : Whence did the early inhabitants of Hissarlik obtain their metals? The answer is, first, that they must have had an abundance of *gold*, since the Troad borders on Phrygia, where mythology localized the legend of Midas and his treasures, and it nearly touches the valley of the Pactolus, which was so famous for its auriferous sands.

Besides, there were, according to Strabo, gold mines in the Troad itself, nay in the immediate neighbourhood of Ilium, for he says : " Above the territory of the Abydians in the Troad lies Astyra, a ruined city, now belonging to Abydos; but formerly the city was independent and had gold mines, which are now poor and exhausted, like those in Mount Tmolus around the Pactolus." [7]

Homer mentions among the auxiliary troops of the Trojans the Halizonians (οἱ ᾿Αλίζωνοι), who came from Alybé (ἡ ᾿Αλύβη), " where is the birth-place of *silver ;*" [8] that is to say, where there are silver mines. Strabo holds these Halizonians to be the later Chalybes on the Pontus called in his time Chaldaeans; he thinks that either the reading has been changed from ἐκ Χαλύβης into ἐξ ᾿Αλύβης, or that the Chalybes had been formerly called Alybans.[9] Other silver mines appear to be indicated by Strabo in the Troad to the right of the Aesepus, between Polichna and Palaescepsis.[10]

Copper mines are mentioned by Strabo in the Troad near Cisthené on the Gulf of Adramyttium,[1] where now stands Cidonia or Cythonies. Strabo also mentions a stone found near Andeira in the mountains of Ida,

[2] Chr. Hostmann, *Zur Geschichte und Kritik des Nordischen System's der drei Culturperioden ;* Braunschweig, 1875, p. 18.

[3] *Fragm.* ap. Augustin. *de Civ. Dei,* vii. c. 24.

[4] *De Mari Erythr.* ap. Phot. c. 29.

[5] Gen. iv. 22.

[6] This must not be pressed too far. The natural meaning is that Tubal Cain was the first who worked in metals *in general,* and the metals specified indicate only the knowledge of the *writer's* age.

[7] xiii. p. 591 : Ὑπέρκειται δὲ τῆς τῶν ᾿Αβυδηνῶν χώρας ἐν τῇ Τρῳάδι τὰ ῎Αστυρα, ἃ νῦν μὲν ᾿Αβυδηνῶν ἐστι, κατεσκαμμένη πόλις, πρότερον δὲ ἦν καθ᾿ αὑτά, χρυσεῖα ἔχοντα ἃ νῦν σπάνιά ·ἐστιν, ἐξαναλωμένα, καθάπερ τὰ ἐν τῷ Τμώλῳ τὰ περὶ τὸν Πακτωλόν.

[8] *Il.* ii. 856, 857 :
αὐτὰρ ᾿Αλιζώνων ᾿Οδίος καὶ ᾿Επίστροφος ἦρχον τηλόθεν ἐξ ᾿Αλύβης, ὅθεν ἀργύρου ἐστὶ γενέθλη.

[9] Strabo, xii. p. 549 : οἱ δὲ νῦν Χαλδαῖοι

Χάλυβες τὸ παλαιὸν ὠνομάζοντο ; and τούτους οἶμαι λέγειν τὸν ποιητὴν ᾿Αλιζώνους ἐν τῷ μετὰ τοὺς Παφλαγόνας καταλόγῳ. Further : ἤτοι τῆς γραφῆς μετατεθείσης ἀπὸ τοῦ " τηλόθεν ἐκ Χαλύβης," ἢ τῶν ἀνθρώπων πρότερον ᾿Αλύβων λεγομένων ἀντὶ Χαλύβων.

[10] Strabo, xiii. p. 603 : ἐν δεξιᾷ δὲ τοῦ Αἰσήπου μεταξὺ Πολίχνας τε καὶ Παλαισκήψεως ἡ Νέα κώμη καὶ ᾿Αργυρία. Now, I believe with Forbiger (*Real Encycl.* s. v. Nea) that instead of ἡ νέα κώμη we have, according to the· parallel passage (in Strabo), p. 552, to read Αἴνεα or ῎Ενεα κώμη καὶ ἀργύρια, and not ᾿Αργυρία. Forbiger identifies this Αἴνεα κώμη with the present town of Iné, where silver mines are mentioned by Chandler, i. p. 142 ; Pococke, iii. p. 160.

[1] xiii. p. 606 : ἔξω δὲ τοῦ κόλπου (τοῦ ᾿Αδραμυττίου) καὶ τῆς Πυρρᾶς ἄκρας ἥ τε Κισθήνη ἐστι πόλις ἔρημος ἔχουσα λιμένα. ὑπὲρ αὐτῆς δ᾿ ἐν τῇ μεσογαίᾳ τό τε τοῦ χαλκοῦ μέταλλον, κ. τ. λ.

which when burned became iron; when melted with a certain earth, zinc (ψευδάργυρος) flows forth from it; whilst, copper being added to it, it becomes brass (κρᾶμα), called by some people ὀρείχαλκος. Zinc is also found in the neighbourhood of Tmolus.[2]

Phrygia was also the country of the Idaean Dactyli, the fabled sons of Rhea, who in her flight to Mount Ida in Crete rested her hands on the mountain and so gave birth to her child (Zeus); and from the impression of her hands sprang the Curetes or the Corybantes, who were called Idaean Dactyli.[3] This tradition is also mentioned by Nonnus.[4] These Phrygian Dactyli were celebrated as metallurgists, and were said to have discovered iron in Crete.[5] According to the Scholiast on Apollonius Rhodius, Sophocles also called the Dactyli Phrygians.[6] Diodorus Siculus also, who seems to have copied largely from Ephorus, says that there are many, and among them Ephorus, who affirm that the Idaean Dactyli dwelt around Mount Ida in Phrygia and passed over to Europe with Mygdon. They were enchanters, and practised spells, religious ceremonies, and mysteries; and, residing in Samothrace, they greatly excited the astonishment of the inhabitants by these arts.[7] The Phrygian origin of the Dactyli is also confirmed by Clemens Alexandrinus, who calls them Phrygians and barbarians.[8] Strabo says: " As some say, the first inhabitants of the slopes of Ida were called Dactyli, because the slopes of the mountains are called their feet, and the summits are called the crowns of their heads, and thus all the spurs of Ida which are sacred to the mother of the gods are called Idaean *Dactyli* or ' toes.' But Sophocles believes the first Dactyli to have been five men, who discovered iron and first worked it, and invented many other things useful for life: they had five sisters, and from their number they were called Dactyli (*i.e.* ' toes '). But others relate other fabulous stories, heaping absurdity on absurdity; but they also state the names and number (of the Dactyli) differently: calling one of them Celmis and the others Damnameneus, Heracles and Acmon (the anvil). Some say that they were natives of Ida, others report that they were immigrants, but all maintain that by them iron was first worked in Ida: all suppose them to have been enchanters employed in the service of the Mother of the Gods, and residing in

---

[2] xiii. p. 610 : ἔστι δὲ λίθος περὶ τὰ Ἄνδειρα, ὃς καιόμενος σίδηρος γίνεται· εἶτα μετὰ γῆς τινος καμινευθεὶς ἀποστάζει ψευδάργυρον, ἣ προσλαβοῦσα χαλκὸν τὸ καλούμενον γίνεται κρᾶμα, ὃ τινες ὀρείχαλκον καλοῦσι· γίνεται δὲ ψευδάργυρος καὶ περὶ τὸν Τμῶλον.

[3] Diomed. p. 474, ed. Putch : " Aiunt Opem in Idam montem insulae Cretae fugiendo delatam manus suas imposuisse memorato monti, et sic infantem ipsum edidisse, et ex manuum impressione emersisse Curetas sive Corybantas, quos a montis nomine et a qualitate facti Idaeos Dactylos appellant."

[4] Dionys. xiv. 25 seq. :

　　. . . . Ὄν ποτε Ῥείη
ἐκ χθονὸς αὐτοτέλεστον ἀνεβλάστησε γενέθλην.

[5] Plin. *H. N.* vii. 57 : " Aes conflare et tem-perare Aristoteles Lydum Scythen monstrasse; Theophrastus Delam Phrygem putat; aerariam fabricam alii Chalybas, alii Cyclopas; ferrum Hesiodus in Creta eos qui vocati sunt Idaei Dactyli."

[6] *Ad Argonaut.* i. 1129 : Σοφοκλῆς δὲ αὐτοὺς Φρύγας καλεῖ ἐν Κωφοῖς Σατύροις.

[7] Diod. Sic. v. 64 : ἔνιοι δ' ἱστοροῦσιν, ὧν ἔστι καὶ Ἔφορος, τοὺς Ἰδαίους Δακτύλους γενέσθαι μὲν κατὰ τὴν Ἴδην τὴν ἐν Φρυγίᾳ, διαβῆναι δὲ μετὰ Μύγδονος εἰς τὴν Εὐρώπην ὑπάρξαντας δὲ γόητας ἐπιτηδεῦσαι τάς τε ἐπῳδὰς καὶ τελετὰς καὶ μυστήρια, καὶ περὶ Σαμοθράκην διατρίψαντας οὐ μετρίως ἐν τούτοις ἐκπλήττειν τοὺς ἐγχωρίους.

[8] *Stromat.* i. p. 360, ed. Pott : Φρύγες δὲ ἦσαν καὶ βάρβαροι οἱ Ἰδαῖοι Δάκτυλοι.

Phrygia in the district of Ida; for they call the Troad Phrygia, because the neighbouring Phrygians took possession (of it) after the destruction of Troy." [9]

The Cabiri, who were likewise celebrated metallurgists, came also from Phrygia, and were said to owe their name to the mountains of Phrygia, whence they passed over to Samothrace.[10] According to Pausanias,[1] the country inhabited by the Pergamenes was anciently sacred to the Cabiri. Strabo informs us that, according to Pherecydes, from Apollo and Rhytia sprang nine Corybantes, who lived in Samothrace, but from Cabiro, daughter of Proteus, and Hephaestus, three Cabiri and three Cabirian nymphs; both brothers and sisters enjoyed divine worship. They were especially venerated in Imbros and Lemnos, but also in some places in the Troad.[2] Though there is no tradition that the Cabiri were also sons of Rhea, the tutelary deity of Phrygia, we see them in the service of that goddess[3] in Samothrace.

We have seen that they were sons of Hephaestus, who, according to Diodorus Siculus, was the inventor of all works in iron, copper, gold and silver, and in all other substances which are wrought by means of fire.[4] We have also seen (p. 253) that there were mines of gold, copper, and silver, in the Troad, and no doubt there were still richer ones in Phrygia, because it is to Phrygia that tradition attributes the discovery of the art of fusing metals by the accidental melting of them in a forest fire.[5]

Strabo quotes the opinion of Posidonius, who believed in the story that, the forests having once caught fire, the earth beneath, containing silver and gold, became liquefied, so that these metals boiled forth to the surface.[6]

---

[9] Strabo, x. p. 473: Δακτύλους δ' Ἰδαίους φασί τινες κεκλῆσθαι τοὺς πρώτους οἰκήτορας τῆς κατὰ τὴν Ἴδην ὑπωρείας· πόδας μὲν γὰρ λέγεσθαι τὰς ὑπωρείας, κορυφὰς δὲ τὰ ἄκρα τῶν ὀρῶν· αἱ οὖν κατὰ μέρος ἐσχατιαὶ καὶ πᾶσαι τῆς μητρὸς τῶν θεῶν ἱεραὶ περὶ τὴν Ἴδην . . . . Σοφοκλῆς δὲ οἴεται πέντε τοὺς πρώτους ἄρσενας γενέσθαι, οἳ σίδηρόν τε ἐξεῦρον καὶ εἰργάσαντο πρῶτοι καὶ ἄλλα πολλὰ τῶν πρὸς τὸν βίον χρησίμων, πέντε δὲ καὶ ἀδελφὰς τούτων, ἀπὸ δὲ τοῦ ἀριθμοῦ δακτύλους κληθῆναι, ἄλλοι δ' ἄλλως μυθεύουσιν ἀπόροις ἄπορα συνάπτοντες, διαφόροις δὲ καὶ τοῖς ὀνόμασι καὶ τοῖς ἀριθμοῖς χρῶνται, ὧν Κέλμιν ὀνομάζουσί τινα καὶ Δαμναμενέα καὶ Ἡρακλέα καὶ Ἄκμονα· καὶ οἱ μὲν ἐπιχωρίους τῆς Ἴδης οἱ δὲ ἐποίκους, πάντες δὲ σίδηρον εἰργάσθαι ὑπὸ τούτων ἐν Ἴδῃ πρῶτόν φασι, πάντες δὲ καὶ γόητας ὑπειλήφασι καὶ περὶ τὴν μητέρα τῶν θεῶν καὶ ἐν Φρυγίᾳ ᾠκηκότας περὶ τὴν Ἴδην, Φρυγίαν τὴν Τρῳάδα καλοῦντες διὰ τὸ τοὺς Φρύγας ἐπικρατῆσαι πλησιοχώρους ὄντας τῆς Τροίας ἐκπεπορθημένης.

[10] Apoll. Rhod. ad Argonaut. i. 917: Κάβειροι δὲ δοκοῦσι προσηγορεῦσθαι ἀπὸ Καβείρων τῶν κατὰ Φρυγίαν ὀρῶν, ἐπεὶ ἐντεῦθεν μετηνέχθησαν εἰς Σαμοθράκην.

[1] Pausanias, i. 416: Ἦν δὲ νέμονται οἱ Περγαμηνοί, Καβείρων ἱεράν φασιν εἶναι τὸ ἀρχαῖον.

[2] Strabo, x. p. 473: Φερεκύδης δ' ἐξ Ἀπόλ-

λωνος καὶ Ῥητίας Κύρβαντας ἐννέα, οἰκῆσαι δ' αὐτοὺς ἐν Σαμοθράκῃ· ἐκ δὲ Καβειροῦς τῆς Πρωτέως καὶ Ἡφαίστου Καβείρους τρεῖς καὶ νύμφας τρεῖς Καβειρίδας, ἑκατέροις δ' ἱερὰ γίνεσθαι. μάλιστα μὲν οὖν ἐν Ἴμβρῳ καὶ Λήμνῳ τοὺς Καβείρους τιμᾶσθαι συμβέβηκεν, ἀλλὰ καὶ ἐν Τροίᾳ κατὰ πόλεις.

[3] A grammarian in the Lexicon of Gude, s. v. Κάβιροι, cited by J. P. Rossignol, Les Métaux dans l'Antiquité, p. 47: Κάβιροι δέ εἰσι δαίμονες περὶ τὴν Ῥέαν οἰκήσαντες τὴν Σαμοθράκην.

[4] v. 74: Ἥφαιστον δὲ λέγουσιν εὑρετὴν γενέσθαι τῆς περὶ τὸν σίδηρον ἐργασίας ἁπάσης καὶ τῆς περὶ τὸν χαλκὸν καὶ χρυσὸν καὶ ἄργυρον, καὶ τῶν ἄλλων ὅσα τὴν ἐκ τοῦ πυρὸς ἐργασίαν ἐπιδέχεται.

[5] Lucretius, 1240–1243:
"Quod superest, aes atque aurum ferrumque repertum est,
Et simul argenti pondus, plumbique potestas,
Ignis ubi ingentes silvas ardore cremarat
Montibus in magnis."

[6] Strabo, iii. p. 147: Ποσειδώνιος δὲ τὸ πλῆθος τῶν μετάλλων ἐπαινῶν καὶ τὴν ἀρετὴν οὐκ ἀπέχεται τῆς αὐτῆς συνηθείας ῥητορείας, ἀλλὰ συνενθουσιᾷ ταῖς ὑπερβολαῖς. οὐ γὰρ ἀπιστεῖν τῷ μύθῳ φησὶν ὅτι τῶν δρυμῶν ποτε ἐμπρησθέντων ἡ γῆ τακεῖσα, ἅτε ἀργυρῖτις καὶ χρυσῖτις, εἰς τὴν ἐπιφάνειαν ἐξέξεσε.

Rossignol [7] also cites Clement of Alexandria, who, in establishing a synchronism among the events of sacred history and Greek history, says, "From the deluge of Deucalion to the burning of Mount Ida and the discovery of iron, and to the Idaean Dactyli, 73 years elapsed according to Thrasyllus; and from the burning of Ida to the rape of Ganymedes, 65 years." [8] He further cites Strabo, who mentions that the Titans gave to Rhea, as armed servants, the Corybantes, who, as some said, had come from Bactria; according to others, from Colchis. [9] The reason why they were said to have come from the one or the other of these two countries is, that both were celebrated for the number and the richness of their mines. Rossignol [10] further mentions that "Servius in his Commentary on Virgil, in stating the etymologies which were given of the word Corybantes, says that according to some it was derived from Κόρη, the surname of Proserpine, according to others it is derived from copper, there being in Cyprus a mountain rich in copper, which the Cypriotes call Corium." [1] M. Burnouf mentions to me that Eugène Burnouf has proved the word Corybantes to be identical with the Zend word gĕrĕvantô, which means "mountaineers," and that Orthocorybantes is identical with Ĕrĕdhwagĕrĕvantô, which means "inhabitants of the high mountains." [2]

Like the Cabiri and the Corybantes, the Curetes passed over from Phrygia to Samothrace. This is evident, as Rossignol [3] says, from the Orphic hymn addressed to the Curetes, in which it is assigned to them, as a claim to veneration, that they should make the bronze resound, wear martial arms, and inhabit Samothrace, the sacred land. [4] Some verses further on, the poet, confounding the Curetes with the Corybantes, calls them even kings of Samothrace. [5]

In a long and learned discussion, Rossignol proves beyond all doubt that the Telchines were also famous artists and metallurgists, who passed over to Samothrace; and further that the Dactyli, Cabiri, Corybantes, Curetes, and Telchines, differed, as some believed, merely in name, and formed one identical class of Genii; while, according to others, they were related to one another, presenting only slight differences; that, finally, they are nothing else than the representatives of an identical metallic industry, symbolized in its progressive developments; that the religion of Samothrace was in the beginning nothing but a simple institution of mysteries founded on metallurgy, and presided over by Rhea, whose priests were in fact metallurgists. These ministers, having transmitted the blessing of the goddess to other men, were deified from gratitude. In this manner Samothrace became the isle of pious priests, and the sacred asylum against revenge for bloodshed. But it was not every

[7] Les Métaux dans l'Antiquité, p. 50.

[8] Strom. i. 21, p. 401, ed. Pott.

[9] Strabo, x. p. 472: οἱ δ' ὑπὸ Τιτάνων 'Ρέᾳ δοθῆναι προπόλους ἐνόπλους τοὺς Κορύβαντας ἐκ τῆς Βακτριανῆς ἀφιγμένους, οἱ δ' ἐκ Κόλχων φασίν.

[10] Les Métaux dans l'Antiquité, p. 77.

[1] Ad Aen. iii. 111: "Alii Corybantes ab aere appellatos, quod apud Cyprum mons sit aeris ferax, quem Cyprii Corium vocant."

[2] See Eugène Burnouf, Commentaires sur le Yaçna.

[3] Les Métaux dans l'Antiquité, p. 88.

[4] Hymn. Orphic. xxxviii. 4: οἵ τε Σαμοθρῄκην, ἱερὴν χθόνα, ναιετάοντες.

[5] 21, 22: Κουρῆτες Κορύβαντες, . . . ἐν Σαμοθρῄκῃ ἄνακτες.

homicide that could obtain absolution there ; for the cases were heard, justice was administered, and he who had maliciously done a wicked deed was condemned and cast out. Ancient metallurgy gives us an insight into the life of the men of bygone times ; the metals are the material and instrument of the arts, the spring of all political activity, the soul of civilization.[6]

According to Sir John Lubbock : [7] "It is probable that gold was the metal which first attracted the attention of man ; it is found in many rivers, and by its bright colour would certainly attract even the rudest savages, who are known to be very fond of personal decoration. Silver does not appear to have been discovered until long after gold, and was apparently preceded by both copper and tin ; for it rarely, if ever,[8] occurs in tumuli of the Bronze age. But, however this may be, copper seems to have been the metal which first became of real importance to man ; no doubt owing to the fact that its ores are abundant in many countries, and can be smelted without any difficulty ; and that, while iron is hardly ever found except in the form of ore, copper often occurs in a native condition, and can be beaten at once into shape. Thus, for instance, the North American Indians obtained pure copper from the mines near Lake Superior and elsewhere, and hammered it at once into axes, bracelets, and other objects.

"Tin also early attracted notice, probably on account of the great heaviness of its ores. When metals were very scarce, it would naturally sometimes happen that, in order to make up the necessary quantity, some tin would be added to copper, or *vice versâ*. It would then be found that the properties of the alloy were quite different from those of either metal ; a very few experiments would determine the most advantageous proportion, which for axes and other cutting instruments is about nine parts of copper to one of tin. No implements or weapons of tin have yet been found, and those of copper are extremely rare, *whence it has been inferred that the art of making bronze was known elsewhere before the use of either copper or tin was introduced into Europe.* Many of the so-called ' copper ' axes, &c., contain a small proportion of tin ; and the few exceptions indicate probably a mere temporary want, rather than a total ignorance, of this metal."

But this I must most decidedly deny, for implements and weapons of pure copper are found all over Hungary, and M. Pulszky Ferencz,[9] president of the committee of organization of the Pre-historic Exhibition of 1876 at Buda-Pesth, had all their different types represented in two large glass cases, in order that they might serve as proofs of the existence of a Copper age, which he authenticated in his lecture before the Congress.[10]

---

[6] Rossignol, *Les Métaux dans l'Antiquité*, pp. 99–148.
[7] *Pre-historic Times*, pp. 3, 4.
[8] A. W. Franks, *Horae ferales*, p. 60.
[9] This is the Hungarian name, which would be in English, Francis or Frank Pulszky.

[10] Joseph Hampel, *Catalogue de l'Exposition préhistorique des Musées de Province et des Collections particulières de la Hongrie ;* Buda-Pesth, 1876, pp. 138–140 : and Joseph Hampel, *Antiquités préhistor. de la Hongrie ;* Esztergom, 1876, Pl. vii., viii.

If among numerous bronze implements there had been found one of
copper, this latter might indeed indicate a mere temporary want of tin ;
but all the objects from the first and second cities of Hissarlik being
proved, upon Professor W. Chandler Roberts's highly important analysis,
to consist of pure copper, we must naturally infer a total ignorance of
tin on the part of their inhabitants.

Sir John Lubbock repeatedly states that silver and lead do not
occur in the Bronze age,[11] which appears to imply that still less can
they be found in the Stone age. But I found these metals, in smaller or
larger quantities, in all the five pre-historic cities of Hissarlik. It is true
that in the *first* and *second* cities lead only occurred in small shapeless
lumps, but these are sufficient to attest that the primitive inhabitants
were acquainted with it. In the third pre-historic city we shall pass in
review an idol and several other objects of lead. In the gilded knife,
No. 120, we have the proof, that even the inhabitants of the first city of
Hissarlik were acquainted with gold, and knew how to work it. Homer
mentions the plating of silver with gold: "But as when gold is fused
around the silver by an experienced man, whom Hephaestus and Pallas
Athené have instructed in all kinds of arts, that he may execute graceful
works, so did the goddess pour gracefulness around his head and
shoulders."[1]

According to Pliny,[2] one ounce of gold could be beaten out to more
than 600 leaves, each being four fingers square. In our own days the
same quantity could be beaten into three times that number of leaves.

My friend, Professor A. Sprenger of Berne, endeavours to prove, in
his famous work *Die alte Geographie Arabiens*, that in remote antiquity
the bulk of the gold was brought by the Phoenicians from Arabia,
which had twenty-two gold mines,[3] and was the ancient Eldorado and
proverbial for its wealth of gold in all antiquity down to the Middle Ages.
"Thus William, the biographer of Thomas a Becket, uses the expression
'Arabia sends us gold.' Is this only a fiction, or was Arabia indeed
the California of antiquity, and was especially Dzahaban (Dzahab
_ ذهب, 'gold'), which is only at a distance of 500' from Berenice,
the port where gold was bartered?" He goes on to prove that the
famous *Ophir*, which scholars have for a long time past identified with
Abhîra in India, is nothing else than the Arabic word for "red." "By
the Hebrews the 'gold of Ophir' was especially valued. Agatharchides
states that the gold nuggets found in the district of Debai consisted of
pure metallic gold, and did not need to be purified by fire, in consequence
of which this gold was called ἄπυρον, 'untouched by fire.' This word,
therefore, would answer to the Arabic *tibr ;* for while *dzahab* means gold
generally, unmelted gold is called *tibr* and *tibra*, a 'gold nugget.' The
greater part of the gold existing in antiquity was derived from nuggets,

[11] *Pre-historic Times*, pp. 21, 38.
[1] *Od.* vi. 232-235 :
ὡς δ' ὅτε τις χρυσὸν περιχεύεται ἀργύρῳ ἀνήρ
ἴδρις, ὃν "Ηφαιστος δέδαεν καὶ Παλλὰς 'Αθήνη

τέχνην παντοίην, χαρίεντα δὲ ἔργα τελείει,
ὡς ἄρα τῷ κατέχευε χάριν κεφαλῇ τε καὶ ὤμοις.
[2] *H. N.* xxxiii. 19.
[3] Paragraphs 53, 54-58.

which were sometimes of enormous size. Idrysy (i. 2) reports that the
king of Ghâna preserved as a rarity a nugget weighing 30 *ratl* (75 lbs.).
It is very probable that the Greeks had also a special word for *tibr*,
'nugget.' Nevertheless, I do not believe in the assertion of Agatharchides ; I hold ἄπυρον to be a bastard word of Semitic origin, which has
been græcized. The finest gold is designated by Hamdâny and Abûlfidâ,
p. 157, as *red gold*, ذ هـب اُ حـمـر, and the Persians call the gold pieces
which are coined therefrom *Dynârisurch,* '*red* Aurei.' In Iklyl (viii. p. 77),
it is related that on the corpse of a woman, exhumed at Dhahr, there
were found gold ankle-rings weighing 100 *mithqâl*, and that the metal
was *red* gold. Such 'treasure trove' was so frequent, that this fine sort
of gold was also called 'tomb gold' (ذ هـب ذ هـب قـبـور or ذ هـب قـبـوري).
It is reported in Iklyl (viii. p. 52), that especially in the ruins in and
between Gauf and Mârib much tomb gold was discovered. In Pliny [4]
apyron has the signification of 'red gold.' If *Magi* is the subject
of *vocant*, then the expression *apyron* was also in use among the Persians. At all events, the *Apyron* is hardly different from the gold
of Ophir, qualified in the Bible as 'good.' According to a well-known
phonetic change, *ôfir* must be pronounced *âfir* in the Central Arabian
dialect ; but according to Ibn Mârûf (*apud* Golius) *afira* signifies tran-
sitively, 'splendidum clarumque effecit,' and intransitively, 'manifestus
evasit.' The participle of this verb is *âfir*. In the South-Arabic dialect
this word, differently pronounced, is the common word for *red*. According to a vocabulary,[5] *red* is called *ophir* (sic !) in Socotra. In other
dialects the word for 'red' is pronounced, according to Maltzan,[6] *ôfer*,
ohfar, *afûr*, and so forth. Now I imagine that, according to their
custom, the Greeks have given a Greek origin to the word *âfir*, *ôfir*.
In Job (xxii. 24) *Ophir* is used for 'gold' without the additional word
zahab ; and the passage from Pliny warrants the conclusion that *apyron*
was used in the same manner. Besides, Ophir occurs in the Bible as
the name of a people and a country. Where this half-mythic land was
first thought to exist is a point on which I have no doubt. In Genesis
(x. 29) Ophir is mentioned between Sheba and Havilah. In the story
of Solomon, the narrator passes twice or thrice backwards and forwards
to and from the Queen of Sheba and the Ophir expedition, and in
1 Kings x. 15 'all the kings of Arabia' come between. Ophir was consequently thought to be on the coast of Arabia, or rather the Hebrews
called the *Litus Hammaeum* Ophir. In the famous question about Ophir,
far too little weight is laid on the fact that, in many passages in the
Bible, Ophir appears as the California of antiquity, and far too much
importance is given to Solomon's expedition to Ophir. I neither doubt
that the Phoenicians navigated the Red Sea, nor that Solomon associated

---

[4] *H. N.* xxi. 11, p. 66 : "Heliochrysos florem
habet auro similem . . . . Hoc coronare se Magi,
si et unguenta sumantur ex auro, quod *apyron*
vocant, ad gratiam quoque vitae gloriamque

pertinere arbitrantur."
[5] *Journ. As. Soc. Beng.* B. iv p. 165.
[6] *Z. D. M. G.* 27, p. 230.

with King Hiram and bartered gold in Dzahaban; but the story, as it is told, is not free from fictions invented to glorify the great king. In 1 Kings ix. 28 it is stated that the servants of Hiram and Solomon fetched 420 talents of gold; here Ophir is still simply the land of gold. In x. 11, again, the result is spoken of, and then it is said that the gold-ships also brought sandal-wood and precious stones. We cannot object to this, for the narrator confines himself here at least to Arabian articles. Precious stones are also mentioned elsewhere in the Bible, as articles of trade with the Arabian merchants. The genuine sandal-wood, it is true, does not occur in Arabia, but Hamdâny (333) speaks of Mount Hanûm as situated near Chaulân, on which also the Chaulânites live, and says: 'There grows a plant which resembles the white sandal-wood, and comes near to it in smell. The wood serves instead of the Indian sandal-wood.' In 1 Kings x. 22, the produce fetched from Ophir is mentioned for a third time, with the addition of silver and ivory, and of rarities such as monkeys and peacocks.[7] Here it is also stated that the ships came once in three years; and in this way Ophir is removed to an endless distance and made a fairy-land. This version, as well as the story of the Queen of Sheba, I hold to be a fiction of later origin. The idea that Ophir also exported silver is by no means happy, this metal having always been dear in Arabia. Even in Mohammed's time, when the gold mines were for the most part exhausted, only seven and a half pounds of silver were given for one pound of gold. If, with Lassen, we relegate Ophir to India (of whose *natural* wealth in gold I never heard), we do not gain much; because here also the value of silver in proportion to that of gold was always greater than in the West."

Sprenger further points to a passage in Strabo, which corroborates his opinion that the Phoenicians, in times of remote antiquity, lived on the Arabian coast of the Persian Gulf, whence they emigrated to the coast of the Mediterranean; and this view is now very generally accepted. After having spoken of the city of Gerrha, which, he says, lies in a deep bay of the Arabian coast on the Persian Gulf, Strabo goes on: "Those who proceed with their ship see two other islands—Tyrus[8] and Aradus,[9] whose temples resemble those of the Phoenicians; the inhabitants at least maintain also that the islands and cities of the Phoenicians, called by the same names, are their colonies."[10]

My friend the Assyriologist, Professor Julius Oppert, informs me that in the Assyrian cuneiform inscriptions, the island of Tyrus (in cuneiform writing, *Tilvun*) is mentioned as the seat of a very ancient worship. The island of Tylus (for Tyrus) is mentioned by Arrian[11] and Pliny[1] as producing pearls and cotton.

---

[7] I might here call attention to the fact that in the Bible the names of the monkeys and peacocks are Sanscrit and Tamil. The monkey is called in Sanscrit *Kapi*, the peacock in Tamil *Togei*.

[8] According to Sprenger's map, this is now called Owal (Bahrayn).

[9] According to Sprenger's map, Moharrag.

[10] Strabo, xvi. p. 766: Πλεύσαντι δ' ἐπὶ πλέον ἄλλαι νῆσοι Τύρος καὶ Ἄραδος εἰσίν, ἱερὰ ἔχουσαι τοῖς Φοινικικοῖς ὅμοια· καὶ φασί γε οἱ ἐν αὐταῖς οἰκοῦντες τὰς ὁμωνύμους τῶν Φοινίκων νήσους καὶ πόλεις ἀποίκους ἑαυτῶν.

[11] *Anab.* vii. 20, § 6.

[1] *H. N.* vi. 32. 6; xii. 22. 1.

Mr. Philip Smith observes to me that: "In the ancient Egyptian records we have accounts of immense quantities of gold levied by the great king Thutmes III. of the Eighteenth Dynasty (in the sixteenth century B.C.), as tribute from the land of *Zahi* (that is, Phoenicia). Gold is also named among the tributes of *Punt*, the Egyptian Ophir, which Brugsch-Bey holds to be on the African coast of Somauli, opposite to Arabia. But the chief supply was derived from the southern lands of *Kush* (Nubia), which Brugsch-Bey calls the Egyptian California. Gold was obtained from this region as early as the Twelfth Dynasty, and the gold-washings in the desert valley of *Akita* (Wady Alaki) were the objects of special care to the great kings of the Nineteenth Dynasty, Ramses II. and his father Seti."[2]

Under No. 123 I represent a needle of bone with a perforated head.

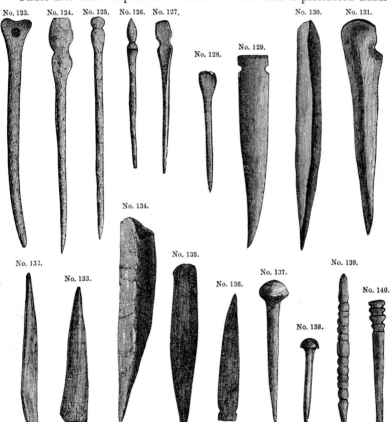

No. 123.   No. 124.   No. 125.   No. 126.   No. 127.   No. 130.   No. 131.

No. 128.   No. 129.

No. 134.

No. 132.   No. 135.   No. 139.

No. 133.   No. 136.   No. 137.   No. 140.

No. 138.

Nos. 123–140.   Pins, Awls, and Needles of bone and ivory, from the lowest stratum.
(Half and 3 : 4 actual size. Depth, 40 to 52 ft.)

[2] Brugsch's *Hist. of Egypt under the Pharaohs*, vol. i. pp. 379, 383 ; vol.ii. pp. 81 f., Eng. trans., 2nd ed.—The Egyptian records of the productions brought from Punt furnish a remarkable parallel to the account of the Ophir-voyages of Solomon's fleet (*op. cit.* vol. i. pp. 352 f.).

Nos. 124, 125, 126, 127, and 128 are rudely-ornamented bone needles without holes; Nos. 129, 130, 131, 132, 133, 134, 135, and 136 are pointed instruments of bone, which may have been used as awls, with the exception perhaps of Nos. 129 and 136, which are quite flat. The objects Nos. 137 and 138 are of ivory; as the latter is in the shape of a nail, it may probably have been used as a brooch. Nos. 139 and 140 are carved implements of bone, probably for female needle-work. Similar awls and needles of bone occur in large numbers in the *débris* of the four lowest pre-historic cities at Hissarlik. Awls and needles of bone, even needles with perforated heads, are found plentifully in the cavern-habitations in the Dordogne, and may be seen in the Museum of St. Germain-en-Laye, where are also exhibited a number of them found in French Dolmens. They were, as Prof. Virchow informs me, in use in Germany in every period down to the twelfth century A.D., and are found there in abundance. They are also frequent in the Swiss Lake-dwellings,[3] in the Lake-dwellings in the Lake of Constance,[4] in the caverns of Inzighofen,[5] in the pre-historic settlements in Hungary,[6] on ancient sites in the Aleutian Islands, in Kentucky, in San Miguel Island, California, &c.;[7] in Denmark on sites of the Stone age,[8] and elsewhere. The object No. 141 represents

No. 141. Object of Ivory.
(Half actual size.
Depth, 48 ft.)

No. 142. Curious Object
of Ivory, probably an Idol.
(Half actual size. Depth, 46 ft.)

No. 143. Huckle-bone
(Astragalus). (Half actual size.
Depth, about 50 ft.)

a flat trapezium of ivory, almost in the shape of a playing card, with eight little stars or small suns. We see a similar ornamentation on each side of the very curious object of ivory No. 142, which, in my opinion, is a primitive female idol, of which the two barb-like projections may indicate the arms, and the stroke across the body the girdle. I call attention to the similarity of the little stars or small suns to the breasts with which the whole body of the Ephesian Diana was covered; and have not the horn-like projections on the head the shape of the crescent?

---

[3] Ferdinand Keller, *Mittheilungen der antiquarischen Gesellschaft, Pfahlbauten,* 7ter Bericht; Zürich, 1876, Plate ii.

[4] L. Lindenschmit, *Die Vaterländischen Alterthümer,* p. 180, and Plate xxviii.

[5] *Ibid.* p. 180, and Plate xxv.

[6] Joseph Hampel, *Antiquités préhistoriques,* Plate ii.

[7] *Smithsonian Contributions to Knowledge,* No. 287, *The Archæological Collection of the U.S. National Museum;* Washington, 1876, pp. 63 and 64.

[8] J. J. A. Worsaae, *Nordiske Oldsager,* Pl. xvii.

As huckle-bones (ἀστράγαλοι), like that represented under No. 143, occur in this first city, as well as in all the other pre-historic cities of Hissarlik, I think there can be no doubt that they were used by children for playing, the more so as most of them are much worn, and appear as if they had been in use for a long time. The game of astragals is mentioned by Homer, who makes Patroclus appear to Achilles in a dream, and say that he had to fly from his native land, having involuntarily killed a boy in anger when playing with astragals.[9] This game was practised by children throughout antiquity.[10] I call attention to the beautiful sculpture of an ἀστραγαλίζουσα in the Museum of Berlin; also, to the famous group of sculpture in the palace of Titus, representing two boys playing with astragals,[1] probably a copy of the celebrated bronze group by Polycletus, the subject of which was no doubt taken from the fatal quarrel of the young Patroclus with his playfellow.

A fractured marble group of the same kind, in the Townley Collection of the British Museum, represented (when perfect) two boys quarrelling over the game. The figure of one is gone, except the fore-arm, which the other is biting; the huckle-bones are seen lying on the ground.

---

[9] *Il.* xxiii. 87, 88:
Ἤματι τῷ ὅτε παῖδα κατέκτανον Ἀμφιδάμαντος,
νήπιος, οὐκ ἐθέλων, ἀμφ' ἀστραγάλοισι χολωθείς.
" In the day when I slew the son of Amphidamas, fool that I was, not wilfully, flying into a passion about huckle-bones."

[10] See, for example, Pseudo-Plat. *Alcib.* i. p. 110, B.: ὁπότε (παῖς ἂν) ἀστραγαλίζοις ἤ ἄλλην τινα παιδίαν παίζοις.
[1] Pliny, *H. N.* xxxiv. 8. 19; Pauly's *Real Encyclopädie*, s. v. Polycletus.

CHAPTER VI.

THE SECOND CITY ON THE SITE OF TROY.

Whether the inhabitants of the first city quietly abandoned their homes and emigrated, or whether their city was captured and destroyed by an enemy, we are unable to discover from the ruins ; at all events, the first town was not destroyed by fire, for I found no marks of a general, or even of a partial, conflagration. It is further quite certain that the first settlers were succeeded by a different people : this is proved by the architecture as well as by the pottery, both of which are totally different from what we see in the first city.

I have already said that these second settlers built both their houses and their walls of large stones. The remains we now see of these dwellings are, of course, only the substructions, but the really enormous masses of loose stones contained in the strata of this second city testify to the fact, that the walls of the houses were built of stone. Not all the houses, however, were built of this material, for we see here and there the *débris* of houses which must have had walls of clay.

It is only to these second settlers that we can attribute the wall B represented in the engraving No. 2 (see p. 24), which I brought to light on the north side of the hill. It is 10 ft. high and 6½ ft. thick, and is built in the so-called Cyclopean manner, in regular layers of large but slightly wrought quadrangular blocks of limestone, which are joined together by small ones. As already stated, its top is just 34 ft. below the surface. As is attested by the layers of *débris* which extend in an oblique direction below it, it was originally erected on the steep slope of the hill. It is therefore evident that, since its erection, the hill has here increased 44 ft. in height ; but it has also increased at this point 131 ft. in width, such being the distance in a horizontal line from the wall to the present slope. The quantity of similar blocks lying beside this wall seem to prove that it was at one time much higher. It was much longer when I first brought it to light at the end of July, 1872. I removed part of it in February, 1873, in order to bring to light the curious retaining wall [1] already described, which rises at an angle of 45°, 6 ft. below it, and served to sustain an isolated sandhill which reaches to within 20 ft. of the surface and appears to be 20 ft. high. This retaining wall we may, as I have before explained, attribute with all probability to the first city.

To these inhabitants of the second city we may further, with every

---

[1] See the wall A in the engraving No. 2, p. 24.

probability, attribute the great internal wall marked *c* on the accompanying view, No. 144, and *a* on the little sketch No. 145. This wall also

No. 145. The great External and Internal Walls, called together the Tower.

consists of large blocks of stone, and slopes to the south at an angle of
45°. But it is only on the south side that it consists of solid masonry;
on the north side it is built of stone for only four or five courses deep,
and is supported here by a large rampart of loose stones and *débris*
marked *r*, of which also its interior, to a great extent, consists. Immediately south of this large wall is a wall of equal size marked *b* on the
accompanying view (No. 144) and *c d* on the sketch (No. 145), which was
evidently built by the third settlers, and of which I shall speak hereafter. After having proceeded for some distance in an easterly direction,
the great internal wall shrinks to a wall of solid masonry 11¾ ft. high,
6 ft. thick at the top, and 12 ft. thick at the base, which turns at a
certain point abruptly to the north north-west.[2] Its builders did not
take the trouble to clear the rock of soil, for the wall is erected on a
layer of earth from 1 ft. 9 in. to 2 ft. deep, with which the rock is
covered. To the inhabitants of this second city evidently belongs also
the erection of the Gate (marked *a* on Plan I.), with its paved street, which
runs down to the plain in a south-westerly direction; for the lower part of
this gateway, as well as the walls which I brought to light in removing
some of the flags of the street, show precisely the same kind of architecture
of large blocks of white limestone. As the keen eye of my sagacious
friend, Professor Sayce, discovered at once, this street was made by the
second settlers, by heaping a mound of *débris* against what had until then
been a steep slope; and the walls which cross the street beneath its
pavement can have had no other object than to consolidate this mound of
débris. All the fragments of pottery contained in the mound belong to
the second city; I have not found a single potsherd there of the thick
lustrous-black terra-cottas of the first city, nor any fragment of the pottery
of the subsequent " burnt city."

The street was paved by the inhabitants of the second city with large
flags of white limestone, in which, however, I failed to discover any ruts
of chariot-wheels. For this reason I think that the street only served
for pedestrians, the more so as it slopes to the plain at an angle of a little
less than 70°, and is, therefore, too steep for chariots. But still the flags
are much worn and denote long use. For this reason they were covered
by the builders of the following, the third or burnt city, with new flags of
a reddish sandstone, which may still be seen *in situ* on the lower part of

---

[2] See Plan I. (of Troy) at the place marked *f h*, close to the wall marked *b*.

the street as far as it is uncovered. Those of the upper part, near the gateway, looked quite as fresh as the rest when I brought them to light at the beginning of May 1873 ; but, when exposed to the sun, they speedily became decomposed and crumbled away, which circumstance can leave no doubt that they had been exposed to an intense heat. The parapets of the gate must have been almost completely destroyed on the arrival of the third settlers, the builders of the burnt city, for—as a glimpse at the accompanying view (No. 144) will show—only the lower part of them denotes by its large slabs of white limestone the architecture of the second settlers ; whereas all the upper part of them, and the whole of the masonry of small stones of reddish colour to the right of the Turk with his spade, are the work of the third settlers, by whom were also built the quadrangular projections of the parapets, between which were the wooden gates. These projections stand in pairs opposite each other.[3] Those of the first gate, in ascending from the plain, project, the one $2\frac{1}{2}$ ft., the other $2\frac{3}{4}$ ft. : both are $3\frac{1}{4}$ ft. high and $3\frac{3}{4}$ ft. broad ; the wooden gate between them was $12\frac{1}{4}$ ft. broad. The street paved with the large flags of limestone ends at this first gate, and the road from this to the second gate, which is situated a little more than 20 ft. further to the north-east, is very roughly paved with large unhewn stones. The pavement has probably become uneven through the masses of burning *débris* which fell upon it during the great conflagration of the third city.

The two following projections, between which was the second gate, are 2 ft. high, above 3 ft. broad, and project about $2\frac{1}{2}$ ft. A few yards further to the north-east a wall of large stones, with a recess on its south-east side, crosses the street, protruding only slightly above the pavement. This wall undoubtedly marks the site of the third gate with a wicket. This third gate is $17\frac{1}{4}$ ft. broad ; beyond it the parapets of the road continue 10 ft. further in a north-easterly direction. That these three gates really existed, every visitor acknowledges ; but how they were put up—that, I think, nobody can explain, there being no holes for the hinges either in the projections of the parapets or in the stones between them. But, as the masonry of the parapet has a smooth surface and has evidently never been higher than it now is, we may take it as certain that it only served as a substruction to a large and high tower of but slightly-baked bricks, and that wood entered largely into its construction. Only in this way are we at all able to explain the intense heat which destroyed the flags of the street before the gates, and to which every stone in the parapets bears witness, as well as the enormous masses of reddish or yellow or black wood-ashes and broken bricks, which obstructed the street, to a depth of from 7 to 10 ft., when I brought it to light. It was in the masonry of this tower, through which the street passed, that the gates must have been fastened.

But the inhabitants of the second stone city, which now occupies us, used no bricks at all ; besides, the three gates, of which I have spoken, evidently belong to the third settlers. It would, therefore, be out of

---

[3] See the engravings No. 10, p. 35, and No. 13, p. 37, as well as Plan I. under the letter *a*.

place to speak of them here were it not that, by giving my opinion as to the architecture of the gates, when in use by the third settlers, I hope to convey to the reader an idea of their condition in the time of the second settlers. In fact, the courses of large white stones in the lower parts of the parapets, as well as of the same sort of stones in the lower part of their four quadrangular projections, can leave no doubt that the architecture of the substructions to the gate-tower was identical with that used in the second city; besides that the wall, which denotes the existence of the third gate with its wicket, belongs evidently to the second settlers, who in all probability built their gate-tower of wood. As the masonry of large blocks built by the second settlers is far more solid than that of small stones or slightly-baked bricks used by the third people, the latter would undoubtedly have taken care to preserve the parapets of the street and their projections, had they found them entire. Moreover, had these structures been destroyed in a siege and capture of the second city, the large stones at least would have remained on the spot or near at hand, and they would have been used by the third settlers for restoring the destroyed masonry. But as this has not been done, we may conclude, with all probability, that the second city must have been abandoned for a long time ere it was colonized by the third settlers. M. Burnouf has come to the very same conclusion, from the large funnel-shaped holes and deep ravines filled with stones, which so frequently occur in the layers of *débris*, from 12 to 16 ft. deep, of the second city, and of which visitors will see many in my trenches, particularly in my great northern trench.[4] He thinks that these large funnel-shaped hollows or ravines in the *débris* could only have been produced in the course of ages by rain-water, and that they were filled with stones by the third settlers, who completely levelled the area of the city before they began to build their own town. Professor Virchow does not admit that these hollows could have been produced by the action of the rain-water in the midst of the *débris*; but I think it most likely, considering the really enormous masses of loose stones contained in the layers of *débris* of the second city. Only I am not of M. Burnouf's opinion, that ages would necessarily be required to produce such ravines. I even think that the rains of a single winter might possibly be sufficient to produce large and deep funnel-shaped holes in such huge masses of *débris*, consisting of loose stones and clay.

To this second city evidently belongs also the large wall which continues from the gate in a north-westerly direction, and which is but a prolongation of the great internal wall marked *c* on the view, No. 144, and *a* on the little sketch, No. 145. Like the internal wall *c*, this is more like a rampart than a mere wall: in general its western and north-western slope consists of solid masonry to a depth of 3 or 4 ft.; but it is intersected by a number of regular walls, which can have had no other object than to consolidate it. This rampart wall, which is in some places 30 ft. thick, is paved with small flags or irregularly shaped

---

[4] These funnel-shaped hollows, filled with stones, are marked by the letter *q* on Plan III., Section X–Y.

stones; but this pavement was covered 3 ft. deep with *débris* when the third city was built, for all the fragments of pottery contained in it are of the second city, to which also belong all the potsherds contained in the *débris* below the pavement.   Now, this rampart resembles an esplanade; but cities so small as the pre-historic towns of Hissarlik can have no esplanades.   Neither did it look as it does now when I first brought it to light; for it was encumbered with crumbling brick walls, mournful remnants of the towers and other works of fortification of the third city. But the masses of saddle-querns, pottery, shells, &c., contained in the *débris*, can leave no doubt that these Trojan works were many storeys high, and served both as fortifications and dwelling-houses for the inhabitants.   We must probably presume, that the works erected on these ramparts by the inhabitants of the second stone city served a like purpose; but, as they certainly were not of brick, they must have been of stone. This seems also to be proved, with all probability, by the stupendous masses of loose stones which occur at the foot of the walls, as well as in and on the ruins of the houses, and which are sometimes 12 or 14 ft. deep. The following settlers found these masses of stones ready at hand, but they did not care to use them: only here and there they built the substructions of their houses with them; all the rest, and in fact generally even the substructions of their houses, they built of slightly-baked brick.

As to habitations on city walls, my dear, my honoured, my learned, my deeply-mourned friend, Dr. Edward Moss, of Arctic celebrity—who, when Staff-surgeon on board H.M.S. *Research*, lying in the autumn of 1878 in Besika Bay, came daily to visit my works at Troy, and who later, as Staff-surgeon on board H.M.S. *Atalanta*, perished with that unfortunate vessel—called to my remembrance that in this respect Troy resembled several cities in Scripture: thus, for example, the Book of Joshua (ii. 15) describes the house of Rahab as situated on the wall of Jericho.

As I have said, the great internal wall [5]—which, on the south side, was the external wall of the inhabitants of the second stone city—(the wall marked *b* on No. 144, and *c d* on the sketch No. 145, having been subsequently built by the people of the third city)—slopes at an angle of 45°, and its western prolongation from the gate at an angle of about 15°; consequently these walls could easily be scaled, and they can only have served as substructions to the works of defence erected upon them.

To this second city also belongs the irregular wall on the north side to the left of the entrance to my great northern trench (marked V on Plan III., Section X-Y). M. Burnouf, who carefully examined this wall, made the following observations on it :—" At the north angle, close to the large ruined brick wall, we see again for a distance of 12 mètres or 40 ft. the more or less damaged courses of blocks of the great wall of the second city, which, like the wall *c* on No. 144 and *a* on the sketch No. 145, consists only on the outside of real masonry, and for the rest of loose stones. In the ditch dug at the foot of the rampart, visitors may

---

[5] See No. 144 *c*, and sketch No. 145, *a*, p. 265.

see the lower courses of this wall, which consist of very large blocks of limestone."

On this rampart, as on the two which we have already passed in review, were no doubt built the works of fortification, which served at the same time as habitations. Visitors will see there a number of substructions of large stones belonging to this second city, to which belongs also the large building (marked R on Plan III., Section X–Y), whose slightly dislocated thick walls will be seen further on to the left in my great northern trench, at a depth of from 33 to 40 or 43 ft. below the surface of the hill. I call particular attention to the layers of *débris* (marked P on the same plan), which slant at an angle of 45° from the top of this building towards the great internal wall (*c* on No. 144), and which go far to prove that this building is much more ancient than the latter, and that the rampart-like walls were not built till ages after the foundation of the second city. What has this large building been ? This edifice seemed to me important to preserve; but as all the stones of its walls are slightly dislocated, just as if shaken by an earthquake, I could not possibly excavate it ; for, unless supported, its walls would have fallen at once. I was therefore forced to leave it embedded as it was, with only the edges of its walls peeping out from the east side of my trench. I call the attention of visitors to the ponderous blocks composing what appears to be its flat roof.

The inhabitants of this second city, like their predecessors and successors, used to a large extent cakes of clay (*galettes*), in order to level the ground and consolidate it for their ponderous stone buildings. In this second city I found the *débris* of three houses, which had evidently been destroyed by fire. One of them, which is immediately to the north-west of the well,[6] may be easily examined by visitors, in accordance with the following description of M. Burnouf :[7] —

" I. *The Area.*—The substratum is formed of superposed compact strata containing earth, ashes, bones, shells, stones, and other *débris* belonging to the first city. This substratum is from 8 to 10 ft. deep in the great trench. The area established on this substratum is made solely of bruised and compressed brick matter ; its thickness is 0·05 m. (2 in.). The burning material which in the conflagration has fallen on this soil has, first, vitrified the surface of the area from 1 to 2 millimètres (1-25th to 2-25ths in.) deep (this thin layer is of a greenish colour) ;[8] secondly, it has completely baked the brick-stratum to a depth of 0·02 m. = 0·8 in. (this layer is light yellow); lastly, it has burnt the layer below black to a depth of from 10 to 15 centimètres = 4 to 6 in.

" II. *The Débris.* — Over the area we see : (1) a uniform stratum of very light charcoal, 0·01 to 0·02 m. deep: (2) a stratum of brick-earth, which has in the centre a depth of half a mètre = 20 in. : this proves that in the middle of the house there has been much more of this matter

---

[6] Marked *a* Z on Plan I. (of Troy).
[7] See the Section, No. 146, p. 270.
[8] The centimètre (0·01 m.) = 0·4 in. nearly ;

the millimètre (0·001 m.) = 0·04 in., or 1-25th in. See the Table of French and English Measures.

than elsewhere ; it is the base of this stratum of brick-earth which, by its heat, has vitrified the soil of the area.   Above it are strata of a brownish or light colour, forming the arc of a circle ; of which the upper layer (*a*) is of a brown colour ; it contains small yellow clay-cakes (*galettes*) which have fallen almost without breaking : (3) a sporadic stratum of pretty large flat pieces of charcoal, 0·10 to 0·12 m. = 4 to 4·8 in. long and broad : (4) a thick party-coloured stratum, from 0·70 to 0·80 m. = 28 to 32 in. deep of clay-cakes (*galettes*), and blackish, brown, grey or

No. 146.   Section of a burnt House on the north-west side of the Well (*a* Z on Plan I.).

reddish substances more or less mixed with straw.   This stratum contains fragments of pottery, shells, bones, &c.   This last stratum appears to be derived from the terraced roof ; the large pieces of charcoal are from the beams and joists.   The inferior strata of light earth have fallen first through the burning timber-work ; they appear to be derived from the floor, the light wood of which has produced the first stratum of *débris*. Thus the house appears to have had probably a ground-floor and one upper storey.   Contrary to the general architecture of the second city, there is no trace of walls in this house.   Were they perhaps of clay ? "

I would further call the particular attention of visitors to the several house-walls of this second city, which peep out from below the large house of the third city to the north-west of the gate (see the engraving No. 188, p. 325).   As nine out of the ten treasures which I discovered were found in or close to that house, I hold it to be the house of the town-chief or king ; and so the walls, which we see below it, may perhaps belong to the mansion of the chief or king of the second city.   As they are below the level of the rampart wall, they may perhaps claim a greater antiquity than the latter.

To the north of the great wall *c*, in excavating the great trench, I struck, on the 2nd of August, 1872, a stone house of the second city, which had evidently also been destroyed by fire, because it was filled, to the depth of 6 or 7 ft., with yellow or brownish wood-ashes, in which I found the tolerably well-preserved skeleton of a human being.   The colour of the bones, as well as the strange position in which the body[9] was found, can leave no doubt that the person had been overtaken by the fire and burnt to death.   This seems to be the more certain, as all the pre-historic peoples, who succeeded each other in the course of ages on the hill of Hissarlik, used cremation of the dead.   The smallness of the skull led me at once to think that it was that of a woman ; and this opinion seems to

[9] The body was found nearly standing, and but slightly inclined backward.

be corroborated by the gold ornaments which I picked up by the side of the skeleton, and which I shall presently describe.

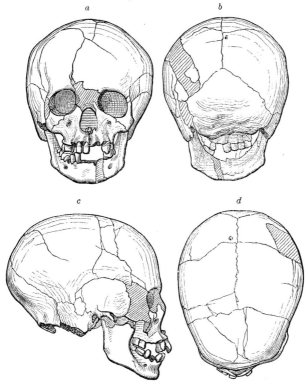

No. 147.   Different Views of the Skull of a Girl, whose skeleton was found in a burnt house at a depth of 42 ft.
a. Front.   b. Back.   c. Side.   d. Top.

The skull was unfortunately broken in the excavation, but it has been recomposed. Professor Virchow, who made the accompanying geometrical drawing (No. 147) of it, writes to me as follows on the subject :—

"Length of the skull . . . . 180·5
Greatest breadth of the skull 149
Auricular height 116
Lower frontal breadth 93
Height of the face 104
Breadth   do. 90
   Do.   of the lower jaw . . . . 82·5
Eye-hole, height 29
   Do.   breadth 38
Nose, height . . . . 48?
   Do.   breadth . . . . 23·3
Height of the alveolar apophysis of the upper jaw 17
Horizontal circumference of the skull 522

" From this the following indices may be calculated :—

"Longitudinal index . . . . 82·5
Auricular index . . . . 64·2
Nasal index . . . . 48·5
Orbital index . . . . 76·3

"This skull is brachycephalic, and decidedly a female one; it is particularly distinguished by strongly-developed prognathism. Though it is badly recomposed, yet it is so far reconstructed, that the above measures may be considered as approximately accurate. The teeth, particularly the upper incisors, are large; the enamel is everywhere very white and furrowed lengthwise; the crowns are but little wasted, and the wisdom teeth not yet cut. It belonged, therefore, to a girl. As the *basis cranii* is missing, nothing more can be said of the age. On the whole, the skull is broader and higher than it is long; the frontal and parietal protuberances are well developed; the forehead is full; the occiput is broadly expanded. The face is somewhat broad, with low eye-holes and moderately broad nose. The chin is retracted; the middle of the lower jawbone is low, the processes steep and broad. When looked at from behind, the skull appears low and flattened."

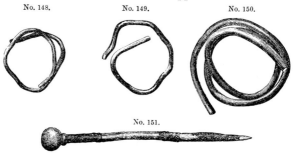

No. 148.   No. 149.   No. 150.

No. 151.

Nos. 148–151.   Gold Rings and Brooch of Electrum, of very primitive workmanship.
(Actual size.   Depth, about 42 ft.)

With regard to the jewels found by the side of the skeleton, the two ear-rings, Nos. 148 and 149, are of a very primitive kind, consisting of simple gold wire 0·0015 m. thick; in fact, it is impossible to imagine anything ruder or more primitive. The finger-ring, No. 150, is of the same rude workmanship; it consists of a treble gold wire 0·0025 m. thick. Compared with these, the third gold ear-ring, like No. 694, is a real work of art; it is composed of six gold wires of equal thickness, which form a leaf. The electrum brooch, No. 151, has that primitive form of which we have passed several specimens of bronze in review (see Nos. 106, 107), in discussing the objects found in the first city, and which existed before the invention of the fibulæ. The body must have worn some more female ornaments, for I collected by its side several plain gold beads, only 1 millimètre in diameter (like Nos. 913–915), as also a very thin oval gold ring, only 1-4th of an inch long.

Electrum occurs several times in the third Trojan city. It is mentioned by Homer together with bronze, gold, silver, and ivory as an ornament of walls: "Consider, O son of Nestor dear to my heart, the gleam of the bronze, the gold, the electrum, and the ivory in the resounding hall."[1] In this instance electrum certainly means an alloy

[1] *Od.* iv. 71–73:
φράζεο, Νεστορίδη, τῷ ἐμῷ κεχαρισμένε θυμῷ,   χαλκοῦ τε στεροπὴν κατὰ δώματα ἠχήεντα,
                                                χρυσοῦ τ᾽ ἠλέκτρου τε καὶ ἀργύρου ἠδ᾽ ἐλέφαντος.

of gold and silver. But the word occurs twice more in Homer, where nothing else than amber can be meant by it.[2]

In speaking of the ingots which Croesus sent to the Oracle of Delphi, Herodotus says: " The number of ingots was 117, four being of refined gold, in weight 1½ talents each; the others were half-tiles of pale gold, and in weight 2 talents each."[3] There seems to be every probability that by the pale gold electrum is meant; for we cannot suppose that the pale gold was inferior to that of the Lydian coins, which are certainly of electrum, though the quantity of silver contained in them seems to exceed the proportion indicated by Pliny in the following most interesting passage:[4]—" Omni auro inest argentum vario pondere, alibi decuma, alibi nona, alibi octava parte. In uno tantum Galliae metallo, quod vocant Albicralense, tricesima sexta portio invenitur: ideo caeteris praeest. Ubicumque quinta argenti portio est, electrum vocatur. Scobes eae reperiuntur in Canaliensi. Fit et cura electrum argento addito. Quod si quintam portionem excessit, incudibus non resistit. Et electro auctoritas, Homero teste, qui Menelai regiam auro, electro, argento, ebore, fulgere tradit. Minervae templum habet Lindos, insulae Rhodiorum, in quo Helena sacravit calycem ex electro. Adjicit historia, mammae suae mensura. Electri natura est, ad lucernarum lumina clarius argento splendere. Quod est nativum, et venena deprehendit. Namque discurrunt in calycibus arcus, caelestibus similes, cum igneo stridore; et gemina ratione praedicunt."

We gather from this passage of Pliny that the ancients gave the name of " electrum " particularly to a natural alloy, containing the requisite proportions, which, according to another passage, they found out by the touchstone:[5] " Auri argentique mentionem comitatur lapis, quem coticulam appellant, quondam non solitus inveniri, nisi in flumine Tmolo, ut auctor est Theophrastus : nunc vero passim: quem alii Heraclium, alii Lydium vocant. Sunt autem modici, quaternas uncias longitudinis, binasque latitudinis non excedentes. Quod a sole fuit in his, melius quam quod a terra. His coticulis periti, quum e vena ut lima rapuerunt experimentum, protinus dicunt quantum auri sit in ea, quantum argenti vel aeris, scripulari differentia, mirabili ratione, non fallente."

Strabo had apparently only a confused idea of electrum, for, speaking of the gold of Spain, he says: " When gold is melted and purified with a certain aluminous earth, there remains a residue which is electrum. If this residue, which contains gold and silver, is remelted, the silver is consumed and the gold remains as a residue."[6] Pausanias mentions the two kinds of electrum in speaking of a statue of Augustus of amber: " That electrum of which the statue of Augustus has been made, inasmuch

---

[2] *Od.* xv. 460:
χρύσεον ὅρμον ἔχων, μετὰ δ' ἠλέκτροισιν ἔερτο·
and xviii. 296:
χρύσεον, ἠλέκτροισιν ἐερμένον, ἠέλιον ὥs.

[3] i. 50: ἀριθμὸν δὲ ἑπτακαίδεκα καὶ ἑκατόν·
καὶ τουτέων ἀπέφθου χρυσοῦ τέσσαρα, τρία ἡμι-
τάλαντα ἕκαστον ἕλκοντα, τὰ δὲ ἄλλα ἡμιπλίνθια
λευκοῦ χρυσοῦ σταθμὸν διτάλαντα.

[4] *H. N.* xxxiii. 23.
[5] *Ibid.* xxxiii. 43.
[6] iii. p. 146: ἐκ δὲ τοῦ χουσοῦ ἐψομένου καὶ
καθαιρομένου στυπτηριώδει τινὶ γῇ τὸ κάθαρμα
ἤλεκτρον εἶναι· πάλιν δὲ τούτου καθεψομένου,
μῖγμα ἔχοντος ἀργύρου καὶ χρυσοῦ, τὸν μὲν
ἄργυρον ἀποκαίεσθαι τὸν δὲ χρυσὸν ὑπομένειν.

as it is only found native in the sands of the Eridanus, is exceedingly scarce, and is highly prized by man; but the other kind of electrum is gold alloyed with silver." [7] Eustathius, who mentions three sorts of electrum, declares the alloy of gold and silver to be the principal one.[8]

From a depth of 26 to 40 ft. below the surface I excavated a third house, destroyed by fire and belonging to this second city, just in front of the long marble slab marked f on No. 144 (p. 265). It is built entirely of small stones joined with clay; an architecture exactly such as we see in the pre-historic buildings found beneath three layers of pumice-stone and volcanic ashes on the Island of Thera (Santorin). The horizontal row of large holes, at a certain height all round its four walls, marks the places of the beams, and proves that the house was at least two storeys high. The walls are still partially covered with a coating of yellow clay, which had been whitened with a wash of white clay. Every stone of its walls, nay, every particle of *débris* contained between them, bears traces of the intense heat to which it has been exposed, and which has so completely destroyed everything that was in the rooms, that we only occasionally found charred fragments of pottery among the yellow and brownish wood-ashes and *débris*, with which the spaces were filled.

In digging down in the centre of this house, below the level of the base of its walls, we found, curiously enough, other house-walls, which must certainly be still more ancient; and these, too, showed indications of having been exposed to a terrible heat. But, owing to the fragile condition of the upper walls, I could bring to light hardly more than the surface of these lower walls. I must, therefore, leave it undecided whether the house, to which these more ancient walls belong, was destroyed by fire, or whether the marks of intense heat, which were conspicuous upon its walls, were produced by the conflagration of the upper house, which might certainly have been the case if the surface of the more ancient walls had protruded just below the wooden floor of the upper house. That this lower floor really was of wood is apparent from the charred remains of it, in a horizontal line all along the four walls of the upper house. But these calcined remains clearly show that the whole floor consisted of beams, and not of planks. The people must have had very great difficulty in cutting down the trees with their stone axes and getting rid of their branches. They must have had still greater difficulty in cleaving them, as no tree has a straight cleavage so that planks can be cloven out of it. With their silex saws, only 2 or 3 in. long, they could only saw bones or small pieces of wood, not beams. They had no bronze axes; for if such had existed I should have found them, especially in the third, the burnt city, which, as the ten treasures found in it go far to prove, was suddenly and unexpectedly destroyed by fire. They had no bronze saws for sawing wood; for in all the five pre-historic cities only the fragment of one thin bronze saw was found ($8\frac{2}{3}$ in. long and nearly

---

[7] Paus. v. 12, § 6 : τὸ δὲ ἤλεκτρον τοῦτο οὗ τῷ Αὐγούστῳ πεποίηνται τὴν εἰκόνα, ὅσον μὲν αὐτόματον ἐν τοῦ Ἠριδανοῦ ταῖς ψάμμοις εὑρίσκεται, σπανίζεται τὰ μάλιστα καὶ ἀνθρώπῳ τίμιον

πολλῶν ἐστιν ἕνεκα· τὸ δὲ ἄλλο ἤλεκτρον ἀναμεμιγμένος ἐστὶν ἀργύρῳ χρυσός.

[8] Ad Odyss. iv. 73, p. 1483 : μάλιστα δὲ μῖγμα χρυσοῦ καὶ ἀργύρου.

2 in. broad), which I at first thought to be a sword. It was contained in the large treasure found by me in May 1873, which circumstance seems to prove that it was a rare object. It is to be seen in my Trojan collection in South Kensington Museum.

The floors were covered with clay, which filled all the interstices and hollows between the beams, so as to make a smooth surface. As the walls of this third burnt house have been so much deteriorated by the confla-gration, they would soon crumble away if they remained exposed to the air. I have therefore thought it in the interest of science to fill this excavation up again, in order to preserve the house for future times. But whoever wishes to see it may easily excavate it with ten workmen in one day. I repeat, it is in the large trench, just below the marble block marked *f* on No. 144.

As, in speaking of the objects found in this Second City, I began with metals, I may say that I found there the same kind of rude brooches with a globular head or with a head in the form of a spiral of copper, as well as the same kind of needles of that metal, as in the First City (see Nos. 104, 105, 107, and 108).[9] I have not noticed in the second city either lead or silver; but, as gold and electrum were found, those metals were undoubtedly known and in use there.

I also collected there an abundance of saddle-querns of trachyte, as well as globular corn-bruisers and rude hammers of gneiss, granite, diorite, &c.; the same kind of axes of blue serpentine rock, gabbro-rock, diorite, &c.; also two small axes, which Mr. Thomas Davies found to consist of green jade (nephrite). I may here add that, according to Dr. William Humble's *Dict. of Geology and Mineralogy* (Lond. 1860), s. v. 'Nephrite,' "This name of the mineral is derived from νεφρίτης (from νεφρός, a 'kidney'), because it was formerly worn from an absurd notion that diseases of the kidney were relieved by its presence. It is a sub-species of jade, possessing the hardness of quartz, combined with a peculiar tenacity, which renders it difficult to break, cut, or polish. It is unctuous to the touch; fracture splintery and dull; translucent. Colours green, grey, and white. Specific gravity from 2·9 to 3·1. Constituents, silex 53·80, lime 12·75, soda 10·80, potash 8·50, alumina 1·55, oxide of iron 5·0, oxide of manganese 2·0, water 2·30."

Under the word 'Jade,' Dr. Humble says: "It is the Nephrit of Werner; Nephrite of Jameson; called also nephrite stone, nephrite, and axe-stone. Brochant states its fresh fracture to present a paler green than that of its surface. Before the blow-pipe it fuses easily, and with a slight ebullition, into a bead of white semi-transparent glass. In con-sequence of its tenacity, it has been wrought into chains and other delicate work."

The perforated stone hammers of this second city are also identical with those of the first city. I represent here one of them under No. 152. I did not find here entire long stone axes, only two halves, which I represent

---

[9] Nos. 113, 114, and 115, which belong to this second city, have been engraved with those belonging to the first city, at p. 250.

under Nos. 153 and 154. The upper one shows the perforation, of which there is no trace on the lower one; besides, the upper one consists of

No. 153.

No. 152. Perforated Stone Hammer. (Half actual size. Depth, about 35 ft.)

No. 154.

Nos. 153, 154. Stone Axes. (Half actual size. Depth, 35 ft.)

No. 155. Object of Stone: a *phallus*. (Half actual size. Depth, 42 ft.)

grey diorite; the lower one of gabbro-rock: therefore these two fragments belong to different axes.

There was also found in this second city the object No. 155, of grey granite, which, by its shape, I hold to represent a *phallus*, the more so as objects of an identical shape are frequent in the subsequent cities; while, further, the god Priapus was fabled to have been born of Aphrodité and Dionysus in the neighbouring city of Lampsacus,[10] where, as well as in his homonymous city, Priapus, he had in historical times a celebrated cultus, and was venerated more than any other god. It deserves, however, particular notice that this god is not mentioned either by Homer or by Hesiod, or by any of the other poets. According to Strabo, Priapus was the son of Dionysus and a nymph.[1] Athenaeus

[10] Paus. ix. 31, § 2 : Ἐνταῦθα καὶ Τηλέφῳ τῷ Ἡρακλέους γάλα ἐστὶν ἔλαφος παιδὶ μικρῷ διδοῦσα, καὶ βοῦς τε παρ' αὐτὸν καὶ ἄγαλμα Πριάπου θέας ἄξιον. τούτῳ τιμαὶ τῷ θεῷ δέδονται μὲν καὶ ἄλλως, ἔνθα εἰσὶν αἰγῶν νομαὶ καὶ προβάτων ἢ καὶ ἐσμοὶ μελισσῶν· Λαμψακηνοὶ δὲ ἐς πλέον ἢ θεοὺς τοὺς ἄλλους νομίζουσι, Διονύσου τε αὐτὸν παῖδα εἶναι καὶ Ἀφροδίτης λέγοντες.

Diodor. Sic. iv. 6 : μυθολογοῦσιν οὖν οἱ παλαιοὶ τὸν Πρίαπον υἱὸν εἶναι Διονύσου καὶ Ἀφροδίτης, πιθανῶς τὴν γένεσιν ταύτην ἐξηγούμενοι· τοὺς γὰρ οἰνωθέντας φυσικῶς ἐντετάσθαι πρὸς τὰς

ἀφροδισιακὰς ἡδονάς· τινὲς δέ φασι τὸ αἰδοῖον τῶν ἀνθρώπων τοὺς παλαιοὺς μυθωδῶς ὀνομάζειν βουλομένους Πρίαπον προσαγορεῦσαι. ἔνιοι δὲ λέγουσι τὸ γεννητικὸν μόριον, αἴτιον ὑπάρχον τῆς γενέσεως τῶν ἀνθρώπων καὶ διαμονῆς εἰς ἅπαντα τὸν αἰῶνα, τυχεῖν τῆς ἀθανάτου τιμῆς.

Tibull. 1, 4, 7 ; Schol. ad Apollon. Rhod. Argonaut. 1, 932.

[1] Strabo, xiii. p. 587 : ἐπώνυμος δ' ἐστὶ τοῦ Πριάπου τιμωμένου παρ' αὐτοῖς, εἴτ' ἐξ Ὀρνεῶν τῶν περὶ Κόρινθον μετενηνεγμένου τοῦ ἱεροῦ, εἴτε τῷ λέγεσθαι Διονύσου καὶ νύμφης τὸν θεὸν

says that " Priapus was with the Lampsacenes originally an epithet of Dionysus, like θρίαμβος and διθύραμβος, and that he is identical with him." [2]

According to Eduard Meyer,[3] " Priapus, the principal god of Lampsacus, was a Bebrycian deity. This is evident from the fact that as a native god he is (*i.e.* in historic times of antiquity) still found in Bithynia. The primitive inhabitants of Bithynia were Bebrycians ; the Bithynians were later Thracian immigrants : we must, therefore, presume that they took Priapus from the religion of the primitive Bithynians. Lucian relates that, according to the Bithynian legend, Priapus was a warlike god, to whom Heré gave Ares to educate ; and he taught him dancing before teaching him fighting. Arrian related, in his Bithynian history, that Priapus (whom he calls Πρίεπος) signifies the Sun, on account of his generating power.[4] This is undoubtedly right. Priapus is by his origin undoubtedly an ithyphallic sun-god, like Amon (Chem) and the Horus bull of the Egyptians. On the other hand, the Sun-god easily becomes a warlike deity. The poets relate a legend, according to which, at the feast of the Mother of the Gods, Priapus lay in wait for Vesta (who is she?) ; but that the ass of Silenus betrayed him by his bray. For this reason the Lampsacenes used to sacrifice an ass to Priapus.[5] The Greeks explained the worship of Priapus on the coast of the Hellespont by the abundance of wine in the country.[6] From his worship at Lampsacus he had the epithet 'Hellespontiacus.' " [7]

He was the protector of the fields,[8] the dispenser of fertility, the tutelary deity of shepherds and goatherds, of the rearing of bees, of horticulture, the cultivation of the vine, and of fishery.[9]

I may here add, that the phallus (φαλλός) was the symbol of the procreating power of nature, whose worship extended, according to Witzschel,[10] " through all natural religions from their rudest beginning until the decay of heathenism. In the Egyptian sculptures we frequently see ithyphallic gods. At the feasts of Dionysus-Osiris the women carried round to the villages puppet-like figures a cubit high, with a not much shorter phallus, which they pulled by strings.[1] Herodotus adds, that the

---

ὁρμησάντων ἐπὶ τὸ τιμᾶν αὐτὸν τῶν ἀνθρώπων, ἐπειδὴ σφόδρα εὐάμπελός ἐστιν ἡ χώρα καὶ αὕτη καὶ [ἡ] ἐφεξῆς ὅμορος, ἥ τε τῶν Παριανῶν καὶ ἡ τῶν Λαμψακηνῶν.

[2] Athenaeus, i. 54 : τιμᾶται δὲ παρὰ Λαμψακηνοῖς ὁ Πρίαπος ὁ αὐτὸς ὢν τῷ Διονύσῳ, ἐξ ἐπιθέτου καλούμενος οὕτως, ὡς θρίαμβος καὶ διθύραμβος.

[3] Geschichte von Troas ; Leipzig, 1877, p. 43.

[4] Lucian. de Saltat. 21 : τὸν Πρίαπον δαίμονα πολεμιστήν, τῶν Τιτάνων οἶμαι ἕνα ἢ τῶν Ἰδαίων Δακτύλων (?) ; Arrian, Frag. 32, edit. Müller ex Eustath. ad Il. vii. 459 : Πρίεπος παρὰ Ἀρριανῷ ἐν Βιθυνιακοῖς, παρ' ᾧ καὶ εἰς "Ηλιον ἀλληγορεῖται διὰ τὸ γόνιμον.

[5] Ovid. Fast. vi. 319–346 ; Lactant. de falsa Rel. i. 21 ; differently Ovid. Fast. i. 391–440.

[6] Strabo, xiii. p. 587 ; Thucydides, i. 138 : ταύτης γὰρ ἦρχε τῆς χώρας, δόντος βασιλέως αὐτῷ

Μαγνησίαν μὲν ἄρτον, ἢ προσέφερε πεντήκοντα τάλαντα τοῦ ἐνιαυτοῦ, Λάμψακον δὲ οἶνον (ἐδόκει γὰρ πολυοινότατον τῶν τότε εἶναι), Μυοῦντα δὲ ὄψον.

[7] Ovid. Fast. i. 440 ; vi. 341.

[8] Voss, Myth. Briefe, ii. p. 344 ff.

[9] Paus. ix. 31, § 2 ; Ovid. Fast. i. 415 ; Anthol. Pal. x. 7, 8 ; Voss, ad Virg. Ecl. vii. 33 ; Georg. i. 110 ; Voss, Myth. Brr. ii. p. 37 ; Pauly, Real Encyclopädie, s. v. Priapus.

[10] Pauly, op. cit. s. v. Phallus.

[1] Herodot. ii. 48 : τὴν δὲ ἄλλην ἀνάγουσι ὁρτὴν τῷ Διονύσῳ οἱ Αἰγύπτιοι, πλὴν χορῶν, κατὰ ταῦτα σχεδὸν πάντα "Ελλησι· ἀντὶ δὲ φαλλῶν, ἄλλα σφί ἐστι ἐξευρημένα ὅσον τε πηχυαῖα ἀγάλματα νευρόσπαστα τὰ περιφορέουσι κατὰ κώμας γυναῖκες, νεῦον τὸ αἰδοῖον οὐ πολλῷ τέῳ ἔλασσον ἐὸν τοῦ ἄλλου σώματος.

seer Melampus was said to have transplanted to Greece[2] the worship of Dionysus with the phallic processions. But, according to another passage of the same author,[3] the worship of the phallus was practised by the Pelasgians in the remotest antiquity, and from them the Athenians learned to make ithyphallic Hermae.[4] For this reason the phallus is not only found on the islands inhabited by Pelasgians,[5] Lemnos and Imbros,[6] but also on the cyclopean walls of Alatri and Terni,[7] on the substruction of a house in the Pelasgian (afterwards Samnite) Saepinum, and elsewhere. On the tomb of Alyattes in Lydia there stood a colossal phallus, the head of which, 40 ft. in circumference and 12 ft. in diameter, is still extant.[8] In Greece the phallic processions ($\phi\alpha\lambda\lambda\alpha\gamma\dot{\omega}\gamma\iota\alpha$, $\phi\alpha\lambda\lambda\eta$-$\phi\dot{o}\rho\iota\alpha$) were general.[9] Before the temple of Dionysus in Syria there stood, according to Lucian,[10] two phalli, with the inscription, 'Dionysus has dedicated them to his step-mother Heré.' Their height is given (c. 28) as 300 fathoms, which number Palmerius has corrected to 30. In the Dionysiac procession of Ptolemaeus Philadelphus at Alexandria a phallus figured, 120 (sic) cubits high, ornamented with a crown embroidered with gold and with a gold star on the top. We see in sculptures and paintings a series of the most varied formations of the phallus, extending from these monstrous works to the amulets for suspension, 2-3 in. long. At Lavinium, during the whole month which was sacred to Liber Pater, the phallus was carried in procession through the villages, for warding off enchantment from the fields.[11] At weddings the newly-married woman was obliged to sit on the phallus, in order to present, as it were, her chastity to him.[1] Considering, therefore, that this worship extends through the whole history of natural religion from beginning to end, we must see in it an originally harmless veneration of the generating principle."[2]

Professor Sayce kindly sends me the following interesting note :— "Last year I discovered on the northern cliff of Mount Sipylus in Lydia, about half a mile to the east of the pre-historic figure of Niobe, the representation of a large phallus, with two artificial niches on either side and two pit tombs in front. It had evidently been a place of pilgrimage, like a similar figure in a hollow on the summit of one of the lower Pyrenees, near Bidarray, which I once visited, and which is still venerated by the Basque women."

In treating now of the pottery of this Second Stone City, I repeat that both in fabric and shape it is altogether different from that of the first city. It therefore gives us the most certain proof that the inhabitants

[2] Herodot. ii. 49.

[3] *Ibid.* ii. 51: ταῦτα μὲν νῦν καὶ ἄλλα πρὸς τούτοισι τὰ ἐγὼ φράσω, "Ελληνες ἀπ' Αἰγυπτίων νενομίκασι· τοῦ δὲ 'Ερμέω τὰ ἀγάλματα ὀρθὰ ἔχειν τὰ αἰδοῖα ποιεῦντες οὐκ ἀπ' Αἰγυπτίων μεμαθήκασι, ἀλλ' ἀπὸ Πελασγῶν, πρῶτοι μὲν 'Ελλήνων ἁπάντων 'Αθηναῖοι παραλαβόντες, παρὰ δὲ τούτων ἄλλοι.

[4] Gerhard, *de Religione Hermarum*, 1845, p. 3.

[5] Herodot. vi. 137 ; v. 26.

[6] K. O. Müller, *Etrusker*, i. p. 77.

[7] Micali, *Monum. per la Stor. de' Ant. pop.* xiii. a ; Göttling, *Geschichte d. Röm. Staatsverf.* p. 28.

[8] K. O. Müller, *Arch. d. Kunst.* p. 304.

[9] Herodot. ii. 49; Aristoph. *Acharn.*

[10] *De dea Syr.* c. 16.

[11] Augustin. *de Civit. Dei*, vi. 9. 3.

[1] Augustin. *Ibid.* i. 6, vii. 24. 2 ; Lactant. i. 20. 39 ; Arnob. iv. 7.

[2] J. Grimm, *Deutsche Mythol.* ii. p. 1209.

of the second city were altogether a different people from those of the first city, for, as my friend Mr. George Dennis [3] observes : " The several styles of art of the same race at different periods are bound to one another like the links of a chain ; and it is impossible for a people, after having wrought out a style of pottery which had acquired among them a sacred and ritual character, to abandon it on a sudden, and adopt another style of a totally different character. A people may modify, develop, perfect, but can never utterly cast aside its own arts and industry, because in such a case it would deny its own individuality. When we find, therefore, between two styles of art so many and such strongly pronounced discrepancies, that it becomes impossible to perceive the most remote analogy between them, it is not enough to attribute such diversities to a difference of age, or stage of culture ; we can only ascribe them to different races."

The large lustrous-black bowls, with long horizontal tubular holes for suspension on both sides in the rim, which are so very abundant in the first city that I was able to collect thousands of fragments of them, never occur in the second city ; neither do the vases with double vertical tubular holes on each side, which are plentiful in the first city. On the other hand, we find in the second city those gigantic terra-cotta jars—5 or 6½ ft. high, from 3 to 5 ft. in diameter, and from 2 to 3 in. thick in the clay—which are altogether wanting in the first city. It is true that I found there now and then fragments of coarse pottery ; but as they are usually less than half an inch thick, and as none of them has a thickness of 1 in., the jars (*pithoi*) to which they belong cannot have been large.

Certainly the large jars (*pithoi*) of the second city are rudely made : where they are broken, we see an enormous mass of pieces of silicious stone, or mica, many of them a quarter of an inch thick ; but nevertheless, as his Highness Prince Otto Bismarck, the Chancellor of the German Empire, ingeniously remarked to me, in July 1879, at Kissingen, the manufacture of these large jars proves already a high degree of civilization, for to make them is just as difficult as to bake them, and they can, consequently, only have been manufactured by a people who had an experience of centuries in the potter's art. The Prince thinks that they must have been made in the following manner :—" The shape of a *pithos* was first made of willow rods or reeds, around which the clay was built up gradually, beginning with the base. When finished, the *pithos* was filled with wood ; a large pyre of wood was also heaped up around it. The wood was simultaneously kindled inside and outside the jar, and thus, by the double fire from within and from without, a very great heat was produced. This operation being several times repeated, the jar became at last thoroughly baked." I feel sure that Prince Bismarck's opinion is perfectly correct ; for, whilst even the smallest and thinnest clay vessels are at the most only half baked, the large jars, though from 2 to 3 in. thick, are always perfectly baked ; and as the pre-historic peoples had—as I have explained (p. 219)—no kilns, and had to bake all their pottery at

---

[3] *The Cities and Cemeteries of Etruria ;* 2nd edit., London, 1878.

an open fire, a heat great enough to do this could, I think, only be produced by a double fire several times repeated. I may add that the thorough baking of these large jars was a necessity ; for, owing to their great size and ponderous weight [4] (sometimes nearly a ton), they could not have been moved without breaking to pieces had they been as imperfectly baked as all the other pottery. It is from this thorough baking also that these large *pithoi* have always a pretty dark-red colour.[5]

In the accompanying engraving (No. 156) I represent a fragment of a *pithos* of this second city, the terra-cotta of which is $2\frac{1}{2}$ in. thick. It is

No. 156.   Fragment of a large Jar.   (1 : 4 actual size.
Depth, about 42 ft.)

decorated with two projecting bands, of which the upper one is composed alternately of the fish-spine or herring-bone ornament and a row of circles, the lower one also of fish-spines, to which, however, the primitive artist has added a stroke in another direction, in order to make his decoration more varied and attractive. All this ornamentation looks as if it had been impressed ; but on closer examination one finds that it has been incised before the first baking of the jar. Prof. Sayce remarks to me regarding this fragment that " the band with circles may be compared with the necklace of the pre-historic head from Boujah, near Smyrna, now in the British Museum. This head displays a very strange and barbarous style of art, and a very peculiar type of countenance."

The large jars, πίθοι, are only once mentioned in Homer.[6] Just as we find them standing in rows in the store-rooms on the ground-floor of the

---

[4] A *pithos* of this kind, found in the third (the burnt) city, which I presented to my worthy collaborateur, Professor Rudolf Virchow, for the Royal Museum of Berlin, was so heavy that fourteen of my very strongest workmen, who had put it on two poles, laboured a whole day in carrying it a distance of 150 yards.

[5] Professor Virchow remarks to me that the baking of the *pithoi* could also be effected with cow-dung in a closed pit. But I cannot accept his theory, thoroughly baked pottery being always much more solid, pretty, and valuable than slightly baked pottery. If, therefore, a thorough baking of the immense *pithoi*, whose clay is from 2 to 3 in. thick, could be obtained in this way, the same could certainly have been obtained at once for the small vessels whose clay

has a thickness of from 3 to 4 mm. (1-8th to 1-6th in.). But it is a fact that, however thin the clay of the small vessels may be, it is only baked to one-third, seldom to one-half, of its thickness. The baking can consequently only have taken place in an open fire ; in fact, only by this theory we can explain the total baking of the *pithoi* and the partial baking of the thin pottery.

[6] *Il.* xxiv. 527–533 :

δοιοὶ γάρ τε πίθοι κατακείαται ἐν Διὸς οὔδει
δώρων οἷα δίδωσι, κακῶν, ἕτερος δὲ ἑάων.
ᾧ μέν κ' ἀμμίξας δώῃ Ζεὺς τερπικέραυνος,
ἄλλοτε μέν τε κακῷ ὅ γε κύρεται ἄλλοτε δ' ἐσθλῷ·
ᾧ δέ κε τῶν λυγρῶν δώῃ, λωβητὸν ἔθηκεν
καί ἑ κακὴ βούβρωστις ἐπὶ χθόνα δῖαν ἐλαύνει,
φοιτᾷ δ' οὔτε θεοῖσι τετιμένος οὔτε βροτοῖσιν.

houses in the four upper pre-historic cities in Hissarlik, so the poet represents to us two such πίθοι standing on the ground-floor in the hall of the palace of Zeus. In these two πίθοι lay stored the gifts of good luck and the gifts of misfortune, the bitter and the sweet, like apples or pears, or rather like two sorts of wine, so that the poet considers the μοῖρα as a substance which Zeus can employ and distribute according to his pleasure,—an allegorizing naïveté such as we find in the legend of Pandora.[7] In relating this legend, Hesiod represents a jar standing in the house of Epimetheus, full of diseases and evils for mankind, which fly out when Pandora, through curiosity, opens the jar; but Hope alone remained under the edge of the jar, for, before she could fly out, Pandora clapt the lid on again.[8]

I may here also mention the terra-cotta plates, from half to two-thirds of an inch thick, which are peculiar to this second city, and which are not found anywhere else. They consist of the same sort of clay mixed with crushed granite, as the vases; but being *thoroughly* baked and having evidently been repeatedly dipped in a wash of fine pure clay before the baking, they are perfectly smooth on both sides and have a lustrous dark-red colour. As they are completely flat, and only increase almost imperceptibly in thickness towards the middle, they cannot possibly be fragments of vessels. As I never found such a plate entire, I cannot judge of their original size. I am puzzled as to what may have been their use. Were they perhaps employed as decorations of the internal house-walls? I cannot think that they can have been used for paving the floors of the houses, as in that case they would have marks of having been so used. I call the particular attention of visitors to these flat terra-cottas, which peep out everywhere in my trenches from the strata of the second city. They strike the eye by their lively red colour on both sides, which has of course been produced by the oxide of iron contained in the clay; they glitter all over with sparkles of mica, which appears to have entered very largely into their composition.

The most interesting vases in this second city, as well as in the three following pre-historic cities at Hissarlik, are undoubtedly those with an owl's head and the characteristics of a woman. Considering the great similarity of the owl's faces on the vases to these on the idols (such as Nos. 205, 212), we may suppose with much probability that these vases had a sacred character, and were used for religious rites, the more so as the vases themselves have the shape of the idols. I call particular attention to the fact, that the only Trojan statue mentioned by Homer, that of Athené, as well as all the idols of marble, bone or terra-cotta, and all the owl-vases, are *female*, and that they are placed in apparent relation with Athené through her favourite bird the owl.

In January 1874[9] I made bold to declare that the hundreds of female idols and vases with owl-heads, found in the pre-historic cities of Hissarlik, could represent but one goddess, and that this goddess could be

[7] V. H. Koch, *Homer's Iliade*; Hannover, 1873, ii. p. 137, foot-note.

[8] Hesiod, *Op. et Di.* vv. 50 ff.

[9] In my book *Trojanische Alterthümer*, Leipzig, 1874; *Troy and its Remains*, London, 1875.

none other than Athené, the tutelary goddess of Troy; all the more so as Homer continually calls her γλαυκῶπις (that is, literally translated, "with the face of an owl"), and never gives this epithet to any other goddess or mortal woman. Thereupon I was challenged by my honoured friend, Professor Max Müller [10] of Oxford, who evinced his readiness to accept my interpretation, provided I proved that Heré βοῶπις was represented as a cow-headed monster. I eagerly accepted the challenge, and began the excavations at Tiryns and Mycenae, with the most perfect confidence that I could there solve the problem for ever, as both these ancient cities lie close to the celebrated Heraeum, and as even the name of Mycenae appeared to me to be derived from the lowing of the cow (μυκᾶσθαι, but always μυκᾶν in Homer).[11] The result of my researches certainly far exceeded my expectations, for I found there thousands of cows of terra-cotta, also 56 cow-heads of gold, one of silver with gold horns, some cow-heads engraved on gems, many hundreds of female idols with two pro-jections like cow-horns, in the shape of the crescent, proceeding from the breasts, also females with cow-heads.[1] In consequence of these dis-coveries, I think it has been universally admitted that the original mean-ing of the epithet βοῶπις is cow-faced. Upon this subject Mr. Gladstone says in his Preface to my *Mycenae* :[2]

"He (Schliemann) presents to us the rude figures of cows; and upon a signet ring (No. 531) and elsewhere, cow-heads not to be mistaken. He then points to the traditional worship, from the first, of Hera in Argolis; and he asks us to connect these facts with the use of *Boöpis* (cow-eyed) as a staple epithet of this goddess in the poems; and he might add, with her special guardianship of Agamemnon in his interests and his personal safety (*Il.* i. 194-222).

"This appears to me a reasonable demand. We know that upon some of the Egyptian monuments the goddess Isis, mated with Osiris, is represented in human figure with the cow's head. This was a mode of exhibiting deity congenial to the spirit of an Egyptian [3] immigration,[4]

---

[10] In the *Academy* of 10th January, 1874.

[11] Professor Sayce is not of my opinion. He thinks that, if Greek, the name Μυκῆναι would be derived from μυχός. But I think there can be no doubt regarding the derivation from μυκᾶν, perf. μέμυκα, μεμυκέναι, this active form being exclusively used in Homer, and having undoubt-edly been used also in a pre-Homeric time. Professor Max Müller writes me on this subject as follows :—"I do not venture to speak posi-tively about the name of Μυκῆναι. Words end-ing in ηνη are derived both from nouns, like ὑηνός, ψεφηνός, and from verbs, like τιθήνη. Philologically, therefore, a derivation of Μυ-κῆναι from μυκάω is not impossible. But names of towns are ticklish subjects for etymologists. Professor Curtius, of Leipzig, admits a possible etymology of Μυκῆναι and Μυκάλη from μύσσω. All I can say is, that your etymology from μυκάω is equally possible, but no more."

[1] See my *Mycenae*, Plate A, figs. *a, b, d;* Plate B, figs. *e* and *f;* Pl. C, fig. *k;* Pl. D, fig.

n, o, p; and pp. 216 and 217, Nos. 327 and 328; p. 218, Nos. 329, 330; p. 309, No. 471; p. 360, No. 531; p. 362, No. 541.   [2] Pp. vi.–viii.

[3] M. Burnouf observes to me : "It is not only in Egypt that the gods were represented with animal heads : the Vêdas perpetually repre-sent divine beings by animals; the sun by a horse, mother earth by a cow, &c. And do not the ten incarnations of Vishnu also present striking examples of this fact? It was there-fore a custom of the greatest human races in antiquity."

[4] "Since this preface was put in type, the fragments of an ostrich egg, originally mistaken for an alabaster vase, have been tested and verified. This object seems to afford a new indication of pre-historic relations between My-cenae and Egypt." But Professor Sayce observes on this that "it rather points to Phoenician trade. Elsewhere ostrich eggs, covered with stucco, have been found among Phoenician remains."

such as might, compatibly with the text of Homer, have taken place some generations before the *Troïca*. But it was also a mode against which the whole spirit of Hellenism, according to the authentic type of that spirit supplied in the poems, utterly revolted. We find there a Hera, who wore, so to speak, the mantle of Isis, besides carrying the spoils of one or more personages enrolled in the Golden Book of the old Pelasgian dynasties. Nothing could be more natural than a decapitation of the Egyptian Isis, not penally but for her honour. She might consequently appear with the human head ; but, not to break sharply with the traditions of the people, the cow-head, and even the cow-figure, might nevertheless be retained as symbols of religion. And the great Poet, who invariably keeps these symbols so to speak at arms' length, in order that he may prevent their disparaging the creed of which he was the great doctor, might nevertheless select from the bovine features that one which was suited to his purpose, and give to his Hera, who was never a very intellectual deity, the large tranquil eye of the cow. The use of the epithet for Hera in Homer is not, indeed, exclusive, and I admit that he may have inherited that use. But, though not exclusive, it is very special ; and this speciality is enough to give a sensible support to the doctrine of our famous explorer."

Another honoured friend, and one of the highest authorities in ancient Oriental literature, M. François Lenormant, writes : [5] " Schliemann is right to insist upon the fact, that the greater part of the rude *figurines* found by him at Mycenae represent positively a cow. In Argolis we are in the very land in which, in the remotest antiquity, there prevailed the worship of a female deity in the form of a cow, who afterwards, reduced to the proportions of a heroine, became Iö in poetical fable." Further on, M. Lenormant admits that Heré's epithet Boôpis can only refer to the primitive cow-head of this goddess.

I may here refer to a principle conspicuous in Homer's language, which at once disposes of the most formidable objection to my view. When asked, whether Homer himself conceived of Athené as a owl-headed monster, and of her image in her temple on the Pergamus as nodding its owl-head in response to the prayers of the Trojan women,—I reply, in the words already used in the Preface to *Troy and its Remains*, that " one of the most striking characters of his language is the use of *fixed epithets*," which are constantly repeated without any regard to their fitness on each particular occasion of their use. Thus, like his heroes in general, Aegisthus is still " blameless " (ἀμύμων)[6] even in the mouth of Zeus, denouncing his crimes as the climax of human impiety. And as of persons, so of things : for example, the colonnade (αἴθουσα) round the front court of the palace, as the resort of the people who came to wait upon the king by day, obtained the fixed epithet of ἐρίδουπος, " very noisy ; " and so by night guests were lodged " under the *very noisy* colonnade " (ὑπ' αἰθούσῃ ἐριδούπῳ), a somewhat inhospitable entertain-

---

[5] *Gazette des Beaux Arts*, Feb. 1, 1879, p. 108.

[6] *Od.* i. 29. Whether or no " blameless " be the exact meaning, the epithet is at all events one of dignity and respect.

ment, if the *sense* of the epithet held good![7]   This point, which many
modern scholars have overlooked, was recognized by the poetic instinct of
Alexander Pope. Speaking, in the Preface to his *Iliad*, of the importance
of placing ourselves at the poet's point of view, so remote in every respect from our own, he says : " This consideration may further serve to
answer for *the constant use of the same epithets* to his gods and heroes ;
such as the ' *far-darting* Phoebus,' the ' *blue-eyed* Pallas,' the ' *swift-footed*
Achilles,' &c., which some have censured as impertinent, and tediously
repeated. Those of the gods . . . . had contracted a *weight and veneration*
from the rites and solemn devotions in which they were used : they were
*a sort of attributes with which it was a matter of religion to salute them on
all occasions, and which it was an irreverence to omit.*"

I think it not out of place to repeat here what I have written on this
important subject : [8] " It is not difficult to prove that Hera had originally
a cow's face, from which her Homeric epithet βοῶπις was derived.   When,
in the battle between the gods and the giants, the former took the shape
of animals, Hera took the form of a white cow, ' nivea Saturnia vacca.' [9]
We find a cow's head on the coins of the island of Samos, which had the
most ancient temple of Hera, and was celebrated for its worship of this
goddess.[10]   We further find the cow's head on the coins of Messene, a
Samian colony in Sicily.[11]   The relation of Hera to the cow is further
proved by the name Εὔβοια,[1] which was the name of one of her nurses,[2]
the name of the island in which she was brought up,[3] and the name of
the mountain at the foot of which her most celebrated temple (the
Heraeum) was situated.[4]   But in the name Εὔβοια is contained the word
βοῦς.   Hera had in Corinth the epithet βουναία,[5] in which the word βοῦς
may also be contained.[6]   Cows were sacrificed to Hera.[7]   The priestess
rode in a car drawn by bulls to the temple of the Argive Hera.[8]   Iö,
the daughter of Inachus, the first king of Argos, was changed by Hera
into a cow.[9]   Iö was priestess of Hera,[10] and she is represented as the
cow-goddess Hera.[1]   Iö's cow-form is further confirmed by Aeschylus.[2]

[7] *Od.* iii. 399 ; vii. 345.

[8] See my *Mycenae*, pp. 19–22.

[9] Ovid. *Metam.* v. 330 :

" Fele soror Phoebi, nivea Saturnia vacca."

[10] Mionnet, *Descr. des Méd. Ant.* Pl. lxi. 6.

[11] Millingen, *Anc. Coins of Greek Cities*, tab. ii. 12.

[1] Paus. ii. 17, § 2 : τὸ γὰρ δὴ ὅρος τοῦτο
ὀνομάζουσιν Εὔβοιαν, λέγοντες Ἀστερίωνι γενέσθαι τῷ ποταμῷ θυγατέρας Εὔβοιαν καὶ Πρόσυ-
μναν καὶ Ἀκραίαν, εἶναι δὲ σφᾶς τροφοὺς τῆς
"Ηρας.

[2] Plut. *Quaest. Conviv.* iii. 9, § 2 : δοκοῦσιν
αὐτῷ καὶ οἱ παλαιοὶ τοῦ μὲν Διὸς δύο ποιεῖν
τιθήνας, τὴν Ἴτην καὶ τὴν Ἀδράστειαν, τῆς δὲ
"Ηρας μίαν τὴν Εὔβοιαν.

Etym. Mag. 388. 56.

[3] Plut. *Frag. Daedal.* 3 : ἱστοροῦσιν τὴν "Ηραν
ἐν τῇ Εὐβοίᾳ τρεφομένην ἔτι παρθένον, ὑπὸ τοῦ
Διὸς κλαπῆναι.

[4] Paus. *ibid.*

[5] Paus. ii. 4, § 7 : ταύτῃ καὶ τὸ τῆς Βουναίας
ἐστὶν "Ηρας ἱερόν. ·

[6] Professor Sayce thinks the etymology of
βουναία is from βουνός, the temple being on
a hill on the way to Acrocorinthus.

[7] Paus. ix. 3, § 4 : αἱ μὲν δὴ πόλεις καὶ τὰ
τέλη θήλειαν θύσαντες τῇ "Ηρᾳ βοῦν ἕκαστοι
καὶ ταῦρον τῷ Διΐ, κ.τ.λ.

Hesych. s. v. ἄγαν χαλκεῖος.

[8] Herod. i. 31 : ἐούσης ὁρτῆς τῇ "Ηρῃ τοῖσι
Ἀργείοισι, ἔδεε πάντως τὴν μητέρα αὐτῶν ζεύγεϊ
κομισθῆναι ἐς τὸ ἱρόν· οἱ δέ σφι βόες ἐκ τοῦ
ἀγροῦ οὐ παρεγίνοντο ἐν ὥρῃ.

[9] Lucian. Θεῶν Διάλ. 3 :

Ζεύς. Οὐκέτι παῖς ἐκείνη ἐστίν, ἀλλὰ δάμαλις
. . . . Ζηλοτυπήσασα ἡ "Ηρα μετέβαλεν αὐτήν
(τὴν Ἰώ).

[10] Aesch. *Suppl.* 291, 292 :

Κληδοῦχον "Ηρας φασὶ δωμάτων ποτέ
Ἰὼ γενέσθαι τῇδ' ἐν Ἀργείᾳ χθονί.

Apollodor. ii. 1. 3 : φωραθεὶς δὲ ὑφ' "Ηρας, τῆς
μὲν κόρης ἁψάμενος εἰς βοῦν μετεμόρφωσε λευκήν.

[1] Creuzer, *Symbolik*, ii. 576.

[2] *Prom.* 589, Tauchn. edit. :

κλύεις φθέγμα τᾶς βούκερω παρθένου.

The Egyptian goddess Isis was born in Argos, and was identified with the cow-shaped Iö.[3] Isis was represented in Egypt as a female with cow-horns, like Iö in Greece.[4] " The cow-shaped Iö was guarded in Hera's sacred grove at Mycenae by the hundred-eyed Argus, who was killed by Hermes, by order of Zeus; and Hera next persecuted Iö by a gad-fly, which forced her to wander from place to place.[5] Thus Prometheus says: ' How should I not hear the daughter of Inachus, who is chased around by the gad-fly?'[6] But the wandering of Iö is nothing else than the symbol of the moon, which moves restlessly in its orbit. This is also shown by the very name of Iö ('Ιώ), which is derived from the root Ya (in εἶμι, 'I go'). Even in classical antiquity Iö was still frequently represented as a cow; as at Amyclae.[7] Iö continued to be the old name of the moon in the religious mysteries at Argos.[8] Apis, king of the Argive realm, was the son of Phoroneus, and thus the grandson of Inachus, and the nephew of Iö. From Apis the Peloponnesus and also Argos were called *Apia*; after his death he was worshipped under the name of Serapis.[9] According to another tradition, Apis ceded his dominion in Greece to his brother, and became king of Egypt,[10] where, as Serapis, he was worshipped in the shape of a bull. Aeschylus makes the wanderings of Iö end in Egypt, where Jove restores her to her shape, and she bears Epaphus, another name for the bull-god Apis. The cow-horns of the Pelasgian moon-goddess Iö, who became later the Argive Hera and is perfectly identical with her, as well as the cow-horns of Isis, were derived from the symbolic horns of the crescent representing the moon.[11] No doubt the Pelasgian Iö, the later Hera, had at an earlier age, besides her cow-horns, a cow's face. Hera, under her old

---

[3] Diod. Sic. i. 24, 25 : φασὶ δὲ καὶ τὸν Περσέα γεγονέναι κατ' Αἴγυπτον, καὶ τῆς Ἴσιδος τὴν γένεσιν ὑπὸ τῶν Ἑλλήνων εἰς Ἄργος μεταφέρεσθαι, μυθολογούντων τὴν Ἰὼ τὴν εἰς βοὸς τύπον μεταμορφωθεῖσαν.

Apollod. ii. 1, 3 : Ἱδρύσατο δὲ ἄγαλμα Δήμητρος, ἣν ἐκάλεσαν Ἶσιν Αἰγύπτιοι, καὶ τὴν Ἰὼ Ἶσιν ὁμοίως προσηγόρευσαν.

Hygin. 145 : " Deamque Aegyptorum esse fecit quae Isis nuncupatur."

[4] Herodot. ii. 41: τὸ γὰρ τῆς Ἴσιος ἄγαλμα ἐὸν γυναικήϊον βούκερών ἐστι, κατάπερ Ἕλληνες τὴν Ἰοῦν γράφουσι.

[5] Apollod. ii. 1, 3 : Φωραθεὶς δὲ (Ζεὺς) ὑφ' Ἥρας, τῆς μὲν κόρης ('Ιοῦς) ἁψάμενος εἰς βοῦν μετεμόρφωσε λευκήν, ... φύλακα αὐτῆς κατέστησεν Ἄργον τὸν πανόπτην. .... Διὸς δὲ ἐπιτάξαντος Ἑρμῇ κλέψαι τὴν βοῦν, μηνύσαντος ἱέρακος, ἐπειδὴ λαθεῖν οὐκ ἠδύνατο, λίθῳ βαλὼν ἀπέκτεινε τὸν Ἄργον, ... Ἥρα δὲ τῇ βοῒ οἶστρον ἐμβάλλει.

[6] Aeschyl. *Prom.* 585 :
πῶς δ' οὐ κλύω τῆς οἰστροδινήτου κόρης τῆς Ἰναχείας.

[7] Paus. iii. 18, § 13: τὰ δὲ ἐν Ἀμύκλαις θέας ἄξια .... Ἥρα δὲ ἀφορᾷ πρὸς Ἰὼ τὴν Ἰνάχου βοῦν οὖσαν ἤδη.

[8] Eustath. *ap.* Dionys. Perieg. 92, 94 : Ἰὼ γὰρ ἡ σελήνη κατὰ τὴν τῶν Ἀργείων διάλεκτον,

on which Heyne, *ad* Apollod. p. 100, says: " Fuisse suspicor nomen hoc caputque feminae cornutum symbolum Lunae apud Argivos antiquissimum." See also Jablonsky, *Panth.* ii. p. 4 ff.

[9] Apollod. ii. 1. 1 : Ἄπις μὲν οὖν εἰς τυραννίδα τὴν ἑαυτοῦ μεταστήσας δύναμιν, καὶ βίαιος ὢν τύραννος, ὀνομάσας ἀφ' ἑαυτοῦ τὴν Πελοπόννησον Ἀπίαν, ὑπὸ Θελξίονος καὶ Τελχῖνος ἐπιβουλευθείς, ἅπαις ἀπέθανε, καὶ νομισθεὶς θεὸς ἐκλήθη Σάραπις.

Schol. Lycophr. 177 : Ἄπις οὖν τυραννικῶς ζῶν ἀναιρεῖται ὑπὸ Θελξίονος καὶ Τελχῖνος, ἀφ' οὗ καὶ ἡ χώρα Ἀπία ἡ τῆς Πελοποννήσου.

Schol. Apoll. Rhod. iv. 263 : Ἀπιδανήων δέ, τῶν Πελοποννησίων, ἀπὸ Ἄπιδος τοῦ Φορωνέως.

Steph. Byz. s. v. Ἀπία.

[10] Euseb. *Chron.* pars i. pp. 96, 127, 130, ed. Aucher; Augustin. *de Civit. Dei,* xviii. 5.

[11] Diod. Sic. i. 11 : κέρατα δὲ αὐτῇ (τῇ Ἴσιδι) ἐπιτιθέασιν ἀπό τε τῆς ὄψεως ἣν ἔχουσα φαίνεται καθ' ὃν χρόνον ὑπάρχῃ μηνοειδής. Plut. *de Is. et Os.* 52, compare c. 39 : τὴν δὲ Ἴσιν οὐχ ἑτέραν τῆς σελήνης ἀποφαίνοντες καὶ τῶν ἀγαλμάτων αὐτῆς τὰ μὲν κερασφόρα τοῦ μηνοειδοῦς γεγονέναι μιμήματα. Macrob. *Sat.* i. 19; Aelian. *Hist. Anim.* x. 27 : καὶ αὐτὴν τὴν Ἶσιν Αἰγύπτιοι βούκερων καὶ πλάττουσι καὶ γράφουσιν.

moon-name Iö, had a celebrated temple on the site of Byzantium, which city was said to have been founded by her daughter Keroëssa—i.e., 'the horned.' According to Stephanus Byzantinus, it was founded by Byzas, son of Keroëssa and Poseidon.[1] The crescent, which was in all antiquity and throughout the Middle Ages the symbol of Byzantium, and which is now the symbol of the Turkish empire, appears to be a direct inheritance from Byzantium's mythical foundress, Keroëssa, the daughter of the moon-goddess Iö (Hera); for it is certain that the Turks did not bring it with them from Asia, but found it already an emblem of Byzantium. But M. Burnouf remarks that, long before Byzantium was founded, it existed in Babylonia and Assyria, where it is most frequently found; he therefore suggests that it may have thence been imported to Byzantium. Hera, Iö, and Isis must at all events be identical, also, with Demeter Mycalessia, who derived her epithet, 'the lowing,' from her cow-shape, and had her temple at Mycalessus in Boeotia. She had as doorkeeper Hercules, whose office it was to shut her sanctuary in the evening and to open it again in the morning.[2] Thus his service is identical with that of Argus, who in the morning unfastens the cow-shaped Iö, and fastens her again in the evening to the olive-tree,[3] which was in the sacred grove of Mycenae, close to the 'Ηραῖον.[4] The Argive Hera had, as the symbol of fertility, a pomegranate, which, as well as the flowers with which her crown was ornamented, gave her a telluric character.[5]

"In the same way that in Boeotia the epithet Mycalessia, 'the lowing,' a derivative from μυκᾶσθαι,[6] was given to Demeter on account of her cow-form, so in the plain of Argos the name of Μυκῆναι, a derivative from the same verb, was given to the city most celebrated for the cultus of Hera, and this can only be explained by her cow-form. I may here mention that Μυκάλη[7] was the name of the mount and promontory directly opposite to, and in the immediate neighbourhood of, the island of Samos, which was celebrated for the worship of Hera.

"In consideration of this long series of proofs, certainly no one will for a moment doubt that Hera's Homeric epithet βοῶπις shows her to have been at one time represented with a cow's face, in the same way as Athena's Homeric epithet γλαυκῶπις shows this goddess to have once been represented with an owl's face. But in the history of these two epithets there are evidently three stages, in which they had different

---

[1] O. Müller, Dorier. i. 121; Steph. Byz. s. v. Βυζάντιον: καὶ οὕτως ἐκτίσθη ἀπὸ Βύζαντος τοῦ Κεροέσσης, τῆς Ἰοῦς θυγατρός, καὶ Ποσειδῶνος.

[2] Paus. ix. 19, §4: Μυκαλησσὸν δὲ ὁμολογοῦσιν ὀνομασθῆναι διότι ἡ βοῦς ἐνταῦθα ἐμυκήσατο ἡ Κάδμου καὶ τὸν σὺν αὐτῷ στρατὸν ἄγουσα ἐς Θήβας. Professor Sayce remarks to me that here we have a reference to " Astarte with the crescent horns " of the Cadmeian Phoenicians. Europa on the bull is another form of Astarte or Ashtoreth, the Assyrian Istar.

[3] Ovid. Metam. i. 630.

[4] Apollod. ii. 1, 3: οὗτος ἐκ τῆς ἐλαίας ἐδέσμευεν αὐτήν, ἥτις ἐν τῷ Μυκηναίων ὑπῆρχεν

ἄλσει.

[5] Panofka, Argos Panoptes (1837), tab. ii. 4; E. de Cadalvène, Recueil de Méd. Gr. Pl. iii. 1; Müller, Denkmäler, xxx. 132; Duc de Luynes, Études Numismat. pp. 22–25.

[6] I again call particular attention to the fact that this verb only occurs in Homer in the active form, μυκᾶν.

[7] Professor Sayce holds Μυκ-άλη to be a Lydo-Karian and not a Greek word. But I point to the remarkable fact that we find names beginning with the syllable Μυκ- always close to a Heraeum.

significations. In the first stage the ideal conception and the naming of the goddesses took place, and in that naming, as my honoured friend Professor Max Müller rightly observed to me, the epithets were figurative or ideal; that is, natural. Hera (Iö), as deity of the moon, would receive the epithet βοῶπις from the symbolic horns of the crescent moon and its dark spots, which resemble a face with large eyes; whilst Athena, as goddess of the dawn, doubtless received the epithet γλαυκῶπις to indicate the light of the opening day, γλαυκός being one of the forms of λευκός, which is an adjective of λύκη, in Latin lux.

" In the second stage of these epithets the deities were represented by idols, in which the former figurative intention was forgotten, and the epithets were materialized into a cow-face for Hera and into an owl-face for Athena; and I make bold to assert that it is not possible to describe such cow-faced or owl-faced female figures by any other epithets than by βοῶπις and γλαυκῶπις. The word πρόσωπον for ' face,' which is so often used in Homer, and is probably thousands of years older than the poet, is never found in compounds, whilst words with the suffix -ειδης refer to expression or likeness in general. Thus, if Hera had had the epithet of βοοειδής, and Athena that of γλαυκοειδής, we should have understood nothing else but that the former had the shape and form of a cow, and the latter that of an owl. To this second stage belong all the pre-historic ruins of Hissarlik, Tiryns, and Mycenae.

" The third stage in the history of the two epithets is when, after Hera and Athena had lost their cow and owl faces, and received the faces of women, and after the cow and the owl had become the attributes of these deities, and had, as such, been placed at their side, βοῶπις and γλαυκῶπις continued to be used as epithets consecrated by the use of ages, and probably with the meaning ' large-eyed ' and ' owl-eyed.' To this third stage belong the Homeric rhapsodies."

I may add here what M. François Lenormant has written [8] regarding my interpretation of γλαυκῶπις as the epithet of Athené: " The images with owl-heads, which Schliemann sees on the idols and vases of Hissarlik, are represented by him as the type of the representation of Athené Ilias, the tutelary deity of Priam's city. In his opinion, contrary to the generally admitted ideas, Athené γλαυκῶπις was originally not a goddess ' with blue eyes ' of the colour of the luminous sky which she personifies, but a goddess ' with an owl-face,' just as Hera βοῶπις became a goddess ' with the face of a cow,' and no longer ' with large eyes,' wide open, like those of a heifer. This idea has roused a real tempest. It has appeared to some persons a sort of crime of high treason against Hellenism. That the Greeks could, at any epoch, have conceived in their imagination gods with animal heads, like those of Egypt and like certain gods of Asia, is a thing which was too great a shock to preconceived æsthetic theories of the genius of the Hellenic race, which, as was affirmed à priori, could have admitted in some figures the mixture of animal and human forms, only by always reserving to humanity the head, the noblest part, the

---

[8] Les Antiquités de la Troade; Paris, 1876, pp. 21–23.

seat of thought. I must confess that this kind of argument, belonging to a philosophy more or less shallow, touches me very little; for, in my opinion, it should give place to the reality of archæological observation. The idea of a primitive Athené with an owl-head or a Heré with a cow-head, like the Egyptian Hathor, or like certain forms of the Syro-Phoenician Astarté, has nothing which scandalizes me or appears impossible to me. It is true that there is some philological difficulty in the view that epithets like γλαυκῶπις or βοῶπις apply rather to an aspect of the face than to the eye. It appears, however, to me that this difficulty has been exaggerated; and that, for instance, when Empedocles, in a celebrated verse, qualified the moon as γλαυκῶπις, he alluded to the appearance of the lunar face, and not to an eye.

"Besides, monumental examples altogether positive prove to us that the Greeks of the remotest times, who copied their first works of art from Asiatic models, borrowed from those models, and themselves represented, figures with animal heads on human bodies. Mr. Newton has pointed out a little figure found in Cyprus, which represents a woman with a ram's head, probably an Aphrodité. On an archaic painted vase from Camirus, preserved in the Louvre, is represented a man with a hare's head. When Onatas, the great sculptor of Aegina, who lived in the beginning of the fifth century B.C., executed for the people of Phigalia the statue of their Demeter Melaena, he copied faithfully from a painting the consecrated type of the ancient image of this goddess, which had a monstrous appearance. Thus he put on the shoulders of her female body a horse's head, accompanied by serpents and other monsters. The book of the *Philosophumena*[9] has preserved to us the description of one of the symbolical paintings which decorated the family sanctuary of the sacred race of the Lycomids at Phlya in Attica. The great Themistocles had caused these paintings to be restored, and Plutarch devoted a special treatise to their explanation. Among them was represented a winged ithyphallic old man pursuing a woman with a dog's head. Herodotus says that Pan had sometimes the face as well as the feet of a he-goat, and this assertion is confirmed by a bronze figure discovered in the Peloponnesus and preserved at St. Petersburg.

"The Minotaur, who is originally the Baal-bull of the ancient Phoenician worship of Crete, always keeps his animal head in the works of the best period of Greek sculpture. A painted cylix with red figures, of the best epoch, which may be seen in the *Cabinet des Médailles*, in the collection of the Duc de Luynes, represents Dionysus-Zagreus as a child sitting on the knees of his mother Persephoné; he has a bull's head like a little Minotaur. It is, therefore, not the notion of an Athené with an owl's head which staggers me, and which could prevent my accepting Schliemann's theory, the more so as there would, properly speaking, be no question here of Greek productions, but of those of Asia Minor.

---

[9] Mr. Philip Smith remarks to me that this work, formerly ascribed to Origen, is now known to have been written by Hippolytus, bishop of Portus (at the mouth of the Tiber), in the first half of the third century after Christ.

For me the whole question is to know whether there are really owls' heads on the vases and idols of Hissarlik."

Another honoured friend, Professor Otto Keller,[10] writes as follows on the Athené γλαυκῶπις : "The attribution of the owl to Athené is explained [11] by a *jeu de mots* between γλαῦξ and γλαυκῶπις, and it is asserted that it has arisen only in a post-Homeric time, *as it were by a misunderstanding of the epithet* γλαυκῶπις. This view is certainly in a high degree far-fetched, unnatural, and improbable. The non-Hellenic origin of Athené's owl appears also to be proved by her double head at Sigeum and Miletopolis, both of which are in close proximity to Ilium.[1]. To recal a parallel case, I cite the equally non-Hellenic attribution of the mouse to Apollo Smintheus, which is also found in the Troad. The mouse loves the heat of the sun, and thus it prospers under the rays of Phoebus Apollo. The owl is first of all nothing else than the bird and symbol of night : this is its most natural signification, and of most primitive growth ; from this we have to proceed. Herewith coincides in a remarkable manner a point in which the Ilian Athené differs altogether from the common Hellenic Athené ; indeed, a certain coin of Ilium represents the Trojan Palladium as Athené Ilias (ΑΘΗΝΑΣ ΙΛΙΑΔΟΣ), having the Phrygian cap on her head ; in her right hand she brandishes the spear, in her left she holds a burning torch, whilst close to her is sitting the owl.[2] In the same manner another type of coin from Ilium represents the Palladium with the spear in the right hand, the torch in the left ; *in front of it a cow is being sacrificed.* Here is more than that far-fetched *jeu de mots* theory : as the torch illumines the darkness, so the owl's terrible eyes lighten through the night ; her eyes (ὄμματα) are γλαυκότερα λέοντος καὶ τὰς νύκτας ἀστράπτοντα (as Diodorus says of a horrible animal, iii. c. 55). Thus probably the Ilian Athené, or Até, was originally far from being that peaceful Hellenic goddess of art and industry who issued from the head of Zeus, an emanation from the supreme wisdom of the highest god. She was rather the goddess of the night and terror, also of the din of battle and the evils of war : she therefore brandishes the spear and torch, and has the owl. She has become the Amazon of Olympus on Asiatic soil, whence also the Amazons descended. I need cite no proofs for the owl as the bird of night. As a death-announcing bird, it sat on the spear of Pyrrhus when he advanced against Argos.[3] By the Ionian Hipponax [4] it is considered as the messenger and herald of death. As birds of death, two owls (γλαῦκες) sit to the right and left of a Siren, the songstress of the death-wail, on a sepulchre.[5] On a vase painting of a very ancient style (brown figures on a dead yellow ground) with figures of

---

[10] *Die Entdeckung Ilion's zu Hissarlik;* Freiburg, 1875, pp. 56, 57.

[11] Welcker, *Griech. Götterlehre*, i. 303 f.

[1] Mionnet, *Médailles nouv. Gal. myth.* 16.7, 8 ; Eckhel, *Doctr. Numm.* i. 2, 488, 458.

[2] Mionnet, Pl. 75, 6 ; see Eckhel, *Doctr. Numm.* ii. 484 ; and E. Gerhard, *Ueber die Minervenidole Athens*, Tfl. iv. 11, 12.

[3] Aelian. *Hist. Anim.* x. 37 : Ἡ γλαῦξ ἐπί τινα σπουδὴν ὡρμημένῳ ἀνδρὶ συνοῦσα καὶ ἐπιστᾶσα

οὐκ ἀγαθὸν σύμβολόν φασι, μαρτύριον δέ, ὁ Ἠπειρώτης Πύῤῥος νύκτωρ εὐθὺ τοῦ Ἄργους ᾔει, καὶ αὐτῷ ἐντυγχάνει ἥδε ἡ ὄρνις καθημένῳ μὲν ἐπὶ τοῦ ἵππου, φέροντί γε μὴν τὸ δόρυ ὀρθόν. εἶτα ἐπὶ τούτου ἑαυτὴν ἐκάθισεν, οὐδὲ ἀπέστη, δορυφοροῦσα οὐ χρηστὴν τὴν δορυφορίαν ἡ ὄρνις ἡ προειρημένη τήνδε.

[4] *Frag.* 54.

[5] Painting on a Lekythos ; Müller and Oesterley, *Denkmäler alter Kunst*, ii. 59, 751.

animals, we find, with other animals of a religious signification, bulls, panthers, winged sphinxes and griffins, and also the owl.[6] The owl also appears *as a divine being* on a vase painting of the most ancient style, surrounded by a nimbus.[7] Nor must we leave unnoticed the passage in the *Odyssey*,[8] where Athené goes off φήνη εἰδομένη, though the signification of ‘owl’ for φήνη is not ascertained with certainty. The gods of the north put on the plumage of eagles, crows, and hawks, when they are in haste; so, in Homer, Athené puts on winged shoes when speed is necessary. The winged shoes of Perseus also may originally have signified his complete metamorphosis into the bird.[9] In the Homeric language γλαυκῶπις is ‘owl-eyed’ or ‘with glancing eyes:’ the notion ‘bluish,’ found in γλαυκός, appears to belong to the post-Homeric development of the language. For the rest, I hold the whole question treated here an open one, so long as no excavations have been made in the Samian Heraeum down to the pre-Hellenic stratum, which must probably exist there also. As Schliemann has instinctively felt, it is only the parallel of the βοῶπις πότνια Ἥρη that can offer the solution of the problem.”

I may remind the reader that Professor O. Keller wrote all this in January 1875, whereas my excavations at Tiryns and Mycenae, close to the great Heraeum of Argolis, went on from the 31st July to the 6th December, 1876. As by the many hundreds of idols, of gold, silver, or terra-cotta, in the form of cows, cow-heads, or women with cow-horns or cow-heads, which I found there, I have solved for ever the problem of the βοῶπις πότνια Ἥρη, on which, as Professor Max Müller and Prof. Otto Keller *wisely* remarked, the parallel of the θεὰ γλαυκῶπις Ἀθήνη depends, my interpretation of the latter should now be universally accepted.

No. 157 represents a vase with an owl’s

No. 157. Vase with Owl’s Head. (1 : 3 actual size. Depth, 36 to 40 ft.)

---

[6] King Ludwig’s *Collection of Vases*, No. 953.
[7] Stephani, *Nimbus und Strahlenkranz*. The nimbus is considered by F. Wieseler (*Phaethon*, p. 26) to be an allusion to the brilliancy of her eyes. [8] *Od.* iii. 372.
[9] Wackernagel, ἔπεα πτερόεντα, 34.

head from the second city; but it must be distinctly understood that the neck with the owl's head was found separate and does not belong to the lower vase, on which I have merely put it, as it can thus be the better preserved. No doubt the neck has belonged, as is always the case, to a vase with the characteristics of a woman. It is hand-made, and has a dark-red colour, produced by the oxide of iron contained in the clay. It was discovered in the calcined *débris* of the burnt house, in which I found the skeleton of the woman. Owing no doubt to the intense heat to which it had been exposed in the conflagration, it is thoroughly baked. The cover may or may not belong to it. As I found it in the same house, I have put it on the head, the rather as this sort of cover with a curved handle seems to belong to the vases with owl-heads. I am confirmed in this belief by the incisions on the forepart of these covers, which, like those on the idols Nos. 205, 206, 207, 216 (pp. 334, 336), appear to indicate the hair of the goddess. On many vase-covers on which the owl's face is modelled, and which evidently belong to vases with the characteristics of a woman, the hair is indicated either by long vertical scratches or tresses in relief, on the nape of the neck; it is indicated by such vertical scratches on the idols Nos. 194, 196, 239, and on the remarkable ball Nos. 1997, 1998. The shape of the little curved handle on the vase-cover before us may probably have been copied from that of the ridge (φάλος) on the helmets, into which the crest was sunk.

I represent under No. 158 another vase of this description, which was found at the foot of the fragmentary wall of large blocks B on No. 2 (p. 24). It is much injured by fire, so that its primitive colour

No. 159. Terra-cotta Vase, with the characteristics of a woman and two handles in the form of wings. (1 : 3 actual size. Depth, 19 ft. The cover is from a depth of 42 ft.)

No. 158. Vase with Owl's Face, two female breasts, and two upright wing-like excrescences. (About 1 : 4 actual size. Depth, 48 ft.)

cannot be recognized; its handles, in the form of wings, are partly restored. The face of the bird is here represented very rudely, the eyes being put in the same line as the lower part of the beak. The curved handle of the cover is broken.

Of No. 159 only the vase-cover belongs to this second city, the vase itself to the fourth city; but this being the only vase with the female characteristics on which this small cover fits, I thought it necessary to represent it here, in order to show the reader the cover in its proper place. Of the face we see here only the eyes. The vase-cover is of a dull black colour and but very imperfectly baked. These Trojan vases with owls' faces are, as far as I know, unique; no similar ones have ever been found elsewhere. But funeral urns, with rudely-modelled human faces, have been found in the Prussian province of Pommerellen, near Dantzig. They are always found in stone boxes composed of five flat stones, hardly deserving the denomination of coffins, containing the ashes and bones of the deceased. This funeral urn stands either alone in a stone box, or in the midst of six, eight, ten, twelve, or even fourteen, empty common vases. The clay of the funeral urns is either yellow or brown or black, sometimes of good quality and well burnt, sometimes very rough and but little baked. Up to August 1875, when I visited Dantzig, there had been discovered in all fifty-seven such urns, all of them hand-made, but only thirty of them are preserved there; two are at Neu Stettin, and the remaining twenty-five are in the Berlin and other Museums. It is important to notice that, with the exception of one funeral urn with a human face found at Sprottow in Silesia, another found at Gogolin (in the district of Culm, West Prussia [10]), a third found in the province of Posen, and a fourth found in the province of Saxony, no such urn has ever been found anywhere but in Pommerellen.[1] Of course I do not speak here of the Roman urns with human faces, of which some have been found on the Rhine, and large numbers in Italy. The characteristics of the Pommerellen urns, which distinguish them from the Trojan owl-faced vases, are these: that their manufacturers have evidently always intended to represent the human face, however roughly and incompletely; that they never have either the wing-like excrescences or the female organ or breasts, which are nearly always conspicuous on the Trojan vases; that they have always been used as funeral urns, whereas the Trojan vases can, on account of their small size, never have been employed for such purposes, and have probably only served as idols or sacred vases; and, finally, that they have covers in the form of common caps, whereas the Trojan vases have covers in the shape of helmets, on which the female hair is often indicated. And with regard to the age of these Pommerellen face-vases, the glass beads with which they are ornamented, and the iron with which they are constantly found, cannot possibly authorize us to ascribe to them a higher antiquity than the beginning of our era, or, at the very utmost, the first or the second century B.C.; whereas I now agree, I think, with all archæologists, in claiming for the Trojan vases the very remote antiquity of 1200 to 1500 B.C. I will here describe some of the human-faced vases of the Dantzig collection:—

---

[10] See the *Report of the Berlin Society of Anthropology, Ethnology, and Pre-historic Archæology*, Session of Jan. 18, 1879, p. 2.

[1] Professor Virchow kindly informs me that he has proved that a series of transitions into "ear- and cap-urns" can be followed up from the province of Pommerellen to the river Oder.

1. A vase with two eyes, a nose, but no mouth, and two ears, which have three perforations ornamented with bronze rings, on which are fastened beads of glass and amber. The ornamentation of the neck is formed by six stripes of incised ornaments representing fish-spines. Below is the monogram of an animal with six legs. The cap has also incised ornaments.

2. A vase with *no* eyes, but a nose and a mouth; the ears have four perforations ornamented with bronze rings; a bronze chain fastened to the ears hangs down on the breast.

3. A vase with a nose and mouth, but no eyes; ears with two perforations; ear-rings of bronze with beads of amber. In this vase was found an iron breast-pin.

4. A vase with ears *not* perforated; eyes, long nose, a mouth, and a beard; a girdle indicated by points.

5. An urn with nose, eyes, and a mouth with teeth; ears with six perforations, each ornamented with a bronze ring, on which are a large number of small rings of the same metal.

6. An urn without eyes or mouth, but with a pointed nose; two ears, each with four perforations, which are ornamented with iron rings.

7. A very rough urn with eyes and nose, but no mouth; ears not perforated.

8. Urn with eyes, nose, and mouth; but ears not perforated.

9. Urn with eyes, mouth, and nose; ears with three perforations.

10. Urn with nose and eyes; no mouth; an iron ring is fastened round the vase.

11. A very remarkable urn with a falcon's beak, and large eyes; ears with three ear-rings in each, which are ornamented with brown and blue glass beads. This urn, as well as its cover, is decorated all over with incised ornaments. A certain number of the Pommerellen urns, with human faces, preserved in the Royal Museum at Berlin, of which Dr. Albert Voss is the learned keeper, are very remarkable for the brooches with spiral heads, like No. 104, or linear animals similar to those on the Trojan whorls (see Nos. 1881–1884), which we see rudely incised on them.

I cannot leave unnoticed the flagon-shaped vessels (*oenochoae*) found in the pre-historic habitations, below the deep strata of pumice-stone and volcanic ashes, in the islands of Thera (Santorin) and Therasia.

On several of these two large eyes are painted near the orifice, as well as a necklace of large dots at the base of the neck, whilst two female breasts are modelled on the upper part of the body; each breast is painted brown, and is surrounded by a circle of dots. On none of them is a human face painted or modelled; but still it is certain that it was the primitive potter's intention to imitate in these *oenochoae* the figure of a woman. From these barbarous *oenochoae* of Thera may be derived, as M. Fr. Lenormant[2] suggests, the beautifully painted *oenochoae* of Cyprus with the head of a woman.[3] But as these Cyprian vases belong to the

---

[2] *Antiquités Troyennes*, p. 43.
[3] See General Louis Palma di Cesnola, *Cyprus*; London, 1877, p. 394, Pl. xlii. xliii. pp. 401, 402.

historical period, and are perhaps a thousand years later than the owl-vases of Hissarlik, I cannot discuss them here. I would only add that on nearly all the Cyprian *oenochoae*, with a trefoil mouth, though without any characteristics of the human figure, two eyes are painted. This is not the place to discuss the Roman urns with human faces, which occur at Oehringen in Würtemberg,[4] near Mainz; at Castel, opposite Mainz;[5] and elsewhere.

In the burnt house described above, together with the remains of the woman, there was also found the tripod terra-cotta vessel in the shape of a sow, No. 160. It is of a lustrous dark-brown colour, $8\frac{2}{3}$ in. long, 7 in. high, and nearly 6 in. thick in the body. It has a projecting but closed head, and three feet. The orifice of the vessel is in the tail, which is connected with the back by a handle. Similar vessels in the form of animals, with

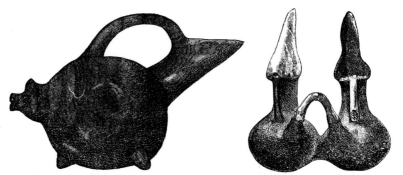

No. 160.   Terra-cotta Vessel in the shape of a Sow.
(1 : 4 actual size. Depth, 42 ft.)

No. 161.   Two conjoined *Oenochoae*. (1 : 4
actual size. Depth, about 40 ft.)

three or with four feet, are frequent in the third and fourth pre-historic cities of Hissarlik. They are very abundant in Cyprus,[6] and may be seen in the collections of Cypriote antiquities in the British Museum, the South Kensington Museum, the Louvre, and the Musée de St. Germain-en-Laye. There are also a number of similar vessels in the collections of Peruvian and Mexican antiquities in the British Museum.

Of the pottery of this second city I mention further the curious lustrous-red vessel, No. 161, in the form of two separate *oenochoae* with long and perfectly upright beak-shaped mouths; the two jugs being connected with each other at the bulge as well as by a handle. Terra-cotta vessels, with the same system of separate jugs connected at the bulge, occur in all the subsequent pre-historic cities of Hissarlik, and we shall have to pass several more of them in review. Vessels of terra-cotta made on the same principle are found in Rhodes, in Egypt, and in Cyprus. The collection of antiquities from a tomb at Ialysus, in the British Museum, contains four conjoined cups; the Egyptian collection, two conjoined flasks; the collections of Cypriote antiquities, both in the British Museum

[4] O. Keller, *Vicus Aurelii*, 1871, Pl. vii. 2.
[5] L. Lindenschmit, *Die Alterthümer unserer heidnischen Vorzeit;* Mainz, 1860.

[6] General di Cesnola's *Cyprus;* London, 1877, Plate viii.

and in the South Kensington Museum, contain vessels forming two conjoined flasks with one handle.   Another vessel with three or four
conjoined cups is represented by General di Cesnola.[7]   The small collection of pre-historic antiquities, found under the deep layers of pumice-
stone and volcanic ashes in Thera, preserved in the French School at
Athens, contains also two conjoined jugs with a trefoil mouth.   I may
also mention a vessel formed of two pitchers, joined both at the bulge and
by a handle, in the Egyptian Collection in the Louvre.   A vessel with
three conjoined cups is certainly also indicated by the object No. 3 on
Pl. xii. in Dr. Victor Gross's Atlas of antiquities found in the Lake-
habitations of Moeringen and Auvernier in Switzerland.   I may also
mention a vessel with two conjoined flasks in the Peruvian Collection in
the British Museum.   Professor Virchow kindly informs me that similar
conjoined vessels are very common in the ancient tombs in the provinces
of Lusatia (Lausitz) and Posen.

No. 162 is a lustrous-black vase, $9\frac{1}{2}$ in. high, with a long tubular hole
for suspension on each side.   The body, of globular form, is ornamented
with incised zigzag lines ; the neck is very wide, in the form of a chimney,
and ornamented with incised dots ; the bottom is flat.

No. 162.   Vase with tubular holes for suspension. Ornamentation : zigzag and points.
(About 1 : 4 actual size.   Depth, 42 ft.)

No. 163.   Tripod Vase, with incised ornamentation, and
a similar system for suspension.
(1 : 4 actual size.   Depth, about 42 ft.)

No. 163 represents a lustrous dark-brown tripod, with tubular holes
for suspension ; the long chimney-like neck has an incised ornamentation,

---

[7] *Cyprus*, p. 406, No. 25.

resembling fish-spines. A similar tripod-vase, of a dull blackish colour, with incised circular bands, is represented under No. 164.

No. 164. Globular Tripod Vase, with tubular holes for suspension. Ornamentation of circular bands. (1 : 4 actual size. Depth, 35 ft.)

No. 165. Globular Vase, with tubular holes for suspension. Ornamentation: triangles. (1 : 4 actual size. Depth, 35 ft.)

No. 165 is a very pretty little dark-yellow vase of an almost globular shape, which has also tubular holes for suspension and an incised ornamentation of triangles.

All the vases of the second city which we have hitherto passed in review are hand-made; but wheel-made pottery occurs here also, though rarely. A wheel-made vase, for example, is shown under No. 166; it is a

No. 166. Wheel-made Tripod Vase, with incised bands and tubular holes for suspension. (About 1 : 4 actual size. Depth, 35 ft.)

tripod of a blackish colour, with incised circular bands, and has tubular rings for suspension. The cover may probably not belong to this vase. All these vases I can only represent, not compare with others, as no vases of anything like a similar type occur elsewhere. But to my list of the collections in which vases with vertical loopholes for suspension occur (see p. 222) I have to add the Museum of Stockholm, in which there are three vases, found in Dolmens of the Stone age, which are ornamented with incised patterns; two of them having on each side two, the third on each side four, vertical perforations, for suspension with a string. I saw in the Museum of Copenhagen, besides the vase already mentioned,[8] two vases with incised patterns, having on each side two vertical tubular loopholes, which are not in projections, as on the Trojan vases, but in the clay of the body of the vase itself; both of them have also tubula loopholes in the covers, which correspond with those in the body. There must have been a time when similar vases with holes for suspension were in more general use in Denmark, for I saw in the same museum sixteen vase-covers of the same system.

---

[8] See No. 100, p. 20, in J. J. A. Worsaae's *Nordiske Oldsager*.

Under No. 167 I represent a handsome black hand-made vase with two handles; under No. 168, a dull brownish wheel-made pitcher or goblet,

No. 167.   Black Jug, with two handles.
(About 1 : 4 actual size.   Depth, 39 ft.)

No. 168.   Double-handled Pitcher or Goblet.
(Nearly 1 : 3 actual size.   Depth, 39 ft.)

No. 169.   Oval Vase, with three handles.
(Nearly 1 : 4 actual size.   Depth, 42 ft.)

No. 170.   Large lustrous-black Vase, with two handles
and pointed foot.   (1 : 6 actual size.   Depth, 33 ft.)

likewise with two handles. No. 169 is a lustrous dark-red wheel-made vase of oval form, with three handles. As it has a convex bottom, it cannot stand without support.

The shapes of these last three vessels are very frequent here, but I have not noticed them in other collections. As on most vases with handles the ends of these latter project slightly on the inside of the vessels, it is evident that the handles were only made after the vases had been modelled, and that holes were then cut in them in which the handles were fastened.

No. 170 is a hand-made lustrous-black vase, with a pointed foot and two handles, between which on each side is a projecting decoration in the form of the Greek letter *Lambda*, or the Cypriote character *go*. Similar vases are rare in the second city, but very frequent in the following, the burnt city. I would suggest that the early inhabitants of Hissarlik, who used these vases with a pointed foot, must have had in their rooms heaps of sand into which they put them. Or might they perhaps have used as stands for this kind of vase the large stone discs, from 6 to 8 in. in diameter, with a round perforation in the centre, 2 to 3 in. in diameter, of which so many are found in the pre-historic cities of Hissarlik? This idea was suggested to me by Dr. Victor Gross, who, in his beautiful Atlas of the objects found in the Lake-habitations at Moeringen and Auvernier, has on Pl. xii., No. 22, put a vase with a pointed foot into a large ring, which appears to be of slightly-baked clay. But as clay rings of such large size are very rare at Hissarlik, the large perforated stone discs may have been used in their stead. Mr. Philip Smith mentions to me that in chemical laboratories in England earthenware rings are used in the same way, as supports for basins, flasks, &c.

No. 171 represents a hand-made lustrous dark-brown vessel with a convex base, two handles, and a spout in the rim.

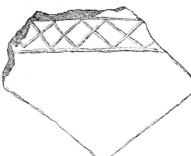

No. 171.   Vase with spout and two handles.
(1 : 4 actual size.   Depth, 48 ft.)

No. 172.   Fragment of lustrous-grey Pottery, with an
incised ornamentation.
(2 : 3 actual size.   Depth, 33 ft)

No. 174.

No. 175.

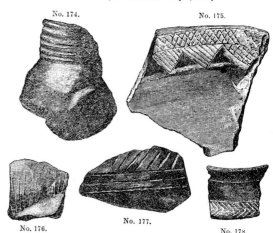

No. 173.   Fragment of lustrous-black
Pottery, with incised signs resembling
written characters.   (2 : 3 actual size.
Depth, 33 ft.)

No. 176.

No. 177.

No. 178.

Nos. 174-178.   Fragments of Pottery, with an incised ornamentation.
(Nearly hal actual size.   Depth, 42 ft.)

Nos. 172–178 represent seven fragments of lustrous yellow or black pottery, with an incised ornamentation. Nos. 172, 175, and 176 are fragments of flat bowls. No. 178 is the fragment of a small vase. The ornamentation of these four pieces is filled in with white chalk. Nos. 174 and 177 are fragments of vases. No. 173 seems to be the fragment of a vase-handle; the incised signs thereon appear to be written characters, to which I call very particular attention.[9]

In the strata of ruins of the second city there also occur the terra-cotta goblets in the form of a champagne glass, with a pointed foot and two enormous handles, like No. 179, but they are rare here. Almost all of them have a lustrous-black colour. In the three following pre-historic cities they are of a lustrous-red colour, and so frequent that I was able to collect about 150 of them. Again they occur of a dull blackish colour (see No. 1393) in the *débris* of a settlement, which succeeded the latest pre-historic city, but preceded the Aeolic Ilium, and which for this reason I call the sixth city. There consequently appears to be every probability that this form of goblet was still in common use on the

No. 179. Goblet with two handles, the Homeric δέπας ἀμφικύπελλον. (1 : 3 actual size. Depth, 35 ft.)

coast of Asia Minor at the time of Homer, who by his δέπας ἀμφικύπελλον cannot possibly mean anything else than a goblet with two handles. The universal explanation of the δέπας ἀμφικύπελλον as having an upper and a lower cup, like an hour-glass with the ends opened out, seems to me to be altogether erroneous. As a goblet of such a description could, at all events, be filled only on one side at a time, there would be no *raison d'être* for the two cups in opposite directions. Moreover, whenever a goblet with wine is presented by one person to another, Homer clearly always meant it to be understood that it is a δέπας ἀμφικύπελλον, namely, that it is double-handled, and that, being presented by the one handle, it is received by the other. I may mention, besides, that no goblet with an upper and a lower cup has ever yet been found, while I found at Troy twenty differ-ently-shaped terra-cotta goblets with two handles, among them one of gold, and at Mycenae a large number of double-handled goblets, of terra-cotta or gold, all of which can be nothing else than δέπα ἀμφικύπελλα. I think, therefore, that Aristotle was wrong in his theory, that the ἀμφι-κύπελλον had the shape of a bee's cell:[10] " The cells for the honey and for the drones have openings on both sides; for on one bottom are two cells, like those of the *amphikypella*—the one inward, the other outward."

The best judge, nay the highest authority, for the form of the Homeric δέπας ἀμφικύπελλον must necessarily be Homer himself; and, according to him, the δέπας ἀμφικύπελλον is always synonymous with ἄλεισον ἄμφωτον,

---

[9] The inscription is discussed by Professor Sayce in his Appendix.

[10] *Hist. Animal.* ix. 27: Αἱ δὲ θυρίδες καὶ αἱ τοῦ μέλιτος καὶ αἱ τῶν σχαδόνων, ἀμφίστομοι· περὶ μίαν γὰρ βάσιν δύο θυρίδες εἰσίν, ὥσπερ τῶν ἀμφικυπέλλων, ἡ μὲν ἐντός, ἡ δ' ἐκτός.

a "two-eared goblet" (literally, "with an ear *on both sides*," for this is the exact meaning of ἀμφί). Thus, for instance, in a passage of the Odyssey, *one and the same goblet* is called twice δέπας, once ἄλεισον, and once δέπας ἀμφικύπελλον:[11] "Then he gave them part of the entrails, and poured wine in a golden goblet (δέπας), and, pledging her with outstretched hand, he called upon Pallas Athené, daughter of Aegis-bearing Zeus : ' Pray now, O stranger, to king Poseidon, because to him is sacred the meal at which you find us, as you come here. And after having made libations and prayed, as is the custom, then give the cup (δέπας) of sweet wine also to this man to make a libation ; for I think that he also prays to the immortals ; because all men stand in need of the gods. But he is younger (than thou art) and of my age. I therefore give the golden goblet (ἄλεισον) first to thee.' Having spoken thus, he put the cup (δέπας) of sweet wine into her hands, and Athené was pleased with the prudent just man, because he had given her first the golden goblet (ἄλεισον), and she at once offered many prayers to king Poseidon : ' Hear, O earth-containing Poseidon, do not refuse us, who beseech thee to accomplish these deeds. Above all, to Nestor and his sons give glory; and afterwards to others grant a gracious recompense, to all the Pylians, for the magnificent hecatomb. Grant also. to Tele-machus and to me to return after having accomplished that for which we came hither in the swift black ship.' Thus she prayed and fulfilled all herself. She then gave to Telemachus the beautiful double-handled cup (δέπας ἀμφικύπελλον)."

See further *Od.* xxii. 8–11 :[1] " He spake, and directed the bitter arrow against Antinous. He was indeed about to lift a beautiful golden double-eared goblet (ἄλεισον ἄμφωτον); and had already seized it with his hand that he might drink of the wine."

See again *Od.* xxii. 17, where the very same goblet, which in verses 9 and 10 was called ἄλεισον ἄμφωτον, is simply called δέπας : " He sank sidewards, and the cup (δέπας) fell from his hand."[2]

See further *Od.* xxii. 84–86, where a δέπας ἀμφικύπελλον is mentioned, which is not indeed the identical ἄλεισον ἄμφωτον spoken of before and called also simply δέπας, but which is most assuredly of an identical form, namely, a goblet with two handles :—

---

[11] *Od.* iii. 40–63 :
δῶκε δ' ἄρα σπλάγχνων μοίρας, ἐν δ' οἶνον ἔχευεν
χρυσείῳ δέπαϊ · δειδισκόμενος δὲ προσηύδα
Παλλάδ' Ἀθηναίην, κούρην Διὸς αἰγιόχοιο ·
" Εὔχεο νῦν, ὦ ξεῖνε, Ποσειδάωνι ἄνακτι ·
τοῦ γὰρ καὶ δαίτης ἠντήσατε, δεῦρο μολόντες.
αὐτὰρ ἐπὴν σπείσῃς τε καὶ εὔξεαι, ἣ θέμις ἐστίν,
δὸς καὶ τούτῳ ἔπειτα δέπας μελιηδέος οἴνου
σπεῖσαι · ἐπεὶ καὶ τοῦτον ὀΐομαι ἀθανάτοισιν
εὔχεσθαι · πάντες δὲ θεῶν χατέουσ' ἄνθρωποι.
ἀλλὰ νεώτερός ἐστιν, ὁμηλικίη δ' ἐμοὶ αὐτῷ ·
τοὔνεκα σοὶ προτέρῳ δώσω χρύσειον ἄλεισον."
Ὣς εἰπών, ἐν χερσὶ τίθει δέπας ἡδέος οἴνου ·
χαῖρε δ' Ἀθηναίη πεπνυμένῳ ἀνδρὶ δικαίῳ,
οὕνεκα οἷ προτέρῃ δῶκε χρύσειον ἄλεισον.
αὐτίκα δ' εὔχετο πολλὰ Ποσειδάωνι ἄνακτι ·

" Κλῦθι, Ποσείδαον γαιήοχε, μηδὲ μεγήρῃς
ἡμῖν εὐχομένοισι τελευτῆσαι τάδε ἔργα.
Νέστορι μὲν πρώτιστα καὶ υἱάσι κῦδος ὄπαζε,
αὐτὰρ ἔπειτ' ἄλλοισι δίδου χαρίεσσαν ἀμοιβήν
σύμπασιν Πυλίοισιν ἀγακλειτῆς ἑκατόμβης.
δὸς δ' ἔτι Τηλέμαχον καὶ ἐμὲ πρήξαντα νέεσθαι,
οὕνεκα δεῦρ' ἱκόμεσθα θοῇ σὺν νηῒ μελαίνῃ."
Ὣς ἄρ' ἔπειτ' ἠρᾶτο, καὶ αὐτὴ πάντα τελεύτα ·
δῶκε δὲ Τηλεμάχῳ καλὸν δέπας ἀμφικύπελλον.

[1] Ἦ, καὶ ἐπ' Ἀντινόῳ ἰθύνετο πικρὸν ὀϊστόν.
ἤτοι ὁ καλὸν ἄλεισον ἀναιρήσεσθαι ἔμελλεν,
χρύσεον ἄμφωτον, καὶ δὴ μετὰ χερσὶν ἐνώμα,
ὄφρα πίοι οἴνοιο.

[2] ἐκλίνθη δ' ἑτέρωσε, δέπας δέ οἱ ἔκπεσε
χειρός.

" And, rolling over with the table, he fell staggering; and he poured the viands on the ground and the double-handled goblet (δέπας ἀμφικύπελλον)." [3]

By the above citations we have therefore proved, that in Homer a δέπας is identical with ἄλεισον and with δέπας ἀμφικύπελλον; further that δέπας is identical with ἄλεισον ἄμφωτον. Consequently ἄλεισον ἄμφωτον is also identical with δέπας ἀμφικύπελλον. Now, as ἄλεισον ἄμφωτον most undoubtedly means a double-handled goblet, δέπας ἀμφικύπελλον must just as undoubtedly mean a double-handled goblet. I could multiply these examples, but I think them perfectly sufficient to do away with an absurd interpretation of an important Homeric text, and to make the false theory fall to the ground, that there could ever have existed in antiquity goblets with a cup at both ends, and thus identical in form with the vessels which are to the present day used in the streets of London for measuring a penny or halfpenny worth of nuts.

But who tells us that, by comparing the bees' cells to the ἀμφικύπελλα, Aristotle had in view a vessel with a drinking cup at each end? He could only designate by ἀμφικύπελλον a thing so named, which had a real existence at his time. Now such a goblet with a cup at each end never occurs in any classical author; it has never yet been seen in sculptures or wall- or vase-paintings; no specimen of it has ever been found; and consequently it can never have existed. Besides, Aristotle does not call the object of his comparison a δέπας ἀμφικύπελλον: he merely calls it an ἀμφικύπελλον. But what does a κύπελλον mean? In Homer and other poets it is certainly a goblet, but it also means a milk-vessel in Quintus Smyrnaeus; [4] nay, Athenaeus[5] says that, according to Philetes, the Syracusans called the crumbs of bread, which remained on the table after meals, κύπελλα. I would therefore suggest that, just as now in the streets of London, so in the time of Aristotle hazel-nuts and other commodities were sold in the streets of Athens in wooden vessels in the shape of a bee-cell, which measured an obol's or two obols' worth of them, and that such a vessel was called ἀμφικύπελλον. Besides, in speaking of the shape of the Homeric δέπας ἀμφικύπελλον, Athenaeus does not even state that Aristotle compares it to the bee's cell, but he cites the opinion of Asclepiades of Myrlea, who says that ἀμφικύπελλον does not mean anything else than that the goblet is ἀμφίκυρτον.[6] But the phrase which follows can leave no doubt that the latter word signifies " with two handles," and this is confirmed by Passow's Greek Lexicon (ed. Rost and Palm). In another passage (xi. 65) Athenaeus asks: " What does κύπελλον mean? Is it identical with ἄλεισον and δέπας, or is only its name different? Or was its type different, and not like that of the δέπας and the ἄλεισον ἀμφικύπελλον, but only curved? For from the curved shape (κυφότης) the κύπελλον as well as the ἀμφικύπελλον (have their names), either because,

---

[3] . . . . . περιρρηδὴς δὲ τραπέζῃ
κάππεσε δινηθείς, ἀπὸ δ' εἴδατα χεῦεν ἔραζε
καὶ δέπας ἀμφικύπελλον.

[4] vi. 345: πλήθεϊ δ' αὖτε κύπελλα βοῶν

γλάγος ἠδὲ καὶ οἰῶν.

[5] xi. 65.

[6] Athen. xi. 24: ἀμφικύπελλον δὲ λέγων αὐτό, οὐδὲν ἄλλο σημαίνει ἢ ὅτι ἦν ἀμφίκυρτον.

being similar in shape to milk-pails, they were more narrow in the curve; or the ἀμφικύπελλα have their name, like the ἀμφίκυρτα, from their handles, because they are made of the same form. For the poet also mentions a golden ἄμφωτον." "Silenus says that the κύπελλα are ἐκπώματα, similar to the σκύφοι, as Nicander the Colophonian says, 'The swineherd distributed κύπελλα.' Eumolpus says that the κύπελλα are a kind of ποτήριον, because they are curved. Simaristus says that the Cypriotes call the double-handled ποτήριον a κύπελλον; the Cretans call the double-handled cup as well as that with four handles by the same name."[7] I may here add that δέπας, from the root δαπ, is related to δεῖπνον, and is always the goblet of the wealthier class.

The only cup discovered elsewhere, which shows any resemblance to the Trojan δέπας ἀμφικύπελλον, was found at Vulci, and is represented in Mr. George Dennis's famous work, *The Cities and Cemeteries of Etruria*, p. cxviii. No. 43. It has a pointed foot and two enormous handles, but the whole cup is not higher than the diameter of its mouth. From its resemblance to a woman's breast, Mr. Dennis identifies it with the ancient goblet called *mastos*, a name given to it by the Paphians.[8] This name (μαστός) being Greek, there can be no doubt that goblets of this form existed in Greece also; but they were probably but little in use, for the above cup represented by Dennis appears to be unique.[9]

The fanciful vase, No. 180, was found in the town-chief's house in the third, the burnt city; but as fragments of similar vases—usually of a lustrous-black colour—are abundant also in the second city, I prefer representing it here. It is 25 in. high, and has a convex bottom and two handles, besides two projections in the form of wings, at each side of which is a spiral ornament in relief. The wing-like projections are hollowed, and taper away to a point; they are, consequently, not adapted to be used as handles; nay, they would break away if a full vase were lifted by them. Are they then mere ornaments, or are they meant to show the sacred

---

[7] Athenaeus, xi. 65:

Κύπελλον. τοῦτο πότερόν ἐστι ταυτὸν τῷ ἀλείσῳ καὶ τῷ δέπαϊ, ἢ ὀνόματι μόνον διαλλάσσει;

τοὺς μὲν ἄρα χρυσέοισι κυπέλλοις υἷες Ἀχαιῶν δειδέχατ' ἄλλοθεν ἄλλος ἀνασταδόν.

ἢ διάφορος ἦν ὁ τύπος, καὶ οὐχ ὥσπερ τὸ δέπας καὶ τὸ ἄλεισον ἀμφικύπελλον οὕτω δὲ καὶ τοῦτο, κυφὸν δὲ μόνον; ἀπὸ γὰρ τῆς κυφότητος τὸ κύπελλον ὥσπερ καὶ τὸ ἀμφικύπελλον· ἢ ὅτι παραπλήσιον ἦν ταῖς πέλλαις, συνηγμένον μᾶλλον εἰς τὴν κυφότητα· ἢ ἀμφικύπελλα οἷον ἀμφίκυρτα ἀπὸ τῶν ὤτων. διὰ τὸ τοιαῦτα εἶναι τῇ κατασκευῇ. φησὶ γὰρ καὶ ὁ ποιητής 'χρύσεον ἄμφωτον.' Ἀντίμαχος δ' ἐν πέμπτῳ Θηβαΐδος·

πᾶσιν δ' ἡγεμόνεσσιν ἐποιχόμενοι κήρυκες χρύσεα καλὰ κύπελλα τετυγμένα νωμήσαντο.

Σειληνὸς δέ φησι 'κύπελλα ἐκπώματα σκύφοις ὅμοια, ὡς καὶ Νίκανδρος ὁ Κολοφώνιος· κύπελλα δ' ἔνειμε συβώτης.' Εὔμολπος δὲ ποτηρίου γένος ἀπὸ τοῦ κυφὸν εἶναι. Σιμάριστος δὲ τὸ δίωτον

ποτήριον Κυπρίους, τὸ δὲ δίωτον καὶ τετράωτον Κρῆτας. Φιλητᾶς δὲ Συρακουσίους κύπελλα καλεῖν τὰ τῆς μάζης καὶ τῶν ἄρτων ἐπὶ τῆς τραπέζης καταλείμματα.

[8] Apollod. Cyren. *ap.* Athen. xi. 74.

[9] Considering the relations, now well established, of the people of Palestine and Phoenicia with Asia Minor, it is very interesting to find, among the spoil taken by the Egyptian king Thutmes III. from Megiddo, "a great flagon with two handles, *a work of the Khal*, i.e. *Phoenicians*," which reminds us of the silver vases named in *Il.* xxiii. 741–43; *Od.* iv. 615–19. This is named among objects of gold and silver; and, later on, among the spoils of Kadesh, the capital of those very Kheta, or Hittites, whom we have already seen in connection with Troy, we find golden dishes and *double-handled jugs*, besides vessels of gold and silver *wrought in the land of Zahi*, i.e. Phoenicia. (Brugsch, *Hist. of Egypt under the Pharaohs*, vol. i. pp. 374, 379, 385, Engl. trans., 2nd ed.)

character of the vase ? On the top of it I have put the bell-shaped cover
with a double handle in the form of a crown, which was found close by,

No. 180. Large lustrous-black Vase, found in the Royal House. (About 1 : 8 actual size. Depth, 30 ft.)

and may possibly have belonged to it. Similar vase-covers, always of a
lustrous-black colour, occur in the second city, but they are rare here, as
compared with the abundance of them found in the upper pre-historic
cities, and particularly in the third or burnt city.

There was, no doubt, in the second city a vast variety of other pottery,
but I have not been able to collect more types than those I have represented, because, owing to the immense superincumbent masses of stones,
nearly all the pottery has been smashed to small fragments.

Of terra-cotta whorls, I have been able to collect a good number in the
débris of the second city, though they are far less abundant here than
in the subsequent pre-historic cities. They are also much smaller than
those of the first city, and their incised ornamentation is identical with
that of the whorls in the upper cities ; the only difference is, that all the
whorls of the second city, like those of the first, are of a black colour.

The shallow as well as the deep plates are here all wheel-made, and
precisely of the same rude fabric as those of the third city (see Nos. 461–
468, p. 408) ; the only difference being in the colour, which is here
brownish, whereas it is light yellow in the following city. In fact, except
a certain class of yellow pitchers, which are plentiful in the following
cities, and of the same rude fabric as the plates, these plates, though
wheel-made, are almost the rudest pottery found at Hissarlik. My friend
Mr. Joseph Hampel, keeper of the collection of coins and antiquities of
the Hungarian National Museum in Buda-Pesth, informs me that plates

of an identical shape and fabric have been found frequently at Magyarad in Hungary.

But there also occur in all the strata of the second city large quantities of fragments of hand-made lustrous-black deep plates; but, as has been said, none of them has here a trace of those horizontal tubular holes for suspension in the rim which characterize the bowls and plates of the first city.

I never found a trace of columns in any one of the five pre-historic cities of Hissarlik; hence it is certain that no columns of stone existed there. Moreover, the word κίων never occurs in the *Iliad*, but only in the *Odyssey*, where columns of wood seem to be meant. In a house, at a depth of about 40 ft., I found a prettily-carved and very hard piece of limestone

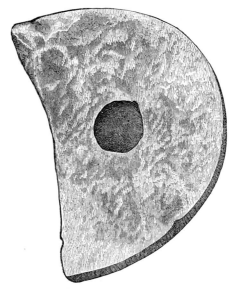

No. 181.   Block of Limestone, with a socket, in which the pivot of a door
may have turned.   (About 1 : 7 actual size.   Depth, 40 ft.)

in the form of a crescent, with a round hole 1½ in. deep in the centre of it, and I suppose that it may have been used as the support for the fold of a door ; I represent it here under No. 181.

CHAPTER VII.

THE THIRD, THE BURNT CITY.

I HAVE already shown that the site of the second city must have been deserted for a long time before it was again built upon. The new settlers began, as M. Burnouf remarks, " with levelling the *débris* upon the ruins of the Second City : they filled the cavities and ravines with stones and other material, in many places only with ashes or clay, interlaid with clay cakes (*galettes*)."

The great wall *c* on the view No. 144, which their predecessors had built on the south side, did not appear strong enough to them, because it sloped at an angle of 45°, and could, consequently, be very easily scaled. They therefore built just before it, on the south side, the large wall marked *b* on No. 144, which slopes to the south at an angle of 15° from the vertical line, whilst on the north side, where it faces the old wall *c*, it was built up vertically. In this manner there was formed between the two walls a great triangular hollow, which was filled up with earth. My excavations in this hollow have proved that it is pure earth, without any intermixture of *débris*. But, like the wall *c*, this second wall *b* does not consist altogether of solid masonry. Two walls, each from 4 to 6 ft. thick, were erected, the one vertically at the foot of the sloping wall *c*, the other at a distance of from 4 to 6 ft. to the south of the former, ascending on the south side at an angle of 75°, the space between the two walls being filled up with loose stones. In this way the outer wall, the southern face of which ascends at an angle of 75° with the horizon, or slopes at an angle of 15° from the vertical line, served as a sort of retaining wall for the loose stones, whose ponderous pressure it could probably not have sustained had it been built perpendicularly. Both these walls consist of small stones joined with clay ; they do not appear to contain a single wrought stone : but the flattest side of the stones having been put outside, the face of the wall presents a tolerably smooth appearance. The top of this wall was, like that of the wall *c*, paved with larger stones ; and, the two walls *c* and *b* being of equal height, and the hollow between them being filled up with earth to a level with the surface of the coping of the walls, a flat terrace was obtained, 100 ft. long by 40 ft. wide on the east, and 23 ft. on the west side. I found this flat space covered to the height of from 7 to 10 ft. with ruins of buildings, of slightly-baked bricks, which, having been exposed to an intense heat in the great conflagration by which this third city was destroyed, had been partly vitrified by means of the silica they contained. These bricks had suffered so much from the fire that they had decayed into formless masses, among which I rarely found entire bricks well preserved. The really enormous masses of pottery, saddle-querns of trachyte, whorls, &c., contained in these shapeless masses of bricks and red wood-ashes, can leave no doubt that they belonged to tower-like inhabited buildings, which served both as an ornament and as works of defence for the walls.

As I have before stated, to these third settlers is also due all the masonry of small stones of a reddish colour, which we see on both sides of the entrance to the gate. The work of their predecessors, the people of the second city, can easily be recognized by the large blocks of white lime-stone with which they built, and which may be seen in the lower courses of the parapets on the view No. 144. As has been before explained, to the second settlers must also be attributed the pavement of the road, consisting of large flags of white limestone, whereas to the third settlers evidently belongs the superposed new pavement of large flags of a reddish colour, which visitors will easily discern on the whole of the lower part of the road; while on the upper part of it the reddish flags have crumbled away from contact with the air, as they had been exposed to an intense heat in the conflagration. The reddish flags of this second pavement rest upon the white flags of the whole road; there is no earth or *débris* between them.

I have not been able to trace the handiwork of the third settlers in the building of the large wall, which continues from the gate in a north-westerly direction, and which is but a prolongation of the great internal wall, marked *c* on No. 144, and *a* on the little sketch No. 145. But the shapeless crumbling masses of slightly-baked bricks, mixed with large quantities of wood-ashes and stones, with which both this wall and the gate were covered to a depth of 7 and 10 ft., testify to the vastness of the works of defence which had been erected here by the third settlers; because they, and they alone of all the different pre-historic peoples who lived here, used bricks. The masses of objects found in these heaps of brick-*débris* in the gate, as well as on the wall which proceeds in a north-westerly direction from it, can leave no doubt that here, as well as on the great flat space formed by the walls *b* and *c* on No. 144, were tower-like, densely-inhabited, works of defence.

If, as there can be no doubt, the wall of large boulders on the north side (B, in the engraving No. 2, p. 24) belongs to the second city, then certainly the third city, which now occupies us, was on the east side much smaller than its predecessor, because its walls, which I have brought to light throughout their whole circuit, stop 230 ft. short of the wall of large boulders.[1] To the south, on the contrary, it is somewhat larger, because, while the prolongation of the wall *c* on No. 144 continues to the east, the prolongation of the wall *b* on the same plate continues at first in a south-easterly direction, where it forms the projection marked *d*, which was a buttress; it runs thence some distance to the east, and then bends at a sharp angle to the north-west.[2] The prolongation of this wall consists of only a few courses of slabs, which have been laid on the *débris* of the second city. For this reason, and from the consequent weakness of the

---

[1] See Plan I. (of Troy).   [2] See Plan I. (of Troy).

stone wall, the brick walls by which it was surmounted were not built directly upon it. An agglomeration of clay cakes (*galettes*) was first laid on this wall to give it greater solidity, and on these clay cakes the brick walls were built. M. Burnouf, who studied this singular sort of construction for a long time, has given me the following interesting details on the subject:—

"*Clay Cakes (galettes)*.—Yellow clay is still employed to the present day in the villages of the Troad to form the coatings of the house-walls, and even the house-walls themselves.

"The agglomeration of clay cakes (*galettes*) represented under No. 182 may be seen on the large southern wall, at the angle of the trench in

No. 182. Different Layers of Clay Cakes on the great Southern Wall, at the angle of the Trench opposite the nine Jars.

front of the nine jars.[3] It is surmounted by solid brickwork *in situ*, which constituted part of the brick wall.[4] Above this remnant of brick wall are house-walls of the following city; they are inclined, and in a ruined condition; above them is the Hellenic wall. The clay cakes (*galettes*) may be also seen to the west and east of this point. They appear to have been used in the whole of the ancient stone wall, and to have belonged to the brick city. Has the legend of Apollo and Poseidon been applied to this construction with dried clay? There are also, indeed, clay cakes (*galettes*) in the first two cities, but they are there embedded in a dark-grey mass, and not employed, as they are here, as part of a general architectural system. The jars (the nine on the south side and the three at the south-western angle of the city) rest on a soil of yellow or dark-grey or ash-coloured clay cakes (*galettes*). The same may be said of the houses of the unburnt part of the city, where we find yellow clay cakes (*galettes*) still at a depth of 3 mètres (10 ft.) below the surface of the hill. Above these clay cakes there is a stratum of grey earth, which has been formed from the *débris*, and on this stratum the last houses were built. At the north-west angle of the great rampart wall, where the last treasure was found,[5] there is also a mass of clay cakes (*galettes*) belonging to the wall, and this mass was much larger before the last excavation.

"In the gate, at the northern projection (*jambage*), the clay cakes are mixed with the stones; they are here made of yellow earth or of brown ashes, and they are covered by a burnt yellow stratum, which is derived from bricks. The mass of *débris* is composed of stones and ashes, which buried the gate in the conflagration, and have enlarged the city in that direction.

[3] See Plan I. (of Troy), s.
[4] See the engraving No. 183, which represents this corner.

[5] About twenty yards to the north of the place marked Δ on Plan I. (of Troy).

"The system of the clay cakes (*galettes*) has been applied on a large scale in the mound to the north-west, behind the quarter of the well below the Hellenic wall.[6] The clay cakes (*galettes*) are very large there, and sometimes 1 mètre (3 ft. 4 in.) long. At the eastern angle of this mound we again see these clay cakes of the common size.

"We also see clay cakes on the top of the great brick wall[7] of the city, at the north angle, where they served to obtain a solid basis for the houses which we see built upon them; we perceive the same system below the adjoining houses. But these houses, as well as the clay cakes on which they rest, belong to the following or fourth city.

"We also see clay cakes below the little walls[8] to the east of and adjoining the gate. They are mixed with black ashes and fragments of burnt bricks.

"In short, the clay cakes (*galettes*) appear to have been a system of building which was generally employed in the first three, and even in the first four, Trojan cities, but particularly in the Third City, in which they served for the large constructions."

M. Burnouf goes on to describe the remains of the brick walls of this third city; his description is so clear and precise that visitors can have no difficulty in finding them out.

"*The Brick Walls.*—No. 183 represents that portion of the brick wall which is in front of the nine jars (s on Plan I.). At A are sixteen courses

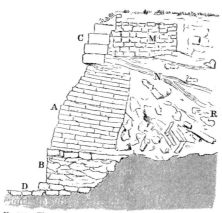

of bricks, joined with a paste made of crushed bricks. These courses of bricks reach nearly up to the Hellenic wall c. They are inclined on the outside; the mass of clay cakes (*galettes*), B, on which they rest, is 1·70 m. (5 ft. 8 in.) thick; they are separated from it by a course of limestone. The mass of clay cakes, B, rests on the large wall D, which is the circuit wall of the citadel. Later on the city was enlarged by the mounds of *débris* thrown outside the walls. R marks one of these mounds of *débris*,

No. 183. The portion of the brick Wall in front of the nine Jars.

which contains a layer of black ashes, N. M is the wall of a house which leans against the Hellenic wall c.

"This brick wall continued in an easterly direction. We find it again, with its exterior coatings, in the ramp which M. Schliemann has left standing to the west of the quadrangular Hellenic structure.[9] Here also

---

[6] This Hellenic wall is marked z o on Plan I. (of Troy); see also the engraving No. 186 (p. 311).

[7] Marked H on Sectional Plan III.

[8] In the place marked o on Plan I.

[9] This ramp is distinctly indicated by the letter T on Plan I., and by the letter R on Sectional Plan IV.

the faces of this brick wall are inclined; the latter forming, at the angle of the citadel, a large solid mass of masonry, probably a tower or a buttress.

"In the massive block of bricks at the north angle of the fortress,[10] it may be discerned, first, that the courses of bricks are inclined to that side on which the conflagration was severest, namely, to the east; secondly, that the exterior coatings on the wall indicate its thickness and direction.

"*The first massive block of bricks on the north side.*[11]—Instead of the stone wall we have here only one course of large flags, on which the brick wall rests. This course of flags passes below the first block of bricks, and penetrates below the second. It rests on a thin horizontal layer, formed of a more or less ashy earth and yellow clay. The surface of this wall is burnt.

"On the stone wall or pavement is (1) a grey or black layer 6 to 10 ctm. (2·4 to 4 in.) deep, of burnt shells; (2) a layer 2 to 3 ctm. (·8 to 1·2 in.) thick, of yellow-red brick matter; (3) the massive block of bricks (*e, a, d,* on the engraving No. 184). At the foot of the east front of the block of bricks, for a length of 1·50 m. (5 ft.) is a *coating* of a paste of crushed bricks, and of several very thin layers of fine earth, which are polished on the outer side. This coating is *in situ*, and inclined to the outside. It has sustained the action of an intense heat, whose black vapour (*buée noire*) has penetrated far into the wall. As the coating is at the foot of the massive block of bricks, and in an exact line with the course of large flags which constitutes its base, this latter was evidently the foundation of the brick construction. Above this brick construction is a layer of ashes mixed with the stones of subsequent houses, and remnants of house-walls [1] rise again on these ruins. Visitors will see this observation confirmed by examining the neighbouring houses, whose stone walls rest on ashes, which are frequently consolidated by the system of clay cakes (*galettes*).

"The north side presents a vertical white coating (*c,* in the engraving No. 184), similar to that on the east side. Like the latter, it is inclined and parallel to a third intermediate front, *b.* We therefore recognize here two parallel walls of bricks, the space between which is filled in with broken

No. 184.   The great brick Wall, North side. This engraving serves to explain the first, the second, and the third massive blocks of bricks, which are remnants of the city wall.

bricks. The whole rests on the course of large flags already mentioned. The front *d* is uncertain, as it has been demolished.

"The proportions of the walls represented in the engraving No. 184 are:—

"*The first block of bricks:*[2] from *a* to *b*, 1·17 m. (3 ft. 11 in.); from *b* to *c*, 53 ctm. (1 ft. 9 in.); from *c* to *d*, 1·37 m. (4 ft. 6·8 in.).

"*The second massive block of bricks.*—The course of large flags continues to serve as the base of the wall. The aforesaid coating of a paste of

[10] Marked H on Plan III. (Section X–Y).
[11] Marked H on Plan III.; also represented by the engraving No. 184.

[1] Marked T on Plan III. (Section X–Y).
[2] The three blocks of bricks are marked II on Plan III. (Section X–Y).

crushed bricks continues here on the east front of the wall; as does also
the filling up of the interval between the two walls with crushed bricks.
Also the above-mentioned white coating c, as well as the wall c d, whose
front d is demolished, continues here. We likewise see here on the top of
the brick construction the same layer of ashes mixed with the stones of
subsequent houses, and on these again remnants of later house-walls.[3]

"*The third massive block of bricks.*—We see here the continuation of the
coated front a, against which lean ashes which have fallen from above.
Behind the coating we perceive the continued action of the black vapour
(*buée noire*) of the intense heat which has penetrated far into the wall. We
see the continuation of the fronts b and c, between which the space is filled
with *débris*. The mark of the black vapour (*buée noire*) below this filling
seems to prove that the interval between the two walls was empty before
the conflagration, and that it served as a passage. The wall c d continues.
The front d does not exist in the massive block; it appears to have been
defaced by time, for on this side the bricks are *shapeless*. Outside we see
ashes, fragments of pottery, shells, fragments of bricks, &c., accumulated
against the front a.

"Having excavated between the second and third massive blocks
of bricks, I have found, on the regular level, the course of flags on which
the brick wall rests; further, the filled-up interior passage and the
coatings of the fronts.

"*Important remark.*—The east coating, which is marked a, is alone
burnt; it is, in fact, vitrified, and has behind it the marks of the very
dark black vapour (*buée noire*), which has penetrated to a great depth
between the courses of bricks. On the other hand, the coatings b and c
have not been touched by the fire. Besides, the matter which fills the
passage contains fragments of bricks, pottery, stones, bones, shells, &c.,—
all *débris* of the Trojan stratum.

"If from the first massive block of bricks we look across the great
northern trench on the other part of the town, we clearly discern the
level of the buildings. It is marked by a black layer, which descends
like black vapour (*buée noire*). Above it we perceive a yellow stratum of
matter burnt by a white heat; then a grey stratum, upon which are built
the houses of the following city. Close to the gate we see the ruins of
houses founded on a single layer of stones; in this way the large house[4]
close to the entry of the citadel has partly been built.

"The site of the city was raised *on an average* 2 to 3 m. (6 ft. 8 in. to
10 ft.) by the conflagration; it was also considerably enlarged in all directions by the enormous masses of ruins and *débris* thrown down from the
walls. What remained of the brick walls and the houses was buried in the
new soil, which was composed for the most part of ashes and bricks, and of
objects broken or defaced by the fire. This new soil is often consolidated
by clay cakes (*galettes*), or by a judicious employment of the materials
which lay on the surface. On it was built the Fourth City. I call the particular attention of visitors to the enormous mass of *débris* of the third, the

burnt city, thrown from within into and before the gate. This *débris* consists for the most part of ashes and calcined stones from the neighbouring
houses. This mass of burnt *débris* covered the gate, and increased the
city considerably to the south.
On this accumulation the new
settlers built, to the right
and left from the points A and
B (No. 185), houses the walls
of which may still be seen
in the massive block of *débris*
in front of the gate.[5] The
form of the strata of *débris*

No. 185. *Débris* of the Burnt City at the Gate.

before the gate shows a depression, which goes far to prove that the
inhabitants of the fourth city continued to go in and out by the very
same road. But this is not at all surprising, because the roads to the
country commenced and ended at this point."

The engraving No. 186 represents the north-west angle of the great
wall built by the second settlers, and which continued to be used by the

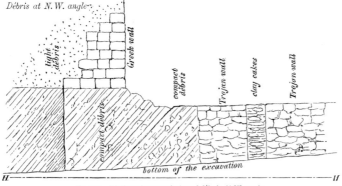

No. 186. Walls and accumulation of *débris*, N.W. angle.

inhabitants of the third, the burnt city, as the substruction for their brick
work of defence. The reader will be astonished to see in this wall a
passage filled with clay cakes, which could have no other object than to
consolidate it. To the left of the wall are slanting layers of *débris*, which
descend at an angle of exactly 45°, and of which a small portion close to
the wall contains fragments of pottery peculiar to the second city, and
must, consequently, belong to it. Then follow the slanting strata of
débris of the third, the burnt city, which visitors recognize at a glance by
their calcined condition. All these layers of *débris* are very compact, and
almost as hard as limestone. The great Hellenic wall, which we see
to the left, could therefore be erected upon them without any foundations.
To the left of the Hellenic wall are masses of light *débris* intermixed with
fragments of pottery of the Roman period.

---

[5] This massive block of *débris* is marked F on Plan I. ; see also Plan IV., Section Z'–Z'.

From this north-west angle the great wall of the second city proceeds in an easterly direction; its prolongation may be followed up as far as my great northern trench, beyond which it appears again. The third settlers, the inhabitants of the burnt city, used it only as a substruction for their brick fortifications as far as the first massive blocks of bricks, to the left in entering the great trench from the north side.[6] Whilst the great wall of the second city continues in the same direction eastward, the brick wall of the third, the burnt city, ran from this point in a south-easterly direction, as represented by the accompanying Section No. 187 and the Plan I. (of Troy). It must, however, be distinctly understood that for some distance from the block *a* on No. 187 the brick wall rested only on a single course of large unwrought flags of limestone. A little further on (probably already before the block marked G on the same Section), the great substruction wall of stones, which I have brought to light from the point B to the point D, where it was accidentally demolished, begins again. It may be seen peeping out of the ruins a few yards beyond the point G in the direction of B, but I suppose it must begin again a few yards from G, in the direction towards A.

It appears strange indeed that this great substruction wall should be missing for a short distance. Can the inhabitants have been forced by the approach of an enemy to hurry the building of the wall, so as to construct their brick wall for a short distance merely on a single course of flags?

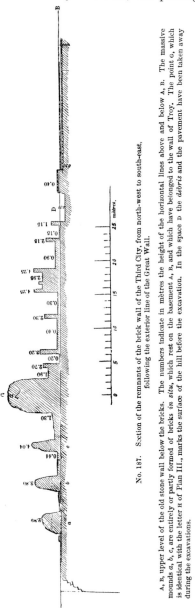

No. 187.   Section of the remnants of the brick wall of the Third City, from north-west to south-east, following the exterior line of the Great Wall.

A, B, upper level of the old stone wall below the bricks. The numbers indicate in mètres the height of the horizontal lines above and below A, B. The massive mounds *a*, *b*, *c*, are entirely or partly formed of bricks *in situ*, which rest on the basement A, B, and which have belonged to the wall of Troy. The point G, which is identical with the letter H of Plan III., marks the surface of the hill before the excavation. In the space D the *débris* and the pavement have been taken away during the excavations.

---

[6] See the engraving No. 184.   The block is marked H on Plan III. (Section X–Y).

As will be seen by the Plan I. (of Troy), this Third City was of triangular form. Its south-east corner alone has not been reached by the flames, but all the rest has been burnt. M. Burnouf remarks, that " during the conflagration the wind must have driven the flames from the south-west (that is, from the direction of the gate) to the north-east, because nearly all the treasures were found on the south-west side. In that part of the city which lies towards the middle of the eastern wall, was one of the great centres of the conflagration. In the *débris* of this centre we see, one above the other, (1) the black vapour (*buée noire*), which has deeply impregnated the soil; a heap of *débris*, which has been exposed to an intense heat, and which, in falling, has broken some large jars into fragments; a layer of ashes mixed with stones, bones, burnt shells, &c.: (2) a second time the marks of the black vapour (*buée noire*), with a series of beams; then a second layer of *débris*, reduced by an intense heat; ashes; a black line; finally, brick earth which has been exposed to an intense heat, and on the top earth which also shows the action of fire. All these *débris* together are 4 mètres (13 ft.) deep; the house from which they are derived must have been two, perhaps three, storeys high: it was sustained on the south side by a wall 1 mètre (3 ft. 4 in.) thick."

The ground-floors of the houses consist generally of clay laid on a bed of *débris*, and in this case they are nearly always vitrified and form a porous mass with a lustrous green glassy surface, but sometimes the clay is laid on large horizontal flags, and in this case they have exactly the appearance of asphalt floors. In the former case they are generally 0·40 in. to 0·60 in., in the latter 0·35 in., thick. In many cases the heat has not been intense enough to vitrify more than the surface of the ground-floors, and in this case the rest resembles pumice-stone in appearance and hardness.

For a very long distance on the north side there was, at a depth of from 26 to 30 ft., a sort of vitrified sheet, which was only interrupted by the house-walls, or by places where the clay had been laid on flags. All the floors of the upper storeys, and even the terraces on the top of the houses, consisted of beams, laid close together and covered with a similar thick layer of clay, which filled all the interstices between the beams, and was made to present a smooth surface. This clay seems to have been more or less fused in the great catastrophe by the burning of the beams, and to have run down; in fact, only in this manner can we explain the presence of the enormous mass of vitrified lumps in the ruins, which are either shapeless or of a conical form, and often from 5 to 6 in. thick. My lamented friend, the late Staff-surgeon Dr. Edward Moss, who, as before mentioned, when on board H.M.S. *Research* in Besika Bay, frequently visited my excavations in October and November 1878, maintained that these vitrified floors had been produced by the action of intense heat on the surface of the underlying clay, the straw in the latter supplying the silica for the formation of an alumina glass. He informed me further that he exposed to a white heat a fragment of this clay, and even some of the fragments of the very coarsest pottery, and that they vitrified at the corners. But it still remains unexplained, why the clay floors

laid on the large flags should in no instance have been vitrified. I
presume that their asphalt-like appearance is merely due to the black
vapour (*buée noire*) by which they are impregnated. The action of the fire
upon them has been so great that even the flags below them bear the
marks of the intense heat to which they have been exposed; but still
the clay is black throughout, and neither baked nor vitrified. Like the
present village houses of the Troad, the Trojan houses must have had a
very thick terrace of clay to protect them against the rain, and all this clay
has contributed largely to produce the enormous accumulation of *débris*.

According to M. Burnouf's measurement, the ordinary dimensions of
the bricks of this third city are 52 ctm. × 43 × 13½ (20·8 in. × 17·2 ×
5·4). The cement with which the bricks are joined is made of brick
matter, probably of crushed bricks and water, and is generally from
0·4 in. to 2 in. thick. The bricks are invariably mixed with straw,
but they show different degrees of baking: some appear to have been
merely dried in the sun and not to have been baked at all; others are
slightly baked; others, of a reddish colour, are more thoroughly baked.
M. Burnouf even found some bricks in the interior of the great wall
which had been over-baked, for they are vitrified on the surface without
having been exposed to the intense heat of the conflagration. But it
must be distinctly understood that, as there were no kilns, the bricks
were baked in an open fire, and hence none of them have either the
appearance or the solidity of the worst of our present bricks. All the
bricks which have been exposed to the intense heat of the conflagration
are, of course, thoroughly baked, or rather thoroughly burnt, for they
have lost their solidity by their exposure to the intense heat.

"The architecture of the houses of this third city is," as Virchow [7]
observes, "exactly the prototype of that architecture which is still in use
in the villages of the Troad. If we ride through such a village and enter
one or more of the houses, we get a series of views which correspond with
what we see in the ancient city. But this is not surprising, for it must
be considered, in the first place, that, owing to its insalubrity, the Plain
of Troy could never be the field of a great colonization. There are neither
important remains of ancient settlements, nor are the few places now
inhabited of any significance. On the contrary, they are poor little
villages with wide lands attached. The few inhabitants have evidently
also contributed but little to introduce a new culture. They have almost
no connection with abroad; roads, in the modern sense of the word, do not
exist, and probably never have existed, in the Plain of Troy. This fact
agrees with the peculiarities of the soil, which nearly everywhere engenders
malaria. But just in proportion as a richer colonization, a more perfect
agriculture, and in general a greater development of the higher arts of
peace, are rendered difficult by the soil, in the same proportion have the
inhabitants, though they are no nomads, always preferred the occupation
of the herdsman. This is the second circumstance which explains the

---

[7] See his Lecture to the Anthropological Congress at Strassburg, Aug. 13, 1879, and his
Beiträge zur Landeskunde der Troas; Berlin, 1879.

continuance of primeval habits. Herdsmen have slighter pretensions to domestic settlement than agriculturists and artisans. They live much in the open air ; the house is of secondary interest to them. The herds of the Trojans consist, to the present day, just as Homer described them, of a multitude of horses, sheep, and goats. Horned cattle, and especially hogs, are out of all proportion rarer. But horses are still bred in such multitudes, that the Homeric description of the wealth of king Erichthonius, who had 3000 mares, is still applicable to certain regions. There are probably in the Troad more horses than men; it is, consequently, never difficult to get a horse.

" Under such circumstances, and as if it were an expression of the conservative disposition of the population, the *ancient architecture* has been preserved. On the levelled soil the house-walls of unwrought quarry-stones are generally built up to a little more than a man's height. These walls enclose store-rooms which are used as cellars, as well as stables for domestic animals. Sheep and goats are not housed in such stables ; for the winter and very bad weather there are half-open shanties or sheds, under which they are driven. Even camels remain in the open air ; they may be seen lying in large troops in the night in the courtyards or in the streets, and on the public places, always with those wooden fastenings on the back, on which saddle and luggage are put. Stables are, therefore, only kept for horses and cows, as well as sometimes for hogs.

" Above this stone ground-floor is raised the storey containing the habitation, the *bel étage* proper. Its walls consist, as they consisted of old, of clay bricks, which far exceed in size those we are accustomed to see. They are large quadrangular plates, sometimes a foot in length and breadth, and from 3 to 4 in. thick ; commonly but slightly baked, or dried in the sun. The clay of which they are made has been previously, and often very abundantly, kneaded with the cuttings of straw, which are obtained by the mode of threshing in use here. The clay is taken just as the heavy land offers it ; the dirt of the street, so abundant in wet weather, is used as cement. The substance of both bricks and cement is, therefore, not very different ; but the one may easily be distinguished from the other by the mixture of the straw cuttings with the clay bricks. These latter receive from it a lighter colour, whilst the cementing dirt exhibits a darker grey or bluish colour and a more equal quality.

" The enclosing walls of the courts and gardens are made in a like manner. Sometimes they consist of stones, and in that case they often contain fragments of ancient house or temple buildings, blocks of marble, sometimes still bearing inscriptions. But most frequently they also are made of clay bricks ; the top of the walls is protected by a cover, generally of a vegetable nature. On the shore sea-weed is employed ; in the neighbourhood of the forest, the bark of trees ; elsewhere, reeds and shrubs. These court and garden walls are commonly joined to the house-walls. As they are nearly always of much more than a man's height, the whole presents the character of a small fortress.

" Clay walls are, of course, much exposed to destruction. Fortunately, on the whole, it does not rain much in the Troad. For comparatively a long time there is dry weather, the effect of which, however, is in some degree compensated by the very constant sea-winds. Strictly speaking, there is scarcely a single wind in the Troad which is not a sea-wind; almost all winds are wet, which circumstance makes the climate, even in the hot days, very agreeable. The prevalent dry weather preserves the clay walls of the houses. They are, besides, protected by the wide projecting roof, as well as by the galleries which are built all round the *bel étage*, and particularly on the west side.

"This mode of building explains two things: there is no need for direct access to the ground-floor; people descend into it from above, as into an underground cellar. For this reason very commonly the stone walls run on without interruption, having no other entrance than the yard-gate. The access to the habitation is by a staircase, which leads at once into the house, and onto the universal verandah or terrace, which is raised upon the stone wall at the level of the *bel étage*: it is the place where part of the household work is done, and where the inmates remain in the cooler time of the day.

"Owing to the neglected condition of the country, one has not seldom the opportunity of seeing such houses in decay; in fact, modern ruins. Of this I saw the most striking example in Yerkassi Kioi, situated just opposite to Hissarlik on the western side of the plain, which always lay before our eyes as the dominating point of the landscape. There is a large old castle there. I was told that it had been built by an Armenian; but, though it had been arranged like a fortress, he had nevertheless thought it advisable to withdraw from the unsafe country. So the property had passed over for a trifle into the hands of the Turkish Government. At present it is managed as a farm on behalf of the Minister of War, or rather the chief of artillery, and partly by soldiers. The consequence is that, for the most part, the houses have been abandoned and fallen into ruins. Here, therefore, was an excellent object of comparison with Hissarlik.

"When it rains in the Troad, it pours in torrents. When the roof of a house is destroyed, the rain gradually washes down the clay bricks, and finally there remains nothing standing but the stone wall, which ultimately also begins to collapse. The ruins of Yerkassi Kioi, therefore, presented exactly the appearance of the excavations at Hissarlik.

"In the house of the king the stone walls are proportionally high and more carefully joined, but they also consist of unwrought irregular quarry-stones. This material is evidently not fetched from a distance. The whole ridge, on the last spur of which Hissarlik lies, consists of tertiary and principally fresh-water limestone, which forms horizontal strata. These can easily be broken into large fragments; and such fragments, as rude as when they come from the quarry, are used in the walls of the ancient cities of Hissarlik. Only the stones which were required for particularly important points, such as corner-stones, have been in some places a little wrought. For the rest, there is no trace of a regular manipulation, or of the working of smooth surfaces, on any of these stones. Everywhere the same rude form appears, just as it is used at the present day by the inhabitants of the Troad.

" Many of the house-walls form enclosed squares without any entrance; others have a door. The former were, therefore, evidently stores, into which access was only possible from above; that is, from the house. In these more or less cellar-like recesses are the jars, which are often so large that a man can stand upright in them without being seen, and which are often ranged in rows of 4 or 6 in one cellar. Many of them have been destroyed by the falling of the houses or by the fire, and only a few have been preserved intact. In a few instances only these jars were found partly filled with burnt grain; but there can be no doubt that all of them served for the preservation of food, wine, or water. Those lower recesses must, therefore, be considered as store-rooms, in which the inmates of the houses put all they needed for their sustenance. The habitation proper was evidently on the *bel étage*, and, therefore, in rooms whose walls consisted essentially of bricks. But one thing remained for some time unintelligible to me. In several places we found in the walls large quadrangular or cubical hollow places, which contained large masses of burnt matter, particularly calcined vegetables. The enigma was solved when I saw the internal arrangement of the present houses, in which the fireside is still established in a niche of the house-walls. There can, consequently, be no doubt that the firesides were arranged in the same manner in the third or burnt city of Ilium.

" But, in many places, parts of the clay brick walls form shapeless masses. This has been produced in a twofold manner. One part has been exposed to the conflagration, and has been changed by it in very different degrees. We see there all the transitions from the common effects of fire to complete combustion. Most frequently the clay masses have been fused to a glassy flux. In proportion to the vehemence of the heat, the fusion has penetrated to various depths. For the most part, the clay bricks have only externally a sort of surface glaze, but sometimes the interior is also vitrified, or has even become a sort of pumice-stone, like sponge, full of blisters. Finally, in many places there has occurred only that little change which is produced by the baking of our bricks. These burnt masses have a great extent. It is in the highest degree surprising to see what piles of them lie one upon the other. It must have been a fearful conflagration which has destroyed nearly the whole city.

" The other kind of change which the bricks have undergone has been their disintegration, such as I saw in its first stage at Yerkassi Kioi. When the roofs had fallen in or had been burnt, and when the masonry had been freely exposed to the influences of the atmosphere, the clay bricks of the walls were gradually softened, disintegrated, and dissolved, and from them has been essentially formed the greater part of the unstratified masses of earth, which, to the wonder of all who see them, have in some places accumulated to enormous masses, and have pushed themselves in between the remnants of the buildings.

" In all the strata of ruins and *débris* of Hissarlik there is found a

large mass of remnants of food. Some of these are better, others worse
preserved. The best preserved of all are the Conchylia. I have made, as
far as possible, a complete collection of all the species which occur, and
M. von Martens has had the kindness to identify them.[8] A glance at this
collection suffices to show that the Trojans were very dainty. There are
oysters and sea-mussels, especially oysters in such masses that whole
strata consist almost exclusively of them. This cannot astonish us. We
must consider what a quantity of oysters is required to satisfy one's
hunger at a meal. Such Conchylia are found already in the *débris* of the
first city. I even collected some specimens near the virgin soil. The
Conchylia which were eaten here in antiquity are, however, generally the
same as those which are still eaten on the shores of the Hellespont, and
which we had frequently on our table. Thus Cardium especially is much
eaten raw; on the banks of the Kalifatli Asmak I have seen at different
places whole heaps of empty shells. They are also very plentiful in the
third or burnt city, and, like the oyster-shells, they are for the most part
blackened by the fire. I seldom found closed shells. At all events, the
Cardium-shells form by far the greatest part of these kitchen remains.
But in general the oysters preponderate in the strata of all the pre-
historic cities here. It is different with the fancy shells. Apart from
certain ornamental shells, like Columbella, Trochus, and Pectunculus,
whose shells are perforated at the lock, like the shells in certain South
European caverns, the purple fish deserves particular mention. This
occurs more particularly in the highest stratum below the wall of Lysimachus, at a time when the painted pottery was in fashion. At one place
I found a whole layer formed exclusively of cut or crushed murex-shells.
Otherwise they occurred but seldom, and always mixed up with other *débris*.
Remains of fish are likewise extraordinarily abundant. Accumulations
of fish-scales and small fish-bones, vertebræ, &c., particularly of Percoidae,
formed sometimes whole layers a hand high. I found less frequently
vertebræ of very large tunny-fish and sharks. I was much surprised at
seeing that remains of tortoises were altogether missing. This animal
(according to Mr. Peters, *Testudo marginata*, Schöpf) is so plentiful in
the Troad, that one can hardly take a step in the country without seeing
it. On the banks of the rivers, in the rivers themselves, on the fields
and heaths, it can be seen in large numbers, particularly when the sun
shines; and when it is pairing time, there are most ridiculous scenes,
particularly among rivals. But just as the present Trojan never thinks
of eating tortoises or of using their shell, so was it with his predecessors
in ancient times.

" The bones of higher vertebrate animals are more abundant in the
ruins of Hissarlik. Of birds there are but few. Though I carefully
collected every bird's bone that I met with, yet I could not obtain many.
Mr. Giebel, of Halle, who has kindly identified them, recognized bones of
Cygnus olor, *Anser cinereus*, and *A. segetum*, as well as of a small kind of
Falco or Circus. These are all wild birds. I endeavoured in vain to find

---

[8] See in pp. 114–116 the names of all the species which have been collected by Prof. Virchow.

a bone of a domestic bird, especially of a domestic fowl. I believed I could the more certainly hope to find such, as I saw in Mr. Calvert's possession at Thymbra (Batak), among the objects collected at the Hanaï Tepeh, an egg, which I held to be a hen's egg. At all events, I found nothing of the kind at Hissarlik. It, therefore, appears that the domestic fowl was not used there.

"In moderate quantities, but in all the strata, occurred bones of domesticated mammalia; but not by any means in such large quantities that the inhabitants of the ancient cities could be credited with being essentially meat-eaters. Nevertheless, there could be gathered a supply of bones large enough to give specimens of them to all the museums of Europe. But as the greater part of these bones were crushed, and as it was not my principal object to make osteological investigations, I have brought away with me only a small number of bones that can be distinctly identified, especially jaw-bones. From these it can be recognized that the domestic animals chiefly represented here are the sheep and the goat, and next to them horned cattle. Of pigs, horses, and dogs I only found traces now and then. From this it is evident that, the cat excepted, all the essentially domestic animals existed, but that—as is still the case in the East, and even in Greece—oxen were only slaughtered exceptionally, and therefore that the meat which served for food was by preference taken from sheep or goats. I do not, of course, maintain that horses or dogs were eaten: their presence within the old ruins only shows that the inhabitants did not take the trouble to throw the carcases out of the city.

"Of wild mammalia, I found bones of stags and hares. Horns of fallow-deer and boar-tusks have been collected in large numbers. Generally speaking, the study of the animal matter which I collected in the strata of Hissarlik proves the stability of the Trojan manner of life with reference to the culture of husbandry. To the present day, as has been already stated, herds of sheep and goats, next to those of horses and horned cattle, form the chief wealth of the Trojans. Camels and buffaloes were probably introduced at a later period; but they are still possessed only by the more wealthy, whilst the common peasant does without them.

"From the bones were made quantities of small instruments, especially scrapers, awls, and needles. But their forms are so trivial, that they might belong with equal right to any pre-historic settlement. Nothing could be more easy than to pick out from the ruins of these ancient cities a collection of bone and stone instruments, which, if they were found alone, would suffice to allot to these strata a place among the beginnings of civilization.

"But the vegetable food found along with them, and that in a surprising quantity, proves to us that even the most ancient layers belong to a settled, that is, an agricultural population. Especially in the third, the burnt city, there are found in some places very large quantities of burnt grain, whole coherent layers, partly in their original position, but frequently in such a manner as to make it evident that, in the breaking down of the buildings, the grain fell from higher places into lower. Thus, the bottom of some of the holes, resembling fireplaces, was especially covered with large layers of carbonized grain. Among this grain the most abundant is wheat, of which very large quantities could have been gathered. The grains of it are so small that it comes very near to rye.[9] Much more rarely, but in several places at some distance from each other, I found in the burnt city, in small quantities, but also in heaps, a leguminous plant, whose calcined, roundish, angular grains reminded me somewhat of pease. But Dr. Wittmack has determined them to belong to the bitter vetch (*Ervum Ervilia*, L.). Hence may be decided the old question of the signification of the word ἐρέβινθος. Manifestly the first two syllables correspond to *Ervum*. Certainly the words *Erbse* ('pease') and ὄροβος ('chick pease')[10] belong to the same family of languages, but at an early epoch a certain distinction had been established in their employment, and the pease proper ought to be excluded from the ancient Trojan agriculture.[11]

[9] Dr. Wittmack (*Monatsschrift des Vereins zur Beförderung des Gartenbaues in den Königl. preussischen Staaten*, October 1879) has examined this wheat and recognized in it a particular variety, which he calls "Triticum durum, var. trojanum."

[10] Victor Hehn, *Kulturpflanzen und Hausthiere in ihrem Uebergang aus Asien nach Griechenland und Italien, sowie in das übrige Europa*; Berlin, 1874, p. 187.

[11] In the Appendix to his *Beiträge zur Landeskunde der Troas* Prof. Virchow proves, however, that pease (*Erbsen*) really existed at Troy. I give here a literal translation of the whole Appendix, as it contains a great deal of interesting information :—

"Somewhat late there has arrived here a parcel of seeds from the Troad, which I had ordered in order to compare them with the carbonized seeds of the *burnt* city at Hissarlik. Dr. Wittmack has had the kindness to determine them. I add here a specification of them.

"1. *Ervum Ervilia* L., *Ervilie*, lentil-vetch.

"2. *Dolichos melanophthalmus* D. C., black-eyed long bean.

"3. *Phaseolus vulgaris albus* Haberle, common white bean, of various sizes, mixed with some *Ph. vulg. glaucoïdes* Alef. (*Ph. ellipticus amethystinus*, v. Mart.), some *Ph. vulg. ochraceus* Savi, and one *Ph. vulg. Pardus carneus*, v. *Mart.* (light-coloured panther-bean). (Transitions frequently occur with beans.)

"4. *Vicia Faba* L., hog's bean, for the most part very large.

"5. *Cicer arietinum* L., *album* Alef., chick-pea, white.

"6. *Lathyrus sativus* L., chickling-vetch; white, with more or less rust-coloured dapples (in German, *Schecken*), which proceed from the navel, and cover, in some cases, the whole seed-corn. It thus shows the transition from *L. sat. albus* Alef. to *L. sat. coloratus* Alef.; but the

rust-brown dapples (in German, *Schattirung*) are also frequent on pure *L. sat. albus*.

"7. *Avena orientalis?*, *flava*, Körnicke, brown-yellow oats. Mixed with this: 1, barley ; 2, rye ; 3, *Lolium temulentum* L. ; 4, one single very small wheat-grain, of *Triticum sativum* L. ; 5, one single larger (eviscerated) grain of *Tr. durum* Desf. ; 6, a grain of *Bromus secalinus* L. ? ; 7, a fruit of *Alopecurus* ; 8, a fruit of *Anchusa* sp., belonging to the section *Buglossum* — perhaps *A. Italica* Retz, perhaps *A. Barrelieri* D. C., the granulation of the little nut being missing ; 9, a fruit of *Alsinearum* sp.

"8. *Sorghum vulgare*, Pers. *Durrha*, millet of Mauritania, white (*Andropogon Sorghum album*, Alefeld).

"9. Yellow maize (Indian corn), with 14 lines or rows, *Zea Mays autumnalis* Alef. ; clubs 24½ centimètres (nearly 10 in.) long ; below the rows are irregular, and the diameter is there 6 centimètres (2¹⁄₁₀ in.), above 3·7 centimètres (nearly 1½ in.) ; grains for the most part very regular, somewhat flatly pressed.

"10. Red maize, with 14 lines or rows, *Zea Mays rubra* Bonaf.: clubs shorter than the former, 15¼ centimètres (6⅛ in.) long : the upper end for 1½ centimètre (⅗ in.) naked ; diameter, below 5·35 centimètres (2¹⁴⁄₁₀₀ in.), above 3·1 centimètres (1²⁴⁄₁₀₀ in.).

"11. *Gossypium herbaceum* L., cotton.

"12. *Hordeum vulgare* L., *genuinum* Alef., barley, with 4 lines. With it : 1, the above-mentioned oats (No. 7) in some grains ; 2, *Sinapis arvensis* L., Ackersenf ; 3. *Triticum durum*, a grain ; 4, *Coronilla* sp. ; 5, several other weed-seeds (three grains).

"Among these seeds the pease as well as the vetch are missing. On the other hand, the *Ervilia* is represented, which was also found in the burnt city. The probability that ἐρέβινθος is to be interpreted as 'pease' would be somewhat

"The very poetical passage in the *Iliad*,[1] in which ἐρέβινθοι are men-tioned, in a metaphor taken from the process of fanning, names both this vegetable and the bean : 'As from a broad fan on a large threshing-floor black-skinned beans or pease leap forth, driven by a shrill wind and by the winnower's power.' The 'black-skinned' bean is the hog's bean (*Vicia Faba*, L.),[2] which is still cultivated in the Troad as one of the most common products of the soil. I collected an abundance of carbonized beans in different parts of the burnt city, and, in particular, very well preserved ones in a place immediately before the city wall, to the left of the gate ; whether it were that a building had fallen over the wall, or that the beans belonged to a still more ancient epoch.

"It is certainly absolutely necessary that the two kinds of testimonies, of which I am treating here, should be rigorously distinguished. It is self-evident that the testimony of the *Iliad* proves nothing directly for the culture of a vegetable by the inhabitants of ancient Ilium, and least of all in a metaphor, the prototype of which may very well have been taken from Greece. On the other hand, the testimony of the carbonized seed is a positive one. Whether the old fortress were called Ilium or not, we now know undoubtedly that wheat, beans, and *erva* were cultivated in the plain, before the great conflagration destroyed the whole city. We know this with the same certainty as we now know that sheep and goats, horned cattle, hogs and horses, were already at that time pastured in the Troad ; that hares,[3] stags and fallow-deer, geese and swans, were at that time hunted. Whether the agreement of the poem with the real con-dition of the Troad, as it was preserved for a long time afterwards, and partly up to the present day, is to be rated higher or lower, I leave to the judgment of philologists. For the historian of human progress these testimonies may at all events have some importance.

"With regard to the social condition of the ancient population, we have now the certainty : first, that they were agriculturists, which agrees with the Homeric representations ; secondly, that to a large extent they busied themselves with the breeding of cattle and fishing : this latter industry they carried on, not only in the rivers, but more particu-larly in the sea, and from both sources they derived rich results. For

---

strengthened by this, if the last parcel from Hissarlik had not contained also carbonized seeds. When these grains came before me, I held them at once to be pease. (*Zeitschr. für Ethnologie*, 1879, vol. xi. ; *Verhandlungen der anthrop. Gesellschaft*, p. 50.) But the small samples of burnt seeds which I had brought with me seemed to contradict this interpreta-tion, because Dr. Wittmack recognized only *Ervum Ervilia* L., and perhaps *Lathyrus Cicera* L. By the last parcel only has Dr. Wittmack become convinced that *Pisum sativum* L. abun-dantly exists. It can, therefore, be considered now as firmly established, *that the pease was already in use in the burnt city, if not earlier in the Troad.* Consequently the interpretation of ἐρέβινθος ought to be made in the contra-

dictory sense, and the word ought to be referred to the pease.

"At all events the old botanical dispute as to the knowledge of the pease by the ancients has now been definitely decided. Among the car-bonized seeds from Hissarlik there occurred, besides, especially hog's beans and *Triticum durum*, whereas, strange to say, barley has not been found."

[1] *Il.* xiii. 588–590 :

ὡς δ' ὅτ' ἀπὸ πλατέος πτυόφιν μεγάλην κατ' ἀλωήν
θρώσκωσιν κύαμοι μελανόχροες ἢ ἐρέβινθοι
πνοιῇ ὕπο λιγυρῇ καὶ λικμητῆρος ἐρωῇ . . .

[2] Hehn, p. 485.

[3] *Il.* x. 361 :

ἢ κεμάδ' ἠὲ λαγωὸν . . .

reasons easily to be conceived, fishing is not mentioned in the *Iliad*: if the coast was occupied by the Achaeans, it became impossible. Much more copious is the information of the *Iliad* as to the pastoral life of the ancient Trojans: the king himself had his principal wealth in the herds which his sons tended. In the main this condition has not changed much, down to the present day. The population still consists half of agriculturists, the other half of herdsmen; and fishing is carried on with success in the Hellespont, as well as in the Aegean Sea."

The late Staff-surgeon Edward L. Moss—who, as I have said, frequently gave me the pleasure of his company at Hissarlik in October and November 1878, and who for a great many days studied the osteology of this most remarkable third or burnt city—sent me the following highly interesting information from on board the ill-fated *Atalanta*, under date of 5th November, 1879:—"I cannot leave England without sending you a note about the bones I collected from the 'burnt layers' with my own hands, and which, by-the-bye, so nearly brought me to grief in the Scamander.[4] Since the animals are well known, I give the popular names: moreover, the bones are too much burnt and broken to make very certain of variety or species. Many of the bones are marked by sharp-cutting instruments, especially near their articular extremities, as if the carver had missed the joint. Others have been gnawed by dogs. The shin-bone of a deer has been used as a handle for some tool, is bored and notched at the lower end to receive a flint or bronze head, and is much worn by the hand. The marrow-bones are all broken open. The bones represent:—

"*Ox*; a small deer-like species, probably 'longifrons:'—*deer*; there are several cast antlers of red deer with the tip of the brow-tine sawn off; bones are numerous:—*goat*:—*sheep*:—*pig*; more abundant than any other bones; the large proportion of *very young* animals points to domestication; bones and tusks of large boars were common:—*dog*; part of the skull and paw:—*weasel*; a skull:—*birds* are represented by the tibia of a Teal and wing-bones of a Wader.

"*Fish*; vertebræ of Tunny, and of a small bony fish; also vertebræ of a large cartilaginous fish, and palate teeth of a Ray.

"*The mollusca* include almost all the kinds now used for food in the Levant:—*cockles*:—*oysters*:—*mussel*:—*scallop*:—*limpet*:—*razor shell*:—*whelk*. There is, in addition, a fragment of a *Trochus*; one or two specimens of a *Cerithium vulgatum*; and a *Columbella rustica*; the latter bored as if to string it.

---

[4] The Scamander being suddenly swollen by the heavy rain during Dr. Moss's visit at Hissarlik, he had, on his return, a very narrow escape. His horse having lost its footing, he abandoned the animal in order that it might return to Hissarlik, and, being an excellent swimmer, he swam through the torrent-like river and went on foot to Besika Bay. Whoever has seen the swollen Scamander with its powerful current will wonder how it was ever possible that even the best swimmer in the world could swim through it. I am a good swimmer myself, but failed to cross even the Jordan at Easter 1859, though this latter river is hardly half as broad as the Scamander, while its current is less rapid. After having escaped thousands of dangers in the Arctic seas, and after having miraculously saved himself from the Scamander, it was destined for Dr. Moss to perish in the *Atalanta*.

" I saw no human bones except those of an unborn child of about six months lying in an earthen pot, on a quantity of much-charred fragments of other bones."

Having submitted to Professor W. H. Flower, of the Royal College of Surgeons of England, eight vertebræ of fish found by me in the third or burnt city, for identification, he declares one of them to be the caudal vertebra of *Delphinus Delphis*, the common Dolphin of the Mediterranean; two others he finds to be the *dorsal vertebræ* of the Tunny (*Thynnus vulgaris*); and five he recognized to be the vertebræ of a small species of *Shark*.

A very curious petrified bone, found in the "burnt city," was submitted by me to Mr. Wm. Davies, of the Fossil Department of the British Museum, who writes to me on the subject as follows:—

" The fossil bone submitted to me for examination is a middle caudal vertebra of an extinct Cetacean, allied to the Delphinidae or Dolphin family. It is completely mineralized, and was probably obtained by its ancient owner from a Miocene tertiary deposit, either in the Troad or in Greece. Fossil remains were objects of attraction to pre-historic man, as they are occasionally found—the smaller forms frequently perforated for ornamental wear—associated with bone and flint implements, in caves and Lake-dwellings, though not always derived from deposits in the immediate locality of such dwellings."

As Dr. Moss mentions in his letter the embryo child whose bones he saw in my possession, I may here say that I found besides it, and also besides the one discovered in an urn on the virgin soil (see p. 227), the bones of two more embryo children, both together with ashes on the bottom of fractured jars. It appears wonderful that the bodies of these unborn children should have been preserved, whilst all other bodies were burnt. In the opinion of Prof. Aretaeos, who kindly recomposed the first skeleton of the embryo (as I have said before), its presence in an urn filled with human ashes can only be explained by supposing that, the mother having died from the effect of her miscarriage, her body was burnt and her ashes put into a funeral urn, into which the unburnt body of the embryo was also thrown. But if this occurred in the case of the embryo found in the first city, may we not suppose that it was a custom so general in high antiquity as to survive the first two cities, and to be still practised by the inhabitants of the third city?

As I have before mentioned,[5] besides the large street, which leads from the plain to the gate, I brought to light only one more street, or rather lane; it is 1·20 m. = 4 ft. broad, and paved with large flags of limestone.[6] Visitors will easily find it on the east side of my great northern trench. There is, besides, a passage only 2 ft. broad between the Trojan houses, running off at right angles from the street *d* to the N.E.

Among the many problems which the ruins of the burnt city present, there is one which has puzzled us very much indeed. It is the shape of a large quadrangular chest, which is most distinctly seen in the more

---

[5] See p. 54.   [6] This street is marked *d* on Plan I. (of Troy).

northerly of the two large blocks of *débris* which mark the original height of the hill before my excavations, on the east side of my great central trench, and whose height is indicated as 8 mètres.[7] It contains at its bottom a large quantity of carbonized grain; the rest of the chest-like quadrangular space being filled with ashes and bricks, which have evidently fallen from above. The shape of the chest is distinctly marked by lines of charcoal. Now the most embarrassing thing is, that the layers of grain and *débris* in the chest continue, for some distance outside of it, with no other interruption than the carbonized lines. On carefully examining the lines of charcoal, M. Burnouf found the matter to consist of a burnt texture, probably of reed, and he recognized on either side of it a layer of earth vitrified by the conflagration.

M. Burnouf now writes to me that he finds the following in the work of Xavier Raymond on Afghanistan:—" The grain is shut up in large baskets placed on wooden feet, and coated over with earth, to preserve it from the contact of the air, and to protect it against humidity; it is also preserved in large jars of raw earth, and in bags of camel's hair." M. Burnouf thinks that this account of X. Raymond might explain the above enigma. I admit that it must indeed have been a large basket in the form of a chest, coated outside and inside with earth, but I do not understand how this can explain the existence of the same strata of grain and *débris* outside and inside of the chest!

By far the most remarkable of all the houses which I have brought to light in the third, the burnt city, is undoubtedly the mansion immediately to the north-west of the gate, which I attribute to the town-chief or king: first, because this is by far the largest house of all; and secondly, because, as before stated, I found in or close to it nine out of the ten treasures which were discovered, as well as a very large quantity of pottery, which, though without painting and of the same forms as that found elsewhere, was distinguished, generally speaking, by its fabric. A good view of this royal mansion is given in the engraving No. 188, from a drawing made by my late lamented friend Dr. Edward Moss in November 1878, when the buildings in the foreground, which appear to be its dependencies, had not yet been excavated. Just in front of the entrance to the chief or king's mansion is an open place: this is the only open place in the town, and may therefore have been the Agora. This would agree with Homer, who tells us that the Trojans, young and old, were assembled in the Agora before the king's doors.[8] In another passage the poet tells us that the Trojans held a tumultuous and stormy Agora before the king's door in the Acropolis of Ilium.[9]

What the reader sees of the town-chief's mansion in the engraving are merely the walls of the ground-floor, 4 ft. 4 in. high on the average, which consist of small uncut stones joined with earth, and also (as M. Burnouf finds), " with ashes containing charcoal, shells, fragments of pottery, and

[7] See Plan III., Section X–Y.

[8] *Il.* ii. 788, 789:

οἳ δ' ἀγορὰς ἀγόρευον ἐπὶ Πριάμοιο θύρῃσιν
πάντες ὁμηγερέες, ἠμὲν νέοι ἠδὲ γέροντες.

[9] *Il.* vii. 345, 346:

Τρώων αὖτ' ἀγορὴ γένετ' Ἰλίου ἐν πόλει ἄκρῃ,
δεινὴ τετρηχυῖα, παρὰ Πριάμοιο θύρῃσιν.

broken bones; with brick-matter mixed with grey earth, and with a *magma* of yellow earth and ashes. There are also in these house-walls fragments of bricks, more or less baked, as well as fragments of large jars supplying

No. 188. Ground-floor of the Royal Mansion of Troy, in or about which Nine Treasures were found. The Building is looking south. Drawing made by Staff-surgeon Edward Moss, then of H.M.S. *Research*, late of the *Atalanta*, in which he perished.

sometimes the place of stones (in the second and third walls). The base of the walls is composed of small clay cakes, yellow earth, grey or brown or black ashes, and fragments of bricks laid in all directions. There are also large pieces of charcoal, marking the place of the beams of which the floor seems to have consisted.

" The coatings of the walls are composed of the same *magma* as the matter with which the stones are joined. The finest coatings are smoothed, not with a trowel, but with a sort of whitish-yellow clay-milk, which has left a layer as thick as paper; there are coatings of two or three such layers. This *painting*, if we may call it so, follows all the sinuosities of the coating, which itself follows those of the wall. This clay-milk has not a uniform colour; it borrows its colour from the ground which it covers; it consequently seems to have been made simply with water, with which the surface of the coating has repeatedly been washed.

" The coatings which are less fine (second chamber) are composed of the same materials, mixed with straw, of which the projections and the hollows may be seen on the surface of the coating. This process is still in use in the country.

" The walls of this house have not been built on a burnt soil, but have themselves been exposed to an intense heat in the great conflagration. The black vapour of the intense heat has here and there penetrated far into them, particularly in the lower part."

In the absence of cellars, this ground-floor served as a store-room. A similar practice of using the ground-floor as a store-room appears to have existed at the time of Homer, for we see in the *Iliad*[10] that Hecuba *descends* to the store-room, where the skilfully embroidered vestures were stored. Had the store-room been on the floor inhabited by the family, the poet would not have said that the queen descended. If asked:—Is this Priam's palace as described by Homer—" But when he came to Priam's splendid house, adorned with polished corridors, in which were fifty chambers built of polished stone, all side by side. There the sons of Priam slept with their wedded wives. Facing these on the other side of the court within were built twelve covered chambers, side by side, of polished stone. There the sons-in-law of Priam slept beside their chaste wives : "[1]—I would answer with the verse of Virgil,

" Si parva licet componere magnis."[2]

But Homer can never have seen the Troy whose tragic fate he describes, because at his time, and probably ages before his time, the city he glorifies was buried beneath mountains of *débris*. In his time public edifices, and probably also royal mansions, were built of polished stones; he therefore attributes the same architecture to Priam's mansion, magnifying it with poetic licence.

---

[10] vi. 288, 289 :

αὐτὴ δ' (Ἑκάβη) ἐς θάλαμον κατεβήσετο κηώεντα,
ἔνθ' ἔσαν οἱ πέπλοι παμποίκιλοι, ἔργα γυναικ-
    ῶν . . .
[1] *Il.* vi. 242–250 :
ἀλλ' ὅτε δὴ Πριάμοιο δόμον περικαλλέ' ἵκανεν,
ξεστῆς αἰθούσῃσι τετυγμένον—αὐτὰρ ἐν αὐτῷ
πεντήκοντ' ἔνεσαν θάλαμοι ξεστοῖο λίθοιο,

πλησίοι ἀλλήλων δεδμημένοι· ἔνθα δὲ παῖδες
κοιμῶντο Πριάμοιο παρὰ μνηστῇς ἀλόχοισιν.
κουράων δ' ἑτέρωθεν ἐναντίοι ἔνδοθεν αὐλῆς
δώδεκ' ἔσαν τέγεοι θάλαμοι ξεστοῖο λίθοιο,
πλησίοι ἀλλήλων δεδμημένοι· ἔνθα δὲ γαμβροὶ
κοιμῶντο Πριάμοιο παρ' αἰδοίῃς ἀλόχοισιν.
[2] *Georgic.* iv. 176.

This building has towards the gate a corridor 40 ft. 8 in. long by 6 ft. wide, leading to a chamber only 7 ft. 6 in. long by 4 ft. 6 in. broad, in which the ingenious Dr. Moss discovered a gutter of hemispherical form; this room is nearly filled up by a huge jar 5 ft. 6 in. high and 4 ft. 6 in. broad in the body. By a doorway only 1 ft. 10 in. wide, this chamber communicates with another and larger one, which is 12 ft. 3½ in. long and 7 ft. 4 in. broad, and contains three immense jars of precisely the same size as that just referred to, and a somewhat smaller one: the pottery of the jars is upwards of 2 in. thick. From this room we enter by a doorway, 3 ft. 2 in. wide, into a larger one, which runs parallel with the aforesaid corridor, and is 24 ft. 4 in. long and 12 ft. broad, and leads to another chamber 10 ft. long and 8 ft. broad. This is the best preserved part of the mansion, to which—as above said—must also belong the buildings which separate it from the northern part of the great wall.

This large house, as well as its dependencies to the north, was buried 9 and 10 ft. deep in mounds of bricks and yellow wood-ashes, which cannot but belong to the walls of the upper storeys, and go far to prove that these buildings had many upper floors and were perhaps five or six storeys high. I therefore do not see any reason why the mansion, with its dependencies, may not have had even more than 100 rooms, smaller or larger.

The bricks are nearly all broken; I secured, however, some entire ones, which are 2 ft. long, 1 ft. 3 in. broad, and 3½ in. thick, and which have been converted by the conflagration into a sort of baked brick. But far from rendering them more solid, the intense heat has made them for the most part very fragile, and it has more or less vitrified a vast number of them.

As I have said before, in several directions beneath the royal mansion we see the walls of a much more ancient house, which we cannot but ascribe to the second city erected on this sacred site, because all the fragments of pottery which we find in the chambers of this ancient mansion, immediately below the stratum of the third or burnt city, have on both sides that peculiar lustrous red, black, or brown colour, which is no longer found in the layers of the third or of the following cities.

One of the most curious objects ever found in my excavations is undoubtedly a distaff, 11 in. long, around which is wound lengthwise a large quantity of woollen thread, as black as coal, evidently from being charred. I discovered it in the royal mansion at a depth of 28 ft. below the surface. According to Dr. Moss, the wood of the distaff was the stem of a very young tree.

As a general rule, I may say that the stratum of this third, the burnt city, begins at a depth of from 22 to 23 ft., and reaches down to a depth of from 30 to 33 ft. But there are exceptions; as, for example, immediately outside the city, on the north-east side of the city wall,[3] we brought to light, at a depth of only 12 to 13 ft., a great many buildings

---

[3] See Plan I. (of Troy), *e e, N N, n a*.

which evidently belonged to a suburb. The enormous masses of calcined matter and partly vitrified bricks, with which the stone ground-floors of the houses were filled; as well as the pottery, all of which bore marks of the conflagration; and finally a treasure of gold ornaments, which was found there at the depth of 13 ft. on a house-wall, and which in quality and fabric perfectly agrees with the gold ornaments found in nine different places in or near the royal mansion;—all these facts leave no doubt that a suburb extended on that side. This suburb seems to have been inhabited by poor people, for the scarcity of objects found there is remarkable. On the ruins of these burnt buildings of the suburb are superimposed the buildings of the succeeding town, on which follow abruptly the vast substructions of the Hellenic city. Under the temple of Athené, of which several walls may be seen in Plan IV. (Section Z–Z, under the letter υ), the ruins and *débris* of the burnt city follow almost abruptly below these walls; a fact of which visitors will have no difficulty in convincing themselves. As before stated, we find it difficult to explain this otherwise than by supposing that the site where this temple stood was once much higher, and that it had been artificially levelled to build the edifice.

I also repeat here that all the peoples who succeeded each other on Hissarlik were in the habit of shooting a great part of their rubbish and *débris* from the slopes of the hill, partly perhaps merely to get rid of them, partly to extend the site for building upon. Besides, in the great conflagration large masses of crumbling bricks and other ruins must have fallen from the tumbling towers or houses with which the walls were surmounted, and perhaps still larger masses of *débris* of the burnt city were shot on the slope by the new settlers. For all these reasons the ruins and *débris* of the third, the burnt city, extend for some distance, and sometimes for more than 60 ft. beyond its walls. But the quantity of *débris* and rubbish shot on the slope by the people of the four subsequent towns, and consequently the increase in width of the hill of Hissarlik, has been so enormous, that even if we sank a shaft 100 ft. deep on the brink of the present north-eastern, northern, or north-western slope, we should find no *débris* at all of the burnt city; nay, we should probably find there nothing else than *débris* and ruins of the upper or Hellenic city. I cannot, I think, illustrate this better than by the accompanying engraving No. 189,

No. 189. Mound of *débris* c of Plan I. (of Troy), forming the east side of the great northern trench. This engraving represents its west side. A marks the present slope of the hill. The layers of *débris* to the left appear to date from the construction of the marble temple. The upper house-walls, as well as those near the slope, likewise belong to Novum Ilium. These walls have given way under the lateral pressure of the *débris*. The stones in the middle appear to have formed the floor of a large room.

which represents the mound of *débris* (c on Plan I., of Troy), which visitors see to the east in entering my great trench from the north.

A marks the slope to the north. The whole upper portion of this mound, as well as the upper walls and the layers indicated by slanting lines, contain ruins and *débris* of the Hellenic time. Then follow in the lowest layers of *débris* to the right, fragments of house-walls of the latest pre-historic city. There are in this mound no remains of the fourth or the third, the burnt city: to find these latter we should have to dig down at the right-hand corner, probably for 10 ft. or 20 ft. more. Thus it is not always by the depth that we can determine what belongs to the one or to the other city; for Hellenic figurines, which occur on the mound close to the surface, may be found on the slopes at a depth of 100 ft. But with the exception of the site of the temple of Athené, the layers of *débris* WITHIN the city walls succeed each other regularly; and if we take as a standard the appearance, shape, and fabric of the pottery found there in the stratum of the third, the burnt city, at a depth of from 22 to 33 ft., we may easily discover what of the pottery, found elsewhere in a greater or a lesser depth, belongs to this same city. I say we may judge from its *appearance*, because the pottery which has sustained the intense heat of the conflagration bears the most distinct marks of it and can at once be recognized.

The pottery of this third city is nearly all hand-made, and, having been baked at an open fire, it was certainly not more baked than that of all the other pre-historic cities at Hissarlik. The intense heat of the conflagration has sufficed to bake it thoroughly in a great many instances, but by no means always; nay, as we distinctly see in the fracture, by far the greater part of the pottery is not thoroughly baked. Among that thoroughly baked is certainly all the broken pottery, which was so exposed to the fire that the intense heat reached it on both sides; but wherever this has not been the case, the original baking of the pottery was only increased by the fire, still remaining incomplete in a great many instances. The conflagration, however, has sufficed to give to most of the pottery a red tinge or a lustrous light or dark red colour, from the oxide of iron contained in the clay.

In treating now of the various kinds of pottery of this third city, I begin with the owl-faced idols and vases, and I would repeatedly call very particular attention to the fact, that the idols, of which I collected about 700, are all of the same shape; that they represent in the rudest possible outlines a female form; and that, therefore, they cannot but be copies of the ancient Palladium, which was fabled to have fallen from heaven with joined feet. Now the feet cannot be imagined to be more joined than they are here, where the whole inferior part of the body is represented by a large lump. I further lay stress on the fact, that the shape of the idol is as truly as possible copied on and imitated by the vases, with the sole difference that here the characteristics of a woman are more distinctly shown. Either, therefore, the owl-headed vases were also idols; or—and this is more likely—they were sacred vases, and only used for the service of the goddess.

The assertion is gratuitous, though it has been repeatedly made, that we have here merely rude representations of a woman made by a primitive

people, who did not know how to model anything better.   But that they
were perfectly able to model symmetrical human faces, is a fact which
I could not show better than by representing here, under No. 190, a vase-

No. 190.   Head of a Vase, with Man's Head.
(Half actual size.   Depth, 26 ft.)

No. 191.   Figure of Terra-cotta.   (2 : 3 actual size.
Depth, 26 ft.)

head found in the burnt city at a depth of 26 ft., on which is modelled a
man's head with perfectly symmetrical features.   I call attention to its
Egyptian type.   The mouth and the nose are very small in proportion to
the eyes.   It is of a lustrous-brown colour, and bears the marks of the
conflagration by which it has been thoroughly baked.   The terra-cotta
figure No. 191 also represents a regular man's face; it is of a dull yellow
colour, and also thoroughly baked in the conflagration.   The remarkable
female figure of lead, No. 226, which I shall more amply discuss in the
subsequent pages, represents again a complete female figure.   I now beg
the reader to compare these two figures of men and the one of a woman
with the rude owl-faced woman on the idols Nos. 193–223, represented in
the ensuing pages; and those modelled on the vases Nos. 227, 228, 229,
231, 232, 233, 238 :—and then to consider whether there is any possibility
of admitting that a people, which could model those regular human figures,
should have been unable to make anything better than the hideous owl-
faced vases and idols, which far exceed in rudeness anything hitherto found
elsewhere.   But there were powerful reasons why they continued to make
the stone idols and the owl-faced vases always of the same rude form, and
why their successors and the successors of their successors carefully
imitated them ; nay, in the last, the uppermost pre-historic city, the
fifth in succession from the virgin soil, owl-vases as rude as No. 229 and
idols like Nos. 202–222 are even more plentiful than in any of the preceding cities.

     Why then did they continue, from the beginning to the end, to make
such monstrous representations of their tutelary deity, if they were perfectly able to represent her, both in stone and clay, in tolerable imitation
of nature ?   It was because they clung with fervent zeal to the shape of
their Palladium, which had become consecrated by the precedent of ages.
This is by no means an isolated case, peculiar to the five Trojan cities.
Very numerous Hera-idols of gold in the shape of cows or cow-heads, as
well as Hera-idols in the form of a woman with a very compressed head
and two cow-horns, were found by me in the ancient royal sepulchres of

Mycenae ;[4] for which, agreeing, I think, with all archæologists, I claim the date of 1500 to 1200 B.C. Cow-shaped Hera-idols, as well as Hera-idols in the form of a horned woman or other monstrous forms, of terra-cotta, were also found at Mycenae, in the very lowest strata outside the sepulchres and in all the successive layers, without the slightest alteration in form or even in colour.[5] Thus it is evident that the cow-shaped Hera, or Hera in the form of a horned woman, was worshipped there until the final destruction and abandonment of Mycenae. My explorations at Tiryns have brought to light similar rude idols in all the layers of rubbish which cover the site.[6] But we need not go so far back. Both in Russia and in Greece, the most archaic images of Christ and the Holy Virgin are always the most prized by all true believers, and they are objects of peculiar veneration. We cannot, therefore, wonder at seeing the Trojans of the five pre-historic cities, which succeeded each other in the course of ages on the hill of Hissarlik, copying and re-copying on their idols and sacred vases the figure of their owl-headed διϊπετές Palladium.

No. 192. Rude figure of Terra-cotta ; probably a child's toy. (About half actual size. Depth, 30 ft.)

Of idols of other forms, only two were found in the five cities ; for I hold the terra-cotta figure No. 192 to be a toy for children and no idol. Our present children would hardly model a better figure. One of the peculiar forms of idols referred to, No. 226, has to be described presently ; the second is represented under Nos. 193, 194 ; and even this latter—from the breasts and the long hair on the back—appears to represent a female goddess.

I further call attention to the idols Nos. 195 and 196, 199, 200, and 201, on which the projections on the sides are likewise indicated. If these projections on the idols are not made upright, as on the vases like No. 227, it is probably owing to their fragility, Nos. 195, 196 being a flat idol of clay, Nos. 199, 200 flat idols of bone, and No. 201 a flat idol of trachyte. I also call attention

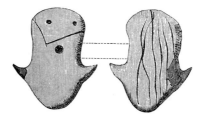

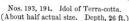

Nos. 193, 194. Idol of Terra-cotta.
(About half actual size. Depth, 26 ft.)

Nos. 195, 196. Idol of Terra-cotta.
(About half actual size. Depth, 23 ft.)

to the cover of the vase No. 227, the handle of which seems to imitate the crest of a helmet, or the little tube (λόφος) into which the horse-

[4] See my *Mycenæ*, pp. 216–218, Nos. 327, 328, 329, 330 ; Plate xvii. Nos. 94–96.
[5] See my *Mycenae*, Pl. xvii. No. 98 ; Pl. xviii.
Nos. 99–101 ; Pl. xix. Nos. 103–110 ; and Coloured Plates A–D.
[6] See my *Mycenae*, pp. 10–12, Nos. 2–11.

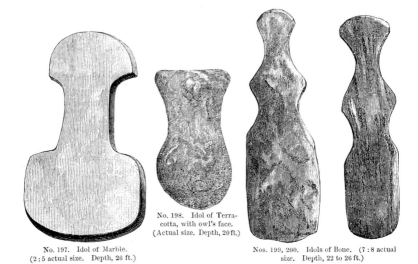

No. 198. Idol of Terra-
cotta, with owl's face.
(Actual size. Depth, 20 ft.)

No. 197. Idol of Marble.
(2 : 5 actual size. Depth, 26 ft.)

Nos. 199, 200. Idols of Bone. (7 : 8 actual
size. Depth, 22 to 26 ft.)

hair crest (ἱππουρις) was fastened; finally, to the incisions in the edge
of the vase-cover, which cannot but be meant to indicate the hair. The
hair is indicated in like manner on the forehead of the idols Nos. 205, 206,
207, 216, whereas on Nos. 194, 196, 200, and 239 it is indicated on the back.

No. 201. Idol of Trachyte. (About 1 : 3 actual size.
Depth, 26 ft.)

Nos. 193 and 194 show the front and back of a broken figure of terra-cotta; the breasts appear to indicate that a woman was intended to be represented; four strokes on the neck seem to denote her armour; only one of the arms has been preserved, which is in an upright position; two lines proceeding from the arms, and crossing each other over the body, give her a war-like appearance; her long hair is distinctly marked on the back of the head. Nos. 195, 196 represent the very rude terra-cotta idol referred to before; it is so rudely made that the eyes, for instance, are above the eyebrows, and the vulva just below the beak, but still the form is that of all the other idols: the long scratchings on the back,

indicating the hair, are very characteristic.   No. 197 represents, in about
2 : 5 size, a marble idol 5¼ in. long and 3 in. broad.   No. 198 is the above-
mentioned idol of terra-cotta, which is bulged on both sides, and has two
large eyes and an owl-beak slightly protruding.   Nos. 199 and 200 are the

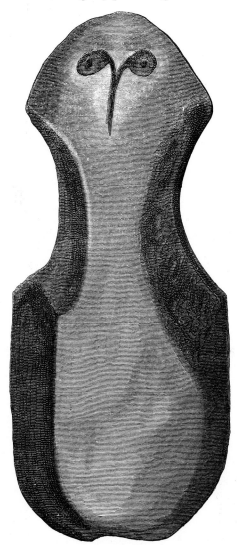

No. 202. Marble Idol. (Actual size. Depth, about 28 ft.)

above-mentioned two flat idols of bone.   Of a similar shape to No. 195, but
very thick and somewhat bulged, is the idol No. 201 (referred to above),
which is of trachyte, 9½ in. long and 6 in. broad.   This is the second
largest idol of trachyte found by me at Hissarlik, the usual material of
the idols being white marble; those of mica-schist, bone, or terra-cotta,

are comparatively rare.   No. 202 is an idol of marble, on which the owl-figure is merely marked with black clay.

No. 203 represents the fragment of a terra-cotta idol with the owl-head : the three strokes on the neck may probably be intended to indicate the necklace : the hair is indicated on the back.

No. 203.   Figure of Terra-cotta.   (Actual size.   Depth, 26 ft.)

The accompanying figures (Nos. 204–211) represent eight marble idols which certainly belong to the third or burnt city.   Of these there

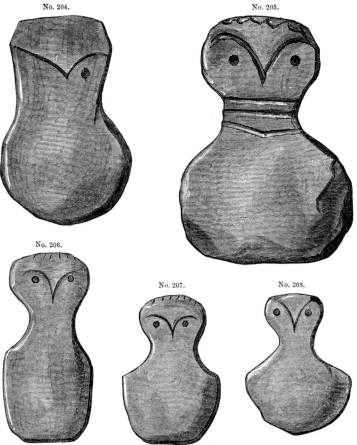

No. 204.   No. 205.

No. 206.

No. 207.   No. 208.

Nos. 204–208.   Marble Idols from the stratum of the third, the burnt city.   (Actual size.)

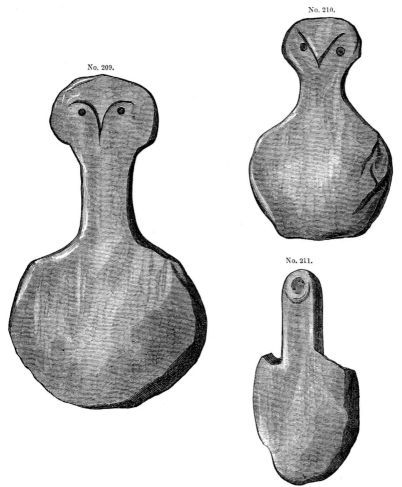

No. 210.

No. 209.

No. 211.

Nos. 209-211. Marble Idols from the stratum of the third, the burnt city. (Actual size.)

are only two—Nos. 204 and 205—on which the owl-face is engraved; on the latter the hair and the girdle are also distinctly marked. On five others the owl-face is indicated with black colour, which I take to be black clay, viz. Nos. 206–210; on the two first of these, besides the owl-face, the hair is delineated. Professor Virchow suggests that the black colour with which the owl-face is indicated may be soot. On another one, No. 211, instead of the face, there is an incised circle.

Nos. 212–220 are nine flat idols of marble, on eight of which the owl's head is incised. On Nos. 212 and 213 the girdle is indicated by a single stroke; on No. 214, by seven strokes; on No. 215, by two lines and five points; on No. 216, again, by three strokes; and on No. 218, by one stroke. Very remarkable are the ten points below the hair on the fore-

head of the idol No. 214; are they meant to indicate a frontlet? On
No. 215 we see a point on the forehead. On No. 220, the eyes seem
to be indicated by two concentric circles, and the beak by a third. Ruder

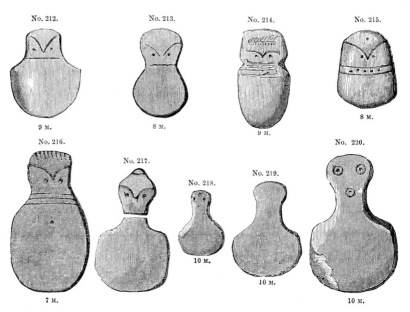

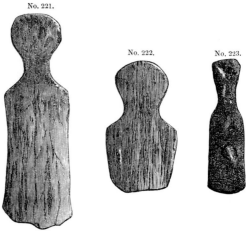

Nos. 212–220. Rude Idols of Marble. (About half actual size.)

than all the rest is the idol No. 218, on which eyes and nose are indicated
by points close to one another, that indicating the nose being above the
eyes; breasts are also indicated on this idol with points.

Under Nos. 221, 222, 223 I represent three flat idols of bone.

Nos. 221–223. Idols of Bone. (7 : 8 actual size. Depth, 26 to 32 ft.)

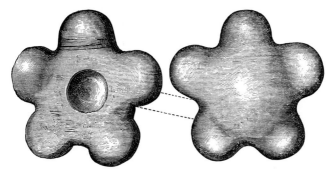

Nos. 224, 225. Remarkable object of Diorite, perhaps an Idol. (Nearly 2 : 3 actual size. Depth, 23 ft.)

Nos. 224, 225 are the front and back views of a very curious, heavy object of diorite, having in the centre a groove; it has five globular projections, around one of which are four incised lines. Can this be an idol, and can the incised lines be intended to indicate necklaces ?

I now pass to the description of the very remarkable figure No. 226, which is of lead, and was found in the burnt city at a depth of 23 ft. Professor Chandler Roberts, who, at my request, cut a minute fragment from the base of this figure to analyse it, kindly gave me the following note on the subject :— "The minute fragment of metal (weighing 0·0352 gramme) proved, on analysis, to be lead. It was submitted to cupellation, but no trace of silver could be detected by the microscope. The amount of metal examined was, however, too small to render the detection of silver probable."

To what lucky accident the preservation of this lead figure is due, I am at a loss to tell. The eyes and nose are very well proportioned; the mouth is rather too far below the nose; the chin also is too broad. The hair is well indicated on the head, on either side of which long goat-horns are represented; the right one is broken off in the middle. Around the neck we see five necklaces. The shoulders have a rectangular shape, like those of the Mycenean hunters or warriors.[7] The two hands touch the breasts, probably as a symbol of the generative power. The navel

No. 226.   Idol of Lead.   (Double size, Depth, 23 ft.)

[7] See my *Mycenae*, No. 140, p. 81; Nos. 334, 335, p. 223.

also is well indicated. The vulva is represented by a large triangle, in the upper side of which we see three globular dots; we also see two lines of dots to the right and left of the vulva. The most curious ornament of the figure is a ⊓, which we see in the middle of the vulva. I shall revert to this important sign in the subsequent pages. The feet are closely joined, but they are indicated by two dots for the knees and two small grooves at the lower extremity.

This figure is probably meant to represent an Aphrodité, which would explain the goat's horns. The ram and the he-goat were sacred to this goddess, as is well known from the Aphrodité of Scopas at Elis, and from the Ἀφροδίτη ἐπιτραγία at Athens.[8] Mr. Newton has pointed out a figure from Cyprus, representing a woman with a ram's head, probably an Aphrodité;[9] also in Di Cesnola's *Cyprus*[10] a woman is represented with two ram's horns, touching her breasts with the hands: but this is the first time the goddess has been found with two he-goat's horns. So far as we know, the only figures to which the idol before us has any resemblance are the female figures of white marble found in tombs in Attica and in the Cyclades. Six of them, which are here (at Athens) in the Museum of the Βαρβάκειον, were kindly shown to me by its keeper, my friend M. Athanasios Koumanoudes. They represent a naked woman, with her arms crossed on the stomach below the breasts; the eyes, nose, and mouth are indicated as on our lead idol; the vulva is represented on the six figures by a large triangle; the feet are separated. Four similar figures of white marble, found in ancient tombs at Trymalia on Naxos, to which my friend Professor Ulrich Köhler (Director of the Imperial German Archæological Institute at Athens) kindly called my attention, are represented on Plate v. in Dr. Karl G. Fiedler's *Reise durch alle Theile des Königreichs Griechenland;* Leipzig, 1841. On two of these figures the face is perfectly smooth, and not even the nose is indicated; on the other two the nose only is represented. All these four figures have separated feet. The triangular vulva is not indicated, but probably only because it had not been noticed by Fiedler, for it exists on all similar white marble figures found in the Cyclades, and preserved in the British Museum. M. Fr. Lenormant writes[11] of these figures as follows:—" In the most ancient sepulchres in the Cyclades, in company with stone arms (principally arrow-heads of obsidian from Milo), and with polished pottery without paintings, there are found statuettes of Parian marble, all of which represent a naked woman, with her arms crossed on the breast. They are the shapeless work of a more than barbarous art; but, in spite of their rude workmanship, it is impossible not to recognize in them an imitation of the figures of the Asiatic Venus, in the same attitude as that in which they are found in such large numbers

---

[8] Plutarch. *Theseus,* 18: Λέγεται δὲ αὐτῷ τὸν μὲν ἐν Δελφοῖς ἀνελεῖν θεόν, Ἀφροδίτην καθηγεμόνα ποιεῖσθαι καὶ παρακαλεῖν συνέμπορον. Θύοντι δὲ πρὸς θαλάσσῃ τὴν αἶγα οὖσαν, αὐτομάτως τράγον γενέσθαι· διὸ καὶ καλεῖσθαι τὴν θεὸν Ἐπιτραγίαν.

[9] F. Lenormant, *Les Antiquités de la Troade,* p. 23.

[10] Plate vi., in the second row of figures to the right.

[11] *Les Antiquités de la Troade;* Paris, 1876, p. 46.

from the banks of the Tigris to the Island of Cyprus, through the whole extent of the Chaldeo-Assyrian, Aramaean, and Phoenician world. Their prototype is the Babylonian Zarpanit or Zirbanit, so frequently represented on the cylinders and by terra-cotta idols, the fabrication of which begins in the most primitive time of Chaldea and continues among the Assyrians. The statuettes of the Cyclades in the form of a naked woman appear, therefore, to be the rude copies made by the natives, at the dawn of their civilization, from the images of the Asiatic goddess, which had been brought by Phoenician merchants."

This appears to be perfectly correct, because the three or four Babylonian Aphrodité-idols of terra-cotta preserved in the Museum of the Βαρβάκειον at Athens show a far more advanced art: on these, as on the Trojan lead-idol, the goddess touches both breasts with her hands; the vulva is indicated by the usual triangle, but this latter is ornamented with five horizontal strokes and with a large number of very small circles, which are no doubt meant to indicate gold ornaments.

Proceeding now to the terra-cotta vases of this Third, the burnt, City: the lustrous-red vase, No. 227, gives the most usual type of the hand-made owl-headed vases. They have an owl-head modelled on the upper part of the neck, which is the head of the vase itself; on the sides of the head are two projecting ears; the face is composed of a double arch representing eyebrows; below each arch is a hemispherical eye, and in the middle of the face a prominent owl's beak. The breasts are protruding and conspicuous, and the vulva[1] is represented by a large circle in relief. On some owl-vases this protruding circle is ornamented with an incised cross (see *e.g.* No. 986 and No. 991, pp. 521 and 523), which can leave no doubt as to its character. Very curious are the upright projections on the sides, which in the large vases are concave on the inside and very long, and have such sharp edges that they can never have served as. handles; besides, they are found very frequently even on those owl-vases which have large handles of the regular form. I ask if these long concave projections may not perhaps be meant to represent wings, and if, in that case, the small upright projections which we see on the sides of No. 227 can represent anything else? I call particular attention to the fact, that these upright projections are never in any case perforated; further that, at variance with all other Trojan vases, these owl-headed vases have never in any case the system of tubes for suspension.

No. 228 is the upper part of a hand-made, lustrous-red owl-headed vase, which appears to have been almost of an identical shape with No. 987 (p. 521). The mouth of these vases is in the form of a cup with two projections on the sides.

No. 229 represents another hand-made lustrous dark-brown owl-headed vase with a cover; it has two handles; the vulva is here represented between the breasts in the middle of the body.

---

[1] M. Burnouf writes to me: "I have always been of opinion, and I still believe, that this circle in relief indicates the navel; the character of the umbilical cord is very important in the ancient theory as a life-transmitting channel. See Vêda, i. 164, 34 and 35."

No. 227. Terra-cotta Vase with owl's head.
(1 : 4 actual size. Depth, about 28 ft.)

No. 228. Upper part of a Vase with
owl's head. (1 : 3 actual size. Depth, 20 ft.)

No. 229. Terra-cotta Vase, with the characteristics of a woman and owl's head.
(1 : 3 actual size. Depth, 32 ft.)

No. 230 is the fragment of a vase with an incised ornamentation representing a flower, probably a rose.

No. 231 represents one of the numerous hand-made Trojan vases, with female characteristics and a plain neck, to which belongs a cover with

an owl's face, similar to that which we see here. The vase before us is
of a dark-brown colour, and has on each side an upright projection,

No. 230. Fragment of a Vase.
(Half actual size. Depth, 26 ft.)

No. 231. Vase with the characteristics of a
woman, and Cover with owl's head.
(The Vase was found in 13, the Cover in
26 ft. depth. 1 : 3 actual size.)

from which issues on either side a spiral ornamentation in relief.
The cover is also hand-made, of a lustrous-yellow colour, and has
a handle of the usual crest-shaped form.[2] Professor Sayce observes
to me that the ornaments below the breasts of this vase resemble
the *lítui* carried by Hittite figures at Boghaz Kioi (near the Halys)
and elsewhere.

No. 232 represents the interesting hand-made black owl-faced vase, in
which quite a treasure of gold ornaments was found. I shall pass these
in review in discussing the metals of the burnt city. The wing-like
upright projections of this vase were broken off; the female breasts are
peculiarly large, and unusually wide apart; the vulva is represented by
a projection with a cavity. In fabric and colour this vase resembles a so-
called " Gesichtsurne " found in a tomb at Golencin, near Posen.[3] The
difference is that on the Golencin urn the eyes are not protruding, as on
our Trojan vase, and that each of its two ear-like projections has three
perforations for suspending ornaments in them. There is this further
difference, that the Golencin urn has neither female breasts, nor vulva,
nor wing-like projections on the sides. Besides, its bottom is flat, whilst
that of our Trojan owl-vase is convex.

---

[2] This owl-headed cover belongs to the third
or burnt city; but not so the vase, which was
found in the ruins of the fourth city. But I
represent it here, as it is the only one on which
the cover fits.

[3] See F. L. W. Schwartz, *II. Nachtrag zu den
" Materialien zur prachistorischen Kartographic*

der Provinz Posen ; " Posen, 1880, Pl. i. No. 4.
This most able dissertation having been sent
to me by its author (Professor Dr. F. L. W.
Schwartz, director of the Royal Friedr.-Wil-
helms-Gymnasium in Posen), I herewith most
gratefully acknowledge his kind attention.

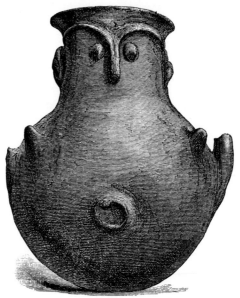

No. 232.   Terra-cotta Vase, with owl's head, in which were found a
great many gold ornaments.   (1 : 3 actual size.   Depth, 30 ft.)

The vase No. 233 is decorated on either side with a curved ornament
in the form of the Cypriote character for *ko*, or of a character which is
found in the alphabets of Caria and Pamphylia, as well as in Hittite
inscriptions: it has two handles.   The head was found separate, and does
not belong to this particular vase.   I only put it here in order to save it.

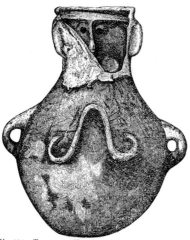

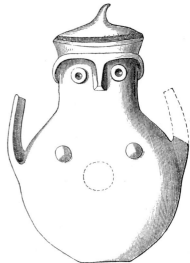

No. 233.   Terra-cotta Vase.   (1 : 5 actual size.   Depth,
26 ft.)   The ornament on the body of the vase resembles a character found in the alphabets of Caria and
Pamphylia, and in the Hittite inscriptions, as well as
one form of the character *go* or *ko* in the Cypriote
syllabary.

No. 234.   Vase with owl's face.   (1 : 4 actual size.
Depth, about 26 ft.)

No. 234 represents another hand-made vase, like No. 227, but it has been so much exposed to the intense heat of the conflagration, that it is difficult to recognize its original colour.

No. 235.   Vase with owl's face, found in the Royal House.
(1 : 8 actual size.   Depth, 28 ft.)

No. 236.   Vase Cover with owl's face.]
(About half actual size.   Depth, 27 ft.)

No. 235 represents probably the most remarkable hand-made owl-headed vase I ever found at Hissarlik. I discovered it at a depth of 8½ mètres, or 28 ft., on the ground-floor in the royal house of the third or burnt city; it is of a lustrous-brown colour, and 25 in. high.   In spite of the intense heat to which it had been exposed in the conflagration, it is not thoroughly baked. It has two breasts and two handles : a very pretty necklace is represented around the neck by a series of grooves and projecting circles. The beauty of this vase is enhanced by the scarf which we see in relief across its body.

No. 236 represents another of those pretty lustrous dark-yellow vase-covers with owl-faces, of which we showed one under No. 231. The cover before us was found in a large red urn at a depth of 27 ft., on the great wall close to the gate : hence its good preservation.

No. 237 represents one more vase-cover, with an owl's head modelled

No. 237.   Vase Cover with owl's face.   (1 : 5 actual size.   Depth, 23 ft.)

on it, belonging to the same class of vases, with a smooth neck like Nos. 231 and 240, having the characteristics of a woman, and usually two wings.

I further call the reader's very particular attention to the terra-cotta ball, No. 1997,[4] on which we see in the middle an owl's face in monogram; to its right a wheel, which may mean the sun; to its left, three concentric circles, which may represent the moon, and below a small circle, perhaps intended to represent the morning star. All these representations can be best distinguished in the developed pattern (No. 1998). On the back the female hair is indicated by deep scratchings. As the hair cannot be distinguished in the engraving, I strongly advise the reader to see the ball itself in my collection in the South Kensington Museum.[5] This owl's face, between the sun and moon and morning star, proves better, I think, than all the vases and idols, that the owl's head is the symbol of the Ilian Athené.

I have still to represent here, under Nos. 238, 239, a curious hand-made vessel of terra-cotta, which was found at a depth of 30 ft. It has been thoroughly baked in the conflagration. It has a distinctly indicated owl's face, below which are three horizontal strokes, probably meant

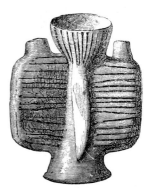

Nos. 238, 239. Front and back View of a curious Vessel, with owl's face. (Half actual size. Depth, 30 ft.)

to represent necklaces. Below the latter, the front part of the body is covered by a long shield, and on the back the long female hair hangs down, like that of the Caryatides in the Acropolis of Athens. On each side is a separate vessel, which does not communicate with that of the main body. Very characteristic are the nine rows of points on the shield, which, like those which we see on the coats of mail and the casques of the six warriors painted on a Mycenean vase,[6] are no doubt meant to indicate the splendour of brass. This vessel is unique; no second one has been found like it.

---

[4] On the last of the lithographed plates at the end of the volume.

[5] M. Burnouf writes to me: "This ball (No. 1997) gives probably the explanation of a great part of the Trojan symbolism, because it is most evident that the *female in the centre* represents here the dawn. The signs on the whorls are nearly all astronomical."

[6] See my *Mycenae*, p. 133, No. 213.

No. 240 is a lustrous dark-red hand-made vase, with two large breasts and a large projecting vulva. Besides two handles, it has two upright

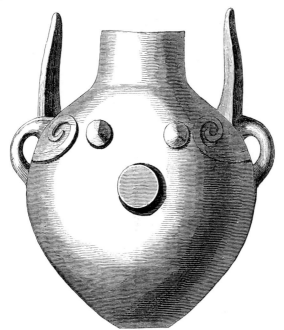

No. 240.   Large Vase, with the characteristics of a woman.   (About 1 : 5 actual size.   Depth, 26 ft.)

wing-like projections, from each of which issues on either side a spiral ornament in relief, resembling, as Professor Sayce observes, the *lituus* or crooked staff carried by certain figures in the Hittite sculptures of Boghaz Kioi or Pteria and elsewhere.   I remind the reader that the owl-faced, cap-like covers, such as No. 236, belong to this sort of vase.

No. 241 is a hand-made light-brown vase, with two breasts on each side and two projections; it is ornamented with grooves and incised lines.

No. 241.   Terra-cotta Vase, with incised ornamentation and female breasts on either side. (1 : 3 actual size.   Depth, 32 ft.)

No. 242.   Terra-cotta Vase, with two projections in the form of birds' heads at the rim. (1 : 3 actual size.   Depth, 26 ft.)

No. 242 is also a hand-made vase, with two perforated projections in the form of birds' beaks at the rim.

It is now time to explain the curious signs 卐 and 卍, which we have seen on the vulva of the lead idol No. 226, and which occurs many hundreds of times on the whorls and other objects of this third or burnt city, and of the two following pre-historic cities (see, for instance, Nos. 1855, 1858, 1859, 1870, 1873, 1874, 1894, 1919, 1947, 1949, 1982, 1988, 1989, 1991, 1999). This sign was evidently brought to Hissarlik by the people of the Third City, for it never occurs on objects from the first or second city. I find it in Émile Burnouf's Sanskrit Lexicon under the denomination " svastika," and with the signification εὖ ἐστι, or as the sign of good wishes.

My honoured friend the celebrated Orientalist, Professor Max Müller, of Oxford, wrote to me some time ago: " *Sv-asti-ka* is derived from *su*, ' well,' and *as*, 'to be,' and would be in Greek εὐεστική. It is always directed towards the right, ⊔╥ ; the other, directed towards the left, ╥⊓, is called *Sauvastika*." He afterwards kindly sent me the following most valuable and highly interesting dissertation on the subject :—

" I do not like the use of the word *Svastika* outside of India. It is a word of Indian origin, and has its history and definite meaning in India. I know the temptation is great to transfer names, with which we are familiar, to similar objects that come before us in the course of our researches. But it is a temptation which the true student ought to resist, except, it may be, for the sake of illustration. The mischief arising from the promiscuous use of technical terms is very great. Travellers, whenever they meet with two or three upright stones and a capstone above, talk of *Cromlechs ;* and if they meet with a holed stone, it is a *Dolmen*. But *Cromlech* and *Dolmen* are Celtic words (*crom*, ' bent,' *leh*, ' slab ;' *toll*, ' hole,' *mên*, ' stone '),[7] and they have a definite meaning among Celtic antiquarians, and, strictly speaking, *cromlech* and *dolmen* imply the workmanship of Celts. After travellers have written for some time of *Cromlechs* and *Dolmens* in India, Africa, and Australia, an impression spreads that all these monuments are real Celtic monuments ; and the next step is that we hear of Celts as the first inhabitants and builders in countries where Celts have never set foot.

" Another objection to the promiscuous use of the word *Svastika* is, that *svastika* in Sanskrit does not mean the cross with crampons, *crux ansata*, in general, but only the cross with the crampons pointing to the right, ⊔╥ ; while the cross with the crampons pointing to the left, ╥⊓, is called *Sauvastika*.

" The occurrence of such crosses in different parts of the world may or may not point to a common origin. But if they are once called *Svastika*, the *vulgus profanum* will at once jump to the conclusion that they all come from India, and it will take some time to weed out such a prejudice.

" Very little is known of Indian art before the third century B.C., the period when the Buddhist sovereigns began their public buildings. The name *Svastika*, however, can be traced a little further back. It occurs, as

---

[7] Max Müller, *Chips from a German Workshop*, vol. iii. p. 283.

the name of a particular sign, in the old grammar of Pânini, about a century earlier. Certain compounds are mentioned there, in which the last word is *karna*, ' ear.' Cattle, it would seem, were marked on their ears with signs indicating their owners. The custom prevailed even during the Vedic times, for in the Rig-veda (x. 62, 7) we meet with *ashtakarní*, as applied to cows marked with the figure 8, whatever that figure may then have been, probably not more than eight lines, or two crosses. In later Sanskrit *athtakarna* is a name of Brahman, who had eight ears, because he had four faces (K*aturmukha*). The same custom of marking cattle is alluded to in the Atharva-veda (xii. 4, 6), and it is more fully described in the Sânkhâyana-gr*i*hya-sûtras (iii. 10, ed. Oldenberg, p. 77), and the Gobhila-gr*i*hya-sûtras (iii. 6. 5). Here an instrument made of copper (*audumbaro 'asi*h) is recommended for marking cattle.

"One of the signs for marking cattle was the *Svastika*, and what Pânini teaches in his grammar is that, when the compound is formed, *svastika-karna*, i.e. 'having the ear marked with a Svastika,' the final *a* of *Svastika* is not to be lengthened, while it is lengthened in other compounds, such as *Dátrá-karna*, i.e. 'having the ear marked with the sign of a sickle.'

"Originally *svastika* may have been intended for no more than two lines crossing each other, or a cross. Thus we find it used in later times also with reference to a woman covering her breasts with crossed arms, *Bálarám.* 75,16, *svahastasvastika-stani*, and likewise with reference to persons sitting cross-legged.

"Etymologically, *svastika* is derived from *svasti*, and *svasti* from *su*, ' well,' and *as*, ' to be.' *Svasti* occurs frequently in the Veda, both as a noun in the sense of happiness, and as an adverb in the sense of ' well,' or ' hail !' It corresponds to the Greek εὐεστώ. The derivative *svasti-ka* is of later date, and it always means an auspicious sign, such as are found most frequently among Buddhists and Jainas. It occurs often at the beginning of Buddhist inscriptions, on Buddhist coins, and in Buddhist manuscripts. Historically the *svastika* is first attested on a coin of Kra*n*anda, supposing Kra*n*anda to be the same king as Xandrames, the predecessor of Sandrokyptos, whose reign came to an end in 315 B.C. (See Thomas, *On the Identity of Xandrames and Krananda*.) The palæographic evidence, however, seems rather against so early a date. In the foot-prints of Buddha the Buddhists recognize no less than sixty-five auspicious signs, the first of them being the *Svastika*.[8]

No. 243.
The Nandyávarta.

The fourth is the *Sauvastika*, 卐 ; the third, the *Nandyávarta* (No. 243), a mere development of the *Svastika*.

"Among the Jainas the *Svastika* was the sign of their 7th Jina, *Supár8va*.[9]

---

[8] See Eugène Burnouf, *Lotus de la bonne Loi*, p. 625.

[9] Colebrooke, *Miscellaneous Essays*, ii. p. 188.

"In the later Sanskrit literature *Svastika* retains the meaning of an auspicious mark, and thus we see in the Râmâya*n*a (ed. Gorresio, ii. p. 348) that Bharata selects a ship marked with the sign of *Svastika*.

"Varâhamihira in the B*ri*hat-sa*m*hitâ (med. saec. vi. p. Ch.) mentions certain buildings, called Svastika and Nandyâvarta (53. 34, seq.), but their outline does not correspond very exactly with the forms of these signs. Some Sthûpas, however, are said to have been built on the plan of a *svastika*.

"That signs identically the same as the *Svastika* and the *Sauvastika* occur elsewhere, in China, in Asia Minor, in Etruria, and among the Teutonic nations, is perfectly true. Comparative archæology may point out this fact, but there it must rest for the present. Identity of form does as little prove identity of origin in archæology as identity of sound proves identity of origin in etymology. Comparative studies are very useful, so long as they do not neglect the old rule, *Divide et impera*, Distinguish, and you will be master of your subject!

"Quite another question is, Why the sign ⌐⌐ should have had an auspicious meaning, and why in Sanskrit it should have been called *Svastika*. The similarity between the group of letters *sv* in the ancient Indian alphabet and the sign of *Svastika* is not very striking, and seems purely accidental. A remark of yours in your book on Troy (p. 38), where you speak of the *Svastika* as a wheel in motion, the direction of the motion being indicated by the crampons, contains a very useful hint, which has been confirmed by some important observations of Mr. Thomas, our distinguished Oriental numismatist. He has clearly proved that on some of the Ândhra coins, and likewise on some punched gold coins, depicted in Sir W. Elliot's Plate ix. *Madras Journ. Lit. and Science*, vol. iii., the place of the more definite figure of the sun is often taken by the *Svastika*, and that the *Svastika* has been inserted within the rings or normal circles representing the four suns of the Ujjain pattern on coins. He has also called attention to the fact that in the long list of the recognized devices of the twenty-four Jaina Tîrthankaras the sun is absent; but that while the 8th Tîrthankara has the sign of the half-moon, the 7th Tîrthankara is marked with the *Svastika*, i.e. the sun.

"Here then, I think, we have very clear indications that the *Svastika*, with the hands pointing in the right direction, was originally a symbol of the sun, perhaps of the vernal sun as opposed to the autumnal sun, the *Sauvastika*, and therefore a natural symbol of light, life, health, and wealth. That in ancient mythology the sun was frequently represented as a wheel is well known. Grimm identifies the Old Norse *hjol* or *hvel*, the A.-S. *hveohl*, English 'wheel,' with κύκλος, Sk. K*a*kra, 'wheel;' and derives *jôl*, 'yule-tide,' the time of the winter solstice, from *hjol*, 'the (solar) wheel.'

"But while from these indications we are justified in supposing that among the Aryan nations the *Svastika* may have been an old emblem of the sun, there are other indications to show that in other parts of the world the same or a very similar emblem was used to indicate the earth.

Mr. Beal, in the same number of the *Indian Antiquary* which contains Mr. Thomas's remarks on the *Svastika* (March, 1880), has shown that in Chinese ⊞ is the symbol for an enclosed space of earth, and that the simple cross (+) occurs as a sign for earth in certain ideographic groups. Here the cross was probably intended to indicate the four quarters, N. S. E. W.; or, it may be, more gene-
rally, extension in length and breadth. That the cross is used as a sign for 'four' in the Bactro-Pali inscriptions,[10] is well known; but the fact that the same sign has the same power elsewhere, as for instance in the Hieratic numerals, does not prove by any means that the one figure was derived from the other. We forget too easily that what was possible in one place was possible also in other places; and the more we extend our re-searches, the more we shall learn that the chapter of accidents is larger than we imagine."

No. 244.   The Foot-print of Buddha.

The cut No. 244, for which I am indebted to my honoured friend Mr. James Fergusson, represents the foot-print of Buddha, as carved on the Amarâvati Tope, near the river Kistna.

Nos. 245, 246 represent the opposite hemispheres of a terra-cotta ball, which is divided by fourteen incised circular lines into fifteen zones, of

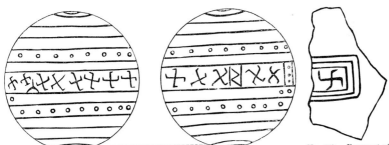

Nos. 245, 246.   Terra-cotta Ball, representing apparently the climates of the globe.
(Actual size. Depth, 26 ft.)

No. 247.   Fragment of Pottery, with the *Svastika*. (Half actual size.)

which two are ornamented with points, and the middle zone, which is the largest of all, with 卐 and 卐. Professor Sayce remarks that " the central ornament ⋈ is the Cypriote character *ki*."

No. 247 is the fragment of a lustrous-black vase with a 卐 in the

---

[10] Max Müller, *Chips from a German Workshop*, vol. ii. p. 298.

middle of three concentric rectangles: the ⊔╥, as well as all the other lines, are incised and filled with white chalk in order to strike the eye.[1]

The ⊔╥ and ╓⊔ are extraordinarily frequent on the Trojan terra-cotta balls, as well as on the whorls, immense numbers of which are ornamented with them (see Nos. 1826, 1838, 1849, 1850, 1855, 1861, 1864, 1865, 1866, 1868, 1871, 1872, 1873, 1874, 1876, 1878, 1879, 1894, 1905, 1911, 1919, 1947, 1949, 1954, 1982, 1983, 1987, 1988, 1989, 1990, 1991, 1999).

On the whorls Nos. 1872 and 1911 we see the ⊔╥ and ╓⊔, together with linear representations of burning altars; on Nos. 1879, 1919, 1947, 1949, 1991, along with the zigzags, which we see also in the hands of the two Phoenician gods represented on a lentoid gem found near Mycenae,[2] and which are generally believed to form the symbolic sign for lightning. The representation of the burning altar has also been found incised on the bottom of a vase in the excavations made by Miss Sofie von Torma in the valleys of Maros and Cserna in Transylvania (Siebenbürgen).[3] The ⊔╥ or ╓⊔ also occurs very frequently on the Trojan whorls in conjunction with rude linear representations of stags, above whose backs are rows of points;[4] it also occurs in conjunction with the sign ⊔⊔.[5] This latter sign is very frequent on the Trojan whorls.[6] Now this very same sign occurs over the opening of three hut-urns found under the ancient lava near Marino.[7] It occurs also among the devices in punched work on the flags in the interior of the tomb of Ollam Fodhla, traditional monarch and lawgiver of Ireland, which is computed to be upwards of 3000 years old;[8] further, on a girdle-buckle of iron plated with silver, found in a tomb at Hedingen, near Sigmaringen.[9] In these two latter cases we see the symbol or character in conjunction with the zigzag, which is interpreted as the symbolic sign of lightning. Finally, we see this sign on six vase-bottoms discovered by Miss Sofie von Torma in the valleys of Maros and Cserna in Transylvania.[10]

We find the ╓⊔ in Ezekiel ix. 4, 6, where—in the form of the old Hebrew letter Tau—it is written as the sign of life on the forehead, like

---

[1] This potsherd as well as another one with a ╓⊔ having been picked up in 1872 at a much greater depth in my excavations, I held them to belong to the first city. But after carefully examining the clay and fabric of these fragments, I feel convinced that they belong to the third or burnt city, and that they must have fallen from a higher level into my excavations. I feel the more certain on this point, as the ⊔╥ or ╓⊔ never again occurred in the *débris* either of the first or of the second city, whereas they occur many hundreds of times in the third as well as in the two subsequent pre-historic cities of Hissarlik.

[2] See my *Mycenae*, No. 540, p. 362.

[3] Carl Gooss, *Bericht über Fräulein Sofie von Torma's Sammlung praehistorischer Alterthümer aus dem Maros- und Cserna-Thal Siebenbürgens*, p. 16, No. 12.

[4] See No. 1879.

[5] See No. 1905.

[6] See Nos. 1912, 1936, 1939.

[7] *Notes on Hut-urns and other Objects from Marino near Albano.* By Sir John Lubbock and Dr. L. Pigorini. London, 1869. Two of the hut-urns represented in the work of Sir John Lubbock and Dr. Pigorini have the sign ⊔⊔ above the door. The third hut-urn with the sign ⊔⊔ above the door is preserved in the Royal Museum at Berlin.

[8] *Discovery of the Tomb of Ollam Fodhla.* By Eugène Alfred Conwell. Dublin, 1873.

[9] Ludw. Lindenschmit, *Die Vaterländischen Alterthümer*, Pl. v. No. 4.

[10] Carl Gooss, *op. cit.* p. 16, Pl. iii. Nos. 8, 9, 10, 13, 14, and 17.

its corresponding Indian symbol. We find it twice on a large piece of ornamented leather contained in the celebrated Corneto treasure preserved in the Royal Museum at Berlin; also on ancient pottery found at Königsberg in the Neumark, and preserved in the Märkisches Museum in Berlin, and on a bowl from Yucatan in the Berlin Ethnological Museum. We also see it on coins of Gaza, as well as on an Iberian coin of Asido;[1] also on the drums of the Lapland priests.[2] It is just such a troublesome puzzle as the Nile-key or *crux ansata*, that symbol which, as a hieroglyph, is read *ankh* ("the living one"), which very frequently occurs in the inscriptions in the Nile valley, and which we see of exactly the same form on a sepulchre of Northern Asia Minor.[3]

The 卍 is a sort of cross, whose four arms are bent at a right angle; it resembles four conjoined Greek Gammas.

Burnouf thinks that "the 卐 and 卍 represent the two pieces of wood which were laid crosswise upon one another before the sacrificial altars, in order to produce the sacred fire (*Agni*), and the ends of which were bent round at right angles, and fastened by means of four nails 卍, so that this wooden scaffolding might not be moved. At the point where the two pieces of wood were joined, there was a small hole, in which a third piece of wood, in the form of a lance (called *Pramantha*), was rotated by means of a cord made of cow-hair and hemp, till the fire was generated by friction. Then the fire (*Agni*) was put on the altar close by, where the priest poured the holy *Sôma*, the juice of the tree of life, over it, and made, by means of purified butter, wood and straw, a large fire."[4]

Burnouf further maintains that the mother of the holy fire was *Mâyâ*, who represents the productive force.[5] If his views are correct, they would go far to explain the presence of the 卍 on the vulva of the idol No. 226. They would also show that the four points which we so frequently see under the arms of the 卍 or 卐 indicate the wooden nails with which this primitive fire-machine was fixed firmly on the ground; and, finally, they would explain why we so frequently see the 卍 or the 卐 in company with the symbol of lightning or burning altars. The other cross too, which has also four points, ✠, and which occurs innumerable times on the whorls of the three upper pre-historic cities of Hissarlik, might also claim the honour of representing the two pieces of wood for producing the holy fire by friction. Burnouf asserts that "in remote antiquity the Greeks for a long time generated fire by friction, and that the two lower pieces of wood, that lay at right angles across one another, were called σταυρός, which word is either derived from the root *stri*, which signifies lying upon the earth, and is then identical with the Latin *sternere*, or it is derived from the Sanskrit word *stâvara*, which means

---

[1] Zobel, *de Zangronis*, 1863, Pl. 1 and 3, and p. 397.
[2] Rochholz, *Altdeutsches Bürgerleben*, p. 184.
[3] Guillaume and Perrot, *Exploration archéo-*logique *de la Galatie et de la Bithynie*, Atlas, Pl. ix.
[4] See Émile Burnouf, *La Science des Religions*, p. 256.
[5] Émile Burnouf, *op. cit.*

'firm, solid, immovable.' After the Greeks had other means of producing fire, the word σταυρός passed simply into the sense of cross."

The ᛘ or ᛘ may be found in nearly all countries of Europe, and in many countries of Asia. We see them on one of three pot-bottoms [6] found on Bishop's Island, near Königswalde, on the right bank of the Oder,[7] as well as on a vase found at Reichersdorf near Guben.[8] A whole row of them may be seen round the famous pulpit of Saint Ambrose in Milan. The sign occurs a thousand times in the catacombs of Rome; [9] we find it very frequently in the wall-paintings at Pompeii, even more than 160 times in a house in the recently excavated street of Vesuvius; we see it in three rows, and thus repeated sixty times, upon an ancient Celtic funeral urn found at Shropham, in the county of Norfolk, and now in the British Museum.[10] I find it also very often on ancient Athenian [1] and Corinthian vases, and exceedingly frequent on the jewels in the royal tombs at Mycenae; [2] also on the coins of Leucas and Syracuse, and in the large mosaic in the royal palace garden at Athens. The Rev. W. Brown Keer, who visited me in 1872 at Hissarlik, assured me that he has seen it innumerable times in the most ancient Hindu temples, and especially in those of the Jainas. I see also a ᛘ on a vase [3] which was found in the county of Liptó, in Hungary, and is preserved in the collection Majláth Béla; further, on terra-cottas found in the cavern of Bará-thegy, in Hungary.[4]

Since the appearance of my work *Troy and its Remains,* I have been favoured with letters from correspondents who have observed the ᛘ and ᛘ in various parts of the old world, from China at the one extremity to Western Africa at the other. Dr. Lockhart, of Blackheath, formerly medical missionary in China—to whom I am indebted for other interesting communications [5]—says that "the sign ᛘ is thoroughly Chinese." [6] Major-General H. W. Gordon, C.B., Controller of the Royal Arsenal at Woolwich, wrote, with reference to the nations amongst whom I have traced the ᛘ, "You may to these nations add the Chinese, since upon the breech-chasing of a large gun lying outside my office, and which was captured in the Taku Forts, you will find the same identical sign." For the very interesting discovery of the symbol among the Ashantees, I am

[6] *Zeitschrift für Ethnologie, Organ der Berliner Gesellschaft für Anthropologie und Urgeschichte,* 1871, iii.

[7] *Third Sessional Report of the Berlin Society for Anthropology, Ethnology, and Pre-historic Researches,* of 1871.

[8] *Sessional Report of the Berlin Society for Anthropology, Ethnology, and Pre-historic Researches,* of July 15, 1876, p. 9.

[9] Émile Burnouf, *op. cit.*

[10] A. W. Franks, *Horae ferales,* Pl. 30, fig. 19.

[1] G. Hirschfeld, *Vasi arcaici Ateniesi;* Roma, 1872, Tav. xxxix. and xl. G. Dennis, *The Cities and Cemeteries of Etruria,* p. xci.

[2] See my *Mycenae,* p. 259, figs. 383, 385, and in many others.

[3] No. 3, Pl. xx. in Dr. Joseph Hampel's *Anti-quités préhistoriques de la Hongrie;* Esztergom, 1877.

[4] Joseph Hampel, *Catalogue de l'Exposition préhistorique des Musées de Province;* Budapest, 1876, p. 17.

[5] For example, the Chinese sacrificial cup, engraved under No. 774 (p. 466), resembling the double-handled gold cup of the large treasure. Dr. Lockhart finds various indications of Chinese influence among the Hissarlik antiquities, and traces Chinese letters on some of the whorls: but I do not now enter into that question.

[6] M. Burnouf asks me whether it has not been imported into China by the Buddhists.

indebted to Mr. R. B. Æneas Macleod, of Invergordon Castle, Ross-shire, who wrote: "You may judge my surprise when, a few weeks ago, on looking over some curious bronzes captured at Coomassie during the late Ashantee war by Captain Eden, son of Bishop Eden, of Inverness, and now in his possession, I observed the same symbol, with some others, as was usual in Asia Minor so many thousand years ago. I enclose photographs of the three bronzes with the symbol in high relief, and of nearly the natural size."

No. 248. No. 249. No. 250.

Nos. 248–250. Bronzes bearing the 卐, taken at Coomassie in 1874.

Professor Sayce observes to me: "It is evident that the sign found at Hissarlik is identical with that found at Mycenae and Athens, as well as on the pre-historic pottery of Cyprus,[7] since the general artistic character of the objects with which this sign is associated in Cyprus and Greece agrees with that of the objects discovered in Troy. The Cyprian vase figured in Di Cesnola's *Cyprus*, Pl. xlv. 36, which associates the *swastika* with the figure of an animal, is a striking analogue of the Trojan whorls on which it is associated with the figures of stags. The fact that it is drawn within the vulva of the leaden image of the Asiatic goddess (No. 226) seems to show that it was a symbol of generation. I believe that it is identical with the Cypriote character ʃʃʃ or ▪|▪ (*ne*), which has the form ɔ⊦ in the inscriptions of Golgi, and also with the Hittite ▪ʃ▪ or ▪|▪, which Dr. Hyde Clarke once suggested to me was intended to represent the organs of generation."

Mr. Edward Thomas kindly sends me a copy of his most able dissertation on the 卐 and 卍,[8] in which he says: "As far as I have been able to trace or connect the various manifestations of this emblem, they one and all resolve themselves into the primitive conception of solar motion, which was intuitively associated with the rolling or wheel-like projection of the sun through the upper or visible arc of the heavens, as understood and accepted in the crude astronomy of the ancients. The earliest phase of astronomical science we are at present in a position to refer to, with the still extant aid of indigenous diagrams, is the Chaldean. The representation of the sun in this system commences with a simple ring or outline circle, which is speedily advanced towards the impression of onward revolving motion by the insertion of a cross or four wheel-like

[7] Di Cesnola, *Cyprus*, Pl. xliv., xlv., xlvii.

[8] *The Indian Swastika and its Western Counterparts*; London, 1880.

spokes within the circumference of the normal ring. As the original
Chaldean emblem of the sun was typified by a single ring, so the Indian
mind adopted a similar definition, which remains to this day as the
ostensible device or caste-mark of the modern Sauras, or sun-worshippers.
The tendency of devotional exercises in India, indeed, seems from the first
to have lain in the direction of mystic diagrams and crypto symbols
rather than in the production of personified statues of the gods, in which
it must be confessed that, unlike the Greeks, the Hindus did not attain
a high style of art."

I now come to the tripod-vases, of which a *really enormous* number
was found. In fact, most of the Trojan vases are tripods. I found, in my
excavations in the Acropolis of Mycenae, a few fragments of terra-cotta
tripods,[9] but never an entire one. Besides, the Mycenean tripods are
very different from the Trojan; for they have two large handles, which, as
well as the three feet, have each two, three, four, or even five perforations,
for suspension with a string. On the contrary, the feet of the Trojan
tripods are never perforated, but there is on either side of the body a
projection with a vertical tubular hole, and, in the same direction, a hole
in the rim and the cover. The string was drawn on each side through
the tubular holes of the projections, and a knot being made below, as I
have shown in No. 252, the string was drawn through the tubular holes
of the neck or the cover. It deserves attention that whenever a vase
has a cover with long tubular holes, such as No. 252, there is no perforation in the vase-neck;
and there being none in
the tripod-vase No. 251,
it must have had a cover
similar to that of No. 252.
In fact, vases with pro-
jections on the rim and
long tubular holes in these
projections, a system such
as we see it on No. 253,
always pre-suppose flat
vase-covers perforated on
either side. In either way,
—by means of the cap-
like covers with tubular
holes, such as we see on
No. 252, or by means of
perforated flat covers, such

No. 251. Ornamented Tripod Vase, with tubular holes for suspension.
(2 : 5 actual size. Depth, 27 ft.)

as there must have ex-
isted on No. 253,—the vase could be shut close, and it could be carried
by the string.

But if, as is evident from the fragments I discovered at Mycenae, the
tripod form of vase was in use in Greece from a very remote antiquity, it

---

[9] See my *Mycenae*, p. 69.

most certainly was no longer in use there or elsewhere in the so-called Graeco-Phoenician period, and far less in later times. The best proof of this is, that neither the Museums of Athens, nor the British Museum, nor the Louvre, nor any other museum in the world, can boast of possessing a tripod-vase of terra-cotta, except one found at Ialysus, preserved in the British Museum, two from Etruria (one of them in form of an animal from Corneto) as well as one from Peru in the Royal Museum of Berlin,[10] one apparently of a late period in the Museum of Leyden,[11] and three bronze tripod-vases of a late time in the Middle Ages in the Museums of Neu Strelitz, Stralsund, and Brandenburg. We must also, of course, except the censers, consisting of a very flat bowl with three very long, broad feet, which occur among the Graeco-Phoenician as well as the Corinthian pottery, and of which the Museum of the Βαρβάκειον in Athens, as well as all the large European museums, contain a few specimens.

No fragment of a tripod-vase of either terra-cotta or bronze has ever been found in the Lake-dwellings;[1] nor, indeed, so far as I know, has any bronze or copper tripod-vase ever been found anywhere, except the above, and one which I discovered in the fourth royal sepulchre at Mycenae, and of which I gave an engraving, No. 440, p. 278 of my *Mycenae*. But as tripods are continually mentioned by Homer, the fact now mentioned goes far to prove that he either flourished in Greece at that remote age to which the Mycenean sepulchres belong, or that he lived in Asia Minor, where tripods may have been still in use at the time usually attributed to the poet (the ninth century B.C.). But my excavations at Hissarlik have *not* proved that tripods were still in use so late: for no trace of them was found either in the layer of *débris* of the sixth city, which I hold to be a *Lydian settlement*, or in the most ancient strata of the Aeolic Ilium.

Tripods of copper (or bronze) were used in the Homeric times for various purposes. In the *Odyssey*,[2] as well as in the *Iliad*,[3] we find them given as presents of honour. In the *Iliad*[4] one is offered as a prize in

---

[10] The Royal Museum of Berlin contains also a terra-cotta vase with four feet, but I have not been able to learn where it was found.

[11] L. J. F. Janssén, *De Germaansche en Noordsche Monumenten van het Museum te Leyden ;* Leyden, 1840.

[1] Professor Virchow informs me that in the peat-moors of Northern Germany are often found copper kettles with three feet, which belong, however, to a late period, and probably to the Middle Ages. Two such tripod-vases—the one of iron, the other of brass or bronze—are represented in the *Sessional Report of the Berlin Society of Anthropology, Ethnology,* &c., of July 11, 1874, Pl. xi. Nos. 4 and 5.

[2] *Od.* xiii. 13 :
ἀλλ' ἄγε οἱ δῶμεν τρίποδα μέγαν ἠδὲ λέβητα . . .
Od. xv. 82–84 :
. . . . . οὐδέ τις ἡμέας
αὔτως ἀππέμψει, δώσει δέ τι ἕν γε φέρεσθαι,
ἠέ τινα τριπόδων εὐχάλκων ἠὲ λεβήτων.

[3] *Il.* viii. 289–291 :
πρώτῳ τοι μετ' ἐμὲ πρεσβήϊον ἐν χερὶ θήσω,
ἢ τρίποδ' ἠὲ δύω ἵππους αὐτοῖσιν ὄχεσφιν
ἠὲ γυναῖχ', ἥ κέν τοι ὁμὸν λέχος εἰσαναβαίνοι.
Il. ix. 121–123 :
ὑμῖν δ' ἐν πάντεσσι περικλυτὰ δῶρ' ὀνομήνω,
ἕπτ' ἀπύρους τρίποδας, δέκα δὲ χρυσοῖο τάλαντα,
αἴθωνας δὲ λέβητας ἐείκοσι, . . .
[4] *Il.* xi. 700, 701 :
. . . . . περὶ τρίποδος γὰρ ἔμελλον
θεύσεσθαι·
Il. xxiii. 262–264 :
Ἱππεῦσιν μὲν πρῶτα ποδώκεσιν ἀγλά' ἄεθλα
θῆκε γυναῖκα ἄγεσθαι ἀμύμονα ἔργα ἰδυῖαν
καὶ τρίποδ' ὠτώεντα . . .
Il. xxiii. 485 :
δεῦρό νῦν, ἢ τρίποδος περιδώμεθον ἠὲ λέβητος . . .
Il. xxiii. 512, 513 :
δῶκε δ' ἄγειν ἑτάροισιν ὑπερθύμοισι γυναῖκα
καὶ τρίποδ' ὠτώεντα φέρειν·
Il. xxiii. 717, 718 :
οἱ δὲ μάλ' αἰεί
νίκης ἱέσθην τρίποδος πέρι ποιητοῖο.

the games, and the tripod also occurs as an ornament of the rooms,[5] and, further, for the heating of water and for cooking.[6] To indicate its use for these latter purposes, Homer [7] gives also to the tripod the epithet ἐμπυριβήτης, "set on the fire."

It is very remarkable that, with all the many hundreds of terra-cotta tripod-vases, no trace of a copper or bronze tripod was found in any one of the five pre-historic cities at Hissarlik. This is all the more astonishing, since the ten treasures found in the third or burnt city appear to prove that the city was suddenly and unexpectedly destroyed by a fearful catastrophe, so that the inhabitants had no time to save anything. Besides, the largest treasure, that one which was found by me at the end of May 1873, contained three copper vessels and some more in fragments, but not one of these was a tripod. The existence, therefore, of terra-cotta and copper tripod-vessels in Mycenae at that remote antiquity to which the royal tombs belong;—their non-existence in Greece at any later period;—the abundance of copper (or bronze) tripod-vessels in the time of Homer;—the general use of terra-cotta tripod-vessels in all the five pre-historic cities at Hissarlik;—the total absence there of copper tripods of any kind:—this series of facts presents just as many problems which bid fair to occupy the scientific world for a long time to come.

In order to avoid continual repetition, I here state that, unless I mention the contrary, all the Trojan vases may be regarded as *hand-made*.

I have still to describe more fully the tripod-vases already mentioned, Nos. 251, 252, and 253. As may be seen, the vertical tubular holes of No. 251 are very long; the three feet, of which only one is visible in the engraving, are very short and thick. On either side of the globular body we see two narrow strips with dots, and two broad ones with an incised ornamentation in the shape of fish-spines. This latter decoration is seen on several gold goblets [8] found by me at Mycenae in the royal sepulchres, as well as on a marble slab found outside of them; [9] it also occurs on terra-cotta vases found in Dolmens of the Stone age in Denmark; [10] on a vase found in Hungary,[11] and elsewhere.

No. 252 is a very remarkable lustrous light-red tripod-vase. Around the body we see a deep furrow, the two edges of which are perforated vertically for suspension; but the usual projections on either side of the body are missing here. Not less curious is the cover, in the form of a Phrygian cap, having on each side a tubular hole more than 2 in. long, by means of which it was fastened on the vase with a string, as I have shown in the engraving. There are similar very long vertical tubular

---

[5] *Il.* xviii. 373, 374 :

τρίποδας γὰρ ἐείκοσι πάντας ἔτευχεν
ἑστάμεναι περὶ τοῖχον ἐϋσταθέος μεγάροιο, . . .

[6] *Od.* viii. 434 :

ἀμφὶ πυρὶ στῆσαι τρίποδα μέγαν ὅττι τάχιστα.

Il. xviii. 344, 345 :

ἀμφὶ πυρὶ στῆσαι τρίποδα μέγαν, ὄφρα τάχιστα
Πάτροκλον λούσειαν.

[7] *Il.* xxiii. 702 :

τῷ μὲν νικήσαντι μέγαν τρίποδ' ἐμπυριβήτην, . . .

In *Il.* xxii. 163, 164, it is called τρίπος instead of the usual form τρίπους :

. . . . . τὸ δὲ μέγα κεῖται ἄεθλον,
ἢ τρίπος ἠὲ γυνή, . . .

[8] See my *Mycenae*, No. 319, p. 206, and No. 453, p. 292.

[9] *Ibid.* No. 215, p. 140.

[10] J. J. A. Worsaae, *Nordiske Oldsager* ; Copenhagen, 1859, p. 19, fig. 95, and p. 20, fig. 100.

[11] Joseph Hampel, *Antiquités préhistoriques de la Hongrie*, Pl. xxi. No. 7.

holes in the projections near the rim of the pretty grey tripod-vase
No. 253, which has smaller projections with vertical tubular holes, in

No. 252. Ornamented Tripod Vase, with tubular rings for suspension. (2 : 5 actual size. Depth, 26 ft.)

No. 253. Ornamented Tripod Vase, with tubular rings for suspension. (2 : 5 actual size. Depth, 26 ft.)

the same direction, in its globular body, which is decorated with wedge-shaped incisions and points.

Another tripod-vase with the suspension system is No. 254, the neck of which is ornamented with 8 circular bands. The body is divided by three bands into four fields, of which the upper one is decorated with the

No. 254. Ornamented Tripod Vase, with tubular holes for suspension. Incised ornamentation. (About 1 : 4 actual size. Depth, 26 ft.)

No. 255. Ornamented Tripod Vase, with tubular holes for suspension. Incised ornamentation. (About 1 : 4 actual size. Depth, 26 ft.)

very common incised zigzag ornament, the two following with small incised strokes; the lower field has no ornamentation. No. 255 is a similar tripod-vase, with an almost identical ornamentation.

No. 256 represents a very characteristic specimen of a Trojan terra-cotta tripod-vase: it is of a light-brown colour, and has two handles,

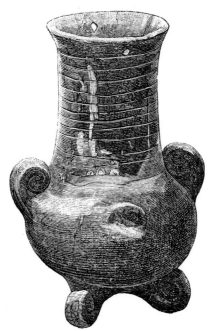

which, as well as the three feet, are of a spiral form. Between the two handles there is, on either side of the body, a large projection with a vertical tubular hole, one of which is just in front, and in the same direction a hole in the rim for suspension. The long funnel-shaped neck is decorated with simple circular bands.

A very elegant red tripod-vase with two perforated handles is represented under No. 257. On each side of its globular body we see an incised decoration of three branches, of which the middle one has on each side a zigzag line, the two others plain lines.

The tripod-vase No. 258 is very curious, on account of its fanciful feet, which, as well as the projections on the sides of the body, are ornamented with incisions; the whole upper part

No. 256. Pretty Tripod Vase, with two handles of spiral form and vertical tubular holes for suspension. (2 : 5 actual size. Depth, 28 ft.)

of this vessel is restored. The only peculiarity in the globular tripod-vase, No. 259, is a projection on the body, the upper part of which is

No. 257. Globular Tripod, with perforated handles for suspension and incised ornamentation of plants or palm-leaves. (1 : 3 actual size. Depth, 26 ft.)

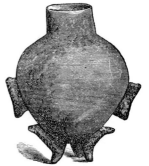

No. 258. Tripod Vase. All the upper part restored with gypsum. (Nearly 1 : 3 actual size. Depth, 26 ft.)

ornamented with a zigzag line between two circular bands. Much prettier is the little globular tripod-vase, No. 260; which has on each side the usual perforated projection for suspension. The body is decorated with an incised band of a horizontal fish-spine-like ornamentation, parallel to which we see a band of strokes round the neck. This latter band is

No. 259. Globular Vase, with three feet and tubular holes for suspension. (About 1 : 4 actual size. Depth, 26 ft.)

No. 260. Globular Tripod, with holes for suspension and incised fish-spine-like ornaments. (Nearly 1 : 3 actual size. Depth, 26 ft.)

joined to the lower one on each side by a row of fish-spine incisions. The neck straitens towards the top.

The tripod No. 261 has two handles of a spiral form, which, as a rare exception to the rule, are not perforated. The globular body is divided by seven parallel circular bands into six fields: of these the larger central one is divided on each side by fifteen vertical lines into sixteen small fields, four of which are ornamented with incised circles, and four others with strokes. No. 262 is another tripod-vase, with tubular holes for

No. 261. Tripod Vase, with incised ornamentation. (Half actual size. Depth, 23 ft.)

No. 262. Tripod Vase, with incised ornamentation. (Half actual size. Depth, 25 ft.)

suspension. The upper part of the globular body, as well as the neck, is ornamented with incised parallel bands, of which two are ornamented with horizontal strokes, the third with an incised zigzag line.

The tripod-vase No. 263 is very similar to No. 252, with the difference that the neck of the latter straitens, while that of No. 263 widens towards the top. On neither of these two vases are there perforated projections for suspension. On No. 263, the edge of the bottom, the projecting edge on the middle of the body, as well as the upper part of the neck and the cover, are perforated on each side for passing the string through.

I call the reader's very particular attention to the curious light-red tripod-box Nos. 264 and 265, the former being the cover and the latter

No. 264.

No. 265.

No. 263. Tripod Vase, with tubular holes for suspension in the lower part of the body, the rim, and the cover. (1 : 3 actual size. Depth, 26 ft.)

Nos. 264, 265. Tripod Box, with holes for suspension. A cuttle-fish is painted on the cover. (Nearly 1 : 3 actual size. Depth, 26 ft.)

being the lower part. The three feet are of a spiral form. On each side of the bottom, as well as on two sides in the rims, there is a perforation for suspending the box and fastening the lid on it. On the top of the

No. 266.

latter the reader sees a curious ornamentation, painted with dark-red clay, in which the keen eye of my friend Mr. Charles Newton, of the British Museum, has recognized a cuttle-fish, and this is in fact most certainly represented here. The same ornamentation occurs at Mycenae and in the Phoenico-Greek remains at Rhodes. The same ornamentation is very frequent on the objects of gold found by me in the royal sepulchres of Mycenae,[1] also on the pottery from a tomb at Ialysus in Rhodes preserved in the British Museum. No. 266 is the cover, and No. 267 the lower part, of a lustrous-black box of terracotta, made of a very compact graphite clay mixed with so much mica that it glitters all over with thousands of sparkles, like gold or silver. I found it on the wall

No. 267.

Nos. 266, 267. Lustrous-black Box, with Cover of Terra-cotta. (Half actual size. Depth, 28 ft.)

near the royal house, together with the curious object of Egyptian porcelain No. 548, and a lustrous-black vase with an owl's head and the characteristics of a woman, in a large broken funeral urn, which

---

[1] See my *Mycenae*, No. 240, p. 166, and Nos. 270, 271, p. 181.

was filled with different sorts of carbonized material and ashes of animal matter. Though the box has evidently been exposed to a great heat, yet it is hardly half-baked, probably because it was shut. But still the heat has been so great in the box that all its contents have been carbonized. In these Professor X. Landerer recognizes grain, remnants of cotton or linen cloth, beads of glass paste, and animal charcoal of bones and flesh. Thus we may with all probability suppose that the funeral urn contained the ashes of a deceased person, to which were added several articles, to one of which the object of Egyptian porcelain belonged; also the box before us, which seems to have contained a dress ornamented with beads of a glass paste, and some food, grain, and animal matter. Unlike the box Nos. 264, 265, the black box before us has no holes for suspension, and the lid is so large that it covers the lower part or box proper entirely.

No. 268 represents a lustrous-black tripod-vase with the system for suspension ; it has on each side of the body three linear projections and two

No. 268. Globular Tripod, with perforated projections for suspension. Ornamentation, 6 linear projections. (1 : 4 actual size. Depth, 32 ft.)

No. 269. Vase, ornamented with incisions.
(1 : 4 actual size. Depth, 26 ft.)

lines incised round the neck. No. 269 is a little grey vase decorated with three lines round the neck, and a series of circles and a zigzag ornamentation round the body. Nos. 270 and 271 are two globular tripod-

No. 270.

No. 271.

Nos. 270, 271. Two Tripod Vases, with tubular holes for suspension and ornamented with incisions. (1 : 4 actual size. Depth, 26 ft.)

No. 272. Tripod Vase, with holes for suspension, also projections on either side (About 1 : 4 actual size. Depth, 26 ft.)

vases of a blackish colour, with tubular holes for suspension ; the former is ornamented with three lines round the neck, and various other rude incised patterns on the body ; the upper part of No. 271 is decorated all round with 7 bands of dots.   No. 272 is a lustrous-black tripod-vase with a ring for suspension on either side, and two small projections on each side of the body.

I pass over to the unornamented tripod-vases, simply placing before the reader nine specimens of lustrous black, brown, or red colour (Nos. 273 to 281), as their several forms may be easily studied from the

No. 273.   Tripod Vase, with perforated projections for suspension.   (1 : 4 actual size. Depth, 32 ft.)

No. 274.   Tripod Vase, with tubular holes for suspension.   (1 : 4 actual size. Depth, 26 ft.)

No. 275.   Tripod Vase, with holes for suspension. (Nearly 1 : 3 actual size. Depth, 26 ft.)

No. 276.   Tripod Vase, with tubular holes for suspension.   (1 4 actual size. Depth, 26 ft.)

excellent engravings.   All of them have two vertically perforated projections for suspension with a string.   In the engravings Nos. 273 and 274 the perforations for the string in the rim are also easily to be discerned. The feet of No. 276 form curves; those of No. 277 are in the form of spirals.

No. 277. Globular Tripod Vase.
(Nearly 1 : 3 actual size.
Depth, 32 ft.)

No. 278. Globular Tripod,
with tubular holes for suspension.
(About 1 : 4 actual size. Depth, 26 ft.)

No. 279. Tripod Vase, with
holes for suspension.
(1 : 4 actual size. Depth, 26 ft.)

No. 280. Tripod Vase, with tubular holes for
suspension. (1 : 4 actual size. Depth,
32 ft.)

No. 281. Terra-cotta Tripod Vase, with
perforated projections on the sides for suspension.
(Half actual size. Depth, 30 ft.)

I now proceed to the vases without feet.   No. 282 is a lustrous dark-
brown globular vase, with a short neck and *double* rings for suspension on

No. 282. Vase with two tubular holes for
suspension on each side. (About 1 : 4 actual size.
Depth, 32 ft.)

No. 283. Spout of a black Vase, with two holes
for suspension. (2 : 3 actual size. Depth,
26 ft.)

each side.   Similar vases with double rings on each side are general in the
first city, but they hardly ever occur in the higher strata ; in fact, in all

my excavations I found only two of them in the third or burnt city.[2]
But No. 283 is a vase-spout with two perforations in the rim. It evidently belongs to a vase with such a spout on each side of the body:
I shall have occasion to represent such a vase on a subsequent page.
No. 284 is a lustrous-black globular vase, with the usual vertical tubular
holes for suspension. As to Nos. 285 and 288, I have nothing particular
to add to the mere view of the objects.

No. 284. Globular Vase, with tubular holes.
(About 1 : 4 actual size. Depth, 32 ft.)

No. 285.   Globular Vase, with tubular holes for
suspension. (Nearly 1 : 3 actual size. Depth, 32 ft.)

No. 286. Bottle with tubular holes for suspension.
(About 1 : 4 actual size. Depth, 26 ft.)

No. 287.   Globular Bottle, with tubular holes for
suspension. (Nearly 1 : 3 actual size. Depth, 26 ft.)

Nos. 286 and 287 are in shape much like our present bottles; but
the projections with the vertical tubular holes on the sides betray at once
their remote antiquity. No. 289 is a large yellowish vase of oval form,
having on the sides the like projections with perforations. No. 290 is a
lustrous-black globular vase with perforated projections for suspension.

---

[2] A hand-made vase similar to this, and also
with two rings for suspension on either side,
is in the remarkable collection of pre-historic
German pottery of Professor Virchow at Berlin.
Great praise is due to this friend for the extensive excavations he has undertaken in company
with his highly talented children, his daughter
Adèle and his son Dr. Hans Virchow, in the
vast graveyard of Zaborówo in the province of
Posen, and of which his very curious collection is
the result. But, unlike the Trojan vases, which
invariably have vertical perforations for suspension, the perforations on the above vase in Prof.
Virchow's collection are in a horizontal position,
like those of all the German vases; but he
possesses one vase found at Belgard in Pom-
mern, which has on each side a vertically perforated excrescence. Another rare exception is a
vase in the Märkisches Museum at Berlin, which
has also a vertical perforation on either side.

No. 288. Vase with tubular holes for suspension.
(About 1 : 4 actual size. Depth, 32 ft.)

No. 289.   Vase of oval shape, with tubular holes for
suspension. (About 1 : 4 actual size. Depth, 26 ft.)

A vase similar to this, but with horizontally perforated excrescences on the sides, is in Professor Virchow's collection.

No. 290. Globular Vase, with
holes for suspension.
(1 : 4 actual size. Depth, 29 ft.)

No. 291. Globular Vase, with
tubular holes for suspension.
(1 : 4 actual size. Depth, 26 ft.)

No. 292. Globular Vase, with holes
for suspension and incised ornamentation. (About 1 : 4 actual size.
Depth, 26 ft.)

No. 293. Globular Vase, with holes
for suspension and incised flowery
ornamentation. (About 1 : 4 actual
size. Depth, 32 ft.)

No. 294. Cup with fish-spine ornamentation. (About 1 : 4 actual size.
Depth, 26 ft.)

No. 291 is remarkable for the shape of its very long perforated projections for suspension. No. 292 is a globular vase, rudely decorated with a linear ornamentation and dots. No. 293 is a grey globular vase with the suspension system, ornamented on each side with six very neatly-incised palm-branches. No. 294 is a lustrous dark-red goblet without handles; it is decorated with an incised band of the fish-spine ornament, encompassed on both sides by double lines, below which we see an engraved branch all round the vase. The perforated projections on the sides of the lustrous dark-brown globular vase, No. 295, are in the shape of ears. No. 296 represents a vase with perforated projec-

No. 295.   Globular Vase, with tubular holes for
suspension. (About 1 : 4 actual size. Depth, 29 ft.)

No. 296.   Vase with linear ornamentation and tubular
holes for suspension. (About 1 : 4 actual size.
Depth, 29 ft.)

tions for suspension; it has a rude linear ornamentation on the body. Professor Virchow calls my attention to the great similarity between the cover of this vase and that of the covers on the Pommerellen vases with human faces. No. 297 is of a lustrous-brown colour; its neck

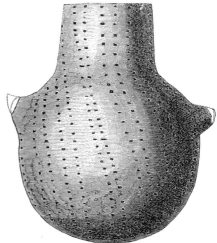

No. 297.   Vase with tubular holes for suspension.
(1 : 4 actual size. Depth, 26 ft.)

No. 298.   Black Vase, with a convex bottom and tubular holes
on the sides for suspension, covered all over with dots.
(1 : 3 actual size. Depth, 23 ft.)

widens slightly towards the top. No. 298 is a lustrous-black vase, with a globular base and the usual perforated projections for suspension; it is covered all over with rows of dots.

The globular lustrous dark-brown vase, No. 299, with its long perforated and deeply-fluted projections for suspension, is very remarkable.

No. 300 is of the same colour, and has the usual system for suspension. It is decorated with a waving line and dots.

To the list of vases found elsewhere, with vertical tubular holes for suspension, I may add two small conical vases from Nimroud, in the British Museum, each of which has four such holes.

No. 301 is a blackish globular vase, with perforated projections on the body as well as in the rim, for suspension. It has a rudely-incised ornamentation filled up with white chalk.

No. 299.   Globular Vase, with tubular holes for suspension. (About 1 : 4 actual size. Depth, 26 ft.)

One of the most interesting objects ever found at Hissarlik is the

No. 300. Vase with holes for suspension, and incised ornamentation. (About 1 : 4 actual size. Depth, 32 ft.)

No. 301. Globular Vase, with tubular holes in the rim and body for suspension; incised ornamentation. (1 : 4 actual size. Depth, 29 ft.)

beautiful lustrous dark-yellow vase No. 302 (p. 368), which has on the sides long projections perforated with tubular holes for suspension; each of these projections is ornamented with four horizontal parallel lines. The surface of the body is divided on each side by two vertical lines into three fields: in the middle field, which is by far the largest, we see on each side a tree with ten branches, a decoration which is very frequent on the Trojan whorls and balls (see Nos. 1899–1904, 1910, 1993, 1999, and 2000). But I remind the reader that this, like all other patterns on the pre-historic pottery of Hissarlik, is incised. If we examine these incisions with a lens, we conclude from their rudeness and irregularity that they must have been made with pointed pieces of silex or hard wood, or with bone-needles, before the pottery was baked for the second time, or, more probably, before it was brought to the fire for the first time. The vase before us (No. 302) has been exposed to the full heat of the conflagration; for, although the clay is very thick, it is thoroughly baked. This vase evidently had a cover like that which we see on No. 252.

Another highly interesting vase is represented by No. 303 (p. 368); it is of a lustrous-black colour, and but slightly baked. Like many other black vases, it would most probably have become quite red had it been exposed to the intense heat of the conflagration, and so been thoroughly

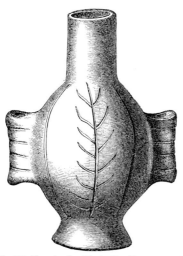

No. 303. Vase of polished blackish Terra-cotta, with tubular holes for suspension. Incised plant-like ornamentation. (Half actual size. Depth, 33 ft.)

No. 302. Vase of well-polished yellow Terra-cotta, with an incised ornamentation and long tubular holes for suspension on either side. (About 1 : 3 actual size. Depth, 26½ ft.)

baked. It has on both sides pointed projections with perforations for suspension. Like the foregoing vase (No. 302), it has a small hollow foot; its shape is globular; it is decorated on each side with two reversed branches, each with 18 leaves and surrounded by dots; there is also a plant-like ornamentation above the projections. A similar ornamentation is very frequent on the whorls (see Nos. 1901 and 1904).

The lustrous-red vase No. 304 is of an oval shape. This also has a small hollow foot and a short neck, which widens towards the mouth; it has the usual tubular holes on the sides, and holes in the rim in the same direction. The body is ornamented all round with rudely-incised vertical lines, just as if the primitive potter had intended to imitate a melon. The neck is ornamented with horizontal parallel lines. This vessel has been exposed to the intense heat of the conflagration, by which it has been thoroughly baked. The crown-shaped cover which we see on the vase is very curious. Unlike the usual covers with a similar crown-like handle, this cover is not intended to be put over the neck of the vase, but to be put into it, like a stopper, because its lower part is hemispherical and hollow, with a wide orifice in the middle. By this contrivance the cover could be put on the vase even when it was full, because the liquid would enter into the hollow. While all the vases which I have hitherto passed in review, and all those which I shall pass in review without a special notice to the contrary, are hand-made, this vase-cover is wheel-made, a circumstance which appears to prove that it does not belong to this particular vase.

Under No. 305 I represent a globular lustrous-yellow vase found in the royal house; it has the usual perforated projections for suspension on

No. 305. Inscribed Terra-cotta Vase, from the royal house. (1 : 4 actual size. Depth, 26 ft.)

No. 304. Lustrous-red Vase of oval shape, with rude linear ornamentation, having long perforated projections on the sides. (Half actual size. Depth, 24 ft.)

No. 306. Vase of oval form, with a hollow foot, tubular holes for suspension, and a projecting ornamentation. (1 : 4 actual size. Depth, 26 ft.)

the sides, and holes in the rim; its bottom is flat. Around the upper part of the body is what has been taken for an incised inscription, which Professor Sayce has discussed in his dissertation on the Trojan inscriptions.[3]

The red vase No. 306 is of an oval shape, and has the same system for suspension as all the foregoing, a hollow foot, and a small neck; it has on each side of the body a spiral decoration in relief, like the Cypriote character *ko*.

Of a far ruder fabric is the little vase No. 307, which has on each side two projections in the form of female

No. 307. Small Vase, with tubular holes for suspension and two breasts on either side. (About 1 : 4 actual size. Depth, 29 ft.)

---

[3] See his Appendix.

breasts, and four vertical lines; the small curved projections on the sides
are perforated for suspension. Very curious in its ornamentation is the

No. 308. Vase of Terra-cotta, with incised
decorations. (About half actual size. Depth, 26 ft.)

No. 309. Vase Cover, with a small handle, decorated
with an incised ornamentation. (About 1 : 3 actual
size.)

globular vase No. 308, which has only two holes for suspension in the rim,
and none on the sides. The surface of the body is divided by horizontal

No. 311.

No. 310.

No. 312.

No. 314.

No. 313.

No. 315.

No. 316.

No. 318.

No. 317.

Nos. 310–318. Fragments of Pottery with incised ornamentation. (Nearly half actual size. Depth, 22 to 32 ft.)

parallel lines into six or seven zones, most of which are decorated with
rude vertical, slanting, or horizontal incisions; on each side of the body

there is a projection which, however, is not perforated. The only pre-historic vases, whose incised decoration offers some resemblance to that on this vase, are those found in Hungary, and represented on Pl. vi. Nos. 4, 6, 7, 8, and 9, in Dr. Joseph Hampel's *Antiquités préhistoriques de la Hongrie.*[4]

Under No. 309 I represent a vase-cover with a small handle; it is rudely decorated with incisions representing lines, small concentric circles, and spirals.

Nos. 310, 313, 314, 315, and 318 are fragments of vases with various rudely-incised patterns. No. 311 is a vase-foot ending in a spiral. Nos. 312 and 316 are fragments of vase-covers. No. 317 is the handle of a vase with curious signs.

The engravings Nos. 319 to 323 represent five of the long lustrous-red goblets, with two enormous handles and a pointed or convex foot, on account of which they cannot be put down except on the mouth; there-

No. 319. Goblet with two handles, δέπας ἀμφι-κύπελλον. (About 1 : 4 actual size. Depth, 29 ft.)

No. 320. Goblet with two handles, δέπας ἀμφι-κύπελλον. (About 1 : 4 actual size. Depth, 32 ft.)

fore, whoever held such a goblet in his hand, when filled with liquid, was forced to empty it before putting it down. In this way the goble was always kept clean. I have tried to prove in the preceding chapter (pp. 299–302) that the Homeric δέπας ἀμφικύπελλον could not possibly have been anything else but a single goblet with two handles. Nos. 319 and 320 are represented upright, as when held in the hand; Nos. 321, 322, and 323, as standing on the mouth. These goblets are sometimes very large; two of those in my collection, with a pointed foot and handles, like No. 319, are 12 inches long, and have a mouth 6 inches in diameter. But there also occur two-handled goblets of a different shape in this third,

---

[4] Esztergom, 1876.

No. 321.

No. 322.

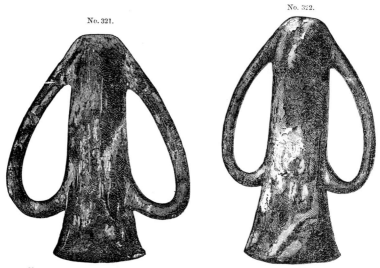

Nos. 321, 322. Goblets with two handles (δέπα ἀμφικύπελλα), (About 1 : 4 actual size. Depth, 29 ft.)

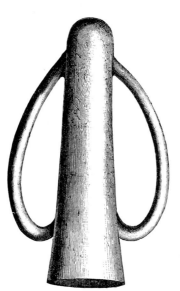

No. 324. Cup with two handles. (1 : 3 actual size.
Depth, 26 ft.)

No. 323. Goblet with two handles (δέπας ἀμφικύπελλον).   No. 325. Goblet with two handles. (1 : 3 actual size.
(About 1 : 4 actual size. Depth, 26 ft.)   Depth, 26 ft.)

the burnt city. The shape represented by No. 324 also occurs very frequently, and still more abundant is the form No. 325, which in the upper
pre-historic cities has sometimes three feet. With rare exceptions, all
the goblets, of whatever form, are of a lustrous-red colour ; the only other
colour which sometimes, but very seldom, occurs on the goblets, is a
lustrous black.

I further represent here, under No. 326, a cup with three feet and two handles; it is of a lustrous-black colour, and decorated all round with parallel horizontal lines. Only two specimens of this type have been found in the third city; but it is very frequent in the following city. But still more frequent in the latter is a double-handled cup of the very same shape, but without the tripod feet; indeed, this shape is so abundant there, that I was able to collect many hundreds of specimens; but it never occurs in the third, the burnt city. I may add that none of these various forms of goblets have ever been found elsewhere.

No. 326. Lustrous-black Tripod Cup, with two handles.
(About 1 : 5 actual size. Depth, 30 ft.)

No. 327.   Very curious sieve-like perforated Tripod-
vessel.   (Half actual size. Depth, 24 ft.)

No. 327 is a very curious tripod-vessel in the form of a one-handled pitcher, which stands on its side, supported by three feet, and is pierced all over with holes like a sieve. Similar vessels are not rare, either in the third or the following city; but their use is a mystery to us. All of them have been made on the potter's wheel, are unpolished, and of the rudest fabric. All the holes have evidently been made before the vessel was baked. But the baking is not thorough. Similar vessels have never been found elsewhere. Professor Helbig[5] suggests that the large sieve-like perforated terra-cotta vases found in the Italian terramare may have served for separating the liquid honey from the wax. May the vessel before us have served for a like purpose?

Nos. 328–330 represent three vase-covers, whose tripod-like handles with a large knob make a very pretty appearance, and resemble crowns. But still more elegant is the vase-cover No. 331, the handle of which consists, as it were, of two arches; its form can best be explained by comparing it to two single handles put cross-wise, one over the other,

---

[5] Wolfgang Helbig, *Die Italiker in der Poebene;* Leipzig, 1879, p. 17. Professor Helbig says, p. 6: "The word Terramare or Terramara is an expression corrupted from Terramarna by the peasants of the province of Parma, and signifies originally every stratum of earth which is mixed with organic matter, and is therefore appropriate for manuring. Now, as the soil of the Emilia contains the remains of many old settlements, remains consisting of manufactures as well as of decomposed organic bodies, the denomination Terramare has in a more narrow sense been transferred to the strata containing such remains."

and joined together by a very large nail.   Both sorts of handle are very
abundant in the third city, as well as in the two succeeding pre-historic

No. 329. Vase Cover with a crown-shaped handle.
(1 : 4 actual size.   Depth, 26 ft.)

No. 328. Vase Cover with a crown-shaped handle.
(About 1 : 4 actual size.   Depth, 26 ft.)

cities, though they have certainly never been yet found elsewhere.   But
my friend Mr. Philip Smith calls my attention to the similarity of these

No. 331. Vase Cover with a crown-shaped handle.
(1 : 4 actual size.   Depth, 26 ft.)

No. 330. Vase Cover with a crown-shaped handle.
(1 : 4 actual size.   Depth, 23 ft.)

Trojan handles to the crown-like form of the modern Phrygian water-
vessels.   He cites the following passage on the subject from page 101 of
the Rev. E. J. Davis's *Life in Asiatic Turkey*.   Writing from Hierapolis,
he says: "Here I saw for the first time the wooden vessels used for
carrying water.   They are made of a section of pine : the inside is
hollowed out from below, and the bottom is closed by a piece of wood
exactly fitted into it.   These vessels are very durable and strong."   On
the opposite page he gives two engravings, according to which these

Phrygian water-vessels have a very great resemblance to the Trojan vase-covers in the form of a crown.

Vase-covers with a simple handle, like No. 332, occasionally occur, but they are not nearly so frequent as the forms before described.

No. 332. Vase Cover with a simple handle. (1 : 4 actual size. Depth, 32 ft.)

The only vase-handles I noticed which have some analogy to these were found at Szihalom in Hungary, and are shown under Nos. 26 and 27 in the glass case No. IX. of the National Museum of Buda-Pesth. The only difference is that, instead of covering the vase-neck like a cap, as at Troy, they were intended merely to shut the orifice: for, as Dr. J. Hampel informs me, the lower part of No. 26 is tapering, and its flattened foot is divided by a cross-like groove into four pivots; the lower part of No. 27 is globular. The handle is on the slightly hollow upper side. Therefore, like the Mycenean vase-covers,[6] these Szihalom vase-covers were kept in place on the orifice by their protruding flat rim, their tapering or globular lower part entering into the neck of the vase, like a stopper.

I now proceed to the description of some vessels in the form of animals. No. 333 represents a lustrous-green globular tripod-vessel with a ram's head; instead of the tail we see a long and large spout,

No. 333. Globular Tripod, with a ram's head.   No. 334. Vessel with three feet in form of a hedgehog.
        (1 : 3 actual size. Depth, 26 ft.)   (1 : 4 actual size. Depth, 23 ft.)

which is joined by a handle to the back of the vessel: the upper part of the body is ornamented with bands of incised lines. No. 334 is a brown tripod-vase of a dull brown colour, with the head of a hedgehog: the

_____

[6] See my *Mycenae*, p. 256, Nos. 373, 374.

primitive potter may have meant to represent the spines of the animal by the three bands of incised strokes with which the body of the vessel is decorated. Here also the mouthpiece is on the back part, and joined to the back by a handle. No. 335 is a lustrous-brown vase, in the form of a fat sow with three feet. No. 336 is a lustrous-brown vessel, in the shape of a sheep with four feet. No. 337 is a lustrous dark-brown tripod-vase, in the shape of a hog. No. 338 is a lustrous-brown tripod-vase, in the form of a mole; this latter vessel has been made so that it can be set upright on the muzzle and the two fore feet.

No. 335. Tripod-vessel in the form of a fat sow. (Half actual size. Depth, 30 ft.)

No. 336. Vase in the shape of a sheep with four feet.
(1:4 actual size. Depth, 32 ft.)

No. 337. Vase in the form of a hog; the upper part
restored. (About 1:4 actual size. Depth, 32 ft.)

No. 339 again represents a hedgehog, but its four feet are too short to set it on, the base being convex. Unlike the other vases, the mouth is

No. 338.   Tripod-vessel in the form of a mole.
(1 : 4 actual size. Depth, 23 to 26 ft.)

No. 339.   Vase in the form of a hedgehog, with four
short feet. (1 : 3 actual size. Depth, 23 ft.)

here over the neck. The only ornamentation of this vessel consists of five horizontal incisions on each side.

No. 340 is of lustrous-red terra-cotta; it has four feet, and can hardly represent anything else than a hippopotamus. It is hollow; on its left side are the most distinct marks of its having been joined to another vessel, which of course must have had an identical form; the neck of the twin vessel may have been in the middle between the two hippopotami. The existence of the figures of hippopotami in the third, the burnt city, at a depth of 23 ft. below the surface, is extremely

No. 340.   Vessel in the form of a hippopotamus.
(About 2 : 3 actual size. Depth, 23 ft.)

remarkable—nay, astonishing; for this animal, as is well known, is no longer met with even in Upper Egypt, and occurs only in the rivers in the interior of Africa. In the time of the Old Empire, however (about B.C. 5000–3500, according to Mariette), the hippopotamus still lived in the Delta, as is shown by a painting in the tomb of Ti at Sakkarah. Ti was an official of the Fifth Dynasty (about B.C. 3950–3700), and is represented as hunting hippopotami among the papyri of the Delta. According to Herodotus,[7] they were worshipped as sacred animals in the Egyptian nome of Papremis only; and in the time of Pliny (*H. N.* xxviii. 8) they still existed in Upper Egypt. At all events, as appears to be evident from the existence of Egyptian porcelain here, this third city of Troy must have been commercially connected with Egypt; but, even so, it is still an enigma how the animal was so well known here as to have been made of clay in a form so faithful to nature. We may compare the vases similarly made in the form of animals found by General di Cesnola in Cyprus.[8]

Professor Virchow informs me that a vase in the form of a hog is in the Museum of Jena, and that vessels in the shape of animals, for the

---

[7] Herod. ii. 71 : Οἱ δὲ ἵπποι οἱ ποτάμιοι νομῷ   Αἰγυπτίοισι οὐκ ἱροί.
μὲν τῷ Παπρημίτῃ ἱροί εἰσι, τοῖσι δὲ ἄλλοισι   [8] Di Cesnola, *Cyprus*, Pl. viii.

most part of birds, are not rare in the tombs of Lusatia (Lausitz) and
Posen. He adds that many of them are mere rattle-boxes for children,
but that there also occur open ones. The Royal Museum at Berlin
contains a terra-cotta vessel without feet, with an animal's head. the
funnel-shaped orifice being in the back; also a terra-cotta tripod-vessel
from Corneto, with an animal's head, the funnel-like orifice being in the
place where the tail ought to be; the handle is on the back. A terra-
cotta vessel in the shape of an ox, with four feet, having the orifice in the
middle of the back, was found in a tomb of the graveyard of Kaźmierz-
Komorowo, in the province of Posen.[9] A similar animal-shaped vessel,

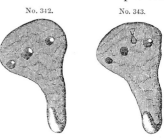

No. 342.   No. 343.

No. 341. Object of Terra cotta representing a fantastical
animal with six feet. (1:3 actual size. Depth, 23 ft.)

Nos. 342, 343. Two Hooks of Terra-cotta, with three
perforations. (1 : 3 actual size. Depth, 26 ft.)

with four feet, having its orifice on the back, is in the Museum of
Neu Brandenburg in Mecklenburg.

No. 344. Large Jar of Terra-cotta, with
polished surface and two projections in
the form of handles. (1:43 actual size.
Depth, 23 ft.)

No. 341 is a strange animal figure, solid,
except for a tube passing through the body
and open at both ends, so that it cannot
have been a vessel. It has six feet and a
tail; but we see on its body four upright
projections, which may also serve as feet if
the animal is put upside down. It is of a
yellowish colour.

Under Nos. 342 and 343 we see two
hooks of terra-cotta, each with three perforations, by which they were nailed to the
wall. Although but slightly baked, twenty-
five pounds' weight might be suspended on
either of them without danger of breaking
the hook, because the blackish clay they are
composed of is very tough and compact.
These hooks may have served for hanging
up clothes.

Under No. 344 I represent, in 1-43rd
of its actual size, the large Trojan jar
which I presented to Professor Virchow for the Royal Museum at
Berlin, where it is preserved in the Ethnological section. Like all the

---

[9] F. L. W. Schwartz, *II. Nachtrag zu den " Materialien zur praehistorischen Kartographie der
Provinz Posen;"* Posen, 1880, p. 6, and Pl. ii. fig. 6.

large jars, it is of a red colour, thoroughly baked, and has a polished surface. Unlike most Trojan jars, it has no handles and merely two small projections which have the shape of handles, but are not perforated. This jar is further distinguished from most other Trojan jars by its straight form, to which its good preservation is probably due. But its safety may also have been partly owing to the circumstance, that it was not exposed to the great heat of the conflagration, because it was found in the south-east corner of the third city, which was not reached by the fire. In fact, in the course of my long excavations at Hissarlik, I have taken out, besides this jar, only two smaller ones intact from the third, the burnt city; they were only 3½ ft. high and 26¾ in. in diameter; their sole decoration was a rope-like band in relief. Of the large jars, from 5 to 8 ft. high and 4½ to 5 ft. in diameter, I have not been able to take out a single one entire. For the most part, they had suffered so much from their long exposure to the intense heat of the conflagration, and from the ponderous weight of the ruins which pressed upon them, that they either already had cracks when I brought them to light, or they cracked as soon as they were exposed to the sun. Others, which were intact, broke as they were being removed.

As I have before mentioned, a compartment of a house in the burnt Trojan stratum below the Temple of Athené appears to have been a wine merchant's magazine,[10] for in it I brought to light nine large jars of various forms, six of which may be seen in the engraving No. 8; the other three are out of view. This magazine was close to the southern brick wall; the nine jars are marked s on Plan I. As may be seen from the engraving, only two of the six jars which are visible were broken; a third is cracked, and the other three are only slightly injured in the rim. The mouths of all these nine jars had been left open, and hence they were filled with débris. I could perhaps have saved these as well as the other three, which are hidden from view in the engraving, but a religious fear prevented me from trying to do so, for I hoped that they might be preserved in situ. But no sooner had I gone than the Turks of the neighbouring villages, who suspected the jars might contain treasure, knocked them partly to pieces.

The number of large jars which I brought to light in the burnt stratum of the third city certainly exceeds 600. By far the larger number of them were empty, the mouth being covered by a large flag of schist or limestone. This leads me to the conclusion that the jars were filled with wine or water at the time of the catastrophe, for there appears to have been hardly any reason for covering them if they had been empty. Had they been used to contain anything else but liquids, I should have found traces of the fact; but only in a very few cases did I find some carbonized grain in the jars, and only twice a small quantity of a white mass the nature of which I could not determine.[1]

---

[10] See p. 32. Professor Virchow suggests to me that it might have been a royal wine-cellar.

[1] With regard to the storage of wine in underground jars in Western Asia, I may add a further illustration from the records of the Egyptian conqueror Thutmes III. When he

For the most part the large jars have no decoration; and when there is any, it is nearly always limited to rope-like bands in relief, or to bands in relief from 2 to $2\frac{1}{2}$ in. broad, ornamented with incised fish-spine decorations, common geometrical patterns, or mere impressed circles. The coarse but very excellent clay, which has been used for the manufacture of these jars, is abundantly mixed with crushed quartz, silicious stone, and mica, of which latter the gold- or silver-like sparkles glitter wherever one looks. Most of the large jars have been carefully polished and abundantly coated with a wash of clay containing peroxide of iron, for they generally have a lustrous-red colour and are perfectly smooth; whereas they show in the fracture an infinity of small fragments of quartz, silicious stone, and mica with sharp edges. The manner in which these jars were made has been minutely explained in a previous passage.[2]

The shape of the vase which comes nearest to that of the large jars is represented by the pear-shaped jug No. 345. It is of a fine lustrous-brown colour. Very characteristic is the shape of the head, from which a

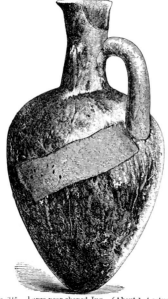

No. 345. Large pear-shaped Jug. (About 1:4 actual size. Depth, 32 ft.)

No. 346. Tripod Vase, with incised bands and bell-shaped cover. (1:4 actual size. Depth, 29 ft.)

hemispherical piece is cut out on the side over the handle. Jugs and pitchers with a similar mouth are frequent in the third and fourth cities at Hissarlik, but they have never yet been found elsewhere. The lustrous-grey, nearly globular, tripod-vase No. 346 is *wheel-made*, while its one-handled cover is hand-made: the vase has no handle; its ornamentation consists of three parallel incised lines, which surround it.

---

went through the land of Zahi (the maritime plain of Palestine), he says, "Their wine was found *stored in cellars*, as well as in skins."

(Brugsch, *Hist. of Egypt*, vol. ii. p. 376, Engl. trans. 2nd ed.)

[2] See p. 279.

The long pitcher, No. 347, is one of the rudest vessels I ever found at Hissarlik, and yet it is most certainly wheel-made. Mr. A. S. Murray,

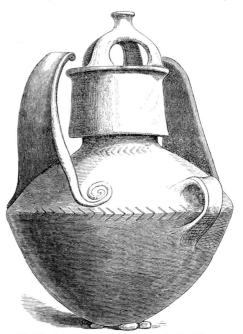

No. 347. A curious Trojan Pitcher of
Terra-cotta. (About 1 : 5 actual size.
Depth, 26 ft.)

No. 349. Splendid Terra-cotta Vase, from the Royal House.
(1 : 4 actual size. Depth, 28 ft.)

of the British Museum, calls my attention to the perfect similarity of this vessel to the ancient Egyptian buckets, which were let down by a rope into the wells to draw water. This sort of vessel is frequent here; most probably they were used in Troy, as in ancient Egypt, for drawing water from the well. Two things seem to corroborate this supposition: first, the very heavy weight of their lower part, which must have been intended to keep them upright; and, secondly, the grooves or furrows on the inner side of the handles, which can apparently have been made only by the rope by which they were let down into the well.

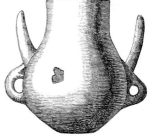

No. 348. Grey Vase, with two handles and
two wing-like projections.
(1 : 3 actual size. Depth, 26 ft.)

No. 348 represents a grey vase, with two handles and two upright projections. To this vase belongs a cover such as we see on Nos. 346, 349, and 350. No. 349 represents one of the most interesting vases ever found at Troy; it has a lustrous-red colour and is thoroughly baked. It has a pointed base, and is here represented with the pebbles used to support it. It has two handles and two long upright slightly-incurved projections, which are hollow on the outside and have the shape of wings. They taper out in a spiral at the top; from their base also a spiral in relief extends on either side. The neck is ornamented with the fish-spine pattern, which we also see on

No. 350. Globular Vase, with two handles and two wing-like projections. Cover in the form of a crown. (About 1 : 4 actual size. Depth, 26 ft.)

No. 351. Globular Vase, with two curved handles and two straight wing-shaped projections. Cover in the shape of a crown. (About 1 : 4 actual size. Depth, 26 to 29 ft.)

the edge of the body all round. The crown-shaped cover was found close to the vase, and may have belonged to it. Of a similar form but of a ruder fabric is the dark-brown vase No. 350, whose upright projections

No. 352. Vase with two handles and two straight wing-like projections. (1 : 3 actual size. Dep h, 25 ft.)

are also curved on the outside; from the base of each of them a spiral in relief runs out on both sides. Of the same form, only with a more pointed foot, is the black vase No. 351, which has some little ornamentation of incised lines and dots on or about the handles. Of the same shape, finally, is the pretty little vase No. 352, which is ornamented all over with dots. The upright wing-like projections of these four vases can never have been intended for handles, because they are too fragile and their edges are too sharp; all of them have two regular handles in addition to the wings. I call particular attention to their great resemblance to the upright wing-like projections on the vases with owl-heads.

No. 353 represents a lustrous-red globular tripod-vase, decorated on both sides with engraved branches, zigzags, and straight lines. On either

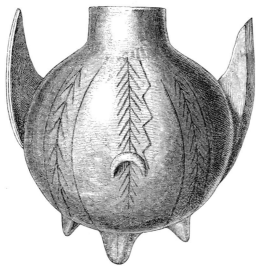

No. 353.   Globular Tripod Vase, with incised ornamentation.   (Half actual size.   Depth, 26 ft.)

No. 354.   Vase with two handles and a spiral ornamentation in the form of a pair of spectacles, or the Cypriote character *ko*.   (1 : 4 actual size.   Depth, 30 ft.)

side is a solid upright projection, with a vertical perforation for suspension; between these there is a crescent-shaped projection on each side. Another very pretty lustrous-red vase is represented in the engraving No. 354. It has a convex foot and two handles, between which we see on each side a high projecting spiral ornament, like a pair of spectacles, or the Cypriote character *ko*. Above this is an inverted branch; below it the body forms an edge which is ornamented with an incised fish-spine pattern. Similar to this is the lustrous dark-brown vase No. 355; only its base is still more pointed and its body more bulged. This also has two handles and two spiral ornaments in relief in the form of spectacles, or the Cypriote character *ko*.

Under No. 356 I represent a tripod-vessel of blackish colour, formed of three separate cups, which are joined together at the body, and of which each has one foot. To the list given in the preceding pages of the places

No. 356. Tripod Vase, consisting of three separate cups. (1 : 4 actual size. Depth, 26 ft.)

No. 355. Vase with pointed bottom, two handles, and projecting ornament in the form of a pair of spectacles, or Cypriote *ko*, on either side. (1 : 5 actual size. Depth, 24 ft.)

No. 358. Tripod Jug with two necks. (Nearly 1 : 3 actual size. Depth, 22 to 26 ft.)

No. 357. Globular Jug. (1 : 3 actual size. Depth, 22 to 26 ft.)

where similar conjoined vessels may be seen, I may add the Museum of the Βαρβάκειον in Athens, which contains a pre-historic hand-made terra-cotta vessel from Thera, consisting of two separate cups which are joined in three places. Professor Virchow's remarkable collection of German pre-historic antiquities contains a double drinking-horn, a vessel with two and another with three cups of terra-cotta, from his excavations in the graveyard of Zaborowo, in the province of Posen. The Märkisches Museum at Berlin contains also a vessel consisting of twin cups and another with three cups. Professor Virchow assures me that vessels consisting of two, three, or more conjoined cups, are not rare in the ancient Germanic sepulchres in Lusatia and the Mark of Brandenburg. The collections of Peruvian antiquities in the Royal Museum at Berlin and the British Museum also contain pottery consisting of two conjoined vessels. No. 357 is a single-handled jug of a yellow colour, with a convex bottom.

No. 358 is a curious tripod-jug of greyish yellow colour, having a globular body, from which project two separate spouts, one of which has a handle. As the one spout stands in front of the other, the liquid could only be poured out by the foremost, so that the other was of no use: these double spouts appear, therefore, to have been a mere fancy of the

No. 359. Curious double-necked Jug. (About 1:4 actual size. Trojan stratum.)

primitive potter. The black flagon (*oenochoë*), No. 359, has likewise two separate spouts, the handles of which are joined at the body. But here the spouts stand side by side, so that the liquid could be poured simultaneously through both of them. Similar *oenochoae*, with two spouts, occur also in the following, the fourth city, but they have never hitherto been found elsewhere, except in Cyprus, Germany, and Hungary. The collection of Cypriote antiquities in the British Museum contains an *oenochoë* with double spouts, each of which is joined by a separate handle to the body; but this vessel may be of a much later period, as it is wheel-made and painted. My friend General di Cesnola represents in his excellent work, *Cyprus*, two similar *oenochoae* with double spouts, one of which he found in his excavations at Alambra, and the other at Dali.[3] A somewhat similar *oenochoë* was found in the village of Tököl, on the island of Csepel in the Danube.[4] I may still mention a terra-cotta vessel with two vertical spouts in the Märkisches Museum at Berlin.

No. 360 represents a pretty lustrous-red pear-shaped *oenochoë*, with a long upright neck and trefoil mouth, joined by a long handle to the body, on which we see small handles to the right and left: round the lower part of the neck we discern three bands in relief; the bottom is flat. Similar to this is the pear-shaped red *oenochoë*, No. 361, which has only one handle. No. 362 is of a dark-red colour, and oval-shaped: it has

[3] See General di Cesnola's *Cyprus;* London, 1877, Plates vii. and ix.

[4] Joseph Hampel, *Antiquités préhistoriques de la Hongrie;* Esztergom, 1876, Plate v. No. 3.

No. 360. *Oenochoë* with three handles and long neck.
(About 1 : 3 actual size. Depth, 26 ft.)

No. 361. *Oenochoë* with long neck.
(Nearly 1 : 4 actual size. Depth, 26 ft.)

No. 362. Vase of oval form, with long neck.
(1 : 5 actual size. Depth, 26 ft.)

No. 363. Vase of lenticular shape, with long neck.
(1 : 5 actual size. Depth, 26 ft.)

also a trefoil mouth and one handle; its base is convex. No. 363 is of a similar form, but of a dark-brown colour; its mouth runs out almost straight, like a bird's beak; its bottom is convex. Professor Virchow observes to me that from the shape of these vases the widely-spread beak-shape of the Etruscan bronze jugs has evidently been developed.

Of *oenochoae* similar to these, I mention first an excellent hand-made specimen in the Museum of Boulogne-sur-mer, the director of which, in his ignorance of pre-historic pottery, thinks it to be Roman, and has therefore put it among the Roman pottery, though it is worth more than the whole collection of Roman terra-cottas in the museum. May this notice reach him, and may it be the cause of the precious *oenochoë* receiving at last the place it deserves!

I further mention three *oenochoae* of nearly the same shape, but with a short neck, in the archaic Greek Collection in the British Museum; also an *oenochoë* of a similar form in the Cypriote Collection in the same museum. Three *oenochoae* of a similar shape found in Thera, below three strata of pumice-stone and volcanic ashes, and believed to date from the 16th or 17th century B.C., are preserved here at Athens in the small collection of the French School. Another, likewise found below three strata of pumice-stone and volcanic ashes on the island of Therasia, and believed to be of the same age, is here in my own collection. But these four latter *oenochoae* have an ornamentation of black paint, whereas the Trojan vessels are unpainted. I have still to mention an *oenochoë*, also very ancient, of a similar form, but with a painted plant-like ornamentation, in the Museum of the Βαρβάκειον at Athens. Finally, I have to mention the three pretty jugs of a similar form (viz. with a spout bent backward) found by me in my excavations in the Acropolis of Mycenae, and preserved in the Mycenae Museum at Athens. All three are decorated with a painted ornamentation of birds, patterns borrowed from woven fabrics, or spiral lines. There are, besides, a few similar jugs in the Etruscan Collection of the Vatican Museum at Rome.

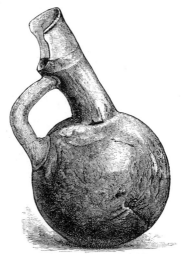

No. 364. Globular *Oenochoë*, with neck bent back-ward. (Nearly 1 : 4 actual size. Depth, 29 ft.)

No. 364 is an *oenochoë* of lenticular form and of a lustrous dark-yellow colour, with a neck and spout much bent backward. It has the same peculiar cut in its mouth which we have also seen in No. 333 and No. 357. The lustrous-yellow jug, No. 365, has also the same form of mouth. All these last four jugs have a convex bottom.

A similar shape, with the neck bent backwards, is seen also in the oviform jug No. 366, which is of a lustrous-black colour, and ornamented with lines filled with white chalk; it has a trefoil mouth. But only the upper part is genuine; the lower has been restored with gypsum. No. 367 represents a similar red jug of globular form.

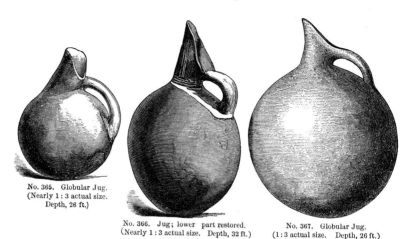

No. 365. Globular Jug.
(Nearly 1 : 3 actual size.
Depth, 26 ft.)

No. 366.   Jug; lower   part restored.
(Nearly 1 : 3 actual size.   Depth, 32 ft.)

No. 367.   Globular Jug.
(1 : 3 actual size.   Depth, 26 ft.)

No. 368 is a yellow jug of globular shape, with the neck also bent backwards; the shape of the mouth is again like that of Nos. 333, 357, 364, and 365.

No. 368.   Globular Jug.   (1 : 3 actual size.
Depth, 23 ft.)

No. 369.   Jug with three projections in the shape of
breasts.   (About 1 : 4 actual size.   Depth, 32 ft.)

Of *oenochoae* with an upright spout, I further represent the lustrous dark-brown jug No. 369, which is ornamented with three breast-like protuberances; the black jug No. 370, which is the first wheel-made vessel we have for a long time passed in review; Nos. 371 and 372, which latter has again a trefoil mouth. Similar in shape are also Nos. 373, 374,

No. 370. Globular Jug. (About 1 : 4 actual size.
Depth, 26 ft.)

No. 371. Globular Jug. (About 1 : 4 actual size.
Depth, 29 ft.)

No. 372. Jug; mouth restored.
(1 : 3 actual size. Depth, 26 ft.)

No. 373. Globular Jug, with straight neck.
(1 : 4 actual size. Depth, 26 ft.)

No. 374. Pear-shaped Jug.
(Nearly 1 : 3 actual size. Depth, 29 ft.)

No. 375. Globular Jug.
(About 1 : 4 actual size. Depth, 26 ft.)

375, 376. A vase of the same shape as No. 376 was found by me at Mycenae, and is now here at Athens in the Mycenae Museum.

No. 376. Globular Jug. (About 1:4 actual size. Depth, 26 ft.)

No. 377. Globular Bottle; upright neck. (Nearly 1:4 actual size. Depth, 26 ft.)

No. 378. Globular Jug, with projections like ears. (About 1:4 actual size. Depth, 26 ft.)

No. 377 represents a lustrous dark-red globular bottle, with a long narrow upright neck. Such bottles are not frequent at Troy. Two hand-made terra-cotta bottles of the same shape, the one yellow, the other black, found in tombs near Bethlehem, are in the British Museum, which also contains, in its Assyrian Collection, a wheel-made bottle of a similar form from Nimroud. Wheel-made terra-cotta bottles of a like shape are likewise found in tombs in Cyprus, as well as in ancient Egyptian sepulchres, and the British Museum contains several specimens of them in its collections of Cypriote and Egyptian antiquities. Several terra-cotta bottles of a similar shape were also found by General di Cesnola in

No. 379.

No. 380.

No. 381.

Nos. 379–381. Jugs of globular form, with one handle. (1:4 actual size. Depth, 22 to 32 ft.)

Cyprus.[5] I may mention one more such terra-cotta bottle from Cyprus, in the South Kensington Museum at London.

Somewhat similar to No. 377 is the jug No. 378, which has on either side below the rim a projecting ornament in the form of an ear.

Three very pretty lustrous yellow or red oval-shaped jugs, with spouts upright or slightly turned back, are represented under Nos. 379, 380, and 381; all of them have a convex bottom. No. 379 has on each side of the orifice a round excrescence, in the form of an eye. No. 381 has a rope-formed handle, and above the body a projecting band, ornamented with vertical strokes. Two similar jugs, but wheel-made, are in the Egyptian Collection of the British Museum. Jugs of a similar shape are frequent at Troy, but, except the two Egyptian specimens, I am not aware that they have ever been found elsewhere.

No. 382 is a pretty lustrous dark-grey *oenochoë*, with a trefoil mouth; it is ornamented with ten incised parallel bands. An *oenochoë* of the same shape, found by me at Mycenae, is represented at p. 65, No. 26, in my *Mycenae*.

No. 382. *Oenochoë* of Terra-cotta, with incised ornamentation. (Half actual size. Depth, 26 ft.)

Nos. 383 to 388 are all bottle-shaped jugs of red, yellow, brown, or

No. 383. Jug.
(Nearly 1 : 3 actual size. Depth, 26 ft.)

No. 384. Jug of a globular form.
(About 1 : 4 actual size. Depth, 26 ft.)

[5] General di Cesnola, *Cyprus*, Pl. vii.

black colour. No. 387 has the best fabric and the prettiest shape of all, with its long neck and widely-stretched handle. Its body is divided by two incised horizontal parallel lines into two fields, which are ornamented with incised vertical strokes. The Märkisches Museum at Berlin contains two jugs similar in shape to No. 383. No. 388 is decorated with seven incised horizontal parallel lines.

No. 385. Globular Jug.
(1 : 4 actual size. Depth, 26 ft.)

No. 386. Globular Jug.
(About 1 : 4 actual size. Depth, 26 ft.)

No. 387. Jug of Terra-cotta, with an incised ornamentation. (Half actual size. Depth, 26 ft.)

No. 388. Jug with incised bands.
(About 1 : 4 actual size. Depth, 22 to 30 ft.)

No. 389. Pitcher with a fluted body and a band imitating a plant. (About 1 : 4 actual size. Depth, 26 ft.)

One of the finest specimens of Trojan pitchers is represented by No. 389, which is of a brown colour, and is decorated with a plant-like ornament round the neck; its whole body is decorated with very symmetrical vertical concave flutings. Under Nos. 390 to 393 I represent four common pitchers of rude fabric. In looking at them, we involuntarily

No. 390.

No. 391.   No. 392.

No. 393.

Nos. 390-393.   Pitchers of different shapes.   (1 : 4 actual size.   Depth, 22 to 26 ft.)

think we have seen such forms often before; but, though they are very abundant in the third and fourth pre-historic cities of Hissarlik, I am not aware that they have as yet been found elsewhere, except a pitcher similar to No. 393, which was found by me at Mycenae.[6]

Under Nos. 394 to 400 I represent seven more red, yellow, or brown pitchers of a larger size, of which No. 397 is wheel-made. Of wheel-made pitchers similar to this one, some hundreds were found in the third, the burnt city, as well as in the fourth and fifth cities, but

No. 395.

No. 394.

Nos. 394, 395.   Pitchers of different shapes.   (1 : 4 actual size.   Depth, 22 to 32 ft.)

especially in the fourth. In general these wheel-made pitchers are of a very rude fabric, are but slightly baked, have the yellow colour of the clay itself, and are not at all polished. But in a great many instances they have been polished both inside and outside, and by a wash of fine clay and a little more baking they have in this case acquired a fine appearance. Such polished wheel-made pitchers are in many instances very light, and sometimes even as light as Roman or Greek pottery. But it deserves peculiar attention that these polished wheel-made pitchers

---

[6] See my *Mycenae*, p. 163, No. 237.

No. 397. Pitcher with globular base.
(About 1 : 4 actual size. Depth, 23 ft.)

No. 396. Pitcher of very rude fabric.
(1 : 4 actual size. Depth, 32 ft.)

No. 400.

No. 399.

No. 398.

Nos. 398–400. Pitchers. (1 : 4 actual size. Depth, 26 to 32 ft.)

are peculiar to this third, the burnt city, and that they do not occur in the fourth or the fifth city.   No. 399, which is very heavy, is of the rudest fabric.

Of pitchers of the same shape I have been able to detect elsewhere only a wheel-made one in the British Museum, which was found in a tomb near Bethlehem.   Two more wheel-made ones, found in ancient Egyptian sepulchres, are also in the British Museum ; and one found in Cyprus is preserved in the Louvre.   I further mention, as of similar type, the pitcher No. 11 on Pl. vi. in Dr. Joseph Hampel's *Antiquités préhistoriques de la Hongrie ;* also the pitchers in the National Museum of Buda-Pesth, which were found at Szihalom, and are represented on Pl. ix., Nos. 10, 20, and 21 of the photographs, corresponding to the numbers of the glass cases in which they are preserved.

I further represent under Nos. 401, 402, and 403 three large one-handled pitchers of very rude fabric, having convex bottoms.   I need only show them here, as their shape has not been found elsewhere.   They are very common at Troy.

No. 404 is a large dark-brown *oenochoë* with a bulbous body.   No. 405 represents a single-handled bowl with a spout.

Under Nos. 406 to 412, I represent seven black, grey, or red terra-cotta bottles, globular or egg-shaped, without handles, all of which are wheel-made, and have a convex or pointed foot.   Bottles of these shapes

No. 401. Pitcher; convex bottom. (About 1:4 actual size. Depth, 23 to 29 ft.)

No. 402. Pitcher; convex bottom. (About 1:4 actual size. Depth, 26 ft.)

No. 403. Very rude Jug; convex bottom. (1:4 actual size. Depth, 26 ft.)

No. 404. Jug with a pointed foot. (Nearly 1:5 actual size. Depth, 32 ft.)

No. 405. Bowl with a spout and handle. (1:4 actual size. Depth, 22 ft.)

No. 406. Globular Vase. (1:4 actual size. Depth, 29 ft.)

No. 407. Bottle of Terra-cotta. (1:4 actual size. Depth, 29 ft.)

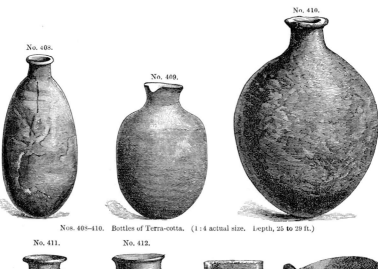

Nos. 408–410. Bottles of Terra-cotta. (1 : 4 actual size. Depth, 25 to 29 ft.)

Nos. 411, 412. Bottles of Terra-cotta. (1 : 4 actual size. Depth, 22 to 32 ft.)

No. 413. Cup with three breast-like excrescences. (1 : 4 actual size. Depth, 22 to 32 ft.)

No. 414. One-handled Tripod Basin. (1 : 4 actual size. Depth, 22 to 32 ft.)

are not rare in the third, the burnt city; they also occur sometimes in the following, the fourth city; but, except the form of the vase No. 411, of which there is an analogous one in the Museum of Leyden,[7] I am not aware that similar vessels have been ever found elsewhere in the remains of pre-historic ages.

Nos. 413 and 414 are also both wheel-made. The former is a cup with three round excrescences, which may represent a nose and two eyes. No. 414 is a tripod-pan or bowl with an open handle.

Nos. 415 and 416 represent black jugs of a peculiar shape, which I merely show here, as I have not noticed analogous ones elsewhere.

No. 415. Pitcher. (About 1 : 4 actual size. Depth, 26 ft.)

No. 416. Globular Pitcher. (1 : 4 actual size. Depth, 26 ft.)

[7] L. J. F. Janssen, de Germaansche en Noordsche Monumenten van het Museum te Leyden, Pl. ii. No. 46.

Nos. 417 and 418 are large red bowls with two handles. A bowl of a
shape like No. 417, and likewise hand-made, was found in Hungary, and

No. 417.   Large double-handled Bowl.   (1 : 3 actual size.   Depth, 26 to 30 ft.)

No. 418.   Large double-handled Bowl.   (1 : 3 actual size.   Depth, 26 to 30 ft.)

is represented in Pl. vi., No. 10, of Dr. Joseph Hampel's *Antiquités préhistoriques de la Hongrie*.

No. 419 represents, in 1–5th of the actual size, a large yellow double-
handled amphora with a convex bottom. I have put on it one of the
crown-shaped vase-covers. Of a similar shape are the dark yellow or
brown amphorae, Nos. 420, 421, 422. This last has on the body a long
excrescence in the form of a breast or teat curved downward. As a
very great number of the large Trojan jugs have a similar excrescence,
always curved downward, I would suggest that these excrescences,
which have almost the form of hooks, served as an additional support
for the rope with which the Trojan women fastened the jugs on their
backs when they fetched water from the springs. Amphorae like these
are very abundant in all the three upper pre-historic cities at Hissarlik,

but, strange to say, the shapes of Nos. 419, 420, 421, 422 have never yet
been found elsewhere.

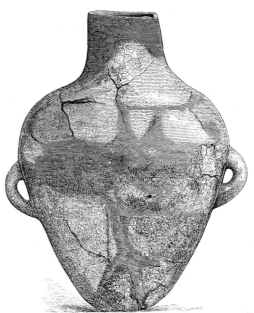

No. 420.   Jar with two handles.   (1 : 4 actual size.
Depth, 26 ft.)

No. 419.   Jar with two handles ; Cover in form of a
crown.   (1 : 5 actual size.   Depth, 26 ft.)

No. 421.   Jar with two handles.   (1 : 5 actual size.   Depth, 26 ft.)

No. 422.   Jar with two handles.   (1 : 6 actual size.
Depth, 28 to 32 ft.)

No. 423.   Large Amphora.   (1 : 7 actual size.
Depth, 26 ft.)

No. 423 represents a Trojan amphora of a different form, like one specimen, preserved in the little collection in the French School here at Athens, found on the island of Thera (Santorin), below three layers of pumice-stone and volcanic ashes, and, like No. 423, it is just 2 ft. high.

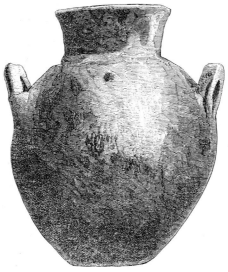

No. 421.   Vase of globular shape, with two handles.   (1 : 4 actual size.   Depth, 26 ft.)

Further varieties of large Trojan vessels with two handles are represented by the dark-red or lustrous blackish specimens Nos. 424, 425, and 426. No. 425 is decorated on each side with an excrescence; No. 426

No. 425. Vase with two handles. (1 : 4 actual size.
Depth, 26 ft.)

No. 427. Amphora of oval shape, with two
handles. (1 : 4 actual size. Depth, 32 ft.)

No. 426. Large Vase with two handles. (1 : 10 actual size.
Depth, 26 ft.)

No. 428. Jar with two handles.
(1 : 4 actual size. Depth, 26 ft.)

represents the usual shape of the funeral urns in the third, the burnt city; and No. 424, the usual shape of the funeral urns in the following, the

No. 429. Vase with two handles. (1 : 4
actual size. Depth, 29 ft.)

fourth city. Only two urns of this identical form were found, at a depth of from 26 to 28 ft., of which we can be pretty certain that they belong to the third or burnt city. The closest analogy to these vases is afforded by a lustrous-red hand-made vase found on the island of Thera (Santorin), below the strata of pumice-stone and volcanic ashes, and preserved in the collection of the French School here at Athens.

No. 427 is a large wheel-made lustrous-brown terra-cotta amphora of oval form, with two handles. A terra-cotta amphora of like shape, found in a tomb at Ialysus on the island of Rhodes, is in the British Museum. Of a somewhat similar shape is No. 428, which is a hand-made black vase with two handles. The oval vases, Nos. 429–432, are wheel-made. No. 429 is a lustrous black vessel with two handles, having in other respects most analogy to a black wheel-made vessel found in Thera (Santorin), and preserved in the French School here ; the only difference is that this latter vessel has only one handle. Nos. 430 and 431 are amphorae of a dark-red colour and have two large handles, which

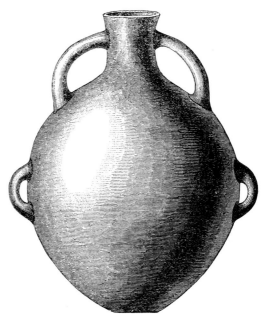

No. 430.   Large Oval Amphora with four handles.   (1 : 5 actual size.
Depth, 26 ft.)

join the spout to the body, and two small handles on the latter. Of the same colour is also No. 432, which has four handles. The amphora No. 433 is

No. 431.   Amphora with four handles.
(1 : 6 actual size.   Depth, 26 to 33 ft.)

No. 432.   Oval Amphora, with four handles.
(1 : 6 actual size.   Depth, 26 ft.)

not oval, but rather of lenticular form; it is of a lustrous dark-green
colour, and has only one large handle, which joins the spout to the body,

and two small ones on the
narrow sides of the latter. I
have found in no museum anything to compare with the
shape of these amphorae, but
that shape is frequent here.

The hand-made terra-cotta
bottles, Nos. 434, 435, and 436,
are of a dark-red or brown
colour, of lenticular form, and
resemble our hunting flasks.
No. 434 has no handles, and
is decorated with four breast-
like excrescences; the other two
are double-handled. No. 435
is decorated round the neck
with a protruding band, ornamented with vertical cuts.
Terra-cotta bottles of an identical shape, found in ancient
Egyptian tombs, are preserved

No. 433. Lustrous dark-green Amphora, of lenticular form,
with three handles. (1 : 4 actual size. Depth, 26 ft.)

in the Egyptian collections of the British Museum and the Louvre.
The collection of Cypriote antiquities in the British Museum also con-

No. 435.

No: 434.

No. 436.

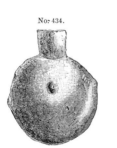

Nos. 434-436. Flat Jugs in the form of hunting flasks. (About 1 : 4 actual size. Depth, 26 ft.)

tains several specimens of a similar shape, but with a somewhat longer
spout. There are also in the Assyrian Collection in the British Museum
a large number of such terra-cotta bottles, found at Nimroud and elsewhere.

No. 437, as well as No. 438, are mixing vessels (κρατῆρες, called by
Homer κρητῆρες). Both are hand-made; the former has two, the latter
four handles; both are of a rude fabric, but little polished, and more
than usually baked. Mixing vessels like No. 437 are not rare; but large
ones of the size of No. 438 occur so seldom that I collected only eight
of them.

Mixing vessels were in general use throughout antiquity; for the ancients—wiser than we are—never drank wine unless mixed with water.[1] We find the word κρητήρ mentioned fourteen times in the *Iliad*,[2] including three instances in the plural. But terra-cotta mixing vessels being too cheap and common for heroes, the poet must have had in view κρητῆρες of metal—namely, gold, silver, or perhaps bronze or copper; for once he expressly says that Achilles, holding in his hand a double-handled goblet (δέπας ἀμφικύπελλον), poured all night wine from a golden mixing vessel (κρητήρ) on the earth and moistened it with the libation.[3] Another time he makes Achilles set a silver κρητήρ as a prize for the foot-race at the funeral games.[4] A third time he makes Hector order the herald Idaeus to bring from Troy a shining mixing

No. 437.   Mixing Vessel (Crater) with two handles.
(About 1 : 4 actual size. Depth, 32 ft.)

No. 438.   Large Mixing Vessel (Crater) with four handles, 1 ft. 9 in.
in diameter. (1 : 9 actual size. Depth, 23 ft.)

---

[1] We see pure wine (οἶνος ἄκρατος) used in the Homeric poems only for libations; so *Il.* ii. 341, and iv. 159:

σπονδαί τ᾿ ἄκρητοι καὶ δεξιαί, ἧς ἐπέπιθμεν.

The Romans certainly occasionally drank *merum*. I will not dispute that the Greeks may, in later times, have also occasionally used ἄκρατος. Mr. Philip Smith makes the ingenious observation : "To drink wine without water was of itself a sign of intemperance, marking a curious connection between two words of quite different origin — the ἄκρατος οἶνος and the ἀκρατὴς ἀνήρ who drank it."

[2] I deem it my most agreeable duty to make here a warm acknowledgment to my honoured friend Mr. Guy Lushington Prendergast, for the immense service he has rendered to science by composing a *Concordance to the Iliad of Homer* (London, 1875), which is a wonderful work for completeness and scholarship. For thirteen long

years has he laboured on this great work, having no other stimulus than his admiration for Homer and his desire to become instrumental in propagating the universal love for his divine poems. Mr. Prendergast could not have shown his noble aim and his disinterestedness better than by not publishing the fruit of his long labours for sale. But he generously presents it to Homeric scholars, or to those who make it their life's aim to show that the divine poems are based on real facts. May Mr. Prendergast's noble example be imitated also for the *Odyssey* !

[3] *Il.* xxiii. 218–220:

. . . . ὃ δὲ πάννυχος ὠκὺς Ἀχιλλεύς
χρυσέου ἐκ κρητῆρος, ἑλὼν δέπας ἀμφικύπελλον,
οἶνον ἀφυσσόμενος χαμάδις χέε, δεῦε δὲ γαῖαν, . . .

[4] *Il.* xxiii. 740, 741:

Πηλεΐδης δ᾿ αἶψ᾿ ἄλλα τίθει ταχυτῆτος ἄεθλα,
ἀργύρεον κρητῆρα τετυγμένον·

vessel (κρητῆρα φαεινόν) and golden goblets.[5] Thus there can be no doubt that the κρητήρ was in this case also of metal, but we are left in doubt as to the sort; for it may have been simply bronze or copper. I find the word κρητήρ also twelve times in the *Odyssey*, where Ulysses receives a silver κρητήρ as a present from the priest Ismarus;[6] one of Circé's maids mixes wine in a silver κρητήρ;[7] and Menelaus presents to Telemachus a silver κρητήρ with a gilded rim.[8] The mixing vessel stood on a tripod in the extreme corner of the great hall of the men.[9] Semper says:[10] "Herodotus distinguishes the Lesbian κρητήρ from the Argolic κρητήρ, but he describes only the latter in detail. It was decorated all round with projecting griffins' heads, and it stood on three kneeling colossi of bronze, seven cubits high.[11] Besides these, the Laconian and the Corinthian mixing vessels are mentioned as different kinds. Mixing vessels with tripods representing colossi, like that consecrated to Hera in the Samian temple and described by Herodotus, are represented in Egyptian reliefs. A small Etruscan clay model represents also similar sumptuous vessels, which were in general use throughout antiquity."

No. 439 is a dark-yellow terra-cotta vessel in the form of a barrel with a short spout. A similar barrel-shaped terra-cotta vessel is seen in the dark-brown tripod No. 440, whose spout is joined to the barrel by a handle. Similar barrel-shaped terra-cotta vessels may be seen in the collections of Cypriote antiquities in the Louvre and the British Museum ; but, except in Cyprus, I think, similar vessels have never yet been found. Mr. Philip Smith remarks to me that "such little barrels (called wooden bottles) are commonly taken to the hay and harvest fields by English labourers, filled with beer or

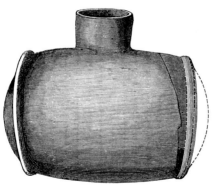

No. 439.   Curious Terra-cotta Vessel in the form of a cask, from the Royal House. (1 : 6 actual size. Depth, 26 ft.)

[5] *Il.* iii. 247, 248 :
. . . . . φέρε δὲ κρητῆρα φαεινόν
κῆρυξ Ἰδαῖος ἠδὲ χρύσεια κύπελλα, . . .

[6] *Od.* ix. 203 :
δῶκε δέ μοι κρητῆρα πανάργυρον, . . .

[7] *Od.* x. 356, 357 :
ἡ δὲ τρίτη κρητῆρι μελίφρονα οἶνον ἐκίρνα
ἡδὺν ἐν ἀργυρέῳ, νέμε δὲ χρύσεια κύπελλα·

[8] *Od.* iv. 615, 616 :
δώσω τοι κρητῆρα τετυγμένον· ἀργύρεος δέ
ἔστιν ἅπας, χρυσῷ δ' ἐπὶ χείλεα κεκράανται·

[9] *Od.* xxi. 145, 146 :
παρὰ κρητῆρα δὲ καλόν
ἷζε μυχοίτατος αἰεί·
xxii. 332, 333 :
ἔστη δ' ἐν χείρεσσιν ἔχων φόρμιγγα λίγειαν

ἄγχι παρ' ὀρσοθύρην· δίχα δὲ φρεσὶ μερμή-ριζεν, . . .
xxii. 340, 341 :
ἥ τοι ὁ φόρμιγγα γλαφυρὴν κατέθηκε χαμᾶζε
μεσσηγὺς κρητῆρος ἰδὲ θρόνου ἀργυροήλου, . . .

[10] G. Semper, *Keramik, Tektonik, Stereotomie, Metallotechnik*; München, 1879, p. 16.

[11] Herodot. iv. 61 and 152 : ἔπειτα ἐσβάλλουσι, ἣν μὲν τύχωσι ἔχοντες, ἐς λέβητας ἐπιχωρίους, μάλιστα Λεσβίοισι κρητῆρσι προσεικέλους, χωρὶς ἢ ὅτι πολλῷ μέζονας . . . . οἱ δὲ Σάμιοι τὴν δεκάτην τῶν ἐπικερδίων ἐξελόντες ἓξ τάλαντα, ἐποιήσαντο χαλκήϊον, κρητῆρος Ἀργολικοῦ τρόπον· πέριξ δὲ αὐτοῦ γρυπῶν κεφαλαὶ πρόκροσσοί εἰσι· καὶ ἀνέθηκαν ἐς τὸ Ἡραιον, ὑποστήσαντες αὐτῷ τρεῖς χαλκέους κολοσσοὺς ἑπταπήχεας, τοῖσι γούνασι ἐρηρεισμένους.

cider, and that they are now also made of polished wood for tourists' bottles."

No. 441 is a brown globular tripod-vessel, the body of which is divided by incised lines into five large and five small fields, alternating in regular succession. All the large fields are filled with dots. The mouth of the spout is only 1-3rd in. in diameter. I presume that this small and pretty Trojan tripod may have been used by ladies for holding scented oil, which, as we know from Homer, was applied after the bath. It cannot have been used as a lamp: first, because it is not adapted for that use; and secondly, because lamps appear to have been totally unknown in Greece and Asia Minor before the sixth century B.C. Not to speak of lamps in pre-historic cities, I have found no trace of them even in the archaic strata of the Hellenic or Aeolic Ilium. Lamps of terra-cotta are, indeed, numerous in the layer of ruins of Novum Ilium, but they nearly all appear to be of the Roman time; there is hardly one among them which might claim to be of the Macedonian period. In fact, even in Greece I never saw a terra-cotta

No. 440.   Curious Tripod Vessel in form of a cask.
(1 : 4 actual size. Depth, 23 ft.)

No. 441.   Tripod Globular Vase, with incised
ornamentation.   (1 : 4 actual size. Depth, 29 ft.)

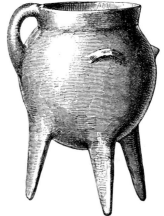

No. 442.   Wheel-made Tripod.   (1 : 3 actual size.
Depth, 23 ft.)

lamp to which archæology could attribute a higher antiquity than the fifth century B.C. Certainly in all antiquity previous to the fifth century B.C. people used torches for lighting. We find them mentioned by Homer[1] on the occasion of the wedding represented by Hephaestus on the shield of Achilles. They most probably consisted here of nothing else than pieces of pine or other resinous wood, called δαΐδες by the poet (from δαίω): hence the word δᾴς for "torch." For lighting the houses fire-pans or basins (λαμπτῆρες) were used, of which three in the great hall of the palace of Ulysses are mentioned, and in which dry wood was burned.[2]

_____

[1] *Il.* xviii. 492, 493:
νύμφας δ' ἐκ θαλάμων δαΐδων ὕπο λαμπομενάων
ἠγίνεον ἀνὰ ἄστυ, πολὺς δ' ὑμέναιος ὀρώρειν, . . .

[2] *Od.* xviii. 307–310:
αὐτίκα λαμπτῆρας τρεῖς ἵστασαν ἐν μεγάροισιν,
ὄφρα φαείνοιεν· περὶ δὲ ξύλα κάγκανα θῆκαν,
αὖα πάλαι, περίκηλα, νέον κεκεασμένα χαλκῷ,
καὶ δαῖδας μετέμισγον·

No. 442 is a *wheel-made* tripod-vessel, with a handle and two projecting ornaments in the form of ears.

Under No. 443 I represent a large lustrous dark-brown vase, with a spout in the body and two handles. As the spout is in the lower part of the body, I cannot explain the use of this vase otherwise than by supposing that it was placed below a fountain, the water of which ran through the orifice into the vase, and that the "thirsty souls" put their mouths to the small spout to drink.

The small yellow tripod pitcher, No. 444, has two handles in the form of horns, and a spout in the upper part of the body. I suppose that

No. 444. Tripod Vase, with two horn-like handles and a spout in the body. (Actual size. Depth, 26 ft.)

No. 443. Vase with two handles and spout.
(1 : 7 actual size. Depth, 23 ft.)

this vessel, as it is but very small, may have served as a baby's feeding bottle. Its only ornamentation consists of two incised lines round the neck.

No. 445 is a lustrous-yellow jug with a trefoil mouth, one handle, and a spout in the body. Very curious is the basket shape of the red cup No. 446, with its handle over the mouth and its spout in the lower part of the body. A terra-cotta vessel, with a similar handle over the mouth and a spout in the body, was found by me in my excavations at Tiryns. It is preserved in the Mycenean Museum at Athens. Equally curious is the light-red little vase No. 447, which has a large spout on one side. All these three last vessels can, in my opinion, have served for nothing else than babies' feeding bottles. Similar small terra-cotta vessels, with a spout in the body, are frequent in the tombs of Cyprus, as well as in ancient Egyptian sepulchres, and may be seen in the collections of Cypriote and Egyptian antiquities in the Louvre and the British Museum, which latter contains also two similar vessels, found in a tomb at Ialysus, in Rhodes.

No. 448 is a small pitcher without a handle. Hand-made pitchers of a similar shape were found at Szihalom, in Hungary, and are exhibited under Nos. 15–18 in the glass case No. IX. in the National Museum of

Buda-Pesth. Wheel-made ones of this form are also found in Holland, and, as Professor Virchow informs me, they are very common in Lusatia

No. 448.

No. 449.

No. 450.

No. 451.

No. 452

No. 445.

No. 446.   No. 453.   No. 447.

Nos. 445–453. Babies' Feeding Bottles, Cups, &c.   (1 : 4 actual size. Depth, 19 to 26 ft.)

(Lausitz). No. 449 is a small cup with two handles; No. 450, a very small cup with a large curved handle: two cups of a similar shape, but of a larger size, are in the collection of Professor Virchow, having been found by him in his excavations in the graveyard of Zaborówo. No. 451 is a small pitcher: hand-made pitchers similar to this, found at Szihalom, are likewise in the National Museum of Buda-Pesth, under Nos. 10, 14, 20, 21 in the glass case No. IX. No. 452 is a small tripod-vase, with per-forated projections for suspension; No. 453, a small cup, like No. 11 found at Szihalom ; No. 454, a small globular tripod-vase, with two dots on the body.

No. 454. Globular Tripod Vase. (1 : 4 actual size. Depth, 29 ft.)

I now come to the plates, which are nearly all wheel-made, and, when so, are always but slightly baked, unpolished, and exceedingly rude ; but there occur also a great many plates which are hand-made, and these are always well polished and a little more baked. The wheel-made plates have always the yellow colour of the clay, and are generally but small; the hand-made ones are either dark-brown or red, and usually of a larger size. The wheel-made plates never have handles ; but the larger hand-made ones have usually one or two handles. Nos. 455 to 460 represent five of the rude wheel-made plates, with a large hand-made one with one handle on the top of them. Nos. 461 to 468, again, represent eight of the rude wheel-made plates.

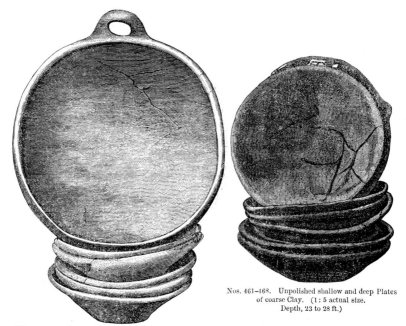

Nos. 461–468. Unpolished shallow and deep Plates
of coarse Clay. (1 : 5 actual size.
Depth, 23 to 28 ft.)

Nos. 455–460. Unpolished shallow and deep Plates of coarse
Clay, with a polished hand-made one on the top.
(1 : 5 actual size. Depth, 23 to 28 ft.)

Similar very rude unpolished wheel-made plates may be seen in the collections both of Assyrian and Cypriote antiquities in the British Museum. As Dr. Joseph Hampel kindly informs me, they are also frequently found in the excavations at Magyarád, in Hungary. Professor Virchow writes to me that plates of the same shape but superficially polished are very common in Germany. None of the wheel-made Trojan plates show the marks of wear and tear. This is the more astonishing, as, on account of their rudeness and fragility, any knife-cut would have made a deep mark on them. As the Greeks in Homer's time, οἱ δ' ἐπ' ὀνείαθ' ἑτοῖμα προκείμενα χεῖρας ἴαλλον, so certainly the Trojans also used no knives or forks, but only the hands in eating, and therefore there may have been nothing to cut on these plates; but still, I think, they should naturally have borne the marks of long use. These wheel-made plates are very abundant: on the little plateau formed by the external and internal walls, which I used to call the Tower, I found, on a space 20 ft. square, 13 entire plates, and 12 broken ones which I could easily recompose. It deserves particular notice that these wheel-made plates are very rare in the *débris* of the following, the fourth city, in which, on the other hand, the hand-made plates are very numerous.

No. 469 represents a crucible of terra-cotta with four feet, but slightly baked, which my friend the celebrated metallurgist, Dr. John Percy, declared to be one of the most valuable objects of my whole Trojan collection. He probably prizes it so highly on account of the residues of fused metal and spangles of gold which are contained in it. Professor W. Chandler Roberts, who examined this object most carefully, and analysed some of the metal it contains, kindly gave me the following note on the subject :—" The vessel appears to be of clay, containing grains of quartz. It has probably been used in some operation connected with the metallurgy of gold, as spangles of that metal may be readily detected on the inner surface. One portion of the vessel is covered with a vesicular slag, and it contains a fragment of carbonate of copper mixed with crystals of red oxide of copper. It is possible that this saucer-like vessel may have been filled with bone-ash, and used as a 'test' for cupelling gold or silver; but I have not yet detected the presence of any lead-compound, which would have made this view almost a certainty."

The crucibles were made of coarse clay, mixed with cow-dung, in order to make them stronger.

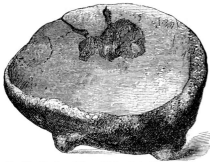

No. 469. Crucible of Clay, with four feet. It has particles of copper and gold still sticking to it. (Nearly half actual size. Depth, 23 ft.)

No. 470. Crucible of Clay. (Nearly half actual size. Depth, 26 ft.)

No. 470 is also a slightly-baked saucer-like crucible, but it has no feet. Nos. 471, 472, and 473 are small boat-like cups of but slightly-baked clay, which, in the opinion of Dr. Percy and Professor Roberts, have also been used in metallurgy, and particularly for refining gold or silver. For

No. 471.

No. 472.   No. 473.

Nos. 471–473. Small boat-like Basins of sun-dried Clay. (Nearly half actual size. Depth, 22 to 26 ft.)

this purpose four times the quantity of lead is now added to the precious metal, and it is left in the fire until the lead evaporates. There can hardly be a doubt that the refining process has been much the same at all times in antiquity. I call the reader's particular attention to the shape of the vessel No. 471. As it runs out to a point to the right, does it not appear to be the facsimile of an ancient ship, the oars being indicated on each side by four incised vertical strokes? A vessel somewhat resembling this was found at the station of Locras in the Lake of Bienne.[3]

Very curious are the little terra-cotta spoons Nos. 474 and 475, which, as they are also but very slightly baked, may likewise have been used by the Trojan metallurgists. Similar spoons are very rare at

No. 474.

No. 475.

Nos. 474, 475. Spoons of Terra-cotta. (Half actual size. Depth, 22 to 26 ft.)

No. 476. Funnel of Mica-schist. (Half actual size. Depth, 26 ft.)

No. 477. Large semi-globular Funnel of Terra-cotta, with sieve-like holes. (Half actual size. Depth, 26 ft.)

Hissarlik, but so they are elsewhere. A broken spoon of an identical shape was found in the settlement of the Stone age at Inzighofen.[4] Three other similar specimens were found at Dozmat in the county of Vas, and at Tisza Ugh in the county of Heves, in Hungary.[5] A broken terra-cotta spoon, found at Szihalom, is exhibited under No. 38 in the glass-case No. IX. in the National Museum of Buda-Pesth. Two such terra-cotta spoons were found in the Lake-dwellings of the Stone age, at the station of Auvernier in the Lake of Neufchâtel,[6] and at the station of Gérofin in the Lake of Bienne.[7] Professor Virchow informs me that spoons of baked clay now and then occur in ancient tombs in the east of Germany.

No. 476 represents in half-size a funnel of mica-schist. Funnels of terra-cotta of the same shape are numerous in all the three upper prehistoric cities at Hissarlik; but the funnel before us is the only one of stone that I ever found. I presume these funnels have been used in

[3] Victor Gross, Les dernières Trouvailles dans les Habitations lacustres du Lac de Bienne; Porrentruy, 1879, Pl. ii. No. 11.

[4] Ludwig Lindenschmit, Die Vaterländischen Alterthümer; Mainz, 1860, Pl. xxvi. No. 1.

[5] Jos. Hampel, Antiquités préhistoriques de la Hongrie, Pl. xiii. Nos. 18, 20, 22.

[6] Victor Gross, Deux Stations lacustres, Moeringen et Auvernier; Neuveville, 1878, Pl. xii. 4.

[7] Idem, Les dernières Trouvailles dans les Habitations lacustres du Lac de Bienne; Porrentruy, 1879, Pl. ii. No. 12.

metallurgy. Professor Sayce observes to me that a similar funnel of terra-cotta, marked with Cypriote characters, was found by the late Mr. George Smith under the floor of Assurbanipal's palace at Kouyunjik, and he fancies it served as a measure. Two funnels of terra-cotta of the very same form, each marked with the character ⊓, were found by me in the fifth pre-historic city of Hissarlik. They are represented in their place.[8] No. 477 and No. 478 are large well-polished lustrous dark-yellow funnels of terra-cotta, of semi-globular form, with sieve-like holes.

No. 478. Large semi-globular Funnel, with sieve-like perforations. (Half actual size. Depth, 26 ft.)

No. 479. A piece of Terra-cotta, with two holes slightly sunk in front like eyes, and a hole perforated from side to side. (Half actual size. Depth, 26 ft.)

No. 479 is a solid piece of terra-cotta, with a perforation from side to side; in front are two cavities, but slightly sunk, in the form of eyes. This object may have served as a weight for the loom or for fishing-nets.

No. 480 is a slightly-baked object of terra-cotta, in the form of a goblet, with sieve-like perforations; it cannot be anything else but a censer. Two similar vessels, held by Professor Virchow to be censers,

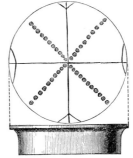

No. 480. Censer of slightly-baked Clay in the form of a goblet, with sieve-like perforations. (Half actual size. Depth, 23 ft.)

No. 481. Vessel in the form of a flower-saucer, with incised decoration. (1 : 6 actual size. Depth, 26 ft.)

---

[8] See Nos. 1338, 1339, p. 582.

are in his collection of antiquities from Zaborówo in Posen. Similar censers are preserved in the Märkisches Museum at Berlin.

No. 481 is a very pretty lustrous-red vessel, in the form of a flower-saucer. Its flat bottom is ornamented with linear decorations and a cross of dots. The engraving represents a side view of this curious vessel, whose decoration is given separately above it. This vase-cover finds its analogue in that which we see on a vase found near Guben in Lusatia, and represented under No. 5 on Pl. xvii. in the *Sessional Report of the Berlin Society for Anthropology*, 21st July, 1877.

Nos. 482 and 483 are fragments of a very large red vase, decorated alternately with broad bands filled with fanciful strokes, and with rows of

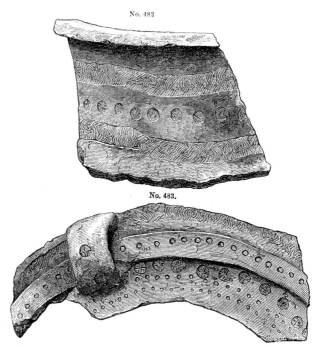

No. 482

No. 483.

Nos. 482, 483. Fragments of a large red Vase, with a curious impressed decoration.
(Nearly 1 : 5 actual size. Depth, 26 ft.)

small or large stamps representing crosses in relief; even the handles are decorated with stamps containing similar crosses. These fragments have evidently been exposed to an intense heat in the conflagration, for they are thoroughly baked. Professor Sayce remarks to me that "the circles with crosses within them resemble the Babylonian rosette, a favourite Babylonian and Hittite decoration." Professor Virchow mentions to me that he noticed a similar ornamentation on terra-cotta vessels found at Bologna.

No. 484 represents the fragment of a grey vase-cover, with the incised linear representation of a stag and another animal, probably intended for a cuttle-fish; but Professor Virchow thinks the primitive Trojan artist

intended to represent a tortoise. We see on it also a plant-like ornament, perhaps meant for a tree. Similar incised ornaments are very

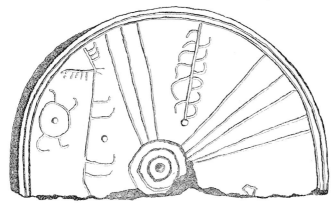

No. 484.   Vase-cover of Terra-cotta, with an incised ornamentation representing a tree, a stag, and probably a
cuttle-fish.   (Half actual size.   Depth, 26 ft.)

common on the Trojan whorls.[9] No. 485 represents a top of terra-
cotta; No. 486, a curious rattle of black terra-cotta, ornamented with
incised lines; the handle is perforated for suspension. There are small
pieces of metal in this rattle; it may have been a child's toy. No. 487
is another rattle with pieces of metal inside it; like the other, it has no

No. 485. Top of Terra-
cotta. (Half actual size.
Depth, 23 ft.)

No. 486. Curious Rattle of
Terra-cotta. (Half actual
size. Depth, 23 ft.)

No. 487. Rattle-box of Terra-cotta, in the form of
a woman; head missing. (2 : 3 actual size. Depth,
20 ft.)

opening. It is in the form of a woman, who holds her hands on the
breast; the head is missing; the necklace is indicated by three horizontal
strokes, and the breast-ornament by six vertical strokes. Though it was
found at a depth of 20 ft., it certainly belongs to the third or burnt
city, both because of its character and because it bears the marks of
the conflagration to which it has been exposed.

[9] See Nos. 1867, 1879, 1880, 1881, 1882, 1885, 1886, 1951, and 2000.

Nos. 488 and 489 represent brush-handles of a peculiar kind of compact and very clean yellow clay, with a perforation for suspension; the many small holes seen in the lower part of No. 488, and which also exist in No. 489, served for fixing in the bristles or whatever else the brush may have been composed of. Professor Landerer, who examined these brush-handles very carefully, writes to me the following note on the subject:—" I succeeded in extracting from three of the small holes some residue which, when put into a platinum spoon and burnt, gave the smell, not of animal, but of vegetable, matter. I therefore believe that little stalks of plants, like those which are now used as toothpicks, as *e.g.* the corolla of Foeniculum, were put into the holes and constituted the brush proper. Besides, the holes are too large for bristles, unless several were fixed in one hole." [10]

It deserves particular attention that these clay brush-handles were merely dried in the sun and that none of them have been baked, except those which have been exposed to an intense heat in the conflagration, in which many of them have been more or less burnt. I have further to notice that these clay brush-handles are frequent in the third or burnt city, but that they never occurred in any of the other pre-historic cities.

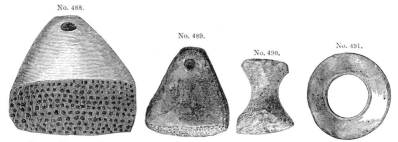

No. 488. Terra-cotta Handle of a Trojan Brush, with the holes in which the bristles have been fixed. (Half actual size. Depth, 33 ft.) Nos. 489–491. Brush-handle of dried Clay, Object of Terra-cotta, and Ring of Mother-of-pearl. (1 : 3 actual size. Depth, 26 to 32 ft.)

No. 490 is an object of slightly-baked clay, which may probably have been used for heckling yarn. No. 491 is a ring of mother-of-pearl.

Nos. 492–499 are eight seals of very slightly-baked clay. The seal No. 492 has in the handle a perforation for suspension with a string. Very curious are the signs which we see incised on it, and which resemble written characters. Professor Sayce remarks to me: " The signs all represent the same symbol, which is identical in form with a character met with in both the Hittite and the Cypriote inscriptions, in the latter of which it has the value of *ne*, and which may be the origin of the Trojan *swastika*." On the seal No. 493 we see two crosses, of which the one is incised, the other marked with dots. On No. 494 are incised zigzag lines and some straight strokes; No. 495, again, has incised crosses. On No. 496 we see a ⊐⊔, with its arms curved into spirals; on No. 497, nothing but dots; and on No. 498, an incised cross and

---

[10] This is no objection, as ordinary brushes are always made with a bunch of bristles in each hole.

dots. My friend Mr. Panagiotes Eustratiades, Director-General of Antiquities in Greece, remarks to me that No. 493 may not be a seal,

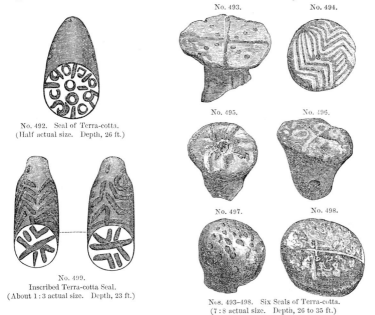

No. 493.   No. 494.

No. 492. Seal of Terra-cotta.
(Half actual size. Depth, 26 ft.)

No. 495.   No. 496.

No. 497.   No. 498.

No. 499.
Inscribed Terra-cotta Seal.
(About 1 : 3 actual size. Depth, 23 ft.)

Nos. 493–498. Six Seals of Terra-cotta.
(7 : 8 actual size. Depth, 26 to 35 ft.)

but the button or handle of a vase-cover. That may be so, but all the rest are certainly seals.

The most curious of all is the terra-cotta seal No. 499, which has a perforation for suspension. Its handle has on two sides an incised herring-bone ornamentation, and on the third side, the one to the right in the cut, an incised inscription, in which, as Professor Sayce says, " characters also found in the Cypriote syllabary can be easily recognized. The Cypriote character representing *e*, in an older form than any met with in Cyprus itself, is engraved on the die of the seal." Both the inscription on the handle and that on the seal are discussed by Prof. Sayce in his Appendix on the Trojan inscriptions.[11] The most striking analogy to the Trojan seals is offered by the terra-cotta seals found at Pilin in Hungary,[1] on which we see circles, stars, crosses, rhombs, and other figures.

Nos. 500 and 501 show the two sides of a perforated cylinder of terra-cotta, with an incised decoration, representing a tree and linear orna-

No. 500.   No. 501.

Nos. 500, 501. Cylinder of Terra-cotta with an incised decoration, from the Stratum of the Burnt City.
(Half actual size.)

---

[11] See Prof. Sayce's Appendix, where also a more perfect engraving of the seal is given.

[1] Joseph Hampel, *Antiquités préhistoriques de la Hongrie*, Pl. xiii. Nos. 4–9.

ments. Nos. 502 and 503 are the two sides of a cylinder of blue felspar,
engraved on one side with a double flower, surmounted by a half-diamond
or arrow-head, and on the other with signs (perhaps the name of the
owner) within a cartouch.[2] It was found in the royal house. Under

Nos. 502, 503.   Engraved Cylinder of blue Felspar.   From the Palace.   (Actual size.   Depth, 30 ft.)

Nos. 504 and 505, I represent two double whorls, in the shape of tops,
which are made of a very fine dark-yellow clay, and are well polished.
No. 504 is decorated on the upper and lower parts, No. 505 on the upper

Nos. 504, 505.   Double Whorls of lustrous-yellow colour, from the Stratum of the Burnt City.
(Half actual size.)

part only, with an incised ornamentation, which may be intended to
represent flowers. Similar double whorls are not frequent. I collected
in all only twenty-five of them.

Nos. 506 to 511A, B, represent the ornamentation of seven terra-cotta
whorls. No. 511 was found in the royal house: the numerous little figures
upon it, resembling faces, are very curious. The different forms of the
whorls which occur in this third, the burnt city, may be seen on the
lithographed plates at the end of the volume, under Nos. 1806, 1807,
1808, 1810, 1812, 1815. All these forms occur in really enormous abundance, except that of No. 1806, which is rare, and is only found unornamented; nearly one-half of all the whorls found have incised patterns,
of which I give the principal examples in the plates. The depth at
which each whorl was found is marked in mètres; and thus all those
which are marked from 7 to 10 M. (23 to 33 ft.), inclusive, may be considered to have been collected in the third or burnt city. Among the most
frequent patterns are those of Nos. 1817 and 1818, representing crosses
with a large dot in each arm, and the pattern No. 1820, which also
shows a cross. The pattern No. 1822 occurs but seldom, as also
No. 1825; that of No. 1824 is frequent. There is only one example of
No. 1826, which represents two *swastikas* and other inexplicable signs.
I call attention, however, to the similarity of the upper figure to that
which we see below in No. 1883, which is certainly meant to represent
a man with uplifted arms. The patterns on No. 1827 are very frequent

---

[2] A more exact representation of these signs is given by Professor Sayce in his Appendix.

on the whorls; those of Nos. 1830, 1831, 1832, 1834, and 1836, occur only once. A very abundant pattern is that of No. 1833, the idea

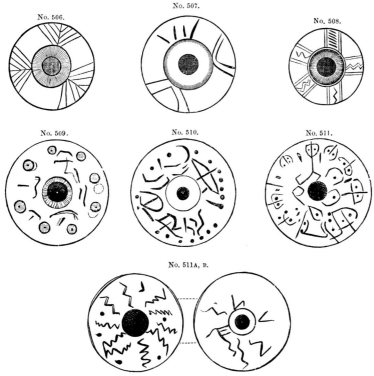

No. 507.

No. 506.

No. 508.

No. 509.

No. 510.

No. 511.

No. 511A, B.

Nos. 506–511A, B. Seven Whorls of Terra-cotta with incised decoration.
(Actual size. Depth, 26 ft.)

of which may have been taken from a moving wheel. Patterns like Nos. 1840, 1841, and 1848, are frequent, particularly the last, which occurs many hundreds of times in the third city, as well as in the two following ones. Nos. 1842 and 1843 occurred only once; No. 1844 occasionally; No. 1846 only once. No. 1853 also occurred only once; whereas the patterns with the ⛨, Nos. 1851, 1855, and 1859, are very frequent. The pattern No. 1856 is found many times, but those of Nos. 1857 and 1860 only once; the latter seems to have written characters. In the pattern No. 1862 we again see the sign ⛨ five times repeated; only its branches are here curved, and the centre of this curious cross is occupied by a circle with a point. This pattern is not rare. We again see the ⛨ with its branches in spirals in No. 1868; this pattern also occurs often. The signs on No. 1869, which seem to be written characters, as well as those on No. 1870, occur only once. The pattern No. 1872, in which we see the ⛨ in conjunction with burning altars, occurs several times; those of Nos. 1873, 1874, 1875, 1876, and 1878, only once : in all these we see the 卐 or 卍 with other signs. A frequent pattern is No. 1877, in which we see four animals, probably intended to be hares.

On No. 1881 we see a very rude linear representation of three quadrupeds with horns, probably meant for stags. Three stags are, no doubt, also intended to be shown in the curious pattern No. 1883, although two of them have only three legs. Similar very rude linear representations of stags, or other animals, are scratched on some of the vases with human faces found in the province of Pommerellen near Dantzig, which are for the most part preserved in the Museum at Dantzig ; others are in the Royal Museum at Berlin.

In perfect analogy with the rude drawing of the stags is the linear representation of the man with uplifted arms, which we see on the same whorl, No. 1883. Similar linear representations of stags, but with four legs, are also seen in No. 1884 ; whorls decorated with these animals are frequent. The rudest representation imaginable of animals is given on No. 1885 ; where one has only three feet, another only one horn. Again, we see three quadrupeds a little better made on No. 1886 : one of them has a tolerable bird's head ; only one of them seems to have horns.

The patterns on the whorls Nos. 1887, 1888, 1890, and 1891 occur frequently. The pattern No. 1892 is unique ; those of Nos. 1893 and 1896 are very common. On No. 1894 the primitive engraver doubtless intended to make four *swastikas*, but with one of them he did not succeed. A curious pattern is No. 1897, with its triangles and 15 zigzag lines ; further, those with plant-like ornaments, Nos. 1898, 1899, 1900, 1901, 1903, 1904. A similar punched decoration is seen engraved on the flags of native Lower Silurian grit, in the interior of the sepulchre of Ollam Fodhla, the famous monarch and lawgiver of Ireland,[3] in which we also find the ornament represented in the upper and lower field of No. 1907, and in the upper field of No. 1908. The whorls are rarely ornamented on more than one side ; but No. 1902 is decorated on both sides—on the one with an incised floral ornamentation, on the other with incisions in the form of crescents. No. 1909 shows in the upper field the form of an altar with flames : we again see four such altars with flames on No. 1914, six more on No. 1913, five on No. 1915, three on No. 1916. On No. 1912 we again see, five times repeated, that curious written character which the late Orientalist, Martin Haug of Munich, read *si*. No. 1919 is ornamented all over with zigzag lines ; it has also one 卐 and one 卍. There is no other example of the exact pattern of either of the Nos. 1918, 1919, 1920, 1921, 1922. In No. 1921 we again see zigzag lines, and also in No. 1923 : this pattern, as well as that of No. 1925, occurs several times ; also that of No. 1924, in which we again see an altar with flames. No. 1926 is decorated with zigzag lines and crosses. The patterns of No. 1927 and No. 1932 are very fre-

---

[3] *Discovery of the Tomb of Ollam Fodhla.* By E. A. Conwell. Dublin, 1873.

quent; that of No. 1930 occurs many times; also that of No. 1933.
Nos. 1934, 1935, 1936, and 1938 occur only once. On the latter whorl
we again see Dr. Haug's character *si*. I call the reader's particular
attention to the beautiful ornamentation of No. 1940, which occurs many
times; also to that of No. 1945, which occurs only once. Nos. 1941,
1943, and 1944 are often found: the pattern No. 1942 does not occur
again. Very curious is the decoration of No. 1946, in which we see a
burning altar, a ⊔ᒣ, a sun, four dots and strokes. This pattern, as well
as those of Nos. 1948 and 1947, in which latter we also see two ⊔ᒣ and
one ᒉᒐ, occur only once. The signs on No. 1949, in which we see again
a zigzag line, probably the symbol of lightning, and a ᒉᒐ, occur many
times; the patterns also on No. 1950 are frequent. There are only single
examples of the patterns of Nos. 1956 and 1959, which are in the form
of a disc, and of No. 1957. That of No. 1958 occurs often; also that
of No. 1964, in which we see three flowers, but not that on the opposite
side. Nos. 1961, 1962, and 1963 occur only once. The patterns of
Nos. 1966, 1968, 1969, and 1971 occur only once; that of No. 1968 is
very remarkable, for it shows in a sort of monogram five birds with very
long necks and beaks. There can be hardly any doubt that the primitive artist intended here to represent *storks*, which must have been at the
Trojan epoch just as abundant in the Troad as they are now.

But still more interesting is the figure which we see on No. 1971;
for if we compare it with that at the top of No. 1826, and with that in
the lower part of No. 1883, which latter cannot possibly be anything
else than a man in monogram, we may be pretty certain that here too
a man with uplifted arms was meant to be represented, his feet being
indicated by two slanting strokes. Rude and even horrible as these
representations of our species are, they are of capital interest to us if we
look upon them as the predecessors of the masterpieces of art in the time
of Pericles. But we have seen that the Trojans were perfectly able to
model in clay tolerably good representations of men and animals (see
Nos. 190, 191, 226, and Nos. 333 to 340): why then did they incise on their
whorls such monstrous figures of men and animals, figures which far
exceed in rudeness the rudest drawings of the wild men of Africa? Is
there any analogy whatever between this monstrous art and the other
handiwork of the Trojans? If we look at the rude but symmetrically
shaped pottery, or if we contemplate the masses of gold ornaments which
reveal so much artistic skill, and which can only have been the work of a
school of artists centuries old,—is it possible to suppose that a people
so far advanced in civilization could have made such rudest of rude representations of man and animal, unless these latter had been conventional
figures, intended as votive offerings to the tutelary deity, figures consecrated by the use of ages? This supposition seems certainly to be
confirmed by the figures themselves, all of which are equally monstrous.
Nay, the anomaly would otherwise be quite inexplicable, because, if this
explanation were not correct, there would at least be a difference in the
style of the figures, some of which might be bad, others better, and others

tolerably good. But, just as the inhabitants of the four upper prehistoric cities adhered with fervent zeal to the modelling of the traditional and conventional hideous owl-heads on their sacred vases, in the same way did they adhere with fervent zeal to the traditional and conventional scratchings of monstrous manikins and hideous animal forms on their *ex-votos* to their patron goddess. This at least appears to me to be the only way of explaining the strange facts before us, for which we have no analogy whatever.

The whorl No. 1970 was found at a depth of 12 mètres or 40 ft., and, therefore, most probably belongs to the second city. But its pattern occurs also in the third and fourth cities. The patterns Nos. 1974 and 1975 occur only once; I call attention to the curious sign in the latter, which may be a written character. We again see the written character, Haug's *si*, on No. 1976. The two patterns of No. 1977, as well as that of No. 1978, which represents a flower, are very frequent; the same may be said of that which we see on Nos. 1979 and 1981. That of No. 1980 with zigzag lines occurs several times. On No. 1982 we again see three *swastikas*. One of the most common patterns is that of No. 1985. No. 1986 represents a ball of terra-cotta with a circle on each pole and a zone round the middle, in which we see on both sides a round groove; the two grooves are joined by a curved line; the whole ball is, besides, ornamented with dots. Similar balls, but without the grooves and the curved line, are very frequent. In the pattern No. 1987 we see, besides the usual curved lines, a ⊐ with curved arms radiating from a circle in the middle. There is a similar ornamentation on the whorl No. 1989, but here the ⊐ has straight arms: the pattern of this latter whorl is common. The exact pattern of No. 1988, with two *swastikas*, three curved lines and three rows of dots, occurs only once. So also does the pattern of the whorl No. 1992, in which we see a number of spirals and 13 bundles, each consisting of three strokes intersected by lines of five dots. Very remarkable are the signs which we see on the whorl No. 1994, some of which may be written characters; but if we turn the page a little to the left, we easily recognize once more, in the large sign to the right, the rude representation of a man in monogram, with uplifted arms and the feet extended to the right and left; nay, here the representation of our species has been more successful than in the three examples already described, for the figure is incised with much more symmetry. On the whorl No. 1996 are written characters which will be explained in the Appendix on the Trojan Inscriptions. The pattern which we see on the whorl No. 1995 is very common.

The most remarkable of all the terra-cotta balls found is no doubt No. 1997, which I have discussed before.[4] We see there on the side *b* two large owl's eyes with their eyebrows distinctly incised, as on many of the idols and on some of the owl-vases; the beak is indicated by a stroke which descends vertically from between the eyes: to the left of the owl-

---

[4] See page 344.

face we see (at *a*) a wheel with six spokes; to the right of the owl-face (at *c*) is a large circle with a small one, and below the circle, between it and the vertical stroke, is a small circle : on the back a number of vertical strokes seem, as on many idols, to indicate the female hair. This hair is not represented in the engraving; all the rest may be seen at *a*, *b*, *c*, as well as in the detailed drawing below them, No. 1998. May not the owl's face be symbolic of the morning springing up between the sun, represented by the wheel, and the moon, indicated by the concentric circles, having below it the morning star indicated by the small circle?

Very curious is also the terra-cotta ball No. 1999, which is divided by incised lines into eight fields, developed under No. 2000, in one of which we see a ⊐⊔, in another a tree, and in all clusters of dots. Professor Sayce observes to me that, judging from the analogy of the Babylonian cylinders, the latter would represent the planets or stars.

The whorls are all perforated; and, though they are made of the same coarse clay, mixed with crushed mica, quartz, and silicious stone, yet as they are well polished and have evidently been repeatedly dipped in a wash of fine clay before baking, they generally have a lustrous surface, and are of red, yellow, black or grey colours. All those of the third city, which were exposed to the intense heat of the conflagration, are thoroughly baked, and can generally be at once recognized by their colour; but even in the other pre-historic cities there may be found a great many thoroughly baked whorls, a fact which is not astonishing, as, owing to their small size, the fire could reach them on all sides. But in general the whorls of the other pre-historic cities are, like the vases, only half baked. The clay of many of those that are well baked, and particularly of the black ones, is so compact, that every one thinks it is stone.

All this may also be said of the balls. The ornamentation has usually been incised with a sharp or pointed instrument of bone, wood, or silex, before the first baking, and filled in with white chalk so as to strike the eye. On many whorls and balls this white chalk has disappeared from the decorations; but, as we see on many hundreds of whorls the ornamentation filled with the white chalk, we may with all probability suppose that all the ornamented whorls were treated in the same way. But we often see whorls with ugly scratches which can only have been made with pointed silex after baking. On many whorls the incised decoration is remarkable for its fineness and symmetry, as, for instance, on Nos. 1825, 1895, 1902, 1921, 1940, 1945; but in general it is as rude as if it were the primitive artist's first essay in *intaglio*-work.

All the drawings of the whorls and balls have been made by M. Burnouf and his accomplished daughter, Mdlle. Louise Burnouf, to whom I here make the warmest acknowledgment. All the whorls and balls are represented of the actual size. As to the few whorls to which the depth in mètres is not affixed, it is unknown.

For what purpose this really stupendous mass of whorls was used, is a problem not yet definitely settled among scholars. But as nearly all of them are so well preserved, and as comparatively but few of them bear marks of having ever been used, I suppose that all, or at least all the decorated ones, served as offerings to the tutelary deity of the city, to the Ilian Athené Ergané, whose Palladium, as before mentioned, was fabled to have fallen from heaven, with a distaff in one hand and a lance in the other.

Of perforated whorls of steatite there were found in all only fifty, and of these only one has a decoration of incised circles; whereas, as has been said, of ornamented and unornamented terra-cotta whorls together, I collected more than 18,000. In my excavations at Mycenae some hundreds of stone whorls, for the most part of steatite, were found, and only five unornamented ones of terra-cotta. The little terra-cotta discs, from $1\frac{3}{4}$ to 3 in. in diameter, of which many hundreds of specimens were found in all the five pre-historic cities of Hissarlik, appear to have served as spindles. As they are only 1-5th or 1-6th of an inch thick, and slightly concave, there can be no doubt that all of them were cut out of broken pottery. They have all a perforation in the middle. Similar discs, found at Szihalom in Hungary, may be seen in the glass case No. IX., Nos. 2 and 4, in the Buda-Pesth National Museum. Similar discs have also been found at Pilin[5] and in German tombs.[6] We may also compare the so-called Kimmeridge coal-money.

I have still to describe the singular object No. 1809, which is represented on the first plate at the end of the book in half-size. It is of a lustrous-yellow colour, and quite flat on the lower side; it has an upright handle, decorated with an incised tree and a flower. Close to the handle, on the right side, is a hollow to put the hand in; I presume, therefore, that this instrument may have served for polishing the newly-made and still unbaked pottery.

Of various objects of clay from this third, the burnt city, I finally represent under No. 512 a scoop, but slightly baked, with a trefoil mouth and a small handle; under No. 513, a small cup of a very rude fabric, unpolished and but slightly baked; a cup of a like shape, contained in a tomb of Corneto, is in the Royal Museum at Berlin. No. 514 represents a vase-lid of a very remarkable and unique form: it is of massive yellow clay, not polished, and bears the marks of the intense heat to which it has been exposed in the conflagration. Its lower part was sunk like a stopper into the vase, so that its projecting upper part completely covered the orifice and shut it almost hermetically by the weight of the lid, which exceeds three pounds. We have seen a similar vase-lid in No. 304, but of this latter the whole lower part was of a semi-globular form and hollow. These two vase-lids or stoppers (Nos. 304 and 514) find their analogy in the vase-covers before described, found at Szihalom in Hungary, and exhibited under Nos. 26 and 27 in the glass case No. IX. in the Buda-Pesth National Museum.

Under No. 515 I represent a curious object of terra-cotta, with four feet and an incised linear ornamentation; it is solid, and may have served

[5] Joseph Hampel, *Ant. préh. de la Hongrie*, Pl. xiii. No. 37.

[6] Similar discs are preserved in the Märkisches Museum at Berlin, in the Grand-ducal Antiquarium in Schwerin, and elsewhere.

No. 512. Scoop of baked Clay. (Half actual size.
Depth, 23 to 26 ft.)

No. 513. Small Cup of baked Clay. (2 : 3 actual size.
Depth, 23 to 26 ft.)

No. 514. Curious Vase-lid of baked Clay.
(Half actual size. Depth, 23 to 26 ft.)

as an *ex-voto*. Under No. 516 is represented a fish of wood found in a
burnt house at a depth of 26 ft. ; how it could ever have escaped being
burnt is inexplicable. The head shows
on both sides a lustrous-black colour,
the body a lustrous yellow : both these
colours may have been produced by
the intense heat of the conflagration.

No. 515. Solid Object of Terra-cotta, with four
feet and incised linear ornamentation.
(Actual size. Depth, 30 ft.)

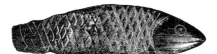

No. 516. Fish of Wood. (7 : 8 actual size. Depth, 26 ft.)

The scales are rudely indicated by small lozenges, produced by cross lines.
The fish resembles a carp, but as there are no carp in the Troad, it is
doubtful whether the primitive artist intended to represent that kind
of fish. But rude as this wooden fish is, it is a real masterpiece of art
when compared with the representations of men, of which we have passed
four in review.

No. 517 is a very curious object of ivory, found in the large house close

No. 517. Object of Ivory in the form of a crouching animal. (Actual size. Depth, 28 ft.)

to the gate. It represents a crouching hog rudely carved, with the hind
legs under the body and the fore legs under the head. The representa-

tion is identical on both sides; it reminds us vividly of the gold lions at Mycenae,[7] though these latter certainly show more artistic skill. The back part of our ivory figure runs out into something like a fish's tail, which has a vertical opening, 0·7 in. long, and is perforated, leading us to suppose that the object must have been used in some way or other in weaving. Time, and probably also the heat of the conflagration, have given to our ivory hog a dark tint; the head and back are nearly black. Professor Virchow writes to me: "It appears to me doubtful whether the figure No. 517 represents a hog. The position of the feet and the shape more resemble those of a dog."

Under Nos. 518 and 519 I represent two objects of ivory, each belonging to a lyre with only four strings, and under No. 520 another

No. 519. Piece of Ivory, belonging to a Trojan Lyre with four strings. (1 : 5 actual size. Depth, 26 ft.)

No. 518. Fragment of a Lyre with four chords. (7 : 8 actual size. Depth, 26 ft.)

No. 520. Ornamented Piece of Ivory, belonging to a Trojan Seven-stringed Lyre. (Actual size. Depth, 23 ft.)

object of ivory, belonging to a lyre with seven strings; all these three pieces are ornamented with incisions. No. 518 has the herringbone ornamentation within a border formed by two lines; No. 519 is merely decorated with straight lines. The decoration of No. 520 is very pretty, having at the edge, where the perforations are, a border of only one line; on the two other edges borders formed by two lines, and decorated with a waving pattern; the surface is ornamented with spirals, in which we likewise see wave or zigzag patterns.

The lyre (φόρμιγξ) was the most ancient stringed instrument of the Greek singers; it is frequently mentioned by Homer, with whom it is especially the musical instrument of Apollo;[8] but the singers play on it also at meals and on other occasions.[9] The φόρμιγξ is mentioned

[7] See my *Mycenae*, Nos. 263, 470, 471.

[8] *Il.* i. 603:
οὐ μὴν φόρμιγγος περικαλλέος, ἣν ἔχ᾽ Ἀπόλλων.
Il. xxiv. 63:
δαίνυ᾽ ἔχων φόρμιγγα, κακῶν ἕταρ᾽, αἰὲν ἄπιστε.
Od. xvii. 270, 271:
ἐπεὶ κνίσση μὲν ἀνήνοθεν, ἐν δέ τε φόρμιγξ
ἠπύει, ἣν ἄρα δαιτὶ θεοὶ ποίησαν ἑταίρην.
Hymn. Hom. Apoll. 184, 185:
τοῖο δὲ φόρμιγξ
χρυσέου ὑπὸ πλήκτρου καναχὴν ἔχει ἱμερόεσσαν.
verse 515:
φόρμιγγ᾽ ἐν χείρεσσιν ἔχων, ἐρατὸν κιθαρίζων.

[9] *Od.* viii. 67, 69, 70:
κὰδ δ᾽ ἐκ πασσαλόφι κρέμασεν φόρμιγγα λίγειαν,
. . . .
. . πὰρ δ᾽ ἐτίθει κάνεον καλήν τε τράπεζαν,
πὰρ δὲ δέπας οἴνοιο, πιεῖν ὅτε θυμὸς ἀνώγοι.
viii. 99:
φόρμιγγός θ᾽, ἣ δαιτὶ συνήορός ἐστι θαλείη.
xxi. 430:
μολπῇ καὶ φόρμιγγι· τὰ γάρ τ᾽ ἀναθήματα δαιτός.
xxii. 332, 333:
ἔστη δ᾽ ἐν χείρεσσιν ἔχων φόρμιγγα λίγειαν
ἄγχι παρ᾽ ὀρσοθύρην·
and others.

together with flutes (αὐλοί); [10] it was often decorated with gold, ivory, precious stones, and intaglio-work—hence its epithets περικαλλής, δαιδαλέη, χρυσέα.[11] It had at first four, but afterwards seven strings : [1] to play on the φόρμιγξ was called φόρμιγγι κιθαρίζειν [2] and φόρμιγγα ἐλελίζειν.[3] It was a kind of large guitar, with a cross-bar which joined both arms (ζυγόν),[4] and had pegs (κόλλοπες), by which the strings were tuned.[5] It was hollow (γλαφυρή),[6] like our harp, but lighter, for the word φόρμιγξ signifies the portable κιθάρα, from φέρω, φορέω, φόριμος, because it was suspended by a girdle on the shoulder, and was held in the hand when it was played.[7] Professor Rhousopoulos kindly calls my attention to Plutarch,[8] where lyres (φόρμιγγες) with four chords are mentioned.

No. 521 is an object of ivory of unknown use ; its upper part is on both sides divided by a band of three lines into two fields, of which the one is decorated with fourteen, the other with twelve, small circles having

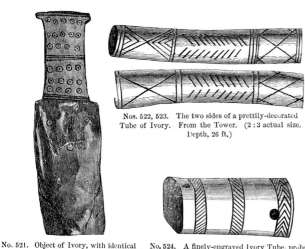

Nos. 522, 523. The two sides of a prettily-decorated Tube of Ivory. From the Tower. (2 : 3 actual size. Depth, 26 ft.)

No. 521. Object of Ivory, with identical ornamentation on both sides. (7 : 8 actual size. Depth, 33 ft.)

No. 524. A finely-engraved Ivory Tube, probably part of a Flute. Found on the Tower. (2 : 3 actual size. Depth, 26 ft.)

No. 525. A piece of Bone, curiously engraved. (2 : 3 actual size. Depth, 23 ft.)

---

[10] *Il.* xviii. 495 :

αὐλοὶ φόρμιγγές τε βοὴν ἔχον.

[11] *Il.* ix. 186, 187 :

τὸν δ' εὖρον φρένα τερπόμενον φόρμιγγι λιγείῃ
καλῇ δαιδαλέῃ, · · · ·

Pindar. *Pyth.* i. 1–3 :

χρυσέα φόρμιγξ, Ἀπόλλωνος καὶ ἰοπλοκάμων

· · · · · · · · · · · · ·
σύνδικον Μοισᾶν κτέανον.

[1] Pind. *Pyth.* ii. 129, 130 :

θέλων ἄθρησον χάριν ἑπτακτύπου
φόρμιγγος ἀντόμενος.

Pind. *Nemea*, v. 42–45 :

μοισᾶν ὁ κάλλιστος χορός · ἐν δὲ μέσαις
φόρμιγγ' Ἀπόλλων ἑπτάγλωσσον
χρυσέῳ πλάκτρῳ διώκων
ἀγεῖτο παντοίων νόμων.

[2] *Il.* xviii. 569, 570 :

τοῖσιν δ' ἐν μέσσοισι πάϊς φόρμιγγι λιγείῃ
ἱμερόεν κιθάριζε · · · ·

[3] Pind. *Ol.* ix. 21 :

ἀνδρὸς ἀμφὶ παλαίσμασιν φόρμιγγ' ἐλελίζων.

[4] *Il.* ix. 186, 187 :

· · · · · φόρμιγγι λιγείῃ
· · · · · ἐπὶ δ' ἀργύρεον ζυγὸν ἦεν.

[5] *Od.* xxi. 406, 407 :

ὡς ὅτ' ἀνὴρ φόρμιγγος ἐπιστάμενος καὶ ἀοιδῆς
ῥηϊδίως ἐτάνυσσε νέῳ περὶ κόλλοπι χορδήν.

[6] *Od.* xvii. 261, 262 :

περὶ δέ σφεας ἤλυθ' ἰωή
φόρμιγγος γλαφυρῆς.

[7] Hesychius, s. v. φόρμιγξ · ἡ τοῖς ὤμοις φερομένη.

[8] *Opp. Moralia*, pp. 1021 E, 1029 A B, 1137 D, 1139 B, 1143 E, 1145 C ; ed. Wyttenbach.

a dot in the centre; on the lower part there are three such circles on each side. The reader will observe the similarity of these circles with those on the curious object No. 142 (p. 262), which is probably an idol.

Nos. 522, 523 and No. 524 are two perforated pieces of ivory decorated with linear incisions; No. 524 has two holes: both these tubes appear to be parts of flutes. The same is probably the case with the prettily-

No. 526. Ornamented Ivory Tube, probably a Trojan Flute. (2 : 3 actual size. Depth, 26 ft.)

engraved bone No. 525. No. 526 is a curiously decorated tube of ivory, in all probability a flute. The bone tubes Nos. 527 and 528 may also

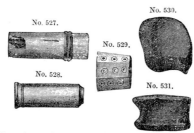

Nos. 527-531. Fragments of a Flute, two Astragals (Huckle-bones), and object of Ivory with ornaments all over. (Half actual size. Depth, 26 to 30 ft.)

be parts of flutes. No. 529 is a perforated piece of ivory cut into a polygonal prism, of which each side is decorated with three small circles, having a dot in the centre like those on No. 142 and No. 521. A similar object of ivory, with an almost identical decoration, was found in a tomb at Ialysus in Rhodes, and is preserved in the British Museum.

Nos. 530 and 531 are hucklebones (*astragali*), of which a large number have been found. I have discussed the use of these bones in a preceding chapter (see p. 263). Nos. 532 to 535 are objects of ivory, rudely ornamented with incisions evidently made with a silex-saw. Two similar objects, found at Ialysus, are in the British Museum. Of ivory also is the object No. 536, which resembles the bar of our watch-chains, as well as the object No. 537, which has four perforations; No. 538, which has the shape of a fish; and No. 539. This latter has a curious engraved pattern, which, however, has probably no symbolical signification. Prof. Sayce

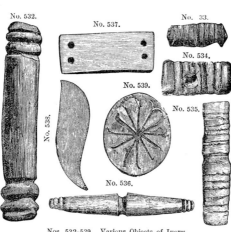

Nos. 532-539. Various Objects of Ivory.
(7 : 8 actual size. Depth, 20 to 26 ft.)

observes to me: "These ivory objects indicate trade with the East. On the Black Obelisk of the Assyrian king Shalmaneser (b c. 840) the people of Muzri on the south-west of Armenia are represented as bringing among other tribute an elephant, which must have been imported from Bactria." On the same obelisk is a two-humped Bactrian camel.

Of ivory are further the curious objects Nos. 540 and 541, which are decorated on both sides with a number of small circles with a point in

No. 540.

No. 541.

Nos. 540, 541. Objects of Ivory, probably for ornamenting a horse-harness. (7 : 8 actual size. Depth, 24 ft.)

the centre, and have a perforation at each end. I would suggest that all these ten objects (from Nos. 532 to 541), and perhaps also Nos. 521 and 529, served as ornaments for horse-trappings. That ornaments of ivory were used in this way is seen from the famous passage in the *Iliad*: "As when some Maeonian or Carian woman stains with purple the ivory, designed to be the cheek-piece of horses. As it lies in the chamber it is coveted by many horsemen; but it lies, a king's boast, to be both an ornament to the horse, and an honour to the charioteer." [9] An object of bone or ivory similar to Nos. 540 and 541, also ornamented with small circles, was found by Dr. V. Gross of Neuveville in the Swiss Lake-dwellings at Moeringen, and is in his collection.[10] No. 542 is the bone handle of a knife or some other instrument, which was fastened in it with three copper pins, of which we still see one in the upper one of the three perforations; on one side of this handle many cuts are visible.

No. 542. Bone Handle of a Knife or some other instrument. (Half actual size. Depth, 26 ft.)

Nos. 543, 544, and 545 are of bone,[1] and cannot but have served as handles of sticks or staves (σκῆπτρον, from σκήπτω, *to prop*, hence Midd. σκήπτομαι, *to lean upon*). No. 546 is also the knob of a stick or staff, a fact of which its two perforations can leave no doubt; but it is of terra-cotta. It has, but only on one side, that double spiral in the form of spectacles, which we have repeatedly seen on the vases. Generally Homer means by σκῆπτρον nothing else than a common staff,

---

[9] *Il.* iv. 141–145 :

ὡς δ' ὅτε τίς τ' ἐλέφαντα γυνὴ φοίνικι μιήνῃ
Μῃονὶς ἠὲ Κάειρα, παρήϊον ἔμμεναι ἵππων·
κεῖται δ' ἐν θαλάμῳ, πολέες τέ μιν ἠρήσαντο
ἱππῆες φορέειν· βασιλῆϊ δὲ κεῖται ἄγαλμα,
ἀμφότερον, κόσμος θ' ἵππῳ ἐλατῆρί τε κῦδος.

[10] Dr. V. Gross, *Résultats des Recherches dans les Lacs de la Suisse occidentale*; Zürich, 1876, Pl. i. No. 26.

[1] I see a similar staff-handle of bone, found

by Dr. Gross in the Swiss Lake-dwellings at Sutz, represented on Pl. ii. No. 28 of his work; but, strange to say, it is explained on p. ii. as a small hammer (*Résultats des Recherches*, &c.). Professor Virchow observes to me that it is not at all astonishing that Dr. Gross should have mistaken the staff-handle No. 28 for a hammer, since perfectly similar hammers of stag-horn frequently occur.

for we see it used alike by kings, heralds, judges, and beggars.[2] But in other passages σκῆπτρον means a royal sceptre, as the sign

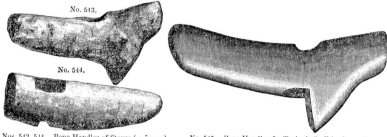

No. 543.

No. 544.

Nos. 543, 544. Bone Handles of Staves (σκῆπτρα).
(Nearly half actual size. Depth, 23 ft.)

No. 545. Bone Handle of a Trojan's Staff (σκῆπτρον).
(Half actual size. Depth, 23 ft.)

of power and dignity, and in such cases it was adorned with golden studs,[3] or was of artistic metal-work.[4] Nor are there wanting, among the remains of Troy, objects well suited to have formed the heads of such sceptres of state. No. 547 is such a sceptre-handle of fine rock-crystal, representing a rudely-carved lion's head: the large hole in the lower side into which the staff was stuck, as well as the perforation on

No. 546. Terra-cotta Knob of
a Staff. (Half actual size.
Depth, about 26 ft.)

No. 547. A Lion-headed Sceptre-handle
of the finest crystal; found on the Tower.
(Half actual size. Depth, 28 ft.)

No. 548. A curious Object, probably a Staff-handle of Egyptian
porcelain. (Half actual size.
Depth, 26 to 28 ft.)

each side, can leave no doubt as to its use. It was found at a depth of 28 ft., on the plateau formed by the two walls which I used to call

[2] Il. xviii. 416, 417 :
. . . ἕλε δὲ σκῆπτρον παχύ, βῆ δὲ θύραζε
χωλεύων· ὑπὸ δ' ἀμφίπολοι ῥώοντο ἄνακτι.
Od. xvii. 199 :
Εὔμαιος δ' ἄρα οἱ σκῆπτρον θυμαρὲς ἔδωκεν.
Od. xiii. 437 :
δῶκε δέ οἱ σκῆπτρον καὶ ἀεικέα πήρην.
Od. xiv. 31 :
. . . . . αὐτὰρ Ὀδυσσεὺς
ἕζετο κερδοσύνῃ, σκῆπτρον δέ οἱ ἔκπεσε χειρός.
Od. xviii. 103, 104 :
. . . . καί μιν ποτὶ ἑρκίον αὐλῆς
εἷσεν ἀνακλίνας, σκῆπτρον δέ οἱ ἔμβαλε χειρί.
Mr. Philip Smith remarks to me : " In the etymological sense, it is simply a thing to support oneself with, or to lean upon, from σκήπτω, ' support ' or ' prop up,' Midd. σκήπτομαι, I support myself (with), i.e. lean (upon), with -τρον

(Lat.-trum), termination of an instrument. Thus the dying Jacob rose in bed to bless his children, leaning upon the top of his staff. (Gen. xlvii. 31; Heb. xi. 21.) Among the spoil taken by King Thutmes III. in Syria, we find ' a beautiful cubit-staff of zagu wood,' ' wands or staves, with heads upon them of ivory, ebony, and cedarwood, inlaid with gold,' also ' one staff of the king,' made in the fashion of a sceptre, entirely of solid gold.' (Brugsch, Hist. of Egypt, vol. i pp. 374, 385, Engl. trans. 2nd ed.)"
[3] Il. i. 245, 246 :
. . . . . ποτὶ δὲ σκῆπτρον βάλε γαίῃ
χρυσείοις ἥλοισι πεπαρμένον.
[4] Il. ii. 101 :
ἔστη σκῆπτρον ἔχων, τὸ μὲν Ἥφαιστος κάμε τεύχων.

the Tower. Not only this lion's head, but the illustrations drawn from the lion, which occur repeatedly in the *Iliad*, make it seem extremely probable that in remote antiquity lions existed in this neighbourhood. Homer could not possibly have described the characteristics of this animal so excellently had he not had frequent opportunity of watching them, and his geographical knowledge of southern countries is too slight for us to suppose that he had visited them, and had there become intimately acquainted with the characteristics of the lion.

No. 548 is of green Egyptian porcelain ; it was found, together with an owl-headed vase and the black box Nos. 266, 267, in a very large broken funeral urn on the wall itself, immediately to the west of the royal house. It has evidently served as the handle of a staff, for it has on the opposite side a quadrangular hole 1 in. long, 0·6 in. deep, and 0·4 in. broad, which gradually diminishes in size towards the end. On each side there is an incision lengthwise, in the middle of which is a perforation, which communicates with the quadrangular hole, and can only have served to fasten the staff inserted in the latter by means of a nail. On the outside we see a quadrangular projection with two furrows. As Egyptian porcelain is too fragile to serve for the knobs of staves, the staff it decorated may perhaps have been a ceremonial one used in funeral services. It is quite vitrified on the lower side, and bears all over the marks of the fire it has been exposed to; fine black ashes stick to it everywhere. Another object of Egyptian porcelain is lying before me while writing this ; it is also in the form of a staff-knob, but it has a large perforation lengthwise. It has suffered so much in the conflagration, that its green colour has crumbled away, and it looks as if it were a decayed white glass paste. All the Egyptian porcelain, as well as the ivory, point to relations between Troy and Egypt.

Nos. 549 and 550, the latter perforated lengthwise, are also apparently knobs of staves or stick-handles, and are of a green glass paste. Both have a decoration of white or yellow spirals, which is not painted

Nos. 549-551. Glass Buttons. (Half actual
size. Depth, the one to the right 6 ft.,
the other two 26 ft.)

Nos. 552-555. Three glass Balls and one glass Bead.
(3 : 4 actual size. Depth, 26 to 33 ft.)

on the glass, but contained in it. No. 551 consists of a green glass paste, ornamented with regular white strokes; it is also perforated and almost in the form of a whorl, but it does not properly belong here, as it was found at a depth of only 6 ft.

Under Nos. 552, 553, and 554 I represent three small balls; under No. 555 a bead of white glass. I call particular attention to the fact that the three balls, the bead, and the two staff-handle knobs are the only glass objects found by me in all my excavations at Hissarlik ; further, that these six objects occurred in the third or burnt city, and that no trace of glass was found in any of the lower or upper pre-historic cities, unless, indeed, No. 551 belongs to the last pre-historic city, which appears to me doubtful. I rather think it belongs to the still later city, the sixth in succession from the virgin soil, which I may be permitted to believe to be of Lydian origin. It is therefore very probable, that all these objects were imported by the Phoenicians to Troy.

No. 556 is a prettily-shaped egg of aragonite. No. 557 represents an object of diorite, of unknown use. There were also found several unpolished hexagons of crystal, as well as a small finely-polished crystal plate with four perforations, which may have belonged to a lyre.

Passing from these ornaments to more useful objects : No. 558 repre-

No. 557.　　　　　　　　　　　No. 558.

No. 556.

No. 556. Egg of Aragonite. (7 : 8 actual size. Depth, 26 ft.)
No. 557. Object of Diorite ; use unknown. (Half actual size. Depth, 26 to 28 ft.)
No. 55×. Comb of Bone. (7 : 8 actual size. Depth, 23 ft.)

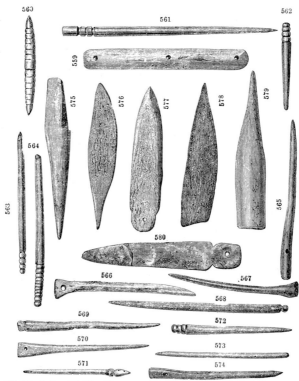

Nos. 559–580. Awls and Needles of Bone and Ivory. (About half actual size. Depth, 22 to 33 ft.)

sents a very primitive comb of bone, whose teeth may have been sawn with the common saws of chalcedony.

In the accompanying group, No. 559 is an object of ivory with three perforations, which may have served as an ornament for horse-trappings. Nos. 560–574 are needles, or other implements of bone or ivory for female handiwork. As I have said before, similar needles of bone are found in the caverns of Dordogne in France, as well as in the Swiss Lake-dwellings (see p. 262). They are also frequent in tombs in Germany. Nos. 575 to 580 are awls of bone, such as I have discussed before (see *ibid*). Nos. 581 to 584 are four more awls of bone. Nos. 585 to 587

No. 581.   No. 582.   No. 583.   No. 584.   No. 585.   No. 586.   No. 587.

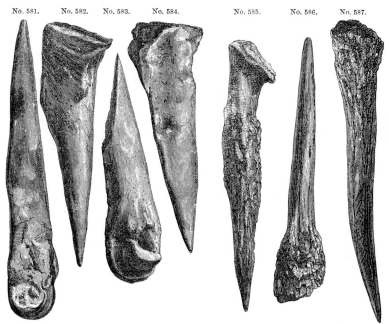

Nos. 581–584. Awls of Bone.   Nos. 585–587. Horns of Fallow Deer, sharpened and probably used as awls.
(Nearly half actual size.   Depth, 16 to 26 ft.)

are, according to Professor Virchow, horns of the fallow deer, sharpened to a point, to be used as awls. Similar horns are frequent in the three upper pre-historic cities of Hissarlik.

Nos. 588–590 are boars' tusks, of which the last two are sharpened to a point. But it appears doubtful whether they were sharpened artificially; they seem rather to have been sharpened by the boar himself. Boars' tusks are very frequent in the *débris* of all the pre-historic cities at Hissarlik. Professor Otto Keller [5] remarks on the subject: "Boar-hunting is an object of great importance in the narrations and plastic representations of the heroic ages. To judge from the boars' tusks found, it was also the favourite occupation of our European Lake-

[5] *Die Entdeckung Ilion's zu Hissarlik;* Freiburg, 1875, p. 46.

dwellers and Cavern-inmates.[6]   To the present day the boar is frequent in the Troad and the adjoining country.[7]   Between Adramyttium and

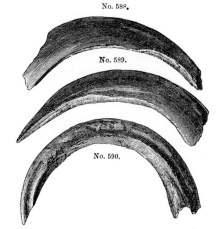

Nos. 588-590.   Boars' Tusks.   (Half actual size.   Depth, 16 to 26 ft.)

Assos, and in other parts of the Troad, the boar leaves every morning traces on the ground where he has wallowed.   The boar is frequent in the forests of the Mysian Olympus, that is, close to the Troad;[8] and in very early times the mythic boar which lacerated Idmon, son of Apollo—an episode in the legend of the Argonauts[9]—and the terrible boar which devastated the land of Croesus,[10] broke forth from those forests.   And in the oak forests of Ida—acorns being their favourite food—many a superb boar may have fattened himself for the ancient Trojans.   They may also have existed in the swamps in the plain."[1]

Nos. 591 to 598 represent objects which, according to Professor W. H. Flower of the Royal College of Surgeons of England, are vertebræ of the tunny and small sharks.

Nos. 591-598.   Vertebræ of Sharks, Dolphins, and Tunnies.   (Half actual size.   Depth, 16 to 33 ft.)

I now come to the Trojan moulds, of which about ninety in all were found, almost all more or less in fragments; nearly all are of mica-schist,

[6] "See Lubbock, Pre-historic Times, 3rd ed. p. 210."

[7] "Fellows, Tagbuch einer Reise in Kleinasien (Germ. trans.), pp. 45, 73."

[8] "Hamilton, Reisen in Kleinasien (Germ. trans.), i. p. 79."

[9] "Hyginus, Fab. c. 14, p. 44; c. 18, p. 47."

[10] "Herodot. i. 36: ἐν τῷ Μυσίῳ Οὐλύμπῳ ὗς χρῆμα γίνεται μέγα."

[1] "Strabo, xiii. p. 595; see also Columella, de Re Rust. vii. 9."

a few are of baked clay, and only one is of granite. Nos. 599 and 600 represent two such stones, with moulds on six sides for casting battle-axes and knives, as well as other implements or weapons unknown to us.

No. 599.   A Mould of Mica-schist, for casting various metal Instruments.   Found on the Tower.
(1 : 4 actual size.   Depth, 26 to 28 ft.)

No. 600.   A Mould of Mica-schist, for casting several metal Instruments.
(Half actual size.   Depth, 28 ft.)

Of these large moulds I only succeeded in collecting four intact, or nearly so. Without any fear of being contradicted, I may fairly say that these moulds with beds on six sides are unique, and have never been found elsewhere; but that such moulds, with beds for weapons or implements on their six sides, were in general use at Troy, is attested by the large quantity of broken ones. The moulds found in the Swiss Lake-dwellings,[2] as well as those found in Hungary[3] and elsewhere, have beds only on one side.[4] In Mycenae I found two moulds, one of them with beds on six sides, but only for casting ornaments.[5] These Trojan moulds are further distinguished by the depth of the beds, which exactly corresponds to the size of the battle-axes, knives, &c., which had to be cast. It is therefore evident that these beds were simply filled with fused metal, and then covered with a flat stone until the newly-cast objects had become cold. In the moulds found elsewhere the casting process was different. There were two stones containing the form of the weapon to be cast, but the beds in each of them represented only one-half of its thickness : these two stones having been joined, so that both beds fitted exactly on each other, the mould for the entire object was formed. As we have seen in the mould No. 103 (p. 248), of the first city, each of the two stones generally had two perforations, by means of which they were fastened together :[6] in each stone was a little furrow leading from the border to each bed ; and when both stones were joined, and consequently the two furrows fitted exactly on each other, they constituted together a small funnel-like tubular hole, through which the liquid metal was poured into the mould. But, as the reader sees in the engravings, these large Trojan moulds have no such furrows through which the metal could have been poured ; it is therefore evident that the process of casting was here the most simple imaginable, the metal being merely poured into the moulds, and these then covered with a flat stone.

The only moulds I ever saw which are somewhat similar to the Trojan moulds were found in Sardinia, and are preserved in the Museum of Cagliari. A good specimen of them is represented under No. 7 on Plate ii. of Vincenzo Crespi's work, *Il Museo d' Antichità di Cagliari.* It is a parallelopiped, said to consist of trachyto-porphyric stone (*sic*), and has beds for weapons on two sides : on one side, a bed for a double-edged battle-axe, with a perforation in the middle, like No. 958 (p. 506) ; on the other, beds for weapons very similar to the common Trojan battle-axes, like Nos. 806 to 809 (p. 476) and No. 828 (p. 486). There is *no* channel by which the fused metal might have been poured into the beds. It is therefore evident that here, as in the Trojan moulds, the fused metal was poured directly into the beds, and the mould was then probably covered with a perfectly smooth stone so as to make the weapons even.

In exactly the same way the battle-axes must also have been cast in

---

[2] See V. Gross, *Résultats des Recherches dans les Lacs de la Suisse occidentale*, Zürich, 1876, Pl. xvii. Nos. 1–12 ; and V. Gross, *Les dernières Trouvailles dans les Habitations lacustres du Lac de Bienne*, Porrentruy, 1879, Pl. i. Nos. 6–8, 10.

[3] Joseph Hampel, *Antiquités préhistoriques de la Hongrie* ; Esztergom, 1877, Pl. xiv. Nos. 1–25.

[4] Professor Virchow, however, observes to me that moulds with beds on two sides also

occur in Europe, but they differ from the Trojan moulds, inasmuch as they have a channel by which the fused metal could be poured in from the border.

[5] See my *Mycenae*, pp. 107–109, Nos. 162 and 163.

[6] There are, however, often found stone moulds without these two perforations.

the mica-schist mould of No. 601, as well as the curious objects, the moulds of which are seen in the stone No. 602, also of mica-schist. The round mould in this latter is also seen in Nos. 599 and 600, but not the mould of a miniature hammer, which we see here, and which is very curious indeed. On the other hand, in the mica-schist mould, No. 603, which has the mould of an arrow-head, like those represented under Nos. 931, 933, 942, 944, and 946 (p. 505), we see the system exactly as described above, because the stone has two perforations and the point of the bed touches the edge of the stone; consequently, another mould of an identical form having been fastened upon No. 603, by means of the perforations, the liquid metal was poured in through the small channel or funnel from above.

No. 604 is a broken mould for casting arrow-heads of a triangular shape, but without barbs: here also the furrow of each arrow-head reaches the border; so that the liquid metal could be poured in with ease. Close

No. 602.   A Mould of Mica-schist for casting copper Implements. (About 1 : 3 actual size.   Depth, 26 ft.)

No. 603.   Mould of Mica-schist for casting arrow-heads of primitive form. (Actual size. Depth, 28 ft.)

No. 601.   Mould of Mica - schist.   (Half actual size.   Depth, 26 ft.)

No. 605.   Mould of baked Clay. (1 : 4 actual size.   Depth, 26 ft.)

No. 604.   Fragment of a Mould of Mica-schist, for casting arrow-heads. (Half actual size. Depth, 26 ft.)

to the left lower corner is one of the holes by which this mould was fixed to another of the same shape which was put upon it; the other perforation has probably been in the missing part of the stone. The mould No. 605 is of very rude clay, which has been much exposed to the conflagration and is thoroughly baked. Here, again, there are no perforations nor funnel-shaped holes through which the metal might have been poured into the beds; it is therefore certain that the beds were in this case simply filled with liquid metal and covered with a flat stone. The moulds of this stone represent merely bars; similar moulds occurred half-a-dozen times.

A mould of *sandstone* similar to No. 601 was found at Pilin,[7] and Dr. J. Hampel informs me that such also occur at Szihalom; but these Hungarian moulds are all of the category before described, the fused

No. 606. Spit of Mica-schist. (Half actual size. Depth, 32 ft.)

No. 607. A perforated and grooved piece of Mica-schist, probably for supporting a Spit. Found on the Tower. (1 : 5 actual size. Depth, 26 ft.)

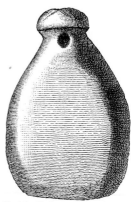

No. 608. Perforated Object of green Gabbro-rock, probably a weight. (2 : 3 actual size. Depth, 30 ft.)

metal being poured in between two moulds, each of which had exactly one-half of the form of the object to be cast. I may add that *before the fused metal was poured into the moulds these had to be exposed to a heat as great as red-hot iron.* Nos. 606 and 607 are of mica-schist; they are doubtless supports for the spit-rests.

Similar spit-rests of mica-schist, as well as of clay, occur often. As all of them have a furrow on the top, and in an opposite direction a perforation through the middle, it appears that two such supports were placed at the fireside and joined by a copper bar so as to give stability to both; besides, as the furrow for the spit is always along the narrow side, the spit could never have been turned on one support standing alone, for it would at once have fallen.

No. 608 is a perforated object of green gabbro-rock, probably a weight. Under Nos. 609 to 616 I represent eight Trojan sling-bullets of loadstone or hæmatite; except No. 616, which is of green diorite. All of them are well polished; and, with the rude implements which the Trojans had at their disposal, it must have been tremendous work to cut and smooth the hard stone into the cylindroid shape of the bullets before us. In fact, labour must have had very little or no value at that time, for otherwise it is impossible to imagine that whole months should have been wasted on the manufacture of one bullet, which was lost as soon as it was slung. Similar sling-bullets have never been found except in Assyria and in a sepulchre at Camirus in Rhodes. The British Museum contains a number of such bullets from Assyria, of hæmatite and magnetic iron, also two which seem to be of granite; besides one of loadstone

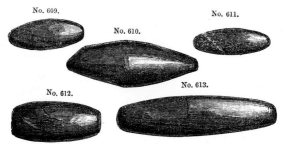

No. 609.   No. 610.   No. 611.

No. 612.   No. 613.

Nos. 609–613. Sling Bullets of Hæmatite or Loadstone. (7 : 8 actual size. Depth, 26 t) 29 ft)

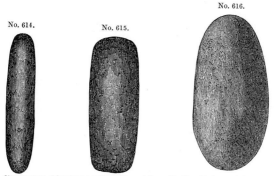

No. 616.

No. 614.   No. 615.

Nos. 614–616. Sling Bullets of Loadstone or Hæmatite and Green Diorite. (3 : 4 actual size. Depth, 30 to 33 ft.)

from Camirus. It deserves particular attention that the sling is only once mentioned by Homer, and that we never find it used as a weapon in the poems: "Then he tied the hand with twisted sheep's wool, torn from a sling, which the attendant carried for his lord."[8]

The sling was a common weapon throughout antiquity, and was still used in the Middle Ages. Among the Greeks, the Acarnanians and the Aetolians were celebrated as slingers (σφενδονῆται), like the inhabitants of the Balearic Islands in the later Roman age. In the time of the Roman Emperors, Vegetius distinguishes two kinds of slings : the *fustibalus*, in which the thongs were joined to a staff, and which was merely discharged by a jerk; and the sling called *funda*, consisting of thongs or twisted hair, sometimes human hair, which was swung over the head before the cast. Acorn-like lead-bullets (*glandes*), or round pebbles (*lapides missiles*), were slung from both with such violence that they crashed through shields and morions. Among the Greeks and Romans the slingers (σφενδονῆται) formed, with the javelin-men (ἀκοντισταί, *jaculatores*) and archers (τοξόται, *sagittarii*), the three kinds of light infantry.

---

[8] *Il.* xiii. 599, 600 :
αὐτὴν δὲ [χεῖρα] ξυνέδησεν ἐϋστρεφεῖ οἰὸς ἀώτῳ,
σφενδόνῃ, ἣν ἄρα οἷ θεράπων ἔχε, ποιμένι λαῶν.

Nos. 617, 618, and 619 are, according to Mr. Davies of the British Museum, of brown hæmatite. Similar well-polished stones are frequently

No. 617.   No. 618.   No. 619.

Nos. 617–619. Well-polished Sling Bullets of brown Hæmatite. (3 : 4 actual size. Depth, 30 ft.)

found in the stratum of the third or burnt city: as they are very heavy, these also may have served as sling-bullets. Bullets of brown hæmatite of an identical shape, and equally well polished, are frequently found in Greece.

No. 620 represents a well-polished battle-axe of green gabbro-rock, with two edges and a perforation in the middle for the handle. Stone

No. 620. Perforated Axe of green Gabbro-rock. (2 : 3 actual size. Depth, 30 ft.)

battle-axes of a perfectly identical form are found in Denmark.[9] Professor Virchow tells me that they also occur in Germany. Axes of this form are very frequent at Troy, but nearly all the specimens are fractured.

No. 621 is another battle-axe of grey diorite, of a ruder fabric and but little polished. It has only one sharp edge; the opposite end runs

No. 621. Stone Axe, with a groove in the middle. (Half actual size. Depth, 26 ft.)

out nearly to a point; a shallow groove in the middle of each side proves that the operation of drilling a hole through it had been commenced, but was abandoned.

[9] P. Madsen, *Antiquités préhistor. du Dane-marc;* Copenhagen, 1873, Pl. xxxi. No. 12.   J. J. A. Worsaae, *Nordiske Oldsager;* Copenhagen, 1859, p. 13, No. 38.

No. 622 is a polished perforated stone hammer of black diorite: similar perforated stone hammers are found in England and Ireland,[10] and are also represented in the Märkisches Museum at Berlin.

No. 623.

No. 622.

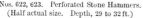

Nos. 622, 623.   Perforated Stone Hammers.
(Half actual size. Depth, 29 to 32 ft.)

No. 624.   Stone Hammer with groove.
(Half actual size. Depth, 29 ft.)

No. 623 represents a hammer of porphyry of a very curious form, the perforation being at the thick end and not drilled, but evidently punched out with a chisel.   A very remarkable form of hammer is also represented by No. 624, which is of green gabbro-rock: here also the drilling of the hole, as the grooves on both sides denote, had commenced, but was again abandoned.   I have not noticed that this peculiar shape with a furrow for fastening the hammer to the handle with a thong ever occurs elsewhere.   No. 625 represents another form of perforated hammer, of polished porphyry: as the reader will see, the hole here tapers towards the middle of the stone.   Hammers similar to this have been found in England.[1] Professor Virchow assures me that they are frequent in Germany.

No. 626 is a hammer of silicious rock, of the same shape; but here again the perforation has been merely commenced on both sides, but is not completed.   Of nearly identical form is the polished hammer of diorite No. 627, on which likewise the drilling of the hole has not been completed: the lower end of this hammer shows that it has been much used.   A similar hammer, in which the drilling had been commenced on both sides, but remained incomplete, was found by Miss Adèle Virchow in the excavations she made with her father in the graveyard of Zaborówo. No. 628 is an unpolished hammer of serpentine, with very deep grooves on both sides, but the perforation is not completed.   No. 629 is a small hammer of limestone, likewise with a groove on each side.   A hammer of identical shape was found in Denmark;[2] another one, found on the

---

[10] John Evans, *Ancient Stone Implements, Weapons, and Ornaments;* London, 1872, pp. 199, 200.

[1] John Evans, *Ibid.* p. 204.
[2] J. J. A. Worsaae, *Nordiske Oldsager,* p. 12, fig. 33.

Island of Sardinia, is in the Museum of Cagliari.[3] The shape of the hammers Nos. 622, 625–628 is very plentiful at Troy. Specimens of

No. 625. Perforated Stone Hammer. (Half actual size. Depth, 32 ft.)

No. 626. Stone Hammer with a groove on either side. (Half actual size. Depth, 26 ft.)

No. 627. Stone Hammer, with a groove on both sides. (Half actual size. Depth, 30 ft.)

No. 629. Small Hammer of Limestone. (Half actual size. Depth, 9 ft.)

No. 631. Object of Gneiss; use unknown. (Half actual size. Depth, 29 ft.)

No. 628. Stone Hammer with a deep groove on either side. (Half actual size. Depth, 22 ft.)

No. 630. Ring of Terra-cotta. (Half actual size. Depth, 26 ft.)

similarly shaped hammers may also be seen in the Märkisches Museum at Berlin.

No. 630 is a ring of baked clay, which must have served as a support for vases with a convex bottom. Twenty-six similar rings, found at Kanya, county of Bars, in Hungary, are in the National Museum at Buda-Pesth;[4] they are also found in the Swiss Lake-dwellings and elsewhere. They are very frequent in the third and fourth pre-historic cities at Hissarlik; a fact explained by the many hundreds of vases with a convex bottom.

It is doubtful whether the object of gneiss No. 631 represents a hammer; it has a furrow round the middle, and may have served as a weight for a loom or a door.

[3] Vincenzo Crispi, Il Museo d' Antichità di Cagliari; Cagliari, 1872, Pl. i. No. 3.

[4] Joseph Hampel, Antiquités préhistoriques de la Hongrie, Pl. xiii. fig. 34.

The very large hammer No. 632, which, according to Mr. Davies, is of porphyry, has round its middle the marks of the rope by which it was attached to the handle ; but as the stone weighs more than fifty pounds troy, the handle must have been very thick : its upper end seems to show long use. Prof. Virchow suggests that this instrument has probably been a club for crushing and bruising granite and silicious stone, for mixing it with the clay for making pottery. No. 633 is of diorite, of a conical shape, and well polished ; both extremities show long use ; it was probably

No. 634. Hammer or Bruiser of Diorite. (Half actual size. Depth, 29 ft.)

No. 633. Pestle of Diorite for bruising. (Half actual size. Depth, 26 ft.)

No. 632. Large Hammer of Porphyry. (1 : 4 actual size. Depth, 33 ft.)

used only as a pestle or bruiser. No. 634 is one of the finer specimens of the common hammers, which occur by many hundreds in all the four lowest pre-historic cities, and are particularly plentiful in the third and fourth cities, for in these two cities alone I could have collected some thousands of them. Mr. Davies, who examined all the specimens of them contained in my collection at the South Kensington Museum, declares them to consist of diorite, porphyry, serpentine, hornblende, gneiss, brown hæmatite, silicious rock, or gabbro-rock. Most of these rude stone hammers bear the marks of long use, but a great many others appear to be quite new. Similar rude hammers are found in almost all countries, but certainly nowhere in such an enormous abundance as at Hissarlik. The shape of one such rude hammer, found at Scamridge, Yorkshire, and represented by Mr. John Evans,[5] is the most frequent at Troy.

Nos. 635 and 636 are two perforated and well-polished balls of serpentine ; but on the ball No. 637 the drilling of the perforation has only commenced and then been abandoned. The use of these serpentine balls

[5] *Ancient Stone Implements*, &c., p. 221, fig. 166.

is a riddle to us; may they perhaps have been attached to lassos for catching cattle? I am not aware that they have been found in Europe,

No. 635. Perforated Stone Ball.   No. 636. Perforated Stone Ball.   No. 637. Stone Ball, with a deep groove
(Half actual size. Depth, 32 ft.)   (Half actual size. Depth, 32 ft.)   on both sides. (Half actual size.
                                                                                          Depth, 26 ft.)

but they occur in Cyprus; there are several specimens of such perforated serpentine balls in the collection of Cypriote antiquities in the Louvre. Similar perforated balls of greenstone were found in Santa Rosa Island, California.[6]

Nos. 638 and 639 are again two of those spherical stones which we have discussed before,[7] and of which such enormous numbers are found in the *débris* of the four lower pre-historic cities of Hissarlik, and

No. 638. Round Stone for bruising.   No. 639. Stone Ball for bruising grain.
(Half actual size. Depth, 26 ft.)   (Half actual size. Depth, 26 ft.)

particularly in the third, the burnt, and fourth cities. Mr. John Evans [8] shares my opinion that they were used as pounders or bruisers. About fifty similar pounders were found by me at Mycenae. Dr. Joseph Hampel writes to me that similar corn-bruisers are pretty frequent at Szihalom, Tószeg, Magyarád, &c. Professor Virchow informs me that they are also very frequent in Germany, and he showed me a number of them in the Märkisches Museum at Berlin. There is also one in his private collection.

No. 640 represents an implement of limestone grooved round the middle, for fastening the strings or thongs by means of which it was connected with the net. Similar implements are found in America [9] and

[6] Charles Rau, *The Arch. Collection of the U.S. National Museum, in charge of the Smithsonian Institution;* Washington, 1876, p. 31, No. 125.

[7] See page 236.

[8] *Ancient Stone Implements,* p. 224.

[9] See No. 107, p. 27, of *The Archæological Collection of the United States National Museum, in charge of the Smithsonian Institution,* by Chas. Rau; Washington, 1876.

in Denmark.[10]   Nos. 641, 642, and 643 are three objects of steatite, of which the first has three holes, the two others only one, through the

No. 611.

No. 642.   No. 643.

No. 640. Stone Implement, with a deep furrow round it.   Nos. 641–643. Perforated Objects of Steatite.
            (Half actual size. Depth, 23 ft.)   (7 : 8 actual size. Depth, 22 to 26 ft.)

centre. The first two are flat; the last has the shape of a whorl. In reviewing, in company with my friend Mr. Athanasios Koumanoudes, Assistant-Keeper of the Museums at Athens, the antiquities excavated by me four years ago at Mycenae, I find, as before mentioned, that I collected there more than 300 whorls of blue stone, of this shape or of a conical form. But, as I have said before, stone whorls are rare at Troy.

Nos. 644 and 645 are whetstones of green stone; the former has a furrow around its broader end, the latter a perforation for suspension. Similar whetstones occur frequently in all the pre-historic cities of Hissarlik. At Mycenae I found only four of them. I have in the preceding pages[1] enumerated the other sites where they are found, and

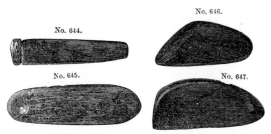

No. 646.

No. 644.

No. 645.   No. 647.

Nos. 614–647. Whetstones of Green Stone and polishing Stones of Jasper. (Half actual size. Depth, 28 to 32 ft.)

I may add that a similar whetstone, found in a sepulchre at Camirus in Rhodes, is in the British Museum. Similar whetstones are also found at Szihalom in Hungary, and two of them are in the glass case X. Nos. 82 and 83, in the National Museum of Buda-Pesth. A whetstone of granite, preserved in the collection of the French School here at Athens, was found in the pre-historic city, below the strata of pumice-stone and volcanic ashes, on the Island of Thera (Santorin).

Under Nos. 646 and 647 I represent two specimens of polishing stones of jasper, and under Nos. 648, 649, 650, and 651, four more of the same

---

[10] J. J. A. Worsaae, *Nordiske Oldsager*, p. 18, fig. 88.   [1] See p. 248.

stone, of diorite, and of porphyry, all used for polishing pottery.
Polishing-stones of a similar shape, of jasper, silicious stone, porphyry,

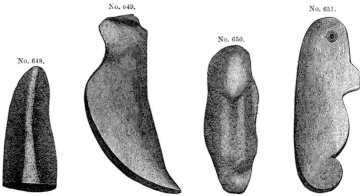

Nos. 648–651. Polishing Stones of Porphyry, Diorite, or Jasper. (2 : 3 actual size. Depth, 23 to 33 ft.)

&c., are very numerous at Troy. Of a very peculiar shape is No. 651,
which is well polished and has almost the shape of an animal, whose eyes
may be represented by a groove on either side of the head. On the back
of this object is incised the sign ⊞ or *mo*, which also occurs on two
funnels of the fifth city and on other objects.

Nos. 652, 653. Little Pyramid of Gabbro-rock and perforated Stone Implement. (Half actual size. Depth, 28 to 32 ft.)

Under No. 652 I represent a small pyramid, which, according to Mr.
Davies, consists of gabbro-rock; it is of a variegated colour, green and
black, and has through the middle a tubular hole filled with lead. We are
at a loss to guess what it could have been used for. No. 653 is a perforated object of very hard limestone, of a yellowish colour.

Nos. 654, 655. Perforated Stone Implements, perhaps Weights. (Half actual size. Depth, 26 ft.)

Nos. 654 and 655 are two objects of silicious stone: the latter has two
perforations, the former only one; both may have served as weights for
doors or looms.

Under Nos. 656 to 659 and 663 to 665 I represent seven more saws of chalcedony or silex, of which several—as, for example, Nos. 656

Nos. 656–664. Saws of Chalcedony or Flint, and Knives of Obsidian. (Half actual size. Depth, 24 to 33 ft.)

No. 667.

No. 665. Silex Saw. (Half actual size.
Depth, 30 ft.)

No. 666.

Nos. 666, 667. Stone Axes. (Actual size. Depth, 26 ft.)

and 665—bear the marks of having been fixed in a wooden handle. Nos. 660, 661, and 662 are knives of obsidian ; but, as I have fully discussed similar objects in the preceding pages, I shall not speak of them here any further, merely adding that knives of obsidian have also been found in the pre-historic city on the Island of Thera (Santorin).

Nos. 666 to 677 represent twelve axes or chisels which, according to Professor Maskelyne and Mr. Davies, are of blue serpentinous rock, green

No. 668.   No. 669.

No. 670

Nos. 668–670. Stone Axes. (Half actual size. Depth, 26 to 32 ft.)

671

672   673   674

675

676   677

Nos. 671-677. Stone Axes and Chisels. (Half actual size. Depth, 22 to 32 ft.)

gabbro-rock, grey diorite, dark-green hornstone, and jade or nephrite. The chisel No. 672, and the axes Nos. 671, 675, 676, and 677, consist of the latter rare and precious stone. Though I have discussed the jade axes at great length in the preceding pages, yet I cannot refrain from copying here in a foot-note, from the *Times*, three most interesting letters on the subject, written by Professor Max Müller and Mr. Story-Maskelyne, as well as the very ingenious editorial article of the *Times* which accompanies the former friend's last letter.[2]

---

[2]   Jade Tools in Switzerland.

(*To the Editor of the Times*: Dec. 18, 1879.)

Sir,—The account sent by your correspondent at Geneva (December 15), of a scraper made of jade, lately found in the bed of the Rhone, is very important. But your correspondent is hardly quite right in calling this scraper a solitary specimen. Scrapers or cutting instruments made of real jade are very rare, in Switzerland and elsewhere, but I have myself seen several beautiful specimens—among the rest, one found by Dr. Uhlmann of München-buchsee, whose collection of lacustrine antiquities, all taken out by his own hand from one and the same small lake, the Moossee-dorfsee, is perhaps the most authentic and most instructive collection in the whole of Switzerland.

Your correspondent asks whether, as true jade is never found in Europe, the Aryan wanderers could have brought that scraper from the cradle of their race in Asia. Why not? If the Aryan settlers could carry with them into Europe so ponderous a tool as their language, without chipping or clipping a single facet, there is nothing so very surprising in their having carried along, and carefully preserved from generation to generation, so handy and so valuable an instrument as a scraper or a knife, made of a substance which is *acre perennius*.

Oxford, Dec. 17, 1879.   F. Max Müller.

Jade as an old-world Mineral.

(*To the Editor of the Times*: Jan. 1, 1880.)

Sir,—The space you have given in your columns to the curious question discussed by Professor Rolleston and Mr. Westropp regarding the sources of pre-historic jade, emboldens me to hope that you may not reject another letter on the subject.

I believe Professor Rolleston is right in asserting an Oriental, possibly a single Oriental, source for the pre-historic jade of the Europ-Asiatic continent. I think so for these reasons :—Jade celts are very rare ; they are found, however, few and far between, from Mesopotamia to Brittany ; and they evince the passion of every race of mankind for the possession of green stones as objects endowed with an intrinsic preciousness. Now, if jade was a native product of all or of several of the numerous countries in the buried dust of which these jade implements are thus sporadically scattered, how comes it to pass that so remarkable a mineral has never been lit upon

by the races of men who have lived and died in those countries since the "old men" wandered over them? One does, indeed, see a small jade celt once worn in a necklace by a Greek girl still pendant, as a talisman probably, from that specimen of antique gold jewellery in the British Museum. But it is a celt, not an object of Roman workmanship. One single cylinder among the hundreds of Assyrian and Babylonian cylinders in the same great repository attests the exceptional character of jade as a material among the peoples who inhabited Mesopotamia, where, however, jade celts have been found of still older date. But among the numerous materials of Egyptian ornamental and sacred art, jade is, I believe, unknown. There is no evidence that Greeks or Romans ever employed jade or (*pace* Mr. Westropp) had even a name for it. Had it been a product of the rivers or of the quarries of the Roman world, specimens of it would certainly have survived as the material of gems or in some other form of art. It may seem a startling proposition to maintain that the jade mines of the Kara Kash river, in the Kuen Luen range, north of the mountains of Cashmere, should have been the sources of the jade celts found over the whole of Europe. The difficulty of believing this seemed all the greater, for that, while white as well as green jade may be quarried there, it was only the green jade, and not the white, which thus permeated the pre-historic world. But a few months ago Dr. Schliemann asked me to look at some of the strange stones which he had lit upon in the oldest of the cities of Hissarlik, and there, with several specimens of green jade—one of them being a beautifully translucent specimen of the stone—was a single celt of fine white jade, just such as might have been dug from one of the pits above the Kara Kash, or fashioned from a pebble out of its stream.

In contemplating these venerable treasures ·from that old town or fortress, one had to recognize that Dr. Schliemann had lit upon a place of importance, perhaps a sort of emporium planted on the stream of a pre-historic commerce, and situated just at one of the points where Asiatic products might collect previously to their being distributed by a process of barter among the peoples of the West. Or was it a halting-place at which some great wave of emigration was arrested for a time by the barrier of the Dardanelles? At any rate, there in considerable numbers were the green jade celts, the

No. 678 is a saddle-quern of trachyte.   I have discussed saddle-querns

No. 678.   Saddle-quern of Trachyte.   (1 : 4 actual size.   Depth, 33 ft.)

kind, no doubt, more valued on account of their colour; and there too was this solitary white celt, their companion probably from a common far-distant home in the Kuen Luen Mountains.

To what cause is the failure in the supply of jade to the world lying to the south and west of the Pamir, after pre-historic times, to be attributed? I do not attempt to answer this question; I would only suggest the apparent evidence of such a failure. It is far from improbable that the green jade implement had in some sense a sacred character in pre-historic times, and was borne westwards by emigrating peoples, as they might bear their household gods, while by a slow process of barter specimens might have penetrated from the Hellespont to the Atlantic sea-board. And it may be that in even that remote age, or towards the close of it, people of Chinese race came to dominate over the district that produced the jade and closed the rugged passes that led south and west from that inhospitable region; and so, while China has from time immemorial had jade in plenty, the rest of the Asiatic continent may have been cut off from the source of its supply. Or, possibly, the geological changes that have raised the level of the lands to the north and east of Persia may have been still in action, and were gradually increasing the inhospitable features of the district towards the close of the period which we call the pre-historic period in Asia. It is probable that other sources of jade further north may have contributed some of the material borne westward in the form of celts. The Amoor in the far north rolls down jade pebbles from the Yablono Mountains of the Trans-Baikal district of Siberia, and the Chinese have probably some sources of green jade unknown to us. Their jadeite, a different mineral from jade, is supplied, though probably not exclusively, by mines in the mountains to the north-west of Bhamo in the Lao State of Burmah.

The introduction of jade, or at least its use as

a material for artistic workmanship, in India, dates almost from yesterday, since it belongs to the time of the early Mogul Emperors of Delhi. "The magnificent son of Akbar," Jehanghir, and Shah Jehan seem to have taken pleasure in jade cups and ornaments; and the art of inlaid work that found such exquisite expression in the Taj Mahal was copied under their munificent auspices in the most precious materials, rubies and diamonds and other precious stones being inlaid in jade of various colours, which was cut in delicate openwork and adorned with enamels, in the production of which India is still unrivalled. The collection of these beautiful productions of Indian art contained in the India Museum is the finest ever brought together. It was purchased, at a suggestion from myself, when the present Chancellor of the Exchequer [Sir Stafford Northcote] was Secretary of State for India; a selection having been made by the late Sir Digby Wyatt and me from an unique collection of jade vessels of all sorts, formed at great expense and trouble by the late Colonel Charles Seaton Guthrie.

But these may be said to be the only forms in which civilized man beyond the confines of China has made jade the material for carving artistic creations.

The Mexicans worked a kind of jadeite. The Maoris worked jade, which is a native mineral in their hornblendic rocks; and the inhabitants of New Caledonia, and indeed of Polynesia generally, have fashioned jade or some varieties of jadeite into implements, useful, ornamental, and perhaps too, in some sense, sacred.

Jade is erroneously supposed to be a very hard substance. It is by no means so. Its most remarkable property—a property eminently fitting it for an implement—is an extraordinary toughness. Like well-tempered steel, in which toughness is combined with only enough hardness to do the work of cutting and to retain an edge, the implement of jade shared with the implement of

in the preceding pages : I repeat that they are very abundant in the

fibrolite an unique combination of these qualities, essential alike in a weapon and in a working
tool.   I am, Sir, your obedient servant,
NEVIL STORY-MASKELYNE.
British Museum, Dec. 30, 1879.

JADE TOOLS.

(*To the Editor of the Times :* Jan. 15, 1880.)

SIR,—The interesting and instructive letters
on jade tools, to which you have lately granted
admission in your columns, will, I hope, have
convinced most of your readers that the theory
which I tried to uphold in my letter, published
in the *Times* of December 16, was not quite so
wild as at first sight it may have appeared.
What are called wild theories are in many cases
very tame theories. Students at first laugh at
them, turn their backs on them, and try every
possible exit to escape from them. But at last,
when they are hemmed in by facts on every
side, and see that there is no escape, they tamely
submit to the inevitable, and after a time the
inevitable is generally found to be the intelligible and the reasonable.

The problem of the jade tools is really very
simple. Mineralogists assure us that jade is a
mineral the identity of which, if properly tested,
admits of no doubt, and they tell us with equal
confidence that Europe does not produce true
jade. These two statements I accept as true till
they are upset by competent authorities. If,
therefore, jade tools of exquisite workmanship
are found in Europe during what is called the
Stone age, I do not see how we can escape from
the conclusion that these tools were brought
from those well-defined areas in Asia—I suppose
I may leave out of consideration America and
Oceania—where alone jade has been found, and
where it is still worked to the present day.
Some of these are not so very distant, for true
jade is found in the Caucasus and the Ural
Mountains. I do not deny that at first one feels
a little giddy when, while handling one of those
precious scrapers, one is told that the identical
scraper was the property of the first discoverers
of Europe. And it was chiefly in order to
remove that feeling of giddiness that I wished to
call attention to another class of tools, equally
ancient, possibly even more ancient, which were
likewise brought into Europe from Asia by our
earliest ancestors, and which we use every day
without feeling the least surprise. Though no
one nowadays doubts that our language came
from the East, yet we do not always realize the
close continuity between ancient and modern
speech and the unbroken chain that holds all
the Aryan dialects together from India to
Ireland. We wonder how jade tools should
have been brought from the East and passed
from hand to hand during many thousands of
years, " before pockets were invented," and yet
every word of our language came from the East

and must have passed from hand to hand
during thousands of years before pocket dic-
tionaries were invented. If we take such useful
tools as our numerals, and consider what is presupposed by the fact that, making allowance for
a certain amount of phonetic wear and tear,
these numerals are the same in Sanskrit and in
English, we shall, I think, feel less upset, even
when brought face to face with the jade tools in
the lacustrine dwellings of Switzerland. Aye, I
go a step further. Let us look at the fact
that, of all the numerals from one to ten in
Sanskrit, *saptá* (seven) and *ashtáu* (eight) alone
have the accent on the last syllable, and then
turn our eyes to ancient and even to modern
Greek, and observe exactly the same exceptional
accentuation there. Any one who can look without a tremor into the depth thus suddenly
opened before our eyes will hardly feel a swim-
ming of the head when examining the wildest
theories that have been founded on the jade tools
unearthed in Switzerland and other parts of
Western Europe.

It is not necessary to enter here on the question, whether these jade instruments were
brought into Europe by Aryan or pre-Aryan
colonists. It is certainly strange that there is
no ancient Aryan name for jade, but neither is
there a pre-Aryan or Turanian name for it in
any of the ancient Indo-European languages. I
have collected elsewhere (*Lectures on the Science
of Language*, vol. ii. p. 251, 9th ed.) some facts
which make it seem not unlikely that Aryan languages were spoken in Europe during the age of
stone and the prevalence of the Scotch fir, and I
may add that the nature of the arguments
brought forward against that hypothesis has
strengthened rather than weakened my own confidence in it. Yet it is an hypothesis only. But,
whether brought by Aryan or pre-Aryan settlers,
certain it is that these jade tools were not made
in Europe, and that, though jade is softer *in situ*,
they testify to a high degree of humanity and
mechanical skill among the people who made
them.

My friends Professors Rolleston and Maskelyne
have left me but little to add in support of the
foreign origin of the jade tools. Two facts only
I may still mention, because they may help
others, as they helped me, in forming their own
opinion on the subject.

It is a fact, I believe, that with a few and
somewhat apocryphal exceptions, such as the
finds at Potsdam and Schwemsal, no raw or unworked jade has ever been met with anywhere
in Europe. This, to my mind, speaks volumes.

It is another fact that there is in Europe no
ancient name for jade. If on page 311 of H.
Fischer's excellent work on *Nephrit und Jadeit*,
1875, we consult the chronological list of writers
by whom jade is mentioned, we find in ancient
times the name of *jaspis, jaspis virens, jaspis*

four lower pre-historic cities, particularly in the third and fourth ; nay,

---

viridis, but nothing to enable us to identify that name with true jade. *Jaspis* itself is a name of Semitic origin. In Chinese, on the contrary, we find from the most ancient to the most recent times the recognized name for jade—viz. *yu* or *chiù*. It is mentioned as an article of tribute in Professor Legge's translation of the Shû-King (*Sacred Books of the East*, vol. iii. p. 72), and it is curious to find in that, as we are told, most ancient among ancient books, articles such as " gold, iron, silver, steel, copper, and flint stones to make arrow-heads," all mentioned together as belonging to the same period, and all equally acceptable as tribute at the Imperial Court. *Forsan et haec olim meminisse juvabit!* The word jade is not met with before the discovery of America. The jade brought from America was called by the Spaniards *piedra de yjada*, because for a long time it was believed to cure pain in the side. For similar reasons it was called afterwards *lapis nephriticus* (nephrite), *lapis ischiadicus, lapis divinus, piedra de los reñones, piedra ischada, pietra del fianco*, kidney-stone, *Lendenhelfer*, &c. The first who introduced this new nomenclature into Europe seems to have been Monardes, in his *Historia Medicinal de las Cosas que se traen de las Indias Occidentales*; Sevilla, 1569. The name which he uses, *piedra de yjada*, is meant for *piedra de ijada*, i.e. groin-stone, or a stone supposed to remove pain in the groin. The Spanish *ijada* is, according to the Dictionary of the Spanish Academy, *il lado del animal debuxo del vientre junto al anca*, and there can be little doubt that it is derived from the Latin *ilia*. *Iliaco* in Spanish is *il dolor colico*. As the name *ijada, jada*, or jade, and the belief in its healing powers, came from America, it can only be an accidental coincidence if, as Professor Skeat tells us in his excellent *Etymological Dictionary*, there existed in Sanskrit Buddhist texts the word *yedâ* as a name of a material out of which ornaments were made.

This is the state of the question of the jade tools at the present moment. To those who wish to study its history in all its bearings, Fischer's exhaustive work on *Nephrit und Jadeit* will give the necessary information. His survey of the literature on a subject apparently so abstruse and remote from general interest fills no less than 248 pages.—Your obedient servant,
Oxford, Jan. 10, 1880.   F. MAX MÜLLER.

EDITORIAL ARTICLE, *Times*, Jan. 15, 1880.

" Swiss dredgers did something more last December than bring up from the bed of the river Rhone a piece of polished carved stone. They uncovered the very foundations of history. It is as if the channel of the Calabrian river had been laid bare, and the tomb of the Visigoth conqueror of Italy revealed, with all its pomp of pillaged gold and gems. Only, the jade

scraper found among the lacustrine dwellings of Switzerland is the key, not to mere dead remains of a vanished civilization, but to the languages living men speak and to the thoughts they think. Professor Max Müller, in the letter we publish to-day, opens up so many suggestive and profound ideas, that the question on the nature and origin of manufactured jade, which was the basis of them all, is in some danger of being buried under the pile of riches of which it has unlocked the doors. Yet, were there nothing beside and beyond it, the inquiry would be sufficiently intricate, how this Rhone jade scraper came among the Alps, whence was brought the mineral, and whence the skill which sculptured it, why it was valued, and in what way it was used. At every turn the history of jade involves us in a dense thicket of problems. The further the explorer advances, the more entangled he finds himself.

" The Chinese have possessed jade from before the beginning of human records. In ' the most ancient among most ancient books ' jade is enumerated as an article of tribute to sovereigns of China. Throughout the thousands of years of human history until the discovery of New Zealand the only known worked mines of pure jade were on the river Kara Kash, in the Kuen Luen Mountains. Over that region China was suzerain ; and thus the source of Chinese jade can be traced. The strange thing is that, though Europe also has possessed jade, no one can say on more than theoretical evidence whence the European jade came. The lake-dwellers of Switzerland were discovered in possession of it. It is found, however, rarely, among the ornaments of Roman ladies. Dr. Schliemann has dug it up in the ruins of his Ilium. It is never found among pre-historic monuments except with marks of manufacture upon it ; but the manufacture testifies, often unmistakably, if not always, not to European art, but to Eastern. This jade scraper, or *strigil*, from the Rhone could neither have been wrought nor, it may be supposed, used by its lacustrine owner. It would have had its meaning in a Pompeian mansion or in an Oriental vapour-bath, but not amid the forests and torrents and glacial atmosphere of the Alps. As the inquirer advances into the domain of history, jade advances with him. But the secret of its presence in Assyrian and Greek and Roman palaces is no more plainly solved than among stone pile hovels. The ancients, though they esteemed it very precious, had not even a distinct name for it. They called it jasper, though jasper it clearly is not. The Middle Ages of Europe valued the stone, but had no more understanding of the process by which it came into their hands than Greeks and Romans. India itself, while it made much account of it, received it as something strange and mysterious. The Mogul Emperors of Delhi had the jade, which

that I could have collected thousands of them.   To the list of localities in

came they hardly knew whence, cut and jewelled and enamelled.   They called Italian artists from Venice and Genoa, and bid them work it into the exquisite shapes which drive European jade collectors mad after a special form of insanity. But the spring and fountain-head of the material which their artists wrought upon remained hidden in the clouds of legend and fable.   Before, however, the Moguls had transformed a cult into a passion and a fashion, veins of a mineral resembling jade had become known to Europe, though not to Asia.   The Spaniards, when they occupied the southern regions of the New World, found there, too, not indeed pure jade, but a stone of similar properties, prized and reverenced.   The Aztecs wore jadeite ornaments carved after their manner, and reposed faith in them as charms against disease.   Their conquerors soon learnt where they obtained the substance itself, and then for the first time jade acquired a real European name.   As if to confirm faith in the occult powers of the mineral, when Oceania was explored, pure jade deposits were discovered ; and it was discovered, also, that the Maoris credited the stone with the same healing qualities as the natives of Spanish America.

"Here, then, is a mineral which four out of the five divisions of the globe have agreed to covet and adore without understanding in the least why or wherefore. Africa alone has resisted the worship of jade. It does not appear among the treasures of the Pharaohs. The stone in its natural state has distinctive merits. The colour, shading from dark green to milky white, is seductive to artistic eyes. It possesses also, as Professor Story-Maskelyne has told us, the virtue of an extraordinary toughness.   Easy to work when freshly extracted from the stratum, it hardens just sufficiently to do the work of cutting yet retain an edge.   On that account New Zealanders used jade as well for tomahawks as for amulets, and the jade relics disinterred in Switzerland are often in the shape of hatchets. Yet, throughout the early stages of the world, there was clearly another use of jade, independent of the commonplace necessities of life, and which made its value higher in the eyes of primitive man.   When Akbar's son and his luxurious successors accumulated their exquisite carvings in jade, the texture would seem to have constituted the stone's essential attraction. What, however, had at first fascinated the world's regard was not toughness and texture or even beauty ; it was some recondite association with a sentiment and a legend which had engrafted itself for once and for all on human nature.   There is one problem of jade ; another, not altogether disconnected from that, is the difficult question whence and how the mineral has wandered from its only known sources.   It cannot have been extracted from European rocks, or modern traces of it would have been before

this time unearthed.   Jade hatchets have been found in Brittany, and even in Ireland, as well in Switzerland.   If European mines had supplied the material of the ubiquitous relics, it would be one more enigma added to the rest, that in the countless ages since these treasures of museums were hammered and carved, modern Europeans should never have lighted upon a single unworked morsel of the vein whence they were hewed.   By a species of exhaustive process of argument, the mind is forced to one particular inference.   Bretons of Brittany, Celts of Ireland, lake-dwellers under the shadow of Mont Blanc, must have conveyed with them their jade ornaments and utensils from the far-away home of themselves and jade in Central Asia, for the simple reason that they could have found the material nowhere in their new country.   An Oriental or Greek or Roman scraper found in the Rhone might conceivably have been the fruit of old plundering forays across the Alps into Italy. But jade hatchets could not have been robbed from classical Italy.   Greeks and Romans knew nothing of the traces of the Stone age which students have now discovered alike in the learned dust of Italy and the primeval forests of America.

Professor Max Müller's argument leads us into a loftier region of speculation.   There may be no alternative for the hypothesis that European barbarians brought with them from Asia the jade which archæologists have traced to their possession.   But at first sight the explanation appears to be itself inexplicable.   Tossed over such an ocean of deserts, forests, wildernesses, frozen mountains, and parched plains, as those poor wanderers, our European forefathers, had to traverse, they might be imagined cast up on the desolate extremities of the world without a single recognizable trace of the similitude they bore when launched on their woful journey.   That these tempest-buffeted Aryans should, when recovering from their swoon of bewilderment at the strange land on which their feet at last were resting, have found in their hands a jade hatchet or jewel which they had prized as a charm, whether against earthquakes or disease, in the depths of torrid Asia, doubtless seems as absolutely impossible as that a child drowned in the Tay bridge should be washed on shore holding the toy it was playing with at the moment of the plunge into the abyss.   Professor Müller would allow it to be impossible if a more impossible phenomenon had not proved itself possible.   A language is the growth of circumstances.   No circumstances could be less alike than those which environed Indo-Europeans when they were Asiatics and when they became Europeans.   As they passed from their first country to their last all must have been tempting them to forget their early language and to frame their tongues to a new speech.   Gradually, it might have been

which similar saddle-querns are found, I may add the Italian terramare[3] and Holyhead[4] in England. No. 679 is a large piece of granite, flat on the lower side, with a large hole through the centre. The hole is too large for us to suppose that the stone could, by means of a wooden handle, have been used as an upper millstone; I rather think that it served as a support for vases with convex bottoms. Similar to this are the stone discs, which are plentiful in the four lowest prehistoric cities; they are of course quite round, and have a large hole through the centre.

No. 680 marks a massive hammer of

No. 679. Perforated Object of Granite.
(About 1 : 5 actual size. Depth, 33 ft.)

expected, first one turn of expression, one tone would have dropped away, and then another, till nothing of the old survived. On the contrary, they brought with them, wherever their lot was cast on this wide world, their vocabulary almost intact. So careful were they to lose nothing that, though everything counselled change, so delicate a thing as an accent on a couple of numerals has withstood what might have seemed the irrepressible genius of Attic and Doric and Ionic Greek. If they could transport their Aryan speech to the banks of the Rhone, they might, yet more easily, urges Professor Müller, transport a few fragments of stone. They might as easily, he might have proceeded to argue, transport the undefined instinct and the religion which made those fragments of stone precious in their eyes. It is a wide field of thought to which the Professor has led us. Traversing it we feel composite beings, centos and compilations, ourselves and all our belongings, of the dead past, which in us lives and breathes. In one respect Professor Müller is even too successful in meeting the argument of the supposed impossibility of the transport of jade by the more than equal hypothetical impossibility of the transport of a language. In the case in point the jade has been conveyed; the name for jade, the Professor himself tells us, was not conveyed. If any addition were needed to the many physical and historical and philosophical mysteries of this strange mineral, there it is."

JADE.

(*To the Editor of the Times:* Jan. 19, 1880.)

Sir,—It is curious to find the remark in a leading article in the *Times* of Thursday to the effect that the ancients had no distinct name for jade confirmed also in the case of the Chinese. They call it *Yuh* or *the* gem, and they have classified the different kinds known to them under seventy-seven headings, but for the mineral itself they have no distinct generic name. Unlike, however, the admirers of jade in other countries, they have at least tried to explain why, to use the words of the leading article, they " covet and adore it." According to the celebrated philosopher Kwan Chung, who wrote in the seventh century B.C., the contemplation of a piece of jade opens to the eyes of a true Chinaman a whole vista of poetic visions. In it he sees reflected nine of the highest attainments of humanity. In its glossy smoothness he recognizes the emblem of benevolence; in its bright polish he sees knowledge emblematized; in its unbending firmness, righteousness; in its modest harmlessness, virtuous action; in its rarity and spotlessness, purity; in its imperishableness, endurance; in the way in which it exposes its every flaw, ingenuousness; in that, though of surpassing beauty, it passes from hand to hand without being sullied, moral conduct; and in that when struck it gives forth a note which floats sharply and distinctly to a distance, music. " It is this," adds the philosopher, " which makes men esteem it as most precious, and leads them to regard it as a diviner of judgments, and as a charm of happy omen."

Other philosophers who have dived into the depths of the very being of this mysterious mineral have pronounced it to be no other than the essence of heaven and earth. Hence its enhanced title to honour, and its supposed potency as a charm. That the veneration shown for jade in China rests on no more substantial basis than the visions of mystics need not surprise us. Are not most of the beliefs which lead men captive founded on dreams?—I am, Sir, your obedient servant, ROBERT K. DOUGLAS.

5, *College Gardens, Dulwich, Jan. 17.*

[3] W. Helbig, *Die Italiker in der Poebene;* Leipzig, 1879, pp. 17, 101.

[4] See Mr. Owen Stanley's paper in the *Archæological Journal.*

diorite.   Nos. 681 to 684 are objects of white marble or compact limestone, and probably *phalli* or *priapi*.

No. 681. Probably a Priapus.
(Half actual size. Depth, 29 ft.)

No. 680. Massive Hammer of
Diorite. (1 : 4 actual size.
Depth, 33 ft.)

No. 682. Object of white Marble,
probably a Priapus. (Actual size.
Depth, 30 ft.)

No. 684. Object of Stone, probably a Priapus.
(Half actual size. Depth, 26 ft.)

No. 683. Object of Stone, probably a Priapus.
(Half actual size. Depth, 26 ft.)

As I have had occasion to mention before,[5] Prof. Sayce writes to me :
"When travelling in Lydia last year (September 1879), I discovered a
curious monument hidden in bushes on the northern slope of Mount
Sipylus, about half a mile to the east of the famous statue of Niobé, and not
far from the top of the cliff. It was a large phallus, with a niche cut out
of the rock on either side of it, and two pit-tombs in front similar to
the pit-tomb in front of the statue of Niobé. The phallus was a natural
formation, like that near Bidarray in the Pyrenees, which I once visited,

---

[5] See p. 278.

and which is still an object of veneration and a place of pilgrimage among the Basque women. The natural formation, however, had been assisted by art. The artificial niches at the side were each about half a foot from the image. It must plainly have been a place of pilgrimage in the pre-historic days of Lydia, and the Lydian women may have visited it, just as the Basque women still visit the so-called 'Saint of Bidarray,' in the hope of getting offspring. I noticed my discovery in a letter to the *Academy* of October 18th, 1879."

I now come to discuss the metals of this third, the burnt city, and I begin with the objects contained in the large Treasure discovered by me on the great wall close to the ancient royal mansion to the north-west of the gate, at the place marked Δ on Plan I. I shall here first name the various articles contained in the Treasure in the order in which I took them out :—

1. The copper shield, No. 799.
2. The copper cauldron, No. 800.
3. The copper plate, No. 782.
4. A fractured copper vase.
5. The globular gold bottle, No. 775.
6. The large δέπας ἀμφικύπελλον, Nos. 772 and 773.
7. Six silver *talents*, Nos. 787 to 792.
8. Three silver vases, Nos. 779, 780, 781.
9. One silver vase-cover, No. 778.
10. A silver cup, No. 785.
11. A silver cup or dish (φιάλη), No. 786.
12. Two silver vases, Nos. 783 and 784.
13. Thirteen bronze lance-heads, of which I represent six in the engravings Nos. 801 to 805 and 815.
14. Fourteen battle axes of bronze, of which five are represented under Nos. 806 to 809 and 810.
15. Seven double-edged bronze daggers ; see the four represented under Nos. 811 to 814, and the two curious bronze weapons Nos. 816, 817.
16. A bronze knife, like No. 956 or No. 967.
17. The copper (or bronze ?) key, No. 818.
The silver vase, No. 779, was found to contain on the bottom :—
18. A gold diadem (πλεκτὴ ἀναδέσμη), Nos. 685 and 686.
19. Another such diadem, No. 687.
20. A gold fillet, No. 767.
21. Four gold ear-rings with pendants, Nos. 768–771.
Among and upon these lay :—
22. The fifty-six gold ear-rings, like Nos. 694, 695, 698–704, 752–764.
23. The 8700 small gold rings, perforated prisms, dice, gold buttons, small perforated gold bars, small ear-rings, &c., represented by the separate cuts Nos. 696, 697, 705 to 738, 765, 766, and by those of the thirteen necklaces, Nos. 739–745 and Nos. 746–751.
Upon these lay :—
24. The six gold bracelets, No. 689, four of which are shown separately, Nos. 690 to 693.

And on the top lay :—

25. The gold goblet, No. 776.

26. The goblet of electrum, No. 777.

As I found all these articles together, forming a quadrangular mass, or packed into one another, it seems to be certain that they were placed on the city-wall in a wooden chest (φωριαμός), such as those mentioned by Homer as being in the palace of King Priam : "And he opened the beautiful lids of the boxes; he selected from out of them twelve gorgeous garments, then twelve simple vestures and as many carpets, also as many mantles and as many tunics. Weighing then the gold, he took ten full talents; also two shining tripods and four cauldrons; also a most beautiful goblet, a rich possession which the men of Thrace had presented to him when he went thither as ambassador : even this the old man did not spare now in the palace, but he excessively desired in his mind to ransom his beloved son."[6] The contents of Priam's chests may, therefore, well be compared with the articles of the treasure before us.

It is possible that in the conflagration some one hurriedly packed the treasure into the chest, and carried it off without having time to pull out the key; that when he reached the wall, however, the hand of the enemy or the fire overtook him, and he was obliged to abandon the chest, which was immediately covered to a height of from 5 to 6 ft. with the reddish or yellow ashes and the bricks of the adjoining royal house. This was certainly my opinion at the time of the discovery; but since then I have found, in the presence of Professor Virchow and M. Burnouf, on the very same wall, and only a few yards to the north of the spot where the large treasure was discovered, another smaller treasure, and three more treasures on and near the walls of the adjoining royal house. I, therefore, now rather believe that all these treasures have fallen in the conflagration from the upper storeys of the royal house.

This appears to be the more likely, as, a few days previously to the discovery of the large treasure, I found close to it a helmet in fragments and the silver vase No. 793, with the goblet of electrum No. 794, all of which articles I shall discuss in the subsequent pages.

On the wood-ashes and bricks, which covered the treasure to a depth of 5 or 6 ft., the people of the following, the fourth city, erected a fortification wall, 20 ft. high and 6 ft. broad, composed of large hewn and unhewn stones and earth : this wall, which has been demolished in the subsequent excavations, extended to within 3¼ ft. of the surface of the hill.

The gold diadem (πλεκτὴ ἀναδέσμη),[7] No. 685, of which No. 686

---

[6] *Il.* xxiv. 228–237 :

Ἦ, καὶ φωριαμῶν ἐπιθήματα κάλ' ἀνέῳγεν,
ἔνθεν δώδεκα μὲν περικαλλέας ἔξελε πέπλους,
δώδεκα δ' ἁπλοΐδας χλαίνας, τόσσους δὲ τάπητας,
τόσσα δὲ φάρεα καλά, τόσσους δ' ἐπὶ τοῖσι
      χιτῶνας.
χρυσοῦ δὲ στήσας ἔφερεν δέκα πάντα τάλαντα,
ἐκ δὲ δύ' αἴθωνας τρίποδας, πίσυρας δὲ λέβητας,
ἐκ δὲ δέπας περικαλλές, ὅ οἱ Θρῇκες πόρον
      ἄνδρες

ἐξεσίην ἐλθόντι, μέγα κτέρας · οὐδέ νυ τοῦ περ
φείσατ' ἐνὶ μεγάροις ὁ γέρων, περὶ δ' ἤθελε θυμῷ
λύσασθαι φίλον υἱόν.

[7] Mr. Gladstone has ingeniously suggested that these gold diadems, Nos. 685 and 687, must be identical in form with the πλεκτὴ ἀναδέσμη which Andromaché casts from her head in her profound grief over the death of Hector; the order of the words implies that this ornament was worn over the κρήδεμνον: " Far from her

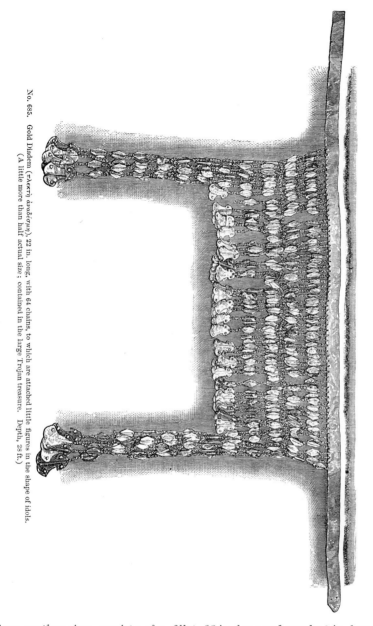

No. 685. Gold Diadem (πλεκτὴ ἀναδέσμη), 22 in. long, with 64 chains, to which are attached little figures in the shape of idols. (A little more than half actual size ; contained in the large Trojan treasure. Depth, 28 ft.)

gives another view, consists of a fillet, 22 in. long and nearly ½ in. broad, from which there hang on either side 7 little chains to cover the

head she threw the glistening adornments, the fillet, the net, and the beautifully entwined diadem, also the veil which golden Aphrodité had presented to her."

Il. xxii. 468–470 :

τῆλε δ᾿ ἀπὸ κρατὸς βάλε δέσματα σιγαλόεντα,
ἄμπυκα, κεκρύφαλόν τε ἰδὲ πλεκτὴν ἀναδέσμην
κρήδεμνόν θ᾿, ὅ ῥά οἱ δῶκε χρυσέη ᾿Αφροδίτη.

temples, each of which consists of 50 double rings, and between every 4 of these rings is suspended an hexagonal leaf having a groove lengthwise:

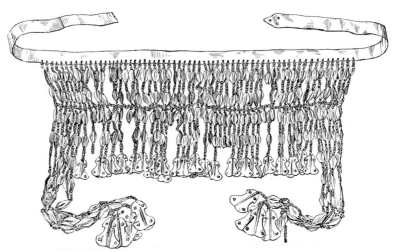

No. 686.   Another View of the same Diadem.

these chains are joined to one another by four little cross chains. At the end of each of the side chains hangs a figure similar in shape to the Trojan idols. Indeed, after having looked over the whole series of Trojan idols, no one can suppose that the primitive goldsmith could have intended to represent here anything else but idols. The only difference between these and the stone idols is that the eyes and the beak, instead of being incised, are here given in relief, and that the latter reaches down to the bottom; further that the knees (or feet ?) are indicated here, like the eyes, by protruding points, and that both eyes and knees are surrounded by circles of small dots. Each idol is nearly an inch long; their breadth at the lower end is about 3-4ths in. The entire length of each of these chains, with the idols, amounts to 10·4 in. Between these ornaments for the temples there are 50 little pendant chains, each of which consists of 21 double rings, and between every 4 of these rings is an hexagonal leaf. At the end of each little chain hangs an idol of identical form, 3-5ths in. high; the length of these short chains with the idols is only 4 in. The number of double rings, of which the 64 chains of this diadem is composed, amounts to 1750, and the number of hexagonal leaves to 354; the number of suspended idols is 64.

The other gold diadem (πλεκτὴ ἀναδέσμη), No. 687, is 20·4 in. long across the top. Instead of a fillet, as in No. 685, it consists of a gold chain, composed of 295 rings of double gold wire, from which are suspended on each side 8 chains, 15·8 in. long. Each of these consists of 360 rings made of double gold wire, and between every 3 of such rings is fastened a lancet-shaped leaf. At the end of each of these chains is suspended a figure 1·3 in. long, in which we again recognize the usual form of the idol; but here no face is indicated: we only see one dot where the forehead ought to be, another in the middle, and three below; each idol is also ornamented with lines of points. Between these ornaments

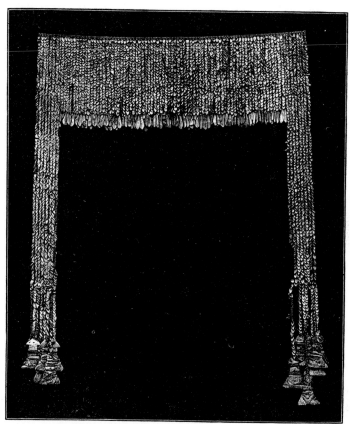

No. 687. Gold Diadem (πλεκτὴ ἀναδέσμη). Length 20·4 in., with 74 short and 16 long chains, contained in the large Trojan treasure. (1:3 actual size. Depth, 28 ft.)

for the temples there are likewise 74 small chains, 4 in. long, each of which consists of 84 rings of double gold wire, and is adorned with 28 lancet-shaped leaves. At the end of each chain is suspended a large leaf of a similar form. Let us compute the number of double rings and leaves of this wonderful head-dress:—

	Rings.	Leaves.
In the upper chain: double rings	295	...
In each of the 16 temple chains:		
360 double rings: (16 × 360)	5760	...
Small lancet-shaped leaves		1920
In each of the 74 short forehead chains:		
84 double rings: (74 × 84)	6216	...
Small lancet-shaped leaves		2072
Besides these: large lancet-shaped leaves		74
Total of rings and leaves	12271 & 4066	
Grand total of pieces (with the 16 idols)	16,353	

All the leaves are suspended by holes to the wires.

My friend Mr. Carlo Giuliano, the celebrated London goldsmith of antiques, who kindly devoted six hours of his precious time to examining the Trojan jewels with me, explains to me that all the idols and leaves of both diadems (Nos. 685 and 687) were cut out with a bronze punch from thin gold plate. To make the very thin wire the Trojans could have

used only ingots of very pure gold, which they forced through the holes of the draw-plate, and which they could gradually and easily reduce to an extreme fineness. Alloyed gold could not have been used to make such very fine wire.

Our illustration No. 688 represents the diadem No. 687 as it might have been worn by a Trojan lady.

No. 689 represents the entangled mass of six gold bracelets precisely in the state in which I found them. Two of these bracelets, represented separately under Nos. 690 and 691, are double, 1-4th in. thick, but quite plain, and have at each end a knob similar to that which we see at one end of the bracelet No. 918.

No. 688.   The Diadem (No. 687) shown as it was worn.

Two others, of which I represent one under No. 692, are only 1-6th in. thick; they are also simple and closed: a fifth is likewise closed, but consists of an ornamented band 1-25th in. thick and 1-3rd in. broad. According to Mr. Giuliano, this has been made in the following way:—Two gold wires were twisted in opposite directions, the one to the right, the other to the left; then a gold wire was soldered to the twist on each side, as is evident from the many places where the soldering is deficient. I do not give here a separate engraving of this bracelet, as the photograph has not succeeded. The sixth bracelet, which I represent under No. 693, is double, and consists of a quadrangular wire which has been twisted. I call particular attention to the small

No. 689.   Six Gold Bracelets, all stuck together in one packet, as they were found in the large Trojan treasure. (About 1 : 3 actual size. Depth, 28 ft.)

size of these bracelets, especially to that of the bracelets Nos. 692 and 693, which seems to denote that the Trojan ladies had astoundingly small arms.

No. 690.

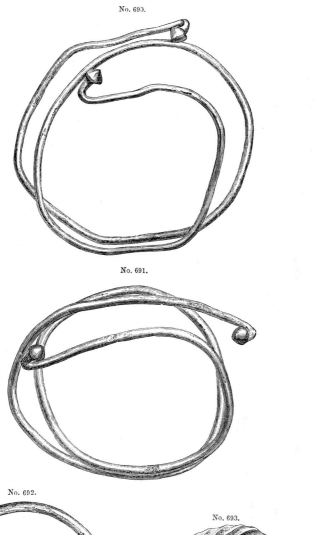

No. 691.

No. 692.

No. 693.

Nos. 690–693 represent in actual size four of the six Bracelets contained in the packet No. 689.

Of the 56 gold ear-rings, I represent the different shapes under Nos. 694, 695, Nos. 698 to 704, and Nos. 752 to 764. With the excep-

No. 694.

No. 695.

Nos. 694, 695. Two of the Gold Ear-rings from the small Gold Jewels in the Silver Jug (No. 779) of the large Treasure. (Half actual size. Depth, 28 ft.)

tion of Nos. 703 and 704, all these ear-rings consist of solid gold wires, which were soldered together, one end being beaten out into a ring and point; then grooves were sunk to receive the beads which we see on Nos. 698, 700, 701, and 702. The curious ear-ring No. 703 is in the form of two serpents, and No. 704 in form of three such serpents. They consist, as Mr. Giuliano explains, of as many plates as there are serpents: these plates were bossed out, and rows of grooves made in each of them; then the two bossed plates were joined together and the lines of grooves filled with globular grains; after that a gold bead was soldered to each end; into the bead at the one extremity was then soldered a globular piece of gold, such as we see it on the thick end of the ear-ring No. 841, whereas a gold wire was soldered to the other side to form the ear-ring. Here, therefore, we see for the first time granular work.

Very simple but highly curious are the gold ear-rings Nos. 705 and 706, of which about a dozen were found. They are nearly in the form of our modern shirt studs, and are 0·3 in. long. They are, however, not

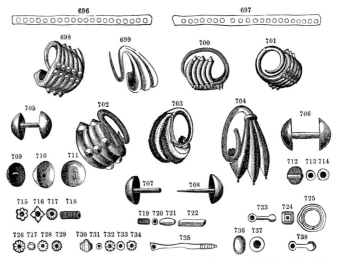

Nos. 696–738. Selection from the small Gold Jewels in the Silver Jug (No. 779) contained in the large Trojan treasure. (About 2 : 3 actual size. Depth, 28 ft.)

soldered, but simply stuck together; for, as we see in No. 707, from the cavity of the one-half there projects a tube (αὐλίσκος) 1-4th in. long, and from the other, No. 708, a pin (ἔμβολον) of the same length, and the pin was merely stuck into the tube to form the ear-ring. Each half of these ear-rings consists of two small gold plates, of which the one has been hammered into a miniature bowl, the other turned into a small tube or into a pin. Then the little tube was soldered into one of the little bowls, the pin was soldered into the other, and the ear-ring was formed by merely putting the pin of the one half into the tube of the other.

My friend Professor Wolfgang Helbig [8] does not admit that jewels such as Nos. 694, 695, 698, 700, 701, 702, and 752 to 764 can have been used as ear-rings. He is of opinion that they served as ornaments for the hair. Professor Virchow observes to me that they look more like nose-rings than like ear-rings. But I certainly believe they were used as ear-rings, and for nothing else.

Very curious also are the gold studs, 1-5th in. high, of which I represent three under Nos. 709 to 711; they have in their cavity a ring 1-8th in. broad for sewing them on: of these studs about a dozen were found.

Under Nos. 712-738 I represent the various shapes of the 8700 small objects of gold, already mentioned as having been found in the silver vase, No. 779. I have strung these in two sets; one of which, consisting of 4610 objects, is represented by the 13 necklaces, Nos. 739 to 745 and Nos. 746 to 751. The other set of 12 necklaces, containing 4090 objects, is precisely similar. The reader sees here gold rings only 1-8th in. in diameter; perforated dice, either smooth or in the form of little indented stars, about 1-6th in. in diameter; gold perforated prisms, 0·1 in. long and 1-8th in. broad, decorated longitudinally with eight or sixteen incisions; and small longitudinally perforated leaves, like No. 712, consisting of very fine double plates, which were made, as Mr. Giuliano explains, by placing the mandril between them, pressing on both sides, and soldering. The gold square prisms, like No. 722, are so perfect that they must have been drawn through a metal drawplate. This was done by bending the fine gold plate into the form of a long pipe, then drawing it through the square holes of the metal plate and soldering it afterwards; but for the most part these prisms are merely bent over, and are not soldered.

To make the little indented wheels and stars, like Nos. 714-717, 726, 728, 729, 732, 734, the Trojan goldsmith took a piece of gold, put it on charcoal, and melted it with the blow-pipe, thus making a globular grain; then he perforated it with a round punch, placed it on a mandril, and cut out the grooves with another oblong punch; but before doing so he beat it square.

Mr. Giuliano further explains that the Trojan goldsmith, in order to make the very small plain gold rings or beads, like No. 731, took a long gold wire, wound it round a copper or bronze mandril, and cut off the rings; he then put the latter on charcoal in long rows, and soldered the two ends of each of them separately with a minute portion of solder in order not to increase the bulk of the wire. He could do this because the gold was more malleable than ours, through being very pure. To make

---

[8] Volfango Helbig, *Sopra il Trattamento della Capellatura e della Barba all' epoca Omerica;* Roma, 1880.

objects like No. 723, he took a small bar of gold, beat it out at one end, and flattened and perforated it with a punch; to the other end he soldered a thick bead. As Mr. Giuliano has shown me, the singular rings, like

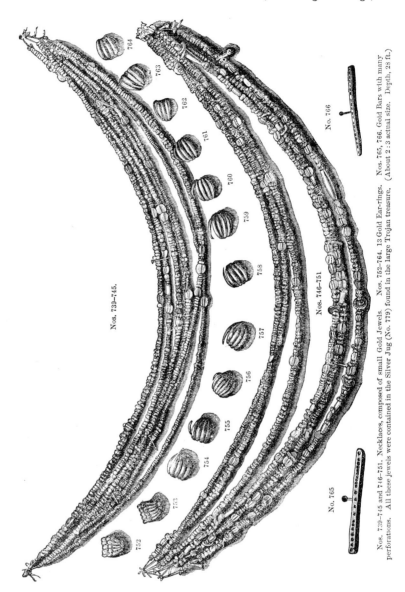

Nos. 739–745 and 746–751. Necklaces, composed of small Gold Jewels.   Nos. 752–764. 13 Gold Ear-rings.   Nos. 765, 766. Gold Bars with many perforations.   All these jewels were contained in the Silver Jug (No. 779) found in the large Trojan treasure.   (About 2 : 3 actual size.   Depth, 28 ft.)

No. 725, consist of two spirals of gold wire, each with three or four turns. These two spirals were placed one upon the other and soldered together; but so that a hole remained on either side between them, for stringing the object on the thread of the necklace.

The large gold beads, like No. 736, were made in the following manner:—Two small cups were beaten out of fine gold plate, a piece having first been cut out from each of them, on either side, one-half of the size the hole was to have; and then the two cups were soldered together. Objects like Nos. 718 and 719 consist of from eight to sixteen small gold rings, like No. 720, which were soldered together. Objects such as No. 735 were made of a gold bar, of which one end was flattened and perforated; the other end was made pointed, and ornamented with seven circular cuts. This object looks like a screw, but it is not one. Objects like No. 730 were thus made:—A piece of gold was put on burning charcoal, and by means of the blowpipe it was melted into a bead, which was perforated, and then hammered and punched into the desired form. Files were certainly unknown, for I found no trace of them in any of the pre-historic cities of Troy, nor at Mycenae.

How the primitive goldsmith could do all this fine work, and particularly how he could accomplish the minute granular work on the ear-rings Nos. 703 and 704, where grains of gold infinitely minute were to be soldered into the microscopic grooves—how he could do all this without the aid of a lens—is an enigma even to Mr. Giuliano.[9] But it was done, and with a powerful lens we can easily distinguish the soldering, even on the smallest rings of a less size than No. 720.

The objects Nos. 696, 697, 765, and 766 consist of long flat pieces of gold with a large number of perforations, on which ornaments composed of small objects like Nos. 712–738 were no doubt suspended.

I represent under No. 767 the golden fillet ($ἄμπυξ$) of the Treasure,

No. 767. Golden Fillet ($ἄμπυξ$), above 18·4 in. long, contained among the Jewels in the Silver Vase No. 779. (Depth, 28 ft.)

which is 18·4 in. long and 0·4 in. broad. It has at each end three perforations for fastening it round the head, and is ornamented all round with a border of dots in punched work. Eight quadruple rows of dots divide it into nine compartments, in each of which there are two large dots.

Of the four ear-rings with pendants, Nos. 768–771, only two, Nos. 768 and 769, are exactly alike. Each of them is composed of 16 round gold wires, soldered together and bent round into the form of a basket, to the upper part of which three gold wires are soldered horizontally in parallel lines, thus forming two fields, in the upper of which are soldered 12, in the lower 11 gold beads. To the lower part of the baskets is soldered a small flat plate of gold, on which 6 rings are soldered; and from each of these is suspended a gold chain made of links of double gold wire, each adorned with 6 quadrangular gold rings,

---

[9] Professor Virchow remarks to me that in the Mexican gold jewels there may be seen granular work of equal fineness.

between every two of which there is a cylinder made of thin quadrangular gold plate, which is merely bent over and not soldered together.

No. 768.   No. 769.   No. 770.   No. 771.

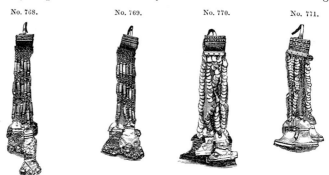

Nos. 768–771. Four Gold Ear-rings, with Pendants or Tassels (θύσανοι), each 3½ in. long,
from the small Jewels in the Silver Jug (No. 779), found in the Trojan treasure. (Depth, 28 ft.)

At the ends of the chains are suspended little figures of gold plate, similar in shape to the usual form of the idols; but they have only one dot on the head, and three on the lower part. To the middle of the basket described above was soldered the hook of the ear-ring with a sharp end.

Still more remarkable are the gold ear-rings Nos. 770 and 771; for their upper basket consists of 40 round gold wires; 18 very fine wires being on each side, and in the centre a bunch of 4 thicker wires which have been beaten flat. All the 40 wires are soldered together, and the 4 central ones are ornamented with linear patterns. On the upper part of this basket are soldered horizontally three parallel wires, thus forming two fields, into each of which are soldered 7 or 8 rosettes, composed of large gold beads surrounded by a number of minute beads. To the lower part of the baskets is attached a gold plate with incised linear patterns, and 5 perforations, in which are suspended 5 chains, formed of links of double gold wire. Every chain is adorned with 23 gold leaves, each having two holes, by which they were suspended on the wire of the links before its ends were soldered together. At the end of each chain is suspended an idol-like figure, cut out of thin gold plate and adorned by the punch with 4 large dots, around each of which is an infinite number of small ones: but this punched work is only on the idols of No. 770; those of No. 771 are quite plain.

I now come to the large double-handled gold goblet, the δέπας ἀμφικύπελλον, Nos. 772 and 773, which Mr. Giuliano declares to be 23 carats fine. It weighs exactly 600 grammes (about 1 lb. 6 oz. troy); it is 3·6 in. high, 7·5 in. long, and 7·3 in. broad. It is in the form of a ship; its handles are very large; on one side there is a mouth 2·8 in. broad for drinking out of, and another at the other side, which is 1·4 in. broad. As my friend, Professor Stephanos Koumanoudes of Athens, remarks, the person who presented the filled cup may have first drunk from the small mouth, as a mark of respect, to let the guest drink from the larger mouth; or, as suggested in the *Quarterly Review* for April 1874, a person, holding the cup before him by the two handles, may have poured a libation from the further spout and then have drunk out of the nearer. Thus Achilles used a choice goblet (δέπας) for pouring libations to Zeus.[10] The

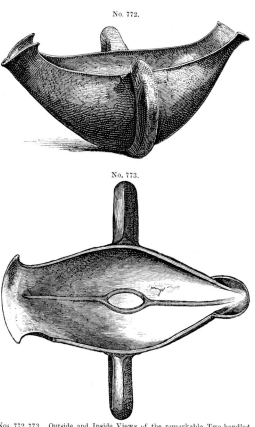

No. 772.

δέπας ἀμφικύπελλον has a foot, which projects about 1-12th in. and is 1·4 in. long and 4-5ths in. broad. Mr. Giuliano declares this cup to have been beaten out of a single plate of gold, but that the two handles, which are hollow, have been beaten out of separate plates of gold, the edges being then soldered together and the handles also joined by soldering to the cup. He explains that this soldering could only be done by mixing silver with gold, by beating the mixture very fine, and by cutting it into very small pieces which would melt, whilst the pure gold would not melt; thus the soldering could easily be made by means of the mixture and a little borax: instead of borax, glass might have been used.

No. 773.

Nos. 772, 773. Outside and Inside Views of the remarkable Two-handled Cup of pure Gold (δέπας ἀμφικύπελλον), weighing about 1 lb. 6 oz. troy, contained in the large Trojan treasure. (Depth, 28 ft.)

[10] *Il.* xvi. 225-227 :

ἔνθα δέ οἱ δέπας ἔσκε τετυγμένον, οὐδέ τις ἄλλος
οὔτ᾽ ἀνδρῶν πίνεσκεν ἀπ᾽ αὐτοῦ αἴθοπα οἶνον,
οὔ τέ τεῳ σπένδεσκε θεῶν, ὅτε μὴ Διΐ πατρί.

But we do not see here that Achilles himself drank after the libation. We are indebted to Mr. J. W. Lockhart for the following account of the double-spouted boat-shaped bronze vessel, used in a similar manner in the Chinese temples, and represented in the engraving No. 774:—"In China there is a vessel of very nearly the same shape, but with ears prolonged till they rise an inch above the cup. The cup stands on three legs, and is, in fact, a tripod. Such cups are used in the temples, especially in the ancestral temples of the real religion of China, when offerings are made to the *manes* of ancestors. The cups are filled with wine when placed on the altar before the idol-shrine, or before the

ancestral tablet; and the wine is afterwards partly drunk and partly poured out as a libation." Such vessels are used in pairs, and our drawing is made from one of a pair in Mr. Lockhart's possession. It is of *bronze*, 6 in. long and 6½ in. high, including the legs. The width is 2 in. between the upright ears, and 2¾ in. at the broadest part. There is only *one* handle. Mr. Lockhart calls attention to the "key" ornament round the cup, which is so well known in the purest Greek art, as a sign of Chinese influence on the art of Western Asia and Europe. Mr. Lockhart also reads Chinese characters on some of the Trojan whorls. I am under a deep obligation to Mr. Lockhart for his spontaneous offer of this very interesting illustration of one of the most striking and unique objects discovered by me at Troy.

In this soldering process the Trojans seem to have been far more advanced than the Myceneans, for on the gold vessels I found in the royal tombs at Mycenae the handles had not been soldered, but merely joined with pins.[1] In fact, the only objects of gold found at Mycenae on which soldering is perceptible are the greaves.[2]

No. 775 represents the globular gold bottle of the treasure. Mr. Giuliano declares this bottle to be of gold, 20 carats fine, and says that it has been beaten out of a single plate of gold with punches and hammers. When the bottle was ready as far as the neck, it was filled with cement or clay, and the neck was then beaten out and its rim turned back and bent

No. 774. Bronze Cup used in China for Libations and Drinking.

over again. This bottle weighs 403 grammes (6220 grains, or nearly 1 lb. 1 oz. troy); it is exactly 6 in. high, 5·6 in. in diameter, and has a zigzag decoration on the neck, which, however, is not continued all round.

The second gold goblet is represented under No. 776. According to Mr. Giuliano, it is 23 carats fine; it weighs 226 grammes (7¼ oz. troy); it is 3·6 in. high and 3·1 in. in diameter; it has 16 flutings, which were obtained by filling the goblet with wood or clay and then beating it with a hammer. I further represent under No. 777 a small goblet of the treasure, which, according to Mr. Giuliano, is of gold, 18 carats fine, mixed with silver. It consists therefore of electrum. It weighs 70 grammes (2¼ oz. troy), and is 3·4 in. high and above 2·6 in.

No. 775. Globular Bottle of Gold, weighing about 1 lb. troy; contained in the large Trojan treasure. (Depth, 28 ft.)

Note.—The objects seen below are merely pieces of wood to support it.

[1] See my *Mycenae*, pp. 232, 233, Nos. 340–343.   [2] See my *Mycenae*, pp. 328, 329.

broad; its foot is only 4-5ths of an inch high, 1 in. broad, and not level; so that the goblet can hardly stand on it, and appears to be

No. 776. Gold Goblet, weighing 7¼ oz. troy; contained in the large Trojan treasure. (Depth, 28 ft.)

No. 777. A small Cup of Electrum (*i.e.* 4 parts of Gold to 1 of Silver); contained in the large Trojan treasure. (Depth, 28 ft.)

intended to be put down on the mouth: like the goblet No. 776, it has 16 flutings. Its foot has been beaten out of a separate plate, and has not been soldered to the bottom, but merely overlaps it. It bears the marks of the great heat to which it has been exposed in the conflagration.

As nothing similar to any one of these various articles of gold has been ever found elsewhere, it will for ever remain a riddle to us whether they were home-made or imported; but if we compare them with the rude works of terra-cotta or the implements and weapons of stone or bronze found in the third city, we certainly feel inclined to think that they were imported.

The small silver vase-cover No. 778 is ornamented with an incised zigzag line.

Under Nos. 779, 780, and 781, I represent the three silver vases of the treasure. The largest of them, No. 779, which contained all the small gold articles, is 8·4 in. high and 8 in. in diameter, and has a hollow handle, 5·6 in. long by 3·6 in. broad. Its lower part is globular, and the foot convex; the neck

No. 778. A small Silver Vase Cover; contained in the large Trojan treasure. (Depth, 28 ft.)

No. 779. Large one-handled Silver Jug, contained in the large Trojan treasure, in which the small Ornaments were found. (Depth, 28 ft.)

varies slightly from the cylindrical form. It has been beaten entirely out of a silver plate into its present form; there is no soldering except that of the huge handle, the soldering of which to the body of the vase is distinctly visible. This handle itself must certainly have been hammered out of a silver plate and soldered together; but no soldering is perceptible, even with a powerful lens. The silver vases Nos. 780

and 781 are also globular, with a neck varying from the cylindrical form. The former is 7·4 in. high and 6·4 in. in diameter. The foot

No. 780. Silver Vase, with a quantity of copper fixed to its bottom by the fire; found in the large Trojan treasure. (Depth, 28 ft.)

No. 781. Silver Vase, to which part of another Silver Vase is attached by the cementing power of the chloride of silver; contained in the large Trojan treasure. (Depth, 28 ft.)

of this vase is convex, and has a great deal of copper fused on to it, which must have dripped from the copper objects contained in the treasure during the conflagration. No. 781 is 7 in. high and 6 in. in diameter; the foot is flat. Another silver vase, of which, however, only portions have been preserved, is cemented upon it.[3] All these three silver vases have on the outside a thick incrustation, which Professor Roberts of the Royal Mint has found "to consist of chloride of silver, which can, in most instances, be easily cut with a knife, and resembles horny chloride of silver, which may be deposited from solution in translucent layers." To this chloride of silver adhere wood-ashes, clay, and very small stones, probably the detritus of bricks.

Another fractured silver vase, 4¾ in. high and broad, with tubular holes for suspension on the sides, may be seen cemented to the copper plate, No. 782. This plate is 2-5ths. in. thick, 6·4 in. broad, and 17·6 in. long; it has a rim 1-10th in. high; at one end of it there are two immovable wheels with an axle-tree. The plate is very much bent in two places; the curvatures can only have been produced by the heat to which the object was exposed in the conflagration.

This remarkable object lay on the top of the whole mass; hence I suppose it to have been the support to the lid of the wooden chest in which the treasure was packed, and that the two immovable wheels served as hasps. Professor Roberts, who examined this object carefully and analysed a fragment of the silver vase, writes to me as follows on the subject:—"The small portion of metal 1 mm. thick from the fractured silver vase, No. 782, consists of three layers; a central one of

---

[3] The cause of this cementing will be explained presently.

silver, about 0·2 mm. thick, the external layers being chloride of silver, in which grains of sand and earthy matter are imbedded. The cementing

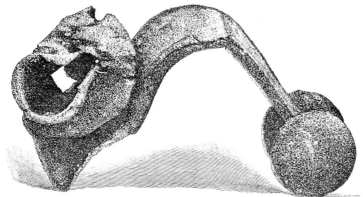

No. 782. Curious Plate of Copper, having probably served as a support of the wooden lid of the chest, with two immovable discs, which may probably have served as hasps. A Silver Vase is cemented on it by the action of the chloride of silver and the oxide or carbonate of copper. Found in the large Trojan treasure. (Depth, 28 ft.)

action of this chloride, so beautifully shown in many of the silver articles, is interesting, and is specially remarkable in this object, in which a vase of silver is cemented to an article of copper. In other examples sand, charcoal, and shells adhere tenaciously to silver articles by the pseudo-morphous layer of chloride of silver in which they are imbedded."

Nos. 783 and 784 represent the two pretty silver vases of the treasure, which have rather an Egyptian form. They are, however, Trojan, for the former has on each side of the body and of the cap-like cover one

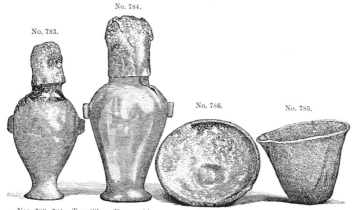

No. 784.

No. 783.

No. 786.   No. 785.

Nos. 783, 784. Two Silver Vases, with caps, and tubular rings for suspension with strings.
No. 785. A Silver Cup, 3⅓ in. high and nearly 4 in. wide.
No. 786. A Silver Dish (φιάλη), with a boss in the centre.
These four objects were contained in the large Trojan treasure. (Depth, 28 ft.)

vertical tubular hole, while the second has on each side of the body and the cap two vertical tubular holes, for suspension with a string, a system which is not found in Egypt. Both vases have been hammered out from plates of silver in the manner already described. There is no soldering about them, except the projections with the tubular holes on the sides. The caps only are covered with chloride of silver; the vases themselves are free from it. The smaller vase is 6·8 in. high and 3·2 in. thick in the body; the larger, 8 in. high and 3·6 in. thick in the body.

The silver goblet, No. 785, is 3⅓ in. high, and has a mouth 4 in. in diameter. It is thickly covered with chloride of silver. Much better preserved is the flat silver cup or dish (φιάλη) No. 786, which is 5½ in. in diameter, and has a boss (ὀμφαλός) in the middle; it has little or no chloride of silver.

The next object I took out was a package of the six blade-like ingots of silver, which I represent here under Nos. 787–792, which were stuck

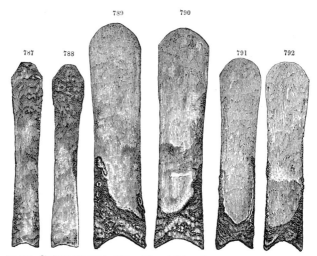

Nos. 787–792.   Six blade-like Ingots of Silver (Homeric Talents?), contained in the large Trojan treasure.
(Depth, 28 ft.)

together by the cementing action of the chloride of silver; I have separated them not without difficulty. Professor Roberts, who kindly analysed a small portion of one of them, sends me the following note:—

"Weight of portion submitted to analysis: 0·6408 gramme.

Analysis:—		
Silver ..	.. ..	95·61
Copper	.. ..	3·41
Gold ..	.. ..	17
Iron ..	.. ..	38
Lead ..	.. ..	22
Nickel	.. ..	traces.
		99·79

The amount of lead present points to the silver having been purified by cupellation. Alloys of silver are known to vary in composition throughout the mass, but it is probable that the results of the analysis fairly indicate the amount of precious metal in the talent."

The six pieces of silver before us are in the form of large knife-blades, having one end rounded, and the other cut into the form of a crescent; they have all been wrought with the hammer. The two larger blades are 8·6 in. long and 2 in. broad, and weigh respectively 190 and 183 grammes. The next two pieces are 7·4 in. long and 1·6 in. broad; one of them weighs 174, the other 173 grammes. The two remaining pieces are nearly 7 in. long and 1·2 in. broad; one of them weighs 173, the other 171 grammes.[4]

Are we to see in these six ingots of pure silver Homeric "talents"? These latter could only have been small, as, for instance, when Achilles offers for the first prize in the chariot-race a woman, for the second a horse, for the third a cauldron, and for the fourth two gold talents.[5]

Professor Sayce sends me the following interesting note on the subject of these six curious silver wedges: —

"In the *Academy* of Nov. 22, 1879, Mr. Barclay V. Head shows that 'the silver mina of Carchemish,' the Hittite capital, mentioned on an Assyrian tablet, is identical on the one side with the Babylonian silver mina of about 8656 grains troy (561 grammes), and on the other with the mina in use in Asia Minor. The Lydian silver money of Croesus, says Mr. Head, 'follows this so-called Babylonic silver standard, fifty staters of Croesus, each weighing 173 grains (11·2 grammes), making one Babylonic silver mina of 8656 grains.

"'Nevertheless, that this Babylonic silver mina was in use throughout Asia Minor long before the age of Croesus for weighing bullion silver, may, I think, be inferred, not only because the earliest silver coins of nearly the whole of Asia Minor are regulated by it, but from the fact that it was also in use among the Phrygio-Thracian mining tribes, who must have brought it over with them from Asia, together with the worship of the Phrygian Bacchus, when they separated from their brethren of the same stock who remained behind. More than this, I believe that there is proof positive that this weight was used in the Troad at the period of the burial of the treasure discovered by Dr. Schliemann. There are in that treasure six wedges or bars of silver, about 7 or 8 in. long by about 2 in. in breadth. These weigh respectively 171, 173, 173, 174, 183, and 190 metric grammes. The heaviest and best preserved appears to have gained slightly by oxydization and incrustation at one end to the amount of about 40 or 50 grains troy. Supposing its original weight to have been about 187 grammes, or 2885·4 grains troy, what else can this be but precisely the third part of the Babylonian silver mina of 8656 grains? That these bars or wedges are thirds and not halves or fourths is, to my mind, a

---

[4] The two largest weigh, respectively, a little over and a little under 6 ozs., and the other four are a little over 5½ ozs. troy. The gramme is 15·43235 grains; that is, a little less than 15½ grains.

[5] *Il.* xxiii. 262-270:

Ἱππεῦσιν μὲν πρῶτα ποδώκεσιν ἀγλά' ἄεθλα
θῆκε γυναῖκα ἄγεσθαι ἀμύμονα ἔργα ἰδυῖαν

καὶ τρίποδ' ὠτώεντα δυωκαιεικοσίμετρον,
τῷ πρώτῳ· ἀτὰρ αὖ τῷ δευτέρῳ ἵππον ἔθηκεν
ἑξέτε', ἀδμήτην, βρέφος ἡμίονον κυέουσαν·
αὐτὰρ τῷ τριτάτῳ ἄπυρον κατέθηκε λέβητα
καλόν, τέσσαρα μέτρα κεχανδότα, λευκὸν ἔτ'
αὔτως·
τῷ δὲ τετάρτῳ θῆκε δύο χρυσοῖο τάλαντα,
πέμπτῳ δ' ἀμφίθετον φιάλην ἀπύρωτον ἔθηκεν.

strong point in favour of their being fractions of the Babylonian mina, the shekels of this standard being very generally divided by three, while those of the Phoenician standard are halved and quartered.

" 'Dr. Schliemann calls his wedges Homeric talents, but, be this as it may, they are certainly thirds of the Babylonic silver mina of from 8645 to 8656 grains. If my proposed identification of the mina of Carchemish with the mina in use in the Troad about the fourteenth century B.C. be accepted, may it not prove suggestive when considered in connection with the Egyptian text (the poem of Pentaur), in which the people of Ilion, Pedasos, Dardanos, Mysia, and Lycia are mentioned as allies of the Kheta (Hittites) in their wars with Ramses II. about the same period? . . . When, therefore, we find a particular silver mina specified in Assyrian documents as the mina of Carchemish, I think we shall not be wrong in concluding that this is the weight which the Hittites used in their commercial transactions with the peoples of Cilicia, Pamphylia, Lydia, Phrygia, the Troad, &c., and that this name was given to it in Assyria to distinguish it from the other heavier silver mina of about 11,225 grains used in Phoenicia. . . . The earliest coined money on this standard is the Lydian electrum of the time of Gyges. Croesus appears to have been the first to strike silver coins on the same standard; and, as town after town begins to coin money, we perceive that from the Gulf of Issus in the east to Phaselis in the west, as well as in Lydia, and here and there in Ionia, in Cyprus, and perhaps even in Crete, the earliest coins are staters of 173 grains or fractions of such staters.' "

Under No. 793 I represent the silver vase found a few days previous to the discovery of the large treasure, and very close to it; its lower part is of globular shape, and its neck slopes outward, like part of an inverted cone. It has been damaged by the pickaxe of the labourer who found it. Like the other large silver vases, it is covered with chloride of silver; it is 7·2 in. high and 5·6 in. broad. It deserves particular attention that all these silver vases are only covered with chloride on the outside, and that they are exempt from it on the inside. The vase No. 793 contained the

No. 793.

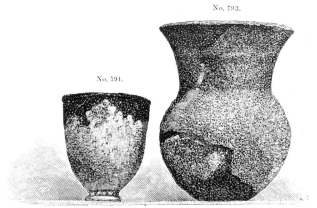

No. 791.

Nos. 793, 794.   No. 791 is a Goblet of Electrum, which was contained in the Silver Vase No. 793, found near to the large Treasure, at a depth of 28 ft.

elegant cup of electrum, No. 794, which is 4·4 in. high and 3·6 in. wide
at the mouth. This cup bears the marks of the intense heat to which it
was exposed in the conflagration, but otherwise it is exceedingly well
preserved. Only its upper part is externally covered with a thick incrustation; for the rest it is of a dazzling white, both outside and inside.
Electrum, which, as before mentioned, occurs three times in the *Odyssey*,
is a word unknown to the *Iliad;* but we find in the latter [6] the word
ἠλέκτωρ for " sun." It, therefore, appears that the poets intended to
indicate by ἤλεκτρον a substance capable of being compared in brilliancy
with the sun.

Together with this latter vase was found a helmet, but so much
destroyed by the chloride of copper, that it fell into minute fragments
when it was being taken out, and it cannot be recomposed. Only its
upper portions, Nos. 795 and 796, have been preserved. I shall revert to
these in the subsequent pages, when I come to discuss similar portions

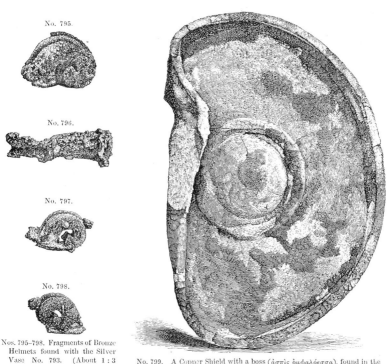

No. 795.

No. 796.

No. 797.

No. 798.

Nos. 795–798. Fragments of Bronze
Helmets found with the Silver
Vase No. 793. (About 1 : 3
actual size. Depth, 28 ft.)

No. 799. A Copper Shield with a boss (ἀσπὶς ὀμφαλόεσσα), found in the
large Treasure. (Depth, 28 ft.)

of another helmet, represented under No. 979. Nos. 797 and 798 appear
to be also fragments of the upper portions of helmets.

No. 799 represents the large copper shield of the treasure (the ἀσπὶς
ὀμφαλόεσσα of Homer) in the form of an oval salver, in the middle of
which is a large boss encircled by a small furrow (αὖλαξ). This shield is

———————

[6] *Il.* vi. 513; xix. 398.

a little more than 20 in. in diameter. It is quite flat, and is surrounded by a rim (ἄντυξ) 1½ in. high. The boss (ὀμφαλός) is 2·4 in. high and 4·4 in. in diameter ; the furrow encircling it is 7·2 in. in diameter, and is 3–5ths in. deep. It has evidently been composed of four and perhaps five pieces. First the high projecting boss (ὀμφαλός) was beaten out of a plate, with the furrow and a high border round it ; round this was soldered a plate in the form of a flat ring, and round it the high protruding rim (ἄντυξ), on which a narrow strip of thin copper plate was again soldered all round.

This shield of copper, with its central boss and the furrow and rim so suitable for holding together a covering of ox-hides, reminds us irresistibly of the seven-fold shield of Ajax : "Ajax came near, bearing before him his tower-like copper shield, covered with seven layers of ox-hide, the work of Tychius, the best of artificers that wrought in leather ; he had his home in Hylé. He made him the easily-wielded shield with seven-fold hides of fat bulls, and laid over them an eighth plate of copper." [7]   It is equally striking to compare this shield of the treasure with the description of Sarpedon's shield, with its round plate of hammered copper, and its covering of ox-hides, fastened to the inner edge of the rim by long golden rods.[8]

No. 800 marks the copper cauldron of the treasure, with two horizontal handles, which certainly gives us an idea of the Homeric λέβης. It is

No. 800.   Great Copper Cauldron (λέβης), contained in the large Trojan treasure ; found at a depth of 28 ft.

16·8 in. in diameter and 5·6 in. high ; the bottom is flat, and is 8 in. in diameter. This cauldron shows the marks of the fearful conflagration, and near the handle, on the left side, are seen two fragments of bronze weapons (a lance and a battle-axe) firmly fused into it. It deserves particular attention that whilst in Mycenae there is hardly any soldering, and

[7] Il. vii. 219-223 :

Αἴας δ' ἐγγύθεν ἦλθε φέρων σάκος, ἠΰτε πύργον,
χάλκεον, ἑπταβόειον, ὅ οἱ Τυχίος κάμε τεύχων,
σκυτοτόμων ὄχ' ἄριστος, Ὕλῃ ἔνι οἰκία ναίων,
ὅς οἱ ἐποίησεν σάκος αἰόλον ἑπταβόειον
ταύρων ζατρεφέων, ἐπὶ δ' ὄγδοον ἤλασε χαλκόν.

Compare also vv. 245-247.
[8] Il. xii. 294-297 :

αὐτίκα δ' ἀσπίδα μὲν πρόσθ' ἔσχετο πάντοσ' ἐΐσην
καλὴν χαλκείην ἐξήλατον, ἣν ἄρα χαλκεὺς
ἤλασεν, ἔντοσθεν δὲ βοείας ῥάψε θαμείας
χρυσείης ῥάβδοισι διηνεκέσιν περὶ κύκλον.

the different pieces of which the copper cauldrons consist are all joined together with pins, here at Troy we see only soldering, and nothing fastened together with pins. As the two handles of the cauldron before us were too thick to be easily soldered on, the two ends of each of them were sawn into or split, and then the rim of the vessel was placed in the opening and soldered on.

We find λέβητες mentioned ten times in the *Iliad*, usually as prizes in games ;[9] also as presents.[10] The λέβης had the value of an ox ;[11] only once we find it used as a cauldron.[1] In the *Odyssey* it is for the most part used as a washing bowl, in which the hands were washed before the meal and at the sacrifice. It was often of silver and ornamented ;[2] it was also of copper and used for a foot-bath.[3] Mr. Philip Smith observes to me, that "among the tribute received by Thutmes III., apparently from Western Asia (the name of the country is imperfect in the record), was 'a brass cauldron, the work of Kefthu.'[4] This special mention of it, as an article of foreign workmanship, may be compared with the value evidently set on the Trojan cauldron, by its preservation in the treasure."

Upon and beside the gold and silver articles, I found in the treasure thirteen bronze lance-heads, more or less fractured, five of which are shown under Nos. 801–805 and one under 815. They are from 7 to above 12½ in. in length, and from 1·6 to 2·4 in. broad at the thickest point. At the lower end of each is a perforation, in which, in most cases, the nail or peg which fastened the lance-head to the wooden handle is still sticking. The pin-hole is clearly visible in the lance-head No. 805, which the conflagration has fused on to a battle-axe.

The Trojan lance-heads were therefore quite different from those of the Myceneans,[5] as well as from all those found in the Swiss Lake-dwellings,[6] in the tombs of Fronstetten,[7] in those of Hedingen,[8] Ebingen,[9] Rothenlachen,[10] Laitz,[1] and many other sepulchres in Germany, Austria, and Italy,[2] at Hallstatt,[3] in Denmark,[4] and in Hungary,[5] all of which have

[9] *Il.* xxiii. 259 :
νηῶν δ' ἔκφερ' ἄεθλα, λέβητάς τε τρίποδάς τε.
xxiii. 485 :
δεῦρό νυν, ἢ τρίποδος περιδώμεθον ἠὲ λέβητος.
[10] *Il.* ix. 263, 265 :
. . . ὑπέσχετο δῶρ' Ἀγαμέμνων,
αἴθωνας δὲ λέβητας ἐείκοσι, δώδεκα δ' ἵππους.
[11] *Il.* xxiii. 885 :
κὰδ δὲ λέβητ' ἄπυρον, βοὸς ἄξιον, ἀνθεμόεντα.
[1] *Il.* xxi. 362 :
ὡς δὲ λέβης ζεῖ ἔνδον, ἐπειγόμενος πυρὶ πολλῷ.
[2] *Od.* i. 136–138 :
χέρνιβα δ' ἀμφίπολος προχόῳ ἐπέχευε φέρουσα
καλῇ χρυσείῃ ὑπὲρ ἀργυρέοιο λέβητος,
νίψασθαι ·
and *Od.* iii. 440, 441 :
χέρνιβα δέ σφ' Ἄρητος ἐν ἀνθεμόεντι λέβητι
ἤλυθεν ἐκ θαλάμοιο φέρων.
[3] *Od.* xix. 386, 387 :
Ὡς ἄρ' ἔφη · γρηῢς δὲ λέβηθ' ἔλε παμφανόωντα,
τοῦ πόδας ἐξαπένιζεν, ὕδωρ δ' ἐνεχεύατο πουλύ.

Od. xix. 469 :
ἐν δὲ λέβητι πέσεν κνήμη, κανάχησε δὲ χαλκός.
[4] Brugsch, *Hist. of Egypt*, vol. i. p. 385, Eng. trans., 2nd ed.
[5] See my *Mycenae*, pp. 278, 279, fig. No. 441.
[6] Victor Gross, *Moeringen et Auvernier*, Pl. iv., Nos. 1, 8–13. Ferdinand Keller, *Pfahlbauten*, vii. Bericht, Pl. iii. Nos. 14, 18.
[7] L. Lindenschmit, *Die Vaterländischen Alterthümer*, Pl. iii. Nos. 27 and 28.
[8] *Ibid.* Pl. iv. Nos. 2, 9, 10, 13, 14.
[9] *Ibid.* Pl. vii. Nos. 3, 4, 9, 11, 12.
[10] *Ibid.* Pl. xii. No. 10.
[1] *Ibid.* Pl. xii. Nos. 5-7. [2] *Ibid.* Pl. xxxix.
[3] Ed. Freih. von Sacken, *Das Grabfeld von Hallstatt*, Pl. vii. Nos. 1, 3–6.
[4] J. J. A. Worsaae, *Nordiske Oldsager*, Pl. 38 and 82.
[5] Joseph Hampel, *Antiquités préhistoriques de la Hongrie*, Pl. ix. Nos. 1–6, and Pl. xv. No. 1 : and *Catalogue de l'Exposition préhistorique*, p. 25, No. 10 ; p. 27, Nos. 13, 14.

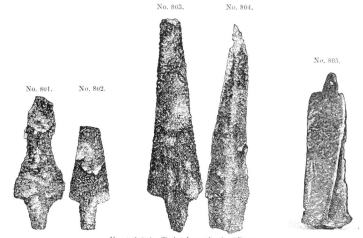

Nos. 801–804. Trojan Lance-heads of Bronze.
No. 805. Bronze Lance and Battle-axe fused together by the conflagration. The pin-hole of the lance is
visible. (Nearly 1 : 3 actual size. Depth, 28 ft.)

Nos. 806–809. Trojan Battle-axes of Bronze.
Nos. 807 and 809 have pieces of other weapons fused on to them by the fire.
(Nearly 1 : 3 actual size. Depth, 28 ft.)

a tube in which the wooden lance-shaft was fixed. The Homeric lance-
heads seem to have had a similar tube in which the shaft was fixed, for

the poet says: "And the brain ran out from the wound along the tube of the lance."[6] But the British Museum and the Louvre contain in their collections several specimens of bronze lance-heads found in tombs in Cyprus, which are identical with the Trojan lance-heads.[7]

No. 810.   Trojan Battle-axe.
(Nearly 1 : 3 actual size. Depth, 28 ft.)

I further took out from the treasure four-teen battle-axes of bronze, of which I represent four entire ones under Nos. 806–809 and a fractured one under No. 810. They are from 6·4 to 12·4 in. long, from half an inch to 4-5ths in. thick, and from 1·2 to 3 in. broad. The largest of them weighs 1365 grammes, or about 3 pounds avoirdupois. M. Ernest Chantre, Assistant Director of the Museum at Lyons, sent me the result of the analysis of these battle-axes made by the famous chemist, M. Damour of Lyons. I had drilled two of them and sent him the drillings:—

No. 1.—Drillings from one of the battle-axes of the treasure:—

		Grammes.
For analysis	.. ..	0·3020
Deducting the sand contained in it	.. .. ..	0·0160
Analysed metal ..	..	0·2860

	Grammes.	In 1·0000 part.
This consists of copper	0·2740 =	0·9580
Do. do. tin	0·0110 =	0·0384
	0·2850 =	0·9964

No. 2.—Drillings of another battle-axe from the treasure:—

		Grammes.
For analysis	.. ..	0·2970
Deducting the sand contained in it	.. .. ..	0·0020
Analysed metal ..	..	0·2950

	Grammes.	In 1·0000 part.
This consists of copper	0·2675 =	0·9067
Do. do. tin	0·0255 =	0·0864
	0·2930 =	0·9931

I have still to mention a curious sling-bullet of copper ore which was analysed by M. Damour of Lyons with the following result:—

---

[6] *Il.* xvii. 297 :
ἐγκέφαλος δὲ παρ' αὐλὸν ἀνέδραμεν ἐξ ὠτειλῆς.

[7] Professor Virchow kindly calls my attention to Evans, *Petit Album de l'Age du Bronze de la Grande Bretagne*, London, 1876, Pl. xi., where a series of similar blades, called there "couteaux de poignards," are represented. But, in my opinion, similar weapons can never have been used for anything else than lances; for a dagger we necessarily must suppose a handle such as we see on the real daggers Nos. 811–814, 901, and 927. As the blades before us (Nos. 801–805) do not fulfil this indispensable condition, they cannot be daggers. Professor Virchow adds that similar blades occasionally occur also in Germany, but that the lower end of them is usually broad and has two perforations for fixing in the lance-shaft. He showed me, however, in his own collection a lance-head found on the island of Rügen, which is perfectly similar to the Trojan lance-heads.

" Drillings of one of the Trojan sling-bullets, externally covered with verdigris, and internally of the colour of iron.

ANALYSIS.

					Grammes.		
Quantity of analysed metal	..	..	..	0·2410			

							In 1·0000 part.
Consisting of sulphur	..	..	..	..	0·0470	=	0·1950
Do.	copper	..	..	..	..	0·1920	= 0·7966
Do.	iron	..	..	..	..	0·0002	= 0·0008
Do.	quartzose	..	..	..	..	0·0005	= 0·0020
					0·2397	=	0·9944 "

Professor W. Chandler Roberts, of the Royal Mint, who also bored two of these battle-axes and analysed the drillings, writes to me that one axe gave—   and the other—

95·41 copper.   93·80 copper.
4·39 tin.   5·70 tin.

99·80   99·50

He adds that he found them free from zinc.

The lance-heads have not been analysed, but we may with all probability suppose that they are of bronze, since the battle-axes, which are fifty times heavier, are of that metal.

Professor Virchow kindly calls my attention to the *compte rendu* of the Berlin Anthropological Society of 29th July, 1876, p. 8, where a perfectly similar battle-axe is represented, which was found, together with five similar ones, at a depth of 3 ft., at Bythin, in the duchy of Posen. All these six axes consist of pure copper. Virchow says of them: " Their form approaches most to that of the ancient stone axes. It is true that they are not so massive as the stone axes generally are, but this was not necessary when metal was used. Such a form might pass as an excellent proof of how the stone form has gradually been transferred into a metal form, and how people manufactured of metal an implement analogous to the stone axe."

Battle-axes of a like form, of pure copper, were also found in Hungary.[8] My honoured friend, Professor James D. Butler, LL.D., kindly sends me his learned dissertation[9] on the pre-historic antiquities of Wisconsin, illustrated by excellent photographic plates, on which seven similar battle-axes of *pure copper* found in Wisconsin are represented.

Similar battle-axes occur, though very rarely, in company with silex saw-knives and axes of diorite, in India. The British Museum contains in its collection of East Indian antiquities 9 perfectly similar bronze battle-axes, found at Gungeria in the Mhow Talook district of Burrha, in Central India; their length is from 20 to 28 in. The British Museum contains also 2 bronze battle axes, in all respects like the Trojan, found at Tel-Sifr in Babylonia. The Ethnographical and Pre-historic Collection of

[8] Joseph Hampel, *Antiquités préhistor. de la Hongrie*, Pl. viii. Nos. 13, 15.

[9] James D. Butler, *Pre-historic Wisconsin*, Annual Address before the State Historical Society of Wisconsin, in the Assembly Chamber, February 18, 1876.

General Lane Fox in the South Kensington Museum contains 7 bronze battle-axes of an identical shape, found in tombs in Cyprus. Further, 2 exactly similar battle-axes, found in ancient Egyptian tombs, are preserved in the Egyptian Collection in the Louvre. At Mycenae I found only one such battle-axe [10] and the fragment of another. These Trojan bronze battle-axes are nothing but exact copies of the primitive stone battle-axes; only they have been made longer for greater convenience and usefulness, as they could then be more easily fastened to the wooden shafts and could be used on both sides.

Having described the battle-axes of the Trojan Treasure, which have been proved to consist of bronze, it may not be out of place to discuss here the important question, whence the pre-historic peoples, and particularly those who now occupy us—the inhabitants of the third, the burnt city of Hissarlik—obtained their tin. M. Burnouf,[1] judging from the resemblance of the Greek word for tin (κασσίτερος) to the Sanscrit "kastira," thinks it probable that they received it from India. But Professor Sayce observes to me: "Kastira is as little a Sanscrit word as κασσίτερος is a Greek one, and both seem borrowed from the same source. In Arabic kazdir is 'tin,' in Assyrian kizasaddir, and in the primitive Accadian of Babylonia kasduru or kazduru. The Arabic and Assyrian may be borrowed from the Accadian, but more probably both words, together with the Accadian, the Sanscrit and the Greek, have been imported from a common source, which was perhaps one of the early languages of the Caucasus, where ancient tin mines have been found." Sir J. Lubbock, on the other hand, thinks it more probable that the ancients obtained tin through "the Phoenicians from Cornwall:" he says, "As Cornwall, Saxony, and Spain[2] are the only known European sources from which tin can be obtained in any quantity, the mere presence of bronze is in itself a sufficient evidence, not only of metallurgical skill, but also of commercial intercourse." [3]

Again, in another passage: "Unless the ancients had some source of tin with which we are unacquainted, it seems to be well established, and is indeed admitted even by Sir Cornewall Lewis, that the Phoenician tin was mainly derived from Cornwall, and consequently that, even at this early period, a considerable commerce had been organized, and very distant countries brought into connection with one another. Sir C. Lewis, however, considers that the tin was 'carried across Gaul to Massilia, and imported thence into Greece and Italy.' [4] Doubtless much of it did in late times come by this route, but the Phoenicians were in the plenitude of their power 1200 years B.C., while Massilia was not built until 600 B.C. Moreover Strabo expressly says that in early times the Phoenicians carried on the tin trade from Cadiz, which we must remember was nearer to Cornwall than to Tyre or Sidon. We are, therefore, surely quite

---

[10] See my *Mycenae*, p. 306, No. 463.

[1] *Mémoires sur l'Antiquité*; Paris, 1879.

[2] Tin is said to have been anciently obtained in Pannonia, near the modern Temesvar, but I do not know whether the mines were extensive. See Howorth, *Stockholm Pre-historic Congress*, p. 533.

[3] *Pre-historic Times*, p. 47.

[4] Mr. Philip Smith observes to me "that the account of the overland traffic between Britain and the Greek cities of Southern Gaul, given by Diodorus and Strabo, refers clearly to the time of those writers, and we have no evidence of its high antiquity."

justified in concluding that between b.c. 1500 and b.c. 1200 the Phoenicians were already acquainted with the mineral fields of Spain and Britain. Under these circumstances, it is, I think, more than probable that they pushed their explorations still farther, in search of other shores as rich in mineral wealth as ours. Indeed, we must remember that amber, so much valued in ancient times, could not have been obtained from any nearer source than the coast of the German Ocean."

I may add that the general use of tin in remote antiquity could not be better proved than by its frequent mention in the Homeric poems, as well as in the Old Testament. That its mixture with copper was also known at a very remote age, could not be better shown than by the weapons of bronze found even in the third, the burnt city of Hissarlik. But in the classics the fact of its being a mixture of tin and copper is seldom mentioned. Polyaenus informs us that Perdiccas being short of silver coins had a coin made of tin mixed with copper.[5] Aristotle mentions that the copper of the Mossynoeci was said to be very brilliant and very white, not because tin was mixed with it, but because a sort of earth was added to it and calcined with it. It was said that the inventor of this alloy did not teach it to any one: for that reason the first works of copper made in that country were superior; those which succeeded were not so good.

Copper (probably bronze) was highly prized in remote antiquity, and constituted, next to gold, or perhaps even more than gold, the principal form of wealth. Thus we see in the *Iliad* Ulysses offering to Achilles on the part of Agamemnon, in order to appease his anger, to fill his ship after the capture of Troy with all the gold and bronze it could carry.[6] But Achilles refuses, saying that he will take with him gold and red bronze, as well as women and grey iron, which fell to his lot.[7] According to Lucretius,[8] bronze was in remote antiquity valued even more highly than gold or silver.

Rossignol[9] is of opinion that "to consecrate the remembrance of the services which the primitive copper had rendered, and the high value which men had attached to it, religion affected at a later time to use it, as Macrobius says.[10] A law of Numa ordered the priests to cut their hair with scissors of copper, and not of iron."[1] Rossignol[2] also explains the etymology of the word "bronze" from *brunus aes*.[3]

[5] iv. 10. 2 : Περδίκκας, Χαλκιδεῦσι πολεμῶν ἀργυροῦ νομίσματος ἀπορούμενος χαλκόκρατον κασσίτερον ἐχάραξε, καὶ οὕτως ἦν μισθοφορὰ τοῖς στρατιώταις.

[6] *Il.* ix. 279, 280 :
νῆα ἅλις χρυσοῦ καὶ χαλκοῦ νηήσασθαι
εἰσελθών, ὅτε κεν δατεώμεθα ληΐδ' Ἀχαιοί.

[7] *Il.* ix. 365–367 :
ἄλλον δ' ἐνθένδε χρυσὸν καὶ χαλκὸν ἐρυθρόν
ἠδὲ γυναῖκας εὐζώνους πολιόν τε σίδηρον
ἄξομαι, ἄσσ' ἔλαχόν γε.

[8] Vv. 1268–1273 :
"Nec minus argento facere haec auroque parabant,
Quam validi primum violentis viribus aeris :
Nequicquam, quoniam cedebat victa potestas,

Nec poterant pariter durum sufferre laborem ;
Nam fuit in pretio magis aes, aurumque jacebat
Propter inutilitatem, hebeti mucrone retusum."

[9] *Les Métaux dans l'Antiquité*, p. 219.

[10] *Saturn.* v. 19. 11: "Omnino autem ad rem divinam pleraque aenea adhiberi solita, multa indicio sunt." Professor Sayce suggests to me that *aenea* must mean here "bronze," not "copper."

[1] Lydus, *de Mens.* i. 31: Καὶ τοῦτο δὲ πρὸς τοῦ Νουμᾶ διατέθειται, ὥστε τοὺς ἱερεῖς χαλκαῖς ψαλίσιν, ἀλλ' οὐ σιδηραῖς ἀποκείρεσθαι. Here no doubt, also, bronze is meant.

[2] *Op. cit.* p. 271.

[3] " *Brunus*, fuscus, subniger, nigricans. Gall. *Brun*, Ital. *Bruno*, Germ. *Braun* . . . Sic

François Lenormant[4] is of opinion that "the Aryan tribes which peopled Greece and Asia Minor seem to have had almost no knowledge of metals at the time of their arrival. We have the proof of this in their language, in which the names of the metals are not those found among the other peoples of the same race and which all have in common ; in fact, their names for metals have for the most part been borrowed from foreign sources. So χρυσός, 'gold,' is the Semitic hharouts, and was manifestly imported by the Phoenicians. The name even of the mine and of metal in general (μέταλλον) is the Semitic matal. No satisfactory Aryan etymology can be found for χαλκός, 'bronze,' while this word has a quite natural relation—and this is a fact accepted by philologists as strict as M. Renan—with the Semitic root hhalaq, indicating 'metal worked by the hammer.' The origin of the name χαλκός would thus appear to indicate the source whence the Graeco-Pelasgic peoples received a knowledge of the real alloy of bronze, after a first age of pure copper and a certain number of attempts to find the proportion of tin which was to be mixed with it,—attempts which must have resulted from the desire to imitate more perfect models of metallurgy, which had probably been brought from another quarter. I may add that the very fact, that there was tin to alloy with copper in more or less suitable proportions, proves that the people whose vestiges we are studying had a foreign commerce. Tin is one of the metals which are the least generally diffused in nature. At Hissarlik, the two nearest points from which its ore could be imported were the Caucasus and Crete, where deposits are found in the mountains of Sphakia. I am inclined to think that it was brought from Crete, this being the nearest point. For the rest, it is certain that from the remotest antiquity there was a certain maritime intercourse, by means of a coasting trade still in its infancy, from isle to isle, and from cape to cape, between the populations whose civilization was on the same level, and which extended at that time from Cyprus to the Troad."

But, besides the alloy with tin, the ancients had still another way of hardening their copper, namely, by tempering it in water. We find this method mentioned by Homer : "As the coppersmith dips into cold water the great axe or the hatchet, which violently hisses, tempering it (for this gives new strength to iron itself)."[5]

In the same way Virgil represents the Cyclopes plunging the hissing copper into water :—

> ". . . Alii stridentia tinguunt
> Aera lacu."[6]

Pausanias, also, in speaking of the fountain of Pirene at Corinth,

---

forte dictus a prunorum colore, ut censet Octavius Ferrarius, vel quod *Bruniae*, seu loricae, colorem referat ; unde nostri *Bronze* pro aere, ex quo Bruneae et statuae conficiuntur, a cujus colore subfusco, *Bronzer* dicimus, Itali *Abbronzare*, fusco colore illinire, depingere." (Glossarium mediae et infimae latinitatis conditum a Domino Du Cange : Parisiis, 1840, t. i. p. 788.)

[4] *Les Antiquités de la Troade*, p. 11.
[5] *Od.* ix. 391–393 :

ὡς δ' ὅτ' ἀνὴρ χαλκεὺς πέλεκυν μέγαν ἠὲ σκέπαρνον
εἰν ὕδατι ψυχρῷ βάπτῃ μεγάλα ἰάχοντα
φαρμάσσων· τὸ γὰρ αὖτε σιδήρου γε κράτος ἐστίν·

[6] *Aen.* viii. 450 ; *Georg.* iv. 172.

says that bronze was dipped into it while it was still ignited and burning.[7] Rossignol[8] quotes Pollux, "who confirms the passage of Pausanias by a remarkable example. Noticing the use of βάψις instead of βαφή, Antiphon, he observes, speaks of the tempering (βάψις) of copper and iron." [9]

I have further to mention the 7 large double-edged bronze daggers of the Treasure, of which I represent one under No. 811, 11 in. in length and 2·2 in. broad at the broadest part. A second dagger, No. 812, which is 1¾ in. broad, has had the point broken off, and is now only 9 in. long, but it appears to have been 11 in. long. A third dagger (not engraved) is 8·6 in. long, and measures 1½ in. across at the broadest part. A fourth, No. 813, has become completely curled up in the conflagration, but appears to have been above 11 in. long. Of the fifth, sixth, and seventh daggers

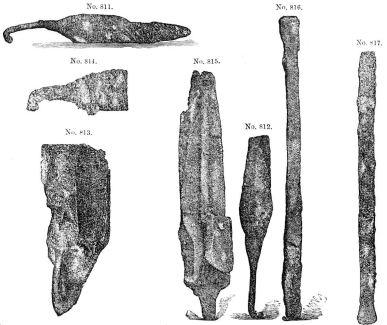

No. 811. No. 816. No. 817.

No. 814. No. 815.

No. 813. No. 812.

Nos. 811–814. Trojan two-edged bronze Daggers, with hooked stems that have been fastened into wooden handles; the Dagger No. 813 is curled up by the conflagration. No. 815. Six Battle-axes, Daggers, and Lance-heads molten together. Nos. 816, 817. Quadrangular bronze Bars, probably weapons, with a sharp edge at the end. (1 : 5 actual size. Depth, 28 ft.)

I only discovered fragments, such as No. 814: these are from 4 to 5½ in. long. But in the mass of lance-heads and battle-axes, No. 815, which have been fused together by the intense heat of the conflagration, another entire dagger is visible in the front of the engraving. All these daggers have handles from 2 to 2·8 in. long, the end of which is bent round at a right angle. These handles must at one time have been

---

[7] ii. 3. 3 : Καὶ τὸν Κορίνθιον χαλκὸν διάπυρον καὶ θερμὸν ὄντα ὑπὸ ὕδατος τούτου βάπτεσθαι λέγουσιν.

[8] Les Métaux dans l'Antiquité, p. 241.

[9] vii. 169 : Ἀντιφῶν δὲ εἴρηκε βάψιν χαλκοῦ καὶ σιδήρου.

encased in wood; for, if the cases had been made of bone, they would have been still wholly or partially preserved. The handle was inserted into a piece of wood, so that the end projected half an inch beyond it, and this end was simply bent round. I can only represent these singular Trojan daggers to the reader, as similar ones have never yet been found elsewhere.

Of common one-edged bronze knives, like No. 956 or No. 967 (pp. 505, 507), I only found one in the Treasure.

I also thought at first that I had found in the Treasure a fragment of a bronze sword; but, as visitors to the South Kensington Museum may see in my collection, the object referred to is no sword, but merely a very thin bronze *saw*: the fragment is nearly 9 in. long and 2 in. broad. If swords had been in use at all, I should probably have found some of them in this Treasure, among so many other weapons; or at least I should have found them elsewhere in this third city, which was destroyed so suddenly and unexpectedly by a fearful catastrophe, that the inhabitants had not the time even to save their treasures, of which ten were left for me to discover. Even with the skeletons of men, apparently warriors, I found only lances; never even so much as the trace of a sword. Neither did I find a trace of a sword even in the ruins of the two upper pre-historic cities. Moreover, had swords been in use, I should probably have found the moulds in which they were cast; but among the 90 moulds or thereabouts, which I collected, and which have forms for all the weapons I discovered, as well as for others which I did not find, there is not one for a sword. This absence of swords is the more astonishing to me, as I found hundreds of bronze swords in the royal tombs of Mycenae. Their non-existence at Hissarlik, even in the latest of its pre-historic cities, is the clearest proof of the very high antiquity of these ruins, and of the great distance of time which separates them from Homer, with whom swords are in common use. But if from the absence of this weapon, seemingly so indispensable, we might be forced to infer a low state of barbarism at Troy, our minds are bewildered when we look at the Trojan gold ornaments, which in artistic execution come fully up to those contained in the Mycenean treasures; and we are still more bewildered when we consider the Trojan inscriptions, since written characters were altogether unknown at Mycenae. I may here add that no swords have ever been found in the ancient British tumuli of the Bronze period.

But I return to the description of the Trojan Treasure, from which I also took out the four-cornered bronze bar No. 816, which ends in an edge; it is 15 in. long, and may have served as a weapon. The bronze bar No. 817, which likewise ends in a sharp edge, was found elsewhere in the burnt city.

No. 818. Copper or Bronze Key supposed to have belonged to the Treasure-chest. (Nearly 1 : 4 actual size. Depth, 28 ft.)

Perhaps the most curious object I found in the Treasure is the copper (or bronze?) key No. 818, which is 4·2 in. long, and has a head 2 in. in length and breadth; it greatly resembles a large key of an iron safe. Curiously enough, this key has had a wooden handle; there can be no doubt of this, from the fact that the end of the stalk of the key is bent round at a right angle, as in the case of the daggers. We read in Homer of a bronze key (κληΐς), with a handle encased in ivory, in the hand of Penelope; but that was not like the key before us, because it was in the form of our pick-locks, having, instead of the head, a crooked hook.[10] With this key—by means of a hole into which it was stuck—the bar (or bolt) of the door was pushed back.[1] On the other hand, in the *Iliad* the κληΐς is merely the bolt or bar which fastens two folding doors.[2] Of such a κληΐς I found four specimens in the third, the burnt city; two of them, which have been already engraved in the Introduction,[3] I picked up at the gate itself, the larger one between the two first projections of masonry in coming up from the plain, the other between the two next

No. 820.   Large Silver Vase found in the Royal House.
(About 1 : 3 actual size. Depth, 28 ft.)

No. 819.   Trojan Key in form of a Bolt.
(Actual size. Depth, 28 ft.)

---

[10] *Od.* xxi. 6, 7:
εἵλετο δὲ κληῖδ' εὐκαμπέα χειρὶ παχείῃ,
καλὴν χαλκείην · κώπη δ' ἐλέφαντος ἐπῆεν.
[1] *Od.* xxi. 47, 48:
ἐν δὲ κληῖδ' ἧκε, θυρέων δ' ἀνέκοπτεν ὀχῆας
ἄντα τιτυσκομένη.
Mr. Philip Smith observes to me that "the form

of the ancient Egyptian keys was similar to this. (See Wilkinson's *Ancient Egyptians*, vol. i. p. 354, No. 123, new edit.)"
[2] *Il.* xiv. 167, 168:
. . . πυκινὰς δὲ θύρας σταθμοῖσιν ἐπῆρσεν
κληῖδι κρυπτῇ · τὴν δ' οὐ θεὸς ἄλλος ἀνῷγεν.
[3] See Nos. 11 and 12, p. 36.

projections. Of this latter κληΐς a piece is broken off. A third bronze (or copper?) κληΐς, found in a house of the third, the burnt city, at a depth of 28 ft., is represented under No. 819. Both these κληῖδες are of quadrangular shape; at one end thick and gradually tapering towards the other.

Of objects found in the Treasure, and not represented here, I may mention a copper vase 5½ in. high and 4⅓ in. in diameter.

No. 820 is another silver vase found in the royal house.

I now come to the three smaller treasures, found at the end of March 1873, at a depth of 30 ft. on the east side of the royal house and very close to it, by two of my workmen, one of whom lives at Yeni Shehr, the other at Kalifatli. One of them was found in the owl-headed vase No. 232, which was closed by the pointed foot of another vase; the two other little treasures were found, together with the battle-axe No. 828, close by. But as the statements of the labourers differ as to the particular objects contained in each treasure, I can only describe them here conjointly. The two workmen had stolen and divided the three treasures between them-selves, and probably I should never have had any knowledge of it, had it not been for the lucky circumstance that the wife of the workman of Yeni Shehr, who had got as his share of the plunder all the articles Nos. 822–833, besides two more pendants like Nos. 832 and 833, had the boldness to parade one Sunday with the ear-rings and pendants Nos. 822 and 823. This excited the envy of her companions; she was denounced to the Turkish authorities of Koum Kaleh, who put her and her husband in prison; and, having been threatened that her husband would be hanged if they did not give up the jewels, she betrayed the hiding-place, and thus this part of the treasure was at once recovered and is now exhibited in the Imperial Museum of Constantinople. The pair also denounced their accomplice at Kalifatli, but here the authorities came too late, because he had already had his part of the spoil melted down by a goldsmith in Ren Kioi, who, at his desire, had made of it a very large, broad, and heavy necklace, with clumsy flowery ornaments in the Turkish fashion. Thus this part of the treasure is for ever lost to science. I can, therefore, represent here only that part which was taken by the Yeni Shehr thief, because it exists, and everybody can see it in the Constantinople Museum. As both thieves declared separately on oath before the authorities of Koum Kaleh that the owl-vase No. 232, with part of the gold, was found by them immediately to the west of the well (marked a z on Plan I. of Troy), and that the two other treasures were found close by, and indicated the exact spot of the discovery, there can be no doubt as to its accuracy.

No. 821 is a bar of electrum, 6½ in. long, weighing 87·20 grammes.

Each of the ear-rings, Nos. 822 and 823, consists of 23 gold wires, which are soldered together and bent round in the form of a basket; the middle wire, which is beaten flat and is as broad as three of the other wires, is ornamented with horizontal incisions; the wire baskets are decorated with four horizontal plates ornamented with vertical incisions; to the middle of the upper part of the baskets are soldered the ear-rings, which are flat at the top and decorated with incised vertical and horizontal strokes. To the lower part of the baskets is soldered a gold plate decorated with linear patterns; and to this latter are soldered 6 rings, rom which are suspended as many long chains ornamented with leaves

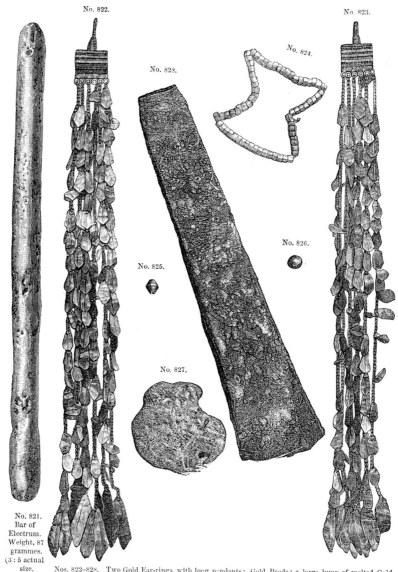

No. 822.

No. 823.

No. 824.

No. 823.

No. 826.

No. 825.

No. 827.

No. 821.
Bar of
Electrum.
Weight, 87
grammes.
(3 : 5 actual
size.
Depth, 30 ft.)

Nos. 822–828. Two Gold Ear-rings, with long pendants; Gold Beads; a large lump of melted Gold, with traces of Charcoal in it, and a bronze Battle-axe. (Nearly 3 : 5 actual size. Depth, 30 ft.)

of lancet form, in precisely the same way as those of the πλεκτὴ ἀναδέσμη, No. 687, with the sole difference that the leaves are here larger. A large double leaf of lancet form is suspended at the end of each chain. The length of each of these ear-rings with the pendants is 10 in.

The necklace No. 824 consists of 70 quadrangular gold beads. The large gold beads, Nos. 825 and 826, are in the form of whorls. No. 827 is a lump of melted gold weighing 97·30 grammes, or a little less than 3 oz. troy. Several pieces of charcoal are visible in it: a large one is seen in front. No. 828 is a bronze battle-axe, similar to those we have passed in review.[4] The thieves asserted that they had found the battle-axe together with one of the treasures. No. 829 is a gold bracelet, 3 in. in diameter; it is merely bent together. At the place where the two ends join is a soldered plate of oval form, decorated with incised linear patterns. Nos. 830 and 831 are two ear-rings in the form of serpents; they are hollow, and have been punched out of thin plates of gold and soldered. On the thick end was soldered a thick quadrangular bead, and on it a grain of gold in the form of a button. On the upper and lower parts three rows of small holes were punched, into which were soldered small grains of gold; to the thinner end of the serpents was soldered the ear-ring proper. Nos. 832 and 833

No. 832.   No. 833.

No. 829.   Bracelet of Gold, with an ornamented oval plate.   (3:4 actual size.   Depth, 30 ft.)

No. 830.   No. 831.

Nos. 830, 831.   Gold Ear-rings, in the form of serpents.   (3:4 actual size.   Depth, 30 ft.)

Nos. 832, 833.   Pendants of Gold.   (3:4 actual size.   Depth, 30 ft.)

are gold pendants, consisting alternately of leaves and chains made in the same manner as those of Nos. 685 and 686, which we have explained above (pp. 455, 456). At the end of each is suspended a figure similar in shape to those of No. 687 (p. 457). As already stated, there are four of these pendants or hangings.

Both thieves concur in their statement that the other part of the treasures, which was melted down, contained, amongst other jewels, a pair

---

[4] See Nos. 806–809.

of golden ear-rings with long pendants, like Nos. 822 and 823, and a very
large round plate of gold with most curious signs engraved on it. The
loss of this latter object grieves me more than anything else.

Of gold ear-rings of an identical shape with those figured under Nos.
830 and 831, I found one at a depth of 30 ft. in a large bundle of 25 silver
bracelets, which were cemented together by the chloride of silver: this
bundle contained also 4 or 5 ear-rings of electrum, in form like Nos.
752 to 764.

The pretty golden hair or breast pins, Nos. 834 and 849 (p. 489)[5] were
found by me in my north-western trench, at a depth of from 46 to 48 ft.,
exactly 16 ft. below the

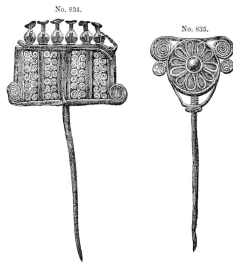

No. 834.

No. 835.

Nos. 834, 835. Brooches of Gold. (3 : 4 actual size.
From the Trojan stratum.)

great Hellenic wall attributed to Lysimachus. The
stratum of the third, the
burnt city reaches at this
point much deeper than
usual, and the two brooches
certainly belong to it.
No. 834 is 3 in. long and
very massive, consisting,
according to Mr. Carlo
Giuliano, of gold 23 carats
fine. It is ornamented with
a quadrangular plate of
gold, 1½ in. long and 0·7 in.
broad, the lower side of
which is soldered on a
band of gold, which has
been turned at both ends
into spirals with 7 wind-
ings. On the top has been
soldered another flat gold band, on which again are soldered 6 vases of
solid gold, each with 2 handles, placed in such a way that each vase
is turned with one handle towards the front; the covers of these vases
are circular. The surface of the plate is divided by five vertical flat
bands, soldered on it, into four vertical fields, each of which is filled up
with a spiral ornament made of thin gold wire and soldered on. These
ornaments are identical with those found by me in the third royal tomb
at Mycenae;[6] but to enhance the beauty of this ornamentation the
Trojan goldsmith, or whosoever may have been the maker of this brooch,
has taken care to represent the spirals in two columns with their heads
upwards, and in two others head downwards. The 6 little gold vases
have exactly the shape of the terra-cotta vase No. 261, if we suppose
its three feet removed.

I found the other gold brooch, No. 849, hardly 1 ft. distant from

No. 834; it is somewhat longer, but lighter and simpler. Its upper end is ornamented with a solid gold ball, both below and above which is a spiral decoration, precisely like a Mycenean ornament,[7] with the sole difference that here each spiral has only four turns. The top ends in

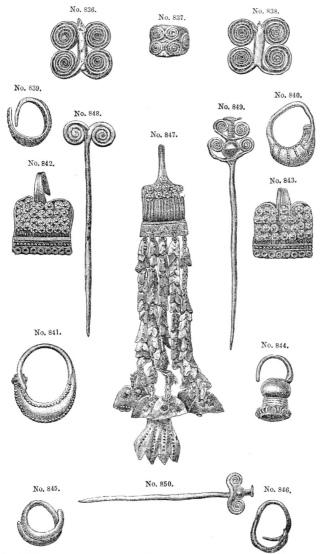

Nos. 836-850. Gold Ornaments: Beads for Necklaces, Ear-rings, Ear-rings with pendants, Hair-rings, and Brooches.
(About 3 : 4 actual size. Depth, about 26 to 28 ft.)

an object which has a large flat cover, and looks much like a screw; but on closer examination we find that it is merely ornamented all round with six horizontal parallel incisions.

---

[7] See my *Mycenae*, p. 196, No. 295.

Another treasure was found by me on the 21st October, 1878, at a depth of 26 ft. 5 in., in the presence of seven officers of H.M.S. *Monarch*, to the north-east of the royal house (in the place marked *r* on Plan I.), in a chamber of the buildings which may have been its dependencies. It was in a broken wheel-made vessel of terra-cotta, containing a good deal of powder, chiefly snow-white, but here and there bluish, which lay in an oblique position, about 3 ft. above the floor, and must have fallen from an upper storey. The jewels consisted of 20 gold ear-rings, of which 16 are precisely similar to those found in the large treasure, which are represented under Nos. 694 and 695. The other 4 ear-rings, of which No. 840 is one, are similar in form to those given under Nos. 830 and 831. There were also 4 very pretty gold ornaments, of which I represent 3 under Nos. 836, 838, 853. Precisely similar gold ornaments were found by me in the third royal sepulchre at Mycenae.[8] They must have been used for necklaces, as they have in the middle a long tubular hole. They were made in the following manner :—To each end of a small gold tube were soldered two thin gold wires, which were on either side turned five times round, and the spirals thus formed were soldered together, the outside twist of each being also soldered to the tube. Of the like pattern is the gold hairpin No. 848, from the top of which runs out on either side a gold wire, forming spirals with 4 turns. Of a similar pattern is another gold hairpin, No. 850, the top of which is ornamented with a solid gold ball, and with spirals on both sides : on the ball is soldered a piece of round gold wire, covered with a round plate, so that the object resembles a bottle.

There was also found a very large quantity of gold beads of the various shapes represented under Nos. 851 and 854–858, as well as of those

No. 851.   No. 853.   No. 852.

Nos. 851–853. Objects of Gold and Cornelian for necklaces.
(About 3 : 4 actual size. Depth, 26 to 28 ft.)

found in the large Treasure and represented under Nos. 708–738 (p. 460). The shape of the buttons on the necklace No. 858, of which Nos. 859 and 860 are two separate specimens, were found here for the first time. They are made of gold plate, hammered out in the shape of a boss, and

---

[8] See my *Mycenae*, p. 196, Nos. 297, 299.

in the centre of the hollow an ear is soldered; the row of dots is of punched work. To this treasure belonged also the bracelets of electrum,

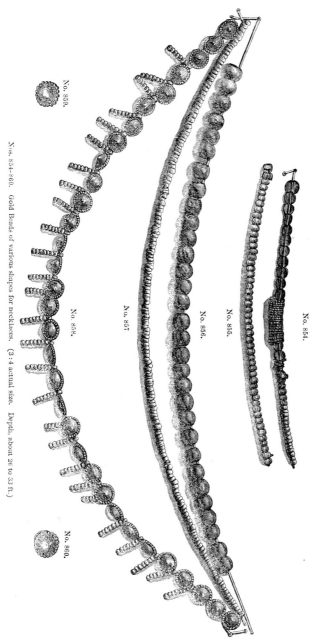

Nos. 854–860. Gold Beads of various shapes for necklaces. (3 : 4 actual size. Depth, about 26 to 33 ft.)

Nos. 861 and 862. The former is composed of three turns; it is 0·16 in. thick, and so small that it could only fit a child's arm. To this bracelet one of the gold ear-rings had been fused in the great conflagration, as well as a large number of the gold beads, and parts of a necklace of

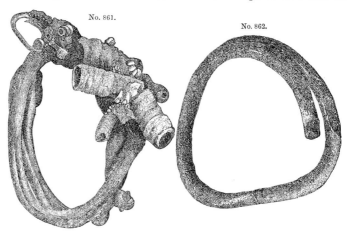

No. 861.

No. 862.

Nos. 861, 862. Two Bracelets of Electrum, to one of which a large number of silver rings and gold beads, also a gold ear-ring, were fused in the conflagration, and have been firmly attached together by the cementing agency of the chloride of silver. (3 : 4 actual size. Depth, 28 ft.)

small silver rings, which are also cemented together by the chloride of silver; all these objects form, as it were, one solid mass with the bracelet.

The little treasure further contained 11 silver ear-rings of the same form as Nos. 694, 695 (p. 460), and 754–764 (p. 462), except one which resembles a pair of tongs. This latter is attached by the chloride of silver to another silver ear-ring, and to two gold beads. Of the other silver ear-rings also, four are cemented together by the chloride in one packet, and three in another. There are, besides, 20 parts of necklaces, like Nos. 863

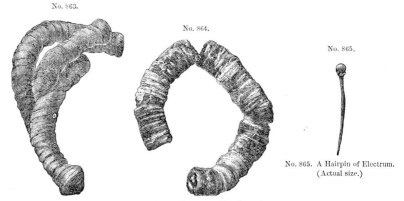

No. 863.

No. 864.

No. 865.

No. 865. A Hairpin of Electrum. (Actual size.)

Nos. 863, 864. Parts of Necklaces, consisting of innumerable silver rings cemented together by the chloride of silver and strung on sticks of ivory. (3 : 4 actual size. Depth, 28 ft.)

and 864, consisting of innumerable silver rings, each 0·28 in. in diameter, which are stuck together by the cementing action of the chloride. They are strung on pieces of a substance which I believe to be ivory, and my lamented friend Dr. Edward Moss (in 1878 of H.M.S. *Research*) fully confirmed this. All the parts of necklaces form curves, and seem to have retained the shape they had when in use. In one instance two of these parts of necklaces are cemented together by means of a silver ear-ring. I further counted 158 similar silver rings, either single or joined by the chloride. In a like manner there were also many parts of necklaces composed of silver beads, cemented together by the chloride, to which are attached numerous gold beads. I further mention a cylindrical bar of electrum, 1-9th in. long, as well as a hairpin of the same metal, which I represent under No. 865 : it has nearly the common form of the bronze brooches, being in the form of a nail with a globular head.

To the west of the gate visitors see the longest wall of the house of the king or town-chief. It runs parallel with the great city wall (see Plan I., of Troy), and is 53 ft. 4 in. long and 4 ft. 4 in. high. Near the north-western extremity of this wall, and just 3 ft. above the ground,[7] I found in a layer of grey ashes two more small treasures, both contained in broken hand-made terra-cotta vases, with a good deal of the same white powder which I noticed in the other treasure. Of these vases, the one lay in an oblique, the other in a horizontal position, from which circumstance I conclude that both had fallen in the catastrophe from an upper part of the house ; the orifices of the two nearly touched each other. The vase which lay in a horizontal position contained 6 round and 4 oval beads of cornelian, like those under No. 852 (p. 490) ; a flat plain gold frontlet, having at each end three perforations for stringing them together ; 43 large globular gold beads, like those under No. 856 (p. 491), and innumerable small gold beads of various shapes ; the gold bar No. 866, with 18 perforations, apparently for suspending ornaments, probably chains with pendants ; a gold plate, ornamented with zigzag lines and crowns of tolerable intaglio-work, but, either by the action of the fire or by the hand of man, this plate has been folded together four or more times, and, as it is very thick, it is impossible to unfold it with the hand.

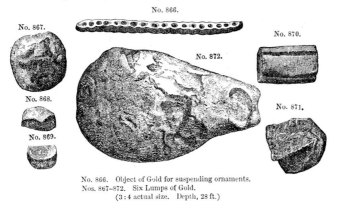

No. 866.   Object of Gold for suspending ornaments.
Nos. 867–872.   Six Lumps of Gold.
(3 : 4 actual size. Depth, 28 ft.)

There were also large and small lumps of gold, Nos. 867, 868, 869, 870, and 871 ; also a very large one, No. 872, which seems to have been inten-

---

[7] At the point marked *t* on Plan I.

tionally melted into the shape of a bell: to this lump has been fused in the conflagration a good deal of silver, now turned into chloride. I have also to mention a nugget of silver, which latter has turned into chloride, to which are cemented ten gold beads of different forms; a long quadrangular gold wire, almost in the form of an ear-ring; 14 gold ear-rings of the common Trojan type, like Nos. 694, 695, 754–764; a gold ear-ring in the form of a serpent, like Nos. 840, 841 (p. 489); and a gold ear-ring in the shape of an inverted vase, to the mouth of which a gold wire with 21 windings is soldered (see No. 844). There was also a gold ear-ring with a plain pendant and two pointed ends, so that it could be put through the ear by either of them; further, a pretty gold ear-ring, in the shape of No. 847, formed of 14 gold wires, which had been bent over in the form of a basket and soldered together; the inner side had then been smoothed and polished. On one of the external sides it is ornamented with one row, on the other with two rows, of 5 rosettes, with one rosette at the top. To the lower part is soldered a small gold plate, ornamented with five triangles between two lines—all of intaglio-work; and below each triangle is a perforation: from each of these latter is suspended a gold chain, covered with 16 gold double leaves ornamented with dots, and at the end of each chain hangs a gold ornament, much like a Trojan idol, but terminating in four leaves decorated with dots. This and all the other articles of gold and silver I can unfortunately only show as they are; for, except the spirals and rosettes, which occur frequently in Mycenae, and also abundantly in Assyria and Babylonia, nothing like these Trojan gold articles has been ever found elsewhere. Professor Sayce thinks the ornamentation with rosettes to have been invented in Babylonia, to have passed into the handiwork of the Phoenicians, and to have been brought by them to the West.[8]

I further mention an ear-ring of electrum, ornamented with a little crown, in which is fixed a pendant, apparently of silver, for it is much destroyed by the chloride; to this latter object have been cemented a silver ear-ring and innumerable silver beads: also a pendant of electrum, to which are attached numerous gold and silver beads: also about ten silver ear-rings, all cemented together by the chloride, and covered with gold beads, which likewise stick firmly to them; these ear-rings have the usual Trojan shape (see Nos. 694, 695, 754–764): also a gold disc with 18 incisions. Close to the two vases with the jewels there lay embedded in the ashes a bronze battle-axe, $9\frac{1}{3}$ in. long, of the common Trojan shape (see Nos. 806–809 and 828), and two of those strange weapons represented by Nos. 816 and 817 (p. 482).

Only 3 ft. from this discovery, but on the house-wall itself, and at a depth of 26 ft. below the surface, there was found another and larger treasure of bronze weapons and gold jewels:[9] these latter again more or less embedded in the same sort of white powder. The weapons consisted of two lance-heads, like Nos. 803 and 804, a knife like No. 964 (p. 506), and two small weapons like Nos. 816 and 817—all fused together in the conflagra-

---

[8] *Contemporary Review*, December 1878.
[9] The place where this treasure was found is marked s on Plan I.

tion ; further, a battle-axe, like those previously described ; also a broken copper vessel, with many gold beads cemented to the oxide on its surface. It contained the two heavy gold bracelets Nos. 873 and 874, each of which weighs nearly as much as 18 sovereigns, and is, according to Mr. Giuliano, of the fineness of 23 carats. They are almost an inch broad, and consist of a thick gold plate, which on No. 873 is piped with gold wire, on No. 874

No. 873.

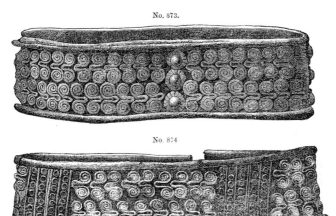

No. 874

Nos. 873, 874.   Gold Bracelets, found on the wall of the Royal House.   (7 : 8 actual size.   Depth, 26 ft.)

with silver wire. The outside of the former is divided by four vertical rows of three rosettes in each, into four nearly equal fields, which are filled up by two rows of the spiral ornamentation which we see on the Mycenean jewels ; [10] and, to enhance the beauty of the bracelets, the primitive artist has taken care to represent the ornament in one row with the head up- wards, and in the other with the head downwards. The one row contains 8, the other 9, of such spiral ornaments ; there is, besides, a vertical row of four of them, and thus all round the bracelet there are 72 such ornaments, made of gold wire and soldered on the plate. The ornamentation of the other bracelet, No. 874, is almost identical with this, the only difference being that, instead of rosettes, the vertical columns are filled with beads. These vertical columns, of which 5 are to the right of the spectator, 4 to the left, and another 4 on the other side, are bordered by vertical gold wires soldered to the plate of the bracelet. In each central column there is a border of double wires. Each of these vertical columns has 8 rings, except one which has only 7 ; thus they contain 103 rings altogether. The number of spiral ornaments is 54, there being 18 in each field. I may also mention large lumps of melted gold, one of which is similar to the gold nuggets found in mines ; also a lump of gold, evidently cut from a bar, similar to Nos. 869 and 870.

Together with these objects was found the lower half of one of those large Trojan goblets of terra-cotta with two handles (δέπα ἀμφικύπελλα),

---

[10] See my *Mycenae*, p. 196, No. 295.

from which 16 bars of gold protruded, each being 4·33 in. long, and having from 52 to 60 horizontal incisions.

I represent here under Nos. 875–877 three of these gold bars. I

Nos. 875–877.   Three Bars of Gold, with 52 to 60 horizontal incisions.   (About 7 : 8 actual size.   Depth, 26 ft.)

again ask, if the 6 blades of pure silver (Nos. 787–792) are not Homeric talents, have we to recognize the latter in these 16 gold bars ? Professor Roberts, of the Royal Mint, who kindly analysed a portion of one of them, writes to me the following note on the subject :—

"A very small portion cut from the end of one of the gold rods was scraped clean and submitted to analysis, the weight of metal examined being 2·536 grains. It was found to contain 65·10 per cent. of gold and 33·42 per cent. of silver, together with minute traces of lead, copper, and iron, but the amount of these metals collectively does not exceed 1·5 per cent. The alloy of which the talent is composed is, therefore, electrum."

Having pulled these 16 bars out of the goblet, I found below them two pairs of very heavy gold ear-rings, of which I have represented one pair under Nos. 842 and 843 (p. 489). Each of them is made of 40 gold wires, soldered together, beaten round, and cut out in the upper part, so as to have the shape of a crown, in the middle of which was soldered the hook or ear-ring proper, at first flat and ornamented with vertical incisions, and tapering gradually to the point. On the inner side the wires were polished to a smooth surface ; on the outer side of each ear-ring basket were soldered four rows of 7 rosettes, making in all 28 rosettes on each, except on one of them, which has only 27. To render the ear-rings more solid, a gold wire, which may be easily discerned in places where it is detached, was soldered all round the edges. To the lower part of each basket were soldered two gold plates : on that in front we see, between an upper border of two flat gold stripes and a lower one of a very narrow stripe, a row of 18 beads soldered into grooves ; the other gold plate is not orna-mented, as it was on the side of the head. To each of these plates are fastened 8 rings, made of double gold wire, so that, as there are 16 rings, we may with all probability suppose that to each of these ear-rings were suspended 16 chains, which must, however, have been strung on thread, because they have disappeared ; but the many hundreds of gold beads which have remained are silent witnesses to their splendour. The beads are either quadrangular and ornamented with incisions, like those shown at No. 855, or of round or oval form, like No. 857 or No. 721 ; or they consist of long and very thin rings, like Nos. 894–897.

I represent the other pair of ear-rings under Nos. 881 and 882. Both were made of gold plate, to either side of which were soldered 13 gold wires ; then the whole was turned round into the form of a basket, the hook or ear-ring proper being soldered on the top in the middle, and decorated at its lower end with 20 beads soldered into grooves. Each side of both ear-rings was then decorated with 5 rows of 25 beads, soldered

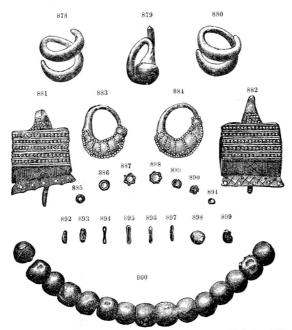

Nos. 878–900. Three Rings for fastening and ornamenting the tresses or locks of hair, four richly ornamented Ear-rings, and Beads for pendants and necklaces—all of gold. (3 : 4 actual size. Depth, 26 to 33 ft.)

into grooves, between 6 borders of double horizontal wires : thus there were in all, on both sides of each ear-ring, 270 beads. Very simple linear patterns are incised on both sides of the plate in the middle, as well a on the plate soldered below : in this latter there are 5 holes for suspending ornaments. M. Alessandro Castellani thinks that "the primitive goldsmiths imitated the types of the Diademiae, the pseudo-Diademiae, and the family of Echinae, covered as these aquatic creatures are with a variety of lines and raised points. It is natural that artistic decoration should derive its elements from surrounding nature."[11]

Mr. Giuliano estimates the fineness of these two pairs of ear-rings to be 23 carats. But the gold beads are of different degrees of fineness ; Mr. Giuliano considers some to be 20, others 18 or only 16 carats fine. This agrees with the analysis made by Prof. Roberts, who writes to me : " 0·0910 gramme of gold beads were found by assay to contain 67·91 per cent. of gold. A single bead, weighing 0·0920 gramme, of richer colour than the rest, contained 75·8 per cent. of gold. The standard of these beads varies, therefore, from 16 to 18 carats. In all the beads submitted to me the colour of the surface of the metal appears to have been brought out by artificial means, and it may be well to remember that the Japanese,

[11] Alessandro Castellani, at the German Archæological Institute in Rome, Jan. 3, 1879.

who employ an interesting series of gold alloys, use plum-juice vinegar for this purpose."

There were further found in this treasure 9 simpler gold ear-rings, one of which, No. 837 (p. 489), is ornamented with four rows of two spirals in each, resembling those on the second Mycenean tombstone.[1] Another, No. 879 (p. 497), has a pendant in the shape of a bell-clapper. Three others have the usual Trojan form of Nos. 694, 695, and 754–764. The remaining four, of which I represent two under Nos. 878 and 880, are merely spirals with two twists, and, on closer inspection, I find both extremities of them far too thick to be put into the lobe of the ear. They must, therefore, have been used for holding together the locks of the hair, and they may, in my opinion, perfectly explain the passage in Homer : " Dabbled with blood were his locks, which might vie with the Graces, and the braids twined with gold and silver." [2]   I suppose the curious ring No. 879, which has no point, could also not have been anything else but an ornament of the hair.

I further collected from the Treasure two gold bars like No. 866, the one with 18, the other with 20 perforations for suspending ornaments; also 45 gold buttons of a semi-globular form, like those marked Nos. 858, 859, 860, with an ear in the hollow and a border decorated with 25 dots of punched work ; also a small plain hairpin, like No. 865, but with an octagonal head.

I have still to mention another smaller discovery of gold, made by me in November 1878, in my excavation on the north side of the hill, exactly at the north-east corner of the brick wall.[3] It consisted merely of a pair of heavy massive ear-rings, like No. 841, in the shape of a serpent decorated with three rows of beads soldered into grooves, a small object of silver with six perforations, and a silver plate of oval form measuring 2·4 in. in its broadest part : its length cannot be well determined, as it has been folded in the fire and both ends are bent over, but it appears to have been about 5 in. long. Together with these objects were found hundreds of gold beads, among which are many in the form of leaves, like No. 912, with tubular holes in the middle. Finally, I have to record the finding of the pretty gold hairpin, No. 835 (p. 488), which exhibits on each side a rosette with eleven flower-petals ; but this round part with the two rosettes consists of two distinct gold discs with no punched work. They were made in the following way :—A small semi-globular gold plate was soldered in the centre, and around it a border of gold wire ; then the leaves were formed of gold wire and soldered on symmetrically. When the two discs had been thus decorated, they were joined by a broad flat gold band, which projects slightly over both of them. Then this double disc was soldered on the long pin, the upper part of which is decorated with incisions. The pin was then stuck through a flat gold band, which was soldered on both sides of the double disc, and coiled at both ends into a spiral with three turns. The pin was further pierced

---

[1]. See my *Mycenae*, p. 81, No. 140.

[2] *Il.* xvii. 51, 52 :

αἵματί οἱ δεύοντο κόμαι χαρίτεσσιν ὁμοῖαι
πλοχμοί θ᾽ οἳ χρυσῷ τε καὶ ἀργύρῳ ἐσφήκωντο.

[3] See Plan I. (of Troy) and Sectional Plan III. II.

through a small gold disc, which we see soldered below the gold band. Lastly, a gold band was soldered on the top of the disc, and turned on either side into spirals of five turns.

I have further to mention among the discoveries of 1878 the remarkable *silver dagger*, No. 901, which was discovered in the royal house at a depth of 28 ft. The good preservation of this object, its horizontal lines and its black colour, would lead any one to believe that it was of meteoric iron. But Professor Roberts of the Royal Mint, who scraped off a little of the thin black layer with which the dagger is covered and analysed it, proved it to be chloride of silver. I may also state that the metal below the black layer is perfectly white; there can, therefore, be no doubt that Professor Roberts's analysis is correct, and that we have here a silver and not an iron dagger.

Mr. Gladstone thinks the silver dagger must have been a ceremonial weapon. It is 6 in. long, double-edged, and pretty sharp. Near the lower end of the blade are two openings, 0·53 in. long and 0·12 in. broad, which have probably been made only for the sake of ornament. The end of the long handle is bent round at a right angle, which proves that it has been cased in wood; it can hardly have been cased in ivory, as all the ivory I found in the burnt city is so well preserved. I have

No. 901. Dagger of Silver, probably a ceremonial weapon. (Actual size. Depth, 28 ft.)

to add that this silver dagger has precisely the form of the daggers found in the large Treasure (see Nos. 811–814). We may probably recognize another ceremonial weapon in the gold arrow-head, No. 902, which was found on the plateau of the two large walls (the Tower).

No. 902. Flat Piece of Gold, in the form of an Arrow-head. From the Tower. (Nearly actual size. Depth, 26 ft.)

Of precious metals, I also discovered two small treasures during my excavations in 1879. The first of these was found in April, on the north side of the hill, about 66 ft. outside the brick city wall (see Plan I., of Troy, the place marked *n a*), at a depth of only 13 ft. below the surface; it lay on a fallen house-wall, and had probably dropped from an upper storey. As explained in the preceding pages, the stratum of the third, the burnt city does not always occur at the same depth below the surface: within the precincts of the burnt city it is generally reached at a depth of 23 ft., but, for reasons before explained, it is also struck immediately below the foundations of the Temple of Athené; and, on the north-east and east sides, outside the brick wall of the burnt city, it generally occurs at so small a depth as

12 ft.   Visitors will have no difficulty in convincing themselves of this fact in my trenches.   At all events, this appears to be confirmed by the shape of the gold ornaments contained in this small treasure, all of which are perfectly similar to those found in the treasures discovered near the royal house in the city proper, except the gold discs Nos. 903 and 904, of which three were found, and which now occurred here for the first time.   But similar gold discs were abundant in the royal sepulchres of Mycenae ; where, in the third tomb alone, I collected 701 of them.[4]   No. 903 represents a pretty star flower within a small border, and we see a similar one in No. 904 within a treble border, all in repoussé·

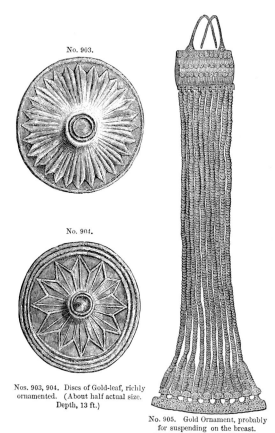

No. 903.

No. 904.

Nos. 903, 904.   Discs of Gold-leaf, richly
ornamented.   (About half actual size.
Depth, 13 ft.)

No. 905.   Gold Ornament, probably
for suspending on the breast.
(1 : 4 actual size.   Depth, 13 ft.)

work.   It is difficult to explain how the Trojans produced such patterns. Mr. Giuliano thinks with Mr. Landerer that the gold plate was laid on a block of lead and the ornamentation hammered or pressed into it.   In the treasure was also the gold breast ornament No. 905, which is 18 in. long.   The upper part, in the form of a basket, is 1·8 in. long and 1½ in. broad ; it consists of twenty-five gold wires, which were beaten flat, soldered together, bent over, and joined by means of a small gold plate, 0·12 in. broad, and of two gold pins ; to the upper border were soldered two gold hooks, 2½ in. long.   One side of the gold basket is ornamented with three rows of eleven gold rings, and two more such rings are seen on the lower part of the hooks.   All these rings were filled up with a substance like white glass, which seems to have once had another colour, and may probably have been blue. At the lower end is soldered a gold plate, with ten holes, from which ten chains hang down, consisting of double rings of gold wire, and on

[4] See my *Mycenae*, pp. 165–172.

each link is fixed a leaf of gold, 0·2 in. in diameter. Each gold chain has 155 such links and 155 such leaves, and there are, consequently,

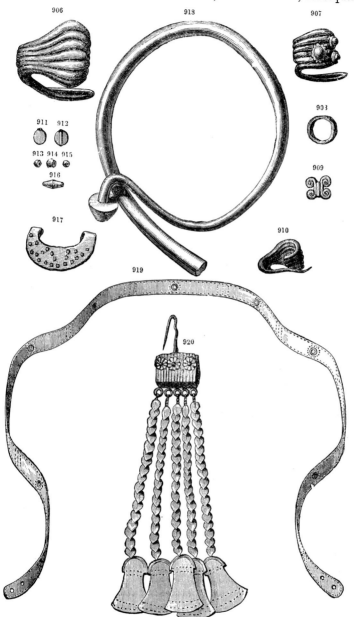

Nos. 906–920. Ear-rings, Bracelet, Fillet, Beads for necklaces, Ear-ring with pendant, all of gold.
(3 : 4 actual size. Depth, 26 to 33 ft.)

1550 double rings or links, and 1550 leaves. At the end of each chain is suspended a gold idol of the usual form, with two eyes well indicated. This ornament had not come under the notice of the labourers, and, with other *débris*, it had been put on the wheelbarrow to be shot over the incline; but it was discovered by the keen eye of Professor Virchow, who lifted it from the wheelbarrow and saved it from certain destruction. There were also found the fragments of seven much larger gold idols.

Another treasure was found by me, in the presence of M. Burnouf and Professor Virchow, at a depth of 33 ft. below the surface (in the place marked v to the north of the place marked Δ on Plan I., of Troy), on the slope of the great Trojan wall, close to the house of the ancient town-chief or king, and close to the spot where the large Treasure was found in 1873. It consisted of two gold ear-rings, of which I represent one under No. 920. Both have the usual basket form, and are ornamented with three rosettes. To the basket is soldered a gold plate, ornamented with very simple incised linear patterns. To this gold plate are fixed, on the one ear-ring five, on the other only four, gold rings; from which are suspended gold chains covered with leaves.

I further mention the very large gold ear-rings of the common form, Nos. 906 and 907, of which the latter is ornamented with three rosettes: —another gold ear-ring, just like No. 920, but without pendants:— two more small gold ear-rings of the usual form, of which I represent one under No. 910:—a small gold ring, like Nos. 878 and 880, for holding the hair locks or braids: —one plain gold fillet, 21 in. long, which I represent under No. 921; it has at one extremity three perforations, and on the other one perforation, for fastening it round the head:—nine gold ornaments with four spirals, like Nos. 836 and 838; and some smaller ones of the same kind, like No. 909. Similar ornaments are very abundant in the royal tombs of Mycenae.[5]

No. 922. Six Silver Ear-rings, fastened together by the cementing action of the chloride of silver, many gold beads sticking to them. (Half actual size. Depth, 28 ft.)

No. 921. Fillet of Gold. (Half actual size. Depth, 33 ft.)

This treasure further contained two very large and heavy gold bracelets, of which I represent one under No. 918. It consists of a very thick round gold rod, having at one extremity only an ornament in the form of a flower-button. In the treasure were also hundreds of gold beads, in the form of rings or leaves, with a tubular hole, like Nos. 911–916, and 885–899; the six silver ear-rings, No. 922, which are fastened together by the cementing action of the chloride of silver, and to which also many gold beads are stuck; and the large silver spoon, No. 923, of good repoussé-

---

[5] See my *Mycenae*, No. 297.

work. Like the shield, No. 799, this spoon has in the centre a large navel-like boss (ὀμφαλός), surrounded by a furrow (αὖλαξ) and by a projecting border. The handle has a floral orna-mentation in intaglio; its end is per-forated, and has a large ring for sus-pension. The large size of this spoon, and particularly its boss, make it pro-bable that it had a sacred use, and was employed for libations. Further, the treasure contained the pretty gold fillet, No. 919, which has two perforations at each end. It is decorated, in punched work, with a border of dots, 9 double concentric circles, and 27 vertical rows of dots. There were also found nine gold ear-rings of the shape represented by No. 917, which had never yet occurred except of silver (see No. 122, p. 250). They have the form of a primitive boat, and consist of simple gold plate. The two ends are turned round in the form of spirals, and by the holes of the latter they were suspended in the ear by means of a thin gold wire. Each of these boat-like ear-rings is ornamented with 21 dots made with the punch. There are gold ear-rings similar to these in the gold room of the British Museum, but I could not find out where they came from.

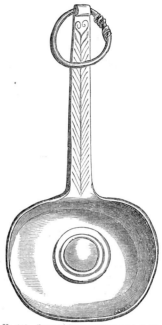

No. 923.   Spoon of Silver, with a large ὀμφαλός in the middle. The handle is ornamented ; a ring for suspension is attached to its end. (Half actual size. Depth, 33 ft.)

I have further to mention gold rings with a spiral ornamentation like No. 839 and No. 845, the thick ends of which can leave no doubt that they served to fasten and ornament the hair-tresses. Also plain ear-rings like No. 846, and ear-rings in the form of a serpent, with a granular orna-mentation like Nos. 883 and 884.

Among the gold objects found I have finally to mention the pretty eagle, which I represent in three different positions, under Nos. 924, 925, 926. Its form resembles a pigeon, but the head is decidedly that of an eagle. It is nearly 2 in. long and 1¾ in. broad ; the tail has a breadth and length of 0·6 in. It is made of two gold plates joined by two gold pins,[6] and presents an example of pretty good repoussé-work. In the lower part of the hollow belly (see No. 925) is a round hole, which makes it likely that the eagle was fixed on an object of wood. The upper side is ornamented with linear patterns of intaglio-work ; the wings and tail have also an incised decoration on the reverse side. The ornamentation of the wings reminds us of that of the double-headed eagle in the Hittite sculptures of Boghaz Kioi and Eyuk.

---

[6] This is the only instance at Troy in which we see metal plates *not* soldered, but joined with pins.

No. 924.

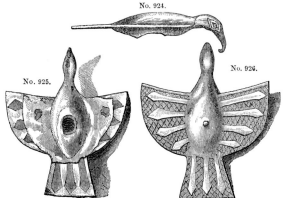

Nos. 924–926. Eagle of Gold. (7 : 8 actual size. Depth, 20 ft.)

At a depth of from 30 to 33 ft., immediately to the east of the royal house, was found the remarkable bronze dagger, No. 927, which is

8·2 in. long, very well preserved, and of a dark grey colour, just like iron. The blade is 4·2 in. long, and nearly 1⅓ in. wide at its thickest part. The handle is quadrangular, and is decorated with incised triangles, which makes it probable that it was not cased in wood. The end of the handle is ornamented with a couchant cow or ox with long horns. I hold with Mr. Gladstone that this also was a ceremonial dagger, as, on account of the cow, it seems too unhandy to have served for common use. By the cementing power of the chloride of copper there stick to this dagger five glass beads, which are now white, but which have apparently once been blue. Most certainly these glass beads have never served as ornaments of the dagger; they can only have come in contact with it accidentally: but their presence seems to prove that they were in general use here. But were they imported by the Phoenicians or home-made ?

Under Nos. 928–930, 934–936, 940, 941, and 945, I represent some of the common bronze pins or brooches, which are found in large quantities in the burnt city, and also frequently in all the other pre-historic cities of Hissarlik; they have a globular head, and were in use before the invention of the fibula. Nos. 939, 947, and 951 are similar; the only difference is, that the head is here turned in the form of a spiral; but this is hardly visible, owing to the oxide or carbonate of copper with which the brooches are covered. No. 932 is a brooch

No. 927. Dagger of Bronze; with a hilt in the form of a cow with long horns. (Half actual size. Depth, 30 to 33 ft.) with a double spiral.

Nos. 931, 933, 942, 944, and 946 are primitive arrow-heads of bronze or copper. No. 937 is a fish-hook; No. 938, a curious object of lead in the form of an ear-ring, but, being far too thick to be stuck into the ear, it very probably served to fasten and ornament the hair.   Nos. 943, 948, and 949 are

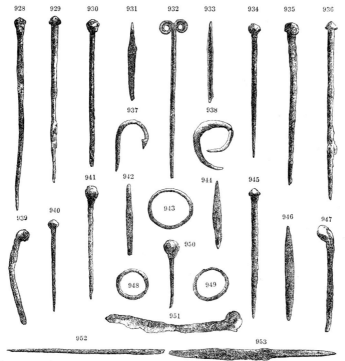

Nos. 928–953. Primitive Brooches, Arrow-heads, a Punch, Rings, &c. of Bronze. (About half actual size. Depth, 24 to 32 ft.)

rings; No. 952 is a needle, and No. 953 a punch of bronze. Nos. 954 and 956 are bronze knives; in the handle of the former may be seen one,

Nos. 954–957. Knives, Arrow-head, and Lance-head of Bronze. (Half actual size. Depth, 22 to 32 ft.)

in that of the latter two round heads of the pins by means of which the handles were fixed in the wooden casing.

No. 955 is the only bronze arrow-head with barbs ever found by me in this third, the burnt city, all the other arrow-heads being of the shape described before. But that similarly shaped arrow-heads were in use, though *without* barbs, seems also to be proved by the mould No. 604, which has the forms for casting them.

No. 957 is another lance-head of bronze. In its handle may be seen two pin-heads, by which it was fastened to the shaft. No. 958 is a bronze battle-axe, with a perforation for the handle. Only four were found by me of the like shape, and all of them in the burnt city. Similar battle-axes of bronze have been found on the Island of Sardinia, and are preserved in the Museum of Cagliari.[6] Numerous battle-axes of a similar

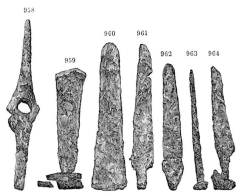

Nos. 958–964. A Battle-axe perforated in the middle, two common Battle-axes, three Knives, and another instrument—all of bronze. (1 : 6 actual size. Depth, 23 to 33 ft.)

shape, but of *pure copper*, were found in Hungary.[7] Nos. 959 and 960 represent two more of the bronze battle-axes of the common Trojan shape. Nos. 961, 962, and 964 are bronze knives; No. 963, a pointed implement of bronze.

Under Nos. 965 and 966 I represent two bronze knives of a remarkable form; both run out into a spiral. No. 965, which is single-edged, has evidently had its handle encased in wood; No. 966 is double-edged: the singular shape of its handle makes it hardly possible that it can have been cased in wood. Mr. Basil Cooper calls my attention to the exact Egyptian type in the form of these two knives. I represent under No. 967 one more one-edged knife of the common form. The Trojan knives had in no instance the shape of our present pocket-knives; they were much longer, had handles of wood, and were worn attached to the belt, as we see in Homer.

No. 968 is again a bronze lance; in its lower end may be seen the

[6] See Vincenzo Crespi, *Il Museo d'Antichità di Cagliari;* Cagliari, 1872, Pl. ii. Nos. 4, 5, 6. On the same plate we also see represented, under No. 7, a mould, with a bed for casting a similar battle-axe.

[7] See Joseph Hampel, *Catalogue de l'Exposition préhistorique des Musées de Province et des Collections particulières de la Hongrie,* Buda-Pesth, 1876, pp. 139, 140, Nos. 146, 150, 152; and Joseph Hampel, *Antiquités préhistoriques de la Hongrie,* Esztergom, 1876, Pl. vii. Nos. 4, 7, 8, 9, 10, 13, 14, 15.

holes for the pins by which it was fastened in the shaft. It was picked up by the side of one of the two entire skeletons of men, which I found in the room of a house to the east of the plateau of the Tower, immediately

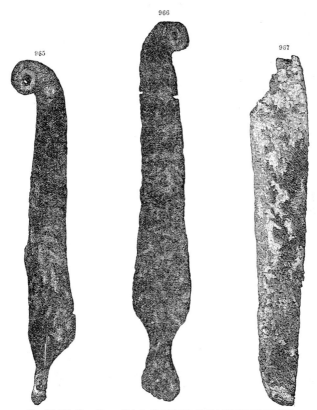

Nos. 965–967. Three Bronze Knives, of which two are of a very remarkable form. No. 965. Actual size. Depth, 24 ft.   No. 966. Actual size. Depth, 24 ft.   No. 967. 2 : 3 actual size. Depth, 23 ft.

to the north of the nine jars (see Plan I., of Troy, the place marked *e* s), and which appear to be those of warriors, as they had helmets on their heads. One of the skulls was fractured, the other was uninjured; but

No. 968.   Bronze Lance of a Trojan Warrior, found beside his Skeleton. (Half actual size. Depth, 23 ft.)

this latter was also fractured on its way to London. Professor Virchow, who kindly recomposed both skulls and made the accompanying excellent geometrical drawings of them (Nos. 969–972 and Nos. 973–976), has sent me the following interesting note.

"Dimensions of the Two Skulls (in Millimètres).

	Nos. 969–972.	Nos. 973–976.
Length of the skull	193	191
Greatest breadth of the skull	132·5?	141
Auricular height	110	110
Breadth of the frontal bone at its base... ...	90	99
Height of the face	104·5	106
Breadth „	—	89
„ of lower jaw	88?	77?
Orbit, height	—	30
„ breadth	—	38
Nose, height	47?	49
„ breadth	23	26
Height of the alveolar apophysis of the upper jaw	15	16
Horizontal circumference of the skull	521	537

" From which the following indices may further be calculated :

	Nos. 969–972.	Nos. 973–976.
Longitudinal index	68·6	73·8
Auricular index	56·9	57·5
Nasal index	48·9	53·0
Orbital index	—	78·9

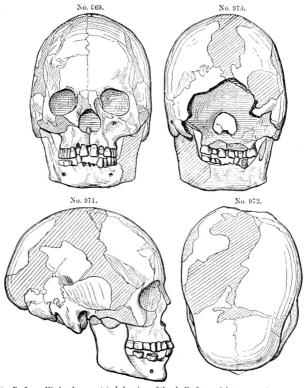

No. 969.   No. 970.

No. 971.   No. 972.

Nos. 969–972. Professor Virchow's geometrical drawing of the skull of one of the two warriors found, with helmets on their heads and a lance-head, in the room of a house of the burnt city. (Depth, about 26 ft.) The deficiencies replaced by gypsum are indicated by *oblique* lines.

" The skull Nos. 969–972 is evidently that of a male ; judging from the good preservation of the teeth-crowns, it belongs to a young man, who, however, has had time to wear deeply down the edges of the incisors. The forehead is broad ; the glabella moderately deepened. The vertical curve (curve of the vertex) is long and well shaped, with a rapid falling off of the occiput, which for the rest is rounded ; lambdoidal suture serrated. The eyebrow projections are strongly developed ; maxillary bones quite orthognathous ; the chin projecting, broad and angular. The middle of the lower jawbone above the chin is inflected ; the upper alveolar process very low. The upper part of the nose is narrow, the spine much developed. The face is somewhat coarse and narrow, with deep *Fossae caninae.*

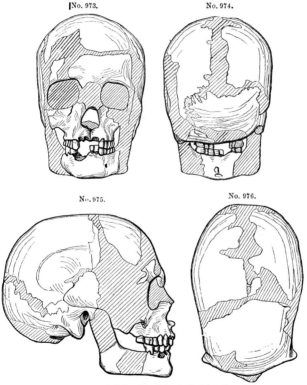

No. 973.   No. 974.

No. 975.   No. 976.

Nos. 973–976. Professor Virchow's geometrical drawing of the skull of the other of the two warriors found, with helmets on their heads and a lance-head, in the room of a house of the burnt city. (Depth, about 26 ft.) The deficiencies replaced by gypsum are indicated by *oblique* lines.

" The skull Nos. 973–976 is probably that of a young man, though it has a very delicate appearance. The superciliary arches are slight ; the frontal and parietal tubera distinct, but not strongly protruding ; the teeth but little worn down. It is distinguished by a continuous frontal suture and prognathism pretty strongly developed. Though almost the whole occiput and the right side had to be artificially reconstructed, in consequence of which the uncertainty of the measuring is great, yet the chief results may be considered as trustworthy. On the whole, the skull is narrow and high; its greatest height is two finger-breadths behind the coronal suture. Owing to the restoration, it broadens perhaps more than is necessary towards the back and below. In the *Norma temporalis* it appears high and long. The face is moderately high; less coarse than the preceding, but not pretty. The nose appears to be broad; its back especially is somewhat flattened at its beginning. The eye-holes are low; the *Fossae caninae* deep; the incisors large; the alveolar apophysis of the upper jaw projects obliquely. The lower jaw is strong; the chin broad and projecting; the alveolar part of the lower jaw is on the whole somewhat bent forward; high processes; low coronoid apophysis.

" While the two male skulls have many resemblances to each other, they are essentially distinguished from the female skull (No. 147). This is *brachycephalic* (index 82·5), while the two others are distinctly stamped *dolichocephalic*, with an index of 68·6 in the first, of 73·8 in the second. Probably their narrowness has been partly caused by the pressure of the masses of earth which lay upon them, and somewhat higher numbers ought to be taken; but this makes no difference in the contrast between the skulls. It is only in the prognathism that the skull Nos. 973–976 approaches the female skull No. 147, whilst the strongly orthognathic skull Nos. 969–972 is in contrast with both.

" The question whether all three skulls belong to the same people, is difficult to decide on account of such great differences. If the prognathism is regarded as an ethnological criterion, then the conclusion must be that the male skull, Nos. 969–972, must belong to a people different from the other two. On the other hand, it is evident that the form of the skull indicates rather a relation between the two male skulls than between them and the female skull. It is true that the female sex inclines more to prognathism, and in many races the female calvaria appears shorter and broader than the male; but still the difference in the cephalic index $(82·5 - 73·8 = 8·7)$ is so considerable that it cannot be referred to a mere difference of sex. Thus we are led naturally to the question, whether we have not here before us the remains of a mixed race. In this respect it must not be overlooked that all three skulls present in a striking manner the appearance of the bones of a race in an advanced state of civilization. Nothing of the savage, nothing massive in the formation of the bones, no particularly strong development of the apophyses of the muscles and tendons, can be observed. All the parts have a smooth, fine, almost slender appearance. It is true that all three skulls have belonged to youthful persons, or at least to persons but little advanced in age, and many a protuberance would perhaps have been further developed had they grown older. But with savage races the bones acquire earlier a greater thickness and ruggedness, and it is therefore most natural to infer that the ancient owners of these heads belonged to a settled people, who were acquainted with the arts of peace, and who, through intercourse with distant races, were more exposed to being mixed in blood.

" Of course these remarks can only be offered with great reserve, as in all three skulls decay had reached such a degree, that the recomposition of the fragments, particularly of the face, by no means excludes the possibility of arbitrariness. Each of the two male skulls has, under my direction, been taken to pieces and recomposed six or seven times; nevertheless I cannot say that I am satisfied with the result. But at last I have terminated the attempts at restoration, because, as large pieces are missing, a certain arbitrariness on the part of the restorer cannot be avoided; besides, at least in the main points, it cannot be perceived that a fresh restoration would give an essentially different result. The dolichocephalism of the male and the brachycephalism of the female skulls would surely as little disappear as the orthognathism of the one and the prognathism of the two other skulls.

"The temptation is very great to make further suppositions regarding the extraction of the individual persons and their social position. This temptation, I believe, I must resist, because our real knowledge of the craniology of ancient peoples is still on a very small scale. If it were correct that, as some authors suppose, the ancient Thracians, like the modern Albanians, were brachycephalic, we might perhaps connect with them the people represented by the brachycephalic head from Hissarlik. On the other hand, the dolichocephalism of Semites and Egyptians would permit us to go with our dolicephalic skulls from Hissarlik to so distant an origin. But if besides the skull index we take into consideration the entire formation of the head and the face of the dolichocephalic skulls, the idea that those men were members of the Aryan race is highly pleasing. Hence I believe the natural philosopher should stop in the face of these problems, and should abandon further investigation to the archæologist."

The skull Nos. 977, 978, which was found in the third, the burnt city, in a jar, together with ashes of animal matter, is, as Prof. Virchow informs me, that of a woman, probably of a "young maiden. Its type is a very characteristic female one: the bones are fine; the form is very pleasing. Corresponding to the pronounced *dolichocephalic* index of 71·3 (greatest length 188, greatest breadth 134 mm.), the *Norma verticalis* is long and oval; the *Norma temporalis* extended, with a long and somewhat flat vertex-curve. The auricular height is 111 mm.; according to this, the auricular index amounts to 57, which is a very low measure. In the same way the Lambda-angle is low and very obtuse; the forehead low, falling off distinctly and rapidly from the vertex-curve; the orbital edges quite smooth. The *Sutura frontalis* is continuous. Compared with the other skulls, we find a great contrast to the female skull, No. 147, which is brachycephalic; but, on the other hand, a near approach to the two male skulls, especially to Nos. 969–972. There can, therefore, be no objection to join these three skulls in one group. In connection with this it is not without importance that the new skull, as well as the skull Nos. 973–976, has an open *Sutura frontalis*.

"Regarding this skull, I can only repeat what I said of the first skulls; namely, that the bones give one the impression of a delicate, civilized, settled population. If this population were pre-eminently a *dolichocephalic* one, then we have the choice between Aryan, Semitic, and perhaps Hamitic races. A definite decision on this point cannot yet be made from a purely anthropological point of view, but I may say that the last skull can hardly be distinguished in the midst of ancient Greek skulls."

No. 977.

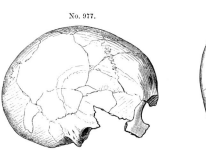

No. 978.

Nos. 977, 978. Skull found in a jar, together with ashes of animal matter, probably human ashes, at a depth of 23 ft.

Professor Virchow kindly sent me also the following note on the skeleton of a fœtus which was found in a vase in the third or burnt city : —" This skeleton is very defective, because there are only a few fragments of the head, breast, pelvis, hands and feet. On the other hand, the upper and lower extremities as far as the hands and feet are pretty complete. Their bones give the following measurements :—

	mm.				mm.
" Os humeri	. . . 36		Os femoris	. . .	37
Ulna	 34		Tibia	. . . .	34
Radius	 31		Fibula	. . . .	33

" It may, therefore, be a fœtus of from 6 to 7 months."

Unfortunately both the helmets, which were on these skulls, had been so much destroyed by the chloride of copper, that they could only be taken out in small fragments, which are too much corroded and too fragile to be recomposed.

The upper portions of both helmets have, however, been well preserved; and these parts form the ridge (φάλος), in which the horsehair plume (λόφος ἵππουρις), so frequently mentioned in the *Iliad*, was fixed.[8] In both cases the φάλος consists of two pieces, such as we have seen under Nos. 795-798, and as I have recomposed them in No. 979. The reader

---

[8] iii. 362 ; iv. 459 ; vi. 9 ; xiii. 132 ; xvi. 216. Mr. Philip Smith says in his foot-note at p. 281 of *Troy and its Remains :* " Few coincidences have struck us more than the comparison of these helmet-crests with the frequent allusions in Homer, especially where ' Hector of the dancing helmet-crest ' (κορυθαίολος Ἕκτωρ) takes off the helmet that frightened his child (*Il.* vi. 469, foll.):

τὰρβήσας χαλκόν τε ἰδὲ λόφον ἱππιοχαίτην,
δεινὸν ἀπ' ἀκροτάτης κόρυθος νεύοντα νοήσας.

(' Scared at the brazen mail and horsehair plume, That waved terrific on the crested helm.')

" No such plumed helmets are found among the remains of ' pre-historic ' barbarous races. The skeletons, with the helmets and lances beside them, bear striking witness to a city taken by storm. In Homer, the Trojans, under the command of the ' crested Hector,' are ' valiant with lances ' (μεμαότες ἐγχείησιν, *Il.* ii. 816-818)."

will see in the lower portion a round boss; this is the head of the copper nail by which the piece is transfixed: the point of the nail on the other

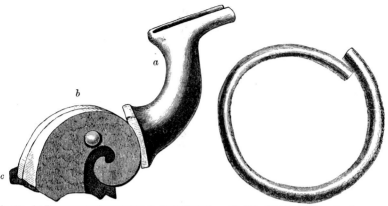

No. 979. (a) The upper and (b) lower pieces of a Trojan Helmet-crest (φάλος) placed together. (c) A small piece of the Helmet remains adhering to the lower part of the Crest. A pin, fastened to the front of the part b, may be seen protruding on the opposite side. (About half actual size. Depth, about 23 ft.)

No. 980. Great Copper Ring, found near the Helmet-crest. (About half a‧tual size. Depth, about 23 ft.)

side is merely bent round. As to the place into which the λόφος ἵππουρις was inserted and fixed there can be no doubt, for the opening at the top of the ridge can have served no other purpose.[9] By the side of one helmet I found the copper ring No. 980, by the side of the other the fragment of a similar ring. I am at a loss to say how these rings could have been connected with the helmets.

Under No. 981 I represent six primitive bronze brooches, of which only two have globular, the others flat heads. They had been stuck

No. 981. Six Bronze Brooches, stuck together in the hollow of a bone, and cemented together by the oxide or carbonate of copper. (2 : 3 actual size. Depth, 26 ft.)

together into a hollow bone, and are consolidated by the cementing action of the oxide or carbonate. This is the sole instance of brooches with flat heads in the burnt city.

No. 982 marks an object of bronze in form like a small coin. On the front side it is slightly concave, and represents in very low relief a little figure, in which, by the help of what we have learned from those on the whorls Nos. 1826, 1883, 1971, 1994, we see a man with uplifted arms. On the reverse side this object is quite flat; we only see there a single dot. I think that, with all its resemblance to a coin, this object cannot be one, for nothing else like it has ever been found in any one of the

---

[9] A similar contrivance is also seen on the helmet of a warrior in the *intaglio* of a Mycenean gold bead and a gold ring. See my *Mycenae*, p. 174, No. 254; p. 223, No. 335.

pre-historic cities of Hissarlik. Besides, coined money was still unknown even in the time of Homer.

No. 982. Object of Bronze in shape of a coin. (Actual size. Depth, 23 ft.)

No. 983. Curious Object of a white substance, with three perforations.
(3 : 4 actual size. Depth, 26 to 33 ft.)

No. 983 is a very curious object of a perfectly white substance, with traces of blue colour on the outside. It has nine semi-globular projections, a linear ornamentation, and at one end one perforation, at the other two, by which it was pinned on another object. I, therefore, hold it to have served as an ornament of a wooden box. In the fracture it has quite the appearance of gypsum, and it is much softer and lighter than Egyptian porcelain. As nothing like a similar paste has ever been found by me, and also on account of its blue colour, which never occurs elsewhere at Hissarlik, I think it to be of foreign importation.

No. 984 represents a plain perforated lentoid gem of cornelian, found in the royal house; its sole decoration is an incised line, which goes round

No. 984. Plain Lentoid Gem of Cornelian.
(3 : 4 actual size.
Depth, 28 ft.)

it lengthwise. A perfectly similar gem of cornelian, found in a tomb at Camirus in Rhodes, is in the British Museum.

I cannot conclude this chapter on the third, the burnt city, without examining once more the question, whether this pretty little town, with its brick walls, which can hardly have housed 3000 inhabitants, could have been identical with the great Homeric Ilios of immortal renown, which withstood for ten long years the heroic efforts of the united Greek army of 110,000 men, and which could only at last be captured by a stratagem.

First, as regards the size of all the pre-historic cities, I repeat that they were but very small. In fact, we can hardly too much contract our ideas of the dimensions of those primeval cities.

So, according to the Attic tradition, Athens was built by the Pelasgians, and was limited to the small rock of the Acropolis, whose plateau is of oval form, 900 ft. long and 400 ft. broad at its broadest part; but it was much smaller still until Cimon enlarged it by building the wall on its eastern declivity and levelling the slope within by means of *débris*.[10] The Ionians, having captured the city, forced the Pelasgians to settle at the southern foot of the Acropolis. According to Thucydides, Athens was only enlarged by the coalescence of the Attic demi there (συνοικισμός)

---

[10] Paus. i. 28, § 3: Τῇ δὲ ἀκροπόλει, πλὴν ὅσον Κίμων ᾠκοδόμησεν αὐτῆς ὁ Μιλτιάδου, περιβαλεῖν τὸ λοιπὸν λέγεται τοῦ τείχους Πελασγοὺς οἰκήσαντάς ποτε ὑπὸ τὴν ἀκρόπολιν · φασὶ γὰρ Ἀγρόλαν καὶ Ὑπέρβιον. πυνθανόμενος δὲ οἵτινες ἦσαν, οὐδὲν ἄλλο ἐδυνάμην μαθεῖν, ἢ Σικελοὺς τὸ ἐξαρχῆς ὄντας Ἀκαρνανίαν μετοικῆσαι.

effected by Theseus.[1] In like manner Athens ('Αθῆναι), The Mycenae (Μυκῆναι), and all the other cities whose names plural form, were probably at first limited to their stron πόλις, and had their names in the singular ; but the cities enlarged, they received the plural name, the citadel being Acropolis, and the lower town πόλις. The most striking pr the name of the valley " Polis " in Ithaca, which, as I have is not derived from a real city, or acropolis,—for my excavations there have proved that this *single* fertile valley in the island can never have been the site of a city,—but from a natural rock, which has never been touched by the hand of man. This rock, however, having—as seen from below—precisely the shape of a citadel, is for this reason now called *castron*, and was no doubt in ancient times called *Polis*, which name has been transferred to the valley.

The ancient Polis or Asty (ἄστυ) was the ordinary habitation of the town-chief or king, with his family and dependants, as well as of the richer classes of the people ; it was the site of the Agora and the temples, and the general place of refuge in time of danger. We have traces of this fact in the extended sense of the Italian *castello*, to embrace a town, and in the Anglo-Saxon *burh ;* also, as Professor Virchow suggests to me, in the Slavish *gard = hortus* (Burgwall). " What, indeed," says Mr. Gladstone, " have we to say when we find that, in the period of the *incunabula* of Rome, the Romans on the Palatine were probably faced by the Sabines on the hill of the Capitol ?"[3] It is, therefore, not the small-ness of the third, the burnt city, which can prevent us from identifying it with the Homeric Troy, because Homer is not a historian, but an epic poet. Besides, he does not sing of contemporaneous events, but of events which happened probably 600 or 700 years before his time, and which he merely knew from hearsay :—

ἡμεῖς δὲ κλέος οἶον ἀκούομεν, οὐδέ τι ἴδμεν.[4]

" If," as Professor Sayce observes,[5] " Greek warriors had never fought in the Plain of Troy, we may be pretty sure that the poems of Homer would not have brought Achilles and Agamemnon under the walls of Ilion." Great national heroic poems always rest on the foundation of great decisive national combats and definite regions which had become famous for these combats. The whole of Greek antiquity, and at its head the greatest of all historians, Thucydides, never doubted of such combats at the entrance of the Hellespont. " The capture of Troy is," as M. Lenormant says,[6] " one of the five or six primitive reminiscences of the Greeks, which seem to refer to real facts, and which, in spite of the exuberant mythological vegetation in the midst of which they appear, throw into the dark night of the heroic ages a light on the successive phases of growing civilization. Such are, the foundation of the kingdom of Argos by the early Pelasgic dynasty of Inachus ; its replacement by

---

[1] Thucyd. ii. 15 : τὸ δὲ πρὸ τούτου ἡ ἀκρόπολις ἡ νῦν οὖσα πόλις ἦν, καὶ τὸ ὑπ' αὐτὴν πρὸς νότον μάλιστα τετραμμένον.   [2] See Introd. p. 46.
[3] *Homeric Synchronism*, p. 39.   [4] *Il.* ii. 486.
[5] *Contemporary Review* of December 1878.
[6] *Antiquités de la Troade*, pp. 35, 36.

the new dynasty of Danaus ; the power of the monarchy of the Pelopids ; and, in another part of Greece, the Phoenician colonization of Thebes. The Greeks always considered these events as marking the principal and decisive epochs of their primitive annals and their pre-historic traditions. For the Trojan war there is a remarkable unanimity of tradition, a unanimity too decisively marked not to be founded on a positive fact. I am particularly struck by the constancy with which, in the midst of the infinite divergence of the heroic legends of the Greeks, there is always maintained the same space of time between the capture of Troy and the Dorian invasion, which is placed a little less than a hundred years later, and opens the historical ages."

In the catalogue of ships [7] the poet mentions "the lower Thebes" (Ὑποθῆβαι), because the upper town, the Cadmea, destroyed by the Epigoni, had not yet been rebuilt. His mention of the lower town only seems, therefore, to confirm another ancient tradition.

Mr. Gladstone writes : [8] "As to the question what light Schliemann's discoveries throw upon the question, whether Troy had a real or only a mythical existence, it is difficult to suppose that the mythical theory, always wofully devoid of tangible substance, can long survive the results attained. In the Plain where the scene of the *Iliad* is laid, upon the spot indicated by the oldest traditions, which for very many centuries were never brought into question, and which, as testifying to a fact the most simple and palpable, were of high presumptive authority ; at a depth of from 23 to 33 ft., with the *débris* of an older city beneath it, and of three more recent successive towns above it ; has been found a stratum of remains of an inhabited city, which was manifestly destroyed by a tremendous conflagration."

As we have seen in the preceding pages, the third city of Hissarlik perfectly agrees with the Homeric indications as to the site of Troy ; and the fact, that there is no second place in the Troad which could possibly vie with it, goes far to prove its identity, the more so as the third city has, like the Homeric Ilios, been destroyed by the hand of an enemy in a fearful catastrophe, which fell on it so suddenly that the inhabitants had to leave even a large part of their treasures behind. In this respect also the third city agrees with the Homeric description, because the poet says : " Priam's city used to be far-famed for its wealth in gold and bronze, but now the precious wealth has disappeared from its houses." [9] If, therefore, in spite of its exhaustion by a long-protracted siege, the third city of Hissarlik was still so rich that I could find in it ten treasures, this is an additional proof of its identity with the poet's Ilios.

In proportion to the wealth and power of Ilium it was but natural that the sudden catastrophe, by which this rich and famous capital of the Trojan kingdom perished, should have made a very deep impression on the minds of men, both in Asia Minor and in Greece, and that it should at once have been taken up by the bards. But while, as Mr.

---

[7] *Il.* ii. 505 :
οἳ θ᾿ Ὑποθήβας εἶχον, ἐϋκτίμενον πτολίεθρον.
[8] *Homeric Synchronism*, p. 20.

[9] *Il.* xviii. 288–290 :
πρὶν μὲν γὰρ Πριάμοιο πόλιν μέροπες ἄνθρωποι
πάντες μυθέσκοντο πολύχρυσον πολύχαλκον ·
νῦν δὲ δὴ ἐξαπόλωλε δόμων κειμήλια κ᾿᾿λά.

Gladstone says, the local features of the site and Plain of Troy were given sufficiently for a broad identification, the bards handled them loosely and at will in point of detail. They treated the Plain without any assumption of a minute acquaintance with it, like one who was sketching a picture for his hearers, boldly but slightly, and not as one who laid his scene in a place with which he was already personally acquainted, and which formed by far the most famous portion of the country he inhabited. The ruins of the burnt Ilium having been completely buried under the ashes and *débris*, and people having no archæological desire for the investigation of the matter, it was thought that the destroyed city had completely disappeared. The imagination of the bards had, therefore, full play; the small Ilium grew in their songs, in the same proportion as the strength of the Greek fleet, the power of the besieging army, and the great actions of the heroes; the gods were made to participate in the war, and innumerable legends were grouped around the magnified facts.

I wish I could have proved Homer to have been an eye-witness of the Trojan war! Alas, I cannot do it! At his time swords were in universal use and iron was known, whereas they were totally unknown at Troy. Besides, the civilization he describes is later by centuries than that which I have brought to light in the excavations. Homer gives us the legend of Ilium's tragic fate, as it was handed down to him by preceding bards, clothing the traditional facts of the war and destruction of Troy in the garb of his own day. Neither will I maintain that his acquaintance with the Troad and with Troy was that of a resident; but certainly he was not without personal knowledge of the localities, for his descriptions of the Troad in general, and of the Plain of Troy in particular, are too truthful for us to believe that he could have drawn all his details from the ancient myth. If, as appears likely, he visited the Plain in the ninth century B.C.,[10] he would probably have found the Aeolic Ilium already long established, having its Acropolis on Hissarlik and its lower town on the site of Novum Ilium. It would, therefore, be but natural that he should depict Priam's Troy as a large city, with an acropolis called Pergamos, the more so as in his time every larger city had its Acropolis. My excavations have reduced the Homeric Ilium to its real proportions.

I have never called in doubt the unity of the Homeric poems, and have always firmly believed both the *Odyssey* and the *Iliad* to be by one author, except perhaps—partly or entirely—the 24th Rhapsody of each poem, on account of the contradictions they contain with the preceding text. Besides—to use Mr. Gladstone's words,[1]—" If I consider how much learning and ingenuity have been expended in a hundred efforts (scarcely any two of the assailants, however, agreeing except in their negative or revolutionary criticism) to disintegrate the Homeric poems, to break up into nebulous fragments the Sun of all ancient literature,"—I think it idle on my part to attempt a task already marked by so many failures; and I rest content with those immortal epics as they stand—the first-fruits of the noblest literature of the world, and the fount of poetic inspiration for all later ages.

---

[10] Professor Sayce observes to me that, according to Euphorion and Theopompus, Homer was a contemporary of Gyges of Lydia.   [1] *Homeric Synchronism*, p. 7.

CHAPTER VIII.

THE FOURTH CITY ON THE SITE OF TROY.

As we have seen in the preceding pages, the inhabitants of Novum Ilium held, according to an ancient legend, that Troy, the city of Priam, had not been entirely destroyed by the united Greek army under Agamemnon, and that it had never ceased to be inhabited. This legend is certainly confirmed by Homer, who, when Aeneas was on the point of being killed by Achilles in single combat, makes Poseidon say : " It is fated that Aeneas should be saved, in order that the race and the name of Dardanus may not utterly disappear—Dardanus, whom Zeus loved most of all the sons he begat of mortal women ; because the race of Priam has now become odious to the son of Kronos : *now, therefore, shall the mighty Aeneas reign over the Trojans, and the sons of his sons hereafter to be born.*" [1]

This legend has apparently been also confirmed by the *criticism of my pickaxe and spade,* for—as visitors can easily convince themselves with their own eyes—the south-eastern corner of the Third, the *brick city,* has not been destroyed by the conflagration. I must further say that this legend is also confirmed by the relics I have discovered, for—as the reader will see in the succeeding pages—we find among the successors of the burnt city the very same singular idols ; the very same primitive bronze battle-axes ; the very same terra-cotta vases, with or without tripod feet ; the very same double-handled goblets (δέπα ἀμφικύπελλα) ; the very same battle-axes of jade, porphyry, and diorite ; the same rude stone hammers and saddle-querns of trachyte ; the same immense mass of whorls or balls of terra-cotta with symbolical signs. The only difference is that, in general, the pottery of this fourth city is coarser and of a ruder fabric ; and that we find here an infinitely larger quantity of rude wheel-made terra-cottas and many new forms of vases and goblets. Besides, the quantity of rude stone hammers and polished stone axes is here fully thrice as large as in the third city ; also the masses of shells and cockles accumulated in the *débris* of the houses are so stupendous, that they baffle all description. Visitors can best see them in the great block of *débris* which I have left standing close to the " great tower." A people which left all their kitchen-refuse on the floors of their rooms must have lived in a very low social condition.

This low state of civilization seems also to be proved by the absence of large city walls. The large stone walls built by the inhabitants of the

---

[1] *Il.* xx. 302–308 :

. . . . μόρμον δέ οἵ ἐστ' ἀλέασθαι,
ὄφρα μὴ ἄσπερμος γενεὴ καὶ ἄφαντος ὄληται
Δαρδάνου, ὃν Κρονίδης περὶ πάντων φίλατο
παίδων,

οἳ ἔθεν ἐξεγένοντο γυναικῶν τε θνητάων.
ἤδη γὰρ Πριάμου γενεὴν ἤχθηρε Κρονίων·
νῦν δὲ δὴ Αἰνείαο βίη Τρώεσσιν ἀνάξει,
καὶ παίδων παῖδες, τοί κεν μετόπισθε γένωνται.

second city and used by the people of the third, the burnt city, as sub-structions for their huge brick walls, were buried beneath the mounds of ruins and *débris* produced by the conflagration; and, as is amply proved by the undisturbed state of these ruins and *débris*, the people of the fourth city did not attempt to bring them to light and to use them. Visitors can convince themselves of this by a glance at the accumulation of the

No. 985. Accumulation of *débris* before the Gate. The form of the strata of *débris* indicates that after the great conflagration the Trojans continued to go in and out on the same spot as before, although the paved road A was deeply buried under the ashes.

calcined *débris* of the third city in front of the gate, because, as M. Burnouf has ingeniously found out, and as he shows by the sketch which I give here, the form of the strata of the burnt *débris* indicates that, after the great conflagration, the inhabitants continued to go in and out at the same place as before, although the paved road A was buried 10 ft. deep under the ashes and *débris*. If a part of the old inhabitants remained in the city after the conflagration, they certainly went in and out by the same way, because they were accustomed to it. If the city were re-colonized by another people, the new comers may have used the same road because it was less steep and therefore easier, for everywhere else the descent must have been at an angle of 45°, this being always the slope the rubbish will adopt when shot from a height and left to itself, or, as engineers say, its angle of repose. Besides, the road through the old gate must, at a short distance, have joined the country-roads in the plain. Thus the mere fact that the gate-road, though at a high level, continued to be used by the inhabitants of the fourth city, neither proves that these latter were the former people nor that they were new comers.

There were certainly walls of defence: as, for example, one, 6½ ft. high and 4 ft. thick, immediately to the north-west of the tower road, and which seems to have run parallel with it down to the plain; another, 20 ft. high and 5 ft. thick, built of large stones and earth, on the burnt material which covered the west side of the great ancient wall to a depth of 6½ ft.; further, an ancient enclosure wall, 5 ft. high, with a pro-jecting battlement, on the north-west side of the hill; and two more on the south-eastern side, the one 5¼, the other 10 ft. thick, and nearly as high. As all these walls are outside the precincts of the third city, and as they are certainly pre-historic and are in the strata of *débris* of the fourth city, I believe them to belong to it. As, however, they are so entirely different in size, and as there is no continuity between them, I cannot possibly regard them as parts of a city wall; but I consider them to have been erected merely for the defence of certain special points. Now, if the people of the third, the burnt city had continued to reside there, it would appear wonderful why they should not have continued to surround themselves with new brick walls of defence, for they had passed all their lives within such brick fortifications, which could so easily have been erected. But there is no trace of such city walls of brick. Neither is there a trace of brick in the houses of the fourth city. As we have seen, only the ground-floors of the third, the burnt city are of stones joined with earth ; all the upper part of the houses was built of slightly-baked bricks, rarely of mere clay. Now, if the Trojans had continued to reside in their city, it is difficult to admit that they could have suddenly abandoned their mode of architecture and have adopted a different one. But that the architecture of the fourth city was a different one, is a fact of which visitors can easily convince themselves in the great block of *débris* which I have left standing. They will see there, in the strata of *débris* succeeding those of the burnt city, house-walls 10 or 12 ft. high, built of stones joined with clay ; they will also see many such stone walls of this height in my excavations to the east of the brick wall of the third city. This would lead us to suppose that all the house-walls were built of stones. This mode of architecture seems also to be proved by the very large masses of loose stones which occur in the strata of the fourth city. But as the people had neither planks nor tiles, it is more than probable that, like the present inhabitants of the Troad, they covered in their houses with terraces of earth. I readily admit that in many houses the stone walls may have been superseded by walls of clay, for in that case we should have no difficulty in explaining the thickness of the stratum of *débris* of this fourth city, which is generally from 12 to 13 ft. deep. But at all events no bricks, or traces of bricks, ever turned up there; and this is the principal reason which gives the preponderance of argument against our tendency to believe that this fourth city might have been inhabited by the people of the preceding, the burnt city.

But on this point I differ from my friend Professor Virchow, who writes to me : "I do not dare to contradict, but I would maintain that the present sun-dried bricks of the Troad are decomposed by air and rain without leaving a trace of their shape. Had the fourth city been destroyed by fire, the bricks would have been preserved longer. But this not having been the case, I do not see how the fact that no trace of them can now be found can militate against their former existence."

If the pottery of the fourth city does not differ much in shape from that of the third, the burnt city, it certainly differs much from it in colour and general appearance ; because the pottery of the fourth city has been only half or less than half baked at an open fire,[2] whereas the pottery

---

[2] Professor Virchow remonstrates against my belief that the pre-historic peoples baked their pottery at an open fire, for he thinks they performed this operation with animal dung in closed pits. But I can so much the less accept his theory, as he claims the same manipulation for the baking of the large *pithoi*. But this is contradicted by the fact that these latter are always thoroughly baked ; whilst all the other pottery, and even the very thinnest, whose clay is not more than $0 \cdot 003$ or $0 \cdot 004$ thick, is baked on an average only to one-third of the thickness of their clay.

of the third city, after having passed through the same operation, has been exposed to the intense heat of the conflagration, which in a very great many cases has completed the thorough baking and has given to it a much finer colour, except in cases where, the heat having continued too long or having been too intense, the vessels have been more or less destroyed by it. Thus we have before us, in this fourth city, a pottery very inferior in fabric to that of the first and second cities, but a pottery which would have been but slightly inferior to that of its predecessor, the third city, had it not been through the accidentally superior baking of the latter in the conflagration.

Under No. 986 I represent a pretty lustrous-yellow owl-headed vase, of a globular shape but flat-bottomed, with the characteristics of a woman and two wing-like vertical projections : the vulva, with its incised cross and the four dots, is of special interest. Very interesting is also the globular red vase No. 987, which has also a flat bottom, and on

No. 986. Terra-cotta Vase, with an owl's head, the characteristics of a woman, two wings and a cross with points on the vulva. (1 : 6 actual size. Depth, 20 ft.)

No. 988. Terra-cotta Vase, with an owl's head, the characteristics of a woman, and two wings. (1 : 3 actual size. Depth, 22 ft.)

No. 987. Curious Vase, with an owl's head, holding a double-handled cup. (About half actual size. Depth, 15 ft.)

which we see the large owl-eyes still more distinctly marked. The figure has on its head a basin, which forms the orifice ; four necklaces are indicated round the neck. In its hands it holds a double-handled cup, which communicates by a hole with the principal vase. Owl-headed vases

of an identical shape also occur in the third city: the fragment represented under No. 228, p. 340, is the mouth-piece of a similar vase.

No. 988 is a pear-shaped lustrous-black vase, with wing-like vertical
projections, an owl's head, and the characteristics of a woman; there is a
slight hollow in the vulva. Owl-vases of this shape are the most frequent.
Of the same colour and of nearly an identical shape, but much larger, is
the vase No. 989. Of the same colour is also the owl-vase No. 990, which

No. 990. Vase with an owl's head, two breasts, and
handles in form of wings. (1:4 actual size.
Depth, 22 ft.)

No. 989. Vase with an owl's head, the characteristics
of a woman, and two wing-like handles. (1:4 actual
size. Depth, 22 ft.)

has no vulva. Of still greater interest is the pear-shaped lustrous dark-
brown vase No. 991, which has an incised cross on the vulva, no vertical
projections, but two handles. Here the neck is plain, and was evidently
intended to be crowned with a cover on which the owl-head is modelled,
like that which I have put on it, but certainly not this particular one, as
it is too narrow. Of an identical shape and colour is the vase No. 992.
Of a very rude fabric is the pear-shaped yellow vase No. 993, on which
the characteristics of a woman are indicated by shapeless excrescences.
The usual wing-like projections, instead of being upright, are here bent
towards the neck of the vase; the bottom is flat. All these vases are
hand-made.

To this fourth city also belong the idols Nos. 994 and 995; both
are very curious, as they approach nearer to the human shape than any
other of the stone idols. No. 994 is of fine white marble, and differs

also from the other idols by its bulky form, approaching to the round ; it has a rudely-incised owl-face. A necklace is indicated by a horizontal stroke, and the hair by vertical scratches on the hinder part of the neck.

No. 991. Vase with two handles and the characteristics of a woman ; cover with an owl's head. (1 : 4 actual size. Depth, 13 ft.)

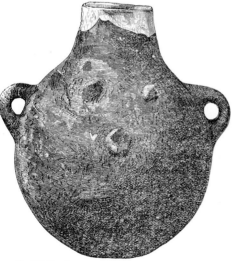

No. 992. Two-handled Vase, with the characteristics of a woman. (1 : 4 actual size. Depth, 13 ft.)

No. 993. Vase of Terra-cotta. (Half actual size. Depth, 16 ft.)

The vulva is indicated, considerably below its natural place; the whole body has been decorated with formless scratches, which seem to have no signification. I call attention to the great resemblance of this idol to a Babylonian image of the goddess Nana in the

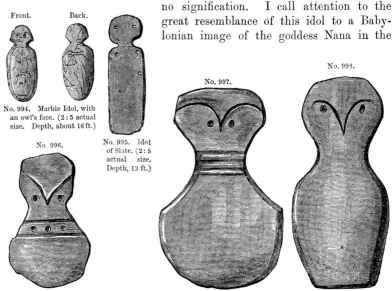

Front.   Back.

No. 994.   Marble Idol, with an owl's face. (2 : 5 actual size. Depth, about 16 ft.)

No. 995. Idol of Slate. (2 : 5 actual size. Depth, 13 ft.)

No. 996.

No. 997.

No. 998.

Nos. 996–998. Owl-faced Idols of Marble. (Actual size. Depth, 13 to 20 ft.) No. 996 has a girdle; No. 997, four necklaces; on No. 998 the owl's face is painted.

British Museum. The idol No. 995 is of slate and flat; of the face, only the two eyes are marked. A necklace is indicated by two horizontal strokes. Through the inability of the primitive artist, the breasts are indicated on the shoulders, and the vulva on the left side.

I have further to mention, as belonging to this fourth city, the marble idols Nos. 996, 997, 998. On the first two the owl-head is rudely incised. No. 996 has a girdle indicated by two horizontal strokes and three points. No. 997 has on the neck four horizontal strokes, probably indicating the necklaces. On the idol No. 998, the eyes and beak of the owl are rudely painted with a black colour, probably with black clay.

No. 999 is a fragment of the side of a vase with an incised linear ornamentation, on which we see the projection with a tubular hole for

No. 999.

No. 1000.

No. 1001.

Nos. 999–1001. Fragments of Pottery, with incised ornamentation. (Nearly half actual size. Depth, 13 to 19 ft.)

suspension. No. 1000 is the fragment of a vase-handle; No. 1001, the fragment of a vase-neck, with a linear decoration.

Nos. 1002 and 1003 represent the upper part of a lustrous-black vase, with a rude but very curious deeply-incised decoration. On No. 1002 we

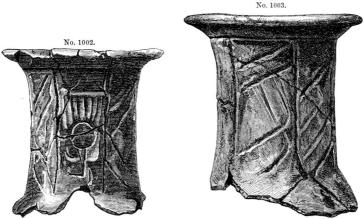

No. 1003.

No. 1002.

Nos. 1002, 1003. Front and back views of a Vase-neck, with very curious incised signs and perhaps a man with uplifted arms. (Half actual size. Depth, about 17 ft.)

see, perhaps, the very rude figure of a man with uplifted arms, whose head is almost as large as the whole remainder of the body. I do not attempt to explain the rest of the decoration. On No. 1003 the sign in the middle resembles a written character. The clay of this vase-head is

No. 1005. Vase, with tubular holes for suspension. (Nearly 1 : 3 actual size. Depth, about 22 ft.)

No. 1004. Small Vase, with double holes for suspension on each side. (Actual size. Depth, about 20 ft.)

No. 1006. Globular Vase, with tubular holes for suspension. (1 : 4 actual size. Depth, about 19 ft.)

but very slightly baked. No. 1004 is a small vase with vertical tubular holes for suspension. No. 1005 is a small pear-shaped vase of a blackish colour, with tubular holes for suspension. No. 1006 is a globular lustrous dark-brown vase, with a convex bottom and tubular rings for suspension; it has a breast-like excrescence in front. The vase No. 1007 is wheel-made and of a dark-red colour; its handles are in the form of spirals,

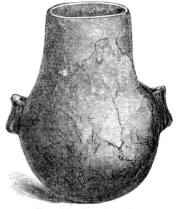

No. 1007. Vase with tubular holes in the handles for suspension. (About 1 : 4 actual size. Depth, about 19 ft.)

No. 1008. Vase with tubular holes for suspension. (1 : 4 actual size. Depth, about 16 ft.)

and are perforated vertically for suspension with a string. No. 1008 is pear-shaped, with a convex bottom and a long neck tapering towards

No. 1009. Vase with two handles and tubular holes for suspension. (About 1 : 4 actual size. Depth, about 19 ft.)

the mouth; on each side is a long projection with a perforation for suspension. Vases of this shape are very frequent. No. 1009 is a pretty lustrous-red wheel-made vase, with two handles in the form of spirals, and between them, on each side, a perforated projection for suspension; in the same direction there are perforations in the rim: the only ornamentation consists of four impressed horizontal lines round the neck.

No. 1010 represents a dark-red hand-made vase, with a hollow bottom and perforated projections for suspension on the sides; there is besides, on either side, a protuberance in the form of a handle, but it is not really such. On the upper part of the body we see all round the vase, between borders of incised lines and dots, a row of strange signs, which may be written characters; the neck of the vase is fractured. No. 1011 represents this same vase from the other side, and with a restored neck. I also give separately the supposed inscription or mere decoration as copied by M. Burnouf (No. 1012). But Prof. Sayce does not think it to be an inscription. Professor Virchow calls my attention to some resemblance which he finds in the decoration of this vase to that on a vase found in Reichersdorf in Lusatia (Lausitz).[3]

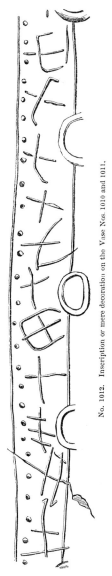

No. 1012. Inscription or mere decoration on the Vase Nos. 1010 and 1011.

No. 1010. A Terra-cotta Vase, with two little ears and two large perforated handles, marked with eleven strange characters. (About 1 : 4 actual size. Depth, about 18 ft.)

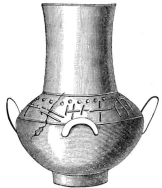

No. 1011. The foregoing Vase, with a restored neck.

No. 1013 is another suspension vase, with a long neck decorated with four incised horizontal lines; the bottom is flat. I repeat that all vases are hand-made, unless I distinctly state the contrary. No. 1014 is dark-red, of a globular shape, with a hollow foot and a cylindrical neck. The neck is deco-rated with horizontal, the body with vertical, incised lines: the projections on the sides are perforated for suspension. No. 1015 is a small black globular suspension vase, with deeply incised spirals and wave-lines. No. 1016 is a wheel-made globular lustrous-black vase, in the shape

---

[3] This Lusatian vase is represented in the *Sessional Report of the Berlin Society for Anthropology, Ethnology*, &c., of July 15, 1876, p. 9.

of a bottle, with perforated protuberances for suspension ; it has round
the body an incised zigzag ornament, with accompanying dots.   No. 1017

No. 1013.   Vase with tubular holes for suspension
and incised bands.
(About 1 : 4 actual size.   Depth, about 22 ft.)

No. 1014.   Vase with linear ornamentation.
(About 1 : 4 actual size.   Depth, 18 to 22 ft.)

is also a suspension vase of a dull yellow colour ; it is ornamented with
four parallel horizontal lines, forming three fields, which are filled up with
zigzag lines.   No. 1018 is a little black tripod-vase with two handles,

No. 1015. Globular Vase, with tubular
holes for suspension and incised
ornamentation of spirals. (About
1 : 4 actual size. Depth, 13 ft.)

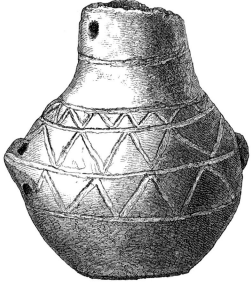

No. 1016.   Vase for suspension,
with incised zigzag ornamentation. (1 : 4 actual size. Depth,
19 ft.)

No. 1017.   Vase of grey Terra-cotta, with perforated tubular holes on the
sides and holes in the rim for suspension. Incised zigzag
ornamentation. (Actual size. Depth, 16 to 20 ft.)

and an incised zigzag decoration round the body.   No. 1019 is a small
yellow tripod-vase of an oval shape, having perforated protuberances

for suspension on the sides ; it is decorated with incised vertical strokes between horizontal parallel lines. No. 1020 is a one-handled pitcher,

No. 1019.

No. 1018.

No. 1020.

No. 1021.

No. 1022. Vase with three different flat bottoms, on each of which it may be put down in turn. (1 : 4 actual size. Depth, 13 ft.)

Nos. 1018–1021. Vases of various shapes, having an incised ornamentation. (About 1 : 4 actual size. Depth, 16 to 19 ft.)

with an incised linear decoration; No. 1021, a small suspension vase, decorated with dots. No. 1022 is a very curious little yellow suspension vase, with three different flat bottoms, on each of which it may be put down in turn.

No. 1023 is a very pretty vase, whose surface is divided by five parallel horizontal bands into four fields, filled with strokes, turned in opposite directions. No. 1024 is a little vase, covered all over with a very pretty incised ornamentation.

One of the most curious vases is No. 1025 ; it is a yellow tripod, and has on each side a handle of spiral form, with a tubular hole for sus-

No. 1023. Vase with a curious incised ornamentation. (About 1 : 4 actual size. Depth, about 13 ft.)

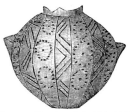

No. 1024. Vase decorated with incisions. (Half actual size. Depth, about 20 ft.)

No. 1025. Tripod Vase, with perforated projections for suspension, and a small Vase on its body. Linear ornamentation. (About 1 : 4 actual size. Depth, about 16 ft.)

pension; just in front of the handle to the right of the spectator is a small projecting jug, which does not communicate with the vase. The vase is decorated on the neck with incised horizontal lines, under the lowest of which may be seen incised vertical lines, below each of which is a dot.

No. 1026 is a lustrous-black tripod, of globular form, with perforated projections for suspension; the upper part of the body, as far as the neck, is decorated with dots.   No. 1027 is another globular black tripod,

No. 1026. Tripod Globular Vase, with tubular holes for suspension, and an ornamentation of points. (About 1 : 4 actual size. Depth, about 19 ft.)

No. 1027. Tripod Vase, with tubular holes for suspension and incised ornamentation. (1 : 4 actual size. Depth, about 22 ft.)

with large perforated projections for suspension; the upper part of the body has also a linear decoration.   Another black tripod-vase for suspension is represented by No. 1028; the neck is decorated with impressed horizontal furrows.   A similar black suspension tripod is No. 1029, the

No. 1028. Tripod Vase, with tubular holes for suspension. (About 1 : 4 actual size. Depth, about 16 ft.)

No. 1029. Tripod Vase, with tubular holes for suspension. (About 1 : 4 actual size. Depth, about 22 ft.)

body of which has an incised wedge-shaped ornamentation. The black suspension tripod No. 1030 again is similar to it, but has much longer feet.

No. 1031 is a wheel-made yellow vase-cover, having on each side a perforation in the rim for suspension; one of the holes is seen in front The most curious thing on this vase-cover is the three feet on its top, which make us suppose that it was also used as a cup. At all events, this tripod vase-cover is unique; no second specimen like it has occurred. No. 1032 is a wheel-made single-handled grey tripod, with long feet; it has ear-shaped protuberances in front and on both sides. Of an identical

No 1030. Tripod Vase, with holes for suspension.
(Nearly 1 : 3 actual size. Depth, about 19 ft.)

No. 1031. Vase Cover, with three feet and two tubular
holes for suspension. (1 : 4 actual size.
Depth, about 19 ft.)

No. 1033. Terra-cotta Vessel with three feet, a handle,
and two ear-like ornaments. (1 : 6 actual size.
Depth, 16 ft.)

No. 1032. Tripod with handle and three projecting
ear-like ornaments. (About 1 : 4 actual size.
Depth, 13 ft.)

No. 1034. Globular Triped, with tubular holes for suspension. (1 : 4 actual size. Depth, 22 ft.)

No. 1035. Tripod Vase, with tubular holes for suspension. (1 : 4 actual size. Depth, about 22 ft.)

shape is the tripod No. 1033. No. 1034 is a black globular bottle-shaped
tripod, with tubular holes for suspension. No. 1035 is a lustrous-black

tripod-vase, with perforated projections for suspension: tripod-vases of this shape are frequent. No. 1036 is a small tripod-vase for suspension, and No. 1037 is a similar tripod-vase. No. 1038 is a red globular tripod for suspension; No. 1039, a red flat jug in the form of a hunting-bottle; No. 1040, a grey tripod *oenochoë*. No. 1041 is a red suspension tripod

No. 1036. Tripod Vase, with tubular
holes for suspension.
(Nearly 1 : 3 actual size.
Depth, about 22 ft.)

No. 1037. Globular Tripod,
with tubular holes.
(About 1 : 4 actual size.
Depth, about 22 ft.)

No. 1039. Flat Jug in form of a
hunting-bottle. (1 : 4 actual size.
Depth, about 19 ft.)

No. 1038. Globular Tripod, with
tubular holes for suspension.
(About 1 : 4 actual size. Depth,
about 22 ft.)

No. 1041. Tripod Vase, with tubular
holes for suspension.
(About 1 : 4 actual size. Depth,
about 22 ft.)

No. 1043. Tripod Pitcher.
(About 1 : 4 actual size.
Depth, about 22 ft.)

No. 1042. Tripod, with tubular
holes for suspension.
(Nearly 1 : 3 actual size.
Depth, about 22 ft.)

No. 1044. Tripod Vase, with spiral
handles. (1 : 4 actual size.
Depth, about 20 ft.)

No. 1045. Rude Pitcher.
(1 : 4 actual size.
Depth, about 20 ft.)

with cover: a similar red tripod is seen in No. 1042. No. 1043 is a red wheel-made tripod-pitcher; No. 1044, a dark-red tripod-vase, with handles in the form of spirals; No. 1045, a rude unpolished wheel-made pitcher, of a form which is very abundant. No. 1046 is a lustrous-black single-handled globular *oenochoë*, with a long upright neck: this sort of jug is very frequent. No. 1047 is a red one-handled wheel-made cup, with two ear-like protuberances, and a breast-like projection in front.

No. 1040. Tripod *Oenochoë*.
(1 : 4 actual size. Depth, 13 ft.)

No. 1046. Globular *Oenochoë*, with straight neck.
(1 : 4 actual size. Depth, about 22 ft.)

No. 1048 is a one-handled tripod-jug; No. 1049, a red tripod-vase, with handles in the form of spirals. No. 1050 is a rude unpolished wheel-made pitcher: this sort of pitcher is so abundant in the fourth

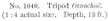

Nos. 1047–1050. Tripod Vases and Pitchers. (1 : 4 actual size. Depth, 13 to 19 ft.)

Nos. 1051–1053. Rattle-box, Cup, and Tripod Pitcher. (1 : 4 actual size. Depth, 16 to 22 ft.)

city that I collected more than 400 of them. No. 1051 is a very rude rattle-box, with pieces of metal inside; rattle-boxes of clay, but of different shape, occur also in the Lake-habitations in the Lake of Moeringen.[4] No. 1052 is a very rude cup; No. 1053, a very rude tripod-pitcher.

[4] V. Gross, *Résultats des Recherches dans les Lacs de la Suisse occidentale;* Zürich, 1876, Pl. xix. Nos. 3, 4.

No. 1054 is the lower part of a rude tripod-box ; it is here represented head downwards; it is on the same principle as the tripod-box Nos. 264-5, p. 360. No. 1055 is a little pitcher without a handle. No. 1056 is a small tripod-cup; No. 1057, a small vessel with a pointed foot, having exactly the form of the large jars : a vessel of an identical shape was found in the ancient settlement on the rock near Inzighofen.[5] No. 1058 is a small cup. Nos. 1059, 1061, 1062, 1064, 1066, 1067, 1075, 1076 are small rude vases with perforated projections for suspension ; No. 1076 only is a tripod. Nos. 1060, 1063, 1065, 1070, 1072 are small, very rude one-handled pitchers : the first of them (No. 1060) is decorated

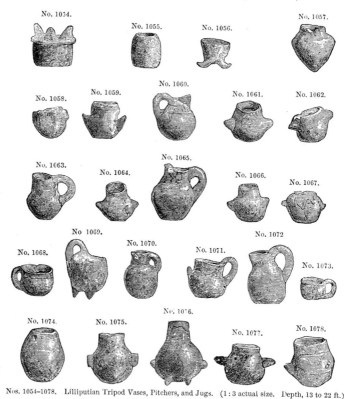

No. 1054.   No. 1055.   No. 1056.   No. 1057.

No. 1058.   No. 1059.   No. 1060.   No. 1061.   No. 1062.

No. 1063.   No. 1064.   No. 1065.   No. 1066.   No. 1067.

No. 1068.   No 1069.   No. 1070.   No. 1071.   No. 1072   No. 1073.

No. 1074.   No. 1075.   No. 1076.   No. 1077.   No. 1078.

Nos. 1054-1078. Lilliputian Tripod Vases, Pitchers, and Jugs. (1 : 3 actual size. Depth, 13 to 22 ft.)

with two parallel horizontal lines, between which the space is filled with strokes. Nos. 1068 and 1073 are small one-handled cups. No. 1069 is a small, very rude tripod-pitcher. The little pitcher No. 1071 has an upright handle which joins the rim to the body, and a horizontal one on the body. No. 1074 is a rude vessel with two holes for suspension in the rim ; No. 1077, a rude little vessel with two straight projections ; No. 1078, a rude pitcher, with the handle broken off. Lilliputian vases, jugs, cups, and pitchers like these (Nos. 1054-1078) are very abundant

---

[5] L. Lindenschmit, *Die Vaterländischen Alterthümer*, Pl. xxvi. No. 5.

in this fourth and in the fifth pre-historic cities at Hissarlik, and appear to have been used as toys for children. They are rare in the third, the burnt city, and, when they occur there, they are of a better fabric, or at least they are of a much neater appearance, which is no doubt due to the intense heat they have been exposed to in the great conflagration.

No. 1079 is a one-handled lustrous-red pitcher, of a form which occurs very abundantly in this fourth as well as in the burnt city. The same

No. 1080. Cup in the shape of an hour-glass. (1 : 3 actual size. Depth, 19 ft.)

No. 1079. Pitcher with one handle. (1 : 4 actual size. Depth, 22 ft.)

shape rarely occurs in the fifth city, and is there generally of a ruder fabric. No. 1080 is a very pretty wheel-made black double-handled goblet (δέπας

No. 1081. Two-handled Goblet (δέπας ἀμφικύπελλον). (1 : 4 actual size. Depth, 22 ft.)

No. 1082. Goblet with two handles (δέπας ἀμφικύπελλον). (1 : 4 actual size. Depth, 22 ft.)

ἀμφικύπελλον), in form like an hour-glass, decorated with four incised lines round the middle. This form of goblet occurs solely in the fourth and fifth cities; it never occurs in the third, second, or first cities. It is perhaps the prettiest of all the different sorts of δέπα ἀμφικύπελλα. It deserves attention that in the fourth city this sort of goblet is of a black, in the following city generally of a red, colour; it is always wheel-made. Nos. 1081 and 1082 are two more of the common red δέπα ἀμφικύπελλα, which I have discussed before. Goblets of this shape are found here in great abundance. They also frequently occur in the following, the fifth city, but they are there generally of a much smaller size. Many of these long goblets are hand-made, but there are also a vast number of wheel-made ones; and I think I am near the mark if I express the opinion that one-half of the whole number are wheel-made. The remarkable red double-handled goblet (δέπας ἀμφικύπελλον), No. 1083, is hand-made; its shape reminds us of the form of the small white bread (*Semmel*) used in Mecklenburg-Schwerin: this shape of goblet occurs only once. No. 1084 is a pretty hand-made, double-handled lus-

No. 1083. Curious large two-handled Goblet (δέπας ἀμφικύπελλον). (1:4 actual size. Depth, 13 to 20 ft.)

No. 1084. Double-handled Goblet, ornamented with points. (Nearly 1:3 actual size. Depth, 16 ft.)

No. 1085. Cup with two handles. (1:3 actual size. Depth, 19 ft.)

No. 1086. Cup with two handles. (1:3 actual size. Depth, 16 ft.)

No. 1087. Jug with two handles. (1:4 actual size. Depth, 22 ft.)

trous-red goblet, with 6 indented spots on either side: this same shape, but without spots, is not rare. No. 1085 is a rude red hand-made cup, of a similar shape; No. 1086, a frequently-occurring pretty hand-made one, of a lustrous dark-brown colour. No. 1087 is a red wheel-made vase with two handles; No. 1088, a similar, but unpolished, very rude hand-

No. 1088. Jug with two handles.
(1 : 4 actual size. Depth, 22 ft.)

No. 1089. Jug with two handles.
(1 : 4 actual size. Depth, 13 ft.)

made one, of a thick clay. Another rude unpolished hand-made one is No. 1089; and Nos. 1090 and 1091 are two larger lustrous-red hand-made

No. 1090. Vase with two handles.
(1 : 4 actual size. Depth, 16 ft.)

No. 1091. Jug with two handles.
(1 : 4 actual size. Depth, 22 ft.)

vases of a similar shape. No. 1092 is a dull black hand-made one, having an incised linear ornamentation. To the same kind of jugs belongs also the hand-made one, No. 1093, on which I have put a cover with a handle running out into three spirals.

All these shapes of vessel, from No. 1088 to No. 1093, are frequent in the fourth and third cities; but more frequent than any other form is the two-handled cup, No. 1094, which, as has been before said, only came into use in this fourth city, for it only twice occurred as a tripod in the third, the burnt city. These cups are so abundant that I collected more than

400 of them, yet I never found a single wheel-made one among them; all are hand-made, generally red, but very frequently also of a black colour.

No. 1092. Pitcher with two handles, and impressed
linear ornamentation.
(1 : 4 actual size. Depth, about 22 ft.)

No. 1094. Cup with two handles.
(Half actual size. Depth, about 19 ft.)

No. 1093. Jug with two handles, and Cover
in the form of a crown.
(1 : 4 actual size. Depth, about 16 ft.)

On account of the abundance of these cups I believe them to have been used also as wine-cups. I am not aware that double-handled cups of an

No. 1095.   No. 1096.   No. 1097.

No. 1098.   No. 1099.   No. 1100.

Nos. 1095-1100. Six Cups, each with one handle. (Nearly 1 : 3 actual size. Depth, 13 to 22 ft.)

identical shape have ever been found elsewhere, except in Mycenae, where I found four of them in the royal tombs.[6] But just as frequent as these

---

[6] See my *Mycenae*, No. 349, p. 240.

are the single-handled lustrous red or black hand-made cups Nos. 1095–1100, and particularly the shapes of Nos. 1096 and 1099.   All these forms are also very frequent in the following, the fifth city, so that I have been able to collect more than 500 of them.   Frequent also, but far less abundant than the form No. 1094, are the large double-handled cups,

No. 1101.   Large Cup or Bowl, with two handles.   (1 : 4 actual size.   Depth, 16 ft.)

No. 1102.   Globular Cup or Bowl, with two handles.   (About 1 : 4 actual size.   Depth, 22 ft.)

No. 1103.   Globular Urn, with two handles.   (1 : 4 actual size.   Depth, 26 ft.)

Nos. 1101 and 1102, which are generally red, and are also always hand-made.   The red urn No. 1103, which has two handles, is also hand-made,

No. 1104. Tripod Pitcher, with two handles.
(1 : 4 actual size. Depth, 18 to 22 ft.)

No. 1105. Double-handled Tripod Pitcher. (About
1 : 4 actual size. Depth, about 22 ft.)

No. 1106. Tripod Cup, with two handles. (Nearly
1 : 3 actual size. Depth, 13 to 20 ft.)

No. 1107. Tripod Cup, with two handles.
(1 : 3 actual size. Depth, 18 to 22 ft.)

No. 1108. Terra-cotta Tripod Cup. (1 : 4 actual size.
Depth, 10 to 16 ft.)

No. 1109. Small Vase with two handles.
(1 : 4 actual size. Depth, about 14 ft.)

No. 1110. Curious Tripod drinking Vessel, consisting
of three cups issuing from a circular tube.
(1 : 4 actual size. Depth, 13 ft.)

No. 1111. Tripod Vessel, consisting of a circular tube
with four cups. (1 : 4 actual size. Depth, 20 ft.)

as are likewise the double-handled tripod-pitchers Nos. 1104 and 1105,
as well as the red double-handled tripod-cups, Nos. 1106, 1107, and 1108.
No. 1109 is a vase with two handles, of a shape which often occurs.

No. 1110 marks a very curious lustrous-brown tripod-goblet, consisting of a circular tube with three cups. This goblet could serve for three persons sitting round a table, each of whom could drink from a separate mouth of the goblet. A similar vessel is indicated by No. 1111; it also consists of a tube resting on three feet, and having four cups, one of which is larger than the rest. No. 1112 is a large rude urn with two handles, of a common shape. No. 1113 is a rare lustrous-brown double-handled bottle, with a rather flat body and a convex bottom; No. 1114, a globular two-handled red vase with a hollow foot; No. 1115, a flat double-

No. 1112.   Large Urn with two handles.   (1 : 6 actual size. Depth, 22 ft.)

No. 1115.

No. 1116.

Nos. 1115, 1116. Lentil-shaped Bottle and Jug, with two handles. (1 : 4 actual size. Depth, about 16 ft.)

No. 1113.   Lentil-shaped Bottle, with two handles. (1 : 4 actual size. Depth, 18 to 22 ft.)

No. 1117. Vase with two handles, and projecting ornament in the form of spectacles on either side. (1 : 4 actual size. Depth, 19 ft.)

No. 1114. Globular Vase, with two handles. (1 : 4 actual size. Depth, 18 to 22 ft.)

handled lustrous-red vessel in the form of a hunting-bottle, with a convex bottom : such bottles are not rare here. No. 1116 is a vessel with a convex bottom, and perforated projections on the sides for suspension. No. 1117 is a double-handled vase, decorated on either side with a projecting double spiral : vases with the same spiral decoration are frequent in the third and fourth cities. No. 1118 is a red double-handled vase of a common shape, with a convex bottom : the bell-shaped cover is of a dark-red colour ; it does not belong to this particular vase. No. 1119 is a large

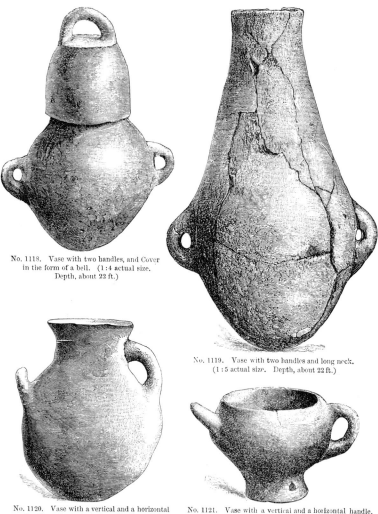

No. 1118. Vase with two handles, and Cover in the form of a bell. (1 : 4 actual size. Depth, about 22 ft.)

No. 1119. Vase with two handles and long neck. (1 : 5 actual size. Depth, about 22 ft.)

No. 1120. Vase with a vertical and a horizontal handle. (1 : 6 actual size. Depth, 19 ft.)

No. 1121. Vase with a vertical and a horizontal handle. (1 : 4 actual size. Depth, 16 ft.)

unpolished double-handled vase with a convex bottom : vases of this shape are common in this and in the preceding city. No. 1120 marks a large vase of a rude fabric, having one handle joining the neck to the body, and a smaller handle on the opposite side. The rude vessel, No. 1121, has its two handles in similar positions ; the foot is hollow, and has two perforations. Vessels like these are very rare. No. 1122 is a wheel-made black bottle ; its foot is convex, and almost pointed. The grey bottle, No. 1123, is also wheel-made ; its foot is hollow. No. 1124 is a wheel-made black bottle with a pointed foot : similar terra-cotta bottles are not rare here, but they do not occur in the subsequent city.

No. 1124. Terra-cotta
Bottle with convex
bottom. (About 1 : 4
actual size. Depth,
about 16 ft.)

No. 1123. Terra-cotta Bottle with
hollow foot. (1 : 4 actual size.
Depth, about 19 ft.)

No. 1122. Terra-cotta Bottle with pointed
foot. (1 : 4 actual size. Depth, 22 ft.)

No. 1125 is a lustrous-brown wheel-made globular vase, with four breast-like protuberances on the body; the bottom is flat. A vase very similar to this, found by Professor Virchow in his excavations in the graveyard of Zaborówo, is in his collection. The curious vessel, No. 1126,

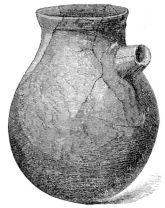

No. 1125. Globular Vase, with four breast-like projections. (About 1 : 4 actual size. Depth, 16 ft.)

No. 1126. Vase with spout. (About 1 : 4 actual size.
Depth, 16 ft.)

has a globular base, and a spout in the upper part of the body. It is wheel-made, but of a rude fabric. No second specimen of this shape was found.

The terra-cotta plates of this fourth city are of two sorts. They are either wheel-made, and in this case they are always shallow, very rude, often of irregular form, always unpolished, and perfectly similar in shape to those of the third, the burnt city, of which I have represented some under Nos. 455 to 468 (p. 408). Or they are hand-made, and in this case they are from 2 to $2\frac{1}{2}$ in. deep and nearly 8 in. in diameter, made with great symmetry, well polished, and of a lustrous dark-brown or red colour; nay, on account of their depth they might rather be called bowls than plates. They have generally no handle, but sometimes they have one, and even two. There also occur double-handled bowls, 18 in. in diameter, and from 7 to 8 in. deep. The wheel-made plates have always a flat bottom; the hand-made ones always a convex one. There also occur very rude wheel-made tripod plates, with sieve-like perforations. I represent here under No. 1127 a dark-brown hand-made plate or bowl of the usual form with one handle, and under No. 1128 a hand-made lustrous-red plate of a different shape, having a large cross painted with dark-red clay in its

Nos. 1127-1132.   Bowls, Tripods, Bottle, and Vase of Terra-cotta.   (1 : 4 actual size.   Depth, 13 to 19 ft.)

hollow: this cross was evidently painted there before the plate was baked. Similar deep dishes or bowls, but wheel-made, found in Cyprus, are in the British Museum. The bottle, No. 1129, is hand-made. The pretty tripod No. 1130 is wheel-made; the feet and the handle were added after the upper vessel had been fashioned; holes were made into which they were stuck, and in which they were consolidated with clay. In all vessels whose orifice was large enough to introduce the hand, the places where the feet or handles had been stuck in were smoothed, so that nothing appears of them on the inside of the vessels; but in the vessels with a narrow mouth the feet and handles were often left protruding on the inside.

No. 1131 is another hand-made lustrous-red double-handled tripod-

cup; No. 1132, a hand-made vase of the same colour, with two handles;
No. 1133, a brown wheel-made jug, of a globular form, with one handle.

No. 1133. Globular Jug. (About 1 : 4 actual
size. Depth, about 22 ft.)

No. 1134. Curious lustrous-black Jug, having a
bottom with eleven perforations.
(Half actual size. Depth, 16 ft.)

No. 1134 is a very massive lustrous-black jug, having a flat bottom with
eleven perforations. Though but slightly baked, it is very solid; it has

Nos. 1135, 1136. Large Vessels of lustrous-black Terra-cotta, with four handles.
(1 : 8 actual size. Depth, 14 to 20 ft.)

a trefoil orifice and a rope-like handle; it has round the neck an incised zigzag decoration, from which bands of a rude linear ornamentation extend downwards, right and left. All these incised ornaments seem to have been made with pointed flints; they are filled in with white chalk, in order to strike the eye. The peculiar sort of clay of this jug, its shape, fabric, and deeply-incised decoration, are widely different from all that we are accustomed to find here. I only found the very same clay and fabric in the vase-head Nos. 1002 and 1003, in the terra-cotta ball No. 1993, and in the vases Nos. 1135 and 1136. If the clay of which these five objects were made, and the potter who made them, had belonged to Troy, we should undoubtedly have found more specimens of such ware. I therefore feel bold to attribute to these objects a foreign origin.

The vases Nos. 1135 and 1136 are 2 ft. 2 in. high, wheel-made, very imperfectly baked, well polished, and of a lustrous-black colour. Very characteristic are the four thin handles and the very wide protruding border all round the orifice in both. The bottom is flat. Of this same form only three vases were found; it does not occur in any of the other cities.

No. 1137 is a rude hand-made one-handled yellow pitcher: No. 1138,

No. 1137.   Pitcher with one handle.   (1 : 4 actual size.   Depth, 19 ft.)

No. 1138.   Jug with one handle.
(1 : 6 actual size.   Depth, about 22 ft.)

a dark-brown hand-made jug or bottle, of irregular form, with one handle; its bottom is convex. All the following jugs (Nos. 1139 to 1147) are wheel-made, except No. 1144, which is hand-made. Nos. 1139 and 1140 are one-handled yellow globular jugs. No. 1141 is a lustrous-red jug, with a convex base and three handles, of which two are on the body and one joins the neck to the body. The pretty little vase, No. 1142, has four handles. No. 1143 represents a pear-shaped lustrous-yellow *oenochoë*, with a convex bottom and a trefoil orifice; it has a large handle joining the neck to the body, and two small ones on the body. The red hand-made vase, No. 1144, has a pointed foot and two handles; it has a spiral ornament on each side. No. 1145 is a pretty red pear-shaped vase, with three handles and a cover of crescent form, which reminds us of the vase-handles of crescent form found in the Italian terramare; No. 1146, a large dark-brown jug, with a convex bottom and three handles. This last vase, as well as the three foregoing ones, were found in the large house which

No. 1139. Globular Jug. (Nearly 1:3 actual
size. Depth, about 22 ft.)

No. 1141. Jug with three handles.
(Nearly 1:4 actual size. Depth, about 19 ft.)

No. 1140. Globular Jug.
(About 1:4 actual size.
Depth, about 16 ft.)

No. 1142. Vase with four handles.
(About 1:4 actual size.
Depth, about 16 ft.)

No. 1143. Globular *Oenochoë*
with three handles. (1:4 actual
size. Depth, about 13 ft.)

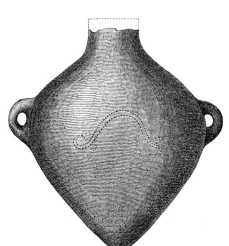

No. 1144. Large double-handled Vase, with pointed foot.
(1:4 actual size. Depth, about 20 ft.)

No. 1146. Vase with convex bottom and three handles.
(1:4 actual size. Depth, about 20 ft.)

No. 1145. Vase with three handles, and Cover with a handle of crescent form. (1 : 4 actual size. Depth, about 20 ft.)

No. 1147. Oval Vase, with four handles. (1 : 7 actual size. Depth, about 13 ft.)

was built on the top of the old royal house. No. 1147 represents, in 1-7th of its size, a large egg-shaped vase of a blackish colour, with four handles.

No. 1148 is a globular wheel-made lustrous-brown *oenochoë*, with a flat base and a long upright neck; it has three breast-like protuberances. The red globular *oenochoë*, No. 1149, is likewise wheel-made; the bottom is flat; the mouthpiece is restored. The grey *oenochoë*, No. 1150, with

No. 1148. Globular Jug, with long neck and breast-like projections. (About 1 : 4 actual size. Depth, about 20 ft.)

No. 1149. Globular Jug; mouthpiece restored. (About 1 : 4 actual size. Depth, about 22 ft.)

No. 1150. Jug with long neck. (About 1 : 4 actual size. Depth, about 15 ft.)

a long neck, is hand-made. The pretty red tripod *oenochoë*, No. 1151, is hand-made. The blackish *oenochoë*, No. 1152, is wheel-made. No. 1153, again, is hand-made. No. 1154 is a pretty hand-made pear-shaped red *oenochoë*, decorated with incised lines round the neck; the mouth has a trefoil shape, and so also has the mouth of the pretty red *oenochoë* No. 1157. No. 1155 is also hand-made; but the red *oenochoë*, No. 1156,

No. 1151. Tripod *Oenochoë*, with one handle and trefoil mouth. (1 : 4 actual size. Depth, 13 to 20 ft.)

No. 1152. Jug with a long neck. (About 1 : 4 actual size. Depth, about 19 ft.)

No. 1153. Jug with a long neck. (Nearly 1 : 3 actual size. Depth, about 19 ft.)

No. 1154. *Oenochoë* with straight neck. (Nearly 1 : 4 actual size. Depth, 18 to 22 ft.)

No. 1155. Oval Jug or *Oenochoë*. (Nearly 1 : 4 actual size. Depth, 19 to 22 ft.)

is wheel-made. The globular *oenochoë*, No. 1158, is wheel-made; it has a protuberance on the fore-part of the neck, and a small one on each side of it: these protuberances may have been intended to represent a face. All the following jugs or *oenochoae*, Nos. 1159–1169, are hand-made.

No. 1156.   *Oenochoë* with one
handle.   (1 : 4 actual size.
Depth, about 19 ft.)

No. 1158.   Globular *'Oenochoë*, with
a curious neck.   (About 1 : 4
actual size.   Depth, 16 ft.)

No. 1157.   *Oenochoë* with upright neck.
(About 1 : 4 actual size.
Depth, about 16 ft.)

No. 1159.   Jug.   (Nearly 1 : 3 actual size.
Depth, 16 ft.)

No. 1160.   Jug.   (About 1 : 4 actual size.
Depth, about 22 ft.)

No. 1163.   Jug of globular form, with one handle.
(1 : 4 actual size.   Depth, about 13 ft.)

No. 1164.   Jug with long perpendicular neck.
(1 : 4 actual size.   Depth, 19 ft.)

No. 1161. Globular *Oenochoë*, with straight neck.
(Nearly 1 : 4 actual size. Depth, 16 ft.)

No. 1162. Globular *Oenochoë*, with upright neck.
(About 1 : 4 actual size. Depth, 20 to 22 ft.)

No. 1159 is a pretty black jug, of a form which very frequently occurs. The forms of the jugs or *oenochoae*, Nos. 1161, 1162, and 1163, are also frequent, particularly the last.

No. 1165. Globular Jug, with a straight neck.
(Nearly 1 : 3 actual size. Depth, 19 ft.)

No. 1166. Jug with long neck. (1 : 4 actual size.
Depth, 18 to 22 ft.)

I have discussed in the preceding pages the different places where jugs with a narrow upright neck, like Nos. 1164 to 1168, occur elsewhere, and shall, therefore, not repeat what I have said. The black jug No. 1169, again, is wheel-made; it is decorated on the neck with three impressed lines. All the following jugs, from No. 1170 to No. 1178, are hand-made.

No. 1167. Globular Jug. (About 1:4 actual size. Depth, 18 to 22 ft.)   No. 1168. Globular Jug, with straight neck. (About 1:4 actual size. Depth, about 13 ft.)   No. 1169. Jug. (About 1:4 actual size. Depth, 13 ft.)

Very curious is the shape of the blackish jug No. 1170, with its neck bent backward and ornamented with a protuberance, its trefoil mouth, long

No. 1170. Jug of Terra-cotta, with spout in the body. (2:3 actual size. Depth, 16 ft.)   No. 1171. Remarkable lustrous-yellow Vessel, with a small orifice (No. 1172) and a sieve-like bottom (No. 1173). (About half actual size. Depth, 16 ft.)

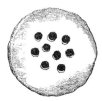

No. 1172. Half actual size.   No. 1173. Half actual size.

handle, and the spout in its body. But still more remarkable is the lustrous-yellow jug No. 1171, of which I represent under No. 1172 the very curious orifice, and under No. 1173 the flat sieve-like bottom. No. 1174 is a pear-shaped dark-red jug, with a hemispherical bottom and two distinct upright necks. A similar but globular dark-brown jug with a flat bottom is represented under No. 1175; it has also two distinct

No. 1174. Jug of oval form, with two distinct necks.
(Nearly 1 : 4 actual size. Depth, 18 to 22 ft.)

No. 1175. Globular Vase, with two separate necks.
(Nearly 1 : 4 actual size. Depth, 18 to 22 ft.)

upright necks, joined by a handle to the body. No. 1176 is a globular yellow jug, likewise with two upright spouts; but here the spouts stand one before the other, so that, when the liquid was being poured out, it could only run from the foremost (to the right in the engraving), and thus the hinder one was of no use. These two conjoined spouts seem, therefore, to have been only a fancy of the primitive potter, as we have seen in the case of No. 358, p. 384. This particular shape of double spout is unique; other shapes of double-spouted jugs are not rare here, but, as has been already said, they have never occurred elsewhere except in Hungary and in Cyprus.

Very curious and unique is the red vase No. 1177, which has, both to the right and left of its large mouth, a spout slightly bent forward; the cover which I have put on the large mouth may or may not have belonged to it: this vessel has on each side a breast-like protuberance, which cannot have been intended for a handle. No. 1178 represents a one-handled jug of very coarse grey clay, covered all over with protuberances, which may have been intended to imitate birds' feathers; on either side is an ear-like projection.

Under No. 1179 I represent one more of the common wheel-made pitchers which are so abundant here. No. 1180 is a small hand-made, one-handled basin; No. 1181, a hand-made red pitcher with a very small

No. 1176. Globular Vase, with two distinct necks.
(Nearly 1 : 4 actual size. Depth, about 19 ft.)

No. 1177. Vase with three mouths and two handles.
(About 1 : 4 actual size. Depth, 13 ft.)

No. 1179. Pitcher.   No. 1180. Bowl.
(1 : 4 actual size. Depth, 18 to 22 ft.)

No 1178. Jug of coarse grey clay, covered all over with
protuberances ; having one handle, and an ear-like projection on either side. (1 : 4 actual size. Depth, 20 to 22 ft.)

No. 1181. Pitcher.
(About 1 : 4 actual size.
Depth, 13 ft.)

No. 1182. Cup. (About
1 : 4 actual size.
Depth, 16 ft.)

handle. No. 1182 is a lustrous-red one-handled wheel-made cup : this
shape does not occur in the third, the burnt city, but it is very frequent
in the fourth as well as in the fifth pre-historic city of Troy.

No. 1183 is a one-handled red hand-made pitcher, with two breast-like
excrescences. No. 1184 is a one-handled wheel-made vessel of cylindrical
shape; it is of very thick unpolished clay and very rude fabric : like the
vessels of this shape found in the third city (see No. 347, p. 381), it is
particularly massive and heavy in its lower part. The deep impressions
made by a rope may be seen in the handle of a similar specimen which
lies before me as I write ; I, therefore, readily accept the suggestion of
Mr. A. S. Murray of the British Museum, that, as in Ancient Egypt,
vessels of this sort may have served as buckets for drawing water from
the wells.

No. 1183. Pitcher with one handle, and   No. 1184.   Vessel of   No. 1185.   Censer of Terra-cotta, of very
     two breast-like projections.   cylindrical shape.   rude fabric.
(About 1 : 4 actual size. Depth, 19 ft.)   (1 : 4 actual size. Depth, 22 ft.)   (1 : 4 actual size. Depth, 13 ft.)

The vessels Nos. 1185–1187 are also hand-made.   No. 1185 is a very
rude brown, unpolished, but massive censer, with a hollow foot decorated

No. 1186.   Globular Bowl, with one handle.
(1 : 4 actual size. Depth, 19 ft.)

with four lenticular perforations.   This shape of vessel is unique.   But
who knows whether the lustrous-black vessels of the first city, of which
only a vast number of feet have been found, had not a similar shape?   I
remind the reader that all those feet are hollow, and that, as in the censer
before us, they are decorated with large perforations.   Professor Virchow
informs me that censers of a similar shape are found in tombs in Lusatia
(Lausitz) and in the duchy of Posen, and calls my attention to a censer
of this kind found at Reichersdorf, between the little rivers Neisse and
Lubs.[7]   He has in his own collection some such censers, which he found
in the graveyard of Zaborówo, and many others, found elsewhere in

[7] See the *Sessional Report of the Berlin Society of Anthropology, Ethnology*, &c. of July 21, 1877,
p. 23, and Pl. xvii. No. 7.

Germany, are in the museums of Berlin. Under No. 1186 I represent a large single-handled red globular bowl, with a hollow foot; under No. 1187, a single-handled red globular cup, with a convex bottom.

No. 1189.   Vase with
incised ornamentation.
(1 : 4 actual size.
Depth, 16 ft.)

No. 1187.   Large Globular Cup.
(About 1 : 4 actual size.   Depth, 19 ft.)

No. 1188.   Vase of globular shape,
with two curved handles and two straight
ones in the form of wings.
(About 1 : 4 actual size.   Depth, 13 ft.)

Cups of this shape are very common in the fourth and also in the fifth cities. No. 1188 is a globular black vase, with a convex bottom and two curved handles of the usual shape; it is decorated, besides, with two wing-like upright projections and with dots all round. Similar vases, but of a light red colour, are not rare, but they are much more frequent in the preceding city. No. 1189 marks a small hand-made globular lustrous-black vase, with perforated projections on the sides for suspension; it is decorated on both sides with strokes.

No. 1190.   Bowl, perforated all over
in the form of a sieve.
(1 : 4 actual size.   Depth, 16 ft.)

No. 1192.   Jug with sieve-like
perforations. (1 : 4 actual size.
Depth, about 19 ft.)

No. 1191.   Vase with two handles, covered with
sieve-like perforations.
(About 1 : 4 actual size.   Depth, about 22 ft.)

No. 1190 is a sieve or colander of terra-cotta, in the shape of a bowl: like all the following sieve-like vessels, Nos. 1191 to 1196, it is of

coarse clay, unpolished and of rude fabric. Even if we could explain the use
of this sieve, we can hardly explain that of the sieve-like double-handled

No. 1193. Two-handled Globular Vase, the body of which is perforated all over.
(1 : 5 actual size. Depth, about 22 ft.)

vessel No. 1191, which has the shape of a wine-cup, or of the perforated
vase No. 1192, or of the large double-handled sieve-like perforated vases

No. 1195. Tripod, with mouth on the side,
and perforated all over. (About 1 : 4 actual
size. Depth, about 22 ft.)

No. 1194. Two-handled Vase, with sieve-like perforations.
(About 1 : 4 actual size. Depth, about 20 ft.)

No. 1196. Cup, perforated in the form of a sieve.
(1 : 4 actual size. Depth, 13 ft.)

Nos. 1193 and 1194. We experience a like difficulty in explaining the
use of the sieve-like tripod vessel, perforated all over, No. 1195, which

resembles a pitcher standing on one side, and of the perforated cup No. 1196. Of these different shapes of sieve-like vessels, those of Nos. 1193, 1194, and 1195 occur oftener than the others, but they are by no means very frequent.[8]

The British Museum contains a jug and a tripod of terra-cotta with similar sieve-like perforations, which were found in sepulchres at Ialysus in Rhodes. Another vase with sieve-like perforations may be seen in the Phoenician Collection in the Louvre, at Paris. Similar sieve-like perforated vases were also found at Szihalom in Hungary,[9] as well as in the Lake-dwellings in the Lake of Bienne; and Dr. V. Gross suggests that they may have served for draining out honey from the comb.[10] A like use is suggested by Professor W. Helbig for the vases of terra-cotta with perforated bottoms found in the Italian terramare.[11] The Royal Museum at Berlin contains a sieve-like bowl like No. 1190, as well as a one-handled jug, perforated all over like No. 1191. Professor Virchow suggests that they may have been used to preserve fruits; and probably he is right.

No. 1197. Crucible of Clay. (Nearly half actual size. Depth, 19 ft.)

No. 1197 is a crucible of but slightly-baked clay, which, as Mr. Giuliano says, was mixed with cow-dung to make the vessel stronger and better able to resist the fire. No. 1198 is another crucible. No. 1199 marks a smaller boat-like vessel, of a similar clay and fabric, which must also have been used in Trojan metallurgy.

Nos. 1200 and 1201 represent perforated cylinders of grey clay, which have evidently been only sun-dried, and never baked. Clay cylinders of this shape are frequent in the fourth city, but they are still much more abundant in the third, the burnt city, where, owing to the intense heat to which they have been exposed in

No. 1198.

No. 1199.

Nos. 1198, 1199. Crucibles of Clay. (Nearly half actual size. Depth, 13 to 19 ft.)

the conflagration, they always have a yellow colour. It deserves attention that these clay cylinders occur neither in the following, the fifth city, nor in the first or the second city, and that they are peculiar to the third and fourth. Those of the third, the burnt city have for the most part become

---

[8] A vessel like No. 1195 was found in the Third City: see No. 327, p. 373.

[9] See Nos. 23 and 36 in the glass case No. IX. in the National Museum of Buda-Pesth.

[10] V. Gross, *Résultats des Recherches dans les Lacs de la Suisse occidentale*, p. 23.

[11] Wolfgang Helbig, *Die Italiker in der Poebene*; Leipzig, 1879, p. 17.

so fragile by the conflagration that they easily dissolve in the rain. Those of the fourth city have not been exposed to the conflagration, and are for that reason much more compact and solid. Clay cylinders of the same shape

No. 1201.   Cylindrical Piece of Clay, with perforation.
(Half actual size. Depth, 19 ft.)

No. 1200.   Perforated Clay Cylinder.   (Half actual size.
Depth, 13 ft.)

and fabric are found in the Lake-dwellings in the Lake of Constance,[1] and, as Professor Virchow informs me, they are found in tombs in many regions of Germany. I also saw several specimens of them in the Museum of the Lacustrine Antiquities at Zürich, though I do not see them represented in Ferd. Keller's *Pfahlbauten* (7ter Bericht). The use of these cylinders is unknown to us. We cannot admit Lindenschmit's[2] opinion, that they served as weights for fishing-nets, as they are not baked, and would,

No. 1202.   Implement of Clay, with perforation.
(Half actual size. Depth, 19 ft.)

No. 1203.   Perforated Implement of Clay.
(Half actual size. Depth, 19 ft.)

consequently, dissolve in the water. Of precisely the same fabric are the nearly flat objects of sun-dried clay, like No. 1202, which are also very fre-

---

[1] L. Lindenschmit, *Die Vaterländischen Alterthümer*, Pl. xxx. No. 16.   [2] *Ibid.* p. 218.

quent, not only in the third, the burnt, and the fourth cities, but also in the fifth: they have a perforation near the smaller end; in a few cases they have a furrow all round the edge, or only on the edge of the smaller end. Similar objects of clay occur also in the uppermost or seventh city; but there they are thoroughly baked, and have a more symmetrical shape. An object of baked clay of an identical shape was found below the strata of pumice-stone and volcanic ashes in Thera (Santorin), and is in the collection of the French School at Athens. An object of clay, similar to No. 1202, found at Nimroud, is in the British Museum; several similar pieces are in the Museum of Saint Germain-en-Laye, and in the Royal Museum at Berlin. Lastly, I have to mention the quadrangular objects of the very same clay and fabric, like No. 1203, which are perforated through the smaller side. They are likewise very abundant in the third as well as in the fourth and fifth cities.

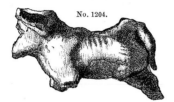

Nos. 1204, 1205.   Cows of Terra-cotta.   (3 : 4 actual size.   Depth, 16 ft.)

No. 1206.   Ox of Terra-cotta.   (3 : 4 actual size.   Nos. 1207, 1208.   Dogs of Terra-cotta.   (3 : 4 actual size.
Depth, 16 ft.)   Depth, 16 ft.)

Nos. 1204–1206 represent oxen or cows, Nos. 1207 and 1208 dogs, of slightly-baked clay. Such animal figures were found exclusively in this fourth city. A large number of similar figures, found at Szihalom, are in the National Museum at Buda-Pesth,[3] where similar ones found at Pilin may also be seen.[4] The Trojan cows before us correspond very well with those found by me in such abundance at Mycenae,[5] with the difference that the Mycenean cows are thoroughly baked, and have always a painted ornamentation. I may add that there is in the British Museum a cow of terra-cotta found in a tomb at Ialysus in Rhodes.

No. 1209 is a funnel-like object of terra-cotta of unknown use; it is of very thick clay, and has one perforation in the bottom and two on either side.

No. 1210 is a fragment of a six-stringed lyre of terra-cotta. No. 1211 is a ring of clay, but slightly baked; similar rings are abundant in the

---

[3] In the glass case No. X. under Nos. 85–100.
[4] See Joseph Hampel, *Antiquités préhistoriques de la Hongrie*, Pl. xiii. Nos. 10–15; and *Catalogue de l'Exposition préhistorique des Musées de Province*, pp. 118, 119.
[5] See my *Mycenae*, Plate A.

third and fourth cities. They were probably used to support vases with a convex or pointed bottom. Similar terra-cotta rings, found at Pilin, are in the National Museum at Buda-Pesth.[6]

Under Nos. 1212 and 1213 I represent two seals of terra-cotta; the former with a linear decoration. The ornamentation of No. 1213 seems to be floral: this latter seal has a perforated handle. Prof. Virchow

No. 1209.   Curious Object of Terra-cotta, having a perforation in the bottom and two on either side. (Actual size. Depth, 13 ft.)

No. 1210.   Fragment of a Lyre with six chords, of Terra-cotta. (7 : 8 actual size. Depth, 16 ft.)

suggests to me that No. 1212 may not be a seal, but the button of a vase-handle : as the lower part is fractured, this is possible, but it is certainly not the case with No. 1213, which is entire.

No. 1212.   No. 1213.

No. 1211. Ring of Terra-cotta. (2 : 5 actual size. Depth, 22 ft.)

Nos. 1212, 1213.   Seals of Terra-cotta. (7 : 8 actual size.   Depth, 10 to 16 ft.)

No. 1214. Small massive quadrangular Object, with incised ornamentation. (Nearly half actual size. Depth, 20 to 22 ft.)

No. 1216.

No. 1215.

No. 1217.

Nos. 1215–1217.   Curious cubical Object of black clay, having on one side a deep, wide, smooth hole, and an incised ornamentation on four sides. (Almost actual size. Depth, 13 ft.)

[6] Joseph Hampel, *Antiquités préhistoriques de la Hongrie*, Pl. xiii. No. 34.

A striking analogy to these Trojan seals is offered by the terra-cotta seals found at Pilin in Hungary,[7] on which the sign of the ⊔╆ or ⊓╆ predominates; in fact, there are no fewer than seven seals with such signs; one seal has even two ⊓╆ and two ⊔╆.

No. 1214 is a solid object of terra-cotta, with four feet, having on the top and on the four sides an incised linear ornamentation. Nos. 1215, 1216, and 1217 represent three sides of a very curious object of black slightly-baked clay, in the form of an inkstand; it is ornamented on one side (1215), within a border of incised hooks and strokes, and an incised circle, enclosing a sign resembling the ⊓╆, with curved arms, and the middle arms turned downward into spirals; the other sides are decorated with incised strokes or lines. No. 1218 is a pretty lustrous-red vase-cover

No. 1218. Terra-cotta Vase Cover, perforated for
tying down to the Vase.
(Half actual size. Depth, 10 ft.)

No. 1219. Small Tripod Dish, with an
incised ornamentation.
(Half actual size. Depth, 10 ft.)

of terra-cotta, with perforated projections for tying it down to the vase, which could then be hung up by the same string.[8] This cover has an incised ornamentation representing within a border of strokes a circle with a cross, each arm of which ends in a small circle: between the arms of the cross are three ⊓╆ and one ⊔╆. Professor Virchow calls my attention to the similarity which exists between this vase-cover and a vase-cover found near Guben in Lusatia.[9] This latter has also a richly incised decoration of concentric circles, crosses and dots, but it has not the two perforated projections of our vase-cover No. 1218.

No. 1219 is a little tripod-dish of terra-cotta, with an incised ornamentation representing a caterpillar, a tree, and a cross. No. 1220 represents the decoration of a whorl with three ⊔╆; No. 1221, the incised decoration of another whorl. Under Nos. 1222 to 1224 I represent three more whorls, calling very particular attention to the signs on Nos. 1222, 1223,

[7] Joseph Hampel, *Catalogue de l'Exposition préhistorique des Musées de Province*, pp. 120, 121.

[8] See the explanation of the method, verified from Homer (p. 221).

[9] See *Sessional Report of the Berlin Society of Anthropology, Ethnology*, &c., of July 21, 1877, Plate xvii. No. 5A.

No. 1220.

No. 1221.

Nos. 1220, 1221. Whorls of Terra-cotta. (Half actual size. Depth, 13 and 16 ft.)

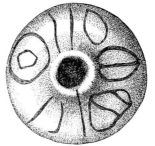

No. 1222. Whorl of Terra-cotta, with curious signs, perhaps written characters. (Actual size. Depth, 20 ft.)

No. 1223.

No. 1224.

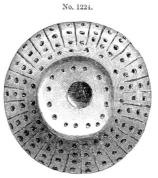

Nos. 1223, 1224. Whorls of Terra-cotta, with incised ornamentation. (Actual size. Depth, 20 ft.)

No. 1225.

No. 1226.

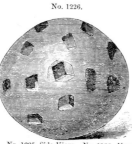

No. 1227.

Nos. 1225–1227. Terra-cotta Ball. No. 1225. Side View. No. 1226. Upper Hemisphere. No. 1227. Lower Hemisphere, with the signs. (Actual size. Depth, 13 ft.)

No. 1228.

No. 1229.

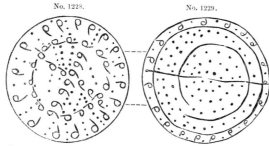

Nos. 1228, 1229. A remarkable Terra-cotta Ball. (Actual size. Depth, 20 ft.)

which may be written characters. Nos. 1225, 1226, and 1227 represent
the three sides of a ball of terra-cotta, with incised signs, which may be
written characters. Nos. 1228 and 1229 represent the incised decoration
of the two hemispheres of another terra-cotta ball, decorated with a great
number of signs resembling the Greek ρ.

Of knives, several were found of the same shape as before represented.
Of a different shape is the bronze knife No. 1230, which has been worn

No. 1230. Knife of Bronze. (Nearly half actual size. Depth, 16 ft.)

down by long use. Nos. 1231 to 1243 are brooches of bronze, of which
nine have globular heads and four have the head turned into a spiral.
These brooches, as Mr. John Evans points out to me, consist of the
needle (*acus*) without the support (*fibula*). No. 1244 is a bronze wire.
Nos. 1245–1247 are bronze arrow-heads. No. 1248 is of bronze, and probably the handle of a small box. Nos. 1249, 1250, and 1251 are bronze

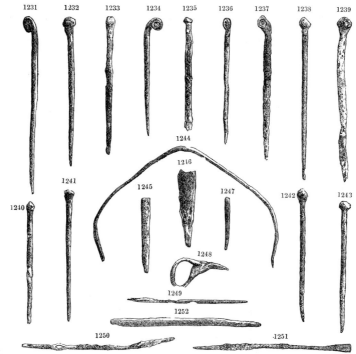

Nos. 1231–1252. Primitive Brooches, Arrow-heads, &c., of Bronze. (Nearly half actual size. Depth, 13 to 29 ft.)

needles, 3–3½ in. long, with eyes for threading. The needles Nos. 1249
and 1250 have two pointed ends. Very remarkable are the forms of the

last-named needle No. 1250, the eye of which is not in the head, but nearly an inch distant from it, and of No. 1251, the head of which has been beaten flat, and then perforated. The object under No. 1252 is of bronze, and may be an awl or punch.

Of bronze battle-axes of precisely the same shape as those found in the burnt city, and represented under Nos. 806–809, only five were found in the fourth city, but all of them a smaller size. Bronze lances or daggers were not found there.

No. 1253 is a wheel with four spokes of lead, and may be an *ex-voto*. But there can hardly be a doubt that this wheel was copied from the wheels existing at the time it was made. Wheels with four spokes were also in use at Mycenae, for they are seen in the three chariots represented on the tombstones of the royal sepulchres,[10] as well as in the chariot represented on one of the gold rings.[11] I also found at Mycenae two wheels of bronze [1] and six wheels of gold with four spokes.[2] In the Swiss Lake-dwellings at the station of Corcelettes were found two ornaments of bronze in the shape of a wheel with four spokes, and two others of gold with six spokes;[3] also an ornament of tin, and another of bronze, in the form of wheels with four spokes, at the station of Auvernier.[4] We see also wheels with four spokes on two miniature bronze chariots found at Burg in the bed of the river Spree, and of which one is in Professor Virchow's collection, the other in the Royal Museum at Berlin; and also on two other chariots of bronze, one of which was found at Ober-Kehle, the other near Drossen, in Prussia. I shall revert to these four chariots in the subsequent pages. The Trojan wheel before us (No. 1253) is unlike the wheels (κύκλα) of Homer's chariot of the gods, which had eight spokes round the axle.[5]

No. 1253.   Wheel of Lead.
(2:3 actual size. Depth, 16 ft.)

No. 1254 is the fragment of a flat disc of ivory, decorated with incised circles, each with a dot in the centre. Nos. 1255, 1256 are also flat

---

[10] See my *Mycenae*, p. 52, No. 24; p. 81, No. 140; p. 86, No. 141.

[11] *Ibid.* p. 223, No. 334.

[1] *Ibid.* p. 74, No. 120.

[2] *Ibid.* p. 203, No. 316.

[3] V. Gross, *Résultats des Recherches exécutées dans les Lacs de la Suisse occidentale;* Zürich, 1876, Pl. viii. Nos. 9, 16, 18, 19.

[4] V. Gross, *Deux Stations lacustres, Moeringen et Auvernier;* Neuveville, 1878, Pl. vii. Nos. 31, 61.

[5] *Il.* v. 722, 723:

Ἥβη δ' ἀμφ' ὀχέεσσι θοῶς βάλε καμπύλα κύκλα
χάλκεα ὀκτάκνημα, σιδηρέῳ ἄξονι ἀμφίς.

My friend Mr. W. S. W. Vaux calls my attention to the fact that the four-spoked chariot-wheel is characteristic of the earliest Greek coins. The early Egyptian, Ethiopian,

and Assyrian wheels have six spokes. The Persian Achaemenid sculptures show chariots with eight-spoked wheels. Professor Sayce observes: "The wheels of the Hittite chariots, however, are represented on the Egyptian monuments with only four spokes. The wheels of the Egyptian chariots also sometimes have only four, sometimes eight; and a Persian chariot-wheel given by Ker Porter has eleven." (See Wilkinson's *Ancient Egyptians*, i. pp. 223–241, new edit., 1879.) In two of the earliest representations of chariots in Egypt, in the same tomb at Thebes, of the time of Amenhotep II., two chariots have wheels with six spokes, but another chariot has wheels with four. (Villiers Stuart, *Nile Gleanings*, Pl. xxxviii. xxxix. pp. 294, 295.)

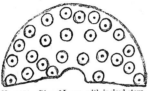

No. 1254.   Disc of Ivory, with incised stars.
(2 : 3 actual size.   Depth, 16 ft.)

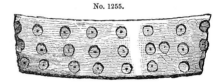

No. 1256.

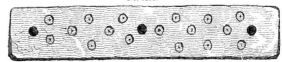

Nos. 1255, 1256.   Objects of Ivory, with incised stars, probably ornaments of a
horse's harness.   (Actual size.   Depth, 20 ft. and 13 ft.)

objects of ivory, ornamented on both sides with similar circles; the latter
has three perforations.   These three objects may have served as ornaments on horse-trappings.

No. 1257 is of bone and has three perforations.   Mr. John Evans holds
it to be a guard or bracer used by archers, to prevent the wrist from
being hurt by the bow-string; he adds that the Esquimaux use to the
present day similar guards or bracers of bone.   The guards or bracers
found in England are of stone, and have three perforations at each end.

Nos. 1258–1260 are ribs of animals sharpened to a point, and probably

No. 1258.   No. 1259.   No. 1260.

No. 1261.

No. 1262.

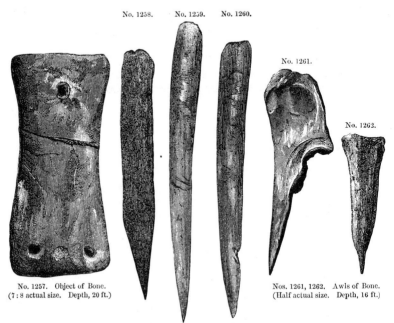

No. 1257.   Object of Bone.
(7 : 8 actual size.   Depth, 20 ft.)

Nos. 1261, 1262.   Awls of Bone.
(Half actual size.   Depth, 16 ft.)

Nos. 1258–1260.   Ribs of Animals, sharpened
to a point, and probably used as awls.
(Nearly half actual size.   Depth, 13 to 18 ft.)

used as awls. Nos. 1261 and 1262 are awls of thicker bone. Nos. 1263 and 1264 are very rude staff-handles of stag-horn; both of them having

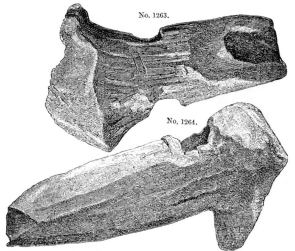

No. 1263.

No. 1264.

Nos. 1263, 1264. Staff-handles of Bone. (Nearly half actual size. Depth, 16 to 20 ft.)

quadrangular perforations. A similar staff-handle, of better fabric, found at Inzighofen,[6] is considered to be a small hammer. But this I cannot admit, stag-horn being ill-suited for hammers. Under No. 1265 I represent in double size a whetstone, which, according to Mr. Davies,

No. 1265. Whetstone of porphyry, with an inscription. (Double actual size. Depth, about 22 ft.)

is of red porphyry; it has an incised inscription, to which I call very particular attention. Professor Sayce discusses this object in his Appendix on the Trojan inscriptions.[7]

No. 1266 is a piece of mica-schist, with the bed for a very curious instrument, which is altogether unknown to me. No. 1267 is another mould of mica-schist, with the bed for casting a rude leaf. I represent under No. 1268 a third mould of mica-schist. The object to be cast in it seems to be a large ring with a handle: this mould has two perforations, by which it was fixed to another mould which had the same form. A perfectly similar mould of green basalt, found at Nimroud, is in the Assyrian Collection of the British Museum.

---

[6] L. Lindenschmit, *Die Vaterländ. Alterth.* Pl. xxv. No. 2.

[7] The characters are not quite correctly copied here. A facsimile will be found in the Appendix.

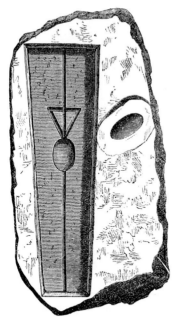

No. 1267. Mould of Mica-schist. (Half actual size.
Depth, 9 ft.)

No, 1266. Mould of Mica-schist. (Half actual
size. Depth, 16 ft.)

No. 1268.   Mould of Mica-schist. (Half actual
size. Depth, 13 to 16 ft.)

Nos. 1269 to 1272 are, according to Mr. Davies of the British
Museum, hammers and axes of porphyry, diorite, brown hæmatite, and
silicious rock.

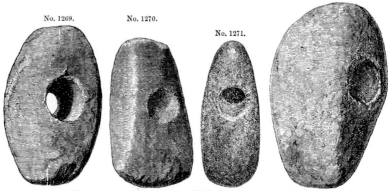

Nos. 1269–1272. Stone Hammers. (Half actual size. Depth, 13 to 22 ft.)

No. 1269 is a perforated hammer of a common type; the perforation
has been worked from both sides, narrowing towards the centre. No. 1270
is a hammer with grooves on both sides: similar grooved hammers occur
in England [8] and Denmark. [9]   No. 1271 is a perforated hammer of a form

---

[8] John Evans, *Ancient Stone Implements;* London, 1872, pp. 215, 217.
[9] J. J. A. Worsaae, *Nordiske Oldsager,* p. 12, No. 33.

which is also found in England.[1] No. 1272 is a perforated axe, of a form which has also been found in Hungary.[2] Nos. 1273 and 1274 are two

No. 1273. Stone Hammer, with groove in the middle. (Half actual size. Depth, 22 ft.)

No. 1274. Stone Hammer, with groove in the middle. (Half actual size. Depth, 19 ft.)

No. 1275. Axe of Stone. (Half actual size. Depth, 19 ft.)

more grooved hammers, of a shape which I have not noticed elsewhere. No. 1275 is a very rude axe of diorite. Nos. 1276–1281 are six axes,

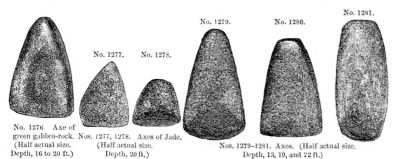

No. 1276. Axe of green gabbro-rock. (Half actual size. Depth, 16 to 20 ft.)

Nos. 1277, 1278. Axes of Jade. (Half actual size. Depth, 20 ft.)

No. 1277.   No. 1278.

No. 1279.   No. 1280.   No. 1281.

Nos. 1279–1281. Axes. (Half actual size. Depth, 13, 19, and 22 ft.)

of which, according to the investigations of Mr. Davies, Nos. 1277 and 1278 are of green jade. I have discussed the jade axes at length in the preceding pages.[3] Of the four other axes, according to Mr. Davies, one is of green gabbro-rock, two are of diorite, and one is of blue serpentinous rock. No. 1282 is, according to Mr. Davies, a pear-shaped object of polished crystalline limestone. No. 1283 is another of those round corn-bruisers which we have discussed before, and which are found here in very large masses. These round corn-bruisers are also found in the *débris*

---

[1] John Evans, *op. cit.* p. 203.

[2] Joseph Hampel, *Collection de l'Exposition préhistorique des Musées de Province ;* Buda-

Pesth, 1876, p. 67, Nos. 34, 38.

[3] See pp. 240–243 and 446–451.

of the Stone age in Egypt,[4] and in the pre-historic city below the strata of pumice-stone and volcanic ashes on the island of Thera.[5] With reference to the stone balls for bruising corn, I am informed that the process may still be seen among the Indians of the Yosemite Valley in California. Their squaws pound acorns with round stone mullers on a granite rock, the flat surface of which is worn into holes by the operation. The same Indians offer another parallel to my discoveries at Troy in the beautiful little arrow-points of obsidian, which they make and use for small game, though they have rifles for large game,—a remarkable

No. 1282. Pear-shaped Object of Stone. (Half actual size. Depth, 9 ft.)

No. 1283. Stone Ball for bruising grain. (Half actual size. Depth, 13 ft.)

No. 1284. Implement of Stone. (Half actual size. Depth, 18 to 22 ft.)

example of mixed states of civilization. No. 1284 is an instrument of hæmatite: as the upper side is well polished and perfectly smooth, it may have served, as Professor Virchow suggests, for smoothing cloth or other textures, while the other side may have been used as a hammer. This is one of the better specimens of the rude stone hammers, which occur by thousands at Hissarlik. No. 1285 is a hollow object of granite,

No. 1285. Hollow Instrument of granite, of globular form, with large perforation in the bottom. (1 : 5 actual size. Depth, about 13 ft.)

No. 1286. Stone Implement. (Half actual size. Depth, about 16 ft.)

No. 1287. Quadrangularly cut Lime-stone with a semi-globular hollow. (1 : 6 actual size. Depth, 22 ft.)

of globular form, with a large perforation in the bottom; its use is unknown. Of granite also, according to Mr. Davies, is the implement No. 1286, which has a deep groove all round it, and which may have

---

[4] Friedrich Mook, *Aegypten's Vormetallische Zeit ;* Würzburg, 1880, Pl. xii. Nos. 4–6.

[5] Some specimens of them are in the small collection in the French School at Athens.

served as a weight for fishing-nets. Similar stone implements are found in Denmark,[6] in Georgia, and in Rhode Island.[7] No. 1287 is a quadrangular piece of limestone, with a semi-globular hollow; its use is a mystery to us. Polishing stones of jasper are frequent.

There were also found in the fourth city many needles of bone for female handiwork, boar-tusks, spit-rests of mica-schist, whetstones of slate, porphyry, &c., of the usual form, hundreds of small silex saws, and some knives of obsidian. Stone whorls, which are so abundant at Mycenae, are but rarely found here : all those which occur are, according to Mr. Davies, of steatite. On the other hand, terra-cotta whorls, with or without incised ornamentation, are found by thousands; their forms hardly vary from those found in the third, the burnt city, and the same may generally be said of their incised ornamentation, of which a fair selection may be seen in the Plates at the end of the volume. The depth at which each whorl has been found is always marked in mètres; and, as a general rule, all the whorls which are marked as from 4 to 6 M., may with great probability be supposed to belong to the fourth city. But of course this can never be said with certainty, because a whorl belonging to the fifth city may by some accident be found in the *débris* of the fourth, or even of the third city. The only thing of which I can assure the reader with certainty is, that I have spared no care and pains to avoid mistakes. Regarding the whorls with patterns which are found of an identical shape in the third, the burnt, and in the fourth cities, I may say that, for example, the cross patterns Nos. 1817, 1818, 1820, &c., which are frequent in the third, abound also in the fourth city. I can only lay before the reader all the incised patterns of the whorls, leaving it to him to see or not to see in them symbolical signs. I shall remark on those only which, in my opinion, deserve very particular attention. Among these are No. 1838, on one side of which we see three burning altars and a large number of dots, on the other a 卐 and three such altars. On No. 1852, again, we see three 卍; on No. 1860, probably, written characters; on No. 1863, again, a 卐 and a 卍, and similar signs on Nos. 1865, 1866, 1871. More curious is the incised ornamentation of No. 1867, in which we recognize four hares with a dot below each of them; and still more so that of the whorls Nos. 1879 and 1880. On the former we see a number of 卐 and 卍, a burning altar, a zigzag line generally thought to be the sign of lightning, and three male animals with dots over the back. On No. 1880 we see on each side of the circle a singular sign, which is probably intended to represent a man; each of these figures is touched by the horns of a large quadruped. In marked contrast with these rudest of rude linear representations of man and animal is the very symmetrical ornamentation on many of the whorls; as, for example, that on No. 1895. I again call attention to the curious written character which we see on No. 1905 on the top of four 卍

[6] J. J. A. Worsaae, *Nordiske Oldsager*, p. 18, No. 88.

[7] Charles Rau, *The Archæological Collection of* the U.S. *National Museum;* Washington, 1876, p. 27, Nos. 107 and 108.

and one ⊔̸. It also occurs on Nos. 1912, 1936, and 1939. On No. 1911 we again see three ⊔̸, and as many burning altars. May the curious figure on the side of the whorl No. 1951, to the right, be perhaps meant to represent a cuttle-fish? From the experience we have gathered of the rude linear representations of men, we venture to propose to the reader to recognize also a human figure in the strange sign on No. 1954. We believe we see written characters on No. 1972, but they still await their decipherer. On No. 1990, again, we see three ⊔̸, alternately with three circles. Under No. 1991 we represent a curiously engraved ball with two ⊔̸, and on the side shown in the upper row to the right a strange figure, which tempts us to ask whether it is not also meant to be a cuttle-fish. The most curious of all the terra-cotta balls is no doubt No. 1993, which is divided by incised lines into eight equal fields, in three of which we again see the same very strange figure; we again ask the reader if we are permitted to recognize also in these three figures the primitive artist's representation of a cuttle-fish?

CHAPTER IX.

THE FIFTH PRE-HISTORIC CITY OF TROY.

ABOVE the stratum of ruins of the Fourth City there is a layer of *débris* about 6 ft. thick, evidently consisting of the remains of houses built of wood and clay. That the people of the Fourth City, of which we see innumerable house-walls, should suddenly have abandoned the architecture they were accustomed to, and have built their houses of wood or mud, or of both conjoined, seems incredible. Besides, the rude stone hammers, which are found in such enormous quantities in the fourth city, are no longer found in this stratum; nor do the stone axes, which are so very abundant there, occur again here. Instead of the hundreds of axes I gathered in the fourth city, I collected in all only two here; but one of these—the axe of white jade represented under No. 1288 – is, in the opinion of Mr. Story-Maskelyne, the most precious of all my thirteen Trojan jade axes, on account of its extreme rarity. I attribute it to this Fifth City, as it was found at a depth of only 6 ft. The saddle-querns of trachyte, which occurred in the fourth city by hundreds, were very rarely met with here. The forms of the terra-cotta whorls, too, are in innumerable instances different here. These objects are of a much inferior fabric, and become more elongated and pointed. Forms of whorls like Nos. 1801, 1802, and 1803, which were never found before, are here very plentiful.

No. 1288. A very rare Axe of white Jade. (Half actual size. Depth, 6 ft.)

Nos. 1289 and 1290 represent two whorls, the former of which is decorated with three linear quadrupeds in rude incised work. Two of them

No. 1289. A Whorl with three animals. (Actual size. Depth, 10 ft.)

No. 1290. A Whorl with curious signs. (Actual size. Depth, 10 ft.)

are no doubt intended to be stags with long horns; the third is perhaps a roe. In the decoration of the other whorl there is nothing intelligible.

We continue to find here the same patterns of pottery, hand-made or wheel-made, but they manifest a general decline. We also find here a large quantity of plain wheel-made pottery, which looks quite modern when compared with that of the preceding city. Moreover, the mode of life of the people to which this stratum belongs was entirely different from that of their predecessors : instead of throwing all their kitchen-remains on the floor of their rooms, they carried them away and shot them from the mound, since we but very rarely see in this stratum of *débris* the shells of oysters or mussels, which visitors may see in such really stupendous masses in the houses of the fourth city.

Now that a people should on a sudden have completely changed their mode of life, appears perhaps still more impossible than that they should on a sudden have changed their mode of architecture, or that they should on a sudden have thrown away their numberless stone implements and weapons, and have used in their stead implements and weapons of bronze. This series of facts seems to present as many proofs that the stratum of *débris*, which we are now to discuss, belongs to a new people, among whom, however, part at least of the old inhabitants

No. 1291. Vase with two breasts and two wing-like handles ; the Cover has an owl's face. (1 : 4 actual size. Depth, 13 ft.)

continued to live. We shall, therefore, call this settlement the Fifth Pre-historic City of Troy. Whether the old settlement was conquered, or peacefully taken possession of by the new settlers, must for ever remain uncertain. At all events, there are no traces of a catastrophe ; besides, as we have seen in the preceding pages, the inhabitants of the fourth city can only have had partial works of defence ; they had no regular city walls, like their predecessors.

It is difficult to say whether the inhabitants of the fifth city had walls. I certainly brought to light small works of defence in several places, but these may equally well have belonged to the sixth as to the fifth city. It may be that the fifth city had regular walls, but that these were destroyed by the next settlers, or even by the builders of the later Aeolic Ilium.

In describing those of the objects found which deserve particular attention, I begin again with the owl-headed vases, which in all probability must

have had a sacred character. *All of them, without exception, are wheel-made, of a rude fabric, and unpolished.*[1]   One which I represent under No. 1291
has only two female breasts
and two upright projections.
The very conspicuous owl's
face is modelled on the cover,
which has a crest-like handle.
May not these strange vase-
covers have been copied from
the ancient helmets? Of much
inferior fabric is the vase
No. 1292, on which the owl's
face has been rudely modelled ;
in fact, the inability of the
primitive potter was such that
he made the beak above the
eyes. On this vase, besides
the breasts, the vulva is indicated : to this vase belongs a
flat cover with a crest-like
handle, like that I have put
on it.

No. 1292.   Vase with an owl's head, the characteristics of a
woman, and two wing-like handles.
(1 : 4 actual size. Depth, 6 ft.)

The owl-features and the
characteristics of a woman have been much more symmetrically modelled
on the vase No. 1293, to which also belongs a flat cover such as the reader

No. 1293. Vase with an owl's head and the characteristics of a woman   (1 : 4 actual size.
Depth, 10 ft.)

No. 1294.   Vase with the characteristics of a
woman and Cover with an owl's head.
(1 : 3 actual size. Depth, 6 to 9 ft.)

---

[1] Only the owl-vases are altogether unpolished in this city. Of all the other pottery the greater
part is polished.

sees on it. No. 1294 is again a vase with the characteristics of a woman ;
to it belongs a cover with an owl's face, like the one I have put on it :
the wing-like upright projections are here merely indicated. The face
we see on the vase-cover No. 1295 resembles a human face. Very characteristic owl-heads are seen again on the vase-covers Nos. 1296, 1297,

No. 1296.

No. 1297.

No. 1295. Vase-
cover. (About 1 : 6
actual size. Depth,
10 ft.)

Nos. 1296, 1297. Vase-covers with owl-heads.
(About 1 : 4 actual size. Depth, 6¼ to 10 ft.)

No. 1298. Owl-headed Vase-cover.
(About 1 : 4 actual size.
Depth, about 10 ft.)

and 1298. No. 1299 marks another vase with the characteristics of a
woman, to which has belonged a cover like that which we see on No. 1294.
No. 1300 is a very rude terra-cotta idol, on which the owl's beak is
indicated by two scratches, and the eyes by two dots ; the hands, which
are broken off, appear to have projected. No. 1301 represents one more

No. 1299.   Terra-cotta Vase with
the characteristics of a woman.
(1 : 4 actual size. Depth, 6½ ft.)

No. 1300. Idol of Terra-cotta,
with owl's head. (Half actual
size. Depth, 6⅓ ft.)

No. 1301. Marble Idol, with owl's head
and girdle. (Nearly actual size.
Depth, about 8 ft.)

No. 1301A. Marble Idol,
with owl's head and girdle.
(2 : 3 actual size. Depth,
6 to 10 ft.)

No. 1302. Two-handled Cup (δέπας
ἀμφικύπελλον). (1 : 4 actual size.
Depth, about 6¼ ft.)

No. 1303. Sieve-like perforated Terra-
cotta Funnel. (About 1 : 3 actual size.
Depth, 6¼ ft.)

of the common idols of marble on which an owl's head is rudely scratched. On the waist the girdle is indicated by four parallel incised lines. A further very characteristic specimen of an owl-faced marble idol is represented under No. 1301A. Similar owl-faced marble idols are even more plentiful in this fifth city than in any of the preceding cities. No. 1302 is a δέπας ἀμφικύπελλον, belonging to this fifth city. Like all similar goblets found in this stratum, it is but of very small size when compared with the large goblets of the preceding cities. No. 1303 is a large sieve-like perforated funnel, which is represented here head downwards.

No. 1305. Double-handled Goblet.
(Nearly 1 : 3 actual size. Depth, 6 ft.)

No. 1304.   Vase with two handles, two breasts, and incised ornamentation. (About 1 : 4 actual size. Depth, 13 ft.)

No. 1306. Large Jug with straight neck. (1 : 6 actual size.
Depth, 9 ft.)

No. 1307. Jug with long neck.
(Nearly 1 : 3 actual size. Depth, 9 ft.)

No. 1304 is a very rude hand-made double-handled grey vase, having on either side two breast-like excrescences ; its neck is decorated with four rudely-incised lines and signs without signification. The double-handled lustrous-red goblet, No. 1305, is hand-made and well polished ; its type but rarely occurs in this stratum.

No. 1306 is a wheel-made globular lustrous-yellow jug, with an upright spout and trefoil orifice, such as we have already passed in review ; the bottom is convex. Wheel-made also is the dark-red jug No. 1307, with an upright spout of a peculiar shape, such as we have never seen before. A spout of an identical shape is seen on the wheel-made tripod-jug No. 1308. No. 1309 is a grey hand-made jug of a very

No. 1309.   Jug.   (About 1 : 4 actual size.
Depth, 10 ft.)

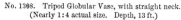

No. 1308.   Tripod Globular Vase, with straight neck.
(Nearly 1 : 4 actual size. Depth, 13 ft.)

rude fabric, with a convex bottom ; No. 1310, a wheel-made black tripod-jug, with a trefoil mouth. No. 1311 is a very large wheel-made globular well-polished lustrous-yellow jug, with a trefoil mouth ; No. 1312, a red wheel-made bottle ; No. 1313, a hand-made jug, with a long spout and one handle ; No. 1314, a wheel-made black bottle, with a convex bottom ; No. 1315, a wheel-made red globular vase, with a long cylindrical neck and convex bottom.

Very frequent in this fifth city is the shape of the one-handled lustrous-red pitcher No. 1316, as well as that of No. 1317, both of which may probably have been used as drinking cups. Cups already shown under Nos. 1094 to 1100 are very abundant in this city also. No. 1318 is a brown hand-made basin, with one handle ; No. 1319, a rude hand-made

No. 1310.   Tripod Jug.   (About 1 : 4 actual size.
Depth, 9 ft.)

No. 1311.   Globular lustrous-yellow Vase.
(1 : 8 actual size.   Depth, 13 ft.)

No. 1312.   Jug or Bottle with long neck.   (1 : 4 actual
size.   Depth, 9 ft.)

No. 1313.   Jug.   (About 1 : 4 actual size.
Depth, 6 ft.)

No. 1314.   Globular Bottle.
(About 1 : 4 actual size.
Depth, 9 ft.)

No. 1315.   Globular Vase,
with a long vertical neck.
(1 : 4 actual size.   Depth, 9 ft.)

No. 1316.   No. 1317.

Nos. 1316, 1317.   Pitcher in the form of an
hour-glass and a common Pitcher.   (Nearly
1 : 3 actual size.   Depth, 9 ft.)

No. 1318.   Cup with one handle.   (1 : 4 actual size.
Depth, 6 ft.)

No. 1319.   Ladle of Clay.   (Nearly half actual size.
Depth, 9 ft.)

No. 1321.   Rude Censer.   (1 : 4 actual size.
Depth, 13 ft.)

No. 1320.   Vase with incised ornamentation.   (1 : 4
actual size.   Depth, 6 ft.)

ladle; No. 1320, a pretty little lustrous-black wheel-made vase, with an incised zigzag ornamentation round the neck; No. 1321, a very rude un-polished censer. No. 1322 is a large wheel-made globular yellow vase, with double upright curved handles. The fabric and form of this vase, as well as the clean though very common clay of which it is made, appear very modern when com-pared with any of the other vases found in this last pre-historic city, or in any of the preceding ones. The cover is also wheel-made, of a lustrous dark-red colour, and has a pretty handle in the form of a crown; it is decorated with two parallel incised lines. This par-ticular sort of vase-cover does not occur any more, but vases of the shape of that before us are frequent in this fifth city.

No. 1322.   Globular Vase, with two handles and Cover in form
of a crown.   (About 1 : 4 actual size.   Depth, 9 ft.)

No. 1323 is a wheel-made one-handled jug, of an oval form, with a flat bottom; it is of a rude fabric, and badly polished; the rim of the orifice is bent over. Jugs of this form are not rare.

No. 1323.   Jug with one handle.
(1 : 4 actual size.   Depth, 9 ft.)

No. 1324.   Globular Jug, with a projection on the
neck.   (About 1 : 4 actual size.   Depth, 6 ft.)

No. 1324 is a wheel-made one-handled grey jug, of a globular form, with a flat bottom; it has a trefoil mouth and a curious boss on the neck. No. 1325 is a red one-handled hand-made cup, with an ear-like protuberance on either side: cups of a similar shape are not rare. No. 1326 is a grey hand-made vase, with a flat bottom and tubular holes for suspension on the sides, as well as near the mouth.

No. 1325.   Globular Vase, with projecting ornament on
either side in the form of a horse-shoe.   (1 : 4 actual
size.   Depth, 9 ft.)

No. 1326.   Vase with tubular holes for
suspension.   (About 1 : 4 actual
size.   Depth, 13 ft.)

The pottery shown under Nos. 1327 to 1330 is all hand-made and of a rude fabric: the shapes of the jug No. 1327, and of the pitcher No. 1328,

No. 1327.

No. 1328.

No. 1329.

No. 1330.

Nos. 1327–1330.   Three Pitchers and a Baby's Feeding Bottle.   (1 : 4 actual size.   Depth, 6 to 10 ft.)

are frequent. Very remarkable and unique is the cup No. 1330, with its handle above the mouth and the spout in the body; it is probably a baby's feeding bottle. The black double cup, No. 1331, with flat bottoms, is also wheel-made, as well as the double cup No. 1332, which has four feet.

No. 1331.   Terra-cotta Vessel, composed of two separate cups. (1 : 4 actual size. Depth, 6 ft.)

No. 1332.   Terra-cotta Vessel, with four feet, forming two Vases. (1 : 4 actual size. Depth, 6 ft.)

Both of these vessels are partly restored with gypsum. No. 1333 is a hand-made bowl of a dark-brown colour : similar bowls frequently occur here. It deserves peculiar attention that there are *no* wheel-made dishes in this city. One might suppose that the people had become disgusted with the rude unpolished dishes of the two preceding cities, and preferred to use hand-made ones, which are much more solid and prettier.

Nos. 1334 to 1336 are three very small, rude, very slightly-baked clay cups, with convex bottoms and flat covers. These lilliputian vessels

No. 1334.   No. 1335.   No. 1336.

No. 1333.   Dark-brown Bowl.   (1 : 4 actual size. Depth, 10 ft.)

Nos. 1334–1336.   Small Terra-cotta Cups, with flat covers. (Nearly half actual size. Depth, 6 ft.)

only occur in this fifth pre-historic city, but they are found here in large numbers, sometimes by the dozen together : their use is an enigma to us. Professor Roberts thinks they may possibly have been crucibles. No. 1337 is a seal of terra-cotta, with a perforated handle for suspension ; it is badly baked and of a rude fabric, with a rudely-incised linear decoration and four dots. Nos. 1338 and 1339 are two funnels of slightly-

No. 1339.

No. 1338.

No. 1337.   Terra-cotta Seal.   (About half actual size. Depth, 3 ft.)

Nos. 1338, 1339.   Two little Funnels of Terra-cotta. (About half actual size. Depth, 10 ft.)

baked clay, of a lustrous-brown colour. On both of them we again see the
written character *mo*, which so frequently occurs in the preceding cities.
As Prof. Sayce shows in his Appendix, these funnels are almost identical in
shape, material, and character with a funnel found by Mr. George Smith
under the floor of the palace of Assur-bani-pal or Sardanapalus at Kouyunjik, and inscribed with Trojan characters, which was probably brought
to Nineveh by the Lydian ambassadors of Gyges. They seem to have
been used as measuring vessels, and the word *mo* with which they are
inscribed may be derived from the Aryan root *mâ*, "to measure."
No. 1340 is another terra-cotta seal, better baked, but decorated merely
with small concentric circles.[2]

No. 1341 is a perforated object of stone of unknown
use. No. 1342 is a large saw of silex, with marks on
its upper part of its having been cased in a wooden
handle. To the many localities enumerated in the
preceding pages where similar flint saws are found,
I can now also add Egypt; for in Fr. Mook's *Aegyptens
Vormetallische Zeit*[3] I find a great many silex saws

No. 1340. Seal of Terra-cotta.   No. 1341. Object of Stone.
(7 : 8 actual size. Depth, 6 to 10 ft.)

No. 1342. Silex Saw.
(Half actual size.
Depth, 6 ft.)

represented, also one (Pl. xiii. 8) made of jasper found at Helwan in
Lower Egypt, which is nearly of an identical shape with the saw before
us (No. 1342). But I must add that in the fifth pre-historic city of Troy
I found only two saws of this shape and not one of any other shape,
though the silex saws occur in such vast abundance in the preceding
cities, and particularly so in the fourth.

No. 1343 is a curious well-shaped hammer of diorite; it has no hole.
This is the only specimen of a hammer found in the fifth city. I do not
find that hammers of a like shape have ever occurred elsewhere; but Prof.
Virchow observes to me that stone hammers of a somewhat similar shape
have been found in Oregon. No. 1344 is one of the very few stone
grain-bruisers of this fifth city. I do not think I found more than three

---

[2] In terminating with this seal my review of
the pottery of the five pre-historic cities of Troy,
I beg leave to say that, in spite of the most
scrupulous attention devoted by me to the subject, it may be that there are a few vessels belonging to the third city which have been classed
under the fourth, and again a few belonging to
the fourth which have been classed under the
fifth city, or *vice versâ*; indeed, this is almost
unavoidable, owing to the inequality of the level

of these last three cities. But if there be any
confusion, it can only be in a few instances.
There can be no mistake in the pottery of the
two lowest cities, the types being so vastly
different from each other, and also from the
pottery of all the following cities. The depth
was carefully noted on each object, either by
my overseers or myself, when it was found.

[3] Würzburg, 1880.

of them in all here, whilst, as has been said, they occur by thousands in the preceding cities, and particularly in the fourth. Besides the many places enumerated in the preceding pages in which they have been

No. 1345. A Stone
Implement of unknown

No. 1343. Hammer of
Diorite. (Half actual
size. Depth, 6 ft.)

No. 1344. Stone Ball for
bruising grain. (Half actual
size. Depth, 6 ft.)

use. Weight, 472 grammes.
(Half actual size. Depth,
6 to 8 ft.)

No. 1346. Object of Stone :
a Phallus? (Half actual
size. Depth, 9 ft.)

met with, they are found in Egypt.[4] No. 1345 is an instrument of silicious stone, which may have served as a weight for fishing-nets. Similar stone instruments are found in Denmark.[5] No. 1346 is of white marble, and from its shape we are led to think that it may be a symbol of Priapus. I have discussed this subject in the preceding pages. Similarly-shaped stones occur in all the five cities.

No. 1347 is a perforated disc or quoit of granite, the only one found in this fifth city, but similar discs occur in all the four other pre-historic

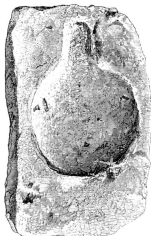

No. 1347. Stone Disc or Quoit. (Half actual size.
Depth, 9 ft.)

No. 1348. Mould of Limestone, in the shape
of a bottle. (Half actual size. Depth, 6 ft.)

cities of Hissarlik. The game of quoit-throwing was in general use in the Homeric age. The player who threw it farthest gained the prize;[6] hence

[4] F. Mook, *Aegyptens Vormetallische Zeit*,
Pl. xii. Nos. 4–6.

[5] J. J. A. Worsaae, *Nordiske Oldsager*, Pl. xviii.

No. 88.

[6] *Il.* ii. 774 :

δίσκοισιν τέρποντο καὶ αἰγανέῃσιν ἱέντες.

the word δίσκουρα, signifying the distance of a quoit's throw :—" For although at first he remained a quoit's throw behind, yet quickly he came up with him."[7] Also δίσκου οὖρα, to express the same thing.[8] The word δίσκος may be derived from δικεῖν, δείκ-νυμι, the Sanscrit diç, for δίκyos. The quoit was always round and smooth, usually of stone, but also of wood, and once in the *Iliad* of iron, and was then called σόλος,[9] connected with σάλος, σαλεύω, σαλαγή, Lat. *salum*, Germ. *schwellen*, English *swell* ; it was usually perforated in the centre, in order that, by means of the hole and a strap fixed in it, it might be thrown to the greatest possible distance, but sometimes it had no hole. Discs of silex also occur in the dolmens of the Stone period in Denmark as well as in Holstein.[10] Unperforated discs of stone, up to 9 in. in diameter, also occur in England.[1] There is a perforated disc of shelly limestone, 5½ in. in diameter and 3-4ths in. thick, in Mr. John Evans's collection.[2]

No. 1348 is a piece of limestone, of nearly quadrangular shape, with a mould in the form of a bottle. No. 1349 is a small disc of ivory, with a border on the side shown in the engraving.

No. 1349.   Disc of Ivory.   (7 : 8 actual
size.   Depth, 13 ft.)

No. 1350 is a brooch of bronze, with a double globular head ; No. 1351, a bronze brooch, with its head of a spiral form ; and No. 1352, a bronze needle with a long hole in the upper end. Nos. 1353 and 1355 are bronze brooches with globular heads. No. 1354 may be a primitive pair of pincers or tweezers ; it consists of two short rods of bronze cased in a hard substance. No. 1356 is a needle of bronze, with two pointed ends and a hole near the end to the right. No. 1357 is an object of silver, in the form of a dog's or rather antelope's head with long ears ; No. 1358, an object of bronze, which may have served for an ornament on horse-trappings. No. 1359 is a bronze ring. No. 1360 is a small curved knife of bronze. No. 1361 is an object of lead.

There were also found in the fifth city knives and battle-axes of bronze, of the usual Trojan form, which I do not represent here, as I have repeatedly brought similar ones before the reader's notice (see Nos. 806–

[7] *Il.* xxiii. 523, 524 :
. . . ἀτὰρ τὰ πρῶτα καὶ ἐς δίσκουρα λέλειπτο,
ἀλλά μιν αἶψα κίχανεν·
[8] *Il.* xxiii. 431 :
ὅσσα δὲ δίσκου οὖρα κατωμαδίοιο πέλονται, . . .
[9] *Il.* xxiii. 826, 827 :
αὐτὰρ Πηλείδης θῆκεν σόλον αὐτοχόωνον,
ὃν πρὶν μὲν ῥίπτασκε μέγα σθένος Ἠετίωνος·

[10] A. P. Madsen, *Antiquités préhistoriques du Danemarc*, Pl. xli. Nos. 1, 2. J. J. A. Worsaae, *Nordiske Oldsager*, Pl. xviii. No. 86.
[1] John Evans, *Ancient Stone Implements of Great Britain* ; London, 1872, p. 394.
[2] *Ibid.*

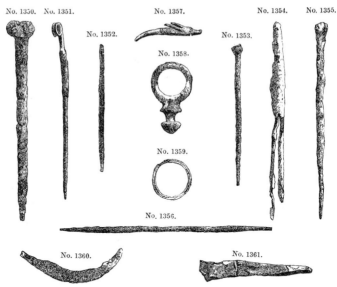

Nos. 1350–1361. Dog's Head of silver ; primitive Brooches ; Ring, Knife, &c., of bronze, and an object of lead.
(Half actual size.   Depth, 3 ft.)

809).   The only difference is, that the battle-axes found here are shorter than those found in the third, the burnt city, and they do not generally exceed 6 in. in length.   Needles of bone, like Nos. 566–574, occur here, but they are by no means so plentiful as in the former cities.

CHAPTER X.

THE SIXTH CITY, MOST PROBABLY A LYDIAN SETTLEMENT.

ABOVE the stratum of the Fifth pre-historic city, and just below the ruins of Novum Ilium, I found a vast quantity of very curious pottery, partly hand-made, partly wheel-made, which in shape and fabric, in colour and in the clay, is so utterly different from all the pottery of the preceding pre-historic cities, as well as from the pottery of the upper Aeolic Ilium, that I hesitate whether to refer it to pre-historic or to historic times. Such pottery is particularly plentiful on the slopes of the hill; and as, for reasons before explained, the stratum of the Greek city reaches in those places down to much more than the usual depth, it is found there even at 10 and 20 ft. below the surface. But the usual depth at which it is found on the hill is on an average 6 ft.; sometimes, however, it occurs at a depth of only 3 or 4 ft. below the surface. As neither the Greeks, nor the pre-historic peoples who succeeded each other on the hill of Hissarlik, ever made such pottery, and especially as this pottery occurs in such abundance, it evidently points to a settlement of a different people. But who were they? From the great resemblance this pottery has to the hand-made vases found in the cemeteries of Rovio, Volterra, Bismantova, Villanova, and other places in Italy, which is held to be either archaic Etruscan or præ-Etruscan pottery, we think it likely that there may have been a Lydian settlement on Hissarlik contemporary with the colonization of Etruria by the Lydians, asserted by Herodotus, and that the Lydian dominion may have been established over the whole Troad at the same epoch; and this the more as we have the certainty that the Troad was subject to the Lydian dominion under king Gyges (698–660),[1] and there is every probability that this dominion commenced at a much earlier period. We may remind the reader of the ancient legend, told by Herodotus, of the emigration of one-half of the whole population of Lydia to Umbria in Italy, under the leadership of Tyrsenus, son of their king Atys.[2] This mythical account seems to become an historical fact by my discovery, and I may, therefore, be permitted to call this sixth settlement on the hill of Hissarlik the Lydian City.

But all I am able to show of this city is its pottery: there is no wall of defence, nor even any house-walls which I could with any degree of

---

[1] Strabo, xiii. p. 590: Ἄβυδος δὲ Μιλησίων ἐστὶ κτίσμα ἐπιτρέψαντος Γύγου τοῦ Λυδῶν βασιλέως· ἦν γὰρ ἐπ᾽ ἐκείνῳ τὰ χωρία καὶ ἡ Τρῳὰς ἅπασα, ὀνομάζεται δὲ καὶ ἀκρωτήριόν τι πρὸς Δαρδάνῳ Γύγας.

[2] Herodotus, i. 94, quoted above, pp. 128, 129. As Professor Sayce observes to me : "According to Herodotus, the colonization took place in the mythical age of Lydia, before the rise of the Heraclid dynasty (circ. B.C. 1200)."

probability attribute to it.   On the contrary, it is very likely that the
Aeolian Greeks, who did not continue to use Hissarlik as the site of their
city, but as their Acropolis and as the sacred precinct of their sanctuaries,
levelled the ground and used the stones for the erection of their sacred
edifices.   That such a levelling really took place is, as we have before
repeatedly mentioned, proved with certainty by the site of the temple of
Athené, the builders of which cut away so much of the ground that they
were able to lay the foundation of this shrine immediately on the *débris*
of the third, the burnt city.   This is a fact of which every visitor may
easily convince himself with his own eyes.   Had the Aeolians been a pre-
historic people, they would have left *in situ* all the ruins they found, and
they would have levelled them by filling them up with *débris* or clay
cakes.   But they were a civilized people, and therefore they levelled the
ground by destroying the walls that they found standing, and by
throwing the *débris* from the slope of the hill.   That they proceeded in
this way seems to be proved by the fact, that most of the Lydian pottery
is found immediately outside of the *débris* of the preceding pre-historic
city, just below the Greek stratum, and in places where the declivity of
the hill must at that time have commenced.

I begin the description of the pottery with the large *pithos*
No. 1362, which I found embedded in a vertical position, the orifice being
6 ft. below the surface.   It is made of a coarse red clay, which, like that
of all the other *pithoi*, is mixed with crushed silicious stones and syenite
containing much mica, to give it greater solidity.   It is thoroughly baked,
which, as Prince Bismarck suggested to me,[3] could, in the absence of
kilns, only have been effected by filling and surrounding the *pithos* with
wood, and by kindling a fire simultaneously both inside and outside of
it.   It is unpolished, has no handles, and is ornamented all round with
four broad projecting bands.   It was lying in 1872 and 1873, for
fourteen months, before my house at Hissarlik, and was always used as
a lodging by one of my workmen; it even lodged two of them in rainy
weather.

Nearly all the smaller pottery is hand-made, and abundantly mixed with
crushed silicious stones and syenite containing much mica.   The vessels
are in general very bulky; and as they have been dipped in a wash of the
same clay and polished before being put to the fire, besides being but
very slightly baked, they have a dull black colour, which much resembles
the colour of the famous Albano hut-urns.[4]   (But there also occur a few
vases of a dull yellow or brown colour.)   This dull black colour is, however, perhaps as much due to the peculiar mode of baking as to the
peculiar sort of clay of which the pottery is made, because there occur
in all the five pre-historic cities of Hissarlik many vases but very slightly
baked, and yet none of them have the dull colour of these Lydian terra-
cottas.   Besides, the shape and fabric are totally different from those of
any pottery found in the pre-historic cities, or in the upper Aeolic Greek

---

[3] See p. 279.
[4] L. Pigorini and Sir John Lubbock, *Notes on
Hut-Urns and other Objects from Marino near*
Albano; London, 1869, pp. 2, 13.   See also the
Albano hut-urn in the Royal Museum at Berlin.

city. The reader will recognize this great difference in shape and fabric in the case of every object of pottery which I pass in review.

No. 1362. Pithos. (About 1 : 13 actual size.   Depth, 6 ft.)

I begin with the dull blackish tureen, No. 1363, which is wheel-made and has two handles. The large one-handled cup No. 1364 is also wheel-made and of the same colour; as is the very large vase No. 1365, with four handles, on two of which are small breast-like protuberances.

No. 1363.   Black Tureen, with two handles.   No. 1364.   Vase of globular shape, with one handle.
(1 : 6 actual size.   Depth, 6 ft.)   (1 : 4 actual size.   Depth, 6 ft.)

N o. 1365.   Large Vase, with four handles and impressed ornamentation.   (1 : 8 actual size.   Depth, 7 ft.)

No. 1366.   Jug with an impressed ornamentation.
(1 : 4 actual size.   Depth, 6 ft.)

This vessel is decorated all round with four parallel bands, each of three lines, of a wave-pattern, rudely incised before the baking took place. Of the same colour, and also wheel-made, is the jug No. 1366, with three such bands of incised wave-lines, and an orifice of trefoil form; as well as the two-handled globular vase, No. 1367.

No. 1368 marks a hand-made cup of the same colour and clay, with an incised ornamentation of zigzag lines, which seems to have been copied from the decorations of tapestry or embroidered vestures.

Cups of an identical shape were found in the excavations of Felsina at

No. 1367. Globular Vase, with two handles.
(1 : 4 actual size. Depth, 9 ft.)

No. 1368. Cup with incised ornamentation of
zigzag lines. (1 : 4 actual size. Depth, 6 ft.)

Bologna.[5] A cup of a similar shape, but without any decoration, found at Corneto in Italy, is in the Royal Museum at Berlin. Another very similar one, at least in shape, is in Prof. Virchow's collection at Berlin. There also occur among the Lydian pottery plain hand-made one-handled cups of the same dull blackish colour. A number of cups of an identical form have been found in the excavations at Villanova.[6]

No. 1369 is a large one-handled hand-made vase of a dull yellow colour, with three long rams' horns, which may perhaps explain the three or four

No. 1369. Large Vase, with three handles in the shape of rams' horns, and one common handle.
(1 : 8 actual size. Depth, 10 ft.)

excrescences which we nearly always see on the vases found in the ancient tombs of Bismantova,[7] as also on a vase in the Etruscan Museum in the

---

[5] Giovanni Gozzadini, di alcuni Sepolcri della Necropoli Felsinea, p. 6.

[6] La Necropoli di Villanova, per Giovanni Gozzadini ; Bologna, 1870, p. 33.

[7] Chierici, in the Bullettino di Paletnologia Italiana, 1875, Pl. ii. Nos. 3-5; 1876, Pl. viii. Nos. 1, 2, 4, 7, 8.

Vatican,[8] and on another from the station of Demorta in the district of Mantua.[9] At all events, the three long rams' horns on No. 1369 seem to explain the *three* horn-like or breast-like excrescences or bosses which we see on the heavy hand-made dull blackish pitchers Nos. 1370, 1371, 1372, 1374, 1375, and 1377. For the rest, vases with bosses or excrescences like horns or breasts are also frequent in Germany. Prof. Virchow found one such vase in the pre-historic graveyard of Zaborówo, and he calls my attention to two more represented under Figs. 9 and 10, Pl. xxv. in the *Sessional Report of the Berlin Society of Anthropology, Ethnology, &c.*, of Nov. 18, 1876.

No. 1370. Cup with three horns or breast-like projections. (1 : 4 actual size. Depth, 6 ft.)

No. 1371. Cup with three breast-like projections in the body. (1 : 4 actual size. Depth, 6 ft.)

No. 1372. One-handled Jug, with three projections in the form of female breasts. (1 : 4 actual size. Depth, 6 ft.)

No. 1373. Vase with three breast-like projections and zigzag ornamentation. (1 : 5 actual size. Depth, 7 ft.)

No. 1374.

No. 1375.

Nos. 1374, 1375. Cups with impressed linear ornamentation. (1 : 4 actual size. Depth, 6 ft.)

---

[8] L. Pigorini and Sir John Lubbock, *Notes on Hut-Urns*, &c., Pl. x. No. 10.

[9] Chierici, in the *Bullettino di Paletnologia Italiana*, 1877, Pl. v. No. 15.

I have succeeded in collecting about forty similar pitchers, with three horns or breast-like bosses; most of them have all round the body a decoration of vertical concave incisions or impressions, and many have each of the protuberances surrounded by three or four concentric circles of concave lines. The slight baking of these pitchers could not be better shown than by the variety of colours we often see on one and the same pitcher, for it is of a dull blackish colour where it is but very slightly baked, pale yellow in places where it has been a little more exposed to the fire, and reddish or brown where it has been long in a great heat. Apart from the three breast-like or horn-like excrescences, these pitchers have, in respect to shape, fabric, and ornamentation, a great resemblance to vases found in sepulchres at Rovio in Italy.[10] We see the three breast-like excrescences also on the large hand-made, heavy, dull blackish jug No. 1373, which has one handle and an incised decoration of zigzag lines, with a horizontal band of lines round the neck.

No. 1376. Two-handled Cup, with impressed linear ornamentation. (1 : 4 actual size. Depth, 6 ft.)

The heavy hand-made, double-handled cups Nos. 1376 and 1377 are likewise of a dull blackish colour, and seem to be in shape, clay, and ornamentation, the exact counterparts of two similar double-handled cups found at Volterra, and of many others found by Zannoni in his excavations at the necropolis of Felsina at Bologna.[11] A double-handled cup of an identical form, found at Corneto in Italy, is in the Royal Museum at Berlin.

No. 1378 marks a hand-made double-handled bowl of the same clay and colour. Nos. 1379, 1380, and 1381 are hand-made cups of the same

No. 1377. Double-handled cup, with breast-like excrescences. (About 1 : 4 actual size. Depth, 4 to 6 ft.)

No. 1378. Double-handled Bowl. (1 : 3 actual size. Depth, 4 to 6 ft.)

[10] Pompeo Castelfranco, in the *Bullettino di Paletnologia Italiana*, 1875, Pl. iii. Nos. 1, 2.

[11] Pompeo Castelfranco, *Ibid.* p. 61, Pl. iii. Nos. 3a, 3b.

clumsy heavy fabric and clay, with two very long handles. No. 1379 is
decorated on the body with incised vertical strokes, which here, as on

Nos. 1379, 1380.   Cups with two large handles.   (1 : 4 actual size.   Depth, 6 ft.)

many others of these vessels, are filled in with white chalk in order to
strike the eye. My honoured friend M. Alexandre Bertrand, director of
the Musée de Saint Germain-en-Laye, calls my attention to the fact that
the custom of filling the incised ornamentation on pottery with white
chalk was practised by the Gauls before the time of Julius Caesar's
campaigns.

Double-handled cups like these are frequent in this sixth city, and

they remained in use in Etruria for many
centuries. Similar cups can be seen in all
Etruscan collections. The shape of the hand-
made double-handled cups Nos. 1382 and
1383 may also be seen in nearly all collections of Etruscan pottery.

Nos. 1381–1390.   Terra-cotta vessels of different shapes.   (1 : 4 actual size.   Depth, 6 to 13 ft.)

Double-handled cups of this peculiar form do not occur in Greece, but they seem to have given to the Greeks the idea of their *kantharos* and *skyphos*, which are much more refined both in shape and fabric, but still have some resemblance to them.   These two cups are very frequent in Etruscan tombs of a later time.   Mr. George Dennis,[1] who figures two specimens of them, writes : " The most common cups in Etruria were the *kantharos* and the *skyphos*.   The *kantharos* was a two-handled cup sacred to Dionysos (Pliny, xxxiii. 53 ; Macrob. *Sat.* v. 21), in whose hands it is generally represented on painted vases.   The cup itself is rarely found decorated with paintings, at least in Etruria, where it is generally of plain black ware.   This vase is supposed to take its name from some resemblance in form to that of the beetle—κάνθαρος—but it more probably took it from the boat or vessel of the same name.[2]

No. 1384 is a large, heavy, one-handled cup or bowl.   No. 1385 is a vessel, probably a goblet, rudely shaped like a horse, or, still more probably, like a dog, as Professor Virchow suggests ; the spout, which is in the place of the tail, is joined by a handle to the neck.   This may be compared with No. 1391, the fragment of a vessel, probably a cup, in the form of an animal's head with two horns.   I thought it might be a horse's head ; but a horned horse being without example, Professor Virchow suggests that it may represent a young roe-buck or even a giraffe.   Professor Sayce remarks that this animal-head has a striking resemblance to the vases with animals' heads brought by Phoenician tributaries to the Egyptian kings of the Eighteenth Dynasty and de-

No. 1391.   Fragment of a Terra-cotta Vessel, in the shape of a horse's head.
(About half actual size.   Depth, 6 to 8 ft.)

picted on the monuments.   Goblets terminating in a horse's head were very frequent among the Etruscans, and Mr. G. Dennis[3] identifies them with the Greek goblet called *rhyton*, which, according to Theophrastus,[4] was given to heroes alone.   But the head before us has the peculiarity that it is perforated lengthwise, and has a spout in the mouth.   It can therefore only have served as the spout of a goblet, the shape of which is unknown ; perhaps it had another, wider opening, by which it could be easily filled, for it would have been difficult to fill it by the narrow spout in the head.   The Berlin Märkisches Museum contains two somewhat similar goblets in the shape of horns, one of which runs out in an

---

[1] *The Cities and Cemeteries of Etruria*, p. cxvii. Nos. 36, 37.   [2] Athenaeus, xi. 47, 48.
[3] *Op. cit.* p. cxxii. No. 60.   [4] *Ap.* Athenaeum, xi. 4.

animal's head.   Several vases with horses' heads are in the collection of antiquities from Chiusi in the British Museum.

No. 1386 is a small hand-made vase with three protuberances; No. 1387, a whorl with an incised ornamentation filled with white chalk. No. 1388 is a vase-bottom with an incised ornamentation.   No. 1389 is a hand-made *oenochoë* with a trefoil mouth.   The form of this vessel, but slightly changed, is also found in Etruria, in the trefoil-mouthed Lekythos.[5] No. 1390 is a hand-made vase, with a vertically perforated protuberance for suspension on each side.   All this pottery is of the same dull blackish clay as the preceding vessels.   Of the same clay is also the remarkable vessel No. 1392, which is in the shape of a bugle with three feet.   It has

one handle, and probably served as a goblet.   A similarly shaped vessel, found in a tomb at Camirus, in Rhodes, is in the British Museum. Of two similar vessels found in Cyprus, one is in the British Museum, the other is in the Louvre at Paris. From the form of these bugle-cups, which occur several times among the pottery of the Lydian settlement at Hissarlik, we may perhaps derive the Greek and Etruscan Aryballos,[6] which has the same shape, with the sole difference that it has no feet, and that the spout is in the side of the circular tube.

No. 1392.   Remarkable Terra-cotta Vessel, in the shape of a bugle with three feet.
(About 1 : 3 actual size.   Depth, 6 ft.)

The goblet No. 1393, which is represented upside down, belongs to this sixth, the Lydian city, as is proved by its clay, its colour, and its fabric.   Though only a couple of vessels of this form were found in

No. 1393.   Double-handled Cup (δέπας ἀμφικύπελλον), represented here upside down.
(2 : 5 actual size.   Depth, about 6 ft.)

No. 1394.   Oenochoë with one handle.
(1 : 4 actual size.   Depth, 9 ft.)

---

[5] George Dennis, *op. cit.* p. cxxiv. No. 66.   [6] *Ibid.* No. 70.

this city, they prove at least that it was in use there also. It is therefore highly probable that this form of goblet still existed at the time of Homer, and that it is to this very same sort of double-handled cup that he gives the name δέπας ἀμφικύπελλον. But if we compare this rude bulky cup with the fine goblets of the same shape from the third, the burnt city, we see that it has enormously degenerated.

No. 1394 is a pear-shaped one-handled *oenochoë*, with a conical excrescence on each side of the head. If we compare this jug or *oenochoë* with the Cypriote *oenochoae* or the jugs from the pre-historic cities on the island of Thera (Santorin), on most of which a human eye is painted on either side of the orifice, we become convinced that the conical excrescences on the jug before us (No. 1394) cannot mean anything else than rude representations of human eyes. No. 1395 is a pitcher with a spout in the body; perhaps a baby's feeding-bottle.

No. 1396. Pitcher with impressed ornamentation, filled with white chalk. It belongs to a vessel of which the other half is broken off.   (1 : 4 actual size. Depth, 6 ft.)

No. 1395.   Pitcher with spout in the body. (1 : 4 actual size. Depth, 9 ft.)

No. 1396 is a cup with a decoration of vertical concave incisions round the body, and a band of oblique incisions filled with white chalk round the neck: the base is convex. To the left, this vessel has a large broken projection, proving that, like so many cups and vases in the preceding pre-historic cities, it has been joined to another cup of exactly the same shape. A similar vessel, consisting of two cups joined together and decorated with linear incisions, is among the ancient pottery said to have been found below the stratum of peperino near Marino.[7]

In this Lydian city vases were still in use, with vertically perforated projections for suspension by strings, for, besides the vase No. 1390, I can also point to Nos. 1397 and 1398, which have similar perforations; both are decorated with rudely-incised zigzag lines.

No. 1397.   Vase with incised ornamentation, and two tubular holes for suspension. (1 : 4 actual size. Depth, 13 ft.)

No. 1398.   Vase with incised ornamentation. (1 : 4 actual size. Depth, 29 ft.)

[7] L. Pigorini and Sir John Lubbock, *Notes on Hut-Urns*, &c., Pl. x. No. 15.

Nos. 1399 to 1404 are rude two-horned serpent-heads of the slightly-baked dull blackish clay which is peculiar to this city. These horned

No. 1400.

No. 1401.

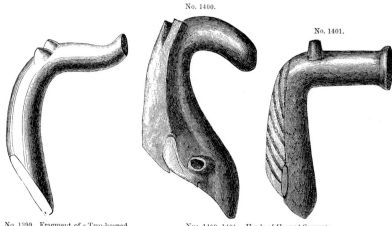

No. 1399. Fragment of a Two-horned
Serpent (κεράστης) in Terra-cotta.
(About half actual size.
Depth, 8 to 10 ft.)

Nos. 1400, 1401. Heads of Horned Serpents.
(No. 1400 may perhaps represent an elephant's trunk.)
(About half actual size. Depth, 12 ft.)

No. 1403.   No 1404.

No. 1402. A Serpent's Head, with horns on
both sides, and very large eyes.
(About 1 : 3 actual size. Depth, 18 ft.)

Nos. 1403, 1404. Head of an Asp in Terra-cotta
(both sides).
(About 1 : 3 actual size. Depth, 12 ft.)

snake-heads appear to be an ancient and significant Lydian symbol of great importance, since even now there is in the Troad a superstition that the horns of serpents, by merely coming into contact with the human body, cure a number of diseases, and especially epilepsy; also that, when they are dipped in milk, it is instantly turned into cheese; and other notions of the same sort. On account of the many wholesome and useful effects attributed to the horns of serpents, they are regarded as immensely valuable, and one of my workmen was once accused by a jealous comrade of having found two serpents' horns and made off with them. All my assurances that there are no such things as serpents' horns failed to convince the men, and they still believe that their comrade has robbed me of a great treasure.

The serpent's head Nos. 1403 and 1404 seems to represent the poisonous asp. I call particular attention to the horn-like excrescences to the right and left of the head. This head has a number of dots above the mouth, and the head and back are divided by cross lines into sections which are filled with dots. On the opposite side are lines running longitudinally, like female hair. It deserves particular attention that no such horned serpent-heads have ever been found of a clay or fabric that I could possibly attribute to any one of the preceding pre-historic cities. The shape of these serpent-heads induces me to think that they have served as handles to vases. This even appears certain from the shape of No. 1400, which, contrary to *all* the other vases found at Hissarlik, has a *horizontal* perforation; but no second specimen with a horizontal hole has been found. A vase with a horizontal perforation occurs, however, among the pottery from Marino.[8] Professor Virchow calls my attention to the peculiar shape of No. 1400, which, in his opinion, resembles an elephant's trunk more than a serpent's head.

Vase or cup handles with tolerably well-modelled heads of cows or oxen with long horns occur frequently among the pottery of the Lydian city. I represent one of them here under No. 1405. I shall not attempt to decide the question whether here, as at Mycenae, the cow's head is the symbol or image of Heré; *but as the cow's head occurs here so often, and always on vase-handles, I suggest that it explains to us the two-horned vase-handles which are found in such rich abundance in Italy from the trans-Padane region to the Abruzzi.* They are further found in the Lake-dwellings in the districts of Mantua and Vicenza, in the terramare of the Emilia, in a tomb and in fields in the district of Bologna, in the tombs of Volterra, and in fields in the valley of Vibrata. A large cup with three excrescences, having a handle with two such horns, was also found below the foundations of a house on the Esquiline, near the church of Sant' Eusebio, in Rome; but this is as yet the first specimen of such a horned vase found in Latium.

No. 1405. Vase-handle with a cow's head. (Half actual size. Depth, about 18 ft.)

Chronologically, therefore, it belongs to the Bronze age in the terramare of the Emilia, and perhaps to the Stone age in the Lake-dwellings on the other side of the Po; but it belongs to the first Iron age in the tombs and fields in the district of Bologna, and in the tombs of Volterra; to the Bronze age, in the fields of the Abruzzi; and to the Bronze age, also, on the Esquiline.[9]

These two-horned vase handles have called forth many learned discussions, but it never yet occurred to any one that they might be the inheritance of the Lydian vase-handles with cow-heads. I feel sure that the explanation I now offer will at once be universally adopted. I may add that cow-heads never occur in any of the first five pre-historic cities of Hissarlik; and also that among the pottery from Chiusi in the British

[8] L. Pigorini and Sir John Lubbock, *op. cit.* No. 6.
[9] Pigorini, in the *Bullettino di Paletnologia Italiana* of January 1878, p. 16.

Museum there are some terra-cotta vases having handles ornamented with heads of horses or cows.[10]

I remind the reader that cow-heads of gold or terra-cotta, and particularly those of gold, are very frequent at Mycenae, where I found fifty-six solely of the shape represented in my *Mycenae*, p. 218, Nos. 329, 330, and numerous fragments of others. They also occur of bronze in Germany. Thus, for instance, Professor Virchow calls my attention to a small two-wheeled chariot of bronze in his collection, which is decorated with three cow-heads and as many birds; also to a three-wheeled chariot of bronze, decorated with two cow-heads and three birds, which is in the Royal Museum at Berlin. Both chariots were found in the bed of the river Spree, near Burg, in Lower Lusatia.[11] He further recommends to my notice a third two-wheeled chariot of bronze, found near Ober-Kehle, in the district of Trebnitz (Lower Silesia), and preserved in the Breslau Museum, which is likewise decorated with two cow-heads and three birds, and to a fourth similar one found at Frankfurt on the Oder, and preserved in the Museum of Neu Ruppin. Professor Virchow further mentions a cow-head of bronze with long horns, found near Gr. Pankow in Westpriegnitz, near Pritzwalk, and a three-horned cow-head of bronze with a bird's beak, preserved in the Museum of Copenhagen; the horns are long, and strongly bent forward. He also draws my attention to two cows or oxen of pure copper found near Bythin, in the district of Samter, in the province of Posen. Professor Virchow writes on them: "The length of the horns and their wide span decidedly point to southern prototypes. So far as it is known, such long-horned cattle have never existed in our country; even now we do not see them before coming to Moravia, Hungary or Italy. The pointed heads do not permit the idea that buffaloes might be intended."[1] The Märkisches Museum at Berlin also contains a vase found in Germany with handles in the form of two cow-horns, similar to the vase-handles found in Italy. Some small cow-heads of gold have also been found in Scythian tombs in the south of Russia. Perhaps the most remarkable vessel I ever saw is a terra-cotta vessel with a well-formed cow-head[2] in Professor Virchow's collection. It was found by the sagacious Miss Adèle Virchow, in the excavations she undertook, as before mentioned, in company with her father and her brother, in the pre-historic graveyard of Zaborówo, in the province of Posen.

I cannot conclude the discussion on pre-historic heads of cows or oxen without calling particular attention to the marvellous collection of bronzes found in the island of Sardinia, and preserved in the Museum of Cagliari. Among the numerous animals represented there, we see

---

[10] Among the spoil taken from the Shasu Arabs by King Thutmes III., we find "*one silver double-handled cup, with the head of a bull*"—probably, like other objects mentioned in the same record, of Phoenician workmanship. (Brugsch, *Hist. of Egypt*, vol. i., p. 383, Eng. trans. 2nd ed.)

[11] See *Auszug aus dem Monatsbericht der König-*

lichen Akademie der Wissenschaften in Berlin, November 16, 1876.

[1] *Sessional Report of the Berlin Society of Anthropology, Ethnology*, &c., of December 6, 1873.

[2] See *Sessional Report of the Berlin Society of Anthropology, Ethnology*, &c., of May 10, 1873, Pl. xiii. fig. 1.

bulls and cows;[3] we also recognize some cow-heads among the horned animal heads which decorate the very curious miniature round boats of bronze, called in the Sardinian dialect *Cius* (perhaps a corruption of the Greek κύαθος, cup), and supposed to be votive offerings.[4] We also see there an object of bronze representing a woman riding on a cow,[5] as well as a large number of female idols with cow-horns on their heads,[6] or with cow-horns proceeding from the shoulders,[7] like those on most of the Mycenean idols.[8] As these Sardinian idols have the arms well formed, there is no possibility that the cow-horns (or perhaps symbolic horns of the crescent) might be mistaken for arms, as has been the case with those of the Mycenean idols.

I may add that the remarkable Museum of Cagliari contains also horned man's heads.[9]

No. 1406 represents a brooch of ivory, ornamented with a bird.

No. 1407 is a small disc of ivory exhibiting in intaglio-work a scorpion, on each side of which is an animal. One of these is represented

No. 1408. Watch-shaped Object of Terra-cotta, with two perforations. (About half actual size. Depth, 5 to 8 ft.)

No. 1406. Brooch of Ivory. (2 : 3 actual size. Depth, 5 ft.)

No. 1407. Object of Ivory. (Double size; found on the surface.)

with three teats, and is turned upwards; the other is turned the reverse way. They resemble fitchets or polecats, though the primitive artist may have intended to represent lions or dogs: that this latter animal was intended to be represented is the opinion of Professor Virchow. The scorpion was, in Egyptian mythology, the symbol of the goddess Selk. I picked up this curious disc of ivory on the surface of the ground on the high plateau of the hill, where excavations were going on at a depth of from 6 to 12 ft.: it must therefore have fallen from a cart-load. As nothing like it was found in the *débris* of any of the first five prehistoric cities or in the ruins of the Aeolic Ilium, whilst in the artistic style of the intaglio there is at least some analogy to that of the head No. 1391, and the cow-head No. 1405, I attribute it with much confidence to the Lydian city.

No. 1408 displays the same dull black colour and the same fabric as all the pottery of this Lydian city; it is of the size and shape of our watches,

---

[3] Vincenzo Crespi, *Il Museo d' Antichità di Cagliari*; Cagliari, 1872, Pl. v. figs. 7, 8.
[4] *Ibid.* Pl. vi.
[5] *Ibid.* Pl. iv. fig. 10.
[6] *Ibid.* pp. 52, 53, 54, figs. *c, e, f, g, k.*

[7] *Ibid.* p. 52, fig. *b.*
[8] See my *Mycenae*, p. 12, figs. 8, 10; Pl. xvii. figs. 94, 96; Coloured Pl. A, fig. *d*, Pl. B, figs. *e, f.*
[9] Vincenzo Crespi, *op. cit.* Pl. iii. fig. *k.*

and has two perforations.   It is remarkable for the character or symbol incised on it, which so very frequently occurs on the Trojan whorls; and, curiously enough, also over the doors of three of the hut-urns found in the ancient necropolis below a stratum of peperino near Marino,[10] as well as over the door of a similar hut-urn from the same necropolis, preserved in the Royal Museum at Berlin.   It also occurs seven times on the bottoms of vases found by Miss Sofie von Torma in her excavations in the Maros and Cserna valleys in Siebenbürgen (Transylvania).[11]

Whorls are frequent in the sixth city; all of the very same slightly-baked, dull blackish clay of which all the vases consist.   They have for the most part the form of Nos. 1802, 1803, and 1805, and have generally only an incised linear decoration filled with white chalk; but there are also some whorls ornamented with ⌐┘ or ⌐┐ and other signs, which may have a symbolical meaning.

No. 1411.   Die of Stone.
(7 : 8 actual size.   Depth, 13 ft.)

No. 1409.   Marble Knob of a Stick.
(2 : 3 actual size.   Depth, 10 ft.)

No. 1410.   Marble Knob of a Stick.
(Half actual size.   Depth, 5 ft.)

No. 1409 and No. 1410 are marble knobs of sticks; No. 1411, a die of silicious stone.   Herodotus[1] attributes to the Lydians the invention of dice.

No. 1412 is of the same clay, and is probably a female idol.   All the marks we see on it—eyes, nose, mouth, &c.—have been incised before the

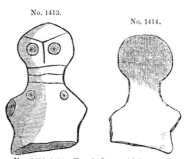

No. 1413.

No. 1414.

No. 1412.   Figure of Terra-cotta, probably a female idol.
(2 : 3 actual size.   Depth, 13 ft.)

Nos. 1413, 1414.   Female figure with large eyes.
No. 1413.   Front.   No. 1414.   Back.
(Nearly 2 : 3 actual size.   Depth, about 9 ft.)

---

[10] L. Pigorini and Sir John Lubbock, op. cit. Pl. ix., Nos. 7–9; only on No. 8 the sign has one vertical stroke more than on the two others and on the object before us.
[11] Carl Gooss, Bericht über Fräulein Sofie von

Torma's Sammlung praehistorischer Alterthümer aus dem Maros- und Cserna-Thal Siebenbürgens; Hermannstadt, 1878, Nos. 8, 9, 10, 13, 14, 17.
[1] i. 94: ἐξευρεθῆναι δὴ ὧν τότε καὶ τῶν κύβων.

baking : the horizontal line above the eyes may indicate the frontlet; the necklace is indicated by another horizontal line, with three ornaments, hanging down from it. The figure has a projection to the right and left to indicate the arms. These are joined by a third horizontal line. In its middle is a dot, perhaps intended to mark the vulva.

No. 1413 is probably another female idol, for two breasts are indicated. The eyes are particularly large; the eyebrows and the nose are marked in the rudest way. The mouth is not indicated as in the owl-headed vases and images, or the rude idols found in the Aegean islands. Three horizontal lines on the neck seem to denote necklaces. The arms are represented by small projections to the right and left. Vertical scratchings on the back of the head (No. 1414) indicate the female hair.

The bronze brooch, No. 1415, as well as the fragment of another brooch, No. 1416, were found by a shepherd in digging a furrow a few

No. 1415. Primitive Bronze Brooch, with a file of gold beads attached to it. (Actual size.
Found near the surface.)

No. 1416. Fragment of Bronze Brooch, with two files of gold beads attached to it. (Actual size.
Found near the surface.)

inches deep round a barrack of wood and straw which he had built for me at the western foot of Hissarlik. I attribute these objects to the Lydian city only because the inhabitants of the succeeding Aeolic Ilium were too civilized to use such rude nail-like brooches with flat heads, and I do not see how these objects could lie so close to the surface if they belonged to any one of the pre-historic cities. That they were used as brooches is evident from the gold beads, of which twenty-five adhere to the large brooch and twenty-two to the fragment. Professor W. Chandler Roberts of the Royal Mint, who examined these objects, is of opinion that the gold beads must have been suspended by a string to the brooches, and must have become attached to them by the cementing action of the oxide and carbonate of copper. Professor Virchow suggests to me that No. 1415 might have been a hair-pin. But I hardly think this possible, on account of its heavy weight and its length of 0·12 mètre, or nearly 5 in.

No. 1417 is a knife of bronze plated with gold, but in many places

No. 1417. Knife of Bronze, thickly gilt. (Actual size. Depth, 6¼ ft.)

covered with oxide and carbonate of copper. Nos. 1418 to 1420 are crooked
bronze knives : in No. 1418 may be seen the hole by which it was fastened

No. 1418.

No. 1419.   No. 1420.

Nos. 1418-1420. Three Knives of Bronze. (Nearly half actual size. Depth, 3 ft.)

in the wooden handle. No. 1421 is an iron knife, with a ring for suspension. A nail, the head of which is clearly seen in the engraving, can leave

No. 1421. Iron Knife, with ring for suspension and a rivet of the wooden handle.
(About 2 : 3 actual size. Depth, 13 ft.)

no doubt that the handle was enclosed in wood. This knife was found at a
depth of 13 ft. below the surface, and, judging from the depth alone, it
ought to belong to the fourth or fifth pre-historic city. But as not the
slightest trace of iron has ever been found by me in any of the five pre-
historic cities of Troy or in Mycenae ; as, moreover, the shape of this knife
is so widely different from the shape of all other knives found in those
cities, whilst it has the very greatest similarity to the Etruscan knives,
and also to the blade of a bronze knife found in the necropolis of Rovio,[2]
as well as to a bronze knife found in the tombs of Soldo near Alzate
(Brianza),[3] I am forced to attribute it to the Lydian city. The weight
of the iron would easily account for its having sunk to the depth at which
it was found.

No. 1422 is evidently also an arrow-head with two barbs, but we are
at a loss to say in what manner it could have been fastened to the shaft.
No. 1423 is a bronze arrow-head without barbs. Similar arrow-heads
are found in Denmark.[4] No. 1424 is a lance-head of bronze. Unlike all
the lance-heads found in the third, the burnt city,[5] this lance-head has a

[2] *Bullettino di Paletnologia Italiana*, 1875,
Pl. iv. No. 1.

[3] *Ibid.* January and February, 1879, Pl. i.
No. 11. The knife before us resembles likewise
some of the bronze knives found in the Swiss
Lake-dwellings (see V. Gross, *Résultats des*

Recherches dans les Lacs de la Suisse occidenta'e ;
Zürich, 1876, Pl. v.).

[4] J. J. A. Worsaae, *Nordiske Oldsager*, Pl. xxxii.
No. 145.

[5] In the other four pre-historic cities of Hissarlik no lance-heads of bronze were found.

tube, in which the wooden shaft was fixed. As I have already stated, all the Homeric lances seem to have had a similar tube for the shaft. Moreover, all the lance-heads found by me at Mycenae are similar to that before us.

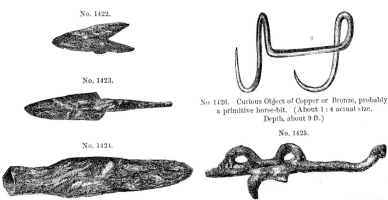

No. 1422.

No. 1423.

No 1426. Curious Object of Copper or Bronze, probably a primitive horse-bit. (About 1 : 4 actual size. Depth, about 9 ft.)

No. 1425.

No. 1424.

Nos. 1422–1425. Lance, Arrow-heads, and Fragment of Bridle of Bronze. (Nearly half actual size. Depth, 6 ft.)

The object No. 1425 is also of bronze, with three rings, of which the lower one is broken; it seems to be part of a bridle. This is also the opinion of Mr. John Evans, who has in his collection a similar object, with the sole difference that the rings, instead of protruding as on the Hissarlik bridle, are here in the centre of circular projections in the rod of the bridle. Moreover, a bronze bridle was found by Dr. V. Gross in the Lake-dwellings at the station of Moeringen, in the Lake of Bienne, composed of two pieces almost perfectly similar to that of the object before us; the bit for the mouth of the horse was fixed in the middle ring in both cases, the sole difference being that the rings from Switzerland form long ovals.[6] Professor Virchow calls my attention to two objects of bronze, each with three protruding rings, strikingly similar to the bridle-fragment No. 1425, which were found at Seelow, in the district of Lebus, near the Oder.[7] Only here each piece is in the form of a lizard, and has four feet. The curious instrument of copper or bronze (No. 1426), in the shape of a bar with the two ends turned into pointed hooks, has also the appearance of a bit.

No. 1427 is a small bronze cup, perforated like a colander. No. 1428 is a bronze cup on a tall stem, but without handles, and with a very large foot. A cup of a perfectly identical shape is in the Museum of Verona.[8] The cup No. 1428 is also very similar in form to the Greek and Etruscan cup called *holkion* by Mr. Dennis.[9]

Nos. 1429 and 1430 represent a curious sort of large double-edged bronze battle-axe, of which I found four at a depth of 6 ft. As I never found

[6] V. Gross, *Résultats des Recherches dans les Lacs de la Suisse occidentale*, Pl. xv. No. 1.

[7] See *Sessional Report of the Berlin Society of Anthropology, Ethnology*, &c., of April 17, 1875.

[8] Pigorini, in the *Bullettino di Paletnologia*, Feb. 1877, Pl. ii. No. 3.

[9] *The Cities and Cemeteries of Etruria*, p. cxxi. No. 55.

No. 1428.

No. 1427.

Nos. 1427, 1428. Goblet and sieve-like Cup of Bronze. (Nearly half actual size. Depth, 6 ft.)

No. 1429.

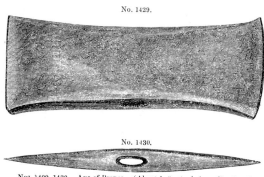

No. 1430.

Nos. 1429, 1430. Axe of Bronze. (About 1 : 3 actual size. Depth, 6 ft.)

this shape in any of the other pre-historic cities, I attribute them with much probability to this Lydian city. I found two double-edged bronze hatchets of a perfectly identical shape at Mycenae.[10] A similar double-edged axe of copper was found in Hungary.[1] These double-edged axes are characteristic of Asia Minor, and Zeus Labrandeus of Caria derived his name from *labranda*, which meant a double-edged battle-axe in the Carian language. They also frequently occur in Greece and Assyria, as well as in Babylonia. A similar double-edged axe, but of copper, was found in the Lake-dwellings at Lüscherz;[2] another on the Lower Danube.[3] A similar double-edged axe, also of pure copper, was found by Dr. V. Gross in the Lake-dwellings at the Station of Locras, in the Lake of Bienne in Switzerland.[4] I also found them very frequently represented on the gold jewels in the royal tombs of Mycenae; as, for example, between the horns of fifty-six cow-heads;[5] also two such double-edged axes are

---

[10] See my *Mycenae*, p. 111, No. 173.

[1] See Joseph Hampel, *Catalogue de l'Exposition préhistorique des Musées de Province*, p. 139, No. 147.

[2] See *Sessional Report of the Berlin Society of Anthropology, Ethnology*, &c., of October 18,

1879, Pl. xvii. Nos. 2*a*, 2*b*.

[3] *Ibid.* Nos. 3*a*, 3*b*.

[4] V. Gross, *Les dernières Trouvailles dans les Habitations lacustres du Lac de Bienne*; Porrentruy, 1879, Pl. i. No. 1.

[5] See my *Mycenae*, p. 218, Nos. 329, 330.

represented on the gold seal-ring in the archaic Babylonian style,[6] and
one on the remarkable gem of agate.[7]

M. Ernest Chantre, assistant director of the Museum of Lyons, has
sent me the analysis of one of these battle-axes made by the celebrated
chemist, M. Damour of Lyons. I had drilled the axe, and sent him the
drillings :—

					Grammes.
Analysis	..	..	..	..	0·5280
Deducting the sand contained in it	..	..	..	0·0070
					0·5210

					In 1·0000 part.
This consists of copper..	..	..	..	..	0·4810 = 0·9232
„ tin	..	..	..	..	0·0385 = 0·0739
					0·5195 = 0·9971

Now, regarding the chronology of this Lydian city, I think every
archæologist will admit that all the articles which we have passed in
review, and particularly the pottery, denote an early state of civilization.
Moreover, here were still in use the vases with long rams' horns and the
vase-handles with long-horned cow-heads, from the former of which the
bosses on the most ancient Etruscan vases seem to have originated, while
from the long-horned cow-heads we may trace the famous two-horned or
crescent vase-handles found in the terramare and elsewhere in Central
Italy. No vases with rams' horns, or handles with long-horned cows'
heads, have ever been found in the terramare; but this does not by any
means prove that the Lydian city on Hissarlik must be anterior to the
Lake-dwellings by which the terramare were formed; because vases with
bosses or with crescent handles may have existed for centuries in the
Italian terramare, whilst the ram-horned vases and the cow-headed
handles, from which they were derived, continued to be used in the
Lydian settlement at Hissarlik. But it is pretty certain that the immigration of the Etruscans into Italy took place before the Dorian invasion
of the Peloponnesus,[8] which, as explained in the preceding pages, became
the cause of the Aeolian emigration to the Troad.

Having to the best of my knowledge and belief selected and described
the objects belonging to the Lydian city from among those found in the
strata between the fifth pre-historic city and the ruins of the Aeolic
settlement, I now proceed to the description of the seventh city, the
Greek Ilium.

---

[6] See my *Mycenae*, p. 354, No. 530.   [7] *Ibid.* p. 362, No. 541.
[8] Wolfgang Helbig, *Die Italiker in der Poebene;* Leipzig, 1879, p. 100.

CHAPTER XI.

THE SEVENTH CITY: THE GREEK ILIUM; OR NOVUM ILIUM.[1]

§ I. Remains of the City.

The founders of Novum Ilium built their city both to the east and to the south of Hissarlik,[2] and used this hill as their Acropolis and the seat of their sanctuaries. They did so probably for three reasons: first, because they were conscious of the fact, that here had once stood the sanctuary of Athené as well as the houses of Troy's last king and his sons, and that here the fate of sacred Ilios had been decided, and therefore a religious reverence deterred them from giving up the place to profane use; secondly, because Hissarlik had strong natural defences, and was admirably situated for an Acropolis; and, in the third place, because the new settlers were too numerous to build their town on so small a space. This explains the thinness of the Greek stratum of *débris* on Hissarlik, the scarcity of objects of human industry, even of fragments of pottery, and the abundance of terra-cotta figurines and round pieces of terra-cotta, in the form of watches, with two perforations, which here replace the pre-historic whorls, and seem, along with the figurines, to have served as votive offerings. In commemoration of the Acropolis of old, erroneously attributed to Ilium by Homer, and probably believed by the new settlers to have occupied this identical hill, Hissarlik was thenceforth called Pergamus, or Priam's Pergamon, as Herodotus[3] names it.

Of the first sacred buildings erected here by the new settlers nothing is known to us. The first mention made of a temple is by Herodotus, who relates that Xerxes, on his expedition to Greece (480 B.C.), went up hither to sacrifice to the Ilian Athené.[4] Strabo says that this temple, up to the time of Alexander the Great, was but small and insignificant (μικρὸν καὶ εὐτελές).[5] To this, and to other old temples built by the Aeolian settlers, probably belong the very numerous wrought blocks of lime-stone, often with rude sculptures, which I found embedded in walls of a later time.

Of the later costly temple of Athené built by Lysimachus, destroyed partly or entirely by Fimbria, and restored by Sulla,[6] but little had escaped the pious zeal of the early Christians, and no trace of it was visible above ground. The drums of its Corinthian columns, with their

---

[1] I once more remind the reader that no ancient author calls this city by any other name than simply Ἴλιον, Ilium, or, sometimes poetically, Troja. "Novum Ilium" is merely a modern *customary name*, which I reluctantly adopt as a convenient abridgement of the phrases used by Strabo to distinguish the Greek city from Homer's — τὸ νῦν Ἴλιον, τὸ σημερινὸν Ἴλιον, ἡ νῦν πόλις.

[2] See Plan II. (of the Hellenic Ilium).
[3] Herod. vii. 43.   [4] *Ibid.*
[5] Strabo, xiii. p. 593.   [6] See pp. 176–178.

beautiful capitals, all of white marble, had been used to build a wall of defence, the drums being joined with cement. In my trench on the south-east side I have been obliged to break through this wall, which visitors will recognize to the right and left of that excavation.[7] The drums which I took out may be seen standing upright at the entrance of the trench.

Of the temple itself, I found only the foundations *in situ;* they nowhere extended deeper than 6½ ft. The floor, which consisted of slabs of limestone, and which rested upon double layers of the same stone, was covered with vegetable soil, from 1 to 3 ft. deep. This explains the total absence of entire sculptures; for whatever sculptures there were, remained lying on the surface, till they were destroyed by fanaticism or wantonness. This explains also the enormous mass of fragments of statues which cover the entire hill. Judging from the foundations, the temple was 288 ft. long by 72½ ft. wide; its direction is E.S.E. ½ E. In order to excavate the pre-historic cities, I have been forced by dire necessity to destroy the greater part of these foundations, of which, however, visitors will see some remains on the north-east and south-west sides of my great trench, which cuts the hill from south-east to north-west. The long Hellenic wall on the south side (see Sectional Plan No. IV., under the letter υ) also belongs to this temple, and seems to have been its wall of enclosure; so too does the quadrangular Hellenic substruction in the form of a tower; but I am at a loss to say of what use this latter can have been to the temple. Visitors will see that it rests directly upon the calcined ashes and *débris* of the third, the burnt city. Of other temples I found only the large ruins of the Doric temple of Apollo, on or close to the slope, on the north side;[8] but, strange to say, not one stone of it *in situ.* One beautiful triglyph block of this temple, hereafter to be described, was found at a depth of 3 ft. below the surface, on the northern slope; another unfinished triglyph block on the plateau, near the surface. I struck besides, in my excavations on the plateau of the hill, the foundations of many other buildings of large wrought stones, one of which was 59 ft. long and 43 ft. broad. This latter, in or near which I found three inscriptions which seem to have been put up in it, appears to have been the Bouleuterion or Senate-house. Other buildings may have been temples or the houses of high priests. But as my object was to excavate Troy, and as I could not possibly do so by tunnels or leave all these ruins hanging in the air, over our heads, I have—much to my regret—been obliged to destroy them, and to save of them only what I thought of great interest to science.

Of works of defence, which I might attribute to a time anterior to the Macedonian period, I can only mention the lower courses of a large tower, which I struck in my north-west trench.[9] All the upper portion of this tower consisted of large wrought stones, probably of the time of Lysi-machus. A portion of it may still be seen on the south-west side of the

---

[7] See point z East on Sectional Plan IV.

[8] The site of this temple is marked v on Plan I.

[9] The trench is marked z′ on Plan I., and z′ West on Sectional Plan IV.

same trench.[10]   As the great wall built by Lysimachus round the hill was
entirely covered up, it was well preserved ; it is generally 12 ft. high and
10 ft. thick ; it consists of large well-hewn blocks of limestone, laid one
upon another without any kind of cement, and generally bearing a monogram.[1] As the letter is not always the same, there being, for example, on
one stone a Σ, and upon another an Υ or a Δ, I presume that they are
quarry-marks. In order to open trenches, I have unfortunately been obliged
to break through the wall in many places, as, for example, at the points
z East and z' West and R on Plan I. In other places I have been forced
to remove it entirely for long distances, as, for example, at N N and V
(Plan I.) ; but even so all the injuries I have inflicted on it together
affect only one-sixth of its entire circuit round Hissarlik. Whoever, therefore, may take pleasure in bringing the remainder to light, will find more
than five-sixths of it well preserved. A fine specimen of the architecture
of the time of Lysimachus may be seen in the tower in the west side of
my great northern trench, as represented under letter F on the accompanying woodcut (No. 1431). D marks a wall of a later time. Visitors will see
that the tower has been erected on the *débris*, which covered to a depth of
35 ft. the top of the ancient wall marked B and the retaining wall marked
A on the woodcut No. 2, p. 24. I particularly recommend visitors to
examine the slanting layers of *débris*, which are indicated in the engraving
No. 1431, together with their thickness and the material of which they
are composed. As all the layers in which marble occurs belong to Novum
Ilium, it will be seen that the accumulation of Greek remains is here particularly great. Probably all the marble splinters date from the time
when the marble blocks were cut for the Corinthian temple of Athené
and the Doric temple of Apollo. Of the walls round Ilium, built by
Lysimachus, and probably only repaired by Sulla, portions only are here
and there preserved ; but, with the aid of the potsherds and fragments of
marble with which the whole site of Novum Ilium is strewn, they will
suffice to enable the visitor to follow up the entire circuit of the city.

Besides the outer walls, there are traces of an inner wall, connecting
two quadrangular forts, of which large ruins remain.[2] One of these forts
is close to the road to Chiblak, the other on the east border of the city.

The vast extent of the city ; the masses of marble or granite columns
which peep out from the ground ; the millions of fragments of sculptures
with which the site is strewn ; the many large heaps of ruins ; the mosaic
floors brought to light in various places ; the gigantic aqueduct which still
spans the Thymbrius, and by which Ilium was provided with water from
the upper part of that river ; and last, not least, the vast theatre, capable
of seating 5000 spectators, which visitors will see cut in the slope,
immediately to the east of Hissarlik ;[3]—all this testifies to the large size,
the wealth, and the magnificence of the town. The marble seats have
disappeared from the theatre ; but in a small trench, which I dug in the

---

[10] Sectional Plan IV., z' West, and Plan I. (of
Troy), z'.

[1] Sectional Plan IV., z' West and z East, and
Plan I. (of Troy), K, N O, Z O, R, Y.

[2] See Plan II. (of the Hellenic Ilium). One of
the quadrangular forts is marked 43, the other
37, which means their height in mètres above
the sea.   [3] See Plan II.

orchestra, I brought to light numerous fragments of marble sculptures which testify to its grandeur.

As before mentioned, I have sunk on the site of Novum Ilium, outside of Hissarlik, 20 shafts, the sections and depths of which are accurately

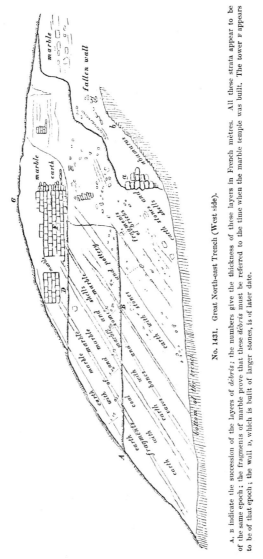

No. 1431. Great North-east Trench (West side).

A, B indicate the succession of the layers of *débris*; the numbers give the thickness of these layers in French mètres. All these strata appear to be of the same epoch; the fragments of marble prove that these *débris* must be referred to the time when the marble temple was built. The tower F appears to be of that epoch; the wall D, which is built of larger stones, is of later date.

given on the Plan of the Hellenic Ilium (Plan II.); it will be seen from them that the accumulation of the *débris*, at a short distance to the west and south-west of Hissarlik, is from 5 to 5·30 m. (16 ft. 5 in. to 17 ft. 5 in.), but that more to the south and south-east it falls off to 2 or 2·50 m. (6 ft. 7 in. to 8 ft. 2 in.). The depth of the *débris* on the plateau above the theatre also does not exceed 8 ft. 2 in., and further on to the east it diminishes still more. These *débris* abound with fragments of pottery of all epochs, from the foundation of the city by the Aeolian colonists down to its decay in the fourth and its abandonment in the fifth century of our era. But I infer this decay and abandonment solely from the absence of coins later than Constans II., and from the entire absence of pottery or ruins of the Byzantine period, of which no trace was found in my 20 shafts. I have no other proofs.[4] As already stated, E. Meyer[5] mentions that " Constantinus Porphyrogennetus (911–959 A.D.) still cites most of the cities of the Troad as bishoprics : Adramyttium, Assos, Gargara, Antandrus, Alexandria-Troas, Ilium, Dardanus, Abydus, Lampsacus ; Parium even as seat of an archbishop.[6] But may not the bishopric of Ilium have been on another site ? "

The mass of coins picked up from the surface by the shepherds on the site of Novum Ilium is really astounding ; but they are all of bronze : the oldest of them do not go further back than the Macedonian period. For the most part they are coins of Ilium itself, but those of Alexandria-Troas are also very frequent ; while those of Sigeum, Dardanus, Tenedos, Ophrynium, Gergis, Elaeussa, Abydus, Lampsacus, Heracleum, Smyrna, Ephesus, Adramyttium, Assos, &c., are rarer. I found also coins of all these places in my excavations on Hissarlik, and a very large number of Ilian coins, or coins of Alexandria-Troas. Silver tetradrachms of Ilium are very rare ; I never found one. Incised gems are also frequently found by the shepherds. I myself picked up sixteen of them in my trenches. They are for the most part of the Roman time. I attribute only six of them with much confidence to the Macedonian period ; none of them are of great artistic value. They represent a warrior on a chariot with four horses, an Artemis with a crescent and the morning star, an Isis, a Pan with a bunch of grapes in his hand, or busts—apparently portraits—of men and women. The fact that these gems are always found without rings can, I think, be only explained by the supposition that the rings were of tin, a metal which disappears without leaving a trace. Similar incised gems were highly prized in antiquity. According to Professor Rhousopoulos, Athenaeus mentions that an *intaglio* of great artistic skill was sold for five talents. King Mithridates VI. had a collection of 2000 gems with *intagli ;* the Emperor Hadrian also was a great admirer of similar jewels, and spent large sums of money on them.

I represent here a few fragments of the more characteristic archaic Greek pottery found in the hill of Hissarlik itself.

The hand-made fragment, No. 1432, represents, in black colour on a light-red dead ground, the upper part of a winged female figure, with a long pointed nose and chin ; the long hair hangs down on the back ; the eye is very large ; the head is covered with a short cap, to which is attached a very long tail or crest, the end of which, branching into two

---

[4] That Ilium was still flourishing in the time of the immediate successors of Constantine the Great, is proved by the letter of Julian, quoted in the chapter on the History of Troy (pp. 181–2).

[5] *Geschichte von Troas ;* Leipzig, 1877, p. 97.

[6] Const. Porphyr. *de Caerem.* ii. 54, p. 792, 794 f.

spirals, is particularly curious. Before the figure, in the right-hand corner, we see again the curious symbol found on the Italian hut-urns

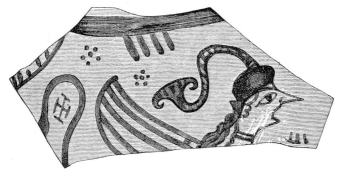

No. 1432. Painted Archaic Pottery. (About half actual size. Depth, about 5 ft.)

and the Trojan whorls, and which the late Professor Martin Haug of Munich read *si*, and thought to be the first syllable of the Trojan god or hero Sigo or Siko, which he found repeatedly in the Trojan inscriptions. Behind the figure we see a curious object with a *swastika* in the form of a Maltese cross. I also call attention to the two clusters of dots, which, as Prof. Virchow presumes, may be meant to represent flowers.

No. 1433 is a wheel-made potsherd, having an ornamentation painted with black colour on a dead white ground; it consists of nine waving lines, and, between two borders, an arrow-like decoration. No. 1434 is

No 1433. Painted Archaic Greek Pottery.
(About half actual size. Depth, about 6 ft.)

No. 1434. Painted Archaic Pottery. (Actual size. Depth, 6 ft.)

a fragment of the upper part of a wheel-made bowl, decorated on the outside with plain dark-brown bands, on the inside with the winged female figure before us, painted with brown colour on a light-yellow dead ground. The hair is very luxuriant, bound up by a frontlet of dark-red colour, which seems to hang down far below the wings; the features of the figure are archaic; behind the head is a curious triangle, with an ornamentation that is frequent on Assyrian sculptures.

No. 1435 is a broken terra-cotta figure, probably of a priestess, with

Assyrian features; the hands have evidently been projecting. This
figure is decorated all over with painted red ornaments, probably meant to
indicate the clothing. No. 1436 is a fragment of the border of a plate,
with a key-pattern decoration, painted in dark-brown colour on a light-
green background; just below the border are two perforations for suspension. No. 1437 is a vase-spout in the form of an animal's head,
painted dark-red.

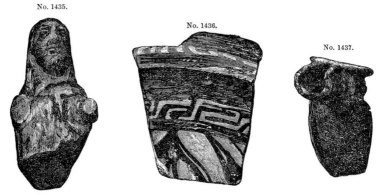

No. 1435.   No. 1436.   No. 1437.

Nos. 1435–1437. Figure of a Priestess in Assyrian style and painted Archaic Pottery. (Half actual size. Depth, 6 ft.)

No. 1438 is the head of an archaic vase, with vertically perforated projections for suspension, and a painted linear decoration in black on a dead

No. 1438. Head of an Archaic Vase, with tubular holes
for suspension. (Nearly half actual size. Depth, 6 ft.)

white ground. No. 1439 is the outside of the rim of a hand-made vessel,
with a net-like decoration, painted in dark-brown on a white dead ground.
No. 1440 is a fragment of the inner side of a hand-made vase or bowl with
a primitive key-pattern decoration, painted in dark brown on a light-
yellow dead ground; above and below are bands of dark brown alternated
with violet. No. 1441 is a fragment of a small wheel-made vase which,
exactly like a vase found by me at Mycenae,[7] represents, in dark brown
on a light-yellow dead ground, warriors with lances and enormous oval
shields. Nos. 1442, 1443, and 1444 are fragments of wheel-made vessels
with a painted spiral or circular ornamentation. Nos. 1445 and 1446 are
fragments of hand-made bowls, profusely painted on the inner side; on
both we recognize part of an animal, probably a horse. On the outside

_____

[7] See my *Mycenae*, p. 68, No. 80.

Nos. 1439–1446. Fragments of painted Archaic Greek Pottery. (Half actual size. Depth, 4 to 6 ft.)

these bowls are decorated with plain red, brown, or black bands. Fragments of archaic pottery with a painted linear decoration are abundant, but I obtained only one entire vase of this description.

No. 1447 is a flat object of red terra-cotta, representing in relief a pretty woman with long hair and a rich Oriental head-dress; she seems to hold her hands clasped on her breast. According to all appearance,

No. 1447. Object of Red Terra-cotta, representing in relief an Asiatic goddess with a rich Oriental head-dress. Probably an idol. (2 : 3 actual size. Depth, 5 ft.)

No. 1448. Figure with Child, holding a book on her lap. Best Hellenic period. (Nearly half actual size. Depth, 3 ft.)

this is an idol, and has been encased in wood. I call attention to the four excrescences at the sides of the figure. No. 1448 is a seated terra-cotta figure, having to her left a child, and holding a book on her lap; both figures are of masterly work, and may belong to the end of the fifth or the beginning of the fourth century B.C. No. 1449 is a rudely-modelled lion of terra-cotta. No. 1450 is a fairly well modelled pig, curiously

No. 1449.   Lion of Terra-cotta.
(2 : 5 actual size.   Depth, about 3 ft.)

No. 1450.   Pig of Terra-cotta, curiously marked
all over with stars.   (Actual size.   Depth, 12 ft.)

decorated with dark-red stars on a light-red dead ground. No. 1451 is a tablet of terra-cotta representing a painted draped figure with a long beard, on horseback; the head is covered with a cap.

No. 1451.   Tablet of Terra-cotta, with a horseman in relief.   (Actual size.   Depth, 2 to 3 ft.)

No. 1452 is an object of terra-cotta, representing in relief the bearded figure of an old man with a Phrygian cap on his head. Professor Sayce remarks to me regarding this object : " The figure is in the Assyrian style. On each side of the head is a winged thunderbolt, such as is found on the coins of Elis and Sicily. It has been explained by Mr. Percy Gardner in the *Numismatic Chronicle*, N. S. xix. (1879). We shall find it again on the terra-cotta *plaques* figured under Nos. 1459–1461." No. 1453 is a bearded head covered with a cloth. Nos. 1454, 1455, and 1456 are very pretty

No. 1452. Curious Object of Terra-cotta, with an archaic figure in relief. (Half actual size. Depth, 3 ft.)

female heads of terra-cotta, which may be of the Macedonian period; the face of No. 1455 is partly veiled. As Professor Rhousopoulos mentions to me, Dicaearchus affirms that the Theban women covered their heads with the gown to such a degree that nothing of the face was visible.

No. 1453. Bearded Head, with a curious head-dress. (Half actual size. Depth, 2 to 3 ft.)

No. 1454. Very beautiful Female Head. (Half actual size. Depth, 2 to 3 ft.)

No. 1455. Very pretty veiled Female Head. (Half actual size. Depth, 2 to 3 ft.)

No. 1456. Female Head; probably Macedonian time. (Nearly half actual size. Depth, 2 ft.)

No. 1457. Cup-bottom, representing in relief two boys kissing each other. (Nearly half actual size. Depth, 2 ft.)

No. 1457 is the fragment of a cup-bottom, representing in relief two boys kissing each other. This object finds its analogue in the fragment of a vase from Tarsus (Cilicia) in the Louvre, on which two youths kissing each other are likewise represented in relief.

No. 1458. Terra-cotta Mould, representing a man and a woman; probably late Roman time. (Nearly half actual size. Depth, 1 to 2 ft.)

No. 1458 is a mould of terra-cotta, representing a woman and a man; the latter seemingly with a halo of glory round the head. A two-handled vessel is represented between their heads, with flowers below it. This mould seems to be of the late Roman time.

Nos. 1459–1464 are six terra-cotta tablets, the first three of which represent, in the opinion of Prof. Virchow and Prof. Sayce, the winged thunderbolt of Zeus in low relief. Professor Virchow sees in No. 1462 the representation of a quiver for arrows. Nos. 1463 and 1464 are more difficult to explain. These tablets, of which a large number were found, have probably served to ornament boxes or furniture.

No. 1459.   No. 1460.   No. 1461.

No. 1462.   No. 1463.   No. 1464.

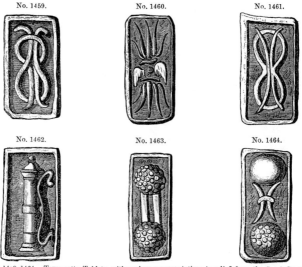

Nos. 1459–1464. Terra-cotta Tablets, with curious representations in relief, from the Greek Stratum. (Half actual size. Depth, 2 ft.)

No. 1465 is the fragment of a painted Hellenic vase, with curious signs resembling Egyptian hieroglyphs.

Whorls of clay still occasionally occur in the stratum of Novum Ilium, but all of them are thoroughly baked, and have never any incised or painted ornamentation. But much more abundant here are the objects of terra-cotta, but slightly baked, in the form of our watches, with two perforations near the border. Many of these objects are round; in many others the border, just above the two perforations, is flattened. In most instances these objects are decorated with a stamp, in which we see a dog's head, a bee with extended wings, a flying figure, a swan, &c. : this stamp is sometimes in the middle of the object, sometimes on the flat border. But many of them have no stamp, and in this case they are generally much larger, more bulky, of coarser clay and fabric, and more thoroughly baked. Those with stamps are usually of a much better fabric and less baked, probably in order that the stamp might not be injured by long exposure to the fire. Of this latter class I represent seven under Nos. 1466 to 1472. We see in the stamp on

No. 1465.   Fragment of painted Greek Pottery.   (Half actual size. Depth, 2 to 3 ft.)

No. 1466.   Object of Terra-cotta, with two perforations, representing a swan and an ibex. (Half actual size.   Depth, 2 to 6 ft.)

No. 1467. Object of Terra-cotta, with two perforations, representing curious signs.   (2:3 actual size. Depth, 2 to 5 ft.)

No. 1469.   Object of Terra-cotta, with two perforations, representing a pigeon. (Half actual size. Depth, 2 to 6 ft.)

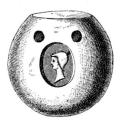

No. 1468.   Object of Terra-cotta, with two perforations, representing the bust of a man.   (Half actual size.   Depth, 2 to 6 ft.)

No. 1466 an ibex and a swan; in that of No. 1467, curious signs resembling Egyptian hieroglyphs; in that of No. 1468, the bust of a young man with a helmet on his head; in that on No. 1469, a pigeon; on No. 1470, a naked woman; on No. 1471, two ibexes; on No. 1472, a horse.

No. 1470.   Curious Object of Terra-cotta, with two perforations, representing a naked woman.   (Half actual size. Depth, 2 to 5 ft.)

No. 1471.   Object of Terra-cotta, with two holes, representing two quadrupeds, probably meant to be ibexes. (Half actual size.   Depth, 2 to 5 ft.)

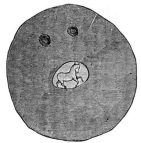

No. 1472. Object of Terra-cotta, with two holes, representing a horse. (Actual size. Depth, 2 to 5 ft.)

Similar objects are found all over the Troad; I picked up some of them from the surface on the sites of Aeanteum and Rhoeteum. They are also frequent in Greece, but there they do not occur with stamps. I am not aware that they have been found elsewhere. It has been suggested that they were used as weights for fishing-nets; but this is contradicted by the neat appearance of these objects, for none of them show marks of wear and tear; besides, the slightly-baked ones would at once deteriorate in the water, while the delicate figures in the stamps are ill adapted for submersion. I would therefore suggest that, like the ornamented whorls in the five pre-historic cities, these neat objects with double perforations served in the Aeolic Ilium as *ex-votos* to the tutelary divinity, the Ilian Athené.

Of the Greek terra-cotta lamps found in the ruins of Novum Ilium, I represent one, No. 1473, which has a pillar-shaped foot, 7 in. long.

No. 1475A.   No. 1475B.

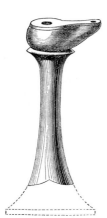

No. 1473. A Greek Lamp on a tall foot. (1 : 4 actual size. Depth, 5 ft.)

No. 1474. Lead Weight, with a hog's head in relief. (Nearly half actual size. Depth, 6 ft.)

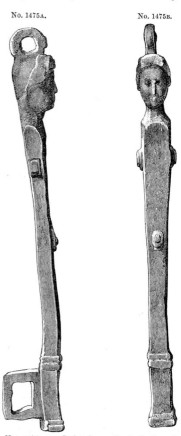

Nos. 1475A, B. Curious bronze Key in the form of a Hermes. (Actual size. Depth, about 4 ft.)

As mentioned in the preceding pages, lamps were entirely unknown in all the pre-historic cities, unless certain little bowls served the purpose, like the *candylia* still used in Greek churches. Homer only knew λαμπτῆρες, fire-vessels or cressets, of which three stood in the great hall of the palace of Ulysses. They consisted of pans of terra-cotta or copper, probably placed on pedestals, in which very dry wood mixed with resinous wood [8] (δαΐς) was burned. The Homeric torches, δαΐδες,[9] were therefore nothing else than pieces of resinous wood. From δαΐς originated the later word δᾴς, for " torch," which is used by Thucydides, Polyaenus, Plutarch, and others.

No. 1474 is a quadrangular object of lead, representing a boar's head in relief; it was found in my shaft [10] sunk at the eastern extremity of the town, near the road to Chiblak. It weighs 18 ounces avoirdupois, and recals to mind the ¼ Attic dimnaeon, on which likewise heads of animals are usually represented. Nos. 1475A and B represent a very curious key of bronze, with a ring for suspension. Professor Athanasios Rhousopoulos, who examined this key carefully, writes to me the following valuable note on the subject :—" I do not remember having ever seen anything like this key, either in private collections or in museums. It has the shape of the so-called quadrangular images of Hermes, with an altar-like base forming one piece with the body, to which a quadrangular projection is fixed on the back, with a hole corresponding to the lock-bolt. Without this it would not be easy to find out the use of the object, and one might think it to be rather an *anathema* than a key. The body of the Hermes increases in width towards the top, as is often the case with similar objects ; it has in the middle the phallus, which is indispensable in every Hermes, on account of its symbolical signification. It has also the quadrangular shoulder-projections, which are often conspicuous on the stone Hermae, and which were used for suspending wreaths. You may see this custom in a wall-painting from Herculaneum, in K. O. Müller's *Denkmäler der alten Kunst*, i., Pl. i. No. 3. The Hermes body is surmounted by a female head, having two tufts of hair above the forehead, which seem to indicate that it was intended to represent Ariadne or a Bacchante ; otherwise we should recognize in it a head of Pallas, and call the whole figure a Hermathené. From the head projects a ring for suspending the key. The whole length of the key is 0·115 mètre (about 4½ in.). You may see such forms of stone Hermae at Athens, in the Patesia Street National Museum, near the Polytechnic School, of which I have published the best in the *Archæological Ephemeris*, New Series, 1862-1863, pp. 183 and 205, Pl. xxx., xxxi., and xxxiii."[1]

---

[8] *Od.* xviii. 307–310 :
αὐτίκα λαμπτῆρας τρεῖς ἵστασαν ἐν μεγάροισιν,
ὄφρα φαείνοιεν · περὶ δὲ ξύλα κάγκανα θῆκαν,
αὖα πάλαι, περίκηλα, νέον κεκεασμένα χαλκῷ,
καὶ δαΐδας μετέμισγον ·

[9] *Il.* xviii. 492, 493 :
νύμφας δ' ἐκ θαλάμων δαΐδων ὕπο λαμπομενάων
ἠγίνεον ἀνὰ ἄστυ, . . .

[10] Marked A on Plan II. (of the Hellenic Ilium).

[1] I give here the original text of Prof. Rhousopoulos's valuable note, as I am sure it will interest the intelligent English student much more than the translation :—

'Ρουσόπουλος Σχλιεμάννῳ χαίρειν.

Οὐ μικρᾶς, ὡς ἔοικε, δεῖται ἀποκρίσεως τὸ ἐν τῷ ἐπιστολίῳ ἐρώτημα περὶ τῆς χαλκίνης κλειδός, ἥν ἐκ Τροίας κομίσας διὰ Πέλοπος, τοῦ σοῦ ὑπηρέτου, συναπέσταλκάς μοι, μαθεῖν τι περὶ αὐτῆς βουλόμενος · ἐγὼ γὰρ πολλὰς μὲν ἐν ἰδιωτῶν συλλογαῖς ἰδών, πλείστας δὲ ἐν μουσείοις, οὐ μέμνημαι ὁμοίᾳ τῇ σῇ κλειδὶ ἐντυχών.

Ἔστι μὲν οὖν τὸ ὅλον αὐτῆς σχῆμα ἑρμοῦ

No. 1476 represents an iron key, with three teeth and a ring for suspension. There are similar keys in all museums of Greek antiquities.

No. 1477.   No. 1478.

Nos. 1477, 1478. Orna-
mented Glass Beads. (Half
actual size. Depth, 3 ft.)

No. 1476. Iron Key, with three teeth and a ring for suspension.
(Half actual size. Depth, 1 to 2 ft.)

No. 1477 is a green glass bead decorated with small yellow concentric circles; No. 1478, a blue glass bead with vertical flutings.

No. 1479 is the splendid block of triglyphs, which I have already mentioned, 6½ ft. in length and 2 ft. 10 in. in height, with a metope which represents Phoebus Apollo with the four horses of the Sun. The grandeur and classical beauty of the style, the happy character of the composition, the life and the movement of the horses—all is admirable. This is a master-piece of the first order, worthy of being compared with the best Greek sculptures. A cast of this metopé, which I presented to the British Museum, has been put up by Mr. Newton close to the Elgin antiquities, where it holds an honourable place even in the neighbourhood of the Parthenon sculptures, and of those from the Temple of Artemis at Ephesus. "The composition as a work of art shows," as Heinrich Brunn remarks to me, "the greatest skill in solving one of the most difficult of problems : for the team of four horses ought not to move on the surface of the relief, but to appear as if it came out of it at a half-turn. This has been achieved principally by pressing back the right hinder thigh of the horse in the foreground, while the left foot steps forward; at the same time the same horse is slightly foreshortened, and the surface of the thigh lies deeper than the upper surface of the triglyphs; while, on the other hand, the surfaces of the withers and of the neck are higher, and the head, in conformity with the rules of Greek reliefs, is again almost level with the base. For this reason there is no indication of a chariot,

τῆς τετραγώνου καλουμένης ἐργασίας, μετὰ βάσεως βωμοειδοῦς συμφυοῦς τῷ σώματι, ἣ προσκεκόλληται κατὰ τὴν ὀπισθίαν πλευρὰν τετραγωνικὴ ὀπὴ ἐπιτηδεία εἰς τὸν μοχλὸν τοῦ κλήθρου, ἧς ἄνευ οὐκ ἂν ἐξευρίσκετο ἡ χρῆσις τοῦ σκεύους καὶ εἴκασεν ἄν τις ἀνάθημα μᾶλλον ἢ κλεῖδα εἶναι τὸ πρᾶγμα. αὐτὸ δὲ τὸ σῶμα τοῦ ἑρμοῦ πλατύνεται μὲν προϊὸν εἰς τὰ ἄνω, ὥσπερ πολλάκις καὶ ἐν ἄλλοις ὁμοίοις, ἔχει δὲ τὸν ἀναγκαῖον παντὶ ἑρμῇ φαλλὸν ἐν τῷ μέσῳ, ἔχει δὲ ἔνθεν καὶ ἔνθεν καὶ τὰς μασχαλιαίας τετραγωνικὰς ἐξοχάς, ὥσπερ καὶ ἐπὶ τῶν λιθίνων ἑρμῶν πολλάκις πρὸς ἀνάρτησιν στεφάνων, ὥσπερ ἰδεῖν σοι πάρεστι εἰκόνα τοιχογραφικὴν τοῦ ἐθίμου ἐξ Ἡρακλείου ἐν Müller-ου Denkmäler der alten Kunst τόμῳ Α΄, πίνακι ά, ἀριθμῷ 3. ἐπί-

κειται δὲ τῷ σώματι τοῦ ἑρμοῦ κεφαλὴ γυναικός, ἧς ἡ κόμωσις δύο κορύμβους ὑπεράνω τοῦ μετώπου ἔχουσα Ἀριάδνην τινα ἢ Βάκχην ὑποσημαίνει, ἄλλως γὰρ ἂν προσείκασα αὐτὴν τῇ τῆς Παλλάδος καὶ Ἑρμαθήνην ἂν τὸ ὅλον ἐκάλεσα. ἔπεστι δὲ τῇ κεφαλῇ κρίκος συμφυὴς πρὸς ἀνάρτησιν τῆς κλειδός · τὸ μῆκος ὅλον τῆς κλειδὸς 0·115 γαλλικοῦ μέτρου· ἴδοις δ᾽ ἂν τοιαῦτα σχήματα ἑρμῶν λίθινα ἐν Ἀθήναις ἐν τῷ κατὰ τὴν ὁδὸν Πατησίων ἐθνικῷ μουσείῳ τῷ πρὸς τῷ Πολυτεχνείῳ, ὧν τὰ κάλλιστα δεδημοσιευμένα κεῖται ὑπ᾽ ἐμοῦ ἐν τῇ Ἀρχαιολογικῇ Ἐφημερίδι, περιόδῳ δευτέρᾳ 1862–1863, σελίδι 183 καὶ 205 καὶ πίνακι Λ΄ καὶ ΛΑ΄, πρβλ. καὶ ΛΓ.

Ἐν Ἀθήναις τῇ Β΄ τοῦ μηνὸς τοῦ ΙΒ΄, ἔτους ͵αωοθ΄.

which has to be imagined as concealed by the foremost horse. Moreover the position of the god is half turned forwards, slightly following that of the head, and here also the arm is again strongly turned inwards, but not

No. 1479. Block of Triglyphs, with Metope of the Sun-God. From the Temple of Apollo in the ruins of the Greek Ilium. (1 : 13 actual size. Depth, 3 ft.)

so as to bring the position into conflict with the rules of relief. If the encroachment of the head on the upper border of the triglyph is considered inaccurate, we find in this a very happy thought, which may remind us of the differently conceived pediment of the Parthenon, where only the head and shoulders of Helios rise out of the chariot still under the ocean. Helios here, so to speak, bursts forth from the gates of day, and sheds the light of his glory over the universe. These are beauties peculiar only to Greek art in the fulness of its power."

"The sculpture has also," as my friend M. Fr. Lenormant remarks to me, "a real importance for the history of art: it marks a particular phase of it, which is also indicated by the numismatic monuments and the vase-paintings of Greece. This results from the intentional disposition, by which the sculptor has presented nearly the full face of the god's figure, as well as of the whole composition, instead of giving it in profile, as may be seen, for example, in the celebrated bas-reliefs of Florence, representing the like subject. A disposition like this is very rare in Greek art. Numismatists agree that there was an epoch at which all the cities of the Greek world adopted almost simultaneously the custom of placing on their coins an effigy with a full or three-quarters' face, instead of the head in profile which had been in use before. This was in the time of Alexander, tyrant of Pherae in Thessaly, who himself participated in the new fashion by coining a superb silver medal bearing the head of Artemis with a full face: this was also the time when the victories of Epaminondas and Pelopidas gave Thebes for a while the supremacy over the rest of Greece. In the same century, if we may judge from the style of the coins, Larissa in Thessaly, Amphipolis in Macedonia, Clazomenae in Ionia, Lampsacus in Mysia, Sigeum in the Troad, Thebes in Boeotia, Rhodes, Velia, Croton, Heracleum in Italy, Syracuse and Catania in Sicily, Barca in the Cyrenaica, and many more obscure cities, represented their tutelary divinities with the full face on their coins. In point of material perfection this was the furthest point of progress attained by monetary art. It was the application to this branch of art of the discovery made by Cimon of Cleonae in painting, who was the first to represent heads with the full face, or with three-quarters of the face, which even Polygnotus and Micon themselves had not dared to attempt; and the discovery passed rapidly over into the domain of sculpture. Until then artists had not ventured to draw or model in the flat a figure with the full or three-quarters' face: this was indeed at first a very difficult enterprise, in which the Greeks had no predecessors. In painting and relief the figures were represented in profile. The school of Phidias itself had not dared to represent them otherwise, except in the sculptures of nearly full relief, like the metopes of the Parthenon or the frieze of the Temple at Phigalia. The invention of Cimon of Cleonae consequently appeared marvellous, and the fashion to which it gave birth is borne witness to by the painted vases with full and three-quarter faces. It has also been found in works of sculpture, and the metope before us must henceforward be reckoned among the number of these monuments. But the new fashion passed rapidly away. The exquisite taste of the Greeks made them soon feel how far, merely from the point of view of the laws of art, the use of the profile was superior to that of the face on coins. At the same time it was found that, in order to place on them heads of this kind, it was necessary to give to the monetary types a relief which, being worn off by constant friction, exposed them to rapid and prejudicial deterioration. Hence, from the time of Alexander people had almost everywhere, except in a few places, such as Rhodes, returned to profiles, the moderate reliefs of which secured for the coin a longer duration with a less rapid diminution of weight. In sculpture in low-relief, also, artists returned, though perhaps a little less promptly, to the habit of representing figures generally in profile, without, however, renouncing completely the new resources at their command, and the element of variety furnished to the artist by the step of progress realized by the Peloponnesian painter."

As to the halo of rays which we see on the head of Phoebus Apollo, it first occurs about the time of Alexander the Great. The special form of long and short rays is found on the coins of Alexander I., of Epirus, and of Ceos (Carthaea), mentioned by Curtius. Archæologists universally agree in claiming for this metope the date of the fourth century B.C.

About 60 yards to the west of the spot where this monument was found, I came upon a second Doric triglyph-block,[2] with a metope representing warriors fighting; but this sculpture is much mutilated and had evidently never been finished, and is therefore of no interest to science. Visitors will see it lying in my large northern trench.

About 200 yards to the west of Hissarlik, at a place where the site of Novum Ilium slopes gently down to the plain, is a protruding rock crowned with three fig-trees, which have grown up from the same root. Beneath this rock only ten years ago a hole was visible, said to be the

No. 1480.   Cavern with a spring, to the left on leaving Troy. The water of this spring runs in the direction of the ancient Scamander. The tree above it is a wild fig-tree.

entrance to a passage called *lagoum* by the villagers; but now this hole had been entirely filled up. Mr. Frank Calvert, who crept in about twenty years ago, when the hole was still large, saw before him a long passage; but several villagers, who pretended to have done the same,

---

[2] This second triglyph-block was found at the place marked P P.

assured me that they had seen in it a great many marble statues, standing upright.

Wishing to clear up the mystery, I resolved to excavate the cavern, but in spite of all the kind endeavours of my honoured friend, Sir Henry Layard, it took a long time to obtain the necessary permission from the Sublime Porte. Having at last got this, I set ten labourers to work with pickaxes, shovels, and wheelbarrows, to excavate it. To facilitate the excavation, I made them first dig a trench before the cavern, so as to be able to work it at once on the virgin soil. The proprietor of the land had consented to the excavation, under the condition that he should be one of the workmen and receive treble wages. I found a vaulted passage, 8 ft. 4 in. broad and $5\frac{1}{2}$ ft. high, cut out in the limestone rock.

About 30 ft. from the entrance a vertical hole, $2\frac{1}{2}$ ft. in diameter, has been cut through the superincumbent rock. It reminded me vividly of a similar hole cut through the rock above the Grotto of the Nymphs in Ithaca, in order to serve as a chimney for the smoke of the sacrifices (see p. 49). But the hole in this Trojan cavern can hardly have been made for such a purpose, for I found in the cavern nothing but potsherds of a late epoch and some bones of animals. I therefore think that the chimney-like hole must have been cut merely for letting in fresh air and light. At a distance of 55 ft. from the entrance the large passage divides into three very narrow ones, only large enough for one man to enter, and of which one turns to the north-east, the second to the east, and the third to the south-east. In the floor of each of these narrow passages a small trench has been cut in the rock, from which water flows. The water of the three trenches unites in a larger trench cut in the floor of the large passage, from which it flows into an earthen pipe. According to Virchow's observation, the water has a temperature of $15°\cdot6$ centigr. $= 60°\cdot08$ Fahr.

As the reader will see from the engraving, No. 1480, the rock which covers the entrance to this passage looks as if it had been artificially cut : but this is not the case ; it is a natural formation. At a short distance to the right and left of it are the remains of a large city wall, which has evidently passed over it. Thus the entrance to the passage was immediately below the wall, but outside of it ; a fact inexplicable to us. We, therefore, presume that there has been a second larger city wall still further to the west, where the road now runs from Hissarlik to Kalifatli. This certainly appears to be confirmed by the potsherds and marble fragments, which reach down as far as that road.

§ II. The Greek Inscriptions found at Novum Ilium.

Of Greek inscriptions six were found among the ruins of the Temple of Athené. The largest of them, on a marble slab in the form of a tomb-stone, 5¼ ft. long, 17½ in. broad, and 5¾ in. thick, is as follows :—

```
    ΜΕΛΕΑΓΡΟΣΙΛΙΕΩΝΤΗΙΒΟΥΛΗΙΚΑΙΤΩΙΔΗΜΩΙΧΑΙ
    ΡΕΙΝΑΠΕΔΩΚΕΝΗΜΙΝΑΡΙΣΤΟΔΙΚΙΔΗΣΟΑΣΣΙΟΣΕΠΙ
    ΣΤΟΛΑΣΠΑΡΑΤΟΥΒΑΣΙΛΕΩΣΑΝΤΙΟΧΟΥΩΝΤΑΝΤΙΓΡΑ
    ΦΑΥΜΙΝΥΠΟΓΕΓΡΑΦΑΜΕΝΕΝΕΤΥΧΕΝΔΗΜΙΝΚΑΙΑΥ
  5 ΤΟΣΦΑΜΕΝΟΣΠΟΛΛΩΝΑΥΤΩΙΚΑΙΕΤΕΡΩΝΔΙΑΛΕ
    ΓΟΜΕΝΩΝΚΑΙΣΤΕΦΑΝΟΝΔΙΔΟΝΤΩΝΩΣΠΕΡΚΑΙΗ
    ΜΕΙΣΠΑΡΑΚΟΛΟΥΘΟΥΜΕΝΔΙΑΤΟΚΑΙΠΡΕΣΒΕΥΣΑΙΑ
    ΠΟΤΩΝΠΟΛΕΩΝΤΙΝΑΣΠΡΟΣΗΜΑΣΒΟΥΛΕΣΘΑΙΤΗΝ
    ΧΩΡΑΝΤΗΝΔΕΔΟΜΕΝΗΝΑΥΤΩΙΥΠΟΤΟΥΒΑΣΙΛΕΩΣΑΝ
 10 ΤΙΟΧΟΥΚΑΙΔΙΑΤΟΙΕΡΟΝΚΑΙΔΙΑΤΗΝΠΡΟΣΥΜΑΣΕΥΝΟΙ
    ΑΝΠΡΟΣΕΝΕΓΚΑΣΘΑΙΠΡΟΣΤΗΝΥΜΕΤΕΡΑΝΠΟΛΙΝΑ
    ΜΕΝΟΥΝΑΞΙΟΙΓΕΝΕΣΘΑΙΑΥΤΩΙΠΑΡΑΤΗΣΠΟΛΕΩΣΑΥ
    ΤΟΣΥΜΙΝΔΗΛΩΣΕΙΚΑΛΩΣΔΑΝΠΟΗΣΑΙΤΕΨΗΦΙΣΑΜΕ
    ΝΟΙΤΕΠΑΝΤΑΤΑΦΙΛΑΝΘΡΩΠΑΑΥΤΩΙΚΑΙΚΑΘΟΤΙΑΝ
 15 ΣΥΓΧΩΡΗΣΗΙΤΗΝΑΝΑΓΡΑΦΗΝΠΟΗΣΑΜΕΝΟΙΚΑΙΣΤΗ
    ΛΩΣΑΝΤΕΣΚΑΙΘΕΝΤΕΣΕΙΣΤΟΙΕΡΟΝΙΝΑΜΕΝΗΙΥΜΙΝ
    ΒΕΒΑΙΩΣΕΙΣΠΑΝΤΑΤΟΓΧΡΟΝΟΝΤΑΣΥΓΧΩΡΗΘΕΝΤΑ
    ΕΡΡΩΣΘΕ            ΒΑΣΙΛΕΥΣΑΝΤΙΟΧΟΣΜΕΛΕΑ
    ΓΡΩΙΧΑΙΡΕΙΝΔΕΔΩΚΑΜΕΝΑΡΙΣΤΟΔΙΚΙΔΗΙΤΩΙΑΣΣΙΩΙ
 20 ΓΗΣΕΡΓΑΣΙΜΟΥΠΛΕΘΡΑΔΙΣΧΙΛΙΑΠΡΟΣΕΝΕΓΚΑΣΘΑΙ
    ΠΡΟΣΤΗΝΙΛΙΕΩΝΠΟΛΙΝΗΣΚΗΨΙΩΝΣΥΟΥΝΣΥΝΤΑΞΟΝ
    ΠΛΑΡΑΔΕΙΞΑΙΑΡΙΣΤΟΔΙΚΙΔΗΙΑΠΟΤΗΣΟΜΟΡΟΥΣΗΣΤΗΙ
    ΓΕΡΓΙΘΙΑΙΗΤΗΙΣΚΗΨΙΑΙΟΥΑΝΔΟΚΙΜΑΖΗΙΣΤΑΔΙΣΧΙΛΙΑ
    ΠΛΕΘΡΑΤΗΣΓΗΣΚΑΙΠΡΟΣΟΡΙΣΑΙΕΙΣΤΗΝΙΛΙΕΩΝΗΤΗΝ
 25 ΣΚΗΨΙΩΝ   ΕΡΡΩΣΟ   ΒΑΣΙΛΕΥΣΑΝΤΙΟΧΟΣΜΕΛΕ
    ΑΓΡΩΙΧΑΙΡΕΙΝΕΝΕΤΥΧΕΝΗΜΙΝΑΡΙΣΤΟΔΙΚΙΔΗΣΟ
    ΑΣΣΙΟΣΑΞΙΩΝΔΟΥΝΑΙΑΥΤΩΙΗΜΑΣΕΝΤΗΙΕΦΕΛΛΗΣ
    ΠΟΝΤΟΥΣΑΤΡΑΠΕΙΑΙΤΗΝΠΕΤΡΑΝΗΜΠΡΟΤΕΡΟΝ
    ΕΙΧΕΝΜΕΛΕΑΓΡΟΣΚΑΙΤΗΣΧΩΡΑΣΤΗΣΠΕΤΡΙΔΟΣ
 30 ΕΡΓΑΣΙΜΟΥΠΕΘΡΑΧΙΛΙΑΠΕΝΤΑΚΟΣΙΑΚΑΙΑΛΛΑ
    ΓΗΣΠΛΕΘΡΑΔΙΣΧΙΛΙΑΕΡΓΑΣΙΜΟΥΑΠΟΤΗΣΟΜΟ
    ΡΟΥΣΗΣΤΗΙΠΡΟΤΕΡΟΝΔΟΘΕΙΣΗΙΑΥΤΩΙΜΕΡΙΔΙΩΙ
    ΚΑΙΗΜΕΙΣΤΗΝΤΕΠΕΤΡΑΝΔΕΔΩΚΑΜΕΝΑΥΤΩΙΕΙ
    ΜΗΔΕΔΟΤΑΙΑΛΛΩΙΠΡΟΤΕΡΟΝΚΑΙΤΗΓΧΩΡΑΝΤΗΝ
 35 ΠΡΟΣΤΗΙΠΕΤΡΑΙΚΑΙΑΛΛΑΓΗΣΠΛΕΘΡΑΔΙΣΧΙΛΙΑ
    ΕΡΓΑΣΙΜΟΥΔΙΑΤΟΦΙΛΟΝΟΝΤΑΗΜΕΤΕΡΟΝΠΑΡΕΣ
    ΧΗΣΘΑΙΗΜΙΝΤΑΣΚΑΤΑΥΤΟΝΧΡΕΙΑΣΜΕΤΑΠΑΣΗΣ
    ΕΥΝΟΙΑΣΚΑΙΠΡΟΘΥΜΙΑΣΣΥΟΥΝΕΠΙΣΚΕΨΑΜΕΝΟΣ
    ΕΙΜΗΔΕΔΟΤΑΙΑΛΛΩΙΠΡΟΤΕΡΟΝΑΥΤΗΗΜΕΡΙΣΠΑ
 40 ΡΑΔΕΙΞΟΝΑΥΤΗΝΚΑΙΤΗΝΠΡΟΣΑΥΤΗΙΧΩΡΑΝΑΡΙΣ
    ΤΟΔΙΚΙΚΙΔΗΙΚΑΙΑΠΟΤΗΣΒΑΣΙΛΙΚΗΣΧΩΡΑΣΤΗΣΟΜΟ
    ΡΟΥΣΗΣΤΗΙΠΡΟΤΕΡΟΝΔΕΔΟΜΕΝΗΙΧΩΡΑΙΑΡΙΣΤΟΔΙ
    ΚΙΔΗΙΣΥΝΤΑΞΟΝΚΑΤΑΜΕΤΡΗΣΑΙΚΑΙΠΑΡΑΔΕΙΞΑΙ
    ΑΥΤΩΙΠΛΕΘΡΑΔΙΣΧΙΛΙΑΚΑΙΕΑΣΑΙΑΥΤΩΙΠΡΟΣΕΝΕΓ
```

45 ΚΑΣΘΑΙΠΡΟΣΗΝΑΜΒΟΥΛΗΤΑΙΠΟΛΙΝΤΩΝΕΝΤΗΙΧΩΡΑΙ
ΤΕΚΑΙΣΥΜΜΑΧΙΑΙΟΙΔΕΒΑΣΙΛΙΚΟΙΛΑΟΙΟΙΕΚΤΟΥΤΟ
ΠΟΥΕΝΩΙΕΣΤΙΝΗΠΕΤΡΑΕΑΜΒΟΥΛΩΝΤΑΙΟΙΚΕΙΝΕΝΤΗΙ
ΠΕΤΡΑΙΑΣΦΑΛΕΙΑΣΕΝΕΚΕΣΥΝΤΕΤΑΧΑΜΕΝΑΡΙΣΤΟ
ΤΟΔΙΚΙΔΗΙΕΑΝΑΥΤΟΥΣΟΙΚΕΙΝ   ΕΡΡΩΣΟ
50 ΒΑΣΙΛΕΥΣΑΝΤΙΟΧΟΣΜΕΛΕΑΓΡΩΙΧΑΙΡΕΙΝΕΝΕΤΥΧΕΝΗ
ΜΙΝΑΡΙΣΤΟΔΙΚΙΔΗΣΦΑΜΕΝΟΣΠΕΤΡΑΝΤΟΧΩΡΙΟΝΚΑΙΤΗΓ
ΧΩΡΑΝΤΗΝΣΥΓΚΥΡΟΥΣΑΝΠΕΡΙΗΣΠΡΟΤΕΡΟΝΕΓΡΑΨΑΜΕΝ
ΔΙΔΟΝΤΕΣΑΥΤΩΙΟΥΔΕΤΙΚΑΙΝΥΝΠΑΡΕΙΛΗΦΕΝΑΙΔΙΑΤΟΑΘΗ
ΝΑΙΩΙΤΩΙΕΠΙΤΟΥΝΑΥΣΤΑΘΜΟΥΕΠΙΚΕΧΩΡΗΣΘΑΙΚΑΙΗΞΙ
55 ΩΣΕΝΑΝΤΙΜΕΝΤΗΣΠΕΤΡΙΤΙΔΟΣΧΩΡΑΣΠΑΡΑΔΕΙΧΘΗΝΑΙ
ΑΥΤΩΙΤΑΙΣΑΠΛΕΘΡΑΣΥΓΧΩΡΗΘΗΝΑΙΔΕΚΑΙΑΛΛΑΠΛΕ
ΘΡΑΔΙΣΧΙΛΙΑΠΡΟΣΕΝΕΓΚΑΣΘΑΙΠΡΟΣΗΝΑΜΒΟΥΛΗΤΑΙ
ΤΩΜΠΟΛΕΩΝΤΩΝΕΝΤΗΙΗΜΕΤΕΡΑΙΣΥΜΜΑΧΙΑΙΚΑΘΑ
ΠΕΡΚΑΙΠΡΟΤΕΡΟΝΕΓΡΑΨΑΜΕΝΟΡΩΝΤΕΣΟΥΝΑΥΤΟΝ
60 ΕΥΝΟΥΝΟΝΤΑΚΑΙΠΡΟΘΥΜΟΝΕΙΣΤΑΗΜΕΤΕΡΑΠΡΑΓΜΑ
ΤΑΒΟΥΛΟΜΕΘΑΠΟΛΥΩΡΕΙΝΤΑΝΘΡΩΠΟΥΚΑΙΠΕΡΙ
ΤΟΥΤΩΝΣΥΓΚΕΧΩΡΗΚΑΜΕΝΦΗΣΙΝΔΕΕΙΝΑΙΤΗΣ
ΠΕΤΡΙΤΙΔΟΣΧΩΡΑΣΤΑΣΥΓΧΩΡΗΘΕΝΤΑΑΥΤΩΙ
ΠΛΕΘΡΑΧΙΛΙΑΠΕΝΤΑΚΟΣΙΑΣΥΝΤΑΞΟΝΟΥΝΚΑΤΑ
65 ΜΕΤΡΗΣΑΙΑΡΙΣΤΟΔΙΚΙΔΗΙΚΑΙΠΑΡΑΔΕΙΞΑΙΓΗΣ
ΕΡΓΑΣΙΜΟΥΤΑΤΕΔΙΣΧΙΛΙΑΚΑΙΠΕΝΤΑΚΟΣΙΑΠΛΕ
ΘΡΑΚΑΙΑΝΤΙΤΩΝΠΕΡΙΤΗΝΠΕΤΡΑΝΑΛΛΑΕΡΓΑ
ΣΙΜΟΥΧΙΛΙΑΠΕΝΤΑΚΟΣΙΑΑΠΟΤΗΣΒΑΣΙΛΙΚΗΣΧΩ
ΡΑΣΤΗΣΣΥΝΟΡΙΖΟΥΣΗΣΤΗΙΕΝΑΡΧΗΙΔΟΘΕΙΣΗΙ
70 ΑΥΤΩΙΠΑΡΗΜΩΝΕΑΣΑΙΔΕΚΑΙΠΡΟΣΕΝΕΓΚΑΣΘΑΙ
ΤΗΝΧΩΡΑΝΑΡΙΣΤΟΔΙΚΙΔΗΝΠΡΟΣΗΝΑΝΒΟΥΛΗΤΑΙ
ΠΟΛΙΝΤΩΝΕΝΤΗΙΗΜΕΤΕΡΑΙΣΥΜΜΑΧΙΑΙΚΑΘΑ
ΠΕΡΚΑΙΕΝΤΗΙΠΡΟΤΕΡΟΝΕΠΙΣΤΟΛΗΙΕΓΡΑΨΑ
ΜΕΝ ΕΡΡΩΣΟ[3]

Μελέαγρος Ἰλιέων τῇ βουλῇ καὶ τῷ δήμῳ χαίρειν. Ἀπέδωκεν ἡμῖν Ἀριστοδικίδης ὁ Ἄσσιος ἐπι-
στολὰς παρὰ τοῦ βασιλέως Ἀντιόχου, ὧν τἀντίγρα-
φα ὑμῖν ὑπογεγράφαμεν· ἐνέτυχεν δ' ἡμῖν καὶ αὐ-
5 τὸς φάμενος, πολλῶν αὐτῷ καὶ ἑτέρων διαλε-
γομένων καὶ στέφανον διδόντων, ὥσπερ καὶ ἡ-
μεῖς παρακολουθοῦμεν διὰ τὸ καὶ πρεσβεῦσαι ἀ-
πὸ τῶν πόλεων τινὰς πρὸς ἡμᾶς, βούλεσθαι τὴν
χώραν τὴν δεδομένην αὐτῷ ὑπὸ τοῦ βασιλέως Ἀν-
10 τιόχου καὶ διὰ τὸ ἱερὸν καὶ διὰ τὴν πρὸς ὑμᾶς εὔνοι-
αν προσενέγκασθαι πρὸς τὴν ὑμετέραν πόλιν. Ἃ
μὲν οὖν ἀξιοῖ γενέσθαι αὐτῷ παρὰ τῆς πόλεως, αὐ-

[3] " Meleager greets the Council and the people of Ilium. Aristodicides, of Assos, has handed to us letters from king Antiochus, the copies of which we have written out for you. He (Aristodicides) came to meet us himself, and told us that though many other cities apply to him and offer him a crown, just as we also understand because some have sent embassies to us from the cities, nevertheless, prompted by his veneration for the temple (of the *Ilian Athené*), as well as by his feeling of friendship for your town, he is willing to offer to you the land which king Antiochus has presented to him. Now, he will communicate to you what he claims to be done for him by the city. Thus you would do well to vote for him every kind of hearty friendship,

τὸς ὑμῖν δηλώσει· καλῶς δ' ἂν ποήσαιτε ψηφισάμε-
νοί τε πάντα τὰ φιλάνθρωπα αὐτῷ καὶ καθ' ὅτι ἂν
15 συγχωρήσῃ τὴν ἀναγραφὴν ποησάμενοι καὶ στη-
λώσαντες καὶ θέντες εἰς τὸ ἱερόν, ἵνα μένῃ ὑμῖν
βεβαίως εἰς πάντα τὸγ χρόνον τὰ συγχωρηθέντα.
ἔρρωσθε.   Βασιλεὺς Ἀντίοχος Μελεάγρῳ χαίρειν. Δεδώκαμεν Ἀριστοδικίδῃ τῷ Ἀσσίῳ
20 γῆς ἐργασίμου πλέθρα δισχίλια προσενέγκασθαι
πρὸς τὴν Ἰλιέων πόλιν ἢ Σκηψίων. Σὺ οὖν σύνταξον
παραδεῖξαι Ἀριστοδικίδῃ ἀπὸ τῆς ὁμορούσης τῇ
Γεργιθίαι ἢ τῇ Σκηψίαι, οὗ ἂν δοκιμάζῃς τὰ δισχίλια
πλέθρα τῆς γῆς καὶ προσορίσαι εἰς τὴν Ἰλιέων ἢ τὴν
25 Σκηψίων. ἔρρωσο. Βασιλεὺς Ἀντίοχς Μελεάγρῳ χαίρειν. Ἐνέτυχεν ἡμῖν Ἀριστοδικίδης ὁ
Ἄσσιος ἀξιῶν δοῦναι αὐτῷ ἡμᾶς ἐν τῇ ἐφ' Ἑλλησπόντου σατραπείαι τὴν Πέτραν, ἣμ πρότερον
εἶχεν Μελέαγρος καὶ τῆς χώρας τῆς Πετρίδος
30 ἐργασίμου πέθρα⁴ χίλια πεντακόσια καὶ ἄλλα
γῆς πλέθρα δισχίλια ἐργασίμου ἀπὸ τῆς ὁμορούσης τῇ πρότερον δοθείσῃ αὐτῷ μεριδίῳ·
καὶ ἡμεῖς τήν τε Πέτραν δεδώκαμεν αὐτῷ, εἰ
μὴ δέδοται ἄλλῳ πρότερον καὶ τὴγ χώραν τὴν
35 πρὸς τῇ Πέτραι καὶ ἄλλα γῆς πλέθρα δισχίλια
ἐργασίμου, διὰ τὸ φίλον ὄντα ἡμέτερον παρεσ-
χῆσθαι ἡμῖν τὰς κατ' αὐτὸν χρείας μετὰ πάσης
εὐνοίας καὶ προθυμίας. Σὺ οὖν ἐπισκεψάμενος
εἰ μὴ δέδοται ἄλλῳ πρότερον αὕτη ἡ μερίς, πα-
40 ράδειξον αὐτὴν καὶ τὴν πρὸς αὐτῇ χώραν Ἀρισ-
τοδικικίδῃ⁵ καὶ ἀπὸ τῆς βασιλικῆς χώρας τῆς ὁμορούσης τῇ πρότερον δεδομένῃ χώραι Ἀριστοδικίδῃ σύνταξον καταμετρῆσαι καὶ παραδεῖξαι
αὐτῷ πλέθρα δισχίλια καὶ ἐᾶσαι αὐτῷ προσενέγ-

---

and, whatever concession he may make, do you put it on record, engrave it on a stone slab, and set it up in the temple, in order that the concession may be safely preserved to you for ever. Farewell.

"King Antiochus greets Meleager. We have granted to Aristodicides, the Assian, two thousand plethra of arable land, for him to confer on the city of *Ilium*, or on the city of Scepsis. Order therefore that the two thousand plethra of land be assigned to Aristodicides, wherever you may think proper, of the land which borders on the territory of Gergis, or on that of Scepsis, and that they be added to the city of the Ilians, or to that of the Scepsians. Farewell.

"King Antiochus greets Meleager. Aristodicides, the Assian, came to meet us, begging that we would give him, in the satrapy of the Hellespont, Petra, which Meleager formerly had, and in the territory of Petra one thousand five hundred plethra of arable land, and two thousand plethra more of arable land bordering on the portion which had been given to him first as his share ; and we have given Petra to him, provided it has not yet been given to some one else ; and we have also presented to him the land near Petra, and two thousand plethra more of arable land, because he is our friend and has supplied to us all that we required, as far as he could, with kindness and willingness. Do you then, having examined if that portion has not already been given to some one else, assign it to Aristodicides, as well as the land near it, and order that of the royal domain which borders on the land first granted to Aristodicides two thousand plethra be measured off and assigned to him, and leave it to him to confer the land on what town soever in the country or confede-

---

⁴ Sic.   ⁵ Sic.

45 κασθαι πρὸς ἣν ἀμ βούληται πόλιν τῶν ἐν τῇ χώραι
τε καὶ συμμαχίαι· οἱ δὲ βασιλικοὶ λαοὶ οἱ ἐκ τοῦ τόπου, ἐν ᾧ ἐστὶν ἡ Πέτρα, ἐὰμ βούλωνται οἰκεῖν ἐν τῇ
Πέτραι ἀσφαλείας ἕνεκε, συντετάχαμεν Ἀριστο-
τοδικίδη⁶ ἐὰν αὐτοὺς οἰκεῖν.   ἔρρωσο.

50 Βασιλεὺς Ἀντίοχος Μελεάγρῳ χαίρειν.   Ἐνέτυχεν ἡ-
μῖν Ἀριστοδικίδης, φάμενος Πέτραν τὸ χωρίον καὶ τὴγ
χώραν τὴν συγκυροῦσαν, περὶ ἧς πρότερον ἐγράψαμεν
διδόντες αὐτῷ, οὐδ᾽ ἔτι καὶ νῦν παρειληφέναι, διὰ τὸ Ἀθη-
ναίῳ τῷ ἐπὶ τοῦ ναυστάθμου ἐπικεχωρῆσθαι, καὶ ἠξί-
55 ωσεν ἀντὶ μὲν τῆς Πετρίτιδος χώρας παραδειχθῆναι
αὐτῷ τὰ ἴσα πλέθρα, συγχωρηθῆναι δὲ καὶ ἄλλα πλέθρα δισχίλια προσενέγκασθαι πρὸς ἣν ἀμ βούληται
τῶμ πόλεων τῶν ἐν τῇ ἡμετέραι συμμαχίαι, καθάπερ καὶ πρότερον ἐγράψαμεν.   Ὁρῶντες οὖν αὐτὸν
60 εὔνουν ὄντα καὶ πρόθυμον εἰς τὰ ἡμέτερα πράγμα-
τα, βουλόμεθα πολυωρεῖν τἀνθρώπου, καὶ περὶ
τούτων συγκεχωρήκαμεν.   Φησὶν δὲ εἶναι τῆς
Πετρίτιδος χώρας τὰ συγχωρηθέντα αὐτῷ
πλέθρα χίλια πεντακόσια.   Σύνταξον οὖν κατα-
65 μετρῆσαι Ἀριστοδικίδη καὶ παραδεῖξαι γῆς
ἐργασίμου τά τε δισχίλια καὶ πεντακόσια πλέθρα καὶ ἀντὶ τῶν περὶ τὴν Πέτραν ἄλλα ἐργασίμου χίλια πεντακόσια ἀπὸ τῆς βασιλικῆς χώρας τῆς συνοριζούσης τῇ ἐν ἀρχῇ δοθείσῃ
70 αὐτῷ παρ᾽ ἡμῶν· ἐᾶσαι δὲ καὶ προσενέγκασθαι
τὴν χώραν Ἀριστοδικίδην πρὸς ἣν ἂν βούληται
πόλιν τῶν ἐν τῇ ἡμετέραι συμμαχίαι, καθάπερ καὶ ἐν τῇ πρότερον ἐπιστολῇ ἐγράψαμεν.   ἔρρωσο.

This inscription, the great historical value of which cannot be denied,
seems with certainty to belong to the third or second century B.C., judging
from the subject as well as from the form of the letters, for the king

---

racy he pleases. Regarding the royal subjects
in the estate in which Petra is situated, if for
safety's sake they wish to live in Petra, we have
recommended Aristodicides to let them remain
there. Farewell.

"King Antiochus greets Meleager. Aristodicides came to meet us, saying that Petra, the
district and the land with it, which we gave
to him in our former letter, is no longer
disposable, it having been granted to Athenaeus,
the commandant of the naval station; and he
begged that, instead of the land of Petra, the
same number of plethra might be assigned to him
(elsewhere), and that he might be permitted to
confer another lot of two thousand plethra of land
on whichsoever of the cities in our confederacy
he might choose, according as we wrote before.
Now, seeing him friendly disposed and zealous

for our interests, we wish to show great regard
for the man's interest, and have complied with
his request about these matters. He says that
his grant of land at Petra amounts to fifteen
hundred plethra. Give order therefore that the
two thousand five hundred plethra of arable
land be measured out and assigned to Aristodicides; and further, instead of the land
around Petra, another lot of fifteen hundred
plethra of arable land, to be taken from the
royal domains bordering on the estate which we
first granted to him. Let now Aristodicides
confer the land on whichsoever of the cities in
our confederacy he may wish, as we have written
in our former letter. Farewell."

⁶ Sic.

Antiochus, who is repeatedly mentioned, must be either Antiochus I., surnamed Soter (281 to 260 B.C.), or Antiochus III., the Great (222 to 186 B.C.). Polybius, who was born in 210 or 200 B.C. and died in 122 B.C., speaks indeed in his History[7] of a Meleager who lived in his time, and was an ambassador of Antiochus Epiphanes, who reigned from 174 to 164 B.C., and it is quite possible that this Meleager afterwards became satrap of the Hellespont. But in the first letter of Antiochus to his satrap Meleager, he gives him the option of assigning to Aristodicides the 2000 plethra of land, either from the district bordering upon the territory of Gergis or upon that of Scepsis. The town of Gergis, however, according to Strabo, was destroyed by king Attalus I. of Pergamus, who reigned from 241 to 197 B.C., and transplanted the inhabitants to the neighbourhood of the sources of the Caïcus in Mysia. These sources, as Strabo himself says, are situated at a great distance from Mount Ida, and therefore also from Ilium. Two thousand plethra of land at such a distance could not have been of any use to the Ilians ; consequently, it is impossible to believe that the inscription can be speaking of the new town of Gergitha, which was rising into importance at the sources of the Caïcus. Thus the old town of Gergis must be meant, whose ruins are probably those on the height of the Bali Dagh beyond Bounarbashi.   Livy[8] gives an account of the visit of Antiochus III., the Great, to Ilium. I also find in the *Corpus Inscriptionum Graecarum* (No. 3596), that this Antiochus had a general called Meleager, who may subsequently have become satrap of the Hellespont. On the other hand, Mr. Calvert calls my attention to Chishull, who, in his *Antiquitates Asiaticae*, says that Antiochus I., Soter, on an expedition with his fleet against the king of Bithynia, stopped at the town of Sigeum, which lay near Ilium, and that the king went up to Ilium with the queen, who was his wife and sister, and with the great dignitaries and his suite. There is, indeed, nothing said of the brilliant reception which was there prepared for him, but there is an account of the reception which was arranged for him at Sigeum. The Sigeans lavished servile flattery upon him, and not only did they send ambassadors to congratulate him, but the Senate also passed a decree, in which they eulogized all the king's actions, and proclaimed that public prayers should be offered up to the Ilian Athené, to Apollo (who was regarded as his ancestor), to the goddess of Victory, and to other deities, for his and his consort's welfare ; that the priestesses and priests, the senators and all the magistrates of the town, should carry wreaths, and that all the citizens and all the strangers settled or temporarily residing in Sigeum should publicly extol the virtues and the bravery of the great king ; further, that a golden equestrian statue of the king, raised on a pedestal of white marble, should be erected in the Temple of Athené at Sigeum, and that it should bear this inscription : " The Sigeans have erected this statue to king Antiochus, the son of Seleucus, for the devotion he has shown to the temple, and because he is the benefactor and the saviour of the people : this mark of honour is to be proclaimed in the popular assemblies and at the public games."

---

[7] xxviii. 1, and xxxi. 21.   [8] xxxv. 43.

It is very probable that a similar reception awaited Antiochus I. in
Ilium, so that he kept the city in good remembrance. That he cherished
kindly feelings towards the Ilians is proved also by the inscription
No. 3595 in the *Corpus Inscriptionum Graecarum*. But whether it is he
or Antiochus the Great that is referred to in the newly-found inscription,
I do not venture to decide.

Aristodicides, of Assos, who is frequently mentioned in the inscription,
is utterly unknown, and his name occurs here for the first time. The
name of the place Petra also, which is mentioned several times in the
inscription, is quite unknown: it must have been situated in the neighbourhood, but all my endeavours to discover it in the modern Turkish
names of the localities, or by other means, have been in vain.

Another inscription is on a marble slab 2 ft. broad and 3 ft. long, and
runs as follows :—

```
                          ΩΝΙΟΥΤΟΥΕΥΔ
        ΟΣΜΕΝ            ΟΥΚΑΜΕΝΑΧΟΣΓΛΑΥΚΟ
ΕΠΕΓΡΑΨΑΜΕΝΕΙΣΣΤΗΛΗΝΚΑΤΑΤΟΝΝΟΜΟΝΕΡΓΟΦΙΛΟΝΠΑΤΡΟΣΟΥ
ΧΡΗΜΑΤΙΣΖΗΕΖΗΜΙΩΜΕΝΟΝΥΠΟΤΩΝΠΡΟΤΑΝΕΩΝΤΩΝΠΕΡΙΔΙΟ
5 ΦΑΝΗΝΗΓΗΣΙΔΗΜΟΥΟΦΙΛΟΝΤΑΤΟΥΣΚΑΤΑΤΟΝΝΟΜΟΝΣΤΑΤΗΡΑΣΔΥΟ
ΚΑΙΜΗΝΟΓΕΝΗΝΜΝΗΣΑΡΧΟΥΚΑΙΑΡΤΕΜΙΔΩΡΟΝΦΑΝΙΑΚΑΙΔΙΟΜΗΔΗΝ
ΑΠΟΛΛΩΝΙΟΥΕΖΗΜΙΩΜΕΝΟΥΣΥΠΟΤΩΝΠΡΥΤΑΝΕΩΝΤΩΝΠΕΡΙΔΙΟΦΑΝΗΝ
ΗΓΗΣΙΔΗΜΟΥΥΠΟΗΜΕΡΑΣΤΡΕΙΣΟΦΙΛΟΝΤΑΣΕΚΑΣΤΟΝΑΥΤΩΝΣΤΑΤΗΡΑΣΔΥΟ
ΜΗΝΟΔΟΤΟΝΜΗΝΟΔΟΤΟΥΚΑΙΗΡΑΚΛΕΙΔΗΝΚΑΙΜΗΝΟΔΟΤΟΝΤΟΥΣΗΡΑΚΛΕΙ
10 ΔΟΥΕΖΗΜΙΩΜΕΝΟΥΣΥΠΟΤΩΝΠΕΡΙΦΑΙΝΩΝΑΚΤΑΕΥΔΗΜΟΥΠΡΥΤΑ
ΝΕΩΝΟΦΙΛΟΝΤΑΕΚΑΣΤΟΝΑΥΤΩΝΣΤΑΤΗΡΑΣΔΥΟ
ΑΡΤΕΜΙΔΩΡΟΝΜΗΝΟΦΑΝΤΟΥΕΖΗΜΙΩΜΕΝΟΝΥΠΟΤΩΝΝΟ
ΜΟΦΥΛΑΚΩΝΤΩΝΠΕΡΙΙΠΠΑΡΧΟΝΗΓΗΣΙΔΗΜΟΥΟΦΙΛΟΝ
ΤΑΣΤΑΤΗΡΑΣΔΥΟ
```

. . . . ωνίου τοῦ Εὐδ . . . .
. . . . . . οσμεν . . . . ουκαμεναχος Γλαυκο . .
ἐπεγράψαμεν εἰς στήλην κατὰ τὸν νόμον Ἐργόφιλον Πατρόσου (?)
Χρήματις[1] ζη[2] ἐζημιωμένον ὑπὸ τῶν προτάνεων[3] τῶν περὶ Διο-
5 φάνην Ἡγησιδήμου, ὀφίλοντα[4] τοὺς κατὰ τὸν νόμον στατῆρας δύο
καὶ Μηνογένην Μνησάρχου καὶ Ἀρτεμίδωρον Φανία καὶ Διομήδην
Ἀπολλωνίου, ἐζημιωμένους ὑπὸ τῶν πρυτάνεων τῶν περὶ Διοφάνην
Ἡγησιδήμου ὑπὸ ἡμέρας τρεῖς ὀφίλοντας[4] ἕκαστον αὐτῶν στατῆρας δύο.
Μηνόδοτον Μηνοδότου καὶ Ἡρακλείδην καὶ Μηνόδοτον τοὺς Ἡρακλεί-
10 δου ἐζημιωμένους ὑπὸ τῶν περὶ Φαινώνακτα Εὐδήμου πρυτάνεων, ὀφίλοντα[4] ἕκαστον αὐτῶν στατῆρας δύο.
Ἀρτεμίδωρον Μηνοφάντου ἐζημιωμένον ὑπὸ τῶν νο-
μοφυλάκων τῶν περὶ Ἵππαρχον Ἡγησιδήμου, ὀφίλοντα στατῆρας δύο.

In the inscription quoted in the *Corpus Inscriptionum Graecarum* under
No. 3604, which is admitted to belong to the time of Octavianus Augustus,
Hipparchus is mentioned as a member of the Ilian Council; and as on
line 13 the same name occurs with the same attribute, I do not hesitate
to maintain that the above inscription belongs to the time of Augustus.

---

[1] *Sic.*   [2] *Sic.*   [3] *Sic.*   [4] *Sic.*

In the first wall of the temple I found a marble slab nearly 1 ft. thick, 32½ in. broad, and 3½ ft. long, with the following inscription :—

ΗΒΟΥΛΗΚΑΙΟΔΗΜΟΣ
ΓΑΙΟΝΚΑΙΣΑΡΑΤΟΝΥΙΟΝΤΟΥΣΕΒΑΣ
ΤΟΥΤΟΝΣΥΝΓΕΝΗΚΑΙΠΑΤΡΩΝΑΚΑΙΕΥ
ΕΡΓΕΤΗΝΤΗΣΠΟΛΕΩΣ

'Η βουλὴ καὶ ὁ δῆμος
Γάϊον Καίσαρα τὸν υἱὸν τοῦ Σεβαστοῦ τὸν συγγενῆ καὶ πατρῶνα καὶ εὐεργέτην τῆς πόλεως.

The person praised in this inscription can by no means have been the Emperor Caligula, for in that case the title αὐτοκράτωρ would have been added. But as this word is wanting, the person meant is certainly Caius Caesar, the son of Marcus Vipsanius Agrippa and of Julia, the daughter of Augustus. He had a brother called Lucius. Both were adopted by Augustus, and, owing to this adoption, they received the title of υἱοὶ τοῦ Σεβαστοῦ, and both were selected by Augustus as his successors. Caius Caesar, born in the year 20 B.C., was adopted at the age of three years. He took part in the Trojan games, which Augustus instituted at the dedication of the Temple of Marcellus. At the age of fifteen he was appointed Consul, and when nineteen he was made Governor of Asia. During his administration there he became involved in a war with Phraates, king of Armenia, was wounded, and died in the year 4 after Christ, on the 21st of February, at the age of twenty-four.[5] As in the inscription he is called the kinsman, the benefactor, and the patron of Ilium, it is probable that he often came here during his administration : at all events, he took great interest in the city, and lavished favours upon it. The family of the Julii always attached great importance to their descent from Iülus (or Ascanius), the son of Aeneas ; and the political object of Virgil's *Aeneid* was to prove and glorify their genealogy. This explains the favours which the Julii lavished upon Ilium, and their hatred against the Greeks, because they destroyed Troy, and also because they had espoused the cause of Mark Antony.

I am indebted to the kindness of Mr. Frank Calvert for a squeeze of another inscription engraved on a marble slab, which he found on his field at Hissarlik after my departure thence in the summer of 1873. It has been carefully re-copied from the squeeze by my friend Professor Stephanos Koumanoudes, who, judging from the shape of the characters, thinks that this inscription dates from the time of Antigonus Doson, who died in 221 B.C.

(Γνώμη τῶν συνέδρ)ων· ἐπειδὴ Μαλούσιος Βακχίου
(Γαργαρεὺς ἀνὴρ ἀγ)αθὸ(ς) ὢν διατελεῖ περὶ τὸ ἱερὸν τῆς Ἀθ-
(ηνᾶς τῆς Ἰλιάδος καὶ) περὶ τὰς πόλεις, καὶ πρότερόν τε πολλὰ χρησ(ά-)

---

[5] Velleius Paterculus, ii. 102.

(μενος τῷ τε) συνεδρ(ί)ῳ καὶ ταῖς πόλεσιν εἴς τε τὰ κατασκευάσμα-
5 (τα πάντα τὰ τῆ)ς πανηγύρεως καὶ εἰς τὰς πρεσβε(ί)ας τὰς (ἀ)ποστελ(λο-)
(μένας περὶ) τῶν ἄλλων τῶν συμφερόντων τῇ πανη(γύρει) χρήματα
(ἄτο)κα καὶ τὴν ἄλλην προθυμίαν ἐμ πᾶσι τοῖς (κ)αιροῖς παρεχόμε(νος με-)
(τ)ὰ πολλῆς εὐνοίας, καὶ νῦν εἴς τε τὴν πρεσβείαν τὴν ὕστερον ἀποστ(ελλο-)
(μέ)νην πρὸς Ἀντίγονον ἔδωκεν χρυσοῦς τριακοσίους ἀτόκους καὶ εἰς (τὴν)
10 (τοῦ) θεάτρου κατασκευὴν χρήματα κομίσας εἰς Ἴλιον ἔδωκεν τοῖς ἐγ-
(δό)ταις ὅσων ἐδέοντο χρυσοῦς χιλίους τετρακοσίους πεντήκοντα
ἀτόκους· ἐπειδὴ Μαλούσιος διατελεῖ πράττων καὶ λέγων ἀπροφα-
σίστως ἐμ πᾶσι τοῖς καιροῖς τὰ συμφέροντα τῇ θεῷ καὶ ταῖς πόλεσιν,
ἀγαθῇ τύχῃ, δεδόχθαι τοῖς συνέδροις, ἐπαινέσαι Μαλούσιον
15 Βακχίου Γαργαρέα καὶ στεφανῶσαι αὐτὸν ἐν τῷ γυμνικῷ ἀγῶνι
χρυσῷ στεφάνῳ ἀπὸ δραχμῶν χιλίων, ἀρετῆς ἕνεκεν τῆς περ(ὶ)
τὸ ἱερὸν καὶ τὴν πανήγυριν καὶ τὸ κοινὸν τῶν πόλεων, δεδόσθαι δὲ
αὐτῷ μὲν τὴν ἀτέλειαν καθάπερ δέδοται, δεδόσθαι δὲ καὶ τοῖς ἐκ-
γόνοις αὐτοῦ τὴν ἀτέλειαν ὅτι ἂν πωλῶσιν ἢ ἀγοράζωσιν· τὸ δὲ ψή-
20 φισμα τόδε ἀναγράψαντας εἰς στήλην θεῖναι εἰς τὸ ἱερὸν τῆς
Ἀθηνᾶς, ἐπιμεληθῆναι δὲ τοὺς Γαργαρεῖς, ὅπως ἂν εἰδῶσιν ἅπαντες
ὅτι ἐπίσταται τὸ κοινὸν τῶν πόλεων τοῖς οὖσιν ἀγαθοῖς ἀνδράσιν εἰς
αὑτοὺς χάριν ἀποδιδόναι.—Γνώμη τῶν συνέδρων· ἐπειδὴ Μαλούσιος
ἀποστελλόντων τῶν συνέδρων πρέσβεις πρὸς τὸν βασιλέα (. . . . . ὑπὲρ)
25 τῆς ἐλευθερίας καὶ αὐτονομίας τῶν πόλεων τῶν κοινωνουσ(ῶν τοῦ
ἱεροῦ καὶ τῆς πανηγύρεως ἔδωκεν ἄτοκα χρήματα τοῖς ἀποστ(ελλο-)
μένοις ἀγγέλοις ὅσα ἐκέλευον οἱ σύνεδροι, παρεσκεύασε(ν δὲ) καὶ τὰ (εἰς)
σκηνὴν ἄτοκα χρήματα καὶ τἄλλα δὲ προθύμως ὑπηρετ(εῖ εἰς) ὅτι ἂ(ν πα-)
ρακαλῇ τὸ συνέδριον· ἀγαθῇ τύχῃ, δεδόχθαι τοῖς συνέδροις, ἐπαι-
30 νέσαι τε Μαλούσιον Βακχίου Γαργαρέα, ὅτι ἀνὴρ ἀγαθός ἐστιν περὶ τὸ
ἱερὸν τῆς Ἀθηνᾶς καὶ τὴν πανήγυριν καὶ τὸ κοινὸν τῶν πόλεων καὶ στεφανῶσαι αὐτὸν χρυσῷ στεφάνῳ ἀπὸ δραχμῶν χιλίων ἐν τῷ γυμνικῷ ἀγῶνι, ἀναγράψαι δὲ τὸ ψήφισμα τόδε εἰς στήλην τὴν ὑπὲ(ρ)
τῶν συνεδριῶν τῶν Μαλουσίου μελλουσῶν ἀνατεθῆσε(σθα)ι εἰς τὸ ἱερόν,
35 ἐπιμεληθῆναι δὲ τοὺς Γαργαρεῖς, ὅπως ἂν εἰδῶσιν ἅπαντες, ὅτι
ἐπίσταται τὸ κοινὸν τῶν πόλεων τοῖς οὖσιν ἀγαθοῖς ἀνδράσιν εἰς αὑτοὺς χάριν ἀποδιδόναι.—Γνώμη τῶν συνέδρων· ἐπειδὴ Μαλούσιος κελεύει ἐπαγγεῖλαι αὐτῷ ἤδη τὸ συνέδριον, πόσων δεῖται παρ' αὐτοῦ χρημάτων εἴς τε τὸ θέατρον καὶ εἰς τἄλλα κατασκευάσματα καὶ εἰς τὰ
40 ἱερὰ καὶ εἰς τὴν πρεσβείαν, καὶ φησὶ θέλειν παρόντων τῶν συνέδρων ἤδη δοῦναι πάντα· ἀγαθῇ τύχῃ, δεδόχθαι τοῖς συνέδροις ἐπαγγεῖλαι Μαλουσίῳ, δοῦναι τοῖς ἀγωνοθέταις χρ(υσοῦς)
τρισχιλίους καὶ πεντακοσίους σὺν τοῖς πέρυσι ὀφειλομένοις α(ὐτῷ,)
τοὺς δὲ ἀγωνοθέτας οἷς μὲν ἂν αὐτοὶ χρήσωνται, (τὰ) δ(?)ὲ ἀ(?)(ναλώ-)
45 ματα θεῖναι εἰς τὸ ἱερόν, ἂν δέ τι περιγένηται (ἐκ?) δοθέντ(ων τῶν)
ἔργων, ἀποδοῦναι Μαλουσίῳ.—Γνώμη τῶν συνέδρων· ἐπειδὴ Μαλούσιος Βακχίου Γαργαρεὺς ἀνὴρ ἀγαθὸς ὢν διατελε(ῖ περὶ τὸ)
ἱερὸν τῆς Ἀθηνᾶς τῆς Ἰλιάδος καὶ τὸ συνέδριον, δ(εδόχθαι)
τοῖς συνέδροις, στεφανῶσαι Μαλούσιον χρυσῷ στ(εφάνῳ ἀπὸ)
50 χρυσ(ῶν τριά? κον)τα, καλεῖν δὲ αὐ(τὸν καὶ) εἰς προεδρία(ν σὺν τοῖς συνέδρ- ?)
οις ἐν τοῖς ἀγῶ(?)σιν ὀνομασ(τί . . . .) εἶναι δ(ὲ ἀτέλειαν)

καὶ αὐτῷ καὶ ἐγγόνοις· τὸ δὲ ψή(φισμα τό)δε ἀναγράψαντας (τοὺς ἀγωνο-)
θέτας εἰς στήλην θεῖναι εἰς (τὸ ἱερὸ)ν τῆς Ἀθηνᾶς.—(Γνώμη τῶν συν-)
έδρων· ἐπειδὴ Μαλούσ(ιος) ἀ(νὴρ ἀ)γαθὸς ὢν διατ(ελεῖ περὶ τὸ ἱερὸν)
55 τῆς Ἀθηνᾶς τῆς Ἰλιά(δος) καὶ τὸ κοινὸν τῶν πόλ(εων,)
ἀγαθῇ τύχῃ, δεδόχθ(αι τοῖς) συνέδροις, (α)ἷς τιμαῖς (τετίμηται Μαλού-)
σιος ὑπὸ τοῦ συνε(δρι)ου, ἀναγράψαι ἑκά(στ)ην (τ)ῶν πόλεων τῶν κοινωνου-
σῶν τοῦ ἱεροῦ κ(αὶ τῆ)ς πανηγύρεως κα(.· . . . . καθὼς ἑκάσ-)
τῃ νόμος ἐστ(ί . . .)—Σίμαλος Λαμψακη(νὸς εἶπεν· ἐπειδὴ Μαλούσιος)
60 ὁ Γαργαρεὺς ἐ(πιμεμ?)έληται προθύ(μως . . .)
τὰ ἀναλώ(ματα . . . . . .)
πόλεσιν ε . . . .
ὅτι προθύ(μως) . . . . δεδόχθαι τοῖς συνέδροις
στεφ(ανῶσαι Μαλούσιον Βακχίου Γαργαρέα χρυσῷ στε-)
65 φάν(ῳ) . . . .
. . . .

I also found in the Temple of Athené, besides an inscribed pedestal of black slate, 3 ft. 8 in. high and 20¾ in. broad, the statue of a man, of fine white marble, nearly 4 ft. high. As is proved by the inscription, it was sculptured by Pytheas of Argos, and was erected by the Ilians in honour of Metrodorus, the son of Themistagoras, of whom it is a representation. The figure was in the position of an orator, as is shown by the footmarks on the pedestal. The head and the feet are unfortunately wanting.

The inscriptions run as follows :—

ΟΔΗΜΟΣΟΙΛΙΕΙΩΝ
ΜΗΤΡΟΔΩΡΟΝΘΕΜΙΣΤΑΓΟΡΟΥ

And lower down, on the same side of the pedestal—

ΠΥΘΕΑΣΑΡΓΕΙΟΣΕΠΟΙΗΣΕ

Ὁ δῆμος ὁ Ἰλιείων
Μητρόδωρον Θεμισταγόρου.
Πυθέας Ἀργεῖος ἐποίησε.

There were in antiquity many men named Metrodorus, but only two of them were especially celebrated, and both were natives of Asia Minor. The one, born in Lampsacus, was a pupil of Epicurus ;[6] the other, a native of Scepsis, was a philosopher, orator, and statesman, and was held in high esteem by Mithridates VII. Eupator,[7] who afterwards had him put to death in a horrible manner.[8] The name of the father of this Metrodorus of Scepsis is unknown, and whether he was called Themistagoras or otherwise, is uncertain ; but it is extremely probable that the inscription and the statue were raised in honour of the Scepsian orator, philosopher, and statesman. I find no mention whatever of the sculptor Pytheas of Argos. Only one Pytheas, a silver-chaser, is named by Pliny,[9]

---

[6] Strabo, xiii. p. 589.   [8] Plutarch, Life of Lucullus.
[7] Strabo, xiii. p. 609.   [9] H. N. xxxv. 12, s. 55.

as being a contemporary of Pompey the Great : Pliny, however, does not
state his birth-place. Another Pytheas was a wall-painter and a native
of Achaea. Neither of these can therefore be the Argive sculptor who
carved the statue and put his name on the pedestal. But, as Professor
Koumanoudes, observes to me, it is not astonishing that the name of an
insignificant sculptor should be forgotten, seeing that the names of so
many great kings are lost.

In the same part of the Temple of Athené we found the fragment of
a marble slab, which has evidently been very long, with the following
inscription :—

ΕΠΕΙΤΟΥΑΝΘΥΠΑΤΟΥΓΑΙΟΥΚΛΑΥΔΙΟΥΠΟΠΛΙΟΥΥΙΟΥΝΕΡΩΝΟΣΕΠΙΤΑΞΑΝΤΟΣ
ΤΟΙΣΠΟΙΜΑΝΗΝΩΝΑΡΧΟΥΣΙΝΕΞΑΠΟΣΤΕΙΛΑΙΠΡΟΣΗΜΑΣΕΙΣΠΑΡΑΦΥΛΑΚΗΝ
ΤΗΣΠΟΛΕΩΣΣΤΡΑΤΙΩΤΑΣΚΑΙΕΠΑΥΤΩΝΗΓΕΜΟΝΑΣΠΟΙΜΑΝΗΝΩΝ
ΟΝΤΕΣΗΜΩΝΦΙΛΟΙΚΑΙΕΥΝΟΩΣΔΙΑΚΕΙΜΕΝΟΙΠΡΟΣΤΟΝΔΗΜΟΝΗΜΩΝ
5 ΕΞΑΠΕΣΤΕΙΛΑΝΤΟΥΣΤΕΣΤΡΑΤΙΩΤΑΣΚΑΙΕΠΑΥΤΩΝΗΓΕΜΟΝΑΝΙΚ
ΔΡΟΝΜΗΝΟΦΙΛΟΥΥΙΟΣΚΑΙΠΑΡΑΓΕΝΟΜΕΝΟΣΕΙΣΤΗΝΠΟΛΙΝΗΜΩΝ
ΤΕΕΝΔΗΜΙΑΝΠΟΙΕΙΤΑΙΚΑΛΗΝΚΑΙΕΥΣΧΗΜΟΝΑΚΑΙΑΞΙ
ΡΟΥΔΗΜΟΥΚΑΙΤΗΣΕΑΥΤΟΥΠΑΤΡΙΔΟΣΤΗΝΤΕΤΩΝ
ΕΑΥΤΩΙΝΕΑΝΙΣΚΩΝΕΝΔΗΜΙΑΝΕΥΤ...ΟΝΠ
10 ΤΟΝΚΑΘΑΠΕΡΕΠΙΒΑΛΛΕΙΑΝΔΡ
ΧΕΙΡΙΣΜΕΝΗΝΕΑΤΩΙΠΙ
ΤΗΝΥΠΕΡΤΗΣΦΥΛΑΚ
ΕΙΣΦΕΡΕΤΑΙΣΠΟΥΔ
ΕΚΚΑΙΝΩΝΟΥΔΕΙ
15 ΜΟΝΚΑΙ

ἐπεὶ τοῦ ἀνθυπάτου Γαΐου Κλαυδίου Ποπλίου υἱοῦ Νέρωνος ἐπιτάξαντος,
τοῖς Ποιμανηνῶν ἄρχουσιν ἐξαποστεῖλαι πρὸς ἡμᾶς εἰς παραφυλακὴν
τῆς πόλεως στρατιώτας καὶ ἐπ' αὐτῶν ἡγεμόνας Ποιμανηῶν (οἱ ?)
ὄντες ἡμῶν φίλοι καὶ εὐνόως διακείμενοι πρὸς τὸν δῆμον ἡμῶν
5 ἐξαπέστειλαν τούς τε στρατιώτας καὶ ἐπ' αὐτῶν ἡγεμόνα Νίκ(αν-)
δρον, Μηνοφίλου (υἱ)ὸς καὶ παραγενόμενος εἰς τὴν πόλιν ἡμῶν (τήν)
τε ἐνδημίαν ποιεῖται καλὴν καὶ εὐσχήμονα καὶ ἀξί(αν τοῦ τε ἡμετέ-)
ρου δήμου καὶ τῆς ἑαυτοῦ πατρίδος, τήν τε τῶν (ὑφ' ?)
ἑαυτῷ νεανίσκων ἐνδημίαν εὔτ(ακτ)ον π(αρέχεται καὶ ἑαυ-)
10 τὸν καθάπερ ἐπιβάλλει ἀνδρ(ὶ . . . . . καὶ τὴν ἐξουσίαν τὴν ἐγκε-)
χειρισμένην ἑαυτῷ πι(στῶς καὶ) . . . .
τὴν ὑπὲρ τῆς φυλακ(ῆς) . . . .
εἰσφέρεται σπουδ(ὴν)
ἐκ καινῶν οὐδει . . . . .
15 μον καὶ . . . . . .

The Proconsul Caius Claudius Nero, the son of Publius, who is praised
in this inscription, ruled over the province of Asia from 674 to 675 after
the foundation of Rome (80–79 B.C.). Hence he lived in the time of
Cicero, who mentions him in his orations against Verres.[10]

The Poemanenians (Ποιμανηνοί) are the inhabitants of the fortress of
Poemanenon, to the south of Cyzicus.[11]

[10] Waddington, Fastes des Provinces Asiatiques
de l'Empire Romain ; Paris, 1872, pp. 43, 44.

[11] Pape-Benseler, Lexikon der Griechischen
Eigennamen.

To judge from the form and thickness of the stone, this inscription must have been very long and have contained more than 70 lines. But even the fragment is of historical value, and all the more as we know for certain that it comes down to us from the year 80 B.C.

Upon the site of the Doric Temple of Apollo, on the north side of the hill, I found at a depth of 6½ ft. a block of marble, 5¼ ft. high and 2¾ ft. both in breadth and thickness; it weighs about 50 cwt. and bears the following inscription :—

```
    ΗΒΟΥΛΗΚΑΙΟΔΗΜΟ
    ΙΛΙΕΩΝΕΤΙΜΗΣΑΝΑΥ
    ΚΛΑΥΔΙΟΝΚΑΙΚΙΝΑΙ
    ΑΙΟΝΚΥΖΙΚΗΝΟΝΑ
  5 ΤΑΛΟΓΙΣΤΗΝΥΠΟΤΟ
    ΟΤΑΤΟΥΑΥΤΟΚΡΑΤΟΡΟ
    ΣΑΡΟΣΤΙΤΟΥΑΙΛΙΟΥΑΔ
    ΝΟΥΑΝΤΩΝΙΟΥΣΕΒΑ
    ΕΥΣΕΒΟΥΣΚ..ΙΠΟΛΛ
 10 ΜΕΓΑΛΑΤΗΙΠ(Ο)ΛΕΙΚΑΤΟ
    ΣΑΝΤΑΚΑΙΓ..ϽΑΣΧΟΝΤ
    ΤΕΤΗΛΟΓΙΣΤ..ΙΑΚΑΙΣΥ
    ΓΟΡΙΑΙΣΑΝΔ...ΠΑΣΗΣΤ
    ΑΞΙΟΝΑΡΕΤΗ..ΕΝΕΚΕΝΚ
 15 ΕΥΝΟΙΑΣΤΗΣΠΡΟΣΤΗ
        ΠΟΛΙΝ
```

The first name occurring in this inscription, of which the syllable ΑΥ is preserved, is probably ΑΥΛΟΣ. The word ΚΑΙΚΙΝΑΙ should no doubt be ΚΑΙΚΙΝΑΝ, *Caecinam*. Whether the other name, of which ΑΙΟΝ remains, is intended for ΓΑΙΟΝ, I do not venture positively to decide, but I consider it to be probable. For the inscription, which I read as follows, is written in bad Greek, especially towards the end :—'Η βουλὴ καὶ ὁ δῆμο(ς) 'Ιλιέων ἐτίμησαν Αὖλον Κλαύδιον Καικινὰν Γάιον (?) Κυζικηνὸν ἄ(ρχον)τα λογιστὴν ὑπὸ το(ῦ θει)οτάτου αὐτοκράτορο(ς Καί)σαρος Τίτου Αἰλίου 'Αδ(ρια)νοῦ 'Αντωνίου Σεβα(στοῦ) Εὐσεβοῦς κ(α)ὶ πολλ(ὰ καὶ) μεγάλα τῇ πόλει κατο(ρθώ)-σαντα καὶ παράσχοντά τε τῇ λογιστείᾳ καὶ συ(νη)γορίαις ἄνδ(ρα) πάσηϲ τ(ιμῆς) ἄξιον ἀρετῆς ἕνεκεν κ(αὶ) εὐνοίας τῆς πρὸς τὴν πόλιν.

The emperor mentioned in this inscription is of course Antoninus Pius, whose reign began in the year 138 A.D., and who died in 161 A.D. ; it is merely by an error that he is here called Antonius. He took the name of Hadrian from his adoptive father, the Emperor Hadrian, and assumed the name of Aelius after the death of Hadrian's first adopted son, Aelius Caesar. Upon the upper end of the block of marble there are two foot-marks, the one considerably in advance of the other. Each of them being 15⅓ in. long, they leave no doubt but that upon this block the

colossal statue of the Cyzicene, who is praised in the inscription, stood in
the attitude of an orator. In the hinder foot-mark there is a hole, 1⅕ in.
square, in which was placed the iron rod for fixing the statue. To judge
from the size of the foot-marks, the statue must have been more than 8 ft.
high; and, as the marble block is 5¼ ft. in height, the whole must have
been at least 13¼ ft. high, and hence we may conclude that the Temple of
Apollo in which this work of art stood was very spacious.

In the quadrangular building of large wrought stones, 59 ft. long and
43 ft. broad, the foundations of which I had brought to light in October
1871, I found, at a depth of about 5 ft., a slab of marble 25·6 in. in
length, the upper part of which is 13·6 in. in breadth, and the lower part
15·36 in. It contains the following inscription:—

'Επειδὴ Διαφένης Πολλέως Τημνίτης, διατρίβων παρὰ τῷ βασιλεῖ,
φίλος ὢν καὶ εὔνους διατελεῖ τῷ δήμῳ, χρείας παρεχόμενος προθύμως εἰς
ἃ ἄν τις αὐτὸν παρακαλῇ, δεδόχθαι τῇ βουλῇ καὶ τῷ δήμῳ ἐπαινέσαι μὲν
αὐτὸν ἐπὶ τούτοις, παρακαλεῖν δὲ καὶ εἰς τὸ λοιπὸν εἶναι φιλότιμον εἰς τὰ
τοῦ δήμου συμφέροντα, δεδόσθαι δὲ αὐτῷ πολιτείαν, προξενίαν, ἔγκτησιν,
ἀτέλειαν ὧν καὶ οἱ πολῖται ἀτελεῖς εἰσι καὶ ἔφοδον ἐπὶ τὴν βουλὴν πρώτῳ
μετὰ τὰ ἱερὰ καὶ ἄφιξιν καὶ ἐμ πολέμῳ καὶ ἐν εἰρήνῃ ἀσυλεὶ καὶ ἀσπονδεί·
ἀναγράψαι δὲ τὰ δεδομένα αὐτῷ ταῦτα εἰς στήλην καὶ (ἀνα)θεῖναι ε(ἰς . . . .

The king spoken of in this inscription must have been one of the kings of
Pergamus, and from the character of the writing I believe that it must be
assigned to the third century before Christ.

At about the same depth, and by the side of the building, I found
a second marble slab, 16·5 in. in length and 13·4 in. in breadth. The
inscription runs as follows:—

'Ιλιεῖς ἔδοσαν Μενελάῳ 'Αῤῥαβαίου 'Αθηναίῳ εὐεργέτῃ γενομένῳ αὐτῶν
καὶ περὶ τὴν ἐλευθερίαν ἀνδρὶ ἀγαθῷ γενομένῳ προξενίαν καὶ εὐεργεσίαν.

This second inscription, to judge from the form of the letters, appears
to belong to the first century B.C. 'Αῤῥαβαῖος here occurs for the first
time as an Attic name.

At the same depth, and likewise by the side of the foundations of the
same building, I found a third marble slab, nearly 15 in. long and about
14 in. broad, bearing the following inscription:—

Μηνόφιλος Γλαυρίου εἶπεν· ἐπειδὴ πλείονες τῶν πολιτῶν ἐπελθόντες ἐπὶ
τὴν βουλήν φασιν Χαιρέαν τὸν τεταγμένον ἐπ' 'Αβύδου εὔνουν τε εἶναι τῇ
πόλει ναὶ ἐνίοις πρεσβευομένοις ὑπὸ τοῦ δήμου πρὸς αὐτὸν βουλόμενον τῇ
πόλει χαρίζεσθαι τὴν πᾶσαν σπουδὴν καὶ πρόνοιαν ποεῖσθαι καὶ τοῖς συναν-
τῶσιν αὐτῷ τῶν πολιτῶν φιλανθρώπως προσφέρεσθαι, ἵνα οὖν καὶ ὁ δῆμος
φαίνηται τὴν καθήκουσαν χάριν ἀποδιδοὺς τοῖς προαιρουμένοις τὴν πό(λιν)
. . . . δεδόχθαι.

This third inscription also appears to belong to the first century B.C.

It is probable that the building in which I discovered these three inscriptions was the Town-hall or Bouleuterion of Ilium ; at all events, it does not appear to have been a temple.

The following inscriptions were found at a depth of from 19 in. to 3½ ft. below my wooden house on Hissarlik :—

```
. . . . . . . . . . . . . . . . . . . . . . . . . . . . . . . . . . . . . . .
. . . . . . . . . . . . . . . . . . . . . . . . . . . . . . . . . . . . . .
. . . . . . ΣΑ . . . . . . . . . . . . . . . . . . . . . . . . . . . . . . .
. . . ΕΣΑΙ . . . . . . . . . . . . . NOY . . . . . . . . . . . . . . . . .
5 . . . . . . ΑΒΟΥΚΟΛ . . . . . . ΕΤΡΑΝΦ . . . . . . . . . . .
. . . . ΣΚΑΤΑΠΛΗΘΟΣΕΙΣΟΙΝΙΣΤΡΑ . . . . .
. . ΤΩΝΕΨΗΦΙΣΘΑΙΣΚΑΔΡΕΙΣΟ . . . . .
. . ΣΑΝΔΡΑΣΤΟΥΣΣΥΝΘΗΣΟΜΕΝ . . . . .
. . . . ΕΡΟΝΥΠΗΡΧΕΝΚΑΙΣΤΗΛΩ . . . . .
10 . . . . ΙΕΝΤΩΤΩΝΣΑΜΟΘΡΑΚ . . . . . . . . .
. . . . ΙΣΑΠΟΚΑΘΙΣΤΑΜΕΝΟ . . . . . . . . . .
. . . . ΕΝΟΥΣΤΗΝΣΥΝΘΕΣΙΝ . . . . . . . . . .
. . . . . . ΜΟΛΟΓΙΑΣΤΟΑΝΤΙΓΡΑ . . . . . . . . .
. . . . . . ΟΙΚΗΣΟΝΤΕΣΗΡΕΘΗΣ . . . . . . . . . . .
15 . . . . . . ΟΠΕΙΘΟΥΜΙΛΗΣΙΟΣ . . . . . . . . . . . . . .
. . . . . . ΘΟΥΔΙΟΠΕΙΔΗΣΒ . . . . . . . . . . . . . . . .
. . . . . ΤΙΦΑΝΗΣΑΠ . . . . . . . . . . . . . . . . . . . . .
```

```
. . . . . . . . . . . . . . . . . . . . . . . . . . . . . . . .
. . . . . . . . . . . . . . . . . . . . . . . . . . . . . . . .
. . . . . . . . . . . . . . . . . . . . . . . . . . . . . . . .
. . . . . . σα . . . . . . . . . . . . . . . . . . . . . . . .
. . . . εσαι . . . . . . . . . . . . . . . νου(ς) . . . . . .
5 . . . . . . . . αβουκολ . . . . . . ετραν φ . . . . .
. . . . ς κατὰ πλῆθος εἰς οἴνιστρα . . . . . . . . . . .
. . των ἐψηφίσθαι Σκαδρεῖς ο . . . . . . . . . . . .
. . ς ἄνδρας τοὺς συνθησομέν(ους) . . . . . . . . . . .
. . . . ερον ὑπῆρχεν καὶ στηλω . . . . . . . . . . . .
10 . . . . ι ἐν τῶ¹ τῶν Σαμοθράκ²(ων) . . . . . . . . . .
. . . . ις ἀποκαθισταμένο . . . . . . . . . . . . . . .
. . . . ενους τὴν σύνθεσιν . . . . . . . . . . . . . . .
. . . . . . . (ὁ)μολογίας τὸ ἀντίγρα(φον) . . . . . . .
. . . . . . . οἰκήσοντες ἡρέθησ³(αν) . . . . . . . . . . .
15 . . . . . . (Δι)οπείθου Μιλήσιος . . . . . . . . .
. . . . . . θου Διοπείδης Β. . . . . . . . . . . . . .
. . . . . . (Ἀν)τιφάνης Ἀπ . . . . . . . . . . . . . .
```

This inscription contains a contract for a settlement and gives the names of the men selected for founding it. Σκαδρεῖς is an unknown word, which has never before been met with.

---

¹ *Sic.*   ² *Sic.*   ³ *Sic.*

```
        \XN
       ΩΣΧΙΛΙΑΣ
    ΩΣΤΗΣΔΟΘΕΙΣΗΣ
   ΕΙΠΕΝΤΕΚΑΙΟΥΕΛΑΒΟ
5  ΒΑΛΛΟΝΤΩΙΕΝΙΑΥΤΩ
   ΤΗΝΣΥΝΕΔΡΕΙΑΝΟΥΚΑ
   ΤΗΣΒΟΟΣΤΗΝΤΙΜΗΝΥ
   ΤΩΓΚΡΕΩΝΤΑΣΛΟΙΓΑ
   ΤΡΩΒΟΛΟΝΤΗΝΓΟΛΙΝΤΗΜ
10 ΚΑΣΑΝΤΟΥΣΤΟΚΟΥΣΤΟΥΣ
   ΚΟΣΙΑΣΤΕΣΣΑΡΑΚΟΝΤΑΓΕ
   ΘΕΤΟΣΔΙΑΚΟΣΙΑΣΤΕΣΣΑ
   ΚΑΙΟΤΙΤΗΝΣΥΝΕΔΡΕΙΑΙ
   ΤΕΙΛΑΝΠΕΝΤΑΚΟΣΙΑΣΚΑΙΤΗ
15 ΡΗΜΕΝΗΣΤΗΣΤΙΜΗΣΤΩΓΚΡΕ
   ΤΑΔΥΟ
```

. . . . χν . . . .
. . . . ως χιλίας . . . .
. . . . ως τῆς δοθείσης . . . .
. . . . . ει πέντε καὶ οὗ ἔλαβο(ν) . . . .
5 . . . . (τὸ ἐπι)βάλλον τῷ ἐνιαυτῶ(ι) . .
. . . . τὴν συνέδρειαν οὐ κα . . . .
. . . . τῆς βοὸς τὴν τιμὴν ὑ . . . .
. . . . τῶγ κρεῶν τὰς λοιπὰ(ς) . . . . . .
. . . . (τε) τρώβολον τὴν πόλιν τημ . .
10 . . . . (ἠνάγ ?)κασαν τοὺς τόκους τοὺς. .
. . . . (α)κοσίας τεσσαράκοντα πέ(ντε) .
. . . . θετος διακοσίας τεσσα(ρα) . . . .
. . . καὶ ὅτι τὴν συνέδρεια(ν) . . . . . .
. . . (ἀπέσ)τειλαν πεντακοσίας καὶ τη .
15 . . . ρημένης τῆς τιμῆς τῶγ κρε(ῶν) . . .
. . . (τάλαν ?)τα δύο . . . .

§ III. The Coins found at Novum Ilium. By M. Achilles Postolaccas, Keeper of the National Collection of Coins at Athens.

According to the testimony of the famous numismatologist Eckhel,[4] all the known coins of Ilium belong to Novum Ilium, and are either autonomous or imperial. Of these, the autonomous are either of silver or copper, and belong to the Macedonian period or to the succeeding times; the imperial coins occur only in bronze, and date from Augustus to Gallienus and his wife Salonina.

Of the autonomous silver coins we only know of tetradrachms of an artistic style, belonging to the Attic metrological system, bearing on one side the head of Athené with a three-crested helmet crowned with laurel, and on the other side the legend ΑΘΗΝΑΣ ΙΛΙΑΔΟΣ, the name of

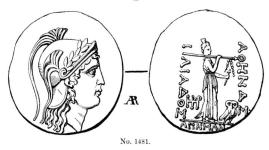

No. 1481.

the archon, and the image of the standing Athené holding on her right shoulder a spear, and a distaff in her left hand;[5] on the field are mono-grams and accessory symbols (No. 1481). The tetradrachms in question were struck, according to the illustrious Cavedoni,[6] under the reign of Mithridates Eupator, king of Pontus and the Cimmerian Bosporus (123–64 B.C.).[7]

No. 1482.   No. 1483.

The types of the bronze coins have on one side a head or bust of Athené, a turretted head of the personified Rome with the legend ΘΕΑ ΡΩΜΗ (No. 1482), and a she-wolf suckling Romulus and Remus (No. 1483); on the other side the following devices:[8]—a standing Athené, like that on the above tetradrachms (see No. 1481);[9] a standing Apollo, dressed

---

[4] *Doctrina Num. Vet.* ii. p. 483.

[5] Pausanias, vii. 5, § 4, describing the statue of Athené Polias at Erythrae in Ionia, says: ἠλακάτην ἐν ἑκατέρᾳ τῶν χειρῶν ἔχει. According to Apollodorus (iii. 12. 3), the Palladium, which had fallen from heaven, held in the left hand a distaff and a spindle.

[6] *Spicilegio numismatico*, p. 152.

[7] 121–63 B.C. according to Eduard Meyer, *Geschichte des Königreichs Pontos*; Leipzig, 1879, 8vo. p. 56.

[8] It is to be understood that the following descriptions and cuts are of the *reverses* of the medals.

[9] Choiseul-Gouffier, *Voyage pittoresque de la Grèce*.

in a long chiton and holding a patera and a lyre ; or Ganymedes carried away by the eagle of Zeus (No. 1482).

No. 1484.   No. 1485.   No. 1486.   No. 1487.

Hector standing, with his head turned aside, holding in his right hand a lance, in his left a sword, with the legend ЄΚΤШΡ (Nos. 1484 and 1485). Hector walking, his right hand uplifted, holding in his left a shield and a lance, and the legend ΕΚΤΩΡ or ΕΚΚΤΩΡ (sic) (No. 1486). Hector naked, walking, having a helmet on the head, a sword in the uplifted right hand, a shield in his left, with the legend ΕΚΤΩΡ ΙΛΙΕΩΝ.

Aeneas walking, carrying Anchises on his back and holding Ascanius by the hand. Aeneas flying with Anchises and Iülus.[10] Aeneas going on board a ship, carrying Anchises on his back and leading Ascanius by the hand (No. 1487).

The legends and types of the imperial coins are more numerous and more varied ; the most important and curious of them are the following :—

No. 1488.   No. 1489.   No. 1490.

ΔΙΑ ΙΔΑΙΟΝ ΙΛΙΕΙС or ΙΛΙΕΩΝ. Zeus Nikephoros seated, holding in his right hand a spear ; sometimes, instead of Niké, he holds the Palladium : on coins of the younger Faustina, of Commodus (in the collection of Dr. Schliemann), of Crispina and of Julia Domna (No. 1488).

ΔΑΡΔΑΝΟС ΙΛΙΕΩΝ. Dardanus seated, holding in his left hand a sceptre, with a woman standing by : on the coins of Crispina (No. 1489). The type in question represents, according to Cavedoni,[11] the colloquy of Dardanus about his marriage with Batieia, daughter of Teucer, king of the Troad ;[1] or, according to another tradition,[2] with Teucer's wife Chrysé, who brought him the Palladium as a dowry.

ΕΙΛΟС ΙΛΙΕΩΝ or ΙΛΙΕΩΝ. Ilus standing, wearing an upper garment (ἱμάτιον), and sacrificing on an altar before a column on which stands the Palladium : on a coin of Julia Domna (in Dr. Schliemann's collection) and of Caracalla (No. 1490).

The following coins, all of which have only the legend ΙΛΙΕΩΝ or ΙΛΙΕΩΝ, have these types :—

---

[10] According to Sestini, Descriptio Num. Vet. p. 305, No. 1.
[11] Op. cit. p. 153.   [1] Apollodorus, iii. 12. 1.   [2] Dionys. Halicarn. Antiq. Roman. i. 68, 69.

A man (Ilus) riding on a bull, which is jumping near a tree; in front the Palladium on a column: on a coin of the younger Faustina (No. 1491). Athené on a column, towards which a cow is approaching: on a coin of the same empress. Ilus leading a cow to the statue of Athené Ilias on a small column; in the field is a column: on a coin of Gordianus III. (No. 1492).

No. 1491.

No. 1492.

These four types find their interpretation in Apollodorus,[3] who relates that Ilus travelled to Phrygia, carried off the victory in the sacred games, and, having consulted an oracle, received the answer that he must follow " a speckled cow," and build a city on the spot where she might lie down. This took place on the so-called hill of Até, where Ilus built a town called by him Ἴλιος. Praying to Zeus to grant him a favourable sign, he saw falling from heaven before his tent the Palladium, which for that reason was called διιπετές : hence the reason is evident why the Ilian Zeus holds the Palladium on his hand.[4]

No. 1493.

ANXEICHC AΦΡΟΔΕΙΤΗ or ANXEICIC AΦΡΟΔΙΤΗ IΛΙΕΩΝ. Aphrodité, wearing a long chiton, and Anchises are standing joining hands: on coins of Julia Domna (No. 1493). This type may be interpreted by the verses in the Homeric Hymn :[5]—

τὸν δὴ ἔπειτα ἰδοῦσα φιλομμειδὴς Ἀφροδίτη,
ἠράσατ᾽, ἐκπάγλως δὲ κατὰ φρένας ἵμερος εἷλεν.

Compare also what Apollodorus says.[6]

ΠΡΙΑΜΟC IΛΙΕΩΝ or IΛΙΕΩΝ. Priam, wearing a Phrygian cap, seated and holding a spear in his left hand: on coins of Commodus and Crispina (No. 1494).

ΝΕCΤΩΡΗC IΛΙΕΩΝ. Nestor, clad in an upper garment (ἱμάτιον), is sacrificing with his right hand on an altar before the statue of Athené, and holding in his left a spear in an oblique position: on a coin of Caracalla.

No. 1494.

ΕΚΤΩΡ IΛΙΕΩΝ or ΕΚΤΩΡ or ΕΚΤWΡ IΛΙΕΩΝ. Hector's ideal youthful head covered with a helmet: on a coin of the younger Faustina. Hector standing, armed with lance and shield: on a coin of Maximinus I., the Thracian. Hector standing before a burning altar, holding in his right hand a patera, in his left a lance and shield: on a coin of Julia Domna, in the collection of Dr. Schliemann. Hector standing, wearing a helmet; his head is turned aside; in his right hand he holds a shield: on a coin of Septimius Severus with Geta. Hector standing, naked, wearing

<hr />

[3] iii. 12. 3.   [4] Cavedoni, *op. cit.* p. 153.   [5] *In Aphrodit.* iv. 56, 57.   [6] iii. 12. 2.

a helmet, holding in his right hand a lance, and leaning with his left
on a shield: on a coin of Caracalla and Geta (No. 1495).   Hector

No. 1495.   No. 1496.   No. 1497.   No. 1498.

standing armed before a column with a statue, holding in its one
hand a lance and shield, in the other a small figure: on coins of
Caracalla.   Hector standing armed, holding in his left hand a shield
and spear, and touching with his right the statue of Athené on a column:
on a coin of Caracalla (No. 1496).   Cavedoni observes[7] that the last two
types remind us of the passage in the *Iliad*,[8] where Hector leaves the
camp by the advice of Helenus and goes quickly up to the town, to order
the Trojan matrons to go in suppliant procession to the Temple of Athené
in the Acropolis.   Hector walking, armed: on coins of Faustina the elder
and of Caracalla (No. 1497).   Hector walking, armed; he lifts in his right
hand a spear in the attitude of fighting, and his left hand holds the shield
as if warding off a blow: on coins of Caracalla (No. 1498).   Hector armed,
marching forth to battle: on a coin of Hadrian.

Hector on a chariot drawn by two horses: on a coin of Marcus
Aurelius.   Hector, in full armour, on a chariot drawn by two horses:
on a coin of Gordianus III.   Hector on a chariot drawn by two horses,
holding in his uplifted right hand the whip, and in his left the reins

No. 1499.   No. 1500.

as well as lance and shield: on coins of Marcus Aurelius and Caracalla[9]
(No. 1499).   The last three types are according to the *Iliad*. xix. 399–401:

σμερδαλέον δ' ἵπποισιν ἐκέκλετο πατρὸς ἐοῖο·
Ξάνθε τε καὶ Βαλίε, τηλεκλυτὰ τέκνα Ποδάργης,
ἄλλως δὴ φράζεσθε σαωσέμεν ἡνιοχῆα . . . .

Hector on a chariot drawn by four horses, holding in his right hand
the reins and the shield, in his left the whip: on a coin of Marcus
Aurelius.   Hector on a chariot with four horses: on coins of Commodus,

[7] *Op. cit.* p. 153.   [8] vi. 86 and ff.   [9] Mionnet, *Description de Médailles antiques*, Suppl. v. Pl. 5.

Caracalla, and Gallienus. Hector on a chariot with four horses, holding in his right hand a lance, and in his left a shield and the reins : on coins of Commodus (No. 1500).

No. 1501.   No. 1502.

Hector standing, holding a shield and throwing a burning torch : on coins of Julia Domna and Valerianus I. Hector as on the preceding coin, but armed with a javelin, which he throws upon a ship before him : on a coin of the younger Faustina (No. 1501). In the two last types Hector is represented as fighting (with Ajax), and intending to set the Greek ship on fire. So thinks Cavedoni,[10] having in his mind the following verses of the *Iliad* :—

$$\text{Ἕκτωρ δὲ πρύμνηθεν ἐπεὶ λάβεν, οὔ τι μεθίει}$$
$$\text{ἄφλαστον μετὰ χερσὶν ἔχων, Τρωσὶν δὲ κέλευεν ·}$$
$$\text{Οἴσετε πῦρ, ἅμα δ' αὐτοὶ ἀολλέες ὄρνυτ' ἀϋτήν.}[1]$$

$$\text{. . . . . . ·. τοὶ δ' ἔμβαλον ἀκάματον πῦρ}$$
$$\text{νηΐ θοῇ · τῆς δ' αἶψα κατ' ἀσβέστη κέχυτο φλόξ.}[2]$$

Hector walking, holding in his left hand a shield, and throwing with his right a burning torch upon the two ships before him. On a coin of Elagabalus[3] (No. 1502).

No. 1503.   No. 1504.

Hector armed with a lance and shield, fighting on a chariot with four gallopping horses. Patroclus is lying under the horses, lifting his right arm, and resting the left on the ground ; behind him is his shield :—on a coin of Macrinus (No. 1503). Cavedoni[4] thinks that on this coin Patroclus is represented as uttering to Hector these last words :—

$$\text{ἤδη νῦν, Ἕκτωρ, μεγάλ' εὔχεο · σοὶ γὰρ ἔδωκεν}$$
$$\text{νίκην Ζεὺς Κρονίδης καὶ Ἀπόλλων, οἵ μ' ἐδάμασσαν}$$
$$\text{ῥηϊδίως.}[5]$$

Hector on a chariot with four horses, holding in his right hand a shield and lance, in his left a Niké. On a coin of Septimius Severus (No. 1504).

<hr>

[10] *Op. cit.* p. 153.   [1] xv. 716–718.   [2] xvi. 122, 123.
[3] *Revue Num.* 1852, Pl. iv. fig. 9.   [4] *Op. cit.* p. 153 in note.   [5] *Il.* xvi. 844–846.

This type, which represents Hector's victory, is interpreted by the foregoing verses.

Hector standing in full armour, dragging with his right hand the

lance from the supine corpse of Patroclus, which he spurns with his left foot; in his left hand he holds a shield: to the usual legend is here also added ΠΑΤΡΟΚΛΟC :— on a medallion of Septimius Severus (No. 1505). This very curious type is adapted to the verses of the *Iliad*:—

No. 1505.   No. 1506.

$$\text{ὣς ἄρα φωνήσας δόρυ χάλκεον ἐξ ὠτειλῆς}$$
$$\text{εἴρυσε, λὰξ προσβάς, τὸν δ' ὕπτιον ὦσ' ἀπὸ δουρός.}^{6}$$

This is the excellent interpretation of Mr. Barclay Vincent Head, who has published the medallion in question in the *Numismatic Chronicle*.[7]

Three warriors contending for the corpse of Patroclus: the warrior in the middle seems to represent Ajax coming to the rescue, when the Trojans were dragging away the corpse from the Greeks, as described in the splendid passage of Homer (*Il.* xvii. 274 ff.): on a coin of Macrinus (No. 1506). Although this type is altogether different from the foregoing, it nevertheless has the legend ΕΚΤΩΡ ΙΛΙΕΩΝ.

CKAMANΔPOC ΙΛΙΕΩΝ. The river Scamander personified, recumbent, holding in some cases a reed, and leaning on an overturned vase, from which water flows: on coins of Nero, of Nero and Britannicus, of Vitellius, Marcus Aurelius, Commodus, Caracalla, and Geta (No. 1507).

No. 1507.

ΙΛΙΟΝ ΡΩΜΗ. Two women standing, of whom one (the personified Ilium) is turretted and dressed in a long chiton, and holds in her right hand the Palladium. The other woman (the personified Rome), in a dress fastened with a girdle, is turretted, and holds in her left hand a flag:—on a medallion of Caracalla. The Tychae (Τύχαι, *genii*) of the cities of Ilium and Rome, with joined hands: on a coin of Elagabalus.

ΣΕΒΑΣΤΟΣ ΚΤΙΣΤΗΣ. Head of Augustus: statue of Athené, with the hair bound together on the crown of the head, on a small pedestal, holding in her uplifted right hand the Palladium, in her left a lance: on a coin of Augustus. With regard to this Ilian coin, particular attention is claimed by the epithet of Augustus as founder (κτίστης); but the word is to be understood as *restorer*, it being customary to give this title to benefactors who were deemed worthy of honour.

Besides the types on the imperial coins here represented, there also

---

6 xvi. 862, 863.   7 New Series, viii.; London, 1868, 8vo. p. 326, Pl. xi. 2.

occur the following, which bear merely the legend ΙΛΙΕΩΝ or ΙΛΙΕΩΝ
namely :—

The winged Ganymedes standing, holding in his right hand a bow, in
his left a shepherd's crook: on a coin of Commodus.

No. 1508.   No. 1510.   No. 1509.

The winged Ganymedes, wearing a Phrygian cap on his head, seated
on a rock, and offering drink to the eagle of Zeus, behind which is a tree :
on a coin of Commodus (No. 1508).

The winged Ganymedes, as in the foregoing type, but holding a vase
before the eagle which is caressing him; behind is a column on which
stands a statue: on a medallion of Commodus (No. 1509).[8]

The winged Ganymedes carried away by the eagle, and holding in
his right hand a shepherd's crook: on coins of Commodus and Geta
(No. 1510). The legend of the rape represented on the foregoing coin,
which is not mentioned by Homer, is related by Apollodorus,[9] who says:
τοῦτον (τὸν Γανυμήδην) μὲν οὖν διὰ κάλλος ἀναρπάσας Ζεὺς δι᾿ ἀετοῦ θεῶν
οἰνοχόον ἐν οὐρανῷ κατέστησεν.

Aeneas walking, carrying on his back Anchises, and leading Ascanius
by the hand: on medallions of Commodus and of Caracalla. Homer
says nothing concerning the flight of Aeneas represented in this type,
which is interpreted by the following verses of Virgil:—

No. 1511.

" Ergo age, care pater, cervici imponere nostrae ;
Ipse subibo humeris, nec me labor iste gravabit." [10]

". . . . . . Mihi parvus Iulus
Sit comes et longe servet vestigia coniux." [1]

" Cessi et sublato montes genitore petivi." [2]

The same type; below is a she-wolf suckling Romulus and Remus :
on a coin of Hadrian (No. 1511).

Hector, with a helmet on his head, walking, and throwing with his
right hand a stone; his left is armed with a shield and two lances :
on a coin of Diadumenianus.

Hector in full armour, on a chariot drawn by two horses: on a coin
of Gordianus III.

---

[8] According to Vaillant, *Numismata Graeca*, and Mionnet, *Descr. de Méd.*
[9] iii. 12. 2.   [10] *Aen.* ii. 707, 708.   [1] *Ibid.* ii. 710, 711.   [2] *Ibid.* ii. 804.

CHAPTER XII.

THE CONICAL MOUNDS IN THE TROAD CALLED THE HEROIC TUMULI.

THE traveller who goes by sea from Constantinople to the town of the Dardanelles, sees on both sides of the Sea of Marmora and the Hellespont a number of conical hills, on the origin of which tradition is silent, and which are universally called by the name of "Tepeh," a Turkish word signifying merely a low and small hill, but which in the imagination of men has obtained, like the word "tumulus" in the West, the additional signification of a sepulchral mound, covering the remains of a deceased person, or of more than one.

The first of these Tepehs which tradition has assigned to a particular person, is the tumulus on the Thracian Chersonesus, obliquely opposite the town of the Dardanelles, attributed to Hecuba, of which Strabo says: "Between the two (Dardanus and Abydus) the Rhodius falls into the Hellespont, and directly opposite its mouth the Cynossema (Κυνὸς σῆμα, or Κυνόσσημα, i.e. Dog's monument), said to be the tomb of Hecuba, stands on the Chersonesus."[1]

Proceeding from the Dardanelles by land to the Plain of Troy, the traveller passes another tumulus to his left, near the site of Dardanus; immediately afterwards, a third to his right, and a fourth again to his left, above the village of Ren Kioi. Descending hence to the sea-shore, he passes three more Tepehs on the height which overhangs the little port of Karanlik, and which belongs to the heights of Rhoeteum. To none of the six tumuli last mentioned does tradition attach a name.

To the north of the heights of Rhoeteum he will see, close to the shore, a very low tumulus, to which tradition points as the original sepulchre of Ajax, whose second resting-place is identified with the large tumulus on a lower spur of the heights of Rhoeteum. This latter tumulus is called In Tepeh, which name may be derived from the stem AIANT, seen in the genitive of Αἴας.

Riding thence along the shore of the Hellespont, the traveller reaches on the lower height, immediately to the north-east of Cape Sigeum, the tumulus which tradition throughout historical antiquity claimed as the tomb of Achilles.

Proceeding thence in a southerly direction, on the road which borders the heights of Sigeum and leads to Yeni Kioi, the traveller passes at a distance of only about 350 yds. to the south-east of the latter tumulus another, which is identified with the tomb of Patroclus. But this identifi-

---

[1] Strabo, xiii. p. 595 : μεταξύ τε ὁ Ῥόδιος ἐκπίπτει ποταμός, καθ᾽ ὃν ἐν τῇ Χερρονήσῳ τὸ Κυνὸς σῆμά ἐστιν, ὅ φασιν Ἑκάβης εἶναι τάφον.

Hecuba was fabled to have been changed into a bitch.

cation must be quite modern, it being in perfect opposition to the precise statement of Homer, who puts in the mouth of Achilles the words: "Let us wrap the bones (of Patroclus) in a double layer of fat, and put them in a golden urn, until I also am hidden with Hades. Now do not make the tumulus large, but only of becoming size. Later, you Achaeans, who shall survive me on the ships with many rowing-benches, may make it wide and high."[2] His companions obeyed: having gathered the bones of Patroclus, they wrapped them in a double layer of fat, and put them in a golden urn, which they brought into the tent, and covered with a soft linen cloth. They then marked out the round place for the tumulus, laid the foundations around the funeral pile, and heaped up the earth. Having completed the tumulus, they departed.[3]

Now, in all this there is not a word to show that the golden urn which contained the bones of Patroclus was either deposited in the tumulus, or was meant to be ever deposited there. All we can possibly understand here is that on the death of Achilles his bones should be added to those of Patroclus in the golden urn, and that on that event the tumulus should be enlarged, but there is no allusion whatever to the depositing of the urn in it. Had it been deposited, or had it been destined to be deposited there, Homer would not have kept back from us the important fact. Consequently the tumulus of Patroclus was a mere cenotaph. I wish I could cite, as further evidence, the beautiful passage in the *Odyssey*,[4] where it is said that the bones of Achilles and Patroclus lie together in a golden amphora, in a tumulus on the shore of the Hellespont; and the passage in the *Iliad*,[5] according to which the bones of Hector, after being put in a golden box, were laid in a grave and covered with a tumulus of stones. Unfortunately both these books of the *Odyssey* and *Iliad* are universally acknowledged to be later additions. Consequently all we know from the poet regarding the nature of one of the tumuli in the Plain of Troy is that it was a cenotaph, and this Homeric assertion has been borne out by all the researches hitherto made. But before his funeral Patroclus appeared to Achilles in a dream, and said:

θάπτε με ὅττι τάχιστα, πύλας Ἀΐδαο περήσω.[6]

Now the word θάπτω has always been translated by "bury" or "inter." But as from the foregoing passage it is evident that no real burial took place, I suggest that the meaning of this word, in this instance as well as in three other passages in which it occurs in the *Iliad*,[7] can only be "burn the body and perform the funeral ceremony," without implying that the

---

[2] *Il.* xxiii. 243–248:

καὶ τὰ μὲν ἐν χρυσέῃ φιάλῃ καὶ δίπλακι δημῷ
θείομεν, εἰς ὅ κεν αὐτὸς ἐγὼν Ἄϊδι κεύθωμαι·
τύμβον δ' οὐ μάλα πολλὸν ἐγὼ πονέεσθαι ἄνωγα,
ἀλλ' ἐπιεικέα τοῖον. ἔπειτα δὲ καὶ τὸν Ἀχαιοί
εὐρύν θ' ὑψηλόν τε τιθήμεναι, οἵ κεν ἐμεῖο
δεύτεροι ἐν νήεσσι πολυκλήϊσι λίπησθε.

[3] *Il.* xxiii: 252–257:

κλαίοντες δ' ἑτάροιο ἐνηέος ὀστέα λευκά
ἄλλεγον ἐς χρυσέην φιάλην καὶ δίπλακα δημόν,
ἐν κλισίῃσι δὲ θέντες ἑανῷ λιτὶ κάλυψαν.
τορνώσαντο δὲ σῆμα, θεμείλιά τε προβάλοντο

ἀμφὶ πυρήν· εἶθαρ δὲ χυτὴν ἐπὶ γαῖαν ἔχευαν.
χεύαντες δὲ τὸ σῆμα πάλιν κίον.

[4] xxiv. 76–84.   [5] xxiv. 793–798.

[6] *Il.* xxiii. 71.

[7] *Il.* xxiv. 664, 665:

ἐννῆμαρ μέν κ' αὐτὸν ἐνὶ μεγάροις γοόῳμεν,
τῇ δεκάτῃ δέ κε θάπτοιμεν δαινῦτό τε λαός.

Il. xxiii. 630:

ὡς ὁπότε κρείοντ' Ἀμαρυγκέα θάπτον Ἐπειοί.

Il. xxi. 322, 323:

αὐτοῦ οἱ καὶ σῆμα τετεύξεται, οὐδέ τί μιν χρεώ
ἔσται τυμβοχοῆσ' ὅτε μιν θάπτωσιν Ἀχαιοί.

bones were buried. In this sense I also understand the word θάπτω in
a passage in the *Odyssey*, in which the funeral of Elpenor is described:—
" Then I sent forward my companions to the palace of Circe to bring
the dead body of Elpenor. We at once cut trunks of trees, and, sore
grieved, performed his funeral on the high projecting shore, shedding
abundant tears. And when the body was burnt with his weapons, we
heaped up a tomb, erected a pillar (*stélé*) on it, and put up on its highest
point a well-fitting oar." [8]

But in another passage of the *Odyssey* the word θάπτω must really
mean " to bury in the ground: "—" First came the soul of our companion
Elpenor, for he had not yet been buried below the earth with broad
paths." [9]

In a passage in the *Iliad*, where the funeral of Eëtion is described,
we read:—" He (Achilles) slew Eëtion; but he stripped him not of his
arms, through the restraint of a religious awe, but burnt him there in
his panoply, and heaped up a mound." [10]

Here, as well as in the description of Elpenor's funeral, Homer leaves
us in doubt as to whether the tumulus was heaped over the body of the
deceased, or whether, as in the case of Patroclus, the bones were carried
away, and the tumulus was a mere cenotaph. But I have no reason to
doubt that in a post-Homeric time, and probably as early as the time
when the xxivth *Iliad* and the xxivth *Odyssey* were written, it was really
the custom to heap a tumulus over the remains of great personages. At
all events, in the imagination of Aeschylus, Agamemnon's sepulchre was a
tumulus, for he makes Electra say : " On the tumulus of this sepulchre
I announce this to my father." [11] Further, all the artificial tumuli at
Sardis, as well as on the Crimean coast and elsewhere in the south of
Russia, appear to be real tombs.

Riding for half an hour further south on the road to Yeni Kioi, the
traveller passes to the left of another much higher mound, called Hagios
Demetrios Tepeh, from an open chapel close by, which is dedicated to that
saint. But, as we have seen in the preceding pages, the chapel has
received this dedication from a temple of white marble sacred to Demeter,
which stood on the site, and of whose marbles it is partly built. This
Tepeh, by its high position on the very brink of the lofty shore, overhangs the sea, and it is therefore visible from a great distance out at sea ;
and, as Professor Virchow says, there is no point on land, to a distance
of 9 or 12 miles, from which it cannot be seen.

Proceeding further on, the traveller, after having passed Yeni Kioi,

---

[8] *Od.* xii. 9–15 :

δὴ τότ' ἐγὼν ἑτάρους προΐειν ἐς δώματα Κίρκης
οἰσέμεναι νεκρὸν 'Ελπήνορα τεθνηῶτα.
φιτροὺς δ' αἶψα ταμόντες, ὅθ' ἀκροτάτη πρόεχ'
     ἀκτή,
θάπτομεν ἀχνύμενοι, θαλερὸν κατὰ δάκρυ χέοντες.
αὐτὰρ ἐπεὶ νεκρός τ' ἐκάη καὶ τεύχεα νεκροῦ,
τύμβον χεύαντες καὶ ἐπὶ στήλην ἐρύσαντες
πήξαμεν ἀκροτάτῳ τύμβῳ εὐῆρες ἐρετμόν.

[9] *Od.* xi. 51, 52 :

Πρώτη δὲ ψυχὴ 'Ελπήνορος ἦλθεν ἑταίρου ·
οὐ γάρ πω ἐτέθαπτο ὑπὸ χθονὸς εὐρυοδείης.
[10] *Il.* vi. 416–419 :

. . . . κατὰ δ' ἔκτανεν 'Ηετίωνα,
οὐδέ μιν ἐξενάριξε (σεβάσσατο γὰρ τό γε θυμῷ),
ἀλλ' ἄρα μιν κατέκηε σὺν ἔντεσι δαιδαλέοισιν
ἠδ' ἐπὶ σῆμ' ἔχεεν.
[11] Aeschylus, *Choëphoroe*, v. 4 :

τύμβου δ' ἐπ' ὄχθῳ τῷδε κηρύσσω πατρί.

comes to another tumulus, 60 ft. high, situated on the height close to and north of the Bay of Besika, and called, probably for that reason, Besika or Bashika Tepeh, from the Turkish work Beshik, which means " cradle." It lies immediately to the east of the little promontory called Palaeo-castro, of which we have spoken before.

Still further south, and separated by a deep valley from the heights of Sigeum, there follows a group of tertiary ridges, in the midst of which, and about four miles distant from the sea-shore, rises another gigantic tumulus, 83 ft. high and 433 ft. in diameter at its base, called Ujek Tepeh. To understand well the height of 83 ft. the reader should bear in mind that the highest houses in Broadway in New York are not more than 70 ft. high.

Going on thence to Bounarbashi, and ascending the heights behind it —the Bali Dagh—the traveller sees there four more tumuli, the highest of which consists of loose pebbles, and has for this reason been identified, by the defenders of the Troy-Bounarbashi theory, with the tomb of Hector ; while of the other three, which are much lower, one has been attributed by them to King Priam himself.

Descending again to Bounarbashi and crossing the Scamander, the traveller finds opposite the Bali Dagh—on the slope of the mount which overhangs the river, and which, as before mentioned, is crowned with the ruins of an ancient town—another tumulus [1] of pebbles, which has lost much of its primitive height.   Descending again and riding along the right bank of the Scamander, the traveller sees, at a short distance to the north-west of the confluence of the Scamander and the Thymbrius, on the right bank of the latter, the large tumulus called Hanaï Tepeh, situated on the farm of Mr. Frank Calvert, whom I have helped to excavate it, and who has described the results of our researches in Appendix IV.

Proceeding thence in a north-westerly direction by the road to Hissarlik, the traveller passes to his right another smaller tumulus, called Pasha Tepeh,[2] on a low hill-ridge, which extends from the heights of the tertiary formation pretty far into the plain. Further on, at distances of no more than 200 and 300 yds. to the south of Novum Ilium, he sees to the right and left of the road two still smaller tumuli.

Finally, I have to mention the low tumulus on the right bank of the Kalifatli Asmak, at a distance of about 300 yds. to the north of Koum Kioi.   I have had occasion to mention this tumulus repeatedly in the preceding pages, and have explained the reasons why I hold it to be identical with the tumulus of Ilus, which is mentioned four times in the *Iliad*.

Proceeding now to the history of the researches made in these tumuli of the Troad, generally called " Heroic Tombs," I must begin with that of Ajax, as according to tradition it was first opened, not indeed by the hands of men, but by the waves of the sea.

---

[1] This tumulus, like all the other tumuli, is indicated on the Map of the Plain of Troy.
[2] Marked on the map Pasha Tepeh or Tumulus of Batieia.

1. *The Tumulus of Ajax.*—As before mentioned, the tumulus on the shore of the Hellespont, 600 yds. to the north of the conical hill now universally attributed to Ajax, and called In Tepeh, has had the honour to be indicated by tradition as the original tomb of that hero. According to the legend related by Pausanias, that side of the tumulus which faced the shore having been washed away by the sea, the entrance to the tomb was rendered easy ; the corpse was found to be of so gigantic a size that the bones at the knees, called knee-pans (*patellae*) by anatomists, were of about the size of the quoit (*discus*) of a boy who exercises himself in the *pentathlon*.[3]   This legend is confirmed by Philostratus, who says that, the tumulus of Ajax having been destroyed by the sea, his bones had come to light, denoting a man 11 cubits long, and that Hadrian, on his visit to Troy, embraced and kissed them, and erected over them the present tumulus, now called In Tepeh, in honour of Ajax.[4]   According to M. Burnouf's measurement, the height of this tumulus of In Tepeh above the sea is 131 ft.   Strabo also confirms the fact that in his time the tomb of Ajax was on the shallow sea-shore, for he writes : " Hereupon (after Ophrynium) follows the city of Rhoeteum on a hill, and, adjoining Rhoeteum, the shallow sea-shore, on which is the tomb and the temple of Ajax, as well as his statue, which was taken away by Marcus Antonius and carried to Egypt ; but Caesar Augustus returned it to the Rhoeteans."[5]   Strabo's statement is confirmed by Lucan[6] (38–65 A.D.), who praises the beauty of the statue of Ajax.

It appears incredible indeed that all the archæologists who cite the passage of Philostratus have thought the word περιαρμόζειν meant " restore," and have therefore understood that Hadrian merely restored the tomb and the temple, whereas τάφον περιαρμόζειν τινι can never have meant anything else than " erect a tomb to some one."   Strange to say, even no less an authority than Carl Gotthold Lenz,[7] one of the greatest philologists and Homeric scholars that ever lived, has fallen into this wonderful error.

We shall not attempt to investigate whether the corpse found in the low tumulus on the sea-shore was that of Ajax or not ; at all events, it appears certain that a corpse was found there, and that Hadrian brought it to the spur of the heights of Rhoeteum, now called In Tepeh, and built a small sanctuary over it, which he covered up with a high conical tumulus ; and no doubt in such a manner that nothing of it was visible at the top of

---

[3] Pausanias, i. 35, § 3 : τοῦ γὰρ τάφου τὰ πρὸς τὸν αἰγιαλὸν ἔφασκεν ἐπικλύσαι τὴν θάλασσαν, καὶ τὴν ἔσοδον ἐς τὸ μνῆμα οὐ χαλεπὴν ποιῆσαι, καί με τοῦ νεκροῦ τὸ μέγεθος τεκμαίρεσθαι τῇδε ἐκέλευε · πεντάθλου γὰρ παιδὸς εἶναί οἱ κατὰ δίσκον μάλιστα τὰ ἐπὶ τοῖς γόνασιν ὀστᾶ, καλουμένας δὲ ὑπὸ τῶν ἰατρῶν μύλας.

[4] Philostr. *Heroïca*, p. 137, ed. Kayser : Ἄκουε δή · πάππος ἦν μοι, ξένε, πολλὰ τῶν ἀπιστουμένων ὑπὸ σοῦ γιγνώσκων, ὃς ἔλεγε διαφθαρῆναι μέν ποτε τὸ τοῦ Αἴαντος σῆμα ὑπὸ τῆς θαλάσσης, πρὸς ᾗ κεῖται, ὀστᾶ δὲ ἐν αὐτῷ φανῆναι κατὰ ἑνδεκάπηχυν ἄνθρωπον, καὶ ἔφασκεν

Ἀδριανὸν βασιλέα περιστεῖλαι αὐτὰ ἐς Τροίαν ἐλθόντα καὶ τὸν νυνὶ τάφον περιαρμόσαι τῷ Αἴαντι ἔστιν ἃ καὶ προσπτυξάμενον τῶν ὀστῶν καὶ φιλήσαντα.

[5] Strabo, xiii. p. 595 : Εἶτα Ῥοίτειον πόλις ἐπὶ λόφῳ κειμένη καὶ τῷ Ῥοιτείῳ συνεχὴς ᾐὼν ἁλιτενής, ἐφ' ᾗ μνῆμα καὶ ἱερὸν Αἴαντος καὶ ἀνδριάς, ὃν ἄραντος Ἀντωνίου κομισθέντα εἰς Αἴγυπτον ἀπέδωκε τοῖς Ῥοιτεεῦσι πάλιν, καθάπερ καὶ ἄλλοις, ὁ Σεβαστὸς Καῖσαρ.

[6] *Pharsalia*, ix. 961–979.

[7] See C. G. Lenz, *Die Ebene von Troja* ; Neu Strelitz, 1798, p. 76

the mound. The base of this building was circular, and was, as Choiseul-Gouffier reports, consolidated by a number of curved walls built within the circle, and adapted to support the weight of the edifice. There

No. 1512. Tumulus of In Tepeh, called the Tomb of Ajax, with the Ruins of his Temple built by Hadrian.

appears to have been no other entrance than by a circular passage vaulted all round, 3½ ft. in diameter. This passage is still well preserved, but the foundations of the temple, which probably consisted of large wrought stones, were in 1770 partly taken out by a Turkish officer,[8] who used the materials for building a bridge. Visitors will find in and close to the tumulus large massive blocks of masonry, consisting of small stones joined with chalk. There is every probability that the early Christians who, in their pious zeal, destroyed so many temples and works of art, also destroyed the temple and statue of Ajax, but this could not of course be done without partly demolishing the tumulus. The Turkish officer, therefore, who in 1770 removed the foundations of the temple, only completed the destruction begun probably 1400 years before. On the right bank of the In Tepeh Asmak, close to the shore, visitors will see a large mutilated marble statue, which may perhaps be identical with the statue of Ajax. The sea is 10 ft. lower than the base of the primitive tumulus of Ajax ; but in strong southerly storms the mound is nevertheless flooded, and it is therefore very probable that it may have been washed away by the waves. What now remains of it is not more than 3 ft. 4 in. above the surface, and consists of pebbles with a large number of fragments of marble sculptures. I sank a shaft in the mound, but struck the rock at a depth of 8 ft. 4 in., and found nothing but pebbles and some large bones identified by Professor Virchow as horse-bones. There is no trace of a temple.

---

[8] See C. G. Lenz, *Die Ebene von Troja, nach dem Grafen Choiseul-Gouffier;* Neu Strelitz, 1798, p. 77.

2. *The Tumulus of Achilles.*—The second tumulus in succession, called that of Achilles, was explored in 1786 by a Jew, by order and on account of Choiseul-Gouffier, who was at that time French Ambassador at Con-

No 1513. Tumulus called the Tomb of Achilles.

stantinople. A shaft was sunk from the top,[9] and the virgin soil was reached at a depth of 29 ft. The upper part of the conical tumulus was found to consist of well-beaten clay to the depth of 6 ft.; then followed a compact layer of stones and clay, 2 ft. deep; a third stratum consisted of earth mixed with sand; a fourth of very fine sand. In the centre was found a small cavity, 4 ft. in length and breadth, formed of masonry, and covered with a flat stone, which had broken under the weight pressing upon it. In the cavity were found charcoal, ashes impregnated with fat, fragments of pottery exactly similar to the Etruscan, several bones, easy to distinguish, among which was a tibia, and the fragment of a skull; also fragments of an *iron* sword; and a bronze figure seated on a chariot with horses. Several of the clay vases were much burnt and vitrified, whereas all the painted vessels were unhurt. This is an abstract of the account given of the excavations by Choiseul-Gouffier.[10] But, as no man of experience or worthy of confidence was present at the excavation, scholars seem to have distrusted the account from the first, and to have thought that the Jew, in order to obtain a good reward, had procured and prepared beforehand all the objects he pretended to have found in the tumulus. And all the experience we have now gathered by the exploration of so many similar tumuli is fatal to the Jew's account of his discoveries. As I felt assured that the fragments of pottery contained in the tumulus would give me the key to its date, I was very anxious to explore

---

[9] See C. G. Lenz, *Die Ebene von Troja, nach dem Grafen Choiseul-Gouffier;* Neu Strelitz, 1798, p. 64.   [10] *Ibid.* pp. 60–62.

it; but as the owner of the land, a Turk in Koum Kaleh, would not give me the permission to sink a shaft in it without receiving beforehand a reward of £100, I abstained from doing so.

That this tumulus was considered in the historical times of antiquity as the sepulchre of Achilles, is evident from Pliny (*H. N.* v. 33) and Quintus Smyrnaeus (vii. 402), both of whom place it on the left bank of the Scamander. That Homer knew, from his own eyesight, the tumulus which in his time was considered as the common tomb of Achilles and Patroclus, or at least that he had a particular tumulus in view which he attributes in common to both heroes, appears evident from the verses in which he makes Achilles direct the Greeks to heap up for Patroclus a small tumulus, and to make it larger and higher after his own death.[1] This is also confirmed by the passage in which Patroclus appears to Achilles in his dream, and begs him not to put his bones apart from his own,[2] but to erect a tumulus over the bones of both.[3] I call attention to the word σορός (an ἅπαξ εἰρημένον), used in the latter verse for the usual σῆμα.

3. The next tumulus excavated was that which is situated on the height above Ren Kioi. It was explored by the late Mr. Frederick Calvert, who ascertained that it was an artificial mound, but found neither bones, nor ashes, nor objects of human industry in it.

4. *The Tumulus of Priam.*—The fourth tumulus was excavated by Mr. Frank Calvert, who gives the following account of it:[4]—" According to the description of Forchhammer, three of the four tumuli before Gergis are situated on the summit of the rocky eminence, the Bali Dagh, a little distance outside the thick wall which separates them from the Acropolis; and by the side of each is a deep pit, apparently artificial. The fourth is on the same ridge, more to the west. He is not altogether correct, however, in stating that their materials are all derived from the natural rock on which they stand, for one of them alone is entirely so; namely, the one correctly so described by Lechevalier, and which he names the tomb of Hector. The largest of the other mounds, supposed to be the tomb of Priam,[5] was the one I decided on excavating. It is about 13 ft. in height, and, cropping out on the summit, traces of a quadrangular building were visible. I caused an open shaft to be commenced at the base of the mound, and it was carried along the surface of the natural rock through a mixture of earth and stones, as far as the masonry in the centre, which rested upon the rock. This structure I found to be, as at the top, square in form, and measuring about 14 ft. by 12. It is formed of large irregular stones, roughly hewn on the outward faces alone, and put together without cement. The space in the interior is filled in with small loose stones. A few casual potsherds

---

[1] *Il.* xxiii. 245–248 :
τύμβον δ' οὐ μάλα πολλὸν ἐγὼ πονέεσθαι ἄνωγα,
ἀλλ' ἐπιεικέα τοῖον. ἔπειτα δὲ καὶ τὸν Ἀχαιοί
εὐρύν θ' ὑψηλόν τε τιθήμεναι, οἵ κεν ἐμεῖο
δεύτεροι ἐν νήεσσι πολυκλήϊσι λίπησθε.

[2] *Il.* xxiii. 69–90.

[3] *Il.* xxiii. 91 :
ὣς δὲ καὶ ὀστέα νῶϊν ὁμὴ σορὸς ἀμφικαλύπτοι...

[4] *Contributions towards the Ancient Geography of the Troad*, p. 2.

[5] *Remarks and Observations on the Plain of Troy*, by W. Franklin, p. 19 ; Walpole's *Travels*, i. p. 108.

were thrown out during the excavations, but nothing was found to indicate that this mound had been used as a place of sepulture. It appears rather to have served as a base to some statue or public monument, or, as Dr. Hunt remarks, as a foundation to some altar or shrine."[6]

5. The fifth tumulus explored, likewise by Mr. Frank Calvert, was the conical mound below Yeni Shehr, the so-called Tumulus of Patroclus. He sank an open shaft in it and dug down in the centre to the virgin soil, but found here also neither bones nor ashes nor anything else. Homer says of the cenotaph of Patroclus :

$$τορνώσαντο \; δὲ \; σῆμα, \; θεμείλιά \; τε \; προβάλοντο \; . \; . \; .^7$$

which means, "they traced out the circle for the tumulus, and encompassed it with foundation-stones." This passage leads us naturally to expect to find at least one circle of stones in or around this and the other tumuli ; but nothing of the kind has been found in any one of the tumuli hitherto excavated.

6. *The Tumulus of Hector.*—In October 1872 this tumulus, already mentioned as on the Bali Dagh, was excavated by my honoured friend Sir John Lubbock. It consists entirely of small stones, and was, probably for this reason, attributed by Lechevalier to Hector. But there were found in it neither bones nor charcoal nor any traces of the destination of this tumulus for a funeral mound.

7. *The Pasha Tepeh.*—The seventh tumulus, called Pasha Tepeh, was excavated in the beginning of May 1873 by Mrs. Sophia Schliemann. As I have said in the preceding pages, there can hardly be any doubt regarding the identity of this tumulus with the mound held by Strabo to be the tomb of Aesyetes, mentioned by Homer,[8] for Strabo says that it was situated at a distance of 5 stadia from Novum Ilium on the road to Alexandria-Troas.[9] But Alexandria-Troas lay to the south-west of Ilium, and the road to it, which is distinctly marked by the ford of the Scamander at its entrance into the valley, goes direct south as far as Bounarbashi. Now, Pasha Tepeh is exactly at a distance of 1017 yds. to the south of the southern wall of Novum Ilium, and therefore its situation answers perfectly to Strabo's indication, and even the road close to which it lies is most probably identical with the road of which Strabo speaks. But the identity of this tumulus with the tomb of Aesyetes is quite out of the question, for, according to the above Homeric passage, Priam's son Polites was watching on the tumulus of Aesyetes when the Achaeans should rush forth from the ships, and it must therefore have been situated to the north of Ilium, between the city and the Hellespont, probably about Koum Kioi. If, therefore, Demetrius of Scepsis and Strabo, who adopted his theory, pretended that Pasha Tepeh was identical with the tumulus of Aesyetes, it was merely to uphold their impossible theory that Troy had been situated on the site of Ἰλιέων Κώμη.

But Pasha Tepeh being in front of Ilium and to the side of the Plain,

---

[6] Walpole's *Travels*, i. p. 108.
[8] *Il.* ii. 791–794, already quoted at p. 147.
[7] *Il.* xxiii. 255.
[9] Strabo, xiii. p. 599.

its position corresponds perfectly with the indications which Homer [10] gives us of the position of the monument held by the gods to be the tumulus of Myriné, whereas men believed it to be the sepulchre of Batieia, and there can hardly be any doubt that the poet, in describing this tomb to us, had Pasha Tepeh in view.

No. 1614. The Pasha Tepeh, or Tumulus of Batieia, excavated by Mrs. Sophia Schliemann.

We have seen that Batieia, or Bateia, was the daughter of Teucer, son of the Scamander and the nymph Idaea, and the queen of Dardanus. Myriné, to whom the tumulus was ascribed by the gods, was one of the

<hr>

[10] *Il.* ii. 811–814 :

ἔστι δέ τις προπάροιθε πόλιος αἰπεῖα κολώνη,
ἐν πεδίῳ ἀπάνευθε, περίδρομος ἔνθα καὶ ἔνθα,

τὴν ἦ τοι ἄνδρες Βατίειαν κικλήσκουσιν,
ἀθάνατοι δέ τε σῆμα πολυσκάρθμοιο Μυρίνης·

Amazons who undertook a campaign against Troy.[1] I remind the reader
that, according to Professor Sayce, Myriné is identical with Smyrna,
which was a name of Artemis-Cybele, the Amazons having been in the
first instance the priestesses of this Asiatic goddess.

Mrs. Schliemann sank from the top a shaft $10\frac{3}{4}$ ft. broad and $17\frac{1}{2}$ ft.
long, and found that the layer of vegetable soil is scarcely more than
$\frac{3}{4}$ of an inch thick; then follows brown earth as hard as stone, which
alternates with strata of calcareous earth. At a depth of 15 ft. the white
limestone rock was struck. No ashes or charcoal were found, much less
the bones of a burnt corpse. That Mrs. Schliemann could have missed the
traces of a funeral pyre, if such had really existed, is inconceivable, when
we consider the size of the perpendicular cutting. There were found in
the brown earth some fragments of hand-made pottery similar to that of
the third, the burnt city of Hissarlik, which led me to ascribe a similar
age to the mound. But, after the winter rains had widened the shaft
and brought to light more pottery, I found there also very common
archaic Greek potsherds, which made me at first doubt of the great
antiquity of this tumulus. But having carefully compared them with the
common archaic pottery found in the lowest stratum of Novum Ilium,
as well as with the archaic pottery found in my excavations in Ithaca,
I no longer hesitate to attribute to them a high antiquity, although
their age does not, of course, come up to that of even the latest pre-
historic city of Hissarlik. I therefore find in the pottery no obstacle
to my theory that this tumulus existed at the time of Homer, and that it
gave him the idea for the sepulchre of Queen Batieia or the Amazon Myriné.
As for the fragments of pre-historic pottery contained in the tumulus,
they were no doubt lying on or in the ground with which it was heaped up.

8. *Tumulus of Ujek Tepeh.*—Although my honoured friend Sir Austen
Henry Layard had already in January 1879 obtained for me permission
to explore the remaining tumuli of the Troad, there yet remained a
thousand difficulties to overcome. But by the kind endeavours of Mr.
E. Malet, Minister Plenipotentiary during Sir A. H. Layard's absence,
and of Count Hatzfeldt, the German Ambassador at Constantinople, who
assisted me at the request of Professor Virchow, I obtained my firman on
the 17th of April, and began on the following morning to sink shafts on
the summits of the gigantic tumuli of Ujek Tepeh and Besika Tepeh.
Ujek is the pure Turkish word اوجاق, which means "fireside." The
tumulus is, according to M. Burnouf's measurement, 213 ft. high above
the sea, and it has obtained its name from the strange fact that (probably
from a confusion of the name Ilus with Elias) it is regarded as the
sepulchre of the prophet Elias by the inhabitants of the Troad, who
go thither on pilgrimage on the festival of that saint, on the 1st of
August, to pray to him and to light fires on the top of the tumulus in
his honour. Such fires must have been kindled there by the Christians for
many centuries, for down to a depth of 2 ft. 2 in. I found nothing but
yellow wood-ashes mixed with fragments of uninteresting modern pottery.

---

[1] *Il.* iii. 189, 190; Strabo, xii. p. 573.

I began my excavations by sinking a shaft 10 ft. square. I worked during the first two days with picks and shovels only, with which latter I threw out the earth from the shaft; but the next two days I had to

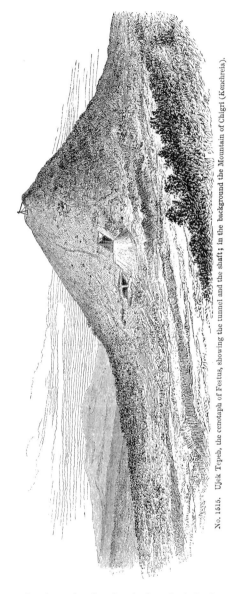

No. 1515. Ujek Tepeh, the cenotaph of Festus, showing the tunnel and the shaft; in the background the Mountain of Chigri (Kenchreïa).

employ baskets, and, when the depth of the shaft had reached 13 ft., to erect a wooden triangle (called by builders shear-legs), by means of which the earth was drawn out in baskets with windlasses. In the accompanying engraving, No. 1515, this tumulus is represented from the north side, which has, according to M. Burnouf's measurement, a perpendicular height of 68 ft. 6 in. ; its greatest height of 83 ft. is on the east side, its lowest of 53 ft. 8 in. on the west side. Another engraving, No. 1516,

No. 1516.   The Scamander below the confluence of the Thymbrius ; in the background the Tumulus of Ujek Tepeh.

represents the tumulus of Ujek Tepeh as seen from the confluence of the Scamander and Thymbrius.

The excavations of both Ujek Tepeh and Besika Tepeh were conducted by my able engineer Mr. M. Gorkiewicz.   The first day I could only work the shaft in Ujek Tepeh with four labourers, but I had to increase the number daily as we went deeper, until I had twelve workmen, which remained the number of hands in the shaft to the end.[2]

I struck, at a depth of 2 ft. 8 in. below the summit, a wall which consists alternately of roughly-hewn stones, large and small, from 1 ft. to 3 ft. long and from 8 in. to 1 ft. 6 in. thick, cemented with a quantity of clay; and, as visitors will see, by a most lucky chance this wall was discovered exactly on the west side of my shaft, so that it was no obstacle to me.   Its direction is from north to south.   Having dug through the layer of ashes, I struck alternately layers of coarse yellow, brown, or whitish clay, which are intersected at intervals of from 4 to 5 ft. by horizontal strata of unwrought stones ; and these could not, in my opinion, have been put there for any other purpose than to consolidate the tumulus.   On reaching a depth of 6 ft., I found that my shaft had been commenced on too large a scale, and I therefore narrowed it to $6\frac{1}{2}$ ft. square.   To avoid fatal accidents I supported the four sides of the shaft vertically as well as horizontally with large beams and thick planks, which were carefully nailed together.   Nevertheless there was always some danger, particularly for the workmen who worked in the shaft, and who always had to be hoisted in and out by the rope of the windlass. I therefore paid somewhat higher wages to those who worked the windlass above, and double wages to those who worked below.   No Greek workman in the Troad ever works on a Sunday or on any of the numerous other

---

[2] The following description is illustrated by Plans V. and VI. at the end of the volume ; the former giving a Plan and the latter a Section of the subterranean buildings within the tumulus.

Greek holidays; but by paying 5 francs to each man who worked on those days, I got them to overcome all their scruples, and always had most assiduous labourers. Thus in four weeks' time I reached, at a depth of 46 ft. 4 in., the virgin soil, consisting of very hard yellow clay mixed with stones. As will be seen from the plan of the excavation (Plans V. and VI.), the large wall on the west side of my shaft is only 11·80 mètres = 39 ft. 4 in. high, and reaches down to a depth of 42 ft. below the surface; consequently, it was not built on the virgin soil, but 4 ft. 4 in. above it. By comparing these figures with the height of the tumulus as given above, the reader will see that the mound was erected on a natural hill.

Simultaneously with this shaft, I dug into the mound from the north side, at a perpendicular depth of 66 ft. 8 in. below the summit, a tunnel 6 ft. 8 in. high, 5 ft. 4 in. broad below and 4 ft. 4 in. above; and I made it vaulted, in order to lessen the danger for my workmen. Owing to the narrowness of the tunnel, there was only room in it for three men, of whom two worked with picks, whilst the third carried out the earth in a wheelbarrow.

I did not begin the tunnel lower down, owing to the rising ground on the west side of the tumulus, which made me afraid that I should strike the natural soil. The earth being as hard as stone, and the tunnel being so narrow, I could not work in it with my usual pick-axes, and had to have a dozen steel picks half their size made in haste, one end of which was pointed and the other 2-3rds in. broad and very sharp. When I had penetrated 29 ft. horizontally into the mound, I came upon the virgin soil, consisting of a yellowish sandy clay and stones. It was covered to the depth of 1 ft. 7 in. with a layer of humus, which was no doubt on the surface when the tumulus was built. This humus was covered, from 1 ft. 2 in. to 1 ft. 4 in. deep, by a layer of brown clay, succeeded by another thin layer of black earth. This latter was followed by a thin layer of white clay, on which again lay a stratum of humus; then followed again a layer of brownish clay, 3 ft. thick. I now at once ordered the tunnel to be raised 6½ ft.; and as, in digging further into the mound, I nevertheless again struck the virgin soil, I was obliged to raise the tunnel 3½ ft. higher, and then to follow the ascending slope of the natural soil in the direction of my shaft, which I at last reached after a month's very hard labour.

The layers of brown, yellow, or white clay succeeded each other continually as I worked on. Visitors will see that their thickness varies, which is natural, for the earth was of course brought gradually from many different places when the mound was heaped up. Fortunately I had no need to support the sides or the roof of the tunnel with wooden beams and planks; for the soil being, as already mentioned, as hard as stone, there was not the slightest danger to my workmen. But the heat in the narrow tunnel was very great, and it was increased by the petroleum lamps; besides, the work being very heavy, I was obliged to pay the workmen 5 francs a head daily. Great was our joy when at last the bottom of the shaft was reached, and a cool draught of air was established through the tunnel. The event was celebrated by my workmen with 13 okes (32½ bottles) of wine and two roasted sheep, which I had given them on the occasion. The tunnel is 96 ft. 8 in. long. By digging galleries to the right and left at the bottom of the shaft, I found that the great wall formed the east side of a gigantic quadrangular mass of masonry, a species of tower, 15 ft. square ; its height being, as already stated, 39 ft. 4 in. I further ascertained that it had been founded directly above a circular enclosure, 4 ft. 4 in. high, consisting of well-cut polygons, from 1½ to 2½ ft. long, 1 ft. 2 in. broad, and 2½ ft. thick, which are so admirably fitted together that the whole enclosure appears to consist of one single block ; its diameter being 34 ft. As will be seen on the plan and section of Ujek Tepeh (Plans V. and VI.), on the north-west side of this circle another wall leans against it, which also forms a curve, but of a greater radius. It is of the same height, and consists of rather small quadrangular wrought stones, joined together without any binding material. Having cut a gallery into the massive square structure, I found in its midst, and 6 ft. above its base, a quadrangular cavity, 3 ft. square and 5 ft. high,[3] filled with fine earth, which must in the course of ages have penetrated through the fissures between the stones. From this cavity I cut a vertical shaft through the masonry down to the virgin soil, without finding anything else than some fragments of pottery, among which late Roman potsherds are conspicuous, and also an iron knife. I also dug galleries above the two circular walls, and was by these means enabled to sink vertical shafts into the circular enclosures. From one of the shafts I also dug a tunnel, and joined it to the shaft sunk in the midst of the massive quadrangular tower; but everywhere I obtained the same result—some fragments of iron implements and pottery of various epochs, among which late Roman pottery is the most abundant. The very same result had been obtained in the large vertical shaft, as well as in the large tunnel.

How difficult it is to dig tunnels in the midst of a huge mound, from these again to sink shafts, and to dig tunnels again from the bottom of these shafts, he who has been an eye-witness of such an undertaking can alone understand.

In the opinion of M. Burnouf and my own, the circular enclosure of polygonal stones, over which the quadrangular tower is built, can have been nothing else than a sacred shrine, and must probably have been built a considerable time before the superincumbent structure and the tumulus were erected. He thinks with me that it is of the Macedonian age, or perhaps of the fifth century B.C.; for as the polygons have been worked with iron pick-hammers, we do not feel ourselves authorized to attribute to it a higher antiquity. Professor Sayce finds the masonry of the circular enclosure to be distinctively Macedonian, and does not think it can possibly be older.

Considering all this, and bearing in mind that history knows only of one single tumulus having been erected here, I do not hesitate to assert

---

[3] See on Plan VI.

that this must necessarily be that very historical monument; namely, the tumulus which, according to Herodian, the Emperor Caracalla (211-216 A.D.) erected in honour of his most intimate friend Festus, whom some believed he had poisoned merely to provide his Patroclus, in order to imitate the funeral celebrated by Achilles to his friend,[4] which Homer describes with so much beauty and precision in the twenty-third book of the *Iliad*.

The tumulus of Patroclus was, as we have seen above, a mere cenotaph; it is therefore obvious that the tumulus of Festus could be nothing else than a cenotaph, because the funeral rites detailed by Homer were, of course, scrupulously observed by Caracalla. The identity of this tumulus with that of Festus is confirmed by its gigantic proportions; for a vain fool like Caracalla, who aped the manners of Alexander the Great, and in cold blood murdered his dearest friend in order to imitate Achilles, could not but erect a funeral mound far exceeding in magnitude all the other tumuli of the Troad.

Of a funeral fire no trace was found either at the bottom of the tower or elsewhere in the tumulus. We may therefore consider it as certain that the corpse of Festus was not burnt on this very spot. But probably it was burnt close by. If Caracalla built the cenotaph right upon the open sanctuary which the two circular enclosures seem to indicate, it may probably have been in order to impart a greater solemnity to his farce.

To many of the fragments of terra-cottas found in this tumulus I would not hesitate to assign the date of the fifth, to some of them even of the sixth or the seventh century B.C.; but it is not to them, but to the abundant late Roman potsherds, that we must look for the key to the date of the monument, for this may be at any time later, but it cannot possibly be older, than the latest pottery found at its bottom. With regard to the great quadrangular tower, it is obvious that it was built for no other purpose than to support the tumulus and to preserve it. All my tunnels, shafts, and galleries in this tumulus remain open to visitors of the present and all future generations, Sir Austen H. Layard having kindly obtained for me permission to that effect from the Turkish Government.

Regarding the quadrangular tower discovered by me in Ujek Tepeh, I call the reader's attention to the similarity of this tumulus with the so-called tumulus of Priam on the Bali Dagh, which, as I have just mentioned, was excavated by Mr. Calvert, and in which also a quadrangular structure was discovered.

My honoured friend Dr. Arthur Milchhoefer, member of the German Archæological Institute in Athens, kindly calls my attention to the

---

[4] Herodian, iv. 8, §§ 3–5: ἀφικόμενος δὴ ἐκεῖ, καὶ ἐς ὅσον ἤθελε τῶν ὀνειράτων ἐμφορηθείς, ἧκεν ἐς Ἴλιον. ἐπελθὼν δὲ πάντα τὰ τῆς πόλεως λείψανα, ἧκεν ἐπὶ τὸν Ἀχιλλέως τάφον, στεφάνοις τε κοσμήσας καὶ ἄνθεσι πολυτελῶς πάλιν Ἀχιλλέα ἐμιμεῖτο, ζητῶν τε καὶ Πάτροκλόν τινα ἐποίησέ τι τοιοῦτον. ἦν αὐτῷ τις τῶν ἀπελευθέρων φίλτατος, Φῆστος μὲν ὄνομα, τῆς δὲ βασιλείου μνήμης προεστώς· οὗτος ὄντος αὐτοῦ ἐν Ἰλίῳ ἐτελεύτησεν, ὡς μέν τινες ἔλεγον, φαρμάκῳ ἀναιρεθεὶς ἵν' ὡς Πάτροκλος ταφῇ, ὡς δὲ ἕτεροι ἔφασκον, νόσῳ διαφθαρείς. τούτου κομισθῆναι κελεύει τὸν νέκυν, ξύλων τε πολλῶν ἀθροισθῆναι πυράν· ἐπιθείς τε αὐτὸν ἐν μέσῳ καὶ παντοδαπὰ ζῷα κατασφάξας ὑφῆψέ τε, καὶ φιάλην λαβὼν σπένδων τε τοῖς ἀνέμοις εὔχετο.

analogy which exists between the tumulus of Ujek Tepeh and the Cucumella at Vulci in Etruria, of which he gives me the following details :—

"The Cucumella is a tumulus now between 40 and 50 ft. high by about 200 ft. in diameter at the base. It was first explored in 1829 by the Prince of Canino, the proprietor of the land. The tumulus was surrounded by a wall of large blocks which is now destroyed, and on which, according to all analogy, must have stood the sculptures of sphinxes and lions, of which several have been found outside. Beneath the wall were found some unimportant tombs, which, in the opinion of Mr. Dennis,[5] belong to servants and slaves. Towards the middle of the tumulus two towers were struck, about 40 ft. high; one quadrangular, the other conical; which are distinguished from everything else of the kind by their careless and irregular masonry. But Micali[6] observes that the conical tower consists of better and larger materials than the other. These towers have, it is asserted, no visible entrance, though an entrance is indicated in the drawing given by Micali.[7]

"Lenoir[8] has already called attention to the tumulus of Alyattes in Lydia, which, according to Herodotus,[9] had on its summit five conical pillars (like the tomb of Porsena, near Chiusi, and the so-called 'tomb of the Horatii and the Curiatii,' near Albano), and he draws from this the conclusion that the towers had been erected in the tumulus of Cucumella to support five similar pillars.

"Of the further discoveries of the Prince of Canino, besides Ed. Gerhard,[1] Mr. Dennis says : 'At the foot of these towers is now a shapeless hollow; but here were found two small chambers constructed of massive regular masonry, and with doorways of primitive style, arched over by the gradual convergence of the horizontal courses. They were approached by a long passage, leading directly into the heart of the tumulus ; and here on the ground lay fragments of bronze and gold plates, very thin, and adorned with ivy and myrtle leaves. Two stone sphinxes stood guardians at the entrance of the passage.'[2]

"It is a remarkable fact that the tomb of Porsena, at Clusium, the only Etruscan tomb of which we have any record, bore a close affinity to the only Lydian sepulchre described by the ancients (that of Alyattes), the square merely taking the place of the circle; for it is said to have had 'five pyramids' rising from a square base of masonry, one at each angle, and one in the centre.[3] And the curious monument at Albano, vulgarly called the tomb of the Horatii and Curiatii, has a square basement of masonry, surmounted by four cones, and a cylindrical tower in the midst. Five, indeed, seems to have been the established number of cones, pyramids, or columnar *cippi*, on tombs of this description ; whence it has been

---

[5] *The Cities and Cemeteries of Etruria*, i. p. 452.

[6] *Storia d' Ant. Pop. It.* iii. p. 103.

[7] *Antichi Monumenti*, 62. 1 ; see also the sketch in the *Monumenti* of the Roman Institute, i. 41. 2.

[8] *Annali dell' Instituto*, 1832, p. 272.

[9] i. 93.

[1] *Bullet. dell' Inst.* 1829, p. 51.

[2] Dennis, *op. cit.* p. 453.

[3] Varro, *ap.* Plin. *H. N.* xxxvi. 19, § 4.

suggested that three other towers are probably buried in the unexcavated part of the Cucumella." [4]

Dr. Milchhoefer adds that, on account of the sphinxes, we cannot ascribe a later date than the fifth century B.C. to the Cucumella. "We have," he says, "in these monuments a new proof of the ancient and direct connection of Asiatic and Tyrrhenian culture. In Asia Minor, and especially perhaps in the necropolis of Sardis, might be found the key to the solution of many of these moot questions."

But the tumulus of Ujek Tepeh seems to have no affinity to any one of these tombs. It was evidently copied by Caracalla from the other tumuli of the Troad, and from the cenotaph of Patroclus as described by Homer. The large size of the quadrangular tower erected just in the centre, and the fact that no other masonry was found in my tunnel, prove that this is the only tower in the tumulus, and that its sole object was to consolidate the mound.

9. *Tumulus of Besika Tepeh.*—Simultaneously with the exploration of Ujek Tepeh, I also investigated the Besika Tepeh, of which I have already spoken. It is not mentioned by ancient writers, but some modern travellers have identified it with the sepulchre of Peneleos.[5] This tumulus is, according to M. Burnouf's measurement, 141 ft. high above the sea, 48 ft. 3 in. in height, and 266 ft. in diameter at its base. Here also I sank from the summit of the tumulus a shaft $6\frac{1}{2}$ ft. square, and began at the same time to dig a tunnel into the mound from the north side. But I gave up this tunnel after a few days, and limited myself to the sinking of the shaft. The earth being very loose, I had constantly to support all the four sides of the shaft, both vertically and horizontally, with beams and planks, in order to avoid accidents. Just as in Ujek Tepeh, I worked here at first with picks and shovels, throwing out the earth on the sides of the mound. But when the depth of the shaft exceeded 6 ft., I had the earth lifted out with baskets, and, when this could no longer be done, I made a wooden triangle of beams over the shaft, and had the earth removed in baskets with windlasses, three men being always occupied at the bottom of the shaft in digging and filling the basket. I began with seven workmen, but had to increase their number gradually to ten. The danger from the loose earth being here still greater than in the Ujek Tepeh, I had to pay as high wages as at the latter tumulus. As in that case, the earth which was brought up was thrown all round the summit, in order to avoid disfiguring the mound. I struck from time to time layers of large stones, which can have had no other purpose than to consolidate the tumulus. In a great many places these stones may be seen peeping out from the slope of the mound.

After incessant labour for twenty-four days, my shaft, at a depth of 44 ft., reached the rock, which consists of limestone. M. Burnouf, who carefully measured and investigated the different strata of earth in the

---

[4] *Ann. Inst.* 1832, p. 273—Lenoir.

Dennis says : "I much doubt this. There may be one or two more, but from the position of the disclosed towers in the mound there can hardly have been five." (Dennis, *op. cit.* i. pp. 453, 454.)

[5] Barker Webb, *Topographie de la Troade,* p. 66.

shaft, found the rock covered with a layer of dark vegetable earth, which was probably there when the tumulus was made :—

							métres.		ft.	in.
1. The thickness of this humus is		..	..		..	1·10	=	3	8
2. A stratum of white earth	..	••	..		..	70	=	2	4
3. A stratum of dark earth	..	..	..		..	80	=	2	8
4. Do.	stones and white earth		..		..	1·0	=	3	4
5. Do.	vegetable earth		..	..	..	1·10	=	3	8
6. Do.	earth with yellow clay and stones		..			70	=	2	4
7. Do.	do. do. do.		to the top	7·80			=	26	0
						13·20	..	44	0

From the depression of the soil at the foot of this tumulus, on the north-east side, it is evident that all the clay and earth for making it has been taken from that place. Further on, in a north-easterly and easterly direction, the rock has evidently been artificially levelled for a distance of about 200 yds. square, and most probably this little plateau has been the site of the prehistoric city to which we are indebted for the strange pottery found in the tumulus.

From the bottom of the shaft I excavated two galleries, which cross each other, and of which each has a length of 18 ft. 4 in. The excavation of these galleries was a very dangerous work, the earth being so loose and full of huge stones, that I could not proceed a single foot without supporting the roof and both sides of my underground passages with beams and planks. Owing to the nature of the soil, I could use large picks here. The *débris*, carried in baskets from the galleries into the central shaft, were poured there into the large basket and drawn up by the windlass. The most curious object I found was the fragment of a vase-bottom

No. 1517. Fragment of a Vase-bottom, with signs, found in the Tumulus of Besika Tepeh. (Actual size. Depth, 43 ft.)

(No. 1517), with incised signs, filled up with white chalk, of which I sent a copy to Prof. Sayce, who answered me : " I do not think it is a real inscription, but it may possibly be a bad attempt to imitate a cuneiform inscription seen by some one who did not understand the latter, like the bad copies of Egyptian hieroglyphics made by the Phoenicians."

In the layers of yellow clay I never found anything, whilst the layers of dark earth, which appear to have been cut away from the surface of the ground when the tumulus was made, contained large masses of fragments of very coarse as well as of better pottery, of a red, brown, yellow, or black colour, which has received a lustrous surface by hand-polishing: all this pottery is hand-made. The coarse pottery, which is sometimes an inch thick, is either quite unpolished or polished on one side, but seldom on both. The largest of the vessels which the fragments of the rude pottery denote, cannot have been higher than about 3 ft. They are sometimes ornamented with a projecting rope-like band round the neck and a handle in the form of a rope. In general, these coarse vessels are baked only to about one-third of the thickness of their clay, and they far exceed in rudeness any pottery ever found by me in any one of the five pre-historic cities of Hissarlik. But, strange to say, some of them have a rude painted ornamentation of large black bands.

The fragments of the better pottery denote smaller vases, and the first impression they make is certainly that they are similar to the pottery of the second city of Hissarlik, and of the same make; nay, some of them appear at first sight to be similar even to the pottery of the first city. But on close examination we find that they are vastly different; for their clay is coarser, and contains much more of the coarsely-crushed silicious stone and syenite, with a far greater quantity of mica; besides, the pottery is evidently altogether different in shape and fabric. It is seldom baked to more than half the thickness of the clay, and generally only to one-third. Nevertheless, having been abundantly dipped in a wash of clay, and having been evidently put twice to the fire, and polished both inside and outside before each baking, the vases are generally smooth on both sides; but a vast number of them have only been polished on the outside, and are rude and coarse on the inside. The vase-bottoms especially are rude and bulky, all of them are flat, and in a very great number of cases they have the impressions of the wicker-work of straw on which the vases had been put after they had been modelled. On most of these vase-bottoms the impression of the wicker-work is so perfect, that one might count in them all the straws of which it was composed. Indeed, it would appear that the impression of the wicker-work was made on purpose to decorate the vase-bottoms. In a few cases the vase-bottoms represent the impression of a wicker-work of rods.

The Besika pottery further differs from that of Hissarlik in the total absence of perforated projections for suspension. Only two fragments with a hole were found; one of them belonging to a bowl, the other being the fragment of a hollow wing-like handle, such as we see on the vases like No. 180, p. 303. Two such wing-like handles were found, which prove that vases similar to those represented under these numbers were in use. There were also found two fragments of a red and a black vase, with a rudely-incised linear decoration representing net-work, which had evidently been made *after* the baking; also two fragments with a concave linear decoration; whereas hundreds of other fragments were brought to light, having a most curious painted decoration, which is for the most

part of a floral kind, representing trees of brown colour on a light-yellow
dead ground, but so rudely made that one doubts after all if the primitive
artist intended to represent trees with their branches, or fish-spines.
Sometimes we see this floral decoration of a lustrous black, on a light-
yellow dead ground; and in such cases, all the rest of the vase being
of the same uniform lustrous black colour, I cannot but think that the
decoration must have been produced without paint, and merely by a
polishing stone. Sometimes we see on the vases a number of parallel
black bands, between which the painted tree or herring-bone decoration
proceeds alternately in opposite directions. At other times we see a
decoration of painted brown bands, vertical or horizontal, on a light-red
dead ground. But it must be well understood that the decoration is, in
the case of the vases or jugs, always on the outside, in that of the bowls
on the inside. There are also bowls which are on the outside of a lustrous
black, on the inside partly of a lustrous dark-red, partly of a light-red,
and decorated with dark-red bands, with the tree or herring-bone ornamentation described above. We also frequently see on the outside, both
of the vases and bowls, which are of a light-brown or dark-red colour,
very curious black signs, resembling written characters; but they are so
indistinct that I believe them to have been painted with black clay. The
same is no doubt the case with the painted floral or other decorations ;
they are too indistinct to be anything else than clay paint. The total
absence of the whorls and the tripod-vessels, which occur in such immense
numbers at Hissarlik, is astonishing.

The vase-handles of Besika Tepeh are usually plain, but there are some
with pointed projections. Of vessels with breast-like projections only two
fragments turned up; one of them has the projection at the very rim.

But not all the pottery is hand-made. In carefully examining one by
one all the thousands of fragments, I found the fragments of two wheel-
made vases, which, as compared with any of the other fragments, are of
very fine clay, but the baking of both is but very slight. One of them is
grey, and is the lower part of a vase ; it is decorated with a hardly perceptible painted black band, probably of clay colour: the other, though
of the same colour, is covered on the outside with a whitish clay, which
gives it the appearance of Egyptian porcelain.

If, at the risk of wearying the reader, I have given a detailed
account of the Besika Tepeh pottery, it is because it is of capital interest
to archæology, no similar pottery having ever come under my notice
elsewhere. All this pottery must have been lying on the north-east side
of the tumulus, on or in the soil with which the latter was made. Here,
therefore, was a town or village, which no doubt extended much further
still to the north-east and east, for, as I have before stated, the projecting
rock there has been artificially levelled. But as to the chronology of this
settlement it is difficult to express an opinion, the more so as, with the
exception of the hollow wing-like vase-handles, the pottery is so totally
different from all the pottery found in the five pre-historic cities of
Hissarlik, and most decidedly denotes an altogether different race of
people. I have vainly endeavoured to find an analogy to it in the British

Museum. The only similar pottery I found there consisted of two brown vase-fragments from Malta; but in these the resemblance is very striking.

Of other objects of human industry found in this tumulus, I can only mention some good polishing-stones for smoothing pottery. Strange to say, not a single flint knife or flint saw turned up, and not even a single stone hammer, bruising-stone, or saddle-quern, which are found in such immense abundance in all the five pre-historic cities of Hissarlik.

Some bones, apparently of animals, were found here and there in the tumulus; also many oyster-shells, a broken murex, and some other shells.

No trace of a funeral fire was found at the bottom or anywhere else in the tumulus.

10. *Hagios Demetrios Tepeh.*—I also explored, in company with Professor Virchow and M. Burnouf, the conical hill, called Hagios Demetrios Tepeh, which I have mentioned in the preceding pages. We found it to consist altogether of limestone-rock. Nevertheless, as M. Burnouf found a small pitcher of the Roman time near the surface, I excavated for two days on its summit, in the hope of finding there at least tombs of the Greek period; but I found the layer of earth to be nowhere deeper than 5 ft., with no trace of sepulchres. As in the days of old the inhabitants went in crowds on the festival of Demeter to the adjoining marble temple of that goddess, of which large ruins still exist, in the same manner they now go on the festival of Hagios Demetrios on pilgrimage to the little open shrine of the saint and kindle on the mound bonfires in his honour.

11. *The Tomb of Ilus.*—I further excavated the repeatedly mentioned σῆμα Ἴλου, or Tomb of Ilus, situated on the right bank of the Kalifatli Asmak, at a very short distance to the north of Koum Kioi. As this tumulus probably consisted of pure earth, and was brought under the plough, it gradually vanished, and its present dimensions are merely 38 ft. 4 in. in diameter and 3 ft. 4 in. in height. There is a circular depression around its centre, which seems to indicate that there has been a round recess, from which the stones have been extracted for building purposes. I merely found there a layer of stones and *débris* 1 ft. 8 in. deep, and not even a fragment of pottery. Below the stones I struck a layer of clay, and then a thick stratum of coarse or fine river sand; and beneath this (at an average depth of from 5 to $8\frac{1}{3}$ ft. below the surface) the very compact brown clay of the plain.

12. At Prof. Virchow's suggestion, I also sank a shaft into the tumulus situated near the southern extremity of Novum Ilium,[6] to the left of the road in going to Pasha Tepeh, but I found there nothing else than a few fragments of Roman bricks, and struck the rock at a depth of about 5 ft.

13. I cannot conclude this discussion of the Heroic tombs in the Troad without discussing the real tomb of Hector. According to the *Iliad*, Hector's corpse was brought out of Troy and put on the pyre raised before the town.[7] The body having been consumed by the fire, the bones

---

[6] See the Map of the Troad.

[7] *Il.* xxiv. 782–787:

ὣς ἔφαθ᾽, οἳ δ᾽ ὑπ᾽ ἀμάξῃσιν βόας ἡμιόνους τε
ζεύγνυσαν, αἶψα δ᾽ ἔπειτα πρὸ ἄστεος ἠγερέθοντο.
. . . .

ἀλλ᾽ ὅτε δὴ δεκάτη ἐφάνη φαεσίμβροτος ἠώς,
καὶ τότ᾽ ἄρ᾽ ἐξέφερον θρασὺν Ἕκτορα δάκρυ χέοντες,
ἐν δὲ πυρῇ ὑπάτῃ νεκρὸν θέσαν, ἐν δ᾽ ἔβαλον πῦρ.

were collected, put into a golden box, and deposited in a grave, which was covered up with large stones, and over these the tumulus was raised. The poet leaves us in doubt of what material this tumulus was made; but as he says that it was raised in haste, we must suppose that it was heaped up with earth. Around it sat watchmen, on the look-out lest the Achaeans might rush forth ere the tumulus was completed. The work being terminated, the men returned to the town.[8]

From both these passages it is evident, that the author of the twenty-fourth *Iliad* had in view, not a cenotaph, but a real tomb, and that this tomb was erected before or close to Ilium. But here I have to repeat that the twenty-fourth *Iliad*, as well as the twenty-fourth *Odyssey*, is generally regarded as pseudo-Homeric and as a later addition. This would at once explain why we see here a real tomb instead of a mere cenotaph, like that which was erected for Patroclus;[9] and further, why we see in the twenty-fourth *Iliad* the tumulus of Ilus on the right bank of the Scamander,[10] whilst according to other passages it was situated on the left bank of that river.[1] Professor Sayce observes to me that "the author of the twenty-fourth *Iliad* seems to have been a native of Smyrna, well acquainted with Lydia (see *Il.* xxiv., lines 544 and 614–617); he may consequently be describing the practice of the Lydians, whose burial mounds exist in such numbers in the neighbourhood of Sardis." In fact, it appears that, if not throughout antiquity, at least from the Macedonian period, the twenty-fourth *Iliad* was considered as apocryphal, for Lycophron already mentions Hector's tomb at Ophrynium:[2] and this is also confirmed by Strabo.[3] But it seems that the Ilians also showed in or near their city a tumulus which they alleged to be Hector's tomb, for Dio Chrysostom[4] relates that Hector's tomb was in high honour by the Ilians. Lucian[5] also mentions sacrifices to Hector at Ilium. Philostratus moreover informs us that Hector had a celebrated statue at Ilium, which wrought many miracles, and was the object of general veneration; games were even held in his honour.[6] I also remind the reader of the Emperor Julian's letter given in the preceding pages,[7]

---

[8] *Il.* xxiv. 792–801:

. . . . αὐτὰρ ἔπειτα
ὀστέα λευκὰ λέγοντο κασίγνητοί θ᾽ ἕταροί τε
μυρόμενοι, θαλερὸν δὲ κατείβετο δάκρυ παρειῶν.
καὶ τά γε χρυσείην ἐς λάρνακα θῆκαν ἑλόντες,
πορφυρέοις πέπλοισι καλύψαντες μαλακοῖσιν·
αἶψα δ᾽ ἄρ᾽ ἐς κοίλην κάπετον θέσαν, αὐτὰρ
    ὕπερθεν
πυκνοῖσιν λάεσσι κατεστόρεσαν μεγάλοισιν.
ῥίμφα δὲ σῆμ᾽ ἔχεαν· περὶ δὲ σκοποὶ εἵατο
    πάντη,
μὴ πρὶν ἐφορμηθεῖεν ἐϋκνήμιδες Ἀχαιοί.
χεύαντες δὲ τὸ σῆμα πάλιν κίον·

[9] *Il.* xxiii. 253–256, as quoted above.

[10] *Il.* xxiv. 349–351:

οἳ δ᾽ ἐπεὶ οὖν μέγα σῆμα παρὲξ Ἴλοιο ἔλασσαν,
στῆσαν ἄρ᾽ ἡμιόνους τε καὶ ἵππους, ὄφρα πίοιεν,
ἐν ποταμῷ·

[1] *Il.* viii. 489–491:

Τρώων αὖτ᾽ ἀγορὴν ποιήσατο φαίδιμος Ἕκτωρ,

νόσφι νεῶν ἀγαγών, ποταμῷ ἔπι δινήεντι,
ἐν καθαρῷ, ὅθι δὴ νεκύων διεφαίνετο χῶρος.
See also 560, 561, and x. 414, 415.

[2] Lycophron, *Alexandra*, 1208 ff.

[3] xiii. p. 595: Πλησίον δ᾽ ἐστὶ τὸ Ὀφρύνιον, ἐφ᾽ ᾧ τὸ τοῦ Ἕκτορος ἄλσος ἐν περιφανεῖ τόπῳ.

[4] *Orat.* xi. 179.   [5] *Deorum Conviv.* 12.

[6] *Heroïca*, p. 295: τὸ ἐν Ἰλίῳ ἄγαλμα τοῦ Ἕκτορος ἡμιθέῳ ἀνθρώπῳ ἔοικε καὶ πολλὰ ἤθη ἐπιφαίνει τῷ θεωροῦντι αὐτὸ ξὺν ὀρθῷ λόγῳ· καὶ γὰρ φρονηματῶδες δοκεῖ καὶ γοργὸν καὶ φαιδρὸν καὶ ξὺν ἁβρότητι σφριγῶν καὶ ἡ ὥρα μετ᾽ οὐδεμιᾶς κόμης. ἔστι δ᾽ οὕτω τι ἔμπνουν, ὡς τὸν θεατὴν ἐπισπάσασθαι θιγεῖν. τοῦτο ἵδρυται μὲν ἐν περιβλέπτῳ τοῦ Ἰλίου, πολλὰ δὲ ἐργάζεται χρηστὰ κοινῇ τε καὶ ἐς ἕνα, ὅθεν εὔχονται αὐτῷ καὶ ἀγῶνα θύουσιν, ὅτε δὴ θερμὸν οὕτω καὶ ἐναγώνιον γίγνεται, ὡς καὶ ἱδρῶτα ἀπ᾽ αὐτοῦ λείβεσθαι.

[7] See pp. 181, 182.

in which he states that first of all he was conducted to Hector's *heroüm*, where his bronze statue stood in a small temple; it was anointed with oil, and there was still a sacrificial fire burning on the altar. But already, perhaps more than 700 years before Julian's time, Thebes in Boeotia had disputed with Ophrynium and Ilium the honour of possessing Hector's bones; for, as Pausanias[8] relates, in consequence of an oracle Hector's bones were brought from Ilium to Thebes, and a tomb was erected over them at the fountain of Oedipus, where they were worshipped. I may still further mention that in the *Peplos* of Aristotle is an epigram:[9]

’Επὶ Ἕκτορος κειμένου ἐν Θήβαις.

Ἕκτορι τόν δε μέγαν Βοιώτιοι ἄνδρες ἔτευξαν
τύμβον ὑπὲρ γαίης, σῆμ’ ἐπιγιγνομένοις.

I give here finally under No. 1518 the engraving of a terra-cotta figure, probably an idol, which was found by a boy near the village of

No. 1518.   Figure of Terra-cotta, with a cap on the head;
found in the Troad, near the surface.   (Actual size.)

Yeni Shehr, and which is remarkable for its resemblance to some of the rudest Mycenean idols.[10]

---

[8] Paus. ix. 18, § 4: Ἔστι δὲ καὶ Ἕκτορος Θηβαίοις τάφος τοῦ Πριάμου πρὸς Οἰδιποδίᾳ καλουμένη κρήνῃ· κομίσαι δὲ αὐτοῦ τὰ ὀστᾶ ἐξ Ἰλίου φασὶν ἐπὶ τοιῷδε μαντεύματι·

Θηβαῖοι Κάδμοιο πόλιν καταναιετάοντες,

αἴ κ’ ἐθέλητε πάτραν οἰκεῖν σὺν ἀμύμονι πλούτῳ,
Ἕκτορος ὀστέα Πριαμίδου κομίσαντες ἐς οἴκους
ἐξ Ἀσίης Διὸς ἐννεσίης ἥρωα σέβεσθαι.

[9] *Appendix Epigrammatum Anthol. Palat.* 9.

[10] See my *Mycenae*, Pl. xviii. and xix.

In closing this account of the result of my researches on the site of "sacred Ilios" and in the country of the Trojans, I would express the fervent hope that historical research with the pickaxe and the spade, which in our time engages the attention of scholars with more curiosity and more diversity of opinion than any other form of study, may be more and more developed, and that it may ultimately bring forth into broad daylight the dark pre-historic ages of the great Hellenic race. May this *research with the pickaxe and the spade* prove more and more that the events described in the divine Homeric poems are not mythic tales, but that they are based on real facts; and, in proving this, may it augment the universal love for the noble study of the beautiful Greek classics, and particularly of Homer, that brilliant sun of all literature!

In humbly laying this account of my disinterested labours before the judgment-seat of the civilized world, I should feel the profoundest satisfaction, and should esteem it as the greatest reward my ambition could aspire to, if it were generally acknowledged that I have been instrumental towards the attainment of that great aim of my life.

I cannot conclude without mentioning with the warmest gratitude the names of my honoured and learned friends Professor Rudolf Virchow of Berlin, Professor Max Müller and Professor A. H. Sayce of Oxford, Professor J. P. Mahaffy of Dublin, M. Émile Burnouf of Paris, Professor H. Brugsch Bey, and Professor Paul Ascherson of Berlin, Mr. Frank Calvert, U. S. Consul of the Dardanelles, and Mr. A. J. Duffield of London, who have favoured me with most learned and valuable Appendices or Notes to the present work. Lastly, I here express my warmest gratitude to the learned publisher of this work, my honoured friend Mr. John Murray, as well as to my honoured and learned friend Mr. Philip Smith, for all the kind services they have rendered me, and all the valuable assistance they have lent me in carrying out the present work.

APPENDIX I.

TROY AND HISSARLIK.

By Professor Virchow.

At the beginning of last year Dr. Schliemann asked my help in his explorations at Hissarlik and in the Trojan plain. The journey to Troy was a considerable one, but, after a good deal of hesitation, I resolved to make it. In fact, I could not refuse.

A journey to Troy—how many heads would be turned by the thought of it! Men of the most various callings offered me their company, when it was known that I meant to visit so rare a spot. And yet this was no Swiss tour, where the attraction is in the scenery, though an occasional visit may be paid to the Rütli and Küsznacht, Sempach and Laupen, Murten and St. Jacob an der Birs. It is the *Iliad* which takes us to Troy. The forms conjured up by the poet fill the traveller's fancy from the first. He wants to see the spots where the long struggle for Helen was fought, the graves where the heroes lie who lost their lives in it. Achilles and Hector stand in the foreground of the vivid picture, which is still engraven, as it was thousands of years ago, on the mind of every educated boy. This picture, it is true, cannot have now all the moving power it had in antiquity. Even Xerxes, as he marched against Greece in the fulness of his might, could not withstand the fascination of these memories. While his army was marching from Adramyttium to Abydos, he sought out the ruins of Ilium, and there offered a thousand bulls to Athené. Alexander again, when his army crossed the Hellespont in its trium-phant progress against Asia, forthwith turned his steps to the funeral mound of Achilles, that it might give him strength and a confident hope of victory. The soil of Troy has had no such mighty visitors since, but any one who treads it feels something of what Xerxes and Alexander felt at the same place. There is an atmosphere of poetry lying over the whole country, and of this atmosphere it cannot be divested.

It is not to be supposed, however, that it is this poetical atmosphere alone which arouses the traveller's interest. Before the *Iliad* arose with all its wealth of stories, there existed a series of popular travellers' stories, in which Troy figured. One of the oldest of Greek myths is connected with the name of the Hellespont. Helle and her brother started from Boeotia over the sea north-eastwards; but when they came to the Trojan coast, Helle fell into the sea (Pontos), and only her brother Phryxus reached the distant Colchis, where he hung up the ram's golden fleece. Then came the Argonauts, to fetch this fleece, and the great Heracles, whose deeds on the Trojan coast bring him into contact with the royal race of Priam. At the north end of Besika Bay there is a steep and almost bare promontory of shelly tertiary rock, where travellers are told that the princess Hesione was exposed to the attacks of the sea-monster until the monster was slain by the roving hero; and there is still visible, though half filled up, a deep trench going crosswise through the headland of Sigeum, on the south side of Hagios Demetrios Tepeh, which is said to have been dug by Heracles in order to drain the Trojan plain.

It is but a short step from the heroes to the Olympian gods themselves. The walls of the ancient city had, as the story went, been built by Poseidon when undergoing a temporary bondage. Ganymede was a member of the Trojan royal family. The union of Anchises with the goddess of beauty herself gave birth to Aeneas, through whom the race of the Julii in Rome could lay claim to descent from the gods. Thus was it that the first emperors arose by the grace of God: the Julii were not unmindful of this descent, and they showered honours and privileges on the late city of New Ilium. Lastly, not to forget the most important of all these legends, it was Priam's son Paris who decided the contest between the three goddesses for the prize of beauty. The apple of Paris won for the judge the beautiful Helen, but brought ruin in the sequel on himself, his family, and his country. In this way does the central fact of the *Iliad* connect it with the doings of the Immortals.

It cannot be pure chance or mere caprice that has associated with this country such a rich store of myths, whether of gods, heroes, or men. No other place has ever gathered around itself a fund of legend so great or so glorious. There must be something in the country, in its natural conditions, some special incentive to poetical creation, to account for this wealth of legend. The place itself must have possessed a special charm for the poet. Nature must have worn an aspect here which gave fire to his fancy. Who can believe that all these memories have been arbitrarily connected with the Hellespont, or that the Troad has been chosen without reference to its real nature, by a sort of geographical

caprice, to be the arena of all these legendary events?

The ordinary traveller, especially if he approaches the country from the sea, will find this riddle hard to read. On the other hand, if he comes, as I did, by way of the Black Sea and the Bosporus to the Dardanelles, and enters the Troad on that side by land, an immeasurably deeper impression is made by the beauty and singularity of the region. Constantine the Great has borne conclusive testimony that this is the case. When he formed the purpose, fraught with such world-wide issues, of transplanting the seat of the Roman Empire from Rome to the East, his thoughts turned first to Ilium. We are told that the building of the new Rome had been actually begun here, when the superiority of Byzantium in natural charms and political importance dawned upon his mind. He built Constantinople, and Ilium was left to fall in ruins. There can be no doubt that if the traveller sails through the southern part of the Hellespont, on one of the steamers which are now almost the only means of transport, especially on a day when the mountain background is hidden, the whole Troad looks uninteresting, dreary, and barren. It is not likely that any one who did no more than coast round the Trojan plain would ever think of making it the scene of action for a great poem or a wide circle of legends.

For all this, scholars dispute as to whether Homer, or, to speak in more general terms, the poet of the *Iliad*, was ever in the country itself. A marvellous dispute this must seem to any one who has not merely seen the country from the sea, but has traversed its interior! I must say I think it impossible that the *Iliad* could ever have been composed by a man who had not been in the country of the *Iliad*.

There is, it is true, a third alternative. It is conceivable that the legend of Ilium, like those of Ganymede and Paris, of Hesione and Heracles, of Laomedon and Anchises, arose and assumed form in the country itself, on a foundation laid by the impressions made by the scenery on the native inhabitants, and that these legends were then, at whatever stage of completeness, put into the hands of the poet of the *Iliad*, who was a native of some other country. Such an assumption, while it recognizes the charms of the country as a cradle of legend, considerably disparages the functions of the poet of the *Iliad*. We have, I believe, no right to make it. The *Iliad* could hardly have preserved so true a local colouring, if a stranger had adopted the native legends and wrought them into his poem, without ever having seen the land itself.

There are instances, it is true, which seem to prove the contrary. Schiller had never been in Switzerland, and yet he produced in his *Wilhelm Tell* a work of art so perfect, that even the man born on the shore of the Lake of Lucerne cannot but wonder at it. In a certain sense, and in the case of Troy itself, Virgil may be added as another example. But we must not forget how different were the conditions under which these poets worked. Both Schiller and Virgil found *written* local legends, and accurate geographical information ready to their hands. In spite of this they were not able to give to their poetry such a specific local colouring, or to find such clearly recognizable localities for all their scenes, as the author of the *Iliad* does. How different is the glowing recollection of ever-fresh passages in the *Iliad*, which arises as we traverse the Troad, to the reminiscences of *Wilhelm Tell* suggested by a sail on the Lake of Lucerne or a clamber about its shore! The power of intuition shown by the poet of *Wilhelm Tell* is marvellous indeed, but it is confined to three or four spots whose situation could be easily grasped with

the help of good maps; while in the *Iliad* we are struck, on the one hand, by the truth of the general impression of what is an extensive district, and on the other by the number of distinct views which present to us ever fresh spots in the landscape. I do not refer merely to Homer's oft-noticed characteristic description of all objects by means of short and apt distinctive epithets, as "Ida rich in springs," "the eddying Scamander," "the windy Ilium," but far more to his almost surprising knowledge of the meteorology of the district, of the flora and fauna, and the social peculiarities of its population. Three thousand years have not sufficed to produce any noteworthy alteration in these things. The clouds are still drawn in the same courses as are described in the *Iliad*, and the storms gather on the same mountain-tops as in Homer's time. The number of wild beasts has grown gradually less, and the camel and the turkey have been added to the tame stock, but the native species are unchanged. The flowers, shrubs, and trees, mentioned in the poem, still grow on the river-banks and the mountain uplands. This is the case, above all, with the people. Immigration has followed immigration: Aeolians and Romans, Turks and Armenians, have come into the country, but the population remains what it has always been. There is but little cultivation, and there are herds in abundance; and this influences not only the social arrangements of the people, but even the nature of the earth's surface. If the Turks were not such an unchangeable race, another mode of life would have been sure to arise in the course of time. It is possible, however, to burn petroleum, and to remain in all else a Homeric Trojan; to build a church or a mosque, and still to hold a proper carriage or a passable high-road in abhorrence.

I do not mean, however, to assert that the poet of the *Iliad* was a native

Trojan, or that he tested every word in his poem by a reference to the realities of nature and human institutions. On the contrary, I acknowledge that there are several passages in the *Iliad* which do not suit the circumstances at all. The two springs of the Scamander, the cold and the warm, placed by the *Iliad* in the plain, are sought there in vain; they are high up on Mount Ida, two days' journey from the plain. But the *Iliad* has not many passages of this kind, and several of these admit of more than one interpretation, while others are very possibly later additions made by some subsequent hand. Trifles such as these are not enough to cloud our conviction of the truth of the general representation. The truth of this warrants us in assuming that the poet did visit the country, though perhaps he may not have stayed there long, and it does not exclude the possibility that a body of legend, though disjointed and incongruous, already existed before his time.

For a bird's-eye view of this mighty arena an eminence must be sought in the interior. This is furnished by the hill of Hissarlik, the scene of Dr. Schliemann's excavations. There are other points admirably adapted for this purpose on the rising ground on the west, along the coast of the Aegean Sea, on the promontory of Sigeum and the ridge of Ujek. A most commanding view may be obtained from the conical sepulchral mound (also recently excavated by Dr. Schliemann) which rises to about 80 feet from a high ridge to the south of Sigeum, about two miles from Besika Bay. This is the Ujek Tepeh, which is seen far out at sea, and is used as a signal by sailors. From its summit we gain a comprehensive view of the whole arena of the *Iliad*.

Immediately at our feet lies the Trojan plain proper, stretching away from the shores of the Hellespont on the north to Bali Dagh on the south.

This plain is an old fiord, which has been filled by river-deposit—especially that of the Scamander—which has produced a rich marshy soil, broken by frequent swamps and occasional deposits of sand. The plain lies so as to correspond in the main to the course of the Scamander, which, rising well to the east, gets nearer and nearer to the western edge of the plain, and flows into the Hellespont close by the Sigean promontory. On both sides of its course, and more particularly on its right, it is joined by a network of branch channels, which in dry seasons are nearly or quite empty, but which, when the river is high, receive the surplus waters of the Scamander and swell to all appearance into independent streams. The lower we get in the plain, the broader and deeper do these become, and near the coast they never run dry, though the inroads of the water of the Hellespont make them more or less brackish.

This complicated network of watercourses, we may say at once, is of considerable significance for the interpretation of the *Iliad*. Beyond a doubt this river is the Scamander of the poem. In spite of all the attempts which have been made to transfer this name to a little rivulet which runs its short course in the western part of the plain by the side of the Scamander—the Bounarbashi Su—an unprejudiced comparison of the Homeric references with the actual phenomena forbids us to look for the "divine" Scamander in a corner of the Trojan plain, and to force the real river of the plain, to which it owes its existence, into a position of fictitious inferiority. It is true that in many points the great river does not correspond to the Scamander of the poem. The Scamander flowed into the Hellespont to the eastward and not to the westward of the plain. It is described as lying between Ilium and the naval camp of the Achaeans; and the battle-field, again, is represented as between the camp and the river's *left* bank. The Bounarbashi brook suits these conditions still less, and this is reason enough for leaving it out of the discussion for the future. Assuming the great river to be the Scamander, we must choose between two explanations of the facts. Either Homer is all wrong about the course of the Scamander—and this would be a strong argument to prove that he had never been in the Troad—or the river has in the course of centuries altered its bed, and its lower course is no longer the same as that of the old Scamander.

I have not space on the present occasion to expound in detail the reasons which to my mind make it in the highest degree probable, if they do not absolutely prove, that the Scamander does flow in a new bed, and that the channels called Asmaks, which are now only used occasionally and are partially filled with salt water, mark different old beds of the Scamander, which it has long since abandoned. In this respect the Trojan plain resembles the deltas of other rivers. Just as the Rhine and the Vistula have changed their estuaries in historical times, and have left extinct watercourses or networks of streams where they used to run, so has it been with the Scamander. Even Pliny, the distinguished Roman author who collected together all the natural science of his time, speaks of a Palaescamander. As early then as the beginning of the Christian era there was an " old Scamander," just as for five centuries past there has been an " old Rhine."

It is probable that this opinion would have found a more ready acceptance if the Trojan plain, like other deltas, had had a free expansion seawards. It has however a peculiarity shared by many estuaries in Asia Minor, Greece, and Turkey, namely, that the formation of the delta has taken place in a fiord, and that it is consequently enclosed by ridges of hills which formed the banks of the old fiord. It would perhaps be more intelligible if we called it a valley rather than a plain, were it not that the level surface is too broad in proportion to the height of the surrounding hills to give the effect of a valley. There is no doubt, however, that if the Trojan " plain " lay on the north coast of Germany, it would be called a valley there. This valley is open towards the Hellespont, and closed in towards the west and south. On its right side, towards the east, there are some side-valleys introduced between the neighbouring upland ridges—two in particular, which are longer than the rest—which in their turn send out a number of small valleys and coves into the mountains. Of these easterly side-valleys the largest runs parallel to the Hellespont, and is separated from it by a mountain ridge which rises higher and higher towards the east. In the midst of this valley flows a narrow mountain stream of but moderate proportions, sufficient however to satisfy the requirements of the Simois of the *Iliad*. Unless then the reader prefers to follow Hercher, in regarding all passages of the *Iliad* which mention the Simois as subsequent spurious interpolations, he may be content, with Demetrius of Scepsis and Strabo, to see the Simois in the brook just described, which in Turkish times has borne the name of Doumbrek Tchai.

This name has misled many in modern times from the resemblance it bears to the Homeric name Thymbra. At the point where the Thymbrius fell into the Scamander the testimony of later writers placed the temple of Apollo, near which Achilles received his mortal wound from Paris, while seeking a lover's meeting with Priam's daughter Polyxena. The position of the Doumbrek Tchai does not suit this story. Numerous local features unite in pointing rather to the most southerly of the above-mentioned side valleys, through which flows the Kemar Su; and hence most modern authorities take this to be the Thymbrius.

This, then, is the extent of the so-called Trojan plain. Except for the two or three miles of coast along the Hellespont, it is surrounded by lines of hills, which are tolerably steep, though their height only ranges from 100 to 500 feet. From the Ujek Tepeh we look over to the greater part of this encircling line. The western boundary of the plain, — the long and somewhat straggling ridge of Sigeum, which stretches along the coast of the Aegean Sea to the Hellespont,—appears to be a continuation of the range from which the Ujek Tepeh itself arises. On the south there advances a stretch of broken upland which rises gradually to above 900 feet in the "black mountain," Kara Dagh. On the east several slightly diverging ridges extend into the plain, enclosing the side-valleys mentioned above.

The most northerly of these eastern ridges keeps close to the coast of the Hellespont, and, ending abruptly towards the plain, forms the promontory of Rhoeteum, facing that of Sigeum on the west. Its extremity in the direction of the plain, and close to the sea-shore, is a half-isolated cone, the so-called grave of Ajax, In Tepeh; while on the other side two other conical tumuli, those of Achilles and Patroclus, stand out from Cape Sigeum. Behind Cape Rhoeteum runs the Doumbrek valley, and to the south of it a second ridge, almost parallel with the coast of the Hellespont, at the west end of which, and separated from it by a slight depression, stands the celebrated Hissarlik, a spacious hill of more than 100 feet in height. From the Ujek Tepeh we look between Hissarlik and the In Tepeh into the Doumbrek valley,

which lies open to our view, even to its very end. At the head of the valley the various ridges—the coast ridge, the Hissarlik ridge, and that to the south—after gradually rising, unite in a kind of knot, called Oulou Dagh. The wooded summit of the Oulou Dagh is the commanding point in this part of the landscape, and hence it agrees much better with what Homer says about the position of the renowned beacon-point Callicolone than does the far lower and much more retired Kara Your, an eminence on the eastern half of the ridge of Hissarlik itself.

The part of the landscape just described wears, not only from the Ujek Tepeh, but from the whole line of Sigeum, the aspect which, according to Homer, the battle-field wore just before the decisive battle. As the mortals advanced to meet on the plain, the Immortals ranged themselves into two groups, according to the side they favoured. The gods on the Trojan side surveyed the fight from Callicolone, those on the Achaean sat on the rampart of Heracles on Sigeum.

All the hills which rise immediately out of the plain consist of limestone of the middle tertiary period, very rich in mussel-shells. This stone must have been formed in a brackish or fresh-water lake, at a time when the Hellespont did not exist. There is only one place, and that is in the Doumbrek valley, where volcanic rock crops out. When, however, we take a wider space within our view, the case is different.

We here encounter a long range of higher mountains, mostly rounded cones, stretching away in a wide sweep from the Oulou Dagh to the Kara Dagh, that is from the Hellespont to the Aegean, and forming a frame for the Trojan plain, or, more correctly speaking, for the whole of the anterior Troad. This range consists throughout of volcanic rock, or at least volcanic rock forms its basis. Trachyte, basalt, serpentine, &c., succeed each other in picturesque variety. Beyond this frame there is no fighting in the *Iliad* between men, with the exception of single expeditions, which are mentioned as having already taken place before the poem opens. All mention of more distant places is either made incidentally, without immediate reference to the Trojan war, or concerns the gods. For it must be understood, once for all, that *the mythological arena of the Iliad is incomparably wider than the strategical.*

At the chain of volcanic rock which stretches from Oulou Dagh to Kara Dagh, we are still far short of Ida proper. Neither in the *Iliad* nor at the present day is this name applied to hills of such a moderate height. The later ancient writers were the first to see Ida itself in these outlying ranges. Nowhere is the contrast between these outlying hills and Ida more clearly visible than in the view from Ujek Tepeh. From this point we see to the south-east a huge cleft in the chain of these hills, to the left of Kara Dagh and to the right of Foulah Dagh. This is the point at which the Scamander breaks in wide curves through the outlying hills and enters the plain. Over this cleft, far away in the distance, Ida (Kaz Dagh) rises over the nearer range in a mighty mass. Between Ida and the northern range of lower hills lies a broad and fruitful valley, the plain of Iné and Beiramich, through the whole length of which, from east to west, flows the Scamander; and there is the less reason for making Mount Ida extend to these lower hills, in spite of the broad intervening plain, because there rises on the west of the plain of Iné an extensive volcanic ridge, the Chigri Dagh, completely isolated from the mass of the Ida range, and much more closely connected with the hills near the Trojan plain. This ridge can be seen from Ujek Tepeh

rising above the Kara Dagh, and commanding, with its spurs, the whole of the coast district to the south.

The view from Ujek Tepeh, however, has been by no means exhaustively described: it extends far beyond the Troad. The whole picture which lies before the eyes of the admiring spectator is embraced by the old poet. To the north of the plain, to begin with, we see a long streak of blue, the Hellespont. The Hellespont is no less an object of wonder to us than it was to the ancients. They saw in it the road which led to the unknown lands of the dark North. It took the traveller to Cimmerians and Hyperboreans, all wrapped in a mist of legend. To our eyes the Hellespont is the common outlet for the waters of an immense range of rivers. The Danube and Pruth, the Dniester and Dnieper, the Don and the Kouban, all roll their waters through the Hellespont into the Mediterranean. Accurately speaking, it is no mere water-way between two seas, but a huge stream which carries off the rainfall of a mighty tract of land. Germany and Austria, Bulgaria and Roumania, Russia and Caucasia, pay their tributes to this stream; and the contemplation of the beholder finds pleasure in following back the course of these tributaries, while he pictures to himself the wanderings of the peoples who have ranged in historic and pre-historic times within the limits of the regions which they drain.

Who could fail to feel the thrilling interest of such a view? From the oldest times the Hellespont has been not merely the boundary, but, in a much higher degree, the connection between Asia and Europe. Here the armies of the two continents met in conflict. What the Persians failed to do, the Turks have done. The enterprise in which Alexander succeeded was attempted over again by the Crusaders. The shores of the Dardanelles provide the easiest passage from Europe to Asia, or from Asia to Europe. History has taught us that the Asiatic stream has, on the whole, been the stronger one. It is probable even that our own ancestors, the Aryan immigrants, came by this passage on their victorious career into Europe, long before the *Iliad* was composed, and still longer before the history of mankind began to be written.

Such thoughts as these were constantly present to my mind as I turned my eyes to the little bit of Europe which was visible from our wooden hut on Hissarlik. A very little bit it was, and I cannot say that I wished it larger. All we saw of it was the southern point of the Thracian Chersonese, a low rising ground beyond the Hellespont, at the south end of which the ancients placed the grave of Protesilaus. In the evening, when I had put out my lamp and looked out once more, the only visible sign which remained to connect me with Europe was the beacon-light at the end of this promontory, which shone straight into my little window. But what a crowd of memories did its beam awaken!

As I looked out in the morning from the same window, I saw stretching far away the deep-blue sea with its islands. In the distance, separated from the Chersonese by a wide stretch of sea, lay rocky Imbros, with its long jagged ridge; and just behind it rose the towering peak of Samothrace. How majestic this island looks from Ujek Tepeh! What Ida is in the far south-east, Samothrace is in the far north-west: the former the seat of Zeus, the mightiest of all the gods; the latter that of the next mightiest, Poseidon.

The Northerner, especially if he lives where the sky is often clouded, finds it hard to understand how the religious ideas of Southern nations attached themselves so prevailingly to the phenomena of the atmosphere, or, to speak more mythologically, of "Heaven." It is necessary to see the wide horizon and the pure blue of the Trojan sky, in order to appreciate the effect produced here by the formation of clouds. When, on a sudden, while sea and land are lying apparently at rest, a dark mass of cloud gathers round the peak of Samothrace, and, sinking deeper every moment, enshrouds one sharp line of rock after another, till the storm at last descends, and, after lashing the sea with its gusts, wraps even it in darkness, we find it easier to see how it was that a childlike spirit looked for the presence of the sea-god himself in the secret recesses of the clouds. And if far away in the south-western sky, in the direction of Greece, a single cloud appears over the Aegean, and gradually rises and spreads, draws nearer and nearer, and at last touches the summit of Ida, there to thicken and cling for hours and even days together, and if then lightning breaks from this cloud-mass whole nights through, while all the face of Nature seems to lie beneath it in fright, who can help thinking of the poet's descriptions of the journey and sojourn of the Thunderer?

From the height of Ujek Tepeh may be seen several other islands of the Aegean, rising high, with clear rock outlines. Close at hand, just opposite to Besika Bay, lies the vine-clad Tenedos, behind which the Achaean fleet hid by way of preparing for their attack on Ilium. Far to the south, though only when the air is very clear, we may see the angular lines of Lesbos, or, as it is called in modern times, Mitylene. Sometimes a cloud rises far out at sea, which makes for Lesbos and Cape Baba, the Lectum of the ancients, and which passes from mountain to mountain till it reaches Ida. It takes exactly the path which Hera took when she sought out her angry spouse on Gargarus, and accomplished the loving reconciliation portrayed in one of the most charming passages in the *Iliad*.

Who would not feel the captivating charm of such scenes as these? and who can fail to see that the great poet has created out of them the magnificent picture he gives us of the ways and workings of the Olympian gods? I will not here describe these natural phenomena in detail. I will even forbear to portray the grand spectacle presented by the lifting and sinking of the clouds at the foot of Mount Ida. But I cannot conceal my amazement that it should have been thought possible to darken the wondrous beauty of the Trojan scenery by the light of the student's lamp, and to call in question the background of reality which gave shape to the visions of the immortal poet.

This attempt would probably never have been made if the site of ancient Ilium had been known. But even in the days of Demetrius of Scepsis, a native of the Troad, who lived about two hundred years before the beginning of the Christian era, not a trace was to be seen of the old city anywhere in the plain. This country was left isolated at an early time by the ruin of many kingdoms; and thousands of years elapsed before the search actually began for the real site of the city. Since the commencement of that search, scarcely a part of the country has been safe from the conjectures of the learned. Beginning with the Gulf of Adramyttium and Cape Lectum, they have sought the city, now here, now there. The points which occupied for the longest time the attention of scholars were Alexandria-Troas, the site of the extensive ruins of a metropolis founded on the Aegean by Antigonus, and so post-Homeric, and Bounarbashi, a wretched Turkish hamlet at the southern extremity of the Trojan plain. It was only fifty years ago that Maclaren first ventured to fix on

the hill and fortress of Hissarlik as the spot where Troy once stood. Others, among whom was Von Eckenbrecher, adopted his view. The first actual excavations were conducted by Mr. Frank Calvert. These excavations, however, were confined to the surface. It has been reserved for Dr. Schliemann, by the application of resources such as can hardly ever have been devoted by a private individual to such an object before, to lay bare, by digging down to an amazing depth, the ruins of settlements of immense antiquity, and thereby to make Hissarlik an object of the highest interest to all educated men.

Does this settle the question about the site of the ancient Ilium? Opponents say, No. And why? While they condemn Schliemann for taking the *Iliad* literally, they think it a sufficient refutation of his views if they prove that the ruins of Hissarlik do not correspond to Homer's descriptions. Correspond they certainly do not. Homer's idea of his sacred Ilios is very different from any conception we can form from the testimony of the ruins.

No one doubts that Ilium was destroyed centuries before the *Iliad* was composed. How many centuries, is a question which divides even those who take Homer's side. Even if the interval were not more than two or three hundred years, still Ilium itself could never have been seen by the poet. *The Ilium of fiction must, under any circumstances, be a fiction itself.* It is possible that legend may have preserved many topographical particulars about the ancient city, but it is not to be imagined there should have been preserved a detailed and authentic description of the city or the fortress as it existed before its destruction. "Grass" had no doubt "grown" meanwhile over the ruins. New settlers had built on the old spot dwellings which had perhaps lain long in ruins themselves when the poet began his work. It is very questionable whether he ever saw with his eyes even the ruins of the fallen city. The place where it stood he saw no doubt, *but the city itself he saw only in a vision.* Just as Zeus and Hera, Poseidon and Athené, Ares and Aphrodité, were creatures of his fancy, so the city of Ilium was itself "a dream." No one can expect the actual ruins to correspond to every imagination of the poet; and when it is established that Homer had in his mind much that never existed, at all events on this spot, it simply comes to this, that the *Iliad* is not an historical work, but a poetical one.

And yet the correspondence of the poetical representation with the local conditions is far from being so imperfect as it is represented. The situation of Hissarlik satisfies in the main all the demands of the Homeric topography. From this spot, as from Ujek Tepeh, we get a view over the whole of the anterior Troad. The plain with its rivers and brooks, the side-valleys, the encompassing hills, the circlet of volcanic mountains, the Hellespont and the Aegean, lie spread out before our eyes as we stand on the height of Hissarlik. The only difference is that we are ever so much nearer to the plain, and especially to that part of it which is best suited for a battle-field, and which, if we overlook the present altered courses of the rivers, completely answers to the topography of the Homeric field of battle. The separate objects on this plain are clearly distinguishable, and it is not quite impossible that Helen should have been able to point out the individual chieftains of the Achaeans to her royal father-in-law. The distance, too, is quite visible enough for the purposes of the Homeric landscapes. We see the Thracian Chersonese, and we have Imbros and Samothrace before us. Further to the left lies Tenedos, and right behind in the south-east

the snowy top of Ida rises above the nearer range of hills. At sunset even the pyramid of Athos may sometimes be seen for a few minutes in the far west.

It is true that the old city did not stand as high as the top of the hill of Hissarlik did before the excavations were begun. Dr. Schliemann had to go deep down—from 25 to 30 feet or more—before he came on the walls and houses of Ilium under the *débris* of later settlements. But even if we sink the level of Ilium to such a depth, it is still high enough to preserve to the city its commanding position. Its houses and towers, even though they were of a very moderate height, must have risen far enough above the surface to reach the level of the later hill. This would still make it a lofty, " windy " fastness. Our wooden huts, which had been put up at the foot of the hill, well below the level of the old city, looked straight down upon the plain from a height of at least 60 feet, and the winds blew about us with such force that we often felt as if our whole settlement might be hurled down the precipice.

The fortress-hill of Hissarlik, as it appeared to travellers before Dr. Schliemann started his huge excavations, was then, properly speaking, an artificial hill, most nearly comparable perhaps with the earth hills of the Assyrian plain which covered the ruins of the royal castles; only it had not been set up on the plain itself, but on the west end of the second ridge of tertiary rock above described. Consequently it lay right over the plain, and must have looked high from the first. Its subsequent increase in height must have been very gradual indeed. In digging down from the surface fresh ruins are constantly encountered, belonging to various epochs. One people has lived here after another, and each fresh one which settled on the ruins of its predecessor levelled the surface anew by clearing away some of the ruins and throwing them over the precipice. In this way the surface of the hill grew gradually in extent, and it is conceivable that, now that last year's excavations have almost completely laid bare the boundaries of the old city, the vast pit should present the aspect of a funnel, at the bottom of which the ruins of Ilium lie within a pretty small compass. We must admit the justness of the objection that this Ilium was no great city, capable of finding room for a great army of foreign warriors in addition to a large population of its own. Such an Ilium as that existed only in the poet's vision. Our Ilium hardly deserves to be called a city at all. In our part of the world we should call such a place a fortress or a stronghold. For this reason I prefer to call the place a *fortress-hill* (*Burgberg*); a term which, strictly speaking, is merely a translation of the Turkish word Hissarlik.

But why take these very ruins at the bottom of the funnel to be Ilium? To this I answer that it is a question again whether there ever was a place called Ilium. Is it not questionable whether there ever was any Heracles or any Argonauts? Perhaps Ilium, Priam, and Andromaché, are just as much poetical fictions as Zeus, Poseidon, and Aphrodité. But this does not amount to saying that we ought not to look for the Ilium of the poet at the bottom of our funnel. There lies a close array of houses surrounded by a mighty wall of rough-hewn stone. The walls of houses and rooms have been preserved to such an extent, that it is possible to give a ground-plan of the place. A pretty steep street, paved with large flags, leads through a single gate on the western side into the fortress. Only a narrow passage is left between the houses. The whole place is full of the rubbish left by a conflagration. Great clay

bricks, half a yard square, have been melted by a fierce heat and turned to a glassy paste. Heaps of corn, especially wheat, pease, and beans, have been turned to charcoal. The remains of animal food, oyster-shells and mussels of all kinds, bones of sheep and goats, of oxen and swine, have likewise been partially burnt away. Of wood-charcoal proper there is but little to be seen, and what there is is mostly oak. The conflagration must have lasted long enough to destroy entirely almost all the woodwork. Even the metal, and especially the bronze, is for the most part molten and reduced by fire to an undistinguishable mass.

It is evident that this fortress was destroyed by a conflagration of great extent, which lasted long enough to destroy utterly all inflammable materials. Such a fire as corresponds to Homer's description has only taken place once in the settlements on Hissarlik. In the numerous strata of ruins which lie one above the other there are several other traces of fire, but none on the scale on which they occur in the "burnt city." Even below it there are still strata, going down at some points to a depth of 20 or 25 feet or more, — for the "burnt city" was not the oldest settlement on Hissarlik,—but even in these oldest strata there is nowhere the trace of such an extensive conflagration.

It is the "burnt city," however, where, among numerous objects of art-work — of pottery especially — some of which are of rare excellence, gold has repeatedly been brought to light, sometimes in connection with objects of silver, bronze, and ivory. All these discoveries have been eclipsed in splendour by the "Treasure of Priam," upon which Dr. Schliemann lighted in the third year of his successful excavations. And not a year has passed since, without the discovery of at least some articles of gold. I was myself an eye-witness of two such discoveries, and helped to gather the articles together. The slanderers have long since been silenced, who were not ashamed to charge the discoverer with an imposture. Especially since the Turkish government, on the occasion of the furtive appropriation of a portion of the discoveries by two of the workmen, has laid an embargo on all objects of the kind,—as is the case with such collections elsewhere, — such envious spite has retreated to the privacy of the family hearth. Since that time, objects of gold of the same type as those from Hissarlik have been found not only in Mycenae, but also in other Greek graves. One of the gold treasures which were excavated in my presence contained stamped plates of gold, the ornamentation of which is in the minutest details the counterpart of that found at Mycenae.

The " burnt city " was then also the " city of gold." It is only in it that we find this wealth of marvellous and at the same time distinctly foreign treasures. For it is clear that we have here no product of native industry, but articles brought from abroad either by trade or plunder. Their character is Oriental, and more particularly Assyrian. Consequently the burnt fortress must have been the seat of a great and prosperous hero— or of the son of such a man—who had amassed treasures of the rarest value in his small but secure home.

The chief treasure was found all together at one spot, in a kind of cupboard. It appeared to have been originally stowed away in a wooden chest. It was near the wall of a very strongly built stone house, in other parts of which were found numerous other treasures, in vases of terracotta, in a good state of preservation, and which was evidently the residence of the prince. For in no other place were any such treasures discovered ; and, as the area of the burnt

city has now been completely brought to light, we may assert definitely that *on this spot was the palace. The old city wall runs close by it, and the street which comes up through the single gate of the fortress leads up to it.*

Was this gate the Scaean gate, and this house the house of Priam ? Dr. Schliemann, overawed by his learned adversaries, now talks only of the house of the " chief of the city " (*Stadthaupt*). But can the " chief of the city," who was master of so much gold at a time when gold was so scarce, have been anything but a prince ? And why not call him Priam ? Whether Priam ever existed or not, the prince of the golden treasure who lived on this spot comes near enough to the Priam of the *Iliad* to make us refuse to forego the delight of giving the place his name. And what harm can there be in assigning to the western gateway, *the only one which exists in the city wall at all*, to which a steep road led up from the plain, the famous name of the Scaean gate ?

Do not let us cut ourselves off from all poetry without the slightest need. Children that we are of a hard and too prosaic age, we would maintain our right to conjure up again before our old age the pictures which filled our youthful fancy. It saddens but it also elevates the soul when we stand on a place like Hissarlik, and read the course of history from the series of successive strata as from a geological disclosure. This history is not written for us, but set bodily before our eyes in the relics of bygone times, in the actual objects used by men who lived in them. Huge masses of ruins are piled in layers above the burnt stronghold, between it and the first layer containing hewn stones and a wall of square blocks. This was perhaps the wall which Lysimachus, one of Alexander's generals, is recorded to have built on Ilium. Anyhow this wall resembles the walls of the Macedonian period, and the corresponding layer conceals Greek walls and pottery. Here then we have a definite limit of time. From this point we have got to reckon the time backwards, and it is easy to see that this reckoning is not unfavourable to our interpretation of the Trojan legend.

Perhaps then Homer's song is not pure fiction, after all. Perhaps it is true that in a very remote pre-historic time a rich prince really dwelt here in a towering fortress, and that Greek kings waged a fierce war against him, and that the war ended in his own fall and the destruction of his city by a mighty conflagration. Perhaps this was the first time that Europe and Asia tried each other's strength on this coast, the first time that the young but more and more independent civilization of the West put to the rough test of force its superiority over the already effeminate civilization of the East. To me this seems a probability, but it is one which I will not press any one else to accept.

Of this we may be sure, that even the oldest and earliest settlement on Hissarlik was made by a people which had already felt the influence of civilization. True, it still used stone weapons, but these weapons were finely polished and bore witness by the delicacy of their outline to a knowledge of metals. In fact, traces of metals are not wanting even in the oldest strata. It is impossible therefore to assign these strata to the Stone age. They are indications of what we may undoubtedly assert to be *the oldest known settlement in Asia Minor of a people of pre-historic times, of some advance in civilization.* Hence the hill-fortress of Hissarlik is certain to hold an enduring place as a trustworthy witness in the history of civilization. It will be to our descendants an important geographical position, and a fixed starting-point for the flights of their fancy. For it is to be hoped that, however the strife may end about the existence of Ilium or of Priam, the young will never lose the *Iliad.*

APPENDIX II.

ON THE RELATION OF NOVUM ILIUM TO THE ILIOS OF HOMER.

By Professor J. P. Mahaffy.

The full and explicit argument of Strabo, in the 13th book of his Geography, has persuaded the philological world pretty generally, from his day to our own, that the Greek Ilium of his time was not the town about which the heroes of the *Iliad* were supposed to have fought their immortal conflicts. I now propose, according to the flattering invitation of Dr. Schliemann, to enquire critically into this argument, and see what foundation it has in real history.

Let me first observe that Strabo is not our original authority for this theory, but that he professedly borrows his arguments from a certain Demetrius of Skepsis (in the Troad), who had written largely on the subject, and who had, in fact, started what I may call the illegitimacy of the Ilium of his day. This Demetrius is described as follows by Strabo (xiii. § 55): Ἐκ δὲ τῆς Σκήψεως καὶ ὁ Δημήτριώς ἐστιν, οὗ μεμνήμεθα πολλάκις, ὁ τὸν Τρωϊκὸν διάκοσμον ἐξηγησάμενος γραμματικός, κατὰ τὸν αὐτὸν χρόνον γεγονὼς Κράτητι καὶ Ἀριστάρχῳ. He was then a grammarian, probably of the Pergamene school of Crates, but versed in Alexandrian criticism, for he cited in support of his theory (Strabo, *loc. cit.* § 36) a learned lady of that school—Hestiaea—who had evidently raised doubts on the same point before him, and among her ἀπορήματα had asked whether the plain below the existing Ilium could be the scene of Homer's battles, sec-

ing that most of it was a late deposit made by the Skamander and Simois. We may be sure from this authority being so carefully cited, as well as that of the orator Lycurgus, who asserts in a rhetorical passage the total destruction and complete disappearance of Ilium, that Demetrius had no older or clearer evidence for his theory in Greek literature. What, then, were his arguments?

(1.) The total destruction of Ilios is stated or implied by Homer himself.

(2.) The sacred image of Athené is apparently in the *Iliad* a sitting figure, whereas that at the existing Ilion was standing.

(3.) Various geographical allusions in the *Iliad*, about the hot and cold springs of the Skamander (§ 43); about the considerable distance of the ships from the town (§ 36); about the look-out of Polites, who ought to have used the acropolis of the town with far more effect, if it were so near (§ 37); about the dragging of Hector round the walls, which could not be done on the rough ground about the present town (§ 37), because the Καλλικολώνη, on which Ares sits, is not near the present town (§ 35); lastly (in order of importance), because the ἐρινεός and φηγός mentioned in the *Iliad*, and which he translated wild fig wood and beech wood (?), were not close to Ilium, but some distance further inland.

From all these hints Demetrius concluded that Homer's Ilios was not on the site of the then existing city, but some 30 stadia higher inland, on the site of what he calls the Ἰλιέων κώμη. Here, he thinks, all the difficulties of allusion can be explained.

In answer to the obvious questions, what had become of the old city? and how did the new one come by the old name? he stated:

(1.) That all the stones of the old city had been carried away to build or restore the neighbouring towns, when they had been sacked (ἐκπεπορθημένων, οὐ τελέως δὲ κατεσπασμένων), whereas this town had been ἐκ βάθρων ἀνατετραμμένη (§ 38).

(2.) On the second point nothing certain could be ascertained. Demetrius considered it was founded by the Aeolic Greeks, "in the time of the Lydian monarchy" (ἐπὶ δὲ τῶν Λυδῶν ἡ νῦν ἐκτίσθη κατοικία καὶ τὸ ἱερόν· οὐ μὴν πόλις γε ἦν, ἀλλὰ πολλοῖς χρόνοις ὕστερον, καὶ κατ᾽ ὀλίγον, ὡς εἴρηται, τὴν αὔξησιν ἔσχε, § 42).

According to others, the town had been changed from one site to another, and finally settled there κατὰ χρησμὸν μάλιστα, from which Kramer conjectures, reasonably enough, κατὰ Κροῖσον μάλιστα.

These arguments so fully persuaded Strabo and others, that the claim of the historical Ilium to prehistoric antiquity was rejected, especially by the pedantic commentators on Homer. Thus from that day to this the Greek Ilium has been set down as a new foundation, perhaps on the old site, but more probably not so; and it has been called Novum Ilium, a name unknown to the Greeks and Romans.

I now come to criticize Strabo's arguments.

(1.) As regards the evidence in the Iliad that the city was entirely destroyed, no passage can be shown which affirms it. The arguments of Demetrius are mere foolish quibbles. He quotes:

ἔσσεται ἦμαρ, ὅταν ποτ᾽ ὀλώλῃ Ἴλιος ἱρή,

and

ἦ γὰρ καὶ Πριάμοιο πόλιν διεπέρσαμεν αἰπήν,

and

πέρθετο δὲ Πριάμοιο πόλις δεκάτῳ ἐνιαυτῷ.

But that these latter need not mean τὸν ἀφανισμόν τῆς πόλεως appears from the frequent use of πορθέω, πέρθω, and its compounds as regards Lyrnessus, Pedasus, Thebé, and other towns of the Troad, as quoted by Strabo (§ 7). The quibbles about Heracles' capture of the town, as compared with that of the Homeric chiefs (§ 32), are too foolish to require comment. The first line above quoted is a mere prophecy of Priam's, pathetic as such, but of no other value. The belief in the total ruin of Homer's Ilios really arose (1) from the Cyclic poems, and from (2) the many tragedies which were based on them.

I do not delay over these points because any serious person requires them to be refuted, but simply to show *the kind of argument* which satisfied Demetrius. I do not think anything more need be said about (2) the sitting image. It would at most prove that the old image had really been carried off from Ilios, as many legends stated.

(3.) The various minute geographical criticisms are more interesting, not from their weight, but because they lead us to discover the whole source of the dispute. But it is quite unnecessary to take them in detail, till we have considered the two broad assumptions involved in them: (a) that the poet (or poets) of the *Iliad* was accurate in all these details, and had a definite picture of the ground before his eye: (β) That the modern names of the places, which were indicated to Demetrius or to travellers in the time of Strabo, were faithfully handed down from other days.

I do not believe that either of these assumptions is at all probable. From what we know of the geography of the *Odyssey*, and still more of the tragic poets, it seems almost a law of Greek poetic art to be negligent of geographical detail, while it is curiously faithful and accurate in the more essential features of poetry. We have, I think, no evidence whatever that any place in the world was bound to correspond accurately in its features to the descriptions of the *Iliad*. I will not even touch on the possible difficulties in such a matter caused by a variety of authors on the *Iliad*.

But supposing even that the allusions in the *Iliad* were consistent, and applicable to a real scene, what authority had the places designated to Demetrius, or to Strabo, to represent them? On this we have happily very clear evidence. The historical Ilion had long been an obscure and half-forgotten place, when Alexander the Great, having sacrificed there, as an omen, on invading Asia, determined after his success (§ 26) to reward this town, and make it again a great city. This he did, and his policy was seconded by Lysimachus. As the town lay on one of the thoroughfares into Asia, it throve and became very populous, and of course crowds of visitors passed through, and desired to see the scenes of the *Iliad*, which they had learned by heart in their youth. Hence the *ciceroni* of the place were bound to satisfy them, and of course they were equal to the occasion. The tomb of Ilos, the beech-tree, the fig-tree, in fact every minute allusion in the *Iliad*, was to be verified on the spot. The places therefore which Demetrius criticized were named by the people of 330–300 B.C., when their city suddenly rose into importance, and when these traditions acquired a pecuniary value. Of course they were ignorantly chosen. In most cases there was no evidence to go upon, and the least unlikely place must be selected. But I need not dilate to any traveller upon the habits of these *ciceroni* in all ages.

But what shall we say of the statement that the historical town was founded in the time of the Lydians?

In the first place, the date is suspiciously vague. Compare, for example, the parallel account of the founding of Abydos in the same book of Strabo (§ 22) : Ἄβυδος δὲ Μιλησίων ἐστὶ κτίσμα, ἐπιτρέψαντος Γύγου, τοῦ Λυδῶν βασιλέως· ἦν γὰρ ἐπ' ἐκείνῳ τὰ χωρία καὶ ἡ Τρωὰς ἅπασα. Or see the still more explicit account of the transfer of Skepsis from its old site Παλαίσκεψις to the historic town (§ 52). The more specific date of Kroesus is only a conjecture, and is qualified by the suspicious μάλιστα.

It is probable then that this statement rested on no definite tradition, but only on reasoning by analogy from the foundation of Abydos and other towns in the Troad by the permission of the Lydians. But why, it may be asked, did Demetrius assign so old an origin to the historical town, if he desired to destroy its claim to any epic importance? He only did so because there was clear evidence of the recognition of Ilion as the genuine city up to the days of Xerxes. Had he attempted to assert a later foundation, he could have been refuted by distinct texts.

I will now therefore trace down the history of the historical Ilium from the earliest evidence we have to the days of Demetrius, and show what were the reasons which determined the theory of the Skepsian critic.

Our earliest allusion is (I think) that in Herodotus, vii. 42, who speaks of τὴν Ἰλιάδα γῆν, and says that Xerxes ἐς τὸ Πριάμου Πέργαμον ἀνέβη, where he sacrificed Ἀθηναίῃ τῇ Ἰλιάδι. There is no suspicion that this was any other than the historical (or Novum) Ilium, and this sacrifice distinctly implies that about 500 B.C. it was already an old and venerable shrine.

Demetrius (or Strabo) admitted that the offering of Locrian virgins to this shrine was as old as the Persian wars; but in fact the origin of the custom was lost in the mists of antiquity.

We find, about the same date as Herodotus, the learned Mitylenaean antiquary, Hellanicus, asserting that the Homeric and historic Ilium were the same. This Demetrius quotes, but sets aside as a piece of favouritism in the historian (§ 42): Ἑλλάνικος δὲ χαριζόμενος τοῖς Ἰλιεῦσιν, οἷος ἐκείνου θυμός, συνηγορεῖ τὸ τὴν αὐτὴν εἶναι πόλιν τὴν νῦν τῇ τότε. But why could he not quote any such ancient and respectable authority on his own side?

I imagine the town to have been of no importance in Xerxes' day except for its shrine; for in the quarrels of the Athenians and Mitylenaeans about Sigeum, settled by the arbitration of Periander (Herod. v. 94), we hear of Sigeum and Achilleum being occupied, but not a word about Ilium. And so through all the history of the Athenian hegemony, till in the closing years of the Peloponnesian war, when Xenophon tells us of Mindarus (Hellen. i. 1. 4) κατιδὼν τὴν μάχην ἐν Ἰλίῳ θύων τῇ Ἀθηνᾷ. The battle was off Rhoeteion. The shrine then had remained there, and the habit of sacrificing at it. But the town must also have been fortified, and no mere κώμη, as Demetrius says. For we are told of Derkyllidas: (Hellen. iii. 1. 16): πέμπων δὲ καὶ πρὸς τὰς Αἰολίδας πόλεις ἠξίου τε ἐλευθεροῦσθαί τε αὐτοὺς καὶ ἐς τὰ τείχη δέχεσθαι. Οἱ μὲν οὖν Νεανδρεῖς καὶ Ἰλιεῖς καὶ Κοκυλῖται ἐπείθοντο· καὶ γὰρ οἱ φρουροῦντες Ἕλληνες ἐν αὐτοῖς, ἐπεὶ ἡ Μανία ἀπέθανεν, οὐ πάνυ τι καλῶς περιείποντο.

So also Demosthenes (in Aristocr. p. 671) speaks of Ilium as opening its gates to Charidemus. It seems accordingly difficult to believe Demetrius of Skepsis, when he says that, visiting it when a child, it was again so decayed that the roofs were not even tiled. Hegesianax, however, is quoted by Strabo as stating that the Galati in their invasion found it ἀτείχιστον, and hence deserted it after

a short occupation. But this points to some sudden decay after the time of Alexander: for he, as we have already noticed, made it an important city, and from this date down to the age of Augustus it remained so, though doubtless with some vicissitudes. Nicolaus Damascenus (Frag. 4, ed. C. Müller) tells us that, with the assistance of King Herod, he saved the Ilians from a fine of 100,000 drachmae, imposed on them by M. Agrippa, because his wife Julia (daughter of the Emperor Augustus) was nearly lost along with her retinue in the Skamander, which had suddenly risen with a flood. The Ilians protested that they had received no notice of her visit (B.C. 17). I fancy that the fine of 100,000 drachmae points to a supposed population of that number, for we know that the town was large and populous, and that Lysimachus had draughted into it the people of neighbouring towns. I need pursue its history no further.

But so much will appear more than probable. By the favour of Alexander and Lysimachus, Ilium assumed a sudden importance, and even asserted authority over the whole Troad. This must have raised up for the Ilians many enemies among the neighbouring towns, especially at Skepsis, which boasted a foundation by Skamandrius, the son of Hektor. Demetrius, whose parents might remember Ilium a decayed and neglected place, lived to see it ousting his own city, and all the others of the Troad, from their former importance, and no doubt the Ilians, like all upstarts under royal favour, were overbearing and insolent. Hence this scholar set himself to work to pull down their historic reputation, and to prove that after all they were people of recent origin, and of no real nobility, as a city. He asserts that Hellanicus favoured them (χαριζόμενος), but this very expression suggests an opposite feeling in his own mind. So he set to work to prove that the places shown by the local guides (καὶ τοὺς ὀνομαζομένους τόπους ἐνταῦθα δεικνυμένους ὁρῶμεν) would not fit the descriptions of the *Iliad*, without moving the city. But he quietly assumes the accuracy of all these special spots, *as then named*, though he rejects the far more trustworthy tradition which attached the name of Ilion to the one historic city.

I see no adequate reason to question this tradition, and believe that whatever the Trojan war may have been, and whatever may be the accuracy of the details of the *Iliad*, the conflict was localized by the poet at the place then and ever after called Ilium, and that no new foundation ever took place.

The argument of Demetrius is merely that of a malevolent pedant, who hated the Ilians, on account of their recent good fortune, and who sought to detract from their respectability on antiquarian grounds.

Having made this examination on purely critical grounds, and having drawn my conclusions from internal evidence as to the value of Demetrius' theory, I appeal to Dr. Schliemann to say whether his researches do not verify them. I believe they do, and that there is clear evidence of an unbroken occupation (except for the disasters of war) on the present site from pre-historic days down to Roman times.

I am thus unfortunate enough to conflict with our Greek evidence as to the destruction both of Mycenae and of Troy. But as I have persuaded Dr. Schliemann and most other competent judges that the accounts of the destruction of Mycenae are false, I may perhaps be able to persuade them that the re-foundation of Ilium rests on no better basis.

APPENDIX III.

THE INSCRIPTIONS FOUND AT HISSARLIK.

By Professor A. H. Sayce.

Not the least interesting and important of the results obtained from Dr. Schliemann's excavations at Hissarlik is the discovery that writing was known in the north-western corner of Asia Minor long before the introduction of the Phoenician or Greek alphabet. Inscribed objects are not indeed plentiful, but sufficient exist to show that the ancient inhabitants of the place were not wholly illiterate, but possessed a system of writing which they shared with the neighbouring nations of the mainland and the adjacent islands. Throughout Asia Minor a syllabary was once in use, which conservative Cyprus alone retained into historical times.

Numerous inscriptions in this syllabary have been found in the latter island. The characters, which amount to at least fifty-seven in number, long resisted all attempts at decipherment, but at last the problem was successfully solved by the genius of the Assyrian scholar, the late Mr. George Smith, with the help of a mutilated bilingual inscription, written in Phoenician and Cypriote. The language concealed under so strange a garb turned out to be the Greek dialect spoken in Cyprus, a dialect full of interesting peculiarities, and especially noteworthy as preserving up to the fourth century B.C. the two sounds of *v* and *y* (or digamma and yod), which had disappeared elsewhere. To the student of Homer the dialect is of considerable importance, since several of the grammatical forms found in the *Iliad* and *Odyssey* can be shown to have had a Cyprian origin.

When the key was once discovered to the Cypriote syllabary—a syllabary being a collection of characters, each of which denotes not a mere letter but a syllable—the task of deciphering it advanced rapidly. Dr. Birch, Dr. Brandis, Dr. Siegismund, Dr. Deecke, M. Pierides, and Prof. Bréal, took it up successfully; General di Cesnola's excavations in Cyprus added a great abundance of new material; and two or three bilingual inscriptions, in Greek and Cypriote, were brought to light. At present, it may be said that two characters only of the syllabary still remain undetermined.

But the origin of the syllabary was an unexplained mystery. Dr. Deecke, indeed, following up a suggestion of Dr. Brandis, made á bold attempt to derive it from the cuneiform characters introduced by the Assyrians during their occupation of Cyprus in the time of Sargon (*circa* B.C. 710). Subsequent investigation, however, has not confirmed the attempt, plausible as it appeared at first, and the evidence we now possess all points to the conclusion, that the syllabary was imported into Cyprus from the mainland of Asia Minor, where it had been previously in use. This conclusion is rendered almost a certainty by Dr. Schliemann's discoveries.

It was the keen insight of the lamented Professor Haug that first detected Cypriote characters on certain objects disinterred by Dr. Schliemann at Hissarlik. Among these a terra-cotta whorl[1] was found at the depth of 24½ ft. (see No. 1524) and inscribed with symbols, which Dr. Schliemann had pronounced to be written characters immediately after their discovery. On this Prof. Haug believed he was able to read the words *ta.i.o. si.i.go*, that is, θείω Σιγῷ, "to the divine Sigo," a deity whose name he thought he saw in Sigeum, Scamander, and Sicyon, as well as upon two terra-cotta funnels dug up by Dr. Schliemann from a depth of 3 mètres, and of which more will be said presently. Dr. Haug published his researches in 1874, in the *Augsburger allgemeine Zeitung*, p. 32.

The enquiry was now taken up by Professor Gomperz of Vienna, who gave an account of his results in the *Wiener Abendpost* of May 6th and June 26th, 1874. He accepted the values assigned by Haug to the characters on the whorl, but, by reading them from right to left instead of from left to right, he obtained the good Greek words *ta.go.i.di.o.i* (ταγῷ δίῳ), "to the divine general." This striking result was communicated to the *Academy* shortly afterwards by Professor Max Müller, and seemed to be "almost beyond reasonable doubt."

At the same time Professor Gomperz proposed tentative explanations of four other inscriptions: one on a terra-cotta seal found at a depth of 7 mètres; another on a whetstone of red slate, also from a depth of 7 mètres; a third round the neck of a vase from a depth of 8 mètres; and a fourth on a whorl from a depth of 10 mètres. The depth at which the latter object was found gives some idea of the antiquity to which a knowledge of writing in the Troad must reach back.[2]

Satisfactory as the readings of Professor Gomperz appeared at first to be, it was not long before it was perceived that they must be abandoned, and their author himself was the first to recognize this necessity. It was, indeed, startling to find good Greek on objects of Trojan manufacture; Greek, too, which was of a later age than that to which the objects themselves probably belonged. But Professor Gomperz had taken his values for the characters from the identifications of George Smith and Brandis, and subsequent investigation showed that many of these were erroneous. Thus, one of two characters read *i* by Smith and Brandis, and consequently by Gomperz after them, is really *ta*, while the other ought to be *vo*. It was clear that no progress had yet been made beyond Haug's discovery that the Trojan inscriptions were written in the characters of the Cypriote syllabary.

Discouraged by this abortive endeavour to decipher them, Professor Gomperz has dropped the whole subject, and it still remains as it was left by him at the end of 1874. The last six years, however, have brought with them important additions to our knowledge both of the Cypriote syllabary and of the modes of writing employed by the populations of Asia Minor; and I hope to show, therefore, that it is not only possible to read many of the characters in the Trojan inscriptions, but also to draw certain inferences from them of considerable historical and palaeographical importance. I have carefully examined all the objects in Dr. Schliemann's collection which bear marks in any way resembling written characters, and have thus been enabled to correct the published copies upon which Professor Gomperz worked, as well as to ascertain that some of the so-called inscriptions are really mere decorative scratchings.

---

[1] This word is used merely for the sake of uniformity, not because I believe the objects in question to have been really employed as whorls.

[2] See *Troy and its Remains*, pp. 367–371.

The first inscription to which I shall draw attention is one on a terracotta seal, which was disinterred at a depth of nearly 23 feet (No. 1519: No. 499, p. 415). Two-thirds of the handle of this are ornamented with the tree-pattern not uncommon on pre-historic Greek pottery, but

No. 1519. Seal with inscription.

No. 1520. The inscription and accompanying tree-pattern.

the rest of the handle, as well as the die, is occupied by an inscription in Cypriote letters, a revised copy of which is here engraved. The die is occupied with a single letter, and three more are incised on the handle. Each is perfectly clear, and corresponds with well-known characters in the Cypriote texts. Reading them in the direction in which they look, that is, from the handle towards the die, we have the name or word *re . ne . ta . e* or *rentae*.[3] The first character has the value of *le* in the inscriptions of Paphos and Kurium, and I fancy that was also its value in Trojan, though elsewhere it stood for *re;* the third character indifferently expressed the sounds of *ta, da,* and *tha.* What the word may mean I have no idea, but an interesting conclusion can be drawn from the form of the character *e* on the die. When compared with the corresponding Cypriote forms, it is clearly seen to be more

[3] It is just possible, however, that the second and third characters are really intended for one only. In this case they would represent an archaic form of *si,* and the word would read *resie* or *lesie,* or conversely *esire* or *esile.* If ⊢ is the single character *ta,* the word could not be read conversely, the rule being that the inscriptions are read in the direction in which the characters look.

primitive, the earliest of the forms met with in the Cypriote inscriptions having a lesser number of lines and being plainly derived from it. It is only necessary to set the two side by side to show that this is the case:

Earliest Cypriote form.   Trojan form.

No. 1521. Forms of the character for E.

This prepares us to expect to find older forms among the Trojan characters than among those found on the monuments of Cyprus.

The seal seems to be a modified imitation of a Babylonian signet-cylinder. That exact imitations of Babylonian cylinders were actually made and used at Hissarlik we know from the results of Dr. Schliemann's diggings. Besides an unadorned cylinder of stone, Dr. Schliemann discovered, at a depth of $29\frac{1}{2}$ ft., a cylinder of blue felspar, on which a native artist has cut rude representations of a flower and a cartouche (No. 1522, No. 503, p. 416). The flower is of the old Babylonian type, but the cartouche reminds us of Egypt, and may possibly contain the name of the owner, symbolized by what looks like a flower tied by a string. The tied string, it may be added, has the shape of the Cypriote character which denotes *ro.* However this may be, in these two cylinders we have manifest indications of Babylonian influence. This influence declined after the rise of Assyria in the fourteenth

No. 1522. Cylinder of Felspar.

No. 1523. Design upon the Cylinder.

century B.C., and was succeeded by the influence of Assyrian art, as modified and propagated by the Phoenicians. We may, therefore, perhaps assign these cylinders to the period between the fourteenth century B.C. and about B.C. 1800, when Sargon I., the king of Northern Babylonia, carried his arms as far as Cyprus. I must add, however, that the Phoenicians were not the only medium through whom the art and civilization of the Assyrians were brought to the West; the Hittites were also potent instruments in carrying out the same work, and there is a good deal in the style of the ornamentation of the cylinder which reminds us of Hittite sculpture. But even if we suppose that the Trojan cylinders are not imitated directly from Babylonian originals, but indirectly through Hittite influence, the fact remains that they are Babylonian rather than Assyrian in style, while I hope hereafter to show that the art which was appropriated by the Hittites, and carried by them through Asia Minor, was the art of Babylonia rather than of Assyria. The leaden figure of the goddess found by Dr. Schliemann during his recent excavations (No. 226) is the Artemis Nana of Chaldea, who became the chief deity of Carchemish, the Hittite capital, and passed through Asia Minor to the shores and islands of the Aegean. Characteristic figures of the goddess have been discovered at Mycenae as well as in Cyprus, and I am strongly of opinion that the rude Trojan figures, which Dr. Schliemann believes to represent the owl-headed Athena, are really barbarous attempts to imitate the images of the goddess who went under the various names of Atargatis, Atê, Kybelê, Ma, and Omphalê.

The next inscription I shall take is one which Professor Gomperz vainly tried to decipher (No. 1524). It is plain that the sign ⟟ is not a double character, as Haug and Gomperz imagined, but a single one. Now Perrot and Guillaume, in their great work, *Exploration de la Bithynie et Galatie* (plate 6), give a drawing of an inscription on the jamb of a rock-cut tomb at Delikli-tash, between Yeni-

No. 1524. An inscribed whorl. (Actual size. Depth, 23 ft.) Also engraved, with its section, under No. 1996.

keui and Mohimul, and near the river Rhyndacus, in Mysia, which is as follows:

Here we have a character which is evidently identical with the problematical one on the Trojan whorl, allowance being made for the fact that the stonecutter has changed curves into angles, and that a fancied similarity of the character to the Latin uncials **A N** may have caused a slight modification of it on the part of the copyist. We have only to turn it round and extend one line a little in order to bring it into exact harmony with the form of the character on the whorl. The only Cypriote character which it in any way resembles is ⟟ or *ye*, which when laid upon its side bears some likeness to it, though a resemblance may also possibly be detected between it and the Cypriote , *la*. But for many reasons it is pretty certain that the characters of the Cypriote syllabary are but selected specimens of a syllabary that originally contained many more, and we may accordingly expect to find characters in the syllabaries in use on the mainland which do not appear in that employed by the Cyprians. For the present, however, we may provisionally give this Trojan character the value of *ye*, in default of anything better.

The character which follows is also found in the inscription of Delikli-tash, but there is no difficulty about identifying it. It is the Cypriote ᴧ, ⋀, or ⋀, which has the variant values of *ko*, *go*, and *kho*. There is more difficulty about the next, ⌐. This may be the Cypriote △ or ᖳ, *ya*, but it may also be a character not used in Cyprus. I do not think there is much doubt about the next letter, ⋔ or ↷, which is also found on the whorl No. 3563,[4] under the forms ↿ and ⇑, as well as on No. 2224. It is the Cypriote ⇑ or ↖, *ti*, rather than ⌐ or ⌐, *vo*.[5] The last character in the inscription is an interesting one. It occurs in the inscription of Delikli-tash under the form of ⋀, in which form it is also found in the Cypriote inscriptions of Golgoi, where it has the value of *re*. The form met with on the whorl (⌐) is similar to that borne by it in the inscriptions of Paphos (⌐), where it has the value of *le*. On the whorl No. 3563 it is written ⌐ and ⌐, on No. 4148 as ⌐, on No. 2224 as ⌐ (a form frequently presented by the character on the Cyprian monuments), and on the whorl No. 3551 as ⌐. The terra-cotta seal given above makes it ⌐.

Where the inscription on the whorl No. 1524 commences it is impossible to say. If we start with the first

character discussed and read the character next but one as *vo*, we shall have *Ye-le-vo ye-go*, which looks curiously like 'Ιλίου for ϜιλιϜου, but unfortunately both conditions are more than doubtful.

Our next inscription is one on a whorl numbered 3559, and found at the remarkable depth of 33 ft. Here the break in the continuity of the letters seems to indicate that the inscription should begin or end with the character ⌐. This may be the Cypriote ⌐, *ka* (*ga* or *kha*), or even ᴗ, *si*, but it is more probably the Paphian ⌐, *le*, mentioned above. The character 𝟩 is plainly the Cypriote *ve*, which appears at Paphos as Z ; the next character is *ko* (*go* or *kho*), and the next the Cypriote *u*, written ⋀ and ⋀ in the inscriptions of Ktima and Paphos, as well as on the monuments of Karia. But again we find ourselves in the presence of an unknown word or name.

The following inscriptions equally indicate the place where the name or word contained in them ends. First of all, one on a whorl numbered 3558, which reads ⌐. All these characters except the last, which is manifestly the Cypriote ⋀, *ti*, are new. The one next to it has no analogue in the Cypriote inscriptions, though a similar letter occurs in the Lykian alphabet with the value of *b*. A similar letter is also found in the alphabet of Karia. The character that follows has likewise no analogue in the syllabary of Cyprus, though it is met with in the Lykian alphabet with the value of *g* (or perhaps *s*), as well as in the Karian and Pamphylian alphabets, and in a curious inscription copied by Hamilton (*Travels*, i. p. 383) at Eyuk, near the Halys. The next character may possibly be the Cypriote ⌐ or ⌐, *me*, while the

---

[4] All the Numbers above 2000, cited in this Appendix, are the numbers affixed to the objects referred to in Dr. Schliemann's Trojan collection, at present in the South Kensington Museum.

[5] Compare, however, the Lykian ⋀ or ↷, *é*.

last is perhaps the indication of a full stop.

On the whorl No. 2461 we have

the first character of which I should read *ye*, and the second possibly *sa*, while the third is a common form of the Cypriote *go* or *ko*. On the whorl No. 2236 is ⟨symbols⟩, where the last character may be the Cypriote ⟨symbol⟩, *ro*, turned upside down, and the middle one is the same as that which I have hesitatingly identified with the Cypriote *ye*, when dealing with the inscription on No. 1524. The first character may be the Cypriote *mo*, which sometimes appears under the form of , but it is more probably a character of undetermined value which is plentiful in the Karian inscriptions.

On whorl No. 3551 we seem to have two words: ⟨symbols⟩.

These we may perhaps read *sa-ye vo*(?)-*go-re* or *le*.

The inscription on whorl No. 2224, ⟨symbols⟩, *go-go-ti-re* or *le*, may be merely intended for ornament, but it may also contain a proper name. The same may be said of the inscription on No. 3563.

⟨symbols⟩,

ti-u-ti-re-re.

It is otherwise with a whorl bearing the inscription given below, and found at a depth of 20 ft. (No. 1525; No. 1222, p. 563). Here the straight line clearly denotes the end of the word, words being similarly divided from one another in the Karian inscriptions, as well as in the inscription copied by Hamilton at Eyuk. I can suggest no explanation of the first character on the left; the next is the Cypriote *mo*, the next *ye*; then comes a letter the phonetic power of which

in Cypriote has not yet been ascertained; then another unknown charac-

No. 1525. An inscribed whorl. (Natural size. Depth, 20 ft.)

ter which may be compared with the first on No. 2236, and lastly *go* or *ko*. It is possible, however, that the straight line which I have supposed to be a mark of division may really belong to the lines adjoining it; in this case we should have the Cypriote character *vo*. This possibility is suggested by a whorl, found at a depth of 13 ft., which contains the following inscription: ⟨symbols⟩.

No. 1526. Inscription on whorl, No. 1860.

Here the second character is the Cypriote *si* (⟨symbol⟩), the third is *mo*, the fourth *u*, and the last *vo*. It is a pity that the value of the first remains unknown, since we seem to have in *si-mo-u-vo* the same root as in Simoeis ($= \Sigma \iota \mu o$-$Fεντ$-$ς$).

There are four other whorls about which I am in doubt. They bear marks which *may* be intended for characters, but if so they are not recognizable, and I am disposed to think that they are mere ornaments. Of course it is always possible that the artist was unskilfully endeavouring to reproduce real characters which he did not understand. Here are the inscriptions:—

⟨symbols⟩

No. 1527. Inscription on whorl, No. 1994 (No. 3544).

⟨symbols⟩

No. 1528. Inscription on whorl No. 1962 (No. 2640).

No. 1529. Inscription on whorl, No 4148.

No. 1530. Inscription on whorl, No. 1972.

No. 1531. An inscribed fragment of pottery.
(2 : 3 actual size. Depth 33 ft.) Already
represented on p. 298, No. 173.

The same uncertainty hangs over a fragment of pottery of which a copy is here given (No. 1531; No. 173, p. 298). The last character on the left looks like one of those in the inscription of Eyuk, and the next two characters *may* be intended for *ye* and *go*.

I feel no uncertainty, however, about the marks which run round two vases and which have been taken for inscriptions. They are manifestly mere decorations, the first consisting of a series of rudely-formed *taus*, the second of crosses. Here are exact copies of them :—

No. 1532. Marks round the neck of the vase, No. 305 (p. 369).

No. 1533. Marks round the neck of the vase, Nos. 1010, 1011, 1012 (p. 527).

I am inclined to think that the signs incised on a whetstone in which Professor Gomperz saw an inscription, as he did also in the first of the vase-markings just given, have likewise nothing to do with written characters. Let the reader, however, judge for himself (No. 1534) :—

No. 1534. Incised signs on the whetstone. No. 1265.

Here, it is true, we have the Cypriote ⋔, *ro*, as upon the terra-cotta seal already discussed, but there is nothing else which can be compared with any of the characters of the Cypriote syllabary, while on the side of the stone there is plainly the representation of a man with his arm outstretched. It is difficult to attach any signification to the other marks.

It is different with the design upon a seal now in the Museum of the Chinili Kiosk at Constantinople. This is as follows : ⋔⋔. The picture of the bull is in the same childish style of art as that with which the terra-cotta whorls discovered by Dr. Schliemann have made us familiar. But it bears in its mouth what may indeed be intended to represent fodder, but is more probably the character *ko* or *go*. If so, we have evidence that the Trojan language denoted the bull by a word of the same origin as the Sanskrit *gaus*, the Greek βοῦς (for γƑοƑ-ς), the Latin *bos*, and the Old High German *chuo* (*cow*). The language of the Lydians, from whom according to Herodotus (vii. 74) the Mysians were descended, represented a guttural followed by a labial by a simple guttural, as may be seen from the word κανδαύλης, translated σκυλλοπνίκτης by Hipponax (*Fr.* 1, Bergk), where καν answers to the Sanskrit *śwan*, the Greek κύων, the Latin *canis*, and the English *hound*.

I believe that significant characters may be read on a small button of the annexed pattern:—

Here we have ⌒ , *re*, or perhaps the Cypriote ⌒ , *lu*, ⌂ , *ye*, and ⌐ of doubtful value.

No. 1535. A button with inscribed characters.

Still more striking is the legend, consisting of a single character, scratched upon two funnel-shaped cones of yellow clay, found at a depth of 10 ft. (Nos. 1338, 1339, p. 582). The character in question is ⊞, *mo*, the name probably of some weight or measure.[6]   We are irresistibly reminded of the Aryan root *má*, "to measure," with its derivatives, the Sanskrit *mátram*, "a measure," the Zend *má*, "a measure," the Greek μέτρον, and the Latin *metare* and *metiri*. But these cones lead us to conclusions even more interesting. A cone of almost exactly the same shape and material was discovered by the late Mr. George Smith under the pavement of the palace of the Assyrian king Assur-bani-pal or Sardanapalus at Kouyunjik. On this is scratched in the same place and in a similar manner as on the cones from Hissarlik the following inscription:

No. 1536. Inscription on an Assyrian cone from Kouyunjik.

These are unmistakably Trojan letters, the first on the left being the familiar *re* or *le*. The second character is either ⌃ or ⌃, more probably the latter, its lower line coinciding with the line along which the engraver drew the characters. If the character is ⌃, it may be an abbreviated form of the Cypriote *to*, which occurs

in some late inscriptions; if it is ⌃, it is the ordinary *ve*. The third character is unfortunately one which is not met with in the Cypriote syllabary, though it occurs in an inscription on a Pamphylian coin. The cone from Kouyunjik cannot be later than B.C. 650, and this gives us an approximate date not only for the period down to which the Cypriote syllabary was in use in the Troad, but also for the relative antiquity of the several strata of remains at Hissarlik.

I do not, of course, mean to say positively that the cone discovered by Mr. George Smith actually came from the Troad, though its remarkable similarity to the Trojan cones in shape, material, and the form of its characters strongly points to such a conclusion; but it must have come from a people who used the same system of writing as the inhabitants of the Troad and were in close contact with them. Early in his reign, which commenced B.C. 668, Assur-bani-pal received tribute from Gugu or Gyges, king of Lydia, a country the very name of which, he says, his fathers had never heard, and it is probable that the cone reached Nineveh through the Lydians. For the present, therefore, we must leave it undecided whether it was of Trojan or of Lydian manufacture. This is a point that can only be settled by excavations on the site of the Lydian capital. But it is at least highly probable that the same system of writing was in use in Lydia as in the Troad, and that the discovery of Lydian inscriptions would pour a flood of light on the enigmatical legends from Hissarlik which I have been discussing.[7]

---

[6] Dr. Schliemann tells me that he has found the same character on a round object of terracotta, as well as on the back of the polishing stone, No. 651, p. 444.

[7] It is probable, however, that a fragment of a Lydian inscription exists on a broken marble base found by Mr. Wood in the temple of Artemis at Ephesus, and published by Mr. Newton in the *Transactions of the Society of Biblical Archaeology*, iv. 2 (1876). The base seems to have belonged to an archaic statue, or more probably to one of the *caelatae columnae* presented by Krœsus. At

One thing at any rate is clear. The use of the so-called Cypriote syllabary was not confined to the island of Cyprus, though it continued to be employed there down to a later period than elsewhere. But there was a time when it was known all over the continent of Asia Minor, and it is to that time that the inscribed monuments of Hissarlik take us back. No inscriptions have hitherto been discovered in other parts of the Peninsula which are older than the period when the Phoenico-Greek alphabet had been introduced and adapted to express the sounds of the various languages spoken there. They are all composed in either the Lykian, the Karian, the Pamphylian, the Kilikian, the Kappadokian, or the Phrygian alphabets. But apart from the Phrygian alphabet, which is purely Greek and must have been borrowed from the Ionic before the latter had lost the *digamma* in the seventh century B.C., each of these alphabets contains convincing evidence that it had been preceded by a syllabary identical in the main with that of Cyprus. Sounds which were not expressed at all in the Greek alphabet, or only inadequately expressed in it, are represented by characters which have the same forms and the same phonetic values as those of the Cypriote syllabary. Thus in Lykian we have the Cypriote ✳ (*khu*), *kh*, ᶌ, *o*, ✥, *e*, and ⊃|⟨ (*va*), *v;* in Karian, ⋀, *mi*, ⌃, *re* (or *le*), ⋂, *ko* (*go*), Ω, *ra*, ✕, *le*, ⊕, *mo*, ⊥, *ve*, and ı/ı, *ne;* in Pamphylian, ᛏ, *ro*, ⋎, *u*, ⋂, *ko*, ⋈, *vu* or *v*, and ᛦ, *ss* (*se*)*;* and in Kilikian, ⊣, *ta*, and ⨆, *se.* Our only

any rate it formed part of the older temple whose foundations and materials were used for the temple built in the time of Alexander the Great. One of the characters contained in the inscription is the Trojan *ve*, spoken of above. Another has the form ⋀, which is also found in a slightly different form at Eyuk, and a third has the same form as the *n* at Eyuk.

knowledge of the Kappadokian alphabet is derived from the inscription copied by Hamilton at Eyuk, which lay within the frontiers of Kappadokia before the settlement of the Gauls in Galatia, and which is as follows :

ᛦ⋀ᛘ|o᛬o)⌐(⋀ᛦ⋂ᶕᶚ

No. 1537. Inscription found at Eyuk in Kappadokia.

This I would read from right to left: *Ri*(?)*-si-p*(?)*-u* [or *sa*] *S* (or *G*)*-ma-o-v-o m-a-n,* " Rispu (son) of Smaovos (am) I." Here at least four letters are Cypriote, and one other (ᛦ) also probably belongs to the old syllabary.

As I have already remarked, the characters found on the monuments of Cyprus are a selected residuum of those once contained in the syllabary which has left scattered memorials of itself in the later alphabets of Asia Minor. I strongly suspect that the Kappadokian ᛦ, which is similar in form to the Trojan character found on the whorl, No. 3558, as well as to a character (⊤) met with on Pamphylian coins and Karian monuments, is one of the characters not represented in Cyprus. The same is certainly the case with the Lykian ⋀ or ⋀, *é* (also found in Karian, and possibly in Trojan), +, *h*, ⊃, *s* (also found in Kappadokian), ⋊, *th* (also found in Karian) ✕ (which resembles one form of the Cypriote ✕, *me*) and ⊥, *ih* (unless this is the Cypriote ✥, *e*), as well as with the Pamphylian ⧫, ⊏, and possibly ⋀. So, too, in Karian we have ᛒ or ᛔ, *ě*, ⋎, *ss*, ⊘, and ⊕. The original syllabary of Asia Minor probably possessed about a hundred characters. It seems to be meant by the famous σήματα λυγρά of Homer (*Il.* vi. 169); though, if so, folded tablets covered with wax were already in use for the purposes of correspondence. These σήματα or "characters" were carried by Bellerophon to Lykia, where, as we have seen, the syllabary of Asia Minor had been long in use.

The origin of this syllabary is still enveloped in obscurity. Five years ago, in the *Transactions of the Society of Biblical Archaeology* (v. i. 1876), I endeavoured to trace it to the still undeciphered Hittite hieroglyphics which have been found at Aleppo and on the sites of Hamath and Carchemish, the Hittite capital, now represented by the mounds of Jerablûs (the Greek Hierapolis) on the Euphrates, 16 miles to the south of Birejik, as well as in Asia Minor. But at that time the only legible Hittite inscriptions known were a few short ones from Hamah (or Hamath), which turn out to be engraved in a later, hieratic form of Hittite writing; while the earliest accessible forms of the Cypriote characters were those found in comparatively late inscriptions from the island of Cyprus. My comparisons, therefore, had to be made between the selected characters of the Cypriote syllabary, with late and special forms, and an equally restricted number of Hittite hieroglyphics, similarly late and special. Moreover, I had not then made the important discovery of the Hittite origin of the sculptures and inscriptions photographed or copied by Perrot and others at Eyuk and Boghaz Kioi (the ancient Pteria) on the Halys, at Ghiaur-Kalessi near the villages of Hoiadja and Kara-omerlu, 9 hours to the south-west of Angora (Ancyra), at a spot which commands the old road by Gordium from Ancyra to Pessinus, and above all at Kara-bel in Lydia, at the junction of the two roads from Ephesus to Phokaea and from Smyrna to Sardes, where in 1879 I had the satisfaction of finding a Hittite inscription accompanying one of the two figures supposed by Herodotus (ii. 106) to have been portraits of the Egyptian Sesostris. In Lykaonia, near the silver-mines of the Bulgar Dagh, Mr. Davis has discovered Hittite sculptures and inscriptions at Ibreez (or Ivris) a little to the south of Eregle,

the ancient Kybistra, and at Bulgar Maden (near Chifteh Khan); while Mr. Edmund Calvert has informed me of another Hittite sculpture, consisting of three figures and accompanied by Hittite characters, near Frehtin in the neighbourhood of Ibreez. In fact, it is plain that Hittite power and influence once made itself felt as far as the Aegean along the two high roads of Asia Minor, one of which ran northwards through Kappadokia, Galatia, and Mysia—being in fact the road traversed by Kroesus when he marched against Cyrus—and the other southwards through Lykaonia to Sardes. This latter road was the one followed by Xenophon and the Ten Thousand on their outward march.

Now Hittite art, which is characterized by thick limbs, a fondness for round ornaments and convolutions, winged solar discs, and figures with tiaraed heads and shoes with turned-up ends, is an art which is Assyro-Babylonian in its origin, but which has been modified in a very special way by the artists of Carchemish. It was carried by the Hittites to the nations of the West, where it became the peculiar art of Asia Minor, and passed over, probably through Lydian hands, to Greece. The hitherto unexplained element in early Greek art, which cannot be traced to Phoenician influence, has really come from this source. Thus the tombstones found by Dr. Schliemann at Mykenae are Hittite in general character; so also are the lions over the principal gate of the Acropolis, which find their analogue in a rock-tomb at Kumbet in Phrygia;[8] while the head-dress of an ivory figure discovered in the pre-historic tombs of Spata in Attica is distinctively Hittite.

The age when the authority and culture of the Hittites extended itself to the far West was probably about

---

[8] Compare especially the forms of the bull and lion copied by Perrot at Eyuk (plate 57) with those found on objects from Mykenae and Spata.

B.C. 1300–1200. Herodotus makes Ninus the son of Belus the ancestor of
the dynasty of the Heraklids in Lydia
which ended with Kandaules. This
was formerly supposed to refer to an
Assyrian occupation of Lydia, but the
supposition is rendered untenable by
the fact that, according to the cuneiform inscriptions, the country westward of the Halys was unknown to the
Assyrians before the reign of Assur-
bani-pal. The legend however may be
sufficiently explained by the arrival of
a culture which had come to the Hittites from Assyria and Babylonia, and
was transmitted by them to Asia Minor. Ammianus Marcellinus (xiv. 8)
calls Hierapolis on the Euphrates, that
is, as we now know, Carchemish, the
"ancient Ninus" or Nineveh (see, too,
Philostratus, *Vita Apoll. Tyan.* i. 19;
and Diodorus, ii. 3, 7). If we may
trust the chronology of Herodotus,
the beginning of the Heraklid dynasty
must be placed about 500 years before
the accession of Gyges, or about B.C.
1200. The date is confirmed by the
fact that the Assyrian monarch, Tig-
lath Pileser I. (B.C. 1130), states that
the Moschi had been sufficiently strong
fifty years previously to wrest the
countries of Alzu and Purukhumzu on
the Upper Euphrates from the Assyrians, the Hittites at the same time
overrunning Subarti or Syria; while
Egyptian annals show that in the time
of Ramses II. (B.C. 1320) Dardanians
and Mysians came to the assistance of
the Hittites, and that under Ramses
III. (B.C. 1200) they were ranged
among the Hittite allies.

We can hardly suppose that, when
the natives of Asia Minor adopted the
art of the Hittites, they did not at the
same time adopt either wholly or in
part the system of writing which accompanied it. When, therefore, the
earliest mode of writing that appears
among them is the peculiar syllabary
generally known as Cypriote, the presumption arises that this syllabary was
derived from the Hittite hieroglyphics.

And the presumption is confirmed by
several facts. First of all the syllabary is distinguished by the remarkable peculiarity of representing the
sounds of *b*, *p*, and *ph*, *g*, *k*, and *kh*,
and *d*, *t*, and *th*, respectively, by the
same characters. That is to say, the
original employers of the syllabary
made no distinction in pronunciation
between the sounds of *b*, *p*, and *ph*, of
g, *k*, and *kh*, and of *d*, *t*, and *th*. So far
as I know, there is only one race in
Western Asia to which such a curious
indistinctness of pronunciation can be
referred. The name of the Hittite
capital is written *Gar-gamis* by the Assyrians, *Car-chemish* by the Hebrews,
and *Karu-kamaisha* by the Egyptians;
in other words, the name was so pronounced that the guttural contained in
it seemed to be *g* to Assyrian ears,
hard *k* to Egyptian ears, and soft *k* (*c*)
to Jewish ears. Secondly, the Hittite
inscriptions are all written in *boustro-
phedon* fashion : this, it would seem,
must have once been the case also
in Karian, since some of the Karian
inscriptions are written from right to
left, while others are written from left
to right. Moreover, while most of the
Cypriote legends run from right to
left, those of Paphos run from left to
right, although Paphos was the centre
of the Semites, whose writing runs
from right to left, while the Assyrian
cuneiform is always written from left
to right. An explanation would thus
be afforded of the otherwise puzzling
fact that, whereas some of the oldest
Greek inscriptions are in *boustro-
phedon*, all Phoenician or Aramean
inscriptions written in the alphabet
afterwards handed on to the Greeks
run from right to left. And thirdly,
we have the two positive facts
that the inscription discovered by
Hamilton at Eyuk was found at a
spot in which Hittite sculpture and
writing have left prominent memorials
of themselves, while a coloured figure
of a warrior copied by Texier (vol. ii.
plate 103) at Konieh or Ikonium is a

specimen of Hellenized Hittite art, accompanied by characters which, if Texier's copy can be trusted, belong to a form of the Cypriote syllabary.

I am strongly inclined to think that the engraving on the whetstone found at Hissarlik is a rude attempt at imitating a Hittite inscription.

So far, therefore, as the evidence goes at present, we are justified in believing that Hittite influence extended throughout Asia Minor in the fourteenth or thirteenth century B.C., and brought with it the art of Assyria and Babylonia as modified at Carchemish, along with the knowledge of writing. It is, of course, impossible to determine whether the artists whose remains have been found in Kappadokia, Lykaonia, and Lydia were actually Hittites proper or the inhabitants of the district which extended from the Black Sea to Syria, on the one hand, and from Armenia to the Halys on the other, all of whom, if we may trust the testimony of proper names, together with the Hittites, belonged to the same race, spoke allied languages, and shared in a common civilization. Two or three considerations, indeed, make it more probable that they were the Hittites themselves. The sculptured rocks at Karabel bear witness to a military invasion and conquest, such as only a powerful people like the Hittites are likely to have made; the connection shown by the Egyptian monuments to have existed between the Hittites and the inhabitants of Mysia points in the same direction; while Mr. Gladstone's identification of the Κήτειοι of Homer (*Od.* xi. 521) with the Hittites has much in its favour.[9] However this may be, a syllabary was derived from the hieroglyphics used and probably invented by the Hittites, which came to be employed throughout Asia Minor. After passing through various changes and undergoing particular modifications in the different

[9] *Homeric Synchronism* (London, 1876), pp. 171 *sq.*

districts into which it had been introduced, this syllabary was carried from Kilikia into Cyprus in a reduced form, and remained in use there down to a comparatively late period.

Its disappearance from Mysia and the Troad belongs to an earlier date. The cone discovered by Mr. George Smith at Kouyunjik shows that it was still employed there about B.C. 650. But it must have been displaced shortly afterwards by the Ionic Greek alphabet, if we may argue from the fact that the Ionic Greek alphabets of Phrygia, Karia, and Lykia, all contained the *digamma*, which had been lost at the time when the Ionian mercenaries of Psammitichus carved their names on the colossi of Abu-Simbel, B.C. 640 (less probably B.C. 595). A remarkable relic of the period of transition has been discovered by Mr. Frank Calvert in one of the tombs in the necropolis of Thymbra. This is a patera of a shape peculiar to the locality, made of the same drab clay as the funnel-shaped cones above mentioned, and belonging to the early Phoeniko-Hellenic period of Greek art. Four Cypriote characters occur on it, two of which are written in combination on opposite sides of the *patera*, and seem to contain the name of the maker or owner. These are 𐊠 𐊹 (the second character taking also the form 𐊹), the first of which is *re* or *le*. The other is apparently the Cypriote 𐊚, the phonetic value of which is unknown, though I am inclined to believe it was *von*, in which case the name would read *Levon* or Λέων. The other two characters are written separately and are evidently used as mere ornaments, one of them, indeed, ✳, being a symmetrical modification of ✳, *e*, for decorative purposes, though the second, 𐊛, *ne*, is unchanged in form. The patera proves that, in the middle of the seventh century B.C., the period to which it belongs, the old syllabary was fast passing out of use and coming to be employed for decorative purposes only.

A good many of the terra-cotta whorls discovered by Dr. Schliemann are similarly inscribed with single characters, whose meaning is merely decorative. Thus we find  and other characters, employed along with rude drawings of animals for this purpose. In some cases it is difficult not to fancy that the designs are intended to be barbarous imitations of the more striking objects represented by the Hittite hieroglyphics. Thus the tree-pattern is very common, and this pattern is not only found among the hieroglyphics of the Hittites, but also forms the ornamentation of the robe worn by a figure on a sculptured monument from Carchemish, now in the British Museum, while the same ornament occurs frequently upon Babylonian seals and other antiquities. A curious phallus of black basalt, for example, lately brought to England from the Island of Bahrein in the Persian Gulf (which was called "the island of the gods" by the early Chaldeans) has the same pattern engraved by the side of a short inscription. In Babylonian art it represents the sacred tree of life.[10]

Among the Hissarlik whorls there are two or three which seem to me to bear marks intended to reproduce cuneiform characters, or rather the wedges of which the characters were composed, and which were wholly unintelligible to the Trojan artists. The Phoenician artists similarly often reproduced the hieroglyphics of the Egyptians, which they did not understand and accordingly miscopied and miscombined. We learn from the Trojan cylinders already discussed, that objects of early Babylonian origin were known to the primitive inhabitants of Hissarlik, and several of the designs on the whorls are obviously imitations of designs on Babylonian cylinders, among which small round holes denoting the stars and planets are especially plentiful. A fragment of pottery excavated by Dr. Schliemann in the Besika Tepeh has markings upon it which also seem somewhat unsuccessful attempts to imitate cuneiform characters (No. 1517, p. 666).

Two more points remain to be noticed before I conclude. One of these is the ingenious endeavour made by Dr. Deecke to derive the Cypriote syllabary from the Assyrian syllabary as it was at the close of the eighth century B.C., when Sargon overran the island of Cyprus. But the fatal objection to this endeavour is the fact that the same syllabary already existed, as we have seen, in an older and fuller form on the mainland, and that consequently it could not have been the invention of a Cyprian of Paphos about 710 B.C. The inscriptions found at Hissarlik show that its characters already existed in an older form far away in the north-west of Asia Minor. Consequently it must have been an importation into Cyprus from the mainland; not a possession peculiar to the island. But there are other objections to Dr. Deecke's theory. Thus the forms of the cuneiform characters that he compares belong to more than one age and district, and were not all in use at one and the same time or in one and the same country, while in several instances he has to imagine non-existent forms intermediate between the supposed cuneiform prototype and its Cypriote equivalent. The phonology of the Assyrian and Cypriote syllabaries, again, does not agree. The Assyrian language has distinct signs for

---

[10] In Phoenician art it seems to denote a palm-branch. On a silver bowl found at Palestrina and bearing a Phoenician inscription, the tails of the horses are artistically represented under the form of these trees or palm-branches.

t and *d* (also for *th*); for *g, k,* and *kh,* and for *b* and *p;* and it is inconceivable that these should have been confounded together in a syllabary meant to express the sounds of two languages, the Phoenician and the Greek, both of which possessed these very sounds. On the other hand, the Assyrians made no distinction between *m* and *v,* as the Cypriote syllabary does, and had no *ye, yi* or *o,* which have special characters to denote them in Cypriote. It may further be added that the only two characters, *e,* ✳, and *pa,* ✝, which display a marked resemblance to cuneiform characters with corresponding phonetic values, lose this resemblance when traced back to the older forms ✳ and ⊤.

The other point to be noticed is unfortunately one upon which very little can be said. Of the language of the Trojans and Mysians we know next to nothing, and it is therefore impossible to explain the words written in Trojan characters, even when they have been deciphered, or to know whether we are dealing with significant words or proper names. All we can say positively is, that the Mysian language was allied to those of the neighbouring populations of Asia Minor. Xanthus, the Lykian historian (*Fr.* 8), makes it half Lydian, half Phrygian, and the words of Herodotus (i. 171) imply the same. Indeed, Herodotus goes so far as to state (vii. 74) that the Mysians were Lydian colonists, though Strabo (xii. pp. 542, 566) calls them Thrakian colonists. But the dialects of Thrace and Western Asia Minor belonged to the same stock, while extant Phrygian inscriptions and glosses show that Phrygian was a sister-tongue of classical Greek. Slight differences, of course, must have existed between Mysian and Phrygian, as indeed is asserted by a passage in the Homeric Hymn to Aphrodité (111–116), quoted by Dr. Schliemann in an earlier part of this volume (p. 120). The differences, however, could not have been great, and it is therefore possible that the meaning of the Trojan inscriptions may yet be cleared up by the discovery of Phrygian and Lydian inscriptions. Hektor was called Dareios "by the Phrygians," which seems to imply that *dareios* was the equivalent of the Greek ἕκτωρ, "a stay," in both Phrygian and Trojan. Paris seems to have been the native name which corresponded to the Greek Ἀλέξανδρος, "defender of men," and it is difficult to separate Paris from Priamos. The Aeolic form of Priamos, Πέρραμος, shows that the original form of the word was Peryamos, which has clearly nothing to do with *pergamos* (? "a citadel"), but seems to be connected with the Lydian πάλμυς, "king."

The four curious passages in which Homer contrasts the language of the gods with the language of men, probably also contain some specimens of the Mysian dialect. The single analogy that can be found for these passages is a very close one from the Old Edda of Iceland. In this we have a poem called the Alvíssmal, or the "Speech of the Allwise," in which the names of various objects are given in the language of men, of the Aesir or gods, and of the Vanir or demigods. It appears that the language of men was the language of ordinary life, while that of the gods was the language of the poets. In the latter language were included many foreign words; thus we are told that what is called *ale* by men is called *beer* by the gods, *ale* being Scandinavian and *beer* the borrowed Anglo-Saxon. The four passages of Homer are explained and cleared up by the Icelandic poem. In Homer, too, the language of men means that spoken by the natives of Asia Minor; the language of the gods that used by the poets of Ionia. Briareus, as he is called by the gods, is called Aegaeon by men (*Il.* i. 403–4), Briareus meaning "the mighty," and Aegaeon being probably connected with the Greek αἰγίς, " tempest " (the Dorian αἶγες, " waves "). In *Il.* ii. 813–4, men are said to term Batieia what the gods call the tomb of the Amazon Myrinê, whose name reappears in those of Smyrna and the Lemnian and Aeolic towns of Myrina. Batieia may be βατιϝεσγα, " the brambly," a good designation for a tumulus which is still covered with bushes. According to *Il.* xiv. 291 and xx. 74, men called κύμινδις and Σκάμανδρος what the gods called χαλκίς and Ξανθός. Κύμινδις is said to have been the Ionic name of the night-jar; but since it has no kindred in Greek, it would seem that it was one of the native words borrowed by the Ionic settlers in Asia Minor. If we can suppose that χαλκίς, " the bronze-coloured," and ξανθός, " yellow," are real equivalents of κύμινδις and Σκάμανδρος, we may infer that a root σκαμανδ or κυμινδ existed in Mysian which had the signification of

" yellow." It must not be forgotten, however, that several of the river-names of Asia Minor, such as Alander and Maeander, the latter of which claims relationship with Maeonia, the Lydian μωῦς, " earth," end with the syllables -ανδρος; while, on the other hand, we have various names like Kadyanda, Labranda (from the Lydian λάβρυς, " hatchet "), Piginda, Alinda (from the Karian ἄλα, " horse ") which have the same termination as κύμινδις. The name of Mysia itself was derived from the Lydian μυσός, which is explained by the Greek ὀξύη, " the beech " (or *Fagus silvaticus*).[1]

---

[1] The following inscription, found by Mr. Frank Calvert in the necropolis of Thymbra, probably contains a specimen of the Mysian dialect spoken in the Troad :—

ΛΙΣΘΕΝΕΙΑΙΕΜΜ(?)ΙΤΟΝΙΚΙΑΙΟΙ-
ΤΟΓΛΥΚΙΟ.

It is given in Le Bas : *Voyage archéologique en Grèce et en Asie Mineure,* v. 1743 m.

APPENDIX IV.

THYMBRA, HANAÏ TEPEH.

By Mr. Consul Frank Calvert.

The first mention of Thymbra is by Homer. Dolon, when he details to Ulysses the position of the Trojan army outside of Troy, places the Ca-rians, Paeonians, Leleges, Caucones, and Pelasgi, towards the sea; the Lycians, Mysians, Phrygians, and Maeonians, towards Thymbra.[1] This

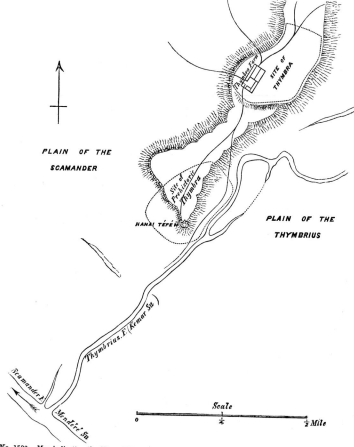

No. 1538. Map indicating the Sites of Thymbra and Hanaï Tepeh, and the junction of the Rivers Thymbrius and Scamander.

[1] *Il.* x. 428.

allocation, though it does not establish the geographical position of Thymbra, yet, taken with the more precise information given by Demetrius of Scepsis, is of value ; it evidences that a direction opposite to the sea, that is, inland, was intended by the poet. The more modern author places the temple of Apollo Thymbraeus at fifty stadia from Ilium (Novum), at the junc-tion of the river Thymbrius with the Scamander.[2] Thymbra was identified by Hobhouse with Akshi Kioi [3] (the present Thymbra Farm), and Barker Webb recognized the Thymbrius in the Kemar Su.[4] My researches have led to the discovery of another ancient site at Hanaï Tepeh, separated from that of Akshi Kioi by an interval of about five hundred yards (see Map,

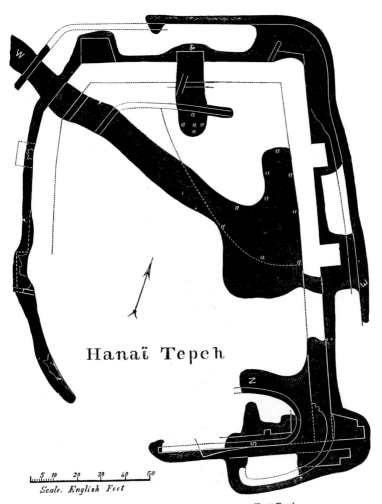

Hanaï Tepeh

Scale. English Feet

No. 1529.   General Plan of Excavation made at Hanaï Tepeh.

[2] Strabo, xiii. p. 598.   [3] *Journey through Albania* ; London, 1813, p. 753.
        [4] *De Agro Trojano* ; Milan, 1821, p. 49.

No. 1538). At Akshi Kioi the remains
are of later date than at Hanaï Tepeh.
The Homeric site of Thymbra would
appear not to be identical with the later
town and temple of the Thymbrean

Apollo of Demetrius; and subsequent
ancient authors appear to have transferred it to Akshi Kioi from Hanaï
Tepeh. Pre-historic Thymbra covered
a considerable surface of land, on

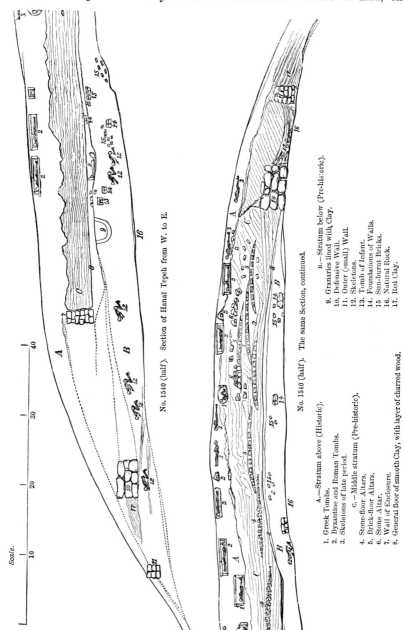

No. 1540 (half). Section of Hanaï Tepeh from W. to E.

No. 1540 (half). The same Section, continued.

A.—Stratum above (Historic).

1. Greek Tombs.
2. Byzantine and Roman Tombs.
3. Skeletons of late period.

C.—Middle stratum (Pre-historic).

4. Stone-floor Altars.
5. Brick-floor Altars.
6. Stone Altar.
7. Wall of Enclosure.
8. General floor of smooth Clay, with layer of charred wood.

B.—Stratum below (Pre-historic).

9. Granaries lined with Clay.
10. Defensive Wall.
11. Outer (small) Wall.
12. Skeletons.
13. Tomb of Infant.
14. Foundations of Walls.
15. Sun-burnt Bricks.
16. Natural Rock.
17. Red Clay.

Scale.

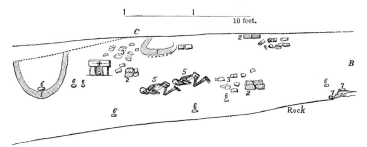

No. 1541. Enlarged portion of Section of Hanaï Tepeh from W. to E.

1. Granaries lined with Clay.
2. Foundations built on with No. 3.
3. Sun-dried Bricks.
4. Tomb of Infant.

5. Skeleton.
6. Stone Axes, Weights, &c.
7. Vases.

which are found hand-mill stones, stone axes, fragments of pottery, whorls, silex flakes, and other relics.

The artificial mound of Hanaï Tepeh, which gives its name to the site, is of remarkable interest. It forms, as it were, the nucleus of the old settlement, and stands out prominently in the plain at the end of a long spur of land which reaches back to Akshi Kioi. My first excavation in this tepeh was made in 1857, and the results and hypothesis founded thereon were published in the *Journal of the Archaeological Institute.*[5] Further researches were made subsequently; latterly with the powerful assistance of Dr. Schliemann. The later and more extensive investigations, as shown in the accompanying General Plan, No. 1539, have led me to relinquish the conviction of the identity of Hanaï Tepeh with the common tomb of the Trojans, published in the above-mentioned journal. A trench, 12 ft. wide, which I made through the mound from west to east, gives a complete section of this artificial hillock (No. 1540). The natural rock rises from the plain to a flat shelly limestone stratum (No. 1540, 16), which forms a plateau on the spur. On this surface are the remains of the original settlers, extending beyond the mound itself (No. 1540, B). The

⁵ Vol. xv. 1858.

débris are composed in great part of sun-dried bricks derived from fallen habitations, wood-ashes, and charcoal (No. 1540, B 15; No. 1541, 3). Marks of fire on many of these bricks and the foundations of houses superposed severally one on the other (No. 1540, B 14), indicate the repeated destruction and reconstruction of the buildings: these dwellings are unfortunately in too great a state of dilapidation to allow their form or size to be traced. The three or four lower courses of bricks were protected by an outer facing of stone (No. 1541, 2), a method of preserving the walls from damp and rain-drip still adopted in the country. These sun-dried bricks are of various dimensions: the largest and best preserved, from the tombs of two infants No. 1540, B 13), measure—

Length, inches.	Breadth, inches.	Depth, inches.
16	8	4
19¼	9½	2¾
19¼	13½	3¼

In the manufacture of the bricks, the yellow loam of the plain was mixed with chopped straw or hay, impressions of which binding-material are quite distinct. Many of these bricks have been burnt red or black by the accidental conflagration of the dwellings. Slime or mortar made of the same materials as the bricks was used as cement; it served also as plaster for the surface of the inside walls, portions of which have been preserved.

In remarkable agreement with the pre-historic cities at Hissarlik is the absence of doors and windows in the habitations. From the numerous indications of fires in both these ancient sites, it would appear that timber was used largely as a building material. This circumstance suggests the hypothesis of an upper story of wood, to which access was gained by means of steps or ladders : for security the ground-floor had no exterior communication, but was entered from above from the wooden story. The unhewn pine-log huts, now in use among the Yourouk tribes in this country, may afford a clue to the kind of superstructure adopted by the pre-historic inhabitants of Hissarlik and Hanaï Tepeh. This kind of hut has a roof made of salt clay laid on branches of trees covered with reeds or seaweed. Masses of clay with impressions of long reeds are found at Hanaï Tepeh, a coincidence which is worthy of remark. No walls of a defensive nature have been discovered in the lowest stratum (No. 1540, B).

Fragments of pottery are very numerous, but entire vessels are rare. These are both hand-made (No. 1541,

No. 1542. Massive hand-made Vase.
(About 1 : 3 actual size.)

7 ; No. 1542) and turned on the wheel. Most of the specimens are hand-polished, an effect produced by rubbing the vase with a hard substance previous to its being baked. The luléhs or pipe bowls now made at Constantinople are polished in this manner, and at the same time a deeper shade is given to the clay by this

rubbing. The prevailing colour of the pottery is black or dark brown, due to the presence of carbonaceous matter; red is comparatively rare. A few fragments show a dark-coloured core with a bright red surface. Many of the vases have horizontal perforations for the purpose of suspension (Nos. 1543, 1544, 1545), a peculiarity

No. 1543. Bowl with horizontal perforations for suspension. (About 1 : 3 actual size.)

No. 1544. Fragments of Bowl, with horizontal hole for suspension, dark-brown, hand-polished.
(About 1 : 3 actual size.)

No. 1545. Fragment of a lustrous black Bowl, with large horizontal tubular hole for suspension.
(About 1 : 3 actual size.)

limited to the original settlement, as these have not been discovered above a foot or two from the rock, nor in the upper part of the stratum B. Some of these perforated handles are of a bright lustrous red, striking in appearance, with some similitude to the claw of a lobster (Nos. 1546, 1547). Ribbed ware is common in the upper part of the stratum B, but does not appear to have been manufactured in the earlier settlements. The most prevalent form is a large, but shallow,

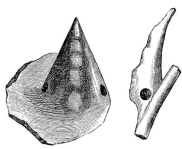

No. 1546. Handle of Vase, horizontally perforated, lustrousred, hand-polished. (1 : 2 actual size.)

No. 1547. Horizontally perforated lustrousred Vase-handle. (1 : 2 actual size.)

circular bowl. Vessels on tripods were not rare; for many fragmentary

No. 1548. Handle or foot of a Tripod Vase, black, hand-polished. (1 : 2 actual size.)

feet (No. 1548) of different shapes have been found close above the rock. Fragments of vases with soot on their exterior show that the use of boiling or stewing in earthenware vessels was not unknown to the inhabitants. Bones of the fallow deer, the roebuck, and the wild boar, which furnished this people with food, are abundant. Besides the produce of the chase, grain of some kind must have been plentiful, judging by the number of hand-mill stones in basalt and syenite.

Beginning with the lowest stratum (B in plan No. 1540), we find at or near the top small granaries, sometimes of a circular, sometimes of a square shape, which have been ex-cavated in the soil and coated with clay plaster (No. 1541, 1). In one of these a stone axe has been discovered.

Since no species of grain is indigenous in the country, it is clear that the original settlers must have brought the cereals they cultivated along with them. The plain of Troy, with its rich and fertile soil, would naturally have attracted them to an agricultural life, and from the first we may assume that agriculture was an important occupation in the Troad. The near neighbourhood of the sea furnished the inhabitants of the district with other articles of food: fish, oysters, mussels, and cockles, entered largely into their diet, but varied at different epochs and in different localities. Thus Professor Virchow has observed that the *Ostrea lamellosa* alone is found at Hanaï Tepeh, whilst *Ostrea cristata* is confined to Hissarlik. The bones that have been discovered and examined, in the lowest stratum at Hanaï Tepeh, prove that the goat was the commonest of the domestic animals, the ox the most rare; while the horse, as Professor Virchow has noticed, is conspicuous by its absence. From this negative evidence we may infer that the latter animal was unknown in the Troad in the pre-historic age, in striking contrast to the age of Homer, who mentions it so frequently. The dog, on the other hand, that faithful friend of man, has left memorials of its presence in its footprints on several sun-dried bricks, made upon them while the clay was still plastic. Bronze is the only metal met with, and that sparingly. In fact, the only specimens of it found in stratum B consist of a hairpin with a double spiral head and two corroded and shapeless fragments.

On the other hand, implements of bone and stone are not uncommon. Thus we have bone awls; a few polished axes made of diorite, serpentine, talc, and other stones (No. 1541,

6); as well as flakes, scrapers, knives, and saws (No. 1549) of obsidian,

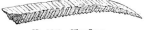

No. 1549. Silex Saws.

quartz, jasper, and other hard stone. One or two specimens of crystal have also been found. The stones of which the implements are made have all come from the neighbourhood : diorite from the valley of the Rhodius ; serpentine and talc from the Foulah Dagh, the Kara Dagh, and the Dumbrek ; obsidian from the vicinity of Saragik, in the valley of the Rhodius, and of Aivajik ; while flint nodules are plentiful in the chalk of the White Cliffs on the Hellespont, and jasper is abundant in many localities, more especially in the Foulah Dagh and between Lampsacus and the town of Dardanelles. Quartz, too, approaching to chalcedony, occurs in nodules in a bed of conglomerate metamorphosed by superposed basalt, at the foot of the Foulah Dagh.

Besides these implements, two objects of mother-of-pearl have been found,—one a small button with a hole in the centre, the other an ornament 2 inches long in the shape of a pear. Spindle whorls of dark-coloured clay which has been baked at a fire are common ; *but no ornamentation occurs on any discovered in stratum* B. Whorls of marble and hard stone are rare, whereas circular potsherds with perforated centres used as substitutes for whorls are plentiful. A couple of reels for winding thread, made of dark-coloured baked clay, and similar to those still employed for the same purpose, also turned up during the excavations, as well as numerous four-sided pyramids of sun-dried clay, which must have served as weavers' weights. These objects indicate a knowledge of textile manufactures on the part of those who used them.

The early people of Hanaï Tepeh were also musicians, since the upper fragment of a bone flute (No. 1550) has been discovered.

No. 1550. Fragment of Flute of Bone.

Their religion may be represented by a small marble foot, with a minute perforation at the knee for suspension, which seems to have been a votive offering. This is not the only object of marble which bears witness to the artistic capacities of the people ; another which is probably intended to represent a flower (No. 1551) has

No. 1551. Flower (?) in Marble.

been found, besides flattened spheres of marble, which may have been weights.

A remarkable feature in this stratum, B (No. 1540, 12 ; No. 1541, 5) is the number of skeletons found in it at every variety of depth. Some were on the rock itself, others under the foundations of later houses, and in what seem to have been the floors of inhabited dwellings. These interments are peculiar to the stratum we are now considering, since as will be shown further on, none were made during the subsequent period represented by the superposed *débris*. The interments on the east side of the mound (No. 1541, 12) were discovered during the excavations of 1857 ; the rest were found last winter (1879). The bodies were buried with the faces downwards, the heads towards the west, and the knees doubled up. The head of one was found resting on a hand-mill stone (No. 1552). Gene-

No. 1552. Skeleton, with Skull resting on hand-mill stone.

rally speaking, they seem to have been interred in the loose earth; at all events, no special graves or tombs

were prepared to receive them. An exception, however, must be made in the case of two infants, whose bones were found in small tombs made of sun-dried bricks. The skeleton of one of these was that of a newly-born babe; it was extended on the back, and the tomb in which it was laid was free from earth (No. 1541, 4, Nos. 1553, 1554). Curiously enough, though the bones show no signs of having been burnt, a quantity

No. 1553.   No. 1554.

Nos. 1553, 1554. Tomb of Infant, made of sun-burnt bricks.

of asbestos was found mixed with them. This was unfortunately too fragile to be removed, but its appearance when first discovered plainly showed that it must have consisted of some woven texture. The interior of the tomb was 18 inches long by 9 broad and 8 high. The body of the other infant was that of a young child (No. 1555), which was laid on the

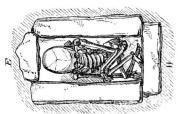

No. 1555. Tomb of Child, made of sun-burnt bricks.

right side, with the knees bent up, the right arm extended, the left crossed over the body, and the head resting upon the breast. It had apparently sunk down from its original position. The right side of the tomb in which it was placed was made of stone instead of brick, and its head was turned towards the east. The interior of the grave measured 16 inches in length, 9 in breadth, and

9 in height. No asbestos was found with this skeleton, nor indeed with any of the others, the body of the newly-born babe alone excepted. As may be seen from the plan, the interments are on the west, rather than on the east, side of the tumulus.

According to Professor Virchow, the race to whom the skeletons belonged was brachycephalic; and the shin-bones have the remarkable peculiarity of being angular,—a peculiarity now confined to the Malay race. He is at present engaged in writing a description of them.

No defensive walls were brought to light in the lower part of stratum B (No. 1540).

On the other hand, the surface of the stratum had been levelled on the western side to a depth of about 3 ft., for the sake of a massive wall of defence, which must have been erected after the accumulation of the soil, and the eastern foundations of which were laid on the rock itself. The wall was supported by a number of buttresses. Its average breadth is from 8 to 10 feet (B, No. 1540, 10), and its greatest present height is 5 feet. Its southern side has disappeared. The largest stone found in the wall is 7 feet long by 2 in breadth, and 2½ in height. All the stones composing it are rough and un-hewn, and are bound together with clay cement. They consist partly of miocene shelly limestone found on the spot, partly of crystalline limestone and basalt from the bed of the Thym-brius.

Besides this inner defensive wall (No. 1540, 10), there was also an outer wall (No. 1540, 11), which sometimes stands detached, with a breadth of two and a half feet, while at other times it is a mere external facing to a rude heap of loose stones. On the east side this wall is of bricks made from the sur-face soil, and the part laid bare by the excavations was well preserved, so far as its form was concerned, though the bricks composing it were disintegrated. Outside the wall, as well as between it and the inner wall, was a quantity of marly red clay (No. 1540, 17); no trace of which, it must be observed, was found on the inner side of the inner wall. The origin of this red miocene clay was at first proble-matical; but a clue was eventually given by the discovery of a brick made of it, built into one of the walls of the habitation near the gateway. The form of this brick was very dis-tinct, though, owing to the absence of straw or any similar binding mate-rial, the clay was disintegrated. It showed clearly that the marly clay, of which such quantities were found, had come from decomposed bricks. These must once have formed the upper part of the massive wall of defence, the stones which now alone mark its course having served as a foundation. As the brickwork crumbled away it fell to the foot of the wall, and there formed the accu-mulation seen in No. 1540, 17. Wood-ashes were occasionally found inter-mixed with it, but otherwise there were no marks whatsoever of fire.

The entrance to the fortress to which these walls belonged lay on the eastern side, and was formed by a narrow passage, 3 feet wide, between two long projecting buttresses. It must have been built upon the tumulus after the accumulation of soil repre-sented by the stratum B. Little addi-tional soil was accumulated within the fortress itself, and the unbroken line of the latter proves incontestably that the interments previously men-tioned must have been made before its construction. One skeleton, in-deed (No. 1540, 12), was actually found under the massive inner wall itself (No. 1540, 10). The inner wall, it may be added, shows in some parts a facing of yellow loam brick on the inside, from 2 to 3 feet in height, and the remains of these bricks c n-stitute in great measure the *débris* within the fortress, which form what we will call stratum C.

The fragments of pottery discovered in stratum B are but few. In the lower part the handle of a vase, made in the shape of a cow or ox (Nos. 1556–1559), was found, while a small hand-made vase with horizontally per-forated excrescences (No. 1560) was met with close to the wall, and frag-ments of lustrous-black ribbed vases were turned up, similar to those found in the stratum C (Nos. 1561, 1562).

It is to this stratum that we must now turn. Here we find ourselves in presence of a sacred enclosure, within which altars once stood, dedi-cated in all probability to that Thym-brean Apollo, whose temple, according to the indications of Strabo, must have stood upon this very spot. On the west side are the remains of a wall two and a half feet in diameter, built on the *débris* of the old fortress, and probably once faced with brick (No. 1540, 7). On the east side, the massive inner wall of the old fortress was converted to the use of the new edifice. On the south-east was a long piece of building, and here too was the entrance, consisting of a narrow passage. The massive wall on the east side shows traces of having

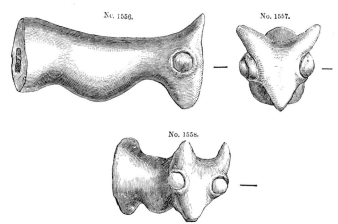

No. 1558.

Nos. 1556–1558. Vase-handle in dark-coloured Clay. (About 1 : 2 actual size.)

been burnt, from which we may infer that the fortress had been successfully stormed and taken by an attacking

No. 1559. Vase-handle of lustrous black Terra-cotta. (About 1 : 3 actual size.)

No. 1560. Small hand-made Vase with perforated excrescences. (About 1 : 2 actual size.)

No. 1561. Handle of a ribbed Vase. (About 1 : 3 actual size)

No. 1562. Fragment of a lustrous-black ribbed Vase. (About 1 : 3 actual size.)

force. The ground within what we may term the sacred enclosure has all been artificially levelled, and a floor formed by a coating of yellow loam plaster from half an inch to one inch thick (No. 1540, 8). Above this floor lies a thin unbroken line of charcoal, testifying to the sacrificial fires that

once burnt within the enclosure, the whole of which would thus have been consecrated to religious uses. Numerous altar-floors of brick occur at various levels (No. 1540, 5), stone taking the place of brick at the northern angle (No. 1540, 4). Their succession is indicated in the section No. 1563,

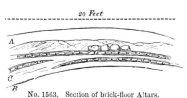

No. 1563. Section of brick-floor Altars.

where a line drawn from B to A shows the limits within which they were found. The fact that they were thus superposed one upon the other points pretty plainly to the long period of time during which the enclosure was employed for sacrificial purposes and the floor gradually covered by successive deposits of ashes. The brick altar-floors are circular in form, from 15 to 20 feet in diameter, each being composed of a single course of sun-dried brick, imbedded in clay cement (No. 1564).

No. 1564. Enlarged portion of Section of brick-floor Altar.

Cement and brick have alike been reduced by the action of fire to one homo-geneous consistency and colour. The altar-floors of stone are made of pebbles of basalt from the river-bed, which have been burnt red. Besides these altar-floors, two altars of stone have been discovered (No. 1540, 6), the stones of which they are built being crystalline limestone, calcined by the great and long-continued heat to which they have been exposed. The altars and altar-floors alike stand in a thick bed of wood-ashes, derived from the sacrificial fires which formerly burnt upon them. This bed forms the accumulation marked in the plan (No. 1540) as stratum c, which has a depth of from 5 to 8 feet. The ashes are partially vitrified, and there is no trace of charcoal among them. The moisture from the surface has been unable to penetrate through them, so that the whole mass was light, and caused much annoyance in working in consequence of the dust.

A few calcined fragments of bone and shell have been found in this bed, the forms of which are preserved, though the bones have been converted into vivianite. But these fragments are few and scattered. As shown by me in the *Journal of the Archaeological Institute* for 1858, the opinion that the accumulation is of an ossiferous character is entirely contrary to the fact. A close examination proves that its origin was a vegetable one, and that the bones and shells found their way into it only, as it were, accidentally. Consequently, the hypothesis that we have here the common tomb of the Trojans must be rejected.

Fragments of ribbed pottery were found in the stratum, similar, as has already been stated, to those found in the upper part of stratum B, but all burnt red or yellow, and vitrified.

At certain points on the north-east side, stratum c covers and extends beyond the massive wall (No. 1540, 10), from which we may conclude that the enclosure continued to be used for sacrificial purposes after the soil within it had grown to such an extent as to cover the upper surface of the old fortress wall. In the trench driven along the eastern wall, as given in section No. 1565, is a remarkable diagonal fissuring of the wood-ashes under the basement of one of the altars, which may possibly be due to lateral pressure.

A fragment of sun-dried brick from one of the altar-floors has four curious marks upon it, evidently imprinted by the hoofs of some animal, probably a kid, while the white clay was still plastic (No. 1566).

Near the gateway the old massive wall has been partly destroyed, and a low wall has been built upon it, in the form of a curve, and crossing both the

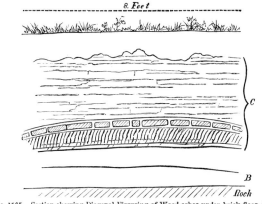

No. 1565. Section showing Diagonal Fissuring of Wood-ashes under brick-floor Altar.

buttresses which flanked the entrance as well as the entrance itself. At the same time, a second inner wall, built partly on the foundations of the massive wall, curves inward, enclosing

No. 1566. Footprints of a Kid on a fragment of sun-dried brick.

a space in the shape of a tongue about 15 feet in diameter. The entrance to the sacred enclosure was formed by a narrow passage between the extremity of this tongue and the massive wall. A quantity of burnt bricks was found

here, as well as outside the low curved wall and also within it.

A section of a portion of the mound from south to north, given in the cut No. 1567, will illustrate the statements just made, and render them easier to understand. We have first of all the natural rock (No. 1567, 1); then comes a stratum of sundried bricks (No. 1567, 2), 1 foot in thickness. The uniformly bright red colour of these shows that they have been subjected to a strong heat. Next (No. 1567, 3) follows a stratum of clay, representing the decomposed sun-dried bricks which have fallen from the walls, of which only the lower part has been preserved. The thickness of the portion of the

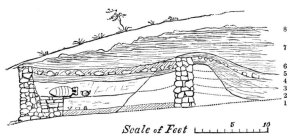

Scale of Feet

No. 1567. Section of Portion of Hanaï Tepeh from S. to N.

1. Natural Rock.
2. Stratum of Bricks burnt bright red.
3. Stratum of sun-dried Bricks.
4. Stratum of Wood-ashes and Charcoal.
5. Layer of Wood-ashes.
6. Sun-dried Bricks and Stones.
7. General Layer of Wood-ashes in connection with C.
8. Surface stratum A. on Plan No. 1540.

stratum on the left of the section is from one and a half to two feet. Some of the bricks whose forms may be traced in it rested on low foundations of stone. The inner side of the walls, as well as the floors, were covered with a plaster of clay and chopped straw, the surface of which has been burnt red. Some of the fallen bricks likewise show the marks of fire. In fact, it is plain that the building to which they belong must have perished in the flames. On the floor was a layer of wood-ashes, in which a number of pyramidal weavers' weights of different sizes were found, as well as some whorls without ornamentation and a minute hand-made vessel with horizontally perforated excrescences, similar to No. 1560. Among

the potsherds were some ribbed fragments similar to Nos. 1561, 1562.

No. 1567, 4, represents a layer of wood-ashes and charcoal, in which we may see evidence of a third conflagration. A building composed of bricks similar to those found below must once have existed here. Resting on the ashes were large jars or *pithoi*, which had the appearance of having been placed in a row along the walls, together with smaller vessels. The majority of the vessels are ribbed, some are dark, while others are of a brilliant red colour. They have all been turned on the wheel. The peculiarity of the *pithoi* is that they have no handles properly so called, a triangular hole below the lip having served as a substitute. Other large jars with ordinary handles and fragments of ribbed cups were also found. This stratum is from one and a half to two feet thick.

We now come to a layer of wood-ashes (No. 1567, 5), which are thoroughly burnt, the layer being 1 foot in thickness. After this is a stratum of sun-dried bricks and stones (No. 1567, 6), 9 inches thick, which contained a few fragments of dark ribbed pottery. Then follows (No. 1567, 7) what we have marked as stratum c in the general plan No. 1540, consisting of wood-ashes, which rises above and beyond the sacred enclosure. The position of this stratum, together with the black line of charred wood (No. 1540, 8), proves that the enclosure was originally built before the huge accumulation of ashes which forms the stratum. Above it is the surface stratum (No. 1567, 8), marked A in the general plan No. 1540.

This stratum carries us into the historic period. We first find sun-dried bricks scattered over the surface of the layer of wood-ashes (c), in No. 1540, proving that a time came when the altar-fires were discontinued, the temple in which they had burned being desecrated, and dwelling-houses erected upon its site. These houses seem to have had neither doors nor windows, or rather these necessary openings were at such a height from the ground that all trace of them has disappeared. A brick wall on the western side, between the massive wall of the old fortress and the inner wall (No. 1540, 7), shows that they were constructed in the same fashion as the earlier brick buildings beneath. The bricks, as will be seen from the following table, were of various sizes :—

10 inches × 8½ × 3.
11¼ ,, × 5½ × 2¾.
10 ,, × 8 × 2⅓.
11 ,, × 10 × 2¾.
19¼ ,, × 12 × 2¼.
18⅓ ,, × 12½ × 2⅔.

It may be noted that one of the bricks has upon it the print of the toes of a child's foot.

Among the pottery found in this upper stratum may be mentioned the fragment of a specimen of the old dark-coloured ribbed pottery, in the shape of the handle, neck, and broken spout of a vase, the spout being adorned with two eyes, in order to avert the evil eye (No. 1568). Frag-

No. 1568.   Upper portion of ribbed Vase, with eyes on Spout.

ments were also found both of archaic and of later Greek painted pottery, as well as sepulchral *pithoi* and cists of the Hellenic period. In fact, a time came when the ancient tumulus of Hanaï Tepeh formed a portion of the necropolis of the historical town of Thymbra, now represented by Akshi Kioi, and groups of tombs are met with all the way to it from the latter spot. Byzantine tombs, too, occur near the surface of the tumulus, some of which contain several bodies, along with vases, beads, and bronze ornaments. These tombs are built of stones, with stone covers, and are ornamented with engraved crosses. Turkish and other undetermined interments have also been found.

A large number of Greek amphorae have been dug up in the surface soil. It is possible that they may have been used for the libations, and they may indicate that traditions of sanctity still lingered around the spot. Indeed it was still known in the days of Strabo that the place had been the site of the legendary temple of the Thymbrean Apollo. A considerable number of circular terra-cotta discs with raised centre and two perforations, which may have been employed as seals, were discovered together with the amphorae (No. 1569). Several of these discs

No. 1569.   Object of Terra-cotta with two perforations.
(1 : 10 actual size.)

have impressed stamps upon them ; one represents the double-headed axe and bunch of grapes which was the emblem of Tenedos. Many, no doubt, served as seals to the amphorae to which they were attached ; and seals of exactly the same form, though without perforations, are still used to the present day in Lemnos. Here they are employed for medicinal purposes, and are polished by rubbing after being impressed with the seal of the governor of Lemnos.

The skulls found in the Greek and Byzantine tombs are dolichocephalic, like those found in stratum B (No. 1540, 12,). We may shortly expect a published account of Professor Virchow's examination of them.

As has been already stated, the historical Thymbra.stood at some little distance from Hanaï Tepeh, and occupied the site of the present Thymbra farm, the predecessor of which was the Turkish village of Akshi Kioi, depopulated by plague several years ago. Thymbra was a walled town, and the rock on which it was built shows traces of having been cut into in various places in order to receive hewn stones. No pre-historic remains have been found on its site. Its necropolis, however, which extended as far as Hanaï Tepeh, has yielded archaic as well as later Greek pottery. Among

the subjects painted upon it may be mentioned the Return of Ulysses, Briseis in the tent of Achilles, Clytaemnestra, the Adventures of Dionysus, and the like. Besides the pottery, glass vases with bands and waves of different colours have been exhumed, as well as sepulchral inscriptions, *pithoi*, and cists. Certain marble blocks on the highest portion of the site of Thymbra probably mark the position of the historical temple of Apollo Thymbraeus, as opposed to that famous one of legend and myth which stood on Hanaï Tepeh, and was believed to have been the scene of the death of Achilles. A mutilated inscription discovered there, and published in Le Bas (*Voyage archéologique*, v. No. 1743 *d*), contains an inventory of the temple treasur

SECTION OF THE TROJAN PLAIN IN THE VALLEY OF THE THYMBRIUS.

The accompanying sketch No. 1570 shows a natural section of the left bank of the river Thymbrius (4) (Kemar Su), about 250 feet from the base of Hanaï Tepeh. Fragments of pottery (2), similar to those to be seen on the site of pre-historic Thymbra (Hanaï Tepeh), are found on the miocene rock (3), upon which there are from 4 to 6 feet of alluvial soil (1). The depth of this soil is relative to the irregular configuration of the rock which formed the actual surface in those pre-historic times. Some other fragments of pottery were discovered in sinking a well in the alluvium, some 600 yards to the east of this locality, and about 20 from the bed of the river, at a depth, from the surface, of 6 to 7 feet. If the arbitrary age of 3000 years be given to this pottery, the rate of increase of allu-

No. 1570.   Section of the Trojan Plain, Valley of the Thymbrius.

vium on the plain would average a foot in 500 years. Too much stress, however, cannot be laid on a uniform rate of deposit as proved by ocular evidence. For instance, a flood covers a large tract on the plain with sand and gravel a foot deep, destroying the land for cultivation ; some succeeding flood removes the whole of the detritus, lays bare the former surface, and perhaps adds a thin stratum of fertile sediment, re-adapting the land to agricultural purposes. The general effect of the floods in the plain of Troy is to elevate the beds and banks of the rivers : the coarser the matter held in mechanical suspension, the nearer it is deposited to the river; thus the Scamander, in the upper part of the plain, has formed two sloping levels from its banks to the hills on either side. The clear streams from the Bounarbashi and Duden springs, with their uniform flow and no tributary torrent to swell their volume or to bring down detritus, have thus had their courses directed along the base of the hills on either lower level of the plain.

NOTE.

From the above description given by my friend Mr. Frank Calvert of his exploration of Hanaï Tepeh, in which I assisted him in 1878 and 1879, it will be seen that all the peoples which succeeded each other on that hill interred their dead, and did not use cremation, which was in general use in all the five pre-historic cities of Hissarlik. The pottery, too, is widely different, for at Hanaï Tepeh all the vases (see the engravings No. 1546, 1547, 1560) have horizontal perforations for suspension with a string, while at Hissarlik all the perforations for suspension are vertical. There is certainly some analogy between the bowls found in the lowest stratum at Hanaï Tepeh and the bowls found in the first and lowest city at Hissarlik, because they have in common long horizontal tubes for suspension. But again, as will be seen by comparing the Hanaï fragments represented in the engravings No. 1543, 1544, and 1545, with similar ones from Hissarlik represented on p. 218, Nos. 39–42, the tubular holes are altogether different in shape and position. Besides, although tripods occur at Hanaï Tepeh, as at Hissarlik, the vase-feet are altogether different in form, and among the thousands of vase-feet at Hissarlik there is not one which resembles the vase-foot from Hanaï Tepeh represented under No. 1548. The same may be said of the vase-handles, which never occur at Hissarlik of the shape of those found at Hanaï Tepeh and represented under Nos. 1546, 1547, 1556 to 1559, and 1561. Conspicuous among the terra-cottas in the second stratum at Hanaï Tepeh is a dull blackish or grey hand-made pottery, which—as, for instance, the vase-fragment 1568—has in colour and fabric a great resemblance to the ancient Lydian pottery found at Hissarlik, immediately below the stratum of *débris* of the Ilium of the Aeolic colony. I may also lay stress on the fact that, among this pottery from the second Hanaï Tepeh stratum vase-handles occur with a cow or ox head, which likewise occurs on vase-handles in the Lydian city at Hissarlik, but never in any one of the five pre-historic cities of Hissarlik.

From all this we may conclude with the greatest certainty, that, although Hanaï Tepeh is only an hour's walk distant from Hissarlik, yet all the peoples which succeeded each other on that peculiar spot were altogether different from the pre-historic inhabitants on Hissarlik, except a Lydian colony, whose existence we infer from the pottery.

HENRY SCHLIEMANN.

APPENDIX V.

MEDICAL PRACTICE IN THE TROAD IN 1879.

By Professor Rudolf Virchow.

When last spring I accepted Dr. Schliemann's invitation to assist him in his excavations in the Troad, I was prompted to do so in no small degree by the hope that, in turning my back on the soil of Europe, I should also for some time turn it upon the whole mass of occupations which threatened to crush me. I did not suspect that the very occupation from which I had gradually withdrawn at home, the practice of medicine, would fall to my lot there in burdensome abundance. But scarcely had I been one day at Ilium, or, to speak less dogmatically, at Hissarlik, when some sick labourers were brought to me from among the large numbers employed by Dr. Schliemann, and this sufficed to spread over the whole of the Northern Troad the report that a newly-arrived Effendi was a great physician. The labourers, numbering from 120 to 150, who came every morning to the excavations from all parts of the neighbourhood, as well as the numerous persons who brought victuals and other necessaries, took care, in a country where foreigners are in themselves a very unusual sight, to excite a general curiosity.

I am at a loss to say whether there is a real physician in the Troad. Though I travelled through the country from the Hellespont to the Gulf of Adramyttium, yet I nowhere met with such a man. Even professional quacks did not come across me. Only the Greek priests practise a little medical manipulation here and there;

especially are they highly dangerous phlebotomists. Dr. Schliemann[1] has rightly denounced this practice, and has mentioned the terrific example of such a priest, who had bled a girl, seventeen years old, seven times in one month.

An apothecary's shop is as unknown in the Trojan land as a physician. We were obliged to send for our medicines to the Dardanelles, a distance of six or eight hours, when we needed to renew our stock; and when, on my journey to the west coast, I came to the village of Ghiekli, and for want of appropriate medicines wrote a prescription for a sick woman, her husband told me, in answer to my question whether he could get it made up, that he would go on purpose for it to the island of Tenedos. But that was a real voyage. Strange to say, the people appeared not even to know domestic remedies. Camomile grows in many places in such great abundance, that the whole air smells of it, like the kitchen of a Western hospital, but nevertheless I had some trouble to make the plant known to the people and to introduce its use. Juniper grows on all the mountain slopes, but nobody had ever made use of its berries. Happily we had an abundance of medicines. Dr. Schliemann had in former years been obliged to treat diseases in the Troad, and his medicine box was abundantly supplied. My friend Liebreich had

[1] *Troy and its Remains;* London, 1875, p. 141.

provided for me a complete travelling apothecary's store; and though I had taken it with me somewhat reluctantly, it rendered good service. Happily I had little need to make use of it for myself. Of the *vaseline* I must make a particular acknowledgment. Not only against the effects of sun-burning on the skin, but also in various other excoriations, especially from riding, it proved to be highly beneficial.

My practice consisted at first solely in receiving out-door patients. Besides our labourers and the other persons engaged on the excavations, people came seeking help from all the neighbourhood for a distance of from two to three hours. They came some on foot, some on horseback, others on donkeys. With the exception of small carts, which have wooden discs instead of wheels, there are still to the present day in the Troad neither vehicles nor real practicable roads. Even the women, therefore, ride when they have to go any long distance. Once only a sick person, a poor consumptive girl, in the last stage of exhaustion, was brought to me in a large basket hung on a horse, and, as usual, balanced by a second basket on the other side of the animal.

In the early morning a whole troop of persons seeking help, men, women, and children, gathered before our wooden barracks. They squatted in a long row in the shade of the kitchen building which was opposite to our barracks, and waited patiently till their turn came. Towards the end of my stay, when my reputation had extended, a second troop came about noon, for the most part from more distant localities.

But to this was gradually added a practice in the patients' houses. This was particularly the case in the nearest Greek village, Kalifatli, situated in the plain, which we had to pass in most of our excursions, especially in our rides to the Heroic tombs

on the west coast. Sometimes on our return late in the evening, people waited for us, and I cannot sufficiently praise the kind patience of my friend Schliemann, who, in spite of the pressing urgency of his affairs, and often in spite of his extreme fatigue, never for a moment grew impatient of acting the onerous part of interpreter, and explaining my prescriptions in a circumstantial and popular way with the greatest care and attention. Wherever we came, sick people gathered around us, their attention having probably been aroused by the communications of our workmen; and even on our journey through the mountains of Ida, the first act in the morning was usually to inspect those who sought help in the open market. Then followed, not seldom, the request to visit more serious cases at home.

For the most part my patients were Greeks, and their homes were principally in the Greek towns and villages; especially (besides Kalifatli) Ren Kioi on the Hellespont, Yeni Kioi and Yeni Shehr on the Aegean Sea. Turks, however, were not wanting. The Turkish official who had been sent by the Ministry to Hissarlik to watch the works, as well as the ten zaptiehs (gensdarmes) whom Dr. Schliemann always kept as an escort and safeguard, furnished from the first a certain contingent. The Turkish villages, especially Chiblak and Koum Kaleh, contributed their patients, and even Turkish women were brought to me. Besides these came Gipsies (Γύφτοι), who live in the country in large numbers, partly as nomads, partly as resident craftsmen, especially smiths. Our labourers were also composed of many nations; among them were Bulgarians, Armenians, and even Persians. It is easy to conceive what a trouble and what a loss of time it was, in this mixture of nationalities and languages, to carry on the examination of the sick and the explanation of the prescriptions, which had often to be done by two or more interpreters. Sometimes we almost despaired of making ourselves understood, for even the modern Greek *patois* of the men does not know many expressions which are current in the more civilized language of Athens. Thus, for instance, we did not succeed in ascertaining whether in this provincial dialect there exists a precise expression for diarrhoea.

On the whole, I was surprised to find a strong and healthy-looking population. Even the appearance of the women exhibited a favourable contrast with what I had seen, though only in the streets, at Constantinople and Scutari. Whilst in these large cities the faces of the women, so far as they were at all visible, exhibited a fearful paleness, nay a very strikingly bloated and anaemic appearance, I found the women of the Troad, even those from the very regions of fever, if not fresh-looking, at least less pale and of a purer complexion than the greater part of the female population of our large cities. Among the men there are a great number of very strong and well-built forms, and in their bronzed faces rosy cheeks are not wanting.

And yet it was a particularly critical time. The forty days' fast of Lent was approaching its end, and the whole Greek population was in a state of exhaustion, which could be very precisely measured by the daily decrease of the work done. When the first sick woman I spoke to, a person worn out by long fever, asked me what she should eat, and I prescribed to her a generous diet, I was not a little astonished to hear that Lent excludes altogether not only the eating of meat but even of eggs and fish, and that there is no dispensation for the sick or even for children. For forty consecutive days Lent is observed with the greatest austerity by the entire population! Such is the

influence of the priests, who are neither educated nor removed from the common pursuits of the people. Nay, I saw one of these gentlemen who kept a frequented inn, and who on Sunday was to be seen sitting in the middle of the bar-room smoking his nargileh.

In addition to Lent, with the atrophy it produces, comes a second mischievous influence, the malaria. The Trojan Plain is a notorious region of fever, nor can any one be astonished at this. Large swamps and marshes extend in all directions. Several rivers and rivulets disappear in them and fill the subsoil with their water. Shortly before my arrival, the Scamander had overflowed its banks and had inundated the plain far and wide. In the first week of April the whole land on its west side was still coated with thick silt and mud; all the roads were covered up, and stagnant water still stood in many places. Then the evaporation commenced, and in the evening a stinking fog lay over the plain. The various arms of the Kalifatli Asmak began soon afterwards to change from flowing watercourses into chains of stagnant pools and tanks. In short, all the conditions were supplied for the formation of malaria, for at the same time the temperature of the air increased rapidly, and at noon we had not seldom in the shade 20°, 22°, and even higher degrees centigrade (68°, 71·6° F., and upwards).

Nevertheless I did not see a single case of malignant fever proper. According to what the people say, it is only June and July that bring this increase of the malarious action. We remained exempt, though we did not follow for a single day the well-known rule, not to stay in the open air after sunset. How often did we ride by starlight or moonlight over the stinking plain! Sometimes after such rides, which were usually very long and fatiguing, I felt on the following morning a slight fulness in the head, so that for precaution's sake I took some quinine, but no trace of fever was observable. Among the population, intermittent fever, for the most part tertian, was the prevailing disease, but generally in lighter forms, though frequently the new attacks were developed on the basis of an old malarious condition, or as gradations of a chronic state of fever which had existed for five, six, or nine months. Tumours of the spleen are common among the people, and the term "spleen" ($\sigma\pi\lambda\dot{\eta}\nu$) is generally employed to express the disease. Many apparently similar diseases of course fall under the same term. Thus, for instance, one day a little boy was brought to me with a large echinococcus, and my assurances that it was no "spleen" were hardly believed. A man whom I consoled with the assurance that his wife had no "spleen," but that she would present him with a child in a few months, was quite panic-stricken, for they had been married for seven years without having any children. I had to refer him to the example of the old patriarch Jacob. Another, who believed himself to be sick of the spleen, had a most developed purpura (*morbus maculosus Werlhofii*); his disease was promptly cured by the administration of sulphuric acid, though at first he was very reluctant to take it. In other cases extraordinarily large spleens occurred. What was most striking, nay, really new to me, were the splenic tumours of the young children. In Kalifatli, which of all the Trojan localities has the most unfavourable situation in the midst of a swampy region, I saw a child of two years, and another of ten months, who had very large and hard splenic tumours; in the case of the latter child, the spleen filled almost the whole anterior part of the abdomen. This was the more remarkable, as with adults large splenic tumours were rare; and in the lighter and more recent cases they were generally hardly perceptible.

Another circumstance also struck me. Shortly before, I had visited the hospitals in Bucharest, and had seen there a larger number of fever-stricken patients. Dr. Glück had pointed out to me several cases in which ascites with chronic hepatitis (cirrhosis) had been engendered as a consequent disease, and he assured me that this is a frequent occurrence in the fever districts of Roumania. In the Troad I did not see a single case of the kind. Nor did even anasarca frequently occur.

At all events, we should have expected that malaria must exercise a great influence on the aspect of the people. If this is by no means generally the case, the reason is not that the number of fever districts is small. It is true that almost all the villages are built on heights, on purpose to avoid the fever. In the plain proper there are in all only three small settlements: the small town of Koum Kaleh at the mouth of the Scamander, and the two villages of Koum Kioi and Kalifatli. But even the villages situated on heights, and in fact always on heights of tertiary or volcanic rock, are not free from fever. Manifestly the malaria is brought to them by the winds. The fact that the inhabitants have nevertheless a decidedly healthy look, I am inclined to ascribe to their passing the greater part of their life in the open air. Many of them wander about with their herds and seldom come home. Almost all carry on agriculture over large tracts, and the women also take part in the work in the open field.

This manner of living of course exposes them to other diseases, especially to colds, and these were the order of the day just at the time when I was in the Troad, — during the whole month of April. Though the days were for the most part warm, and sometimes even hot, yet the temperature frequently fell in the night to 10° C., and lower; a quick change taking place at sunset. At the same time a strong wind generally prevailed, and in particular a cool sea-breeze. Under such circumstances, catarrhs and pneumonia were not to be wondered at. The severest pneumonia I saw was in the case of a man who had passed the nights without shelter in the field. None of these cases, however, terminated fatally. Nevertheless it is not improbable that at least some of the cases of consumption, of which very severe examples were brought to me, are to be attributed to the same cause. I have not been able to authenticate an immunity from consumption.

It deserves particular mention that I met with no trace of acute exanthemata, unless erysipelas should be counted amongst them. I saw neither small - pox, nor scarlet fever, nor measles. It may be that the slight intercourse with the outer world contributes to prevent these contagions. It is still, however, remarkable that such free spots are found on a continent. Of erysipelas I saw some very severe cases, the most severe being that of an elderly man, who had at the same time erysipelas of the face and a large roseolar swelling of both hands and fore-arms, with high fever. He also recovered.

Other contagious diseases, apart from skin affections, were also rare. Of lues I met with a single case (tertiary) in a foreign labourer. Scabies I saw sometimes; tinea (porrigo) also among children, but in slight forms.

A very large number of sick persons sought relief from chronic diseases, which had already subsided, but had been cured imperfectly, especially chronic diseases of the eye and ear. I extirpated an aural polypus; but for the rest I could do but little except that, particularly for the eye-diseases, I put myself in communication with Dr. Mühlig, the physician of the excellent German hospital in Constantinople, asking him to admit them. Of surgical cases but few occurred; but on the other hand a comparatively large number of chronic nervous diseases, particularly spasms and paralysis. Among the more frequent skin diseases, I may mention a remarkable case of *ichthyosis cornea palmaris.*

Finally, a case of particular interest to me was that of a little boy with geophagia. He was a child seven years old, with a somewhat bloated thick face. The abdomen was rather protuberant, though I could not feel any tumour in it, and the mucous membrane of the mouth was entirely anaemic. In the vessels of the neck there was a remarkably loud anaemic murmur. Though he was the son of the shepherd who brought us every morning excellent fresh sheep's milk, and though the opportunity for a similar indulgence was certainly not wanting to him, he nevertheless, "from the time he walked," had preferred to eat earth, that is to say the common earth, consisting of calcareous clay, which forms the soil of the pasture. Formerly he is said to have had a healthy appearance, but now he is small and weak for his age. His parents declared that they had tried in vain to break him of his propensity. Whether the iron powder which I gave him has cured him, I do not know.

On the whole I cannot complain of the results of my medical campaign. The sick were obedient; and, even when I went altogether in opposition to their habits, they were compliant. Schliemann writes to me, in his enthusiastic way, from Ilium (May 10): "All your sick in Kalifatli are perfectly cured, and, blessing you, they exclaim:

ᾧ Τρῶες κατὰ ἄστυ θεῷ ὡς εὐχετόωντο."

At the same time he relates the following story, which is characteristic of the East and its formation of myths. For the purpose of a geological investigation of the soil of the Trojan Plain, I had ordered a hole to be dug in the neighbourhood of Kalifatli, in an ancient river-course. Having little time, I set two labourers to work there, and instructed them to dig on until they reached water. In the meantime I rode with my zaptieh (gendarme) to the Ujek and Besika Tepehs, but was so much hindered that it was after nightfall when I returned to the place. As the matter was important to me, I ordered the servants to light matches, examined the hole attentively, and took away some of the excavated earth. On the following days I again returned to the spot several times, and investigated the condition of the soil. This had evidently excited the curiosity of the people, who did not understand the purpose of the work. Under the date of June 4, Schliemann wrote to me from Troy: " Your excavation in the bed of the Kalifatli has been reverently enclosed by the villagers with a wall of stones; a great magical virtue is attributed to the spring you brought to light in it, which is called τὸ πηγάδι τοῦ ἰατροῦ (the Doctor's spring); all the villagers fetch their water from it."

In this way local legends still originate in the East at the present day. Though it was not possible for me on the island of Kos to seek out the old plane-tree under which the father of medicine, Hippocrates, is said to have received his patients, yet a vivid picture of the old state of things has been disclosed to me. This people is still in many respects just what it was thousands of years ago; especially in point of personal gratitude. Schliemann, who had formerly practised medicine with much success in the Troad, and to whom I had therefore given the name of Machaon, has for a long time been in doubt whether the people were thankful.[2] I myself had the same doubts; but when the people learnt that I gathered flowers daily, no morning passed without our table being covered with fragrant bouquets; and when on my return journey to the Dardanelles I rode through Ren Kioi, so many bouquets of stock gilly-flowers (levkoies) and basilicum (which are grown in flower-pots on the balconies and on the terraces of the houses) were presented to me, that I had great trouble to find a place about me in which to put them.

[2] *Troy and its Remains*, pp. 89, 142.

APPENDIX VI.

CATALOGUE OF THE PLANTS HITHERTO KNOWN OF THE TROAD, COMPILED ACCORDING TO THE COLLECTIONS OF PROFESSOR RUDOLF VIRCHOW AND DR. JULIUS SCHMIDT, AND FROM THE LITERARY SOURCES BY PROFESSOR PAUL ASCHERSON OF BERLIN, PROFESSOR THEODOR VON HELDREICH OF ATHENS, AND DOCTOR F. KURTZ OF BERLIN.

THE Troad [1] belongs in a botanical point of view to the least known countries of Asia Minor. Though this country has been visited or wandered through by several of the most renowned botanical travellers, such as Forskål (1761) and Dumont d'Urville (1819), who merely visited the island of Tenedos, Olivier (1794 and 1798), Sibthorp (1794?), Barker Webb and Parolini (1819), Aucher-Eloy and Gust. Coquebert de Montbret (1833), who explored the Troad proper, yet these explorations did not lead to detailed communications on the plants of the regions visited, because some of the travellers named visited the Troad in an unfavourable season, midsummer or autumn, whilst others did not publish anything on their collections, of which only some species have here and there become known. At least as much, therefore, as to the botanists by profession, if indeed not more, are we indebted for our knowledge of the Trojan flora to travellers, who besides their principal archaeological, geological, or geographical objects of study, paid also attention to the ever-attractive children of Flora; such were Clarke (1801), Tchihatcheff (1849), Julius Schmidt (1864), and Rudolf Virchow (1879); supplementary information has also been received from Frank Calvert (1879 and 1880). The collections of the three last-named explorers are for the most part given here for the first time (that of J. Schmidt according to the communications of Th. von Heldreich). From them and from the sporadic notices contained in botanical literature on collections of former travellers we gather that (including cultivated plants) there are scarcely 500 kinds of plants known to belong to the Troad, which number constitutes at most a quarter or one-third part of the plants existing there. But doubtless in a country which offers such favourable conditions for the vegetation, a country too which—from the sandy and rocky sea-coast and the swampy plain to the lofty summits of the mountains abounding in forests and springs, and only for some months free from snow—offers a manifold variety of situation and geological formation, there are still reserved for the future splendid botanical discoveries.

Since many of the future travellers to the Troad will certainly be active in this direction, an enumeration of the plants hitherto known—however incomplete it must be—seems to be useful in this place.

---

[1] The territory, from which botanical information has been collected in this catalogue, is far more restricted than the area of the Troas as understood at p. 67 of this work. It extends, on the shore, southward as far as Adramyttium (Edremit), northward to the Quarantine (between Rhoiterion and the Dardanelles).

To economize space the names of the more frequently occurring observers are abbreviated, namely—

C = Clarke   T = Tchihatcheff
F = Forskål   V = Virchow
S = Julius Schmidt   W = Barker Webb.

RANUNCULACEAE.

Anemone coronaria, L. In the Troad widely spread, e.g. In Tepeh (C.), Novum Ilium (V.), Bounarbashi (C.), Gargarus (C.).

A. stellata, Lmk. Bali Dagh (C.).

A. formosa, Clarke. Gargarus (C.).

A. blanda, Schott and Kotschy. Bali Dagh (C.), Gargarus (C.).

Adonis aestivalis, L. Tumulus of Achilles (V.), Plain of Troy (V.).

Ranunculus aquatilis, L. In Tepeh Asmak (V.), Kalifatli Asmak (V.).

R. ficariiformis, F. Schultz. Novum Ilium, grove of fig-trees above the springs (V.). ? Tenedos (Virlet).

R. orientalis, L. Ida region (V.).

? *R. Reuterianus*, Boiss. Between Nurlü and Tchaukhlar (T.).

R. velutinus, Ten. Plain of Troy (S.).

R. sceleratus, L. Plain of Troy (S.).

R. ophioglossifolius, Vill. Plain of Troy (S.).

R. trachycarpus, Fisch. et Mey. Plain of Troy (S.).

R. arvensis, L. Plain of Troy (S.).

Ceratocephalus falcatus, Pers. Valley of the Kimar Su (Calvert).

Nigella arvensis, L., var. *involucrata*, Boiss. Tenedos (D'Urville).

N. sativa, L. Troad, cult. (W.).

Paeonia decora, Anders. Below the source of the Scamander (V.).

BERBERIDACEAE.

Leontice Leontopetalum, L. Plain of Troy (V.), e.g. near Bounarbashi (C.).

PAPAVERACEAE.

Papaver dubium, L. Troad (V.).

P. Argemone, L., var. Valley of Aiwajik Su, near Esheklü (V.), Assos (V.).

FUMARIACEAE.

Hypecoum procumbens, L. Plain of Troy (C. W.), Hissarlik (V.).

Corydallis Marschalliana, Pers. ? (*Fumaria bulbosa*, Clarke). Source of the Scamander (C.).

Fumaria officinalis, L. Troad (C.).

F. Vaillantii, Loisel. On the Hellespont, near the Quarantine (V.).

F. parviflora, Lmk. Troad (C.).

F. anatolica, Boiss. Plain of Troy (S.).

F. Gussonei, Boiss., var. *umbrosa*, Hausskn. Plain of Troy (S.).

CRUCIFERAE.

Matthiola tricuspidata, R. Br. Sandy strand of Talian Kioi near Alexandria Troas (V.).

Cardamine hirsuta, L. ? (*C. tenella*, Clarke). Bounarbashi (C.).

C. graeca, L. Troy (V.). Between Kelbi and Tchaukhlar (T.).

Dentaria bulbifera, L. Mountain forests of the Troad (T.).

Arabis verna, R. Br. Upper Scamander valley (V.).

A. albida, Steven. Between Nurlü and Tchaukhlar (T.).

Nasturtium officinale, R. Br. At the springs near Novum Ilium (V.).

Erysimum smyrnaeum, Boiss. Ida region (V.).

Sisymbrium polyceratium, L. Tenedos (F.). In Greek, ἀγριοτιάρα.

Malcolmia flexuosa, Sm. Port of Alexandria Troas (V.). Tenedos (Olivier).

Aubrietia deltoidea, DC. Rock above the Scamander source (C.), Alexandria Troas (V.).

Vesicaria graeca, Reut. Troy (V.).

Alyssum umbellatum, Desv. Troy (V.).

A. campestre, L. Troy (V.).

Koniga maritima, R. Br. Troad (W.).

Draba muralis, L. Kestambul (V.).

Aethionema ovalifolium, Boiss. ? (*Thlaspi saxatile*, Clarke). Scamander source (C.).

Cakile maritima, Scop. Sandy beach opposite Tenedos (F.).

Sinapis arvensis, L. Among oats (Calvert).

CAPPARIDACEAE.

Capparis spinosa, L. Troad (W.), Tenedos (F.). Greek, ῥιμονιαριά.

RESEDACEAE.

Reseda Phyteuma, L. ? (*R. alba trigyna undata*, Forsk.). Tenedos (F.). Greek ἀγριοχάρθαμο.

R. lutea, L. Tumulus of Patroclus (V.).

CISTACEAE.

Cistus villosus, L. Mountains near Ghiekli (V.) ? Scamander source (*C. crispus*, Clarke) (C.). Var. *creticus*, Boiss. Between Nurlü and Akhmetlü (T.).

C. salviifolius, L. Ren Kioi (V.), Troy (V.), Ida district (V.).

Helianthemum guttatum, Mill. Troy (V.).

VIOLACEAE.

Viola silvatica, Fr. Chigri Dagh (V.), Between Nurlü and Tchaukhlar (T.).

Viola olympica, Boiss. Between Nurlü and Tchaukhlar (T.).

SILENACEAE.

Dianthus erinaceus, Boiss., var. *alpinus*, Boiss. (*D. juniperinus*, Webb; *D. Webbianus*, Parol.). On the summit of the Gargarus (W. Parolini).

D. glutinosus, Boiss. et Heldr. (*D. pubescens*, D'Urv.). Tenedos, on sunny hills, not rare (D'Urville).

Tunica velutina, Fisch. et Mey.   Plain of Troy (S.).

T. Sibthorpii, Boiss.   Troad (Olivier).

Saponaria Vaccaria, L., var. *grandiflora*, Boiss.   Plain of Troy (S.)

Silene conica, L.   Plain of Troy (S.).

S. Behen, L.   Plain of Troy (S.).

S. colorata, Poir.   Stomalimne (V.)., Troy (V.). Tenedos (Virlet). Var. *canescens*, Heldr. Plain of Troy (S.).

S. fabaria, Sm.? (*Cucubalus foliis crassis*, Forsk.).   Tenedos, rock (F.).

S. inflata, Sm.   Troad (S.).   Var. *rubriflora*, Boiss.   Troad (S.).

ALSINACEAE.

Alsine setacea, Mert. et Koch.   Var. *anatolica*, Boiss.   Gargarus (Aucher).

A. tenuifolia, Wahlenb.   Troad (S.).

Arenaria leptoclados, Rchb.   Troad (S.).

Stellularia media, Cir.   Plain of Troy (S.).

Moenchia mantica, Bartl.   Troy (S., V.).   Hill at Sigeum (V.).

Cerastium brachypetalum, Desp.   Var. *luridum*, Boiss.   Troad (S.).

PARONYCHIACEAE.

Herniaria incana, Lmk.   Troad (S.).

Paronychia argentea, Lmk.   Troad (W.).

MOLLUGINACEAE.

Mollugo Cerviana, Ser.   Troad (W.).

TAMARISCACEAE.

Tamarix parviflora, DC.   At the Scamander and Simois in the Plain (V.).   The μυρίκη mentioned by Homer.

HYPERICACEAE.

Triadenia Russeggeri, Fenzl.   Adramyttion (Montbret).

Hypericum rhodopeum, Friv.   (*H. recognitum* Fischer et Meyer).   Between Nurlü and Tchaukhlar, in a low stony situation (T.).

?*H. olympicum*, Forsk., hardly L.   Tenedos (F.).   Greek γουδοῦρα, ἀγουδοῦρα or ἀγαθουδέρα.

H. Aucheri, Jaub. et Spach.   Gargarus (Aucher), Adramyttion (Montbret)?   Between Nurlü and Akhmetlü (*H. procumbens*, T., hardly Michx.).

H. supinum, Vis.   On the gulf of Adramyttion, near the ancient Antandros (Parolini).

H. Montbretii, Jaub. et Spach.   Alexandria Troas (V.), Kestambul (V.).

MALVACEAE.

Malope malacoides, L.   Alexandria Troas (V.).

?*Malva Tournefortiana*, Forsk., hardly L.

Tenedos (F.).   Greek, μολλοχά; Turkish, achedjumez.

Abelmoschus esculentus, Mnch.   Troad, cult. (W.).   Greek, βαμιά; Turkish, bamia.

Gossypium herbaceum, L.   Is extensively cultivated in the Plain of Troy (Olivier, W. V.).   In Tenedos, scantily cultivated (F. Olivier).

TILIACEAE.

Tilia intermedia, DC.   Below the Scamander source, very sparingly (V.).

LINACEAE.

Linum alpinum, Jacq.   Besika Tepeh (V.), Chigri Dagh (V.).

GERANIACEAE.

Geranium asphodeloides, Willd.   Valley of the Aiwajik Su near Esheklü (V.).

G. dissectum, L.   Plain of Troy (Calvert).

ZYGOPHYLLACEAE.

Tribulus terrester, L.   Troad (W.).

Peganum Harmala, L.   Troad (W.), Tenedos, on the beach (F.).   Greek, βρομοχόρταρο; Turkish, yserlik.

RUTACEAE.

Ruta chalepensis, L.   Troad (W.).

SAPINDACEAE.

Acer creticum, L., var. *obtusifolium*, Boiss.   Troad (T.).

AMPELIDACEAE.

Vitis vinifera, L.   In the Plain of Troy, very often wild (W.), e.g. at the In Tepeh Asmak, Simois, Thymbrius, Kimar Su (V.); but sparingly cultivated, by the Mahomedans only for the grapes; for the making of wine, only at Yeni Shehr, Yeni Kioi (W.), Ren Kioi (V.).   Chiefly on Tenedos, the wine of which is celebrated.   In this island, viticulture was flourishing already in ancient times, the arms of ancient Tenedos showing a grape.

TEREBINTHACEAE.

Rhus Coriaria, L.   Sumach.   Wild on hills near the sea (W.).

Pistacia Terebinthus, L.   In the Plain of Troy, not rare (W. V.); also near Ren Kioi, and on the Oulou Dagh (V.).

P. Lentiscus, L.   Troad (W.).

PAPILIONACEAE.

Anagyris foetida, L.   Found all over the Troad (C. W. S.), e.g. on the banks of the In Tepeh Asmak, and near Novum Ilium (V.).   Is not eaten by the cattle.

Adenocarpus divaricatus, DC.   Middle region of the Ida above Evjilar (W.).

Calycotome villosa, Lk. (*Spartium spinosum*, Webb).   Troad (W.), e.g. Oulou Dagh (V.).

?*Spartium Scorpius*, Webb.   Troas (W.).

S. junceum, L. Troad (W.). Between Nurlü and Akhmetlü (T.).

Genista lydia, Boiss. Gargarus (Aucher).

Cytisus smyrnaeus, Boiss. Between Nurlü and Tchaukhlar (T.).

Trigonella spicata, Sm. Between Nurlü and Akhmetlü (T.).

T. cretica, Boiss. Between Nurlü and Akhmetlü (T.).

Medicago marina, L. Troad (S.). On the shore of the Hellespont, near Koum Kaleh (V.).

M. orbicularis, All., var. *marginata*, Benth. Plain of Troy (Calvert).

M. coronata, Desv. Troad (S.).

M. hispida, Urb., var. *denticulata*, Urb. Plain of Troy (Calvert).

M. arabica, All. Plain of Troy (Calvert).

M. minima, Bartal. Troad (S.).

Melilotus sulcatus, Desf. Plain of Troy (Calvert).

M. neapolitanus, Ten. Troad (S.).

Trifolium Cherleri, L. Troad (S.).

T. stellatum, L. Troad (S.), e.g. on the Kalifatli Asmak, not far from the mouth of the Simois (V.).

T. scabrum, L. Plain of Troy (Calvert). Between Nurlü and Tchaukhlar (T.).

T. Bocconei, Savi. Plain of Troy (Calvert).

T. spumosum, L. Plain of Troy (Calvert), Ida district (V.).

T. repens, L. Troad (S.).

T. uniflorum L. Bounarbashi (C.), between Nurlü and Tchaukhlar (T.).

  procumbens, L. (*T. agrarium*, Poll.). Plain of Troy (S. Calvert), Alexandria Troas (V.), between Tuzla and Hasii (T.).

Physanthyllis tetraphylla, Boiss. Troad (W.), between Nurlü and Akhmetlü (T.).

Hymenocarpus circinatus, Savi. Plain of Troy (S. V.).

Lotus creticus, L., var. *cytisoides*, Boiss. Troad (S.).

L. belgradica, Forsk. Tenedos (F.) ?

Bonaveria Securidaca, Scop. Between Nurlü and Akhmetlü (T.).

Coronilla emeroides, Boiss. et Spr. (*C. Emerus*, Webb), Troad (W.).

C. glauca, L. Troad (W.).

C. parviflora, Willd. Frequently in the Plain of Troy (S. V.), e.g. on the Kalifatli Asmak (V.). It has yellow and pink, seldom white flowers.

Psoralea bituminosa, L. Troad (S.). Var. *major*, Heldr. Troad (S.).

Glycyrrhiza glabra, L., var. *glandulifera*, Regel et Herd. (*G. hirsuta*, Pall.). Troad (W.).

Astragalus Haarbachii, Sprun. Troad (S.).

A. Virchowii, Aschs. et Kurtz (*A. christianus*, Webb). Yeni Shehr, not far from the tumulus of Achilles (V.).

A. anatolicus, Boiss.? (*A. longiflorus*, Clarke hardly Pallas). Troad (C.).

A. trojanus, Stev. (*A. Tragacantha*, Webb), Troad (Olivier, Aucher).

Onobrychis aequidentata, D'Urv. Troad (S.), e.g. Sigeum (V.), Bali Dagh (V.).

Cicer arietinum, L. Troad, cultivated (W. Calvert).

C. Montbretii, Jaub. et Spach. Ida district (V.), Gargarus (Aucher, Montbret).

Vicia hybrida, L. Troad (S.), e. g. Hissarlik (V.). Tenedos (Virlet).

V. melanops, Sibth. et Sm. Troad (V.).

V. grandiflora, Scop. Between Nurlü and Tchaukhlar (T.) Var. *Biebersteiniana*, Koch. Troad (V.).

V. sativa, L., var. *macrocarpa*, Boiss. Troad (S.).

V. Cosentinii, Guss., var. *amphicarpa*, Heldr. Troad (S.).

V. lathyroides, L. Between Nurlü and Tchaukhlar (T.).

V. cuspidata, Boiss. Troad (V.).

V. peregrina, L. Troad (V.).

V. Faba, L. Troad, cultivated (V.).

V. Cracca, L. Troad (V.).

V. villosa, Rth. Troad (V.).

V. laxiflora, Boiss. Kotch Ali Ovassi (V.).

V. smyrnaea, Boiss. Besika Tepeh (V.).

V. hirsuta, Koch. Troad (S.).

V. Ervilia, Willd. Troad, cultivated (Calvert).

Lens esculenta, Mnch. Troad, cultivated (W.).

Lathyrus Aphaca, L. Troad (S.).

L. sativus, L. Troad, cultivated (Calvert).

L. Cicera, L., var. *pilosus*, Alef. Troad (S. V.).

L. setifolius, L. Troad (S.).

L. saxatilis, Vis. Troad (S).

Orobus sessilifolius, Sibth. et Sm. Troad (S. V.). Between Nurlü and Tchaukhlar. (T.)

O. hirsutus, L. Troad (V.). Between Nurlü and Tchaukhlar (T.) Var. *glabratus*, Gris. Troad (S. V.).

Pisum elatius, M. B. Troad (S.).

Phaseolus vulgaris, L. Troad, cult. (W. Calvert).

Dolichos Lubia, Forsk. Troad, cult. (Calvert).

CAESALPINIACEAE.

Cercis Siliquastrum, L. Alexandria Troas (V.). On the Iné Tchai (V.). Between Nurlü and Akhmetlü (T.).

AMYGDALACEAE.

Amygdalus Webbii, Spach. Bali Dagh (W. V.).

A. communis, L. Cultivated in the vicinity of the villages (V.), e.g. in the Simois valley (C.).

A. Persica, L. Like the foregoing (V.).

POMACEAE.

Pirus communis, L. Forms frequently bushes in the Plain of Troy, more seldom trees, e.g. Koumi Koi (V.). On the In Tepeh Asmak

(V.)   Tenedos (*Prunus oxyacantha*, Forsk.).
Greek, ἀχλάδα; also cultivated.
P. Malus, L.   Aggdagh (T.).   Cultivated in
the neighbourhood of the villages (V.).
Crataegus monogyna, Jacq.   Often in the underwood, of the plain and the mountains (V.),
e. g. Novum Ilium (V.), upper Scamander
valley (V.).

ROSACEAE.

Rosa canina, L.?   In bushes, particularly on
the river-banks, frequent (V.).
Rubus sanctus, Schrb.?   In bushes, particu-
larly on river-banks, frequent (V.).
R. tomentosus, Borkh.   Gargarus (W.).
Potentilla micrantha, Ramond?   (*Fragaria
sterilis*, Clarke, whether L.?)   Gargarus
(C.).
Aremonia agrimonioides, Neck.   Alexandria
Troas (V.).
Sanguisorba spinosa, Bertol.   In the bushes
of the Plain of Troy and the hills, so fre-
quent that it is used for fuel, e. g. near
the In Tepeh, Novum Ilium, Besika Tepeh
(V.).

MYRTACEAE.

Myrtus communis, L.   Troad (W. V.).

GRANATACEAE.

Punica Granatum, L.   Troad, wild and cultivated (W.).

CUCURBITACEAE.

Citrullus vulgaris, Schrad.   Troad, cult. (W.).
Ecbalium Elaterium, Rich.   Hissarlik (V.).
The seed of this plant was found in ex-
cavating.
Bryonia dioeca, Jacq.?   Troad (V.).

CRASSULACEAE.

Umbilicus pendulinus, DC.   Kotch Ali Ovassi
(V.).
Sedum Cepaea, L.   Bali Dagh, "tumulus of
Hector" (C.).

UMBELLIFERAE.

Eryngium campestre, L.   Tenedos (F.).   Greek,
ἀγγαθία.
E. bithynicum, Boiss.? (*E. tricuspidatum*, Sibth.
et Sm, hardly L.).   Plain of Troy (Sib-
thorp).
E. foetidum, Forsk., not L.   Tenedos (F.).
Lagoecia cuminoides, L.   Troad (V.).
Bupleurum trichopodum, Boiss. et Sprun.
Troad (S.).
Apium graveolens, L.   Assos (V.).
Ammi majus, L.   Tenedos (F.).   Greek, ἀσ-
προκέφαλος.
Physocaulus nodosus, Tausch.   Troad (S.).
Anthriscus nemorosa, M. B., var. *anatolica*,
Boiss.   Gargarus (Aucher).
A. vulgaris, Pers., var. *pubescens*, Heldr.
Troad (S.).
Scandix grandiflora, L.   Troad (S.), e. g. His-
sarlik (V.).

`Bifora testiculata*, DC.   Troad (V.).
Smyrnium Orphanidis, Boiss.?   Ruins of Assos
(V.).
Hippomarathrum cristatum, Boiss.?   Troad
(S.).
Echinophora Sibthorpiana, Guss.   Troad (S.),
vineyards on Tenedos frequent (D'Urville).
Oenanthe silaifolia, M. B.   On the Bounar-
bashi Su, near the bridge (V.).
Foeniculum officinale, All.   On the Kimar Su
(V.).
Crithmum maritimum, L.   Rocky coast of the
Troad (W.).
Ferula communis, L.   Troad (S.), e. g. on the
In Tepeh Asmak, above the bridge (V.).
Tordylium officinale, L.   Troad (S.).
T. apulum, L.   Troad (S.), Alexandria Troas
(V.).
Opopanax orientale, Boiss.   Troad (S.).
Daucus Broterii, Ten.?   (*Artedia muricata*,
Forsk.).   Tenedos (F.).   Greek, ἀξιγγάνο.
Caucalis leptophylla, L.   Troad (S.).

ARALIACEAE.

Hedera Helix, L.   Ida district (V.).

CORNACEAE.

Cornus mas, L.   Troad (T., V.).

CAPRIFOLIACEAE.

Lonicera Caprifolium, L.?   Troad (V.).
L. orientalis, Lmk.   Between Karajilar and
Divanjik (T.).

RUBIACEAE.

Rubia peregrina, L.   Troad (S.).
R. Olivieri, A. Rich.   Hedges near Beira-
mitch (V.).
Sherardia arvensis, L.   Plain of Troy (S., Cal-
vert).
Galium Aparine, L.   Troad (S.).
Vaillantia muralis, L., var. *hirsuta*, Guss.
Troad (S.).
V. hispida, L.   Troad (S.).

VALERIANACEAE.

Valeriana Dioscoridis, Sm.   Troad (C.).   Upper
Scamander valley (V.).
Centranthus ruber, DC.   Troad (W.).
Valerianella coronata, DC.   Hissarlik (V.),
Tumulus of Batieia (V.).

DIPSACACEAE.

Knautia hybrida, Coult.   Valley of the Aiwa-
jik Su near Esheklü (V.).
Scabiosa ochroleuca, L., var. *Webbiana*, Boiss.
(*S. Webbiana*, Don).   Ida mountains (W.,
Parolini).

COMPOSITAE.

Bellis perennis, L.   Near the Kalifatli Asmak
(V.).
Asteriscus aquaticus, Mnch.?   (*Buphthalmum
maritimum*, Forsk.).   Tenedos (F.).   Greek,
χόρτο καδιφέ.

Inula heterolepis, Boiss. (*Conyza candida*, Webb, not L.). Troad (W.).

I. viscosa, Ait. Besika Tepeh (V.).

Diotis maritima, Sm. Sea-shore of the Troad (W.).

Anthemis altissima, L. Plain of Troy (Calvert). Tenedos (D'Urville).

A. arvensis, L. Plain of Troy (V.).

Matricaria Chamomilla, L. Plain of Troy (Calvert).

Chamaemelum trojanum, Bory et Chaub. Tenedos (Virlet).

? *C. caucasicum*, Boiss. Between Nurlü and Tchaukhlar (T.).

Artemisia maritima, L. Strand near Koum Kaleh (V.).

Doronicum caucasicum, M. B. Between Nurlü and Tchaukhlar (T.).

Senecio vernalis, W. K. Between Nurlü and Tchaukhlar (T.).

Calendula arvensis, L. Hissarlik (V.).

Echinops viscosus, DC. (*E. sphaerocephalus*, Forsk. not L.). Tenedos (D'Urville). Greek, κάθαρ ἄγγαθο.

E. microcephalus, Sibth. et Sm. ? (*E. strigosus*, Forsk., not L.). Tenedos (F.).

Cardopatium corymbosum, Pers. Troad, Tenedos (Olivier).

Carlina lanata, L. ? (*C. rubra*, Forsk.). Tenedos (F.). Greek, κοκινάγγαθο (that is, red Thistle).

Cynara Scolymus, L. Troad (W.).

Jurinea mollis, Rchb. ? (*Serratula centauroides*, Forsk.). Coast of the Troad, opposite Tenedos (F.).

Centaurea Cyanus, L. Chigri Dagh (V.).

C. lanigera, DC. Between Akhmetlü and Nurlü (T.).

C. polyclada, DC. (*C. arenaria*, D'Urv., not M. B.). Troad ? (Aucher). Dry hills on Tenedos, frequent (D'Urville).

C. spinosa, L. (*Serratula spinosa*, Forsk. ?). Troad (Olivier), Tenedos, on dry uncultivated hills very frequent (D'Urv.). Greek, 'Ιαλαστυβιά, Turk. djevvan. Is fastened on the hedges (F.).

C. solstitialis, L. Troad (W.), ? Tenedos (*C. tomentosa*, Forsk. Greek, ἀτρόγιρα).

C. Parolinii, DC. (*C. aurea*, Webb). Summit of Gargarus (W., Parolini).

Carthamus dentatus, Vahl. Troad (Parolini).

Scolymus hispanicus, L. (*Catananche lutea*, F. not L.). Troad (W.), Tenedos (F.). Greek, σαρδάλρια or κετρινάγγαθο.

Cichorium Intubus, L. Tenedos (F.). Greek, κόρλα.

C. Endivia, L. Tenedos (probably cult.) (F.). Greek ραδίκη ; Turk. hiddiba.

Hedypnois cretica, Willd. Plain of Troy (Calvert), Tenedos (F.). Greek, κολτζίδα.

Tragopogon porrifolius, L. ? Kotch Ali Ovassi (V.), Assos (V.).

Taraxacum officinale, Web. Meadows along the Kalifatli Asmak (V.).

Picridium vulgare, Desf. Tenedos (F.).

Crepis rubra, L. Valley of the Aiwajik Su, near Esheklü (V.).

Rodigia commutata, Spr. Troy (V.).

Lagoseris bifida, Boiss. Tenedos (Virlet).

CAMPANULACEAE.

Campanula lyrata, Lmk. Troad (V.)

C. Erinus, L. Troad (S.).

Podanthum cichoriiforme, Boiss. Troad (S.).

Specularia Speculum - Veneris, Alph. DC. Fulah Dagh near the Thymbrius (Kimar Su), white and blue flower (V.).

Sp. pentagonia, Alph. DC. Troad (V.).

ERICACEAE.

Arbutus Unedo, L. Upper Scamander valley (V.).

A. Andrachne, L. Oulou Dagh (V.), on the Scamander, between Karajilar and Divanjik (T.), upper Scamander valley (C., V.).

Erica arborea, L. Troad (W.), e. g. Oulou Dagh (V.).

Rhododendron flavum Don (*Azalea pontica*, L.). Between Karajilar and Divanjik (T.).

PRIMULACEAE.

Cyclamen europaeum, Webb, hardly L. Troad (W.).

STYRACACEAE.

Styrax officinalis, L. Troad (W., S.), e. g. slopes of Hissarlik towards the Simois valley (V.).

OLEACEAE.

Olea europaea, L. Cultivated in the neighbourhood of the villages (V.).

Phillyrea media, L. Troad (W.).

Fontanesia phillyreoides, Labill. Between Bairamkioi (Assos) and Shubrak (T.).

JASMINACEAE.

Jasminum fruticans, L. Troad (W.), e. g. Hissarlik (V.).

APOCYNACEAE.

Nerium Oleander, L. Troad (W.). Greek, ροδοδάφνη or πικροδάφνη.

ASCLEPIADACEAE.

Periploca graeca, L. Plain of Troy (W.).

SESAMACEAE.

Sesamum indicum, L. Troad, cult. (Olivier, W., Calvert , Tenedos, rarely cultivated and growing wild (F., Olivier, D'Urville). Greek, σισάμι.

CONVOLVULACEAE.

Convolvulus tenuissimus, Sibth. et Sm. Troad (V.).

C. arvensis, L. Plain of Troy (Calvert).

BORAGINACEAE.

Heliotropium europaeum, L.   Troad (W.).
H. sp.   Evjilar (W.).
Cerinthe major, L.   Troad (W.).
Anchusa officinalis, L.   Plain of Troy (V.),
between Nurlü and Akhmetlü (T.).
Onosma stellulata, W. K., var. *pallida*, Boiss.
Alexandria Troas (V.), Kestambul (V.).
Echium plantagineum, L.   Valley of the Thym-
brius (Kimar Su) (V.)?   Tenedos (*E. creti-
cum*, Forsk.'.
Lithospermum apulum, L.   On the Hellespont,
near the Quarantine (V.).
L. purpureo-caeruleum, L.   Upper Scamander
valley (V.).
Alkanna tinctoria, Tausch.   Troad (C., V.).
Myosotis hispida, Schlechtd.   Kalifatli (V.'.
Cynoglossum pictum, Ait.   Valley of the
Thymbrius (Kimar Su) (V.), between Nurlü
and Akhmetlü (T.).
Asperugo procumbens, L.   Valley of the
Thymbrius (Kimar Su) (V.).

SOLANACEAE.

Solanum sodomaeum, L.   Troad (W.).
S. Melongena, L.   Troad, cult. (W.).
Hyoscyamus albus, L.   Tenedos (F.).
H. aureus, L.   Tenedos (F.).   Greek, μελο-
χόρταρο.

SCROPHULARIACEAE.

Verbascum phlomoides, L.   Troad (W.), Tene-
dos (F.).   Greek, φλόμο.
V. sinuatum, L.   Troad (W.).
Linaria Pelicieriana, DC.   Novum Ilium (V.),
Besika Tepeh (V.), valley near Tuzla (T.).
L. arvensis, Desf.   Troad (C.).
Scrophularia canina, L.   Assos (V.).
Veronica multifida, L.   Troad (V.).
Eufragia latifolia, Gris.   Plain of Troy (Oli-
vier, Calvert), e. g. Hissarlik (V.).
E. viscosa, Benth.   Plain of Troy (Olivier).
Trixago apula, Stev.   Plain of Troy (Calvert),
between Nurlü and Akhmetlü (T.).

OROBANCHACEAE.

Phelipaea ramosa, C. A. Mey.   Fulah Dagh
(V.), Alexandria Troas (V.).   Var. *Muteli*,
Boiss.   Assos (V.).
Orobanche pubescens, D'Urv.   Troad (V.'.

ACANTHACEAE.

? *Acanthus mollis*, L.   Troad (W.).

VERBENACEAE.

Vitex Agnus-castus, L.   Troad (W.) e. g.
Valley of the Simois (V.).   Also between
Chigri Dagh and Iné (Sayce).   Greek,
λιγαριά.

LABIATAE.

Lavandula Stoechas, L.   Troad (W.).
Mentha, sp.   On the Kalifatli Asmak (V.).
Origanum vulgare, L., var. *viride*, Boiss.?

Tenedos (F.).   The ὀρίγανον of Tenedos is
praised by ancient classics.
O. Onites, L.   Troad (W.) e. g. at the Scaman-
der source. (C.)
Thymus striatus, Vahl?   (*T. Zygis*, Forsk.)
Tenedos (F.).   Greek, θυμάρι.
Th. hirsutus, M. B.   (*T. vulgaris*, Webb, not
L., *Th. cherlerioides*, Vis.).   Ida mountains
(Parolini).
T. capitatus, Lk. et Hfmg.   Troad (W.)
Satureja Thymbra, L.   Troad (Olivier, W.),
Olivier derives the name of the city Thym-
bra and the river Thymbrius from that of
the plant, which he found abundantly in
the valley of the Simois (Doumbrek Tchai),
which used to be identified with the Thym-
brius.
Salvia grandiflora, Ettl., var. *rotundifolia*,
Boiss. (*S. rotundifolia*, Vis.).   Ida moun-
tains (Parolini).
S. argentea, L.   Troad (S.).
S. verbenaca, L., var. *vernalis*, Boiss.   His-
sarlik (V.).
S. viridis, L.   Hissarlik (V.), between Nurlü
and Akhmetlü (T.).
Stachys orientalis, Vahl.   Between Nurlü and
Akhmetlü (T.).   Var. *pauciflora*, Boiss. ; *S.
pauriflora*, Vis.   Troad (Parolini).
S. cretica, L.?   (*S. tomentosa*, Forsk.).   Tene-
dos (F.).   Greek, μόσχο βόλο χόρταρο.
? *Lamium album*, L.   Between Akhmetlü and
Nurlü (T.).
L. moschatum, Mill.   Troad (S.), e. g. valley of
the Thymbrius (Kimar Su), (V.).
Ballota acetabulosa, Benth.   Troad (V.).
Does *Moluccella fruticosa*, Forsk., Tenedos
(Greek, χαραβό), belong here ?
Phlomis fruticosa. L.   Troad (W.).
Prasium majus, L.   Troad (W.).
Ajuga chia, Schreb.   Troad (V.).
Teucrium Polium, L.   Bali Dagh (C.).

PLUMBAGINACEAE.

Statice sinuata, L.   Shore of the Troad (W.).
Plumbago europaea, L.   Troad (W.).

SALSOLACEAE.

? *Chenopodium album*, L.   Tenedos (F.).   Turk.
siritjam.
C. Botrys, L.   Troad (W.).
? *Atriplex Halimus*, L.   Troad (W.).
Salsola Soda, L.   Coast of the Troad (W.).
S. Kali, L.   Sandy strand opposite Tenedos (F.)

POLYGONACEAE.

Emex spinosa, Campd.   Kestambul, on the
Chigri Dagh (V.).
Rumex pulcher, L.   Plain of Troy (Calvert).
R. tuberosus, L.   Tenedos (Virlet).
R. acetoselloides, Bal.   Plain of Troy (V.).
Polygonum aviculare, L.   Plain of Troy (Cal-
vert), Tenedos, frequent in dry places
(D'Urville).

THYMELAEACEAE.

Thymelaea Tartonraira, All. (*T. argentea*, Clarke). Very frequent near the villages, used as firewood; e. g. in the environs of the In Tepeh (C , V.), Hagios Demetrios Tepeh (V.).

T. hirsuta, Endl. Troad (W.).

ELAEAGNACEAE.

Elaeagnus hortensis, M. B. (*E. angustifolia*, Forsk.). Troad, cult. (W.), Tenedos, cult. (F.). Turk. idae.

LAURACEAE.

Laurus nobilis, L. Troad (W.).

CYTINACEAE.

Cytistis Hypocistis, L. Parasitic on the roots of *Cistus salviifolius*, L., near Ren Kioi (V.).

ARISTOLOCHIACEAE.

Aristolochia Tournefortii, Jaub. et Sp. Troad (Olivier).

A. hirta, L. Ridge of Hissarlik (V.).

EUPHORBIACEAE.

Euphorbia Chamaesyce, L. (*E. polygonifolia*, Forsk.). Coast opposite Tenedos (F.).

E. amygdaloides, L. Between Nurlü and Tchaukhlar (T.)

E. biglandulosa, Desf. Kalifatli (V.).

Crozophara tinctoria, A. Juss. Troad (W.), Tenedos, on fallows (F.). Greek, σκλαρό-χορτο : with the Greek of Natolia, ἄγριο φασουλιά.

URTICACEAE.

Urtica pilulifera, L. Valley of the Thymbrius (Kimar Su) (V.), Tenedos (F.). Greek, ἀτζηκνίδα.

Humulus Lupulus, L. In bushes on the river-banks of the Plain of Troy, frequent (V.).

Morus nigra, L. (Cultivated near the villages
M. alba, L.   { (V.).

Ficus Carica, L. Wild in the Plain of Troy, e. g. in the grove above the springs at Novum Ilium (V.), Bounarbashi (Olivier). Cultivated near the villages. The practice of caprification occurs in this country (W.).

Celtis Tournefortii, Lmk. In the ruins of the thermae ' of Alexandria Troas' (W.).

Ulmus campestris, L. Bushes on the river-banks of the Plain of Troy; e. g. on the Kalifatli Asmak, on the Scamander, Simois, Thymbrius (Kimar Su) (V.), near Bounarbashi (Olivier). The πτελέα mentioned by Homer.

JUGLANDACEAE.

Juglans regia, L. Cultivated near the villages (V.).

PLATANACEAE.

Platanus orientalis, L. Wild in the bushes on the river-banks of the Plain of Troy and in the mountains; e. g. in the lower Simois

valley (V.), at the Scamander source, there also often a tree (C., W., V.); planted in and near the villages. It is the most stately tree of the Troad, e.g. at Kalifatli, in Doumbrek Kioi (V.), Bounarbashi, near Beiramitch (C. W.).

CUPULIFERAE.

Quercus pedunculata, Ehrh. Ida, lower region (W.).

Q. sessiliflora, Sm. Like the former (W.).

Q., var. *pubescens*, Boiss. Plain near Koum Kioi (V.).

Q. lusitanica, Lmk., var. *genuina*, Boiss. (*Q. infectoria*, Oliv.). In the Troad, e. g. Iné (T.), only shrub-like; the gall-nuts are gathered (Olivier, V.), most appreciated are those which are not yet quite ripe, called "green" or "black;" the ripe "white" ones have far less value (Olivier).

Q. Ilex, L. Troad, here and there (W. T.).

Q. coccifera, L. Frequent in the anterior Troad, but only shrub-like (W., T.), e. g. Hissarlik, on the slopes above the springs (V.).

Q. Cerris, L. In the lower range of the Ida, and on the Scamander near Kara Kioi (T.), in the upper Scamander valley from Kushumlü upwards (W.)

Q. Aegilops, L. In the Troad, widely spread ; it gives abundant Valonia (βελανίδια) (Olivier, D'Urville, W., S , V.); particularly remarkable trees near Ren Kioi, Koum Kioi, at the foot of the Fulah Dagh, on the Sudluch Su between Ghiekli and Talian Kioi (V.), and particularly in the ruins of Alexandria Troas (Olivier, W., V.), scantily on Tenedos (Olivier). Here also belong *Q. trojana*, Webb (*Q. aegilopifolia*, Webb) and *Q. Libani*, Tchh. (not Oliv.), the latter between Iné and Kestambul (T.).

Castanea sativa, Mill. Ida district (V.).

BETULACEAE.

Corylus Avellana, L. ? Upper Scamander valley (C., V.).

Carpinus Betulus, L. Spread in the Plain and in the mountains (V.).

C. duinensis, Scop. In the valley of the Eltchi Tchai (T.).

SALICACEAE.

Salix alba, L. Spread in the Plain of Troy as bushes on the river-banks, also a tree, e. g. on the Scamander, Bounarbashi Su, Thymbrius (Kimar Su) (V.), near Bounarbashi (Olivier). The ἰτέα mentioned by Homer.

Populus italica, Mnch. At Ren Kioi and Doumbrek Kioi, planted ; not in the Plain (V.).

TYPHACEAE.

Typha, sp. On the In Tepeh Asmak, above the bridge (V. v.).

ARACEAE.

Dracunculus vulgaris, Schott. On the Kalifatli
Asmak, near the mouth of the Simois, in
the underwood of Elms (V.).

POTAMEAE.

Zostera marina, L. Hellespont (Calvert).
Posidonia oceanica, Del. In the Gulf of Adramyttion, near Bairam Kioi (Assos) (V.).

ORCHIDACEAE.[2]

Aceras pyramidalis, Rchb. fil.   Alexandria
Troas (V.).
Orchis papilionacea, L.   Troad (Olivier),
valley of Yerkassi Kioi (V.).
? *O. longicornu,* Poir.   Between Nurlü and
Tchaukhlar (T.).
O. coriophora, L., var. *sancta,* Rchb. fil.
Troad (Olivier).
O. tridentata, Scop. Yerkassi Kioi (V.).
O. brevilabris, Fisch. et Mey. Between Kara-
jilar and Divanjik on bushy hills (T.).
O. punctulata, Stev. Alexandria Troas (V.).
O. provincialis, Balb. Troy (V.), Alexandria
Troas (V.).
O. heroica, Clarke. Bali Dagh, "tumulus of
Hector" (C.).
O. pseudosambucina, Ten. Oulou Dagh (V.),
between Nurlü and Tchaukhlar (T.).
Ophrys fuciflora, Rchb. Upper Scamander
valley (V.).
O. aranifera, Huds. Yerkassi Kioi (V.), var.
mammosa, Rchb. fil. Upper Scamander
valley (V.).
Cephalanthera Xiphophyllum, Rchb. fil. Yer-
kassi Kioi (V.). Here may belong *C. epipactoides,*
Fisch. et Mey. Between Kestambul and
Tuzla (T.).
Spiranthes autumnalis, Rich. Gargarus, below
the summit (W.).

AMARYLLIDACEAE.

Galanthus nivalis, L. Scamander-source (C.).
Sternbergia lutea, Ker. Troad (W.).
St., sp.? Between Bounarbashi (near Bei-
ramitch) and Aiwajik (W.).
Pancratium maritimum, L. Sea-shore of the
Troad (W.).

IRIDACEAE.

Crocus moesiacus, Ker, var. *Landerianus,* Herb.
Kurshuklu Tepeh (Kushumlü?) (Herbert).
C. gargaricus, Herb. fil. (*C. aureus,* Clarke).
Gargarus (C.).
C. biflorus, Mill., var *nubigenus,* Baker (*C.
vernus,* Clarke? *C. nubigenus,* Herb.)
Summit of the Gargarus (Herbert).
C. Sieberi, Gay. Troad (Olivier).
C. candidus, Clarke. Gargarus (C.).

C. autumnalis, Webb. Gargarus, below the
summit (W.).
Romulea Bulbocodium, Seb. et Maur.   Troad
(C.).
Iris pumila, L. Novum Ilium (V.), Hagios
Demetrios Tepeh (V.).
I. Pseudacorus, L. On the Bounarbashi Su,
not far from the bridge (V.).
Gynandriris Sisyrinchium, Parl. Not rare in
the meadows of the anterior Troad, e. g. in
the bed of the In Tepeh Asmak, on the Kali-
fatli Asmak (V.).

DIOSCOREACEAE.

Tamus communis, L. Ida district, at Erinlü
(V.).

SMILACEAE.

Smilax aspera, L. Troad (W.).
Ruscus Hypophyllum, L. (*R. troadensis,* Clarke).
Scamander-source (C., V.).

LILIACEAE.

Tulipa montana, Lind. Upper Scamander
valley, near Karakioi (T.).
Gagea arvensis, Schult.? (*Ornithogalum a.,*
Clarke). In Tepeh (C.)
G. polymorpha, Boiss. Valley of the Thym-
brius (Kimar Su) (Calvert).
G. lutea, Schult.? (*Ornithogalum l.,* Clarke).
Bali Dagh, on the "tumulus of Hector" (C.).
Fritillaria Pinardi, Boiss. Between Nurlü
and Tchaukhlar (T.).
F. Schliemanni, Aschs. et Boiss. Upper Sca-
mander valley (V.).
Leopoldia trojana, Heldr. Troad (S.), Plain
of Troy (V.), upper Scamander valley (V.),
Alexandria Troas (V.). Here seems also
to belong *Bellevalia comosa,* Tchih. Plain
of Tuzla (T.).
L. Pinardi, Heldr. Troad (S.).
Muscari racemosum, Mill. Plain of Troy (V.),
Bali Dagh, "tumulus of Hector" (C.).
M. paradoxum, C. Koch. Between Nurlü and
Tchaukhlar (T.).
Ornithogalum prasandrum, Gris. Kalifatli
(V.), Alexandria Troas (V.).
O. sulphureum, R. et S. Troad (S.).
O. comosum, L. Troad (S.), e. g. Hissarlik (V.).
Allium nigrum, L. Troad (S.).
A., sp., purple flower. Summit of the Gar-
garus (W.).
Asphodelus microcarpus, Vis. Plain of Troy
(W.), e. g. in the dry meadows on the In
Tepeh Asmak and on the Simois (V.),
Tenedos (F.). Greek, ἀσπουρδοῦλι.
A. luteus, L. Alexandria Troas (V.).

MELANTHIACEAE.

? *Colchicum autumnale,* L., and
C. variegatum, L. Gargarus, below the sum-
mit (W.).
Bulbocodium trigynum, Adam. Valley of the
Thymbrius (Calvert).

---

[2] Virchow's collection has been determined by
Mr. F. Kränzlin.

JUNCACEAE.

Juncus acutus, Lmk.   In Tepeh Asmak, above the bridge (V.).

BUTOMACEAE.

Butomus umbellatus, L.   Plain of Troy (S.)

CYPERACEAE.

Cyperus longus, L.   Plain of Troy (W.).

Galilaea mucronata, Parl.   Sandy strand of the Troad (W.), e. g. to the north of Talian Kioi (V.).

Scirpus Holoschoenus, L.   Plain of Troy, near Bounarbashi (C.).

S. maritimus, L.   Troad (S.).

Carex divisa, Huds.   Troad (S.).

C. divulsa, Good.   Novum Ilium (V.).

C. hispida, Willd.   On the Bounarbashi Su, near the bridge (V.).

C. distans, L.   Plain of Troy (S.), e. g. on the In Tepeh Asmak (V.).

GRAMINEAE.

Phalaris minor, Retz.   Plain of Troy (Calvert).

Sorghum vulgare, Pers.   Troad, cult. (Calvert).

S. halepense, Pers.   Tenedos (F.).   Greek, καλαμάγρα.

Zea Mays, L.   Troad, cult. (Calvert).

Cynodon Dactylon, Rich.   Tenedos (F.).   Greek, ἀγρία or ἀγρίδα.

Phleum tenue, Schrad.   Plain of Troy (S., Calvert).

Ph. pratense, L.   Plain of Troy (Calvert).

Alopecurus utriculatus, Pers.   Plain of Troy (S.).

A. agrestis, L.   Plain of Troy (Calvert).

Avena orientalis, Schreb.   Troad, cult. (Calvert).

A. barbata, Brot.   Troad (S.).

Aera capillaris, Host, var. *ambigua*, Heldr.   Troad (S.).

Arundo Phragmites, L.   Swamps of the Plain of Troy, everywhere (V.).

A. Donax, L.   Plain of Troy, e.g. in the lower Simois valley (W.).

Briza maxima, L.   Troad (S.), quarry at Kotch Ali Ovassi (V.).

B. spicata, Sibth. et Sm.   Troad (S.).

Dactylis glomerata, L.   Troad (S.).

Catabrosa aquatica, P. B.   Plain of Troy (S.)

Festuca ciliata, Danth.   Troad (S.).

Bromus sterilis, L.   Troad (S.).

B. tectorum, L.   Plain of Troy (S., Calvert), Chigri Dagh (V.).

B. madritensis, L.   Plain of Troy (S., Calvert).

B. secalinus, L.   Among oats (Calvert).

B. scoparius, L.   Plain of Troy (S., Calvert).

B. mollis, L.   Plain of Troy (Calvert).

Brachypodium distachyum, P. B.   Plain of Troy (Sibthorp, S.).

Triticum vulgare, Vill., and

T. durum, Desf.   Troad, cult. (V., Calvert).

T. villosum, M. B.   Troad (S.).

Aegilops triaristata, Willd.   Plain of Troy (Calvert).

Secale cereale, L.   Troad, cult. (V.).

Hordeum vulgare, L.   Troad, cult. (V., Calvert).

H. bulbosum, L.   Troad (S.).

H. murinum, L.   Plain of Troy (S., Calvert).

H. maritimum, With.   Plain of Troy (Calvert).

Lolium temulentum, L.   Among oats (Calvert).

GNETACEAE.

Ephedra procera, Fisch. et Mey.   Novum Ilium (W., V.).

CONIFERAE.

Pinus Laricio, Poir.   Mountains above Iné (T.), Ida Mountains (W.).

P. halepensis, Mill.   Near the sea-coast (W.), Tenedos, scantily (Olivier).

P. Parolinii, Vis.   Ida Mountains, forming the main part (W., Parolini).

P. Pinea, L.   Between Iné and Ovajik (T.).

Picea orientalis, Carr. (*Pinus Abies*, Webb).   Ida Mountains (W.), lower mountain range at Tchaukhlar (T.).

Abies alba, Mill.   Ida mountains (W.), Agg-Dagh (T.).

Cupressus sempervirens, L.   In the Middle Troad, on graveyards, not in the Plain (V.) e. g. Iné (C.).

Juniperus Oxycedrus, L.   Troad (W.), e. g. Hissarlik, slopes above the spring (V.).

FILICES.

Polypodium vulgare, L.   Upper Scamander valley (V.).

Pteris aquilina, L.   The same (V.).

Asplenium Trichomanes, L.   Scamander-source (V.).

A. Adiantum-nigrum, L.   Upper Scamander valley (V.).

Ceterach officinarum, Willd.   Gargarus (C.).

Cystopteris fragilis, Bernh.   Scamander-source (V.).

MUSCI.

Cinclidotus aquaticus, Bruch et Schimp.   Overgrows the wet rocks at the Scamandersource (V.).   The same species is also found at the source of Vaucluse (*C. Müller*, Hal.).

LICHENES.

Usnea articulata, Ach.   Gargarus (C.).

APPENDIX VII.

ON THE LOST ART OF HARDENING COPPER.

By A. J. Duffield.

Some years ago, while engaged in writing on the Incas of Peru, their civilization and knowledge of the fine and the industrial arts, I came to doubt what has been so confidently set forth by some historians, that the Children of the Sun knew of a secret in metallurgy that baffles the scientific knowledge of the nineteenth century to discover. It is true that the Incas had their mirrors of polished copper, which their women greatly prized; and did not Humboldt bring to Europe a copper chisel, that was found in a silver mine close to Cuzco? And is it not true that many of the vessels, weapons, tools, and ornaments, which belong to Incarial times and are now and again found in various parts of Peru, are of a brown complexion, and not blue or green with rust? And does not all this prove that the Incas possessed and practised the art of hardening copper?

The Incas were a wonderful people: their system of colonization and settlement is worthy the attention of modern statesmen. Their way of life was admirable and enviable for many things: no one, for example, of their kingdom could die for lack of bread; idleness was punished as a crime; no lawsuit could be postponed longer than five days. Everybody received an education peculiar to his state and condition. The compulsory education of children began at their birth; for no mother was allowed to take her babe in her arms to give it suck, but was to bend over it as it lay on its back, encouraging the infant to an effort which he should never be released from making through the rest of his life—that, namely, of doing something by which to win his daily food. Thieving was punished with the loss of the eyes; the moving of a landmark with death. Water was made the universal servant and slave of man; the soil was divided equally every year between God, the king, and the people; the earth was cultivated with joy and singing; the sun was the image of the Creator, the moon that of his spouse; the rainbow was his messenger, and the stars which hung in the sapphire night inspired a sense of beauty, that refined while it elevated the taste of all observers. But for all that, I do not believe that the Incas knew how, by artificial means, to give hardness to copper. They were a people gifted with a clear insight; they loved and worshipped Nature in her most excellent forms, and imitated her in all things; their kings' gardens were beautiful, not only in exquisite flowers and birds and bright-coloured insects, but also in perfect imitations of these in silver and gold.

Much meditation on the arts of this refined and deeply religious people made me frequently muse and think and mourn, as, wandering among the ruins they have left behind them, I came to indulge in a "lodged hate and a certain loathing" for the immaculate Spanish Christian people who murdered those worshippers of

Nature, trampled their kings' gardens into mud, melted their silver lilies into five-shilling pieces, and their gold primroses and butterflies into *onzas*, buttons for court monkeys, and buckles and bracelets for frivolous women. These and like things being fastened in my revolving mind often shaped themselves as figures are shaped by the idle motion of the kaleidoscope; and some years after, while sojourning in Keewaiwona, once the territory of a race who delighted to make beautiful things out of a beauteous material,—the Huron Indians, who held the south shore of Lake Superior,—I one day caught sight of a large boulder of peculiar shape and colour lying amongst other and different boulders on the lake-shore. It was slightly tinged with a blue-green mould, but its deeply cut crevices were as bright as red-hot wire. Afterwards I picked up some copper daggers of fine shape, and sharp in edge and point. I was also present at the finding, some thirty feet below the level of Lake Superior, of three swords, 20 in., 18 in., and 16 in. long respectively, also complete in bevelled edge and shapeful point, handle and fluting of the sides finely wrought, untouched by the lapse of time, and but little sullied by the presence of an oxide. I subsequently visited the Ontonagon district, where for the first time in my life I saw native copper lying in its rocky womb, twin-born with silver, and shining with a lustre comparable only to that of the heavenly bodies. There is something in the sight and presence of a large massy body shining in the dark of the earth, and retaining its brightness for the eye to take in its fill of beauty, that may be compared to the charm of sustained music unexpectedly heard for the first time; and, in the course of a year's residence in that metallic region, I had abundant opportunities of returning to that comparison and testing its truth.

On my return to England I carried with me many samples of these metals, which were analysed in the usual way; but the gangue of the samples from Keewaiwona carried a number of bright specks visible to the naked eye, which I picked out with a pair of pincers. They were globules of a bright grey-white metal, which had resisted the action alike of nitric acid and aqua regia. Assisted by my late friend Mr. W. Valentin, of the Royal College of Chemistry, 15 grains' weight of these minute specks were treated with an infusion of potassic bisulphate, dissolved in water, precipitated on zinc, and subsequently heated in hydrogen, giving us a dark-grey powdery substance that could be beaten into shape. Professor Frankland subjected a portion of this to spectrum analysis. The left hand of the ribbon was filled in with the bars characteristic of rhodium, and the charcoal finger crucibles carried minute particles of pure metallic rhodium, which I retain. Subsequently to this I was requested by Mr. Valentin to analyse the "impurities" of certain coppers, which I did, not knowing whence the coppers came, or in what part of the world they were found; they yielded us, among other elements, ruthenium and iridium. When I came to learn that these coppers came from the great native copper deposit from which the Incas took their metal for making their edge-tools and weapons, their arrow-heads and vessels, their bright flat reflecting mirrors to give gladness to their women, their concave mirrors by which their priests "drew fire from the sun,"—the whole thing flashed across my mind, that it was to the presence of the metals of the platinum group that the hardness of the copper was due, and not to any art of hardening copper, which was known to the Incas, but is now lost. Then I returned to Lake Superior to hunt for the home of rhodium, sending from time to time to Mr. Valentin for analysis examples of a certain lustrous deeply-dyed native copper, and he always found traces of rhodium.

I come therefore to the conclusion, that all the knowledge which the Incas and the Hurons had on the hardening of copper was due to their love of beautiful things : they came to know by experience that the deep-coloured copper from a certain locality was not only fine of complexion, but very hard : of this, therefore, they made their excellent vessels and their keen-cutting blades.

Professor Roberts, of the Royal Mint, who has taken a deep interest in this matter, has made an experiment with 90 per cent. of copper and 10 per cent. of rhodium, which has yielded an alloy very similar in colour to the native copper of Keewaiwona : the fracture is exactly the same in shade, but of its hardness it is difficult to tell : a portion of the alloy left in the bottom of the crucible was found to be very hard. It is to be hoped that Professor Roberts may yet find time to conduct other experiments which shall throw some light on the amount of rhodium with which Nature used to form that alloy of her own, and from which we may assume that some of her devout children made their most perfect things.

————————

In printing the foregoing communication, I offer my very sincere thanks to Mr. Duffield for his interesting account of a discovery so important in its bearing on the general question of pre-historic metallurgy. The discovery presents an obvious *analogy* to the implements of copper, *harder than ordinary commercial copper*, which I found in the stratum of the first city at Hissarlik (see p. 251); but there has not been time, since my attention was called to it, to decide the question whether the copper found by me is, in fact, a natural alloy similar to that which Mr. Duffield discovered in America. The necessary experiments have still to be conducted ; but meanwhile I feel it an honour and pleasure that the present work should be enriched with a discovery that promises to be fruitful in results to our knowledge of the early Copper Age, which we now know certainly to have preceded that of Bronze (see pp. 257, 258).—H. S.

APPENDIX VIII.

ON HERA BOÖPIS.

By Professor Henry Brugsch-Bey.

In no other land of the ancient world does the worship of the Cow play so important a part as in Egypt. The representations and inscriptions on the oldest monuments already contain copious references to the sacred Cow; but it is only from the monuments of later periods that scientific enquiry is first supplied with clearer information as to the origin of this worship and its connection with a goddess of the Egyptian Olympus of learned investigation. The following account, founded on monumental records, comprises in one view everything that relates to the origin of this worship, and that is calculated to throw light on the nature of this peculiar veneration for the cow.

In the oldest representations, relating to the creation of the world, the cow, coming forth out of the primeval waters, appears on the territory of the Hermopolite nome in Upper Egypt as the mother of the young Sun-god. Clinging to the horns of his parent, the young god kindles the light of day, and the life of all creatures begins with him. To speak in the language of the monuments, Isis (that is, the cow) causes her son Horus (more exactly Harpocrates, that is, "Horus the child") to come into existence first of all, and the visible forms of the world commence the cycle of their earthly course from life to death: Horus becomes Osiris, and, in the eternal revolution of things, from the dead Osiris a new rejuvenated Horus is developed. In

this myth Osiris symbolizes the primeval water, the fertilizing moisture; Isis, under the image of the cow, the receptive and productive power of nature; Horus, the light which is kindled from the moisture, just as in the teaching of Heraclitus, surnamed "the obscure" (ὁ σκοτεινός). This is the esoteric part of the ancient Egyptian doctrines of hoary wisdom, to which a later cycle of myths sought to give an historic foundation.

The more ancient conception, which goes back to the times of the thirteenth century, gives the following solution of the enigmatical representation of the goddess Isis with the head of a cow. Horus (Apollo) and Set (Typhon) fought with one another for the sovereignty over the kingdom of Osiris. Set is defeated. Isis, moved with compassion for the "elder brother" conquered by Horus, frees him from his bonds. Horus, filled with anger and rage, separates the head of Isis from her body. Thot, the Egyptian Hermes, by the aid of the magic power of his charms, replaces it by the head of the (sacred) Cow (tep-ahe). This strange myth is preserved in the Sallier papyrus No. 4, containing an ancient Egyptian calendar of the times of the first Ramessids, according to which this event took place on the 26th day of the month Thot (the 14th of August, according to the Sothis-year, and the 23rd of September,[1] ac-

---

[1] Chabas, Le Calendrier du papyrus Sallier, iv. p. 30.

cording to the Alexandrian calendar). In remembrance thereof, sacrifices for the gods Isis and Thot were prescribed for ever on this day.   Plutarch[2] was acquainted with this legend, of which he says, " The fight lasted many days, and Horus conquered. But Isis, to whose keeping the fettered Typhon had been committed, did not kill him, but freed and dismissed him.   Horus did not bear this patiently ; he even laid hands on his mother, and tore the crown from her head ; but Hermes placed on her a helmet like the head of a cow ($\beta o\acute{v}\kappa\rho a\nu o\nu$ $\kappa\rho\acute{a}\nu o\varsigma$)." The best proof that Isis was in fact worshipped under the local conception of her as Hathor (Aphrodite) in this cow-headed form, is the name of the town dedicated to her, *Tep-ahe* ('cow-head'), called by the Copts, with the article prefixed, *Petpieh*, by the Arabs *Atfih*, the metropolis of the last (the 22nd) Upper Egyptian nome, known to the Greeks under the name of Aphrodito-polis,[3] in which Isis was worshipped as Hathor (Aphrodite).[4]

In another conception (almost a thousand years later) the myth which identifies Isis with the cow is explained in a way that throws the clearest light on its connection with corresponding Greek myths. The goddess Isis, per-secuted by Typhon, retires to the marshes of Buto in Lower Egypt, on the island of Chebi (the Chemmis or Chembis of the Greek authors from Herodotus onward), whose papyrus-beds secured her from the snares of her pursuer. There she brought into the world her son Horus (surnamed Nub, that is, "the golden ").   This is the same island spoken of by Herodotus (ii. 156), according to whom the Egyptians maintained that it had been floating since the time when the goddess Leto of Buto received into her care from Isis-Demeter the young Horus-Apollo. The Egyptian representation of the legend of the journey of Isis to the island of Chebi-Chemmis is found most fully in a part of the remarkable texts which are treated of in the Metternich-Stele of the time of king Nectanebus I. (378–360 B.C.), for the full publication of which, under the title : "The Metternich-Stele published for the first time in its original size " (Leipzig, 1877),[5] science is indebted to the industry of a young Russian Egyptologist, M. Golnisheff. I have published the translation of the part in question in the *Aegyptische Zeitschrift* for 1879, page i.

The Egyptian texts frequently allude in other passages to the wander-ings of Isis, and to the flight of the goddess from Typhon. In these, Isis appears accompanied by her son Horus, whom she seeks to withdraw from the snares of his hostile brother by the use of all kinds of stratagems and magic arts. The most remarkable account is that found on one of the walls of the great temple of Edfou (Apollinopolis Magna in Upper Egypt) regarding the statements of mythical geography about the seven Oases of the Libyan Desert, known to the Egyptians in the times of the Ptolemies.[6]   Under the head which treats of the Oasis of To-ahe, that is " Land of the Cow " (the present Oasis of Farafrah) it is expressly noted that here the worship of Osiris was predominant, in which the great trinity, Osiris, Isis and Horus, was venerated by the inhabitants. On this occasion it is related of the goddess : " She wandered about with her son,

---

[2] *De Iside et Osiride*, c. 19.

[3] See Brugsch, *Dictionnaire géographique*, p. 933.

[4] *Ibid.* p. 1360, xxii.   According to Strabo also (xvii. p. 809), a sacred *white* cow was held in special honour in the Arabian town of Aphro-ditopolis (that is, on the eastern Arabian side of Egypt), and in the nome of the same name.

[5] *Die Metternich-Stele in der Originalgrösse zum ersten Mal herausgegeben ;* Leipzig, 1877.

[6] Published in full in Dümichen's *Die Oasen der libyschen Wüste ;* Strassburg, 1877, plate iv. foll.

the young boy, to hide him from Set (Typhon). This goddess changed herself into the sacred Cow Hor-Secha, and the young boy into the sacred Bull Hapi (Apis, Epaphus). She went with him to this town of Hapi (Apis, in the Libyan nome of Lower Egypt), in order to behold his father Osiris who is there."

Nothing can be plainer, clearer, or more instructive than these few words, which throw such a surprising light on the worship of the Cow in the western parts of the Delta. The geographical researches founded on an almost inexhaustible supply of records from all times of Egyptian history, to which my whole attention has been turned for more than twenty years, afford most important disclosures as to the worship of the Cow in the Libyan nome, inclusive of the nome called Mareotes by the geographer Ptolemy.[7] Three towns, above all, claim our attention in this connection. First the town of Hapi, Apis, the old capital of the Libyan nome, in the neighbourhood of the Lake Mareotis, with the worship of Osiris as a bull; next, the place Tha-ahe, "the Cow-town" par excellence, situated in the neighbourhood of the former; and the place Tha-Hor-Secha, or Tha-Secha-Hor (the Τάχορσα of Ptolemy), the name of which means " Abode or Town of the sacred Cow Hor-Secha.[8] All these designations had their origin in the flight of Isis and her son Horus from the Oasis of the " Cow-land " (Farafrah) to the maritime districts of the Libyan nome situated to the north, the ancient settlements of immigrant tribes, who were wont to direct their course to Egypt on the west by land,

on the north by water, and who were destined to become disagreeable neighbours for the Egyptians. That among these foreigners there were also adventurers of Ionio-Carian descent, is proved by the purely Greek designations of some names and towns situated on this side of Egypt; designations, the origin of which appears to have been connected above all with prominent names in the Trojan legends. Menelaus and his pilot Canobus gave their names, the former to a nome, the latter to the well-known town of Canobus. Helen and Paris, on their voyage to Egypt, landed in the same parts, to claim the hospitality of the Egyptian coastguard. Besides these famous names, other appellations of a Greek form indicate a foreign intercourse, the origin of which must not be first sought in the times of classical antiquity. The designation of the Metelitic Nome, lying upon the sea on the western side of the Canobic branch of the Nile, shows most clearly how regular foreign intercourse must have been in this part of the Delta; for the origin of the name cannot be sought in any Grecized Egyptian word, but in the pure Greek μέτηλυς, "foreign visitor and settler." Thus, then, we obtain the clearest explanation of the fact that, besides the worship of Osiris, the Egyptian monuments attribute to the districts frequented by foreigners a worship of the (Typhonic) Set, which found its sensuous expression in the animals consecrated to this deity, the crocodile and the hippopotamus.[9] While these strangers brought to the Egyptians what the latter were accustomed to comprehend under the general name of SET, that is everything foreign, on the other hand the former received more from the Egyptians than they themselves were in a position to give. In the province of religion, what must have specially struck the foreigners was the

---

[7] Referring to classical accounts, it may be remarked here that, according to Strabo (xvii. p. 80), an Aphrodite, and a cow consecrated to her, were worshipped in the town of Momemphis, belonging to the ancient Libyan nome of the monuments.

[8] See my treatise Le lac Maréotis, in the Revue égyptologique; Paris, 1880, p. 32.

[9] See my Dictionnaire géographique, p. 1305 f.

worship of Osiris, that is, the primitive form of the Egyptian faith, with its peculiar idea of the wandering Isis, who, in the shape of a cow, sought to escape the snares of Set. Even though they may not have known the secret meaning of this myth, which had been developed on the Libyan side of Egypt along the sea-coast, and which denoted the conflict of foreign ideas with the native religion, customs, and views—the former symbolized by the forms of Set and his demoniacal animals, the crocodile and the hippopotamus, the latter by the trinity of Osiris, Isis, and Horus, and by the animal forms of the sacred cow, Hor-secha, and the Apis-bull,—yet the Greek genius breathed its life into these legends of pure Egyptian origin, and modelled them according to special local colouring into special myths, which found their most striking expression in the HERA BoÖPIS, and in the cow-headed Iö, the wandering goddess, whose name is from the root I in εἶμι: and in ancient Egyptian the root i, iu, io, as also the Coptic word i derived from it, denote exactly the same—ire, venire. The migration and transference of this legend from the north-west corner of the Egyptian Delta to the Greek coasts and islands, seems to me to have been conceived under the form of an historical fact, which is best exhibited in the fable of the emigration of the Libyan king Danaüs, the brother of Aegyptus, to Argos.

I am not bold enough to seek an Egyptian origin for the name of Danaüs, according to a method in favour with many scholars nowadays; but I cannot pass over in silence the fact that, among the districts and tribes nearest to the sea-coast of the Libyan nome, there appears the name Tehannu, Thannu, which must have been known down to the time of Ptolemy, since this writer expressly observes, in his enumeration of the regions, nomes, and towns, on the west side of the

Delta: τοῦ δὲ Μαρειώτου τὰ μὲν ἐπὶ θαλάσσῃ καλεῖται Ταινεῖα ἢ Τενεῖα. Regarded from this point of view, the contest for sovereignty, celebrated in the Greek legend, between the two brothers Danaüs and Aegyptus, that is between a Libyan and Egyptian race, would have a deeper historical significance. We know still further from the Egyptian monumental records, that under Mineptah II. (Menephthes, about 1300 B.C.), the son of king Ramses II., there occurred a vast migration, which first made its pressure felt from Libya on the western territory of the Delta,[10] whose nearest border district, lying along the sea-coast, embraced the land and people of the Tehannu or Tehennu (the inserted vowels e and a are doubtful, since they have to be supplied). The name Tehannu, also written simply Tehan or Than, which here appears a second time in a wider sense, is of pure Egyptian origin, and must be referred to the Egyptian root thn, "to glitter, to shine, to flash, to beam," (compare the Coptic ΘΗΝ fulgur); whence also we find the name thn as the designation of a stone, according to Lepsius the yellow topaz, although this latter explanation is not placed beyond doubt. The Egyptian appellation thn, transferred to another and larger territory, reminds us at once of the Greek name Marmarica (Μαρμαρική) for the region which followed immediately to the west of the Libyan nome, and, in the time of the geographer Ptolemy, formed a separate independent nome, belonging to Egypt. Just as the Egyptian root thn, so the Greek μαρμαίρω, μαρμαρίζω, signifies "to glisten, to glimmer, to sparkle, to shine," whence the derivatives μαρμάρεος, "glistening, gleaming," μάρμαρος, "shining stone, marble," and, let us now add, Μαρμαρική, in a sense

---

[10] See my *History of Egypt*, p. 567; vol. ii. p. 122 f., Eng. trans. 2nd ed.

referring to the brightness and glitter of the district, which consists of bright, shining limestone.

Whether we accept the connection of the Greek Danaüs with the name of the larger region (Marmarica) or of the lesser (Ταινεῖα, Τενεῖα), called Thn on the monuments, the Libyan locality of both remains as certain as the Libyan origin of King Danaüs. The statement, accredited by the ancients, that he taught the Argives among other things to build larger and more convenient ships, and to dig wells (we may call to mind the cisterns in Libya, the land of drought), cannot but contribute to give greater force to the probability of this connection; and still more so the circumstance, that Danaüs made good his claim to Argos by proving his descent from Inachus, that is, from the father of Iö, the Libyan Isis, the Cow-Mother of Epaphus-Apis.

The comparison of the Egyptian and Greek accounts concerning the worship of the Cow and of the cow-headed goddess, whatever were the names and local conceptions of her in Greece and Egypt, leads to the following result:—

The Cow (*ahe*), under the peculiar mythological name of Hor-secha or Secha-hor, was regarded on the Libyan side of Egypt—from the Oasis of To-ahe (that is " Cow-land," the Farafrah of our time) to the sea-coast—as the living symbol of the goddess Isis; and was worshipped there in towns and sanctuaries of the same name. She represents the transformed Isis, who in this shape seeks to escape the

persecutions of Set, the Kakodaemon of the Egyptian pantheon. The region of her wanderings is Libya and the Libyan desert in the narrow sense of the word. Her child Hor, the future Osiris-Serapis, appears veiled under the form of a Bull, the Hapi-Apis-Epaphus. The Libyan seat of his worship is the town of Apis, in the neighbourhood of the Lake Mareotis. The Cow-headed (*boöpis*) Isis, or whatever may have been her local designation, or Isis with the horns of a cow and the disc of the moon between them on her head, are stereotyped forms of the Egyptian idols, the origin of which goes back to the most ancient times of Egyptian history. The relationship of these forms with the Hera-Iö, in idea and representation, is indisputable, and comes from a common source, which had its origin from the soil of the Libyan side of the Egyptian Delta—on that territory which, in the earlier times of the history of the Pharaohs, witnessed the development of an active foreign intercourse by sea and land.[1]

Every connection of the Greek γλαυκῶπις, as an epithet of the Homeric Athené, with Egyptian representations, must be rejected. The Egyptians regarded the owl as a bird of ill omen; and no deity, whether male or female, bears the head of this animal.

---

[1] These views of my friend Brugsch agree perfectly with the myth of Iö as given in the *Prometheus* of Aeschylus, and especially with the termination of her wandering in Egypt, where she gives birth to Epaphus.

H. SCHLIEMANN.

APPENDIX IX.

TROY AND EGYPT.

By Professor Henry Brugsch-Bey.

My dear friend Schliemann, — In complying most readily with your wish to do justice to the above title from the point of view of Egyptian antiquity, I am troubled with certain scruples, which I cannot withhold from you in the very beginning of my letter. As I have the accidental merit, by favour only of good fortune, of having moved for a long number of years amidst the world of Egyptian monuments as among old acquaintances, you will perhaps demand from me, as from an initiated priest, disclosures on the relations between Troy and Egypt. You may expect from me the solution of obscure historical enigmas, and rejoice by anticipation at having found at the right hour the right man, who has in this respect succeeded in evoking, as if by enchantment, old life from the ruins of dead monuments. Nothing have I to bring of all that you expect and that I should like to lay at your feet, as the most eloquent testimony of my friendship and high esteem. Is it my fault, is it the fault of the monuments, if I appear before you with a poor gift? I fear the fault lies with both, and, with this frank confession, I transport myself into the midst of the monuments and their inscriptions.

The name of the Hellenes must necessarily have been known to the Egyptians from the time when Hellenes, as pirates or as travellers and cast-away mariners, set foot on Egyptian soil. The latest testimonies to this are furnished, as is self-evident, by the times of the Ptolemies. On the extant stones and in the papyrus-rolls of that epoch, which is comparatively the modern history of Egypt, the Hellenes are called by the name of *Uinen, Ueinen*, which has continued in the Coptic language in the forms of *Ueinin, Ueeinin, Ueeienin*. The word so written and spoken has no linguistic connection either with the 'Iάονες, 'Iωνες, of the Greeks, or with the *Javan* of the Bible (as has been generally assumed), but it is a derivative from the Egyptian root *uni, uini*, preserved also in Coptic in the forms *uoein, uóini, uoeine*, etc., with the significations of the Latin *lumen, lux, splendor*, and, in composition with the verb *er* (= *facere, esse*), it means *fulgere, splendere, illucescere, illuminare*, or participially, *lucidus, splendens*. I observe at once in this place how, in fact, the peoples of the Pulasta (Pelasgians) and Tekkar (Teucrians)[1] are once denoted on a monument, of the times of King Ramses III., with the help of a Semitic word like *taher*, that is in Hebrew טהר, "brilliant," "shining," "conspicuous," "celebrated." That is to say, the above nations, which I have in my mind, are called, some of them, "celebrated peoples on the land," the others "on the sea."

This designation, which implies so much that is flattering for the Hel-

---

[1] *History of Egypt*, vol. ii. p. 153 foll., Eng. trans. 2nd ed.

lenes, can only be established, as I have said, for the later period of Egyptian history. It is said to be peculiar to the *demotic* epoch of writing. It is, however, scarcely to be presumed that the Egyptian proper name *Uinen*, in connection with the Semitic *taher*—both with the sense of "light, luminous, brilliant,"—could have been an invention of the Egyptians. On the contrary, the supposition may be admitted, that the name *Uinen* represented the Egyptian *translation* of a genuine Greek denomination of the Hellenic race, and in this connection I call to mind the name Hellas, Hellen, itself, the root of which seems to me to lie in the Greek stem *sel* (compare σέλας, σελάω, σελάσσομαι, "lustre," "glance," "shine,") with the signification of "to be bright, glance, shine, glimmer." Analogies within Greek itself are not wanting. Let us compare σελ-άνη with ἐλ-άνη, "torch," Σελ-ήνη, "moon," σῦς with ῦς, the name of the race of the Ἑλλοί (Strabo, vii. § 328) with the Homeric Σελλοί (*Iliad* xvi. 234); let us add to this the words in which the Greek aspirate (‘) is equivalent to the Latin *s*, as in ῦς = *sus*, ἕδος = *sedes*, ἅλς = *sal, salum*, ἕρπω = *serpo*, ἑλίκη = *salix*, ἅλ-λομαι = *salio*, ἥλιος = *sol*, ἱδὸς = *sudor*, and many others.

In the existing bilingual and trilingual inscriptions, the demotic *Uinen* uniformly corresponds to a hieroglyphic form *Ha-neb* or *Hau-neb*, which (compound) word has the signification of "those who are behind their chiefs, those who follow their chiefs," consequently foreigners, who choose their chiefs in order to accompany them on warlike expeditions. My explanation of this most ancient proper name is new; but I have confirmed it by the most striking examples of its use. The Hau-neb appear already on the monuments of an early time, even before the epoch of the Eighteenth Dynasty (about 1700 B.C.). They make their appearance in what is called the "List of the Nine Nations," as a distinct group of peoples, whose places of abode are clearly and distinctly indicated by the following words in an Egyptian hieroglyphic text of the Ptolemaic time: "*Hau-neb* is the name of the inhabitants of the islands and coasts of the sea, and the numerous and great (or, the very numerous) peoples of the north." In this geographical conception of the seat of the peoples and races of the north on the soil of Asia Minor, called Hau-neb,—established as it is by the monuments—we have the solid foundation for all the indications of the earlier and later monuments.

With some of these peoples we become first acquainted from the records of the monuments about the campaigns of King Ramses II. Sestura (Sesostris) against the mighty people of the Cheta or Chita, the Hittites, or "children of Cheth," of the Bible. A great confederacy of nations, which extended over Western Asia and Asia Minor, opposed the celebrated Egyptian conqueror, in order to dispute with him the supremacy over the parts of Asia now mentioned. The heroic poem of Pentaur, in glorification of the victories of this Pharaoh over the king of Cheta and his confederates, names as such, first quite generally, "all peoples from the furthest extremities of the sea to the land of Cheta." The region is distinctly indicated: the whole of Asia Minor as far as the Euphrates, on whose banks lay the eastern border districts of QARQAMASHA, Carchemish,[2] and QAZAUANATAN, Gauzanitis, the Go-hen of the Bible. Over against them, as representatives of the western regions of Asia Minor (at the extremities of the sea), appear the peoples of the DARDANI, the Dardanians, MAUNA,

---

[2] The ruins of Carchemish have been lately discovered at *Jerablûs* (Hierapolis) on the Euphrates.

MAUON, the Maeonians or Meonians (the ancient Lydians), MASU, the Mysians, LIKU, the Lycians. The two names of nations mentioned besides, PIDASA and KERKESH or GERGESH remind us, the former of Pedasus, the latter of the Gergithians in the dominion of Troas.[3]

These names, handed down to us with all fidelity, bear upon them an unmistakable mark, namely, that of a close connection founded on a politico-geographical relation. They exhibit the military power of Western Asia in its chief representatives, just as we already have them enumerated by name in Homer in the Catalogue of the allies of Troy. But the ILION to which prominence has been given by E. de Rougé, in his celebrated dissertation on the epic of Ramses—in ancient Egyptian *Iri-una, Iliuna,*—must disappear from the record of the Trojan allies of the Cheta in their contest against Sesostris, for the reading Ili-una has probably to be rectified in respect of the first part of the name, *ili.*[4] It is not to be read *Ili-una,* but *Ma-una,* that is *Maeonia.*

We feel bound to maintain that the whole series of the confederates named, on the west coast of Asia Minor, "beginning from the furthest extremities of the sea," as the texts express themselves, is an historical fact of capital importance. It gives us the certainty that, about a hundred years before the destruction of Troy, the nations enumerated inhabited the same territories which the geographers of classi-

cal antiquity have attributed to them. To these we add, with particular reference to later times, the names of the Shardana (Shairdana) and Turash (Tuirash), generally with the epithet " of the sea"; which denoted nations distinguished by their foreign attire and armament, first as enemies of the Egyptians, but afterwards also as their auxiliaries in the wars of Ramses II., both against the Cheta and against other peoples. It is the warlike races of the Sardians and the Homeric Τρῶες, the inhabitants of Troas, who thus show themselves for the first time on the theatre of the world's history as faithful allies of the Egyptians.

But under the successor of the great Ramses, king Mineptah II. (about 1300 B.C.), the Pheron of Herodotus, the Shardana and Turash appear again as opponents of the Egyptians and as allies of the king of the Libyans, who, from the west, on African soil, made a formidable attack on the region of the Delta. According to the texts relating to them, they appear at one time as "peoples of the sea," at another as "peoples of the north," that is to say, as inhabitants of the coasts of Asia Minor, in brotherly community with the kindred tribes adjacent to their native seats. The inscriptions call them in succession: the " Shairdana, Shakalsha, Akaiuasha, Leku, Turisha,"[5] which we translate: " the Sardians, Shakalsha, Achaeans, Lycians, Trojans."[6] Together with their Libyan friends, they are entirely defeated by the Egyptians in the battle of Prosopis; and

---

[3] Unless we are altogether deceived, both names are derived from Semitic roots. Pedasos reminds of the root *patash* "to hammer," whence *pattish* "iron-hammer;" *gergesh* of *girgash*; Chaldean, *garyeshta*; Arabic, *girgis* "clay, loam—black silt." The change of the Semitic sound *sh* into the Greek *t* can be proved also by other examples: compare *Kadesh,* in Greek Kadytis.

[4] The sign in question is of a polyphonic nature, and can be equally well read *iri, ili,* or *ma* and *mar.* From internal reasons, the statement of which cannot be given here without prolix explanations, I prefer the reading *ma.*

[5] The final syllable *sha* or *ash* of these or other proper names is remarkable, because it represents a termination (the Greek *os*) which does not occur in any ancient Egyptian writings; it is conspicuous in the proper name Mashauasha, also written Mashaua, a Libyan people called Maxyes by the Greeks.

[6] *History of Egypt,* vol. ii. pp. 122, foll., Eng. trans., 2nd ed.

are partly slain and partly carried into captivity.[7]

Under King Ramses III. (1200 B.C.), the Proteus of Herodotus, the contemporary of Alexandros and his beloved Helen, who in their flight are cast away on Egypt, this country is involved in new wars against neighbouring peoples. Large confederations of nations rose up more formidably than ever before, to join in hostile invasions upon Egypt. From the West it was the Libyans (Libu), with their allies, who threatened Egypt's ancient frontiers and independence. Among their allies we cite the Masha-uasha, Asabta, Hasa, and Bakana, since the same forms of names are clearly preserved in the classical designations of the Maxyes, Asbytae, Ausees, and Bakales.[8] From the East "the peoples of the north," "the inhabitants of the isles and the coastlands," at one time also called Hau-neb, directed their attack by water and by land against Egypt. The expedition on the mainland issued from Asia Minor. The peoples and cities, which they touch in their migration, are seized with fear and terror. They settle down in the land of the Amori (Amorites) and establish a fixed camp. Then the warlike attack is again directed against Egypt. At Migdol, on the Pelusian arm of the Nile, they join their confederates, who arriving by sea, had sailed up with their ships into the broad arm of the Nile. A great battle is joined between them and the Egyptians both on land and on the water. The enemy are defeated and killed or captured. Ramses III., the victor, does not omit, in his later expedition against Asia Minor, to wreak vengeance on the enemies of Egypt; and he attacks their cities in their own land, that is to say on the isles and coast-districts of Asia Minor.

This is the brief summary of the rich representations and inscriptions which cover the temple walls of Medinet Abou (in the western quarter of Thebes) and of which the celebrated Harris Papyrus No. 1 contains an epitome.[9]

" The peoples of the north," " the inhabitants of the isles and of the coast districts," appear also in the wall-paintings, in two separate groups, distinguished by their attire and armament. The first includes the peoples called Purosata or Pulosata (Pelasgians — Philistines!), Tekri or Tekkari (Teucrians) and Danau (Danai?). Their armament consists of spears, short swords, round shields, and helmets crowned with feather-like crests. The enemies of the Egyptians designated as Purosata appear on the monuments as the most important and most distinguished people among the nations now mentioned. The termination ta gives to the name a Semitic complexion, and with this agrees the fact, that the root PUROS, PURAS, PULAS, contains a very suggestive meaning; for palas, palash (in Hebrew), falasa (in Ethiopic) means " to make a way for oneself, to depart (abroad), to migrate." The Purosata are, therefore, " the wanderers, foreigners," which name perfectly suits the Pelasgians of the Greek tradition, whom Attic wit conceived as the Pelargoi, that is " the storks," which come and depart again.[10]

---

[9] Op. cit. p. 155.

[10] The name Iö also contains a similar signification, for according to your sagacious judgment (Mycenae, p. 20) it should be referred to the root I (in εἶμι, I go); in stating which I ought not to leave unnoticed the attempt to bring the name of the goddess Io into connection with the Egyptian word Ioh " moon," (but of the masculine gender!). Whether the name of the Ionians is related to Io, as I see from some remarks of learned Hellenists, I would by no means venture to decide. From my Egyptian and Oriental point of view I would rather refer it to the root I, which in Semitic as well as in Archaic-Egyptian (ϊ, ia, ia; plural, iuu, ion) signifies " isle " and " islanders." In the Bible the Iyyim (once

---

[7] History of Egypt, vol. ii. pp. 146, foll., Eng. trans., 2nd ed.   [8] Ibid. pp. 153, foll.

The second group is formed by the kindred peoples of the Shardana, Shakalsha, and Uashash, with the epithet " of the sea," that is valiant warriors on sea. Their armament is essentially distinguished from that of the first group. Helmets surmounted with horn-like crests, coats of mail, armlets, shields with handles and bosses, long swords, sandals on their feet, — all give them a chivalrous appearance, especially in contrast with the Pelasgian group. The Greek type is unmistakable.

A pylon of the above-mentioned temple of Medinet Abou shows the king Ramses III. as vanquisher of the Hau-neb, that is, the Hellenes. He brings to the god Amon of Thebes thirty-nine conquered cities with their inhabitants, the names of which— often of Semitic origin—may be found again on the islands and coasts of Asia Minor.[1] I cite the most striking names in the appended list: No. 5, Tarshcha or Tarshach = Tarsus. No. 7, Salomaski = Salamis in Cyprus. No. 8, Katian = Kition; No. 9, Ai-mar, I-mar

= Marion; No. 10. Sali = Soli, and No. 11, I-tal = Idalion;—all four also in Cyprus. No. 14, Bitar or Bizar, exactly represents the Hebrew bezer, " copper mine." No. 15, Asi, suggests the name of Assos, a Mysian city in Troas, or of Issa, the ancient designation of the island of Lesbos, or of Issus in Cilicia. No. 20, Kerena, Kelena, recals Kolonae in Troas; as does No. 22, Aburot, Aburt, the Mysian district of Abrettene. No. 23, Kabur, Kabul, shows itself again in the Greek Kabalis, the name of a district of Phrygia and Lycia. No. 24, U-lu, if the transcription of the name is right, brings ILIUM to mind. No. 26, Kushpita, Kushpat, recals the Semitic Keseph " silver," as this again reminds us of the silver city Argyrion in Troas. With No. 27, Kanu, might be compared the name of the city of Caunus in Caria, and with L(a)res one of the cities called Larissa. No. 33, Maulnus, otherwise also written in the inscriptions Muaullos, Mulnus, calls to mind the Cilician Mallus, as do No. 38, Atena, and No. 39, Karkamash, the names of the cities Adana and Coracesium, likewise situated in Cilicia.

In this and in all similar lists of nations, countries, and cities, we cannot think of a strictly geographical arrangement. The monuments prove this a hundred times. But, on the other hand, names which have a broad general connection are not separated. The general outline which includes the above-mentioned list of cities is traced out, for the reference is to the islands and coast-cities of Asia Minor, of that region, namely, on which the migrations of Aryan and Semitic groups of nations present a confused scene of movements hither and thither. The fact, that the monuments, which are contemporary with the Trojan epoch begin suddenly to speak and to present the wandering tribes according to their appearance and their names before our astonished eyes, is another witness of

---

also *Iyyin*, in the plural) are a general synonym for the coast-lands and the islands of the Mediterranean. May not the Ionians have represented by their names just the inhabitants of those islands and coasts? At all events, this hint appears to me worthy of examination. The Bible (*Genesis*, x. 4) expressly says of the children of Javan, Elishah, Tarshish, Kittim and Dodanim : " by these were *the isles* of the Gentiles overspread [a], in their lands, each according to their languages, races, and peoples." That the ethnic name Javan is identical with Iaones, Ionians, cannot be a subject of the slightest doubt.[b] But the opinion of a scholiast deserves notice, that the barbarians had denoted the Hellenes by the designation Iaones, as if the name itself had been of a barbarian, that is to say *not Greek*, origin.

[1] For the full list see *Hist. of Egypt*, vol. ii. pp. 158, 159, Eng. trans. 2nd ed.

---

[a] German *ausgebreitet*. A. V. " divided."

[b] This was clearly seen by Milton, who, in his catalogue of the fallen angels (*Par. Lost*, bk. i.) calls the Greek deities "The *Ionian* gods, of *Javan's* issue." In fact IΩN is identical, letter for letter, with יון (Ion : with the added vowel points, Javan).

the certainty of the Greek traditions about the olden time. In this respect the information of the monuments acquires a value beyond all description. Troas, Mysia, Maeonia, Lycia, appear already as the fixed seats of nations bearing the like names, on the west coast and the neighbouring islands of Asia Minor. The statement of the classical writers, that King Ramses II. (Sesostris) advanced on his victorious expedition as far as Thrace, and there set up his last memorial pillars, is therefore no empty tale, invented to glorify the extent of the expeditions of the Egyptian Sesostris. Those conquests belong to the region of facts. The further progress of the study of the monuments will hereafter dissipate the mist which still covers some parts of these expeditions, which have an historical foundation. The broad general fact is proved, that, as early as the fourteenth century before our era, the Greeks and their several tribes were perfectly known to the Egyptians, and carried on intercourse with them. This is already attested by the Greek fables and the classical traditions. Perseus, Danaüs, Menelaus, Archander, Canobus, Paris, Helen, are names which stand in the closest connection with the geography and the history of Egypt at the northwest corner of the Delta, in the neighbourhood of the Canobic mouth, for they refer to times in which Ionians and Carians landed on the same coasts of that region which were marked, at the later epoch of the Ptolemaic age, with the names of the Menelaïte and Metelite nome. I have elsewhere shown [2] how the latter denomination has sprung directly from the Greek μέτηλυς ("immigrant, foreign visitor"). Long before Psammetichus I. had opened the land to Ionians and Carians clad in bronze armour, in order to make use of them as mercenaries and auxiliary troops, the Pharaohs had already, 800 years before, obtained the like service from their ancestors.

There are two tribes especially, which claim our whole attention at that epoch; these are the Shardana and the Shakalsha, the predecessors of the Ionians and Carians of the time of Psammetichus. We meet with them sometimes as auxiliaries in the suite of Libyan kings and as enemies of the Egyptians, sometimes as troops allied with the Egyptians against Libyan and Asiatic despots, as has been stated above (p. 747). Misled by the resemblance in sound, some have wished to recognize in their names the most ancient designations of the Sardinians and the Sicilians. But for all this, it appears to us impossible to sever these tribes from the connection with their neighbours in Asia Minor, among whom they obtained so conspicuous a place through their Hellenic appearance. We believe with M. Maspero,[3] that the names refer to Maeonian tribes, among which were the Shardana, the Lydian Sardians, descendants of Sardos, the *hero eponymus* of the city named after him. When Shardana served in the armies of the Pharaohs, they did not at all renounce the rights of their native home. Maeonia, the country called Mauna in the ancient Egyptian texts, was and still remained their fatherland. The same is true of the peoples called Shakalsha and Uashash, whom we have to regard as tribes akin to the Shardana. I must not omit to mention that, as the former have been regarded as inhabitants of Sicily, so the latter are viewed by some scholars, according to the suggestion of M. Chabas, as the predecessors of the Oscans.

Here then, my dear Friend, you have in bold and rough outline, from the sketch traced on the monuments, the picture of the groups of nations

---

[2] See Appendix VIII., p. 742.

[3] See his *Histoire ancienne des Peuples de l'Orient* (Paris, 1875), p. 249.

who peopled the coasts of Asia Minor about the Trojan times. Among them the *Dardani*, the Dardanians, are not wanting. I have taken pains, as far as I had the ability, to fix clearly the fundamental lines of the picture, and to follow, so far as accorded with my own conviction, the masterly first essays of E. de Rougé and Chabas. The opinions at variance with theirs, which the study of the monuments has forced upon me almost against my will, have respect principally to the country of Asia Minor, which I feel obliged to regard as the common fatherland of those *Hau-neb* or peoples of the islands and coasts to the north of Egypt. I repeat that to recognize the Etruscans in the Tuirsha or Turisha (Trojans), the Oscans in the Uashash, the Siculans in the Shakalsha, and the Sardinians in the Shardana (Sardians), is repugnant to my own geographical convictions.

And where, you will ask me, is the *Egyptian Troy* (Troja), the site, according to classic tradition, of the settlement of the Trojans who followed Menelaus and remained there as captives? Granted that through this story, preserved by Strabo, there shines forth a bright and clear ray of the historical fact of the old relations between the Egyptians and the Trojans (the Turisha of the monuments), confirming what I have maintained above, yet the connection between the names of the two cities of Troy is in no wise established. The Egyptian Troja, situated at the foot of the like-named mountain, on the right bank of the Nile opposite to Memphis, and now called *Turra*, bore in old Egyptian, from the time of the pyramid-building kings,[3] the designation of *tarāu* or *tarāui*, as the mountain bore that of *turāu* or *turāui*, which is of genuine Egyptian origin, and has nothing to do with the foreign name of the Asiatic Troy. The Greeks travelling or settled in Egypt found it easy to take advantage of the similar names of the two places, in order, after their wonted fashion, to add a geographical basis to the old traditions of the wars of the Egyptians against Troas. Accordingly the captive enemies were represented as making a settlement at the place referred to, and calling it Troy in honour of their native city.

With this remark, dear and valued Friend, allow me to close this long epistle. On reading over once more the little that it contains, I feel almost ashamed, in contrast with your brilliant labours and discoveries, so rich in results and consequences, to expose on my part such an evidence of poverty. The reasons for this I have explained in the introduction. Dispose of my slight gift according to your own judgment.

HENRY BRUGSCH.

---

[3] See *History of Egypt*, vol. i. p. 91 (*et alii*), Eng. trans. 2nd ed.

INDEX.

————————

ABBREVIATIONS.

Besides those usual, such as M. = mount; Pr. = promontory; R. = river, &c.: c. = city, cities ; d. = daughter ; f. = father; k. = king; m. = mother; s. = son; N. Ilium, or N. I. = Novum Ilium: Tr. denotes objects belonging to the great Treasure first found; Tr., objects of the 9 other Treasures ; *all* found in the *débris* of 3rd city.

or bowl, 594, 595; horse-shaped, and fragment with horse's head, 594, 595; one of a pair conjoined, 597.

Cups, metal : bronze, 6th c., perforated like a colander; one on a tall foot, like the Etruscan and Greek *holkion*, 605 :— electrum, Tr.; see *Electrum:* silver, Tr.; see *Silver.*

Curetes, mythical metallurgists in Phrygia and Samothrace, 256.

Curtius, E., 'History of Greece,' 121 *et passim ; Lecture on Troy,* 187.

Cuttle-fish (sepia), on a Trojan box, 225 ; on goblets fr. Ialysus, 225 ; painted in dark-red clay, on a terra-cotta box lid, 3rd c., 360 ; (or tortoise ?) on a vase-cover, 413.

Cyclopean Walls (so called), in 2nd city, 24 (see *Walls*) ; in *Ithaca* (*q. v.*);—not necessarily primitive, but used at all periods, 192. (Comp. *Polygonal Masonry.*)

Cylinder, of terra-cotta, perforated, with incised decoration, 3rd c., 415 ; of blue felspar, with remarkable signs, from the royal house, 416 ; the signs discussed ; a mark of Babylonian influence ; resemble the Hittite sculptures, 693, 694.

Cymindis (Κύμινδις, Ion., 'night jar'), native name equivalent to Greek *Chalcis* (*q. v.*) ; κυμινδ connected with σκαμανδ, 113, 705.

Cynossema (" dog's monument "), the traditional tomb of Hecuba, 648.

Cypriote character go, on vases, 298 ; syllabary. See *Inscriptions, Trojan.*

Cyprus, pottery of: flagons with female heads, perhaps derived from Thera, 293 ; animal vases, 294 ; other forms, *passim.*

Cyzicus and Dascylium, Aeolian colonization of, by Archelaus, s. of Orestes, 127.

DACTYLI, the Idaean, mythical metallurgists, 254, 256.

Daggers : bronze, Tr., broken and curled up by the conflagration ; proofs of wooden handles, 482 ; with couchant cow or ox on handle, 3rd c., a ceremonial weapon, 504 ;—none in 4th c., 565 :—silver, royal house, 3rd c., a ceremonial. weapon, 499.

Danaïs, connection with Egypt, 743, 744.

Dardanelles, present town of, 133.

Dardania, the Troad called from Dardanus, 119 ; name also in Samothrace, 124.

Dardania, dominion of Aeneas and the Antenorids, 68, 133 ; defined by Strabo; long and narrow ; its boundaries, 134.

Dardania (or *Dardanus,* 119), c. of Dardanus, at foot of Ida, *before sacred Ilios was founded in the plain,* 134, 194 ; de-

stroyed before Strabo's time, 134 ; not the later Dardanus, 134, 174 *n.*

Dardanian, the Scaean Gate so called, 143.

Dardanians, in the Troad, 123 ; play important part in the *Iliad,* 124 ; dominion of Troy promised to their prince Aeneas, 125 ; akin to, and confounded with, the Trojans, 134 ; the *Dardani* of Egyptian records, 746, 750.

Dardanus, s. of Zeus and Electra, 119 ; crosses from Samothrace to the Troad, 119 ; adopted by Teucer, marries his d. Batieia, and succeeds him, 119, 152, 156, 642 ; or marries Chrysé, who brought him the Palladium, 642 ; builds the c. of Dardanus, 119, 152 (see *Dardania*); not known to Homer as an immigrant, 123 ; oldest name in Homer's Trojan genealogy, 152 ; his sons Ilus and Erichthonius, 152 ; on coins of N. I., 642.

Dardanus, Greek c. on the Hellespont, 134 ; excavations gave only fragments of Greek pottery, 134.

Dareios, the Phrygian name of Hector, 704.

Dascylium. See *Cyzicus.*

Date of Pre-historic Troy, probably 1500–1200 B.C., 292.

Davies, T., on the stone implements, 235.

Davies, Wm., on a Trojan fossil bone, 323.

Davis, E. J., ' Life in Asiatic Turkey,' 374.

Débris, slanting layers thrown down from the hill by successive inhabitants, 64, 328 ; section of, 328. See *Hissarlik.*

Deer, species of, in the Troad, 112.

Deiphobus, s. of Priam, 157 ; marries Helen ; killed by Ulysses and Menelaus, 161.

Demeter, St. Demetrius, confounded, 106.

Demetrius, grammarian of Scepsis (*cir.* B.C. 200–180), Homeric critic, his 30 books of *Commentaries on the Catalogue* (*Il.* ii.), 174 ; visits Ilium, 173 ; first questions identity of site at N. Ilium from jealousy for Scepsis, 168, 174 ; his objections, 174 ; refuted, 175, 686–9 ; explanation of utter destruction of Troy, a gratuitous assumption, 175, 176 ; places the site of Ilios at Ἰλιέων Κώμη, 79 (see *Ilians, Village of the*) ; on source of Scamander, 58.

Dendrinos, Mr. and Mrs., their hospitality to travellers in Ithaca, 50.

Denmark, suspension-vases from, 215, 216 ; other pottery, &c., *passim.*

Dennis, G., ' Cities and Cemeteries of Etruria,' 129 *et passim ;* on pottery as a test of race, 279.

Δέπας Ἀμφικύπελλον. See *Amphikypellon.*

tions, 592–3 ; hand-made, like Etruscan *lekythos*, 596 ; with conical excrescences, intended for eyes, 597 ; similar fr. Thera and Cyprus, 597.

Julia, d. of Augustus, nearly drowned in Scamander, 178.

Julia Domna, coins of, N. I., 642, 643, 645.

Julian (alt. emp.), letter of, describing his visit to N. I., 180 f. ; comments of Dr. Carl Henning, 182 ; his policy towards renegades from Christianity, 182, 210.

Julii, house of ; their favour to the Trojans and hatred of the Greeks, 633.

Juno, prophecy of, in Horace, 204 f. (See *Site of Homer's Ilios.*)

Jutchenko, author's agent at Moscow, 12.

KADESH, on the Orontes, war of Ramses II. against, 123.

Kalifatli, village of, 105.

Kalifatli Asmak, R., ancient bed of the *Scamander* (*q. v.*) ; its two arms, 99 ; its course described, 100.

Kantharos (κάνθαρος), Greek cup sacred to Dionysus, probable origin of, 595. (See *Cups*, 6th c.)

Kara-Euli, hill of, 70.

Kara Your, M., visited, 59 ; height, 59, 71 ; wrongly identified with Callicoloné, 59, 71 ; view from, 71 ; traces of an ancient building on ; desert plateau to Chiblak, 72.

Karanlik (*i. e.* "darkness"), port on the Hellespont, perhaps of Aeanteum and Rhoeteum, 104.

Keller, Otto, '*Die Entdeckung Ilion's zu Hissarlik*,' 154, 189 ; on the owl in connection with Athené, 289.

Kermes, worm of the oak, 114.

Keys (κληΐδες) : copper or bronze, of the treasure-chest, 41, 454, 484 ; more usual form of, a bolt, as in Homer ; 4 such in burnt city, 484 (comp. *Bolts*) ; 2 in the gates ; 1 in loose, 484–5.

Key, bronze, with handle in shape of, and with attributes of, the quadrangular *Hermae*, N. I., 620, 621 ; Prof. Athanasios Rhousopoulos upon, 621 ; iron, 622.

Kheta or *Khita* (Kattaia, Khethites, Hittites ; comp. *Ceteians*), confederates of, in war with Ramses II., 123 ; include peoples of Asia Minor, 746–7.

Ki, Cypriote character, on a terra-cotta ball, 3rd c., 349.

Kiepert, '*Memoir über die Construction der Karte von Kleinasien*,' 187.

Kilns unknown at Troy ; dates of use, 219.

King or Chief, last, of Troy, his house, 51 ;

view of, 35 and 325 (see *House*) ; Virchow's plea for still calling him Priam, 684, *Pref.*

Kitchen refuse, on floors of houses of 4th c. ; shot down the hill from 5th c., 574.

Knife-handle, bone, 3rd c., 427.

Knives used in Homer's time for eating, 408 ; straight, and worn in the belt, 506.

Knives, copper, 1st c. ; one of them *gilt*, 251.

Knives, bronze, 3rd c. ; only one in the great Treasure, 483 ; in other treasures, 494 ; still with pins which fastened them to the wooden handle, 505, 506 ; 2 single and double edged of remarkable form, like the Egyptian, 506 ;—4th c., 564 ;—5th c., 585–6 ;—6th c., one plated with gold, 604 ; one of iron, with ring and rivet, like the bronze Etruscan knives, 604.

Knives of flint, chalcedony and obsidian, in the 4 lowest c., 246–7 ; 3rd c. ; also found at Thera, 445 ;—4th c., 571.

Ko, or *Go*, Cypriote character, ornament like, on vases of 3rd c., 342, 369, 383, 384.

Korax, rock in Ithaca, 50.

Koumanoudes, Ath., assistant keeper of the antiquities at Athens, 338.

Koumanoudes, St., Prof. at Athens, 464, 633.

Koum Kaleh, town on Hellespont, probably site of Achilleum, alluvial deposits at, 104.

Koum Kioi (" Village of Sand "), 103 ; site of *Polium* (*q. v.*).

Kouyunjik (Nineveh), palace of Assurbanipal, funnel with Cypriote characters, like the Trojan of 5th c., found at, 411.

Kuhse, W., author's brother-in-law, 5 *n.*

Kurtz, Dr. F., list of plants of the Troad, 727 f.

LABRANDA, the double-edged battle-axe common in Asia Minor, whence the Zeus Labrandeus of Caria ; like one in 6th c., 606.

Ladle of clay, 5th c., 580.

Laërtes, grandson of Poseidon, a sign of Phoenician relations of Ithaca, 50.

Lake-dwellings, whorls found in, 230 ; other objects, *passim*.

Lambda, ornament on vases in shape of the Greek Λ, or the Cypriote character *go*, 290, 297.

Lampon, s. of Laomedon, 156.

Lamps not in pre-h. cities, except perhaps little bowls like the *condylia* in Greek churches ; not known to Homer, 620, 621, *Pref.* xii. ; unknown in Greece and Asia Minor till 6th cent. B.C. ; those found in N. Ilium nearly all Roman, 405 ; Greek, terra-cotta, one on a long foot, N. I., 620.

---

[1] These are only various readings of the same character, ∿ · See p. 695, a, near the top.

THE END.

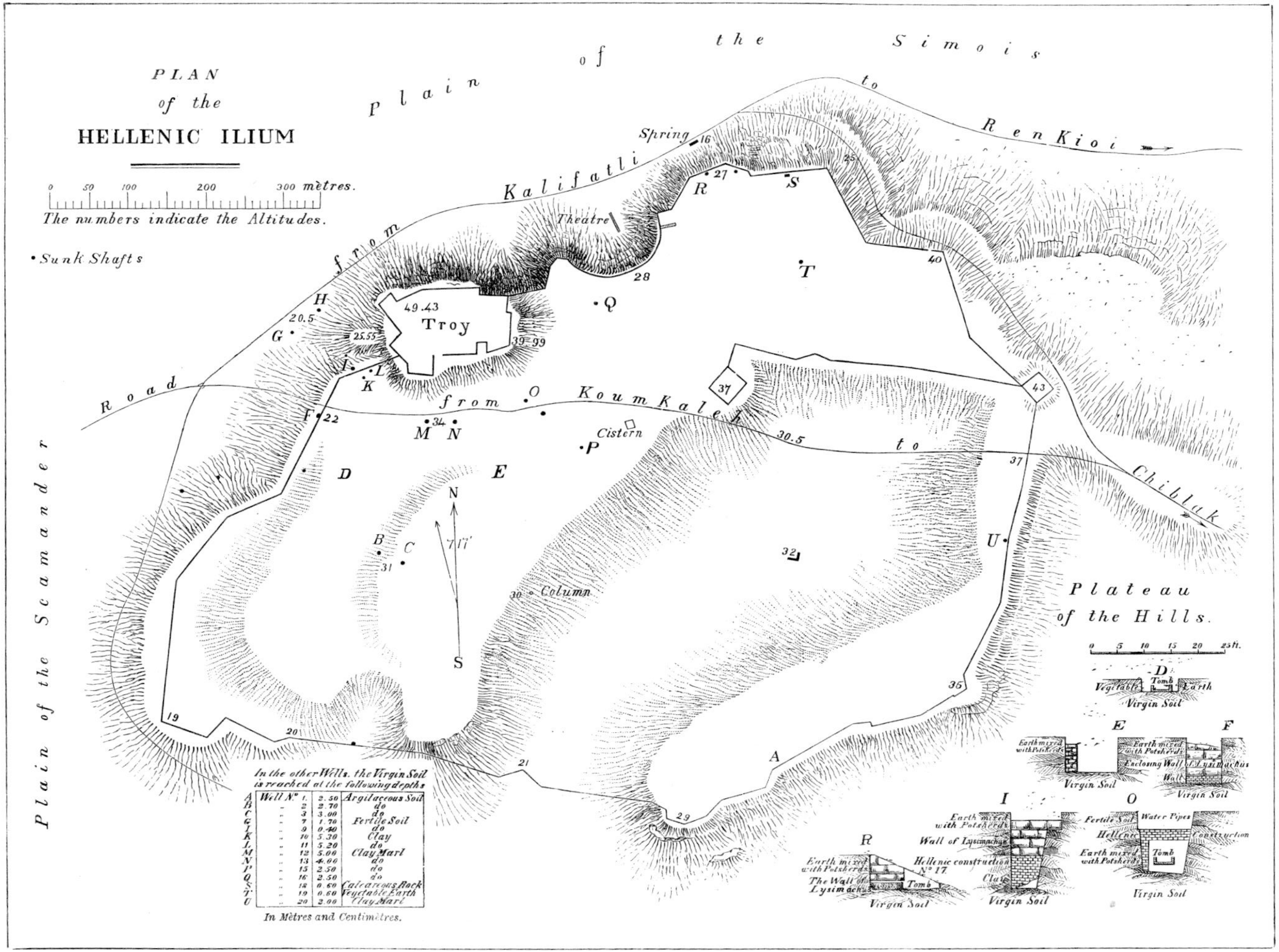

PLAN
of the
HELLENIC ILIUM

The numbers indicate the Altitudes.

• Sunk Shafts

0   50   100   200   300 mètres.

Simois

Ren Kioi

to

the Plain of

Kalifatli

Plain of the Scamander

Chiblak

Plateau of the Hills

Spring

Theatre

Troy

49.43

Koum Kaleh

from O.

to U.

Cistern

• Column

Road from ... Scamander

N
S

In the other Hills, the Virgin Soil is reached at the following depths:

Argillaceous Soil
Fertile Soil
Clay
Chalk Marl
Calcareous Rock
Clay Marl

In Metres and Centimetres.

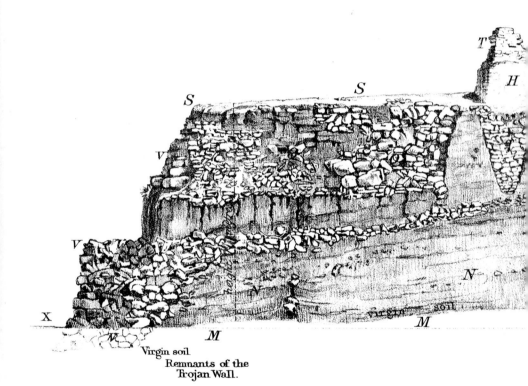

Virgin soil
Remnants of the
Trojan Wall.

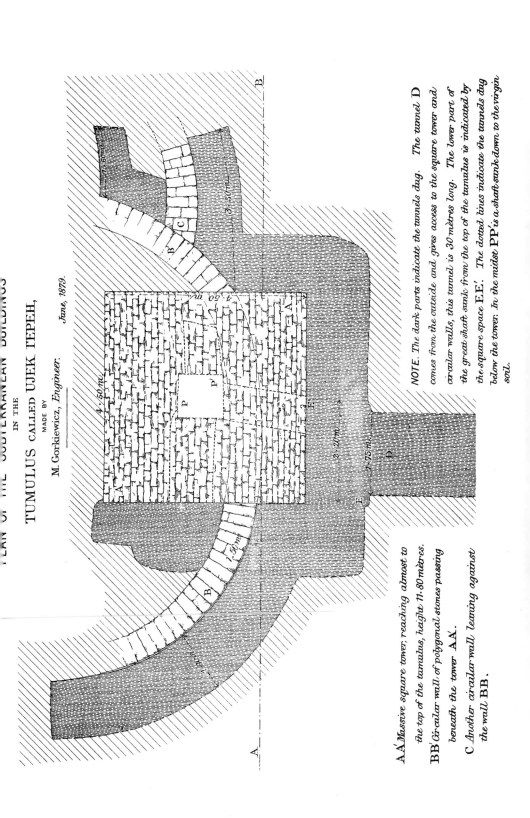

PLAN OF THE SUBTERRANEAN BUILDINGS

IN THE

TUMULUS CALLED UJEK TEPEH,

MADE BY

M. Gorkiewicz, Engineer.   June, 1879.

AA' Massive square tower, reaching almost to
the top of the tumulus, height 11.80 mètres.

BB' Circular wall of polygonal stones passing
beneath the tower AA.

C Another circular wall leaning against
the wall BB.

NOTE. The dark parts indicate the tunnels dug.   The tunnel D
comes from the outside and gives access to the square tower and
circular walls, this tunnel is 30 mètres long.   The lower part of
the great shaft sunk from the top of the tumulus is indicated by
the square space E.E'.   The dotted lines indicate the tunnels dug
below the tower. In the midst P.P' is a shaft sunk down to the virgin
soil.

TRANSVERSE SECTION FOLLOWING THE LINE A_B.

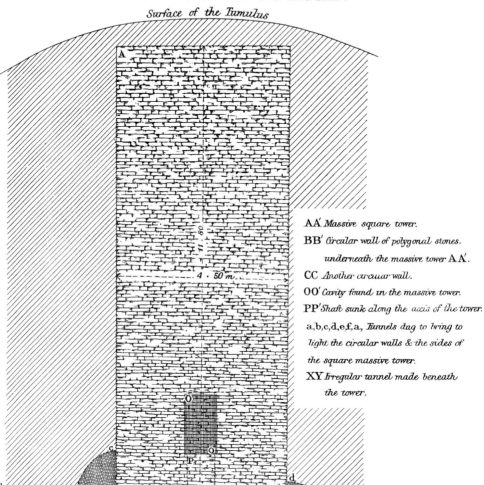

Surface of the Tumulus

4 · 50 m

AA' *Massive square tower.*
BB' *Circular wall of polygonal stones.*
    underneath the massive tower AA'.
CC *Another circular wall.*
OO' *Cavity found in the massive tower.*
PP' *Shaft sunk along the axis of the tower.*
a,b,c,d,e,f,a, *Tunnels dug to bring to*
  light the circular walls & the sides of
  the square massive tower.
XY *Irregular tunnel made beneath*
   the tower.

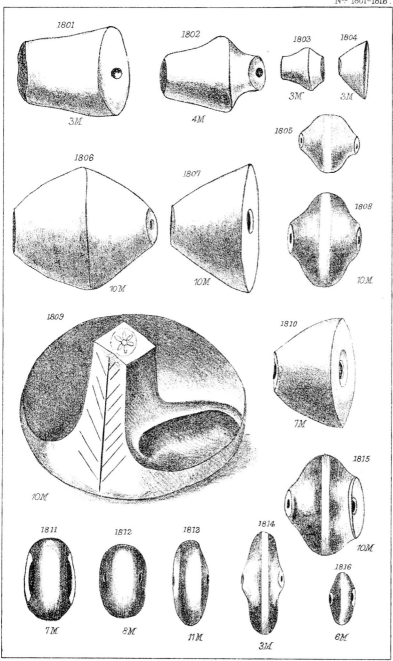

SPECIMEN SECTIONS OF WHORLS DUG UP AT TROY_

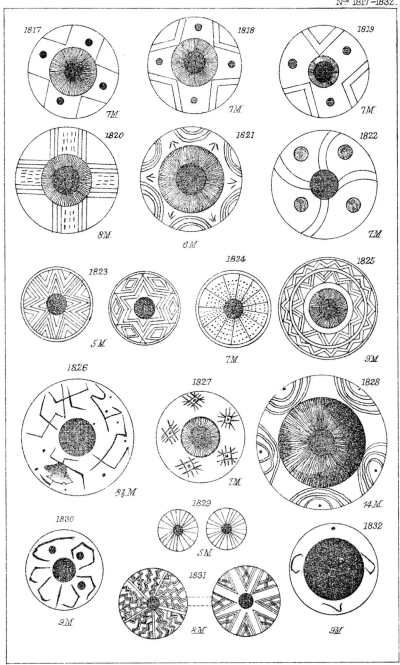

SPECIMEN PATTERNS OF WHORLS DUG UP AT TROY.

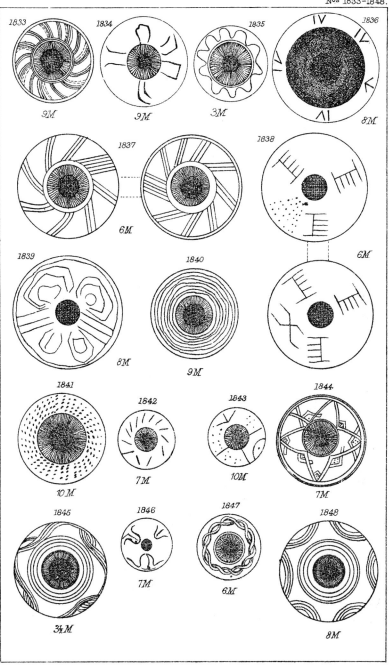

SPECIMEN PATTERNS OF WHORLS DUG UP AT TROY.

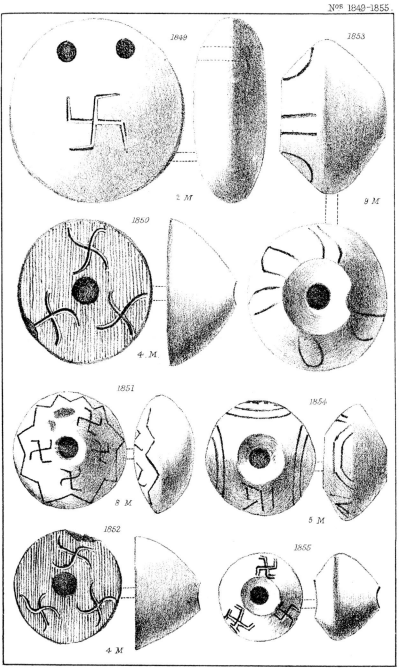

SPECIMENS OF WHORLS, &c. DUG UP AT TROY.

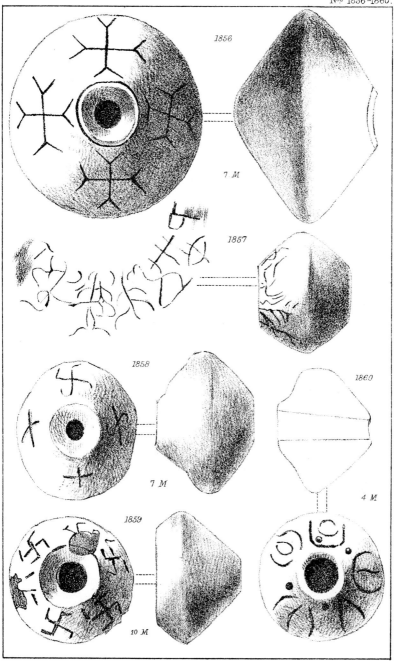

1856

7 M

1857

1858

1860

7 M

4 M

1859

10 M

SPECIMENS OF WHORLS, &c. DUG UP AT TROY.

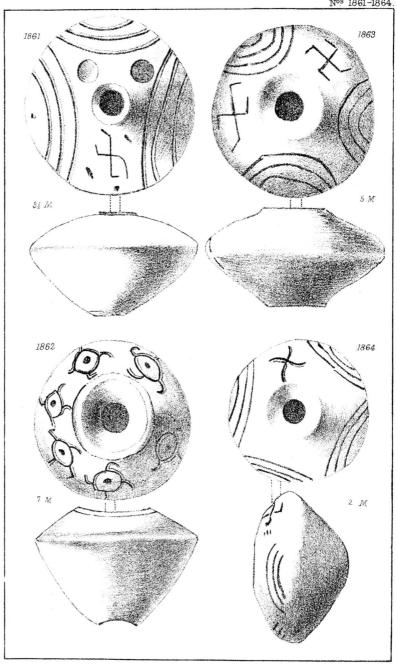

SPECIMENS OF WHORLS, &c. DUG UP AT TROY.

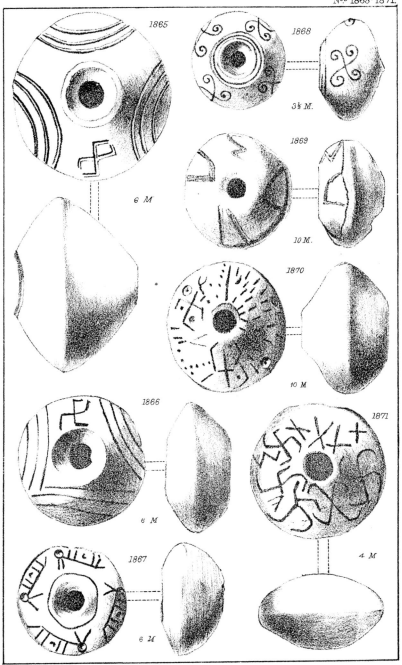

SPECIMENS OF WHORLS, &c. DUG UP AT TROY.

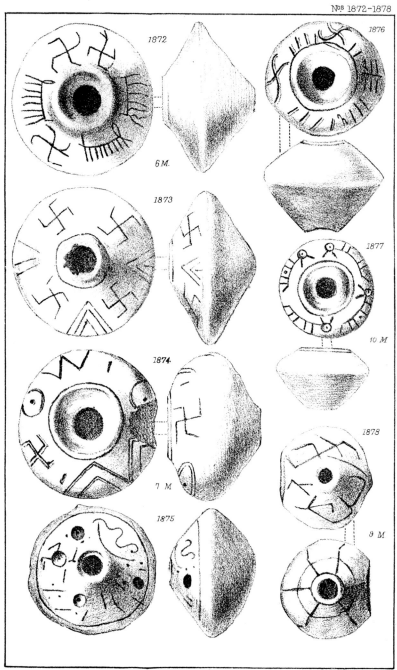

SPECIMENS OF WHORLS, &c. DUG UP AT TROY.

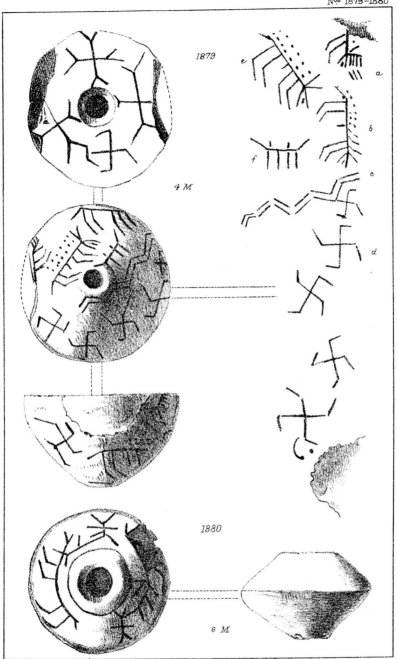

SPECIMENS OF WHORLS, &c. DUG UP AT TROY.

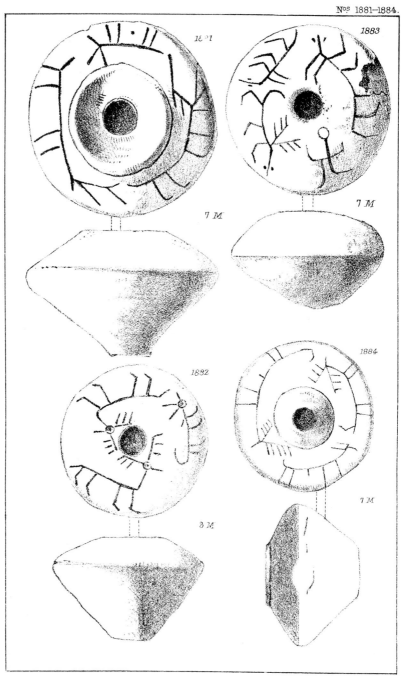

SPECIMENS OF WHORLS, &c. DUG UP AT TROY.

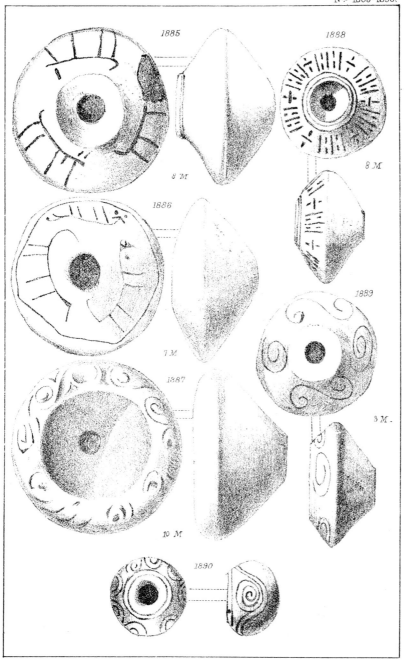

SPECIMENS OF WHORLS &c. DUG UP AT TROY.

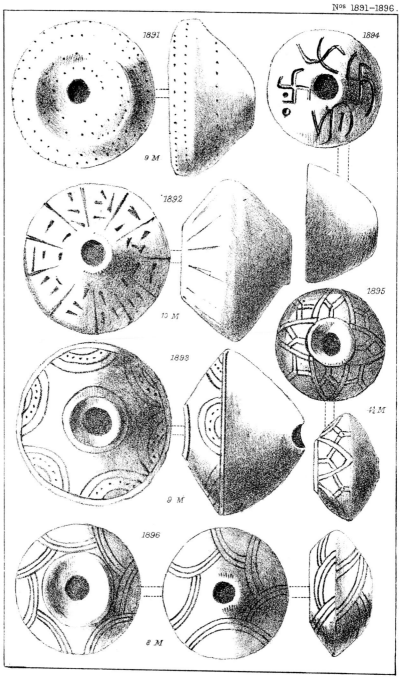

SPECIMENS OF WHORLS, &c. DUG UP AT TROY.

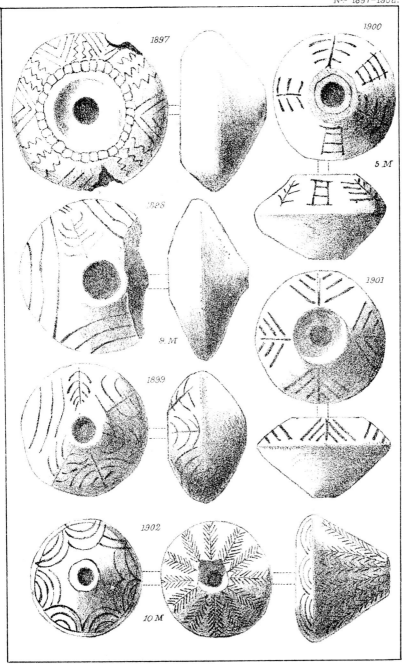

1897

1900

5 M

1898

9 M

1901

1899

1902

10 M

SPECIMENS OF WHORLS, &c. DUG UP AT TROY.

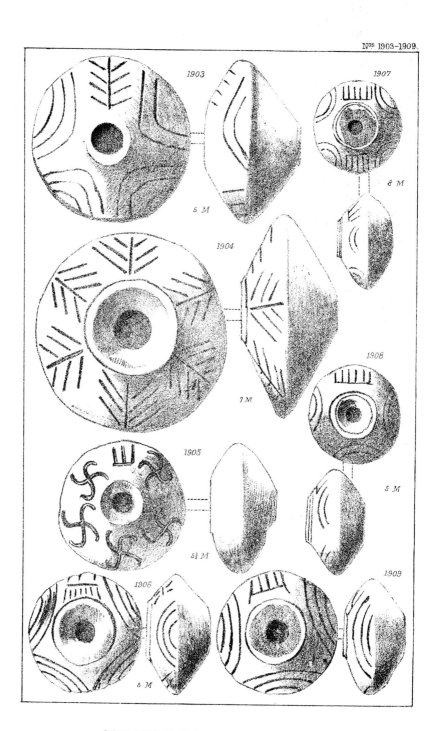

1903
1904
1905
1906
1907
1908
1909
6 M
7 M
5½ M
5 M
8 M
5 M
5 M

SPECIMENS OF WHORLS, &c. DUG UP AT TROY.

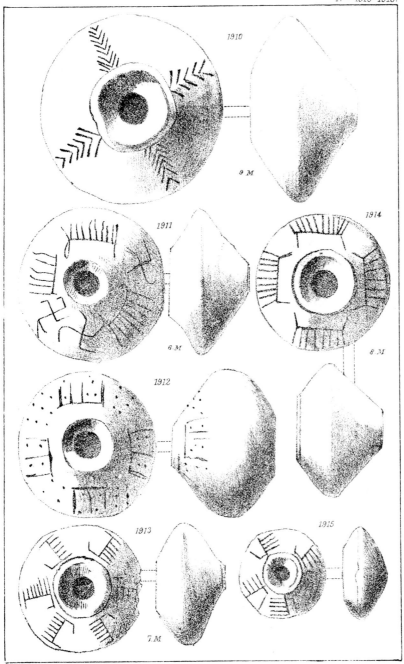

SPECIMENS OF WHORLS, &c. DUG UP AT TROY.

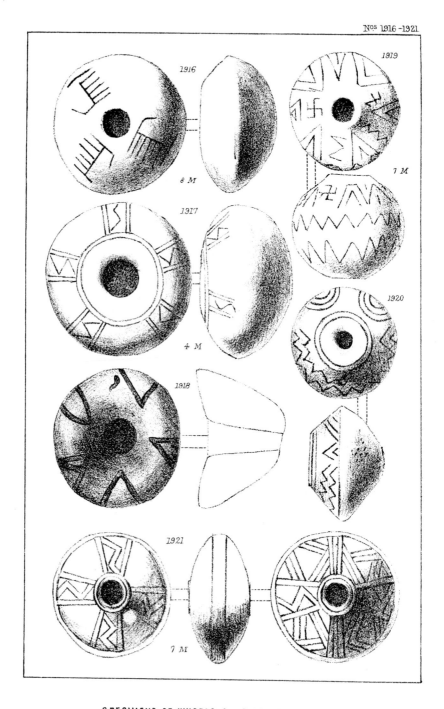

SPECIMENS OF WHORLS, &c. DUG UP AT TROY.

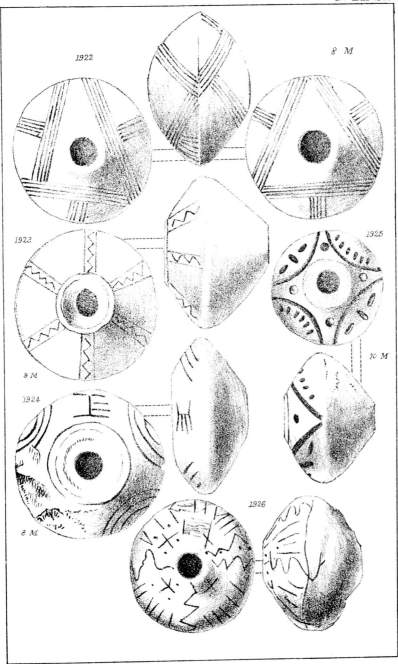

SPECIMENS OF WHORLS, &c. DUG UP AT TROY.

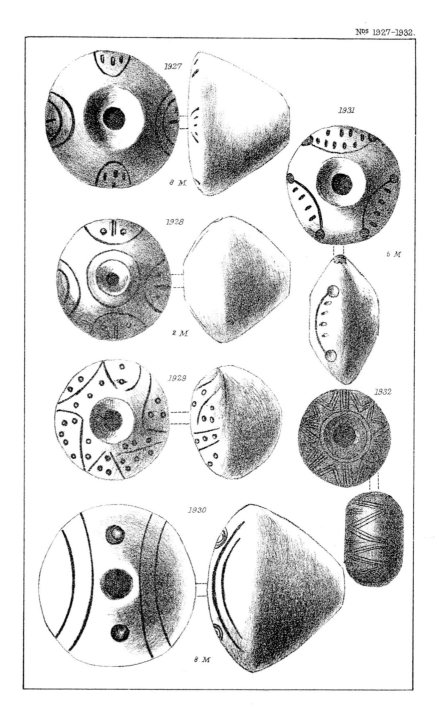

SPECIMENS OF WHORLS, &c. DUG UP AT TROY.

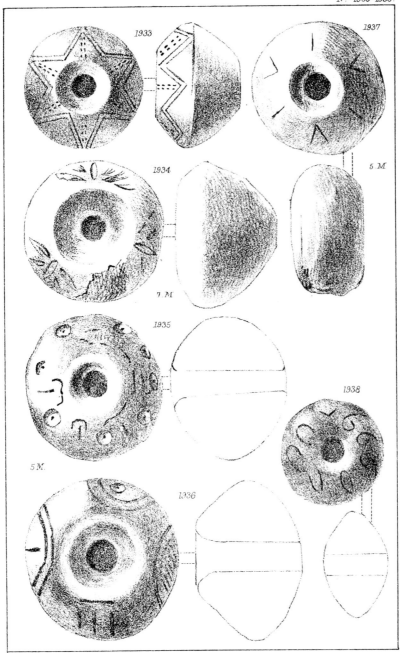

SPECIMENS OF WHORLS, &c. DUG UP AT TROY.

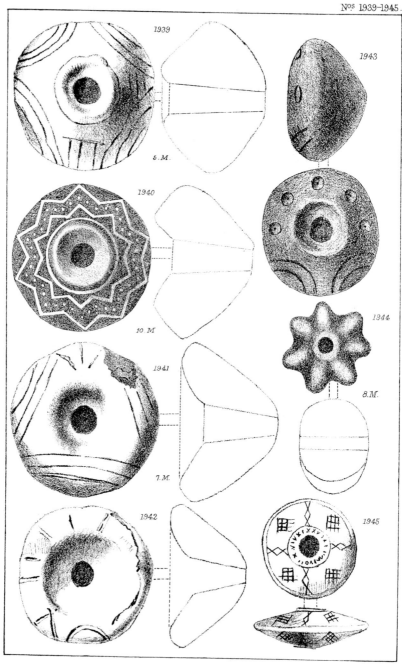

1939

1943

5.M.

1940

10 M

1944

1941

8.M.

7.M.

1942

1945

SPECIMENS OF WHORLS, &c. DUG UP AT TROY.

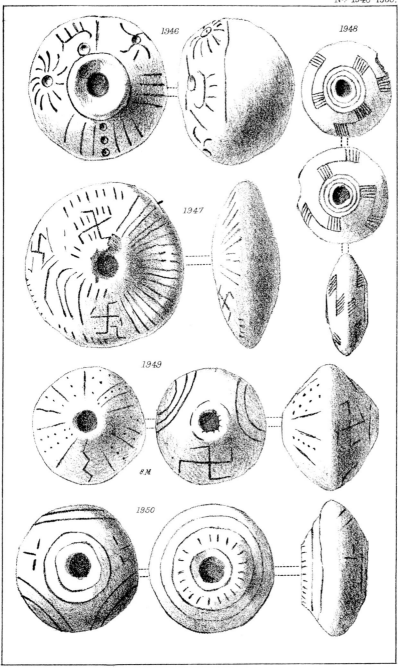

SPECIMENS OF WHORLS, &c. DUG UP AT TROY.

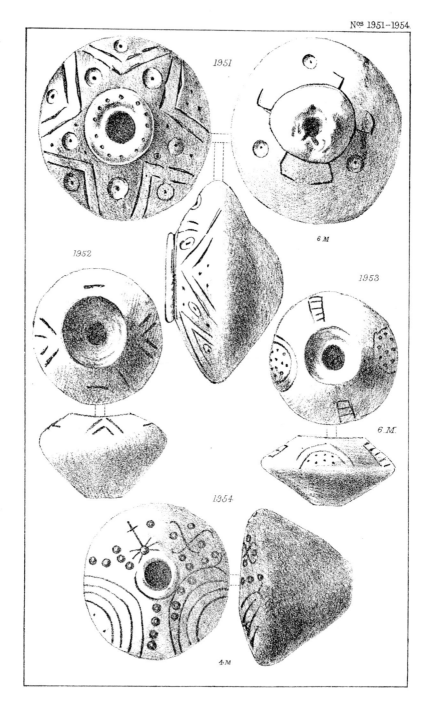

SPECIMENS OF WHORLS, &c. DUG UP AT TROY.

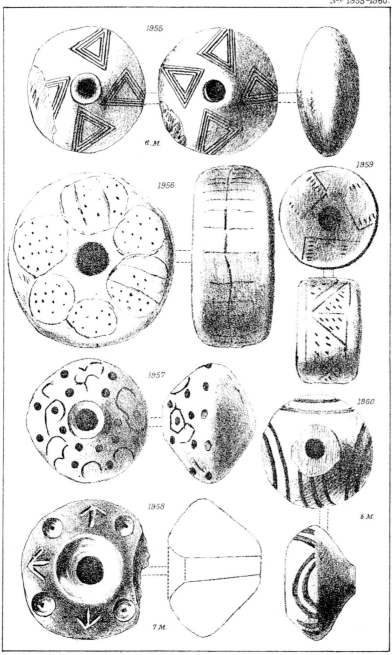

SPECIMENS OF WHORLS, &c. DUG UP AT TROY.

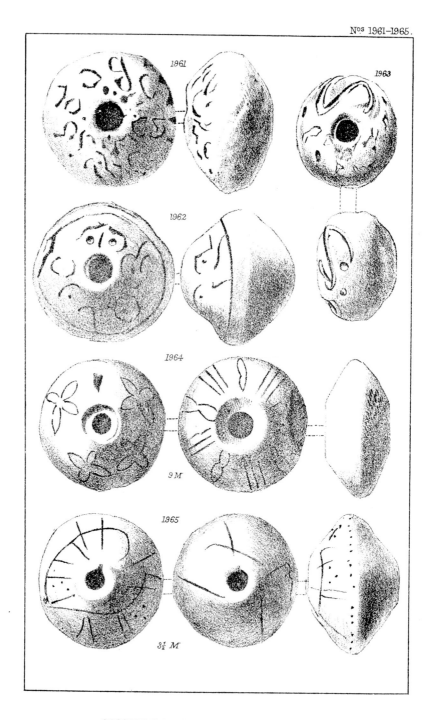

SPECIMENS OF WHORLS, &c. DUG UP AT TROY.

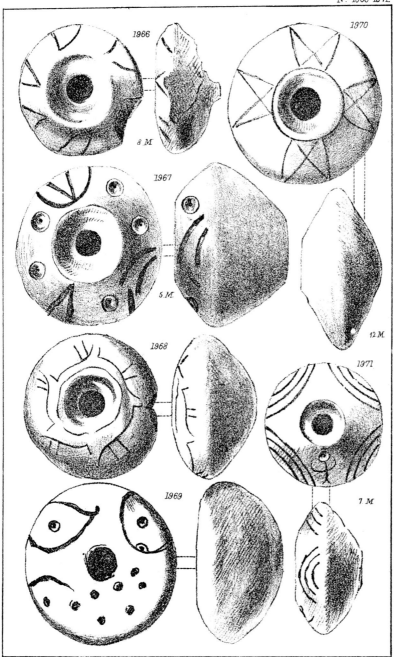

SPECIMENS OF WHORLS, &c. DUG UP AT TROY.

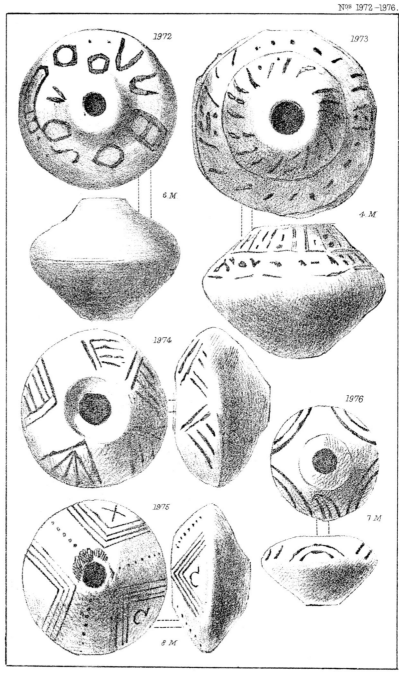

SPECIMENS OF WHORLS, &c. DUG UP AT TROY.

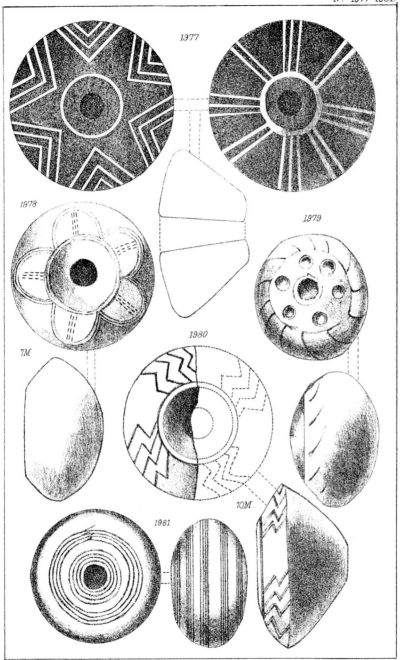

SPECIMENS OF WHORLS, &c. DUG UP AT TROY.

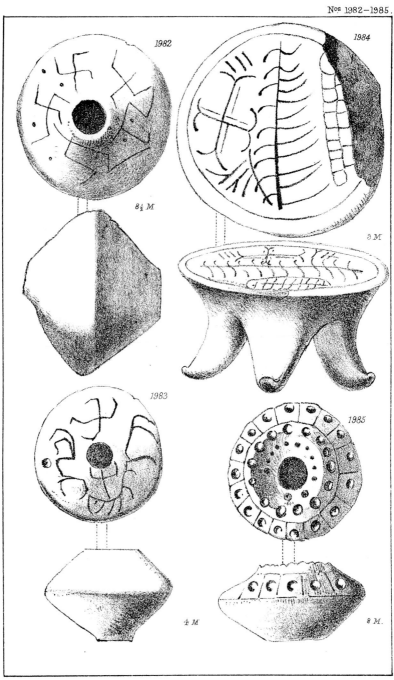

1982

1984

8½ M

3 M

1983

1985

4 M

8 M.

SPECIMENS OF WHORLS, &c. DUG UP AT TROY.

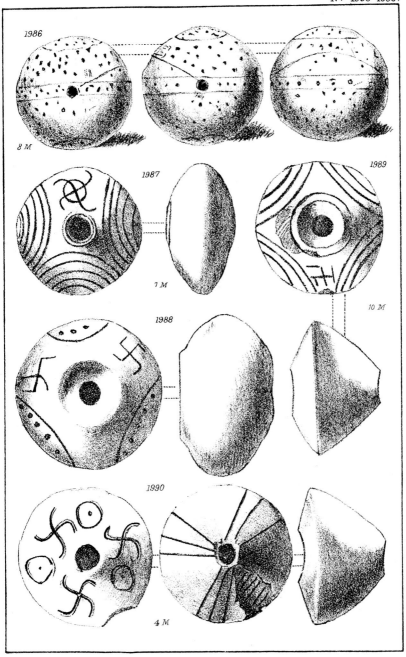

SPECIMENS OF WHORLS, &c. DUG UP AT TROY.

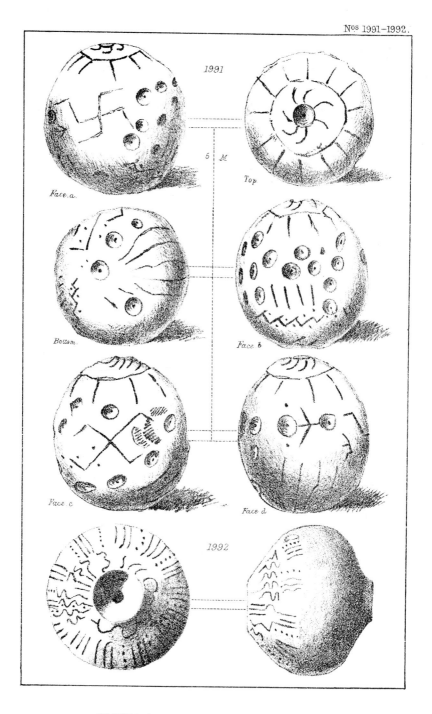

1991

Face.a.

Top

5 | M

Bottom.

Face b

Face c

Face d

1992

SPECIMENS OF WHORLS, &c. DUG UP AT TROY.

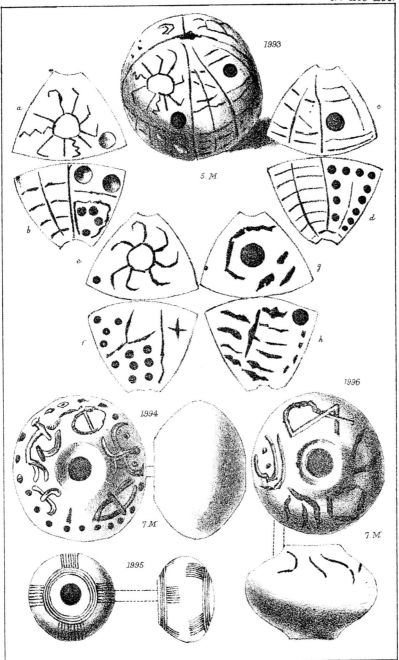

SPECIMENS OF WHORLS, &c. DUG UP AT TROY.

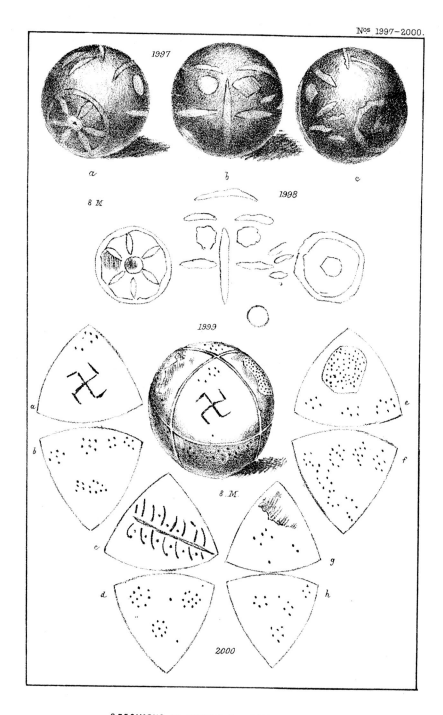

SPECIMENS OF WHORLS, &c. DUG UP AT TROY.